SIXTH EDITION

The Development of CHILDREN

CYNTHIA LIGHTFOOT
Pennsylvania State University, Delaware County

MICHAEL COLE
University of California, San Diego

SHEILA R. COLE

WORTH PUBLISHERS

Senior Publisher: Catherine Woods
Executive Editor: Jessica Bayne
Executive Marketing Manager: Katherine Nurre
Developmental Editor: Randee Falk
Associate Managing Editor: Tracey Kuehn
Media and Supplements Editor: Sharon Prevost
Photo Editor: Ted Szczepanski
Photo Researchers: Christina Micek, Vikii Wong
Art Director and Cover Designer: Babs Reingold
Text Designers: Babs Reingold and Lyndall Culbertson
Project Editor: Kerry O'Shaughnessy
Illustrations: Kim Martens, Chris Notarile, Matrix Publishing Services
Illustration Coordinator: Susan Timmins
Production Manager: Barbara Seixas
Composition: Matrix Publishing Services
Printing and Binding: Quebecor

Credit is given to the following sources for permission to use the part- and chapter-opening photos: p. 2, Brian Cruickshank / Lonely Planet Images; p. 48, Dr. David Phillips / Visuals Unlimited; p. 50, Asian Specialists / Alamy; p. 82, Dr. G. Moscoso / Photo Researchers; p. 120, Gabrielle Revere / Getty Images; p. 122, Shehzad Noorani / Peter Arnold Inc.; p. 160, Nancy R. Cohen / Digital Vision / Alamy; p. 200, Design Pics Inc. / Alamy; p. 232, David Grossman / Photo Researchers; p. 234, Sean Justice / Digital Vision / Getty Images; p. 268, Lawrence Migdale / Photo Researchers; p. 300, Michael Pole /Corbis; p. 338, Suzy Bennett / Alamy; p. 382, Richard Hutchings / Photo Researchers; p. 384, Lori Adamski Peek / Getty Images; p. 424, Pierre Perrin / Agence Zoko; p. 458, © R. Ian Lloyd / Masterfile; p. 496, Jim Craigmyle / Getty Images; p. 498, S. Mitchell / Peter Arnold; p. 542, © Little Blue Wolf Productions / Corbis.

Library of Congress Control Number: 2008935258

ISBN-13: 978-1-4292-0225-1
ISBN-10: 1-4292-0225-4

Worth Publishers
41 Madison Avenue
New York, NY 10010
www.worthpublishers.com

CYNTHIA LIGHTFOOT is Professor and Head of Human Development and Family Studies at the Pennsylvania State University, Brandywine. Her published works focus on the sociocultural contexts of child and adolescent development, most recently, on teen pregnancy, identity development, and youth culture. Lightfoot has served on the editorial boards of Culture and Psychology and Cognitive Development, and as Vice President of the Jean Piaget Society. Her interest in children and adolescents was fueled by experiences working with emotionally disturbed and autistic children in schools and as a child development specialist in a program for teenage mothers.

MICHAEL COLE is an all–University of California Professor of Psychology, Communication, and Human Development. His home base is the University of California, San Diego, where he is the Director of the Laboratory of Comparative Human Cognition. For many years he spent his afternoons participating with children and undergraduates in development-enhancing after-school programs. He is an editor of the journal *Mind, Culture, and Activity*. He has published widely on the role of culture and schooling in development, for which he has been awarded honorary degrees at Copenhagen University and the University of Helsinki. He is a member of the American Academy of Arts and Sciences and the National Academies of Education (of the United States and Russia).

SHEILA COLE is a former journalist who specialized in writing about families, children, development, and education. She is also a children's writer. Her most recent book offers a history of American childhood and is written for young people. She has also authored picture books, historical fiction, and novels for young adults. She participates in literacy programs for homeless adolescents.

The Coles have three grandchildren with whom they like to spend their summers.

brief contents

contents

PART I IN THE BEGINNING

PART II INFANCY

Chapter 9 Social and Emotional Development in
Early Childhood 301

Chapter 10 Contexts of Development 339

PART IV MIDDLE CHILDHOOD

Chapter 11 Boxes

Chapter 12 School as a Context for Development 425

Chapter 13 Social and Emotional Development in Middle Childhood 459

PART V ADOLESCENCE

Welcome to the sixth edition of *The Development of Children*. In my new role as "lead author," I would like to share with you some of the goals that focused our work on this edition. If you are new to the book, we hope you will find it a thorough review of developmental theory and research, presented in a way that engages the interest and intellect of today's students. If you have used previous editions, we think you will be pleased with how we have integrated recent advances in developmental science with central themes that have characterized *The Development of Children* from its inception. More generally, we have made a wealth of changes in content, organization, and style that, while increasing accessibility, also serve to strengthen thematic features that have distinguished the book since its debut in 1989: the interaction of cultural and biological processes throughout development; the integration of theory, research, and practice; and the child as situated within a dynamically changing set of contexts.

Our interest in children's development is the result of years of personal and professional experience. My own interest was sparked during my undergraduate years when I worked in classrooms and programs for autistic and developmentally delayed children. Later, between graduate degrees, I worked in a program for teen mothers and their children, many of whom were Vietnamese and Cambodian refugees. Having spent my adolescence in Japan, I had developed an early interest in the relationship between culture and behavior. Over time, my professional interests focused on development, culture, and issues affecting minority and immigrant children and families.

Similarly, Michael and Sheila Cole's personal interest in children's development extends back to their youth when they worked together as camp counselors. Their years of experience first as parents raising children and now as grandparents have deepened their appreciation for children's development and the changing contexts in which it occurs. Both have also committed their professional lives to children's development: Michael Cole specializes in the study of the role of culture in children's learning and cognitive development; Sheila Cole is a journalist who has written articles about children and books for children.

Beyond our interest in children's development, the Coles and I share a longstanding devotion to undergraduate education. Michael Cole has spent most of his professional life at a "Research 1" university; I have spent most of mine at a small college that is part of a large state university system. He and I alike see our book as a tool for promoting cultural literacy and critical thinking as well as an appreciation for how research can improve the lives of children by leading to programs and policies. The goal of making a positive contribution to our students' development, as well as to the development of the children that they will someday go on to educate, counsel, study, and/or parent, was a high priority for us as we worked on this book. In the sections below, we explain how we have pursued this goal through the book's central themes and by strengthening these themes and making other changes in this new edition.

Theoretical Orientation
A Biocultural Approach

As mentioned, culture and biology have been focuses of this book from the first edition. Integrating some of the most influential and respected work in contemporary developmental sciences, the biocultural perspective presented in this edition is true both to the direction of the field and to our conviction that students' understanding of diversity—of culture, gender, ethnicity, class, religion—is essential to their own development in a rapidly globalizing world. Replacing the bio-social-behavioral shift theme of earlier editions, the biocultural approach enables us to usefully focus the book's content for students in ways that are consistent with recent trends in the developmental sciences. We introduce the perspective in a new chapter (Chapter 2: Biocultural Foundations) that describes cultural as well as biological processes of inheritance and provides a solid conceptual framework for learning about how these processes relate to each other and to the development of individual children. Biocultural foundations are underscored throughout the book in numerous discussions and illustrations, further advancing students' understanding of their relevance to developmental pathways. For highlights of the coverage of culture throughout the book, please see Table 1.

In addition to its relevance to students' understanding of the world around them, the diversity focus inherent to the biocultural perspective speaks directly to our students' personal lives and histories. It is obvious to all that, like our neighborhoods, places of work, and society in general, our student populations are becoming increasingly multiethnic and multilingual. It is equally clear to anyone who has spent much time in the classroom that students naturally seek connections between course material and their own life experience. The diversity focus of our book encourages and rewards such relevance-seeking behavior. As our many years in the classroom have shown us, when students succeed in anchoring course content to their own experience, they are more likely to understand and remember.

Integrating Practice, Theory, and Research

As part of challenging students to look at information critically and skeptically, we promote the understanding that information arises in the context of particular theories and particular research questions and methods of inquiry, and that it should be held to standards of science. For this edition, we have dropped the "theoretical frameworks" scheme, which added an unnecessary layer of complexity, in order to focus more fully on the major developmental theories and research designs. However, along with wanting students to understand the connections among information, theory, and research, we want them to understand that research—its questions and methods—is importantly tied to matters of practice—that is, to the issues, problems, plans, and concerns of the day. To give practice its proper place, as well as for pedagogical reasons, we make certain not to sacrifice the stories of development to disconnected facts and figures but, rather, use such information to help students acquire meaningful, connected, and relevant *knowledge*.

The focus on practice is also consistent with our own scholarly work. We are all actively interested in discovering practical approaches for fostering the development of children, and in engaging our students in this enterprise. Michael Cole's development of the *Fifth Dimension* after-school program is an example, as is my work with teenage mothers, immigrant families, and nutrition education programs for inner-city children. In all cases our students are actively involved in the research process, carrying knowledge from the classroom to the contexts in which children live and develop.

Our belief in the importance of linking practical, theoretical, and research orientations in studying development comes not only from our own experience but

table 1

Highlights of the Coverage of Culture in the Sixth Edition

Culture as a context of development, p. 6
Cultural variations about managing fussiness in children, p. 7
Japanese and American understandings of aggression in children, p. 17
Vygotsky and sociocultural theory, p. 23
Ethnography, p. 34
Cultural inheritance, pp. 53–58
Coevolution of culture and biology, pp. 77–78
Cultural variations in prenatal care, pp. 93–98
Cultural variations in childbirth, pp. 106–108
Newborn functioning in different cultures, p. 112
Parental responses to infants by culture, p. 117
Sleeping arrangements around the world, pp. 151–153
Symbolic cultural tools, p. 197
Cultural and universal emotional expressions, pp. 203–207
Imitative games across culture, p. 208
Cultural variations in attachment, pp. 217–219
Learning two languages, p. 245
Culture and sustained processing of spatial relations, p. 274
The role of language in culture, p. 289, p. 293
Cultural scripts, p. 294
Culturally organized context of children's developing competence, p. 297
The cultural view, p. 308
Cultural variations in the age at which children mask emotion, p. 321
The influence of culture on emotional regulation, p. 323
Family and culture, p. 342
Immigrant families, p. 349
Community and culture, p. 364
Children's literature and culture beliefs, p. 370
Social stereotypes, p. 373
Culture and athleticism in girls and boys, p. 392
Is the acquisition of conservation universal? p. 411
Cultural variations in planning, p. 413
Are IQ tests culturally biased? p. 420
Cultural variations in school, p. 425, 427
Cultural variations in preschools, p. 433
Contemporary challenges in a globalizing world, p. 449
The culture of school, p. 450
Culturally responsive classroom strategies, p. 454
The role of culture in competitive vs. cooperative play, pp. 474–476
Cultural variations in sleep during adolescence, p. 512
Puberty, culture and gender, pp. 513–514
Cultural variations in the sexual debut, pp. 517–518
Teenage pregnancy, pp. 520–521
Cultural variability in formal-operational thinking, p. 527
Cultural variations in moral reasoning, pp. 535–538
Ethnic identity, pp. 566–569
Cultural variations in externalizing problems, pp. 573–575
Cultural issues in emerging adulthood, pp. 577–578

also as a response to the current concerns of developmental science, as well as to the increasing interest in practice and service that we see in our students. It is therefore natural that our book should focus on research as an ethical enterprise, underscoring its implications for defining and creating healthy contexts of development, and preventing and solving problems that threaten children's well-being. Among the many issues we discuss are the benefits of special nutrition programs for children who have experienced malnutrition early in life, methods for assessing the quality of out-of-home care for young children, the importance of extended families in ameliorating the problems facing poor children, the special hazards of teenage pregnancy, and effective means of parenting teenagers. Indeed, we have introduced a new feature, In the Field boxes, to showcase developmentalists whose applied work is being recognized for its important impact on developmental and child-welfare and justice issues. We also include many examples drawn from the everyday lives of children to show how a society's beliefs influence its children's development by shaping both the laws and the social norms that govern child-rearing practices.

A Focus on Dynamic Interaction

The Development of Children combines traditional chronological and topical approaches to the study of development in a deliberate attempt to make as clear as possible the idea that development is a process involving the whole child situated within multiple, interacting contexts. Although the book is chronological in its overall structure and adopts traditional age boundaries for each of its major sections, its organization is topical in two important respects. First, within the traditionally defined age periods, it describes development in physical, cognitive, social, and emotional domains, emphasizing the interaction among domains. Second, it includes several chapters devoted to underscoring the role of contexts in general, and of the special context of school in particular, in shaping developmental pathways.

Our emphasis on development in context is meant to inspire students to look more closely at children, in order to understand their developmental needs and how they experience the world—their peers and parents, their schools and playgrounds, their toys and games, and the monsters under their beds. After all, whether in their personal, professional, or civic lives, our students will influence the contexts of children's development, thereby affecting children's potential for success and happiness. Our goal as teachers is to ensure that they do so mindfully and with purpose.

New to the Sixth Edition

As you'll notice from even the most cursory glance, the sixth edition of this book has been revised from head to toe. From the macro level of a reorganized table of contents to the micro level of more accessible, concrete language, we have examined and revised the entire book.

High points of the revision include:

Reorganized Sections on Infancy and Adolescence

Responding to changes in the field and requests from instructors, the infancy and adolescence sections have been reorganized. Coverage of infancy is now divided into a chapter on the newborn, a chapter on physical and cognitive development, and a chapter on emotional and social development. The adolescent section has been substantially reorganized so that it is easier to teach and learn from.

Reorganization and a Refreshing New Voice Throughout

With students *and* instructors in mind, the book has been reorganized to better emphasize interactions across physical, cognitive, social, and emotional domains of development. In addition to helping students understand the complexity of

table 2

Highlights of the Coverage of the Brain in the Sixth Edition

High-tech research on brain function, development and disorders, p. 35
Brain activity during prenatal development, p. 91
Impact of prenatal nutrition on brain development, p. 94
Impact of teratogens, including marijuana, on brain development, p. 100
Relationship between low birth weight and brain development, p. 114
Neonatal brain development, p. 126
Neurons and neural networks, p. 127
The structure of the central nervous system, p. 128
Experience and development of the brain, pp. 129–130
Infant brain development, pp. 165–166
Implications of infant brain development, p. 197
Intersubjectivity and the brain, p. 208
A brain for language, pp. 239–241
Brain development during early childhood, p. 393
Brain involvement in specific learning disabilities, pp. 441–442
Brain development during middle childhood, p. 493
The influence of the brain on emotional development in adolescence, pp. 507–508

development, the reorganization makes the book easier to fit into a standard course structure. The new coverage and thorough updating throughout enhance the book's characteristic focus on research and culture, while the sentence-by-sentence revision—with more accessible language, briefer text sections, and a more integrated graphic design—make this edition the most lively and student friendly yet. All chapters now begin with compelling vignettes focusing on children from a range of cultures.

Updated Coverage of the Brain

The burgeoning of developmental neuroscience is reflected in expanded coverage of the brain—from infant brain growth to the role of the brain in adolescent risk-taking. Engaging examples and illustrations help students make sense of recent research on brain development and its effects on other developmental domains. For highlights of the coverage of the brain in the sixth edition, see Table 2.

New "In the Field" Profiles

These portraits of developmentalists highlight real-life applications of research and principles of child development. The developmentalists featured are as interesting and varied as, for example, primatologist Elizabeth Vinson Lonsdorf and Inuit midwife Akinisie Quamaluk.

New "Apply, Connect, and Discuss" Exercises

Included at the end of each major section, these exercises ask students, individually or in groups, to reflect and draw on what they have just read—for example, by comparing and contrasting theoretical viewpoints, creating an experiment or intervention, or applying what they have learned to a vignette.

Detailed Chapter Changes

In addition to these changes, all chapters have been extensively revised and updated and many have been reorganized. Highlights of this reorganization are as follows:

1. The Study of Human Development

- Expanded and reorganized coverage of theories of development
- Reconceptualization of treatment of methods, focusing on goals, criteria, and research design as well as data collection
- New final section introducing the book's biocultural approach
- New opening section providing an introduction to developmental science, focusing on the pure and applied goals of developmental science, periods and domains of development, and contexts of development
- Enhanced focus on the social contexts of children and of their study, including a new section on historical beliefs about children and childhood from medieval times through the nineteenth century
- New "In the Field" box: "Probing the Mysteries of Learning," on Elizabeth Vinson Lonsdorf's observations of chimpanzee learning and tool use

2. Biocultural Foundations

- With the new emphasis on a biocultural approach, Chapter 2 has been reorganized, updated and integrated with an introduction to culture. The chapter now gives students an even clearer picture of how biology and culture together shape species and individual development
- New opening vignette on the Laetoli footprints introduces questions about evolution
- New major section on culture including coverage of cultural innovation and evolution among macaque monkeys
- New subsection about genotypes and phenotypes and the operation of natural selection, including on phenotypic traits that are behavioral, such as infant-directed speech
- New "In the Field" box: "Doctor of the Plain People," on D. Holmes Morton's research in the Amish and Mennonite communities on recessive disorders
- New research on the increasing divergence of phenotypic characteristics of identical twins
- New subsection on niche construction and ecological inheritance, focusing on the role of individuals and their environments in shaping individuals' development
- New material on the Baldwin effect and coevolution, with a focus on lactose tolerance and sickle-cell anemia

3. Prenatal Development and Birth

- New opening vignette on the pregnancy and childbirth of Foua Lee, a new mother from Laos

- New "In the Field" box: "Midwifery in the Inuit Villages of Northern Canada," on Akinisie Qumaluk, who draws on traditional Inuit knowledge and modern medical science as part of a new program that has arisen since women insisted on being able to give birth in the community rather than being flown to hospitals in cities

4. The First Three Months

- New opening vignette on M'ama Afwe, a first-time mother, and her newborn

- New major section on physical growth in the first 3 months, including cultural variations and skull shaping

- Updated and reorganized material on brain development

- Restructured beginning of the main section on sensation, with material on methods for evaluating infant sensory capacities split off as a separate subsection

- New material on taste and smell, facial expressions, and the effect of mothers' prenatal diets

- New subsection on intermodal perception

- New material on temperament

- New findings on crying, including cross-culturally and in nonhuman primates, and new material on the evolutionary implications of crying

- New "In the Field" box: "Baby-Friendly Hospitals," on developmental psychologist Heidelise Als's attempts to reshape the environment of NICUs to better support developing behavioral organization and prevent disability

5. Physical and Cognitive Development in Infancy

- Chapter has been completely reorganized to focus on physical and cognitive development

- Expanded coverage of brain development

- Reorganization of major section on motor development

- New "In the Field" box: "The Diaper-Free Movement," including historical and cross-cultural perspectives on the timing of toilet training

- Reorganization of challenges to Piaget on object permanence, with new explanation of Esther Thelen's dynamic systems approach and new material including research by Jeanne Shinsky and Yuko Manakata on the role of experience

- New subsection on recent research on attention and the development of sustained attention

6. Social and Emotional Development in Infancy

- Chapter has been completely reorganized to focus on social and emotional development

- New major section on emotions and emotional expression

- New subsection on intersubjectivity and the brain, relating intersubjectivity to Giacomo Rizzolatti's work on mirror neurons and Andrew Meltzoff and Jean Decety's argument concerning mirror neurons and imitation
- Reorganized coverage of attachment, including new material on Vivian Carlson and Robin Harwood's research on cultural values and maternal sensitivity
- New major section on Erikson's stages of basic trust versus mistrust and initiative versus shame and doubt
- New "In the Field" box: "Children with Reactive Attachment Disorder," on the work of Lark Eshleman, a psychotherapist specializing in treating children who have experienced emotional traumas

7. Language Acquisition

- New main section focusing on the biological and environmental keys to language acquisition, including new material on research using neuroimaging and new discussion of the role of models and motivation
- New research on the emergence of "fast mapping" in toddlers
- Inclusion of "syntactic bootstrapping" and recent related research and its implications
- New example introducing pragmatic development
- New subsection on children's narrative abilities, including extended examples
- Extensive discussion of cultural modeling of narratives, including Carol Lee's work with African American children's narratives
- New "In the Field" box: "A Speech-Language Pathologist in Vietnam," focusing on Charlotte Ducote

8. Physical and Cognitive Development of Early Childhood

- Expanded coverage of physical and motor development, including additional coverage of nutrition, sleep, and food insecurity
- New research on brain development in early childhood
- New "In the Field" box: "Supporting Siblings of Children with Autism," focusing both on a child's support group and on the Autism Genome Project
- New material on cross-cultural challenges

9. Social and Emotional Development in Early Childhood

- New discussion of Erikson's stage of initiative versus guilt
- Revision of coverage of moral development to focus on psychodynamic, cognitive-developmental, and social domain views
- New example to support discussion of heteronomous morality

10. Contexts of Development

- Major reorganization of coverage of contexts and risk and resilience

- New opening vignette on war orphans from Burundi
- Reorganization of section on the family context, highlighting the family and culture and the evolutionary role of the family, with additional coverage of parenting practices and siblings
- New major section on neighborhoods and communities
- Reworking of major section on media contexts, including new discussion of print media and updated coverage of TV and interactive media
- New "In the Field" box: "Louisiana Swamp Nurse," focusing on Luwana Marts, who works with teenage mothers

11. Physical and Cognitive Development in Middle Childhood

- Reorganization of cognition.
- New major section on individual differences in cognitive development
- New opening vignette narrated by a girl from Kukatja Community
- New research relating patterns of cortical development and intelligence
- New data on overweight children in the United States and on sports involvement and self-esteem
- New "In the Field" box: "The Edible Schoolyard: Thinking Outside the Lunchbox," on the problem of childhood obesity and chef Alice Waters' program aimed at changing children's food choices by involving them in growing and preparing their food

12. School as a Context for Development

- New sections focusing on school readiness, classroom organization of learning and individual barriers to learning, and contemporary challenges in a global world
- New chapter opener on the importance of education for girls in sub-Saharan Africa
- New subsection on the role of the family in schooling, including recent research by Jonathan Tudge on differences in family activities across cultures and SES groups, and by Helen Raikes on parents' reading to children
- New subsection on preschools, with recent data on enrollments internationally and in the United States, as well as recent research on preschool participation for U.S. immigrants
- New "In the Field" box: "Learning after School in the Fifth Dimension," on Michael Cole's program to foster learning and intellectual development through computer and other games in an after-school setting with undergraduate mentors

13. Social and Emotional Development in Middle Childhood

- Reorganization of section on peer relationships, including new research on the effects of cultural emphases on independence versus interdependence, and new research on friendship stability

- New subsection on divorce
- In the subsection on self-esteem, incorporation of Erikson's stage of industry versus inferiority

14. Physical and Cognitive Development in Adolescence

- With the reorganization of Part V, this chapter now focuses on physical, cognitive, and moral development
- New opening vignette about Toni, a nurse at a teen mothers program, who discovers that her teenage son, Ryan, is having sex without a condom despite their many frank talks
- New material on evolutionary rationale for delayed maturation in humans
- New subsection on puberty and health, including coverage of nutrition, sleep, and physical activity
- New coverage of the sexual debut, with updates on cultural differences in timing and new information on adolescents' responses to first intercourse
- New coverage on sexual and reproductive health
- New box: "ICONS: Peacekeeping in a Virtual Classroom," looks at the international project that uses computer networks and peer collaboration to promote reasoning about global issues, including developmentalists' studies of the results

15. Social and Emotional Development in Adolescence

- New opening vignette about Kelly, Anna, and Hope and their "Jamboree" tradition, used to introduce adolescents' social and emotional development
- New main section on emotional development in adolescence, with subsections on the experience of emotions and emotion regulation
- New research on the brain development and risk taking
- New "In the Field" box: "Friends with Benefits," focusing on Benoit Denizet-Lewis's research on the adolescent sexual trend of "hooking up" and its implications
- New main section on social and emotional problems, including internalizing and externalizing problems
- New main section on emerging adulthood including discussion of "youth culture" with more recent work, including work on identity issues and on college students' reasoning about the nature of knowledge

Pedagogy

As we mentioned earlier, this new edition introduces two new pedagogical elements—the "In the Field" boxes and the "Apply, Connect, and Discuss" activities, both designed to connect students with the material. In addition, we've tried to highlight high-interest topics in boxes (on everything from correlation and causation to spanking). Each part begins with a prose introduction and a milestone table, which includes relevant sociocultural factors. Each chapter begins with an outline, designed to orient students to the text material that is to come, and ends with a summary and key terms, designed to help them review what they've learned,

Media and Supplements

The sixth edition of *The Development of Children* is accompanied by a number of supplementary materials designed to amplify the themes of the text. These include:

Video Tool Kit for Human Development

The video tool kit spans the full range of topics for the child development course, with 200 brief clips of research and news footage on topics ranging from prenatal brain development, to the experience of child soldiers, to empathy in adolescence. All the video clips can be assigned to students outside the classroom. A selection of these clips are integrated into 45 predesigned interactive activities that are easily assignable and assessable. The student activities are available exclusively online for this edition. More than 200 clips for instructors are available for downloading online, and a subset of more than 100 are available on DVD and CD-ROM.

Instructor's Resource Manual

The *Instructor's Resource Manual* by Jennifer Coots and Ruth Alfaro Piker, California State University, Long Beach, features chapter-by-chapter previews and lecture guides, learning objectives, topics for discussion and debate, handouts for student projects, and supplementary readings from journals. Course planning suggestions and ideas for term projects are also included.

Study Guide

The carefully crafted *Study Guide* by Stephanie Stolarz-Fantino, University of California, San Diego, helps students to read and retain the text material at a higher level than they are likely to achieve by reading the text alone. Each chapter includes a variety of practice tests and exercises to help integrate themes that reappear in various chapters. Each chapter also includes a review of key concepts, guided study questions, and section reviews that encourage students' active participation in the learning process.

Test Bank

Thoroughly revised, the *Test Bank* by Jennifer Jipson, California Polytechnic State University, includes approximately 60 multiple-choice and 70 fill-in, true–false, matching, and essay questions for every chapter. Each question is keyed to the textbook by topic, page number, and level of difficulty.

Computerized Test Bank CD-ROM

This computerized test bank CD-ROM, on dual platform for Windows and Macintosh, offers an easy-to-use test-generation system, allowing instructors to add an unlimited number of questions, select specific questions, edit or scramble questions, format a test, and include pictures, equations, and multimedia links over a secure network. The CD-ROM is also the access point for online testing, as well as Blackboard- and WebCT-formatted versions of the Test Bank.

The accompanying grade book enables instructors to record students' grades throughout the course, and includes the capacity to track student records and view detailed analyses of test items, curve tests, generate reports, add weights to grades, and more.

Online Testing and Quizzing

Online testing, powered by Diploma (www.wimba.net), gives instructors the ability to create and administer secure exams over a network and over the Internet, with questions that incorporate multimedia and interactive exercises. The program allows instructors to restrict tests to specific computers or time blocks, and includes a suite of grade-book and result-analysis features. Online quizzing, powered by Questionmark, can be accessed via the companion Web site at www. worthpublishers.com/thedevelopmentofchildren6e. Instructors can quiz students online using prewritten multiple-choice questions for each text chapter (not from the test bank) which was written and revised by Joy K. Crawford, University of Washington. Students receive instant feedback and can take the quizzes multiple times. Instructor may then view results by quiz, student, or question, or get weekly results via email.

Companion Web Site

The companion Web site, with newly added material from John Wesley Taylor V from Southern Adventist University, can be found at www.worthpublishers.com/thedevelopmentofchildren6e. The new site offers a variety of simulations, tutorials, and study aids organized by chapter with periodic updates (that is, new Web links, exercises, and new developments in developmental psychology). In addition to the online testing, syllabus posting, and Web site building services, the Web site offers the following features: Annotated Web Links; Chapter Outlines; Online Quizzes; Simulations and Demonstrations; Frequently Asked Questions About Developmental Psychology; Interactive Flashcards; and *Scientific American* podcasts.

A password-protected Instructor Site offers a full array of teaching resources, including PowerPoint slides, an online quiz gradebook, and links to additional tools such as WebCT, Blackboard, and the Image and Lecture Gallery.

For Instructors

Readings on the Development of Children, Fifth Edition, edited by Mary Gauvain, University of California, Riverside, and Michael Cole, University of California, San Diego. *Readings on the Development of Children* works as a thought-provoking supplement in a development course. With material ranging from theoretical to empirical, from classic to cutting-edge, this reader provides depth and focus for classroom discussion. The new edition offers 36 articles, 14 new to this edition. New articles were chosen to expose readers to recent research in rapidly changing areas of the field, such as brain development, cognition, socioemotional development, and adolescent well-being.

Acknowledgements

A book of this scope and complexity could not be produced without the help of others. A great many people gave generously of their time and experience to deepen our treatment of various areas of development, particularly the many scholars who consented to review drafts of our manuscript and make suggestions for improvement. The remaining imperfections exist despite their best efforts.

For this edition, we thank **Phyllis Adcock,** University of Nebraska at Omaha; **Kristine Anthis,** Southern Connecticut State University; **Melissa Atkinson,** Surry Community College; **Mita Banerjee,** Pitzer College; **Cheryl Beverly,** James Madison University; **Aviva Bower,** College of Saint Rose; **Chris Boyatais,** Bucknell University; **Dilek Buchholz,** Weber State University; **Jean Burr,** Hamilton College; **Joseph Campos,** University of California, Berkeley; **Caroline Cooke Carney,** Monterey Peninsula College; **Juanita Cole,** University of California, San Diego; **Lisa Comparini,** Clark University; **Dina Cook,** Gainesville College; **Jennifer Coots,** California State University, Long Beach; **Brian Cox,** Hofstra University; **Ron Craig,** Edinboro University of Pennsylvania; **Chrysoula Fantaousakis,** Kean University; **L. Mickey Fenzel,** Loyola College; **Krista Forrest,** University of Nebraska at Kearney; **Jean Louis Gariepy,** University of North Carolina; **Maria Gartstein,** Washington State University; **Amie Hane,** Williams College; **Abraham Hwang,** Messiah University; **Jennifer Jipson,** California Polytechnic State University; **Margaret Kasimatis,** Carroll College; **Marva Lewis,** Tulane University; **Roseanna McLeary,** California State University, Bakersfield; **Judy Neale,** Cameron University; **Harriet Oster,** New York University; **Justina Powers,** Cameron University; **Linda Raasch,** Normandale Community College; **Lisa Scott,** University of Massachusetts, Amherst; **Stephanie Stolarz-Fantino,** University of California, San Diego; **Dennis Thompson,** Georgia State University; **Wadiya Udell,** University of Washington, Bothell; **Deborah Vilas,** Bank Street College of Education; **Kresha Warnock,** Ball State University.

We are also grateful for all those who gave us feedback in our online survey, including **Nameera Akhtar,** University of California, Santa Cruz; **Sumi Ariely,** Massachusetts Institute of Technology; **Joann Benigno,** University of Florida; **Juanita Cole,** University of California, San Diego; **Ramie Cooney,** Creighton University; **Carol Eliot,** National Cathedral School; **Julie Klunk,** University of Massachusetts, Boston; **Janet Oh,** Macalester College; **Christine McCormick,** Eastern Illinois University; **Kathleen McCluskey-Fawcett,** University of Kansas; **Deborah Vilas,** Bank Street College of Education; **Laura Ann Petitto,** Dartmouth College.

We are also grateful to Stacey Alexander, Sharon Prevost, Lorraine Klimowich, Martha Solonche, Anna Paganelli, Alexandra Nickerson, Sharon Kraus, Randee Falk, Jessica Bayne, Babs Reingold, Paul Lacy, Barbara Seixas, Christine Micek, Vikii Wong, Ted Szczepanski, Tracey Kuehn, and Kerry O'Shaughnessy of Worth Publishers.

Cynthia Lightfoot
Exton, Pennsylvania
September, 2008

The Study of Human Development

Early one morning during the cold winter of 1800, a dirty, naked boy wandered into a hut at the edge of a tiny village in the French province of Aveyron to beg for food. In the months before this appearance, some of the people in the area had caught glimpses of the boy digging for roots, climbing trees, swimming in a stream, and running rapidly on all fours. They thought he was inhuman, perhaps a wild beast. When the boy appeared in the village, word spread quickly and everyone went to see him.

Among the curious was a government commissioner, who took the boy home and fed him. The child, who appeared to be about 12 years old, seemed ignorant of the civilized comforts that the people offered to him. When clothes were put on him, he tore them off. He would not eat meat, only raw potatoes, roots, and nuts. He rarely made a sound and seemed indifferent to human voices. In his report to the government, the commissioner concluded that the boy had lived alone since early childhood, "a stranger to social needs and practices. . . . [T]here is . . . something extraordinary in his behavior, which makes him seem close to the state of wild animals" (quoted in Lane, 1976, pp. 8–9).

The commissioner's report caused a public sensation when it reached Paris. Newspapers hailed the child as the "Wild Boy of Aveyron." In the climate that prevailed following the French Revolution, many hoped that the boy could rapidly develop intellectually and socially to demonstrate that even the poor and outcast of a society were as capable as the wealthy if they were provided with a proper education. The Wild Boy seemed a perfect test case because his life had been so devoid of supportive human contact.

Unfortunately, plans to study the Wild Boy soon ran into trouble. The first physicians to examine him concluded that he was mentally deficient and speculated that he had been put out to die by his parents for that reason. (In France in the late eighteenth century, as many as one in three normal children, and a greater percentage of abnormal children, were abandoned by their parents, usually because the family was too poor to support another child [Heywood, 2001].)

Most of the doctors recommended that the boy be placed in an asylum, but one young physician, Jean-Marc Itard (1774–1838), disputed the diagnosis of retardation. Itard proposed that the boy appeared to be mentally deficient only because he had been isolated from society and thereby prevented from developing normally. In support of his view, Itard argued that if the boy had been mentally retarded, he certainly could not have survived on his own in the forest.

Itard took personal charge of the boy, with the goal of teaching him to become fully competent, to master the French language, and to acquire the best of civilized knowledge. To test his theory that the social environment has the power to shape children's development, Itard devised an elaborate set of experimental training

Jean-Loup Charmel, Paris

Victor, the Wild Boy of Aveyron.

Jean-Loup Charmel, Paris

Jean-Marc Itard, who tried to transform the Wild Boy into a civilized Frenchman.

procedures to teach the Wild Boy how to categorize objects, to reason, and to communicate (Itard, 1801/1982).

At first, Victor, as Itard named the Wild Boy, made rapid progress. He learned to communicate simple needs as well as to recognize and write a few words. He learned to use a chamber pot. He also developed affection for the people who took care of him. But Victor never learned to speak or interact with other people normally.

After 5 years of intense work, Victor had not made enough progress to satisfy Itard's superiors, and Itard was forced to abandon his experiment. Victor was sent to live with a woman who was paid to care for him. Still referred to as the Wild Boy of Aveyron, he died in 1828, leaving unanswered the question of what factors prevented him from developing normally. Some modern scholars believe that Victor suffered from autism, a pathological mental condition whose symptoms include a deficit in language and an inability to interact normally with others (Frith, 1989). Others think that Itard may have been right in his belief that Victor was normal at birth but was permanently stunted in his development as a result of his social isolation (Lane, 1976). It is also possible that Itard's teaching methods failed where different approaches might have succeeded. We cannot be sure.

Victor's case became a focal point for debating fundamental questions about human nature and development: To what extent is development determined from birth? To what extent is it influenced by the surrounding environment? What is the role of early experience in shaping later development? Can the effects of negative experience be undone? Although 200 years have passed since the Wild Boy wandered into the village of Aveyron, these questions remain at the forefront of research on children's development.

Developmental Science

This book will introduce you to **developmental science,** a field of study that focuses on the physical, intellectual, social, and emotional changes that children undergo from the moment of conception onward. It is a rich and varied field, encompassing a wide array of theories and methods of study, and covering a broad range of children's characteristics. However, as Victor's story makes clear, the study of children's development has always been driven by two overarching goals. One goal is to understand the basic biological and cultural processes that account for the remarkable complexities of human development. The second goal is to devise effective methods for safeguarding children's health and well-being. These two goals come together in the popular idea, held by developmentalists and the public alike, that conducting scientific research can make the world a better place by fostering the development of its children (Hulbert, 2003).

The field of developmental science has advanced and broadened considerably since Itard's day. As we discuss below, for much of its history the study of children's development was dominated by psychologists. In recent decades, however, the study of development has become increasingly *interdisciplinary,* profiting from the insights of a wide range of disciplines, including psychology, anthropology, biology, linguistics, neuroscience, and sociology. The study of development has also become increasingly *international,* reflecting a growing appreciation of the importance of cultural contexts in the developmental process. In recognition of the broad

developmental science The field of study that focuses on the physical, intellectual, social, and emotional changes that children undergo from conception onward.

scope of modern studies of development, we use the term *developmentalist* to refer to those who contribute to our knowledge of children's development, regardless of their specific discipline or area of expertise.

Not only has the scope of developmental science widened, but so also have the pace and complexity of research. Part of the reason is important advances in technology. The ability to record children's behaviors with video cameras, to obtain images of their brain activity, and to analyze data with powerful computers has revolutionized the way developmentalists do research. Concerns about the welfare of children have also fueled the pace and complexity of research. These concerns have created new questions for researchers—questions on such wide-ranging topics as the influence of maternal stress and nutrition on fetal brain growth, the effects of neighborhoods on family dynamics, the risks attached to medicating children who experience difficulty in school, and the special challenges facing children of immigrant families in their attempts to deal with an alien culture and an unfamiliar language.

Advances in technology allow Dr. Charles Nelson to record how this 18-month-old child's brain changes in response to emotional expressions.

In addition to their roles as researchers looking for answers to these complex questions, developmentalists are often practitioners who strive to promote the healthy development of children. Developmentalists work in hospitals, child-care centers, schools, recreational facilities, and clinics. They assess children's development and make suggestions for helping children who are in difficulty. They design special environments, such as cribs that allow premature babies to develop normally outside the womb. They devise therapies for children who have trouble controlling their tempers, and they develop techniques to help children learn more effectively (Lerner et al., 2003).

Periods of Development

In their research, theorizing, and practice, developmentalists divide the time between conception and the start of adulthood into five broad periods: the prenatal period, infancy, early childhood, middle childhood, and adolescence. Each period is marked by major changes in children's bodies and in how children think, feel, and interact with others. Each is also marked by significant changes in how children are treated by members of their societies as a consequence of cultural assumptions and expectations about what children can and should be doing at different ages. Despite broad cultural differences in the particular tasks that children are expected to master, the institutions (such as school) that they are required to attend, and the rituals that they are made to undergo, most cultures organize the course of childhood in ways that recognize these five general developmental periods.

Domains of Development

As individuals move through each period of development, they undergo remarkable changes in several *domains,* or major areas of development: social, emotional, cognitive (intellectual), and physical. Although developmentalists are interested in the changes that take place within each of these four domains, they also recognize that development in any one of these domains is influenced by and influences development in the others. Consider, for example, how changes in the child's body, including size, strength, and coordination, permit increasingly efficient ways of moving around, exploring, and learning about the world. At the same time, the child's developing knowledge and interest in objects and people in the environment encourage even more exploration, providing additional opportunities for the body to develop greater strength and better coordination.

Michael Benanav

Jean-Marc Bouju / AP

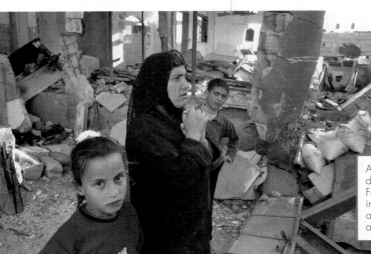

Teun Voeten / Panos Pictures

Contexts of Development

Those who work in the developmental sciences have never been more aware of the relationships between children's development and the *contexts* in which children live. As you will learn throughout this book, contexts of development, including physical environments, cultural beliefs and practices, families and peers, neighborhoods and communities, and institutions such as schools and governments, present children with both resources and risks that profoundly shape the course of their development. Does a child live with a single parent or in a large group of siblings, parents, grandparents, and other kin? Is the neighborhood clean and orderly, or impoverished, disorganized, and dangerous? Will the child attend school, or master skills through apprenticeship? Is it acceptable to spank children when they misbehave, or is physical punishment considered a form of violence that can result in severe psychological and emotional injury to both child and parent?

Answers to such questions begin to define the contexts of the child's development. As you will see throughout this book, researchers often compare children who experience or grow up under different conditions in order to understand the risks and resources provided by various contexts, and how they affect children's development. However, the effects of context are also apparent when children experience radical changes of context, as when divorce leads to family reorganization and a move to a new neighborhood and school, or when war, poverty, or oppression leads to emigration to an entirely new country with a new language, culture, and lifestyle. Thus, although developmentalists remain interested in the fundamental questions raised in Itard's day, it is clear that contemporary researchers, teachers, counselors, and other developmental practitioners are also responding to questions and concerns raised by social forces of our time.

According to the cultural-context framework, children's development is organized by their culture's "design for living." For these children living in Tibet, Rwanda, and Palestine, such influences as their culture's religious beliefs, educational system, and exposure to the consequences of war will significantly affect the paths of their development.

Children, Society, and Science

In order to appreciate contemporary developmental science fully, it is important to understand the cultural and historical forces that have shaped it (Valsiner, 2005). We begin our discussion by exploring beliefs about children, and how these beliefs changed over the course of time and set the stage for the emergence of developmental science. We then trace the history of developmental science from its early stages to its current state.

Historical Beliefs about Children and Childhood

Societies abound with different beliefs about the nature of children and their development. Such beliefs affect every aspect of children's lives, from what behaviors are expected of them at different ages to how they are disciplined, what skills and values they are taught, how they spend their time each day, and with whom they are allowed to socialize (Apple, 2006; Mintz, 2004). Beliefs about children and childhood also differ from one historical era to another. Even within the relatively short span of decades, the pendulum can swing from one view to another about what is good or bad for children, what they should or should not do, and how adults should treat them. For example, not long ago in North America it was thought that picking up crying or fussy babies would make them "spoiled" and demanding, whereas today such practice is considered a sign of positive and responsive caregiving. Likewise, until fairly recently children's play was thought to be important mostly because it promoted physical development. Consequently, children's playgrounds featured gymnastic equipment—ladders, climbing bars, swings. Now, however, play is believed to have much broader implications for development, and playgrounds are built to stimulate the mind and imagination as well as the body (Solomon, 2005).

For historians interested in how social beliefs about children have changed in recent centuries, there is a wealth of information to be found in child-care manuals, books, magazines focusing on parenting, and all sorts of child-rearing paraphernalia (clothing, cradles, toys, feeding utensils, baby-carrying devices, and the like). But such information is much more difficult to come by when it involves reaching back into bygone centuries before social beliefs could be easily preserved in print and the mass production of child-related objects.

THE DANGERS OF INFLATION—By BERNARD M. BARUCH

Ever since developmental science came to public attention, parents have relied on advice books to help them deal with the uncertainties of parenting. Shifting cultural fashions as well as new scientific knowledge have resulted in many changes in the advice parents receive. (Hulbert, 2003.)

Although merry-go-rounds, slides, see-saws, and swings remain popular, early playgrounds (a) emphasized physical play and motor development to the exclusion of all other developmental domains. In contrast, modern playgrounds (b) often include design features intended to foster creativity and social interaction.

(a)

(b)

Erich Lessing / Art Resource, NY

Figure 1.1 Artwork before the 16th century depicts children with adult-like body proportions and clothing, rarely engaged in play or youthful activities. Because age differences between adults and children, and even between younger and older children, are represented simply in terms of relative size, historians describe the period as embracing a "miniature adult" view of childhood.

Historians seeking to unearth beliefs about childhood during medieval times, for example, have had to rely largely on two kinds of sources: art and death reports. Each yields a somewhat different picture of how people viewed children and childhood.

In general, portraiture and other art suggest that before the sixteenth century people did not give much thought to children or their special needs. Many historians have concluded that during medieval times there was no understanding of childhood as a unique period of the life course, and children were considered miniature adults (Ariès, 1965). Accordingly, children were not provided with special toys or clothes and were not educated or cared for in ways that took into account their intellectual abilities and limitations. As illustrated in Figure 1.1, the miniature-adult view was expressed in the typical depiction of children as having adultlike body proportions, wearing elegant and fine, adultlike clothing, and engaging in serious-minded activities. In *Centuries of Childhood,* one of the best known books on the history of childhood, Philippe Ariès notes that artists of the time seemed "unable to depict a child except as a man on a smaller scale" (p. 33). The belief that adultlike capacities, desires, interests, and emotions are present in early childhood is known as *preformationism.* You will see in our discussion below that this belief persisted for hundreds of years, influencing scientists as well as the general public.

Reports written by coroners about the circumstances of children's deaths are a rare exception to the dearth of written documents hinting at social beliefs about children. Barbara Hanawalt (2000), an expert on families in medieval England, found that it was not uncommon for children as young as 3 to be entrusted with the care of little babies. Needless to say, 3-year-olds make poor caregivers, and infants in their charge sometimes died due to their inattention or inability to intervene appropriately when problems arose. It was also relatively common for parents to leave infants and young children entirely alone and unsupervised for extended periods of time while they did chores or worked in their fields. However, even if common, these practices drew criticism in coroners' reports that described young children as "bad custodians" of infants and explained the accidental deaths of unsupervised toddlers as caused by "being left without a caretaker" or being without "anyone looking after" them (p. 177).

A major turning point in the history of Western beliefs about children and childhood came in the sixteenth century with the Protestant Reformation, a religious movement of considerable scope. This movement swept through Europe and crossed the ocean to the "New World," beginning with the Puritans' voyage on the *Mayflower* in 1620. It was associated with harsher child-rearing practices, which followed from the belief that children are born in original sin. In contrast to the medieval Catholic Church, Protestant denominations generally held that original sin could not be washed away by baptism and that salvation would be possible only through obedience and submission to authority—first to one's elders, then to God. Because obedience naturally requires the suppression of individual goals and desires, parents were advised to adopt practices that would encourage compliance and limit arousal.

The legacy of Puritan ideas about children persisted for hundreds of years, as Martha Wolfenstein (1953) discovered when she analyzed manuals on infant care written in the early 1900s. The manuals urged mothers to wage war on their children's sinful and rebellious nature. Masturbation and thumb-sucking were of special concern because they involved "dangerous pleasures" that "could easily grow beyond control." Mothers were encouraged to use a variety of physical restraints, such as tying their children's feet to opposite sides of the crib to prevent their thighs from rubbing together and pinning the sleeves of their nightshirts to the bed to prevent their touching themselves. Stiff arm cuffs were sold through stores and catalogues for the purpose of eliminating thumb-sucking. It was even recommended that rocking cradles be replaced by stationary cribs in order to further reduce experiences that might be stimulating or pleasurable.

Cultural beliefs about children's development influence whether or not certain activities will be encouraged. This child is wearing a special glove manufactured to prevent thumb-sucking, which once was thought to be overly arousing and harmful to children's development.

Although evidence indicates that the idea of childhood as a unique period in development was already taking root in many societies, most historians agree that the modern notion of childhood emerged on a large scale in the late eighteenth and early nineteenth centuries as a consequence of the Industrial Revolution (Sterns, 2006). Taking shape initially in Western Europe and the United States, industrialization transformed the contexts in which children developed in three major ways. First, consistent with a shift from predominantly rural to more urban living conditions, schooling and/or factory work (depending on the family's socioeconomic status) came to replace family farm work as the child's primary social obligation. Secondly, the birthrate dropped significantly, altering family relationships both between parents and their children and between siblings. Finally, the child death rate plummeted, also with impacts on family relationships.

As historian Peter Stearns points out, these three changes were interconnected and had considerable implications for children's lives and experience. With increased schooling, for example, children became economic burdens rather than assets, so family size began to shrink. Increased schooling for girls, by helping to make possible new opportunities for women to work outside the home, played a special role in reducing family size. Beyond reducing the birthrate, girls' education contributed to declining child death rates, because it resulted in mothers' being more knowledgeable about how to ensure the healthy development of their infants and children. The schooling of all children reduced the authority of home and family, bringing children into more contact with other children and increasingly under the influence of peers and nonfamilial adults.

The sweeping changes of industrialization during the 19th century contributed to lengthening the years that most children spend in school, challenging educators to design developmentally appropriate and intellectually engaging curricula.

By the late nineteenth century the industrial age was well under way throughout the world, and children and childhood had begun to receive considerable attention from parents, educators, and scientists.

American Museum of Natural History Library

Charles Darwin and his son, William, who helped inspire his father's interest in the relationship between evolution and human development.

The Emergence of Developmental Science

An effect of industrialization was to drive millions of children to labor in textile factories. The conditions under which they worked became a matter of social concern and soon sparked the attention of the scientific community. The Factories Inquiries Committee in England, for instance, conducted a study in 1833 to discover whether children could work 12 hours a day without being harmed. The majority of the committee members decided that 12 hours was an acceptable workday for children. Others who thought a 10-hour workday would be preferable were concerned less with children's physical, intellectual, or emotional well-being than with their morals. They recommended that the remaining 2 hours be devoted to the children's religious and moral education (Hindman, 2002). Despite its dismal conclusion, this early committee was a start, and concern for children's welfare increased throughout the century as children became ever more visible to both the social and scientific communities.

Also crucial to the rise of scientific interest in children was the work of Charles Darwin. The publication of Darwin's *Origin of Species,* in 1859, set the scientific community on fire and ultimately led to fundamental changes in beliefs about children's development. If human beings had evolved from earlier species, then might not the different stages of children's behavior offer clues to stages of human evolution? It became fashionable, for example, to compare the behavior of children with the behavior of higher nonhuman primates to see if children went through a "chimpanzee stage" similar to the one through which the human species was thought to have evolved (see Figure 1.2). Although such parallels proved oversimplified, the idea that the study of human development is crucial to an understanding of human evolution won general acceptance (Bjorklund & Pellegrini, 2002). Because Darwin's theory of evolution continues to have far-reaching consequences for the way we think about and study children's development, we devote considerable attention to it in Chapter 3.

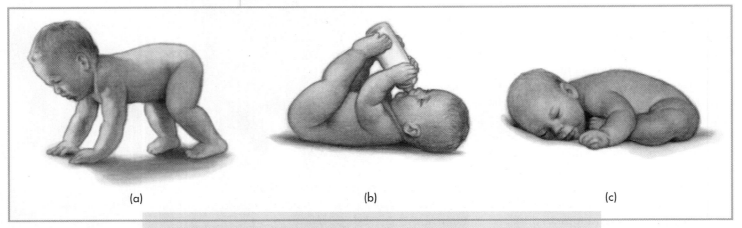

(a)   (b)   (c)

Figure 1.2 Early evolutionists scrutinized the motor development of children for evidence that it recapitulated evolutionary stages. Here an infant (a) crawls about on all fours like many animals, (b) uses its feet for grasping as primates do, and (c) sleeps in an animal-like crouch.

table **1.1**
Preyer's Rules of Observation
• Rely only on direct observations; avoid the reports of "persons not practiced in scientific observing."
• Record observations immediately so that details are not forgotten.
• Make every effort to be unobtrusive, to "observe without the child's noticing the observer at all."
• Avoid any "training" of the young child in order to observe "unadulterated mental development."
• If regular observations are interrupted for more than 1 day, another observer must be substituted, and his or her observations should be checked for accuracy. (Preyer observed and recorded his child's behavior two to three times every day!)
• Everything should be recorded, even behaviors that seem uninteresting at the time.
Source: Preyer, 1890, pp. 187–188.

In the exciting aftermath of the publication of *Origin of Species,* the study of child development grew by leaps and bounds. Some early developmentalists emphasized the importance of using scientific methods of observation to understand fully how the human mind changes over time. William Preyer (1841–1897), for example, wrote the first textbook on child development, proposing the rules of observation summarized in Table 1.1. Preyer used these rules in his examination of the development of emotion, intention, mind, and language. He was particularly eager to identify *sequences of behavior,* because he believed that they would show how new forms of behavior emerged from earlier forms, for example, how walking emerged from crawling. Preyer was also interested in understanding how the child's development was influenced by biological and environmental factors.

Whereas Preyer's greatest contributions to developmental science were his methods of study, other developmentalists focused directly on the process of child development and challenged existing beliefs about the nature of development. Holding a view reminiscent of preformationism, many scientists of the day believed that adult abilities are present and fully formed in the child, just waiting "off stage" for their cue. In effect, the "child mind" was defined in terms of the "adult mind." A striking reversal of this notion was proposed by James Mark Baldwin (1861–1934), who argued that children's abilities progress through a series of specific stages, taking on different forms and undergoing systematic changes before reaching their mature state. Baldwin's proposal represented the first of many *stage theories* of development that would emerge over the next century.

Still other developmentalists directed their efforts to practical applications. One of the best known of these was Alfred Binet (1857–1911), who developed methods of "mental testing" that eventually resulted in the first widely used intelligence tests—the Stanford-Binet. Binet firmly believed that careful testing could reveal individual differences in children's mental abilities and identify schoolchildren who could benefit from special instruction. His work clearly established the role of developmental science in addressing practical problems and issues.

The New Field of Developmental Science

By the early twentieth century, owing in no small measure to the efforts of these pioneers, the study of development had become a recognized field of scientific inquiry. Special institutes and departments devoted to the study of development began to spring up in major universities in the United States. As argued by Cora Bussey Hillis, a child advocate of the time, if research can improve the way we grow corn and raise hogs, why should it not also be used improve the way we bring up our children (Sears, 1975)? Concurring with this kind of logic, government agencies and philanthropic foundations began to support research on child development. Much of this work focused on exploring basic developmental changes over the course of infancy and childhood. But some research involved "special mission" projects on a wide range of topics, including highly gifted children and the effects on children of viewing motion pictures.

To this day, research on children's development continues to be motivated by the twin goals that were present at the discipline's origins: the scientific and philosophic goal of understanding how our biological and cultural heritages combine to shape our development as humans, and the practical goal of understanding how best to promote the health and well-being of children. We now turn to the central issues that continue to guide and inspire developmental science.

||||| **APPLY ━ CONNECT ━ DISCUSS** _

Thumb through some magazines containing images of children (you will likely find a lot of such images in magazines focused on parenting and infant care). How are the children depicted? Describe their clothing, the activities in which they are engaged, and the objects with which and people with whom they are shown. What do the images suggest regarding current conceptions of children and childhood?

The Central Issues of Developmental Science

Despite great variety in the work they do, developmentalists share an interest in four fundamental issues concerning the process of development:

1. *Sources of development.* What do genetic heredity and the environment each contribute to the process of development, and how do they interact?

2. *Plasticity.* To what extent and under what conditions is the course of development plastic, that is, malleable, subject to change as the result of either deliberate intervention or accidental experience?

3. *Continuity/discontinuity.* Is development a gradual, continuous process of change, or is it punctuated by periods of rapid change and the sudden emergence of new ways of thinking and behaving?

4. *Individual differences.* No two human beings are exactly alike. How does a person come to have characteristics that make him or her different from all other people and how stable are these characteristics over time?

Developmentalists' answers to these questions provide insight into principles of development, as well as guidelines for how to promote adaptive developmental outcomes.

Questions about the Sources of Development

What drives development? What, for example, ensures that virtually every human infant will develop the ability to walk on two feet? To use words to communicate with others? To form emotional bonds? What part of these processes is written in our genetic code, and what part is determined by our social and cultural environment? Such questions about the sources of development are often posed as a debate about the relative importance of "nature" and "nurture." **Nature** refers to the individual's inherited biological predispositions. **Nurture** refers to the influences on the individual of the social and cultural environment, particularly the family and the community, and of the individual's experiences. Much of the

nature The inherited biological predispositions of the individual.

nurture The influences of the social and cultural environment on the individual.

argument about Victor, the Wild Boy of Aveyron, was about the relative influences of nature and nurture: Was Victor incapable of speech and other behaviors normal for a boy his age because of a defective biological endowment (nature) or because of his social isolation (nurture)?

Modern developmentalists emphasize that development cannot be understood by considering nature and nurture in isolation from each other because the two are so closely intertwined, continually interacting and mutually influencing each other. Nevertheless, as you shall see, debates about the relative importance of genetic inheritance and experience as sources of development continue to preoccupy developmental science.

Questions about Plasticity

The second major question about development follows from the nature–nurture question and concerns **plasticity,** the degree to which, and the conditions under which, development is open to change and intervention. For different aspects of development, does our experience influence our development significantly or not much at all?

Early ideas about plasticity were influenced by the identification of certain "critical periods" in several nonhuman species. A **critical period** is a period of growth—in some cases only a few hours long—during which a specific kind of experience must occur or an ability or behavior will not develop. In other words, there is plasticity for the particular aspect of development only during this period. For example, in certain species of birds, chicks have a critical period just after hatching during which they become attached to the first moving object they see (usually their mother), which they will thereafter follow wherever it goes. This process is called *imprinting*. If the chicks are prevented from seeing any moving object for a certain number of hours after hatching so that imprinting does not occur, they fail to become attached to anything at all and may wander around alone. As you can imagine, chicks on their own have little chance for survival (Izawa, Yanagihara, Atsumi & Matsushima, 2001).

Examples of such "all-or-nothing" critical periods in any species are rare; in our own species they tend to be limited to specific periods of prenatal development. During the ninth week after conception, for example, the presence or absence of certain hormones will determine whether the fetus becomes male or female. Although there is little evidence of "critical" periods in human development after birth, there is abundant evidence pointing to "sensitive" periods (Gottlieb, 2002a). **Sensitive periods** are defined as times in an organism's development during which a particular experience (or lack of it) has a more pronounced effect on the organism than does exposure to that same experience at another time (Bruer, 2001). For example, children seem to be most sensitive to learning language in the first few years of life, easily acquiring any language to which they are regularly exposed. But even if they are not regularly exposed to language until the age of 6 or 7, it appears they are still capable of acquiring it. Thereafter, however, the risk of failing to acquire language increases (Newport, Bavelier & Neville, 2001).

plasticity The degree to which, and the conditions under which, development is open to change and intervention.

critical period A period during which specific biological or environmental events are required for normal development to occur.

sensitive period A time in an organism's development when a particular experience has an especially profound effect.

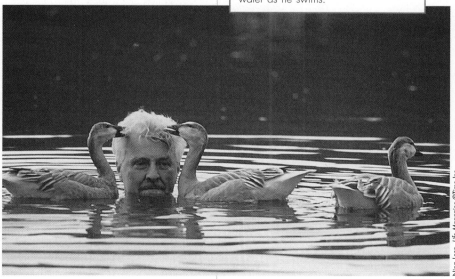

Ethologist Konrad Lorenz proposed the existence of a critical period in the development of newly hatched geese during which they form an attachment to the first moving thing they see. These goslings, which were allowed to see Lorenz rather than an adult goose when they hatched, follow him in the water as he swims.

Nina Leen, *Life Magazine* ©Time Inc.

As with sources of development, questions about plasticity have important real-world implications. The answers are essential to understanding whether and how a child's development can be modified through deliberate intervention, such as therapy or education, or affected by particular experiences, traumatic or otherwise.

Questions about Continuity/Discontinuity

Questions about continuity/discontinuity have to do with the extent to which development tends to be *continuous,* consisting of the gradual accumulation of small changes, and the extent to which it is *discontinuous,* involving a series of abrupt, radical transformations.

As a rule, developmentalists who believe that development is primarily a process of continuous, gradual accumulation of small changes emphasize *quantitative* change, such as growth in the number of brain cells, in memory capacity, or in vocabulary. Those who view development as a process punctuated by abrupt, discontinuous changes emphasize *qualitative* change, or new patterns of behavior emerging at specific points in development, such as the change from babbling to talking or from crawling to walking, or from the ability to reason only in concrete terms to the ability to reason hypothetically. Qualitatively new patterns that emerge during development are referred to as **developmental stages.** The contrast between the continuity and discontinuity views is illustrated in Figure 1.3.

The psychologist John Flavell (1971) suggests four criteria that are central to the concept of a developmental stage:

1. *Stages of development are distinguished by qualitative changes.* The change in motor activity associated with the transition from crawling to walking upright, for example, illustrates what is meant by a qualitative change to a new stage of development. Walking does not arise from the perfection of the movements used to crawl. Rather, the child undergoes a total reorganization of movement, using different muscles in different combinations.

2. *The transition from one stage to the next is marked by simultaneous changes in a great many, if not all, domains of the child's development.* The transition from crawling to walking is accompanied by a new quality of emotional attachment between children and their caregivers as well as the new forms of child–caregiver relations that the child's greater mobility requires.

3. *When the change from one state to the next occurs, it is rapid.* The transition from crawling to walking typically takes place within the space of about 90 days.

4. *The numerous changes across developmental domains form a coherent pattern.* Walking occurs at about the same time as pointing, the ability to follow the gaze of another, the child's first words, and a new relationship between children and their parents.

Supporters of discontinuity and the stage concept argue that the qualitative changes the child undergoes in each new stage alter the way the child experiences the world and the way the world influences the child. For example, infants are especially sensitive to differences in the sounds of language but they do not understand what is being said (Karmiloff & Karmiloff-Smith, 2001). Once they begin to understand and produce language themselves, the way they learn about the world appears to change fundamentally, and so does the nature of their interaction with others. The discontinuity represented by the child's active participation in conversation is so notable that in many societies it marks the boundary between infancy and early childhood.

developmental stage A qualitatively distinctive, coherent pattern of behavior that emerges during the course of development.

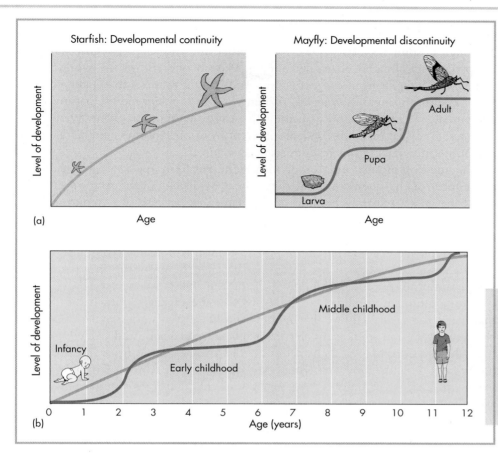

Figure 1.3 (a) The contrasting courses of development of starfish and insects provide idealized examples of continuous and discontinuous development. In the continuity view, development is a process of gradual growth (small starfish, medium-size starfish, large starfish). In the discontinuity view, development is a series of stagelike transformations (larva, pupa, adult). (b) Human development includes elements of both continuity and discontinuity.

Other developmentalists, taking the continuity view, counter that even in this experiencing of the world, continuity prevails. For example, Tamar Kushnir and Allison Gopnik believe that very young children are similar to scientists in the way they learn about the world. That is, young children seem to have *theories* that allow them to explain, predict, and understand other people's behaviors, and they modify their theories when their predictions are incorrect (Kushnir & Gopnik, 2005). In a similar spirit, Elizabeth Spelke and her colleagues have argued that infants perceive essentially the same world as adults (Condry, Smith, & Spelke, 2000).

One major problem for supporters of the stage concept is that contrary to their depiction of qualitatively consistent, across-the-board shifts in behavior and thinking, children often appear to be in one stage on one occasion and in a different stage on another. According to one influential stage theory of cognitive development, for example, 4-year-olds are in a stage in which their thinking is largely egocentric, making it difficult for them to see anything from a point of view other than their own. Consider 4-year-old Nyia, who wanted to give her mother a Bitty Kitty for her birthday. Nyia's birthday present choice indicates that she is, in this case, limited to her own perspective: She wants to give her mother what she herself would enjoy as a present, failing to see that her mother might rather have breakfast in bed. Yet when Nyia talks to her 2-year-old brother, she simplifies her speech, apparently taking the younger child's perspective and realizing that he might otherwise have difficulty understanding her. The fact that at a given point in development a child can exhibit behaviors associated with different stages seems to undercut the idea that being in a particular stage defines the child's capabilities and psychological makeup.

Questions about Individual Differences

Although in some respects you are like all other human beings, in many ways you are psychologically and physically unique, like no one else in the world. What makes you different from everyone else? And will the features that make you different endure throughout your life? When we try to understand the nature of development, we must take into account these two questions about individual differences: (1) What makes individuals different from one another, and (2) To what extent are individual characteristics stable over time?

The question of what makes individuals different from one another is really another form of the question about the sources of development: Are we different from one another mainly because of our nature or because of our nurture? For example, if baby Abdul is unusually fussy, is it primarily because he inherited a tendency to be easily upset or because his parents continually overstimulate him? If baby Soon-Jae becomes an accomplished pianist, is it primarily because she inherited musical talent from her parents or because she grows up in a family that values and promotes the development of musical skills?

The question of stability over time involves the extent to which the features that make you special endure throughout your life. Parents often remark that their children have been friendly or shy since infancy, but scientifically demonstrating the stability of psychological characteristics like these—at least from an early age—has proved difficult. One problem is that measures that seem appropriate for assessing psychological traits during infancy are not likely to be appropriate for assessing the same traits in an 8-year-old or in a teenager. Perhaps for this reason, many studies have found only moderate stability of individual characteristics in childhood (Caspi, Roberts, & Shiner, 2005). There is evidence that, for example, children who were shy and uncertain at 21 months of age still tend to be so at age 12 or later. Similarly, infants who rapidly processed visual information at 7 months of age still tend to be rapid processors at age 11 (Emde & Hewitt, 2001b).

The extent of stability of children's psychological characteristics over time depends in part on the extent of stability in their environment. Studies have found, for example, that children raised in an orphanage that provides adequate physical care but little emotional and intellectual stimulation tend to be lethargic and low in IQ. But if their environment changes—if they are adopted into caring families in their early years—their condition improves markedly, and many of them become intellectually normal adults (Clarke & Clarke, 2000).

The four major issues described above have endured for decades and continue to focus the research efforts of developmentalists. In the next section, we explore the major theories that developmentalists have used to help address these issues.

APPLY ═ CONNECT ═ DISCUSS

The central questions of developmental science are also reflected in the way parents and practitioners (teachers, counselors, and doctors) interpret children's behavior. Identify the central question (nature/nurture, continuity/discontinuity, individual differences, and plasticity) associated with each of the following common phrases.

"Oh, those terrible twos!"

"Don't worry. It's just a phase. She'll grow out of it."

"He's 2 going on 20," or "He's 20 going on 2."

"She's her own little person."

"Of course he's having trouble—his parents work all day and are never home."

"He's been moody since he hit puberty."

Now, drawing on your own experience, think of one or more similar phrases for each of the central questions.

Theories of Development

Many students roll their eyes at the idea that theories are needed to understand children's development. "What's so complicated?" they wonder. "Just observe children and let the facts speak for themselves." But, contrary to popular belief, facts do not speak for themselves. The facts that developmentalists collect add to our understanding of development only when they are brought together and interpreted in terms of a **theory,** a framework of ideas or body of principles that can be used to guide the collection and interpretation of a set of facts. Without the lens of theory through which to observe, we would not know what we were looking at, much less how to characterize it or what to make of it. At the same time, of course, data can be used to test theories, and theories are constantly being revised to better fit the data. In this way, data and theories go hand in hand, each shaping the other.

To see the role of theory, consider a hypothetical example: We observe a little boy running around a preschool classroom, hitting the other children and grabbing toys away from them. How do we interpret this instance of misbehavior? A theory focused on aggression might see it as uncontrolled aggression, whereas one focused on interdependency of group members might see it as the child's having failed to develop a sense of his dependency on others for his well-being. (In fact, for cultural reasons, Americans might tend toward the first interpretation but Japanese might tend toward the second.) The specific observations we make are likely influenced by our theory, as will be our prescriptions for dealing with this behavior.

The preceding example also illustrates a point made by Albert Einstein, namely that theory is present even when we think that we are "objectively observing" the world. We think of our theories as founded on observations, when "[i]n reality the very opposite occurs. It is the theory which decides what we can observe" (quoted in Sameroff, 1983, p. 243).

Einstein's point underscores the importance of theory. A deeper understanding of human development will not automatically come from the continuous accumulation of facts. Rather, it will come through new attempts to make sense of this accumulating evidence in the light of relevant theories. It also raises a caution: As developmental scientists, we need to keep in mind that our theories can bias, or distort, our observations. Throughout this book, you will see examples of both the power and potential problems of theories.

Theory in Developmental Science

There is no single broad theoretical perspective that unifies the entire body of relevant scientific knowledge on human development. Instead, development is approached from several theoretical perspectives that differ in a number of important ways:

1. *Domains of development under investigation.* A theory may be most appropriate for understanding the ways in which children develop cognitively, socially, emotionally, or physically, or it may explore some combination of these domains.

2. *Research methods used.* As you will learn in the next section, particular theories are often associated with particular research methods—observational, experimental, and so forth.

3. *Central issues addressed.* The major theories also differ in their approach to the four central issues we discussed above—the relative contributions of nature and nurture, the degree of plasticity and openness to change, the extent of continuity or discontinuity, and the stability of individual differences.

theory A broad framework or set of principles that can be used to guide the collection and interpretation of a set of facts.

We will begin our discussion of developmental theories by reviewing the "grand theories" that were developed when the field was relatively young. We will then examine several modern theoretical perspectives that the grand theories inspired.

Grand Theories

Most developmentalists would consider four theoretical perspectives to fall into the category of "grand theories"—the psychodynamic, social learning, constructivist, and sociocultural perspectives. These perspectives are "grand" not only because they laid the foundation for the modern theories of development that followed them, but also because they are "grand" in scope, each presenting a sweeping view of various domains of development.

Psychodynamic Theories **Psychodynamic theories** claim a significant place in the history of developmental science, having made the unique contribution of showing how universal developmental processes and stages can be understood by exploring the specific life experiences of particular individuals. Sigmund Freud was the first to develop a psychodynamic theory. Over the years, his theory has been adopted and modified by numerous developmentalists, including his own daughter, Anna. The best known of these modifications is probably that of Erik Erikson, in which culture, in addition to biology, plays a leading role in shaping the path of development.

Sigmund Freud. Trained as a neurologist, Freud (1856–1939) sought to create a theory of personality that would enable him to cure the patients who came to him with such symptoms as extreme fears and anxiety, emotional trauma, and an inability to cope with everyday life. Although many of these symptoms initially appeared similar to those of neurological disorders, Freud found that he could best understand his patients' problems by tracing the symptoms back to unresolved traumatic experiences in early childhood.

On the basis of the clinical data he gathered from his patients, including their recollections of the past and their current dreams, Freud constructed a general theory of psychological development that gave primacy to the ways in which children satisfy their basic biological drives, along with the method of treatment known as *psychoanalysis*. Influenced by Darwin's theory of evolution, Freud reasoned that, whatever their significance for the individual, all biological drives have but a single goal: the survival and propagation of the species. Since reproduction, the necessary condition for the continuation of the species, is accomplished through sexual intercourse, it followed for Freud that all biological drives must ultimately serve the fundamental sex drive.

Freud shocked his contemporaries by arguing that the behavior of children—even infants—is motivated by a need to satisfy the fundamental sex drive. As indicated in Table 1.2, beginning in infancy and moving through adolescence and the advent of adult sexuality, the form of sexual gratification changes, passing through an orderly series of stages related to the parts of the body upon which gratification is focused. Freud (1920/1955) held that each *psychosexual stage* is associated with conflicts between the child's desires and social prescriptions and expectations, and that the way children experience the conflicts at each stage determines their later personality. Perhaps the best known of such conflicts occurs during the anal stage when the child is socially required to control elimination. The strictness of "potty-training" and the severity of consequences for "accidents" have become the stuff of jokes in popular culture.

Another important contribution to understanding development was Freud's belief that the personality is made up of three mental structures: the primitive *id* is

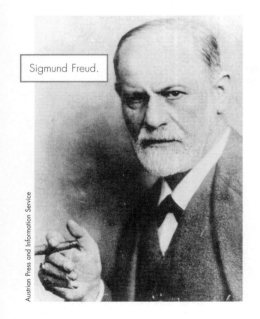

Sigmund Freud.

Austrian Press and Information Service

psychodynamic theories Theories, such as those of Freud and Erikson, exploring the influence on development and developmental stages of universal biological drives and the life experiences of individuals.

table 1.2

Freud's Psychosexual Stages and Erikson's Psychosocial Stages Compared

Approximate Age	Freud (Psychosexual)	Erikson (Psychosocial)
First year	*Oral stage* The mouth is the focus of pleasurable sensations as the baby sucks and bites.	*Trust versus mistrust* Infants learn to trust others to care for their basic needs, or to mistrust them.
Second year	*Anal stage* The anus is the focus of pleasurable sensations as the baby learns to control elimination.	*Autonomy versus shame and doubt* Children learn to exercise their will and to control themselves, or they become uncertain and doubt that they can do things by themselves.
Third to sixth year	*Phallic stage* Children develop sexual curiosity and obtain gratification when they masturbate. They have sexual fantasies about the parent of the opposite sex and feel guilt about their fantasies.	*Initiative versus guilt* Children learn to initiate their own activities, enjoy their accomplishments, and become purposeful. If they are not allowed to follow their own initiative, they feel guilty for their attempts to become independent.
Seventh year through puberty	*Latency* Sexual urges are submerged. Children focus on mastery of skills valued by adults.	*Industry versus inferiority* Children learn to be competent and effective at activities valued by adults and peers, or they feel inferior.
Adolescence	*Genital stage* Adolescents have adult sexual desires, and they seek to satisfy them.	*Identity versus role confusion* Adolescents establish a sense of personal identity as part of their social group, or they become confused about who they are and what they want to do in life.
Early adulthood		*Intimacy versus isolation* Young adults find an intimate life companion, or they risk loneliness and isolation.
Middle age		*Generativity versus stagnation* Adults must be productive in their work and willing to raise a next generation, or they risk stagnation.
Old age		*Integrity versus despair* People try to make sense of their prior experience and to assure themselves that their lives have been meaningful, or they despair over their unachieved goals and ill-spent lives.

present from birth and consists of biological drives; the *ego* begins to emerge in early childhood and is the rational component of the personality; and the *superego* emerges last and assures that the individual behaves in ways that are morally acceptable (we will return to a discussion of these structures in Chapter 9; see p. 314). These three structures are rarely, if ever, in perfect balance. The constant battle among them is the engine of developmental change, which Freud spoke of as *ego development*.

Erik Erikson. Whereas Freud's training was in medicine, Erik Erikson (1902–1994) combined his experience in psychoanalysis with his background in art, teaching, and anthropology. Erikson built on many of Freud's basic ideas of development but departed from him in two significant ways. First, Erikson emphasized social and cultural factors, rather than biological drives, as the major force behind development. Second, he viewed the developmental process as continuing throughout the life span rather than ending in adolescence (the age of sexual maturity).

Erikson believed that the main challenge of life is the quest for identity. Throughout their lives people ask themselves "Who am I?" and at each stage of life they arrive at a different answer (Erikson, 1963, 1968b). For Erikson, each *psychosocial stage* is associated with a particular main task, as shown in Table 1.2. Erikson referred to these tasks as "crises" because they are sources of conflict within the person. The person must in some way accomplish the task, or resolve the conflict, in order to move on to the next stage. The resolution may be more on the positive side or more on the negative side—for example, for the first stage, more toward trust or mistrust. A person's personality and sense of identity are formed in the resolution of these crises.

Erik Erikson.

social learning theories Theories that focus on development as the result of learning, changes in behavior as a result of forming associations between behavior and its consequences.

According to Erikson, each individual's life cycle unfolds in the context of a specific culture. While physical maturation writes the general timetable according to which the components of our personality develop, our culture provides us with the contexts in which we must resolve the crises and the tools with which we can resolve them.

Social Learning Theories As you will learn in later chapters, there are several types of social learning theories. However, all **social learning theories** share the basic idea that learning involves modifying behavior by forming associations between observable behavior and its consequences, favorable and unfavorable. In this respect, social learning theories are quite different from psychodynamic theories, which tend to focus on universal biological drives, the development of internal personality structures, and the resolution of inner conflicts.

In general, social learning theorists explore how certain experiences such as rewards, punishments, and other reinforcers change the likelihood of a child's engaging in a particular behavior. According to this perspective, rewards and punishments gradually shape children to become walkers, talkers, readers, and friends. Indeed, some social learning theories hold the extreme position that development is overwhelmingly the product of nurture—learning—alone. John B. Watson (1878–1958), a leading early theorist, was so certain of the primary role of learning in human development, and of the insignificance of other factors, that he boasted that he could use learning principles to train any infant, regardless of talents, abilities, or family history, to become whatever he wished—doctor or lawyer, even beggar-man or thief (1930, p. 104)!

Since development occurs through learning, developmental change is seen as being gradual and continuous. B. F. Skinner, another leading learning theorist, whose theory of *operant conditioning* is discussed on p. 147, compared development to the creation of a sculpture: The sculptor begins with a lump of clay and gradually shaves away material until the object is complete. In Skinner's words, "the final product seems to have a special unity or integrity of design, but we cannot find a point at which this suddenly appears" (1953, p. 91).

Benjamin Harris

John B. Watson and Rosalie Rayner conducted early experiments in which they induced fear in infants, which they subsequently sought to eliminate through learning. Such research, because it puts the infant at risk should the experimenters fail to extinguish the infant's fears, are no longer considered ethically acceptable.

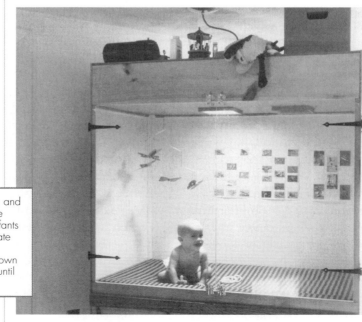

Sam Falk / Photo Researchers

B.F. Skinner designed his famous and controversial "baby box" to make infancy easier for parents and infants by providing a soundproof, climate controlled environment in which clothes were not necessary. His own daughter was raised in the box until the age of two.

Social learning theories have made a number of important contributions to the study of human development, two of which are generally associated with the work of Albert Bandura. One contribution is the concept of *modeling,* the process by which children observe and imitate others. As you will see in later chapters, modeling has proven to be particularly valuable for understanding children's gender role development. Another key concept proposed by Bandura is *self-efficacy,* people's beliefs about their own abilities to deal effectively with the environment (Bandura, 1974/1997). You probably know people who avoid taking on difficult tasks because they don't believe they are capable of doing them well. Or maybe you know people who have a huge amount of faith in their ability to master just about any challenge. Bandura would describe the first group of people as having low self-efficacy, the second group as having high self-efficacy. As we'll see later, in Chapter 9, a child's self-efficacy can have a dramatic effect on learning.

Among Albert Bandura's significant contributions to the discipline is his concept of modeling, in which children observe and imitate others. In the background, you can see a photograph of a child from one of Bandura's studies. After observing a model engage in similar behavior, the boy strikes a Bobo doll with a mallet.

Social learning theorists maintain that many aspects of personality, including personality problems such as aggression and dependency, are learned and therefore can be unlearned. This idea led to the development of *behavior modification,* a technique for breaking the associations between the behaviors and the environmental consequences that maintain them. For example, if a child engages in overly aggressive behavior in the home, a therapist might look into whether the parents were inadvertently rewarding the aggression, perhaps by giving the child a lot of attention. In order to break the association between the behavior and its rewarding consequences, the therapist might then set up a behavioral modification program in which the child is "timed out" for aggressiveness, thereby taking away the reward and substituting a punishment.

Piaget's Constructivist Theory

One of the most influential theories in the history of developmental science is Jean Piaget's theory of children's cognitive, or intellectual, development. Piaget (1896–1980) emphasized children's active role in shaping their own cognitive development. He argued in particular that children do not discover the world and the way it works, but *actively construct* reality on the basis of their experiences with the world. In Piaget's **constructivist theory,** then, gaining knowledge is a creative process of invention, not a process of discovering facts and truths. Children construct successively higher levels of knowledge by actively striving to master their environments.

Piaget believed that children progress through a series of stages of cognitive development (see Table 1.3), and he supported this idea through interviews and experiments. Each stage reflects a unique age-related way of understanding or organizing reality. Imagine, for instance, a 6-month-old baby playing with a set of wooden blocks. She may attempt to chew on some and bang them on the floor. The knowledge she constructs about the blocks—that they are better for banging than for chewing—is entirely different than the knowledge she will construct about them when she is 6 years old and can stack them or throw them at her brother. Another example of how children's stage of cognitive development affects their understanding involves age-related differences in how they tend to explain their parents' divorce. Younger children who, as noted, have a difficult time understanding the perspectives of others, may believe that they themselves were somehow at fault. Older children, in contrast, have reached a stage of development that allows them to understand the divorce from their parents' perspective, that is, in terms of their parents' relationship with each other.

constructivist theory Piaget's theory, in which cognitive development results from children's active construction of reality based on their experiences with the world.

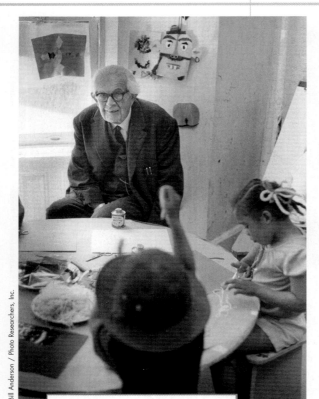

Jean Piaget, whose work has had a profound influence on developmental psychology.

On the basis of data from various cultures, Piaget (1966/1974) believed that development can be speeded up or slowed down by variations in the environment (such as the presence or absence of formal schooling) but that all children go through the same basic stages. In this important sense, a constructivist approach assumes that the processes of developmental change are universal, the same in all human groups.

In Piaget's view, the most basic unit of cognitive functioning is the *schema,* a mental structure that provides a model for understanding the world (Piaget & Inhelder, 1969). Over time, as children interact with their environment, they change—strengthen or transform—their schemas through *adaptation,* which involves processes Piaget termed *assimilation* and *accommodation.*

In *assimilation,* individuals incorporate new experiences into their existing schemas, strengthening those schemas. For example, in Piaget's view, infants have a primitive schema of sucking that enables them to draw milk from a nipple. However, sucking does not remain strictly bound to milk-yielding nipples. Soon babies are likely to find, say, a pacifier, instead of a nipple, touching their lips and start sucking on the pacifier—and in much the same way, as a pacifier is designed to be similar to a nipple. In other words, they assimilate the pacifier, a new object, into their existing sucking schema, which is thereby strengthened.

But pacifiers are not the only objects besides nipples that infants are likely to encounter. And many of these other objects cannot be assimilated into the infant's existing sucking schema. At this point, accommodation becomes relevant. In *accommodation,* individuals modify a schema so it can be applied to both old and new experiences. If an infant encounters her father's shoulder while she is being held, for instance, she may try to suck on it. However, because the qualities of dad's shoulder are so unlike the qualities of a

table 1.3

Piaget's Stages of Cognitive Development and the Sensorimotor Substages

Age (years)	Stage	Description
Birth to 2	Sensorimotor	Infants' achievements consist largely of coordinating their sensory perceptions and simple motor behaviors. As they move through the six substages of this period, infants come to recognize the existence of a world outside themselves and begin to interact with it in deliberate ways.
2 to 6	Preoperational	Young children can represent reality to themselves through the use of symbols, including mental images, words, and gestures. Still, children often fail to distinguish their point of view from that of others, become easily captured by surface appearances, and are often confused about causal relations.
6 to 12	Concrete operational	As they enter middle childhood, children become capable of mental operations, internalized actions that fit into a logical system. Operational thinking allows children to mentally combine, separate, order, and transform objects and actions. Such operations are considered concrete because they are carried out in the presence of the objects and events being thought about.
12 to 19	Formal operational	In adolescence, the developing person acquires the ability to think systematically about all logical relations within a problem. Adolescents display keen interest in abstract ideas and in the process of thinking itself.

nipple or a pacifier, she is unable to assimilate the shoulder into her sucking schema, and must make some accommodation to this new object. That is, she must modify the way she sucks, perhaps by choosing a bit of his shirt and sucking on that, using approximately but not exactly the same schema she had used to suck on a nipple. This transformation of her sucking schema makes it more effective, expanding the universe of suckable objects.

To summarize Piaget's theory, development occurs as the child acts on the world and searches for a fit between new experiences and existing schemas. A lack of fit leads to an imbalance, or disequilibrium, which is corrected through assimilation and accommodation. Piaget believed that this back-and-forth process of the child's search for a fit between existing schemas and new experiences creates a new balance in the child's understanding, which he referred to as **equilibration.** This process of achieving equilibrium between the child's present understanding of the world and his or her new experiences of it creates a more inclusive, more complicated form of knowledge, bringing the child to a new stage of development. Of course, this new balance cannot last for long because the process of biological maturation and the accumulation of experience/knowledge lead to new imbalances and to a search for a new equilibrium and a still higher, more inclusive level of adaptation.

As you will see in later chapters, contemporary developmentalists who follow in the tradition established by Piaget have refined or amended a number of his ideas. Nevertheless, these investigators agree with Piaget's emphasis on the central role of children's active engagement with the world and with his insistence that biology and the environment interact in contributing to developmental change.

Vygotsky's Sociocultural Theory At the same time that Piaget was building the foundation of constructivism, Lev Vygotsky (1896–1934), a Russian psychologist, was at work developing a sociocultural theory of development. Vygotsky agreed that biological and social factors both play a role in development and, like Piaget, believed that children construct their own development through active engagement with the world. But Vygotsky differed from others theorists by claiming that a third force—culture—is part of the mixture. According to Vygotsky's **sociocultural theory,** nature and nurture shape development, not by interacting directly, but by interacting indirectly through culture (Greenfield, Keller, Fuligni, & Maynard, 2003; Rogoff, 2003; Valsiner, 1998; Vygotsky, 1978).

The influence of culture on development can be seen in children's acquisition of mathematical understanding. The kinds of mathematical thinking children develop do not depend only on their ability to deal with abstractions (nature) and on adults' socializing efforts to arrange for them to learn mathematical concepts (nurture). They also depend on the children's cultural heritage. For example, children growing up among the Oksapmin, a group living in the jungles of New Guinea, appear to have the same universal ability to grasp basic number concepts as do children growing up in Paris or Pittsburgh. However, instead of using a formal number system to count, the Oksapmin use a system that refers to 27 specific parts of their bodies. To indicate given amounts, they point to their wrist, their elbow, their ear, and so on. This system would obviously be unwieldy if the Oksapmin had to solve arithmetic problems in school and later in a money economy like that of Western culture, but it is perfectly adequate for dealing with the tasks of everyday life in traditional Oksapmin culture (Saxe, 2002). Thus, culture contributes to the course of development because it is through culture that biological and environmental factors interact.

One of Vygotsky's most important contributions to understanding children's development is his concept of the **zone of proximal development,** defined as

According to Piaget, as a consequence of experience mouthing variously shaped objects, the infant's inborn sucking reflex is transformed into a more general schema. This results in more efficient nursing, and allows the baby to suck happily and well on other objects, such as pacifiers.

Lev Vygotsky, a prominent theorist of the role of culture in development, and his daughter.

equilibration The main source of development, consisting of a process of achieving a balance between the child's present understanding and the child's new experiences.

sociocultural theory The theory associated with Vygotsky that emphasizes the influence of culture on development.

zone of proximal development For Vygotsky, the gap between what children can accomplish independently and what they can accomplish when interacting with others who are more competent.

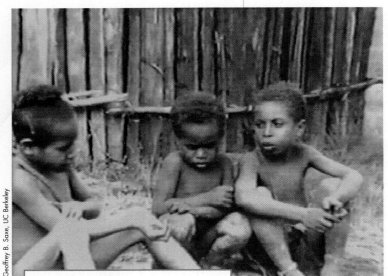

Geoffrey B. Saxe, UC Berkeley

Consistent with the mathematical system of his culture, the Oksapmin child on the left is indicating a number by pointing to a specific place on his body.

the gap between what children can accomplish independently and what they can accomplish when they are interacting with others who are more competent. The term "proximal" (nearby) indicates that the assistance provided goes just slightly beyond the child's current competence, complementing and building on the child's existing abilities. Consider the following scenario:

> Amy, almost 4 months old, is sitting [o]n her father's lap in a booth at the coffee shop. He is talking to a friend, and she is teething on a hard rubber ring. The father holds Amy with his left arm, keeping his right hand free. Twice he uses that hand to catch the ring when it falls from her grasp. When Amy dropped the ring for the third time, her father interrupts his conversation, rolls his eyes and says, "Good grief; not again." He retrieves the ring, puts it on the table, and resumes his conversation. Amy leans forward, reaching excitedly, but both her hands and the ring are covered in drool, and her baby hands and fingers are not yet well coordinated. Her father, still talking to his friend while watching Amy's lack of progress, tilts the ring upward so Amy can get her thumb under it. She grasps the ring, pulls it away from her father, and returns to her enthusiastic chewing. (Kaye, 1982, pp. 1–2)

Here you see that, even with an infant, adults can provide help that enables children to function effectively and learn. Notice that, in keeping with Vygotsky's notion of the zone of proximal development, Amy's father did not put the teething ring in her hand or hold it up to her mouth but, instead, tilted it upward so that she could grasp it herself. To help a child appropriately, the adult must know what the child is trying to do and be sensitive to the child's abilities and signals. Vygotsky attributed great significance to such finely tuned child–adult interactions throughout development. Indeed, as shown in Table 1.4, Vygotsky's theory is unique in its emphasis on social interaction as the primary source of development.

Modern Theories

The grand theories just described continue to exert tremendous influence on thinking about children and their development. At the same time, modern theories of development have generated new and distinctive insights into the fundamental issues that have concerned developmentalists since the field was established. Although the number of developmental theories has expanded significantly in recent decades, four kinds of theories have been particularly influential: evolutionary, information processing, systems theory, and critical theories. Because we will explore these theories in greater detail later in the book, we provide only brief sketches of each here.

Evolutionary Theories **Evolutionary theories** attempt both to explain human behavior in terms of how it contributed to the survival of the species and to address the ways in which our evolutionary past continues to influence individual development (Hernàndez, Blasi, & Bjorklund, 2003). As you will see in Chapter 2, according to evolutionary theory, species develop as they do because individuals with characteristics that favor survival in a particular environment are more likely to reproduce and pass those characteristics on to their offspring. Thus, human characteristics—physical, behavioral, and other—can be understood in terms of their role in contributing to the survival of individuals and the survival and evolution of the species. Of course, evolutionary theorizing about children's development has been around since Darwin. But it has recently emerged as a dominant perspective

evolutionary theories Theories that explain human behavior in terms of how it contributes to the survival of the species and that look at how our evolutionary past influences individual development.

table 1.4

Thumbnail Sketch of Grand Theories

	Psychodynamic Theories	Social Learning Theories	Piaget's Constructivism	Vygotsky's Sociocultural Theory
What develops	Freud: Personality structures of id, ego, superego Erikson: Personality, sense of identity	Patterns of behavior	Knowledge structures (schema)	Cultural knowledge and practices
Source of development	Freud: Biological drives Erikson: Social and cultural factors; tasks, or crises	Learning through social consequences (rewards, punishments)	Lack of fit between existing schemas and new experience (disequilibration)	Social interaction within zone of proximal development
Goal of development	Freud: Survival through sexual reproduction Erikson: Identity; moving through psychosocial stages	Socially appropriate patterns of behavior	Adaptation through balancing schemas and experience (equilibration)	Participation in cultural activities and practices
Main developmental domains addressed	Physical, social, emotional	Cognitive, social	Cognitive	Cognitive, social
Main research methods used	Clinical method	Experimental	Clinical method	Naturalistic
Main research designs used	Longitudinal	Microgenetic	Longitudinal, cross-sectional	Microgenetic
Special topics and applications	Sexuality, aggression, identity	Self-efficacy, gender roles, behavior-modification therapies	Reasoning and scientific thinking	Problem-solving, education

in the discipline, owing largely to advances in sophisticated technologies and research methods that permit more direct measurements of biological processes (see the box "High-Tech Research on Brain Development and Disorders," p. 35).

An evolutionary approach is central in **ethology,** which grew from the field of zoology, and studies behavior in different species in their natural environments (see the box "In the Field: Probing the Mysteries of Learning"). For this reason, naturalistic observation, which we will discuss later, is a major research method ethologists use. Ethology focuses on the development of behaviors that contribute to the survival of the individual and, by extension, the survival and evolution of the species. Consequently, ethologists are interested in how behaviors are adapted to the environment in ways that increase the likelihood that individuals will reach reproductive maturity to have offspring of their own. Ethologists look both at the adaptive behaviors of the young and at the behaviors they elicit in others, asking how both types of behaviors contribute to survival. *Imprinting,* discussed earlier, is an example of such behaviors: By becoming attached to the mother and following her around (and by the mother allowing this behavior), the baby chick is able to survive.

How do human infants and children, like baby chicks, elicit care from their parents? Clearly, human infants and children require considerable parental care and investment if they are to survive to maturity. From an evolutionary perspective, it makes good sense that caregiving should have a strong biological component. A question raised by ethologists is: What products of evolution do children possess that insures they will be cared for? One answer to this question (you will learn of others in later chapters) is found in the infant's appearance. Babies, as we all know, are *cute.* And this cuteness applies not only to our own babies, but to those of many other species. Kittens are cute; puppies are cute; baby lions and tigers and bears are all cute. Cuteness boils down to several key features of appearance, including a relatively large head; large eyes set low on the forehead; short, heavy

ethology An interdisciplinary science that studies the biological and evolutionary foundations of behavior.

In the field ▐ Probing the Mysteries of Learning

Name:	Elizabeth Vinson Lonsdorf
Education:	Undergraduate degrees at Duke University, including summer internships in Hawaii and Florida to study whales and dolphins; Ph.D. at the Jane Goodall Institute Center for Primate Studies at the University of Minnesota
Current Position:	Director of field conservation at Lincoln Park Zoo in Chicago
Career Objectives:	Participate in and support world-wide animal conservation projects

VIDEO CAMERA IN HAND, ELIZABETH Vinson Lonsdorf crouches among the trees of the Gombe National Park in Tanzania. The target of her attention is a mother-daughter pair of wild chimpanzees working to extract termites—a delicacy—from a termite mound. Chimpanzees use tools to gather their food—something that is exceedingly rare among animal species. From vegetation found nearby, they fashion a long tool that can be inserted into the depths of the mound. When the termites attack and cling to the "intruder," the chimpanzees carefully withdraw the tool and feast on the clinging insects. Primatologists refer to this process of foraging as "termite-fishing."

It has been known for some time that chimpanzees engage in tool-assisted foraging. What Elizabeth Lonsdorf wants to know is how chimpanzees learn to use tools in this distinctive way. Her interest is motivated by the understanding that, because chimpanzees are our closest genetic kin, their behavior may shed light on the activities of our earliest evolutionary ancestors (Lonsdorf, 2007). In her words:

I've always been interested in animal learning and tool use—especially the way young animals grow up and learn their way in the world. When you look at chimpanzees, it's so easy to see the link between humans and the rest of the animal kingdom. They make and use tools, conduct warfare, and have very similar mother-child relationships as humans. By studying chimpanzees, we can gain insight into what the activities of our earliest ancestors might have been like.

Her studies of chimpanzee behavior in natural environments suggest that young chimps learn termite-fishing by watching their mothers, much as an apprentice acquires a skills by observing a master. Although chimp mothers provide models of how to fish successfully for termites, and seem remarkably tolerant when youngsters interrupt their foraging with awkward efforts of their own, at no time were the mothers observed to deliberately teach their children how to fish. According to many evolutionary theorists, the deliberate teaching of the young may be a distinctively human trait (see Chapter 2).

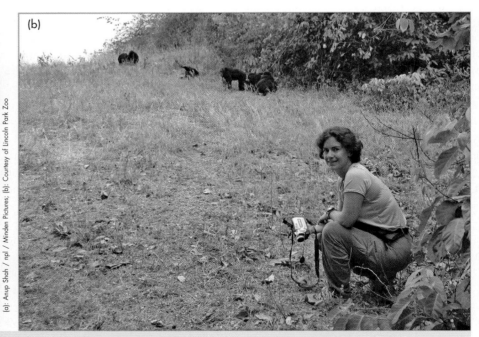

(a): Anup Shah / npl / Minden Pictures; (b): Courtesy of Lincoln Park Zoo

(a) The chimpanzee perched on this termite mound has just slurped ants from the stick used to "fish" them from the mound. (b) Elizabeth Lonsdorf is interested in learning how this tool-using practice, exceedingly rare in the animal kingdom, is transmitted to the young.

limbs; big, round cheeks; a button nose. While ethologists are interested in how these baby features attract the care and attention of others, marketers have used them to sell everything from cars (think VW Bugs) to cartoons.

Some of the other topics addressed by evolutionary theorists that you will encounter later in this book include the development of attachment, aggression and cooperation in peer interaction, and the development of intelligence and learning.

Information-Processing Theories The enormous magnitude of data transfer through high-speed computer technologies and communications systems leaves no doubt that we live in an information age. In addition to introducing significant changes in the ways that people work, live, and learn, the information age has inspired changes in how developmentalists think about the mind. In particular, some developmentalists describe mental functioning in terms of the workings of a digital computer—that is, by taking an information-processing approach to cognition and its development. **Information-processing theories** are concerned with how information flows through the child's developing mental system—how the child comes to process, store, organize, retrieve, and manipulate information in increasingly efficient ways.

As we discuss in more detail in Chapter 9, information-processing approaches distinguish between the "hardware" and "software" of intellectual functioning. In the case of a computer, hardware includes specific *structural* components where data can be stored and retrieved. These structural features set limits on information processing, including storage capacity and speed of processing. The software, on the other hand, includes all those various programs that have been written and loaded for the purpose of moving data through the hardware components, as happens in the process of storing and retrieving data. In the case of the mind, the hardware consists of certain brain structures and neural features, whereas the software consists of strategies and methods that individuals intentionally use to help them process and remember information. Examples of such strategies include rehearsing new information over and over for the purpose of remembering it and tying a string around a finger so as not to forget something.

As you will learn in later chapters, information-processing theories have been especially useful in understanding such topics as how attention and memory develop, how children build information into systems of knowledge, and how children develop and use problem-solving strategies.

Systems Theories As the name suggests, **systems theories** envision development in terms of complex wholes made up of parts—that is, *systems*—and look at how these wholes and their parts are organized and interact and change over time. The particular systems of interest vary. Some systems theorists focus on how specific behaviors of the child, such as walking, become organized and coordinated over time—for these theorists, the behaviors are the systems. Other theorists focus on more general systems, such as systems made up of the contexts in which children live (the family, the community, and so on) and of interrelationships among these contexts. Two types of systems theories have been particularly influential in the past few decades—*dynamic systems theory* and *ecological systems theory*. Despite the considerable differences between them, they share the view that development is best understood as a complex and unified system that is organized and reorganized over time. In the words of Esther Thelen, who devoted her career to exploring the application of systems theory to children's development, a complete understanding of development requires recognizing "the multiple, mutual, and continuous interaction of all levels of the developing system, from the molecular to the cultural" (Thelen & Smith, 1998, p. 563).

information-processing theories Theories that look at cognitive development in terms of how children come to process, store, organize, retrieve, and manipulate information in increasingly efficient ways.

system theories Theories that envision development in terms of complex wholes made up of parts and that explore how these wholes and their parts are organized and interact and change over time.

dynamic systems theory Theory that addresses how new complex systems of behavior develop from the interaction of less complex parts.

ecological systems theory Theory focusing on the organization and interactions of the multiple environmental contexts within which children develop.

Dynamic Systems Theory While information-processing theories have been inspired by computer science, dynamic systems theory has taken leads from physics and mathematics. **Dynamic systems theory** addresses how new complex systems of behavior develop from the interaction of less complex parts. Consider, for example, baby Ryan's ability to reach and grasp a toy that his older brother dangles in front of him. Ryan's reaching-and-grasping system emerged from the development and interaction of several visual and motor (movement) components. First, the visual component of the system must develop to a point that allows Ryan's eyes to follow and fix the toy in his field of vision. Second, the motor component of the system must develop the muscle coordination that allows him to engage in reaching movements with his arms and in grasping movements with his hands. Finally, the visual and motor components must interact in a unified system so that what Ryan *sees* (the toy) is successfully coordinated with what he *does* (reaches and grasps).

With development and experience, the components of Ryan's reaching and grasping will be coordinated into a stable and balanced system, and his reaching and grasping will become second nature, as it is for us. However, as you will learn in Chapter 4, reaching and grasping, as well as many other systems, are initially disorganized and sloppy approximations of what they will become. Dynamic systems theorists are interested in what sparks the beginnings of new systems and in how they develop from initial disorganization and instability to become smoothly functioning and stable.

Ecological Systems Theory The field of biology has been an important source of inspiration to ecological systems theory. *Ecology* is the subfield of biology that studies the relationship between organisms (plants and animals) and their environments. In developmental science, **ecological systems theory** focuses on the organization of the multiple environmental contexts within which children develop.

One of the most influential models of ecological systems was devised by Uri Bronfenbrenner. According to his model, shown in Figure 1.4, the developing child is at the center of a set of four nested, interacting systems:

1. The innermost system, the *microsystem,* includes all of the various settings that the child inhabits on a daily basis—the "face-to-face" settings of home, school, and peer groups.

2. The *mesosystem* is the connective tissue that links the face-to-face settings to one another, such as parents' involvement in their child's school. The strength and nature of these connections are important to children's development. For example, parents, teachers, and peers might be consistent with one another in supporting the child's academic success—or might be in conflict, as would be the case if the parents and teachers were pushing the child toward college but the peers wanted to form an indie-rock band and move to L.A. to play music full time.

3. Part three of Bronfenbrenner's model is the *exosystem,* consisting of settings that affect but do not usually include the child. An example would be the parent's workplace. If a parent's workplace provides good benefits, including good medical benefits and paid leave when children are born or are ill, the parent may be more likely to provide quality care.

4. The fourth and final part of the model is the *macrosystem*—the values, customs, hazards, and resources of the larger culture that shape what happens in all the settings of the systems nested within. The macrosystems of some cultures are very supportive of children's needs, and this may be

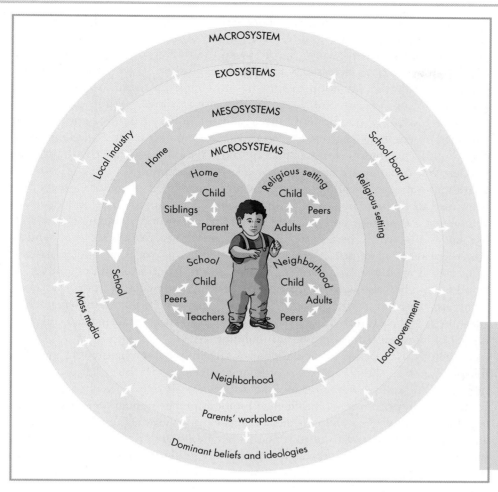

Figure 1.4 The ecological approach sees children in the context of all the various settings they inhabit on a daily basis (microsystems). These settings are related to one another in a variety of ways (mesosystems), which are in turn linked to settings and social institutions where the children are not present but which have an important influence on their development (exosystems). All of these systems are organized in terms of the culture's dominant beliefs and ideologies (the macrosystem).

evident from, for example, child protection laws and resources devoted to providing quality educational and child-care facilities and to ensuring access to health care. As we will see, values regarding such characteristics as race and ethnicity, socioeconomic status, and gender may seriously diminish the quality of care, nurturing, and interaction that children experience.

As in all other systems theories, the four systems here are understood to interact and influence one another. For example, a famous study of the Great Depression found that when the unemployment rate in the United States skyrocketed and parents lost jobs, relationships among family members deteriorated, parenting skills declined, and children's development and well-being were placed at considerable risk (Elder, 1998; Modell & Elder, 2002).

Critical Theories **Critical theories** are distinctive not only in the way they address development, but by the fact that they address—indeed, criticize—cultural biases that may be present in traditional developmental theories (hence the name "critical theory"). For example, feminist approaches explore the ways that both gender and a culture's beliefs about gender are an integral part of children's daily lives and dramatically affect children's development. In the developmental sciences, feminist approaches arose in response to the perception that traditional approaches emphasized the more "masculine" aspects of development. As we saw earlier, science inevitably reflects a society and its beliefs. Feminist theorists point out that developmental science has evolved in a society whose power structure favors men

critical theories Theories that address cultural biases that may be present in traditional developmental theories and that examine power relations between groups and the influence on development gender, race, ethnicity, and socioeconomic class.

hypothesis A possible explanation based on theory that is precise enough to be shown true or false.

and where characteristics that the culture sees as masculine tend to be more valued or simply focused on more. As an example of the feminist critique and approach, consider the following. According to the traditional theories, as children develop, they become increasingly independent of others. Developmentalists have devoted considerable attention to studying how children come to have thoughts and opinions of *their own* and to act on *their own* initiative, without being influenced by the thoughts, opinions, and actions of others. Feminist scholars argue that such an emphasis neglects the importance of connection and relationships to children's development—features that are more typically associated with girls and women, but certainly are far from absent in boys and men.

Although many critical theory approaches have focused on gender, others have been used to examine how race, ethnicity, and socioeconomic class influence development. All of these approaches share an interest in understanding how development is affected by social categories and institutions. In general, they tend to emphasize relations of power between groups—how power is distributed in a society, and how it affects children's physical, social, emotional, and cognitive development. They also agree that many traditional approaches to human development are biased towards studying the emergence of attributes (independence, autonomy, and so forth) that are more common to males than females, or more typical of Western than non-Western cultures.

None of the theories outlined above is sufficiently comprehensive to provide a full picture of all the complexities of human development. But each provides an important and unique frame for looking at certain aspects of development and for formulating **hypotheses,** or possible explanations precise enough to be shown true or false, regarding why children behave as they do, why they change over time, and what practitioners can do to support their health and well-being. In the next section, we explore the research methods typically used to test theoretical hypotheses.

▌▌▌▌ APPLY ▪▪ CONNECT ▪▪ DISCUSS ‒ ‒ ‒ ‒ ‒ ‒ ‒ ‒ ‒ ‒ ‒ ‒ ‒ ‒ ‒

Little Parminder is playing intently with wooden blocks. She puts one on top of another, and looks at her mother, who smiles, claps her hands, and exclaims, "Oh, aren't you clever? You got it on top! Are you a proud little girl?!" Parminder grasps another block and repeats her performance. She smiles broadly at her mother, who again responds with happy excitement. On the third try, however, Parminder topples her tower, and bursts into tears, scattering the blocks. "Poor baby! They fell down and now you're angry," says the mother. "Here, let me help you make the tower."

This scenario can be explored from several different theoretical perspectives. Considering the theories of Erikson, Vygotksy, and Piaget, what would you focus on? How would you interpret the scenario?

Methods for Studying Development

We mentioned previously that different theories tend to rely on different research methods for addressing questions and collecting information about human development. Indeed, the relationship between theory and method is of fundamental importance, and developmentalists take great care to ensure that one follows from the other (Valsiner, 2005). For example, it makes little sense to research children's memory development by collecting only quantitative information (e.g., changes in the number of words remembered from a long list) if, according to your theory, memory development proceeds through a sequence of qualitative stage transitions that are reflected in how memories are *organized*. Individual research methods, like the theories with which they are associated, provide only limited views that are often specific to particular developmental periods or domains. In the sections below, we examine the various goals of conducting research and the different methods by which those goals are accomplished.

The Goals of Developmental Research

Like any other scientists, developmentalists begin their research with particular goals in mind. The goals can range widely. Some seem "purely scientific"—for example, to determine whether the ability to perceive depth is inborn or learned, or to determine whether basic emotions develop universally in all children or emerge differently for children in different cultures. Other goals, however, are inspired by more practical considerations—for example, assessing the effectiveness of different kinds of violence-prevention programs in schools, or whether immigrant children learn better if they are instructed in their native language or in the language of the adopted country. It is helpful to consider three categories of research that differ according to the particular goals that motivate the researcher.

The goal of *basic research* is to advance scientific knowledge of human development. Although its results might be used to help solve practical problems, basic research is undertaken for the simple goal of gaining new knowledge, and it often explores major theoretical issues, such as questions of developmental continuity, plasticity, and sources of development.

In contrast to basic research, *applied research* is designed to answer practical questions related to improving children's lives and experiences. In many cases, applied research also extends basic scientific knowledge. Its primary goal, however, is to benefit society by generating knowledge that can be used in solving specific problems.

Action research is a close cousin of applied research. Also known as "mission-oriented research," action research is designed primarily to provide data that can be used in social policy decision making (Coghlan & Jacobs, 2005). For example, action research has played an instrumental role in programs and policies ranging from the Head Start program to federal regulations regarding the education of children with special needs, toy safety standards, requirements for foster care, and legislation concerning the prosecution of minors who have committed crimes. In contrast to basic and applied research, whose intended audience usually includes

Margaret Beale Spencer conducts basic research on how contextual factors such as minority group status, poverty, and neighborhood dangers influence the learning attitudes of African American youth. She then seeks out the coping mechanisms that such youth develop in order to improve their attitudes and subsequent success in important learning activities.

Sallie Motch is a psychologist with Doctors Without Borders, an organization that recently won the Nobel Peace Prize. She addresses mental stress and trauma issues with Palestinian youths in the area of Hebron in the West Bank. Developmentalists like Motch engage in action research to help government and other organizations develop scientifically based programs that protect children from harm and promote their well-being.

scientists and other developmental practitioners, action research is aimed at legislators and government officials and often meant to sway their opinions.

In recent years, developmentalists have been increasingly drawn to action research. To some extent, this is the result of a growing commitment and sense of social obligation on the part of universities to recognize and serve the needs of their communities better (Caldwell et al., 2005; Jason et al., 2004). Universities and communities across the United States and other nations are forging *university–community partnerships* around specific local issues. For example, the University of California at San Diego has created a charter school both to assist children from poor families that have never had access to higher education and to understand instructional formats that are most helpful to these children (Jones et al., 2002).

Although categorizing research can be helpful, it is important to recognize that the boundaries between basic, applied, and action research cannot be sharply drawn. For example, a research study on the effectiveness of Head Start programs is *basic* in the sense of addressing questions of plasticity such as whether intervention with disadvantaged preschools can have lasting effects on IQ, *applied* in the sense of seeking knowledge to improve the lives of socially disadvantaged children, and *action*-oriented in that its data may influence social policy decisions on program funding and development.

Criteria for Developmental Research

Whether engaged in basic, applied, or action research, developmentalists usually begin their work with commonsense observation and speculation. In this respect, they are like anyone else who might be trying to understand some interesting or puzzling aspect of children's behavior. The difference is that developmental researchers go beyond commonsense observation and speculation—as scientists, they must design research that meets certain specific criteria.

In this information age, in which we are flooded with words from all kinds of sources, it is vitally important to be able to separate casual observation and speculation from scientific evidence. In the aftermath of the Columbine school shooting in 2001 and the several "copycat" attempts that followed in its wake, TV talk shows, documentaries, and newspaper articles showcased a multitude of adolescent problem behaviors—teen violence, pregnancy, drug abuse, school drop out, and so on—and sounded a general alert that such problems were on the rise. Indeed, to the casual observer hearing or reading about teens whose lives had been destroyed by addiction, academic failure, or incarceration, the media glut on adolescent problem behaviors led easily enough to the conclusion that such behaviors must be increasing. Interestingly, however, this conclusion embraced by the media and the general public stood in stark contrast to a wealth of poorly publicized scientific evidence documenting marked *decreases* in adolescent problem behavior at the time (U.S. Department of Health and Human Services, 1999).

The relationship between social science and social issues is complex, as you will see in the chapters to come. For now, it is important simply to understand what distinguishes scientific evidence from speculation and causal observation. Four of the most common criteria used to judge scientific research are *objectivity, reliability, replicability,* and *validity.* Let us look at each in turn.

In a research study, data should be collected and analyzed with **objectivity;** that is, the gathering and analyzing of data should not be biased by the investigators' preconceptions. Total objectivity is impossible to achieve in practice because developmentalists, like everyone else, have beliefs that influence how they interpret what they see. But objectivity remains an important ideal toward which to strive.

objectivity The requirement that scientific knowledge not be distorted by the investigator's preconceptions.

Reliability refers to the consistency of the research findings. Research data should be reliable in two senses. First, investigators should get the same results each time they collect data under the same set of conditions. Second, independent observers should agree in their descriptions of the results. Suppose, for example, that investigators want to determine how upset infants become when a pacifier is taken from them while they are sucking on it (Goldsmith & Campos, 1982). The findings about the degree of an infant's distress are considered reliable in the first sense if the level of distress (measured in terms of crying or thrashing about) is found to be the same when the baby's sucking is interrupted under the same conditions on successive occasions. The findings are considered reliable in the second sense if independent observers agree on how distressed the baby becomes each time the pacifier is taken away.

Replicability, the third criterion, means that if other researchers independently create the same procedures as an initial investigator did, they will obtain the same results. In studies of newborns' ability to imitate, for example, some researchers report that newborns will imitate certain exaggerated facial expressions that they see another person making directly in front of them. However, using the same methods, other investigators have failed to find evidence of such imitation in newborns (see Chapter 6, p. 208). Only if the same finding, under the same conditions, is obtained repeatedly by different investigators is the scientific community likely to regard it as firmly established.

Of the criteria of scientific evidence, validity is in certain respects the most important. **Validity** means that the data being collected actually reflect the phenomenon that the researcher is attempting to study. A study may meet all the other criteria—it may be objective, reliable, and replicable—but still may not meet the criterion of validity, in which case it is of no value. Imagine, for example, a study of infant intelligence. The researchers may be using a particular scale to measure intelligence that is not biased by the researcher's preconceptions (it is objective), that produces the same results when given under similar conditions or when scored by different raters (it is reliable), and that can be used by other researchers to yield the same results (it is replicable). However, imagine that the scale used to measure intelligence is based on hair color. Obviously, hair color has no bearing on intelligence, so the study lacks validity and has no meaning, even though the other criteria have been met. Our example is extreme for purposes of illustration. A vast array of other examples that developmental scientists deal with regularly are much more subtle and controversial. There are, for example, researchers who claim that many laboratory studies of development lack validity because laboratory conditions are artificial and foreign to children's experience. Memory development, they might argue, is best studied in the everyday contexts in which it is used—contexts in which children remember their phone numbers, their friends' birthdays, to brush their teeth and say their prayers—not in sterile laboratory conditions in which children are required to memorize lists of random words.

Methods of Data Collection

Over the past century, developmentalists have refined a variety of methods for gathering information about the development of children. Among the most widely used have been *naturalistic observations, experiments,* and *clinical interviews.* (For a research method that has come to the fore more recently, see the box "Observing the Living Brain.") No single method can answer every question about human development. Each has a strategic role to play, depending on the topic and the goal of the researcher, and each has its advantages and disadvantages (Table 1.5).

reliability The scientific requirement that when the same behavior is measured on two or more occasions by the same or different observers, the measurements be consistent with each other.

replicability The scientific requirement that other researchers can use the same procedures as an initial investigator did and obtain the same results.

validity The scientific requirement that the data being collected actually reflect the phenomenon being studied.

naturalistic observation Observation of the actual behavior of people in the course of their everyday lives.

ethnography The study of the cultural organization of behavior.

table 1.5

Methods of Data Collection

Method	Description	Advantages	Disadvantages
Naturalistic observation	Observing and recording the behavior of people in the course of their everyday lives	Direct way to gather objective information revealing the full complexity of behavior	People might behave differently under observation; expectations may shape observations; information may be lost or time-consuming to analyze
Experiment	Introducing a change in a group's experience and measuring the effects	Best method of testing causal hypotheses	People may behave differently in the experimental setting, distorting the validity of the results
Clinical method	Asking questions tailored to the individual	Possible to probe the child's way of thinking, in order to discover patterns	Reliance on verbal expression makes the method inappropriate with very young children

Often researchers use a process called *triangulation,* in which two or more methods are combined to confirm their conclusions.

Naturalistic Observation The most direct way to gather objective information about children is to study them through **naturalistic observation,** that is, to watch them in the course of their everyday lives and record what happens.

For example, in a study of the role of play in the lives of young Mayan children in a remote farming village in southeastern Mexico, Susan Gaskins (1999) made "spot observations," recording what the children were doing at different times of the day in order to make sure that she captured the full range of their activities. She found that compared with children in the United States, young rural Mayan children spend a great deal of time observing the routine activities of adults and that at an early age they begin to take an active role in daily chores—gathering wood, hauling water, and helping to prepare food. As a result, Mayan children spend considerably less time engaged in pretend play, which is perhaps the dominant activity of young children in industrialized societies.

A special form of naturalistic observation is the **ethnography,** which attempts to go beyond children's naturally occurring behaviors to explain the *meanings* of those behaviors in light of the customs, beliefs, and values of their cultures. For example, researchers have documented how young infants born to the Efe foragers of the Congo's Ituri forest are routinely cared for by many people and are likely to be nursed by several women (Ivey, 2000). This pattern, which seems so at odds with Western ideas about child rearing, is essential to the Efe's foraging way of life and is accepted by Efe children as natural (Ivey, 2000). For the Efe, as well as all other cultural groups, nursing is not just a behavior that feeds an infant; it is a meaningful activity that expresses cultural customs and patterns of life (see

Because Mayan children spend so much time helping adults with chores, they rarely engage in pretend play. However, as illustrated by the two Mayan girls below, children have ways of being playful, even when working.

Russell Gordon / Danita Delimont

Observing the Living Brain

In the not-so-distant past, the only way to examine the brain was to surgically remove it from the skull. Neuroscientists, who study the brain and the rest of the nervous system, have been conducting postmortem research for more than a century in an effort to discover how the brain is designed, how it changes as we grow and age, and how it responds to injury. Although this research has generated a wealth of information on the anatomy, or *structure*, of the brain, it cannot tell us much about the *functions* of the living brain or give us precise information about the link between brain and behavior (Anderson, Damasio, & Damasio, 2005).

Although autopsy specimens continue to provide significant information about the brain and its role in human behavior and development, neuroscientists have benefited from the development of several new research technologies (Nelson, 2001). *Magnetic resonance imaging* (*MRI*) allows scientists to see brain structures in living patients. A scan using magnetic fields and radio waves provides input to a computer that uses the data to construct a three-dimensional image of the brain. The MRI has led to important advances in understanding the development and functions of different structures of the brain (Sowell et al., 2002). It has also helped clinicians estimate the risk of and diagnose at an early stage cer-

tain disorders, such as attention deficit hyperactivity disorder (ADHD) and childhood psychosis (Kumra et al., 2000; Rapoport et al., 2001). More recent technologies, including *positron emission tomography* (*PET*) scans and *functional magnetic resonance imaging* (*fMRI*) scans, have enabled neuroscientists to track the ebb and flow of brain activity under different experimental or disease conditions.

Neuroscience has been described as the "rising star" of developmental science, partly because of its contribution to the nature–nurture debate (Miller, 2002). For example, Helen

This brain scan of an 11-month-old child clearly reveals a large kidney-shaped cyst (the large red area) in the center of the baby's cerebral cortex. Seeing the cyst helps developmentalists to pinpoint its location and size and determine if surrounding brain structures are injured. This information is then used to assist them in devising a plan for treating the child.

Neville (2005) studied the brains of deaf children and found that areas of the brain typically devoted to processing auditory information gradually shift their function to the processing of visual information. Likewise, in blind children, areas of the brain that would normally process visual information shift their function to auditory processing. Neville's work demonstrates how the brain responds and adapts to different forms of sensory experience.

Mehan Kulyk / Photo Researchers.

Chapter 4 for a more detailed discussion of the relationship between culture and infant feeding practices).

Like all methods of data collection, observational research has limitations. It has been demonstrated, for example, that when people know they are being watched, they often behave differently than they normally would (Hoff-Ginsberg & Tardiff, 1995). In addition, despite their best intentions to be objective, research observers often have expectations about what they are going to see and may observe selectively in accordance with those expectations. Another limitation is that an observer cannot write down everything, so information is inevitably lost. Some studies therefore use prearranged note-taking schemes to specify what to look for and how to report it. Recordings of behavior on videotape or film can help preserve information, but they are extremely time-consuming to analyze. Despite their limitations, observational studies are a keystone of child development research and a crucial source of data about children's development.

Experiments A psychological **experiment** is used to study cause–effect relationships, that is, how changing one factor or variable (the *independent variable*) causes a change in another factor or variable (the *dependent variable*). Often times, the

experiment In psychology, research in which a change is introduced in a person's experience and the effect of that change is measured.

experimental group The persons in an experiment whose experience is changed as part of the experiment.

control group The group in an experiment that is treated as much as possible like the experimental group except that it does not participate in the experimental manipulation.

independent variable takes the form of a treatment condition or intervention, whereas the dependent variable takes the form of some behavioral change. To ensure that the change in the dependent variable is in fact caused by a change in the independent variable, and not some other extraneous factor, researchers randomly assign individuals to two different groups. One group, called the **experimental group,** is exposed to the treatment condition; the other, called the **control group,** is not. The two groups are then compared on the dependent variable(s) of interest.

For example, a researcher interested in whether a new drug can increase children's friendliness may go to a school, give all fourth graders a test of friendliness, and randomly assign each child into either the experimental group, which will receive daily doses of the drug, or the control group, which will receive daily doses of a placebo. After a predetermined period of time, the children will again be given the test of friendliness. If the researcher's hypothesis is correct, then the experimental group of children should show significantly higher friendliness scores on the second test, compared to the first test. In contrast, there should be no change in the test scores of children in the control group. (For a discussion of the challenges to determining causation, see the box "Understanding Causes and Correlations.")

Because they are conducted in controlled circumstances, experiments are often preferred in *basic research,* which, as we described previously, is intended to test scientific hypotheses about the causes of behavior. An example of how developmentalists can apply the experimental method is provided by a study that tested the hypothesis that premature babies kept in skin-to-skin contact with their mothers—a practice dubbed "kangaroo care"—will develop more successfully than premature babies kept in bassinets. The latter practice is currently the most common way of caring for premature newborns in locales where sophisticated incubators and highly trained nursing are scarce.

In this study, Nathalie Charpak and her colleagues (Charpak et al., 2001) worked with 764 low-birth-weight infants in a Colombian hospital serving primarily poor and working-class mothers. The infants had weighed 4.5 pounds (2000 grams) or less at birth and by definition were at risk for a variety of developmental problems. Half of the infants were randomly assigned to the experimental group, which received kangaroo care. The other half were assigned to the control group, which received the traditional care of being placed in a bassinet in warm, sanitary conditions.

In the short term, the babies assigned to the experimental group showed more regular breathing and quicker mastery of breast-feeding compared to babies in the control group. In the long term, the experimental-group babies showed significantly shorter hospital stays, less likelihood of illness or death, and faster growth rates. They were also quicker than the control group to reach important developmental milestones, such as raising the head spontaneously while lying on the stomach. These results help confirm the benefits of kangaroo care, which is increasingly being used in many countries around the world, including the United States (Kirsten, Bergman & Hann, 2001).

The clear strength of the experimental method is its unique ability to isolate causal factors. However, experiments also have limitations. One major drawback is that the very control of the environment that the experiments require may distort the validity of the results obtained. As we noted earlier, sometimes people behave differently in an artificial, experimental situation than they would normally. Children are particularly likely to behave unnaturally in an unfamiliar laboratory setting with researchers they have never met before. This, of course, raises doubts about the value of experimental results. When an experimental setting diverges so completely from children's natural environment that children behave differently

Figure 1.5 This South African mother is practicing kangaroo care, which, according to experimental research, increases the likelihood that her premature infant will develop normally.

Eric Miller / Panos Pictures

than they would ordinarily, the experiment is said to lack **ecological validity,** and the results cannot be put to proper use.

Clinical Method The research methods discussed thus far are designed to apply uniform procedures of data collection to every individual observed. In this respect, clinical methods differ fundamentally from the others. The essence of the **clinical method** is to tailor questions to the individual subject. Each question depends on the answer to the one that precedes it, allowing the researcher to follow up on any given question, verify his or her understanding of the subject's responses, and probe more deeply into the subject's thoughts and feelings.

The advantages of the clinical method are particularly evident in the work of Jean Piaget, whose use of the procedure laid a foundation for an entirely new way of understanding the intellectual development of the child. Piaget's goal was to provide an account of how children's thinking becomes organized over time. In one of his early studies, he used the clinical method to focus on how children's understanding of internal mental processes, such as "thinking" and "dreaming," changes as they grow older. In the examples that follow, note how Piaget adapted his questions to the flow of the conversation:

7-YEAR-OLD
Piaget: . . . You know what it means to think?
Child: Yes.
Piaget: Then think of your house. What do you think with?
Child: With the mouth.

11-YEAR-OLD
Piaget: Where is thought?
Child: In the head.
Piaget: If someone opened your head, would he see your thought?
Child: No.

[At this point Piaget changes his line of questioning to get at the child's conception of thinking from a different direction.]

Piaget: What is a dream?
Child: It's a thought.
Piaget: What do you dream with?
Child: With the head.
Piaget: Are the eyes open or shut?
Child: Shut.
Piaget: Where is the dream whilst you are dreaming?
Child: In the head.
Piaget: Not in front of you?
Child: It's as if (!) you could see it.

(Adapted from Piaget, 1929/1979, pp. 39, 54)

Piaget's probing interviews of these and other children revealed two age-related patterns of understanding what thinking is. For the younger child, thinking is a bodily process—the act of speaking. You can see it happening. In contrast, the older child conceives of thinking as a mental process, something invisible and unobservable. Piaget used such data to argue for stagelike changes in the way children understand and experience the world. He believed that not until the age of 10 or 11 are children able to understand thinking as an internal mental process. Younger children, even when given explicit hints and leading suggestions, are not able to express such an understanding:

ecological validity The extent to which behavior studied in one environment (such as a psychological test) is characteristic of behavior exhibited by the same person in a range of other environments.

clinical method A research method in which questions are tailored to the individual, with each question depending on the answer to the preceding one.

Understanding Causes and Correlations

When a window shatters after we have thrown a rock at it, we say that the rock *caused* the window to break. When a light comes on after we have flipped a switch on the wall, we say that the switch (or the electric current it activates) *caused* the light. **Causation** refers to a relationship in which one event (or factor) depends upon the occurrence of a prior event (or factor). In the physical and mechanical worlds of rocks and windows, switches and lights, causal relationships can be identified with relative ease and clarity. In the developmental and behavioral worlds of children, in contrast, identifying causal relationships presents real challenges.

To see the problem, suppose that children who get good grades (do well on a measure of school performance) also have high IQ scores (do well on a measure of intelligence). It might be tempting to conclude that there is a causal relationship between children's intelligence and their school performance—that is, that high intelligence is the prior factor that causes the exceptional school performance. However, another possibility is the opposite causal relationship—that is, working hard to get good grades might cause children's intelligence to rise. Yet another possibility is that some third factor—say, parenting behavior—is operating to cause both children's high intelligence and their school achievement.

As you can see, identifying the causes of behavior and development is not as straightforward as one might expect. Just because two factors occur together does not mean that one caused the other. Indeed, causation is often confused with **correlation,** a relationship in which differences in one factor (intelligence, for example) are associated with differences in another factor (school performance). Although experiments designed specifically to identify causal relationships are used to study children's development (see p. 35), the most frequent type of study by far is one that makes use of correlational methods.

Correlational methods involve measuring two or more factors and then analyzing whether variations in one factor are linked systematically to variations in another factor. If, for example, we are able to measure the quality of a child's relationship with parents, as well as the quality of the child's relationship with peers, we would be able to analyze whether variations (from high to low) in the quality of parent and peer relationships correlate with each other—that is, whether having good (or bad) relationships with parents correlates with having good (or bad) relationships with peers. The degree of association between factors is represented as a **correlation coefficient** (symbolized as r), a number that ranges from -1.0 to $+1.0$ and expresses both the strength (strong or weak) and direction (positive or negative) of the relationship. When $r = 1.00$, there is a *perfect positive correlation* between the two factors, that is, when one factor changes, the other factor changes in the same direction. In our example, a perfect positive correlation would exist when children who have good relationships with their parents also always have good relationships with their peers, and children who have bad relationships with their parents also always have bad relationships with peers. When $r = -1.00$, in contrast, there is a *perfect negative correlation* between the two factors, meaning that as one factor changes in one direction, the other factor always changes in the opposite direction. Thus, a perfect negative correlation between parent and peer relationships would mean that when the parent relationship is good, the peer relationship is inevitably poor, and vice versa. When two factors are uncorrelated, $r = 0$. Correlations, like people, are rarely perfect, and most correlation coefficients fall somewhere between 0 and $+1.0$ or -1.0, with weak associations producing coefficients that are close to 0 and strong associations producing coefficients closer to $+1$ or to -1.

Although correlational methods do not allow us to identify causal relationships, they do permit predictions, and for this reason they are highly valuable. For instance, correlational methods have generated a wealth of information regarding relationships between infant development and maternal behavior during pregnancy (diet, stress, smoking, etc.). The ability to predict developmental outcomes accurately from knowledge of maternal behavior allows us to identify "at-risk" infants and thus to initiate appropriate interventions early on.

causation When the occurrence of one event depends upon the occurrence of a prior event.

correlation The condition that exists between two factors when changes in one factor are associated with changes in the other.

correlation coefficient The degree of association between factors, symbolized as r and ranging between -1.0 and $+1.0$.

Four possible relationships between two variables: (a) As values of x increase, values of y increase, producing a correlation of 1.00. (b) As values of x increase, values of y decrease, producing a correlation of −1.00. (c) As values of x increase, values of y often increase, but there are some exceptions, producing a correlation of .84. (d) As values of x increase, values of y show a weak but noticeable tendency to increase, producing a correlation of .33.

5-YEAR-OLD

Piaget: When you are in bed and you dream, where is the dream?
Child: In my bed, under the blanket.
Piaget: Is the dream there when you sleep?
Child: Yes, it is in my bed beside me.
[Piaget writes: "We tried suggestion:"] Is the dream in your head?
[The child forcefully rejects the possibility]: It is I that am in the dream: it isn't in my head.
(From Piaget, 1929/1979, p. 97)

The strong point of clinical interviews is that they allow the researcher to follow, probe, and challenge the child's way of thinking in order to discover developmental patterns. But the clinical interview method has its limitations, most notably its reliance on verbal expression, which makes it inappropriate for use with very young children. This is especially the case in trying to assess children's cognitive abilities, since young children often understand things well before they can explain or even express their understanding.

Research Designs

Before conducting research, developmentalists must not only select a method of data collection but also develop an overall plan. This plan, referred to as the **research design,** describes how the study is put together—who will be included in the study, how and when data will be gathered from them, and how the data will be analyzed. A wide range of designs is used in the social sciences, although developmentalists tend to favor those that are best suited to the complexities of studying age-related change over time.

Here we will describe the four most basic designs that developmentalists use— longitudinal, cross-sectional, cohort sequential, and microgenetic (in later chapters you will be introduced to a few other designs). As illustrated in Table 1.6, each design takes the passage of time into account in a different way, and accordingly each has certain advantages and disadvantages.

The Longitudinal Design The **longitudinal design** collects information about a group of people as they grow older. For example, in a study of the stability of shyness, Jerome Kagan (2001) led a research team at Harvard University that traced the behavior of a group of children from shortly after birth into early adolescence. This study provided evidence that children who are shy and uncertain at 21 months

research design The overall plan describing how a study is put together; it is developed before conducting research.

longitudinal design A research design in which data are gathered about the same group of people as they grow older over an extended period of time.

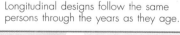

Longitudinal designs follow the same persons through the years as they age.

Courtesy of Sheila Cole (first four photos), Meredith French (last photo)

table 1.6

Research Designs

Design	Description	Advantages	Disadvantages
Longitudinal	Collects information about a group of people over time	Possible to discover patterns of continuity and change over time	Expense; long-term commitment may lead to selective dropout; risk of confounding age differences with cohort differences
Cross-sectional	Collects information about groups of various ages at one time	Relatively less time-consuming and expensive	Disconnected snapshots, requiring inferences about processes of change; if groups differ other than in age, risk of confounding age differences with those differences
Cohort sequential	Combines longitudinal and cross-sectional approaches by studying several cohorts over time	Age-related factors in change can be separated from cohort factors	To a lesser extent, disadvantages of the longitudinal and cross-sectional designs
Microgenetic	Focuses on development over short periods, especially when children are on the threshold of a change	Provides a record of change, revealing change processes	Limited to changes occurring over short periods of time

are likely to show similar traits in their behavior at 12 to 14 years. Without such longitudinal measurements, it would be impossible to discover if there is continuity in behavior patterns and personality traits as children grow older. Other longitudinal studies have dealt with such varied topics as personality, mental health, temperament, intelligence, language development, and social adjustment (Hussong et al., 2005; Troop-Gordon & Ladd, 2005; Shapka & Keating, 2005).

Because it examines development over time, the longitudinal design would seem to be an ideal way to study development. Unfortunately, several drawbacks of the longitudinal design restrict its use. To begin with, longitudinal studies are expensive to carry out. They also require the researcher's long-term commitment to ventures that can be highly uncertain: Some parents, for example, decide that they do not want their children to continue in a lengthy study, or they may relocate, making it difficult for the researchers to stay in touch with the children for later assessments. Such difficulties may be more common with one social, economic, or ethnic group than with others, resulting in *selective dropout,* which creates a biased sample that can greatly reduce the validity of longitudinal work.

Another weakness of longitudinal designs is that they are at risk of confusing differences related to age with differences related to cohort. A **cohort** is a group of persons who were born about the same time and who are therefore likely to share certain experiences that differ from those of people born earlier or later. In longitudinal research, these shared experiences may actually underlie differences that appear to be related to age. Suppose, for example, that a longitudinal study of the development of children's fears from birth onward began in London in 1932. In their early years, the children in this study would have been living through the economic hardships of the Great Depression. At the age of 9 or 10, many of

cohort A group of persons born about the same time who are therefore likely to share certain experiences.

these children would have lost one or both parents in World War II, and many others would have been sent away from their parents to the countryside in an effort to keep them safe from nightly air-raid bombings of the city. If this study found that the children feared mainly hunger in their early years and later, at around age 9, began to fear losing their parents, we could not determine whether these age trends reflected general laws of development, true at any time and in any place, or whether they were the result of children's experiences in this particular time and place, or both (Elder, 1998).

The Cross-Sectional Design The most widely used method for studying development is the **cross-sectional design,** which collects information about people of various ages at one time (see Figure 1.6, which shows the basic differences between the cross-sectional and longitudinal designs). To study the development of memory, for example, a researcher might test 4-year-olds, 10-year-olds, 20-year-olds, and 60-year-olds to see how well they remember a list of familiar words. By comparing how people in the four age groups go about the task and what the results of their efforts are, the researcher could then make inferences about developmental changes in memory processes. In fact, researchers have carried out a great many cross-sectional studies of memory development demonstrating both quantitative and qualitative developmental changes that we will examine in later chapters (Schneider & Bjorklund, 1998).

cross-sectional design A research design in which children of various ages are studied at the same time.

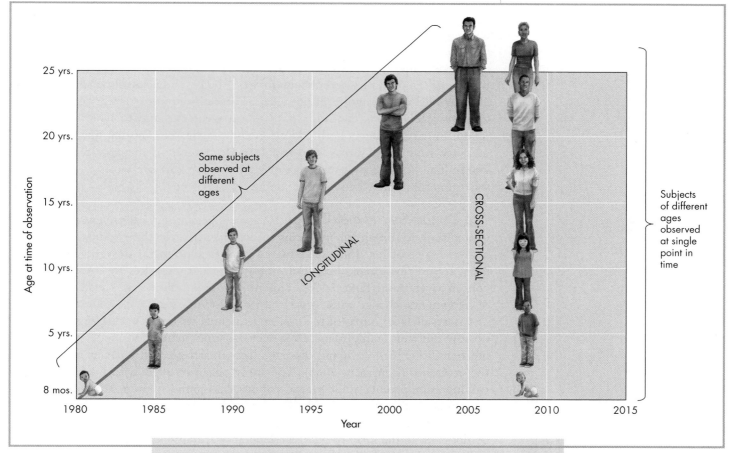

Figure 1.6 The difference between longitudinal and cross-sectional research designs

Because it gathers data on several different ages at once, the cross-sectional design is less time-consuming and expensive than the longitudinal design. The short time commitment required of the participants also makes it more likely that a representative sample will be recruited and that few participants will drop out of the study.

Despite these advantages, cross-sectional studies also have drawbacks. First, by looking at the behavior of different-age people at one time, cross-sectional studies slice up the ongoing process of development into a series of disconnected snapshots, and this is limiting. For example, researchers can contrast the general ways in which 4- and 10-year-olds remember a list of words, but cannot gain direct insights into the developmental process by which memory abilities and strategies change over time because their study is not following the same children over time. Consequently, when theorists make inferences about development on the basis of cross-sectional designs, they must engage in a good deal of extrapolation and guesswork about processes of change.

A second drawback to the cross-sectional design is that, for studies to be properly conducted, all relevant factors other than age must be kept constant. That is, the makeup of all the age groups should be the same in terms of sex, ethnicity, amount of education, socioeconomic status, and so on. If the groups are not the same, findings may reflect these differences rather than age-related change.

In addition, as with longitudinal studies, cohort effects are possible: With the cross-sectional design, differences between the age groups may reflect the groups' different experiences rather than age-related changes. Suppose that, in a study of memory development conducted in 2000, 70-year-olds performed significantly more poorly than 20-year-olds. These results might reflect a universal tendency for memory to decline with age, but they also might reflect differences in the participants' childhood nutrition. Early nutrition has been shown to affect intellectual development (Pollitt, 2001), and the 70-year-olds who were young during the Great Depression were likely to have had poorer nutrition than did the 20-year-olds who grew up in the 1980s. Furthermore, the 70-year-olds are likely to have received less education than the 20-year-olds and to have been out of school for a long time—both education and practice committing new material to memory have been shown to increase performance on memory tests (Rogoff, 2003). The possibility of such cohort effects means that great care must be taken when interpreting cross-sectional studies.

The Cohort Sequential Design Resources permitting, researchers can use various means to minimize problems associated with the longitudinal and cross-sectional approaches. Some have used a **cohort sequential design,** which combines features of longitudinal and cross-sectional approaches by studying several cohorts over time (Figure 1.7). This mixed design allows age-related factors in developmental change to be separated from cohort effects.

An excellent example of the cohort sequential design is Vern Bengston's study of how different family members as well as family generations cope with stressful life transitions such as aging, divorce, and remarriage, and changes in work and the economy (Bengston, 2005). The study began in 1971 with 300 families, including grandparents, middle-aged parents, and grandchildren, and now includes great-grandchildren as well. The longitudinal component allows Bengston to explore how individuals cope with life transitions over time, and the cross-sectional component, in the form of different generations, allows him to examine how these different cohorts adjust to the various transitions.

cohort sequential design An experimental design in which the longitudinal method is replicated with several cohorts.

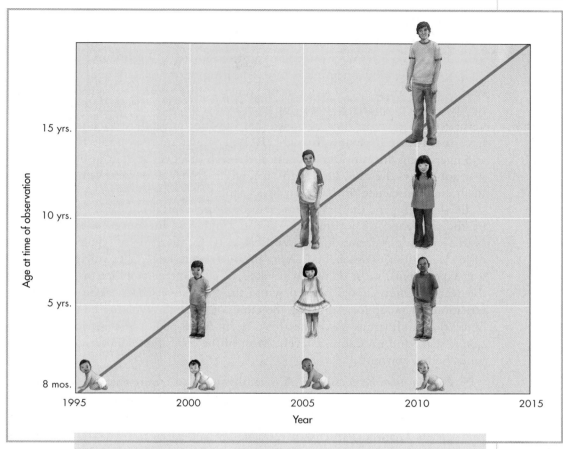

Figure 1.7 By combining features of longitudinal and cross-sectional approaches, the cohort sequential design allows researchers to distinguish between developmental effects and cohort effects.

The Microgenetic Design To try to get closer to observing change processes, developmentalists sometimes use the **microgenetic design,** which focuses on children's development over relatively short periods of time, sometimes only a few hours or days (Lawrence & Valsiner, 2003; Siegler, 2005; Vygotsky, 1978). As a rule, the microgenetic design is used to study children on the threshold of a significant developmental change such as being able to use a new memory strategy or a new adding strategy (e.g., calculating 6 + 2 by counting up from 6 instead of starting at 1 and counting all the way to 8). If researchers give the children concentrated experience in activities that are thought to facilitate the developmental change in questions (such as playing games that involve simple addition), they are sometimes able to observe the change as it actually occurs, thereby learning what factors contributed to it.

Robert Siegler (2005) offers a useful analogy for understanding the advantage of the microgenetic design. Whereas cross-sectional designs provide us with discontinuous snapshots of development, microgenetic designs provide us with a movie, a more or less continuous record of change. In later chapters we will encounter specific examples of what can be learned about children's development through microgenetic designs.

microgenetic design A research method in which children's development is studied intensively over a relatively short period of time.

institutional review boards (IRBs) Groups responsible for evaluating and overseeing the ethical soundness of research practices at an institution.

Ethical Standards

You can see from our discussion above that, in conducting research, developmentalists make a number of important decisions regarding theory, method, and design. The decisions they make have a bearing on the quality and value of their work, and its impact on developmental science. But research is evaluated not only for its scientific quality but also for its ethical soundness. Worldwide, many universities and governmental agencies that conduct research with human subjects have **institutional review boards (IRBs),** which are responsible for evaluating and overseeing the ethical soundness of research practices at their institutions. This was not always the case. Until fairly recently such decisions were left to the judgment and conscience of the individual scientist.

In no small part, the development of uniform ethical standards was prompted by the revelation of horrific experiments conducted in concentration camps by Nazi German physicians during World War II. In the name of science, thousands of Jewish, Polish, Russian, and Gypsy prisoners were forced to participate in medical experiments, most of which resulted in permanent disability or death. After the war, an international council wrote the *Nuremberg Code,* the first formal international standard for evaluating the ethics of research involving human subjects. Since then, numerous guidelines have been developed at the international, national, state, and institutional levels. Most of the ethical guidelines address certain fundamental concerns:

- *Freedom from harm.* Above all, scientists need to ensure that study participants will not be physically or psychologically harmed through their involvement.

- *Informed consent.* Participants must voluntarily agree to be in the study. This means that they must be given a reasonable understanding of what their participation entails, and that their participation must not have been forced, coerced, or based on inappropriate incentives (e.g., the offer of money to low-income participants or higher grades to students). With children, "informed" consent becomes more difficult because young children cannot really understand what their participation entails. Usually, parental consent is required, as well as consent from other child advocates, such as school officials.

- *Confidentiality.* Personal information obtained in the course of research must be kept confidential, that is, confined to scientific uses and not made publicly available in a way that might embarrass or harm the participant. Often, investigators will assign code numbers to the participants to ensure the participants' anonymity. However, investigators sometimes uncover a serious problem that threatens the well-being of the participant, as when a child reports abuse or seems suicidal. Under such circumstances, the higher ethic of the participant's welfare requires that the researcher break confidentiality and inform authorities who are in a position to intervene and protect the child.

Freedom from harm, informed consent, and confidentiality are not accomplished easily. This is particularly true in the case of children. For example, what may be psychologically harmful for a 2-year-old is quite different from what might be harmful for a 12-year-old. In recognition of the unique issues involved in conducting research with child participants, a special set of ethical standards has been devised by the Society for Research in Child Development (see *www.srcd.org*). Institutional review boards in the United States use these guidelines to determine the ethical soundness of all research on children conducted at their universities or agencies.

Your little brother brought home the following letter from school. Evaluate the scientific and ethical merits of the study described. Propose an alternative study that will address the issues.

Dear Parent or Guardian:

In response to the mayor's proposal to re-route a major highway past our elementary school, we will conduct a study of the relationship between road noise and learning in our students. With the assistance of Dr. Heezrite of Baloney University, your child, *Jonathan*, has been randomly assigned to the following group:

☑ During a lesson in mathematics, your child will be exposed to unexpected loud noises, similar to truck horn blasts, after which he/she will be given a test covering the content of the lesson.

☐ After a lesson in mathematics, your child will be given a test covering the content of the lesson.

Thank you for your cooperation in our effort to provide the best learning environment for our children.

Sincerely,

The Principal

Looking Ahead

In the chapters ahead, you will encounter many of the basic theories, methods, questions, and issues that we have outlined in this chapter. Across the five broad periods of child development—the prenatal period, infancy, early childhood, middle childhood, and adolescence—we will trace development in the physical, social, emotional, and cognitive domains. You will also come to understand how development throughout each period and within each domain is shaped by the child's interactions in a range of physical, family, neighborhood, and institutional contexts. To help organize the vast diversity of children's development, we will take a *biocultural approach,* emphasizing how biological and cultural processes intertwine over the course of childhood. Through it all, we will remain true to the two goals that have inspired developmentalists for centuries: the quest for knowledge and the desire to improve children's lives and well-being.

SUMMARY

- One of the earliest efforts in the study of child development involved Jean-Marc Itard's work with the Wild Boy of Aveyron. This unusual case posed fundamental questions: To what extent is development determined from birth, and to what extent is it influenced by the environment? What is the role of early experience in shaping development, and can the effects of negative experiences be undone?

Developmental Science

- Developmental science is an interdisciplinary field of study that focuses on the changes that children undergo from conception onward. Its two goals are to understand the basic biological and cultural processes that account for the complexities of development and to devise ways of safeguarding children's health and well-being.

- Developmentalists divide the time between conception and adulthood into five periods: the prenatal period, infancy, early childhood, middle childhood, and adolescence.

- Developmentalists look at the changes children undergo in several closely interrelated domains—social, emotional, cognitive (intellectual), and physical.

- Children's development is profoundly shaped by the contexts in which they live, including physical environments, cultural beliefs and practices, families and peers, neighborhoods and communities, and institutions such as schools and governments.

Children, Society, and Science

- Developmental science emerged and developed within historical and cultural contexts, including that of changing beliefs about children. In medieval Europe, children evidently were considered miniature adults. In the sixteenth century, the Protestant Reformation led to harsher treatment of children. Nineteenth-century industrialization fundamentally altered family life, education, and work, and changed conditions contributed to the rise of developmental science.

- Darwin's theory of evolution sparked scientific interest in children; by the early twentieth century, developmental science had become a recognized field.

The Central Issues of Developmental Science

- Developmentalists' research is focused on four fundamental issues:

1. *Sources of development.* How do nature and nurture interact to produce development? Developmentalists continue to debate the relative importance of biology and environment.

2. *Plasticity.* To what degree, and under what conditions, is development open to change and intervention? Plasticity is greatest during sensitive periods.

3. *Continuity/discontinuity.* To what extent does development consist of the gradual accumulation of small changes, and to what extent does it involve abrupt transformations, or stages?

4. *Individual differences.* What combination of nature and nurture makes individuals different from one another? To what extent are individual characteristics stable?

Theories of Development

- Theory plays an important role in developmental science by providing a broad conceptual framework to guide the collection and interpretation of facts.

- The grand theories laid the foundation, and each covers various domains; they include:

  - Psychodynamic theories—Freud's theory, in which psychosexual stages are associated with the changing focus of the sex drive, and Erikson's theory, in which psychosocial stages are associated with tasks or crises shaped by social and cultural factors.

  - Social learning theories, which focus on development through learning, behavioral changes resulting from the individual's forming associations between behavior and its consequences.

  - Piaget's constructivist theory, in which children, by striving to master their environments and searching for fits between their existing schemas and new experiences, progress through universal stages of cognitive development.

  - Vygotsky's sociocultural theory, which focuses on the role of culture in development and on children learning through finely tuned interactions with others who are more competent.

- Influential modern theories of development include:

  - Evolutionary theories, which look at how human characteristics contribute to the survival of the species and at how our evolutionary past influences individual development.

- Information-processing theories, which, using computer analogies, look at how children process, store, organize, retrieve, and manipulate information in increasingly efficient ways.

- Systems theories—dynamic systems theory, which focuses on the development of new systems of behavior from the interaction of less complex parts, and ecological systems theory, which focuses on the organization of the environmental contexts within which children develop.

- Critical theories, including feminist approaches, which look at how development is affected by power relations between groups in a society, and at possible biases in traditional theories.

Methods for Studying Development

- Research—whether basic, applied, or action research—must be designed to meet the criteria of objectivity, reliability, replicability, and validity. Research must also be ethically sound.

- Depending on their topic and goal, researchers use one or more methods of data collection, each with advantages and disadvantages:

  - Naturalistic observation involves watching children in the course of their everyday lives and recording what happens.

  - Experiments consist of introducing some change in a group's experience and measuring effects on the group's members, who are compared to a similar group that did not undergo the experience.

  - Clinical interviews allow researchers to tailor data collection to each research participant.

- Researchers also use several designs, or overall plans, intended to capture complexities of age-related change:

  - The longitudinal design studies the same children repeatedly over a period of time.

  - The cross-sectional design studies children of different ages at a single time.

  - The cohort sequential design combines the longitudinal and cross-sectional approaches by studying several cohorts over time.

  - The microgenetic design studies the same children over a short period, often one of rapid change.

Looking Ahead

- Taking a biocultural approach, which emphasizes how biological and cultural processes intertwine, the book will trace development in the physical, social, emotional, and cognitive domains across the periods of childhood.

Key Terms

developmental science, p. 4
nature, p. 12
nurture, p. 12
plasticity, p. 13
critical period, p. 13
sensitive period, p. 13
developmental stages, p. 14
theory, p. 17
psychodynamic theories, p. 18
social learning theories, p. 20
constructivist theory, p. 21
equilibration, p. 23
sociocultural theory, p. 23
zone of proximal development, p. 23
evolutionary theory, p. 24

ethology, p. 25
information-processing theories, p. 27
systems theories, p. 27
dynamic systems theory, p. 28
ecological systems theory, p. 28
critical theories, p. 29
hypothesis, p. 30
objectivity, p. 32
reliability, p. 33
replicability, p. 33
validity, p. 33
naturalistic observation, p. 34
ethnography, p. 34
experiment, p. 35
experimental group, p. 36

control group, p. 36
ecological validity, p. 37
clinical method, p. 37
causation, p. 38
correlation, p. 38
correlation coefficient, p. 38
research design, p. 39
longitudinal design, p. 39
cohort, p. 40
cross-sectional design, p. 41
cohort sequential design, p. 42
microgenetic design, p. 43
institutional review boards, p. 44

Each main section of this book begins with a table, similar to the one shown below, that lists some of the major developments you will learn about in the chapters that follow.

Major Milestones

	Physical Domain	Cognitive Domain	Social and Emotional Domain	
What Develops...	• These milestones relate to the physical body: how it grows, moves, and functions. • Examples: Growth and development of the bones, muscles, and brain; nutrition and sleep requirements of the changing body; hormonal changes and maturation of the reproductive organs; emergence of motor skills such as grasping and walking.	• These milestones relate to intellectual functioning. • Examples: Changes in attention, memory, problem solving; development of scientific reasoning, reasoning about moral issues, and language.	• These milestones relate to the child's social and emotional life. • Examples: Changing relationships with parents and peers; development of the ability to establish and maintain friendships; development of the ability to control emotions and their expression; changes in how the child understands and feels about himself or herself as a person and as a member of a social group.	
Sociocultural Contributions and Consequences...	• Here we highlight aspects of the child's social or cultural context that either contribute to specific developments in the physical domain or are significantly affected by those developments. • Examples: how modern life may affect children's sleep habits; how deprivation affects brain development; how the emergence of new motor skills, such as walking, may require caregivers to modify the child's environment for safety reasons; how the development of breasts or facial hair affects the way others treat the child.	• Here we highlight aspects of the child's social or cultural context that either contribute to specific developments in the cognitive domain or are significantly affected by those developments. • Examples: how formal education or other cultural institutions or practices facilitate certain types of cognitive development; how the social context can affect decision-making; how parents and others respond to intellectual growth by providing the child with increasing responsibilities; how cultural values support various forms of moral reasoning.	• Here we highlight aspects of the child's social or cultural context that either contribute to or are significantly affected by developments within the social and emotional domains. • Examples: cultural values and stereotypes regarding how boys and girls should behave; the conditions under which it is believed appropriate or not appropriate to express particular emotions; cultural support for developing an ethnic or sexual minority identity.	

In the Beginning

The development of every human being starts with the formation of a single cell at the time of conception. However, each individual is but a tiny drop in the vast stream of human life that reaches back through thousands of generations and across millennia. As a result, every human being is a product of the evolutionary past of our species—a past that includes both biological and cultural aspects.

Science views life as a process involving the constant interplay of forces that create order and pattern, on the one hand, and forces that create diversity and variation, on the other. The interaction of these competing forces is the engine of developmental change for the species.

What forces create order and diversity in human development? In Chapter 2 you will see that part of the answer to that question can be found in our biological and cultural heritages. Order arises, on the biological side, from the fact that all human beings share a finite pool of genetic possibilities, and, on the cultural side, from the fact that we all share general ways of learning, communicating, and forming social relationships. Diversity is ever present in the fact that each human being is genetically unique (except in the case of identical twins), and in the fact that each human develops through a unique sequence of experiences associated with the specific features of family life, peer relationships, local environments such as neighborhoods, and cultural values and traditions.

Whereas Chapter 2 focuses on the basic mechanisms of genetic and cultural transmission that enable both order and diversity in the ongoing evolution of our species, Chapter 3 narrows the focus to individual human beings, following development from conception to birth. The process of prenatal development illustrates many of the basic questions about development discussed in Chapter 1. For example, gene-environment interaction in prenatal development relates to questions about sources of development; changes that distinguish the organism five months following conception from the organism at five weeks or five days following conception relate to questions about developmental continuity and discontinuity; critical periods when the organism is highly sensitive to hormonal secretions and to such external agents as drugs and toxins relate to questions about plasticity.

After nine months during which the organism has grown and been nurtured within the mother's body, chemical changes initiate birth—and a radical transformation of the context of development. From the warm, dark womb, the baby crosses into a much richer and more varied environment, filled with new and constantly changing sights, sounds, and smells, and requiring new ways of moving, sensing, and behaving. Thus the cultural and biological forces that have shaped our species begin to orchestrate the development of a single individual, assuring that the newly born infant, while becoming like all other members of the species, will also be unique.

2

Biocultural Foundations

The volcano to the east was active. Its fires dominated the night sky and held the African savannah-woodland in an eerie twilight. By day, the sun barely penetrated the thick fog of smoke and ash, and the details of the landscape were muted by inches of ash that had settled on everything. Then a light rain fell, turning the ash underfoot into a firm, moist clay. Across this surface moved several figures—short, sturdy gray ghosts, fur caked with ash, surveying the world through dark eyes set deeply under thick, protruding brows. The footprints the passersby left behind hardened and were preserved and obscured by the falling ash of the volcano's continuing eruptions. They remained hidden for 3.5 million years, until they were uncovered by natural erosion and then discovered by a paleontologist named Andrew Hill (Leaky & Hay, 1979).

The discovery of these footprints at the Laetoli site in Tanzania is one of archeology's most fascinating finds (Figure 2.1). As any criminologist will tell you, footprints can provide crucial information about the people who left them. Here is what we know about those who left the famous Laetoli prints. Two individuals walked side by side at an unhurried pace. One was about 4 feet tall and weighed about 62 pounds; the other was about 4 feet 8 inches, weighing approximately 100 pounds. Perhaps they were adults, or perhaps an adult and a child. The smaller of the two apparently was burdened on one side by a small load (an infant?). At one point the larger individual turned east, toward the volcano, and then continued on with his or her companion. According to some analysts, there are traces of what may have been a child walking in the prints of the larger two. The most striking feature of the footprints is their resemblance to those of humans: They reveal a forwarding-pointing great toe, a well-rounded heel, a pronounced arch, and a striding bipedal gait. In short, the makers of these footprints walked upright, much as we do.

Although it is impossible to determine exactly *who* the walkers were, there is little controversy about *what* they were—members of the small-brained, apelike hominid species *Australopithecus afarensis,* the same species that produced Lucy, the celebrity skeleton discovered in Ethiopia that has helped us piece together our evolutionary past. *Australopithecus afarensis* lived from about 4 million years ago until about 3 million years ago and may be one of the most ancient ancestors of our species. Recently, a team of Ethiopian scientists undertook a painstaking process of unearthing another remarkable find—a nearly complete fossil of an *A. afarensis* infant that confirms what scientists have inferred from the Laetoli footprints and from bone fragments. *Australopithecus afarensis* had lower limbs much like ours and were capable of walking upright. Their upper body and upper limbs, however, had many apelike characteristics, including broad shoulders and long curving fingers that would have made them effective tree climbers.

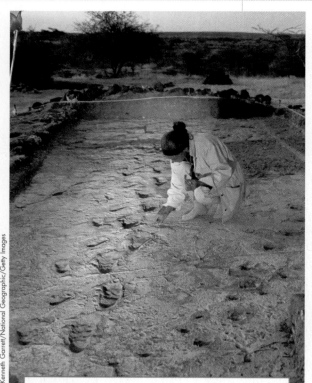

Kenneth Garrett/National Geographic/Getty Images

Figure 2.1 Scientists piece together the biocultural history of our species by examining footprints, skeletal fragments, and tools that have endured for millions of years. The famous Laetoli footprints of Tanzania provide evidence that the uniquely human trait of upright walking emerged 3 to 4 million years ago.

This illustration of a female Australopithecus afarensis carrying an infant is consistent with archeological evidence provided by the Laetoli footprints and skeletal remains of this ancient hominid species.

When we think about the baby fossil and the individuals who left their footprints in volcanic ash 3.5 million years ago, we have a host of questions that extend well beyond our interest in their physical bodies. Were these ancestors of ours generally peaceful or aggressive, solitary or sociable? If sociable, did they live in extended or nuclear family groups? How did they communicate with each other? How did they care for their young? How did they acquire and prepare their food? What risks did they face, and how did they protect themselves? How did they think? What did they feel? And how, from these early beginnings, did biological and cultural processes lead to modern humans and to the developmental path we take from childhood to adulthood?

This chapter will focus on the biocultural foundations of children's development—foundations that were laid in distant times that have left little but bone fragments, cave paintings, primitive tools, and an occasional footprint from which we try to piece together the cultural and biological history of our species, and how it is contained within each one of us. As you will discover, understanding these foundations can tell us a great deal about how and why all children tend to follow a common path of physical, intellectual, social, and emotional development. Indeed, the fact that they do so is something of a miracle when you consider the wildly different and fluctuating environments in which children grow up. Pierre lives in Paris, France; Apatite lives in a Pygmy hunter–gatherer group in the Ituri forest of South Africa. These two children move through their worlds in similar bodies, use language and tools, solve complex problems, and develop social relationships and strong, lasting emotional attachments. Notwithstanding these commonalities, Apatite and Pierre also are different from each other in notable ways—from their height and skin color to the languages they speak, the specific skills they learn, the cultural values and beliefs they adopt, and the types of knowledge about the world they acquire. As you will learn in this chapter, in addition to giving us insight into those aspects of development that all children share, an understanding of the biocultural foundations of children's development sheds light on the sources and significance of developmental diversity.

We begin this chapter by defining and discussing human culture and how it is inherited by each child. We then address the child's genetic heritage and its expression in the particular traits and behaviors the child develops over time. Throughout our discussion, you will see how culture and biology interact in the life of the child, contributing both to the universal pathways of development shared by all children and to the diverse developmental patterns that unfold in relation to the particular circumstances and life experiences of each individual child.

These two photographs record dramatically different cultural rituals in vastly different parts of the world: Holy Communion in France, and a Mbuti pygmy initiation ceremony in the Congo's Ituri forest. The biocultural foundations of children's development include aspects of diversity as well as features that are universal to all members of our species.

Inheriting Culture

Years ago, a team of researchers traveled to a small island in Japan to study macaque monkeys. Their work was difficult because the monkeys spent so much time in the forest, where they were hard to see. In order to lure the macaques into open space, the researchers scattered sweet potatoes on the beach. The bribe worked well, but more remarkably, this seemingly innocent ploy initiated a cascade of new behaviors that entirely changed the monkeys' patterns of daily life. First, a young female named Imo began to wash her potatoes in a nearby stream (apparently, she objected to the dirt that clung to them). Before long, her potato-washing behavior was picked up by other individuals in the group. As more time passed, the monkeys began washing the potatoes in the sea, rather than carrying them to the stream, and would even bite the potatoes first, presumably so the salt would penetrate and season them better (Figure 2.2).

There were other effects as well, and this is where the story gets really interesting. Mothers would carry their babies with them when they went to the sea to collect and wash the food. The babies began to play in the water—swimming, jumping, and diving. The males tended to hang out at the beach but did not participate much in the food preparation activities. They did, however, begin to eat fish discarded by the local fishermen and later began to collect fish and octopus from pools. Thus, the simple act of washing dirt from a sweet potato led to an entirely new pattern of life. The pattern persists to this day. And while baby macaques from this small Japanese island learn how to wash their food and play in water, human observers of their activities are learning much about the meaning of culture and how it influences development.

In simple fashion, the story of the macaques highlights the fact that culture is rooted in everyday activities such as acquiring and preparing food, caring for children, and children's play. It also shows that these activities are interconnected and organized over time, forming complex networks: Once the macaques were drawn out of the forest where they had previously spent

Figure 2.2 This Japanese macaque is washing sand from a sweet potato, a practice that has become part of the culture of everyday life on Koshima Island.

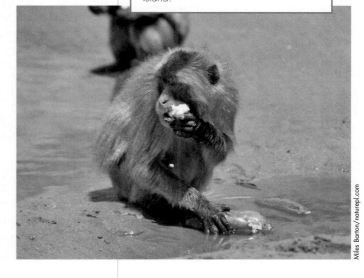

culture Material and symbolic tools that accumulate through time, are passed on through social processes, and provide resources for the developing child.

material tools Cultural tools including physical objects and observable patterns of behavior such as family routines and social practices.

symbolic tools Cultural tools, such as abstract knowledge, beliefs, and values.

most of their time, a whole range of activities gradually emerged related to the beach and the water. But while many developmentalists are willing to grant that nonhuman primate species, including macaques, have evolved some of the rudiments of culture, there is wide agreement that the human species is highly distinctive in how it has developed culture and the means by which it passes culture on to subsequent generations. Although there is a lot of debate about how to best define **culture,** most developmentalists agree that it consists of *material and symbolic tools that accumulate through time, are passed on through social processes, and provide resources for the developing child* (Cole, 2005; Rogoff et al., 2007; Valsiner & Rosa, 2007). We explain the meaning of this complex definition in the sections below.

The Tools of Culture

Several nonhuman primate species are known to use tools of various sorts to reach food, for grooming, or as weapons, and it has even been reported that some have made tools (Savage-Rumbaugh, Toth, & Schick, 2007). However, no other species even remotely compares to humans in the complexity of their tools and extensiveness of tool use. We are indeed a remarkable species in the extent to which tools and technology organize our behavior and modify our relationship to the environment. The briefest reflection should enable you to realize how infused your life is with tools and machines: indeed, there is probably not a moment in the day when you are not using or being affected by them.

Developmentalists recognize that all cultural tools include two principle features: the *material* and the *symbolic* (Cole, 2007) (Table 2.1). Although all tools contain both features, developmentalists may refer to **material tools** when the focus is on *physical objects* (everything from abacuses and axes to zithers and Zip drives) but also *observable patterns of behavior*, such as family routines (how children are "put to bed," how the family organizes dinner time) and social practices (how children are educated, how they celebrate their birthdays). The environment of each and every child is saturated with material tools, which vary from one culture to the next. Born in the countryside of Japan, Kojima lives in a small house with paper walls (shoji screens) separating the rooms. As an infant, he is tightly wrapped in swaddling clothes and sleeps on a mat with his parents; he will never be placed in

Participating in a documentary focused on cultural differences, these two families—one from Japan, the other from Mali—have assembled all their material possessions in front of their homes. As you can see, the material tools of culture reflect enormous differences in how the two families spend their time.

Peter Menzel. Material World: A Global Family Portrait Project

table 2.1

Examples of Cultural Tools

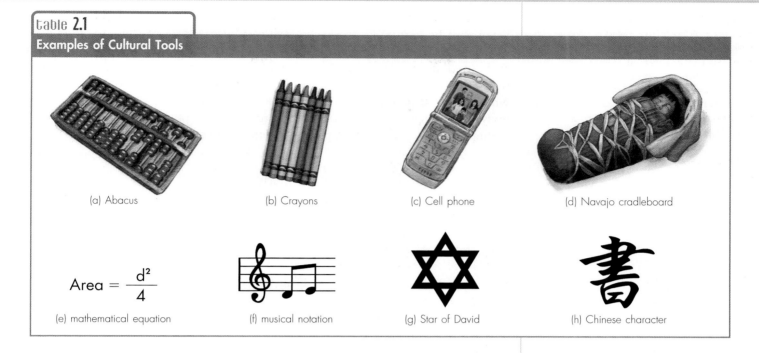

(a) Abacus   (b) Crayons   (c) Cell phone   (d) Navajo cradleboard

$$\text{Area} = \frac{d^2}{4}$$

(e) mathematical equation   (f) musical notation   (g) Star of David   (h) Chinese character

a crib. During mealtimes, he will not be put in a high chair or use a "tippy cup" but will sit in his mother's or older sister's lap and be helped to use "adult" eating utensils. His mother will never use an electronic baby monitor to keep tabs on him during his naptime but will carry him on her back most of the day while she works in the house and the garden. Clearly, the material tools of Kojima's culture influence his behavior and how he interacts with others (Jenkins, 1998; Enfield & Levinson, 2006).

In contrast to focusing on the concrete, material aspects of tools, developmentalists may refer to **symbolic tools** when they want to explore how abstract knowledge, beliefs, and values affect development. For example, Kojima will spend much of his time in school learning mathematics, a symbol system that he ultimately will use in a variety of ways—from measuring the wood for a new tool shed to eventually keeping the books for his family's business. Kojima will also learn his culture's expectations for masculinity and sexuality, including how certain ways of acting and speaking symbolize that he is "male." Raised within the Shinto spiritual tradition, he will come to believe that nature is sacred, that family should be honored, and that physical cleanliness is essential to the purity of spirit. All of these symbolic tools of Kojima's culture—mathematics, gender expectations, religious belief systems—will affect his intellectual, social, and emotional development. As should now be clear, all tools of culture are material and symbolic at the same time. For example, when Kojima accompanies his family to bathe in the river several times a week, he is both engaging in an observable pattern of behavior (an aspect of material culture) and expressing his belief that, as he cleanses his body, he is purifying his spirit (an aspect of symbolic culture).

As they use and acquire the material and symbolic tools of their Shinto religion, these young boys will come to honor family traditions and believe in the sacredness of the natural world.

Chris Steele-Perkins/Magnum Photos

mediation How cultural tools organize people's activities and ways of relating to their environments.

social enhancement The most basic social process of learning to use cultural resources, in which resources are used simply because others' activities have made them available in the immediate environment.

imitation The social process through which children learn to use their culture's resources by observing and copying the behaviors of others.

explicit instruction The social process in which children are purposefully taught to use the resources of their culture.

The material and symbolic tools of a culture have pronounced effects on development because they *organize children's activities and the way they relate to their environments*. Developmentalists call the organization of activity through the use of tools **mediation.** The idea that material and symbolic tools mediate children's behavior and affect their development is at the heart of debates that range from whether toy guns promote aggressive behavior and Barbie dolls promote poor body image to whether the increase in students' disruptive classroom behavior is a symptom of a culture's collapsing educational values.

Processes of Cultural Inheritance

When developmentalists say that material and symbolic tools accumulate over time and are passed on through social processes, thus providing resources for the developing child, they are making claims about how culture is transmitted and transformed from one generation to the next (Rogoff et al., 2007).

Social Processes of Cultural Inheritance

Children inherit culture—that is, they learn to use their culture's material and symbolic resources—through several *social processes*. The most basic of these process is **social enhancement,** in which children use cultural resources simply because the activities of others make these resources available in the immediate environment (Richerson & Boyd, 2005). For example, when 18-month-old Tahira, who has never seen a crayon before, finds one on the family room floor and rubs it on the wall, she is learning through social enhancement that crayons are tools for marking surfaces. The other two processes through which children inherit culture are more complex forms of learning. When children learn by observing and copying the behaviors of others, they are using the social process of **imitation,** which we will describe in more detail in later chapters. When children are purposefully taught to use the material and symbolic resources of their culture, they are learning by **explicit instruction.**

Explicit instruction is the most complex way of inheriting culture for two related reasons. First, unlike social enhancement and imitation, explicit instruction uses *symbolic communication*. The most obvious examples of symbolic communication are written and spoken language, but it also includes drawing, art, and music. Second, because it uses symbolic communication, explicit instruction makes it possible to teach children about things that are not present in their immediate environments. We use history books to teach children about the past; we use stories to teach them moral lessons to apply in the future; we use math to teach children calculations they later can use to figure the number of minutes remaining in their cell phone accounts. With social enhancement and imitation, in contrast, the information learned by the child must be directly available in the child's environment. Researchers have argued that while Imo and her clan may have used these less complex forms to transmit the cultural practice of washing sand from potatoes, cultural transmission by way of explicit instruction is uniquely human.

The Special Role of Symbols and Language

In addition to making it possible to teach children about things that are not immediately present in the environment, symbolic communication permits the expression of abstract ideas, desires, ambitions, and emotions. With astronomical diagrams, for example, we can chart the locations and movement of planets; through music, art, and poetry, we can express an infinite range of thoughts and feelings, both real and imagined; and through our stories and myths, we can learn and convey cultural values and beliefs and an understanding of our relationships to one another and the worlds in which we live. Clearly, symbols and symbolic systems are of tremendous importance to the culture-acquiring child. Symbols in the form of diagrams and stories, no less than toy guns and pencils, are cultural tools. Like all cultural tools, they mediate children's activities and relationships in ways that are central to the process of development (Wells, 2007).

A striking demonstration of how symbols mediate children's activities is provided in a study of young children's self-control (Carlson, Davis, & Leach, 2005). Three-year-olds are famous for acting on impulse rather than thinking things through. Consider the following example: Maria, a typical 3-year-old, is presented with two trays of candy, one of which plainly has more pieces of candy than the other. She is told to pick one tray, with the caution that the tray she chooses will be given away and that it is the other tray that she can keep for herself. According to a recent study conducted by Stephanie Carlson and her colleagues (2005), Maria is very likely to impulsively choose the tray with more candy—and she will continue to do so again and again, even though she sees that her choices leave her with fewer candies. However, Carlson's research suggests that Maria's behavior can be mediated by the use of symbols. In her experiment, the candies were presented in closed boxes instead of on trays (Figure 2.3), with a picture of a mouse placed on top of the box with fewer candies and a picture of an elephant placed on the box with more candies. After being told what the mouse and elephant symbolized (fewer and more candies), 3-year-olds had little trouble choosing the box with fewer candies. The symbols helped them to control their impulses and to organize their behavior to get what they wanted.

Carlson's research illustrates how symbols mediate young children's behavior in the carefully controlled environment of an experiment. In the real world, symbols and symbolic systems are a pervasive and complex part of children's lives and development. A particularly vivid example of this is provided by Alma Gottlieb (2005), an anthropologist who has documented how the use of spiritual symbols pervades the lives of infants and their caregivers in Beng culture in West Africa. The Beng believe that babies are reincarnations of dead ancestors currently dwelling in the "spirit village," where they enjoy rich and full social lives. The invisible spirit world exists side by side with the earthly world of the living, and the boundary between them is fluid and permeable, permitting easy movement from one to the other. Ancestors are believed to visit the world of the living on a daily basis, and some adults are known to have visited the spirit world in their dreams, where they communicate with their ancestors.

Against the backdrop of this complex spiritual belief system is an equally complex system of infant care. Babies are believed to occupy a precarious and risky place as they pass from the spirit village to the world of the living—a journey that does not begin until the umbilical stump drops off (a special drying salve is applied frequently to the stump to hurry the process along), and can take up to seven years to complete. During this time, it is believed, there is a possibility that the infants will return permanently to the spirit village, usually because they miss the wealth, comforts, and friends they had there. Much of Beng infant care is therefore focused on convincing babies to stay by showering them with symbols of wealth. Because cowry shells are believed to be the primary form of wealth in the ancestral village, infants are adorned with cowry shell jewelry as a symbol of their wealth in the land of the living and are promised that they are valued and will be well cared for. They may also be provided with special jewelry or elaborate face paint to combat diseases and disabilities inflicted by ancestral spirits. Gottlieb noted that some babies wear "so many necklaces, bracelets, anklets, knee bands and waist bands that an outside observer might well wonder how the weighed-down infant ever manages to crawl" (p. 113). Infant bathing is highly ritualized, involving symbolic objects and washes, and lasts about an hour. Newborns are bathed four times

(a)

(b)

Figure 2.3 When asked to choose a tray of candy that will be given away, 3-year-olds impulsively choose the tray with more candies (a). However, when the task is modified so the candies are hidden in boxes, one box with a mouse indicating fewer candies, the other with an elephant indicating many candies, children will choose the box with fewer candies, suggesting that their behavior can be symbolically mediated (b).

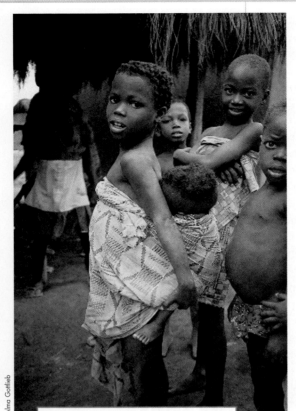

Alma Gottlieb

Because Beng infants are believed to be in transition between a spirit village and the land of the living, they are showered with attention and symbols of wealth. These Beng children began their lives with promises that they will be loved and cared for in the land of the living.

a day; toddlers, twice daily. The purpose is to cleanse the residue of "dirt" from the spirit world. Special care is taken to keep infants and young children away from corpses, which might entice them to join their journey. Beng infant care illustrates some of the same aspects of culture referred to in our discussion of the macaques, including the way that it is rooted in daily life and behavior and the way it forms a complex network of interconnected activities. But it also leads us to recognize that human culture involves other layers of complexity arising from a vast network of beliefs, values, and practices that reflect common human concerns and problems. Like many communities in developing nations, the Beng suffer from high infant mortality rates; about 11 percent of all infants die before the age of 1 year, and about 17 percent die before age 5 (in contrast, the infant mortality rate for infants under 1 year in the United States is about 0.64 percent; see also Chapter 3, p. 96, regarding international infant mortality rates). It makes sense, then, that Beng child-care practices are oriented toward infant survival through cultural practices that follow from their beliefs about the spiritual relationship between life and death.

The Complexity of Culture

Although culture shapes the development of individuals, it is also the case that individuals modify their cultures as they become users of cultural tools in the course of ongoing interactions with the people in their communities. In the words of Barbara Rogoff, "people of each generation, as they engage in sociocultural endeavors with other people, make use of and extend cultural tools and practices inherited from previous generations. As people develop through their shared use of cultural tools and practices, they simultaneously contribute to the transformation of cultural tools, practices, and institutions" (Rogoff, 2003, p. 52). In short, cultures continue to evolve because they are complex, with individuals producing *variations* in the material and symbolic cultural tools that they use. This dynamic process of cultural change through variation is known as **cumulative cultural evolution** (Herrmann et al., 2007; Tomasello et al., 2005).

Developing technologies provide straightforward examples of how cultural resources—in this case, material resources—are modified and accumulate over time. For example, 150 years ago, personal communication was limited to either talking face-to-face or writing and reading letters. The harnessing of electricity in the nineteenth century led to the telegraph and the telephone, and then to the age of computers, fax machines, cell phones, and video conferencing.

In the same way that variations in the material resources of a culture accumulate over time, so, too, do variations in its symbolic resources—its systems of knowledge, beliefs, and values. In many cultures, social beliefs and values about women, marriage, and family have undergone significant changes over time, as has the scientific understanding of everything from the movement of planets and the nature of light to how the brain works and affects behavior.

Based on what you have read so far, you might be inclined to think that cultural evolution represents progress toward ever higher levels of sophistication. Human culture, however, is often a messy affair, riddled with inconsistencies that can be sources of confusion and conflict, sometimes sufficient to inspire cultural evolution or outright destruction (Greenfield et al., 2006). Cultural inconsistencies can be particularly vivid in multicultural societies when the practices, beliefs, and values of different cultures interact in children's lives and experiences.

cumulative cultural evolution The dynamic ongoing process of cultural change as a consequence of variation that individuals have produced in the cultural tools they use.

Through variations, culture is, in the words of Patricia Greenfield, "constantly reinventing itself through the addition of new ethnic groups to multicultural societies, through changes in educational practices, through widening effects of the mass media, and through transformations in economy and technology" (Greenfield, Suzuki, & Rothstein-Fisch, 2006, p. 655). The particulars of variations and changes are impossible to predict. Some cultural practices can persist for generations (Hindu worship practices, for example); others can change in the blink of an eye (the use of the Internet for gathering information). Not only can we not know the timing of such changes, but we cannot know how advantageous a cultural practice will be in the long run or even whether a disadvantageous practice might become advantageous in new circumstances.

As you will see below, variation, inherent in culture and essential to cumulative cultural evolution, is also inherent to the child's biological inheritance and an essential ingredient of biological evolution.

||||| **APPLY ▪ CONNECT ▪ DISCUSS**

As usual, 3-year-old Star is the first in her family to awaken on this Saturday morning. She grabs her teddy bear, kicks off her Barbie-printed covers, climbs out of bed, and paddles down the hallway to the kitchen. She puts Teddy on a chair, instructing, "You wait right here, honey, and *be quiet*." Next, she moves a step stool to the food cupboard, climbs up, and retrieves a box of cereal. She then takes the cereal and the bear to the family room, where she settles on the sofa, and clicks on the TV. The annual MTV Spring Break program fills the screen. Star watches intently, crunching cereal, snuggled up with her bear.

What are some of the material and symbolic tools described in this scene? How do they organize—that is, *mediate*—Star's behavior? What cultural beliefs, values, and practices might she be learning by using these cultural tools? How might her environment be organized differently to reflect a different set of cultural values and beliefs?

Biological Inheritance

In the preceding sections, we made the point that cultural activities are interconnected and organized over time, forming complex networks. The tradition of washing potatoes in the ocean, for instance, emerged as a thread in a complex web of related cultural changes that involved such things as infant play (swimming) and foraging for food (scavenging from fishermen, collecting octopi from pools). Like cultural evolution, biological evolution produces amazing networks in which things often, although not always, go together. As an example, think back to the story of our upright-walking *Australopithecus afarensis* ancestors. Walking upright was associated with a pelvic structure and a birth canal that were narrower than those of the knuckle-walking primates that preceded them. Over the several million years following the emergence of upright walking, however, the brain size of hominid species tripled and the skull enlarged considerably (Brunet et al., 2002; Washburn, 2004). Consistent with this interlocking network of changes in locomotion, pelvic structure, birth canal, brain size, and skull size was a change in the length of pregnancy such that infants were born earlier, in a less developed state.

In order to appreciate how this worked, and its implications for modern children's development and behavior, we need to understand two fundamental issues. The first issue concerns how an individual's genetic endowment is actually expressed in all the physical and psychological traits that he or she displays. The second fundamental issue concerns the way that an individual's genetic endowment and corresponding traits enter into the process of evolution. We will address each of these issues in the following sections.

Genes and Traits

Evolution is made possible by **heredity,** the transmission of biological characteristics from one generation to the next. **Genes**—the basic units of heredity—contain instructions that guide the formation of all the individual's traits—both physical traits (sex, skin and eye color, susceptibility to certain diseases, and so on) and behavioral and psychological traits, including how the individual attends to and responds to the environment, communicates with others, and expresses needs and desires.

The fundamental question for developmentalists is how these instructions become expressed. In addressing this question, developmentalists begin by distinguishing between the individual's *genotype* and his or her *phenotype*. An individual's **genotype** is the exact genetic makeup—the particular set of genes—that the individual has inherited. The **phenotype** represents all the observable physical, behavioral, and psychological traits that the individual actually develops. The distinction between the genotype and the phenotype is important for three reasons. First, our knowledge of an individual's genotype and phenotype comes from different sources of information. Knowledge of the genotype comes from studying the individual's genetic material, whereas knowledge of the phenotype comes from studying the individual's body and behavior. Second, although an individual's genotype and phenotype are related, they do not necessarily coincide. Identical twins, for example, have precisely the same genotype, but their phenotypes—even their fingerprints—are never completely identical, and indeed become increasingly different as the twins age (see p. 65). This is because the phenotype is influenced by the individual's environment, in addition to being influenced by the individual's genotype. Third and finally, the genotype and phenotype enter the process of evolution in distinctive ways, as we discuss below.

Evolution's Process of Natural Selection

Across vast tracts of time, the survival of species, including our own, has been continually threatened by shifting climates and food supplies, natural disasters such as earthquakes and floods, and attacks by other species ranging from microscopic viruses to mighty predators. According to Charles Darwin's famous argument, species survive because of the process of **natural selection.** Through this process, individuals with phenotypes that are adaptive to their particular environmental conditions (i.e., whose traits are well fitted to the environment) have an increased chance of surviving and reproducing. In contrast, individuals whose phenotypes are not adaptive either do not survive or are less reproductively successful. (The fact that the odds of survival are greater for species better fitted to their environment gave rise to the well-known phrase "survival of the fittest.") Thus, those who are phenotypically well adapted to their environment are "selected" by natural conditions to survive and reproduce, passing on to the next generation the genotypes that contribute to the development of adaptive phenotypes.

As Darwin described the process, natural selection requires *phenotypic variation,* that is, heritable variations of particular phenotypic traits that have survival value for the individual and species. Consider, for instance, the phenotypic trait of height in trees growing in a crowded forest. Taller trees may get more sun than shorter trees and are therefore likely to produce more seeds (offspring). You can see that, over the course of many generations, trees with genes for taller height will greatly

heredity The biological transmission of characteristics from one generation to the next.

genes The segments on a DNA molecule that act as hereditary blueprints for the organism's development.

genotype The genetic endowment of an individual.

phenotype The organism's observable characteristics that result from the interaction of the genotype with the environment.

natural selection The process through which species survive and evolve, in which individuals with phenotypes that are more adaptive to the environmental conditions survive and reproduce with greater success than individuals with phenotypes are that less adaptive.

outnumber those with genes for shorter height. Thus, *variations* of phenotypic traits that are adaptive in the existing environmental conditions will increase in the species as a whole while those that are maladaptive will quite literally die out.

The Emergence of Shorter Pregnancies To appreciate how this process works, consider the phenotypic trait of pregnancy duration. In our species, shorter pregnancies evolved as a part of an integrated network of changes related to bipedalism, a smaller birth canal, a larger brain, and increased skull size. The natural selection process resulting in shorter pregnancies probably went something like this. Genotypic variations among females contributed to phenotypic variations in the length of their pregnancies. Females with longer pregnancies, who consequently gave birth to larger infants, were more likely to be damaged during the birth process, less likely to survive, and, therefore, less likely to have additional offspring than were females with shorter pregnancies. Likewise, their infants were more likely to be harmed during difficult deliveries, reducing their chances for reaching reproductive maturity. And those that did live to reproduce were likely to have inherited their mothers' genetic tendency for longer pregnancies, placing both themselves and their offspring at greater risk. In contrast, females whose genotypes favored the development of "shorter pregnancy" phenotypes would have given birth earlier to smaller infants. The mothers would have been more likely to survive and have additional offspring who would inherit the genetic tendency for shorter pregnancies. You can see that over the course of thousands of years, even tens of thousands of years, the average length of pregnancy for the entire species would have shortened as natural selection favored this adaptive phenotypic trait from one generation to the next.

In addition to affecting the evolution of physiological processes such as the length of pregnancy, natural selection works on phenotypic traits that are more behavioral in nature. A particularly interesting example is the very common human behavior of baby-talk, to which we turn next. First, however, it is important to note that arguments regarding the selection of adaptive phenotypes are always tentative, especially in instances involving behavioral phenotypes. In all instances, scientists make inferences about how particular behavioral phenotypes affect the survival of species, inferences that are based on the best available fossil evidence and on the survival value of comparable behaviors in species that are highly similar to humans, such as chimpanzees and bonobos.

The Emergence of Baby-Talk

> Aren't YOU a nice BAby? Good GIRL, drinking all your MILK.
> Look, look, that's a giRAFFE. Isn't that a NICE giRAFFE?
> DOGgie, there's the DOGgie. Ooh, did you see the lovely DOGgie?
> (Karmiloff & Karmiloff-Smith, 2001, p. 47)

It is widely recognized that parents the world over talk to their infants using a special musical speech, known as baby-talk, motherese, or **infant-directed speech.** The melodic, singsong quality of this speech functions to communicate emotion, rather than meaning or grammar (see Chapter 7), and it tends to elicit emotional responses from infants. Baby-talk is found throughout the world, regardless of the specific language used in the community. There is even a sign-language form of baby-talk that signing parents use in communicating with their deaf infants (Spencer & Harris, 2006).

Dean Falk, an anthropologist at Florida State University, suggests that the universality of baby-talk indicates that it evolved through the process of natural selection (Falk, 2004). Her argument takes us back to the emergence of bipedalism

infant-directed speech The special, musical speech used in talking to infants; also known as baby-talk or motherese.

Johner/Getty Images

Infant-directed speech is found throughout the world. Some anthropologists argue that it reflects maternal responsiveness and has evolutionary significance.

in our *Australopithecus* ancestors. Falk notes that the ability to walk upright is at the center of human evolution, because it freed the hands to make and use tools and to carry things such as food and water. It also made it possible for mothers to carry their immature and extremely weak infants, who, unlike infants of earlier ancestral species and contemporary nonhuman primate species, could not cling to their mothers.

Because of their need for frequent feeding and protection from predators, infants had to be in constant close contact with their mother. At the same time, mothers often needed to have their hands free in order to forage for food. Thus, according to Falk, it was advantageous for mothers to "park," or set down, their infants for brief periods while they foraged nearby, rather than constantly carrying them.

Falk argues that the practice of parking probably inspired unhappy, fussy vocalizations on the part of the infants, because babies—human and nonhuman primate infants alike—become distressed when separated from their caregivers. In addition, mothers (and other adults) are highly sensitive to the distress cries of infants, which of course makes good sense in evolutionary terms. So the practice of parking created a context for developing a new way of "keeping in touch" to discourage infant crying during separations. Falk maintains that baby-talk evolved to serve exactly this function. Its soothing, melodic qualities were calming to babies and perhaps even lulled them to sleep, making the baby-talk of our evolutionary ancestors the precursor to our modern lullabies (Dissanayake, 2000).

In the technical language of evolutionary theory, baby-talk is a phenotypic sign of the mother's genetic tendency to be responsive to her infant (there are, of course, many other phenotypic signs of maternal responsiveness, including carrying, grooming, and feeding the child). Maternal responsiveness has obvious adaptive value, ensuring that infants are attended to and well cared for. Mothers who engage in more responsive behavior have more surviving offspring and, through natural selection, pass on to the next generation their genetic tendencies toward responsiveness. To the extent that baby-talk is a phenotypic sign of maternal responsiveness, natural selection will favor the phenotype, increasing the likelihood that offspring will inherit their mothers' genetic tendency to use it.

You now have a grasp of genotypes and phenotypes, and how together they define the biological foundations of each member of our species. In the sections below, we explore in more detail the processes that determine the formation of individual genotypes and the development of specific phenotypes.

Genetic Inheritance through Sexual Reproduction

To ask about the process of genetic inheritance is to ask about how an individual's genotype is formed. The *genotype,* you remember, refers to the individual's genetic endowment, which remains constant over the individual's lifetime. An individual's genotype contains information that defines the individual's membership in the human species, as well as information unique to that individual. In sexual reproduction, all of this information is transmitted through the combination of the mother's egg and the father's sperm.

You may remember from your high school biology class that every human sperm and ovum (egg) contains 23 chromosomes and that a **chromosome** is a single molecule of **DNA** (**deoxyribonucleic acid**). The DNA molecule takes the form of two long, connected strands that spiral around each other—the famous

chromosome A threadlike structure made up of genes. In humans, there are 46 chromosomes in every cell except sperm and ova.

DNA (deoxyribonucleic acid) A long double-stranded molecule that makes up chromosomes.

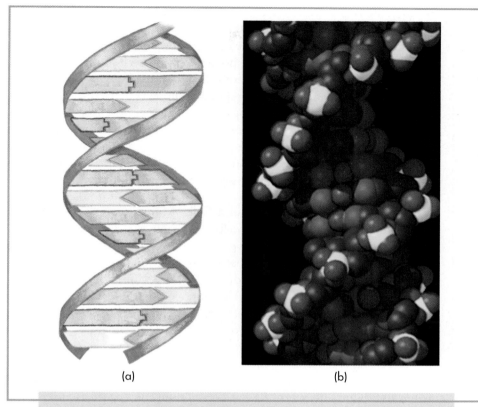

(a)   (b)

Figure 2.4 (a) DNA molecules include two long strands that spiral around each other in a double helix. DNA is a vast database containing all the genetic information a cell will need to develop. (b) A computer-generated color-coded model of DNA allows researchers to rotate the image and study it from various angles.

zygote The single cell formed at conception from the union of the sperm and the ovum.

germ cells The sperm and ova, which are specialized for sexual reproduction and have half the number of chromosomes normal for a species.

somatic cells All the cells in the body except for the germ cells (ova and sperm).

mitosis The process of cell duplication and division that generates all the individual's cells except sperm and ova.

meiosis The process that produces sperm and ova, each of which contains only half of the parent cell's original complement of 46 chromosomes.

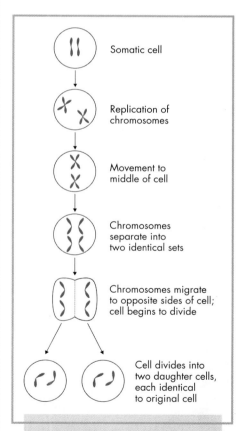

Somatic cell

Replication of chromosomes

Movement to middle of cell

Chromosomes separate into two identical sets

Chromosomes migrate to opposite sides of cell; cell begins to divide

Cell divides into two daughter cells, each identical to original cell

Figure 2.5 Mitosis is the process of cell division that generates new somatic cells. First, all the chromosomes in the cell replicate, producing a new set of chromosomes identical to the first. The two sets then separate and the cell divides, producing two daughter cells. Mitosis ensures that identical genetic information is maintained in the somatic cells over the life of the organism.

double helix (Figure 2.4). Every chromosome contains hundreds or thousands of genes, each of which is a small segment of DNA.

Each gene carries a particular set of instructions for manufacturing the chemicals that are used to create the body's cells and that control how the cells function. The 23 chromosomes in the ovum carry half the genes necessary for the development of a new individual. The other half are carried by the chromosomes in the man's sperm. When conception occurs, the ovum and sperm fuse to form a **zygote,** a single cell containing 46 chromosomes—23 from the mother and 23 from the father—that are arranged in 23 corresponding pairs. This single cell with its 23 pairs of chromosomes is the foundation for all the cells that will ever develop in the individual.

Creating New Cells Our cells are of two types: germ and somatic. **Germ cells** are the sperm and ova, which contain 23 unpaired chromosomes, as described above. **Somatic cells** (or *body cells*) are all the other cells of the body (skin cells, blood cells, bone cells, nerve cells, and so on). Each somatic cell contains 46 chromosomes in 23 pairs, identical to the chromosomes in the zygote. New somatic cells are created through a process called **mitosis.** The process of creating germ cells is called **meiosis.**

Mitosis: A Process of Making New Somatic Cells. In mitosis, the 46 chromosomes in a cell begin by replicating, or producing exact copies of themselves (Figure 2.5). These chromosomes then move to the middle of the cell, where they separate into two identical sets, which migrate to opposite sides of the cell. The cell then divides

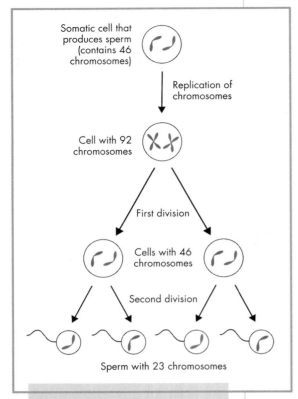

Somatic cell that produces sperm (contains 46 chromosomes)

Replication of chromosomes

Cell with 92 chromosomes

First division

Cells with 46 chromosomes

Second division

Sperm with 23 chromosomes

Figure 2.6 Meiosis is the process of cell division that generates new germ cells (in this case, sperm). Like mitosis, meiosis begins with replication of the cell's chromosomes, but the cell then divides twice. The result is sperm cells, each with just 23 chromosomes.

in the middle to form two daughter cells, each of which contains a set of 46 chromosomes. These two daughter cells go through the same process of replication and division to create two new cells each, which themselves replicate and divide as the process repeats itself again and again.

This process continues throughout the life of the individual, constantly creating new somatic cells and replacing those that die off. Each new somatic cell contains an exact copy of the original 46 chromosomes inherited by the zygote at conception. Thus, under the ordinary conditions of life, our chromosomes and the genes they carry are not altered by the passage of time or by the experiences that shape our minds and bodies; that is, as mentioned earlier, our genotype remains constant.

Meiosis: A Process of Making Germ Cells. Mitosis works very well as a process of creating new somatic cells, each with 46 chromosomes identical to those inherited by the zygote. Germ cells, however, must have only 23 chromosomes each, so that when an ovum and sperm fuse, they create a zygote with 46 chromosomes. This is accomplished through the special cell-division process called *meiosis*.

In the first phase of this process, the 23 pairs of chromosomes in the cells that produce sperm or ova duplicate themselves, just as in mitosis. But then the cell divides not once, as in mitosis, but twice, creating four daughter cells (Figure 2.6). Each of these daughter cells contains only 23 unpaired chromosomes—half the original set from the parent cell. Thus, when the ovum and sperm fuse at conception, the zygote receives a full complement of 46 chromosomes (23 pairs).

Meiosis represents the initial stage of shuffling genetic material from the parent generation to produce new genetic variations in the offspring. Although we receive 23 chromosomes from each of our parents, it is a matter of chance which member of any pair of chromosomes ends up in a given germ cell during meiosis. According to the laws of probability, there are 2^{23}, or about 8 million, possible genetic combinations for each sperm and ovum. Consequently, the probability that siblings will inherit exactly the same genes from both parents is at best 1 chance in 64 trillion! This extreme improbability shows the importance of meiosis as a source of variation, a means of introducing new genetic combinations in the species.

There is one exception to the odds of genetic variability—the special case of **monozygotic (MZ) twins,** who come from a single fertilized egg that, for rea-

Monozygotic twin boys. Despite inhabiting a very similar environment before and after birth, they have distinguishably different facial features. This clearly shows the way in which the phenotype is influenced by the environment.

Because they developed from two separate ova, these dizygotic, or fraternal twins will look no more alike than non-twin siblings.

sons still not understood, divides and develops into two separate individuals. Because they originate from the same zygote, monozygotic twins have identical genetic material, so they potentially could have the same physical and psychological makeup. However, as a result of their encounters with their environments, "identical twins" are never exactly alike in every detail and may even appear far from identical. (Twins that come from two ova that have been fertilized at the same time are referred to as **dizygotic [DZ] twins,** or "fraternal twins," and are no more likely to resemble each other than are any other two siblings.)

Sex Determination Like many other species on the planet, the human species has evolved two sexes—male and female. But what determines whether a given individual is one or the other? In 22 of the 23 pairs of chromosomes found in a human cell, the two chromosomes are of the same size and shape and carry corresponding genes. For chromosomes of the twenty-third pair, however, this is not necessarily the case. This pair of chromosomes determines a person's genetic sex. In females, both members of the twenty-third pair of chromosomes are of the same type, called an **X chromosome** (Figure 2.7). Males, however, have just one X chromosome, which is paired with a different, much smaller chromosome, called a **Y chromosome.** Since a female is XX, each of her eggs contains an X chromosome. Since a male is XY, half of his sperm carry an X chromosome and half carry a Y chromosome. If a sperm containing an X chromosome fertilizes an egg, the resulting child will be XX, a female. If the sperm contains a Y chromosome, the child will be XY, a male. The genetic determination of a person's sex is controlled by a single chromosome; however, other aspects of biology and behavior have more complex origins.

Laws of Genetic Inheritance

The laws of genetic inheritance describe several different ways in which genetic material transmitted by parents can be expressed in the child. In the simplest form, a single pair of corresponding genes, one from each parent, contributes to a particular inherited characteristic. A gene that influences a specific trait (for example, the presence or absence of a cleft in the chin) can have different forms. The specific form of a gene is called an **allele.** When the corresponding genes inherited from the two parents are the same allele (both "cleft" or both "non-cleft"), the person is said to be **homozygous** for the trait. When the alleles are different (one "cleft" and one "non-cleft"), the person is said to be **heterozygous** for the trait. As you will see, whether the allele pairings are homozygous or heterozygous affects the characteristics of the phenotype.

When a child is homozygous for a trait that is affected by a single pair of alleles, only one outcome is possible: The child will display the particular characteristics associated with that allele. When a child is heterozygous for such a trait, one of three outcomes is possible:

- The child will display the characteristics associated with only one of the two alleles. In such cases, the allele whose associated characteristics are expressed is referred to as a **dominant allele,** and the allele whose associated characteristics are not expressed is referred to as a **recessive allele.** Even though individuals may not express a particular characteristic, they may nonetheless pass the recessive trait on to their offspring. Such individuals are referred to as **carriers.** A number of disorders occur when two individuals carrying a recessive allele transmit that allele to a child

Figure 2.7 Human X (above) and Y (below) chromosomes. Note how much larger the X chromosome is. Males have both an X and a Y chromosome, but females have two X chromosomes.

BioPhoto Associates/Science Source/Photo Researchers

monozygotic twins Twins that come from one zygote and therefore have identical genotypes.

dizygotic twins Twins that come from two zygotes.

X chromosome One of the two chromosomes that determine sex; in females, both members of the twenty-third pair of chromosomes and in males one member of the twenty-third pair.

Y chromosome One of the two chromosomes that determine sex; in males, one member of the twenty-third pair of chromosomes.

allele The specific form of a gene coded for a particular trait.

homozygous Having inherited two genes of the same allelic form for a trait.

heterozygous Having inherited two genes of different allelic forms for a trait.

dominant allele The allele that is expressed when an individual possesses two different alleles for the same trait.

recessive allele The allele that is not expressed when an individual possesses two different alleles for the same trait.

carriers Individuals who are heterozygous for a trait with a dominant and recessive allele and thus express only the characteristics associated with the dominant allele but may pass the recessive allele, including for a recessive disorder, on to their offspring.

Figure 2.8 If both parents carry the recessive allele (*r*) for a disorder, a child who gets that allele from both parents (*rr*) will have the disorder; alternatively, a child may get the dominant allele (*R*) from both parents (*RR*) and be unaffected, or may get a dominant and recessive allele (*Rr*) and be unaffected but a carrier.

Unaffected carrier father   Unaffected carrier mother

Unaffected   Unaffected carriers   Affected

(Figure 2.8). Among these *recessive disorders* are phenylketonuria and sickle-cell anemia, both of which we discuss below (see Table 2.2 for other examples).

- The child will be affected by both alleles and will display characteristics that are intermediate between those associated with the two alleles. Thus, with skin color for example, the offspring of a dark-skinned parent and a light-skinned parent may have skin tones in between those of the parents.

- Rather than displaying intermediate characteristics, the child will fully express the characteristics associated with each of the two alleles, an outcome that is called **codominance** (Figure 2.9). For example, children with type AB blood may have a type-A mother, and a type-B father. The blood type of each parent is fully expressed in the AB blood type of the child.

Mutations and Genetic Abnormalities

Despite its fantastic power to produce genetic diversity in human beings, sexual reproduction is restricted to recombining genes that are already present in the human **gene pool,** the total variety of genetic information possessed by a sexually reproducing population. The gene pool can change, however, through **mutation,** an alteration in the structure of an individual's DNA. Mutations can occur for a

codominance Outcome in which a trait that is determined by two alleles is different from the trait produced by either of the contributing alleles alone.

gene pool The total variety of genetic information possessed by a sexually reproducing population.

mutation An alteration in the molecular structure of an individual's DNA.

Figure 2.9 In this illustration of codominance, mom's horizontal stripes and dad's vertical stripes are expressed equally in their youngster's stylish plaid phenotype.

table 2.2

Common Genetic Disorders

	Disorder	Description	Incidence	Prenatal/Carrier Detection?	Treatment and Prognosis
Recessive disorders	Cystic fibrosis	Lack of an enzyme causes a mucus obstruction, especially in lungs and digestive tract	1 in 3000 Caucasian births in U.S.; 1 in 17,000 African American births	Yes/Yes	Medications, treatments, diet used to clear airways, loosen mucus, aid digestion. In U.S., most survive into 30s.
	Phenylketonuria (PKU)	Inability to metabolize phenylalanine, an amino acid, leads to its buildup in the bloodstream, retarding brain-cell development	1 in 10,000–15,000 U.S. infants	Yes/Yes	Treatment by diet beginning in infancy and continuing throughout life can reduce severity of brain damage and mental retardation
	Sickle-cell anemia	Abnormally shaped blood cells cause circulatory problems and severe anemia	8–9% of African Americans; more than 20% of West Africans	Yes/Yes	Organ damage and severe pain can result. Treatment by medication can reduce symptoms and complications.
	Tay-Sachs disease	Lack of an enzyme causes buildup of waste in brain	1 in 3600 among Ashkenazi Jews in U.S.	Yes/Yes	Neurological degeneration leads to death before age 4
	Thalassemia (Cooley's anemia)	Abnormal red blood cells	1 in 500 birth in populations from subtropical areas of Europe, Africa, Asia	Yes/Yes	Listlessness, enlarged liver and spleen, occasionally death; treatable by blood transfusions
X-linked recessive disorders	Duchenne muscular dystrophy	Weakening and wasting away of muscles. Crippling, often fatal by age 20	1 in 3500 males under age 20	Yes/Yes	Crippling, often fatal by age 20
	Hemophilia	Blood does not clot readily. Although usually the result of X-linked gene, also occurs by spontaneous mutation	1 in 10,000 live births of males	Yes/Yes, if not spontaneous mutation	Possible crippling and death from internal bleeding. Transfusions ameliorate effects
Dominant disorders	Neurofibromatosis	Nervous system disorder, causing tumors on nerves and other abnormalities. Usually inherited, but 30–50% of cases arise through spontaneous mutation	1 in 3000 births	Yes/Yes, if not spontaneous mutation	Symptoms are highly variable and may include café au lait spots, benign tumors on peripheral nerves, optic nerve tumors, learning disabilities. Treatment by surgery may be possible
Chromosomal disorders	Down syndrome	Extra copy of chromosome 21 results in mental and physical retardation, distinctive physical characteristics, and susceptibility to certain medical conditions	1 in 1000 live births in U.S.	Yes/n.a.	Medical conditions monitored and treated; special education to develop skills and independence. Depending on severity and complications, survival into 50s is possible
	Klinefelter syndrome	Extra X chromosome in males (XXY) results in incomplete development of sex organs and secondary sex characteristics	1 in every 500–1000 males born in U.S.	Yes/n.a.	Treatment by testosterone replacement therapy at puberty can be beneficial. Most lead normal lives, although with increased risk for certain cancers and heart disease
	Turner syndrome	Lack of an X chromosome (XO) in females. Common symptoms include short stature, failure to develop secondary sex characteristics	1 in 2500 females	Yes/n.a.	Growth hormone and estrogen therapies can facilitate growth and development. Most women lead normal lives, but are infertile

variety of reasons, including errors in the process of chromosome replication during either meiosis or mitosis, and exposure to external agents such as certain chemicals and certain forms of radiation.

When mutations occur in somatic cells, they are not passed on to following generations. However, when mutations occur in germ cells, altering the structure of one or more genes, the changed genetic information may be passed on to the next generation. Geneticists assume that spontaneous mutations have been occurring in germ cells constantly and randomly for millions upon millions of years, introducing new genes into the gene pool of every species and providing a source of variation for the process of natural selection.

The fact that mutations are a natural and fundamental part of life does not, however, mean that they usually benefit the individual organisms in which they occur. Most mutations are lethal, rather than adaptive, and in humans and other mammalian species, result in early miscarriage (Connor & Ferguson-Smith, 1993).

It is estimated that about 3.5 percent of all babies are born with some kind of genetic abnormality (Ward, 1994). Some of the more commonly occurring disorders related to genetic abnormalities are listed in Table 2.2. These disorders are of two main types. Some are a consequence of the specific genetic material inherited by the individual by means of normal processes of inheritance. For example, recessive disorders such as phenylketonuria and sickle-cell anemia, as mentioned above, occur through ordinary processes when both parents transmit the relevant allele. The second type of disorder occurs as result of a breakdown in the process of genetic transmission—the normal process of meiosis, for example, is disrupted for some reason, affecting the structure of chromosomes in the germ cell. Various abnormalities can result, such as Down syndrome and Klinefelter syndrome.

Phenylketonuria: A Recessive Disorder

As a recessive disorder, *Phenylketonuria (PKU)* is an example of a disorder caused by specific genetic material inherited by the individual through the normal process of genetic transmission. PKU is a particularly debilitating condition that leads to severe mental retardation if it is not treated. It is caused by a defective recessive allele that, when inherited from both parents, reduces the body's ability to metabolize phenylalanine, an amino acid that is highly concentrated in foods such as milk, eggs, bread, and fish. When too much phenylalanine builds up in a baby's bloodstream, brain-cell development is retarded (Diamond, 2002). About 1 in every 10,000–15,000 infants born each year in the United States has PKU, and about 1 in 100 people of European descent is a carrier of the recessive allele (Guttler, 1988). The incidence of PKU is lower among blacks than among whites (Connor & Ferguson-Smith, 1993). (For another example of a recessive disorder, see the discussion of GA1 in the box "In the Field: Doctor of the Plain People.")

PKU can be tested for prenatally (Fan et al., 1999), and most states require that all newborns be tested for the disorder. Infants who test positive are treated with diets that are low in phenylalanine. While such treatment significantly reduces the severity of mental retardation, it does not prevent the effects of PKU entirely (Diamond, 2002). The timing of the treatment is crucial. If phenylalanine intake is not restricted by the time an infant with PKU is 1 to 3 months of age, the brain will already have suffered irreversible damage. Genetic testing can identify people who carry the recessive PKU allele, allowing prospective parents who are both carriers to decide whether they want to risk having a child with the disease (see the box "Genetic Counseling").

In the field   Doctor of the Plain People

Name:	Holmes Morton
Education:	High school dropout; undergraduate degree at Trinity College; M.D. from Harvard Medical School; pediatric residency at Children's Hospital of Boston; genetic research at Children's Hospital of Philadelphia
Current Position:	Pediatrician; genetic researcher
Career Objectives:	Understand and treat genetic disorders affecting Amish and Mennonite communities

Dr. D. Holmes Morton practices medicine in the farmlands of Pennsylvania, home to the nation's largest communities of Amish and Mennonites. Collectively called the Plain People because of a lifestyle that shuns technology, the communities have long been the target of genetic research. Their traditions include marrying within their communities, which limits opportunities to introduce genetic variation. As a consequence, children of the Plain People are beset with unusually high rates of rare genetic disorders. Despite their general aversion to modern technologies, the Plain People welcome the assistance of medicines and treatments that can help their children lead healthy, fulfilling lives. And so, using traditional materials of wooden beams and pegs, the Plain People "raised" Dr. Morton's Clinic for Special Children in an alfalfa field. Outside is a hitching post; inside is the most advanced medical machinery available for analyzing children's DNA.

Most of the children treated by Dr. Morton suffer from recessive disorders that interfere with their ability to metabolize proteins, fats, or sugars. An example is GA1, so named because it results in the buildup in the brain of glutaric acid, a by-product of protein. Children who inherit GA1 appear to be healthy at birth. It is only when they contract some common childhood illness like chicken pox or even a common cold that a strokelike event is triggered in their brains, causing severe physical and intellectual damage and sometimes death.

Dr. Morton's research has identified the defective gene responsible for GA1. As with other metabolic disorders, the defect limits the production of an enzyme that the body needs to break down proteins. Dr. Morton has discovered that the best chance for children born with the defect is to have the condition diagnosed at birth, before the newborn is nursed or given protein-rich foods, such as milk. Several procedures can be used to diagnose GA1 in newborns, including analyzing urine for high concentrations of glutaric acid. The preferred procedure, however, is to sample amniotic fluid when labor begins and the water breaks. The amniotic fluid contains fetal skin cells that can be used to analyze the baby's genotype. The advantage of this procedure is that GA1 can be diagnosed before the newborn is damaged by ingesting protein.

As a geneticist and physician, Dr. Morton is dedicating his work to improving the lives of children with genetic disorders.

In addition to developing diagnostic procedures, Dr. Morton has found several ways to keep children with GA1 healthy during the first two years of life, when their growing brains are most vulnerable to damage. For example, when children become ill in ways that can trigger strokelike episodes, infusions of sugar can reverse the buildup of toxic glutaric acid in the brain.

Like many scientist–practitioners engaged in applied research, Dr. Morton is committed to creating knowledge that can improve children's lives and development. There are many ways to gauge his success. For example, when he first began practicing medicine in the Amish and Mennonite communities, 95 percent of children with GA1 suffered devastating physical and intellectual disabilities as a consequence of the disease. Now, in contrast, only 25 percent are severely affected. But the most inspiring measure of his success is found in the exuberant play of healthy toddlers attending the parties that Dr. Morton gives for his 2-year-old GA1 patients. For them, "it truly is a new birth day."

(adapted from Belkin, 2005)

Genetic Counseling

ALTHOUGH EFFECTIVE GENE THERAPIES appear still to be well beyond the horizon of contemporary medicine, thanks to recent advances in the field of genetics, many potential genetic problems can be avoided through genetic testing and counseling (Csaba, 2003). Genetic counselors inform prospective parents about the information they have concerning diagnosed genetic conditions that would put their child at risk. The counseling is ideally done in a way that allows the parents to decide as autonomously as possible about the choices confronting them and the child (Sharpe & Carter, 2006).

Several situations are likely to signal that a couple needs genetic counseling:

1. They have one child with a disorder and are worried that any future children may have the same disorder.
2. They are close relatives of someone who has a genetic disorder.
3. They have had two or more miscarriages, a stillbirth, or an early infant death.
4. They are in their mid-30s or older and want to have children.
5. The woman has been exposed to infections, drugs, or other potentially dangerous substances during pregnancy.

Several inherited disorders are especially likely to be found in specific groups of people. For example, the recessive allele for Tay-Sachs disease, in which a missing enzyme inevitably leads to death before the age of 4, is carried by 1 in 30 Ashkenazi Jews in the United States. Prospective parents who are both genetically linked to a group associated with a particular disorder can clearly benefit from genetic counseling.

In genetic tests, DNA in a person's cells is examined for an abnormality that flags a disease or disorder. The abnormality can be relatively large—a piece of a chromosome, or even an entire chromosome, missing or added. Sometimes the change is very small—as little as one extra, missing, or altered chemical unit within the DNA strand. Genes can be amplified (too many copies), overexpressed (too active), inactivated, or lost altogether. Sometimes pieces of chromosomes switch places or move to an incorrect location.

The alternatives or options that must be explained during genetic counseling often involve important ethical questions, depending upon the particular genetic abnormality, its treatability, and its likely consequences if there is no treatment (Mappes & DeGrazia, 2001). When a genetic disorder is detected, parents usually have only two alternatives: the woman can carry the pregnancy to term and give birth to a child who is genetically defective in some way, or she can terminate the pregnancy. This is not an easy choice, especially since the diagnosis often cannot predict the degree of disability the affected child will suffer or the quality of life that can be expected. The severity of Down syndrome, for example, can vary greatly, and many people who suffer from such defects may lead relatively productive lives.

In recent years, genetic counselors have become sensitive to the fact that the decisions parents face depend importantly on their cultural beliefs, such as the relative roles of men and women in family decision making and the ways in which delicate subjects are most effectively discussed. This recognition has given rise to a new subspecialty, multicultural genetic counseling (Penchaszadeh, 2001; Wang, 2001).

Prenatal diagnosis is a constantly changing field with expanding knowledge and new technologies; thus, any attempt to define the state of the art rapidly becomes outdated. Health-care providers must be aware of the likelihood of changes and the importance of obtaining access to the latest information. For up-to-date information, check the relevant entries at www.thedevelopmentofchildren.com.

Ruby Washington/The New York Times/Redux

This prenatal genetics counselor is talking with a client about options and choices regarding her pregnancy.

Down Syndrome: A Chromosomal Disorder In contrast to disorders such as PKU, which are due to the inheritance of specific genetic material, Down syndrome is a consequence of a disruption in the normal process of genetic transmission. In the vast majority of cases, it results from an error during meiosis that creates extra genetic material on chromosome 21. Indeed, more than 95 percent of the children born with Down syndrome have three copies of chromosome 21 instead of two. (For this reason, the disorder is sometimes called *trisomy 21*.) The effects of this disorder, which occurs at the rate of about 1 of every 1000 births in the United States, include varying degrees of mental and physical retardation, as well as several distinctive physical characteristics: slanting eyes and a fold on the eyelids; a rather flat facial profile; ears located lower than normal; a short neck; a protruding tongue; dental irregularities; short, broad hands; a crease running all the way across the palm; small curved fingers; and abnormally wide-spaced toes. Children with this disorder are more likely than other children to suffer from heart, ear, and eye problems, and they are more susceptible to leukemia and to respiratory infections (Steiner et al., 2005). Although the trigger for the meiotic error that causes Down syndrome is unknown, the disorder is strongly associated with conceptions involving older parents, particularly older mothers (Saltvedt et al., 2005).

How effectively children with Down syndrome function as they grow up depends not only on the severity of their disorder but also on the environment in which they are raised. Supportive intervention that includes special education by concerned adults can markedly improve the intellectual functioning of some of these children, especially when it is begun at an early age (Guralnick, 2005). As you will learn below, even in the case of serious genetic abnormalities such as Down syndrome, variations in the environment can lead to a range of possible phenotypic outcomes.

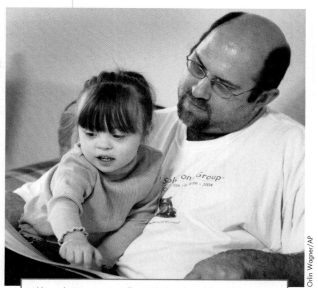

Although Darcie's intellectual development will be limited by Down syndrome, the enriched environment provided by her parents will have a significant impact on what she is able to accomplish as she grows up.

Klinefelter's Syndrome: A Disorder of the Sex Chromosomes

Half of all chromosomal abnormalities in newborns involve the X and Y chromosomes. Occasionally, a boy is born with an extra X or Y chromosome—that is, with an XXY or XYY genotype. Girls are sometimes born with only one X chromosome (X0 genotype) or with three X chromosomes (XXX genotype). Both males and females can be affected by a condition in which the X chromosome, which carries many genes, is brittle and breaks into two or more pieces. Each of these chromosomal abnormalities has different implications for development.

The most common sex-linked chromosomal abnormality is *Klinefelter's syndrome,* the condition in which males are born with an extra X chromosome (XXY). This abnormality occurs in about 1 of every 500 to 1000 males born in the United States (Geschwind & Dykens, 2004). Males who have Klinefelter's syndrome appear to develop normally until adolescence, when they fail to show the typical signs of maturity: their sex organs do not mature; they do not acquire facial hair; their voices do not change; they have low levels of the male hormone, testosterone; and they are sterile. In addition, most have speech and language problems and, as a result, have problems in school (Temple & Sanfilippo, 2003).

The most prevalent treatment for Klinefelter's syndrome is to begin testosterone replacement therapy at age 11 or 12, when testosterone levels begin to rise in normal males. The syndrome is not often diagnosed that early, but even if therapy is started later, it can have positive effects. The benefits include increased facial and pubic hair, a more masculine distribution of body fat, increased strength and bone density, and increased sexual functioning (Smyth & Bremner, 1998).

The Phenotype: From Genes to Traits

Notwithstanding the enormous power of the genotype to influence human development, it does not provide an account of how development actually takes place for each individual, that is, how all the phenotypic traits and characteristics that together define the individual emerge over time. For example, although Down syndrome substantially affects development, the care and support of family members, as well as educational and vocational services provided in schools and communities, can have an enormous impact on the skills and abilities the individual will acquire. The most important question that developmentalists ask about the

Figure 2.10 Waddington's landscape. The rolling ball represents a trait of the developing organism. At each decision point (labeled "This or this"), development of the trait can proceed along either of two diverging pathways. (Adapted from Fishbein, 1976)

development of phenotypic traits concerns the extent to which they are determined by the genotype or are open to influence by the environment.

Phenotypic Plasticity

The degree to which the developing phenotype is open to influence by the environment, rather than determined by the genotype, is referred to as **phenotypic plasticity** (Pigliucci, 2001). In traits with little plasticity, such as eye color, the genotype is strongly influential, and the phenotype develops in a highly predictable manner, irrespective of environmental factors. In contrast, in traits with *high plasticity,* the genotype exerts less pressure, so the phenotype is easily influenced by the environment and develops less predictably, as in the case of intellectual skills and abilities.

Conrad Waddington, a British geneticist, brilliantly captured the basic principles of phenotypic plasticity in his famous landscape of phenotypic development (Figure 2.10). He imagined the development of a phenotypic trait as a journey across a vast landscape of hills and intersecting valleys flowing downward from a high plateau. As shown in the figure, the ball at the top of the plateau represents the particular phenotypic trait in its "infancy"; the valleys represent the possible developmental pathways that lead to various phenotypic outcomes. You can see from the figure that as the ball rolls down the landscape, it sometimes encounters "forks in the road" where more than one valley is available for continuing the journey. You can also see that some valleys are narrow and deep, whereas others are broad and flat.

The particular shape of the landscape—the forks, the hills, the depth of the valleys—is the result of a complex system of interactions between genes and the environment. And because the gene–environment system of interaction changes over the course of a lifetime, *the landscape is not stable over the life course of the individual,* but changes its shape, sometimes dramatically, according to the individual's particular experiences. Exposure to toxins during the prenatal period, for example, can substantially alter the landscape in ways that change the course of developing phenotypes, resulting in physical deformities, mental retardation, and other disorders (see Chapter 3).

The concept of phenotypic plasticity addresses the issue of whether and to what extent different phenotypic forms can develop from a particular genotype. Another equally important issue is the extent to which a particular phenotypic form may develop despite genotypic and environmental variations. The concept of phenotypic canalization will help us to address this issue.

Phenotypic Canalization

We noted earlier in this chapter that development is astonishing in its capacity to generate common developmental outcomes in children despite vast differences in how and where they grow up. In part, this is due to the low plasticity of certain traits, or, in other words, the tight control that the genotype exerts over the developing phenotype. Interestingly, recent research with mice has demonstrated that some traits have such low plasticity that they develop in the same highly predictable ways even when the genotype is altered. Using sophisticated genetic engineering techniques, geneticists conducted "knock-out" experiments, which disable particular genes, and were astonished to find that the organism's developing phenotype was entirely unaffected. There are several reasons why the genotype is able to compensate for disabled genes. First, many genes

phenotypic plasticity The degree to which the phenotype is open to influence by the environment, rather than determined by the genotype.

have duplicate copies, so when one is knocked out, its twin can take over. It also seems that genes that ordinarily perform other functions can step in and assume the functions of a knocked-out gene.

Phenotypic traits that seem unaltered by changes in the environment, or even by changes in the genotype, are said to be **canalized,** a term introduced by Waddington. Like water channeled into a narrow flow by a canal, canalized traits follow a strictly defined path, regardless of most kinds of environmental and genetic variations. Children's acquisition of language is often cited as an example of a canalized developmental process in humans. Only the most severe genetic disorders or prolonged deprivation of language input seems capable of deflecting language development from its species-typical path.

Phenotypic plasticity ensures that each individual is able to adapt to changes in the environment, while canalization ensures that individuals are not thrown off the developmental track by environmental or genetic variations. Together, plasticity and canalization have tremendous power in organizing children's development.

In the next section, we will continue to explore the genotype–phenotype relationship by considering whether and how certain phenotypic traits of parents are likely to occur in the development of their offspring.

Heritability

You have no doubt often seen news reports announcing the discovery of links between certain genes and this or that physical or psychological trait. Although it is tempting to look for genetic causes to explain human characteristics—from physical traits such as height and weight to behavioral traits such as aggressiveness, thrill-seeking, musical talent, intelligence, and so on—developmentalists know that the gene–behavior relationship is usually more complex. In particular, they know that any trait that shows a large range of individual differences—shyness, say—is almost certainly influenced by multiple genes, as well as by characteristics of the environment. Consequently, their conclusions about the role of genes with respect to phenotypic traits are likely to use the phrase "genetically influenced" rather than "genetically caused."

Estimating Heritability
In the broadest sense, the **heritability** of a particular trait is the amount of phenotypic variation in a population that is due to genetic variation. Geneticists who study heritability will often use statistical methods to calculate correlations, or estimates of the association between a characteristic and genetic relatedness (Plomin et al., 2001). High correlations reflect high heritability for the characteristic; low correlations, low heritability.

Consider the example of height, which for North Americans has a heritability of about 90 percent, meaning that for the population as a whole, 90 percent of the variation in height is the result of genetic factors. Keep in mind that heritability estimates are for populations; in another population the heritability of height might be considerably lower. The reason for the high heritability of height in the United States is the relative lack of environmental diversity: Most of the population has access to a reasonable quality of nutrition and health care, so environmental differences play relatively less of a role in height differences, and genetic differences relatively more of a role (Tanner, 1990).

Studying Heritability
To study the heritability of a given trait, developmentalists use **kinship studies,** determining the extent to which relatives of varying degrees of genetic closeness are similar on the trait in question (Emde & Hewitt, 2001). Biological parents and their children share 50 percent of their genes; siblings

---

canalized A trait that is canalized follows a strictly defined path, regardless of most environmental and genetic variations.

heritability A measure of the degree to which a variation in a particular trait among individuals in a specific population is related to genetic differences among those individuals.

kinship studies The use of naturally occurring conditions provided by kinship relations to estimate genetic and environmental contributions to a phenotypic trait.

These Japanese teenagers are clearly enjoying this interactive video game. Research suggests that their enthusiasm may be due to both genetic and environmental factors. Genetic factors may contribute to good eye–hand coordination, enhancing their enjoyment of, and leading them to seek out experiences requiring such skill. At the same time, repeated exposure to such experiences results in even greater skill and, consequently, greater pleasure in challenging experiences.

AFP Photo/Toru Yamanaka/Getty Images

family study A study that compares members of the same family to determine how similar they are on a given trait.

twin study A study in which groups of monozygotic (identical) and dizygotic (fraternal) twins of the same sex are compared to each other and to other family members for similarity on a given trait.

adoption study A study in which genetically related individuals who are raised in different family environments or genetically unrelated individuals living in the same family are compared to determine the extent to which heredity or environment controls a given trait.

(except for identical twins) also share 50 percent of their genes; half siblings share 25 percent of their genes; and so on. If the extent of similarity on the trait correlates strongly with the degree of genetic closeness, it can be inferred that the trait is highly heritable, while weaker correlations indicate lower heritability. The three main types of research designs used in kinship studies are family studies, twin studies, and adoption studies.

In the typical **family study,** relatives who live together in a household—parents, children, stepchildren, half siblings—are compared with one another to determine how similar they are on a given trait. The shortcoming of family studies for estimating the degree of genetic influence is the obvious fact that relatives who live together not only share genes but also participate in the same family environment. Thus, whatever similarities are found among them could be attributed to environmental influences as well as to hereditary ones.

In order to obtain more precise estimates of genetic and environmental contributions to individual differences, researchers capitalize on the other two designs. In a **twin study,** monozygotic twins and dizygotic twins of the same sex are compared with each other and with other family members for similarity on a given trait. Since MZ twins have 100 percent of their genes in common, MZ twins raised together should, to the degree that the trait in question is genetically influenced, show greater similarity on the trait than do DZ twins or other siblings. By the same logic, DZ twins and siblings should be more similar than half siblings.

In an **adoption study,** researchers compare children who have been reared apart from their biological parents. Some adoption studies compare twins or other siblings who have been adopted into different families; others compare children and their adoptive and biological parents. The basic purpose of this strategy is to determine if adopted children are more similar to their biological parents and siblings, who share their genes, or to their adoptive parents and siblings, with whom they share a family environment.

Many family, twin, and adoption studies have shown that the degree of similarity among kin correlates with the degree of genetic similarity. This pattern has been obtained for such varied characteristics as Attention-Deficit/Hyperactivity Disorder (McLoughlin et al., 2007), intelligence (Harden, Turkheimer, & Loehlin, 2007), cheerfulness (Robinson, Emde & Corley, 2001), antisocial behavior (Viding et al., 2008), and susceptibility to schizophrenia (Edvardsen et al., 2008). Table 2.3, for example, shows results from a massive study of the correlations between the personalities of family members of differing degrees of genetic relatedness (Loehlin, 1992). The personality trait studied is "extroversion," which includes general sociability, impulsiveness, and liveliness.

Both genetic and environmental influences are evident in the table. If you focus first on genetic influences, you will see that the correlations for MZ twins are markedly greater than those for DZ twins or other siblings, whether they are raised together in a single family or apart in different families. You can also see that the degree of correlation between personality scores decreases consistently as the degree of genetic relatedness decreases. Environmental influences clearly play a role as well. The correlation between scores for the MZ twins is well below 1.0, although these twins share 100 percent of their genes. In addition, the correlation between biological relatives who are raised together is higher than that between biological relatives raised apart.

Like family studies, twin and adoption studies are not without problems. It is possible, for example, that MZ twins may receive more similar treatment from parents and others than do DZ twins or other siblings, and to the extent that they do, MZ twins may be more alike than DZ twins for environmental rather than genetic reasons (Segal, 1999). In addition, when siblings are adopted by different families and raised apart, the rearing environments may be similar because adoption agencies generally attempt to place children with adoptive parents whose social and cultural backgrounds match those of the biological parents (Joseph, 2001). Thus, the extent to which adopted children are similar to their biological families might not be entirely attributable to the similarity of their genes, but may also be due to environmental similarities.

A further complication for kinship studies is that children within a family do not share the same family environment. Age, birth order, and gender can all affect how children within the same family experience family life, and differences in family-linked experiences may create differences between the siblings (McGuire, 2002; Segal, 1999). For example, not only do parents treat each of their children differently, but siblings offer different environments for each other. In addition, siblings are likely to have different teachers at school, different friends, and different experiences outside the home. The fact that the distinctive environments experienced by different children in the same family can lead to differences in their development in no way minimizes the importance of genetic factors. Rather, it affirms the principle that genes and the environment make essential contributions to phenotypic development.

An excellent illustration of this principle comes from a recent study of identical twins, conducted by Manuel Esteller, at the Spanish National Cancer Center in Madrid (Fraga et al., 2005). At birth, identical twins are on their way to developing identical phenotypes. However, as you already know, even genetically identical individuals develop phenotypic differences. What is particularly interesting about Esteller's research is his demonstration that the phenotypic traits of identical twins become increasingly different as the twins grow older, and become greater still as the twins live apart in adulthood. The increasing divergence of their phenotypic characteristics is due in part to increasing differences in the twins' exposure to environmental and social factors assumed to influence phenotypic development, such as toxins, stress, and nutrition.

table 2.3

Family and Adoption Results for Extroversion

Type of Relative	Actual Correlation	Percentage of Shared Genes
MZ twins raised together	.51	100
DZ twins raised together	.18	50
MZ twins raised apart	.38	100
DZ twins raised apart	.05	50
Parents/children living together	.16	50
Adoptive parents and children	.01	00
Siblings raised together	.20	50
Siblings raised apart	−.07	50

Source: Loehlin, 1992.

Genotypes, Phenotypes, and Human Behavior

At this point, you have a fairly good idea about how phenotypes develop in response to genetic and environmental factors. But Waddington's image of a ball rolling down a landscape, drifting across valleys, and falling into canals is limited in two ways, both of which relate to how the landscape is formed and reformed over the course of development. First, Waddington's account can suggest that developing individuals themselves play but a small role in the process of their own development, when this is far from the case. Second, Waddington's ideas fail to adequately capture how the individual's cultural and social environments form and transform the landscape over the lifetime of the individual. We will now explore these issues in more detail.

niche construction The active shaping and modification of individuals' environments by the individuals' own behaviors, activities, and choices.

co-construction The shaping of environments through interactions between children and their caregivers, siblings, neighbors, and friends.

ecological inheritance Environmental modifications, as a result of niche construction, that affect the development of offspring and descendants.

Niche Construction Developmentalists are becoming increasingly aware of how children actively contribute to their own development. Recall from Chapter 1 that Piaget's theory of development stresses how children *construct* their knowledge of the world through their activities and behaviors. **Niche construction** is the term that developmentalists use to refer to how the behaviors, activities, and choices of individuals actively shape and modify the environments (*niches*) in which they live. For example, an unusually quiet and nondemanding infant may receive little social interaction and stimulation from her busy family simply because she seems content to be by herself. When she enters school, her lack of social and communication skills may make it hard for her to join group play, contributing to her further social withdrawal and isolation. Or think about the 10-year-old boy who wants to be just like his big brother—a gang member. He follows his brother around and hangs out on the fringe of the group, trying to talk, dress, and act in ways that would please them. Naturally, because his time and attention are spent in this way, he is not exposed to alternative contexts that may provide other, more healthy avenues for his development.

In different ways, the behaviors of both these children dramatically affect the very environments in which they are developing. In this respect, the children play active roles in the process of niche construction (Laland et al., 2000; Lewontin, 2000; Parker, 2005). It is important to note, however, that niche construction is a social, not an individual, process. The quiet baby, for example, may have fared quite differently in a less busy family, in which a parent, grandparent, or other caregiver took a great deal of pleasure and time interacting with the quiet, companionable baby. Developmentalists use the term **co-construction** to capture the way that environments are shaped and reshaped through interactions between developing individuals and their caregivers, siblings, neighbors, and playmates.

Ecological Inheritance You know from Chapter 1 that Bronfenbrenner used the term *ecology,* which refers to the relationship between individuals and their environments, to explain how children develop at the center of nested, interacting social systems. Developmentalists interested in the biological foundations of human development have found it useful to return to a more expansive definition of ecology, one that includes not only children's social environments but their physical environments as well. This broader definition has encouraged scientists to explore the complex relationships between children and the environments in which they develop.

The term **ecological inheritance** refers to how niche construction can result in environmental modifications that affect the development of offspring and descendants. Such modifications take place when individuals or families elect to move to new places or when large groups of people migrate from one area to another— a behavior that ecologists refer to as *selection of habitat.* For example, if a young couple moves from a rural to an urban environment (habitat), they reconstruct the niche in which their children, and perhaps many future generations, will live and develop. This reconstruction occurs on a larger level when groups of people migrate to a new land in order to escape environmental disaster, oppression, or violence, or to seek economic, educational, or political advantages.

The modifications that descendants inherit may also come about through *changes to the existing habitat.* Some examples include structural changes such as building homes, subway systems, or schools. Other examples include depleting resources or introducing toxins—frequent consequences of human activity (for example, cutting down forests for building materials or polluting water sources with industrial waste).

Whether through selection of habitat or changes to the existing habitat, it is the niche-constructing behaviors and lifestyles of individuals that bring about the modified environments that are passed on to offspring and descendants through the process of ecological inheritance. Recent research undertaken from an ecological perspective has demonstrated the remarkable and sensitive connections between human behavior and the developing individual's genotype and phenotype. These connections become especially apparent in light of arguments regarding how our biological and cultural inheritances have coevolved.

coevolution The combined process that emerges from the interaction of biological evolution and cultural evolution.

Baldwin effect The role of cultural factors in determining which phenotypes are adaptive.

▌▌▌▌ APPLY ▪ CONNECT ▪ DISCUSS

If you could clone a child from your own exact genes and thereby create a genetic twin, how would this twin be the same as or different from you? Why?

In what ways does your own behavior shape your environment? How might this affect your children?

In human beings, language is a highly canalized trait, whereas intelligence appears to have greater plasticity. Why does this make sense from an evolutionary standpoint?

The Coevolution of Culture and Biology

For many years it was believed that the biological and cultural characteristics of humans developed in a strict sequence: the biological capacities we associate with humanity evolved to a critical point at which humans became capable of developing language and generating culture. Now, however, the situation is believed to have been far more complicated. Contemporary studies of human origins have found evidence that rudimentary forms of culture were already present during early phases of human evolution. *Australopithecus* relatives of those who left the famous Laetoli footprints domesticated fire, built shelters, engaged in organized hunting, and used tools—flint knives, cooking utensils, and notation systems.

Developmentalists are becoming increasingly aware of how culture and biology interact in a process of **coevolution** (Parker, 2005; Richerson & Boyd, 2005; Henrich & Henrich, 2006). Interestingly, the idea is a rather old one in the developmental sciences. James Mark Baldwin, whom we introduced in Chapter 1, proposed that cultural factors may influence the likelihood that people with various mental and physical qualities will survive and reproduce. His idea has been recently resurrected and dubbed the **Baldwin effect** (West-Eberhard, 2003). Cultural evolution and transmission of information about how to obtain and preserve food, how to make shelters, and how to heal the sick and injured are obvious examples of how cultural practices contribute to reproductive success. Individuals who have access to these types of cultural tools are more likely to live to reproductive maturity and to pass on both their genes and their cultural knowledge to the next generation. Insofar as the capacity to engage in cultural activities and make use of culture's material and symbolic tools confers a selective reproductive advantage, it is probable that the more effective users of culture have been more successful in passing on their genes to succeeding generations. In short, the two forms of evolution, biological and cultural, have interacted and coevolved, as we illustrate below with two famous examples.

Quechua chid care practices illustrate the coevolution of culture and biology. In their extremely cold environment, parents who use the cultural practices of infant swaddling and carrying are more likely to have surviving offspring, and thus more likely to pass both their genes and their cultural knowledge to the next generation.

Art Wolfe/Photo Researchers

Lactose Tolerance

Our first example of the coevolution of biology and culture comes from a study of *lactose tolerance*—that is, the ability to digest fresh milk (Durham, 1991; Jablonka & Lamb, 2005). Following the domestication of cattle some 6000 years ago, humans began to use milk, cheese, and other dairy products for food. However, despite the popular notion that milk is the "perfect food," most adults in the world are unable to profit from its nutritional content and get indigestion and diarrhea if they drink it. This is because they cannot produce a sufficient amount of lactase, an enzyme that is needed to break down the milk sugar lactose. The ability to produce lactase is present in virtually all newborn mammals, including humans, but it normally declines after weaning. Nevertheless, some adults, particularly among those of European descent, can digest milk because they have a variant allele of the gene responsible for producing lactase, and this allele overrides the normal postweaning shutdown of lactase production. Interestingly, the variant allele is most likely to occur in cultures that have experienced a selection pressure for adults to benefit from milk consumption. Pastoral nomads of the Middle East and Africa are an example. Hunger and thirst were probably very common among these groups, so animals that had been originally domesticated for meat became a source of food and drink in the form of fresh milk. In these "dairying cultures," those with the variant lactase allele were more likely to survive and have children, thus passing on the genetic capacity for digesting milk.

In Scandinavian countries, more than 90 percent of the adult population has the variant lactase allele. But in this case, the selective advantage is related to the fact that lactose, like Vitamin D, aids in the absorption of calcium. In sunny regions, exposure to the sun produces enough Vitamin D to ensure that individuals absorb sufficient calcium to avoid rickets and other bone diseases. However, in the northern climes of Scandinavia where the hours of sunlight are scant and people are well-bundled against the cold, lactose provides an excellent alternative. Interestingly, many Scandinavian myths and legends feature cows as sacred creatures and milk as a food of the gods and a source of strength.

Pastoral nomads of the Middle East, such as this Bedouin woman and her child, probably evolved the ability to digest milk as a consequence of selection pressure; in a land of food and water scarcity, milk provides both good nutrition and hydration.

Peter Schickert/Peter Arnold

Sickle-Cell Anemia

Another example of the coevolution of biology and culture involves the recessive-gene disorder known as *sickle-cell anemia*. People who inherit the recessive gene for this disorder from both parents, and thus are homozygous for it, have seriously abnormal red blood cells. Normally, red blood cells are disc-shaped, smooth, and flexible, but in people with sickle-cell anemia, they are more rigid and sticky, with a curved, sickle shape (Figure 2.11). Particularly when the supply of oxygen to the blood is reduced, as it may be at high altitudes, after heavy physical exertion, during a fever, or while under anesthesia, these abnormal blood cells tend to clump together and clog the body's smaller blood vessels, damaging affected organs and causing severe pain (Chang, Ye, & Kan, 2006). Because of their characteristics, sickle cells are prone to rupturing and die off much more quickly than normal red blood cells do, often resulting in chronic anemia. Complications of sickle-cell anemia may also lead to early death. People who are heterozygous for the sickle-cell gene are said to have the *sickle-cell trait* and usually do not suffer symptoms.

Sickle-cell anemia is found most prominently among people of African descent. In the United States, the incidence of the sickle-cell trait among African Americans is about 8 to 9 percent. But in West Africa, the incidence of the sickle-cell trait is greater than 20 percent (Serjeant & Serjeant, 2001). This difference is explained in large part by the fact that carriers of the sickle-cell trait are highly resistant to the parasite that causes malaria. Interestingly, much of the West African coast is infested with malaria because the cultural practice of cutting down vast forests has radically increased the habitat and reproductive success of malaria-carrying mosquitoes. Needless to say, West Africans who carry the sickle-cell gene are at a selective advantage because they are less likely to suffer from malaria, which can be deadly, and are more likely to survive to reproduce. Because of this selective advantage, the frequency of the sickle-cell gene has been maintained in the West African population despite the losses caused by the deaths of homozygous carriers. In the United States, where the sickle-cell trait confers no advantage, it is gradually being eliminated from the gene pool.

APPLY ═ CONNECT ═ DISCUSS

Think of some examples from your own cultural practices that may contribute to our species' evolution.

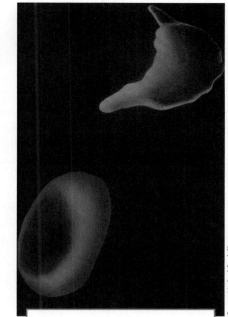

Figure 2.11 A normal, round, red blood cell (bottom) and a sickle-shaped red blood cell (top) from a person with sickle-cell anemia.

Custom Medical Stock Photo

Retracing the Laetoli Footprints

We began this chapter by piecing together a scene from an ancient world. We asked how our evolutionary forebears experienced that world and how their lives and experiences were similar to yet different from our own. An understanding of our biocultural foundations, we argued, provides insight into why all children follow a common path of biological and cultural development, but why each child is nevertheless distinct from all others. Indeed, as we explained throughout the chapter, the complex interplay between commonality and distinctiveness, similarity and diversity, assures that our biological and cultural heritages are passed on to subsequent generations but continue to evolve through time.

Although we have no way of knowing what happened to the individuals whose footprints on the world would survive for 3 million years, it is interesting to speculate about their fate in light of contemporary knowledge of the coevolution of our biological and cultural inheritances. The thick ash that recorded their steps suggests that volcanic activity was affecting their physical habitat, probably limiting food and water resources. So why was their pace so unhurried? Perhaps they, and others like them, were used to volcanic eruptions, and were able, for a time at least, to eke out a life with the food and water resources available to them. We know, however, that under such circumstances their reproductive success would be more restricted than it would be in resource-rich environments, and their contributions to the human gene pool and cultural toolkit more limited. But perhaps they were in the process of migrating to a new habitat with better resources and more opportunities to reproduce—biologically and culturally. If so, was this because the particular individuals were phenotypically uncommonly intelligent or had personality traits that encouraged their migration in the face of environmental destruction?

We may never know the answer to these questions. However, the accumulating knowledge of how biology and culture interact inspires us to consider ourselves in light of our biocultural foundations. The complex interactions between biology and culture are present at the very beginning of each life, when genes in the zygote start to express themselves and guide the creation of new cells that will ultimately result in a unique human being. Chapter 3 follows the course of this development from the moment the genetic material of the mother and father come together. In later chapters, as we follow the general patterns of the development of children, you will encounter many instances of the elegant dance between biology and culture.

SUMMARY

Inheriting Culture

- Culture is defined by the use of material and symbolic tools that accumulate over time, are passed on through social processes, and provide resources for the developing child. Material tools are observable, including manufactured objects and patterns of behavior. Symbolic tools are more abstract, including systems of knowledge, beliefs, and values. Both types of tools provide resources for development by mediating children's behavior—that is, by organizing children's activities, including how children relate to their environment.

- Culture is inherited through social processes whereby children learn to use their culture's tools. These processes include social enhancement, in which children make use of tools simply because they are available; imitation, in which children copy the tool-using behaviors of others; and explicit instruction, which uses language and other symbolic communication. The use of symbolic communication is claimed to be uniquely human, allowing us to teach children about things not immediately present in the environment and about abstractions such as spiritual belief systems.

- Cultures change through the process of cumulative cultural evolution, as individuals produce variations in the tools they use, both material tools (as in the production of new technologies) and symbolic tools (as in changing belief systems and the introduction of new knowledge). This process of change is complex and messy, not a harmonious pattern of progress.

Biological Inheritance

- Biological evolution is made possible by heredity—the transmission of genes from parents to offspring. Genes contain instructions that guide the formation of the individual's traits. The genotype (the individual's particular set of genes) strongly influences the phenotype (the individual's actual traits) but does not completely determine the phenotype, which is also strongly influenced by the individual's environment.

- Natural selection is the process whereby individuals with phenotypes well adapted to the local environment survive and reproduce to a greater extent than individuals with less well-adapted phenotypes, preferentially passing on the genotypes associated with the better-adapted phenotypes. Over many generations, the more adaptive variations of phenotypic traits increase in the species as a whole, while the less adaptive variations decrease. The emergence of shorter pregnancies in our prehuman ancestors is an example of the process of natural selection, and it has been argued that the behavioral trait of baby-talk similarly evolved.

- Humans reproduce through sexual reproduction: The 23 chromosomes in the mother's ovum and the 23 chromosomes in the father's sperm are combined at conception, when ovum and sperm fuse to form a zygote with 23 pairs of corresponding chromosomes, 46 in all. A chromosome is a molecule of DNA; a gene is a segment of a chromosome, a working subunit of DNA.

- The sperm and ova are called germ cells; all the other cells of the body are called somatic cells.

- New somatic cells, each with 46 chromosomes in 23 pairs identical to those in the zygote, are constantly formed through mitosis. New germ cells, each with only 23 chromosomes, are formed through meiosis.

- A child's sex is determined by the chromosomes of the twenty-third pair—females have two X chromosomes, males an X and a Y chromosome.

- A person who inherits the same form of a gene (the same allele) from both parents is homozygous for the trait influenced by that gene; a person who inherits different alleles is heterozygous. When a person is heterozygous for a particular trait, three outcomes are possible:

  - One allele is dominant (the person fully expresses the characteristics associated with that allele) and the other is recessive (its characteristics are not expressed, but the allele can be passed on; if two people are carriers of a recessive allele for a disorder, the child may develop the disorder).

  - The person expresses characteristics intermediate between those associated with each allele.

  - The alleles are codominant (the person fully expresses the characteristics associated with each allele).

- Mutations—alterations in the structure of an individual's DNA—can be passed on to the next generation if they occur in germ cells. Mutation is the only process that can add new genes to the gene pool and thus is an important source of variation of genotypes. However, most mutations are harmful or even lethal, not adaptive.

- Disorders related to genetic abnormalities may result from genes inherited through normal processes of inheritance (for example, phenylketonuria) or from a breakdown in

3

Prenatal Development and Birth

Foua Lee is pregnant for the 10th time. Raised in the Hmong community of Laos, Foua knows that she must pay careful attention to her food cravings to insure the health of her unborn child. If she craves ginger and fails to eat it, the child may be born with an extra finger or toe; if she craves but does not eat chicken flesh, the child may have a blemish near its ear; and if she craves but does not eat eggs, the child may have a lumpy head. When she feels the first pangs of labor, Foua will hurry to her house, or at least to the house of her husband's cousins, because if she gives birth anywhere else she may be injured by an evil spirit. Foua will give birth without an attendant, delivering the baby into her own hands by reaching between her legs to ease out the head and then letting the rest of the body slip out onto her bent forearms. Soon after the birth, the father, Nao Kao, will dig a deep hole in the dirt floor of their home and bury the placenta. Hmong believe that the placenta is a "jacket" for the soul. When a Hmong dies, his or her soul must travel back to the burial place of the placenta, put on the jacket in which it was born and, thus protected, continue its dangerous journey to the land of ancestors from which it will one day be summoned to be reborn as the soul of a new baby. Indeed, a few days after their child is born, Foua and Nao Kao will sacrifice a pig and invite family and friends to witness the soul-calling ritual. Attracted by the sacrifice, as well as promises and prayers from parents and elders, an ancestor will be reborn in their infant's body. (Adapted from Fadiman, 1998.)

oua's beliefs about how to insure a healthy pregnancy and successful delivery, and her experiences giving birth to her children, sound both foreign and familiar to those of us who have been raised in technologically advanced societies. Foua worries that unmet food cravings may result in particular malformations; we worry that nutritional deficiencies or environmental toxins may harm the developing fetus. Foua gives birth at home where she feels protected from malevolent spirits; we give birth in hospitals or birthing centers where we feel safer in the event that medical problems arise. Foua and her family engage in ritual practices that link her newborn to a spiritual ancestral world; our families participate in a variety of ritual practices (circumcision, baptism) to welcome, celebrate, and proclaim our babies as members of specific religious communities.

Regardless of the particular beliefs and practices that each of us embrace as a consequence of our cultural heritage, it is clear that bringing children into the world is a matter of enormous weight and is approached with great care across the globe. The special consideration and care devoted to pregnancy and childbirth are understandable in light of the fact that some of the most eventful and vulnerable periods of human growth and development occur during the 9 months of life in the womb and during the hours spent in transition between the womb and the outside world.

In a traditional Laotian practice, the umbilical cord of this newborn is being cut with a razor-sharp piece of bamboo.

Jim Holmes/World Health Organization

We begin as a **zygote,** a single cell the size of a period on this page, weighing approximately 15 millionths of a gram. At birth, a brief 9 months later, we consist of some 2 billion cells and weigh, on the average, 7 pounds. Along with these remarkable changes in size are truly astonishing changes in form (Figure 3.1) and in behavior. The first few cells to develop from the zygote are all identical, but in a few weeks many different kinds of cells will be arranged in intricately structured, interdependent organs. In a few months, the baby-to-be will move and respond actively to its environment.

The study of prenatal development seeks to explain how these changes in size, form, and behavior take place. Understanding prenatal development is important for both theoretical and practical reasons.

On the theoretical side, many developmentalists consider prenatal development to be a model for development during all subsequent periods, from birth to death, as various principles of development are first seen in action during the prenatal period. For example, development is characterized by changes both in the form of the organism and in the kinds of interactions the changing organism has with its environment. Following discussion of prenatal development, we will outline these principles in Table 3.4 (see page 104).

On the practical side, understanding the prenatal period is important because the developing organism can be positively or adversely affected by the mother-to-be's nutritional status, health, and habits, including whether or not she uses drugs or alcohol. Considerable research is devoted to promoting healthy prenatal development and preventing damage to the growing organism.

In order to understand the relation of prenatal development in the womb to later development in the world, we first must trace the changes that take place as the organism progresses from zygote to newborn and examine the environmental factors that support or threaten development. Then we can consider the circumstances surrounding the newborn's entrance into the world.

Figure 3.1 Changes in the size and form of the human body from 14 days to 15 weeks after conception. (Adapted from Arey, 1974.)

14 days

18 days

24 days

4 weeks

6.5 weeks

8 weeks

9 weeks

11 weeks

15 weeks

The Periods of Prenatal Development

The transformations that occur during prenatal development are nothing short of amazing. Through a microscope, the fertilized ovum, or zygote, appears to be made up of small particles inside larger ones. The chromosomes bearing the genes are contained within the nucleus at the center of the cell. Surrounding the nucleus is the cell matter, which serves as the raw material for the first few cell divisions. Within the first few weeks after conception, this single cell subdivides many times to form many kinds of cells with vastly different destinies. In approximately 266 days, these cells will have been transformed into a wriggling, crying infant.

Developmental scientists often divide prenatal development into three broad periods, each characterized by distinctive patterns of growth and interaction between the organism and its environment: the germinal period, the embryonic period, and the fetal period.

1. The **germinal period** begins when the mother's and father's germ cells are joined at conception, and lasts until the developing organism becomes attached to the wall of the uterus, about 8 to 10 days later.

2. The **embryonic period** extends from the time the organism becomes attached to the uterus until the end of the 8th week, when all the major organs have taken primitive shape.

3. The **fetal period** begins the 9th week after conception, with the first signs of the hardening of the bones, and continues until birth. During this period, the primitive organ systems develop to the point where the baby can exist outside the mother without medical support.

At any step in these prenatal periods, the process of development may stop. One study estimates that approximately 25 percent of all pregnancies end before the woman even recognizes that she is pregnant (Wilcox, Baird, & Weinberg, 1999). If all goes well, however, the creation of a new human being is under way.

zygote The single cell formed at conception from the union of the sperm and the ovum.

germinal period The period that begins at conception and lasts until the developing organism becomes attached to the wall of the uterus about 8 to 10 days later.

embryonic period The period that extends from the time the organism becomes attached to the uterus until the end of the 8th week of pregnancy, when all the major organs have taken primitive shape.

fetal period This period begins the 9th week after conception, with the first signs of the hardening of the bones, and continues until birth.

cleavage The series of mitotic cell divisions that transform the zygote into the blastocyst.

heterochrony Variability in the rates of development of different parts of the organism.

heterogeneity Variability in the levels of development of different parts of the organism at a given time.

The Germinal Period

During the first 8 to 10 days after conception, the zygote moves slowly through the fallopian tube, where fertilization occurred, and into the uterus (Figure 3.2). The timing of this journey is crucial. If the zygote enters the uterus too soon or too late, the uterine environment will not be hormonally prepared and the organism will be destroyed.

The First Cells of Life Recall from Chapter 2 (p. 63–64) that all body cells reproduce through the process of duplication and cell division known as *mitosis*. About 24 hours after conception, as the zygote travels down the fallopian tube, **cleavage** begins—the zygote divides by mitosis into two cells, which then also divide, and so on (see Figure 3.3). Thanks to this repeated duplication, the developing organism will already consist of hundreds of cells by the time it reaches the uterus. An important characteristic of cleavage is that the cells existing at any given moment do not all divide at the same time. Instead of proceeding in an orderly fashion from a two–cell stage to a four–cell stage and so on, cells divide at different rates (Tokita, Kiyoshi, & Armstrong, 2007). This is the first instance of developmental **heterochrony**, whereby different parts of the organism develop at different rates. (*Heterochrony* literally means "variability in time.") This unevenness in rates of development gives rise to **heterogeneity**—variability

Figure 3.2 Development of the human embryo in the mother's reproductive tract from fertilization to implantation. (Adapted from Tuchmann-Duplessis, David, & Haegel, 1971.)

in the levels of development of different parts of the organism at a given time. The fact that a newborn baby's sense of hearing is more advanced than its ability to see, for example, means that it will recognize its mother more readily by the sound of her voice than the way she looks. Both kinds of variability play an important role in the process of development throughout the life of the child.

As illustrated in Figure 3.3, cells formed during the first several cleavages resemble Ping-Pong balls crowded into a balloon. At this very early stage of development, all these cells are **totipotent** ("totally potent") **stem cells,** meaning that each has the potential to grow into an embryo and, ultimately, a normal, healthy baby (Do, Han, & Scholer, 2006). In fact, identical twins develop when this single mass of totipotent cells separates into two cell masses, which then develop into two individual, genetically identical human beings. Such developmental freedom at the cellular level—the ability to develop into virtually any type of human cell and, consequently, into an entirely distinct human being—is unique to this very early period of cell division. The adult body harbors stem cells in various tissues and organs, where they lie dormant until activated by injury or illness; however, these cells are more limited in their developmental potential. A stem cell in the brain, for instance, can become different sorts of neural cells (a neuron or glial cell) but not a bone or liver cell. Because they are capable of becoming different types of cells but not any type of cell, adult stem cells are referred to as *multipotent stem cells.* As you are probably aware, totipotent stem cells have generated considerable interest among scientists, who believe they can be used to replace damaged cells associated with myriad diseases, including heart disease, leukemia and other cancers, Parkinson's disease, and Type I diabetes.

Figure 3.3 A zygote after two cleavages, resulting in four cells of equal size and appearance.

Dr. Yorgos Nikas/Photo Researchers, Inc.

totipotent stem cells Cells that have the potential to grow into a complete embryo and, ultimately, a normal, healthy infant.

implantation The process by which the blastocyst becomes attached to the uterus.

amnion A thin, tough, transparent membrane that holds the amniotic fluid.

chorion One of the membranes that develops out of the trophoblast. It forms the fetal component of the placenta.

placenta An organ made up of tissue from both the mother and the fetus that serves as a barrier and filter between their bloodstreams.

umbilical cord A soft tube containing blood vessels that connects the developing organism to the placenta.

ectoderm Cells of the inner cell mass that develop into the outer surface of the skin, the nails, part of the teeth, the lens of the eye, the inner ear, and the central nervous system.

endoderm Cells of the inner cell mass that develop into the digestive system and the lungs.

mesoderm The cells of the inner cell mass that give rise to the muscles, the bones, the circulatory system, and the inner layers of the skin.

Implantation As the developing cell mass moves farther into the uterus, the outer cells put out tiny branches that burrow into the spongy wall of the uterus until they come in contact with the mother's blood vessels. Thus begins **implantation,** the process by which the developing organism becomes attached to the uterus. Implantation marks the transition between the germinal and the embryonic periods. Like other transitions, such as birth itself, implantation is hazardous for the organism; pregnancy loss during this process is common.

The Embryonic Period

If the developing organism is successfully implanted, it enters the period of the embryo, which lasts for about 6 weeks. During this time, all the basic organs of the body take shape and the organism begins to respond to direct stimulation. The organism's rapid growth during this period is facilitated by the efficient way in which the mother now supplies nutrition and protects the organism from harmful environmental influences.

Sources of Nutrition and Protection Early in the embryonic period, the **amnion,** a thin, tough, transparent membrane that holds the *amniotic fluid,* surrounds the embryo (the amnion and the fluid are often called the "bag of waters"). The amniotic fluid cushions the organism as the mother moves about, provides liquid support for its weak muscles and soft bones, and gives it a medium in which it can move and change position.

Surrounding the amnion is another membrane, the **chorion,** which later becomes the fetal component of the **placenta,** a complex organ made up of tissue from both the mother and the embryo (Figure 3.4). The placenta and the embryo are linked by the **umbilical cord.** Until birth, the placenta acts simultaneously as a barrier that prevents the bloodstreams of the mother and the infant from

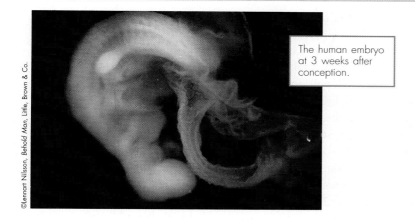

The human embryo at 3 weeks after conception.

©Lennart Nilsson, *Behold Man*, Little, Brown & Co.

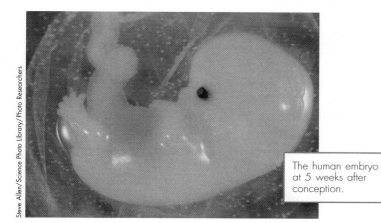

Steve Allen/Science Photo Library/Photo Researchers

The human embryo at 5 weeks after conception.

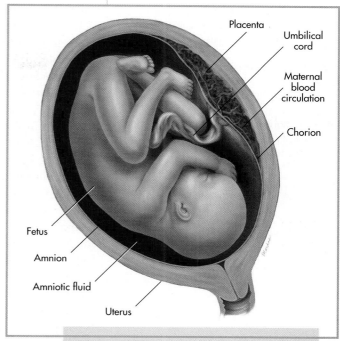

Placenta

Umbilical cord

Maternal blood circulation

Chorion

Fetus

Amnion

Amniotic fluid

Uterus

Figure 3.4 The fetus in its protective environment. (Adapted from Curtis, 1979.)

coming into direct contact with each other and as a filter that allows nutrients and oxygen to be exchanged. It converts nutrients carried by the mother's blood into food for the embryo. It also enables the embryo's waste products to be absorbed by the mother's bloodstream, from which they are eventually extracted by her kidneys. Thus the mother literally eats, breathes, and urinates for two.

Embryonic Growth While the outer cells of the developing organism are forming the placenta and the other membranes that will supply and protect the embryo, the growing number of cells in the inner cell mass begin to differentiate into the various kinds of cells that eventually will become all the organs of the body (Figure 3.5). The first step in this process is the separation of the inner cell mass into two layers. The **ectoderm,** the outer layer, gives rise to the outer surface of the skin, the nails, part of the teeth, the lens of the eye, the inner ear, and the nervous system (the brain, the spinal cord, and the nerves). The **endoderm,** the inner layer, develops into the digestive system and the lungs. Shortly after these two layers form, a middle layer appears, the **mesoderm,** which will eventually become the muscles, the bones, the circulatory system, and the inner layers of the skin (Gilbert, 2001).

One of nature's greatest mysteries is the process through which a few identical stem cells with unlimited developmental capacity evolve into a highly differentiated cell community composed of specialized parts. How does a cell know to act like part of the endoderm, rather than the exoderm or mesoderm? How does a cell know to form skin tissue, rather than blood or liver tissue? Recall from Chapter 2 that each cell contains something

Figure 3.5 Within days of fertilization, a highly organized cell community develops. Distinct parts of the community are identified according to their location and the specialized functions they will develop. The ectoderm (outer layer) will develop functions associated with the growth of the skin, nails, and nervous system. The endoderm (inner layer) will develop functions associated with the digestive system and lungs. The mesoderm (middle layer) will develop functions associated with the growth of bones and the circular system.

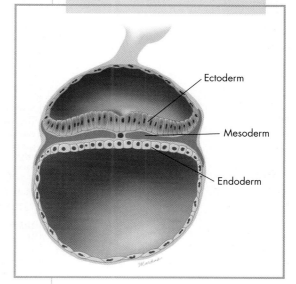

Ectoderm

Mesoderm

Endoderm

epigenesis The process by which a new form emerges through the interactions of the preceding form and its current environment.

cephalocaudal pattern The pattern of development that proceeds from the head down.

proximodistal pattern The pattern of development that proceeds from the middle of the organism out to the periphery.

on the order of 25,000 genes, the vast majority of which it must ignore as it develops into its specialized phenotypic role—as skin, blood, or liver, for example. Current explanations emphasize the idea that each new phenotypic form emerges as a result of the interactions that take place between the preceding form and its environment, a process called **epigenesis** (from the Greek, meaning "at the time of generation") (Gottlieb & Lickliter, 2007). And what is the environment of a cell? In part, a cell's environment consists of surrounding cells, which exchange information and regulate each other's activities. Thus, a stem cell "knows" it should act like part of the endoderm because surrounding endoderm cells have "told" it to do so. Interestingly, the signals from the surrounding cells do not appear to communicate which genes should be turned on, but rather which genes should remain inactive (Boyer et al., 2005). According to the epigenetic explanation of embryonic development, the different interactions that cells have with their environmental conditions (including each other) is what leads to the creation of new kinds of cells and subsequent new forms of interactions between the organism and the environment (Gilbert, 2001).

The embryo develops at a breathtaking pace, as you can see in Table 3.1. The table also reflects two patterns of body development that are maintained until the organism reaches adolescence. In the first, the **cephalocaudal pattern,** development proceeds from the head down. The arm buds, for instance, appear before the leg buds. In the second, the **proximodistal pattern,** development proceeds from the middle of the organism out to the periphery. Thus, the spinal cord develops before the arm buds; the upper arm develops before the forearm; and so on. In general, the process of organ formation is the same for all human embryos, but in one major respect—sexual differentiation—it varies.

table 3.1

Growth and Development of the Embryo

Days 10–13
Cells separate into ectoderm, endoderm, and mesoderm layers. The neural plate, which eventually will become the brain and the spinal cord, forms out of the ectoderm.

Third Week
The three major divisions of the brain—the hindbrain, the midbrain, and the forebrain—begin to differentiate by the end of the third week. Primitive blood cells and blood vessels are present. The heart comes into being, and by the end of the week it is beating.

Fourth Week
Limb buds are visible. Eyes, ears, and a digestive system begin to take form. The major veins and arteries are completed. Vertebrae are present, and nerves begin to take primitive form.

Fifth Week
The umbilical cord takes shape. Bronchial buds, which eventually will become the lungs, take form. Premuscle masses are present in the head, trunk, and limbs. The hand plates are formed.

Sixth Week
The head becomes dominant in size. The halves of the lower jawbone meet and fuse, and the components of the upper jaw are present. The external ear makes its appearance. The three main parts of the brain are distinct.

Seventh Week
The face and neck are beginning to take form. Eyelids take shape. The stomach is taking its final shape and position. Muscles are rapidly differentiating throughout the body and are assuming their final shapes and relationships. The brain is developing thousands of nerve cells per minute.

Eighth Week
The growth of the gut makes the body evenly round. The head is elevated and the neck is distinct. The external, middle, and inner ears assume their final forms. By the end of this week the fetus is capable of some movement and responds to stimulation around the mouth.

Sexual Differentiation As we described in Chapter 2 (p. 65), the genes that influence sexual determination are located on the X and Y chromosomes inherited at conception. Zygotes with one X and one Y chromosome are genetically male, whereas zygotes with two X chromosomes are genetically female. For the first 6 weeks after conception, however, there is no structural difference between genetically male and genetically female embryos. Both males and females have two ridges of tissue, called *gonadal ridges,* from which the male and female sex organs (*gonads*) will develop. Initially, these ridges give no clue to the sex of the embryo.

The genes inherited at conception determine whether the sex glands that develop from the gonadal ridges will be male testes or female ovaries. If the embryo is genetically male (XY), the process of sexual differentiation begins during the seventh week of life, in the transition to the fetal period, when the gonadal ridges begin to form testes (Ostrer, Huang, Masch, & Shapiro, 2007). If the embryo is genetically female (XX), no changes are apparent in the gonadal ridges until several weeks later, when ovaries begin to form.

Following the seventh week, when male gonads begin to form, it is not genes, however, but rather the presence or absence of male gonads that determines whether the embryo develops male or female external genitalia. The male gonads produce male hormones, called *androgens,* chief among which is testosterone. If testosterone is present, a male penis and scrotum develop. Thus, the presence of testosterone determines maleness. If testosterone is not present, female external genitalia are formed. Interestingly, the influence of androgens is not limited to the gonads and the genital tract. For example, during the last 6 months of prenatal development, the presence of testosterone suppresses the natural rhythmic activity of the pituitary gland, located in the brain. If testosterone is absent, the pituitary gland establishes the cyclical pattern of hormone secretion that is characteristic of the female and eventually comes to control her menstrual cycle (Wilson, 1995).

Because the embryo has the potential to develop into either a male or a female, errors in sex development sometimes result in a baby's having sex organs that show characteristics of both sexes. A baby with this condition is called a *hermaphrodite.*

The Fetal Period

The fetal period begins once all the basic tissues and organs exist in rudimentary form and the tissue that will become the skeleton begins to harden, or *ossify* (Gilbert, 2001). During the fetal period, which lasts from the eighth or ninth week of pregnancy until birth, the fetus increases in length from approximately 1½ inches to 20 inches and in weight from approximately 0.02 to 7.1 pounds (Figure 3.6).

Over the course of the fetal period, each of the organ systems increases in complexity. By the tenth week after conception, the intestines have assumed their characteristic position in the body. Two weeks later, the fetus's external sexual characteristics are visible and its neck is well defined. By the end of 16 weeks, the head is erect, the lower limbs are well developed, and the ears, which began to take form in the fourth week, migrate from the neck to the sides of the head. By the end of the fifth month, the fetus has almost as many nerve cells as it will ever have as a person. By the end of the seventh month, the lungs are capable of breathing air, and the eyes, which have been closed, open and can respond to light. By the end of the eighth month, many folds of the brain are present, enabling brain cells to

Figure 3.6 The fetus at the beginning of the fetal period (approximately 9 weeks). The way the umbilical cord is attached to the placenta is clearly visible.

©Lennart Nilsson, *A Child Is Born,* 1990 ed., Dell Publishing Co.

Modern technologies, including the fetal ultrasound used here, produce such high-quality images of the fetus that a variety of disorders can be identified and, in some cases, surgically corrected long before birth.

be packed more efficiently within the skull, and during the ninth month, the brain becomes considerably more wrinkled. In the final weeks before birth, the fetus doubles in weight.

The fetal period marks a critical stage during which the baby-to-be becomes responsive to its environment in new ways. Development is influenced by factors both inside and outside the uterus. Events inside the uterine environment affect the organism in a variety of ways. The mother's digestive system and heart are sources of noise, and her movements provide motion stimuli. The fetus comes in contact with the world outside the mother through the wall of her abdomen and, less directly, through the placenta and umbilical cord. Nutrients, oxygen, some viruses, and some potentially harmful chemicals all cross the placenta to the fetus. Through these various routes, a mother's experiences, illnesses, diet, and social circumstances can affect the child before it is born.

Sensory Capacities Using modern techniques of measurement and recording, researchers have begun to produce a detailed picture of the development of sensory capacities before birth (Lecanuet, Graniere-Deferre, Jacquet, & DeCasper, 2000). This information is essential for determining how the fetus is influenced by the uterine environment. Scientists have discovered the following about the fetus's sensory capacities:

- *Sensing motion.* The vestibular system of the middle ear, which controls the sense of balance, begins to function in the human fetus about 5 months after conception and is fully mature at birth (Lecanuet & Jacquet, 2002). This early maturity means that the fetus is capable of sensing changes in the mother's posture and orienting itself as it floats inside the fluid-filled amniotic sac.

- *Seeing.* Little is known for certain about the extent of the fetus's visual experience. At 26 weeks following conception, fetuses respond to light; it causes their heart rates to change, and it causes them to move (Lecanuet & Schaal, 1996). Aidan Macfarlane (1977) suggested that toward the end of pregnancy the fetus may be able to see light that has penetrated the mother's stretched stomach wall. He likens the fetus's visual experience to the glow seen when the palm of the hand covers the bulb of a flashlight.

- *Hearing.* The fetus is able to respond to sound at 5 to 6 months after conception (Abrams, Gerhardt & Antonelli, 1998). In what will prove essential to language acquisition, the fetus is able respond to *changes* in sound between 6 and 7 months after conception (Draganova et al., 2007). Studies in which tiny microphones have been inserted into the uterus adjacent to the fetus's head reveal that the average sound level inside the womb is approximately 75 decibels, about the level at which we hear the outside world when we ride in a car with the windows up. This background noise is punctuated by the sound of air passing through the mother's stomach and, every second or so, by the more intense sound of the mother's heartbeat. Of all such sounds, the mother's voice is heard best because it is also transmitted as vibrations through her body. When sounds of moderate intensity are presented, it is possible to detect changes in the fetus's heart rate (Kisilevsky, Hains, & Low, 2001; Lecanuet & Schaal, 1996).

Because external sounds must pass through the mother's abdomen and the amniotic fluid before the fetus can hear them, things sound different in the womb than they do outside it. In experiments using recordings of the mother's natural voice and her voice when it has been filtered to resemble how it sounded to the fetus while in the womb, newborns prefer the latter (Fifer & Moon, 1995).

Fetal Activity Just about any pregnant woman will tell you that fetuses do not float passively in amniotic fluid as they await the hour of birth. Women can feel their fetuses moving around, bumping and rolling, sometimes uncomfortably kicking and elbowing. By mid-pregnancy, you can place your hand on a pregnant woman's belly and feel the movements of the fetus.

Modern technologies, such as ultrasound, have revealed that embryos become active within 8 weeks following conception. As the embryo enters the fetal stage, its body movements become increasingly varied and coordinated (Table 3.2; Robinson & Kleven, 2005). At 15 weeks of age, the fetus is capable of all the movements observable in newborn infants, such as head turning and leg flexing (James, Pillai, & Smoleniec, 1995). Toward the end of the fourth month, the fetus is big enough for the mother to feel any movements.

Research has also shown that fetal *inactivity* is important to development. From 24 to 32 weeks after conception, the relatively high rate of fetal activity begins to be interrupted by quiet periods, and there is a gradual decrease in the fetus's movements (Kisilevsky & Low, 1998). These quiet periods are believed to reflect the development of neural pathways that inhibit movement. The appearance of these inhibitory pathways is related to maturation in the higher regions of the brain (Figure 3.7).

Evidence indicates that spontaneous fetal activity plays a significant role in development (Smotherman & Robinson, 1996). Experiments with chick embryos,

table 3.2	
Appearance of Fetal Movements in Early Pregnancy	
Movement	Gestational Age (weeks)
Any movement	7
Startle	8
Generalized movements	8
Hiccups	8
Isolated arm movements	9
Head retroflexion	9
Hand–face contact	10
Breathing	10
Jaw opening	10
Stretching	10
Head anteflexion	10
Yawn	11
Suck and swallow	12

Source: De Vries et al., 1982. Adapted by permission.

30 days

40 days

100 days

5 months
Higher brain regions
have begun to develop

7 months

8 months

9 months

Figure 3.7 The prenatal development of the brain. The primitive parts of the brain are present very early. The cerebral hemispheres, with their characteristic convolutions, do not make their appearance until the middle of pregnancy. (Adapted from Cowan, 1979.)

for example, suggest that prenatal activity is crucial to normal limb development. Under normal circumstances, the spinal cord sends out neurons, or nerve cells, to connect the limbs to the brain—many more neurons than the animal will need when it is fully coordinated. Many of these neurons die off, while the remainder are connected to muscles in an efficient way. If chick embryos are treated with drugs that prevent them from moving, the elimination of excess neurons that ordinarily accompanies neuromuscular development fails to occur. The results are disastrous. In as little as 1 or 2 days, the failure to prune away all but the neurons compatible with coordinated movement causes the joints of the chick embryos to become fixed into rigid structures, a result showing that movement is necessary for normal limb development (Pittman & Oppenheim, 1979). Fetal movements are believed to play a similar role in establishing basic neuronal connections in humans (Robinson & Kleven, 2005).

Breathing movements are another good example of the importance of prenatal activity to the human fetus. The fetus does not breathe in utero. It obtains oxygen through the placenta. Yet certain "breathing" movements with its chest and lungs increase at this time. Without these movements, the muscles necessary for respiration after birth would be insufficiently developed (Wilson, Olver & Walters, 2007).

Learning in the Womb The folklore of many societies includes the belief that the fetus can learn sound patterns of stories and songs while in the womb (Lefeber & Voorhoeve, 1998). Although such beliefs have met with considerable skepticism, there is evidence that the fetus learns from at least some events both inside and outside the mother (Lecanuet, Granier-Deferre, & DeCasper, 2005).

In a particularly well-known study, Anthony DeCasper and Melanie Spence (1986) asked 16 pregnant women to read aloud a particular passage from *The Cat in the Hat,* a rhyming children's story by Dr. Seuss, twice a day for the last month and a half before their babies were due. By the time the babies were born, the passage had been read to them for a total of about 3½ hours.

Two or three days after the babies were born, DeCasper and Spence tested them with a pacifier that had been wired to record sucking rates (Figure 3.8). First the babies were allowed to suck for 2 minutes to establish a baseline sucking rate. Afterward, changes in the rate of sucking turned on or off a tape recording of their mothers reading a story. For half of the babies, increasing their sucking rates turned on the passage from *The Cat in the Hat* that their mothers had previously read aloud, while decreasing their sucking rate turned on a story their mothers had not read. For the other half, increased sucking turned on the new story, while decreased sucking produced *The Cat in the Hat*. The key finding was that the infants modified their rates of sucking to produce *The Cat in the Hat*. The investigators concluded that the babies had indeed heard the stories being read to them by their mothers and that their learning in the womb influenced the sounds they found rewarding after birth. Later research has shown that in the weeks before birth, fetuses prefer the sounds of their native language (Lecanuet et al., 2000).

In addition to showing evidence of learning from auditory input, research indicates that human fetuses also learn through other sensory modalities, including smell and taste, and that such prenatal learning experiences may have consequences for postnatal experiences, including food preferences. We will examine this research in detail in Chapter 4.

Melanie Spence, University of Texas

Figure 3.8 This baby is listening to a recording of its mother telling a story. The apparatus records changes in sucking to determine how newborns react to stories read to them while they were in the womb.

||||| APPLY — CONNECT — DISCUSS

After reviewing the distinction between *continuity* and *discontinuity* presented in Chapter 1 (p. 14), discuss the ways in which prenatal development and activity are both continuous and discontinuous.

Maternal Conditions and Prenatal Development

Although the mother's womb provides a protective and supportive environment for prenatal growth, the baby-to-be is influenced both positively and negatively by the larger world. Outside influences reach the organism through changes in the mother that are then transmitted to the fetus through the placenta. This section focuses on how fetal development may be affected by maternal stress, nutrition, and general health. Then, in a separate section, we will discuss the effects of specific environmental toxins and substances known to adversely impact the developing fetus.

Maternal Attitudes and Stress

Many physicians who care for pregnant women and newborn infants suspect that a woman's feelings of well-being and her attitude toward her pregnancy affect the well-being of the fetus and of the child after birth. Indeed, research indicates a strong relationship between a mother's negative attitudes towards her pregnancy and her infant's risk of low birth weight (Suzuki, Minai & Yamagata, 2007). The clearest evidence that a mother-to-be's negative attitudes can affect her baby's development comes from an extensive investigation conducted in Czechoslovakia in the 1960s and 1970s. Henry David (1981) studied the lives of 220 children whose mothers indicated strong negative attitudes toward having them by twice asking for an abortion. The refusal of the abortion was an indication that medical authorities believed these women to be capable of carrying through the pregnancy and raising the child.

The unwanted children were compared with a carefully matched control group of children whose mothers either had planned for or had accepted their pregnancies. The mothers in the two groups were matched for socioeconomic status and age; the children were matched for sex, birth order, number of siblings, and date of birth. At birth, the unwanted children weighed less and needed more medical help than the children in the control group, even though their mothers had ready access to medical care and were judged to be in good health themselves.

Even when a child is wanted and a pregnant woman has a supportive family, a moderate amount of stress can be expected during pregnancy. The mother-to-be has to adjust her life to accommodate new responsibilities. One who decides to quit her job may have to cope with a reduced income. Another may be working

All cultures have evolved tools and practices that are believed to contribute to the well-being of the fetus. While some societies have high-tech machinery with which to monitor neonatal health, others, such as the Sudanese shown here, monitor the growing fetus with traditional tools.

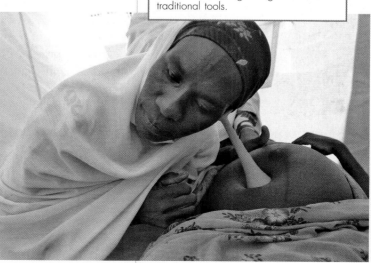

so hard that she feels she does not have enough time to take care of herself, let alone her expected child. And if the pregnancy was unplanned, as many are, the stress that normally accompanies pregnancy may be magnified.

Studies have shown that a mother who is under stress or becomes emotionally upset secretes hormones, such as adrenaline and cortisol, that pass through the placenta and have a measurable effect on the fetus's motor activity (Relier, 2001). These effects can be long lasting (Weinstock, 2005). Elizabeth Susman and her colleagues report that mothers who experienced more stressful environments during pregnancy produced elevated levels of cortisol and that at 3 years of age their children were more aggressive than children of mothers who experienced low stress and produced lower levels of cortisol while pregnant (Susman, Schmeelk, Ponirakis & Gariepy, 2001; Susman, 2006). Stress during pregnancy is also associated with premature delivery and low birth weight (a weight of less than 5 pounds) (Chicz-DeMet et al., 2001).

Nutritional Influences

Fetuses depend on their mothers for the nutrients that keep them alive and allow them to develop. By eating the right foods—in the right amounts—a mother can contribute to her baby's healthy development. In contrast, a deficient diet can have adverse consequences that are difficult or impossible to overcome.

Good Nutrition Research indicates that, whether pregnant or not, a woman who gets moderate amounts of exercise needs to consume between 2000 and 2800 calories daily in a well-balanced diet that includes all the essential vitamins and minerals (Christian, 2002). In addition, pregnant women are advised to increase their intake of folic acid (a member of the vitamin B–complex group commonly found in green vegetables and fruit), calcium, and iron to insure healthy development and prevent certain birth defects (Van Der Put et al., 1997).

Folic acid, for example, is essential to the normal development of the fetus's **neural tube,** an embryonic structure that will later develop into the brain and spinal cord (Yang et al., 2007). Neural tube development takes place between 3 and 4 weeks after conception, often before a woman realizes that she is pregnant. In the absence of enough folic acid, the neural tube may develop serious defects, including *spina bifida,* a disease of the spinal cord and backbone, and *anencephaly,* a disease of the brain and skull. Because the neural tube develops so soon after conception, and because like many other vitamins, folic acid needs time to build up in the woman's system, it is important that women have sufficient folic acid in their diets *before* they become pregnant in order to maximize protection against these conditions. A nationwide study found that most nonpregnant women of childbearing age in the United States reported consuming less than the recommended amount of folic acid, with non-Hispanic black and Hispanic women reporting higher deficiencies than non-Hispanic white women (Yang et al., 2007).

The foods believed to be good for pregnant women are determined by cultural beliefs and practices (Rosso, 1990). Milk is a good source of calcium, and in the United States physicians recommend that pregnant women drink several glasses a day. In China, by contrast, milk is not a part of people's everyday diets (in fact, many Asians are lactose intolerant), so other foods rich in calcium must be substituted for it (Lefeber & Voorhoeve, 2001).

Undernourishment, Malnourishment, and Related Factors Pregnant women with deficient diets often suffer from *undernourishment*—insufficient food intake to develop or function normally—or *malnutrition*—the imbalance between the body's

neural tube An embryonic structure that will develop into the brain and spinal cord.

needs and the intake of nutrients even when calorie intake is within the normal range.

In catastrophic conditions that accompany war and famine (which often occur at the same time), the effects on prenatal development can be profound. The clearest evidence of this effect comes from studies of sudden periods of famine. In September 1941, Leningrad (now St. Petersburg) was encircled by the German army, and no supplies reached the city until February 1942. The standard daily food ration in late November 1941 was 250 grams of bread (four slices) for factory workers and 125 grams (two slices) for everybody else. The bread was 25 percent sawdust. The number of infants born in the first half of 1942 was much lower than normal, and stillbirths doubled. Very few infants were born in the second half of 1942, all of them to couples who had better access to food than did the rest of the population. These babies were, on the average, more than a pound lighter than babies born before the siege, and they were much more likely to be premature. They were also in very poor condition at birth; they had little vitality and were unable to maintain body temperature adequately (Antonov, 1947). Because the timing of the famine in Leningrad was so sudden and precise, it was easy to determine when, in the fetus's development, the severe malnutrition began. Severe nutritional deprivation during the first 3 months of pregnancy was most likely to result in abnormalities of the central nervous system, premature birth, and death. Deprivation during the last 3 months of pregnancy was more likely to retard fetal growth and result in low birth weight.

Loading a cart with fresh veggies; attending a health clinic for pregnant women. Although from vastly different cultures (the United States and Sierra Leon), these women have access to resources necessary to ensure healthy pregnancies.

Studies of the relation between maternal nutrition, prenatal development, and neonatal health suggest that lesser degrees of undernourishment and malnourishment also increase risks to the fetus. Poor maternal nutrition can lead to low birth weight and even miscarriage (Mora & Nestel, 2000; Morton, 2006). There is also some evidence that poor nutrition puts fetuses at greater risk for heart disease, strokes, and other illnesses in later life (Godfrey & Barker, 2000). This association is thought to result from the fetus's adaptation to an inadequate supply of nutrients during a sensitive period in early prenatal life that leads to permanent changes in physiology and metabolism.

However, it is often difficult to isolate the effects of poor nutrition, because undernourished and malnourished mothers frequently live in impoverished environments where housing, sanitation, education, and medical care, including prenatal care, are also inadequate. Expectant mothers with low incomes are more likely to suffer from diseases or simply to be in a weakened state than are women who live in better material circumstances. Their babies are more likely to suffer from a wide variety of birth defects and illnesses and to be born prematurely (Vintzileos, Ananth, Smulian, Scorza, & Knuppel, 2001, 2002). According to a variety of studies conducted in many parts of the world, including the United States, low-income mothers are also more likely to have babies who die at birth or soon after birth (UNICEF, 2003).

Several studies demonstrate that it is possible to prevent or reduce the damaging effects of malnutrition and an impoverished environment. One of the largest intervention programs designed to assess the effects of a massive supplemental food program for women, infants, and children—dubbed WIC—was initiated by the U.S. government in 1972. Low-income women in the program are given vouchers for such staples as milk, eggs, fruit juices, and dried beans. Women who have participated in the WIC program have been found to lose fewer babies during infancy than do comparable women who have not participated in the program (Moss & Carver, 1998). Food supplements during pregnancy have also been found to be important to the baby's postnatal intellectual development. In a study carried out in Louisiana, schoolchildren whose mothers had participated in the WIC program were evaluated on a variety of intellectual measures when they were 6 or 7 years old. Those children whose mothers had received food supplements during the last 3 months of their pregnancies—the period in which the fetal brain undergoes especially rapid development—outperformed the children of mothers who did not receive food supplements until after their children were born (Hicks, Langham, & Takenaka, 1982). Similar results were obtained in studies of food supplement programs in rural Guatemala and Zanzibar (Pollitt, Saco-Pollitt, Jahari, Husaini & Huang, 2000; Stoltzfus et al., 2001).

These conclusions concerning poor maternal and fetal nutrition must be considered with some caution because it is not possible to conduct carefully controlled studies for ethical reasons. However, the overall evidence strongly suggests that millions of children throughout the world are damaged by undernourishment and malnourishment before birth. Moreover, many of these children experience nutritional and other deprivations in childhood: most do not receive food supplements, and even fewer receive high-quality medical and educational help. Thus, they experience a cascade of risk factors, of which poor maternal and fetal nutrition is only one (Figure 3.9). Together, such conditions lead to high rates of infant mortality and shorter life expectancies (Pollitt, 2001).

Figure 3.9 In many countries of the world, poor economic conditions create a set of risk factors. For example, poor health conditions and parents' lack of education negatively influence child health and welfare. (Adapted from United Nations Children's Fund [UNICEF], 1999.)

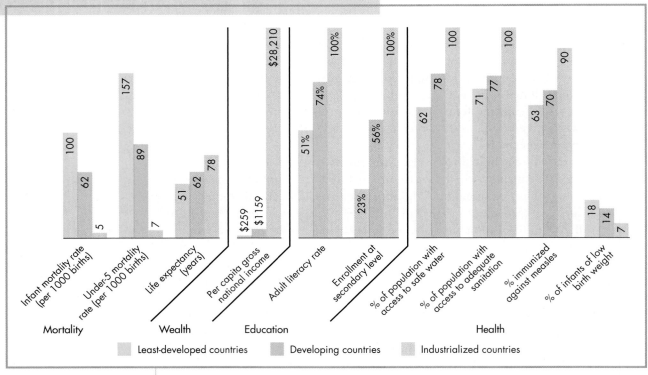

The famous Dutch famine of 1944 has provided a wealth of information for scientists interested in the effects of fetal malnourishment on subsequent development. Conduct some online research and explore some of the projects associated with the Dutch Famine Birth Cohort Study. What are some of the questions currently addressed by the study? What are some of the most recent findings?

teratogens Environmental agents that can cause deviations from normal development and can lead to abnormalities or death.

Teratogens: Environmental Sources of Birth Defects

Other threats to the prenatal organism come from **teratogens**—environmental agents that increase risk of deviations in normal development and can lead to serious abnormalities or death. Although the effects of teratogens on the developing organism vary with the specific agent involved, six general principles apply to all of them (Moore & Persaud 1998):

1. A developing organism's susceptibility to a teratogenic agent depends on its developmental stage at the time of exposure. Overall, the gravest danger to life comes during the first 2 weeks, before the cells of the organism have undergone extensive differentiation and before most women are even aware that they are pregnant (Figure 3.10). During this critical period, a teratogenic agent may completely destroy the organism. Once the various body systems have begun to form, each is most vulnerable at the time of its initial growth spurt. As Figure 3.10 indicates, the most vulnerable

Figure 3.10 The critical periods in human prenatal development occur when the organs and other body parts are forming and therefore are most vulnerable to teratogens. Before implantation, teratogens either damage all or most of the cells of the organism, causing its death, or damage only a few cells, allowing the organism to recover without developing defects. In the figure, the blue portions of the bars represent periods of highest risk of major structural abnormalities; the peach portions represent periods of reduced sensitivity to teratogens. (Adapted from Moore & Persaud, 1993.)

• Indicates common site of action of teratogen

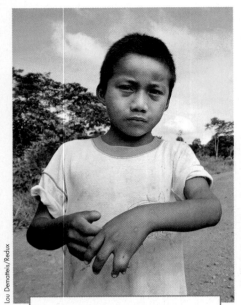

Figure 3.11 Nine-year-old Jairo Yumbo lives in the Amazon rain forest of Ecuador, where vast quantities of petroleum waste were dumped in the 1970s and 1980s, and continue to contaminate the ground and water. It is likely that prenatal exposure to such toxic waste caused his birth-deformed hand.

period for the central nervous system is from 15 to 36 days after conception, whereas the upper and lower limbs are most vulnerable from 24 to 49 days after conception.

2. A teratogenic agent's effects are likely to be specific to a particular organ. Therefore, each teratogen causes a particular pattern of abnormal development. The drug thalidomide, for example, causes deformation of the legs and arms, and mercury compounds cause brain damage that is manifested as cerebral palsy.

3. Individual organisms vary in their susceptibility to teratogens. The way a developing organism responds to teratogenic agents depends to some degree on its genetic vulnerability to these agents. Fewer than one-quarter of the pregnant women who used thalidomide during the period when the embryo's limbs were forming gave birth to malformed babies.

4. Susceptibility to teratogenic agents depends on the mother's physiological state. The mother's age, nutrition, uterine condition, and hormonal balance all affect the action of teratogens on the developing organism. The risk of malformation is highest when the mother is younger than 20 or older than 40. The precise reason is not known. Nutritional deficiency in the mother intensifies the adverse effects of some teratogens. The impact of teratogens also appears to increase if the mother suffers from diabetes, a metabolic imbalance, or liver dysfunction, among other disorders.

5. In general, the greater the concentration of teratogenic agents such as thalidomide or mercury, the greater the risk of abnormal development.

6. Some teratogens such as rubella that have little or only a temporary effect on the mother can lead to serious abnormalities during prenatal development. The most common teratogens include certain drugs and infections, radiation, and pollution (Figure 3.11).

Drugs

Most pregnant women in the United States take some medication during pregnancy, primarily over-the-counter pain relievers, antinauseants, or sleep aids. Fortunately, most of these drugs do not appear to harm the fetus, but there are some that do. It is also estimated that a sizable minority of women use nonmedical substances during pregnancy, ranging from caffeine, alcohol, and tobacco to "hard" drugs such as cocaine and heroin. While most of these drugs appear harmful to prenatal development, it is often hard to isolate the effects of specific drugs because drug-abusing mothers often abuse multiple drugs or are generally poor and undernourished (Orioli & Castilla, 2000).

Prescription Drugs The potential teratogenic effects of prescription drugs first came to light with the drug thalidomide. From 1956 until 1961, thalidomide was used in Europe as a sedative and to control nausea in the early stages of pregnancy. The women who took the drug were unharmed by it, and many of the children they bore suffered no ill effects. Some children, however, were born without arms and legs; their hands and feet were attached directly to their torsos like flippers. Some had defects of sight and hearing as well. About 8000 children with deformities were born before their problems were traced to the drug and it was removed from the market (Persaud, 1977).

Since the disastrous effects of thalidomide were discovered, other prescription drugs have been found to cause abnormalities in the developing organism, including the antibiotics streptomycin and tetracycline; anticoagulants; anticonvulsants; most artificial hormones; Thorazine (used in the treatment of schizophrenia); Valium (a tranquilizer); and Accutane (used to treat difficult cases of acne).

Caffeine Found in coffee, tea, and cola, caffeine is the most common drug used by pregnant women. There is no evidence that caffeine causes malformations in the fetus (Clausson et al., 2002). However, some studies have found that caffeine in large doses is associated with an increased rate of spontaneous abortion and with low birth weight (Klebanoff, Levine, Clemens, & Wilkins, 2002). On this basis, women are advised to limit their caffeine intake during pregnancy.

Tobacco Smoking tobacco is not known to produce birth defects, but it has been found to harm the fetus in a variety of ways. Smoking is related to an increase in the rate of spontaneous abortion, stillbirth, and neonatal death (Chan, Keane & Robinson, 2001). Nicotine, the addictive substance in tobacco, causes abnormal growth of the placenta, resulting in a reduction in the transfer of nutrients to the fetus. It also reduces the oxygen and increases the carbon monoxide in the bloodstreams of both mother and fetus. As a result, mothers who smoke usually have babies whose birth weights are lower than those of infants born to women who do not smoke. The effects of cigarette smoke seem to be dose related: Pregnant women who smoke more have babies who weigh less (Hindmarsh et al., 2008; Wang et al., 2002). Research suggests that even if a pregnant woman does not smoke herself, the health of her baby can be significantly affected by the cigarette smoke of others (Wang et al., 2002).

Alcohol After tobacco and caffeine, alcohol is the most commonly abused drug. About 4 percent of all U.S. women of childbearing age suffer from alcoholism, and many more are "social drinkers" who consume alcohol on a regular basis (Stratton, Howe, & Battaglia, 1996). Women who drink substantial amounts of alcohol while they are pregnant are in danger of having a baby with serious birth defects.

Many studies have found that a large proportion of infants born to mothers who were heavy drinkers during pregnancy—that is, who drank 3 ounces or more of 100-proof liquor a day (the equivalent of 3 shot glasses of whiskey)—were abnormal in some way (see Molina et al., 2007, for a review). Many of these babies suffered from **fetal alcohol syndrome,** a set of symptoms that includes an abnormally small head and underdeveloped brain, eye abnormalities, congenital heart disease, joint anomalies, and malformations of the face (Figure 3.12). The physical growth and mental development of children with this syndrome are likely to be retarded. Women who drink heavily during the first trimester of pregnancy and then reduce their consumption of alcohol during the next 3 months do not reduce the risk of having children with this affliction. Binge drinking—that is, the periodic consumption of 5 or more drinks on a single occasion—early in pregnancy has been associated with a subtle impairment of learning and behavior in adolescence (Kesmodel, 2001).

The effects of lower levels of alcohol consumption on development are not entirely clear, to some extent because they have not been thoroughly studied (Huizink & Mulder, 2006). Research has found that in some cases the equivalent of one or two glasses of wine, either occasionally or daily, causes no discernible harm to the fetus. In other cases, such drinking results in effects that include subtle but measurable deficits in cognitive and motor functioning. Notwithstanding some mixed results, a comprehensive review of the effects of alcohol on human and nonhuman fetal development indicates that

fetal alcohol syndrome A syndrome found in babies whose mothers were heavy consumers of alcohol while pregnant. Symptoms include an abnormally small head and underdeveloped brain, eye abnormalities, congenital heart disease, joint anomalies, and malformations of the face.

This young boy shows facial features typical of those affected by fetal alcohol syndrome, including small eyelid openings, a flattened nasal bridge, a thin upper lip, and a flat skin surface between the upper lip and the nose.

Figure 3.12 Children who suffer from fetal alcohol syndrome do not merely look abnormal (above); their brains are underdeveloped, and many are severely retarded. The brain of a child who suffered from fetal alcohol syndrome (below right) lacks the convolutions characteristic of the brain of a normal child (below left).

alcohol exposure places fetuses at risk for defects—defects that will vary with both the amount of prenatal exposure to alcohol and the timing of the exposure.

Marijuana A national survey of 4 million U.S. women who gave birth in 1992 found that 2.9 percent had used marijuana at some time during their pregnancies. Marijuana has not been definitely found to cause birth defects, but its use is associated with low birth weight, as well as with certain neurological differences that may persist throughout childhood (Smith et al., 2004). Some researchers have also found an increase in premature delivery among women who use marijuana more than once a week. However, it is uncertain whether these effects can be solely attributed to the use of marijuana. Women in the United States who use marijuana during pregnancy tend to be poorer, less educated, younger, single, and more likely to use other illegal drugs than mothers who do not use marijuana. They also receive less prenatal care and gain less weight.

Cocaine A stimulant that rapidly produces addiction in the user, cocaine may result in numerous medical complications for the mother-to-be, including heart attacks, strokes, rupture of the aorta, and seizures (Cunningham et al., 2001). Babies born to cocaine-addicted mothers have a variety of problems. These babies are more likely to be stillborn or premature, to have low birth weights, to suffer from strokes, and to exhibit birth defects (Ursitti, Klein, & Koren, 2001). Babies born to cocaine-addicted mothers are described as being irritable, liable to react excessively to stimulation, uncoordinated, and slow learners (Bendersky & Lewis, 1998; Schuetze, Eiden, & Coles, 2007).

Residual effects of cocaine exposure during the prenatal period may last for several years. For example, preschool-age children prenatally exposed to cocaine exhibit delayed language development and are likely to experience difficulty regulating themselves when presented with novel tasks (Morrow et al., 2003; Noland et al., 2003).

Despite the justified concern about the effects of prenatal exposure to cocaine, some researchers have been critical of claims that cocaine itself is the cause of these problems (Lester & Tronick, 1994). These researchers note that many mothers who use cocaine also drink alcohol and use other drugs. In addition, many of them are poor and live in stressful circumstances. All these factors are known to contribute to symptoms such as those attributed to prenatal cocaine exposure. Consequently, while more recent research continues to show negative impacts on later development, a causal link between prenatal cocaine exposure and later behavior is still not considered ironclad (Bandstra, Morrow, Anthony, Accornero, & Fried, 2001; Morrow et al., 2003).

Heroin and Methadone Babies of mothers who are addicted to the opium derivatives heroin or methadone are born addicted themselves and must be given heroin or methadone shortly after birth to avoid the often life-threatening ordeal of withdrawal. These babies are more likely to be premature, underweight, and vulnerable to respiratory illnesses (Kaltenbach et al., 1998).

While these babies are being weaned from the drugs to which they were born addicted, they are irritable and have tremors, their cries are abnormal, their sleep is disturbed, and their motor control is diminished. The effects of the addiction are still apparent in their motor control 4 months later. Even after a year, their ability to pay attention is impaired (Yanai et al., 2000).

Several studies have also reported long-term developmental problems in children exposed to heroin, methadone, or other opium derivatives in utero, but as with cocaine, whether these problems can be solely attributed to the mother's drug use is still open to question (Jones, 2006).

Infections and Other Health Conditions

A variety of infection-causing microorganisms can endanger the embryo, the fetus, and the newborn. Most infections spread from the mother to the unborn child across the placental barrier. In a few instances, however, the baby may become infected during the passage through the birth canal. Some of the more common infections and other maternal conditions that may affect the developing human organism are summarized below; Table 3.3 summarizes others.

Rubella Rubella, commonly referred to as German measles, is a condition whose symptoms include a mild rash, swollen lymph glands, and a low fever. Researchers have found that rubella also can cause a syndrome of congenital heart disease, cataracts, deafness, and mental retardation in more than half of all babies born to women who suffer from the disease during the first 12 weeks of pregnancy (Bale, 2002). (Thereafter, rubella infections are less likely to have these effects.) The development of a vaccine for rubella in 1969 has greatly reduced the incidence of the disease, but it has not been eradicated. Women are advised to avoid becoming pregnant for at least 6 months after they receive the vaccine. In the United States, several states require a blood test of immunity to rubella before issuing a marriage license.

HIV and AIDS Approximately 30 percent of the babies whose mothers tested positive for the human immunodeficiency virus (HIV) are born with HIV (UNICEF, 2003). The virus, which can lead to acquired immune deficiency syndrome (AIDS), may be transmitted from the mother to her baby either by passing through the placental barrier or by the baby's exposure to the mother's infected blood during delivery. More than 800,000 children were infected in this way in 2001. The risk of transmission increases with the length of time the mother has been infected. There is no known cure for AIDS, now the seventh leading cause of death in children under the age of 4. However, if HIV-positive women receive the drug zidovudine (AZT) during pregnancy and at the time of delivery, the chances of their passing the virus on to their children are reduced by as much as 50 percent (UNICEF, 2003).

AP Photo/Denis Farrell

Whether or not they are infected with AIDS themselves, young children from families in which the parents have AIDS are at risk of homelessness, malnutrition, and disease, in addition to the psychological trauma of losing their parents at an early age.

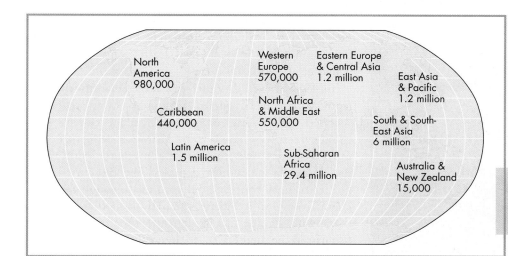

North America 980,000

Western Europe 570,000

Eastern Europe & Central Asia 1.2 million

East Asia & Pacific 1.2 million

Caribbean 440,000

North Africa & Middle East 550,000

South & South-East Asia 6 million

Latin America 1.5 million

Sub-Saharan Africa 29.4 million

Australia & New Zealand 15,000

A total of 42 million adults and children were estimated to be living with HIV/AIDS at the end of 2002. (Adapted from World Health Organization, 2002.)

Rh Incompatibility Rh is a complex substance on the surface of the red blood cells. One of its components is determined by a dominant gene, and people who have this component are said to be Rh-positive. Fewer than 1 in 10 people inherit the two recessive genes that make them Rh-negative (de Vrijer et al., 1999).

When an Rh-negative woman conceives a child with an Rh-positive man, the child is likely to be Rh-positive. During the birth of the baby, some of the baby's blood cells usually pass into the mother's bloodstream while the placenta is separating from the uterine wall. To fight this foreign substance, the mother's immune system creates antibodies, which remain in her bloodstream. If she becomes pregnant again with another Rh-positive child, these antibodies will enter the fetus's bloodstream and attack its red blood cells.

Rh disease can lead to serious birth defects and even death. Fortunately, physicians can prevent Rh disease by giving the Rh-negative mother an injection of anti-Rh serum within 72 hours of the delivery of an Rh-positive child, or by giving the fetus blood transfusions, usually through its umbilical chord (Sommerset et al., 2006). The serum kills any Rh-positive blood cells in the mother's bloodstream so that she will not develop antibodies to attack them. Children who are born with Rh disease can be treated with periodic blood transfusions (Fanaroff & Martin, 1997).

Radiation Massive doses of radiation often lead to serious malformations of the developing organism and in many cases cause prenatal death or spontaneous abortion (Moore & Persaud, 1993). Somewhat lower doses may spare the life of the organism but may have a profound effect on its development. Many of the pregnant women who were within a mile (1500 meters) of the atomic blasts at Hiroshima and Nagasaki in 1945 and survived later lost their babies. Of the babies who appeared to be normal at birth, 64 percent were later diagnosed as mentally retarded.

The effects of low doses of radiation on human beings have not been firmly established. Because X-rays may cause malformations in the embryo, women who need to be X-rayed should inform their doctors if they are or may be pregnant.

Pollution Most of the thousands of chemicals that are present in our environments—in the homes in which we live, the air in which we breath, even the food and water that we consume—have never been tested to see if they are harmful to prenatal development, although some of these substances reach the embryo or fetus through the placenta (Jones, 1997). Many environmental toxins that have been studied, however, are associated with dramatic disruptions and disorders in fetal development, including birth defects, growth retardation, premature birth, and fetal death (Wigle et al., 2008; Yanai et al., 2008).

In 1956 the consumption of large quantities of fish from Minamata Bay in Japan was discovered to be associated with a series of neurological and other symptoms, which have come to be known as Minamata disease. The bay was polluted by mercury from waste discharged by an industrial plant. The mercury passed in increasingly concentrated amounts through the food chain from the organisms eaten by fish to fish to humans who ate the fish. Pregnant women who ate the fish passed the mercury on to their unborn babies. Symptoms in these babies included cerebral palsy (a disorder

Environmental toxins and pollutants have been associated with an array of infant and child health problems ranging from rashes and allergies, to serious deformities and death. This Ukrainian boy is being treated for a skin disease associated with exposure to radiation caused by the famous Chernobyl nuclear plant explosion which, decades later, continues to pollute his community.

Gerd Ludwig/Panos Pictures

table 3.3

Some Maternal Diseases and Conditions That May Affect Prenatal Development

Sexually Transmitted Diseases

Genital herpes	Infection usually occurs at birth as the baby comes in contact with herpes lesions on the mother's genitals, although the virus may also cross the placental barrier to infect the fetus. Infection can lead to blindness and serious brain damage. There is no cure for the disease. Mothers with active genital herpes often have a cesarean delivery to avoid infecting their babies.
Gonorrhea	The gonococcus organism may attack the eyes while the baby is passing through the infected birth canal. Silver nitrate or erythromycin eyedrops are administered immediately after birth to prevent blindness.
Syphilis	The effects of syphilis on the fetus can be devastating. An estimated 25 percent of infected fetuses are born dead. Those who survive may be deaf, mentally retarded, or deformed. Syphilis can be diagnosed by a blood test and can be cured before the fetus is affected, since the syphilis spirochete cannot penetrate the placental membrane before the twenty-first week of gestation.

Other Diseases and Maternal Conditions

Chicken pox	Chicken pox may lead to spontaneous abortion or premature delivery, but it does not appear to cause malformations.
Cytomegalovirus	The most common source of prenatal infection, cytomegalovirus produces no symptoms in adults, but it may be fatal to the embryo. Infection later in intrauterine life has been related to brain damage, deafness, blindness, and cerebral palsy (a defect of motor coordination caused by brain damage).
Diabetes	Diabetic mothers face a greater risk of having a stillborn child or one who dies shortly after birth. Babies of diabetics are often very large because of the accumulation of fat during the third trimester. Diabetic mothers require special care to prevent these problems.
Hepatitis	Mothers who have hepatitis are likely to pass it on to their infants during birth.
Hypertension	Hypertension (chronic high blood pressure) increases the probability of miscarriage and infant death.
Influenza	The more virulent forms of influenza may lead to spontaneous abortion or may cause abnormalities during the early stages of pregnancy.
Mumps	Mumps is suspected of causing spontaneous abortion in the first trimester of pregnancy.
Toxemia	About 5 percent of pregnant women in the United States are affected during the third trimester by this disorder of unknown origin. Most common during first pregnancies, the condition mainly affects the mother. Symptoms are water retention, high blood pressure, rapid weight gain, and protein in the urine. If untreated, toxemia may cause convulsions, coma, and even death for the mother. Death of the fetus is not uncommon.
Toxoplasmosis	A mild disease in adults with symptoms similar to those of the common cold, toxoplasmosis is caused by a parasite that is present in raw meat and cat feces. It may cause spontaneous abortion or death. Babies who survive may have serious eye or brain damage.

Sources: Moore & Persaud, 1993; Stevenson, 1977.

of the central nervous system), deformation of the skull, and sometimes an abnormally small head (Tuchmann-Duplessis, 1975).

The incidence of birth defects is also known to be abnormally high in areas of heavy atmospheric pollution. In the Brazilian industrial city of Cubatão, for instance, the air pollution from petrochemical and steel plants alone exceeds that generated by all the combined industries in the Los Angeles basin of California. During the 1970s, 65 of every 1000 babies born in Cubatão died shortly after birth

table 3.4

Principles of Prenatal Development

Sequence is fundamental. One cell must exist before there can be two. Muscles and bones must be present before nerves can coordinate movement. Gonads must secrete testosterone before further sexual differentiation can occur.

Timing is crucial to development. If the ovum moves too rapidly or too slowly down the fallopian tube, pregnancy is terminated. If exposure to a particular teratogen occurs during a particular stage of development, the impact on the organism may be devastating, whereas if it occurs before or after this stage, there may be little or no impact—a difference that implies the existence of sensitive periods for the formation of organ systems.

Development consists of a process of differentiation and integration. From the single cell of the zygote, division leads to many identical cells, which eventually differentiate into the distinct kinds of cells of all the organs of the body, with the specifics likely the result of cells' interactions with surrounding cells. Arm buds differentiate to form fingers, which will differ from each other in ways that make possible the finely articulate movements of the human hand.

Development proceeds unevenly. From the earliest steps of cleavage, the various subsystems that make up the organism develop at their own rates. An important special case of such unevenness is physical development, which follows cephalocaudal (from the head down) and proximodistal (from the center to the periphery) sequences.

Development is characterized by changes both in the form of the organism and in the ways it interacts with its environment. The embryo not only looks altogether different from the fetus but also interacts with its environment in a qualitatively different way.

Development is epigenetic. Although the development of new phenotypic forms is constrained by genetic materials coded in the zygote, they emerge out of the ongoing organism–environment interactions that sustain and propel development.

because their brains had failed to develop—double the rate of this defect in neighboring communities that were not so heavily polluted (Freed, 1983). Fortunately, strong environmental safety efforts have greatly reduced the pollution in Cubatão, and the death rate of infants there has declined remarkably (Brooke, 1991). However, contaminants still remain in the ground, poisoning local forests (Klumpp, Domingos & Klumpp, 2002).

Atmospheric pollution in many U.S. cities is severe enough to cause concern about effects on prenatal development. One recent study found a strong relationship between air pollutant and infant death rates (Ritz, Wilhelm & Zhao, 2006). There is also a good deal of concern about the risk chemical dumps pose to the unborn children of pregnant women who live nearby. Unfortunately, much more research is required before the risks that these and other such environmental hazards represent for prenatal development can be accurately assessed.

As you may recall, many developmentalists view the prenatal period as a model for all subsequent development because certain principles that apply to prenatal development also appear to explain development after birth. Before we move on to birth, it useful to summarize these principles and illustrate them with examples from our discussion of prenatal development (Table 3.4). Because these principles have been found useful for characterizing development during other periods, you will see them return throughout our study of child development.

||||| APPLY ▪ CONNECT ▪ DISCUSS ▪ ▪ ▪ ▪ ▪ ▪ ▪ ▪ ▪ ▪ ▪ ▪ ▪ ▪ ▪ ▪ ▪ ▪ ▪

Visit the Web site of the Centers for Disease Control and Prevention. Explore their "One Test. Two Lives." initiative. What is the goal of the initiative? How does the CDC hope to implement the initiative? What materials and tools have they developed to move the initiative forward?

Birth

DELLA'S STORY

everything out of sync
   lights on and off
   contractions on top of each other . . .
   nurse never really there—and when she was, she wasn't, reprimanding . . .
   everybody talked to me while I'm blind—increasingly frozen with pain. Even Dr. A trying to extricate himself from my grasp: "you're breaking my hand and if you don't let go I won't be able to deliver your baby". . . .
   then the order to move my legs "square up your knees" the giant operating lights suddenly descending from the ceiling behind Dr. A's head. where am I? my head won't talk to my legs—can't make them move—can't breathe for the pain. . . .
   blue rubbery wet doll on my chest—I wish this gown was off. much to my amazement you are blond! (From Pollock, 1999)

NISA'S STORY

Mother's stomach grew very large. The first labor pains came at night and stayed with her until dawn. That morning, everyone went gathering. Mother and I stayed behind. We sat together for a while, then I went and played with the other children. Later, I came back and ate the nuts she had cracked for me. She got up and started to get ready. I said, "Mommy, let's go to the water well, I'm thirsty." She said, "Uhn, uhn, I'm going to gather some mongongo nuts." I told the children that I was going and we left; there were no other adults around. We walked a short way, then she sat down by the base of a large nehn tree, leaned back against it, and little Kumsa was born. (From Shostak, 1981)

These two descriptions of giving birth are from two vastly different cultures. The first describes the experience of Della, a highly educated, middle-class, urban American woman. The second is provided by Nisa, a woman of the !Kung, a hunting-and-gathering society living in the Kalahari Desert of southern Africa. Each story is unusual in its own way, but neither is unique. In some societies, giving birth unassisted is treated as a cultural ideal that displays the mother's fearlessness and self-confidence. In other societies, birthing has become highly medicalized, while in still others the process is supported by other members of the community, particularly the women in the mother-to-be's family.

Of all life's transitions, birth is the most radical. Before birth, the amniotic fluid provides a wet, warm environment, and the fetus receives continuous oxygen and nourishment through the umbilical cord. At birth, the lungs inflate to take in oxygen and exhale carbon dioxide for the first time. The first breath of oxygen acts to shut off the bypass that shunts blood away from the lungs to the placenta. It also causes the umbilical arteries to close down, cutting off fetal circulation to the placenta. Now the baby must obtain oxygen through the lungs, must work for nourishment by sucking, and no longer has the placenta to provide protection against disease-causing organisms.

The social and behavioral changes that occur at birth are no less pronounced than the biological ones. The newborn encounters other human beings directly for the first time, and the parents get their first glimpse of their child. From the moment of birth, infants and parents begin to construct a social relationship.

The Stages of Labor

The biological process of birth begins with a series of changes in the mother's body that forces the fetus through the birth canal. It ends when the mother expels the placenta after the baby has emerged. Labor normally begins approximately 280 days after the first day of a woman's last menstrual period, or 266 days after conception. It is customarily divided into three overlapping stages (Figure 3.13).

The first stage of labor begins when uterine contractions of sufficient frequency, intensity, and duration begin to cause the cervix (the narrow outer end of the uterus) to dilate. This initial stage continues until the opening of the uterus into the vagina is fully dilated and the connections between the bones of the mother's pelvis become more flexible (Cunningham et al., 2001). The length of this stage varies from woman to woman and from pregnancy to pregnancy: It may last anywhere from less than an hour to several days. The norm for first births is about 14 hours. At the beginning of labor, contractions come 15 to 20 minutes apart and last anywhere from 15 to 60 seconds. As labor proceeds, the contractions become more frequent, more intense, and longer in duration.

The second stage of labor begins as the baby is pushed headfirst through the fully dilated cervix into the vagina. (This passage is facilitated by the fact that the baby's head is comparatively soft because the bones of the skull have not yet fused.) The contractions now usually come no more than a minute apart and last about a minute. The pressure of the baby in the birth canal and the powerful contractions of the uterus typically cause the mother to bear down and push the baby out.

Usually the top of the baby's head and the brow are the first to emerge. Occasionally babies emerge in other positions, the most common being the breech position, with the feet or buttocks emerging first. In cases where babies are born in a breech position, which occurs in 3 to 4 percent of single births, both mother and fetus are at considerably increased risk of serious complications or death (Nkata, 2001).

The third stage of labor, the final one, occurs when the baby has emerged from the vagina, and the uterus contracts around its diminished contents. The placenta buckles and separates from the uterine wall, pulling the other fetal membranes with it. Contractions quickly expel them, and they are delivered as the afterbirth.

Cultural Variations in Childbirth

As a biological process, labor occurs in roughly the same way everywhere. However, as you saw in our descriptions of childbirth for the !Kung and, at the start of the chapter, the Hmong, as well as for a woman in the United States, there are wide variations in cultural practices. Giving birth unassisted is relatively rare but by no means limited to the !Kung (Lefeber & Voorhoeve, 1998). In another variation on unassisted birth, women in the remote Bajura district of eastern Nepal stay alone in an animal shed for childbirth. The shed is separate from the main home and is usually small and dirty. During the delivery, no one helps or touches the mother. The mother must cut and tie the umbilical cord and then care for the baby herself. People believe that if a woman gives birth to a baby inside her home, God will be displeased and will make family members and cattle sicken and die (Sreeramareddy et al., 2006). The same practices and beliefs were common in rural France as late as the end of the nineteenth century (Gelis, 1991).

Figure 3.13 During the first stage of labor, which usually lasts several hours, the cervix dilates, often to 9 or 10 centimeters in diameter. During the second stage, the birth canal widens, permitting the baby to emerge. The final stage (not shown) occurs when the placenta is delivered. (Adapted from Clarke-Stewart & Koch, 1983.)

First Stage of Labor

Birth canal

Cervix

Second Stage of Labor

It is far more common to find several people attending the mother during labor and delivery, although who actually gets to play a role varies across cultures. Among the Ngoni of East Africa, for example, men are totally excluded from the process. The women even conceal the fact that they are pregnant from their husbands as long as they can. "Men are little children. They are not able to hear those things which belong to pregnancy," the women claim (Read, 1960/1968, p. 20). When a woman learns that her daughter-in-law's labor has begun, she and other female kin move into the woman's hut, banish the husband, and take charge of the preparations. They remove everything that belongs to the husband—clothes, tools, and weapons—and all household articles except old mats and pots to be used during labor. Men are not allowed back into the hut until after the baby is born. By contrast, among the Maya of the Yucatán peninsula, in addition to a trained midwife being present to help, the husband is expected to be present both to help his wife and to bear witness to the pain she feels (Jordan, 1993). If the husband is absent and the child dies, its death is likely to be attributed to his failure to participate.

In all industrialized countries, a large proportion of births take place in hospitals, where the process is assisted by a physician or a trained midwife (Gelis, 1991). However, there are wide cultural variations in the place of delivery, the extent to which midwives rather than physicians assist, and in such matters as the use of medication. For example, in Holland, roughly one-third of births take place at home, and the rate of infant mortality is actually lower for home births than hospital births (Jordan, 1993). Moreover, practices are changing, not the least in areas where traditional practices had once been replaced by a more medical model (see the box "In the Field: Midwifery in the Inuit Villages of Northern Canada").

Childbirth in the United States

In the United States there is a strong preference for giving birth in a hospital with the assistance of a physician. According to most recent estimates, 99 percent of all babies in the United States are born in hospitals, and 92 percent are delivered by a physician (Centers for Disease Control and Prevention, 2006a). Three major factors underlie this preference. First, hospitals staffed by trained physicians and nurses are better equipped to provide both antiseptic surroundings and specialized help to deal with any complications that might arise during labor and delivery. Second, many drugs have been developed to relieve the pain of childbirth, and by law such drugs can be prescribed only by physicians. Third, most health insurance policies will not pay for services administered outside hospital settings.

There is no doubt that the lives of thousands of babies and mothers are saved each year by the intervention of doctors and nurses using modern drugs and special medical procedures. However, research indicates that labor and delivery as typically practiced in the United States may lean too heavily on medical procedures and actually place mothers and babies at risk for health problems, especially when medical interventions are used during normal, uncomplicated births (Centers for Disease Control and Prevention, 2007). In general, concerns center on two questions: (1) What is the safest method for dealing with pain during childbirth? (2) What precautions are necessary to ensure the health of the mother and the baby?

Childbirth Pain and Its Medication In industrialized nations, a variety of drugs are used to lessen the pain of labor and delivery when birth takes place at a hospital. They include anesthetics (which dull overall feeling), analgesics (which reduce the perception of pain), and sedatives (which reduce anxiety). Medications seldom threaten the lives of healthy, full-term babies, but the newborns of

In the Field ▮ Midwifery in the Inuit Villages of Northern Canada

Name:	Akinisie Quamaluk
Education:	Trained in both traditional and scientific approaches to pregnancy, childbirth, and infant care
Current Position:	Inuit elder and midwife
Career Objectives:	Preserve and integrate traditional knowledge of health care for the purpose of increasing infant, family, and community well-being.

AKINISIE QUMALUK IS AN INUIT MIDWIFE living in a remote community in the far north of Quebec, Canada. Her craft of assisting women while they are pregnant, delivering their babies, and caring for their newborns draws from modern medical approaches as well as traditional Inuit knowledge. The blending of medical science with Inuit birthing and newborn care traditions is a major innovation in the education and practice of Inuit midwives. But what may be most remarkable is the fact that Akinisie is allowed to practice her craft in the local community. Although midwifery once was an integral part of traditional Inuit culture, in the 1970s the Canadian government began to insist that at 36 weeks gestation, women be flown to a major city in the south in order to deliver their babies in modern medical facilities. As described by a member of the Inuit community, "This intimate, integral part of our life was taken from us and replaced by a medical model that separated our families, stole the power of the birthing experience from our women, and weakened the health, strength, and spirit of our communities" (Van Wagner et al., 2007).

Inuit women did not allow this invasion of their cultural heritage to go unchallenged. A community organization was formed for the purpose of reviving cultural practices, including midwifery, and establishing self-government. As a consequence of the organization's efforts, the first community birth center was opened in 1986. The philosophy of the center was to provide Inuit women and health-care workers with care and education in the community by using traditional midwifery skills and knowledge integrated with modern approaches to care. Today, future midwives are recruited from the local villages to participate in an apprenticeship-style educational program rooted in Inuit teaching methods such as observation and storytelling.

Throughout the process of "returning childbirth to the villages," there was much discussion by women's groups, leaders, elders, and local health-care providers about the capacity and limitations of care in remote village locations and the potential for adverse outcomes should medical complications arise so far from emergency medical services. In response to such concerns, an Inuit elder explains: "I can understand that some of you may think that birth in remote areas is dangerous. (But) you must know that a life without meaning is much more dangerous." Indeed, taking birth out of the community is generally understood as disrespectful of Inuit culture and knowledge, and harmful to women and families. In Akinisie's words:

> With all the changes and women going south, the common knowledge—the things everyone knew abut childbirth and health—began to disappear. . . . People became very dependent on health-care services. . . . We knew birth had to come back to the north. Our aim was to revitalize that common knowledge and community involvement around the birth process—to put the responsibility back in the hands of the Inuit.

Interestingly, when pregnant Inuit women undergo "risk screening" to determine whether they might need to be evacuated to southern medical facilities equipped to deal with complications, the screening includes not only biomedical assessments but social, cultural, and community considerations as well. Conceptualizing risk within this broader context is consistent with Inuit beliefs that good health is not simply an absence of disease but includes positive mental, emotional, and spiritual features and is related to health in the family and community as a whole.

Analyses indicate that the policy of allowing Inuit women to give birth in their own communities, assisted by midwives trained in both modern and traditional approaches, results in fewer labor and delivery complications than the past practice of automatic evacuation. It is, of course, more difficult to gauge additional benefits such as mental, emotional, and spiritual well-being. But according to Inuit midwife Nellie Tukalak, "the midwives have become a voice for our families and our way of life."

(Adapted from Wagner, Epoo & Harney, 2007)

mothers who receive one or another of a variety of drugs during labor and delivery are less attentive and more irritable, have poorer muscle tone and less vigorous sucking responses, and are weaker than those whose mothers receive no medication (Jones, 1997).

Because of their concern about the possible adverse effects of drugs on the newborn, many women use alternative methods of controlling the pain of labor. Typically these methods include educational classes that give the mother-to-be an idea of what to expect during labor and delivery and teach her relaxation and breathing exercises to help counteract pain. Often they also involve having someone—the baby's father, or a sympathetic friend—be at the woman's side during labor to provide comfort and emotional support.

Medical Interventions In addition to administering drugs to ease the pain of labor, doctors may use medical procedures to safeguard the well-being of the mother and child. For example, when the baby is significantly overdue or when the mother is confronted with some life-threatening situation, physicians commonly induce labor, either by rupturing the membranes of the amniotic sac or by giving the mother some form of the hormone oxytocin, which initiates contractions. However, a report issued by the Centers for Disease Control and Prevention (2006a) indicates that the rate of induced labors rose more than twofold between 1990 and 2004, from 9.5 to 21.2 percent, and that much of the increase is not due to medical or obstetric conditions that threaten the baby or mother, but because of physician practice patterns or maternal choice (Figure 3.14). Of special concern is the fact that induced labors are associated with higher rates of cesarean delivery (surgical removal of the baby from the uterus by making an incision through the mother's belly), exposing both mother and child to increased health risks.

The cesarean procedure is typically used in cases of difficult labor, when the baby is in distress during delivery, or when the baby is not in the headfirst position. The number of cesarean sections performed in the United States began to increase significantly during the 1970s. By 2004, more than 29 out of every 100 births in the United States were by cesarean section (Centers for Disease Control and Prevention, 2006). Critics argue that many of the cesarean operations performed in the United States not only are unnecessary but raise the cost of childbirth, expose the mother to the risk of postoperative infection, cause mothers to be separated from their infants while they heal from surgery, and may be detrimental to the babies' well-being. For example, Herbert Renz-Polster and his colleagues report increased susceptibility of children delivered by cesarean section to hay fever and asthma (Renz-Polster & Buist, 2002), while others report increased chances of maternal death (Kusiako, Ronsmans, & Van der Paal, 2000).

Figure 3.14 For reasons that have little to do with threatening medical or obstetric conditions, rates of induced labors in the United States rose dramatically between 1990, when they accounted for 9.5 percent of all births, and 2004, when they accounted for 21.2 percent of all births. Because induced labor is often followed by cesarean delivery, which exposes both mother and newborn to increased health risks, the upward trend in induced labors has been highly criticized.

In many countries, families have choices regarding the context in which their babies will be born. Some prefer highly medical contexts, believing them "safer" in the event of trouble. Other families chose the intimacy of home birth. Still others chose alternatives such as water births, believing that they will relieve some of the stress typically associated with the birth process.

Concerns about unnecessary medical intervention extend to other procedures, such as electronic monitoring of the vital signs of the fetus during labor, which has been associated with the increase in cesarean sections (Martin, 1998). In part because of such concerns, there has been increased interest in alternative ways of giving birth that range from birthing at home with the assistance of a midwife to the use of special birthing centers where family members can also be present. Such centers are often located in or near a hospital in case serious complications arise. Alternative measures are especially popular when prenatal examinations find no indications that the birth will be especially complicated. Moreover, in such cases, the involvement of midwives does in fact appear to reduce the use of medical interventions such as those discussed. For example, a study carried out in Washington State found that in low-risk pregnancies, certified nurse-midwives were less likely to use fetal monitoring than physicians and had lower rates of induced labor. Their patients also were less likely to have spinal injections of anesthesia and cesarean sections than the patients of family physicians and obstetricians (Rosenblatt et al., 1997).

The Baby's Experience of Birth There is no doubt that the process of being born is stressful for babies, even if all proceeds normally. The baby must squeeze through a very narrow opening, and this places a great deal of pressure on the head; if the umbilical cord becomes constricted in the process, the supply of oxygen is reduced. A number of studies document a surge in the fetus's production of stress hormones around the time of birth. In fact, it seems that stress hormones may contribute to initiating the process of labor and delivery (Oh et al., 2006). Hugo Lagercrantz and his colleagues go on to propose that the stress hormones are of vital importance because these hormones prepare the infant to survive outside the womb (Lagercrantz & Slotkin, 1986). In particular, they argue that high levels of the stress hormones in the hours before birth facilitate the absorption of liquid from the lungs and the production of surfactin, both of which allow the lungs to function well. In support of their hypothesis, they point out that breathing difficulties are common among infants delivered by cesarean section, a procedure they believe deprives infants of the experiences leading to the hormonal surge.

Lagercrantz and Slotkin also believe that the stress hormones produce an increase in the newborn's metabolic rate and that they are instrumental in increasing blood flow to such vital organs as the heart, lungs, and brain and thus increase the chances of survival of a baby who is experiencing breathing difficulties. Furthermore, they speculate that the hormonal surge puts the newborn in a state of alertness. Immediately following birth, most normal newborns have a prolonged period of quiet alertness, lasting as long as 40 minutes, during which their eyes are open in a wide-eyed gaze (Klaus, Kennella, & Klaus, 1995).

APPLY ▪ CONNECT ▪ DISCUSS

When it comes to prenatal care, labor, delivery, and newborn care, technologically advanced societies rely heavily on medical science. How would you characterize the culture of medical science (you may want to review the definition of culture presented in Chapter 2, p. 54)? What are some of the costs and benefits of medical science for pregnant women and newborns?

The Newborn's Condition

To first-time parents, especially those who imagine that newborns look like the infants pictured on jars of baby food, the real neonate's appearance may cause alarm and disappointment. The baby's head is overly large in proportion to the rest of the body, and the limbs are relatively small and tightly flexed. Unless the baby has been delivered by cesarean section, the head may look misshapen after the tight squeeze through the birth canal. (The head usually regains its symmetry by the end of the first week after birth.) The baby's skin may be covered with *vernix caseosa,* a white, cheesy substance that protects against bacterial infections, and it may be spotted with blood.

In the United States, neonates weigh an average of 7 to 7½ pounds, although babies weighing anywhere from 5½ to 10 pounds are within the normal range. During their first days of life, most babies lose about 7 percent of their initial weight, primarily because of loss of fluid. They usually gain the weight back by the time they are 10 days old.

The average neonate is 20 inches long. To a large extent, the length of the newborn is determined by the size of the mother's uterus. It does not reflect the baby's genetic inheritance, because the genes that control height do not begin to express themselves until shortly after birth (Tanner, 1990).

Assessing the Baby's Viability

In professionally assisted births, health-care practitioners (midwives, doctors, or nurses) check the neonate for indications of danger so that immediate action can be taken if something is wrong. They take note of the baby's size, check vital signs, and look for evidence of normal capacities. A variety of scales and tests are used to assess the neonate's physical state and behavioral condition (Singer & Zeskind, 2001).

Physical Condition In the 1950s, Virginia Apgar (1953), an anesthesiologist who worked in the delivery room of a large metropolitan hospital, developed a quick and simple method of determining if a baby requires emergency care. The **Apgar Scale,** which is now widely employed throughout the United States, is used to rate babies at 1 minute and again at 5 minutes after birth using five vital signs: heart rate, respiratory effort, muscle tone, reflex responsivity, and color. Table 3.5 shows the criteria for scoring each of the signs. The individual scores are totaled to give a measure of the baby's overall physical condition. A baby with a score of less than 4 is considered to be in poor condition and requires immediate medical attention. According to a recent nationwide study, the proportion of newborns with Apgar scores indicating excellent health declined from 91.1 percent in 2003

table **3.5**			
The Apgar Scoring System			
	Rating		
Vital Sign	0	1	2
Heart rate	Absent	Slow (below 100)	Over 100
Respiratory effort	Absent	Slow, irregular	Good, crying
Muscle tone	Flaccid	Some flexion of extremities	Active motion
Reflex responsivity	No response	Grimace	Vigorous cry
Color	Blue, pale	Body pink, extremities blue	Completely pink

Source: Apgar, 1953.

Apgar Scale A quick, simple test used to diagnose the physical state of newborn infants.

to 88.8 percent in 2004, with non-Hispanic black infants having the highest percent of very low Apgar scores (0–3 points), more than twice the level of Hispanic and non-Hispanic white infants (CDC, 2006).

Behavioral Condition During the past half century, many scales have been constructed to assess the more subtle behavioral aspects of the newborn's condition (Singer & Zeskind, 2001). One of the most widely used is the **Brazelton Neonatal Assessment Scale**, developed by pediatrician T. Berry Brazelton and his colleagues in the late 1970s (Brazelton, 1984). A major purpose of this scale is to assess the neurological condition of newborns who are suspected of being at risk for developmental difficulties. It is also used to assess the developmental progress of infants, to compare the functioning of newborns of different cultures, and to evaluate the effectiveness of interventions designed to alleviate developmental difficulties (Lundqvist & Sabel, 2000).

The Brazelton scale includes tests of infants' reflexes, motor capacities, muscle tone, capacity for responding to objects and people, and capacity to control their own behavior (such as turning away when overstimulated) and attention. When scoring a newborn on such tests, the examiner must take note of the degree of the infant's alertness and, if necessary, repeat the tests when the baby is wide awake and calm. Here are some typical items on the Brazelton scale:

- *Orientation to animate objects—visual and auditory.* The examiner calls the baby's name repeatedly in a high-pitched voice while moving his head up and down and from side to side in front of the baby. Does the baby focus on the examiner? Does she follow the examiner with her eyes smoothly?

- *Pull-to-sit.* The examiner puts a forefinger in each of the infant's palms and pulls him to a sitting position. Does the baby try to right his head when he is in a seated position? How well is he able to do so?

- *Cuddliness.* The examiner holds the baby against her chest or up against her shoulder. How does the baby respond? Does she resist being held? Is she passive, or does she cuddle up to the examiner?

- *Defensive movements.* The examiner places a cloth over the baby's face and holds it there. Does the baby try to remove the cloth from his face either by turning his head away or by swiping at it?

- *Self-quieting activity.* The examiner notes what the baby does to quiet herself when she is fussy. Does she suck her thumb, look around?

In addition to their primary goal of screening for infants at risk, neonatal assessment scales are used to predict aspects of newborns' future development such as their temperaments or typical learning rates. Research over the past decade with neonates thought to be at risk shows that these scales are, in fact, satisfactory guides for determining when medical intervention is necessary, and that they are also fairly good at characterizing whether the baby is developing normally in the period following birth (Hart et al., 1999; Schuler & Nair, 1999). They are less useful when it comes to predicting later intelligence or personality, however.

Problems and Complications

Though most babies are born without any serious problems, some are in such poor physical condition that they soon die. Others are at risk for later developmental problems. Newborns are considered to be at risk if they suffer from any of a variety of problems, including asphyxiation (life-threatening loss of oxygen) or head injury during delivery, either of which may result in brain damage, acute difficulty

Brazelton Neonatal Assessment Scale A scale used to assess the newborn's neurological condition.

gestational age The time that has passed between conception and birth. The normal gestational age is between 37 and 43 weeks.

preterm The term for babies born before the 37th week of pregnancy.

breathing after birth, or difficulty digesting food owing to an immature digestive system (Korner & Constantinou, 2001). These are the kinds of problems that are likely to result in low scores on the Apgar Scale. Most of the newborns who are at risk are premature, abnormally underweight, or both (Singer & Zeskind, 2001).

Prematurity Prematurity is measured in terms of **gestational age,** the time that has passed between conception and birth. The normal gestational age is 37 to 43 weeks. Babies born before the 37th week are considered to be **preterm,** or premature (Figure 3.15). In the United States, the preterm birth rate climbed 18 percent between 1990 and 2004, at which time approximately 12.5 percent of all babies were born before the 37th week (CDC, 2006; Figure 3.16). Disorders related to premature birth are the fourth leading cause of infant mortality. With the expert care and technology now available in modern hospitals (Figure 3.17), mortality rates for premature infants are declining in the United States.

The leading cause of death among preterm infants is immaturity of the lungs (Lee et al., 2006). The other main obstacle to the survival of preterm infants is immaturity of their digestive and immune systems. Even babies of normal gestational age sometimes have difficulty coordinating sucking, swallowing, and breathing during the first few days after birth. The difficulty is likely to be more serious for preterm infants, who may need additional help with all these functions. Their coordination may be so poor that they cannot be fed directly from breast or bottle, therefore special equipment must be used to feed them. Moreover, their immature digestive systems often cannot handle normal baby formulas, requiring that they must be fed special formulas.

There are many potential contributors to prematurity, some of them known. Twins are likely to be born about 3 weeks early, triplets and quadruplets even earlier. Very young women whose reproductive systems are immature and women who have had many pregnancies close together are more likely to have premature

Scott Olson/Getty Images

Figure 3.15 At the time of her birth in 2004, Rumaisa Rahman (which means 'white as milk' in India) weighed 8.6 ounces, making her the smallest known surviving baby in the world. Being born at the Loyola University Medical Center (Illinois, USA) assures that Rumaisa will receive the extensive medical support necessary during the critical first months of her life.

Figure 3.16 In contrast to trends in many other industrialized countries, the preterm birth rate in the United States climbed 18 percent between 1990 and 2004.

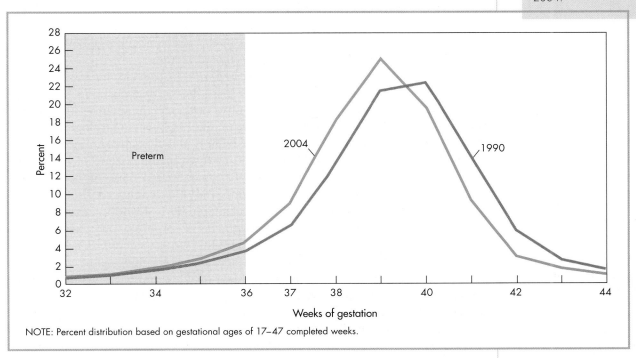

NOTE: Percent distribution based on gestational ages of 17–47 completed weeks.

Sarah Leen/National Geographic/Getty Images

Figure 3.17 The care provided for premature infants in modern hospitals now includes gentle massage in addition to sophisticated medical technologies.

babies. So are women who smoke, who are in poor health, or who have infections of the uterus. The chances of giving birth to a premature infant also vary with socioeconomic status (Joseph et al., 2007). Even in countries with universal health coverage, such as Canada, poor women are significantly more likely than affluent women to give birth to small or preterm infants, or infants who die in the first months of life. This disparity can be explained in part by the fact that poor women are more likely to be undernourished or chronically ill, to smoke, to be overweight, and to experience complications during pregnancy. Cultural factors such as the use of fertility drugs and fasting can also play a role.

Many other causes of prematurity are still not well understood. At least half of all premature births are not associated with any of the identified risk factors and occur after otherwise normal pregnancies to healthy women who are in their prime childbearing years and have had good medical care.

Low Birth Weight Newborns weighing less than 5 pounds, 8 ounces (2500 grams) are said to have **low birth weight.** Often low-birth-weight babies are preterm, but this is not necessarily the case. They may also be **small for gestational age,** with a birth weight that falls in the lowest 10 percent for their gestational age. Small-for-gestational-age infants have usually experienced *intrauterine growth restriction;* in other words, they have not grown at the normal rate. Multiple births, intrauterine infections, chromosomal abnormalities, maternal smoking or use of narcotics, maternal malnutrition, and abnormalities of the placenta or umbilical cord have all been identified as probable causes of intrauterine growth restriction (Meara, 2001).

Developmental Consequences

Intensive research has been conducted on the developmental consequences of prematurity and low birth weight. Both put babies at risk for later developmental problems including delays and disorders in intellectual and language development, attention, and neurological functioning (Aylward, 2006).

Low-birth-weight infants are at increased risk for developmental difficulty, even if they are full term. Two-thirds of the deaths that occur in the period immediately following birth are among low-birth-weight infants. In addition, low-birthweight infants are three times more likely to have neurologically based developmental handicaps than are other babies, and the smaller the baby, the greater the risk (Holcroft, Blakemore, Allen, & Graham, 2001).

Common outcomes for low-birth-weight babies are a decrease in coordination and intellectual capacities. For example, one study that compared 7- to 11-year-olds who had a very low birth weight with children born at a normal weight found that the low-birth-weight children performed more poorly on tests of motor coordination, intelligence, and arithmetic (Holsti, Grunau, & Whitfield, 2002).

The long-term outcome of prematurity appears to be influenced by various factors. Premature babies who are small for gestational age and have medical complications are most likely to have future developmental difficulties. Those premature babies who are of normal size for their gestational age may stand a much better chance of catching up with full-term babies (Lorenz, 2001). However, there is

low birth weight The term used to describe babies weighing 2500 grams or less at birth, whether or not they are premature.

small for gestational age Newborns whose birth weight falls in the lowest 10 percent for their gestational age because they have not grown at the normal rate.

some evidence that even in the absence of any clinically detectable disability, when compared to full-term children, children born prematurely have problems with maintaining attention and with visual–motor coordination when they are school-age (Foreman et al., 1997).

The importance of a supportive environment in overcoming the potential risks of prematurity and low birth weight is underscored by research on the social ecology of the families of premature and low-birth-weight infants. Babies who are raised in comfortable socioeconomic circumstances with an intact family and a mother who has had a good education are less likely to suffer negative effects from their condition at birth than are children who are raised without these benefits (Liaw, Meisels, & Brooks-Gunn, 1995). Low-birth-weight or premature babies who live in impoverished homes or have neglectful parents are more likely to suffer serious developmental problems in later years (Strathearn, Gray, O'Callaghan, & Wood, 2001).

APPLY ▪▪ CONNECT ▪▪ DISCUSS

Low birth weight is one of the leading causes of infant mortality. According to Dr. Alan Brann, a professor of pediatrics at Emory University, birth weight is an important indicator of a community's overall health status. In particular, Dr. Brann argues that low birth weight signals an unhealthy community. In the past 5 years, many southern states have seen a shocking rise in the number of infant deaths. Have birth weights and infant deaths in your community/state/province/nation changed in recent years? How does your community/state/province/nation compare to others on measures of infant birth weight and mortality? What community/state/provincial/national efforts are underway to increase birth weight and/or decrease infant death?

Beginning the Parent–Child Relationship

Because human infants are dependent on the active support and protection of their caretakers for their very survival, the development of a close relationship between infants and their parents is crucial to infants' well-being. However, love and caring between parent and child is neither inevitable nor automatic. The large numbers of infants who are neglected, abused, abandoned, or murdered should convince even the most sentimental and optimistic observer of this harsh fact. How, then, is the bond between parent and child formed? And when no strong attachment develops, what has gone wrong? These are broad questions that you will encounter again and again in subsequent chapters, because a close parent–child relationship is not formed in an instant; it develops over many years. Here we will examine two factors that come into play immediately after birth, helping to set the stage for the future: the initial reactions of the parents to their baby's appearance, and the expectations parents have for their babies.

The Baby's Appearance

In their search for the sources of attachment between mother and infant, some developmentalists have turned to *ethology*—the study of animal behavior and its evolutionary bases. These developmentalists believe that examination of what causes nonhuman mothers to protect or reject their young can shed light on the factors that influence human mothers. As introduced in Chapter 1 (p. 26–27), one important factor that seems to influence animals' responses to their young is their offsprings' appearance (Koyama, Takahashi, & Mori, 2006).

Figure 3.18 Side-by-side sketches of the heads of infants and adults of four species make clear the distinguishing features of "babyness." (From Lorenz, 1943.)

Konrad Lorenz (1943), a German ethologist, noted that the newborns of many animal species have physical characteristics that distinguish them from the mature animal: a head that is large in relation to the body, a prominent forehead, large eyes that are positioned below the horizontal midline of the face, and round, full cheeks (Figure 3.18). This combination of features, which Lorenz called "babyness," and people the world over recognize as "cute," seems to appeal to adults and, more significantly, to evoke caregiving behaviors in them.

Evidence in support of the idea that babyness evokes positive adult responses comes from a classic study by William Fullard and Ann Reiling (1976). These researchers asked people ranging in age from 7 years to young adulthood which of matched pairs of pictures—one depicting an adult and the other depicting an infant—they preferred. Some of the pictures were of human beings; others were of animals. They found that adults, especially women, were most likely to choose the pictures of infants. Children between the ages of 7 and 12 preferred the pictures of adults. Between the ages of 12 and 14, the preference of girls shifted quite markedly from adults to infants. A similar shift was found among boys when they were between 14 and 16. These shifts in preference coincide with the average ages at which girls and boys undergo the physiological changes that make them capable of reproducing.

Appearance may also be an explanation for rejection. Mothers in certain species, including dogs, cats, and guinea pigs, will kill malformed offspring. Though human parents usually do not kill their malformed babies, they do interact less frequently and less lovingly with infants they consider unattractive than with those they consider attractive. They also attribute less competence to unattractive babies (Langlois et al., 2000). This pattern is particularly noticeable for baby girls. While still in the hospital with their newborn girls, mothers of less attractive babies directed their attention to people other than their babies more often than did mothers of attractive babies (Langlois et al., 1995).

Social Expectations

During pregnancy, most parents-to-be develop specific expectations about what their babies will be like, and no sooner does a baby emerge from the womb than the parents begin to examine the neonate's looks and behaviors for hints of his or her future. Will she have her grandmother's high, round forehead? Does his lusty cry mean that he will have his father's quick temper?

One of the most significant characteristics affecting parents' expectations is the sex of the baby (Basow, 2006). Whether their baby is a boy or a girl, the parents' beliefs and expectations begin to shape their responses to the baby even before the child displays any truly distinctive features. One study found that parents shown ultrasound pictures of their babies-to-be tended to rate female fetuses as softer, littler, cuddlier, calmer, weaker, more delicate, and more beautiful than male fetuses (Sweeney & Bradbard, 1988). In another study, first-time mothers and fathers were asked to choose words that described their newborn babies within 24 hours after their birth (Rubin, Provezano, & Luria, 1974). The male and female babies did not differ in length or weight or in their scores on the Apgar Scale. Nevertheless, the parents described their daughters as "little," "beautiful," "pretty," or "cute," and as resembling their mothers, whereas they described their sons as "big" and as resembling their fathers. Fathers, the researchers found, were especially likely to sex-type their babies. Thus, beliefs and expectations shape the way that the parents see the child right from the start—and also the way they treat the child.

There is every reason for their baby's sex to be important to the parents. Children's sex determines what they are named, how they are dressed, how they are treated, and what will be expected of them in later life. But because we like to think of ourselves as individuals to be treated according to who we are rather than what others expect us to be, it can be disconcerting to realize that such expectations held by our parents at the outset may be crucial influences on many aspects of our development.

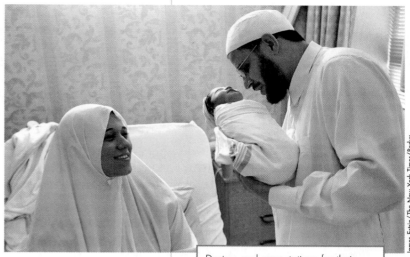

Desires and expectations for their children's futures affect parenting practices, and children's experiences, from the first days of life. This mother is having her newborn blessed by a leader in her religious community.

Unless parental expectations are held so rigidly that they become destructive, parents' responses to their infants do not represent a failing on their part but, rather, reflect the fact that human infants are members of a culture. For their parents and for others in the community, cultural ideas about the experiences that infants are likely to encounter as they grow to adulthood shape the way adults perceive infants and the way they construct the contexts within which children develop. Thus, when differences are found in how boys and girls are treated, they occur not just because parents think that infant boys and girls are different to begin with but, perhaps more significantly, because they believe that their infants will develop into men and women with different roles to play in their society.

Within the context of culture, then, parents organize their infants' activities and environments with an eye to the future (Lyra, 2007). This orientation to the future is expressed in clear symbolic form by the Zincantecos of south-central Mexico (Greenfield, Brazelton, & Childs, 1989). When a son is born, he is given a digging stick, an ax, and a strip of palm used in weaving mats, in expectation of his adult role. When a daughter is born, she is given a weaving stick. Such future orientation is not only present in ritual; it is coded in a Zincantecan saying: "For in the newborn baby is the future of our world."

Ultimately, parents' organization of the present in terms of the future contributes to the powerful role that culture has in development (Valsiner, 2006). Just as infants are born with a set of genetically built-in capacities to learn about and to act upon the world, parents come to this moment with their tendencies to respond in certain ways that have developed through their experience as members of their culture. These tendencies help shape the relationship between child and parents that begins at birth—itself an essential part of the foundation on which development builds.

▌▌▌▌ ▌ APPLY ▬ CONNECT ▬ DISCUSS

Provide some examples of how the relationship between the newborn's characteristics and the care he or she receives is *mediated* by cultural beliefs and values (see Chapter 2, p. 56).

SUMMARY

The Periods of Prenatal Development

- Prenatal development is often divided into three broad periods:

  1. The germinal period begins at conception and lasts until the zygote enters the uterus and becomes implanted there about 8 to 10 days later. Through repeated division, the organism has grown from a single cell to hundreds of cells by the time it reaches the uterus.

  2. The embryonic period extends from implantation to the end of the 8th week. With cell differentiation, by the end of this period, all major organs have taken primitive shape and sexual differentiation has begun. This rapid growth is facilitated by the efficient way the placenta allows the exchange of nutrients and waste products between the mother and the embryo.

  3. The fetal period goes from the 9th week, with the beginning of ossification, until birth. The fetus grows dramatically in size, and the brain and all organ systems increase in complexity to the point where the baby can exist outside the mother. The fetus is subject to environmental influences originating from outside as well as inside the mother. Basic sensory capacities (for sensing motion, light, sound) develop during this period, enabling fetal learning. By 15 weeks the fetus exhibits all movements observable at birth; fetal activity is crucial to neuronal development.

Environmental Conditions and Prenatal Development

- A mother's negative attitudes toward a pregnancy, or stress during pregnancy, may be associated with problems such as low birth weight and certain longer-term developmental risks. The problems may stem from the mother's elevated levels of the hormone cortisol during pregnancy.

- A mother's nutrition is an important factor in fetal development. Pregnant women are advised to consume enough calories in a well-balanced diet and to increase intake of folic acid, calcium, and iron. Extreme maternal undernourishment and malnutrition are associated with low birth weight, prematurity, abnormalities, and death. Lesser degrees also increase risk, although effects can be difficult to isolate.

Teratogens: Environmental Sources of Birth Defects

- Teratogens (environmental agents that can cause deviations from normal fetal development) take many forms. Six general principles apply with all:

  1. The susceptibility of the organism depends on its developmental stage.

  2. A teratogen's effects are likely to be specific to a particular organ.

  3. Individual organisms vary in their susceptibility to teratogens.

  4. The mother's physiological state influences susceptibility.

  5. The greater the concentration of a teratogenic agent, the greater the risk.

  6. Teratogens that have little or no effect on the mother can seriously affect the developing organism.

- Among the common teratogens are drugs, including prescription drugs, caffeine, tobacco, alcohol, marijuana, cocaine, and heroin and methadone. Their effects vary considerably; heavy drinking, for example, is associated with fetal alcohol syndrome. Other teratogenic agents are infections, including rubella and HIV, and radiation or pollution at high levels.

Birth

- Labor begins approximately 266 days after conception and proceeds through three stages, in which contractions cause the cervix to dilate, the baby is pushed through the birth canal and is delivered, and the afterbirth is delivered.

- There are marked cultural variations in childbirth, so that a woman may give birth unassisted, be assisted by a midwife and/or others at home, or be assisted by a physician or midwife in a hospital.

- In the United States, concern about the possible adverse effects of pain medication on the newborn and about overuse of medical interventions, such as induced labor and cesarean section has led to interest in alternatives such as the use of midwives and birthing centers.

- Birth is a stressful experience for the baby, but research suggests that a surge of stress hormones as the process begins protects the baby from the adverse conditions and prepares her to survive outside the womb.

The Newborn's Condition

- The Apgar Scale is used to assess the newborn's physical condition by rating heart rate, respiratory effort, reflex responsivity, muscle tone, and color. Babies with a low score require immediate medical attention. Other scales have been developed to assess behavioral aspects of the newborn's condition.

- Risks are associated with prematurity (birth before the 37th week) and low birth weight (below 5 pounds, 8 ounces [2500 grams]). They are especially great for premature infants who are small for their gestational age and have medical complications.

Beginning the Parent–Child Relationship

- A newborn's appearance plays a significant role in the parents' response to the baby, with "babyness" evidently evoking caregiving behaviors.

- From birth, parents' expectations, influenced by the culture, influence the child's environment in ways that shape the child's development.

Key Terms

zygote, p. 84
germinal period, p. 85
embryonic period, p. 85
fetal period, p. 85
cleavage, p. 85
heterochrony, p. 85
heterogeneity, p. 85
totipotent stem cells, p. 86
implantation, p. 86
amnion, p. 86

chorion, p. 86
placenta, p. 86
umbilical cord, p. 86
ectoderm, p. 87
endoderm, p. 87
mesoderm, p. 87
epigenesis, p. 88
cephalocaudal pattern, p. 88
proximodistal pattern, p. 88
neural tube, p. 94

teratogens, p. 97
fetal alcohol syndrome, p. 99
Apgar Scale, p. 111
Brazelton Neonatal Assessment Scale, p. 112
gestational age, p. 113
preterm, p. 113
low birth weight, p. 114
small for gestational age, p. 114

Major Milestones of Infancy

	Physical Domain	Cognitive Domain	Social and Emotional Domain	
What Develops...	• Rapid growth to about 30–34 inches and 22–27 pounds by end of second year. • Ossification of bones; beginning of ongoing changes in proportions, increase in muscle strength. • Development of cerebral cortex areas, including prefrontal cortex and language-related areas. • Myelination of neurons, including neurons of language-related areas and neurons linking areas of the brain. • Most brain structures present by 2 years of age, with neurons in the cerebral cortex similar to those of adults in length and branching. • Increasing coordination of and control over gross and fine motor behaviors. • Gross motor developments include crawling (around 8–9 months) and walking (around 1 year). • Fine motor developments include perfecting reaching and grasping, and by 2 years, performing movements needed to feed and dress self, etc.	• Behavior becomes increasingly intentional and goal directed. • Emergence of object permanence and representational thinking. • With ability to represent objects and experiences mentally, increased problem solving, symbolic play, deferred imitation, language use. • Development of understanding of cause–effect relationships. • Development of ability to categorize objects according to common features. • Increased ability to control and sustain attention; increased speed of processing information. • Improved memory.	• Basic emotions are present at birth or soon after. • Emergence of primary intersubjectivity. • Increased ability to regulate emotions. • Development of attachment to caregivers (7–9 months); fear of strangers emerges with attachment. • Emergence of secondary intersubjectivity, including social referencing, gaze following, pointing. • Emergence of language comprehension and speech, including recognizing common words and expressions (6–9 months), babbling (7 months), first words (1 year). • Greater ability to share and communicate knowledge, desires, interests. • Emerging sense of self, including self-recognition by 18 months, and associated sense of independence. • Emergence of self-conscious emotions. • Stage of basic trust versus mistrust, in first year; stage of autonomy versus shame and doubt, in second year.	
Sociocultural Contributions and Consequences...	• Factors such as socioeconomic status and diet can contribute to variations in growth. • Cultures vary in how they restrict or encourage specific motor actions, affecting the sequence and timing of gross motor milestones. • Culture influences age of control of elimination. • Child begins to participate in feeding and dressing.	• Motor development coupled with interest in exploring can be risky; parents respond by "baby-proofing" the environment.	• Basic emotions emerge across cultures, facilitating ties to members of the community and, in this way, acquisition of culture. • Cultures differ in ideas about what constitutes sensitive caregiving, including in infancy. • Emotionally warm and responsive interactions generate sense of trust and exploration.	

Infancy

Passing from the birth canal into the hands of the mother or her birth attendant marks the transition from fetal life to infancy. Preparations for this event— perhaps the most radical in the life course of the individual—have been underway for nine months or for millennia, depending on whether they are viewed through the lens of ontogeny (the individual's development) or in terms of the evolution of human species and culture. In either case, the transition from the intrauterine to the extrauterine environment takes place in the context of a facilitating or supportive environment. The birth canal, for example, the channel formed by the mother's cervix, vagina, and vulva, is not simply a physical structure through which the baby passes, but plays a dynamic role in the transition by exerting pressure on the fetus's chest, forcing fluid from airways in preparation for the drawing of the first breath of life. Then the umbilical cord is cut, often with great ceremony, and the infant enters into a fundamentally new relationship with the environment.

The chapters in Part II are organized to highlight the nature of this new relationship and how it continues to change over the course of infancy. Chapter 4 traces development from birth to about 3 months of age, exploring infants' earliest capacities for perceiving and acting on the world, as infants' behavior becomes increasingly organized and integrated. The most obvious requirement of this earliest postnatal period is that infants and their caretakers become sufficiently coordinated in their interactions so that adults can provide infants with enough nourishment and protection to support their continued growth. This requirement is met through a wide variety of cultural systems of infant care that call upon and promote infants' basic capacities to learn from experience.

Chapter 5 examines the marked changes in physical and cognitive development that take place between 3 months and 2 years of age. Increases in physical size and strength are accompanied by increases in motor coordination and control, opening up entirely new opportunities for exploring the world. Both memory and problem-solving abilities improve, providing infants with a finer sense of their environment and how to act upon it. The emergence of imitation and symbol use lays a foundation for new ways of communicating and connecting with others.

The processes through which infants are drawn into the lives of others are the focus of Chapter 6, where we examine the developmental course of infant emotions and emotional expressions, infants' attachments to their caregivers, and the beginnings of language. We discuss why infants become wary of strangers and become upset when left alone. We also explore the budding sense of self, the first glimmer of independence (sometimes described as the "terrible twos"), and the dawning ability to distinguish between "good" and "bad."

Throughout this section, we underscore how interacting domains of development (physical, cognitive, social, and emotional) and the sociocultural contexts in which development occurs jointly contribute to the increasing organization and coordination of the infant's behavior.

4

The First Three Months

On the second day: *M'ama Afwe, a 16-year-old first-time mother, is dozing on her bed with her 2-day-old daughter. They are recovering from the delivery and waiting for the baby's umbilical cord to fall off, the sign in Afwe's West African culture that it is safe to take the newborn outside. When her daughter starts to fuss and cry, Afwe leans over her, trying to get her breast close to the baby's mouth. But her breasts are large and full of milk, and this leaning-over position makes it difficult for the baby to latch onto the nipple. The hungry baby is frustrated and frets. Afwe's grandmother observes the scene and offers some advice: Why not try lying down next to the baby? Perhaps Afwe's nipple will fit into the little mouth that way. Afwe tries out the new position. It works: The baby nurses eagerly.*

In the second week: *After some hours of cycling between fussing and nursing, Afwe's baby girl is sleeping in her grandmother's arms while Afwe naps, tired in the way that new mothers often are. A neighbor comes in to admire the latest addition to the community. She takes the baby from the grandmother to hold and look at her, which rouses the infant from her slumber, and initiates a new bout of fussing. When the baby is returned to her grandmother's arms, she begins to cry vigorously. The grandmother speaks to her in a soft and soothing tone, but the infant is highly agitated, and cries all the more, so the grandmother, who has a nursing toddler of her own, offers the baby her breast. Her granddaughter eagerly accepts it, nurses for a few moments, and then drops off to sleep.*

(Adapted from Gottlieb, 2000.)

ompared with many other animals, which are fairly able to take care of themselves at birth, human beings are born in a state of marked immaturity and dependence. As Afwe quickly learned, she must help her baby to accomplish even such an elementary act as feeding. The relative helplessness of human babies at birth has several obvious consequences. Babies require extensive care and attention. This limits the mother's ability to provide for herself and her other children, and, consequently, increases the importance of child–care assistance from her mate and others in her community. In Afwe's West African culture, extended kin, such as Afwe's grandmother, provide help with infant care. In other cultures or communities, babysitters or day–care providers may give comparable levels of assistance. Moreover, the dependence of human offspring for their survival on the efforts of their parents and other adults lasts for many years. As we discussed in Chapter 2, in order to survive on their own and become integrated into the activities of their community, human children must learn a vast repertoire of knowledge, skills, traditions, and patterns of living that they do not possess at birth.

This chapter describes the capacities and characteristics of children at birth and the processes of developmental change that occur in the initial period of infancy, a period beginning immediately after birth and ending approximately 3 months

growth charts Charts showing average values of height, weight, and other measures of growth, based on large samples of normally developing infants and used to evaluate an infant's development.

fontanels "Soft spots," or spaces separating the bones of the skull prenatally and in early infancy.

later. Examining what babies bring with them into the world, we will see the ways in which newborns' brains and sensory systems allow them to experience the world, the ways in which their specific reflexes and temperamental styles influence how they respond to their experiences, and the ways in which certain innate learning capacities come to affect their early behavior.

In addition to exploring what babies bring with them into the world, we will examine how the world interacts with the newly born through the contexts of family, community, and cultural traditions, and how these contexts and traditions affect the young infant's development. The story of early infancy, as you will see, is a story about organization and coordination: how the brain becomes organized into a highly efficient communication network; how newborn reflexes and sensory systems become organized into more complex systems of behavior; and how these brain and behavioral developments are coordinated with the particular social and cultural environment into which the child is born.

Physical Growth

During the infant's first 3 months, physical growth progresses at an astonishing pace. In just 12 short weeks, the baby will gain approximately 6 pounds and grow more than 4 inches in length. As a consequence of the rapidly developing brain, the circumference of the head will increase by more than an inch. Keeping in mind that the average baby weighs a bit more than 7 pounds at birth, is just 19.5 or so inches long, and has a head circumference of about 14 inches, these changes to the physical body are truly remarkable!

Measuring Body Growth

Pediatricians and other health-care providers for infants closely monitor infants' early physical growth for reassuring signs of normal development—or for early warnings that a problem might exist. Typically, the baby's development is evaluated by using **growth charts,** which depict average values of height, weight, and other measures of growth that have been compiled by studying large samples of normally developing infants. As shown in Figure 4.1 for weight, growth charts indicate the average values as well as various degrees of deviation from the average.

Because growth charts are an integral tool for assessing the health status of the baby, developmentalists are highly invested in assuring their validity. The problems that otherwise can ensue became apparent in recent years when many pediatricians became concerned that some breast-fed babies were malnourished because, according to growth chart averages, they were gaining weight relatively slowly. To compensate for what they believed was inadequate nutrition, some doctors advised mothers to supplement their infants' diets with formula and solid foods. Such advice goes against the recommendation of many infant-health organizations that babies be exclusively breast-fed throughout the first year to optimize healthy development. (Among other long-term benefits, breast-feeding is associated with decreased risk for immune-related diseases, childhood cancers, and obesity, and with improved cognitive functioning [Schack-Neilson, Larnkjaer, & Michaelson, 2005]). As you can see, the pediatricians faced a conflict. On one hand, many breast-fed babies appeared underweight; on the other hand, a trove of evidence indicates that breast-fed babies are generally healthier than their formula-fed peers. The conflict was resolved when it was realized that breast-fed babies typically gain less weight during the first year because they voluntarily take in less milk compared to formula-fed babies, as it is easier to control the flow of milk from a breast than a bottle (WHO,

Perhaps because they have greater control over the milk they drink, breast fed babies tend to gain less weight during the first year compared to their bottle-fed counterparts.

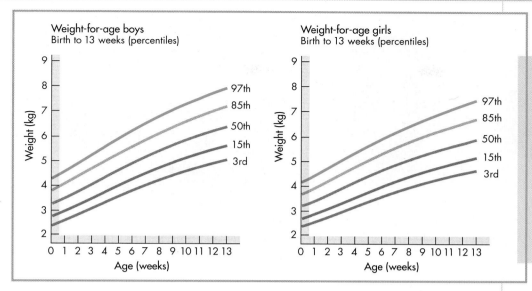

Figure 4.1 Growth charts show age-specific averages as well as variations from averages, helping health-care providers assess whether a child's development is on track or is a cause for concern. The figures to the left illustrate changes in weight averages for boys and girls between birth and 13 weeks of age. As shown in the chart for boys, at 8 weeks of age, 50% of all boys weigh more than 5½ kilograms, and 50% weigh less (illustrated by the purple line). An 8-week-old boy weighing 4 kilograms would be at the 3rd percentile (blue line), suggesting malnutrition and health problems.

2006). However, the growth charts were calculated with data from both breast- and formula-fed babies, so the averages were raised by the heavier, faster-growing (but not necessarily healthier) formula-fed babies.

Faced with mounting evidence that breast-fed and formula-fed babies grow differently during the first year, the World Health Organization (WHO) launched a massive international study to determine optimal standards of physical growth when children are being breast-fed through the first year of infancy and in other respects raised in healthy environments (e.g., with adequate health care and with mothers who did not smoke). Nearly 8500 children growing up in such healthy environments in Brazil, Ghana, India, Norway, Oman, and the United States participated in the study, which resulted in new international standards for evaluating the physical growth of infants and young children. The study indicates that when raised in healthy environments, babies everywhere, regardless of ethnicity or socioeconomic status, show comparable patterns of physical growth (WHO, 2006).

Growth of the Skull

Health-care providers for infants track changes to the baby's head circumference because the primary determinant of the growth and shape of the head is the development of the brain. If you have ever stroked a baby's head, you know the newborn's skull is considerably different than that of an older child or adult. The infant's skull is composed of seven flat membranous bones that are relatively soft and elastic (Margulies & Thibault, 2000). Early in development, the bones are separated by **fontanels,** also known as the "soft spots." Because the bones of the skull are separated, rather than fused together, they are capable of moving in response to external or internal pressure. This trait allows the skull to "mold" during birth in response to external pressure exerted by the relatively narrow birth canal and to expand in response to internal pressure exerted by a rapidly developing brain— an illustration of evolution's marvelous web of adaptations.

During the first months of infancy, the growing brain pushes against the bones of the skull, expanding the infant's head circumference and contributing to its relatively round shape. However, infants who spend most of their sleep time lying in the same position may develop "positional skull flattening" from ongoing external pressure to the same part of the head (this is of special concern given the "back to sleep" campaign intended to reduce the incidence of sudden infant death

(a)   (b)

Hoshower et al., 1995

Figure 4.2 It is likely that some ancient cultures used devices like the one show here (a) to purposefully shape infant skull development. Scholars believe that certain skull shapes (b) probably signaled the individual's kinship ties.

neuron A nerve cell.

axon The main protruding branch of a neuron; it carries messages to other cells in the form of electrical impulses.

dendrite The protruding parts of a neuron that receive messages from the axons of other cells.

synapse The tiny gap between axons and dendrites.

neurotransmitter A chemical secreted by a cell sending a message that carries the impulse across the synaptic gap to the receiving cell.

synaptogenesis The process of synapse formation.

myelin A sheath of fatty cells that insulates axons and speeds transmission of nerve impulses from one neuron to the next.

syndrome by putting babies to sleep on their backs; see the box "Sudden Infant Death Syndrome" on p. 154). The condition is not believed to harm the baby, and it tends to disappear during the second 6 months of infancy, as babies become capable of moving around more and their brains continue to expand, reshaping the skull and reducing the flattening (Piatt, 2003). Interestingly, scholars of ancient cultures have amassed considerable evidence that certain indigenous cultures in the Americas used a variety of methods and devices to intentionally and permanently alter the shape of their infants' skulls as a way of indicating the child's community or kinship ties and family wealth (Figure 4.2; Hoshower et al., 1995).

‖‖‖‖ APPLY ═ CONNECT ═ DISCUSS ─ ─ ─ ─ ─ ─ ─ ─ ─ ─ ─ ─ ─ ─ ─ ─ ─ ─

In societies for which there is a choice, the decision of whether to breast- or bottle-feed newborns is influenced by cultural norms and expectations. Interview your mother and your grandmother about newborn feeding practices common in their generation. (If your mother or grandmother is not available, find another mother of the same generation.) Ask about how newborns were fed, why women might have chosen one method over another, what their own choices were, and so forth. Compare the two women's experiences, and assess them in light of what we now know regarding feeding practices and infants' physical development.

Brain Development

Changes in the brain are associated with many of the developmental changes you will encounter in this chapter. As you saw in Chapter 3 (pp. 90–92), well before full-term babies are born, their brains and central nervous systems support elementary sensory and motor functions: Fetuses respond to distinct sounds, for example, and they move spontaneously. These basic capacities are sufficient for them to learn to recognize the sound of their mothers' voices and of the language spoken around them, and to prepare them physically for their earliest adaptations to their new environment.

At birth, the brain contains the vast majority of all the cells it will ever have—more than 10 billion! Nevertheless, it will become four times larger by adulthood. To understand this growth, we need to look more closely at the nerve cells that transmit information, referred to as **neurons,** and at the brain structures into which neurons are organized.

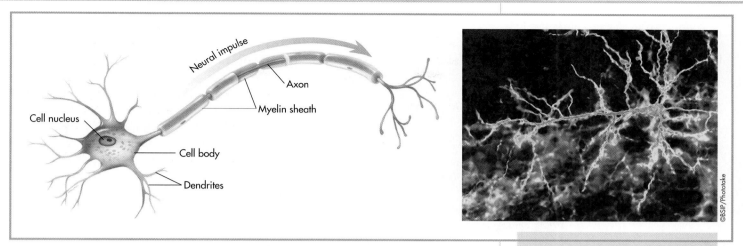

Figure 4.3 The neuron receives information from other neurons through its dendrites and feeds that information to other neurons through its axon. The photograph shows a neuron in the cerebellum.

Neurons and Networks of Neurons

The brain is an enormously complex communication system of neuron networks. Its complexity begins with how neurons transmit information. A neuron accomplishes its basic communication task in two ways: (1) by sending information via small electrical impulses along its **axon,** a branch that reaches out to connect with other brain cells, and (2) by receiving information from the axons of other cells through spiky protrusions called **dendrites** (Figure 4.3).

Between the axons and dendrites of communicating neurons is a tiny gap called a **synapse.** When an electrical impulse from the axon of the sending neuron arrives at the synapse, the sending neuron secretes a chemical, called a **neurotransmitter,** that carries the impulse across the synaptic gap, setting off a reaction in the receiving neuron.

The combination of a sending neuron and a receiving neuron creates the most simple form of a neuronal network. More complex networks are formed as multiple dendrites and axons interconnect. Such multiple forms of connectivity—and the fact that there are billions of neurons—make possible a virtually infinite variety of patterns of brain activity and behavior.

The basic architecture of neurons and neuronal networks suggests two of the reasons for the fourfold growth in brain size that occurs by adulthood. First, there is an increase in the size and complexity of the information-receiving dendrites and the information-transmitting axons (see Figure 4.4 for changes during the first 15 months). As a result of this increase, many new synapses are being formed in a process referred to as **synaptogenesis,** which we discuss in more detail below. The second reason for the growth in brain size is the growth of **myelin,** a sheath of fatty cells that insulates certain axons and speeds the transfer of information from one neuron to the next. Myelinated axons transmit signals anywhere from 10 to 100 times faster than unmyelinated axons, making possible more effective interconnections and communication among various parts of the brain, and more complicated forms of thought and action (Nelson, 2001).

Figure 4.4 These drawings from photomicrographs of infant brain tissue show the marked increases in the size and number of cerebral neurons during the first 15 months of postnatal life. (From Conel, 1939/1967.)

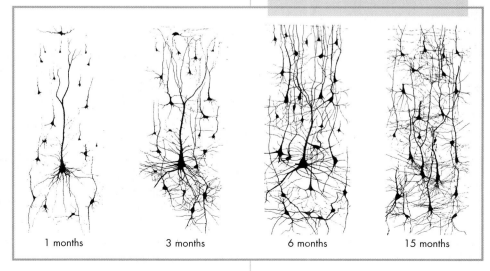

| 1 months | 3 months | 6 months | 15 months |

Figure 4.5 A schematic view of the brain, showing the major lobes, or divisions, of the cerebral cortex (including the areas where some functions are localized), the brain stem, the cerebellum, and the spinal cord. (Adapted from Tanner, 1978.)

The Structure of the Central Nervous System

Because of its association with the most complex behaviors of our species, the system of neural connections of greatest interest to developmentalists is the central nervous system. The central nervous system is conventionally divided into three major sections—the spinal cord, the brain stem, and the cerebral cortex. The **spinal cord,** a tubelike bundle of nerves, is encased in the spinal bones that extend from the base of the brain to below the waist. The nerves of the spinal cord carry messages back and forth from the brain to the spinal nerves that branch out from the spinal cord and communicate with specific areas of the body. Some of these nerves carry messages to the brain from the skin and other body parts and organs; others carry messages from the brain to the various body parts to initiate actions such as muscle movement.

The brain itself grows out of the top of the spinal cord (Figure 4.5). At its base is the **brain stem,** which controls such elementary reactions as reflexive blinking and sucking, in addition to such vital functions as breathing and sleeping. All these capacities can be found in at least rudimentary form during the later stages of prenatal development. At birth, the brain stem is one of the most highly developed areas of the central nervous system.

The **cerebral cortex** is the brain's outermost layer and most complex system, the processing center for the perception of patterns, the execution of complex motor sequences, and planning, decision making, and speech. The cerebral cortex is divided into two hemispheres, each of which is divided into four sections, or lobes, separated by deep grooves. Under ordinary conditions of development, the *occipital lobes* are specialized for vision; the *temporal lobes,* for hearing and speech; the *parietal lobes,* for spatial perception; and the *frontal lobes,* for control and coordination of the other cortical areas to enable complex forms of behavior and thought.

Despite the specialization of areas of the cortex for these functions, many of the functions involve considerable interplay among areas. In addition, the human cortex, unlike that of other animals, has large areas that are not "prewired" to respond directly to external stimulation in any discernible way (Figure 4.6). These "uncommitted" areas provide infants with the capacity to develop brain circuits that grow and change depending upon the experiences they have as they develop, a capacity we referred to in Chapter 1 (p. 13) as *plasticity.* (We will discuss plasticity in greater detail below.)

Figure 4.6 In these six mammalian species, the proportions of the brain mass that are devoted to different functions vary widely. The areas designated "uncommitted cortex" are not dedicated to any particular sensory or motor functions and are available for integrating information of many kinds. (Adapted from Fishbein, 1976.)

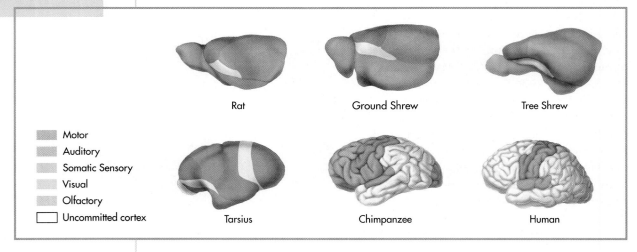

At birth the circuitry of the cerebral cortex is less mature than that of the spinal cord and brain stem (i.e., it has fewer dendritic trees and less myelin) and is poorly connected to the lower-lying parts of the nervous system that receive stimulation from the environment. Because of their relative maturity, the spinal cord and brain stem enable movement, responses to visual stimuli, and even elementary forms of learning without cortical involvement (Woodruff-Pak, Logan, & Thompson, 1990). As the nerve fibers connecting the cortex with the brain stem and spinal cord become myelinated, the infant's abilities expand.

Experience and Development of the Brain

The principle that development emerges from dynamic interaction between the organism and the environment applies no less to the development of the brain than to the development of behavior. Developmentalists distinguish two major classes of brain development, which they refer to as *experience-expectant* and *experience-dependent* (Bruer & Greenough, 2001).

As the name implies, **experience-expectant** processes of brain development are those that seem to *anticipate,* or *expect,* experiences that are universal in all normally developing members of our species (Greenough et al., 1987). For example, the evolution of the visual cortex prepares the baby for certain types of visual experiences such as seeing patterns and borders between light and dark (see p. 133). Likewise, the part of the brain associated with language has evolved in a way that the baby is prepared to process and learn language (see Chapter 7). All human environments are infused with visual patterns and light–dark borders that help us distinguish one object from another. And, of course, all human environments are rich with language. Experience-expectant processes of brain development allow infants to take advantage of their exposure to these features of the environment and use them to acquire the related basic human behaviors and abilities. When such expected experiences are lacking during sensitive periods of brain development, as may happen in the case of blind infants or of babies who have been severely deprived of human contact, then the brain will fail to develop normally (Hubel & Weisel, 2004; Rutter, 2006).

Evidence for experience-expectant brain development is found in an interesting pattern of synaptic proliferation and elimination. At several points during development, different portions of the brain undergo an explosive increase in synapse formation, called **exuberant synaptogenesis,** which produces far more synapses than would be required by the particular experiences the growing organism is likely to encounter. In other words, the profusion of synapse, at different points in development would seem to prepare the brain for a range of possible experiences. Over time, in something like a "use it or lose it" process, synapses that are not used atrophy and die off, a phenomenon referred to as **synaptic pruning** (Webb, Monk, & Nelson, 2001). This is the same process described in Chapter 3 (pp. 91–92), in discussing the importance of movement in chick embryos. It has been estimated that fully 70 percent of the neurons in the human cortex are pruned between the 28th week after conception and birth. Other intensive periods of synaptic pruning have been found in infancy, middle childhood, and adolescence (Giedd et al., 1999) (see Figure 4.7).

spinal cord The part of the central nervous system that extends from below the waist to the base of the brain.

brain stem The base of the brain, which controls such elementary reactions as blinking and sucking, as well as such vital functions as breathing and sleeping.

cerebral cortex The brain's outermost layer. The networks of neurons in the cerebral cortex integrate information from several sensory sources with memories of past experiences, processing them in a way that results in human forms of thought and action.

experience-expectant Development of neural connections under genetic controls that occurs in any normal environment.

exuberant synaptogenesis A rapid growth in synaptic density that prepares the brain for a vast range of possible experiences.

synaptic pruning The process of selective dying off of nonfunctional synapses.

Figure 4.7 The number of synapses in the human visual cortex as a function of age. The first spurt of synaptogenesis peaks at about 1 year of age; through the process of synaptic pruning, the number then declines until about 10 years of age, at which time the number levels off until early adulthood. (From Huttenlocher, 1994.)

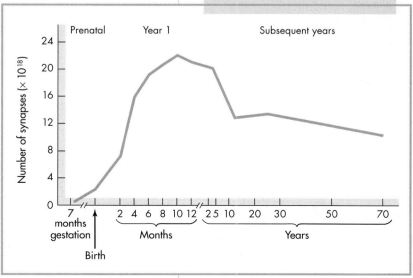

experience-dependent Development of neural connections that is initiated in response to experience.

In contrast to experience-expectant brain development, in **experience-dependent** brain development, synapses are not created in advance of species-universal experiences; instead they are generated in response to the specific experiences of specific individuals. Experience-dependent processes have evolved to allow the organism to take advantage of new and changing information in the environment. It is this experience-dependent brain–environment relationship that allows humans to learn from experience.

An example of experience-dependent brain development comes from pioneering studies by Mark Rosenzweig and his colleagues (Rosenzweig, 1984), in which groups of young male laboratory rats from the same litter were raised in three different environments. Rats in the first two groups were housed individually or together in standard laboratory cages equipped with only food and water dispensers. In contrast, rats in the third group were provided with enriched conditions. They lived together in a large cage furnished with a variety of playthings that were changed daily to keep things interesting. They were also given formal training in running a maze or were sometimes placed in an open field filled with toys.

At the end of the experimental period, which lasted anywhere from a few weeks to several months, behavioral tests and examinations of the animals' brains revealed superior development in the animals raised in enriched conditions. Compared with the other two groups, these rats demonstrated

- Increased rates of learning in standard laboratory tasks, such as learning a maze

- Increased overall weight of the cerebral cortex, the part of the brain that integrates sensory information

- Increased amounts of acetylcholinesterase, a brain enzyme that enhances learning

- Larger neuronal cell bodies and larger glial cells (cells that provide insulation, support, and nutrients to neuronal cells)

- More synaptic connections

These findings have been replicated and extended in numerous experiments (Nelson & Bloom, 1997). As you will see in Chapter 6, they are also consistent with what is known about how the quality of the environment of human infants can affect their brain development, as well as their development in other domains.

▌▌▌▌ APPLY ══ CONNECT ══ DISCUSS

It is widely believed that the developing brain will benefit from an enriched environment and suffer in an environment of deprivation. Using the language and concepts presented in this section, explain what it means for an environment to be "enriched" or "deprived."

Sensing the Environment

Baba is Qalandar, born to a nomadic tribe of entertainers who travel from town to town in Pakistan, exhibiting their dancing bears and monkeys, singing, juggling, and performing magic. As a newborn, when Baba wasn't in the arms of his mother or another tent member, he was placed in a *jhula,* a patchwork cloth hammock suspended a few feet off the ground from the tent ridgepole. Baba swung gently in his *jhula,* where he was out of reach of snakes and insects, and exposed to the smells of animals and traffic, the smiling faces of other tent members as they kissed and tickled him, and the sounds of language and laughter, music and chattering monkeys, and the jingling bells tied to his own ankles and wrists (Berland, 1982).

To what extent was Baba aware of the kaleidoscope of sights, sounds, and smells that surrounded his *jhula*? Did he experience his surroundings as a jumbled confusion, as the philosopher William James (1890) believed infants do—one that he would only gradually made sense of with time and experience? Or was Baba born with fairly sophisticated, even adultlike capacities that allowed him to perceive order and consistency in the world? Did he understand, for example, the connection between the jingling sounds he heard and the movement of his arms and legs?

At present, developmentalists are divided on how to answer such questions (Baillargeon, 2000; Cohen, 2002). This difference of opinion about what perceptual abilities and understandings infants start out with strongly influences the kind of theory needed to explain subsequent processes of developmental change. The idea that infants' perceptions initially amount to total confusion suggests that the world becomes an ordered and predictable place to infants only as they gain experience and learn about the environment. In contrast, the idea that infants are highly competent suggests that biology may play a critical role, endowing infants with special abilities that allow them to tune in to specific features of environment—certain visual patterns or the sound of the human voice, for example. As you will see, most developmentalists take a middle ground, maintaining that initial sensory capacities are biologically determined, but only to the extent that they guide how experience shapes later development.

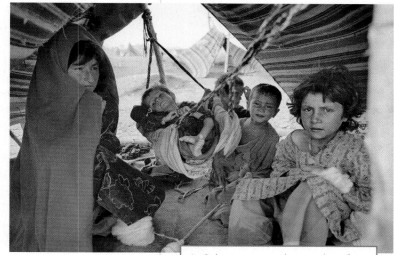

As Pakistani custom dictates, this infant lies in a cloth hammock called a *jhula*, safe from snakes and insects, and close to the faces of older siblings.

Methods of Evaluating Infant Sensory Capacities

You do not have to spend much time with a newborn to understand the difficulties researchers face in assessing infants' initial capacities. Babies sleep a lot—about three-quarters of every day in the first month. When they are awake, they may be drowsy or upset. Even when they appear to be alert and calm, they often do not seem to be paying attention to anything in particular; occasionally something seems to catch their interest, but only fleetingly. These constant fluctuations in newborn states make it difficult for developmentalists to provide reliable and replicable evidence regarding particular newborn capacities.

Normal full-term newborns enter the world with all sensory systems functioning—vision, hearing, tasting, smelling, and touching, among others. However, not all of these systems have developed to the same level. For example, newborns' senses of touch and smell are considerably more advanced than their sharpness of vision. This is not surprising given the relative importance of touch and odor for finding a food source—the breast—and the relative unimportance of vision to the newborn's survival. In addition, this unevenness illustrates the general rules of development of heterochrony and heterogeneity that we remarked on with respect to the fetal period: Different parts of an organism develop at different rates and are therefore at different levels of development at a given time.

The basic method developmentalists use to evaluate infant sensory capacities is to present infants with a stimulus and observe their overt behavioral or physiological responses to it. For example, an investigator might sound a tone or flash a light and watch for an indication that the newborn has sensed it, such as a turn of the head, a variation in brain waves, or a change in the rate at which the baby sucks on a pacifier. Another widely used technique is to present two different

A newborn with a specially designed headpiece that records head turning. In Siqueland's operant-conditioning experiment, head turns of more than 10 degrees were reinforced by the opportunity to suck on a pacifier. (Siqueland, 1968.)

habituation The process in which attention to novelty decreases with repeated exposure.

dishabituation The term used to describe the situation in which an infant's interest is renewed after a change in the stimulus.

phonemes The smallest sound categories in human speech that distinguish meanings. Phonemes vary from language to language.

stimuli at once to determine if the baby will display a preference by looking at one longer than the other. If so, the baby must be able to tell the stimuli apart.

Yet another technique for assessing sensory capacities is to present an infant with a novel stimulus that captures the infant's attention, such as a musical tone or a pictorial arrangement of simple geometric figures, and then continue presenting it until the infant gets bored and stops paying attention to it. The process in which attention to a novel stimulus decreases following continued exposure is called **habituation.** The next step is to change some aspect of the stimulus, such as the pitch of the musical tone or the arrangement of the geometric figures, for example. If the infant shows renewed interest after the change in the stimulus, the infant is said to exhibit **dishabituation,** and the investigator can conclude that the infant perceived the change. The use of such subtle indicators of infants' attention to sensory stimuli provides developmentalists with essential tools for understanding developmental processes at a time when infants are still too immature to make their experiences known through coordinated movement or speech.

Hearing

Since fetuses respond to sounds outside the mother's womb, it is no surprise that newborns respond to sound immediately after birth. Make a loud noise, and infants only minutes old will startle and may even cry. They will also turn their head toward the source of the noise, an indication that they perceive sound as roughly localized in space (Morrongiello et al., 1994). However, newborns' hearing is not as acute for some parts of the sound spectrum as it will be when they are older (Fernald, 2001). (Sensitivity to sound improves dramatically in infancy and then more slowly until the age of 10, when it reaches adult levels.) Significantly, newborns can distinguish the sound of the human voice from other kinds of sounds, and they seem to prefer it over any other. They are especially attuned to the sounds of language. Newborns all over the world are particularly interested in speech directed to them that has a high pitch and slow, exaggerated pronunciation—speech known as "baby talk," "motherese," or "infant-directed speech" (Kitamura,

Figure 4.8 Apparatus for presenting artificially manipulated speech sounds to young infants. The baby sucks on a pacifier connected to recording instruments as speech-like sounds are presented from a loudspeaker just above the Raggedy Ann doll.

James Kilkelly, Scientific American, 252

Thanavishuth, Luksaneeyanawin, & Burnham, 2002). This preference for motherese appears even when the speaker is speaking a foreign language (Werker, Pegg & McLeod, 1994). By the time they are 2 days old, however, babies would rather hear the language that has been spoken around them than a foreign language (Moon et al., 1993).

One of the most striking discoveries about the hearing of very young infants is that it is sensitive to the smallest sound categories in human speech that distinguish meanings. These basic language sounds are called **phonemes,** and they vary from language to language. In Spanish, for example, /r/ and /rr/ are different phonemes (linguists use slashes to denote phonemes); thus, "pero" and "perro," for example, which sound different—"perro" has a rolling *r*—have different meanings. In English, however, there is no such distinction. Similarly, /r/ and /l/ are different phonemes in English but not in Japanese.

In a pioneering study, Peter Eimas and his colleagues demonstrated that 2-month-olds can distinguish among a variety of phonemes (Eimas, 1985). The researchers began by having the infants suck on a nipple attached to a recording device in a special apparatus (Figure 4.8). After establishing a baseline rate of sucking for each baby, they presented the speech sound /pa/ to the babies each time they sucked. At first, the babies' rate of sucking increased, as if they were excited by each presentation of the sound, but after a while they settled back

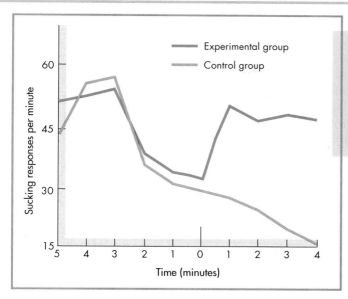

to their baseline rates of sucking. When the infants had become thoroughly habituated to the sound of /pa/, some of them heard a new sound, /ba/, which differed from the original sound in its initial phoneme—/b/ versus /p/. Others were presented with a sound whose initial part differed an equal amount from that of the original sound but remained within the /p/ phoneme category. The babies began sucking rapidly again only when they heard a sound whose initial part belonged to a different phoneme category, an indication that they were especially sensitive to the kinds of differences that languages use to distinguish phonemes (Figure 4.9).

Follow-up studies have shown that very young infants are able to perceive all the categorical sound distinctions used in all the world's languages. Adults, in contrast, perceive only those of their native language. Japanese babies, for example, can perceive the difference between /r/ and /l/; adult speakers of Japanese cannot (Aslin, Jusczyk & Pisoni, 1998). The ability to make phonemic distinctions apparently begins to narrow to just those distinctions that are present in one's native language at about 6 to 8 months of age, the same age at which the baby's first halting articulations of languagelike sounds are likely to begin (Figure 4.10). Given the pattern of infant brain growth during this time, some developmentalists have speculated that the narrowing of the ability to make phonemic distinctions is an example of how cultural experience interacts with the biological process of synaptogenesis and pruning that we discussed earlier (see p. 129; Munakata et al., 2004).

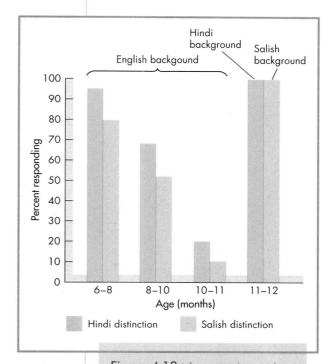

Vision

The basic anatomical components of the visual system are present at birth, but they are not fully developed. The lens of the eye and the cells of the retina are somewhat immature, limiting visual sharpness. In addition, the movements of the baby's eyes are not coordinated well enough to align the images on the two retinas to form a clear composite image. The result is that the baby's vision is blurry. The immaturity of some of the neural pathways that relay information from the retina to the brain further limits the newborn's visual capacities (Atkinson, 1998). Numerous studies have been conducted to determine exactly what, and how well, infants can see.

Visual Acuity

A basic question about infants' vision concerns their **visual acuity,** that is, their sharpness of vision. Estimates of newborns' visual acuity differ somewhat according to the particular measure used, but all suggest that newborns are very nearsighted, with a visual acuity in the neighborhood of 20/300 to 20/600. In other words, they can see at 20 feet what an adult with normal vision can see at 300 to 600 feet (Martin, 1998). (Figure 4.11 indicates what infants can see at different ages.)

Poor visual acuity is probably less troublesome to newborns than to older children and adults. After all, newborns are unable to move around unless someone carries them, and they cannot hold their heads erect without support. Still, their visual system is tuned well enough to allow them to see objects about a foot away—roughly the distance of the mother's face when they are nursing. This level of acuity allows them to make eye contact, which is important in establishing the social relationship between mother and child (Stern, 2002). Between 2 and 3 months of age, infants can coordinate the vision of both their eyes (Atkinson, 1998). By 7 or 8 months of age, when infants are able to crawl, their visual acuity is close to the adult level.

Visual Scanning

Despite their nearsightedness and their difficulty in focusing, newborns actively scan their surroundings from the earliest days of life (Bronson, 1997). Marshall Haith and his colleagues developed recording techniques that allowed them to determine precisely where infants were looking and to monitor their eye movements in both light and dark rooms. They discovered that even in a completely darkened room, neonates scan with short eye movements. Since no light is entering their eyes, this kind of scanning cannot be caused by the visual environment. It must therefore be *endogenous,* originating in the neural activity of the central nervous system. Endogenous eye movements seem to be an initial, primitive basis for looking behavior (Haith, 1980).

Haith's studies also revealed that neonates exhibit an early form of *exogenous* looking, that is, looking that is stimulated by the external environment. When the lights are turned on after infants have been in the dark, they pause in their scanning when their gaze encounters an object or some change of brightness in the visual field. This very early sensitivity to changes in brightness, which is usually associated with the edges and angles of objects, appears to be an important component of the baby's developing ability to perceive visual forms (Haith, 1980).

Figure 4.11 Infants' visual capacity increases dramatically over the first few months of life. By the age of 4 months, a baby can see nearly as distinctly as an adult, as seen in this artist's conception of the appearance of a visual scene for infants of different ages.

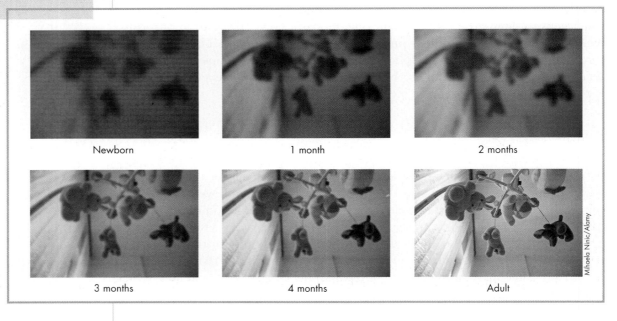

Newborn   1 month   2 months

3 months   4 months   Adult

Mihaela Ninic/Alamy

Color Perception Newborns seem to possess all, or nearly all, of the physiological prerequisites for seeing color in a rudimentary form. When two colors are equally bright, however, they do not discriminate between them. By 2 months of age, infants' ability to perceive different colors appears to approach adult levels (Kellman & Banks, 1998).

Perception of Patterns and Objects What do babies see when their eyes encounter an object? Are they able to see objects much as adults do? Until the early 1960s, it was widely believed that neonates perceive only a formless play of light. Robert Fantz (1961, 1963) dealt a severe blow to this assumption by demonstrating that babies less than 2 days old can distinguish among visual forms. The technique he used was very simple. Babies were placed on their backs in a specially designed "looking chamber" and shown various forms (Figure 4.12). An observer looked down through the top of the chamber and recorded how long the infants looked at each form. Because the infants spent more time looking at some forms than at others, presumably they could tell the forms apart and looked longest at the ones they preferred. Fantz found that neonates would rather look at patterned figures, such as faces and concentric circles, than at plain ones (Figure 4.13). Fantz's findings set off a search to determine the extent of newborns' capacity to perceive objects and the reasons they prefer some forms over others. That research has confirmed that infants visually perceive the world as more than random confusion, but it has also shown that infants' ability to perceive objects is far from adultlike and continues to develop over the first months of life (Johnson et al., 2003).

By 2 months of age, infants begin to show evidence that in some circumstances they see the boundaries between objects and recognize that objects are three-dimensional (Arterberry & Yonas, 2000). These abilities are by no means as elementary as you may think. How, for example, does a newborn who is staring at a cat on a chair know that the cat is not part of the chair? Is it easier for the infant to distinguish between cat and chair if the cat meows, or licks it paw? In a later section we will address the importance of vocalization and movement as important cues in the baby's visual perception of objects. Another important cue, on which we now focus, is contrast—the baby's ability to tell the cat from the chair is enhanced if the cat is black and the chair is white.

A number of studies have shown that the vision of young infants is best under conditions of high contrast, such as when a visual field is divided clearly (like the cat on the chair) into parts that are black and parts that are white (Kellman & Banks, 1998). Gordon Bronson (1991, 1994, 1997) used this property of newborn vision to study the way 2-week-old and 12-week-old babies scan outline drawings of simple figures, such as a cross or a V, on a lighted visual field. When adults are shown such figures, they scan the entire boundary. Two-week-old babies appear to focus only on areas of high contrast, such as black lines and angles on a white background (Figure 4.14). This kind of looking behavior is clearly not random; it shows that infants are born with the ability to perceive basic patterns. At 12 weeks of age, as Figure 4.14 indicates, infants scan more of the figure than at 2 weeks, although their scanning movements are sometimes off the mark and may still be arrested by areas of high

David Linton, Scientific American, 204

Figure 4.12 The "looking chamber" that Robert Fantz used to test newborns' visual interests. The infant lies in a crib in the chamber, looking up at the stimuli attached to the ceiling. The observer, watching through a peephole, determines how long the infant looks at each stimulus.

Figure 4.13 Infants tested during the first weeks of life show a preference for patterned stimuli over plain stimuli. The length of each bar indicates the relative amount of time the babies spent looking at the corresponding stimulus. (Adapted from Fantz, 1961.)

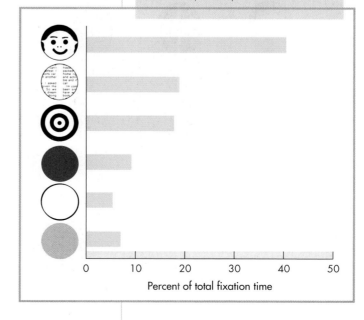

Percent of total fixation time

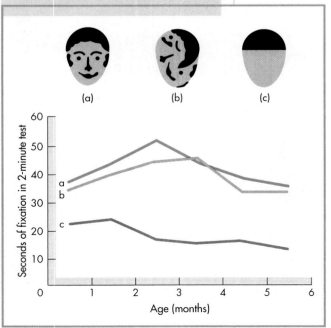

Figure 4.14 Visual scanning of a triangle by young infants. The triangle was mounted on a wall. A video camera was mounted just beneath it, positioned to record the eye movements of infants as they gazed at the triangle. Note that the 2-week-olds concentrated their gaze on only one part of the figure, whereas the 12-week-olds visually explored the figure more fully. Large dots indicate long fixation times; small dots represent short ones. (Adapted from Bronson, 1991.)

Figure 4.15 Visual preferences of infants for (a) a schematic face, (b) a scrambled schematic face, and (c) a nonfacelike figure, all having equal amounts of light and dark area. The infants preferred both facelike forms over the nonfacelike form, and they accorded the "real" face slightly more attention than the scrambled face. (Adapted from Fantz, 1961.)

contrast. In one of his studies, Bronson (1994) found that 13-week-old infants scanned more rapidly and extensively than did infants 10 weeks and under. The developmental change was so marked that Bronson concluded that "by 3 months of age [the] infants appear[ed] to be quite different organisms, at least with respect to their scanning characteristics" (p. 1260). He suggests that as the nervous system matures, it becomes more sophisticated and can begin to control visual scanning.

Perception of Faces In some of his early studies, Fantz presented newborns with a schematic diagram of a human face and a diagram of a facelike form in which facial elements had been scrambled (Figure 4.15; Fantz, 1961, 1963). He found that the infants could distinguish the normal face from the jumbled face, and preferred the normal one. Although the preference was small, the possibility that newborns have an unlearned preference for a biologically significant form like a face naturally attracted developmentalists' interest.

More recent work has shown that a crucial factor in newborns' preference for faces is the presence of more elements in the upper part of the configuration than in the bottom half. This imbalance corresponds to the fact that there are more visual elements in the top half of actual faces, and babies show that they are sensitive to this imbalance. Even a facelike stimulus is not preferred over a scrambled stimulus unless it has more visual elements in the upper half (Turati, Simion, Milani, & Umilta, 2002)

Another key finding is that motion critically influences newborns' perception of faces. In Fantz's studies and other early work, researchers used only stationary schematic representations of faces. Newer studies have shown that babies as young as 9 minutes old will turn their heads to gaze at a schematic face if it moves in front of them and will look at it longer than at a moving scrambled face (Mondloch et al., 1999). In real life, people move both their heads and the features of their faces, such as their eyes and the shape of their mouths. Under these naturalistic conditions, newborns only 2 to 7 hours old recognize, and show a preference for, their mother's face when it is contrasted with that of a stranger, even after a delay as long as 15 minutes between the time that the infant last saw the mother's face and the time that testing commenced (Bushnell, 2001).

Taste and Smell

Neonates have a built-in capacity to discriminate between different tastes and odors, and show strong preferences for things that taste and smell sweet, as does their first natural source of food, breast milk. The newborn's reaction to sweetness, however, extends well beyond simple preference. Research shows that a sweet taste has a calming effect on crying babies, and diminishes indications of pain, both physiological (for example, heart rate and brain excitation) and behavioral, helping babies cope with aversive situations (Fernandez et al., 2003).

Beyond their capacity to distinguish sweet from not-sweet, to what extent do newborns discriminate between different tastes and odors, and why might it be important for them to do so? An influential study conducted by Diana Rosenstein and Harriet Oster (1988) found that babies only 2 hours old produce different facial expressions in response to bitter, sour, and salty tastes. The characteristic facial expressions they make in response to specific tastes, especially those that are bitter and sour, look remarkably like the expressions made by adults when they encounter the same tastes, evidence that these expressions are innate and may have important evolutionary implications (Figure 4.16). Oster, who has done extensive studies of infant facial expressions, suggests that when the face puckers in response to a sour taste (see Figure 4.16c), it stimulates the production of saliva, which has the effect of diluting the pungency of a potentially edible substance. In contrast, the mouth of both newborns and adults alike tends to "gape," or open widely, as though in readiness to eject the food, in response to bitter tastes (see Figure 4.16b), an adaptive response given that bitter substances are more likely to be inedible and potentially harmful (Oster, 2005).

Infants' responses to various tastes goes beyond the innate capacity to make general distinctions between edible and inedible foods. It also involves cultural factors. For example, it has been known for some time that the flavors of the mother's diet during pregnancy are transmitted to the amniotic fluid, which is swallowed by the developing fetus (Hauser et al., 1985). Similarly, flavors from the mother's food enter into her breast milk (Mennella & Beauchamp, 1999). A carefully controlled study suggests that this indirect exposure—prenatally and during breast feeding—to the flavors of food common in the mother's culture affects the newborn's taste preferences (Mennella, Jagnow, & Beauchamp, 2001).

In this study, pregnant women who planned on breast feeding their infants were randomly assigned to experimental and control groups. Those in the experimental group drank a specified amount of carrot juice several times a week in their last trimester of pregnancy and/or during the period in which they breast-fed their newborns. Those in the control group drank water instead. The babies'

Figure 4.16 Newborns respond to different tastes with distinctive facial expressions that have significant adaptive value. In the photographs above, newborns react to tastes that are sweet (a), bitter (b), and sour (c).

(a)

(b)

(c)

taste preferences were tested several weeks after they had begun to eat cereal but before they had any direct exposure to the flavor of carrots. The test involved comparing the babies' reactions to cereal mixed with water and to cereal mixed with carrot juice. Infants who had been exposed to carrot-flavored amniotic fluid or breast milk exhibited fewer negative facial expressions when being fed carrot-flavored cereal then when being fed cereal mixed with water, and they tended to eat more of the flavored cereal. The babies in the control group showed no such preferences.

This research is consistent with that conducted with nonhuman species (rabbits, for example) and suggests that the mother's prenatal diet prepares the offspring for the particulars of the nutritional environment into which it will be born (Jablonka & Lamb, 2005). Interestingly, studies of human young have shown that their food preferences around 4 years of age have been influenced by the flavors of the specific formulas they were fed as infants. More specifically, when exposed to an array of tastes, these children preferred the tastes that were reminiscent of the formula they had been fed as infants, even when the formula tasted a bit like overcooked broccoli (Mennella & Beauchamp, 2005)!

In addition to reacting to different tastes, newborns are known to discriminate between different odors. Within just minutes of being born, infants will turn their heads preferentially toward maternal breast odors, which help guide them toward the nipple (Porter & Winberg, 1999). One test of newborns' capacities for odor discrimination involved holding either an odorless cotton swab or a swab soaked in one of various aromatic solutions under their nose. The infants did not react to the odorless swab but reacted strongly to unpleasant odors, such as garlic or vinegar, by pursing their lips or wrinkling their noses, and they smiled when they smelled something sugary. Like gaping and puckering in response to bitter and sour tastes, newborn (and adult) facial reactions to foul odors have the adaptive consequence of reducing the individual's contact with the unpleasant and potentially unhealthy stimulus. The common reaction of wrinkling the nose is a case in point. Take a deep breath through your nose, and notice how the air flows into your lungs. Now take a deep breath with your nose wrinkled up like you smelled something foul, and notice how the airflow is restricted. Pursing the lips, as the newborns did in the study described above, has the same general affect of inhibiting airflow (try it!).

Intermodal Perception

Thus far, we have been discussing the infant's sensory capacities as if they were relatively independent of each other. Indeed, for the sake of experimental control, researchers of infant perception often try to hold the baby's sensory environment constant while manipulating stimuli in one sensory modality. For example, to study whether newborns prefer to see their mothers' faces over those of strange women, researchers will try as much as possible to eliminate or equalize other sensory cues, such as odors and voices, so that any differences in how long the baby looks at the mother's compared to the stranger's face can be attributed to what the baby is seeing. Of course, outside the laboratory, sensory stimuli are overlapping and interconnected. When looking at the mother, the infant not only sees her face but feels her warmth, smells her, and hears her voice. An important point made in recent research is that infants may be born prepared to perceive certain stimuli as inherently connected to each other (Morrongiello et al., 1998). The simultaneous perceiving of an object or event by more than one sensory system (such as touch, sound, and vision) is known as **intermodal perception** (Gibson & Pick, 2000).

An early demonstration of intermodal perception was provided by a study in which, in a series of trials, 29-day-old infants were given a tiny rubber shape to

intermodal perception The understanding that a certain object or event can be simultaneously perceived by more than one sensory system.

feel with their mouths (Meltzoff & Borton, 1979). After they had "explored" the shape for 90 seconds, the shape was removed carefully so the babies could not see it. When the infants were then shown a pair of shapes (Figure 4.17), they looked longer at the one that they had felt in their mouth, suggesting that they had made an intermodal connection between what they had felt and what they saw.

Figure 4.17 In a study of intermodal perception, infants were given one of two rubber shapes like those shown here to feel with their mouths. When they were later shown the pair of shapes visually, the infants looked longer at the shape that matched the one they had felt in their mouths.

A recent study with newborns provides a fascinating example of how intermodal perception may be a vehicle for learning in the first hours of life (Sai, 2005). You know from our previous discussion that within hours of birth, babies learn the features of their mother's face and prefer looking at their mother's face to looking at a stranger's. However, since in the first few hours of interacting with the mother, the baby not only sees her face but also hears her voice, developmentalists have wondered whether hearing the mother's voice somehow contributes to the baby's ability to learn about the visual features of her face. To tackle this question, researchers compared preferences for the mother's face in two groups of babies 2 to 12 hours after birth. In one group, the infants did not hear their mother's voice prior to the preference tests (a condition ensured by a researcher who stayed with the mother from the birth of the baby until the experimental test). Mothers in the second group interacted with their newborns normally. A standard preference test, in which the infant is presented with the mother and a female stranger, was used to determine whether the babies recognized their mother (Figure 4.18). (The mother and the stranger were both draped in a white cloth to conceal clothing and body features; the stranger's hair length and color matched the mother's; strong air freshener was used to mask body odors.) It was discovered that the babies who had been prevented from hearing their mother's voice were unable to recognize their mother's face in the experimental test, suggesting that the intermodal perception of the maternal face and voice is essential for newborns to learn the unique visual features of their mother's face.

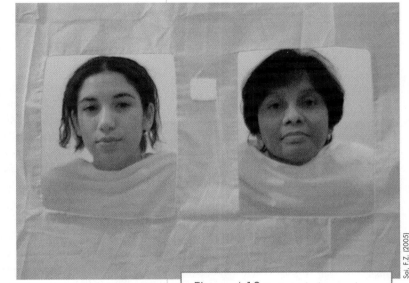

Sai, F.Z. (2005)

Figure 4.18 To test whether newborns can distinguish between the face of their mother and that of a female stranger, researchers attempt to mask as many non-facial cues as possible.

Overall, there is extensive evidence that babies come into the world with sensory capacities in good working order and far more organized than were once thought. (Infants' sensory capacities are summarized in Table 4.1.) The next question is, What capacities do infants have for acting on the world? This is a crucial question, because over the first 3 months of life, infants' growing ability to act in an organized way toward the people and objects in their environment fundamentally changes the nature of their interactions in the world and marks the starting point of postnatal psychological development.

table 4.1

Early Sensory Capacities

Sense	Capacity
Hearing	Ability to distinguish phonemes Preference for native language
Vision	Slightly blurred, slight double vision at birth Color vision by 2 months of age Ability to distinguish patterned stimuli from plain Preference for moving, facelike stimuli
Smell	Ability to differentiate odors well at birth
Taste	Ability to differentiate tastes well at birth
Touch	Responsive to touch at birth
Temperature	Sensitivity to changes in temperature at birth
Position	Sensitivity to changes in position at birth

This section has introduced you to several different research methods that developmentalists use to answer questions about the newborn's sensory systems. Identify and briefly describe four of these methods. Choose one or two of them to design a study addressing some facet of infant sensory capacity.

The Organization of Behavior

As a midwife in a small, rural Turkish village, Fulya is highly knowledgeable and experienced in newborn care. In addition to giving advice on feeding, cleaning, and protecting infants from the evil eye, Fulya tells new mothers how important it is to keep their babies wrapped tightly in cloth:

> Indeed, we continue to swaddle for several months until the baby seems strong and healthy. Swaddling makes the baby feel protected and helps it to sleep. I was shocked when the anthropologist who lived in our village told me how Americans dress their babies—it seems that in summertime the little ones are almost naked, wearing little more than a tiny shirt and diaper. Poor little things with their arms and legs flailing around, they must feel quite unprotected. (Delaney, 2000, pp. 131–132).

The practice of swaddling is very common across cultures and is thought to have a number of benefits. Indeed, in keeping with Fulya's observation that swaddling helps infants sleep, research indicates that newborns who are swaddled tend to be calmer than those who are not swaddled (Giacoman, 1971). Although it is hard to know whether swaddled babies "feel protected," as Fulya believes, it is clear that swaddling reduces opportunities for "arms and legs flailing around," a sign that the baby's behavior has become disorganized, as it does in states of fussiness and agitation.

Developing and maintaining behavioral organization is important for infants because it allows them to interact more effectively and adaptively with the world around them. At birth, babies possess a number of inborn behaviors (reflexes) that provide highly organized ways of responding adaptively to the environment. As development progresses during the early months of infancy, new forms of behavioral organization emerge, expanding infants' capacities for engagement with people and objects in their world. By the age of 3 months, for example, infants' physical control and coordination enable them to raise their heads to look around, smile in response to the smiles of others, and perform deliberate actions, such as shaking a rattle to make a noise. A major goal of the developmental sciences is to explain how biological and cultural processes contribute to the emergence of these new forms of organized behavior. We begin first with infant reflexes, evolution's contribution to the newborn's behavioral organization. We then explore how more complex forms of behavioral organization arise and become coordinated with the particular social world in which the child develops.

Henning Christoph/DAS FOTOARCHIVE

The cultural practices of swaddling and providing pacifiers help this Mongolian baby to maintain behavioral organization, and be calm and quiet.

Reflexes

Newborn babies come equipped with a variety of **reflexes**—specific, well-integrated, automatic (involuntary) responses to specific types of stimulation (see Table 4.2). Some reflexes are clearly adaptive throughout life. One of these is the *eyeblink reflex,* which protects the eye from overly bright lights and foreign objects that might damage it. Other reflexes are adaptive during infancy but disappear over time. For example, the

reflex A specific, well-integrated, automatic (involuntary) response to a specific type of stimulation.

action Complex, coordinated behaviors.

table 4.2

Reflexes Present at Birth

Reflex	Description	Developmental Course	Significance
Babinski	When the bottom of the baby's foot is stroked, the toes fan out and then curl	Disappears in 8 to 12 months	Presence at birth and normal course of decline are a basic index of normal neurological condition
Crawling	When the baby is placed on the stomach and pressure is applied to the soles of the feet, the arms and legs move rhythmically	Disappears after 3 to 4 months; possible reappearance at 6 to 7 months as a component of voluntary crawling	Uncertain
Eyeblink	Rapid closing of eyes	Permanent	Protection against aversive stimuli such as bright lights and foreign objects
Grasping	When a finger or some other object is pressed against the baby's palm, the fingers close around it	Disappears in 3 to 4 months; replaced by voluntary grasping	Presence at birth and later disappearance is a basic sign of normal neurological development
Moro	If the baby is allowed to drop unexpectedly while being held or if there is a loud noise, it will throw the arms outward while arching the back and then bring the arms together as if grasping something	Disappears in 6 to 7 months (although startle to loud noises is permanent)	Disputed; its presence at birth and later disappearance are a basic sign of normal neurological development
Rooting	The baby turns its head and opens its mouth when it is touched on the cheek	Disappears between 3 and 6 months	Component of nursing
Stepping	When the baby is held upright over a flat surface, it makes rhythmic leg movements	Disappears in first 2 months but can be reinstated in special contexts	Disputed; it may be only a kicking motion, or it may be a component of later voluntary walking
Sucking	The baby sucks when something is put into its mouth	Disappears and is replaced by voluntary sucking	Fundamental component of nursing

sucking reflex, of obvious adaptive value to newborn feeding, can be elicited by a touch on the baby's lips. Needless to say, this particular reflex disappears with time.

There are also some reflexes that seem to serve no apparent function. An example is the *Moro reflex,* in which infants make a grasping motion with their arms in response to a loud noise or when suddenly experiencing a feeling of being dropped. Some developmentalists believe that these reflexes currently serve no purpose but were functional during earlier evolutionary stages, allowing infants to cling to their mothers in threatening situations, as do infants of most nonhuman primate species (Jolly, 1999). Others believe that such seemingly useless reflexes may still be functional because they promote a close relationship between mother and infant (Bowlby, 1973; Prechtl, 1977).

Infant reflexes are an important window into the infant's developing brain and can, therefore, be used to diagnose the functioning of the central nervous system. For example, the *absence* of a neonatal reflex, such as sucking, often indicates that the infant suffers some form of brain damage. Brain damage is also indicated when a reflex *persists* beyond the age at which it should have disappeared. For example, the Moro reflex typically disappears in the months after birth. It is seen again only in the event of injury to the central nervous system (Zafeiriou et al., 1999).

From Reflex to Coordinated Action

Virtually all developmentalists agree that reflexes are important building blocks for constructing more complex and coordinated behaviors, often referred to as **action** (Valsiner, 2007). For example, one new action that appears in early infancy is nursing. When we compare the way newborn infants feed with the nursing behavior of 6-week-old infants, a striking contrast is evident. Newborns possess several reflexes that are relevant to feeding: rooting (turning the head in the direction of a touch on the cheek), sucking, swallowing, and breathing. These component behaviors are not well integrated, however. Newborns tend to root around for the nipple in a disorganized way and may lose it as soon as they find it. They also have trouble coordinating breathing with sucking and swallowing, and must frequently break away from sucking to come up for air.

By the time infants are 6 weeks old, a qualitative change is evident in their feeding behavior. For one thing, infants anticipate being fed when they are picked up and can prepare themselves to feed by turning toward the nipple and making sucking movements with their mouths—all without direct stimulation on their cheek or lips from the breast or bottle. Equally significant, they have worked out the coordination of all the component behaviors of feeding—sucking, swallowing, and breathing—so they can perform them in a smooth, integrated sequence (Meyers, 2001). In short, feeding has become nursing. In fact, babies become so efficient at nursing that they can accomplish in 10 minutes what once took them as long as an hour. In the language of *dynamic systems theory* (see Chapter 1, p. 28), the stable and balanced behavioral system of nursing has emerged as its component parts (sucking, swallowing, breathing) interacted over time, became increasingly coordinated with each other, and ultimately unified into a complex system of action. However, as we discuss below, the emergence of nursing as an organized system of action does not happen in a vacuum but is facilitated by the active efforts of the caregiver. (See also the box "In the Field: Baby-Friendly Hospital Care" for procedures used to promote nursing and other aspects of developing behavioral organization in premature infants in intensive care units.)

Whereas the connection between the sucking reflex and the emergence of nursing is readily discernible, the developmental path between other reflexes and subsequent action is less apparent and more controversial. For example, when newborn babies are held in an upright position with their feet touching a flat surface, they make rhythmic leg movements as if they were walking, a form of behavior often referred to as a "stepping reflex" (see Figure 4.19). But they stop doing so at around 3 months of age. Around 1 year of age, babies use similar motions as a component of walking, a voluntary activity that is acquired with practice.

There are competing explanations for the developmental changes in these rhythmic leg movements. According to Philip Zelazo (1983), the newborn's movements are a genuine (i.e., involuntary) reflex, probably controlled by subcortical brain processes. The brain undergoes a period of reorganization as the cortex, the seat of voluntary behavior, develops in the early months, and many lower-level reflexes, including the stepping reflex, disappear. Zelazo maintains that the old stepping behavior reappears in a new form as a voluntary component of walking after this period of brain reorganization.

Esther Thelen and her colleagues reject this explanation (Thelen, 1995). According to these researchers, early stepping disappears, not because of changes in the cortex, but because of changes in the baby's muscle mass and weight that make stepping difficult. In other words, for a period of time, babies' legs are just too heavy for their muscles to lift. In support of their view, Thelen and her colleagues hypothesized that if infants were partially submerged in water and supported in a standing position, stepping would reappear because the buoyancy of the water would counterbalance the infant's increased weight and relative lack of leg strength. They were correct: when infants who had stopped exhibiting stepping were held upright in water up to their waists, the stepping behavior reappeared.

Instead of invoking complex explanations about brain development in order to account for the relationship between early stepping and later walking, Thelen and

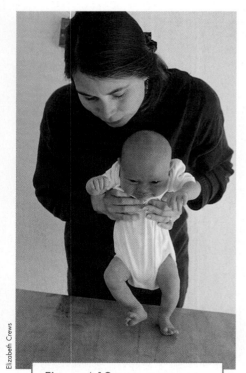

Elizabeth Crews

Figure 4.19 Babies held upright with their feet touching a flat surface move their legs in a fashion that resembles walking. Experts have debated the origins and developmental history of this form of behavior, called the stepping reflex.

Name:	Heidelise Als
Education:	M.S. in education and Ph.D. in human learning and education from University of Pennsylvania; additional training at the Child Development Unit at Children's Hospital Boston
Current Position:	Research associate in Newborn Medicine at the Brigham and Women's Hospital, Boston
Career Objectives:	Develop procedures to minimize newborns' trauma while being treated in hospital intensive care units

HEIDELISE ALS, A DEVELOPMENTAL PSYCHOLOGIST at Harvard Medical School and Children's Hospital, has spent years trying to understand how premature babies experience the world of the traditional newborn intensive care unit (NICU), which may be their home for weeks or even months after their birth (Raeburn, 2005). Emerging from a warm, dark amniotic pool where they had bobbed in warmth, relative quiet, and constant physical and hormonal contact with their mothers, preemies are thrust into the high-tech environment of the NICU, where they lie on their back, with their nose, hands, chest, or feet often pinned with gauze and adhesive tape to hold medical monitors and equipment in place. It is an environment dominated by constant bright lights, the noisy hum and whir of life-support machines, the continual chatter of NICU personnel, and a daily series of by-the-clock feedings, diaper changes, and medical procedures, often painful, in which the fragile newborns are handled on average more than 200 times in a 24-hour period (Sizun & Westrup, 2004). All this, from Als's perspective, overwhelms their immature brains.

Indeed, although it is well-known that premature infants are at risk for a number of neurological problems and have more difficulty maintaining alert states and behavior organization than do full-term infants (see Chapter 3, pp. 114–115), recent research has suggested that the stress of traditional NICUs may actually contribute to babies' difficulties. For example, preterm babies often experience episodes in which the oxygen in their blood drops to dangerous levels. It now appears that routine nursing procedures trigger many of these episodes, as well as increase concentrations of stress hormones in the baby's system (reviewed in Sizun & Westrup, 2004). Moreover, this stress of the NICU is experienced at a critical time in the development of the brain's neuronal circuitry. More specifically, the preterm baby's brain is undergoing the radical synaptic pruning characteristic of the final weeks of pregnancy, and it is thus particularly vulnerable to lasting effects from abnormal sensory input and pain.

Fortunately, as a consequence of Als's impassioned efforts to improve the early experiences of the prematurely born, NICUs throughout the world are beginning to change the way they operate. The busy, stimulus-intense, and medically oriented NICU is being replaced by an NICU that is decidedly more baby friendly. In this new NICU, lights are dimmed and varied to suggest day–night cycles, nurses whisper, and babies are watched for cues that they are hungry or need changing. Stethoscopes are warmed before they are placed on the baby's chest; incubators look more like cozy nests than sterile platforms (see photo); and family members are included in the baby's care.

The individualized developmental care adopted by many modern NICUs also includes procedures used to support developing behavioral organization. For example, babies are given pacifiers to suck, even though, because of their prematurity, many are fed by a tube that delivers nutrients directly into their stomachs. Interestingly, when babies are given pacifiers for sucking, they not only make an easier transition from tube to breast- or bottle-feeding than babies who are not given pacifiers, but they also digest the tube-fed nutrients better, sleep better, and have shorter hospital stays (Pinelli & Symington, 2001). Other procedures used to promote behavioral organization include wrapping babies tightly (swaddling) in order to reduce disorganized motor behavior, such as the frequent occurrence of the Moro (startle) reflex, which often disrupts the baby's sleep.

According to Als, "the neurological disability that many preterms are left with when they leave the NICU may in some ways be preventable" (Cassidy, 2005). That is, the new medical and nursing practices intended to decrease babies' stress may have significant, long-lasting benefits for the developing brain and neurological health of preterm babies (Symington & Pinelli, 2003).

Heidelise Als

Stephanie Mitchell/Harvard News Office

Vincent Laforet/The New York Times/Redux

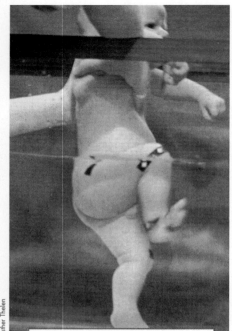

Esther Thelen

Although the stepping reflex seems to disappear around 3 months of age, Esther Thelen and her colleagues demonstrated that it would reappear if babies were given proper support. Here, a baby who no longer exhibits a stepping reflex under normal conditions makes the same stepping motions when partially submerged in water.

her colleagues take a dynamic systems approach. They see walking as a new complex form of behavior that emerges from the interaction of a variety of less complex parts, including the infant's weight and muscle mass.

Reaching

Even from the earliest days of postnatal life, babies' arms are often moving, sometimes allowing them to bring their fingers to their mouths to initiate sucking, and sometimes bringing their hands in contact with objects in the world around them. At first, their contact with objects appears to be totally accidental. Nevertheless, research initiated by Claus von Hofsten (1982, 1984) identified an early form of movement he termed *prereaching,* which he elicited by showing very young infants a large, colorful, slow-moving object such as a ball of yarn. As the object passed in front of them, these newborns reached toward it. However, they were unable to grasp an object even after repeated attempts, because the movements of reaching with the arm and grasping with the hand are uncoordinated and the newborns were unable to get their fingers to close around the object.

At about 3 months of age, a time of maturational changes in the visual and motor areas of the cerebral cortex, *visually guided reaching* emerges. Now, once infants locate an object by either seeing or hearing it, they can use feedback from their own movements to adjust the trajectory of their reach and get their hands close to the object. They are also able to open their fingers in anticipation of grasping the object. Remarkably, they can do this even when a bright object is presented in a darkened room so that they cannot see their own arms, clear evidence that it is feedback from their movement relative to the object that is controlling their reaching and grasping (McCarty, Clifton, Ashmead, Lee, & Goubet, 2001).

In an ingenious experiment, Amy Needham and her colleagues demonstrated that the process of infants' reaching and grasping can be accelerated if infants are given support (Needham, Barrett, & Peterman, 2002). The researchers put specially designed Velcro-covered mittens on the hands of a group of 3-month-old infants, and placed Velcro-covered objects within their reach. The infants' successful experiences connecting their Velcro-covered mittens with objects had fascinating consequences. Compared with a control group of infants who did not have such mittens, those in the experimental group showed greater interest in objects, as well as greater skill in grasping objects when they were later tested without the special mittens.

Piaget's Theory of Developing Action

Jean Piaget, one of the "grand theorists" described in Chapter 1 (see p. 21), provided an impressively comprehensive explanation for the infant's transition from reflexive behavior to coordinated action. As you may recall, Piaget believed that children actively organize an understanding of the world through their engagement with it and that their understanding develops in distinct stages. According to Piaget, the *schema* is the most elementary form of understanding—a mental structure that provides a model for understanding the world. Piaget argued that schemas develop through *adaptation,* a twofold process involving *assimilation* and *accommodation* (see pp. 22–23).

Piaget referred to infancy as the **sensorimotor stage** because during this period, the process of adaptation through which infants gain knowledge of the world consists largely of coordinating sensory perceptions and simple motor responses. Piaget saw the sensorimotor stage as consisting of six substages (Table 4.3). During the first few months of life, infants are said to progress through substages 1 and 2, *exercising reflex schemas* and *primary circular reactions* (substages 3–6 are covered in Chapter 5, on pp. 178–181):

sensorimotor stage Piaget's term for the stage of infancy during which the process of adaptation consists largely of coordinating sensory perceptions and simple motor behaviors to acquire knowledge of the world.

primary circular reaction The term Piaget used to describe the infant's tendency to repeat pleasurable bodily actions for their own sake.

Substage 1: *Exercising reflex schemas.* Piaget believed that in the first 4 to 6 weeks, infants learn to control and coordinate the reflexes present at birth, which provide them with their initial connection to their environments. However, these initial reflexes add nothing new to development because they undergo very little accommodation (they are largely unchanged). In this sense, infants seem to accomplish little more than exercising inborn reflexes.

Substage 2: *Primary circular reactions.* Accommodation first appears in this substage, which occurs from about 1 to 4 months of age. The first hints of new forms of behavior are that existing reflexes are extended in time, as when infants suck between feedings, or are extended to new objects, as when infants suck their thumbs. Piaget acknowledged that babies may suck their thumbs as early as the first day of life (we now know they may do so even before birth), but he believed that the thumb sucking seen during substage 2 reflects a qualitatively new form of behavior. That is, in substage 1, infants suck their thumb only when they accidentally touch their mouth with their hand. During substage 2, in contrast, if a baby's thumb falls from her mouth, the baby is likely to bring the thumb back to her mouth so that she can suck it some more. In other words, infants in this substage repeat pleasurable actions for their own sake. Piaget used the term **primary circular reaction** to characterize such behavior. Behaviors of this type are considered *primary* because the objects toward which they are directed are parts of the baby's own body; they are called *circular* because they circle back to themselves (sucking leads to more sucking, which leads to more sucking, and so on).

Blowing bubbles is an early instance of a primary circular reaction in which an accidental aspect of sucking is prolonged for the sheer pleasure of continuing the sensation.

table 4.3

Piaget's Stages of Cognitive Development and the Sensorimotor Substages

Age (years)	Stage	Description	Characteristics of Sensorimotor Substages
Birth to 2	Sensorimotor	Infants' achievements consist largely of coordinating their sensory perceptions and simple motor behaviors. As they move through the six substages of this period, infants come to recognize the existence of a world outside themselves and begin to interact with it in deliberate ways.	**Substage 1 (0–1½ months)** *Reflex schemas exercised:* involuntary rooting, sucking, grasping, looking **Substage 2 (1½–4 months)** *Primary circular reactions:* repetition of actions that are pleasurable in themselves
2 to 6	Preoperational	Young children can represent reality to themselves through the use of symbols, including mental images, words, and gestures. Still, children often fail to distinguish their point of view from that of others, become easily captured by surface appearances, and are often confused about causal relations.	**Substage 3 (4–8 months)** *Secondary circular reactions:* dawning awareness of the effects of one's own actions on the environment; extended actions that produce interesting change in the environment
6 to 12	Concrete operational	As they enter middle childhood, children become capable of mental operations, internalized actions that fit into a logical system. Operational thinking allows children to mentally combine, separate, order, and transform objects and actions. Such operations are considered concrete because they are carried out in the presence of the objects and events being thought about.	**Substage 4 (8–12 months)** *Coordination of secondary circular reactions:* combining schemas to achieve a desired effect; earliest form of problem solving **Substage 5 (12–18 months)** *Tertiary circular reactions:* deliberate variation of problem-solving means; experimentation to see what the consequences will be
12 to 19	Formal operational	In adolescence, the developing person acquires the ability to think systematically about all logical relations within a problem. Adolescents display keen interest in abstract ideas and in the process of thinking itself.	**Substage 6 (18–24 months)** *Beginnings of symbolic representation:* images and words come to stand for familiar objects; invention of new means of problem solving through symbolic combinations

Over the course of substage 2, primary circular reactions undergo both differentiation and integration. *Differentiation* occurs as actions become increasingly fine-tuned and flexible, so that infants can modify them in response to variations in the environment (for example, sucking on a thumb differently than from a nipple). *Integration* occurs as separate actions become coordinated into new patterns of behavior (for example, reaching becomes coordinated with grasping). Piaget believed that primary circular reactions are important because they offer the first evidence of cognitive development. "The basic law of dawning psychological activity," he wrote, "could be said to be the search for the maintenance or repetition of interesting states of consciousness" (Piaget, 1977, p. 202). By the end of substage 2, infants are ready to direct their attention to the external world.

Learning Theories of Developing Action

Learning theorists argue that new forms of behavioral organization emerge as a consequence of **learning,** a relatively permanent change in behavior brought about when the infant makes associations between behavior and events in the environment. Several types of learning are believed to operate throughout development, including *habituation* (described previously) and *imitation* (which we will explore in Chapter 6), as well as two processes referred to as *classical conditioning* and *operant conditioning.*

Classical Conditioning **Classical conditioning** is learning in which previously existing behaviors come to be associated with and elicited by new stimuli. The existence of this very basic learning mechanism was demonstrated at the turn of the twentieth century by the Russian physiologist Ivan Pavlov (1849–1936). Pavlov (1927) showed that after several experiences of hearing a tone just before food was placed in its mouth, a dog would begin to salivate in response to the tone before it received any food. In everyday language, the dog began to expect food when it heard the tone, and its mouth watered as a result.

In the terminology of learning theories, Pavlov paired a **conditional stimulus (CS)**—a tone—with an **unconditional stimulus (UCS)**—food in the mouth. The food is called an unconditional stimulus because it "unconditionally" causes salivation, salivation being a reflex response to food in the mouth. Salivation, in turn, is called an **unconditional response (UCR)** because it is automatically and unconditionally elicited by food in the mouth. The tone is called a conditional stimulus because the behavior it elicits depends on (is conditional on) the way it has been paired with the unconditional stimulus. When the unconditional response (salivation in response to food in the mouth) occurs in response to the CS (the tone), it is called a **conditional response (CR)** because it depends on the pairing of the CS (the tone) and the UCS (the food). The key indicator that learning has occurred is that the CS (tone) elicits the CR (salivation) before the presentation of the UCS (food) (Figure 4.20).

A number of developmentalists seized on Pavlov's demonstrations as a possible model for the way infants learn about their environments. One of Pavlov's co-workers demonstrated conditioned feeding responses in a 14-month-old infant based on the principle of classical conditioning (Krasnogorski, 1907/1967). The baby opened his mouth and made sucking motions (CRs) at the sight of a glass of milk (CS). When a bell (a new CS) was sounded on several occasions just before the glass of milk was presented, the baby began to open his mouth and suck at the sound of the bell, an indication that classical conditioning built expectations in the infant by a process of association. The crucial point of these observations is that there is no biological connection between the sound of a bell and the

learning A relatively permanent change in behavior brought about by the experience of events in the environment.

classical conditioning Learning in which previously existing behaviors come to be elicited by new stimuli.

conditional stimulus (CS) In classical conditioning, a stimulus that elicits a behavior that is dependent on the way it is paired with the unconditional stimulus (UCS).

unconditional stimulus (UCS) In classical conditioning, the stimulus, such as food in the mouth, that invariably causes the unconditional response (UCR).

unconditional response (UCR) In classical conditioning, the response, such as salivation, that is invariably elicited by the unconditional stimulus (UCS).

conditional response (CR) In classical conditioning, a response to the conditional stimulus (CS).

operant conditioning Learning in which changes in behavior are shaped by the consequences of that behavior, thereby giving rise to new and more complete behaviors.

mouth-opening and sucking responses it elicited. Rather, the fact that the new stimuli elicited these responses shows that learning has occurred.

Operant Conditioning Classical conditioning explains how infants begin to build up expectations about the connections between events in their environment, but it does little to explain how even the simplest new behaviors come into being. The kind of conditioning that gives rise to new and more complex behaviors is **operant conditioning,** in which behaviors are shaped by their consequences. The basic idea of operant conditioning is that organisms will tend to repeat behaviors that lead to rewards and will tend to give up behaviors that fail to produce rewards or that lead to punishment (Skinner, 1938). A consequence (such as receiving a reward) that increases the likelihood that a behavior will be repeated is called a *reinforcement*. Operant conditioning in young infants has been experimentally demonstrated with a variety of reinforcers, such as milk, sweet substances, the opportunity to suck on a pacifier, the sound of a heartbeat or the mother's voice, and the appearance of an interesting visual display (Rovee-Collier & Barr, 2001).

An elegant procedure designed by Rovee-Collier and her colleagues demonstrates how infants will repeat behaviors in order to produce interesting visual effects. The researchers tied one end of a ribbon around an infant's ankle and attached the other end of the ribbon to a mobile hanging above the infant's crib (Figure 4.21). Within just a few minutes the infant learned that kicking would animate the mobile, causing the shapes to shake and spin. The interesting visual effects of the mobile thus acted as a positive reinforcer, prompting the infant to organize her kicking behavior in order to produce additional reinforcements.

Further support for the argument that learning is an important contributor to the development of behavioral organization comes from studies that show that even very young infants are

CS: Light shines   Baby looks, eyes open
(a)

UCS: Hammer hitting gong (loud noise)   UCR: Baby blinks as component of startle reflex
(b)

CS + UCS   UCR: Baby blinks to sound
(c)

CR: Baby blinks to light
(d)

Figure 4.20 In the top panel (a) the sight of a light (CS) elicits no particular response. In (b) the loud sound of a gong (UCS) causes the baby to blink (UCR). In (c) the sight of the light (CS) is paired with the sound of the gong (UCS), which evokes an eyeblink (UCR). Finally in (d), the sight of the light (CS) is sufficient to cause the baby to blink (CR), demonstrating that learning has occurred.

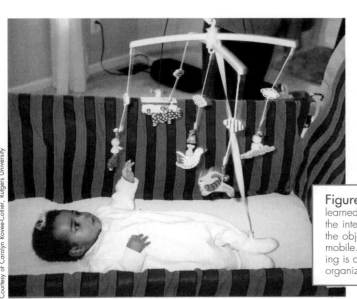

Courtesy of Carolyn Rovee-Collier, Rutgers University

Figure 4.21 This baby has learned that her kicking produces the interesting effect of moving the objects dangling from the mobile. Such operant conditioning is an important process in the organization of infant behavior.

capable of remembering what they have learned from one testing session to the next, a capacity that improves markedly during the first few months of life (Bearce & Rovee-Collier, 2006).

|||||| APPLY ▪ CONNECT ▪ DISCUSS ▪ ▪ ▪ ▪ ▪ ▪ ▪ ▪ ▪ ▪ ▪ ▪ ▪ ▪ ▪

Suppose you have been hired by a local health clinic to lead a class on newborn behavioral organization for expecting parents. How would you describe "behavioral organization" to these parents? How would you explain its importance for development? What sorts of activities or interactions would you recommend to parents for promoting the development of behavioral organization in their newborn?

Temperament

In our discussion of how newborns learn about and become increasingly engaged with the features of their environment, we have focused on universal capacities inherited by each individual infant as a consequence of the evolutionary history of our species. We know, however, that infants are also born with individual differences in how they respond to their environments. Some infants seem to fuss a lot, while others are usually cheerful; some wake at the slightest noise, whereas others seem able to sleep through fireworks. Individual differences such as these relate to variations in **temperament,** an individual's emotional and behavioral characteristics that appear to be consistent across situations and to have some stability over time (Calkins & Degnan, 2006).

Pioneering longitudinal studies of temperament and its role in development were conducted by Alexander Thomas, Stella Chess, and their colleagues (Chess & Thomas, 1996; Wachs & Bates, 2001). They began their research in the late 1950s with a group of 141 middle- and upper-class white children in the United States, and later broadened their study to include 95 working-class Puerto Rican children and several groups of children suffering from diseases, neurological impairments, and mental retardation. Chess and Thomas began their study by conducting structured clinical interviews of the children's parents shortly after the children's birth. They questioned parents about such matters as how the child reacted to the first bath, to wet diapers, to the first taste of solid food. As the children grew older, these interviews were supplemented by interviews with teachers and by tests of the children themselves.

From their data, Chess and Thomas identified nine key traits of temperament: *activity level, rhythmicity* (the regularity or irregularity of the child's basic biological functions), *approach–withdrawal* (the child's response to novelty), *adaptability, threshold of responsiveness* (the minimum intensity of stimulation required to evoke a response), *intensity of reaction, quality of mood* (negative or positive), *distractibility,* and *attention span* or *persistence* (Table 4.4). After scoring the children on each of these nine traits, they found that most of the children could be classified in one of three broad temperament categories:

- *Easy babies* are playful, are regular in their biological functions, and adapt readily to new circumstances.

- *Difficult babies* are irregular in their biological functions, are irritable, and often respond intensely and negatively to new situations or try to withdraw from them.

- *Slow-to-warm-up babies* are low in activity level, and their responses are typically mild. They tend to withdraw from new situations, but in a mild way, and require more time than easy babies to adapt to change.

temperament The term for the individual modes of responding to the environment that appear to be consistent across situations and stable over time. Typically included under the rubric of temperament are such characteristics as children's activity level, their intensity of reaction, the ease with which they become upset, their characteristic responses to novelty, and their sociability.

table 4.4

Basic Indicators of Temperament According to Chess and Thomas

Trait	Definition	Example
Activity level	The level of movement typical of a given child's actions and the relative amount of time spent in action and inaction	Even in the uterus some babies kick and move around a lot, while others are relatively still; similar differences are seen in the level and frequency of arm waving and kicking in early infancy and in the tendency of some young children to spend most of their waking hours in rapid motion
Rhythmicity	The degree of regularity and predictability of basic biological functions	Beginning shortly after birth, marked individual differences can be seen in the ease with which babies adapt to regular feeding and sleeping schedules and to bodily functions such as defecation
Approach–withdrawal	The nature of the baby's initial response to something new	Novel experiences such as the first substitution of a bottle for the breast, meeting a strange person, or the sudden appearance of a jack-in-the-box cause some children to be fearful and withdraw, while others actively explore and seek further stimulation
Adaptability	The ease with which a baby's initial responses to a situation are modified	Whether they initially withdraw from or take to a new experience, babies differ in how rapidly the novelty wears off and how easily they adjust to new circumstances, such as being given solid food in place of milk or being left with a babysitter
Threshold of responsiveness	The intensity level required in order for a stimulus to evoke a response	It takes very little noise to make some babies awaken from a nap or very little moisture in their diapers to make them cry, whereas others appear to react only when the stimulation becomes relatively intense
Intensity of reaction	The energy level of a response	It seems that whatever the circumstances, whether pleasant or unpleasant, some babies remain relatively placid in their responses, cooing when pleased and frowning when upset, whereas others laugh heartily and cry vigorously
Quality of mood	The amount of joyful, pleasant, and friendly behaviors in comparison to unpleasant and unfriendly behaviors	Some babies laugh frequently and tend to smile at the world, whereas others seem to be unhappy much of the time
Distractibility	The extent to which novel stimuli disrupt or alter ongoing behaviors	Parents often seek to distract a crying baby by offering a pacifier or teddy bear, but such tactics work best with distractible babies
Attention span/persistence	The extent to which an activity, once undertaken, is maintained	Some babies will stare at a mobile or play happily with a favorite toy for a long time, whereas others quickly lose interest and move frequently from one activity to another

Source: Chess & Thomas, 1982.

Although the three categories of temperament described by Chess and Thomas are widely used by developmentalists, a number of researchers have tried to create a more refined set of temperament types. For example, Mary Rothbart and her colleagues created a child-behavior questionnaire that provided scores on 195 questions divided into 15 different scales. Parents were asked to decide how well each item applied to their child during the past half year. The results suggested three dimensions of temperamental variation, providing a profile of each child's temperament (Rothbart, Ahadi & Evans, 2000):

- *Reactivity*—the characteristic level of arousal, or activeness
- *Affect*—the dominant emotional tone, gloomy or cheerful
- *Self-regulation*—control over what one attends to and reacts to

There is widespread agreement that genetic factors provide the foundation for temperamental differences (Emde & Hewitt, 2001). For example, working with monkeys, Stephen Suomi (2000) found that an allele on a specific gene is associated with a highly reactive temperament, while a different allele is associated with a calmer temperament. This evidence for a genetic basis to temperamental traits implies that one should expect to find relatively stable "biases" in the way individuals respond to their environment, and thus that it should be possible to predict the characteristic style with which individuals will behave at later stages of development. Indeed, studies conducted in several different societies find evidence of stability in temperamental traits such as irritability, persistence, and flexibility (Emde & Hewitt, 2001).

At the same time, researchers have found ethnic and national differences related to temperamental traits. Comparing large groups of children from the People's Republic of China and the United States, for example, Mary Rothbart and her colleagues found that their three basic dimensions emerged from the data within both countries but also found salient differences (Ahadi et al., 1993). For example, the Chinese children were less active than the American children, a fact they attributed to Chinese child-rearing practices. Chinese parents place a high value on interdependence, and this leads them to discourage high levels of activity and impulsiveness that may be disruptive to others.

In addition to examining the degree of innate temperamental stability, there have been a number of efforts to determine whether certain adjustment problems in childhood or adolescence may be related to temperament in infancy. Several dimensions of temperament reflective of early fearfulness, withdrawal, distress, and lack of adaptability have been linked to later problems with anxiety, depression, and social withdrawal (see Calkins & Degnan, 2006, for a review of these studies). Suppose, for example, that an infant tends to react negatively to new people, objects, and situations with screaming and crying. Because the infant's reactions create a state of behavioral disorganization that severs connections to the baby's environment, the baby loses opportunities to practice more adaptive coping skills such as looking away from the source of distress, sucking a pacifier, or seeking comfort from someone. And because of this failure to develop adaptive coping skills, the world continues to overwhelm the child, who may grow up generally anxious and depressed.

Although evidence supports the idea that temperamental traits are stable over time and may contribute to adjustment problems later in childhood and adolescence, it needs to be emphasized that most studies find only modest correlations of temperament at different ages, indicating that temperament is a complex trait that can be influenced by a variety of factors (Wachs, 2000).

||||| | APPLY ▪ CONNECT ▪ DISCUSS

Developmentalists talk about the importance of "goodness of fit," that is, of the relationship, or "fit," between the child's temperamental traits and the child's environment. A very quiet and passive baby ("slow to warm up") may not receive much attention in a busy household but may be drawn out of her shell by doting, attentive parents. In what context might a fussy, demanding temperament be adaptive?

Becoming Coordinated with the Social World

The indisputable fact that human infants are enormously dependent on others for their survival may lead us to overlook babies' own contributions to the care they receive. Infants' survival and continued development depend not only on the actions of responsive caregivers, but on the infants' ability to coordinate their actions with those of their caregivers. This ability is essential because caregivers cannot always be hovering over their infant, anticipating every need, but have their own rhythms of life and work within the confines of which they must find ways to meet their infant's needs. Most parents, whether they work the land or work in an office, need to sleep at night, and this need is often in direct conflict with their infant's sleep and hunger patterns. As a result, parents may attempt to modify their infant's patterns of sleeping and feeding so that they will fit into the life patterns of the household and the community. In this and other ways, infants become co-ordinated with their social world, as the box "Sleeping Arrangements" shows for sleeping arrangements.

Sleeping Arrangements

LULLABIES, ROCKING CHAIRS, MU-sic boxes, and cuddly stuffed toys are common features of many infants' bedtime routines. But cross-cultural research shows that the use of such objects in bedtime rituals, as well and where and with whom the baby sleeps, are steeped in cultural beliefs, values, and traditional practices.

In a study of 120 societies around the world, 64% of the mothers surveyed reported that their infants sleep in the same bed with them (a practice referred to as *co-sleeping*). Co-sleeping is widely practiced in highly urban, modern communities in countries such as Japan and Italy, as well as in rural communities in many countries including Mexico and China (Wolf et al., 1996). In only a few countries, such as the United States and Germany, are infants expected to sleep in their own beds in a separate room (Valentin, 2005). Within the United States, the practice of having infants sleep separately, while particularly common among college-educated, middle-class families, is far from universal across regions and groups. A study of newborns in eastern Kentucky, for example, found that 48% shared their parents' rooms (and 36% their parents' beds); space did not seem to be the issue (Abbott, 1992). African American babies are more likely than European American babies to have a caregiver present when they fall asleep, to sleep in their parents' rooms, and to spend at least part of the night in their parents' beds (Wolf et al., 1996).

Sleeping practices are related to broad cultural themes regarding the organization of interpersonal relations and the moral ideals of the community (Shweder et al., 1998; Yang & Hahn, 2002). Whereas middle-class U.S. and German mothers emphasize the values of independence and self-reliance, mothers in societies where co-sleeping is the norm emphasize the need for babies to learn to be inter-dependent and to be able to get along with others and be sensitive to their needs. In Ko-

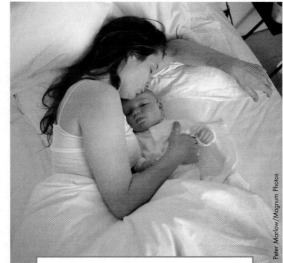

Sleep arrangements vary considerably both within and across cultures. The co-sleeping of this mother and baby is somewhat uncommon in England, where they live.

rea, for example, where nearly all infants sleep with their parents, that practice is considered a natural part of child rearing and an important step in developing family bonds (Yang & Hong, 2002).

These different underlying values are reflected in a study by Gilda Morelli and her colleagues, who interviewed middle-class mothers in the United States and rural Mayan mothers in Guatemala about their infants' sleeping arrangements (Morelli et al., 1992). None of the U.S. parents in the study allowed their infants to sleep with them. Many parents kept the sleeping child in a nearby crib for the first few months but soon moved the baby to a separate room. They gave such reasons for their arrangements as "I think he would be more dependent . . . if he was constantly with us like that," and "I think it would have made any separation harder if he wasn't even separated from us at night." In contrast, the Mayan mothers always had each new child sleep in the bed with them until the next baby was born.

They insisted that this was the only right thing to do. When they were told about the typical U.S. practice, they expressed shock and disapproval at the parents' behavior and pity for the children. They seemed to think that the U.S. mothers were neglecting their children. Similar sentiments have been voiced by mothers from other societies where co-sleeping is a common practice.

Some researchers, in making comparisons between sleeping arrangements, seek to show that one arrangement is better, or worse, for infants. For example, Melissa Hunsley and Evelyn Thoman (2002) report that co-sleeping infants spend more of their time in quiet sleep, which has been associated with slower development. Likewise, a great deal of concern has been raised regarding the possible relationship between co-sleeping and sudden infant death syndrome (see the box "Sudden Infant Death Syndrome" on page 154) because of accidental suffocation (Perrizo & Pustilnik, 2006). In contrast, on the basis of cross-cultural evidence, James McKenna (1996) reports no ill effects associated with co-sleeping and concludes that "infant–parent co-sleeping is biologically, psychologically, and socially the most appropriate context for the development of healthy infant sleep physiology." On balance, it appears that except in rare cases, whether infants sleep in a bed alone or with their mother does not seem to make a great deal of difference (Okami, Weisner, & Olmstead, 2002). All cultural systems are relatively successful in seeing that infants get enough sleep and grow up normally.

However, while co-sleeping or solitary sleeping may not make a big difference, describing cultural differences in family sleeping arrangements highlights the fact that all such arrangements are organized with a view toward ways in which children will be expected to act at a later time—for example, in a way that emphasizes independence or sensitivity to others' needs.

table 4.5

States of Arousal in Infants

State	Characteristics
Non–rapid eye movement (NREM) sleep	Full rest; low muscle tone and motor activity; eyelids closed and eyes still; regular breathing (about 36 times per minute)
Rapid eye movement (REM) sleep	Increased muscle tone and motor activity; facial grimaces and smiles; occasional eye movements; irregular breathing (about 48 times per minute)
Periodic sleep	Intermediate between REM and NREM sleep—bursts of deep, slow breathing alternating with bouts of rapid, shallow breathing
Drowsiness	More active than NREM sleep but less active than REM or periodic sleep; eyes open and close; eyes glazed when open; breathing variable but more rapid than in NREM sleep
Alert inactivity	Slight activity; face relaxed; eyes open and bright; breathing regular and more rapid than in NREM sleep
Active alert	Frequent diffuse motor activity; vocalizations; skin flushed; irregular breathing
Distress	Vigorous diffuse motor activity; facial grimaces; red skin; crying

Source: Wolff, 1966.

Sleeping

As with adults, the extent of newborns' arousal varies from deep sleep to frantic activity. The patterns of their rest and activity are quite different from those of adults, however, particularly in the first weeks after birth. To find out about the range and cycles of newborns' arousal patterns, developmentalists use a variety of methods, including direct observation, video recordings, and sophisticated electronic monitoring devices (Salzarulo & Ficca, 2002). In a classic study in which babies' eye movements and muscle activity were observed over the first several weeks following birth, Peter Wolff (1966) was able to distinguish seven states of arousal (Table 4.5); each state is associated with a distinctive pattern of brain activity (Estevez et al., 2002).

Neonates spend most of their time asleep, although the amount of sleep they need gradually decreases. Several studies have shown that babies sleep about 16½ hours a day during the first week of life. By the end of 4 weeks, they sleep a little more than 15 hours a day, and by the end of 4 months, they sleep a little less than 14 hours a day (Thoman & Whitney, 1989).

If babies sleep most of the time, why do parents lose so much sleep? The reason is that newborns tend to sleep in snatches that last anywhere from a few minutes to a few hours. Thus they may be awake at any time of the day or night. As babies grow older, their sleeping and waking periods lengthen and coincide more and more with the night/day schedule common among adults (Salzarulo & Ficca, 2002; Jenni, Deboer & Achermann, 2006) (Figure 4.22).

Although babies' adoption of the night/day sleep cycle seems natural to people who live in industrialized countries and urban settings, studies of infants raised in other cultures suggest that it is at least partly a function of cultural influences on the infant (Meléndez, 2005). In a widely cited example of the role of social pressure in rearranging newborns' sleep, the development of the sleep/wake behavior of infants in the United States was compared with that of Kipsigis babies in rural Kenya. In the United States, parents typically put their infants to bed at certain hours—often in a separate room—and try not to pick them up when they wake up crying at night, lest they become accustomed to someone attending to them whenever they make a fuss. In rural Kenya, infants are almost always with their mother. During the day they sleep when they can, often while being carried on their mother's back as the mother goes about her daily round of farming, household chores, and social activities. During the night they sleep with their mother and are permitted to nurse whenever they wake up. Among Kipsigis infants, the longest period of sleep reported at 1 month is only about 3 hours; many shorter periods of sleep are sprinkled throughout the day and night. Eventually Kipsigis infants begin to sleep through the night, but not until many months later than American infants begin to do so. Even as adults, the Kipsigis are more flexible than Americans in their sleeping hours (Super & Harkness, 1972).

In the United States, the length of the longest sleep period is often used as an index of the infant's maturation. Charles Super and Sara Harkness (1972) suggest that parents' efforts to get babies to sleep for long periods of time during the early

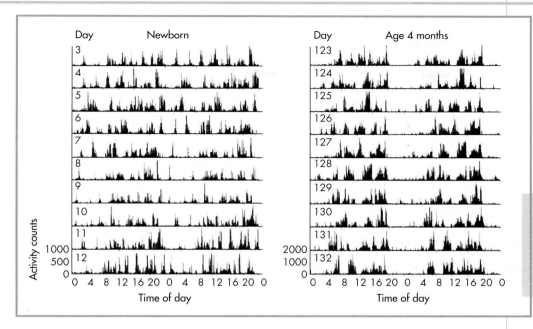

Figure 4.22 These recordings from electronic monitoring devices document significant differences in the activity of a newborn compared to a 4-month-old. Notice how the 4-month-old has both periods of more intense activity, as well as longer stretches of quiet and sleep.

weeks of life may be pushing the limits to which young infants can adapt. They believe that the many changes that occur in a newborn's state of arousal in every 24-hour period reflect the immaturity of the infant's brain, which sets a limit on how quickly the child can conform to an adult routine. This may be the explanation for the failure of some infants in industrialized countries to adopt a night/day pattern of sleeping and waking as quickly and easily as their parents would like them to. (Cultural differences in sleeping practices may also be relevant to differences in rates of infant deaths from a cause known as sudden infant death syndrome; see the box "Sudden Infant Death Syndrome.")

Feeding

As you saw in Afwe's awkward first efforts to feed her baby, in the beginning a new mother's nursing behavior frequently may not be much more coordinated than her infant's (Page-Goertz, McCamman, & Westdahl, 2001). She must learn how to hold the baby and adjust herself so that the nipple is placed at exactly the right spot against the baby's mouth to elicit the sucking reflex, but not press so tightly that the infant's breathing is disrupted.

The coordination of infant and maternal behavior during feeding is also apparent in the physical movements mothers make while they are feeding their infants by either breast or bottle. Kenneth Kaye (1982) and his colleagues found that even during the very first feeding, mothers occasionally jiggle the baby or the bottle. These jiggles come not at random intervals but during the pauses between the infant's bursts of sucking. The jiggles increase the probability of sucking and prolong the feeding session, thereby increasing the amount of milk the neonate receives. Researchers are not certain how such adaptive patterns originated. Kaye calls them "preadapted responses," implying that they may have arisen in the course of human evolution.

Like many other developments that you have encountered in this chapter, the newborn's feeding behaviors are affected by culture as well as by biology. In many parts of the world, such as sub-Saharan Africa, where artificial means of birth control are unavailable, breast feeding babies for 2 or more years is an essential birth control strategy in that it can suppress menstruation for up to 2 years (although

Sudden Infant Death Syndrome

AMONG INFANTS 1 TO 6 MONTHS of age, *sudden infant death syndrome*, often referred to as *SIDS*, is the most common cause of death in the United States, as well as a major cause of infant death in many other countries in the world (Nagler, 2002). In the typical case of SIDS, an apparently healthy infant is put to bed and a few hours later is dead. The infant may be found with clenched fists, discharge from the nose or mouth, and mottled skin, but based on the infant's prior health conditions, the family and its medical history, and the surrounding circumstances, the death is inexplicable.

The first medical report about SIDS was published more than 50 years ago (Garrow & Werne, 1953); since that time there has been an increasingly intense research program to discover its causes and ways to prevent it. Early research suggested that some infants are prone to a condition referred to as *sleep apnea*, that is, irregular breathing due to the brain's periodic failure to activate the muscles controlling the lungs. According to this diagnosis, the most effective prevention is provided by an electronic monitoring device that sounds an alarm whenever an infant experiences an episode of apnea, so that an adult can come and revive the baby in time.

Subsequent research has shown that young infants do indeed experience episodes of apnea during sleep. Postmortem studies of infant brains have shown that insufficient development of a key area in the brain stem called the *arcuate nucleus* is associated with increased rates of apnea and SIDS (Matturri et al., 2002). However, even apparently normal infants still have immature brain structures, and

while they may experience episodes of sleep apnea, they are generally startled awake by such incidents, which cause no lasting harm.

Consequently, researchers began to look at other potential causes, such as accidental smothering when a baby's nose is obstructed by a soft pillow, blankets, or a stuffed animal, or when a baby is sleeping in bed with an adult. Lewis Lipsitt (2003) noted that most deaths from SIDS occur when babies are 2 to 5 months of age. Babies this age are especially vulnerable, he suggested, because they have lost the reflex that causes them to turn their heads when they cannot breathe (which disappears prior to 2½ months) but have not yet developed firm voluntary control of their head movements.

An important turning point in the quest to eliminate SIDS came in 1994 when the American Academy of Pediatrics, in conjunction with the National Institutes of Health and other organizations, began informing parents about SIDS through a campaign called the "Back to Sleep" movement. This clever phrase identified the major strategy upon which the campaign was based: placing babies on their back to sleep instead of having them sleep on their stomach, which greatly increased the chances of accidentally obstructing their breathing. Since the inauguration of this campaign, the rate of SIDS in the United States has been cut in half, from 1.5 per 1000 births to approximately 0.7 per 1000 births. There have been similar reductions in other countries where awareness of the back-to-sleep practice has been increased (Blair et al., 2006).

Nonetheless, SIDS clearly remains a serious threat, so current research is seeking to dis-

cover what additional factors might, either singly or in combination, increase infants' risk. A number of prenatal and postnatal risk factors have been identified (Hauck et al., 2003), including the following:

- Maternal malnutrition and smoking during pregnancy, which increase the risk of prematurity (immaturity of the brain stem is almost certainly involved in apnea episodes)
- Other teratogens
- Postnatal exposure to secondary tobacco smoke—the greater the exposure to tobacco smoke, the greater the risk of SIDS
- Formula feeding of babies, which is associated with a higher SIDS rate than is breastfeeding
- Placing infants to sleep on their stomach on a soft mattress with stuffed animals or other toys in the crib

A great many studies have found different rates of SIDS for different ethnicities (Pollack & Frohna, 2002). For example, Native Americans have a higher rate of SIDS than do European Americans, while Latinos have a lower rate. The incidence of SIDS also varies widely across countries (Bajanowski et al., 2007). Current research strongly suggests that these variations result from cultural differences in eating habits, alcohol and cigarette consumption, and sleeping patterns, not from any group differences in a genetic predisposition for SIDS. Consequently, preventive measures focus on informing local populations of the factors they can change to ensure that their babies will not become victims of SIDS.

---

not reliably in all women), increasing the intervals between the birth of children (LeVine et al., 1994). The Sukuma of Tanzania, for example, try to space pregnancies by 24 to 30 months and describe someone who does not breast-feed for this length of time as a woman who "gives birth like a chicken." The Baganda of Uganda traditionally forbade sexual activity by a new mother because if she has another child too soon, the first child might be deprived of breast milk and be in danger of contracting **kwashiorkor,** an often-fatal form of protein-calorie malnutrition.

Yet another example of culture influencing infant feeding behaviors involves pediatricians' recommendations as to when babies should be fed. Today, pediatricians in the United States often tell parents to feed their newborn baby whenever they think the baby is hungry, perhaps as often as every 2 to 3 hours. But from the early 1920s through the 1940s, pediatricians advised parents to feed their babies only every 4 hours, even if the babies showed signs of hunger long before the prescribed time had elapsed.

kwashiorkor A potentially fatal form of malnutrition in which the diet is extremely low in protein.

For a very small infant, 4 hours can be a long time to go without food, as was demonstrated by a study of mothers and infants in Cambridge, England. The mothers were asked to keep records of their babies' behaviors and their own caregiving activities, including when they fed their babies and the time their babies spent crying. All of the mothers were advised to feed their babies on a strict 4-hour schedule, but not all followed the advice. The less experienced mothers tended to stick to the schedule, but the more experienced mothers sometimes fed their babies as soon as 1 hour after a scheduled feeding. Not surprisingly, the reports of the less experienced mothers showed that their babies cried the most (Bernal, 1972).

What happens if babies are fed "on demand"? In one study, the majority of newborn babies allowed to feed on demand preferred a 3-hour schedule (Aldrich & Hewitt, 1947). The interval gradually increased as the babies grew older. At 2½ months of age, most of the infants were feeding on a 4-hour schedule. By age 7 or 8 months, the majority had come to approximate the normal adult schedule and were choosing to feed about four times a day. (Some parents reported the four feedings as "three meals and a snack.") A more recent study found no difference in growth rate between babies fed on demand and those fed on a strict schedule (Saxon, Gollapalli, Mitchell, & Stanko, 2002).

Crying

One of the most difficult problems parents face in establishing a pattern of care for their babies is how to interpret their infants' needs. Infants obviously cannot articulate their needs or feelings, but they do have one important way of signaling that something is wrong—they can cry.

Crying is a complex behavior that involves the coordination of breathing and movements of the vocal tract. Initially it is coordinated reflexively by structures in the brain stem, but within a few months the cerebral cortex becomes involved, enabling babies to cry voluntarily (Zeskind & Lester, 2001). This change in the neural organization of crying is accompanied by physical changes in the vocal tract that lower the pitch of infants' cries. At this point, parents in the United States begin to report that their infants are "crying on purpose," either to get attention or because they are bored (Lester et al., 1992). Across cultures, and even in chimpanzees, there is a peak in the frequency of infant crying at 6 weeks of age, followed by a decline at approximately 12 weeks (Bard, 2004) (Figure 4.23).

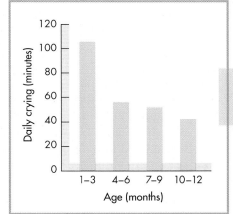

Figure 4.23 Crying decreases substantially between birth and 1 year of age.

Developmentalists with an evolutionary perspective believe that human crying evolved as a signal to promote caregiving when the infant is hungry, in pain, or separated from its caregiver (Zeifman, 2001). Indeed, cross-cultural evidence suggests that infants cry less when their culture's caregiving practices include prolonged holding, frequent breastfeeding, rapid response to infant frets and cries, and co-sleeping with infants at night—all found, for example, in several African cultures, including the !Kung and the Aka (Hewlett et al., 1998; Barr et al., 1991). These practices have been found to different extents in Western cultures, and the differences have similar repercussions for infant crying (St James-Roberts et al., 2006). As shown in Figures 4.24 and 4.25, compared with mothers in London, those in Copenhagen spent significantly more time holding their infants, and in the course of a day their babies cried and fretted significantly less.

Figure 4.24 There are considerable differences within and across cultures in the amount of time that babies are held. In general, those that are held more spend less time fussing and crying.

Figure 4.25 Although many people continue to believe that infants who are held a lot will cry more than those who are held less, research indicates just the opposite. As shown here, the amount of distress during the first 12 weeks of life of infants who are held less (the London group) is significantly higher than that of infants who are held more (the Copenhagen group).

Certainly babies' cries have a powerful effect on those who hear them. Experienced parents and childless adults alike respond to infants' cries with increases in heart rate and blood pressure, both of which are physiological signs of arousal and anxiety (Stallings et al., 2001). When nursing mothers hear babies' cries, even on recordings, their milk may start to flow (Newton & Newton, 1972).

The problem for anxious parents who hear their newborns cry is to figure out the source and seriousness of their baby's discomfort. Research shows that adults are in fact able to make certain distinctions among cries. According to Phillip Zeskind and his colleagues, the higher pitched the cries and the shorter the pauses between them, the more urgent—and unpleasant—adults perceive them to be. In addition, listeners in a variety of cultures can distinguish the cries of normal infants from the higher pitched cries of low-birth-weight babies and babies who have been exposed prenatally to alcohol or the chemicals from cigarette smoke (Worchel & Allen, 1997).

It is widely believed that some children suffer from an unexplained medical condition called *colic,* which causes them to cry excessively. Indeed, excessive infant crying is the most common complaint heard by pediatricians from mothers with infants under 3 months of age (Forsyth, 1989). However, while there are marked individual differences in the amounts that infants cry, the cries of babies thought to suffer from colic are not distinguishable from those of others who cry frequently. Thus, it would appear that it is not the specific sounds of the colicky infant's crying that troubles parents but rather "its unpredictable, prolonged, hard to soothe, and unexplained nature" (St James-Roberts, Conroy, & Wilshir, 1996, p. 375).

Caregivers' efforts to get babies on a schedule for sleeping and feeding and to comfort them when they are distressed continue as the months go by. These parenting activities are so commonplace that it is easy to overlook their significance. They are, however, the first instances of infants' coordination and active participation in the social world.

Parents throughout the world employ a variety of methods to deal with infant cries and fussiness. Holding the baby close, rocking, patting, or making rhythmic sounds, such as clapping, are common. Some child-care practices, including swaddling and carrying, reduce the amount and intensity of fussiness, making it easier for caregivers to soothe their infants.

||||| ▓ APPLY ▬ CONNECT ▬ DISCUSS

How would you respond to a new parent who takes an operant conditioning approach to newborn crying, believing that the baby will cry more if its crying is "reinforced" by the parent's attentions?

Summing Up the First 3 Months

Looking back over the first 3 months of postnatal life, you can see a remarkable set of changes in the organization of infants' behaviors and how they become coordinated with social life.

Babies are born with a rudimentary ability to interact with and learn about their new environment. They have reflexes that enable them to take in oxygen and nutrients and expel waste products. They are able to perceive objects, including people, although they tend to focus on only a part of the entire stimulus. They are sensitive to the sounds of human language, and they quickly develop a preference for the sound of their mothers' voice. Although they sleep most of the time, they are occasionally quite alert.

From the moment of birth, infants interact with and are supported by their parents or other caregivers. Initially, the first interactions of babies and their caregivers are tentative and somewhat uncoordinated, but within a matter of days a process of behavioral coordination has begun that will provide an essential framework for later development.

The developmental changes that characterize the first 3 months of infancy have clear origins in biology and in the physical and sociocultural environment. In the domain of biology, there is rapid maturation of the central nervous system, particularly in the connections between the brain stem and the cerebral cortex. Physically, babies become bigger and stronger; behaviorally, reflexes make way for more sophisticated actions that are increasingly coordinated and responsive to variations in the environment. This responsiveness is assisted by shifts in the infants' arousal states: Less time is spent sleeping and crying, and more time is spent in alert states, where babies can profit from and learn through active engagement with the world. All of these accomplishments converge to position the newborn at a new threshold of cognitive, social, and emotional development.

SUMMARY

Physical Growth

- As growth charts reveal, early physical growth is rapid, with the infant gaining about 6 pounds and growing more than 4 inches in just 12 weeks.

- The growing brain pushes against the bones of the skull, expanding the infant's head circumference.

Brain Development

- At birth, the brain contains most of the cells (neurons) it will ever have, but it will become four times larger by adulthood.

- Increased size results primarily from an increase in the connections among neurons and from myelination, which insulates axons and speeds the transmission of impulses.

- At birth, the cerebral cortex is less mature than the brain stem, which controls reflexes such as sucking and vital functions such as breathing. Development of the cortex occurs through both experience-expectant and experience-dependent processes.

Sensing the Environment

- Although newborns' sensory systems are all functioning, some are more developed than others. Newborns are able to perceive an object or event with more than one sensory system.

- Newborns are sensitive to the differences that distinguish the different sounds of human languages and, although initially able to hear discriminations made in all the world's languages, are soon able to perceive only those made in the language they hear around them.

- Because of immaturity of the eye's structures, newborns are very nearsighted, but visual acuity soon improves. Newborns are able to visually scan their surroundings, are able to perceive patterns and distinguish among forms, and show a preference for faces and the ability to distinguish their mother's face.

- Newborns can distinguish various tastes and smells. They prefer tastes and smells that are sweet, like breast milk, and make characteristic facial expressions in response to sour and bitter tastes and foul odors.

The Organization of Behavior

- Developing and maintaining behavioral organization is important for infants because it allows them to interact more effectively and adaptively with the world around them.

- At birth, reflexes give newborns highly organized ways of responding to the environment.

- Reflexes are building blocks for more complicated, co-ordinated forms of behavioral organization—for example, nursing develops from reflexes such as rooting and sucking. With maturational changes in the cerebral cortex, infants become able to coordinate reaching and grasping.

- According to Jean Piaget, infants gain knowledge largely by coordinating sensory perceptions and simple motor responses. During the first few months, they progress through the first two of the six substages of the sensorimotor stage:

  - In substage 1, infants learn to control and coordinate inborn reflexes.

  - In substage 2, accommodation first appears, with infants' prolonging pleasant sensations arising from reflex actions.

- According to learning theorists, learning, a change in behavior, occurs when the infant makes associations between its behavior and events in the environment. It may take various forms:

  - In classical conditioning, previously existing behaviors come to be associated with and elicited by new stimuli.

  - In operant conditioning, new behaviors may come about as a result of reinforcement and punishment of behaviors.

Temperament

- Infants differ in temperament, emotional and behavioral characteristics that show consistency across situations and some stability over time. Temperament includes such traits as activity level, quality of mood, and attention span.

- The same temperamental traits appear to be found in all cultures. Temperamental differences appear to have both genetic and cultural bases.

Becoming Coordinated with the Social World

- Infants' survival depends not only on the actions of caregivers but also on infants' ability to coordinate their own actions with those of caregivers.

- Newborns sleep approximately two-thirds of the time, but their periods of sleep are relatively brief, so they may be awake at any time. They tend to adapt gradually to adults' night/day sleep cycle, but the specifics depend in part on cultural patterns.

- The maternal–infant coordination that nursing requires has a biological underpinning. However, culture influences the age to which infants breast-feed and their feeding schedules. Newborns tend to prefer a 3-hour schedule, moving to a 4-hour schedule by 2½ months and approximating an adult schedule by 7 or 8 months.

- Infants' crying is a primitive means of communication that evokes a strong emotional response in adults and alerts them that something may be wrong. Infants may cry less in cultures with caregiving practices such as prolonged holding and frequent feeding. Certain distinctive patterns of early cries may indicate difficulties.

Summing Up the First 3 Months

- From birth, infants have a wide range of abilities and interact with their caregivers. Developmental changes in the first 3 months, originating in biology and depending also on the environment, include rapid physical growth and maturation of the central nervous system and a shift from reflexes to complex actions. The 3-month-old is at a new threshold of cognitive, social, and emotional development.

Key Terms

growth charts, p. 124

fontanels, p. 125

neuron, p. 126

axon, p. 127

dendrite, p. 127

synapse, p. 127

neurotransmitter, p. 127

synaptogenesis, p. 127

myelin, p. 127

spinal cord, p. 128

brain stem, p. 128

cerebral cortex, p. 128

experience-expectant, p. 129

exuberant synaptogenesis, p. 129

synaptic pruning, p. 129

experience-dependent, p. 130

habituation, p. 132

dishabituation, p. 132

phonemes, p. 132

visual acuity, p. 134

intermodal perception, p. 138

reflexes, p. 140

action, p. 141

sensorimotor stage, p. 144

primary circular reaction, p. 145

learning, p. 146

classical conditioning, p. 146

conditional stimulus (CS), p. 146

unconditional stimulus (UCS), p. 146

unconditional response (UCR), p. 146

conditional response (CR), p. 146

operant conditioning, p. 147

temperament, p. 148

kwashiorkor, p. 154

Physical and Cognitive Development in Infancy

Two neighbors—Jake, who is about to celebrate his first birthday, and Barbara, his mother—have been out for a walk and have stopped by the house of two of your authors, Mike and Sheila Cole. Sheila is in the kitchen preparing dinner. Jake sits on his mother's lap at the kitchen table, drinking apple juice from a plastic cup while the two women chat. Jake finishes his juice, some of which has dribbled onto his shirt, and puts the cup down on the table with a satisfied bang. He squirms around in his mother's lap so that he is facing her. He tries to get her attention by pulling at her face. When Barbara ignores him, Jake wriggles out of her lap to the floor, where he notices the dog.

"Wuff wuff," he says excitedly, pointing at the dog.

"Doggie," Barbara says. "What does the doggie say, Jake?"

"Wuff wuff," Jake repeats, still staring at the dog.

Following his pointing finger, Jake toddles toward the dog. His walk has a drunken, side-to-side quality, and he has a hard time bringing himself to a stop. Barbara grabs hold of Jake's extended hand, redirecting it from the dog's eyes.

"Pat the doggie, Jake."

Jake thumps the dog's head with a flat hand.

The dog does not like the attention and escapes into the living room. Jake toddles after her like a pull toy on an invisible string. The dog leads him back into the kitchen, where Jake bumps into Sheila's legs and falls to a sitting position.

"Well, hello, Jake," Sheila says, as she bends over and picks him up. "Did you fall down? Go boom?"

Jake, who until now hasn't taken his eyes off the dog, turns, looks at Sheila with a smile, and points at the dog. "Wuff wuff," he repeats.

A t almost 1 year of age, Jake behaves far differently than a 3-month-old. At that earlier age, Jake's main activities were eating, sleeping, and gazing around the room. He could hold his head up and turn it from side to side, but he could not readily reach out and grasp objects or move around on his own. He took an interest in mobiles and other objects when they were immediately in front of him, but he quickly lost interest in them when they were removed from his view, as though they no longer existed for him. His communications were restricted to cries, frowns, and smiles.

The contrast between Jake's behavior then and his behavior at 1 year gives you a hint of some of the amazing changes that occur during the overall period of infancy. Perhaps most obvious are the outwardly visible biological changes: Infants become markedly larger and stronger between 3 and 24 months of age. Essential maturation has also taken place in the central nervous system, particularly the cerebral cortex and other parts of the brain.

Related to these biological changes are the enormous gains that infants make in being able to move their bodies. At 3 months, infants are just beginning to be able to roll over, and their parents can be confident that they will remain more or less wherever they are put down. That soon changes. At about 7 to 8 months, infants begin to crawl; at about 1 year, they begin to walk in the drunken, unco-ordinated fashion demonstrated by Jake; and by the time they are 2, they can run, take a few steps backward, and walk up stairs (with a helping hand). During this period, infants also become much more adept at manipulating objects. At 1 year of age, babies prod, bang, squeeze, push, and pull almost anything they can get their hands on, including the neighbor's dog, and they often put objects into their mouths to learn about them; at 2 years of age, they possess enough control to feed themselves with a spoon, to toss a large ball, to open cabinets, drawers, and boxes, and to pet, rather than poke at or thump, the dog. As infants' mobility, motor control, and curiosity about the world increase, their parents must constantly be on the watch to keep them out of harm's way.

Important changes also occur in infants' cognitive abilities. Older babies learn more rapidly and remember what they have learned for longer periods of time. By the end of the infancy period, babies can remember actions they have observed others perform, in person or on television, and can imitate them days later in play. They can follow simple directions, and they laugh when someone does something silly like wear a cooking pot for a hat. They also begin to use symbols, turning a banana into a telephone or a wooden block into a race car. Of special significance is their emerging mastery of that uniquely human symbol system, language.

These changes in biological makeup, motor behavior, and cognitive capacities interact throughout infancy. We will focus on them in this chapter, and in the next turn to the substantial social and emotional developments that they help make possible.

Physical Growth

The physical differences between a 3-month-old and a 2-year-old are so striking that it's hard to believe that so much could have changed in a scant 20 months (Figure 5.1). There are changes in body size and proportions and in the muscles and bones, as well as in the brain. These changes are connected both with each other and with the development of the new be-havioral capacities babies display. For example, their greater weight requires larger and stronger bones to support them and stronger muscles to enable movement. Their developing cogni-tive capacities make them want to explore new aspects of the world, but to explore the world they must coordinate their con-stantly changing size and strength in new ways.

Figure 5.1 As apparent in this photograph, the body undergoes remarkable changes between 2 and 24 months of age that enable a host of new actions and behaviors, including helping a baby brother with his shoe.

Somos/Veer/Getty Images

Size and Shape

During their first year, most healthy babies triple in weight and grow approximately 10 inches; in the United States, the typical 1-year-old weighs 20 to 22 pounds and stands 28 to 30 inches tall. During the second year of life, children's bodies continue to grow rapidly, though at a much slower rate (Bogin, 2001); in the United States, children on average gain 5 pounds and grow 4 inches, to about 27 pounds and about 34 inches. (This tapering off of the growth rate, apparent in Figure 5.2, continues until

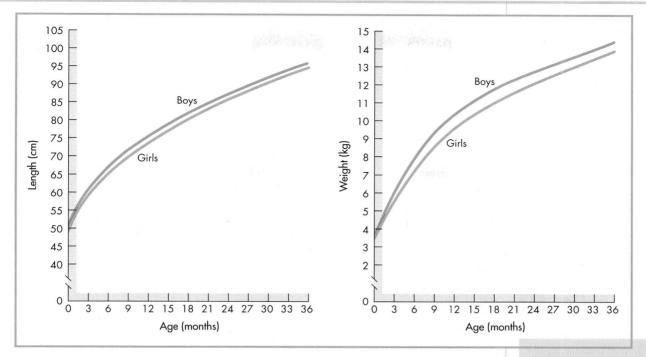

Figure 5.2 U.S. babies' lengths roughly double and their weights increase 5 or 6 times during the first 3 years of life. Note that at this stage, boys tend, on average, to be heavier and taller than girls. (Adapted from the Centers for Disease Control, 2000.)

adolescence, when there is a noticeable growth spurt.) Also by 2 years of age, most children will have all of their baby teeth.

Increases in babies' height and weight are accompanied by changes in their body proportions (see Figure 5.3). At birth, the baby's head is 70 percent of its adult size and accounts for about 25 percent of the baby's total length. By 1 year of age, the head will account for 20 percent of body length, and by adulthood, 12 percent. Infants' legs at birth are not much longer than their heads; by adulthood the legs account for about half of a person's total height. By 12 months, the changes in body proportions have led to a lower center of gravity, making it easier for the child to balance on two legs and begin to walk (Thelen, 2002). As their bodies stretch out, most will lose the potbellied look so characteristic of younger infants: They begin to look more like children than infants.

It should be noted that norms for children's growth, such as those depicted in Figure 5.2, are derived by averaging large samples of children and that individual

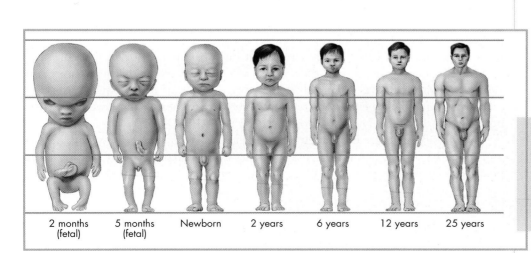

| 2 months (fetal) | 5 months (fetal) | Newborn | 2 years | 6 years | 12 years | 25 years |

Figure 5.3 The proportions of body length accounted for by the head, trunk, and legs at different stages of development. During the fetal period, the head accounts for as much as 50 percent of body length. The head decreases from 25 percent of body length at birth to 12 percent in adulthood. (From Robbins et al., 1929.)

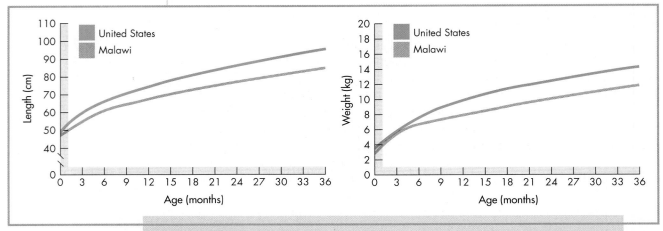

Figure 5.4 Environmental conditions play an important role in infant growth. Babies born in Malawi, a country in southeast Africa, face conditions such as widespread malnutrition, chronic poverty, disease, and a rising HIV/AIDS infection rate. As a result of this complicated array of factors, Malawian infants grow at a slower rate than their American counterparts. These graphs show height and weight curves for the 50th percentile of Malawian and American children. Compared to their American counterparts, the Malawian children were on average 1 inch (2.5 cm) shorter and 1.12 pounds (510 g) lighter. (Adapted from Maleta et al., 2003.)

children normally grow at widely varying rates (Tanner, 1998). Many factors contribute to these variations, including not only genetic factors but also, for example, diet and socioeconomic status (Figure 5.4; Ruel & Menon, 2002).

The Musculoskeletal System

As babies grow, the bones and muscles needed to support their increasing bulk and mobility undergo corresponding growth. Most of a newborn's bones are relatively soft, and they harden (ossify) only gradually as minerals are deposited in them in the months after birth. The bones in the hand and wrist are among the first to ossify. They harden by the end of the first year, making it easier for a baby to grasp objects, pick them up, and play with them. At the same time, infants' muscles increase in length and thickness, a process that will continue throughout childhood and into late adolescence. In infancy, increases in muscle mass are closely associated with the development of the baby's ability to crawl, stand alone, and walk.

Although boys are generally larger than girls, as Figure 5.2 clearly indicates, research supports the common wisdom that girls mature faster than boys. In fact, sex differences in growth rates are apparent even before birth: Halfway through the prenatal period, the skeletal development of female fetuses is some 3 weeks more advanced than that of male fetuses. At birth, the female's skeleton is from 4 to 6 weeks more mature than the male's, and by puberty it is 2 years more advanced. (Girls are more advanced in the development of other organ systems as well. They get their permanent teeth, go through puberty, and reach their full body size earlier than boys do [Bogin, 1999].)

The physical changes of infancy described above open wholly new ways of exploring and learning about the environment. Equally significant in making these possible are the changes taking place in the brain.

║║║║║ APPLY ▪ CONNECT ▪ DISCUSS ─ ─ ─ ─ ─ ─ ─

Provide some concrete examples of how socioeconomic status may affect infants' physical growth.

Brain Development

The development of the baby's brain is as fascinating as it is important. As discussed in Chapter 4 (pp. 129–130), the brain has evolved in such a way that it develops through both experience-expectant and experience-dependent processes. With *experience-expectant* processes, the brain expects that the world will present particular, species-universal experiences—patterns of light and dark, various kinds of tastes and odors, language, and the like—and develops in response to those experiences. With *experience-dependent* processes, development occurs in response to specific experiences—hence the brain's amazing capacity to be changed by the unique experiences of each individual child.

In their efforts to understand infant brain development, researchers have focused on answering two interconnected questions. One concerns the relationship between brain and behavior: What is the relationship between developments in certain parts of the brain and the onset of new skills or abilities? The other key question concerns the relationship between brain and experience: To what extent does experience or the lack thereof (i.e., deprivation) enhance or impede brain development and function?

Brain and Behavior

As we discussed in Chapter 4, the brain undergoes substantial development throughout infancy, although different parts grow at different times and rates. The *cerebral cortex,* as you may recall, is very immature at birth. Because the cortex is associated with such complex functions as voluntary (as opposed to reflexive) behavior, abstract thought, problem solving, and language, its development has been of special interest to researchers eager to understand brain–behavior relationships.

The **prefrontal area** of the cortex, located behind the forehead, plays a particularly important role in the development of voluntary behavior. It begins to function in a new way sometime between 7 and 9 months of age. With this change in functioning comes an increase in infants' ability to regulate themselves (Posner et al., 2007). Infants can stop themselves from grabbing the first attractive thing they see; they can cuddle their teddy bear to keep from being upset when they are put down for a nap. With the emerging ability to inhibit action, they can also better control what they attend to. In effect, they begin to be able to stop and think (Diamond, 2000; Stevens, Quittner, Zuckerman, & Moore, 2002).

Another important development, revealed by brain-imaging techniques, involves the language-related areas of the cortex. These areas, in the frontal and temporal lobes, undergo significant myelination shortly before a characteristic spurt in toddlers' vocabulary (myelin, remember, is the fatty substance that covers axons, speeding the brain's communications) (Pujol et al., 2006; see Chapter 7).

At least as important as the growth of different brain areas is that the different areas increasingly function together (Bruer & Greenough, 2001; Nelson & Luciana, 2001). Once again, myelination plays an important role. For example, myelination of the neurons that link the prefrontal cortex and frontal lobes to the brain stem, where emotional responses are partially generated, creates a new potential for interaction between thinking and emotion. In general, the greater synchrony among brain areas appears vital to the emergence of functions that define late infancy, including more systematic problem solving, the voluntary control of behavior, and the acquisition of language (Richmond & Nelson, 2007).

Toward the end of infancy, the length and the degree of branching of the neurons in the cerebral cortex approach adult magnitudes: each neuron now has multiple connections with others, usually numbering in the thousands. The various

prefrontal area Part of the cortex located directly behind the forehead, and important to the development of voluntary behaviors.

areas of the brain, which have been maturing at very different rates, reach similar levels of development (Nelson, 2001). Most of the brain structures that eventually will support adult behavior are present, and the pace of the brain's overall growth becomes slower and steadier, until adolescence.

Brain and Experience

When we think of how experiences can affect the brain's structures and functions, we are likely to think of intense and traumatic experiences—a blow to the head, high levels of exposure to drugs or toxins, extreme malnourishment, chronic abuse. However, as we discussed in Chapter 4, everyday experience can also affect the brain's structures and functions. Thus, in discussing *exuberant synaptogenesis* and *synaptic pruning* (p. 129), we described how the infant's normal everyday experiences, such as exposure to a specific language, can affect which synapses are strengthened and which are eliminated, or "pruned." (As detailed in the box "Bringing Up Brainy Babies," the idea that brain development is highly sensitive to the baby's experiences has fueled a multimillion dollar industry aimed at making babies smarter.)

If brain development is so readily influenced by the infant's daily experience, how might it be affected by situations in which infants endure prolonged periods of deprivation? The effects of such deprivation have been studied extensively in children from Romanian orphanages who were adopted into families in Western Europe and North America. The adoptions occurred during the early 1990s, after the collapse of a repressive regime, under which the country's orphanages had been little more than human warehouses. Together, the numerous studies of Romanian orphans tell a heart-wrenching story about the conditions that they endured and the severe developmental effects of these conditions. The orphans received basic physical care with little social and intellectual stimulation. Typically, they were confined to cribs for most of each day, with no social interaction and nothing to look at but bare walls. At the time of their adoption, most of the children were physically, cognitively, and emotionally impaired. The question developmentalists were interested in was whether the experience of a normal adoptive home could make up for their previous deprivations.

The most recent research finds that even after the children have spent 7½ or more years in adoptive families and schools, the marks of early deprivation remain, unless the children were adopted in early infancy (Nelson et al., 2007). In particular, the researchers found that while babies who were rescued before 6 months of age seemed to recover fully from their experiences, those who remained in the orphanages beyond 6 months of age showed significant impairments in intellectual functioning.

What accounts for these age differences in recovery, and how, exactly, did deprivation affect the brain development of the orphans? In answering these questions, the researchers point out that the infant brain undergoes considerable development between 6 and 24 months of age and that during such phases of rapid growth, brain structures are particularly sensitive to the infant's experiences. In Chapter 1, we described such phases as *sensitive periods,* or periods of *plasticity,* during which a particular experience (or lack of it) has a more pronounced effect on development than it would at

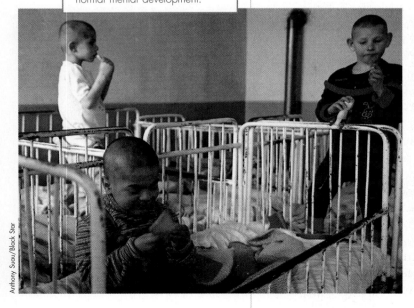

The conditions in orphanages such as this one in Romania provide insufficient stimulation for normal mental development.

Anthony Suau/Black Star

Bringing Up Brainy Babies

PARENTS IN MANY PARTS OF THE world believe that just as nature takes its course, children will develop at their own pace. There is no need for them to force nature's hand (Rogoff, 2003). But American parents have a seemingly unstoppable desire to speed up their offsprings' rate of development. Piaget referred to this parental desire as "the American problem."

One by-product of current research on infant development is a major growth industry in toys, books, DVDs, and computer programs designed to speed up some aspect of young infants' development, in the belief that such acceleration will give them an advantage over their peers in later life. Some of these products (such as attractive mobiles hung over the baby's crib) have a solid foundation in research; others do not (Jones & Zigler, 2002). The range and ingenuity of the products that have been created to speed infant growth are matched only by the enormous amounts of money that have poured into the new "growth industry." At present, the market for development-enhancing products for infants and small children is estimated to be at least $1 billion (della Cava, 2002).

Although the idea that environmental stimulation can enhance young infants' cognitive and social competence has been around since the middle of the twentieth century, the current craze in providing special stimulation for very young infants received a significant boost from various lines of research conducted in the 1980s. First, there were studies showing that newborns learned from the environment outside of their mother's womb (such as the preference for listening to *The Cat in the Hat*) (see Chapter 3). Second, research began to appear on experience-dependent brain growth, showing that animals raised in enriched envi-

A multimillion-dollar toy industry has provided children like 11-month-old Jetta, above, with an array of high-tech toys, including a laptop computer. Despite parents' enthusiasm for such toys, there is little evidence that they are effective in stimulating children's brain functioning or intellectual development.

ronments had more brain development and showed improved problem-solving abilities (see Chapter 4). Third, data appeared showing that young infants learned to categorize alphabet letters and that this learning was retained for sometimes surprisingly long intervals.

Then, in 1993, Frances Rauscher and her colleagues published an article in the prestigious scientific journal *Nature* in which they reported that listening to a Mozart sonata enhanced IQ by an average of 8 to 9 points (Rauscher, Shaw, & Ky, 1993). This report attracted extensive attention and was followed in 1997 by a book, written by a former choral conductor, entitled *The Mozart Effect* (Campbell, 1997). The book was a best seller and was convincing enough for the then-governor of Georgia to propose giving every newborn in the state a classical music CD to enhance the baby's cognitive development. The "brainy baby" movement was well on its way.

Subsequent scientific research has not been kind to the "Mozart effect." When positive effects on intelligence are reported, they are generally short-lived (on the order of a dozen minutes or so), and the number of failures to obtain any effect at all have led many to conclude that it's "curtains for the Mozart effect" (McKelvie & Low, 2002). However, these negative findings have done little to slow the brainy baby movement, which has taken a decidedly electronic turn, producing video game consoles like the V.Smile and Leapster, marketed with such catchy claims as "Turn game time into brain time." While admitting that there is little research to back up claims of their products' educational merits, marketers are quick to point out that there is little research indicating that the products cause young children any harm.

On the other hand, the American Academy of Pediatrics recommends no screen time at all for children under age 2, mainly because it may displace human interaction—a source of essential experiences for infant brain growth and emerging cognitive, social, and emotional development. Indeed, at least one study bears this out. Dan Anderson and his colleagues showed 12- to 15-month-olds how to use a puppet (Anderson & Kirkorian, 2006). One group of babies saw the demonstration live, while another group saw it on a video. Those who saw the live demonstration learned to imitate the action much more quickly than did their video-trained counterparts.

At present it appears clear that environmental stimulation can speed up certain aspects of children's development. But whether or not it provides any lasting benefits for children depends strongly on the nature of the extra stimulation and the cultural context of the infants' later lives.

another point in time (see p. 13). It is likely that during sensitive periods of brain development, the orphans lacked the species-universal experiences required for strengthening and fine-tuning normal experience–expectant neural connections. In addition, the infants' experience–dependent brain development may have been affected by their unique experiences in the deprived conditions of the orphanage.

Aided by new brain-imaging technologies (see Chapter 1, p. 35), developmentalists are gaining spectacular new insights into the relationships between the

Adopted from Romania, Vasile (right) is putting together a puzzle with his friend, Lauren. Research on the development of Romanian orphans indicates that those adopted before 6 months of age usually are able to recover from their early deprivation.

developing brain and the experiences and behaviors of infants. Indeed, brain scans of a group of these orphans showed significant deficits in the functioning of certain areas in the limbic system, which is involved in emotion and motivation (Chugani et al., 2001). Interestingly, work with rats and other animals indicates that the specific limbic areas affected are especially vulnerable to stress, particularly when it is experienced early in development. As the findings involving the orphans suggest, advances in developmental neuroscience hold great promise for exploring how biological and environmental processes interact in the life of the developing child.

APPLY ═ CONNECT ═ DISCUSS

Review the four central issues of developmental science that were discussed in Chapter 1 (pp. 12–16). How does our knowledge of infant brain development shed light on these issues?

Motor Development

One of the most dramatic developments between 3 and 24 months of age is the enormous increase in infants' ability to explore their environments by grasping and manipulating objects and by moving about in their environments. Developmentalists who study motor development typically distinguish between **fine motor skills,** which involve the development and coordination of small muscles, such as those that move the fingers and eyes, and **gross motor skills,** which involve the large muscles of the body and make locomotion possible.

Fine Motor Skills

We pointed out in Chapter 2 that human beings are highly distinctive in their ability to make and use tools. Such tool use would be impossible without the development of fine motor skills that allow us to grasp and manipulate objects. From the perspective of parents and caregivers, increasing fine motor control and coordination means that their baby can participate more fully in such daily activities as feeding and dressing. It also means that babies can get into drawers, cupboards, and other spaces that may contain dangerous objects. Figure 5.5 provides a summary of the major milestones of the infant's fine motor skills.

fine motor skills Motor skills related to the development and coordination of small muscles, such as those that move the fingers and eyes.

gross motor skills Motor skills related to the development and coordination of large muscles; important for locomotion.

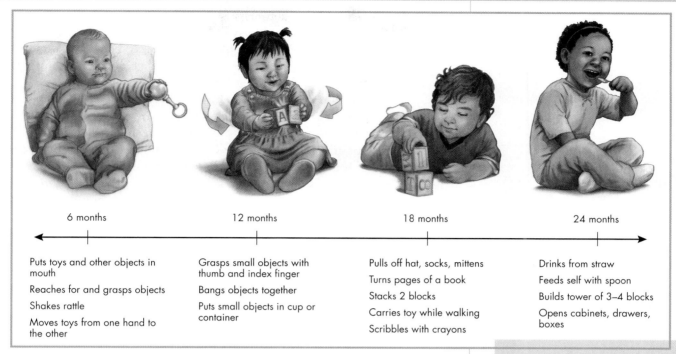

6 months	12 months	18 months	24 months
Puts toys and other objects in mouth	Grasps small objects with thumb and index finger	Pulls off hat, socks, mittens	Drinks from straw
Reaches for and grasps objects	Bangs objects together	Turns pages of a book	Feeds self with spoon
Shakes rattle	Puts small objects in cup or container	Stacks 2 blocks	Builds tower of 3–4 blocks
Moves toys from one hand to the other		Carries toy while walking	Opens cabinets, drawers, boxes
		Scribbles with crayons	

Figure 5.5 The development and coordination of the small muscles that control the fingers and hands are associated with a variety of important skills, and follow a fairly predictable timetable.

Early Skills: Reaching and Grasping Remember from Chapter 4 (p. 144) that very young infants reach for an object moving in front of them, a reflexlike motion we referred to as *prereaching*. At this initial stage, the perceptions and actions involved in reaching and grasping are not yet coordinated. Infants may reach for an object but fail to close their hands around it, usually because they close their hands too soon. Then, around 3 months of age, babies begin to gain voluntary control over their movements, so reaching and grasping occur in the proper sequence. At first, their reaching and grasping is pretty much hit-or-miss (von Hofsten, 2001). With practice, their fine motor coordination gradually improves, although there are marked individual differences in the rapidity and vigor of their reaching movements (Figure 5.6). At about 5 months of age, infants can gauge when an object is beyond their reach, and they no longer attempt to reach for it. By the time they are 9 months old, most babies can guide their reaching and grasping movements with a single glance and execute them in a manner that looks well

Figure 5.6 Three-month-old Lucy (below left) is clearly interested in this brightly colored toy. You can see in the position of her arm and fingers that reaching and grasping is difficult at this age. In contrast, the nine-month-old baby (below right) is able to coordinate reaching and grasping in order to pick up his toy.

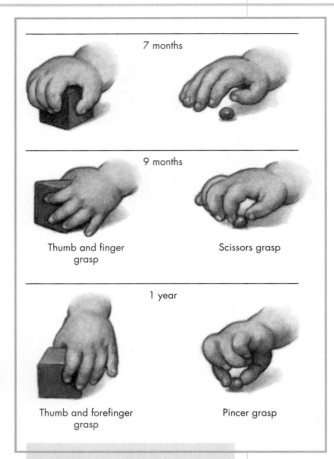

Figure 5.7 Babies find ways to grasp objects from an early age, but good coordination of the thumb and forefinger requires at least a year to achieve. (Adapted from Halverson, 1931.)

integrated and automatic (Smitsman, 2001). This is the time when caretakers need to "babyproof" their homes by putting dangerous or fragile objects out of the infant's reach. They also have to watch out for the sudden appearance of unexpected items in the grocery cart if the baby is along for the ride!

In the period between 7 and 12 months of age, fine motor movements of the hands and fingers become better coordinated. As shown in Figure 5.7, 7-month-olds are still unable to use their thumbs in opposition to their fingers to pick up objects, but by 12 months of age babies are able to move their thumbs and other fingers into positions appropriate to the size of the object they are trying to grasp. As their reaching and grasping become better coordinated and more precise, babies' explorations of objects become more refined. They are increasingly able to do such things as drink from a cup, eat with a spoon, and pick raisins out of a box (Connolly & Dalgleish, 1989).

As babies gain control over their hands, different objects invite different kinds of exploration—banging, shaking, squeezing, and throwing. All of these actions provide the baby with knowledge about the properties of the physical world (Gibson, 1988). Rattles, for example, lend themselves to making noises, while soft dolls lend themselves to pleasurable touching. Perceptual-motor exploration is an all-important way to find out about the environment and to gain control over it.

Later Skills: Manual Dexterity A lot of parents keep pictures of their babies' first efforts to feed themselves—pudgy faces all smeared with food. As amusing as these pictures can be, they illustrate the difficulty in mastering an act as elementary as using a spoon. Figure 5.8 depicts the variety of ways in which infants between 10 and 23 month of age attempt to hold a spoon, and suggests the incredibly precise coordination the effective use of a spoon entails. At 10 to 12 months of age, babies can do only simple things with

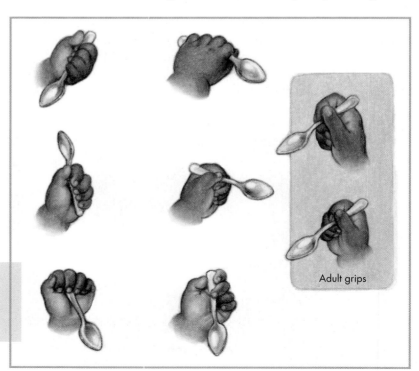

Figure 5.8 Grip patterns. Babies initially grip a spoon in many different ways. As they accumulate experience and gain motor control, they eventually adopt an adult grip.

a spoon, such as bang it on the table or dip it repeatedly into their bowl. Slightly older children can coordinate the action of dipping, opening their mouth, and bringing the spoon to it, but, as often as not, the spoon is empty when it arrives. Once the baby masters the sequence of getting food on the spoon, carrying it to the mouth without spilling, and putting the food in the mouth, the sequence is adjusted until it is smooth and automatic.

Coordination of fine motor movements increases significantly during the second year of life. At age 1, infants can only roll a ball or fling it awkwardly; by the time they are age 2, they are more likely to throw it. By age 2, they can also turn the pages of a book without tearing or creasing them, snip paper with safety scissors, string beads with a needle and thread (although the bead hole usually has to be pretty big!), build a tower six blocks high with considerable ease, hold a cup of milk or a spoon of applesauce without spilling it, and dress themselves (as long as there are no buttons or shoelaces) (Bayley, 1993). Each of these accomplishments may seem minor in itself, but infants' growing ability to manipulate objects with their hands relates to one of the most sophisticated accomplishments of our species and the most effective way of transmitting and transforming culture—using and making tools.

Using a spoon is a lot more complicated than you might think. It will take this baby many more months of practice before the fine motor skills involved in spoon use become smooth and automatic.

Gross Motor Skills

Progress in **locomotion,** the ability to move around on one's own, is a central developmental change that occurs toward the end of the first year. As with fine motor skills, the development of gross motor skills expands infants' opportunities to learn about the world and decreases their dependence on caregivers. Although there is wide variation in the age at which the various gross motor milestones are achieved, most babies throughout the world move through the same sequence of development, which begins with reflexive creeping and ends with purposeful walking, that uniquely human form of locomotion (Figure 5.9).

Creeping and Crawling During the first month of life, when their movements appear to be controlled primarily by subcortical areas of the brain, infants may occasionally creep short distances, propelled by the rhythmic pushing movements of their toes or knees (Figure 5.10). At about 2 months of age, this reflexive pushing disappears, and it will be another 5 or 6 months before babies can crawl about on their hands and knees (WHO, 2006).

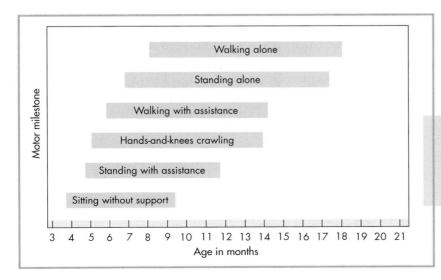

Figure 5.9 Despite wide variation in the ages at which specific gross motor skills are acquired, most children follow the same sequence of motor milestones, from sitting without support to independent walking.

locomotion The ability to move around on one's own.

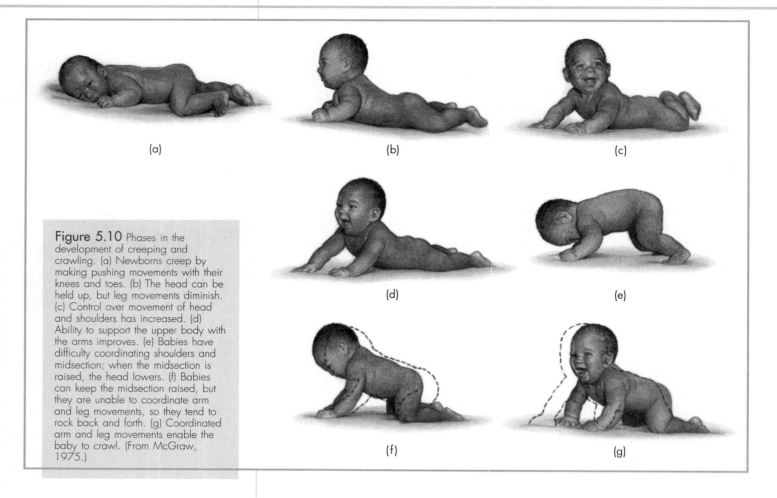

Figure 5.10 Phases in the development of creeping and crawling. (a) Newborns creep by making pushing movements with their knees and toes. (b) The head can be held up, but leg movements diminish. (c) Control over movement of head and shoulders has increased. (d) Ability to support the upper body with the arms improves. (e) Babies have difficulty coordinating shoulders and midsection; when the midsection is raised, the head lowers. (f) Babies can keep the midsection raised, but they are unable to coordinate arm and leg movements, so they tend to rock back and forth. (g) Coordinated arm and leg movements enable the baby to crawl. (From McGraw, 1975.)

By the time they are 8 to 9 months of age, most infants can crawl on flat, smooth surfaces with some skill. The onset of crawling allows babies to explore their environment in a new way and acquire new information about it, thus changing how they respond to the world.

One manifestation of infants' new exploration of and response to the environment is the emergence of wariness of heights, typically, among children in the United States, between 7 and 9 months of age, about the same time that they begin to crawl (Scarr & Salapatek, 1970). This wariness is demonstrated by infants' behavior on a "visual cliff," a specially constructed apparatus that gives the illusion of a dangerous drop-off. As shown in Figure 5.11, the apparatus includes a strong sheet of clear acrylic that extends across two sides—one "shallow," and one "deep." On the shallow side, a checkered pattern is placed directly under the acrylic sheeting, so the surface seems solid and safe. On the deep side, the checkered pattern is placed at a distance below the sheeting, suggesting a cliff. A number of experiments conducted by Joseph Campos and his colleagues have demonstrated that infants are not afraid to cross over to the deep side until they have had a certain amount of experience trying to crawl about on their own (Campos et al., 1992). Appreciating that when

Mark Richards/Photo Edit

Figure 5.11 Despite being encouraged to do so, this little boy is hesitant about crossing the transparent surface of the visual cliff. Associated with learning to crawl, his behavior expresses a fear of heights typical of 7- to 9-month olds.

Usually emerging around 8 to 9 months of age, crawling is a very effective form of locomotion. This photograph was taken at a crawling competition in Hong Kong. The babies are dressed up like panda bears because the competition was part of a celebration of two new pandas arriving at a Hong Kong zoo.

AP Photo/Xinhua, Lui Siu Wai

infants crawl, they not only move across flat surfaces, but gain experience moving—and sometimes falling—over various objects, obstacles, and steps, you can see how crawling may provide children with a clearer understanding of depth and its occasionally unhappy consequences.

Walking A baby's first steps are a source of joy and marvel for caregivers as well as the babies themselves. As infants approach their first birthdays, many become able to stand up and walk, which soon allows them to cover more distance than crawling did, and frees their hands for carrying, exploring, and manipulating objects (Garciaguirre, Adolph, & Shrout, 2007). At first they need assistance of some kind in order to walk. This assistance can come in several forms. Many babies grasp onto furniture to pull themselves into a standing position (Berger & Adolph, 2003). Seeing such attempts, caregivers often help by holding both the baby's arms to support the initial hesitant steps.

No one factor can be considered the key to walking; rather, as dynamic systems theorists point out, walking becomes possible only when all the component

Between the ages of 8 and 14 months, the transition from crawling to walking changes the way these two babies approach the task of going down a ramp. The 8½-month-old (left) sees that there is a slope but plunges down it just the same. The toddler (right) hesitates and feels the incline of the ramp with his foot before attempting to descend it.

Karen Adolph, Carnegie Mellon

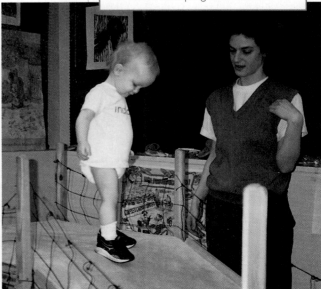

motor skills—upright posture, leg alternation, muscle strength, weight shifting, and sense of balance—have developed sufficiently and when the child has been able to practice combining them (Thelen, Fisher, & Ridley-Johnson, 2002). These new motor skills must then be combined with an increased sensitivity to perceptual input from the environment such as where to walk and what to walk around. Walking ability develops with this sensitivity and with changing size (Adolph & Eppler, 2002).

The Role of Practice in Motor Development

Studies of motor development were among developmentalists' earliest strategies for investigating the relative roles of nature and nurture. During the 1930s and 1940s, it was commonly believed that the attainment of such motor milestones as sitting and walking were dictated by maturation, with learning and experience playing little or no role.

One of the studies cited to support this view was conducted by Wayne and Margaret Dennis among Hopi families in the southwestern United States (Dennis & Dennis, 1940). In traditional Hopi families, babies in the first several months after birth are tightly swaddled and strapped to a flat cradle board. They are unwrapped only once or twice a day so that they can be washed and their clothes can be changed. The wrapping permits very little movement of the arms and legs and no practice in such complex movements as rolling over. The Dennises compared the motor development of traditionally raised Hopi babies with that of the babies of less traditional Hopi parents who did not use cradle boards. They found that the two groups of babies did not differ in the age at which they began to walk by themselves, which is consistent with the notion that this basic motor skill does not depend on practice for its development.

However, observations of babies from other cultural settings provide evidence that practice can affect the age at which babies reach motor milestones and may even alter the sequence of the milestones. Charles Super (1976) reported that among the Kipsigis people of rural Kenya, parents begin to teach their babies to sit up, stand, and walk not long after birth. To teach their children to sit up, for example, Kipsigis parents seat their babies in shallow holes in the ground that they have dug to support the infants' backs, or they nestle blankets around them to hold them upright. They repeat such procedures daily until the babies can sit up quite well by themselves. Training in walking begins in the 8th week after birth. The babies are held under the arms with their feet touching the ground and are gradually propelled forward. On average, Kipsigis babies reach the developmental milestones of sitting 5 weeks earlier and walking 3 weeks earlier than do babies in the United States. (Similar results have been reported among West Indian and Cameroonian children, whose mothers put them through a culturally prescribed sequence of motor exercises during the early months of infancy [Hopkins & Westen, 1988; Keller, 2003]). At the same time, Kipsigis infants are not advanced in skills they have not been taught or have not practiced. They learn to roll over or crawl no faster than children in the United States, and they lag behind children in the United States in their ability to negotiate stairs.

Further evidence for the impact that practice—or lack of it—can have on early motor development comes from the Ache, a nomadic people living in the rain forest of eastern Paraguay. Hilliard Kaplan and Heather Dove (1987) reported that Ache children under 3 years of age spend 80 to 100 percent of their time in direct physical contact with their mothers and are almost never seen more

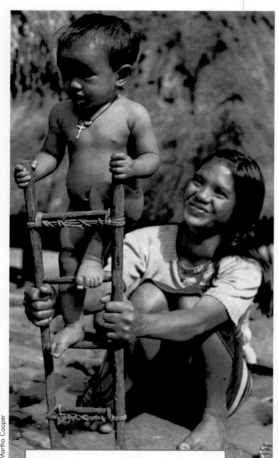

Martha Cooper

Babies who are just beginning to stand up find other people and furniture to be handy aids. This Filipino baby who lives in a house on stilts is being trained at an early age in the essential skill of climbing a ladder.

than 3 feet away from them. A major reason is that Ache hunter–gatherer groups do not create clearings in the forest when they stop to make camp. Rather, they remove just enough ground cover to make room to sit down, leaving roots, trees, and bushes more or less where they found them. For safety's sake, mothers either carry their infants or keep them within arm's reach.

As a result of these cultural patterns, Ache infants are markedly slower than infants in the United States to acquire gross motor skills such as walking. They begin walking, on the average, at about 23 months of age, almost a full year later than children in the United States. At about the age of 5, however, when Ache children are deemed old enough to be allowed to move around on their own, they begin to spend many hours in complex play activities that serve to increase their motor skills. Within a few years they are skilled at climbing tall trees and at cutting vines and branches while they balance high above the ground in a manner that bespeaks normal, perhaps even exceptional, motor skills.

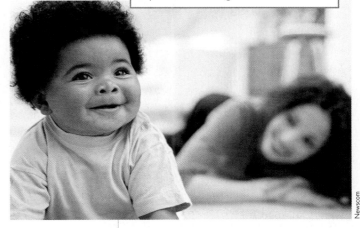

Intended to prevent sudden infant death syndrome, the practice of putting babies to sleep on their backs had the unexpected effect of delaying the onset of crawling. Pediatricians now encourage parents to provide young infants with plenty of "tummy time" in which to gain experiences important to learning to crawl.

The influence of practice, and of cultural norms, on physical development is further highlighted by the recent "back-to-sleep" movement in the United States to eradicate SIDS (see Chapter 4, p. 154). The widespread success of getting parents to put their infants on their back to sleep rather than on their belly has had the unexpected effect of delaying the onset of crawling in North American babies by as much as 2 months or so (Majnemer & Barr, 2005). Since time spent in the prone position (face down) provides babies with their earliest experiences of bearing their body weight with their arms, shifting their weight to reach for a toy, and trying out coordinated movements of their arms and legs, children who spend their waking as well as sleeping hours on their backs miss out on developmentally appropriate experience. As a consequence, pediatricians in the United States are urging parents to provide their young infants with "tummy time to play" so that they can practice pushing themselves up as a precursor to crawling (Pontius et al., 2001).

Control of Elimination

Another significant development in the lives of babies, not to mention their families, is the ability to control the muscles that govern elimination. In the early months of life, elimination is an involuntary act—a reflex. When full, the baby's bladder or bowels stimulate the appropriate sphincter muscles, which open automatically, causing elimination. Before a baby can control these muscles voluntarily, the sensory pathways from the bladder and bowels must be mature enough to transmit signals to the brain. Children must then learn to associate these signals with the need to eliminate. They must also learn to "hold it" by tightening their sphincters to prevent elimination and to loosen them to permit it.

As the box on the Diaper-Free Movement makes clear, learning to control elimination takes place within a historical and cultural context. Until the 1950s, toilet training in many countries was begun as early as possible, not only for convenience in an era before washing machines and disposable diapers but also because early training was believed to ensure bowel regularity, which was considered important for good health. (*Infant Care,* published by the U.S. Children's Bureau in 1914, advised mothers to begin bowel training by the third month or even earlier [Wolfenstein, 1953].) With the advent of washing machines and disposable diapers in the latter half of the twentieth century, parental practices began to change. For example, Remo Largo and his colleagues found that in the 1950s,

In the Field   The Diaper-Free Movement

AT 7 MONTHS, LITTLE HANNAH HAS chubby thighs and a dimpled bottom but lacks her peers' familiar hind-end bulge. She is diaper-free. Her mother, Melinda, has joined a growing number of parents who are starting their children's toilet training at surprisingly early ages—early, that is, by modern, Western standards. Belonging to Internet groups and e-mail lists, and poring over how-to books with such titles as *Diaper Free! The Gentle Wisdom of Natural Infant Hygiene* (Bauer, 2001), these parents are learning about techniques that will encourage their babies—too young to walk or talk—to eliminate in toilets, sinks, or pots. They are also bucking historical trends in the United States according to which the onset of toilet training has been increasingly delayed (see the table).

The Trend in the United States for Beginning Toilet Training

Time period	Starting age
1920–1940	12 months
1940–1960	18 months
1960–1980	2 years
1980–1990	2½ years
1990–present	3 years

Adapted from Bakker & Wyndaele, 2000

The training begins with the parent holding the baby by the thighs in a seated position against their stomachs and making encouraging hisses or grunts. With time, the parent learns the baby's elimination rhythms (babies often go after eating or bouts of activity); meanwhile, the baby learns to eliminate at the sound of the parent's hissing or grunting cues. In Hannah's case, at least, the training was highly effective: she can sleep all night without a diaper and goes in a plastic potty as her mother makes a little "pss-wss-wss" sound. Melinda is pleased. She's saving a bundle in diaper costs, which can reach $3,000 per child, and is helping the environment, which currently sags under the accumulating weight of 22 billion dirty diapers per year. In addition, Hannah is free of diaper rash, and her nursery doesn't smell like a diaper pail.

Although toilet training at such a young age may seem unusual, if not impossible, it used to be common practice in the United States, and it continues to be embraced in many countries across the globe, including India, China, Kenya, and Greenland. Some parents in the United States who adopt children from these countries are startled to discover that that their babies arrive toilet-trained.

Indeed, it has been estimated that more than 50 percent of the world's children are toilet-trained by 1 year of age (de Vries & de Vries, 1977).

Not surprisingly, there is a great deal of controversy regarding the effectiveness of early toilet training, and what, exactly, it means to be "trained." One way of interpreting the difference between reports of early training success and evidence that children are not capable of voluntary control until much later is to argue that it is the parents, not the babies, who have been trained. According to this interpretation, parents become adept at picking up their babies' signals and rhythms and learn when it's time to put their children on the pot. On the other hand, it might be that early training draws upon a different learning mechanism than does later training. Specifically, early training may take advantage of *classical conditioning*, in which a conditional stimulus (Melinda's "pss-wss-wss") is paired with an unconditional stimulus (Hannah's full bladder or bowel) such that over time Melinda's cue is enough to produce the desired response (see p. 146 for a review of classical conditioning). In contrast, later training involves deliberate, voluntary control, requiring the development of sensory pathways in the brain and higher cognitive processes.

Regardless of whether the Diaper-Free Movement is a passing fad or a signal that the historical pendulum of toilet training is about to reverse its direction, it provides an excellent example of how children's development is culturally organized, and of the variety of developmental mechanisms (classical and operant conditioning, for example) that allow children to adapt to radically different rearing conditions (adapted from Kelley, 2005).

Andrea Mohin/The New York Times/Redux

At a "diaper-free baby" meeting in New York, 7-month-old Neshama is sitting on a potty.

96 percent of Swiss parents began toilet training before their infants were 12 months old, but by the mid-1970s, the vast majority of Swiss parents did not begin it until their children were 36 months of age. Significantly, the toilet training of the earlier generation succeeded only in the sense that young infants learned to eliminate when placed on the potty; there was no change at all in the ages at which children gained sufficient control over their bladder and bowel functions to stay dry at night (Largo et al., 1996). Similar trends were found in a study conducted in Belgium (Bakker & Wyndaele, 2000). These results provide strong evidence that the processes of gaining voluntary control over bowel and bladder are under maturational control.

The presence of friends no doubt encourages these young children in their attempts to learn to use the potty.

By the time they are 2 years old, some children are able to remain dry during the day, owing in large measure to the watchfulness of adults who place them on the potty when they show signs of needing it. Many children in the United States and Europe today, however, do not achieve this milestone until sometime later, and most do not manage to stay dry while they are asleep until they are 3½ to 4 years old (Schum, Kolb, McAuliffe, Simms, Underhill & Marla, 2002). The successful completion of toilet training is an important milestone because it allows children a noticeably greater degree of independence.

 APPLY ▪ CONNECT ▪ DISCUSS

Imagine two children—one an early walker, walking well at 9 months of age, the other a late walker, walking well at 15 months. Suppose both children live in the same neighborhood or village and have parents with similar resources and with similar child-rearing practices and beliefs. Explain how the difference in onset of walking may have significant implications for each child's development.

Cognitive Development: The Great Debate

As the physical body, and the ability to control it, continue to mature across the first 2 years after birth, so, too, does the mind. As we shall see in the following sections, developmentalists are engaged in a great debate about how thinking progresses during the first 2 years.

For some developmentalists, such as Piaget, the young child's mind undergoes a radical, discontinuous shift at the end of infancy. According to Piaget's stage theory view, the young infant is limited to sensorimotor intelligence, that is, understands the world only through his or her own actions and perceptions. The infant, therefore, cannot think about people and objects that are not immediately present to be seen, heard, felt, and acted upon. All this changes fundamentally when the child reaches 18 or so months of age and becomes capable of representational thinking, forming mental pictures or images of the world. The ability to form such mental images, and to reason about them, is a significant turning point in cognitive development. Knowledge is no longer tied to the immediate here-and-now. Instead, the infant can hold in mind past experiences, compare and contrast them with each other and with present circumstances, and use them to anticipate the future and guide his or her actions. Developmentalists claim that the emergence of the ability to represent the world mentally results in a mind that is truly *conceptual*, rather than simply "sensorimotor."

On the other side of the debate are developmentalists who maintain that mental development is more continuous than Piaget supposed—that the ability to represent and understand the world conceptually is present very early in development, if not from birth. According to this view, conceptual understanding does not emerge out of sensorimotor knowledge, as Piaget claimed. Instead, young babies are believed to possess at least a rudimentary conceptual system. This system is thought to develop separate from, although in close association with, the sensorimotor system (Mandler, 2004; Moore & Meltzoff, 2004). As you will see below, there is much at stake in this debate regarding the nature and development of the human mind.

Sensorimotor Development

Piaget referred to infancy as the stage of *sensorimotor development* because of his belief that at this early age, infants acquire knowledge exclusively through motor actions that are directed at their immediate environment and guided by their sensory organs. He combined the terms "sensory" and "motor" to emphasize the intimate relationship between sensing the world and acting upon it. Each influences the other: What infants perceive depends on what they are doing, and what they do depends on what they are perceiving at the moment (Piaget, 1973).

You may recall from our previous discussions (Chapter 1, p. 22; Chapter 4, pp. 144–146) that Piaget divided the sensorimotor period into six substages (Table 5.1). During the first substage, the newborn learns to control and coordinate reflexes, and during the second, the newborn begins to modify and repeat behaviors, such as thumb-sucking, simply because they are pleasurable (primary circular reactions). In the following sections we provide an overview of the four remaining substages of sensorimotor development. As you read through them, notice how infants become increasingly flexible, purposeful, and inventive.

Reproducing Interesting Events (Substage 3)

In contrast to the first two substages, in which infants' actions primarily involve their own body, in the third substage, 4- to 8-month-olds begin to direct their attention and their actions to the external world—to objects and outcomes. This new interest in external things gives rise to a characteristic behavior observed in infants during this substage—the repetition of actions that produce interesting

table 5.1

Sensorimotor Substages and the Development of Object Permanence

Substage	Age (months)	Characteristics of Sensorimotor Substage
1	0–1½	*Reflex schemas exercised:* involuntary rooting, sucking, grasping, looking
2	1½–4	*Primary circular reactions:* repetition of actions that are pleasurable in themselves
3	4–8	*Secondary circular reactions:* dawning awareness of relation of own actions to environment; extended actions that produce interesting changes in the environment
4	8–12	*Coordination of secondary circular reactions:* combining schemas to achieve a desired effect; earliest form of problem solving
5	12–18	*Tertiary circular reactions:* deliberate variation of problem-solving means; experimentation to see what the consequences will be
6	18–24	*Beginning of symbolic representation:* images and words come to stand for familiar objects; invention of new means of problem solving through symbolic combinations

changes in the environment. For example, when babies in this substage acciden- tally discover that a particular action, like squeezing a rubber toy, produces an interesting effect, such as squeaking, they repeat the action again and again to produce the effect. Similarly, when babies vocalize by cooing or gurgling and a caregiver responds, they repeat the sound they made. Piaget termed these new, object-oriented actions **secondary circular reactions.** They are "secondary" because they apply to something outside the infant, in contrast to primary circu- lar reactions, which apply to the infant's own body (see p. 145).

The change from primary circular reactions to secondary circular reactions in- dicated to Piaget that infants are beginning to realize that objects are more than an extension of their own actions, that objects have their own, separate identities. In this substage, however, babies still have only a rudimentary grasp of objects and space, and their discoveries about the world seem to have an accidental quality.

The Emergence of Intentionality (Substage 4)

The hallmark of the fourth sensorimotor substage, which occurs between 8 and 12 months of age, is the emergence of the ability to engage in behaviors directed toward achieving a goal. Piaget called this ability **intentionality.** He believed goal- directed behavior to be the earliest form of true problem solving.

Piaget's son, Laurent, provided a demonstration of intentional problem solving of this kind when he was 10 months old. Piaget had given him a small tin con- tainer, which Laurent dropped and picked up repeatedly (a secondary circular re- action characteristic of behavior in substage 3). Piaget then placed a washbasin a short distance from Laurent and struck it with the tin box, producing an interest- ing sound. From earlier observations, Piaget knew that Laurent would repeatedly bang on the basin to make the interesting sound occur (another typical secondary circular reaction). This time Piaget wanted to see if Laurent would combine the newly acquired "dropping the tin box" schema with the previously acquired "make an interesting sound" schema. Here is his report of Laurent's behavior:

> Now, at once, Laurent takes possession of the tin, holds out his arm and drops it over the basin. I moved the latter as a check. He nevertheless succeeded, several times in succession, in making the object fall on the basin. Hence this is a fine example of the coordination of two schemas of which the first serves as a "means" whereas the second assigns an end to the ac- tion. (Piaget, 1952b, p. 255)

In Piaget's view, it is as a result of traversing substages 3 and 4 of sensorimotor intelligence that infants become capable of intentional action directed at objects and people around them. However, these abilities come fully into play only when infants can directly perceive the objects and people in question. Piaget maintained that until substage 4 of sensorimotor development, infants live in a world in which objects come and go from their line of sight, each "a mere image which reenters the void as soon as it vanishes, and emerges from it for no apparent reason" (1954, p. 11). Thus, Piaget believed that for young babies, out of sight is literally out of mind.

Exploring by Experimenting (Substage 5)

The fifth substage of the sensorimotor period, **tertiary circular reactions,** emerges between 12 and 18 months of age and is characterized by an ability to vary the actions of substage 4 systematically and flexibly. This ability makes ex- plorations of the world more complex. Indeed, Piaget (1952b) referred to tertiary circular reactions as "experiments in order to see," because children seem to be experimenting in order to find out about the nature of objects and events (p. 272).

secondary circular reactions The behavior characteristic of the third substage of Piaget's sensorimotor stage, in which ba- bies repeat actions to produce interesting changes in their environment.

intentionality The ability to engage in be- haviors directed toward achieving a goal.

tertiary circular reactions The fifth stage of the sensorimotor period, which is character- ized by the deliberate variation of action sequences to solve problems and explore the world.

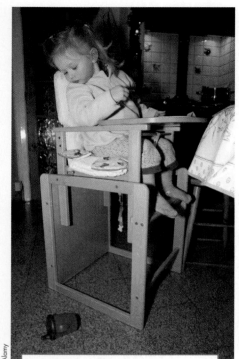

Experimenting with objects, including dropping cups from one's high chair in order to watch them fall and bounce, is typical of Piaget's sensorimotor substage 5.

Here is Piaget's description of this kind of behavior in Laurent, at 10 months and 11 days, lying in his crib:

> He grasps in succession a celluloid swan, a box, etc., stretches out his arm and lets them fall. He distinctly varies the positions of the fall. . . . Sometimes he stretches out his arm vertically, sometimes he holds it obliquely, in front of or behind his eyes, etc. When the object falls in a new position (for example, on his pillow), he lets it fall two or three times more on the same place, as though to study the spatial relations; then he modifies the situation. (p. 269)

According to Piaget's observations, infants in substage 5 cannot seem to be able to reason systematically about actions and anticipate their probable consequences. Theirs is still very much a here-and-now, trial-and-error world. The ability to mentally plan, organize, and otherwise envision their actions and foresee their possible consequences awaits the arrival of *representational thinking*.

Representation (Substage 6)

According to Piaget, the hallmark of substage 6, the final stage of the sensorimotor period, between 18 and 24 months of age, is that babies begin to base their actions on internal, mental symbols, or **representations,** of experience. When they can re-present the world to themselves—that is, when they can present it to themselves over again mentally—they can be said to be engaging in true mental actions.

The infant's ability to represent people, objects, events, and experience mentally has been a central focus for researchers because it has enormous ramifications in other areas of development. For example, once infants are able to represent a sequence of events, they can *solve problems* more systematically, rather than by trial and error. Similarly, once babies become capable of representation, they begin to engage in **symbolic play** (also known as *pretend play* or *fantasy play*), in which one object is used to stand for (represent) another, as when a child combs her baby doll's hair with a twig, or gives her a drink from a small plastic block. Representation also enables **deferred imitation,** the imitation of actions observed in the past, which is of tremendous importance to children's learning and socialization. A child who observes his father having coffee and reading the paper and then later pretends to be drinking coffee and reading is engaged in deferred imitation. Finally, of special significance is the role of representation in *language*, in which words are used to stand for (represent) people, objects, and events.

There is little disagreement about the importance Piaget attached to representation as a foundation for the development of problem solving, symbolic play,

representations The ability to form mental symbols and present experiences to oneself mentally; according to Piaget, emerges during sensorimotor substage 6.

symbolic play Play in which one object stands for, or represents, another.

deferred imitation The ability to imitate an action observed in the past.

At 22 months of age, Laura engages in deferred imitation, feeding her bears in imitation of how she was fed by her mother.

deferred imitation, and language. Nor do developmentalists disagree with Piaget's descriptions of the sequence of behavioral changes that occur as children progress through the early stages of dealing with objects. Indeed, his observations have been widely replicated, not only in Europe and the United States but in traditional societies as well. For example, Baule infants living in rural areas of the West African country of Ivory Coast have been found to proceed through the same sequence of object-related behaviors on almost exactly the same timetable as European children do, despite vast differences in their cultural environments (Dasen, 1973). In fact, research conducted with infant great apes reveals the same pattern of sensorimotor development (Parker & McKinney, 1999). The sequence and timing of sensorimotor stages are so reliable that Piaget's procedures were long ago standardized for assessing the development of children who are at risk because of disease, physical impairment, or extreme environmental deprivation (Uzgiris & Hunt, 1975).

However, in the past two decades there have been challenges both to Piaget's theory and to his methods. In general, these challenges attack the idea that infants are unable to represent objects they cannot see, arguing instead that infants are born with, or quickly develop, a conceptual system with representational powers. As we discuss below, critics argue that infants have representational *competence* but are not always able to express it in their *performance* on traditional Piagetian tests. Using a variety of ingenious methods, the critiques suggest that infants' mental lives are more complex than Piaget believed.

Studies by Andrew Meltzoff (1988) have shown that young infants imitate live models and will also imitate actions they have seen on television. This child observes a televised adult model manipulate blocks, and then immediately the child imitates the adult's actions. Meltzoff also demonstrated that infants who watch a televised model on one day will reproduce the model's behavior 24 hours later.

▌▐▐▌▐ APPLY ▬ CONNECT ▬ DISCUSS ┄┄┄┄┄┄┄┄┄┄┄┄┄┄┄┄┄┄┄┄┄┄┄

Imagine that you have been hired by a company to develop a line of toys appropriate to the ongoing sensorimotor development of infants through age 2. Prepare a presentation of some of your ideas for products, including arguments for how your products will appeal to infants at the various substages of sensorimotor development.

Conceptual Development

Piaget maintained that before the onset of representations, infants' understanding of the world is tied entirely to their direct perceptions and actions; consequently, they have no knowledge that endures beyond the immediate here-and-now. Although they can form primitive associations as, for example, in classical and operant conditioning (see Chapter 4, pp. 146–148), infants not yet at the end of the sensorimotor stage of intelligence lack conceptual understanding of the characteristics of objects and events. The distinction between sensorimotor and conceptual intelligence was cleverly highlighted by Jean Mandler when she characterized the sensorimotor infant as an "absent-minded professor" who, finding herself in the kitchen unable to remember what she wanted there, searches around for a clue and, upon seeing a cup by the sink, thinks, "Aha, I came for coffee!" (2004, p. 21). From Piaget's perspective, the sensorimotor infant can be similarly cued by perceptual features of the immediate environment to "remember" past associations but cannot grasp them conceptually in the absence of such prompts.

In the sections below, we explore the ways that infants demonstrate capacities to understand the world in more conceptual, abstract terms. As you will see, there is strong evidence that Piaget underestimated the conceptual intelligence of infants.

As yet, however, there is no unifying theory that accounts for conceptual development during the first 2 years. Should such a unifying theory take shape, the accumulating evidence indicates that it will need to account for the infant's biological preparedness to construct a typically "human" understanding of the world as well as for the consequences of the infant's experiences in specific contexts.

Understanding the Permanence of Objects

- Observation 1. A baby seated at a table is offered a soft toy. He grasps it. While he is still engrossed in the toy, the experimenter takes it from him and places it on the table behind a screen. The baby may begin to reach for the toy, but as soon as it disappears from sight, he stops short, stares for a moment, and then looks away without attempting to move the screen (Figure 5.12) (Piaget, 1954).

- Observation 2. A baby is placed in an infant seat in a bare laboratory room. Her mother, who has been playing with her, disappears for a moment. When the mother reappears, the baby sees three of her, an illusion the experimenter has created through the use of carefully arranged mirrors. The baby displays no surprise as she babbles happily to her multiple mother (Bower, 1982).

- Observation 3. From the comfort of his mother's lap, a baby follows a toy train with his eyes as it chugs along a track (Figure 5.13). When the train disappears into a tunnel, the child's eyes remain fixed on the tunnel's entrance rather than following the train's expected progress through the tunnel. When the train reappears at the other end of the tunnel, it takes the child a few seconds to catch up with it visually, and the child shows no surprise when the train that comes out of the tunnel is a different color or shape (Bower, 1982).

Each of these observations was recorded in the context of studying **object permanence,** the infant's understanding that objects continue to exist when they are out of sight, and a clear indicator that the development of mental representation is underway. For Piaget, babies demonstrate object permanence only when they begin to search actively for the absent object, as when—in a classic Piagetian test—they uncover a toy they have just seen the experimenter hide under a cloth or behind a barrier. Although this active searching behavior first appears at around 8 months of age, infants' mastery of object permanence is incomplete, according to Piaget. He discovered, for example, that babies between 8 and 12 months tend

Figure 5.12 Instead of searching behind the screen when his toy disappears, this infant looks dumbfounded. This kind of behavior led Piaget to conclude that objects no longer in view cease to exist for infants younger than 8 months of age.

(a)　　　(b)

Denise Goodman/Monkmeyer

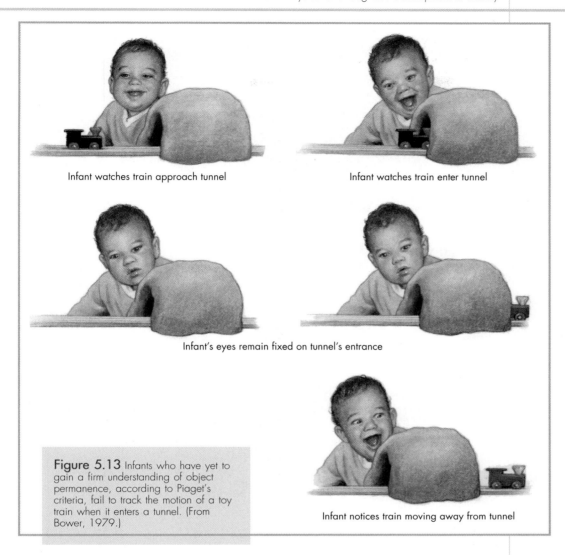

Infant watches train approach tunnel

Infant watches train enter tunnel

Infant's eyes remain fixed on tunnel's entrance

Figure 5.13 Infants who have yet to gain a firm understanding of object permanence, according to Piaget's criteria, fail to track the motion of a toy train when it enters a tunnel. (From Bower, 1979.)

Infant notices train moving away from tunnel

to make a characteristic mistake when searching for objects: If, after they have successfully searched for an object hidden in one location, A, the object is then hidden, *right before their eyes,* in a new location, B (Figure 5.14), they will still search for the object in location A where they previously found it!

Piaget interpreted this pattern of responding—referred to as the **A-not-B error**—as evidence that the child remembers the existence of the object but cannot reason systematically about it. He believed that true representation requires the ability both to keep in mind the existence of an absent object and to reason about that absent object mentally, an achievement he did not think occurs until late in the second year, during the sixth substage of the sensorimotor period.

Alternative Explanations of Infants' Difficulties Other developmentalists have disagreed with Piaget's interpretation of young infants' A-not-B error. They believe that the error is due not to a failure to represent and reason about the object but to other developmental limitations, including limitations of memory or motor skills.

The Role of Memory. In an influential series of studies, Adele Diamond (1991) suggested that young infants may be capable of representation, but fail Piaget's A-not-B task because they simply do not remember where the object was hidden.

object permanence The understanding that objects have substance, maintain their identities when they change location, and ordinarily continue to exist when out of sight.

A-not-B error In an object permanence task, when the child looks in location A, where the object had been previously found, even though the child just observed the object hidden at location B.

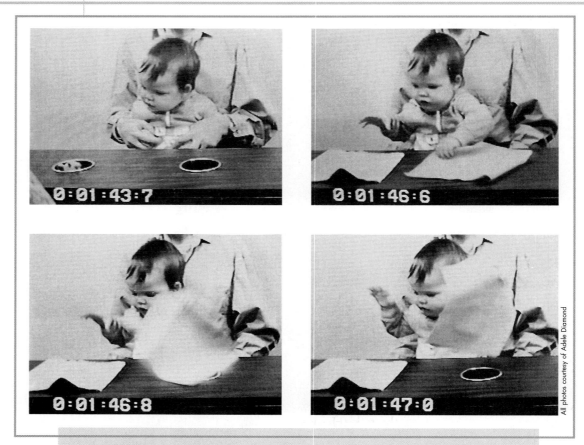

All photos courtesy of Adele Diamond

Figure 5.14 In this movie sequence, an object is placed in the circle on the left (position B), and then both circles (positions A and B) are covered with a cloth while the baby watches. In a previous trial, the object had been placed in the right-hand circle (position A), and the baby had correctly retrieved it. This time, while remaining oriented toward the hidden object at position B, the baby nonetheless picks up the cloth at position A, where the object was hidden before.

Diamond varied the time between the switching an object from location A to location B and the moment when children were allowed to reach for the hidden object (Diamond, 1991, 2000). She found that, if they were allowed to reach immediately, 7½-month-old babies correctly located the object at position B, but if they were prevented from reaching for as little as 2 seconds, they exhibited the A–not–B error. By 9 months of age, infants could withstand a delay of 5 seconds before beginning to make mistakes, and by 12 months of age, they could withstand a delay of 10 seconds. These results suggest that young infants are capable of representing objects they cannot see but quickly forget their location and become confused (the baby in Figure 5.14 is displaying this form of behavior). Other studies documenting a relationship between delay of reaching and successful searching (Bremner et al., 2005; Ruffman, Slade, & Redman, 2005) further suggest that the A–not–B task may impose significant demands on infants' memory system, masking their representational abilities.

The Role of Perseveration. *Perseveration* refers to the persistent repetition of a particular behavior. Diamond believed that young infants may exhibit the A–not–B error not only because of their memory limitations but also because of their tendency to engage in *motor perseveration,* in which they repeat a movement rather than modify it to fit new events. She noted that some infants who make the

A-not-B error in fact look at location B but reach toward location A, as shown in the movie sequence.

Another, similar type of perseveration, not specifically linked to motor behavior, may be involved—babies may reach incorrectly for the object at location A because of their previous success in finding it there. This is an example of a *capture error,* a tendency of people at all ages to continue using a once-successful solution whenever possible, as illustrated in the following task that Renée Baillargeon (1993) conducted with her 2-year-old son:

> Mother: What is an animal with a hump?
> Son: A camel.
> Mother: What is something warm you wear on your feet during the winter?
> Son: Boots.
> (a bit later)
> Mother: What is an animal with a hump?
> Son: A camel.
> Mother: What is something warm you wear on your head during the winter?
> Son: Boots.

Memory limitations, motor perseveration, and capture errors are all explanations for why infants may fail the A-not-B task, even though they may possess the ability to form mental representations. In other words, many developmentalists believe that infants have representational *competence* but lack the *performance* skills required to successfully solve the task (Hespos & Baillargeon, 2006).

Alternative Approaches to Measuring and Understanding Object Permanence

Prompted by evidence that the performance demands of the A-not-B task obscure the young infant's competence about objects, several developmentalists have proposed alternative ways of measuring and understanding object permanence. Some experimenters designed new tests of Piaget's theory, arguing that if infants were not required to demonstrate their understanding by reaching for and manipulating things, it might be possible to show that infants are capable of representational thought at or near birth. Others, however, have taken the more radical stance that the whole idea of competence existing in the absence of performance requires an unnecessary leap of faith. As you will see, these developmentalists do not call for new measures of object permanence as much as for a new theory about how infants behave in various testing situations.

Violation of Expectations Method.

To challenge Piaget's theory of when representation develops, Renée Baillargeon and her colleagues devised an object-permanence test that exploits the well-known tendency of infants—who in this are much like the rest of us—to stare at events that violate their expectations (Hespos & Baillargeon, 2006; Wang, Baillargeon, & Brueckner, 2004). Their new test, the **violation-of-expectations method,** involves a bit of magic. Basically, the method is to habituate babies to a particular event and then present two variants of the event—one that is "possible" under normal circumstances, and one that is "impossible" and comes about only through researcher trickery. The argument is that if infants are capable of mentally representing their experiences, they should develop specific expectations during the habituation phase and then look longer at events that violate those expectations, that is, at the impossible events.

In one study, infants were habituated to two events: in one, a short carrot moved behind a screen and reappeared on the other side; In the other, a tall carrot moved

violation-of-expectations method A test of mental representation in which the child is habituated to an event, and then presented with possible and impossible variants of the event.

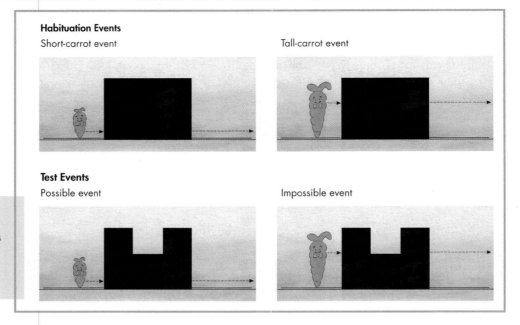

Habituation Events

Short-carrot event

Tall-carrot event

Test Events

Possible event

Impossible event

Figure 5.15 Using this example of the violation of expectations method, researchers find that infants as young as 2½ months of age look longer at the impossible event, suggesting that they are capable of mentally representing their past experiences.

behind the screen and reappeared (Figure 5.15). Once the infants were habituated to these two events, they were presented with the two test events, which differed from the habituation events in that a window had been cut out of the screen:

1. In the *possible event,* a short carrot again moved behind the screen and reappeared on the other side. The window that had been cut out of the screen was high enough that the small carrot would still have been hidden from view as it passed behind.

2. In the *impossible event,* a tall carrot moved behind the screen and reappeared on the other side. The tall carrot *should* have appeared in the window as it passed behind the screen—but magically, in violation of anyone's expectations (except, of course, the crafty researchers'), it did not.

Using this method, Baillargeon demonstrated that infants as young as 2½ months of age looked longer at the impossible event than at the possible event, suggesting that they had, indeed, formed mental representations of their past experiences with the habituation events. As you will see later in this chapter, developmentalists have used similar "magic tricks" to figure out what infants do and do not understand about the physical world.

Dynamic Systems Approach. While many developmentalists have focused on untangling infants' underlying conceptual competence from the performance demands of the tasks, Esther Thelen and her colleagues have offered an entirely different approach to thinking about the nature of knowledge and its development in infants (Thelen, Schoener, Scheier, & Smith, 2001). According to their *dynamic systems* perspective, it is unnecessary to invoke performance limitations to explain infants' failures on the A–not–B task, or to invoke mental concepts such as object permanence to account for infants' ultimate success. In their words, it is not the case that "there lives in the baby's head a creature that is smarter than the body it inhabits" (p. 3). Instead, Thelen and her colleagues view infants' behaviors on tests of object permanence—indeed, all human action in any context—as the result of the dynamics that emerge from the "immediate circumstances and the [individual's] history of perceiving and acting in similar circumstances" (p. 34). Thus, infants' experiences with specific objects, their current memory of those experiences, and their current motor skills all interact in their solving the specific problems posed by whatever task faces them. From this perspective, the critical developmental process is not a shift from sensorimotor intelligence to conceptual intelligence, as it is for Piaget. Rather, it is infants' growing abilities to better coordinate all the various systems involved in both sensorimotor and conceptual intelligence (looking, reaching, perceiving, remembering, and so on) required by the task at hand (Clearfield et al., 2006).

The Role of Experience. Noting that infants' performance on tests of object permanence is highly sensitive to the particulars of the test itself—such as the search method (reaching or looking) and the amount of time between hiding and searching—Jeanne Shinskey and Yuko Munakata (2005) wondered if infants gradually develop stronger representations of objects through their experience with them, and if stronger representations are required for some tasks than for others. In line with the dynamic system approach, the researchers asked about the *process* through which infants build mental representations, instead of focusing on whether, and at what age, infants reliably demonstrate the *capacity* to represent objects mentally. Reasoning that infants' representations of objects gradually strengthen as babies gain experience perceiving and interacting with them, Shinskey and Munakata predicted that object permanence would be stronger for familiar compared to novel objects.

To test their prediction, the researchers used a clever method in which 7-month-olds were presented with novel and familiar objects under "visible" and "hidden" conditions (Figure 5.16). In the "visible" condition, either a novel object or a familiar object was set in front of the babies (an object was made familiar by providing infants several opportunities to reach for it). Infants reached more for the novel object, demonstrating a preference for novelty. In the "hidden" condition— the condition that actually tests for object permanence—the babies were presented with the novel or familiar object and then the lights were turned off, shrouding the room, and the object, in darkness (the babies had been given some experience with the lights going out so that they wouldn't be surprised or scared during the test phase). In this hidden condition, the babies tended to reverse their previous novelty preference, reaching more for the familiar object than for the novel object.

What does this shift from a novelty preference in the visible condition to a familiarity preference in the hidden condition tell us about the process of forming mental representations? As Shinskey and Munakata point out, once infants have mastered information contained in one stimulus, seeking the novelty of a new stimulus is an adaptive strategy for acquiring new information about the world—a strategy that has likely evolved in our species because of its useful role in helping us explore, learn about, and respond to changes in our environments. When the infants in their study showed a preference for the novel object in the visible condition, they were demonstrating that they had processed the familiar object sufficiently well that it had become less interesting to explore, so they were more inclined to reach for the novel object. Furthermore, the fact that the infants were more inclined to reach for the familiar object in the hidden condition suggests that their experience with the object had helped them develop a stronger representation of it

Figure 5.16 Illustrating that mental representations become stronger with experience, 7-month-olds reach for a novel, rather than a familiar, object when both are visible, but reach for the familiar object when both are hidden.

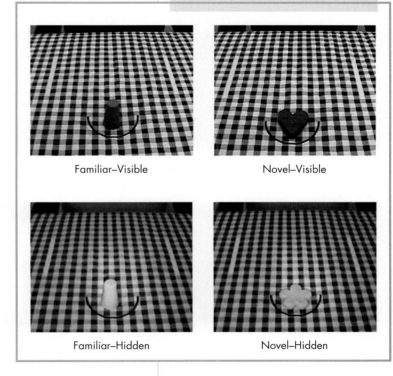

Familiar–Visible

Novel–Visible

Familiar–Hidden

Novel–Hidden

than of the novel object. It is evidence such as this that leads some developmentalists to argue that the formation of mental representations depends heavily on experience (Baillargeon, 2004; Johnson, Amso, & Slemmer, 2003; Kochukhova & Gredebäck, 2007). Thus, it seems likely that infants' developing representations and knowledge of the world is a joint consequence of human evolutionary processes and experiences available to babies in the specific cultural contexts in which they are brought up.

Developmentalists continue to debate questions about when object permanence emerges in development, and whether it is innate, learned through experience, or some combination of the two. As you will now see, these fundamental questions also inspire research on how infants understand other properties of the physical world.

Understanding Other Properties of the Physical World

There are, of course, properties of the physical world other than the fact that objects continue to exist when out of sight. As adults, we are so thoroughly familiar with the properties of our physical world that is it easy for us to overlook their significance for our behavior and development. We walk around obstacles rather than attempting to walk through them; we expect an apple that falls from a tree to land on the ground, and not fly around crazily and hit someone on the nose; we may playfully smack a friend with a pillow but would never do so with a brick; when we reach into the back of a closet, we expect to find a wall, not the land of Narnia.

From where does our knowledge of the physical world come? Are we born with knowledge that objects are solid and conform to physical laws, such as the law of gravity, or does that knowledge emerge from experience? By what process do we come to reason about objects, recognizing that they can be counted, for example, that there are often cause-and-effect relationships between them, or that certain objects share some of their features with other objects and can be categorized accordingly? As with research on the permanence of objects, developmentalists have turned to infants to explore these fundamental questions. And, as with research on the permanence of objects, they have often used the violations-of-expectations method, generally in the form of cleverly crafted magic tricks, to good advantage (Figure 5.17).

A number of such experiments found that between 3 and 9 months of age, and sometimes earlier, infants appear to have at least an initial grasp of a wide variety of physical laws concerning the behavior of objects. An early experiment in a series carried out by Renée Baillargeon and her colleagues (Baillargeon, 2001) tested whether young infants would expect an object that is suspended unsupported in midair to fall (Needham & Baillargeon, 1993). The experimenters repeatedly presented 4½-month-old infants with the event shown at the top of Figure 5.18, in which a hand reaches out and places one block on another before withdrawing. Then they presented either an event that defies the law of gravity, in which the block is left dangling in midair as the hand withdraws (bottom

Figure 5.17 Studies using the violations-of-expectations method find that infants as young as 4 months of age look longer at events that violate certain physical laws, including that objects cannot move through solid obstructions, and that an object inside a container will move if the container is moved.

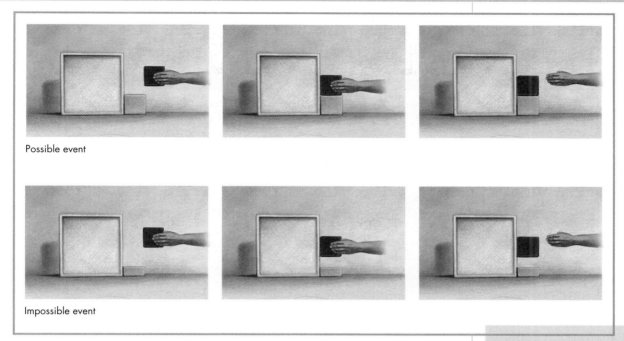

Possible event

Impossible event

Figure 5.18 Evidence that very young infants have some appreciation of the laws of gravity is demonstrated by the fact that they stare longer at impossible events, such as a block remaining suspended in air, than possible events, such as a hand placing an object on a table top.

part of Figure 5.18), or a control event (not shown), in which the hand withdraws partway and continues holding the block unsupported by the bottom block. Infants stared longer only in the case where the block appeared to be suspended in midair without any visible support, a response that indicated to the researchers that the babies expected the block to fall. Similar studies have demonstrated that by 4 months of age, infants appear to believe that objects cannot move through a solid physical obstruction and to believe that if a container with an object inside is moved, the object will move with it (see Figure 5.17) (Spelke, Breinlinger, Macomber & Jacobson, 1992; Baillargeon, 2004).

Reasoning about Objects

An important part of Piaget's theory about knowledge of objects is that even after children begin to be aware of the physical properties of objects, they cannot reason about those objects, for example, they cannot count them, understand cause–effect relations between them, or categorize them according to some feature they have in common.

Counting The question of whether young babies can count was addressed by Karen Wynn (1992), who showed 4-month-old infants the events depicted in Figure 5.19. First, a mouse doll was placed on an empty stage while the baby watched. Then a screen was raised to hide the doll from the baby's view. Next, the baby saw a hand holding a doll identical to the first doll go behind the screen and then reappear without the doll. The screen was then lowered, in half the trials revealing two dolls (the possible outcome) and in the other half revealing only one doll (the impossible outcome). The infants looked longer when there was only one doll, suggesting that they had mentally calculated the number of dolls that ought to be behind the screen. Similarly, when the experiment began with two dolls on the stage and the hand removed one doll from behind the screen, the infants seemed surprised when the screen was lowered to reveal two dolls.

Interestingly, babies seem to "match" number across sensory modalities (see the discussion of intermodal perception, Chapter 4, pp. 138–140). For example, when

Figure 5.19 After 4-month-olds observe the sequence of events depicted at the top of the figure, they show surprise when the screen is removed and only one mouse remains. Apparently the babies not only remember the presence of the first mouse hidden behind the screen but mentally add the second mouse and expect to see it. (After Wynn, 1992.)

Object placed on stage Screen comes up Second object placed behind screen Hand leaves, empty

Outcomes

Possible Impossible

Screen drops . . . revealing 2 objects Screen drops . . . revealing 1 object

7-month-olds hear a recording of three voices speaking, they will look longer at a video that shows three faces than at a video that shows only two (Figure 5.20). Such experiments appear to demonstrate that infants are capable of making simple arithmetical calculations in their heads far ahead of Piaget's timetable regarding their ability to reason about objects.

However, as with other research suggesting precocious, possibly innate, infant abilities (such as whether infants understand the permanence of objects), research claiming to demonstrate that infants can count has not gone unchallenged. For example, Leslie Cohen and Kathryn Marks (2002) found that the infants looked longer the more objects there were and that they looked longer at a familiar display, no matter how many objects were in it. As with research on infants' understanding of object permanence, developmentalists are still working to reach conclusions about competence based on performance, in this case wondering whether young babies are truly able to count objects or only appear to do so in the context of specific tasks.

Cause–Effect Relationships Another way of reasoning about the physical world is through cause–effect relationships. Alan Leslie and his colleagues have contended that primitive knowledge about physical causality is innate and does not require

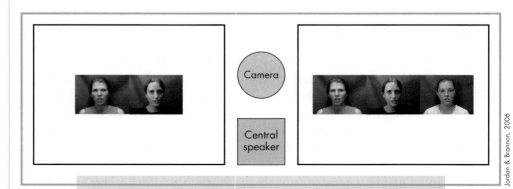

Camera

Central speaker

Jordan & Brannon, 2006

Figure 5.20 When 7-month-old infants hear a recording of three voices speaking (coming through the central speaker), they look longer at a video showing three people speaking than a video showing two people speaking, suggesting that they are capable of simple mathematical calculations.

prior experience of the world to develop (Leslie, 1994, 2002). In an experiment to test this idea, they presented 6-month-olds (the youngest infants they could test reliably) with two computer displays in which one small square appeared to bump into a second square, which then moved. In one, *causal* version, the second square moved immediately, an event that adults perceive as the result of its being bumped by first square. In the other, *noncausal* version, there was a delay in the movement of the second square, suggesting an absence of causation. The researchers showed the infants the causal version several times in a row. Then they showed them either a different causal event or the noncausal version. The infants stared longer at the noncausal event, thus supporting Leslie's contention that they were sensitive to causality as it is manifested in these simplified circumstances, even though the event did not involve their own actions.

Leslie's claim that understanding cause–effect relationships is innate has not gone unchallenged. For example, Lisa Oakes and Leslie Cohen (1990) found that when they replaced Leslie's simple squares with realistic objects in the experiment, 6-month-old infants appeared overwhelmed and no longer could respond on the basis of causality. Such results support the idea that the infants are learning to infer causality and will display such knowledge only under properly arranged circumstances (Cohen, Chaput, & Cashon, 2002)—yet another reminder of the competence–performance debate so central to research on infant cognition.

Categorizing It must be bedtime in 2-year-old Sylvie's playroom. She has put her Dora doll under a cover, along with Bitty Kitty and Pooh Bear. Excluded from the makeshift bed, however, are several other toys that she had just been playing with, among them Dora's truck and Pooh Bear's honey pot. Sylvie has appropriately categorized her toys into two groups: those that need sleep and those that do not.

The process of categorizing, of seeing similarities in different objects and events, is an essential feature of how we make sense of the world. Without the ability to categorize, we would need to learn from scratch about each new detail of our experience. We would not be able to apply knowledge gained in one situation to another, similar situation, and learning about the world would obviously be a very slow and inefficient process. The adults of our species, however, are incredibly adept at categorization. Developmentalists are interested in when this ability emerges and how it changes over time.

Infants display an ability to form categories remarkably early in life. For example, if 3-month-olds are shown a series of pairs of pictures of different cats and then shown a pair consisting of a picture of a cat and a picture of a dog, the infants will look longer at the picture of the dog than they will at the picture of the new cat (Figure 5.21). This preferential looking indicates that the infants had formed a category for what they had been viewing and that a dog did not fit it (Quinn, Eimas, & Rosenkrantz, 1993; Quinn & Eimas, 1996). Brain studies have shown that when young babies form categories, the electrical activity of their brains changes in ways that suggest that basic neurological processes have evolved that support early categorizing abilities (Quinn, Westerland, & Nelson, 2006).

Most research on categorization, however, has been conducted with somewhat older infants and has focused on the bases infants use to form categories. Do they rely primarily on perceptual similarities—that is, on similarities in how objects look, feel, or sound—or are they able to categorize according to more abstract, conceptual features, such as how objects function or behave? The framing of this question may remind you of the general theme that has permeated much of our discussion of infant intelligence: the extent to which an infant's knowledge is primarily perceptual and sensorimotor in nature, or also abstract and conceptual.

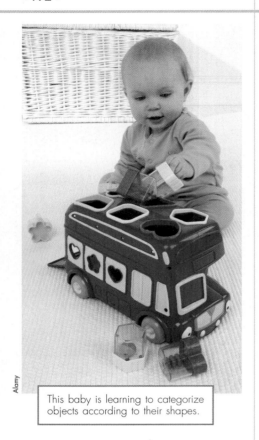

This baby is learning to categorize objects according to their shapes.

Figure 5.21 Three-month-old babies shown a sequence of pictures of cats are surprised when they see a picture of a dog, indicating that they are sensitive to the category of cats.

Trial 1

Trial 2

Trial 3

Test trial

In an early effort to identify the features babies use when they categorize, Jean Mandler and Laraine McDonough (1993) found that 7-month-olds, but not 9- to 11-month-olds, responded to toy birds and toy airplanes as if they were members of the same category. The 9- to 11-month-olds treated toy birds and airplanes as members of different categories despite the perceptual similarities—the toy birds all had outstretched wings and looked like the airplanes (Figure 5.22). Although this research suggests a developmental shift from infants' reliance on perceptual cues to an ability to use more general object features, it nevertheless challenges Piaget's view that infant intelligence is of a sensorimotor nature until 18 or so months of age.

Further evidence that infants form conceptual categories before the first year comes from an intriguing study of "generalized imitation" (Mandler & McDonough, 1996; Mandler, 2004). In this study, 9- and 11-month-old babies observed an adult model performing an action appropriate either to the category of animals or to the category of vehicles—for example, giving a toy dog a drink, or turning a key in a toy car door (Figure 5.23). Then the dog or the car was put away, and a different item was brought out and placed next to the prop (the cup or the key). Sometimes the new item was from the same category as the previous one (a bunny was set next to the cup, or a truck was set next to the key); sometimes it was from the other category (the bunny was set next to the key, or the truck next to the cup). The researchers found that the babies would give the bunny a drink, but not the truck, and likewise would use the key with the truck, but not the bunny. That is, while the babies were likely to imitate the action with the appropriate object, they rarely performed the action on the item from the incorrect category.

There is still uncertainty among developmentalists about the basis for the changes in categorization observed across infancy. Some researchers believe that perceptual similarity remains fundamental to category formation for the entire period. Thus, older infants show improved categorization skills because their sensory systems are more developed and they have greater experience, making them sensitive to more subtle cues (Quinn, 2002). Others believe that before the end of the first year, infants become capable of forming genuine conceptual categories—categories based on such meaningful features as what things do and how they come to be the way they are—in addition to perceptual categories (Mandler, 2004). Taking an information-processing approach, Leslie Cohen and his colleagues have argued that young infants form categories on the basis of specific object features or parts (for example, objects go together because they have wings), but around 10 months of age become capable of processing *relations* among features (objects with wings and feathers are one category; objects with wings and metal are another) (Cohen et al., 2006).

Although developmentalists are continuing to test different theories about how infants form categories, it is clear that by the end of infancy, babies are able to use them to organize their own behavior in relation to their environments, as did Sylvie when she put some of her toys to bed but not others.

APPLY · CONNECT · DISCUSS —

Design an experiment to test whether infants understand the difference between "natural" objects (trees, fish, people, etc.), and "artificial" objects (cars, watches, buildings, etc.).

Jean Mandler and Laraine McDonough

Figure 5.22 Seven-month-old babies treat plastic toy birds or airplanes, which are perceptually similar, as if they were members of the same category. Babies 9 to 11 months old treat them as members of different categories, despite their perceptual similarity.

Figure 5.23 Illustrating the ability to categorize objects, when 7- to 11-month-old babies observe an adult give a toy dog a drink (a), they will not imitate the action with a toy truck (b), but will imitate the adult's action with a toy bunny (c).

The Growth of Attention and Memory

Although we have not yet discussed it specifically, the baby's ability to pay attention to and remember specific aspects of the environment clearly plays an important role in many of the developments described above. Obviously, before babies can figure out whether the wing has feathers or is made of metal, they first need to attend to the object. And it would be impossible for babies to understand cause–effect relationships if, as they were watching some effect, they could not remember the earlier event that caused it.

Developing Attention

The process of attention appears to involve four distinct phases that can be distinguished by changes in infants' heart rates (Figure 5.24) (Courage, Reynolds, & Richards, 2006).

Phase I: Stimulus-Detection Reflex. The stimulus–detection reflex reflects the baby's initial awareness of some change in the environment. In this phase (not labeled in the figure), there is a very brief slowing and then quickening of the heart rate.

Phase II: Stimulus Orienting. During the second phase, the baby's attention becomes fixed on the stimulus. As you can see in the figure, the heart rate slows considerably during this period.

Phase III: Sustained Attention. In the third phase, the heart rate remains slow as the baby cognitively processes the stimulus. The baby's entire body may become still, and it is relatively more difficult to distract the baby with a new stimulus (Richards, 2003). Sustained attention is believed to be a voluntary state; that is, the baby purposefully controls and focuses his or her attention on the stimulus. At this point, the baby is truly *paying attention*.

Phase IV: Attention Termination. In this phase, the baby is still looking at the object but is no longer processing its information (it takes a moment to break contact with the stimulus). The heart rate begins to return to pre-stimulus levels.

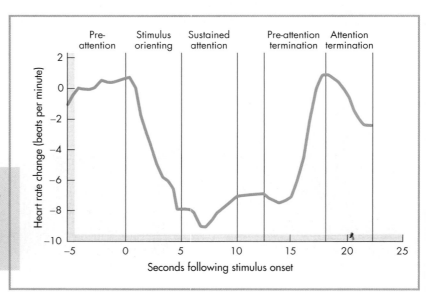

Figure 5.24 Attention is a process involving four phases that can be distinguished by changes in the infant's heart rate. As shown here, the heart rate drops considerably when the infant is engaged in sustained attention.

From the descriptions of these phases, you can imagine why developmentalists are particularly interested in the development of sustained attention. It is the attention phase in which babies actively learn about and remember their experiences. At 3 months of age, babies can sustain their attention only for periods of 5 to 10 seconds. Certainly, one of the most significant developments in the first 2 years is infants' increasing ability to focus their attention in this way.

In addition to getting better at focusing their attention, over the course of the first 2 years, babies get faster at processing information about the targets of their attention. Show a 1-year-old a picture of a bunny, and he is likely to stare with rapt attention for a long period of time. Show the same picture to a 2-year-old, and he may look at it for a few seconds and be done with it. He has processed it, has recognized it, and is ready to turn his attention elsewhere. We know it is not the case that the 1-year-old has better sustained attention than the 2-year-old. Rather, the 1-year-old needs more time to process the information. Indeed, research indicates that with increasing age, there is a decrease in the amount of time that babies will spend looking at simple patterns or figures (Figure 5.25a). It has even been found that 6-month-olds who spend relatively long periods of time looking at simple patterns tend to have lower IQs when they are tested at the age of 11 (Rose et al., 2004). Among other things, all of this means that care must be taken not to confuse *visual attention* (how the baby processes information) with *visual fixation* (the amount of time the baby looks at an object).

While infants' attention to simple visual displays decreases after the first few months of life, attention to complex stimuli increases. Figure 5.25b illustrates the amount of time babies of different ages, ranging from 6 to 24 months, looked at two different videotapes. One videotape showed a computer-generated display of simple geometric patterns. The other was a segment from *Sesame Street*. All of the babies spent about the same amount of time watching the computer-generated film, whereas clear age differences were evident for the *Sesame Street* segment.

As we mentioned earlier, the development of attention, especially focused, sustained attention, is of enormous significance to the infant's emerging ability to remember past events and learn about the environment, a topic that we address next.

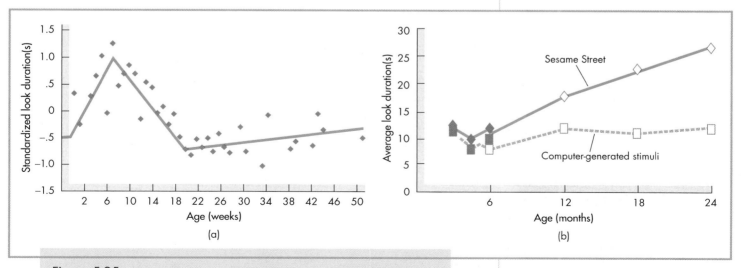

Figure 5.25 Between 6 and 22 weeks of age, there is a significant decline in the amount of time that infants will look at simple geometric figures (a). Between 6 and 24 months of age, however, there is a significant increase in the amount of time that infants will look at complex stimuli, such as Sesame Street videotapes, whereas the amount of time spent looking at simple figures remains stable (b).

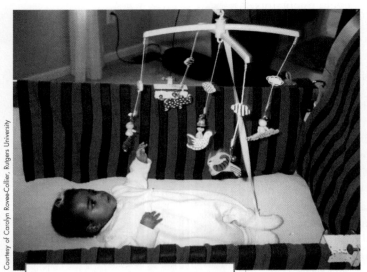

Courtesy of Carolyn Rovee-Collier, Rutgers University

Figure 5.26 Because of the ribbon tied between her ankle and the mobile overhead, this 3-month-old will learn that kicking causes the mobile to move. Research indicates that for several days, she is likely to remember what she learned about the mobile. However, she will probably be at least 6 months old before she can remember the task for 2 or more weeks.

Developing Memory

Carolyn Rovee-Collier and her colleagues have demonstrated that infants' memory increases rapidly during the first year of life (Rovee-Collier & Barr, 2001). In one of their studies, for example, babies from 2 to 6 months were set in a laboratory crib and trained to kick in order to make an attractive mobile move—something they enjoyed watching. (As shown in Figure 5.26, one end of a string was tied to their ankles, and the other was attached to the mobile.) After the training, the babies were returned to the lab after delays of various durations to see if they remembered how to make the mobile move. The researchers found that 2-month-olds started kicking immediately following a 24-hour delay but seemed to forget the procedure if the delay lasted 3 days. Memory for the task was better in 3-month–olds and better yet in 6-month-olds, who remembered their training 2 weeks, although not 3 weeks, later. However, if infants are given a brief visual reminder, they can remember their earlier training much longer (Joh, Sweeney, & Rovee-Collier, 2002; Rovee-Collier et al., 1999).

In an extension of this research, infants from 6 to 18 months of age learned to press a lever to make a train move. As shown in Figure 5.27, with age there was a steady increase in the number of days that infants could remember their prior experiences (Hartshorn et al., 1998).

Rovee-Collier and her colleagues believe that the improvement in infant memory is a continuous process that does not involve any new principles of learning or remembering (Joh et al., 2002; Rovee-Collier, 1997). But just as there are developmentalists who believe that categorization shifts at around the end of the first year to include conceptual categories, so there are those who believe that a qualitative shift in memory occurs at the same time. According to this view, young infants move from relying on **implicit memory,** which allows them to *recognize* what they have experienced before, to acquiring the ability to use **explicit memory,** which allows them to *recall* ("call to mind") absent objects and events without any clear reminder (Bauer et al., 2003; Mandler, 1998).

Figure 5.27 The number of weeks that infants can remember a task climbs steadily and continuously between 2 and 18 months of age.

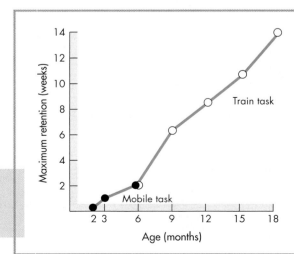

Explicit, or recall, memory is considered an especially important cognitive achievement because it seems to require the conscious generation of a mental representation for something that is not present to the senses. However, as with perceptual and conceptual categories, the task of distinguishing between implicit and explicit remembering in young infants is a tricky one. What is clear in any case is that developments in memory and attention are intertwined with the other cognitive achievements of the baby's first 2 years.

implicit memory The ability to recognize objects and events that have been previously experienced.

explicit memory The ability to recall absent objects and events without any clear reminder.

|||||| **APPLY · CONNECT · DISCUSS** -- -- -- -- -- -- -- -- -- -- -- -- -- --

In what ways might the changes in the brain discussed on pp. 165–168 contribute to the development of attention and memory during infancy?

Implications

It is truly astonishing that babies undergo such enormous physical and cognitive changes in such a brief period of time. Equally amazing are the implications that these changes have for future development. Already, as a consequence of synaptogenesis and selective pruning, the baby's neural pathways are taking shape according to both species-universal and individual experiences. Whereas the crucial biological events during the newborn period (Chapter 4) involved changes in the connections between the sensory cortex of the brain and the brain stem, the remaining months of infancy are marked by increased myelination of the prefrontal cortex associated with voluntary behavior and language, and myelination of pathways connecting different areas of the brain, which allows the brain to work in a more integrated way. Equally important are increases in height and weight, increases in the strength of muscles and bones, and a change in body proportion that shifts the baby's center of gravity—all of which are necessary to support developing motor skills.

As we noted earlier, motor development appears to orchestrate the reorganization of many other functions that have been developing in parallel during infancy. For one thing, the acquisition of new motor skills leads infants to discover many properties of objects in their immediate environment. They become capable of reaching for objects efficiently and picking them up, feeling them, tasting them, moving around them, carrying them, and using them for various purposes of their own. Their growing autonomy and ability to explore the world advances further as gross motor skills emerge, especially the uniquely human form of locomotion—walking.

These experiences would not amount to much, however, if babies were not able to represent them mentally or to remember them. As we mentioned, the capacity to represent objects, people, events, and experiences mentally exerts a powerful influence on other areas of development which we explore in detail in later chapters, including symbolic play, imitation, and language. Indeed, as you will learn in later chapters, mental representation plays a pivotal role in how children make use of the material and symbolic tools of their culture. In the next chapter, we address the social and emotional domains of infancy and how they enter into the biocultural equation of children's development.

SUMMARY

Physical Growth

- Height and weight increase rapidly throughout infancy, especially during the first year. Proportions shift, too, with the head coming to account for relatively less of the infant's length, the legs for relatively more. Soft bones gradually ossify, and muscle mass increases. Although boys tend to be larger, girls tend to develop more quickly.

Brain Development

- Increased myelination of neurons, along with other changes, leads to substantial development of the cerebral cortex, including the prefrontal and language-related areas, and to greater synchrony among the brain areas. These changes appear vital to the emergence in late infancy of more systematic problem solving, voluntary control of behavior, and acquisition of language. By late infancy, most of the brain structures that will support adult behavior are present.

- As shown by studies of Romanian orphans who were adopted, prolonged deprivation in infancy leads to ongoing impairments in intellectual functioning. Because the brain undergoes considerable development between 6 and 24 months, lack of experiences during this sensitive period appears to affect both experience-expectant and experience-dependent brain development.

Motor Development

- Made possible by physical changes, development of fine and gross motor skills enables infants to increasingly explore their environment and reduce their dependence on caregivers.

- During the first year, movements of the hands and fingers become better coordinated, and infants perfect their reaching and grasping. With continuing increases in coordination of fine motor movements, by age 2 infants can do much to feed and dress themselves and can turn book pages, cut paper, string beads, and stack blocks.

- Progress in locomotion leads to the emergence of crawling by 8–9 months, at which time wariness of heights appears. Walking begins at around 1 year, and is made possible by the development of component motor skills and by practice. Studies in different cultures reveal that practice or lack of it can affect the age at which infants reach motor milestones.

- Cultural factors affect the timing of learning to control elimination, but, although young infants can learn to eliminate when placed on the potty, for maturational reasons gaining sufficient control over bladder and bowel functions to stay dry at night generally is not possible before age 3½.

Cognitive Development: The Great Debate

- For some developmentalists, including Piaget, young infants are limited to sensorimotor intelligence until about 18 months, when they become capable of representational thinking—thinking that is truly conceptual.

- For other developmentalists, very early in development, if not from birth, infants are capable of representing and understanding the world conceptually. A rudimentary conceptual system develops separate from, although in close association with, the sensorimotor system.

Sensorimotor Development

- In Piaget's stage of sensorimotor development, infants acquire knowledge exclusively through motor actions directed at their immediate environment and guided by their senses.

- Following the first two substages, in which infants learn to control reflexes and then to modify and repeat actions involving their bodies, infants move through four additional sensorimotor substages:

  - In substage 3, infants of 4 to 8 months become capable of secondary circular reactions, repeating actions that involve objects, not simply their own body.

  - In substage 4, at 8 to 12 months, infants begin to display intentionality, engaging in goal-directed behavior.

  - In substage 5, the stage of tertiary circular reactions, infants of 12 to 18 months deliberately vary their actions, thus experimenting in order to explore the world.

  - In substage 6, between 18 and 24 months, infants begin to base their actions on representations. The ability to represent mentally is crucial to problem solving, symbolic play, deferred imitation, and the use of language.

- The sequence and timing of the behaviors associated with Piaget's sensorimotor stages have been replicated with infants in a wide range of societies. However, critics of Piaget argue that young infants have representational competence that traditional Piagetian tests do not enable them to reveal.

Conceptual Development

- For Piaget, object permanence—the understanding that objects continue to exist when out of sight—emerges only gradually, beginning at about 8 months. Thus, 8- to 12-month-old infants continue to search for an object in a location where they discovered it even when they have then seen it re-hidden in a different location. Piaget claimed that these infants still did not have true representations. Other developmentalists have argued that the infants' behavior reflects not a lack of representational competence but performance problems—specifically, memory limitations or a tendency to perseverate, repeating the same movement or the same successful strategy.

- Using the violation-of-expectations method, in which babies are habituated to an event and then presented with possible and impossible variants, researchers have obtained results suggesting that infants as young as 2½ months are capable of representations.

- According to the dynamic systems approach, cognitive development in infancy involves not a shift from sensorimotor to conceptual intelligence but growing abilities to coordinate all the various systems involved in sensorimotor and conceptual intelligence.

- The formation of representations may depend heavily on experience: In experiments, infants' preference for a familiar object over an unfamiliar object is reversed when the room is darkened, perhaps because experience with an object had led to a stronger representation of it.

- Experiments using the violation-of-expectations method suggest that infants as young as 3 months have an initial grasp of various physical laws concerning the behavior of objects, such as the law of gravity.

- Other experiments using simplified tests suggest that, contrary to Piaget's view, young infants may be capable of understanding basic numbers and cause–effect relationships. Of particular interest is infants' abilities to categorize, evident as early as 3 months. Developmentalists are uncertain whether changes in categorization abilities during infancy simply reflect improved perceptual abilities or signal a change from categorization based only on perceptual features to categorization that is also conceptually based.

The Growth of Attention and Memory

- Developments in attention and memory are crucial to all the other cognitive changes of infancy.

- Infants are increasingly able to sustain their attention; in addition, they are increasingly fast at processing information about the targets of their attention. These changes are reflected in experiments showing that attention to simple visual displays decreases after the first few months but attention to complex stimuli increases.

- Memory increases rapidly during the first year, as shown by the increasing length of time for which infants are able to remember procedures such as how to make a mobile move. The improvement may involve simply a continuous process or may reflect a shift from reliance on implicit memory (recognizing what has been experienced before) to explicit memory (recalling absent objects and events without a reminder). Explicit memory is an important cognitive achievement because it requires generating a mental representation for something not present to the senses.

Implications

- Infancy is a brief period of enormous physical and cognitive changes with enormous implications for development in other domains and for future development. Brain development and increases in height and weight support developing motor skills, which help make the cognitive changes possible. Among cognitive changes crucial to development are the growing capacity to represent mentally and to remember.

Key Terms

6

Social and Emotional Development in Infancy

In a creaky bus bumping along the highway from the airport to the city of Changsha, China, Jeff and Christine take in the passing scenes of marshy rice paddies and smokestacks. They want to remember this landscape so they can describe it someday to their 2-year-old daughter, Jin Yu, whom they are about to meet for the first time. They arrive at a hotel with 25 other new parents from America, all waiting to receive their children. One by one the children are handed over. And one by one they wail in protest. But not Jin Yu. And this disturbs Jeff and Christine. In preparing for this life-altering moment, they learned that such tears are a sign that the child has formed attachments to his or her orphanage caregivers and is therefore capable of forming new attachments to the adoptive parents. Jeff and Christine take Jin Yu to their hotel room, where she sits on the bed, silent and lethargic. They talk to her in soothing tones, stroke her, smile, and reassure her that all is well. But Jin Yu seems untouched and is unresponsive. Jeff and Christine become increasingly concerned. How long has she been like this—so socially and emotionally disconnected? Is her condition temporary or permanent? Then Jeff and Christine discover a ragged scar running across her head. They are frightened—for Jin Yu and for themselves. But she is their daughter now, and committed to this fact, they brace themselves for the unknowable. Back in the United States, doctors relieve their fears; the scar was probably a wound that became infected, but there is no evidence of permanent damage. Most reassuring, however, is Jin Yu's own rapid development. Within 6 months, she has grown 5 inches and gained 5 pounds, and she is taking an avid interest and obvious joy in her toys and playmates. If she becomes frustrated because her parents won't let her handle a cup of hot coffee or a steak knife, she makes an angry face, slams down her hand, and scolds them in Chinese. She has begun speaking in English, too. She requests, "Fries, please," and exclaims, "All done!" And she hums little melodies to herself. Jeff and Christine take great comfort in knowing that someone took time to sing to their baby. Perhaps a caregiver they would never know gave them and Jin Yu the foundation for building loving relationships in their new life together.

(Adapted from Gammage, 2003.)

aced with Jin Yu's initial lack of social and emotional responsiveness, Jeff and Christine were rightly distraught. The ability to respond to others socially and emotionally is crucial to human development because it draws children into the lives of others—and into contact with their knowledge and values, goals and desires, and cultural activities and practices (Trevarthen & Reddy, 2007).

Although we cannot be sure why Jin Yu was so unresponsive and "disconnected" at first, it is clear that within months of her adoption, she has developed a rich emotional life that includes feelings such as interest, joy, anger, and frustration. It is equally clear that she communicates these feelings effectively to others through gesture, facial expression, and language. She has become actively engaged in a social and emotional world that is, most importantly, *shared*.

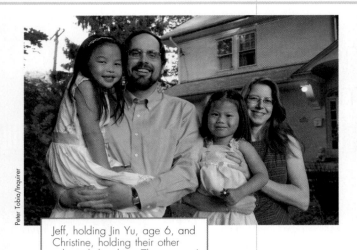

Peter Tobia/Inquirer

Jeff, holding Jin Yu, age 6, and Christine, holding their other adopted daughter, Zhao, age 4.

This chapter explores fundamental developments in the social and emotional lives of babies. We will discuss the range of infants' emotions and where they come from, as well as infants' emotional attachments to caregivers and how they can be affected by experience. We will also examine the changing nature of communication—how babies share their emotions, needs, and interests with others and become interactive partners in an ever-widening sphere of social life. As you will see, the fundamental social and emotional developments of the first 2 years are nurtured and shaped by interacting biological and cultural processes. Thus, some of these developments are universal and deeply rooted in the evolution of our species, and others are specific to the local contexts of children's development.

The Nature of Infant Emotions and Emotional Expressions

When in everyday conversation we talk about emotions, we are usually referring to the feelings aroused by an experience—feelings of happiness and excitement on unexpectedly winning a prize, of sadness on saying good-bye to a loved one whom we will not see for some time, of frustration and anger on being prevented from achieving a goal. But when we think deeply about what it is like to truly *feel* an emotion, it becomes clear that we are dealing with a process of enormous complexity. Our heart pounds; we catch our breath; our palms sweat; we shout or moan; we run away from or rush toward the source of our arousal. Recognizing the complexity of emotion, developmentalists typically define it in terms of the following features (Saarni, Campos, Camras, & Witherington, 2006):

- *A physiological aspect.* Emotions are accompanied by identifiable physiological reactions such as changes in heart rate, breathing, and hormonal functioning.

- *A communicative function.* Emotions communicate our internal feeling states to others through facial expressions, vocalizations, and other distinctive forms of behavior.

- *A cognitive aspect.* The emotions we feel depend upon how we appraise what is happening to us.

- *An action aspect.* Emotions are a source of action. When something causes joy, for example, we laugh or cry or do both at once. When we are scared, we withdraw.

Despite the ease with which we express and share our feelings, developmentalists recognize that emotions are remarkably complex.

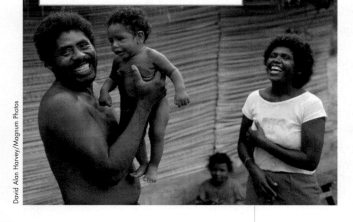

David Alan Harvey/Magnum Photos

Technically speaking then, **emotion** can be defined as a feeling state that involves distinctive physiological responses and cognitive evaluations that motivate action (Saarni et al., 2006). But even this technically comprehensive definition of emotion fails to capture the complexity of the phenomenon fully. Emotions, for example, can emerge slowly, as when a feeling of pleasure blossoms into full-blown elation, or they can emerge rapidly, as in an explosive rage. Emotions can vary in their intensity, as indicated by the different smiles shown in Figure 6.1. Sometimes emotions mix together, as in the joy and sadness many parents feel when their children go off to college. Complicating things further is the fact that people have ways of controlling the emergence and intensity of their own and others' emotions. When an older brother tries to distract his fussy

Oster, 2005

Figure 6.1 Various emotional intensities are clearly apparent in the different smiles shown by this baby.

baby sister with a toy, he is attempting to control her emotions; when the baby sister soothes herself by sucking on her pacifier, she is controlling her own emotions, although probably not intentionally. **Emotion regulation** is the term used by developmentalists to describe how people act to modulate and control emotions. In the sections below, we explore developmental changes in infants' emotions, their expression, and how they are regulated.

Theories of Emotional Development

Most developmentalists agree that there are universal **basic emotions**—joy, fear, anger, surprise, sadness, and disgust—that are expressed in similar ways in all cultures and, for the most part, from birth. For example, adults from vastly different cultures generally agree on which facial expressions represent happiness, sadness, anger, and disgust, and are fairly adept at identifying basic emotions in infants' facial expressions (Figure 6.2; Ekman, 1999). Similarly, research finds that the smiles, distaste expressions and cry faces of babies in different cultures are comparable to those of adults (Camras et al., 2007).

emotion A feeling state that involves distinctive physiological reactions and cognitive evaluations, and motivates action.

emotion regulation Ways of acting to modulate and control emotions.

basic emotions Joy, fear, anger, surprise, sadness, disgust—universal emotions, expressed similarly in all cultures and present at birth or in the early months.

All photos: Carroll Izard

(a)   (b)   (c)   (d)

(e)   (f)   (g)   (h)

Figure 6.2 Images from a videotaped recording of infants' facial expressions used by Carroll Izard and his colleagues to assess the possible universal relation between emotion and facial expression. What emotion do you think each facial expression represents? The responses most of Izard's adult subjects gave are printed upside down below. (Izard et al., 1980.)

(a) joy; (b) anger; (c) sadness; (d) disgust; (e) distress/pain; (f) interest; (g) fear; (h) surprise

Taken together, the cross-cultural and infant research are considered strong evidence for the widely held belief that the basic emotions represent universal adaptive responses that are generated by, and contribute to, the biological and cultural evolution of our species (Panksepp, 2003). From a biological perspective, the basic emotions and their expression both protect children from potential sources of danger and ensure that their basic needs are met, largely by eliciting care and protection. From a cultural perspective, these emotions facilitate social connections to family and community members—connections that are vital to learning about the world and acquiring cultural knowledge and values (Trevarthan, 2005; Tronick, 2005). Indeed, according to Vygotsky's sociocultural theory, introduced in Chapter 1 (pp. 23–24), all complex forms of reasoning and understanding develop as a consequence of the connections formed between individuals (1978).

Although there is consensus on the biological and cultural significance of human emotions generally, developmentalists disagree on several fundamental issues regarding the nature of emotion and its development during infancy. One controversy concerns whether infants' emotions are, from early on, similar to those of adults, or whether they become increasingly adultlike over time. In other words, do infants, like adults, experience distinct emotions such as joy, sorrow, fear, anger, and so on, or does the capacity to feel these specific emotions emerge in the course of infancy and childhood? The second controversy concerns the source of new emotions. That is, assuming that at least some emotions experienced by adults are not present from birth (shame, guilt, and pride are clear examples), do new emotions emerge from more global positive or negative feeling states, or do they emerge full-blown, without precursors, at specific periods of development? We will now consider three different views of early emotional development, each of which takes a different perspective on these two controversial issues.

Theory of Gradual Differentiation

According to the **theory of gradual differentiation,** infants are born with the capacity to express only general emotional reactions that are simply positive or negative. Over the course of the first 2 years, these general reactions—contentment or distress, according to one early theorist (Bridges, 1932)—gradually differentiate into the basic emotions described above. Note that this view emphasizes the *discontinuity* of emotional expression: A young baby's crying signals a general feeling of distress, whereas that of an older infant may be expressing sadness or anger (Sroufe, 2005). The theory of gradual differentiation held sway for many years until it was challenged by a new theory called *differential emotions theory*.

Differential Emotions Theory

Rejecting the view that distinct emotions gradually emerge from general emotional states, Carroll Izard and his colleagues proposed that the basic emotions are biologically innate and present at birth in essentially adultlike form (Izard & Abe, 2004). They called their theory **differential emotions theory** to highlight the idea that infants' early emotions represent a set of distinct emotions comparable to those experienced by adults. In support of their argument, they point to the cross-cultural studies described above which find that people from widely different cultures use similar facial expressions to signal basic emotions and that many infant facial expressions are similar to those of adults. On this view, biology dictates the presence of distinct emotions at birth; the timing at which new, adultlike emotions such as guilt and shame emerge during infancy and childhood (more on this below); as well as the increasing ability to control and regulate emotions (for example, emotion regulation is associated with prefrontal cortex development, which, as you may recall from Chapter 5, is associated with a variety of voluntary behaviors [Panksepp & Smith-Pasqualini, 2005; Trevarthan, 2005]).

theory of gradual differentiation The view that infants are born only with general emotional reactions, which differentiate into basic emotions over the first 2 years.

differential emotions theory The view that basic emotions are innate and emerge in their adult form, either at birth or on a biologically determined timetable.

ontogenetic adaptation Something that has evolved because it contributes to survival and normal development; in one view, infant emotions are ontogenetic adaptations.

primary intersubjectivity Organized, reciprocal interaction between an infant and caregiver with the interaction itself as the focus.

Emotions as Ontogenetic Adaptations The two theories just described tend to focus on whether the basic emotions felt and expressed *by adults* are present from birth or whether they differentiate from general emotional states and gradually become more adultlike. In contrast, the *ontogenetic adaptations* view of emotions takes the infant, rather than the adult, as its starting point (Oster, 2005). According to this perspective, infants' emotions and emotional expressions are **ontogenetic adaptations,** meaning that they have evolved because they contribute to infants' survival and development. Therefore, these developmentalists focus on the circumstances or situations in which babies experience and express different emotions (for example, on the sorts of situations that provoke feelings of fear or joy), and on the ways infants' emotional expressions affect their interactions with their caregiver (Oster, 2005). An illustrative example is the changing nature of the infant's smile.

This very young Congolese infant is demonstrating an endogeneous smile, which was probably a reaction to internal physiological fluctuations.

During the first weeks of life, the corners of a baby's mouth often curl up in a facial expression that looks just like a smile. Most likely to occur when the infant is asleep or very drowsy, these early smiles are called *endogenous smiles* because they seem to be associated with internal, physiological fluctuations rather than with external stimulation from the environment. However, between 1 and 2 months of age, infants begin to smile in response to mild perceptual stimulation, such as when a caregiver talks softly to them or lightly strokes their skin. Then, between 2 and 3 months of age, the infant's smile becomes truly social, both responding to and eliciting the smiles of others. At this point, parents report a new emotional quality in their relationship with their child. The significance of the emergence of the social smile as a marker of a new level of development is reflected in a special celebratory ritual traditionally practiced by the Navajo. When an infant first displays the smile

> [t]he baby's hands are held out straight by the mother, and some member of the family (usually a brother or a sister) puts a pinch of salt with bread and meat upon them . . . . The person who sees the baby smile first should give a present (with salt) to all members of the family. The father or mother will kill a sheep and distribute this among relatives along with a bit of salt for each piece. (Leighton & Kluckhohn, 1947/1969, p. 29)

According to the theory of emotions as ontogenetic adaptations, the changing nature of smiling during these early months of postnatal life demonstrates both continuities and discontinuities in infants' emotions, their origins, and the meanings they have for social interaction.

Infant Emotions and Social Life

> *His eyes locked onto hers for a silent and almost motionless instant, until the mother said "Hey!" opened her eyes wider, raised her eyebrows further, and tossed her head up and toward the infant. Almost simultaneously the baby's eyes widened, his head tilted up, his smile broadened. Now she said, "Well hello! . . . hello . . . heeelloooo!" so that her pitch rose and the "hellos" became longer and more stressed on each successive repetition. With each phrase the baby expressed more pleasure, and his body resonated almost like a balloon being pumped up. (From Stern, 1977, p. 3)*

Around 2 months of age, babies begin to smile in response to the smiles of others. An example of such social smiling is illustrated by this African infant.

We mentioned that infants' emotions play a key role in connecting infants to their social world. The coordination of movement and mood apparent in the interaction described above—the emotional expression of one partner eliciting similar responses from the other—indicates that the mother and baby are each able to recognize and share the emotional state of the other. Colwyn Trevarthen (1998) labeled this kind of well-organized, reciprocal social interaction **primary intersubjectivity.** (It is "primary" in the sense that it is direct face-to-face interaction whose focus is the interaction itself.) The importance of maintaining primary intersubjectivity is nowhere more apparent than in circumstances in which it breaks down, as when interactions between the baby and caregiver are disorganized and out of synch. As we discuss below, the interruption of this synchronous, or coordinated, interaction can take place for a variety of reasons. Mothers who suffer from depression, for example, often have difficulty being emotionally responsive to their babies. But before we discuss such "naturally occurring" influences on primary intersubjectivity, let us first consider what has been found in laboratory settings, when developmentalists experimentally disrupt the emotional connection between babies and their interactive partners.

Figure 6.3 In the still-face method, after a few minutes of normal interaction, the mother is instructed to pose a "still face" and stop responding to her baby. The sequence here shows the baby becoming distressed, a typical reaction.

Edward Tronick, from Nadel & Muir (2005)

Manipulating Intersubjectivity in the Laboratory Developmentalists have experimentally manipulated the synchrony of social interactions in two ways. One of these involves a procedure known as the *still-face method* (Tronick et al., 2005; Tronick, 2007). In this procedure, after a few minutes of normal synchronous interaction with her infant, the mother is cued to pose a neutral "still face" and to stop responding to the baby (Figure 6.3). The other way of disrupting synchrony is by *delayed transmission,* a method that involves the use of TV monitors (Murray & Trevarthen, 1986; Tremblay et al., 2005). In this method, the mother and baby interact naturally and synchronously but they are seeing and hearing each other on the monitors. Periodically, the experimenters make transmissions from the mother's monitor run several seconds behind the baby's, so that her responses are out of synch with the infant's behavior (Figure 6.4). In both the still-face and delayed-transmission methods, babies as young as 2 months of age react to the loss of synchrony by averting their gaze and ceasing to smile. Frequently, the babies become agitated and fussy. These negative emotional responses have been found in babies interacting with mothers, fathers, and even complete strangers in several countries, including the United States, Canada, France, and China (Kisilevsky et al., 1998).

Figure 6.4 In the delayed-transmission method, mother and baby interact by observing each other on monitors, Initially, they see each other in "real time," so their interaction is coordinated and synchronized (a). After several moments, interactional synchrony is disrupted by making the mother's monitor run several seconds behind that of the baby. As illustrated in (b), most babies find this distressing.

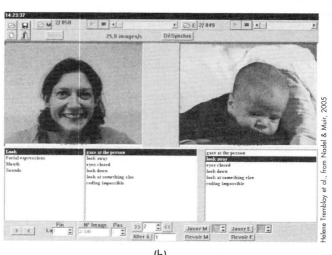

Helene Tremblay et al., from Nadel & Muir, 2005

(a)

(b)

Maternal Depression: An Obstacle to Intersubjectivity Disruptions in infant–caregiver synchrony of course are commonplace outside the lab: Caregivers can be distracted or otherwise busy; babies can be fussy or drowsy. Usually these disruptions are fleeting, and synchrony is quickly restored. However, there are circumstances in which infant–caregiver interactions are routinely disorganized and out of synch. For example, compared to non-depressed mothers, those who suffer from depression may be less sensitive to their infants' emotional cues. In addition to missing opportunities to share emotions, they may "transfer" their unresponsiveness to their babies (Field et. al., 2007a). Indeed, in the still-face procedure, infants of depressed mothers act quite differently than do those of nondepressed mothers (Field et al., 2007b). In particular, although they will avert their gaze when their depressed mothers "still face" (as do infants of nondepressed mothers), they do not fuss and protest. Helene Tremblay and her colleagues believe this reaction suggests not that the babies are undisturbed by their mothers' lack of responsiveness but that they have learned over time to disengage from stressful, unresponsive interactions with their mothers (Tremblay et al., 2005). Developmentalists speculate that many problems frequently observed in children of depressed mothers, such as anxiety and conduct disorders, are due to a history of disorganized and unresponsive emotional interactions (Pelaez et al., 2008).

Emotion Regulation to Maintain Intersubjectivity Based on evidence from the still-face and delayed-transmission methods, it seems that babies have a deeply ingrained need to be emotionally connected to others. Indeed, Harriet Oster (2005) has argued that this need for connection may account for a particularly interesting and very common infant behavior—pouting. Pouting is most common when the infant is just beginning to be upset. The pout is intriguing for two reasons. First, the facial muscles involved in pouting are diametrically opposed to the facial muscles that pull the mouth into a cry face (Figure 6.5), suggesting that pouting is not simply a component of crying. Second, pouting is typically "directed" at a social partner—that is, the baby's eyes tend to remain open and focused on the other individual. In crying, on the other hand, the eyes are usually shut, and the baby's behavior becomes too disorganized for coordinated social interaction. Oster believes that pouting reflects the baby's first efforts (not necessarily intentional) to regulate distress and thereby maintain the social contact that crying would otherwise disrupt. Advocating the position that infant emotions are ontogenetic adaptations, Oster suggests that pouting has evolved as part of an emotion-regulation process because it serves to interrupt intense crying (which can deplete oxygen and lead to physical exhaustion) and also signals the caregiver to provide comfort before the baby begins to cry uncontrollably (Oster, 2005, p. 284). Her account of the evolutionary origins of emotion regulation has its roots in Darwin's observation that some of our most characteristic facial expressions are related to crying and our efforts to control it (Darwin, 1872).

Oster, 2005

(a)   (b)

Figure 6.5 Pouting (a) may be one of the baby's first efforts to regulate distress by signaling to another that help is needed to avoid intense crying (b).

Wicker et al., 2003

Seeking evidence of mirror neurons, scientists compare how a person's brain reacts when the person has a particular experience to how it reacts when the person observes someone else having the experience. In the image shown here, the red color indicates brain activity in response to the individual feeling disgust; the blue indicates activity in response to observing another person express disgust; and the white shows areas of overlap between red and blue.

Intersubjectivity and the Brain

The growing emphasis on the evolutionary origins of emotions has led to an intensive effort to discover how the brain contributes to the experience, expression, and regulation of emotions in infancy. A breakthrough in this quest occurred in a laboratory in Italy on a hot summer day in 1991. A monkey with electrodes implanted in its brain to monitor its brain activity happened to observe a graduate student enter the lab with an ice cream cone. The monkey stared at him, and then the breakthrough moment occurred: When the student raised the cone to his lips, the monkey's brain monitor began registering as if the *monkey* were eating the cone. Subsequent research by Giacomo Rizzolatti, the neuroscientist who heads the laboratory, revealed the existence of special brain cells, called **mirror neurons,** that fire when an animal sees or hears another perform an action, just as they would if the animal were itself carrying out the action (Rizzolatti et al., 1996). Since then, neuroscientists have identified a variety of mirror neuron systems in the human brain that are much more complex and flexible than those found in the brains of monkeys, and which register the intentions and emotions of others as if they were happening to the person who is observing them. According to this evidence, we feel happy when those around us are happy, and sad when others are sad, because the emotional expressions of others trigger the activation of our mirror neurons.

The discovery of mirror neurons has revolutionized developmentalists' understanding of how infants connect emotionally with social partners. As Rizzolatti argued,

> *We are exquisitely social creatures. Our survival depends on understanding the actions, intentions, and emotions of others. Mirror neurons allow us to grasp the minds of others not through conceptual reasoning but through direct stimulation. By feeling, not by thinking. (In Blakeslee, 2006)*

Indeed, Andrew Meltzoff and Jean Decety have argued that mirror neurons very likely contribute to the remarkable ability of newborn infants—within 42 minutes of birth—to imitate certain facial actions or movements of others (Figure 6.6). Meltzoff and Decety consider such imitation in newborns to be innate, governed by brain processes that include mirror neurons (Meltzoff & Decety, 2003). Noting that adults across cultures play imitative games with their children, these researchers suggest that, over the period of infancy, imitation has a special role to play in establishing emotional connections between self and other. Young infants not only imitate the facial expressions of others; they also pay special attention when their own behaviors are imitated. If a young baby sticks out her tongue, for example, and an adult follows suit, the baby will act interested and generate more tongue protrusions. By 14 months of age, the neurological basis of imitation is moderated by other cognitive and social processes. At this age, infants derive a great deal of pleasure from being imitated by adults and, once the "game" is established, will modify their behaviors to make the adult follow their lead (see also Asendorph, 2002; Nadel, 2002). Indeed, they will play such games gleefully for 20 minutes or more—a long time for a 14-month-old to do anything! Meltzoff and his colleagues argue that the joy babies derive from imitative games is a joint function of the emotional connection that comes from understanding the adult is choosing to do "the same as me" and the sense of agency that comes from controlling the behavior of another (Meltzoff, 2007; Repacholi, Meltzoff, & Olsen, 2008). Developing agency is a key feature of an emerging sense of self, a topic we address more fully later in this chapter.

Figure 6.6 Demonstration from one of Andrew Meltzoff and Keith Moore's studies showing that some newborns can imitate adult facial actions.

Enrico Ferorelli

All the research that we have considered in this section points to the importance of well-coordinated, responsive, and synchronous social interactions in establishing emotional connections between babies and their caregivers. In the next section, we examine in depth the development of the infant's first, and what many believe to be the infant's most significant, emotional relationship—that between the baby and his or her primary caregiver. As you will see, the interactive synchrony discussed above is considered an essential ingredient to the formation of this first relationship.

mirror neurons Special brain cells that fire when an individual sees or hears another perform an action, just as they would fire if the individual were performing the same action.

attachment The emotional bond that children form with their caregivers at about 7 to 9 months.

▌▌▌▌ APPLY ▪ CONNECT ▪ DISCUSS

Consider the nature of emotion regulation from a Vygotskian perspective (you may want to review p. 204), and discuss how maternal depression may complicate its development.

The Infant-Caregiver Emotional Relationship

During the second year of life, children find novelty and excitement everywhere. A walk to the corner drugstore with a 1½-year-old can take forever. Each step presents new and interesting sights to explore: A bottle cap lying by the edge of the sidewalk requires close examination; a pigeon waddling across a neighbor's lawn invites a detour; even the cracks in the sidewalk may prompt sitting down to take a closer look.

Even a spoonful of cereal offered by a stranger may evoke wariness in young babies.

Thomas Heinzer

Things that attract babies and young children, however, may also cause them to be wary. Whizzing cars, strange people, and novel objects are often frightening as well as fascinating. There needs to be a balance between interest and fear as infants continue to explore and learn about the world. They cannot spend their entire lives in close proximity to their parents, but they cannot survive for long if they wander off on their own too soon.

Research with both monkey and human mothers and babies indicates how the balance between exploration and safety is created and maintained in ways that allow development to continue. A key element in this process is the emotional bond called **attachment** that develops between children and their caregivers sometime between the ages of 7 and 9 months (Ainsworth, 1982). Developmentalists generally cite four signs of attachment in babies and young children:

1. They seek to be near their primary caregivers. Before the age of 7 to 8 months, few babies plan and make organized attempts to achieve contact with their caregivers; after this age, babies often follow their caregivers closely, for example.

2. They show distress if separated from their caregivers. Before attachment begins, infants show little disturbance when their caregivers walk out of the room.

3. They are happy when they are reunited with the person to whom they are attached.

4. They orient their actions to the caregiver. When they are playing, for example, they watch the caregiver or listen for the caregiver's voice.

Many small children become strongly attached to a teddy bear, a blanket, or some other object. The British psychiatrist D. W. Winnicott (1971) has called such objects "transitional objects." They support children in their attempts to understand and deal with the reality that exists beyond their own bodies. The strong attachment this little girl feels for her teddy bear is written all over her smiling embrace.

Courtesy of Sheila Cole

The special relationship with their primary caregivers that babies begin to display between 7 and 9 months of age undergoes significant changes during the remainder of infancy and beyond.

Explanations of Attachment

The fact that 7- to 9-month-old children everywhere begin to become upset when they are separated from their primary caregivers suggests that attachment is a universal feature of development (Simpson et al, 2007). This possibility has led to a lively debate about the evolutionary reasons for attachment, the causes of changes in attachment behaviors as children grow older, and the influence of the quality of attachment on children's later development. Early on, Sigmund Freud suggested that infants become attached to the people who satisfy their need for food. Although influenced by Freud's ideas, John Bowlby went on to elaborate an alternative theory, according to which infants become attached to those who give them care and protection, providing them with a secure foundation for exploring the world.

Freud's Drive-Reduction Explanation The process of attachment plays an important role in Freud's theory of development. Freud held that the early interactions between children and their social environment, particularly the people who care for them, set the pattern for later personality and social development. In adulthood, Freud wrote, the relationship with the mother becomes "the prototype for all . . . love relations for both sexes" (1940/1964, p. 188).

While Freud's emphasis on the importance of attachment for development is widely shared, his explanation for the causes of attachment is not (Fonagy, 2001). He believed that human beings, like other organisms, are motivated in large part by **biological drives**—the impulses of organisms to satisfy essential physiological needs, such as hunger or thirst, that create tension and a state of arousal in the organism. When such a need is satisfied, the drive is reduced as biological equilibrium is restored, and the organism experiences a sensation of pleasure. In this sense, pleasure-seeking is a basic principle of existence. With respect to attachment in particular, Freud asserted that "love has its origin in attachment to the satisfied need for nourishment" (1940/1964, p. 188). Thus, according to Freud, infants become attached to their mother because she is the one most likely to nourish them. The major problem with this explanation is that research with nonhuman primates has not substantiated Freud's notion that attachment is caused by the reduction of the hunger drive.

In one study that tested Freud's drive-reduction theory of attachment, Harry Harlow and his coworkers (Harlow, 1959) separated eight baby rhesus monkeys from their mothers a few hours after birth and placed each monkey in an individual cage with two inanimate "substitute mothers"—one made of wire, the other of terry cloth (Figure 6.7). These substitute mothers, each of which was equipped with a nipple that produced milk, were the monkeys' sole source of nutrition, with four babies receiving milk from the wire mothers, and four from the terry cloth mothers. The two types of substitute mothers were equally effective as sources of nutrition: All eight babies drank the same amount of milk and gained weight at the same rate.

Nevertheless, over the 165-day period that they lived with the substitute mothers, the baby monkeys showed a distinct preference for their terry cloth mother, regularly climbing on her and clinging to her. Even those who obtained their food from a wire mother would go to it only to feed and would then go back to cling to the terry cloth mother. From the perspective of drive-reduction theory, it made no sense that the four infant monkeys who received their food from a wire mother

Figure 6.7. This baby monkey spent most of its time clinging to the terry cloth substitute mother even when its nursing bottle was attached to a wire substitute mother nearby. This preference indicates that bodily contact and the comfort it gives are important in the formation of the infant's attachment to its mother.

Martin Rogers/Tony Stone

would prefer to spend their time with a terry cloth mother that might feel good but satisfied no apparent biological drive, such as hunger or thirst. Harlow (1959) concluded, "These results attest to the importance—possibly the overwhelming importance—of bodily contact and the immediate comfort it supplies in forming the infant's attachment to its mother" (p. 70).

John Bowlby's Ethological Explanation

John Bowlby's theory of attachment arose from his study of the mental health problems of British children who had been separated from their families during World War II and were cared for in institutions (Bowlby, 1969, 1973, 1980). Bowlby's observations of children in hospitals, nurseries, and orphanages, as well as his analyses of clinical interviews with psychologically troubled or delinquent adolescents and adults, indicated that when children are first separated from their mothers, they become frantic with fear. They cry, throw tantrums, and try to escape their surroundings. Then they go through a stage of despair and depression. If the separation continues and no new stable relationship is formed, these children seem to become indifferent to other people. Bowlby called this state of indifference **detachment.**

In his attempt to explain the distress of young children when they are separated from their parents, Bowlby was particularly influenced by the work of ethologists, who emphasize a broad, evolutionary approach to understanding human behavior (see Chapter 1, pp. 24–27). Ethological studies of monkeys and apes revealed that infants of these species spend their initial weeks and months of postnatal life in almost continuous direct physical contact with their biological mothers. Bowlby noted that these primate infants consistently display several apparently instinctual responses that are also essential to human attachment: clinging, sucking, crying, and separation protest. After a few weeks or months (depending on the species of primate), infants begin to venture away from their mothers to explore their immediate physical and social environments, but they scurry back to the mother at the first signs of something unusual and potentially dangerous (Suomi, 1995). These primate behaviors, Bowlby hypothesized, are the evolutionary basis for the development of attachment in human babies as well.

In contrast to their conclusions regarding Freud's drive-reduction hypothesis, Harlow and his colleagues found strong support for Bowlby's evolutionary theory in their subsequent research with monkeys placed in cages with "substitute mothers" (Harlow & Harlow, 1969). Knowing that normal human and monkey babies run to their mothers for comfort when faced with an unfamiliar and frightening situation, the researchers created such a situation for the monkeys who had received milk from the wire mothers. They introduced into these monkeys' cages a mechanical teddy bear that marched forward while loudly beating a drum. The terrified babies fled to their terry cloth mother, not to the wire one, and began rubbing their body against hers (Figure 6.8). Soon their fears were calmed, and they turned to look at the bear with curiosity. Some even left the protection of the terry cloth mother to approach the object that had so terrified them only moments before.

Harlow concluded that soothing tactile sensations provide the baby with a sense of security that is more important to the formation of attachment than food. However, as Harlow's team discovered, although soothing tactile sensations appear to be necessary for healthy development, they are not sufficient. As these monkeys grew older, they showed signs of impaired development: They were either indifferent or abusive to other monkeys, and none of them could copulate normally. Noting that the substitute mother "cannot cradle the baby or communicate monkey sounds and gestures," the researchers concluded that the physical comfort provided by the cloth-covered mother in the monkey's infancy does not produce a normal adolescent or adult (Harlow & Harlow, 1962, p. 142). Applying the

biological drives Impulses to attempt to satisfy essential physiological needs.

detachment For Bowlby, the state of indifference toward others experienced by children who have been separated from their caregiver for an extended time and have not formed a new stable relationship.

Figure 6.8. (a) This baby monkey clings to its terry cloth substitute mother when it is frightened by the approach of a mechanical teddy bear. (b) After gaining reassurance, the baby monkey looks at the strange intruder. The terry cloth mother, which does not provide nourishment, acts as a secure base, whereas the wire mother, which does provide nourishment, does not. This behavior contradicts drive-reduction theories of attachment.

(a)

(b)

Harlow Primate Laboratory, University of Wisconsin.

concept of *primary intersubjectivity* introduced earlier, we can speculate that the absence of a sensitive and responsive social partner interfered with establishing the infant–mother emotional relationship considered so critical to later social and emotional development.

Phases of Attachment

Bowlby (1969) believed that attachment normally develops through four broad phases during the first 2 years of life, eventually producing a balance between infants' need for the safety provided by the caregiver and their need to explore their world. As you read through the descriptions of each phase, notice how infants take on more responsibility for maintaining the balance of the attachment system as their capacities to act and interact become more sophisticated.

1. *The preattachment phase* (birth to age 6 weeks). In the first few weeks of life, infants remain in close contact with their caregivers and do not seem to get upset when left alone with an unfamiliar caregiver.

2. *The "attachment-in-the-making" phase* (ages 6 weeks to 6 to 8 months). Infants begin to respond differently to familiar and unfamiliar people, and by the time they are 6 or 7 months old, they start to show clear preferences for their familiar caregivers as well as signs of wariness when confronted with unfamiliar objects and people.

3. *The "clear-cut attachment" phase* (ages 6 to 8 months to 18 to 24 months). During this period, the mother becomes a **secure base** from which babies make exploratory excursions and to which they come back every so often to renew contact before returning to their explorations. This is also the time when children display full-blown **separation anxiety,** becoming visibly upset when the mother or another caregiver leaves the room. Once this phase of attachment is reached, it regulates the physical and emotional relationship between children and those to whom they are attached. Whenever the distance between attachment figures and the child becomes too great, one or the other is likely to become upset and act to reduce that distance.

4. *The reciprocal relationship phase* (ages 18 to 24 months and older). As the child becomes more mobile and spends increasingly greater amounts of time away from the mother, the pair enter into a more reciprocal relationship, sharing responsibility for maintaining the equilibrium of the attachment system. When engaged in separate activities, the mother and the child will occasionally interrupt what they are doing to renew their contact. Among humans, this transitional phase lasts several years.

Once achieved, a firm attachment helps infants to retain feelings of security during the increasingly frequent and lengthy periods of separation from their caregivers. It is noteworthy that this phase develops at the same time that infants' powers of mental representation are on the rise (see Chapter 5). Bowlby believed that as a consequence of infants' growing symbolic capacities, parent–child attachment begins to serve as an **internal working model,** a mental model that children construct as a result of their experiences and that they use to guide their interactions with caregivers and others (we will address the implications of the model in detail below).

Patterns of Attachment

The maladaptive social behavior of Harlow's monkeys raised with inanimate substitute mothers, coupled with Bowlby's original observations of detachment in orphans, prompts a question: What kinds of interactions between primary caregivers and children provide the most effective basis for the development of healthy human social relations? (The following discussion is in terms of the mother as the attachment figure because most attachment research has focused on mother–infant pairs.

secure base Bowlby's term for the people whose presence provides the child with the security that allows him or her to make exploratory excursions.

separation anxiety The distress that babies show when the person to whom they are attached leaves.

internal working model A mental model that children construct as a result of their experiences with their caregivers and that they use to guide their interactions with their caregivers and others.

Our use of the word "mother," however, is meant to refer to the person who "mothers" the child and to whom the child becomes attached [Bowlby, 1969].)

Because no two mother–infant pairs are alike and because their environments also vary enormously, we should not expect to find one pattern of attachment that is "right" for social development in all cases. Many investigators believe, however, that it is possible to identify general patterns of mother–child interaction that are most conducive to positive development.

Research on such patterns of mother–child interaction has been greatly influenced by the work of Mary Ainsworth. On the basis of her observations of mother–infant pairs in Africa and the United States, she concluded that there are consistent, qualitatively distinct patterns in the ways mothers and infants relate to each other during the second and third years of infancy (Ainsworth, 1967, 1982). Most of the mother–infant pairs she observed seemed to have worked out a comfortable, secure relationship by the third year, but some of the relationships were characterized by persistent tension and difficulties in regulating joint activities.

To test the security of the mother–child relationship, Ainsworth designed a procedure called the **strange situation.** The procedure takes place in a laboratory playroom and includes eight brief episodes in which the child is observed with the mother present, when left alone with a stranger, when left entirely alone, and when reunited with the mother after a separation. The basic purpose of this procedure is to observe how babies make use of the mother as a secure base from which to explore, how they respond to separation from the mother, and how they respond to a stranger. Ainsworth reasoned that different patterns of reactions would reflect different qualities of the attachment relationship.

On the basis of their findings, Ainsworth and her colleagues initially categorized infants' responses in the strange situation into three types that seemed to reflect the quality of the children's attachment: *secure, avoidant,* and *resistant* (Ainsworth et al., 1971; Ainsworth et al., 1978). Later researchers added a fourth attachment type, *disorganized* (Main & Solomon, 1990). These types of attachment, or *attachment statuses,* and the responses they are associated with in the strange situation, can be described as follows:

- **Secure attachment.** As long as the mother is present, securely attached children play comfortably with the toys in the playroom and react positively to the stranger. These children become visibly and vocally upset when their mother leaves, and they are unlikely to be consoled by a stranger. However, when the mother reappears and they can climb into her arms, they quickly calm down and soon resume playing. This pattern of attachment, which reflects a healthy balance between wanting to be in close contact with the mother and wanting to explore the environment, is shown by about 65 percent of middle-class children in the United States.

- **Avoidant attachment.** During the time the mother and child are left alone together in the playroom, avoidant infants are more or less indifferent to where their mother is sitting. They may or may not cry when she leaves the room. If they do become distressed, the stranger is likely to be as effective at comforting them as their mother is. When the mother returns, these children may turn or look away from her instead of going to her to seek closeness and comfort. About 23 percent of middle-class children in the United States show this pattern of attachment.

- **Resistant attachment.** Resistant children have trouble from the start in the strange situation. They stay close to their mother and appear anxious even when she is near. They become very upset when the mother leaves, but they are not comforted by her return. Instead, they simultaneously

strange situation A procedure designed to assess children's attachment on the basis of their responses to a stranger when they are with their mothers, when they are left alone, and when they are reunited with their mothers.

secure attachment A pattern of attachment in which children play comfortably and react positively to a stranger as long as their mother is present. They become upset when their mother leaves and are unlikely to be consoled by a stranger, but they calm down as soon as their mother reappears.

avoidant attachment The attachment pattern in which infants are indifferent to where their mother is sitting, may or may not cry when their mother leaves, are as likely to be comforted by strangers as by their mother, and are indifferent when their mother returns to the room.

resistant attachment The attachment pattern in which infants stay close to their mother and appear anxious even when their mother is near. They become very upset when their mother leaves but are not comforted by their return. They simultaneously seek renewed contact with their mother and resist their mother's efforts to comfort them.

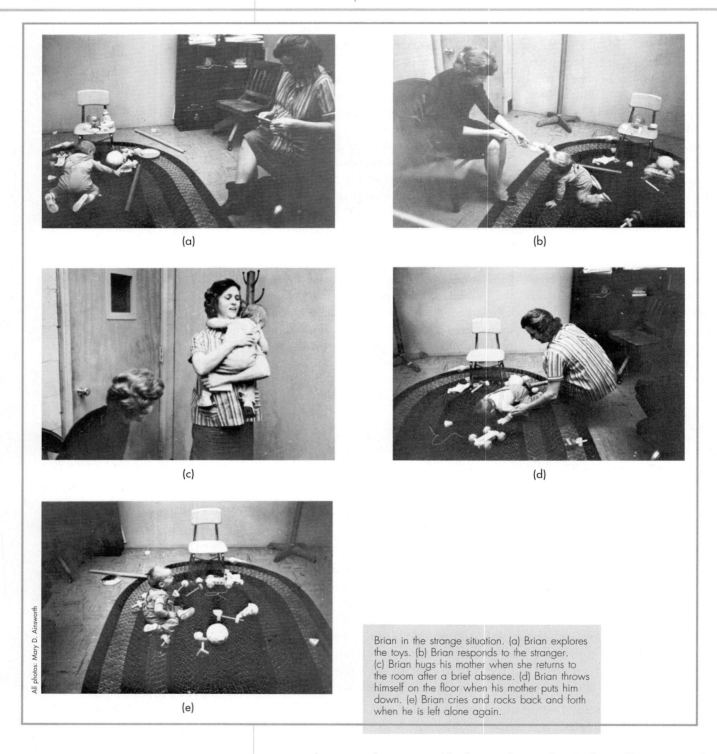

(a)

(b)

(c)

(d)

(e)

All photos: Mary D. Ainsworth

Brian in the strange situation. (a) Brian explores the toys. (b) Brian responds to the stranger. (c) Brian hugs his mother when she returns to the room after a brief absence. (d) Brian throws himself on the floor when his mother puts him down. (e) Brian cries and rocks back and forth when he is left alone again.

disorganized attachment The insecure attachment pattern in which infants seem to lack a coherent method for dealing with stress. They may behave in seemingly contradictory ways, such as screaming for their mother but moving away when she approaches. In extreme cases, they may ~em dazed.

seek renewed contact with the mother and resist her efforts to comfort them. They may cry angrily to be picked up with their arms outstretched but then arch away and struggle to get free once the mother starts to pick them up. These children do not readily resume playing after the mother returns. Instead, they keep a wary eye on her. This attachment pattern is shown by about 12 percent of middle-class children in the United States.

- **Disorganized attachment.** Children who fit this category seem to lack any coherent, organized method for dealing with the stress they experienced. Some cry loudly while trying to climb onto the mother's lap; others may approach the mother while refusing to look at her; still others may stand at the door and scream while she is gone but move away from her silently when she returns. In some extreme cases, the children seem to be in a dazed state and refuse to move while in their mother's presence (Main & Solomon, 1990).

Thus, attachment may be secure or fall into one of three insecure patterns. Over the past several decades, developmentalists have conducted a good deal of research trying to understand the causes of these four basic patterns of attachment behavior (summarized in Cassidy & Shaver, 2001, and Waters & Waters, 2006). Although most of this research has focused on the mother–infant relationship, other attachments that are important in children's lives have also been studied. Moreover, with more mothers of young children in the workforce, research is also increasingly focusing on the effects of child-care on attachment. (See the boxes "Attachment to Fathers and Others" and "Out-of-Home Care: A Threat to Attachment?" for discussion of the findings of both types of studies.)

This baby's attachment to his mother will be strongly affected by the role she plays in providing a secure base from which to explore the world.

Camille Tokerud/Getty Images

Attachment to Fathers and Others

ALTHOUGH MOTHERS CONTINUE TO play the dominant role in rearing the family's children (Hossain et al, 2007), fathers are becoming increasingly involved as parents, and fathers' sensitivity to their children's needs is increasingly recognized as important to children's well-being and attachment and emotional development (Davidov & Grusec, 2006; Ryan, Martin, & Brooks-Gunn, 2006; Stoltz, Barber, & Olsen, 2005; Hawkins et al., 2008).

When fathers spend time with their children, they are most likely to play with them, but in some societies they increasingly take a direct role in routine caretaking as well, a role for which they are by no means lacking in ability (Hawkins et al., 2008; Pleck & Masciadrelli, 2003). Fathers in the United States who have been observed feeding their infants, for example, respond sensitively to the babies' feeding rhythms and engage the babies in social episodes just as often as mothers. Moreover, the infants of fathers who are judged to be sensitive caregivers are likely to be as securely attached to them as they are to their mothers (Howes, 1999), whereas infants of fathers with relatively poor parenting skills develop insecure patterns of attachment (Brown et al., 2007).

The specifics of family relationships play an important role in determining infant–father attachments. In nontraditional American families in which fathers have the role of primary caregiver, babies turn to their fathers, not their mothers, for comfort when they are under stress (Geiger, 1996). A similar pattern has been observed in a vastly different culture, that of

the Aka pygmies, a hunter–gatherer group who live in central Africa. Aka men, women, and children generally forage together, and Aka adult couples spend more time together than do couples in any other documented social group (Morelli et al., 1999). Hewlett (1992) reports that "Aka fathers are within an arms reach of their infants 47 percent of the day and are more likely than mothers to hug or soothe their infants while holding them than are mothers" (p. 238). In contrast with traditional patterns in the United States and many other countries, Aka fathers are more likely than

Among the Aka of the Ituri forests, men play a major role in the care of their young children, promoting close emotional bonds.

Ituri Forest Peoples Fund

their wives to pick up infants who crawl over and request to be held. On the basis of his findings, Hewlett concludes that when cultural patterns lead fathers to be closely involved in their children's upbringing, attachment to the father occurs in the same way as attachment to the mother.

Of course, mothers and fathers are not the only people with whom infants form attachments. Babies also form attachments with non-parental caregivers, including siblings, day-care providers, teachers, and grandparents (Howes, 1999). Studies show that while most children develop positive relationships with their day-care providers, they are less likely to be securely attached to them than they are to their parents. Secure attachments between children and day-care providers are more likely when the child–caregiver ratios are low and the children are younger, female, and from higher socioeconomic backgrounds (Ahnert, Pinquart, & Lamb, 2003).

Many families in the United States, particularly those living close to or below the poverty line, have historically created caregiving systems that include networks of adults, such as grandparents and other kin, to whom children become attached (we will return to this topic in Chapter 10). And in some societies, such as that of the !Kung of the Kalahari Desert, babies are cared for in groups of children beginning around the age of 1 year so that their mothers can resume their work as the society's food gatherers (Konner, 1977). In such circumstances, babies form strong attachments to many older children in the group in addition to adults.

Out-of-Home Care: A Threat to Attachment?

IN MANY PARTS OF THE WORLD, ONE of the most common features of young children's lives is some form of out-of-home care during the first year (Greenspan, 2003). In North American society, this phenomenon is related to two trends: (1) the growing number of single-parent households, and (2) the increasing economic need for both parents to work full time. At present, more than 60 percent of women with children under the age of 6 are employed, and the majority returned to work before their infants were 1 year old (U.S. Department of Labor, 2007; Casper, 1996).

Out-of-home care for infants has been the subject of controversy among developmentalists for several decades (Ahnert, Pinquart, & Lamb, 2006). A prominent voice in this controversy has been that of Jay Belsky, who warned that out-of-home care during the first year of life carries possible developmental risks (Belsky et al., 2007). Belsky's concerns were aroused by evidence that children who had experienced extensive non-maternal care (more than 20 hours a week) during the first year of life were more likely to exhibit insecure patterns of attachment in the strange situation, were less compliant in meeting adults' demands, and were more aggressive in interactions with peers. These concerns were supported by studies that found that firstborn children who had been placed in child-care arrangements before their first birthday were significantly more likely to display insecure forms of attachment when they were 12 to 13 months old than were children who stayed at home with their mothers (Bargelow, Vaughn, & Molitor, 1987).

At 9 months of age, both Samuel and Olivia attend Kids Unlimited, a day-care facility in Oxford, UK. The effects of out-of-home care for infants is a subject of considerable controversy and research.

These findings prompted the U.S. government to initiate a massive study to determine the influence that various kinds of child care during infancy and early childhood have on later development. The study was carried out by a network of leading researchers from centers in 10 different geographical locales. Investigators collect data on the characteristics of the children's families—including their educational and income levels, ethnicity, and size—and on the quality of the care provided—including the ratio of caregivers to children, the size of the care groups, the quality of the facilities, and the quality of caregiving itself. To assess the effects of the care on the children, data was collected on the children's emotional attachment, self-control, compliance with adult demands, mental development, and language development.

As you will see when we discuss the effects of child care in more detail in Chapter 10, the results of these studies indicate that an extensive amount of time in nonparental child care has slight negative effects on children's attachment relationships, as well as on their social behaviors and intellectual development. Much stronger effects are found for "insensitive mothering" and the socioeconomic status (SES) of the family (NICHD, 2003b).

The critical feature that seems to determine to whom infants become attached is whether the caregiving provided plays a positive supporting role in the child's development—a safe base from which to explore the world and a source of comfort. To the extent that such caregiving is restricted to the mother, she is the natural object of attachment. But when caregiving is distributed to include fathers and others, they also become effective attachment figures.

The stakes in assessing the effects of child care are very high. On the one hand, everyone is aware that it is in the interests not only of the children in question but of society as a whole to ensure that children grow up to be emotionally stable and socially competent adults. On the other hand, economic and social pressures are bringing many mothers into the workforce and keeping fathers there. The problem is how best to deal with these conflicting realities to maximize children's life chances, particularly for low-income families who are often unable to afford high-quality care. Belsky suggests that this goal could best be achieved if parents received a subsidy for staying home with their infants during their first year of life. Others argue that what is called for instead is better and more available child care. Proponents of this latter view suggest that responsive, stable, and loving environments can be provided outside the home and point to a number of recent studies indicating that infants and children establish warm, close relationships with a large variety of nonparental figures, including other family members and friends, as well as paid child-care providers (Shonkoff & Phillips, 2000).

Two major questions have dominated the study of attachment patterns. First, what are the causes of variations in the patterns of attachment? Second, do these variations have important consequences for later development?

The Causes of Variations in Patterns of Attachment

Research on what leads to variations in patterns of attachment has focused on three types of contexts that influence the responsiveness and sensitivity of care received by infants: the family; the institutional context—orphanages, in particular; and the child-rearing patterns of the cultural group to which the mother and child belong.

The Family Context In her early studies of the antecedents of attachment, Mary Ainsworth used *ethological* methods (see Chapter 1, p. 25) to examine patterns of attachment in mother–infant pairs in Africa and the United States. Her repeated, detailed observations of mother–infant behavior throughout the first year of life indicated a link between attachment patterns and mothers' sensitivity to their infants' signals of need (Ainsworth & Bell, 1969). Specifically, it was found that 3-month-olds whose mothers responded quickly and appropriately to their cries and were sensitive to their signals of need were likely to be evaluated as securely attached at 12 months.

Over the past several decades many additional studies have examined the relationship between parental sensitivity and attachment status. Michael Lamb and his colleagues reported that parents of securely attached infants are generally more involved with their infants, more in synchrony with them, and more appropriate in their responsiveness (Lamb & Ahnert, 2006). The mother's sensitivity to her infant's distress seems particularly important (McElwain & Booth-LaForce, 2006). This link is especially evident where such sensitivity is low: Maternal depression has been consistently linked to reductions in secure attachment behaviors (Diener, Nievar, & Wright, 2003), and, as might be expected, children raised by extremely insensitive or abusive caregivers are particularly likely to be rated as insecurely attached (Thompson, 1998).

A variety of factors that contribute to stress on parents have also been found to be associated with insecure attachment, including low socioeconomic status (Lyons-Ruth & Jacobvitz, 1999) and marital discord (Belsky, 1999). Researchers believe that these stressors are related to insecure attachment in two ways. First, difficult conditions within the family are likely to increase maternal depression and lower maternal sensitivity. Second, witnessing angry or violent interactions between adult caretakers or experiencing unpredictable changes in caregiving arrangements is likely to make children feel that their caregivers are not reliable sources of comfort and safety.

Although many studies support Ainsworth's hypothesis regarding a relationship between parental sensitivity and attachment, some research has found less than strong evidence for it. An analysis of 65 studies conducted in many parts of the world revealed only a modest correlation between measures of sensitivity and secure attachment, indicating that many factors linking parental behaviors to attachment are still not well understood (De Wolff & van IJzendoorn, 1997).

Institutional Contexts When Jeff and Christine adopted Jin Yu from the orphanage in China, they were particularly concerned about whether she would be able to develop strong emotional attachments to them. Indeed, a large body of research indicates that children who spend their early lives in orphanages may experience significant levels of social-emotional deprivation that impede their ability to form loving relationships with others. (In rare cases, this impeded ability can take the form of reactive attachment disorder, discussed in the box "In the Field: Children with Reactive Attachment Disorder.") The effects that institutional living can have on a child vary dramatically, depending on such factors as the severity of deprivation the child experiences, the length of time the child remained in the orphanage, and the quality of the child's environment after leaving the orphanage.

As you may recall, the cognitive development of children who were adopted from Romanian orphanages where they had experienced severe deprivation depended largely on how old the children were when adopted (see Chapter 5, p. 166). Similarly, when Kim Chisholm (1998) followed the social and emotional development of a group of infants and young children adopted from these same orphanages into Canadian homes, he found that those who were adopted before they were 4 months of age were developmentally indistinguishable from native-born Canadian children who lived in the homes of their biological parents. However, children who had spent 8 months or more in an orphanage showed residual effects of their orphanage experiences. In particular, although all the children had formed emotional attachments to their adoptive parents, they tended to display more evi-

In the Field — Children with Reactive Attachment Disorder

Name:	Lark Eshleman
Education:	B.A. in English and American literature, Utica College of Syracuse University; M.A. in library science, State University of New York at Geneseo; M.A. in psychology, Millersville University; Ph.D. in clinical psychology, Union Institute (also certified in school psychology and play therapy)
Current Position:	Founder, Executive Director, and psychotherapist, Institute for Children and Families, Pennsylvania
Career Objectives:	Help children and families recover from the effects of early childhood trauma, including abuse, neglect, and family upheaval

Lark Eshleman is a child and adolescent psychotherapist specializing in the treatment of children who have experienced early emotional traumas such as exposure to violence, abuse, neglect, or parental separation and loss (Eshleman, 2003). Such children are at risk for reactive attachment disorder (RAD), a severe psychological disorder linked to a disruption in the development of the parent–child attachment relationship (Chaffin et al., 2006).

According to the *Diagnostic and Statistical Manual of Mental Disorders*, the main feature of RAD is extremely inappropriate social relating that takes one of two forms: (1) the child engages in indiscriminate and excessive efforts to receive comfort and affection from any adult, even strangers, or (2) the child is extremely reluctant to seek or accept comfort and affection, especially when distressed, even from familiar adults. Other symptoms used to diagnose this rare disorder include onset before 5 years of age, a history of significant neglect, and lack of a reliable, consistent primary caregiver (APA, 2000). Barbara Braun-McDonald, another attachment therapist, explains that "if a baby cries and he's ignored, and it happens over and over again, at some level he begins to tell himself, 'I can't trust

that the people who are in charge are going to meet my needs'" (in Meltz, 2004, p. H.1).

Eshleman came into the international spotlight for her therapeutic interventions with orphans in Croatia and her advice to parents seeking to adopt them (Eshleman, 2003). Not surprisingly, children who have spent considerable time in orphanages, especially those of poor quality, are at special risk for developing RAD. Significantly, therapies that are specifically linked to attachment theory have been found most effective in healing children whose attachment process has been seriously disrupted by various emotional traumas. As concluded in a major review of research into various therapies for RAD,

> Services for children described as having attachment problems should be founded on the core principles suggested by attachment theory, including caregiver and environmental stability, child safety, patience, sensitivity, consistency, and nurturance. (Chaffin et al., 2006, p. 87)

Especially important to therapeutic success, according to the review, is to focus on the parent–child relationship, rather than on the individual child's pathology, and to teach positive parenting skills that promote a secure attachment relationship between parent and child.

dence of insecure attachment in the strange situation than did the children adopted before the age of 4 months. They also tended to be indiscriminately friendly to strangers, suggesting that they were hungry for attention. Children's social and emotional development seems to suffer even when the orphanages are judged to be of good quality. Barbara Tizard and Jill Hodges studied 65 English children of working-class backgrounds who were raised in high-quality residential nurseries from just after birth until they were at least 2 years old (Hodges & Tizard, 1989a, 1989b; Tizard & Hodges, 1978; Tizard & Rees, 1975). (These nurseries were designed to provide both temporary and long-term care and education for children whose families could not care for them adequately, usually due to ongoing family problems or some type of crisis.) The children in the study were fed well; the staff, consisting primarily of nurses, was well trained; toys and books were plentiful. However, the turnover and scheduling of staff members discouraged the formation of close personal relationships between the staff and children. Tizard and Hodges estimated that by the time the children were 2 years old, each child had been in the care of some 24 nurses, and that by the age of 4½, each had been cared for by as many as 50 nurses. Such circumstances would certainly seem to preclude the kind of intimate knowledge and caring that presumably underlie sensitive caregiving.

Tizard and her colleagues evaluated the developmental status of the children when they were 4½ and 8 years old, and again when they were 16. They found that leaving institutional care had a positive effect on the children, as would be expected, but that how much difference it made depended on what kind of environment they entered. One of the surprising findings was that the children who were restored to their biological families did not fare as well as the children who were adopted, a pattern that persisted even at the follow-up study conducted when the children were 16 years old. Almost all the children who were adopted formed mutual attachments with their adoptive parents, no matter how old they were when they were adopted. This was not the case for the children who returned to their biological parents. The older they were when they left the orphanages, the less likely it was that mutual attachment developed.

One reason the adoptive homes may have produced better outcomes than the biological homes was that many of the families who took back their children were not altogether happy to have them. Many of the mothers expressed misgivings, but they accepted the responsibility because the children were their own. Often the children returned to homes in which there were other children who required their mother's attention or a stepfather who was not interested in them. Most of the adoptive parents, by contrast, were older, childless couples who wanted the children and gave them a good deal of attention. Also, most of the adoptive families were financially better off than the children's biological families had been (Tizard & Hodges, 1978).

Research on the emotional development of children raised in institutions has become especially important in light of the millions of children worldwide who are orphaned because of the HIV-AIDS epidemic. In sub-Saharan Africa alone, there are estimated to be more than 12 million children living as orphans because their parents have died from AIDS (Figure 6.9) (Christian Aid, 2001; Liddell, 2002). In African cultures, orphaned children traditionally would be cared for by extended family. However, the vast and exponentially growing number of parents killed by AIDS has overburdened the extended family system, and the need for orphanages is quickly outpacing the supply (Liddell, 2002; Abebe & Aase, 2007). As you might expect, many AIDS orphans suffer the same effects of institutional care that have been documented in past studies of orphaned children.

Figure 6.9. In some areas of sub-Saharan Africa, more than 15 percent of all children have been orphaned because of AIDS. The crisis has put terrible pressure on the African extended family system, which has traditionally been a refuge for family members in need. The woman in this photograph is the grandmother and now the primary caregiver and provider for six grandchildren whose parents died from the disease. (From UNAIDS, 2004.)

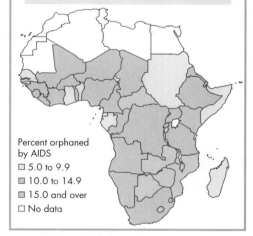

Percent orphaned by AIDS
☐ 5.0 to 9.9
☐ 10.0 to 14.9
☐ 15.0 and over
☐ No data

UNICEF/HQ93-2043/Cindy Andrew

Cultural Contexts At present there is sharp disagreement among developmentalists concerning the extent to which the process of attachment is influenced by cultural variations. Many have argued that attachment is a universal feature of human development and that the emotionally sensitive interactions that nourish attachment are similar across cultures (Posada et al., 2004). Others have argued that there are important cultural variations in attachment and that the very notions of what constitutes sensitive caregiving and secure human relationships are culturally specific (Rothbaum, Weisz, Pott, & Morelli, 2000; Rothbaum & Miki, 2004). Research has produced data that support both positions (Figure 6.10; see van IJzendoorn & Sagi, 2001, for a review of the conflicting evidence).

One of the earliest studies of cultural influences on attachment examined children who from an early age were raised communally on Israeli collective farms called *kibbutzim*. Although these children saw their parents daily, the adults who looked after them were usually not family members, and the children slept together in dormitories. When at the age of 11 to 14 months such communally raised children were placed in the strange situation with either a parent or a caregiver, only 56 percent were classified as securely attached, and 37 percent were classified as resistant (Sagi-Schwartz et al., 2005).

Abraham Sagi and his colleagues suspected that the high rate of insecure attachment among these children was caused by the fact that the communal caregiving, along with staffing rotations, did not allow the caregivers to provide the children with prompt individualized attention. To test this hypothesis, the researchers used the strange situation to compare the attachment behaviors of children raised in the traditional kibbutzim arrangement described above with those of children raised in kibbutzim in which they returned to sleep in their parents' home at night (Sagi et al., 1995). They once again found a low level of secure attachments among the children who slept in communal dormitories. Those who slept at home displayed a significantly higher level of secure attachments, supporting the idea that cultural differences in the opportunities for sensitive caregiving accounted for cultural differences in attachment quality.

While evidence indicates that interactive sensitivity is necessary to the development of secure attachments, it seems that the very nature of "sensitive caregiving" differs depending on the values, beliefs, and socialization goals of the culture. In a study that illustrates this point, Vivian Carlson and Robin Harwood (2003)

Figure 6.10. Secure attachments predominate across cultures, but the percentage of different forms of insecure attachments varies.

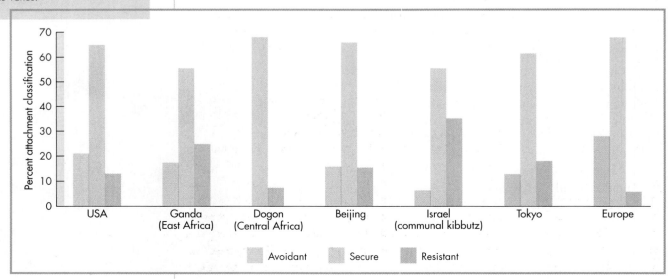

examined maternal sensitivity in mothers from the United States and Puerto Rico, and found that the Puerto Rican mothers exerted significantly more control over their infants—a form of behavior typically judged as "insensitive." Paradoxically, however, the infants of highly controlling mothers were not more likely to be insecurely attached. Carlson and Harwood explained that maternal control is consistent with Puerto Rican cultural values that emphasize the importance of obedience and respect. Mothers who exert this control in order to foster calm, attentive, and well-behaved infants are acting in predictable and meaningful ways that promote their babies' successful integration into the community. Noting that in Ainsworth's description, a sensitive mother is one who establishes a harmonious relationship with her infant, Carlson and Harwood argue that harmonious mother–infant relationships may be best established "by caregiving practices designed to produce culturally valued traits in the growing infant" (p. 69). Thus, while attachment may be universal, this does not exclude the possibility that the development of attachment behaviors, and the caregiving practices that affect their development, differ depending on the nature of the community in which the child is becoming engaged as an active participant (van IJzendoorn & Sagi, 2001; Belsky, 2005).

This child is clearly distressed at the prospect of being separated from his mother while she goes to work.

Attachment Patterns and Later Development

Many developmentalists argue that establishing a secure attachment relationship is crucial not only to infants' emotional well-being but also to the quality of their future relationships (Osofsky & Fitzgerald, 2000; Zeanah, 2000). Supporting this idea, early studies conducted by Alan Sroufe and his colleagues reported that when children who are judged to be securely attached at 12 months of age are assessed at age 3½, they are more curious, play more effectively with their age-mates, and have better relationships with their preschool teachers than do children who were insecurely attached as infants (Erikson, Sroufe, & Egeland, 1985; Frankel & Bates, 1990; Sroufe & Fleeson, 1986). In follow-up observations conducted when the children were 10 years old, and then again when they were 15, researchers found that those who had been assessed as securely attached in infancy were more skillful socially, had more friends, displayed more self-confidence, and were more open in expressing their feelings. (For a recent summary, see Sroufe et al., 2005.)

More recent longitudinal studies also suggest the continuity of attachment from infancy to adulthood. For example, a 20-year longitudinal study conducted by Everett Waters and his colleagues indicated that, as adults, 72 percent of the sample received the same attachment classification (secure or insecure, as assessed through interviews) that they had received as infants (Waters, Hamilton, & Weinfield, 2000a; Waters et al., 2000b).

Researchers who see patterns of attachment as tending to remain consistent throughout development emphasize that such continuity depends on one key factor—how well the individual's *internal working model* functions over time and across situations (Bretherton & Munholland, 1999; Grossmann & Grossmann, 2005). As discussed earlier (p. 212), Bowlby (1969) proposed that on the basis of their interactions with their primary caregiver, infants build up an internal working model of the way to behave toward other people. Enlarging on Bowlby's idea, Inge Bretherton and colleagues (2005) argue that internal working models provide expectations about how others are likely to respond to the child's own behavior and emotional expressions—whether the child will be comforted or rejected, and whether others will be emotionally available to respond when the child expresses his or her feelings. These expectations influence how the child acts in new situations and with new people. The child's actions, in turn, can provoke either positive or negative reactions in others, which can confirm the child's expectations and perpetuate patterns of behavior. Changing a child's internal working model is not accomplished easily and may require an adult who provides experiences that disconfirm the child's expectations. Thus, change and continuity depend on the cumulative outcomes of everyday transactions between children and their environments (Main et al., 2005).

In addition to the effects of the child's internal working model, research also indicates that major changes in the child's life can affect attachment status. In Waters's research cited above, for example, interviews with the mothers of the minority of participants who changed classification from secure to insecure reported at least one of the following negative life experiences:

- loss of a parent
- parental divorce
- life-threatening illness of a parent or child
- parental psychiatric disorder
- physical or sexual abuse by a family member

These and other traumatic events, such as isolation and deprivation, can have a significant impact on a child's attachment status.

|||||| APPLY ▬ CONNECT ▬ DISCUSS

In light of research suggesting that significant out-of-home care during the first year of life may pose some risk for developing insecure attachments, some developmentalists and family advocacy groups have argued for public policy that would grant parents leave for a year after the birth of a child. How acceptable would this policy be to fathers or mothers with strong career goals? Would it be good for infants from low-SES families where mothers might have several small children at home? What other options besides parental leave would serve family needs and be sensitive to the infant's attachment needs?

The Changing Nature of Communication

Seated in his stroller, 12-month-old Juan is enjoying a beautiful spring day with his father. As they stroll through the park, Juan points excitedly and exclaims, "Da!" at a dog, at a bicycle, at another baby in a stroller, each time looking over his shoulder and smiling at his father, who smiles back and says, "Yes, that's a doggie [bicycle, baby]." They come across a small crowd gathered around street performers who are dressed in colorful costumes, entertaining the audience with jokes, juggling, and antics. The performers invite the children to join them—throwing or catching balls, chasing each other around, acting like various animals, and just being generally silly. Juan seems to be enjoying the spectacle—until one of the performers slinks toward him on hands and knees, like a stalking lion. First, Juan leans back into his stroller, stares warily, and looks up at his father, who is scowling at the insensitive performer. The lion-man continues his approach and begins to make growling vocalizations. Then, obviously frightened, Juan bursts into tears and raises his arms toward his father, who picks him up and gives him a reassuring hug.

As you know from our earlier discussions, by 3 months of age infants and their caregivers are jointly experiencing pleasure in simple interactions. This early form of communication, which we referred to as *primary intersubjectivity,* is limited to

secondary intersubjectivity A form of interaction between infant and caregiver, emerging at about 9–12 months, with communication and emotional sharing focused not just on the interaction but on the world beyond.

social referencing A form of secondary intersubjectivity in which infants look to their caregiver for an indication of how to feel and act on encountering an unfamiliar object or event.

direct face-to-face interactions and is supported mainly by the efforts of the caregiver (Trevarthen, 1998). Between 9 and 12 months of age, babies begin to interact with their caregivers in a new and more complex way. This new form of connection is referred to as **secondary intersubjectivity,** because now the infant and the caregiver communicate with each other about the world that extends beyond themselves, such as their pleasure in seeing a passing puppy or their concern over an approaching threat.

The emergence of secondary intersubjectivity marks a major turning point in the infant's development because it brings a new dimension to the communicative process, serving as a foundation for sharing one's thoughts, feelings, and expectations about the world.

The pleasure this child and mother take in their interaction using a fork is an example of the kind of emotional sharing referred to as secondary intersubjectivity.

Social Referencing

An important form of secondary intersubjectivity in infancy is **social referencing,** in which babies look to their caregiver for an indication of how they should feel and act when they encounter some unfamiliar object or event. (Juan's looking up at his father as the street performer slunk toward him was a clear instance of social referencing.) Social referencing becomes a common means of communication as soon as babies begin to move about on their own (Campos et al., 2000). When approaching an unfamiliar object, for example, if they notice that their caregiver is looking at the object and appears to be concerned, they typically hesitate and become wary. If, instead, the caregiver smiles and looks pleased, they continue their approach. (Perhaps if Juan's father had not been scowling at the advancing performer, Juan would not have burst into tears.) As they grow more experienced, babies become increasingly sensitive to where their caregiver is looking and will even check back to see how the caregiver responds to an object after they have made their own appraisal of it (Rosen, Adamson, & Bakeman, 1992; Striano & Rochat, 2000).

Researchers in the United States have found an interesting gender difference in the way infants respond to their caregiver's worried looks in social-referencing episodes: girls are more likely than boys to move away from an object about which their caregivers seem apprehensive. Perhaps as a result, caregivers find it necessary to use more intense facial expressions when communicating concern to boys (Rosen et al., 1992).

Between approximately 9 and 12 months of age, infants' contributions to secondary intersubjectivity become more sophisticated. For example, Tricia Striano and Philippe Rochat (2000) compared the way 7- and 10-month-old infants in a laboratory playroom reacted to the appearance of a remote-controlled toy dog that barked intermittently. An experimenter in the room was instructed either to look at the infant when the dog barked or to look away. The 7-month-olds kept checking with the adult even if the adult ignored them, while the 10-month-olds immediately stopped checking with the adult unless the adult looked at them when the dog barked. Striano and Rochat believe that the 10-month-olds were beginning to engage in "selective social referencing" because the infants knew they could obtain information from the adult only if the adult was attending to them.

In a wonderful illustration of social referencing, this baby checks in with mom before deciding how to react to the medical exam. Mom's reassuring smile will greatly influence how the baby interprets and emotionally responds to this unusual event.

Gaze-following and Pointing

Another way in which infants can communicate with their caretakers once they start moving about is by following the caretaker's gaze to see what the caretaker is looking at and to look at what the caretaker is pointing at. If a mother and her 5-month-old baby are looking at each other and the mother suddenly looks to one side, the infant will not follow the mother's gaze. And if the mother points at some object in the room, the baby is more likely to stare at the end of the mother's finger than to look in the direction the mother is pointing. A month or two later, in similarly simple circumstances, the infant will look in the direction of the mother's gazing or pointing (Butterworth, 2001).

Pointing and gaze-following, like social referencing, become stronger and more reliable means of communication after their initial appearance between 7 and 9 months (Carpenter, Nagell, & Tomasello, 1998), and both are associated with the infant's growing vocabulary (Slaughter & McConnell, 2003). A baby's ability to look in the direction a caretaker points increases rapidly between 10 and 12 months (although the baby's own ability to use pointing will not appear for another several months), while the more subtle form of communication involved in following another's gaze continues to improve well into the second year.

The Beginnings of Language Comprehension and Speech

As babies become more mobile and more likely to wander out of their caregivers' sight and reach, a new means of interaction, one that will allow babies and caregivers to communicate at a distance, becomes an urgent necessity. That new means, of course, is language.

To some extent, all languages are "foreign languages" to young infants. Think about what it is like for you to hear an unfamiliar foreign language. Very probably, it seems like an uninterrupted sound stream; that is, it is difficult to tell where one word ends and another begins. Indeed, one of the first tasks of learning a language is to segment its sounds into distinct words and phrases. Infants are able to recognize their own names and distinguish them from names with similar stress patterns, such as "Amy" versus "Suzie," as early as 4 months of age (Jusczyk, 2001; Nazzi, Kemler Nelson, Jusczyk, & Jusczyk, 2000). By 6 months of age they begin to show the first signs of comprehending words for highly familiar objects, such as "mommy" or "daddy." These new abilities are interesting in their own right, but they also have implications for developing the ability to segment language. In particular, Roberta Golinkoff and her colleagues have found that when babies hear a familiar word—their own name, or "mommy" or "daddy"—the familiar word serves as an anchor for learning the words that immediately precede or follow the familiar word (Bortfeld et al., 2005; Pruden et al., 2006). Thus, it is easier for the baby to learn the word "cup" if it is used in the sentence "Here's your cup, Amy" than if it is used in "Here's your cup." **Perceptual scaffolding** is the term used by developmentalists to describe how the sound of a familiar word serves as an anchor for learning new words.

At about 9 months of age, children begin to understand some common expressions such as "Do you want your bottle?" "Wave bye-bye," and "Cookie?" when they are used in highly specific, often routine, situations. One little girl observed by Elizabeth Bates and her colleagues would bring her favorite doll when she was asked to "bring a dolly," but she did not understand the word "doll" as referring to any doll but her own (Bates et al., 1979).

The ability to produce language follows several months behind the ability to understand it. Its origins can be traced back to the cooing and gurgling noises babies begin to make at 10 to 12 weeks of age (Butterworth & Morisette, 1996). Soon thereafter, babies with normal hearing not only initiate cooing sounds but

perceptual scaffolding The way in which a familiar word serves as an anchor for learning new words that come immediately before or after it.

babbling A form of vocalizing, beginning at around 7 months, in which infants utter strings of syllables that combine a consonant sound and a vowel sound.

also begin to respond with gurgles and coos to the voices of others. When their cooing is imitated, they will answer with more coos, thereby engaging in a "conversation" in which turns are taken at vocalizing. They are most likely to vocalize with their caregivers and other familiar people.

Babbling, a form of vocalizing that combines a consonant and vowel sound, such as "dadadadadadada" or "babababababa," begins at around 7 months of age (Adamson, 1995). Recent research indicates that babbling is controlled by the left hemisphere of the brain; thus, well before recognizable language has begun, the brain areas that will support language are already active and behaving in language-specific ways (Baker, Golinkoff, & Petitto, 2006). At first, babbling amounts to no more than vocal play, as babies discover the wealth of sounds they can make with their tongue, teeth, palate, and vocal cords. They practice making these sound combinations endlessly, much as they practice grasping objects. Early babbling is the same the world over, no matter what language the baby's family speaks; babies produce syllables they have never heard before and will not use when they learn to speak (Blake & De Boysson-Bardies, 1992). At about 9 months of age, however, babies begin to narrow their babbling to the sounds produced in the language that they hear every day (Davis, MacNeilage, Matyear, & Powell, 2000). Since babies often babble when they play alone, early babbling does not seem to be an attempt to communicate. It is almost as if children are singing to themselves using repeatable parts of their language.

This father and his baby girl appear to be engaged in a "conversation" in which they take turns vocalizing about a picture that has captured their attention.

Toward the end of the first year, babies begin to babble with the intonation and stress of actual utterances in the language they will eventually speak. Such vocalizations are called *jargoning*. At this point, as Lauren Adamson (1995) describes it, "a stream of babbling often flows like speech, following its distinctive intonational patterns of declarations, commands, and questions" (p. 163). At about the same time, babies start to repeat particular short utterances in particular situations, as if their utterances have some meaning.

By about 12 months of age, infants are able to comprehend a dozen or so common phrases, such as "Give me a hug," "Stop it!" and "Let's go bye-bye." At about this same time, the first distinguishable words make their appearance, although their use is restricted to only a few contexts or objects (Fenson et al., 1994).

It used to be thought that deaf children babbled, beginning at the same age as hearing children (Lenneberg, 1967). Research has shown, however, that, although deaf infants in their early months do vocalize, they will only progress to babbling if the infants have some residual hearing (Koopmans-van Beinum, Clement, & van den Dikkenberg-Pot, 2001). In the case of totally deaf infants, vocalizations become rare by 1 year of age. However, if their caregivers communicate with each other in sign language, these infants "babble" with their hands—that is, just as hearing infants' babbling comes to have the sounds and sound patterns of the language they hear, so these infants make the movements that will become the elements of sign language (Cormier, Mauk, & Repp, 1998).

After the first year, the baby's ability to understand and produce language accelerates at an astonishing pace. Given the special significance of language development for our species, as well as its importance to advances in various developmental domains, we will devote all of the next chapter to examining the emergence and growth of language competence.

APPLY ▪▪ CONNECT ▪▪ DISCUSS

Social referencing emerges during infancy, and persists throughout life. Give examples of events that might prompt social referencing in an 8-year-old, a 15-year-old, and a 50-year-old. What similarities are there across your three events? What differences are there? How might social referencing have important biocultural implications?

A Sense of Self

Strapped securely in the grocery-cart seat with a bit of a pout on her face, 10-month-old Nadia watched her mother, who had turned away from her to read the nutritional content of a cereal box. All of a sudden, Nadia let out a piercing, heart-stopping screech that could be heard throughout the store. Everyone in the cereal aisle looked at her—and Nadia looked back at them, grinning proudly at her accomplishment. For weeks afterward, Nadia would shriek like that whenever she wanted attention, and acted happy and self-satisfied when she got it. It was as though she were saying, "Look at me!"

Nadia's emotional life has changed considerably since she was a newborn, when her internal feeling states seemed to trigger certain facial and other nonverbal behaviors—smiles, frowns, agitated crying, and so forth. At 10 months of age, she is aware that her emotional expressions affect those around her, and she uses her expressions intentionally to elicit predictable social responses. Moreover, Nadia takes apparent pride in her hugely successful bid for attention. She acts self-satisfied; she shows off. She is, as the saying goes, "full of herself."

By the time they are 6 months old, infants have acquired a great deal of experience interacting with objects and other people and have developed an intuitive sense of themselves as a result (Rochat, 2000). The ability to locomote provides them with still further experience of their separateness from their caregivers and promotes new forms of social relations. Infants at that age begin to learn that they can share experiences and compare reactions, especially through their emerging use of language (Trevarthen, 1998).

Self-recognition

Consciousness of self has been proposed to be among the major characteristics distinguishing human beings from other species and 2-year-olds from younger children. This is an interesting idea, but finding a way to demonstrate it convincingly has been a problem.

Several decades ago, Gordon Gallup (1970) reported an ingenious series of experiments using mirrors with chimpanzees, experiments that have since been replicated with chimpanzees and also used with children. Gallup showed adolescent wild-born chimpanzees their images in a full-length mirror. At first the chimps acted as if they were looking at another animal: they threatened, vocalized, and made conciliatory gestures to the "intruder." After a few days, however, they began to use the mirror to explore themselves; for example, they picked bits of food from their faces, which they could see only in the mirror.

To make certain of the meaning of his finding, Gallup anesthetized several chimps and painted a bright, odorless dye above one eye and on the ear on the opposite side of the head. When they woke up and looked in the mirror, the chimps immediately began to explore the marked spots with their hands. Gallup concluded that they had learned to recognize themselves in the mirror.

This kind of self-recognition is by no means universal among primate species. Gallup gave a wild-born macaque monkey more than 2400 hours of exposure to a mirror over a 5-month period, but the monkey never showed any sign of self-recognition. The problem was not simply dealing with the mirror image, because the monkey quickly learned to find food that it could see only in the mirror. The monkey simply could not recognize itself.

Gallup's procedure has been used in modified form with human infants between the ages of 3 and 24 months (Inoue-Nakamura, 2001). The results

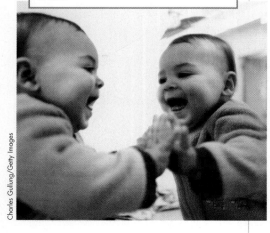

This baby seems delighted to see his own image in the mirror. Developmentalists use infant reactions to mirror images as a way to study the emerging understanding of self.

indicate that there are several stages in learning to recognize oneself in a mirror (Bigelow, 1998). Before the age of 3 months, children held up to a mirror show little interest in their own images or in anyone else's. At about 4 months, if children see another person or a toy reflected in the mirror, they will reach out and touch the mirror image. At this stage, they clearly do not understand that they are seeing a reflection. Ten-month-olds will reach behind them if a toy is slowly lowered behind their back while they are looking in the mirror, but they do not react to the sight of a red spot that has been surreptitiously applied to their nose. Not until children are 18 months old will they reach for their own nose or ask "What's that?" when they see the red spot. Within a few months, whenever someone points to the child's mirror image and asks, "Who's that?" the child will be able to answer unhesitatingly, "Me" (Rochat, 2000).

The Self as Agent

When speech first emerges, most of children's one-word utterances name objects they are looking at. Children point at or pick up an object and say its name. These first descriptions include no explicit reference to the self. Between the ages of 18 and 24 months, about the same time that children begin to use two-word utterances, they also begin to describe their own actions. A child completing a jigsaw puzzle exclaims, "Did it!" or "Becky done." When a tower of blocks falls down, a child exclaims, "Uh-oh. I fix." In these utterances we see not only children's ability to refer to themselves explicitly but also their ability to see themselves as *agents* who exert control and power over their environments. Recall from our discussion earlier in the chapter that this emerging sense of control and mastery underpins the delight shown by infants when their actions are imitated by adults.

The Emergence of Self-Conscious Emotions

The sense of self that arises during infancy changes the nature of the baby's emotional life and experience. Whether they believe that basic emotions (joy, fear, anger, surprise, sadness, and disgust) are present at or soon after birth or develop in the months that follow, developmentalists agree that sometime after the age of 8 months, babies begin to experience new emotions, including embarrassment, pride, shame, guilt, and envy (Reddy, 2005). These new emotions are referred to as **self-conscious emotions** because they depend on babies' newly acquired abilities to recognize, talk about, and think about themselves in relation to other people (Lewis, 2001). That is, whereas basic emotions bear a simple and direct relation to the events that elicit them, self-conscious emotions involve complex combinations of cognition and emotion and cannot appear until children are able to think about and evaluate themselves in relation to other people and the goals they desire. Take pride, for example. To feel pride, babies must be able to judge their own behavior as proper and admirable in the eyes of other people. Feelings of pride take on more complexity around 18 months of age, when babies become capable of thinking about other people's standards and can measure their behavior against the expectations of others (Tomasello, 1999).

Measurement against standards can of course lead to emotions other than pride. Jerome Kagan (1981) explored children's sensitivity to adult standards in a series of studies in which children were encouraged to imitate an adult who performed complex activities. For example, the adult might make one toy monkey hug

self-conscious emotions Emotions such as embarrassment, pride, shame, guilt, and envy, which emerge after 8 months with infants' growing consciousness of self.

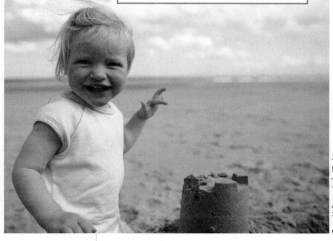

Two-year-old Brooke's obvious pride in her sand castle is a consequence of being able to consider her behavior in relation to the standards and expectations of others.

Zena Holloway/zefa/Corbis

another monkey, or build a stack of blocks, or enact a simple drama using toy blocks as animals. Many of these activities were too complex for the 18-month-old children to imitate. As a result, many of them started to fret, stopped playing, and clung to their mothers. Kagan concluded that their distress signaled a new ability to recognize adult standards, a sense of responsibility to live up to them, and shame or embarrassment when they fail to do so.

As infancy comes to an end, the process of developing a distinctive sense of self undergoes further change comprising several interconnected elements: children's increasing self-awareness, their growing sensitivity to adults' standards of what is good; their new awareness of their own ability to live up to those standards; an ability to create plans of their own and judge them against adult standards; and a strong desire to see that their plans are not thwarted by adults (Harter, 1998; Kagan, 2000). This change is recognized by parents the world over. On the South Pacific island of Fiji, for example, parents say that children gain *vakayalo*—sense—around the second birthday; they can be held responsible for their actions because they are supposed to be able to tell right from wrong. Similarly, the Utku of the Hudson Bay area say that the 2-year-old has gained *ihuma,* or reason. Parents in the United States tend to focus on their infants' newly acquired independence and the dwindling of their own control over them, labeling the change as the onset of the "terrible twos." However parents describe it, the distinctive pattern of infants' behavior at around the age of 2 signals to adults that a new stage of development has been entered. Key to this next stage of development is the growing sense of autonomy that Erikson (1963) says normally characterizes late infancy.

||||| APPLY — CONNECT — DISCUSS _

In what respects might the development of a sense of self contribute to the development of emotion regulation?

Developing Trust and Autonomy

Much of what we presented in this chapter is consistent with Erik Erikson's picture of infancy. As was indicated in Chapter 1 (Table 1.2, p. 19), Erikson divided infancy into two main stages. The first of these he called the stage of **basic trust versus mistrust,** in which the infant determines whether the world is a safe place to explore and discover, or an unpredictable and threatening one, and whether the people in the world are reliable, loving, and kind, or insensitive and hurtful. Consistent with much of the research we have reviewed, Erikson believed that warm and responsive parenting fosters infants' development of trust, and that unresponsive, insensitive, or disorganized parenting fosters a mistrust of people and a wariness about exploring the world.

During the second year, babies enter the stage of **autonomy versus shame and doubt,** during which they develop a sense of themselves as competent or not competent to solve problems and accomplish tasks. In this important period of self-assertion, babies want to do things themselves, often resisting the assistance or control of another. Parents frequently hear the refrain "No! I do it!" (remember Jin Yu, who scolded her parents in Chinese when they tried to keep her from handling dangerous objects). According to Erikson, when parents appropriately structure their children's environments so they can be successful in their early, self-initiated efforts at mastery and control, babies develop confidence in their own abilities and seek challenges. On the other hand, when parents are overly controlling, or fail to create contexts in which their children can demonstrate competence, a sense of doubt and shame may take hold and dampen efforts to achieve.

basic trust versus mistrust For Erikson, the first stage of infancy, during which children come to trust others as reliable and kind and to regard the world as safe or else come to mistrust others as insensitive and hurtful and to regard the world as unpredictable and threatening.

autonomy versus shame and doubt For Erikson, the second stage of infancy, during which children develop a sense of themselves as competent to accomplish tasks or as not competent.

██▌▌ **APPLY ═ CONNECT ═ DISCUSS** ─

Discuss Erikson's notion of trust versus mistrust from the perspective of attachment theory.

Implications

Infancy is a time during which babies and caregivers forge social and emotional ties that provide a foundation for infants' exploring and learning about the world. Consistent with a biocultural perspective, both biological and sociocultural processes contribute to the creation of these ties. On the side of biology, evolution provides infants with certain capacities to express and share their emotions through a variety of facial expressions and behaviors and to form early attachments to social partners. The infant is also biologically endowed with a brain that includes special cells, called mirror neurons, that seem particularly sensitive to the social and emotional behaviors of others.

On the sociocultural side, the infant's emerging emotional and social development and expressiveness are significantly shaped by the nature of early interactions. Social interactions that are well organized and responsive to the baby's cues seem essential to healthy development and to nurturing the baby's sense of trust that the world is a safe and welcoming place to explore. Furthermore, because early interactions are influenced by the values and patterns of life in the infant's culture, they serve to draw the child into the lives of others, laying the foundation for the child's engaged participation in the community.

SUMMARY

The Nature of Infant Emotions and Emotional Expressions

- Emotion can be defined as a feeling state that includes distinctive physiological responses, can be expressed to others, involves a cognitive appraisal, and can motivate action. Through emotion regulation, people modulate and control emotions.

- Certain basic emotions—joy, fear, anger, surprise, sadness, and disgust—appear to be universal and present from birth or early infancy. Several theories explain basic emotions in infancy:
  - According to the theory of gradual differentiation, newborns experience only general emotional states—contentment and distress—from which the basic emotions gradually differentiate.
  - The differential emotions theory argues that at birth or soon after, infants have distinct basic emotions similar to those of adults.
  - Theorists who see infants' emotions and emotional expressions as ontogenetic adaptations believe these evolved because they contribute to babies' development and well-being by eliciting care and protection.

- Through primary intersubjectivity, infants and their caregivers in face-to-face interactions share emotions that focus on the interaction itself. In the laboratory, disruption of the synchrony between infants and their interactive partners results in negative emotional responses in infants. Maternal depression may prove an obstacle to intersubjectivity, as mothers may be less responsive to babies' emotional cues and infants may disengage from stressful, unresponsive interactions.

- Pouting, most common when the infant is beginning to be upset, may have evolved as a form of emotion regulation to maintain the intersubjectivity between infant and caregiver that crying would disrupt.

- Mirror neurons, which evidently fire in the same way when we see another perform an action as when we perform it, may register the intentions and emotions of others as if they were happening to us. Mirror neurons may contribute to newborns' ability to imitate facial actions and, more generally, to the importance of imitation in establishing emotional connections between infants and caregivers.

The Infant–Caregiver Emotional Relationship

- Attachment is an emotional bond between children and their caregivers, which begins to develop at around 7 to 9 months of age. According to Freud's drive-reduction explanation, attachment to the mother originates in the satisfied need for nourishment. Experiments with monkeys have supported not Freud's explanation but the ethological explanation of John Bowlby, according to which attachment provides a sense of security and a safe base from which to explore the world.

- Bowlby described attachment as developing in four phases, with infants ultimately able to retain feelings of security during separations and developing an internal working model for relationships.

- Using a procedure called the strange situation, Mary Ainsworth and other researchers found that the infant's attachment relationship could be one of secure attachment, with a healthy balance between wanting close contact with the mother and wanting to explore, or any of three types of insecure attachment—avoidant, resistant, or disorganized.

- Variations in patterns of attachment may relate to differences in several contexts:
  - Parental sensitivity may correlate with secure attachment, with maternal depression, abusive or extremely insensitive caregiving, and stressors experienced by parents, all possibly linked to insecure attachment patterns.
  - Institutional contexts such as orphanages can negatively affect attachment, with the extent depending on factors such as severity of deprivation, age on leaving the institution, and the quality of the subsequent environment.
  - Cultures may exert an influence, including perhaps through differences about what constitutes sensitive caregiving and secure relationships.

- Establishing a secure attachment relationship may be crucial to later relationships, as there appears to be continuity of attachment status from infancy to adulthood, particularly if the internal working model developed remains unchanged.

The Changing Nature of Communication

- Toward the end of the first year, with the emergence of secondary intersubjectivity, infants and their caregivers interact and share emotions about the world beyond themselves.

- Important forms of communication include social referencing, in which babies look to their caregiver for an indication of how to feel and act on encountering something unfamiliar, and gaze-following and pointing.
- Word comprehension is in evidence by 6 months, and by 9 months children can understand some common expressions. The ability to produce language progresses from early vocalizations through babbling in the sounds and intonation patterns of the surrounding language, to speaking some words at around 1 year, after which the pace of language learning accelerates remarkably.

A Sense of Self

- By about 6 months, experience interacting with objects and people, along with emerging abilities to locomote and to use language, contributes to the infant's new sense of self. The ability to recognize oneself in a mirror emerges gradually and is clearly evident at around 18 months. Children's two-word utterances reflect their ability to see themselves as agents.
- The emergence of a sense of self gives rise to the self-conscious emotions—for example, embarrassment, pride,

shame, guilt, and envy—which require thinking about and evaluating oneself in relation to other people and their standards.
- The end of infancy is marked by patterns of behavior reflecting a sense of self and a new independence.

Developing Trust and Autonomy

- In the first of the two stages into which Erikson divided infancy, that of basic trust versus mistrust, infants may come to see the world as safe for exploration and people as reliable and loving or to see the world as dangerous and people as insensitive and hurtful.
- In the second stage, autonomy versus shame or doubt, infants may acquire a sense of ability to accomplish tasks and tackle challenges or may come to doubt their ability and feel shame.

Implications

- During infancy, babies and caregivers forge social and emotional ties that give infants a foundation for exploring the world. Both biological and sociocultural processes contribute to the creation of these ties.

Key Terms

emotion, p. 202
emotion regulation, p. 203
basic emotions, p. 203
theory of gradual differentiation, p. 204
differential emotions theory, p. 204
ontogenetic adaptations, p. 205
primary intersubjectivity, p. 205
mirror neurons, p. 208
attachment, p. 209

biological drives, p. 210
detachment, p. 211
secure base, p. 212
separation anxiety, p. 212
internal working model, p. 212
strange situation, p. 213
secure attachment, p. 213
avoidant attachment, p. 213
resistant attachment, p. 213

disorganized attachment, p. 214
secondary intersubjectivity, p. 223
social referencing, p. 223
perceptual scaffolding, p. 224
babbling, p. 225
self-conscious emotions, p. 227
basic trust versus mistrust, p. 228
autonomy versus shame and doubt, p. 228

Major Milestones of Early Childhood

	Physical Domain	Cognitive Domain	Social and Emotional Domain	
What Develops...	• Compared to infancy, growth rates of the body and brain slow considerably while the ability to use and control the body increases. • Gross motor developments include running, kicking, climbing, throwing, skipping. • Fine motor developments include unbuttoning, using eating utensils, pouring liquid into a glass, coloring within the lines with crayons. • Brain grows to 90 percent of its full weight. • Myelination and neuronal branching in frontal cortex and other areas important to advanced cognitive functions, including planning and regulating behavior.	• Tendency to confuse appearance and reality. • Difficulty taking the perspectives of others. • Limitations in cause–effect reasoning. • Increased memory ability due to greater efficiency in encoding, storing, and retrieving information. • Increased knowledge of physical laws and properties of objects, such as gravity and inertia. • Development of coherent theories about mental life and activity. • Acquisition of basic vocabulary and grammar of the child's native language.	• Stage of initiative versus guilt, with autonomy asserted but in ways that begin to conform to social roles and moral standards. • Play becomes gender segregated. • Development of concepts of "boy" and "girl," and efforts to match own behavior to concepts. • Emergence of ethnic identity. • Moral judgments often emphasize external consequences rather than motives or intentions. • Increased ability to regulate thought, action, and emotion. • Increasing ability to feel empathy and sympathy toward others.	
Sociocultural Contributions and Consequences...	• The fast pace of modern life may interfere with children's sleep habits. • Changes in access to food and eating behavior associated with globalization may increase risk for obesity, diabetes, and heart disease in children in developing countries. • Certain culturally organized activities may stimulate specific areas of the brain, facilitating growth and synaptic connections that, in turn, support further competence and learning.	• Cultural customs and routines support the development of generalized knowledge and shared understanding.	• Development of gender stereotypes is mediated by social and cultural practices that emphasize gender differences. • Increased cognitive abilities and decreased behavioral problems are associated with parents' socializing pride in ethnic background. • Cultural variations in parenting affect the emergence of self-conscious emotions. • Cultures differ in their tolerance of aggression and violence, affecting the extent to which children behave aggressively.	

part III

Early Childhood

By the age of 2½ or 3, children are infants no longer. It is clear that they are entering early childhood—the period between ages 2½ and 6. They are losing their baby fat, their legs are growing longer and thinner, and they are moving around the world with a great deal more confidence than they did only six months earlier. Within a short time, they can usually ride a tricycle, control their bowels, and put on their own clothes. They can help bake cookies, gather berries, and begin to participate in cultural ceremonies and rituals—as flower girls or ring bearers at a wedding, for example. Three-year-olds can talk an adult's ears off, even if their train of thought is difficult to follow, and they are an avid audience for an interesting story. They can be bribed with promises of a later treat, but they may try to negotiate for a treat now as well. They develop theories about everything, from where babies come from to why the moon disappears from the sky, and they constantly test their theories against the realities around them.

Despite their developing independence, 3-year-olds need assistance from adults and older siblings in many areas. They cannot hold a pencil properly, cross a busy road safely by themselves, or tie their shoes. They do not yet have the ability to concentrate for long on their own. As a result, they often go off on tangents in their games, drawings, and conversations. One minute a 3-year-old may be Dora the Explorer, the next minute a mommy kitty, and the next a little girl in a hurry to go to the toilet.

In early childhood, children still understand relatively little about the world in which they live and have little control over it. Thus they are prey to fears of monsters, the dark, dogs, and other apparent threats. They combat their awareness of being small and powerless by wishful, magical thinking that turns a little boy afraid of dogs into a big, brave, fighter pilot who dominates the playground.

Our discussion of early childhood development covers four chapters. Chapter 7 focuses on language and its acquisition. One of our most significant cultural tools, language is the medium through which children learn about their roles in the world, acceptable behavior, and their culture's assumptions about how the world works. Simultaneously, language enables children to ask questions, to explain their thoughts and desires, and to make more effective demands on the people around them.

Chapter 8 examines physical and cognitive developments during early childhood. The challenge developmentalists face is to explain how children can think and behave logically at one moment and then with complete lack of logic the next. The chapter considers different explanations for the unevenness of young children's cognition.

Chapter 9 shifts attention to social development and personality formation—to children's growing sense of a distinct identity, their ability to control their actions and feelings, their ways of thinking about rules of proper behavior, and their relations with the people around them. Topics focused on include the acquisition of a sense of culturally acceptable sex roles and children's increasing ability to get along with one another as they learn to balance their own desires with the demands of their social group.

With these general characteristics of early childhood as background, Chapter 10 addresses the influence of various contexts on young children's development. Among these are the family, where children first learn about who they are and what adults expect of them; community settings, including day-care centers and preschools; and the media, which link children's experiences in different settings and have important socializing effects.

7

Language Acquisition

Although it has been 15 minutes since her father put her down with her "baby" and gave her a good-night kiss, the Sandman has yet to arrive, and 21-month-old Emily is filling her quiet room with words:

> *baby no eat dinner*
> *broccoli, soup carrots cause rice*
> *baby eat that*
> *baby no in night*
> *broccoli broccoli soup carrots cabbage*
> *no baby sleeping*
>
> *then baby get sick*
> *Emmy no eat dinner*
> *broccoli soup cause*
> *no baby sleeping*
> *baby sleeping all night*

One year later, Emily's bedtime monologue sounds like this:

> *actually it's Stephen's koala bear . . .*
> *when Stephen wakes up I'll have to throw his koala bear in his room*
> *cause it's really Stephen's*
> *as a matter of fact Stephen's*
> *as a matter of fact it's sleeping with me now*

(Levy, 1989, pp. 158 and 169)

A s you can see, the first of Emily's bedtime monologues is barely interpretable. Words are missing or out of the usual order, and the monologue seems a jumble of disconnected statements with no clear meaning. The word "cause" appears in both monologues, but in the first it is next to impossible to figure out the meaning of "broccoli, soup carrots cause rice" and "broccoli soup cause." In fact, the only likely clue to what Emily might mean is the fact that many young children are not big fans of vegetables: she might be reciting her reason for not eating dinner.

By contrast, in the second monologue, Emily's words are far more grammatically organized and more clearly convey her meaning. The groups of words are longer and more like complete sentences now. The word "'cause" expresses a causal relationship ("'cause it's really Stephen's"), and possessive and temporal relationships are also expressed ("it's Stephen's"; "it's sleeping with me now"). It is also clear that Emily has picked up certain speech mannerisms, such as "actually" and "as a matter of fact." Although her language is not fully developed by any means, it is significantly more adultlike and easy to interpret.

The progress Emily has made in her ability to use language during the year separating the two monologues is amazing but by no means exceptional, and similar increases in language-using ability will continue for several years to come. Indeed, by her sixth birthday, Emily's mental and social life will be totally transformed by an explosive growth in the ability to comprehend and use language. Children are estimated to learn several words a day during the preschool years, and by the time they are 6 years old, their vocabularies have grown to anywhere between 8,000 and 14,000 words (Anglin, 1993; Biemiller & Slonim, 2001). They can understand verbal instructions ("Go wash your face—and do not come back until it's clean"), chatter excitedly about the tiger they saw at the zoo, teach friends how to play a video game, or insult their siblings with a variety of colorful labels. In short, 6-year-old children are competent language users. Without this competence, they could not carry out the new cognitive tasks and social responsibilities that their society will now assign them, including acquiring the tools of their culture through formal education or other instruction.

We begin this chapter by reviewing the nature of language as a symbolic system and elaborating on the emerging foundations of linguistic communication that we discussed in earlier chapters. Next, we describe the two main keys—human biological structures and processes, and human social environments—that unlock the door to the world of language. We then trace the course of children's development in the four basic domains of language: the domains of *phonology* (sound), *semantics* (meaning), *grammar,* and *pragmatics* (the uses to which language is put). With the facts of language development in hand, we examine various theories about the processes that underlie this fundamental human capacity. Finally, we explore the unique role of language as a tool for creating and transforming reality.

The Power of Language

The story of Romeo and Juliet has endured for centuries. It was a tragic love, made so by the fact that one was a Montague, the other a Capulet, the names of two families caught in a long and violent feud. In deep despair, Romeo challenges the idea that one's family name could stand as an obstacle to the happiness of a shared life together and asks the famous question "What's in a name? That which we call a rose by any other name would smell as sweet." Romeo suggests that names should not matter; they are just words for things. It is the things themselves that we love or despise, that move us with their sweet scents and beauty. But we know better. Names, like words in general, can carry deep and complex meanings. And when names and other words are woven together into sentences and stories, like Shakespeare's *Romeo and Juliet,* they can move and inspire people for generations.

We made the point in Chapter 2 that language is a *symbolic system* of enormous scope and power (pp. 56–57). It allows us to communicate about the past and the future; permits the expression of abstract ideas, desires, and emotions; and is one of the most significant means of preserving and passing on, and even challenging and transforming, a culture's knowledge, values, and beliefs. We also explained that language, like other tools of culture, profoundly affects development because it organizes or *mediates* our activities, relationships, and thinking—as "Montague" and "Capulet" did for Romeo and Juliet. Alexander Luria (1981, p. 35) beautifully summarized the power human beings possess as a consequence of language:

> In the absence of words, humans would have to deal only with those things which they could perceive and manipulate directly. With the help of language, they can deal with things which they have not perceived even indirectly and with things which were part of the experience of earlier generations. Thus, the word adds another dimension to the world of humans. . . . Animals have only one world, the world of objects and situations which can be perceived by the senses. Humans have a double world.

Although many other species make a variety of communicative sounds and gestures, none has evolved a system of communication as powerful and flexible as human language (Greenspan & Shanker, 2004; Jablonka & Lamb, 2007). Indeed, the evidence presented in previous chapters leaves little doubt that children are born predisposed to attend to language and to communicate with the people around them. At birth they show a preference for speech over other kinds of sounds and are capable of differentiating between two sounds that are distinct *phonemes* (basic sound categories) in any of the world's languages. Within a few days after birth, they can distinguish the sounds of their native language from those of a foreign language. Well before they are able to speak intelligibly, the range of sounds they recognize as distinct becomes narrowed to those that their native language treats as distinct phonemes (Kuhl et al., 2006; Luo & Baillargeon, 2005; see Chapter 6, p. 225). They come to recognize first their own name and words for familiar objects and people and then entire often-heard phrases. Babies make comparable strides in their capacity to produce language. Although newborns' abilities to communicate are limited initially to a small set of facial expressions and crying, soon their sound repertoire expands to include *cooing, babbling,* and then *jargoning* (see Chapter 6, p. 225), with each change bringing the baby closer to producing recognizable words.

At the same time that their capacity to distinguish and produce linguistic signals increases, babies become more adept at interacting with the people and objects around them. In Chapter 6 we explained how infants and their social partners establish *primary intersubjectivity,* sharing feelings as a consequence of well-coordinated and organized face-to-face social interactions (see pp. 205–206). This ability is evident in the rounds of greeting noises and smiling in which caregivers and babies engage, to their mutual delight. We noted, moreover, that between the ages of 9 and 12 months, babies and their partners become able to establish *secondary intersubjectivity*, a crucial precursor to language acquisition because it allows babies and their caregivers to communicate their feelings about objects and events that are the focus of their joint attention (see p. 223).

Somehow, in the space of a very few years, children are launched from these early foundations and enter the world of language (see Table 7.1 for a summary of some of the early developments). We will now examine the special keys that unlock the door to this world.

The face-to-face social interaction enjoyed by this Jordanian mother and baby will expand dramatically as language develops and provides a way of communicating about the world around them.

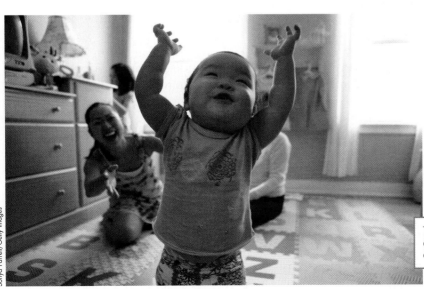

The gesture and vocalizations of this baby communicate very clearly, "pick me up!"

table 7.1

The Progress of Language Development

Approximate Age	Typical Behavior
Birth	Phoneme perception
	Discrimination of language from nonlanguage sounds
	Crying
3 months	Cooing
6 months	Babbling
	Loss of ability to discriminate between nonnative phonemes
9 months	First words
12 months	Use of words to attract adults' attention
18 months	Vocabulary spurt
	First two-word sentences (telegraphic speech)
24 months	Correct responses to indirect requests ("Is the door shut?")
30 months	Creation of indirect requests ("You're standing on my blocks!")
	Modification of speech to take listener into account
	Early awareness of grammatical categories

Keys to the World of Language

Access to the world of language is virtually guaranteed to all who hold two keys: (1) the human biological structures and systems that support language, and (2) participation in a language-using community. Let us consider the biological key first.

The Biological Key to Language

Developmentalists have used two conceptually related approaches to tackle the question of how biology unlocks the door to the world of language. The first is to inquire about the capacities and limitations of other species in producing and comprehending language. If the language abilities of other species depart significantly from those of our own species, then evolutionary forces must have produced the uniquely human biological structures and processes that make language possible. The second, related approach is to try to discover which structures and processes of the human brain support language development and what their special contributions to it are.

Is Language Uniquely Human? Research to determine whether language is uniquely human has a long history (Weiss & Newport, 2006). One early strategy involved experimenters' raising chimpanzees in their home as though they were human children. The hope was that these genetically close relatives (with whom it was then assumed we share 98.5 percent of our genes) would acquire oral language if they were treated just like humans. This research demonstrated that chimpanzees can, in fact, learn to comprehend dozens of spoken words and phrases (Hayes & Hayes, 1951; Kellogg & Kellogg, 1933). But the chimps never *produced* language, at least not in the form of spoken words. Subsequent research that involved manual signing instead of oral speech provided clear evidence that chimps can learn to use signs to refer to and request certain things (such as different kinds of fruit or specific toys). However, the evidence that they can acquire language is still disputed (Savage-Rumbaugh & Fields, 2000; Fields, Segerdahl, & Savage-Rumbaugh, 2007; Tomasello, 2000; Buttelmann, Call, & Tomasello, 2008).

Current enthusiasm for the idea that chimpanzees have the capacity to understand and produce language has been inspired by the work of Sue Savage-Rumbaugh and Duane Rumbaugh (Rumbaugh et al., 1994). The Rumbaughs provided chimpanzees with a "lexical keyboard"—that is, a keyboard that bore symbols that stood for words ("banana," "give," and so on)—and they used standard reinforcement learning techniques to teach the chimpanzees the meaning of these symbols. In addition, the people who worked with the chimpanzees used natural language in everyday, routine activities such as feeding.

The Rumbaughs' most successful student has been Kanzi, a bonobo ape who initially learned to use the lexical keyboard by observing his mother being trained to use it. Kanzi is able to use the keyboard to ask for things, and he can comprehend requests made of him

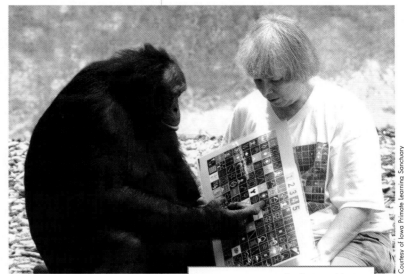

Kanzi uses a specially designed keyboard composed of lexical symbols to communicate.

by researchers using the lexical symbols. He has also learned to understand some spoken English words and phrases (Rumbaugh & Washburn, 2003). For example, when told to "feed your ball some tomato," Kanzi picked up a tomato and placed it in the "mouth" of a facelike soft sponge ball. He has also demonstrated some understanding of syntax: When asked to "give the shot [syringe] to Liz" and then to "give Liz a shot," he correctly handed the syringe to the girl in the first instance and touched the syringe to the girl's arm in the second.

Kanzi's ability to produce language is not as impressive as his comprehension. Most of his "utterances" on the lexical keyboard are single words that are closely linked to his current actions, and they usually involve requests. He also uses two-word utterances in a wide variety of combinations, however, and occasionally makes observations. For example, he produced the request "car trailer" on one occasion when he was in the car and wanted (or so his caretakers believed) to be taken to the trailer rather than to walk there. He has created such requests as "play yard Austin" when he wanted to visit a chimpanzee named Austin in the play yard. When a researcher put oil on him while he was eating a potato, he commented, "potato oil."

Using combinations of visual symbols or gestures, bonobos and chimpanzees can produce language at roughly the level of a 2-year-old child. In their productions, they form telegraphic utterances that encode the same semantic relations as do those of children (for example, a two-symbol combination relating an agent to its action—"Kanzi eat") (Greenfield, Lyn, & Washburn, 2007). Bonobos are also capable of comprehending English speech at roughly the level of a 2-year-old child (Savage-Rumbaugh, 1993). However, in contrast to human children, who acquire complex language with no formal teaching, nonhuman primates develop language ability only in the context of intense explicit instruction provided by their human caretakers. To explore what might account for this dramatic species difference in the ability to learn language, developmentalists have looked to species-unique features of the human brain.

A Brain for Language Scientists have long been aware that the left side of the human brain plays a dominant role in language ability, but it was not until the middle of the nineteenth century that the brain bases of language became an active area of research in medicine and psychology. In particular, it was the work of two physicians, each studying a different form of a speech disorder called *aphasia,* that led to the discovery of language areas of the brain (Luria, 1973).

In 1861, a French surgeon named Paul Broca treated a man who was unable to speak. When his patient died, Broca examined his brain and found damage on the outside surface of the left frontal lobe in an area that came to be known as *Broca's area*. Patients with damage to this area suffer from what is called *Broca's aphasia,* a condition in which speech is either absent or severely disrupted. Individuals with Broca's aphasia may speak with great effort in brief, meaningful phrases that omit small words such as "is," "and," and "the." For example, a person with Broca's aphasia may say "Walk dog" to mean "I will take the dog for a walk." (Those who recover from this disorder often report that they knew what they wanted to say but could not control their speech.) Generally, patients are able to understand individual words but have difficulty understanding more complex structures.

A few years later, Carl Wernicke, a German physician, discovered that damage to an area slightly to the rear of Broca's area results in an inability to comprehend language. People with damage to this area, now called *Wernicke's area,* are often capable of producing language, but much of what they say makes little sense. Patients with what is known as *Wernicke's aphasia* thus often produce long sentences that include unnecessary words and even nonsense words. For example, a person with Wernicke's aphasia may say, "You know that smoodle pinkered and that I want to get him round and take care of him like you want before" to mean "The dog needs to go out so I will take him for a walk" (NIDCD, 2002).

Contemporary studies of the brain and language have shown that in adults, injuries to the left hemisphere in either Broca's or Wernicke's area are overwhelmingly more likely to cause aphasia than are injuries to the corresponding parts of the right hemisphere (Figure 7.1). This evidence appears to confirm the idea that there is indeed a part of the brain that is genetically programmed to produce and comprehend language—an idea that has gained additional support from studies using technologically sophisticated neuroimaging techniques.

Using advanced neuroimaging techniques, researchers from the Max Planck Institute for Human Cognitive and Brain Sciences in Germany tried to determine whether Broca's area has a special role to play in processing complex language (Friederici et al., 2006). Their investigation was inspired by increasing evidence suggesting that although some nonhuman species show at least a rudimentary capacity to process simple sentences (as did Kanzi when he distinguished the difference between "give the shot to Liz" and "give Liz a shot"), they are not able to process more complex sentences. When researchers in the Max Planck study presented participants with both simple and complex speech sequences (for example, a simple sentence like "The song pleased the teacher" and a more complex sentence like "The song that the boy sang pleased the teacher"), they discovered that the complexity of the sequence determined which area of the brain became active. In particular, complex sequences activated Broca's area, a part of the brain that has evolved fairly recently in the history of our species. Simple sequences, in contrast, activated just an evolutionarily older area of the brain, one that we share with other primates. In another line of research using neuroimaging, studies conducted at the University of Barcelona have shown that the characteristic spurt in toddlers' vocabulary (discussed in more detail below) occurs only after substantial myelination of language-related brain regions (Pujol et al., 2006).

Wernicke's area

Broca's area

Figure 7.1 A view of the left hemisphere of the brain that highlights two key areas for normal language processing in adults. Wernicke's area is central to processing sounds and comprehension. Damage to this area results in an inability to comprehend language. Broca's area is central to motor control and language production. For patients with damage to this area of the brain, normal speech is either absent or severely disrupted. (From http://faculty.washington.edu/chudler/lang.html.)

Although Broca's and Wernicke's areas seem to play a significant role in the ability of humans to use and acquire language, recent research with children strongly suggests that it is possible to develop normal, or near-normal, language abilities even if Broca's and Wernicke's areas are damaged, as long as the damage occurs early in life (Bates & Roe, 2001). Data in support of this conclusion come largely from studies of children who, just before, during, or after birth, suffered strokes that cut off the blood supply to the left or right hemisphere of the brain, resulting in damage to the cerebral cortex. These children still acquire language, although their performance may be at the lower end of the normal range. Most important, however, they do so even when the damage occurs in the left hemisphere, where language appears to be localized in adults! Whereas left hemisphere damage would leave an adult considerably more language impaired than right hemisphere damage, for children there is little impairment with damage on either side, as Figure 7.2 shows. This is because of the plasticity of the brain in early development; in infants with left hemisphere damage, parts of the right hemisphere become the brain center for the language.

Some researchers interpret these and similar findings to indicate that, in the absence of any interfering factors, the infant brain is predisposed to ensure the eventual emergence of an area in the left hemisphere of the brain that is specialized to process language (Bates, 2005). Indeed, a fascinating study indicates that when 5-month-old babies babble, their mouths open more on the right side than the left; since the right side of the mouth is controlled by the left side of the brain, this suggests that the left side of the brain has already begun to specialize as a center for language processing (Holowka & Petitto, 2002). On the other hand, evidence that the newborn's brain can compensate for damage caused by strokes indicates that the brain mechanisms supporting language are not fixed at birth. Rather, "learning itself plays a major role in organizing the brain for efficient language use" (Bates & Roe, 2001, p. 305).

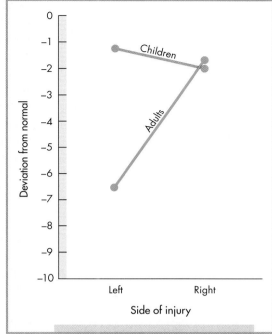

Figure 7.2 The figure shows the difference in the impact of brain injury to left and right hemispheres for adults and children. When adults were presented with novel phrases, the performance of adults with left hemisphere damage was far worse than the performance of those with right hemisphere damage. There was no significant difference in performance between children with left hemisphere damage and those with right hemisphere damage. (After Bates & Roe, 2001.)

The Environmental Key to Language

Sometime before her second birthday, a girl named Genie was permanently locked in her room by her abusive father. For more than 11 years, she spent her days chained to a potty and her nights tied up in a sleeping bag. She lived in almost total isolation, and as far as can be determined, was never spoken to after she was confined. Every time her father came to tie her in for the night or to bring her food, he growled at her like a beast and scratched her with his fingernails. When she was finally liberated from these horrible circumstances at the age of 13, Genie was a pitiful creature. She did not make intelligible sounds, walk normally, chew solid food, or express her emotions appropriately. David Rigler, a scientist, and his wife petitioned the Department of Social Services to become Genie's foster parents and to study her extensively, along with a team of linguists and psychologists. Genie spent 4 years in the Rigler household. During that time she was treated as much as possible like a member of the family. She was taught how to chew solid food, to behave properly at the table, to express her emotions appropriately, and to stop masturbating whenever she felt the urge to. However, despite the special emphasis placed on nurturing her language development, Genie's speech resembled the language used in telegrams. She never learned to ask a real question or to form a proper negative sentence (Curtiss et al., 1974).

Genie's case tells a tragic story of unimaginable deprivation and destruction. It also underscores how participation in a normal social environment is essential to the process of language acquisition (Clark, 2006). In the course of such participation, children are not only exposed to *models* of how language is used and understood; they are also provided with opportunities to communicate with others—opportunities that *motivate* them to be better communicators, that is, to use language to express and share ideas effectively (Hoff, 2006). Clearly, Genie was denied both language models and communication opportunities during the years children acquire language, and these deprivations certainly contributed to her inability to develop normal language. But Genie's horrific deprivations affected every aspect of her health and development, making it impossible to use her case to assess the specific effects that language deprivation can have on children's language development. To do this, researchers have turned to the case of deaf children whose hearing parents do not know sign language and discourage its use (Goldin-Meadow, Mylander, & Franklin, 2007).

Language-Deprived Environments The biological condition of deafness need not be an impediment to normal language acquisition: Deaf children born to deaf parents who communicate in sign language acquire language at least as rapidly and fully as hearing children born into hearing households (Morgan & Woll, 2002; Volterra et al., 2006). Thus, any delays or difficulties in deaf children's language development must result from the way the linguistic environment is organized.

Such difficulties often arise in deaf children whose parents refuse to learn or use sign language because they believe that their children could and should learn to read lips and to vocalize sounds. Although many children raised in these circumstances have significant trouble learning spoken language (Geers et al., 2002), they often develop fairly sophisticated gestural systems that allow them to communicate with others (reviewed in Schick, 2006). In particular, many deaf children raised without exposure to a signed language spontaneously begin to gesture in "home sign," a kind of communication through pantomime (Pizutto et al., 2001).

Goldin-Meadow and her colleagues wanted to find out if the home sign developed by the deaf children displayed the characteristic features of language. They discovered that the gestures these children developed did indeed have certain characteristics of language, even though the children had no one to show them the signs. Home sign begins as pointing. Children then gesture one sign at a time—at the same age that hearing children develop single-word utterances. Home-sign gestures also seem to refer to the same kinds of objects, and to fulfill the same functions, as the early words of hearing children or of deaf children with signing parents. Remarkably, home-signing children go on to make patterns of two, and sometimes three or more, signs around their second birthday, about the same time that hearing children utter multiword sentences. In addition, Goldin-Meadow reports that these deaf children were using complex sentence structures characteristic of all human languages and absent from the communicative system of chimpanzees and other creatures even after long training—the sort of structures that we described above as activating Broca's area, rather than the evolutionarily older part of the brain.

To explore the robustness of home sign, Susan Goldin-Meadow and her colleagues compared its development in deaf children in the United States and in children of Mandarin-speaking parents living in Taiwan, where child-rearing practices and the use of gesture to accompany speech are quite different from those in the United States (Goldin-

Children with hearing impairments acquire language at a comparable rate to hearing children, especially when they receive support from the environment. Here, deaf Palestinian children learn sign language in a special school in the Gaza Strip.

AP Photo/Marco Di Lauro

Meadow & Mylander, 1998; Goldin-Meadow et al., 2007). Despite these cultural differences, the researchers found the same patterns of spontaneous home-sign production, suggesting that universal processes of language creation are at work. (See the box "Children Creating a Language.") However, once the children in both cultures are able to make two- to three-word "utterances" in their home sign and begin to form structurally complex sentences, their language development appears to come to an end. Thus it seems that the mere fact of being raised in an environment where the actions of all the other participants are organized by human language and culture is sufficient to allow the child to acquire the rudiments of linguistic structure, but that without access to the additional information (signed or spoken) provided by accomplished language users in the child's environment, the child has no opportunity to discover the more subtle features of language.

Children Creating a Language

BEFORE THE 1970S THERE WAS NO national education system for deaf Nicaraguans. They were socially isolated and marginalized in Nicaraguan society. But in 1977 a school for 25 deaf children was built in the capital city, Managua. Two years later the school was expanded to admit 100 children; one year later a vocational school was opened for deaf adolescents. These schools served more than 400 students. Within a few years, a community of deaf people ranging in age from childhood to adulthood developed, and with it, a new language. Developmentalist Ann Senghas studied the emergence of Nicaraguan Sign Language within this newly formed community (Senghas & Coppola, 2001). Her findings illustrate that while the child's *capacity* for learning complex language is rooted in the evolutionary history of our species, the acquisition of a fully fledged grammar requires social participation.

In the absence of an organized deaf community in Nicaragua, there had been no Nicaraguan sign language. But when deaf children were brought together on school playgrounds and buses, they began to communicate with one another using the home signs that they had invented before coming to school. Although teachers were instructing children in lip-reading and finger-spelling in Spanish, the children largely ignored these lessons outside the classroom and instead created their very own language community. As children interacted socially, the number and variety of signs that they used increased dramatically, as did the complexity of their communication.

At the start of the second and third school years, new groups of children arrived at the school. With no deliberate instruction, the home signs of individual children mixed with those of others and were conventionalized and

combined, thus becoming a *pidgin language.* Pidgin languages are languages with simplified grammar and vocabulary that emerge in situations of contact between speakers of different languages, most often in situations of slave or immigrant labor. Within a very few years children arriving at school were encountering a pidgin language in place of home signs. Over time, their signs became less like home signs—they became more arbitrary and more stylized and took on more complex grammatical forms. In short, the children began to communicate with each other in a language that exhibits the same structure as any other natural language. Significantly, it was the *youngest* children who elaborated on and enriched the pidgin language they encountered and introduced new grammatical forms that were not present in the signing of the older students (Slobin, 2005; Senghas, Senghas, & Pyers, 2005).

In his review of Senghas's work, Dan Slobin argues the point that children's creation of home signs suggests a human capacity to create the rudiments of a language system but that, for such rudimentary systems to develop further, a community of users, as at the Nicaraguan school, is needed. Slobin writes that "language is like other sorts of human technology; once it is present, it provides a 'niche'—a modified environment—creating new pressures for the refinement of that technology" (2005, p. 280).

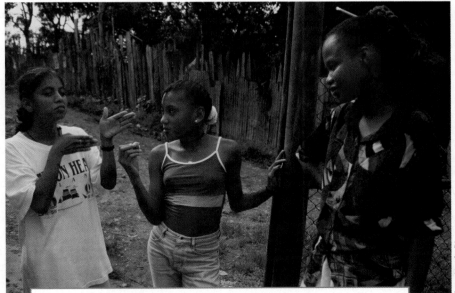

These girls are students at the Esquelitas de Bluefields in Managua, Nicaragua, where they learn sign language, as well as other literacy and academic skills.

Susan Meiselas/Magnum

infant-directed speech (or motherese or baby-talk) Speech adults use with infants, characterized by high pitch, exaggerated intonation, clear boundaries between parts, and simplified vocabulary.

Highlighting this point is the case of a hearing child raised by deaf parents (Sachs, Bard, & Johnson, 1981). This child's parents exposed him to neither conventional oral nor conventional manual language input. He heard English only on TV and during a brief time spent in nursery school. The course of this child's language development was precisely the same as for the deaf children of nonsigning, hearing parents: he developed the basic features of language but not more subtle ones. Once he was introduced to normal American sign language, at the age of 3 years and 9 months, he quickly acquired normal language ability.

Taken as a whole, the research on language-deprived environments suggests that even in the absence of direct experience of language, children will develop the beginnings of language during the first 2 years of life, as long they regularly have the opportunity to communicate with others. However, the language that appears under such linguistically impoverished conditions does not go beyond that of children at the two-word phase. Apparently, to fully acquire language, children must grow up in an environment that provides a language-support system.

Variations in Language Environments Research shows that, even if we look just at "normal" environments, there is enormous variety in the language environments to which children across the globe are exposed. Indeed, some children are exposed to a variety of languages (see the box "Learning Two Languages"). One significant difference concerns the amount of talk that adults direct to infants. North American mothers, for example, are known to talk to their babies from birth, if not before, even using the babies' burps, sneezes, and other noises to engage in "conversation" with them (Snow, 1995; Hoff, 2006). In contrast, adults in cultures such as the Mayan of Mexico and the Walpiri of Australia talk very little to their babies, believing that there is no point in engaging prelinguistic children in conversation (Brown, Blum-Kulka, & Snow, 2002).

In some cultures, adults believe that it is important to actively teach their children how to talk (Ochs & Schieffelin, 1995). The Kaluli of New Guinea, for example, believe that children must be explicitly taught language just as they must be taught other culturally valued forms of behavior. Kaluli parents take their child's first spoken words as a signal that the child is ready to be taught language, and they begin a form of speech activity called *elema*: the mother provides the utterance she wants the child to repeat followed by the command "Elema" ("Say like this"). Eleanor Ochs (1982) described similar practices among Samoans, and Peggy Miller (1982) reported that working-class mothers in Baltimore, Maryland, follow a similar strategy with respect to teaching vocabulary.

Even in societies in which adults do not engage in deliberate language-teaching strategies, many adults are likely to use a special kind of speech when speaking to infants. Dubbed **infant-directed speech,** or more popularly, *motherese* or *baby-talk,* this speech is characterized by a high-pitched voice with exaggerated shifts in intonation, a simplified vocabulary, and an emphasis on the boundaries between meaningful parts of an utterance, all of which help to highlight what the adult wants to communicate (Fernald, 1991; Kitamura et al., 2002; see Chapter 2, pp. 61–62). Such modifications to normal speech are believed to provide a variety of clues that children can use in segmenting the flow of speech to identify words. Indeed, a study conducted by Erik Thiessen and his colleagues demonstrated that 8-month-old babies who heard a string of nonsense words presented in the pitch and intonation characteristic of infant-directed speech were able to learn the words better than were babies who heard them presented in a more monotone fashion (Thiessen, Hill, & Saffran, 2005).

As Table 7.2 indicates, middle-class parents in the United States simplify virtually every aspect of their language when they speak to their children. In addition,

table 7.2

Simplifications Used by Middle-Class U.S. Adults Speaking to Small Children

Phonological Simplifications

Higher pitch and exaggerated intonation

Clear pronunciation

Slower speech

Distinct pauses between utterances

Syntactic Differences

Shorter and less varied utterance length

Almost all sentences well formed

Many partial or complete repetitions of child's utterances, sometimes with expansion

Fewer broken sentences

Less grammatical complexity

Semantic Differences

More limited vocabulary

Many special words and diminutives

Reference to concrete circumstances of here and now

Middle level of generality in naming objects

Pragmatic Differences

More directives, imperatives, and questions

More utterances designed to draw attention to aspects of objects

Source: De Villiers & De Villiers, 1978.

Learning Two Languages

WE LIVE IN AN AGE IN WHICH VAST numbers of people move from one language community to another, rear children with people whose native tongue is different than their own, or grow up in families in which more than one language is spoken. In fact, well over 50 percent of the world's people are *bilingual* or *multilingual*—that is, speak two or more languages (Tucker, 1999). This state of affairs poses interesting questions about language acquisition for parents as well as developmentalists. How does exposure to multiple languages affect a child's language acquisition? Is the child confused by clashing vocabularies and grammars? Is it better for a child to learn one language first before being exposed to another? Despite ample scientific evidence that young children can acquire two or more languages effortlessly (Bialystok, 2001), it is widely believed among North American parents that early exposure to two languages might confuse children and cause them to learn language more slowly or less well than their monolingual peers. As a result of these concerns, many bilingual parents deliberately choose to withhold knowledge of one family language from their children until it is "safe" to add a second language to their repertoire (Petitto et al., 2001).

Psycholinguists who study early bilingualism have been divided in their interpretation of whether, and to what extent, acquiring two languages at the same time differs from acquiring one language and then another. Some adhere to the *unitary language hypothesis*, believing that children exposed to two languages from birth interpret the two languages as part of a single, fused, system. In support of this view, they point to cases where infants in the one-word stage acquire each of their words in just one or the other language. For example, a child who knows the word for dog in one language will not know the word for it in the other language. The fact that children exposed to two languages often use words from both languages in the same sentence is also taken as evidence that they do not distinguish between their two native vocabularies. According to this view, it is not until children are about 3 years old that they become capable of differentiating between two separate languages. The unitary language hypothesis supports those who recommend delaying exposure to a second language in order to avoid confusion and possible language delay.

Those who adhere to the *differentiated language hypothesis,* on the other hand, accept the evidence that children mix two languages but emphasize that children's speech exhibits regular grammatical patterns that are appropriate to both languages they speak. In addition, the language they use is sensitive to the language used by the adults around them. For example, if a young, Chinese–English speaking child is addressed in Chinese, he will respond in Chinese, not English, suggesting that he is able to keep straight which language is appropriate in a given context.

In an effort to find evidence against which to test the two hypotheses, a team of researchers looked at the language acquisition both of hearing children who had deaf parents and were acquiring sign language and French, and of hearing children who were acquiring French and English (Petitto et al., 2001). The researchers found no evidence of language delay in either group; whether the combination of languages was sign–French or French–English, children reached the key milestones of acquiring their first word, their first two-word combination, and their first 50 words at almost precisely the same age as monolingual children. In addition, when the researchers created conditions under which the child was speaking with a person who knew only one of the relevant languages (French, English, or sign), the children almost always used the language that the adult knew, indicating that they differentiated the two languages.

Taken as a whole, these data appear to lay to rest the idea that there is anything harmful about children acquiring two languages simultaneously. Indeed, bilingual children reap surprising rewards. The constant need to grapple with two active language systems—inhibiting one while using the other—may carry over to other areas of intellectual functioning. A case in point is bilingual children's early ability to see multiple images in an ambiguous figure (Bialystok & Shapero, 2005). It is well known that children, particularly those under the age of 5, have difficulty identifying more than one image in ambiguous figures, such as the vase and the faces shown in the figure (Gopnik & Rosati, 2001; Diamond, 2002a, 2002b). Once they see the vase, it is hard for young children to reinterpret the picture and see it in a different way—as a picture of faces (see p. 251 regarding how preoperational children can be "captured" by a specific feature of an object). Bilingual children, however, seem to master such tasks at earlier ages than children learning a single language. Ellen Bialystok and her colleagues believe that this early mastery is due to bilingual children's ability to control their attention to selected aspects of the figure, an ability that stems from their experience in paying attention to and managing two different languages. Thus, in addition to reaping the rewards of being able to communicate in more than one language, bilingual children seem to reap cognitive rewards as well.

In today's world, the ability to not only speak, but also read and write in foreign languages is becoming an increasingly important part of every child's development.

Andy Sacks/Getty Images

At earlier ages than children learning a single language, bilingual children are able to see both the faces and the vase in this ambiguous figure.

several studies have shown that the complexity of adults' speech to children is graded to the level of the complexity of the individual child's speech (Hoff, 2001; Snow, 1995).

Catherine Snow (1972) showed how such tailoring processes can work in the case of a mother's directing a child to put away toys: "Put the red truck in the box now. . . . The red truck. . . . No, the red truck. . . . In the box. . . . The red truck in the box." Note the sequence of the mother's directions. Snow argues that this kind of grading of language, in which statements are gradually simplified and their meaning highlighted, isolates constituent phrases at the same time that it models the whole correct grammatical structure.

In their efforts to aid children's comprehension (and perhaps their discovery of how to use language), American adults not only simplify what they say to children but also often expand upon and reformulate what children say into a grammatically correct adult version (Brown & Bellugi, 1964). A mother whose child says "Mommy wash," for example, might respond with "Yes, Mommy is washing her face"; and to the declaration "Daddy sleep," she might respond "Yes, Daddy is sleeping. Don't wake him up." Recent research conducted by developmental psycholinguist Eve Clark and her colleagues confirmed that the practice of adults' reformulating young children's utterances is widespread, providing novice language learners feedback about the grammar of their language (Chouinard & Clark, 2003).

Despite the common belief that adults' simplifying, highlighting, and reformulating behaviors help children to master language, the necessity of such practices has been the subject of longstanding disagreement among researchers, When Courtney Cazden (1965) attempted to "force-feed" children with a heavy diet of feedback by expanding and correcting their incorrect sentences, she found that these efforts had no special effect on the children's language development. Some subsequent studies have arrived at the same conclusion (Saxton, 1997), but others have not (Valian, 1999). Consequently, no firm conclusions about the influence of deliberate parental feedback are yet possible.

One thing that is clear, however, is that the development of children's vocabulary is affected by the amount of language they hear. This relation was strikingly demonstrated in a study by Betty Hart and Todd Risley (1999) that recorded the language spoken in the homes of welfare families, working-class families, and professional families. The differences in vocabulary exposure and development were quite marked: The 1- to 3-year-old children in welfare homes heard only 33 percent as much language as the children in working-class families, and only 20 percent as much language as children from professional families. The rate at which the children acquired vocabulary closely tracked the amount of language they heard.

But again, rate of vocabulary development aside, several decades of research show that no one method of structuring children's language experience is essential and that the differences in the adults' everyday, intuitive language practices with children appear to make little difference in the rate at which children acquire language. All normally developing children become competent language users.

APPLY ▪ CONNECT ▪ DISCUSS

In describing language as an "instinct," Stephen Pinker (1994) wrote that "people know how to talk in more or less the sense that spiders know how to spin webs . . . spiders spin spider webs because they have spider brains, which give them the urge to spin and the competence to succeed." In what ways might his argument be insufficient for explaining how individual children acquire language?

The Basic Domains of Language Acquisition

The first challenge in understanding a new language is segmenting the stream of sounds into separate and recognizable words. Consider the sentence "Thomas kissed Sylvia, so she slapped his face." If someone read you this sentence aloud, your interpretation would clearly be impaired if you heard something like "To mask issed sylvias oshes lapped hisfa ce." The process through which children acquire knowledge of how to segment strings of speech sounds into meaningful units of language is part of the domain of language acquisition referred to as **phonological development.**

Beyond understanding how to segment the speech sounds of the sentence, it is necessary to understand the meaning of the words that compose the sentence. **Semantic development** refers to this process of learning the meanings of words and word combinations. We know, for example, that the word "kiss" refers to a particular type of action in which the lips are puckered and applied to some person or object. However, the fact that the action resulted in being slapped, which we understand to mean striking another with one's hand, adds another layer of meaning to the kiss: it was unwanted and resented. As this simple example illustrates, word meanings are complex and interact with each other; and as you will see, the meanings of words change for children as they learn and apply them—often in error.

Yet another challenge to interpreting the sentence about Thomas and Sylvia is to understand the rules for how the words are arranged in the sentence. For words to be combined into a comprehensible sentence, they must be related not only to objects and events but to one another. That is, they must be governed by **grammar,** the rules of a particular language for sequencing words in a sentence, and word parts within words. For example, the word sequence "Thomas kissed Sylvia" has a very different meaning from the sequence "Sylvia kissed Thomas." Rules of grammar also lead us to understand that the kissing and slapping are actions that happened in the past (as indicated by the "-ed" ending), and that one action (the kissing) led to the other (the slapping). Thus language acquisition includes the process of learning grammar.

Finally, a full interpretation of the sentence requires that we know something about the connections between the sentence and the social or cultural context in which it occurs. **Pragmatic development,** the process of learning the social and cultural conventions that govern how language is used in particular contexts, is an especially important challenge in children's acquisition of language. Children's failure to appreciate the connections between sentences and their contexts often leads to inappropriate utterances. Indeed, young children are famous for speaking their minds without regard for context, blurting out various facts or opinions at exactly the wrong moment. One of your authors will never forget the time her 4-year-old daughter greeted the somewhat portly chairman of her psychology department with a cheery "Hi, fatso!"

Phonological development, semantic development, grammar, and pragmatic development together represent the basic domains of language acquisition. We explore each of these domains in the sections below. For the sake of clarity we will describe how children become competent in each domain separately. However, it is important to keep in mind that language is a system—each domain is connected to all of the others as well as to the social world of which it is an essential part (de Lemos, 2000).

phonological development Learning to segment speech into meaningful units of sound.

semantic development Learning meanings of words and of combinations of words.

grammar The rules of a given language for the sequencing of words in a sentence and the ordering of parts of words.

pragmatic development Learning the conventions that govern the use of language in particular social contexts.

Phonological Development

As discussed in Chapter 6, in the change from babbling to pronouncing words that occurs late in the first year, children give up their indiscriminate play with sounds and begin to vocalize the particular sounds and sound sequences that make up the words in the language of their community (Kuhl, 2001). The process of mastering the pronunciation of the separate words of a native language takes several years (and can be complicated by, for example, malformation of structures involved in articulation; see the box, "In the Field: A Speech-Language Pathologist in Vietnam"). Children's early pronouncing efforts may be no more than crude stabs at the right sound pattern that frequently leave out parts of words (resulting in "ca" instead of "cat," for example). They may also include using a particular sound pattern for several different multisyllabic words that have sound similarities. For example, a child may use the sound pattern "bubba" to say "button," "bubble," "butter," and "baby." A long word, such as "motorcycle," can come out sounding like almost anything: "momo, "motokaka," or even "lomacity" (Preisser, Hodson, & Paden, 1988).

Children's command of their native sound system develops unevenly. Sometimes children will find a particular sound especially difficult to master, even after they understand many words that employ that sound. At the age of 2½ for example, one of our sons, Alexander, could not pronounce /l/ sounds at the beginning of words, and whenever he referred to his friend's dog, Lucky, it came out "Yucky," much to everyone's amusement.

Alexander's transformation of "Lucky" to "Yucky" generated chuckles because when he changed the phoneme from /l/ to /y/ he changed the *meaning* of the word. As noted in Chapter 6, the close connection between phonemes and meanings becomes clear when one is attempting to learn a foreign language. Some native speakers of Spanish find it difficult to hear or produce the difference between /b/ and /v/, which in English can change meaning, because Spanish has no corresponding distinction in sound. To native English speakers, "boat" and "vote" sound quite different; to Spanish speakers, these two words sound much the same. Likewise, English speakers frequently have difficulty hearing and producing the difference between the French /u/ and /ou/, because that difference, which in French can change meaning, does not exist in English.

While phonemes are the basic units of sound, **morphemes** are the basic units of meaning. Words are composed of one or more morphemes. The word *horse,* for example, consists of one morpheme, which means "a member of the equine family." *Horses,* on the other hand, includes two morphemes: *horse,* meaning "a member of the equine family," plus "-s" meaning "more than one." Until the rules are pointed out, we rarely stop to think about the parts of words or the way we put these parts together. Yet every child must acquire the ability to decipher and reproduce just such intricate interweaving of sound and meaning. By the time they are 8 or 9 years old, children can use knowledge about morphemes to figure out the meanings of made-up words such as "treelet" (Anglin, 1993).

Semantic Development

Semantic development, as you may recall, refers to the process of learning the meanings of words and word combinations. As we described previously through the example of Romeo and Juliet, words refer to something beyond themselves (Hoff, 2001). Indeed, for a child acquiring language, a significant and surprisingly difficult part of the process of learning a new word involves identifying the object to which the word refers, for example, knowing that the fluffy creature with

morpheme The smallest unit of meaning in the words of a language.

Name:	Charlotte Ducote
Education:	B.A. from Louisiana State University; M.A. from Vanderbilt; Ph.D. in speech and hearing sciences from Louisiana State
Current Position:	Ochsner Clinic Foundation as Director of the Division of Communicative Disorders; volunteer for Operation Smile
Career Objectives:	Provide education and services to improve speech and language skills for children with communication disorders

GIANG, A 6-YEAR-OLD VIETNAMESE GIRL, was born in Ho Chi Minh City (Saigon) with a cleft lip and palate, a serious birth defect caused when the structures of the mouth form abnormally during fetal development. As a consequence of the defect, Giang had difficulty eating, communicating, and even breathing. It is estimated that clefting of the lip, palate, or both occurs in 1 to 2.5 of every 1000 births worldwide, making it one of the most common birth defects (McLeod, Arana-Urioste, & Saeed, 2004).

Fortunately for Giang and other children from impoverished areas of the world, a number of humanitarian groups have formed to provide affected children with reconstructive surgery and speech and language therapy.

Charlotte Ducote, a speech-language pathologist, has devoted considerable time to one such group—Operation Smile, a private, not-for-profit medical services organization that has helped tens of thousands of indigent children in more than 20 countries including Bolivia, Brazil, China, the Gaza Strip/West Bank, Russia, the United States, and Vietnam. In addition to volunteering on medical teams that include plastic surgeons, anesthesiologists, pediatricians, nurses, and dentists, Ducote cofounded the Speech Therapy–Vietnam Project, which aims to expand speech therapy services in the country by teaching health-care providers how to screen, evaluate, and treat communication disorders.

Ducote studied Vietnamese and its phoneme system and acquainted herself with the country's customs and culture. Armed with this knowledge and the assistance of a translator, Ducote met Giang, who was brought to the clinic by her mother for

Charlotte Ducote, a speech and language pathologist with Operation Smile.

speech problems that interfered with her being accepted into first grade. Giang's cleft palate and lip had been surgically corrected the previous year, and her mother was convinced that additional surgery would help her daughter speak better. Ducote's evaluation, however, showed otherwise: rather than requiring additional surgery, Giang's speech difficulties could be drastically improved with daily speech therapy. Her mother was skeptical, but finally agreed at the urging of a Vietnamese surgeon. Ducote reports the following instantaneous improvement: *Within minutes of beginning treatment and having success with the child imitating a word that began with a phoneme with which she had particular difficulty, her mother was in tears. "I never thought my child would be able to say that word. How did you do that? It is like magic!"*

Over the course of the next week, Ducote met regularly with Giang and her mother, teaching them how to form phonemes and breathe properly during speech (her mother was to work with Giang every day at home). Ducote also encouraged Giang to open her mouth wider while talking to facilitate airflow and reduce the nasal tone of her voice. Her mother resisted this particular intervention, because she worried that speaking with the mouth more open would make Giang unattractive to future suitors. She relented, however, once she witnessed the dramatic improvement in her daughter's speech.

At last report, Giang is in school and doing very well. Ducote, for her part, continues to volunteer in Vietnam and to mobilize financial and educational resources to help children with communication disorders throughout the world.

One of the most common birth defects, cleft lip and palate is caused by abnormal development of the structures of the mouth during the prenatal period. Without surgery, this baby's health and development would have been seriously affected. Fortunately, a surgical team associated with Operation Smile corrected the defect when the baby was five months of age.

"Vot, sinochik, tam sidit ptitsa."

Figure 7.3 For children just beginning to acquire language, the problem of learning what words refer to is particularly acute. (This father is telling his son to look at the bird.)

the wet nose and wagging tail is the object referred to when the mother exclaims, "Look! It's a *puppy*!"

To get an intuitive feel for just how difficult it may be for a young child to learn the relationship between a word and its referent, examine Figure 7.3. Imagine that you are the child in the picture, and try to decide what the Russian father is saying. It's a puzzle, isn't it? Suppose you know all the words except one: "Look, son, there sits a *ptitsa*." The word *ptitsa* still has various possible referents—the cat, the bird, the helicopter on the roof. At first you may think that the example is unfair because the utterance is in a foreign language. But remember that a baby's native language *is* "foreign" in the beginning and, moreover, that babies must somehow figure out that the sounds they hear are in fact meant to refer to something in the on-going flow of experience—to indicate an actual object, event, or feeling. According to Eve Clark (2006), the process of identifying a word's referent depends critically on the child's ability to establish joint attention with the speaker and to understand that the object or event of joint attention is what the speaker is talking about. As we will see, it takes some years before the child is fully able to appreciate the *referential intentions* of a speaker, which may account for why the child's vocabulary development is initially fairly slow but undergoes a substantial growth spurt during toddlerhood.

It is useful to think of the process of learning the meanings and referents of words as a special sort of joint effort (Tomasello, 2003). Neither the adult nor the child really knows what the other is saying. Each tries to gather in a little meaning by supposing that the other's utterance fits a particular sound pattern that corresponds to a particular meaning. This joint effort may eventually result in something common, a word that both can understand. This process may also fail. As the following examples make clear, the process of learning words can proceed in a variety of ways, depending on how the parent interprets the relation between the child's sounds and actions.

At 8 months of age, Pablo began to say "dahdee." Although this "first" word sounds like "daddy," Pablo used "dahdee" for commands and requests when his father was nowhere to be seen, so it must have had some other meaning for him. Adults interpreted "dahdee" to mean either "Take it from me" (when Pablo said it while he offered something to someone) or "Give it to me"; they ignored the fact that Pablo's first word sounded like "daddy." At about the age of 12 months, "dahdee" disappeared from Pablo's vocabulary (Shopen, 1980).

A different fate befell Brenan's first word, "whey." Around 1 year of age, Brenan began to say "whey" after one of his parents had spoken. In this case, "whey" not only sounded something like "why" but also came at a position in normal conversational turn-taking where "why" would be a possible (if not always appropriate) thing to say. Brenan's parents therefore responded to "whey" as if Brenan had asked a question and rephrased what they had said in order to "answer his question," expanding on their original utterance. Over time, Brenan pronounced and used "whey" more and more like a true "why" until it became a genuine "why" in the English language (Griffin, 1983).

In both of these examples, the child uses a sound pattern that adults might interpret because of its similarity to a word with which they are familiar. But in Pablo's case, the use of "dahdee" did not fit the patterns of usage for its sound-alike, "daddy," so his parents simply ignored it. Brenan's use of "whey" both sounded like "why" and was basically consistent with his parents' guess that he meant "why," so they provided the feedback necessary for Brenan to adjust his pronunciation and use to fit adult norms. Each illustrates the general point that adults collude with each other and their children to create word meanings.

The Earliest Vocabulary Much of the evidence concerning children's earliest words has come from having parents keep records of their children's vocabulary development or by making recordings of children's speech in their homes or in organized play facilities (Dromi, 1999). A number of studies have shown that children typically begin to produce their first comprehensible words around their first birthday and continue to utter single words for several months or more. Although there is a great deal of variation in the ages at which children reach particular levels of language production (Figure 7.4), infants, on average, are able to use approximately 10 words by 13 to 14 months of age, 50 words by the time they are 17 to 18 months old, and approximately 300 words by the time they reach their second birthday. More impressive still is children's *receptive vocabulary*—that is, the vocabulary they understand—which is considerably larger. For example, when they can produce 10 words, they can understand over 100 (Fenson et al., 1994).

The first 100 or so words in young children's vocabularies are predominantly nouns used to label objects, and this is true for children who speak languages as diverse as Spanish, Dutch, French, Hebrew, Italian, Korean, and American English (Bornstein et al., 2004). Many of these nouns refer to objects that children can manipulate or somehow act upon (Mandler, 2006). For example, "hat" and "sock" are common in the initial vocabularies of American children, but "sweater" and "diapers" are not, presumably because little children can put on and take off hats and socks more or less effectively, but cannot do the same with sweaters and diapers. In addition, objects that can change and move and thus capture children's attention (such as cars and animals) are likely to be named; large, immobile objects that are "just there" (such as trees and houses) are not.

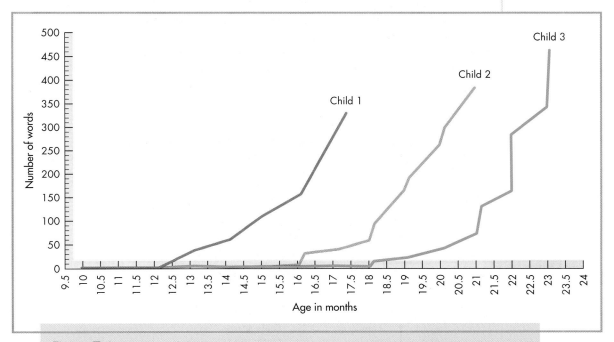

Figure 7.4 There are wide variations in the rates at which young children acquire new words. Each curve indicates the number of words that the designated child spoke while in the one-word phase. Note that despite the variability, each child shows the growth spurt in vocabulary that typically begins shortly before children begin to produce utterances of two or more words. (After Dromi, 1999, p. 104.)

overextension A term for the error of applying verbal labels too broadly.

underextension A term used for applying verbal labels in a narrower way than adults do.

fast mapping The way in which children quickly form an idea of the meaning of an unfamiliar word they hear in a familiar and highly structured social interaction.

As young children's vocabularies grow, there is a rapid increase in the proportion of verbs and adjectives they contain, and by age 2, nouns usually account for less than half of children's vocabularies. Toddlers' growing vocabularies also include a variety of relational words that are used to communicate about changes in the state or location of an object (Gopnick & Meltzoff, 1997). "Gone" and "here," for example, may be used to announce the disappearance and appearance of objects. One of the most useful relational words in children's early vocabularies is "no," which can serve such important communicative functions as rejection, protest, and denial. "No" can also be used to comment on unfulfilled expectations (for example, "no play" when a planned trip to the park is thwarted by rain) and on an object's absence (for example, "no teddy" when a favorite toy goes missing). Given these multiple functions, it is little wonder that "no" is among the earliest and most frequently used words in a child's budding vocabulary (Bloom, 1973).

Allison Gopnik and Andrew Meltzoff (1997) identify an additional class of words that children begin using around the age of 2 years: words used to comment on their successes ("There!" "Hooray!") and failures ("Uh-oh"). The appearance of these words seems to support the idea that children this age become sensitive to social expectations and begin to set standards for themselves (see Chapter 6, p. 227).

Word Errors Along with the first words of language come the first errors of language use. Interestingly, many of the errors made by young children as they acquire language are highly systematic and thus reveal a great deal about language development (Jaeger, 2005). Some errors are so typical and occur so reliably that developmentalists have given them names. One such error is **overextension,** a form of mislabeling in which children use a word to refer to a broader group of objects than the word usually refers to. A 2-year-old who points to a strange man on the street and exclaims "Daddy!" or sees the ocean and says "bath" is displaying the common error of overextension.

Children's early overextensions appear to be strongly influenced by perceptual features of the items named as well as by children's ideas of the items' functions. A word such as "kitty" may be extended to cover a wide variety of small four-legged animals because of their common shape, or it may cover a variety of soft, furry objects because of their similar texture, or it may even refer to other small animals such as rabbits that people keep as pets. (See Table 7.3 for other examples.)

table 7.3

Typical Overextensions in the Speech of Young Children

Child's Word	First Referent	Extensions	Possible Common Property
Dog	Dogs	Dogs, lambs, cats, wolves, cows	Four-legged animal
"'peca"	Wound	Cuts, wounds, Scotch tape, spots on fabric, balloons	Uncertain, partial defect or injury of some kind
Kick	Kicking ball	Cartoon turtles doing cancan, pushing chest against mirror, watching a butterfly	Common movement pattern
"Tik"	Handbag	Folders, nylon bags, plastic sacks, box, hat upside down, pockets	Containing object

Source: Dromi, 1999.

Another reliably occurring error is **underextension,** in which children use words in a narrower way than they are usually meant (Barrett, 1995). It is common, in fact, for children's early words to have a unique referent, often closely associated with a particular context (Golinkoff et al., 1994). For example, a child may use the word "bottle" to label only his or her favorite yellow plastic bottle, not for other kinds of bottles; or use "biddie" to refer to only a special blanket clutched at bedtime and naptime, not for other kinds of blankets. Likewise, it is not uncommon for young children to believe that "cat" applies only to their family's cat, not to cats in the neighborhood or on television.

The Vocabulary Spurt One of the most remarkable features of children's early vocabulary development is the astonishing *growth spurt* of new words that typically occurs during toddlerhood (see Figure 7.4 above). What makes this rapid acquisition possible?

Elsa Bartlett and Susan Carey made use of the normal routine of a preschool to find out what happens when a totally new word is introduced into conversation with children (Bartlett, 1977; Carey, 1978). They chose to study the acquisition of color terms. None of the 14 children in the classroom knew the name of the color that adults call olive: some children called it brown, others called it green, and some did not refer to the color by name at all. Bartlett and Carey decided to give it an implausible name, chromium, just in case some children had partial knowledge of the real name that they had not revealed.

After the children had been tested to determine that they did not know the name of the color olive, one cup and one tray in the classroom were painted "chromium" (olive). While preparing for snack time, the teacher found an opportunity to ask each child, "Please bring me the chromium cup; not the red one, the chromium one," or "Bring me the chromium tray; not the blue one, the chromium one." Despite the fact that the children had never heard the word "chromium" before, all of them picked the correct cup or tray, although they were likely to ask for confirmation ("You mean this one?"). Some of the children could be seen repeating the unfamiliar word to themselves.

One week after this single experience with the new word, the children were given a color-naming test with an array of color chips. Two-thirds of them showed that they had learned something about this odd term and its referents—when asked for chromium, they chose either the olive chip or a green one. Six weeks later, many of the children still showed the influence of this single experience.

As in this experiment, it appears that when children hear an unfamiliar word in a familiar, structured, and meaningful social interaction, they form a quick, "first-pass" idea of the word's meaning (Clark & Wong, 2002). Developmentalists refer to this form of rapid word acquisition as **fast mapping.** Fast mapping has been observed in children as young as 15 months of age in controlled experiments (Schafer & Plunkett, 1998).

An important question for researchers is why fast mapping occurs in toddlerhood but not before. Some developmentalists argue that the answer lies in toddlers' increased abilities to use social cues to infer a speaker's intentions. For example, Shannon Pruden and her colleagues devised an experiment in which younger babies (10-month-olds) were presented with two objects, one boring (like a kitchen cabinet latch) and one interesting (like a sparkle wand) (Pruden et al., 2006). The experimenter uttered nonsense syllables such as "blicket" while looking at the boring object or uttered the nonsense syllables while looking at the interesting object. In both conditions, the babies learned the new word. However, they associated the new word with the interesting object, even when the experimenter applied it to the boring object! Thus, unlike the word learning of toddlers that

metaphor Use of a word in a way that draws a comparison between the thing the word usually refers to and some other, unrelated thing.

syntactic bootstrapping Use of knowledge of grammar to figure out the meaning of new words.

takes into account the speaker's intention, word learning in younger children seems to be indifferent to the social intent of the speaker, and driven instead by the children's own interest and point of view (see also Golinkoff & Hirsh-Pasek, 2006; Poulin-Dubois & Forbes, 2006). The researchers speculate that this form of word learning is necessarily slower than the fast mapping of toddlers because it probably requires repeated word-to-object pairings and may often leave infants with wrong names to unlearn. On the other hand, the pace of word learning should be considerably faster once children are able to use social information to infer a speaker's labeling intent.

Figurative Language Not long after children start to name objects, they begin to use figurative language, specifically, metaphors. A **metaphor** involves the use of a word or a phrase in a way that draws a direct comparison between the thing it ordinarily refers to and some other, seemingly unrelated, thing. When hip-hop artist Big Boi raps about being "cooler than a polar bear's toenails," and Lauryn Hill claims to be "sweet like licorice", they are using metaphors. Likewise, a 2½ year-old may point at his yellow plastic baseball bat and say, "Corn!" or throw Styrofoam bits in the air and shout, "Snow!" Children's use of metaphor provides evidence that language production is a creative process, not simply an imitative one. To generate a metaphor, children must recognize a similarity between two unrelated things and express that similarity in a way that they have never heard before (Dent-Read, 1997; Winner, 1998).

At the same time that young children appear extraordinarily creative in inventing metaphors, they can be very limited in understanding metaphors used by others. An example is the following exchange one of your authors observed at a birthday party: As one 4-year-old girl sat at the table eating cake, another child's mother, evidently a stranger to the girl, reached over and wiped chocolate frosting from the girl's cheek. "Thank you," said the little girl. "I've got your back, sister," said the mother. Obviously shaken by the mother's statement, the little girl replied, "I'm not your sister!" (We can only imagine what she made of "I've got your back.")

The ability to understand and use metaphors develops throughout childhood. During middle childhood, for example, children still have difficulty understanding metaphors that compare people to objects. Metaphors such as "That kid is a bulldozer" are confusing to them because they lack knowledge about personality traits and thus fail to understand the similarity proposed by the metaphor. Not until adolescence will children be able to understand and create metaphors of this nature (Pan & Snow, 1999).

Grammar Development

As noted earlier, a watershed of language development is reached toward the end of infancy, when children begin to produce utterances consisting of two or more words. Significantly, two-word utterances carry more than twice as much information as a single word alone because of the meaning conveyed by the relationship between the two words. With as few as two words, children can indicate possession ("Daddy chair"), nonexistence ("Gone cookie"), and a variety of other meanings. They can also create different meanings by varying the order of words ("Chase Daddy" and "Daddy chase"). This new potential for creating meaning by varying the arrangement of linguistic elements marks the birth of grammar.

Grammar and Meaning As we indicated previously, the rules of grammar play a critical role in interpreting the meaning of sentences. Evidence that children have

Gertner et al., 2006

Figure 7.5 Despite the fact that "gorping" is a nonsense word, 2-year-olds associate the sentence "The duck is gorping the bunny!" with the second photo, demonstrating the importance of grammar in learning and understanding language.

some grasp of grammatical rules fairly early in their language development comes from studies in which young children are asked to interpret grammatically correct sentences that contain nonsense words (Fisher et al., 2006). One such study tested early understanding of syntax by seeing if 2-year-olds could use word order to correctly interpret transitive sentences that had nonsense verbs. In one experiment, the children were shown two pictures of a duck and a bunny interacting (Gertner, Fisher, & Eisengart, 2006). One picture showed the bunny acting on the duck; the other showed the duck acting on the bunny (Figure 7.5). As the children viewed the pictures, they were told "The duck is *gorping* the bunny! See?" Even though "gorping" is a nonsense word, English grammar dictates that if the duck is gorping the bunny, the duck is the active agent and the bunny is the object being acted upon. The 2-year-olds presented with this sentence indicated their knowledge of grammar by looking significantly longer at the picture in which the duck was acting on the bunny. Developmentalists interpret results like this as evidence for an innate universal grammar that helps children interpret the language they hear (Chang, Dell, & Bock, 2006). The process of using grammar to learn the meaning of new words—as the children do with "gorp" in the study—is referred to as **syntactic bootstrapping** (Landau & Gleitman, 1985; Fisher et al., 2006).

Young children also demonstrate their knowledge of grammar through the errors they make when they string words together. Between ages 2 and 3, English-speaking children often make statements like "My doggy runned away" or "Mommy, Johnny camed late." Such errors are so common that it is easy to overlook their significance. Children cannot have been taught to say such things, nor could they have learned them by simple imitation, because they virtually never hear such incorrect sentences uttered. Rather they are revealing their knowledge of the general rule for forming the past tense with regular verbs by misapplying it to irregular verbs.

Increasing Complexity At the same time that children begin to string more and more words together to form complete sentences, they increase the complexity and the variety of words and grammatical devices they use. These changes are illustrated by the following prodigious sentence spoken by an excited 2-year-old girl: "You can't pick up a big kitty 'cos a big kitty might bite!" (De Villiers & De Villiers, 1978, p. 59).

This sentence is by no means typical of 2-year-olds, but it provides a good opportunity to assess how more complex utterances communicate more explicitly. The sentence communicates not only that the little girl does not want to pick up a big cat but also that no one should pick up a big cat; it also conveys her understanding that big cats sometimes bite but do not invariably do so. Such complex sentences communicate shades of meaning that help adults to respond sensitively to children's experiences.

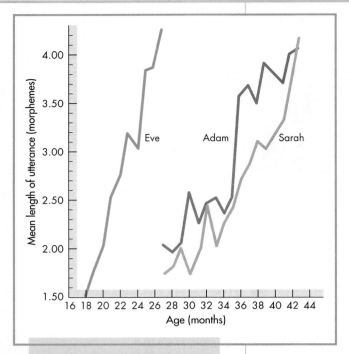

Figure 7.6 This graph shows the rapid increase in the mean length of utterances made by three children from 18 months to 3½ years of age. (From Brown, 1973.)

As Figure 7.6 indicates, the length of the utterances of 2- and 3-year-olds grows explosively, along with their vocabularies and grammatical abilities (Devescovi et al., 2005). Note that the growth in the length of utterances (or the "mean length of utterance") is indicated by the average number of morphemes per utterance rather than by the average number of words. The phrase "That big bad boy plays ball," for example, contains six words and seven morphemes, whereas the phrase "Boys aren't playing" contains only three words but six morphemes ("boy," "s," "are," "not," "play," "ing"). Assessing linguistic complexity by counting morphemes rather than words provides an index of a child's total potential for making meaning in a particular utterance.

The complexity of the little girl's long sentence about picking up cats is attributable in large measure to just those little words and word parts that are systematically absent in two-word utterances. The article "a" ("a big kitty") indicates that it is big cats in general, not just this particular big cat, that are worrisome. The word "'cos" connects two propositions and indicates the causal relationship between them. The contraction "can't" specifies a particular relationship of negation. These elements are a special type of morpheme called **grammatical morphemes** because they create meaning by showing the relations between other elements within the sentence.

Whether the rate of language acquisition is fast or slow, grammatical morphemes appear in roughly the same sequence in the speech of all children who acquire English as a first language. As Table 7.4 indicates, the grammatical morpheme likely to appear first in children's language production is *ing,* used to indicate the present progressive verb tense. This verb form allows children to describe their ongoing activity. Morphemes indicating location, number, and possession make their appearance next. Morphemes that mark complex relations, such as the contraction

table 7.4

Usual Order of Acquiring Grammatical Morphemes

Morpheme	Meaning	Example
Present progressive	Temporary duration	I walk*ing*
In	Containment	*In* basket
On	Support	*On* floor
Plural	Number	Two balls
Past irregular	Prior occurrence	It *broke*
Possessive inflection	Possession	Adam's ball
To be without contraction	Number	There it *is*
Articles	Specific/nonspecific	That *a* book
		That *the* dog
Past regular	Prior occurrence	Adam walk*ed*
Third person regular	Number	He walks
Third person irregular	Number	He do*es*
		She *has*
Uncontractible progressive auxiliary	Temporary duration; number	This *is going*
Contraction of *to be*	Number; prior occurrence	That's a book
Contractible progressive auxiliary	Temporary duration	I'*m* walking

Source: Brown, 1973.

'm in "I'm going" (which codes a relation between the first person singular subject of the action and the present time of the action), are generally slower to emerge.

The appearance of grammatical morphemes is a strong indicator that children are implicitly beginning to distinguish nouns and verbs, because their speech conforms to adult rules that specify which morphemes should be attached to which kinds of words in a sentence. Thus, for example, children do not apply past-tense morphemes to nouns ("girled"), nor do they place articles before verbs ("a walked").

Evidence collected by a number of language-development researchers shows that although children begin to produce grammatical morphemes relatively late in the language acquisition process, they are sensitive to the existence of grammatical morphemes in the language they hear at least by the time they are starting to produce their first multiword utterances (Golinkoff et al., 1999).

Pragmatic Development

Many of us have observed a mother trying to talk to a friend while her child pulls on her pant leg, impatiently intoning "mommy, mommy, mommy." "Not now," the mother may say, or "I'm talking; you need to wait until I'm done." Whether interrupting a conversation or using language that is inappropriate for the context (remember the little girl who greeted her mother's psychology department head with "Hi, fatso!"), young language learners are famous for saying the wrong thing at the wrong time simply because they have not yet mastered *pragmatics,* which include social and cultural conventions of language use in particular contexts. These conventions may vary markedly from one culture to another. In many cultures, children are expected to say "please" when they request something and "thank you" when they are given something. But in certain Colombian communities, such verbal formulas are frowned upon in the belief that "please" and "thank you" signal the speaker's inferiority; obedience, not formulaic politeness, is what these adults expect of their children (Reichel-Dolmatoff & Reichel-Dolmatoff, 1961).

Conversational Acts One important aspect of pragmatics is the use of language as **conversational acts,** actions to achieve goals performed through language and gesture. According to Elizabeth Bates and her colleagues (Bates, Camaioni, & Volterra, 1975), children's earliest conversational acts fall into two categories, *protoimperatives* and *protodeclarative*s. **Protoimperatives** are early ways of engaging another person to achieve a desired goal, for example, holding up a cup and saying "More" to get a refill on juice. **Protodeclaratives** are ways of establishing joint attention and sustaining a dialogue. Perhaps the earliest form of a protodeclarative is the act of pointing, which may be accompanied by words, as when a baby points to a dog and says "Doggie." Young children will often use a succession of protodeclaratives for the purpose of sustaining a dialogue. A common gestural example of this is a child's bringing all his or her toys, one after another, to show to a visitor if each presentation is acknowledged by a smile or a comment (Bates, O'Connell, & Shore, 1987).

In the process of acquiring pragmatics, children also come to understand that a single sequence of words may accomplish several alternative goals and that linguistic and other contexts can be crucial to interpretation. An amusing example of this occurs in a series of incidents in *Higglety, Pigglety, Pop*, Maurice Sendak's tale of an adventurous dog who

grammatical morphemes Words and parts of words that create meaning by showing the relations between other elements within the sentence.

conversational acts Actions that achieve goals through language.

protoimperatives Early conversational acts whose purpose is to get another person to do something.

protodeclaratives Early conversational acts whose purpose is to establish joint attention and sustain a dialogue.

These two girls are making Christmas cookies in Beijing, China. It is likely that the older one is simplifying her language in order to best communicate her cookie-making technique to the younger girl.

blue jean images/Getty Images

chronology A simple story structure used by young children, in which they present a sequence of concrete events.

cultural modeling Culturally specific ways of telling stories.

accepts a job as nanny for Baby, a child caught in the grip of the "terrible twos." At first the dog attempts to get the baby to eat, and the baby says, "No eat!" When the dog decides to eat the food himself, the baby again says, "No eat!" Finally the baby and dog find themselves confronted by a lion, and the baby says for the third time, "No eat!" Baby uses "No eat!" to accomplish various goals and, in view of Baby's imperfect grasp of grammar, understanding its various meanings requires the ability to evaluate the phrase in light of the social context in which it is used.

With adult utterances as well, the listener often needs to be sensitive to social cues in order to get the meaning intended by the speaker. For example, the sentence "Is the door shut?" has the grammatical form of a request for information. But it may be functioning as a request for action or as a criticism—that is, pragmatically equivalent to "Please shut the door" or "You forgot to shut the door again." Marilyn Shatz (1978) found that children as young as 2 years old responded correctly to their mother's indirect commands, such as "Is the door shut?" That is, instead of responding to the surface grammatical form and answering "Yes" or "No," Shatz's toddlers went to shut the door. This finding is consistent with work we described earlier linking toddlers' sensitivity to social cues to the fast mapping of vocabulary growth.

At the same time that children are recognizing that a single phrase can have multiple meanings or goals, they develop the ability to express a single meaning or goal in multiple ways. For example, a 3-year-old observed by John Dore (1979) used three different grammatical forms to achieve a single goal: "Get off the blocks!" "Why don't you stay away from my blocks?" and "You're standing on my blocks."

Viewing communications as conversational acts in which a single phrase can have more than one meaning, and a single meaning can be conveyed in many ways, exposes the complex relationship between the world of language and the world of objects, events, and direct experience. There is no simple and direct correspondence between the two worlds, making the child's apparently easy acquisition of language all the more wondrous. With increasing age, children will become increasingly skilled in their use and understanding of the subtleties of conversational acts—eventually knowing, for example, that despite the difference in language and tone, "I think I need some time to myself to sort things out" and "I'm dumping you" mean the same thing.

Developing Narratives As children's conversational skills develop, so, too, do their abilities to tell stories or *narratives* about their experiences. In a seminal study of developing storytelling abilities, Peterson and her colleagues (2004) asked children to tell them about memorable events such as going to the doctor's office. They found that the stories of young children followed a very simple structure, called a **chronology,** in which children present a sequence of concrete events. For example, 3½-year-old Paul describes a visit to the doctor's office to get stitches as "I get a needle. I get stitches, like first I got a needle, then I got stitches and then go home." As children's narrative abilities mature, their stories become more elaborate and more dramatic in emotional tone, as shown by the following 5-year-old's story about getting stung by a bee:

> I got jabbed with a bee.
> See, I got jabbed on my foot. I was barefooted.
> I screamed and I screamed and I cried and I cried.
> I screamed and I screamed. Until my next door neighbor
> came out and my Dad came out and my brother came out.
> and, they all carried me into the house but after that
> happened I got to sleep overnight with my neighbor.

When children first begin to produce narratives, their stories can be hard to follow because they leave out essential information. A teacher who is approached by a tearful preschooler saying only "He broked it" does not have much to work with until she asks the child to elaborate ("What was broken?" "Who broke it?"). Indeed, adults will often ask young children to expand their stories in an effort to make them more organized and coherent, as the following dialogue between a mother and her 3½-year-old child demonstrates (Nelson & Shaw, 2002, p. 51):

Child: You know something?
Mother: What?
Child: Let me think . . . . What's her name again?
Mother: Who?
Child: That girl.
Mother: Who?
Child: Don't you remember her? You've seen her before.
Mother: Where is she?
Child: I don't know. I don't know her name. Somebody has a rocket. That can turn into a big rocket.
Mother: Who is this person?
Child: I don't know her.
Mother: Where'd you meet her?
Child: At our house!
Mother: Was I home for this?
Child: (shakes head)
Mother: So how would I know who this is?

Although the mother is working hard to help her child develop her story, the child has difficulty understanding that her mother's knowledge of the girl is necessarily limited by the fact that she was not home to meet her, a cognitive limitation we discuss in more detail below.

As they grow older, children's narrative development is also influenced by **cultural modeling,** that is, culturally specific ways of telling stories. Carol Lee's work with African American children has done much to advance our understanding of how children use the storytelling traditions of their culture to form stories of their own (Lee et al., 2004). For example, common features of African American narratives include the following (Lee et al., 2004, p. 47):

- Use of dramatic language
- Use of or description of body language and gesture
- Sermonic tone (a dramatic tone of voice typically used during African American church services)
- References to culturally specific objects, events, and behaviors

To illustrate the cultural modeling of African American children's narratives, Lee and her colleagues showed pictures to 8- to 10-year-old children and asked the children to tell stories about them. One picture, "Jumping the Broom" (Figure 7.7), depicts a custom of great significance in the history of African Americans, dating back to a time when blacks were not allowed legally to marry. To mark the ceremony of entering into the sacred world of marriage, newlyweds would jump over a broom, a custom that endures to this day. One girl who participated in Lee's study told the following story about the picture, giving names to the man and woman being married, and creating a dialogue between them. Notice how she incorporates several of the features of African American narratives described above:

Annie Lee

Figure 7.7 Developmentalist Carol Lee studies cultural modeling, that is, the ways that children draw from cultural traditions to construct meaningful stories of life and experience. To facilitate children's storytelling, Lee makes use of culturally relevant artifacts, such as Annie Lee's painting "Jumping the Broom," which depicts African American marriage traditions.

The wedding looked so pretty. There was dancing [and] Mr. Johnson said to his wife, "I love you." "I love you, too," Ms. Sara Lee said. Mr. Johnson threw up his Bible and said, "Thank you Jesus! For giving me a wonderful ceremony," and Ms. Sara said, "Amen to that." They were both happy. They jumped over the broom. (pp. 52–53)

Whereas Lee's study examined how children incorporate into their stories aspects of their culture and heritage, other developmentalists have used children's story-telling abilities and inclinations as a way of exploring and nurturing their social relationships. For example, Colette Daiute has asked school-age children to tell stories about real and imagined conflicts with friends and has incorporated their storytelling in a violence-prevention program (Daiute, 2004).

▌▌▌▌ APPLY ▬ CONNECT ▬ DISCUSS

Consider the two exchanges below between a mother and her son, Richard, while they were looking at a book, the first when Richard was about 1 year old; the second when he was nearly 2 years old (Bruner, 1983, cited in Clark & Kita, 2003). Analyze each in terms of concepts presented in this section.

First exchange:
Mother: Look!
Richard (touches pictures)
Mother: What are those?
Richard (vocalizes a babble string and smiles)
Mother: Yes, there are rabbits.
Richard (vocalizes, smiles, looks up at mother)
Mother: (laughs) Yes, rabbit.
Richard (vocalizes, smiles)
Mother: Yes. (laughs)

Second exchange:
Mother: What's that?
Richard: *Mouse*
Mother: Mouse, yes. That's a mouse.
Richard (pointing at another picture): *More mouse.*
Mother: No, those are squirrels. They're like mice but with long tails. Sort of.
Richard: *Mouse, mouse, mouse.*
Mother: Yes, all right, they're mice.
Richard: *Mice, mice.*

Explanations of Language Acquisition

During much of the twentieth century, two widely divergent theories dominated explanations of how children acquire language. These theories correspond roughly to the polar positions on the sources of human development—nature versus nurture. Social learning theorists, for example, once attributed language acquisition largely to nurture, especially to the language environment and teaching activities provided by adults. Biological theorists, in contrast, attributed language acquisition largely to nature, assuming that as children mature, their innate language capacity enables acquisition to occur naturally, with only minimum input from the environment and without any need for special training.

In recent decades, both theoretical positions have been modified. On the nurture side, there has been a growing consensus that such mechanisms as learning by association, classical and operant conditioning, and imitation are insufficient to account for how children enter the world of language. Contemporary theorists who emphasize the role of the environment now focus on how social and cultural contexts are organized in ways that draw children into language-using communities. Likewise, theorists who emphasize the biological foundations of language acquisition agree that it is important to specify the ways in which the environment, however minimally, contributes to the developmental process. Thus, as we indicated at the beginning of this chapter, virtually all developmentalists agree that both biology and the environment provide important keys to the world of language. Recently, these two dominant approaches have been joined by a third—one that places emphasis on the distinct role of cognition in language development. We will review each of three approaches in the sections below.

Biological Explanations

For half a century, biological explanations of language acquisition have been dominated by the work of the linguist Noam Chomsky (Chomsky, 2006; Hauser & Chomsky, 2002). According to Chomsky, the fact that children acquire language quickly and effortlessly without any direct instruction and that they produce a vast array of sentences that they have never before heard makes it impossible to claim that language could be acquired primarily through learning mechanisms. Rather, language is innate and develops through a universal process of maturation. Chomsky (1988, p. 134) phrased this idea as follows:

> Language learning is not really something that the child does; it is something that happens to the child placed in an appropriate environment, much as the child's body grows and matures in a predetermined way when provided with the appropriate nutrition and environmental stimulation.

In likening the acquisition of language to the maturation of the body, Chomsky also emphasized that language is a "mental organ." Just as the functions of a physical organ such as the liver are specific, so are the functions of the "mental organ" of language (Chomsky, 1980, p. 52). This view is echoed by psycholinguist Steven Pinker in a book pointedly titled *The Language Instinct*. In Pinker's words, language is a "distinct piece of the biological makeup of our brains . . . distinct from more general abilities to process information or behave intelligently" (2007). The fact that Chomsky describes language as a distinct process does not mean that he denies its connection to other psychological processes or to the environment. Indeed, he explicitly acknowledges that "children acquire a good deal of their verbal and non-verbal behavior by casual observation and imitation of adults and other children" (Chomsky, 1959, p. 49). But such factors, he argued, cannot fully account for language acquisition.

In certain formulations of this theory, Chomsky proposed that children learn language as a result of a mechanism he dubbed the **language acquisition device (LAD).** Through the LAD, the child is, in essence, hard-wired to recognize the abstract grammatical rules (for example, for the order of elements in sentences) of whatever language the child is regularly exposed to. According to Chomsky, at birth, the LAD is in an embryonic state, but as children mature and interact with the environment, maturation of the LAD enables them to use increasingly complex language forms. The eventual result of this process is the adult capacity to use language.

Like Chomsky, those who believe that there must be some preexisting linguistic mechanism that guides children's language acquisition argue that the feedback children get on their early utterances provides insufficient information for them to induce the rules of grammar (Pinker, 2002). One strategy for evaluating this argument is to document how much feedback children actually receive about their

language acquisition device (LAD)
Chomsky's term for an innate language-processing capacity that is programmed to recognize the universal rules that underlie any particular language that a child might hear.

use of language. The answer, based on several decades or research, is "very little" (Valian, 1999). Furthermore, even when parents do attempt to correct erroneous grammar, the effort is likely to fail, as shown in a classic exchange reported by David McNeill (1966, pp. 106–107):

Child: Nobody don't like me.
Mother: No, say "nobody likes me."
Child: Nobody don't like me.

[This interchange is repeated several times. Then:]
Mother: No, now listen carefully; say "nobody likes me."
Child: Oh! Nobody don't likes me.

Michael Newman/PhotoEdit

A great deal of language learning takes place in casual interactions among family members. In the daily conversations of this Asian American family, words from the language of the family's country of origin may smoothly blend with English.

Sequences like this, which are commonplace, seriously undermine the idea that specific teaching is important to language acquisition and bolster the biological view that language acquisition depends only minimally on the environment.

In summary, biological theorists contend that the essential structures that make language acquisition possible—the universals of grammar—are determined far more by the evolutionary history of our species than by the experiential history of particular children. Experience does of course determine which of the many possible human languages a child actually acquires. Children who never hear Chinese spoken will not grow up speaking Chinese, even though they are genetically capable of learning that (or any other) language. According to Chomsky's theory, however, the experience of hearing a particular language does not modify the LAD; it only triggers the innate mechanisms designed for language acquisition and implements the particular language features it encounters.

Social and Cultural Explanations

While acknowledging that innate features of the human brain play an important role in the acquisition of language, many developmentalists stress the fact that language is necessarily a social process. Arguing that children acquire language in the process of using language, these developmentalists emphasize the way the sociocultural environment enters into partnership with the child in the acquisition of language (Karmiloff & Karmiloff-Smith, 2001; Ochs & Schieffelin, 1995; Tomasello, 2003; Vygotsky, 1978).

In an early and influential statement of this position, Jerome Bruner (1982) proposed that the earliest social structures for language development involve what he calls **formats**—recurrent socially patterned activities in which adult and child do things together. In the United States and other cultures, for example, simple formatted activities include such games as peekaboo and the routines surrounding bathing, bedtime, and meals, which provide a structure for communication between babies and caregivers even before babies have learned any language. In this way, formats serve as "crucial vehicles in the passage from communication to language" (Bruner, 1982, p. 8). Bruner argued that, viewed as a whole, the formatted events within which children acquire language constitute a **language acquisition support system (LASS),** which is the environmental complement to the innate, biologically constituted LAD emphasized by Chomsky.

The crucial role of finely tuned and well-timed interaction in supporting word learning is seen in a series of studies by Michael Tomasello and his colleagues (summarized in Tomasello, 2000). These researchers videotaped mothers interacting with their young children in order to identify the precise moment at which the mothers referred to objects in the immediate environment. They found that the

formats Recurrent socially patterned activities in which adult and child do things together.

language acquisition support system (LASS) Bruner's term for the parental behaviors and formatted events within which children acquire language. It is the environmental complement to the innate, biologically constituted LAD.

collective monologues Communications in which young children each voice their own thoughts without attending to what the others are saying.

mothers talked mostly about objects that were already a part of the child's current actions and the focus of the child's and mother's joint attention, thus greatly reducing the child's problem in figuring out the referents of the mother's words. As you recall from a previous discussion, children are much more likely to learn new words for objects they find interesting (see p. 253).

According to theorists who emphasize social and cultural contributions to language development, explicit rewards for learning language are unnecessary. The reinforcement comes from children's increased success at communicating and their enhanced participation with others in valued activities.

Cognitive Approaches

Another approach to understanding language development emphasizes how the child's emerging language abilities follow from the child's increased ability to think and process information (Clark, 2004). Many theorists, including Alison Gopnik and Andrew Meltzoff (1997), suggest that changes in the way children use language arise as a consequence of the kind of cognitive changes described by Piaget. For example, as you saw in Chapter 5 and Chapter 6, sometime around 18 months of age, children begin to reason systematically about hidden objects, deliberately vary their actions to achieve a goal, and display increasing awareness of social standards. Correspondingly, before 18 months of age, children are restricted to words that reflect what they are experiencing at the moment, "social words" such as "Bye-bye" (when Mother is leaving for work) and "Hereyare" (when discovering a searched-for toy). After the age of 18 months, however, they can articulate knowledge of absent objects ("Gone"), describe their own activities ("Done it"), and comment on their perceived failure to meet social expectations ("Uh-oh").

Cognitive development also influences children's emerging conversational skills. Consider the following "conversation" between two preschoolers:

Jenny: My bunny slippers . . . are brown and red and sort of yellow and white. And they have eyes and ears and these noses that wiggle sideways when they kiss.
Chris: I have a piece of sugar in a red piece of paper. I'm gonna eat it but maybe it's for a horse.
Jenny: We bought them. My mommy did. We couldn't find the old ones. These are like the old ones. They were not in the trunk.
Chris: Can't eat the piece of sugar, not unless you take the paper off. (Stone & Church, 1957, pp. 146–147)

Clearly, Jenny and Chris are not having a true conversation. Instead, each is voicing his or her own thoughts without regard for the utterance of the other, a form of communication that Piaget referred to as **collective monologues.** According to Piaget, preschool-age children engage in such talk because they are egocentric and lack the cognitive ability to take into account another person's knowledge, interests, and activities. We encountered a similar example of this cognitive limitation in the dialogue between the mother and the child who were trying to figure out the name of the girl that the mother had never met (see p. 259). This particular cognitive limitation, called *egocentrism,* is discussed in detail in Chapter 8 (pp. 277–278).

Language is acquired in the context of ongoing activity. This mother interacts with her daughter, who is trying to carry her purse.

Stephanie Rausser/Getty Images

It will be several years before these two toddlers develop the cognitive and language skills necessary to engage in true dialogue.

Picture Partners/Alamy

true dialogue A communication in which each person's utterances take into account the utterances of others.

As cognitive development progresses, collective monologues eventually give way to **true dialogue,** in which the utterance of one person takes into account the utterance of another.

Explaining Grammar Because they deny that language acquisition is driven primarily by biological processes, a major challenge for those who adopt a cognitive approach is to explain how children acquire grammar, with its complex rules and structures. Addressing this challenge, Elizabeth Bates and her colleagues propose that the mastery of grammatical structures is a by-product of the growth of vocabulary and of children's attempts to express increasingly complex thoughts (Elman et al., 1996). Evidence for this view comes from research demonstrating a correlation between the size of children's vocabularies and the degree of complexity of the grammatical utterances they can make (Fernald, Perfors, & Marchman, 2006). As we saw earlier (Figure 7.4, p. 251), individual children vary greatly in the rates at which they acquire vocabulary. The same is true for their acquisition of grammar (Fenson et al., 1994). However, when grammatical complexity is related directly to the number of words that children know, there is an almost perfect relationship between vocabulary size and grammatical complexity, regardless of how old the children are. Bates and her colleagues argue that such data clearly demonstrate how grammar develops to deal with a growing vocabulary (Figure 7.8).

Language and Cognitive Impairments Given the extent to which cognitive development is understood to influence language development, researchers and practitioners are naturally interested in how children with various cognitive impairments acquire language. In Chapter 2 (pp. 70–71), we briefly described Down syndrome, a genetic disorder that produces moderate to severe mental retardation. Although children with Down syndrome are able to hold a conversation, their vocabulary is relatively restricted and their talk is grammatically simple. When tested for the ability to produce and comprehend complex linguistic constructions, they fail. Such results suggest that normal language development requires normal cognitive functioning.

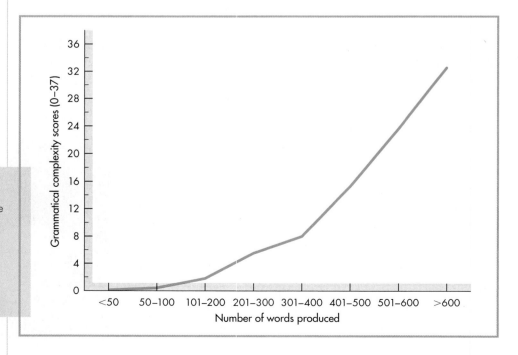

Figure 7.8 When the size of children's vocabulary is plotted against the degree of grammatical complexity of their utterances, there is a clear, positive relationship. These data are used by Elizabeth Bates and her colleagues to argue that grammar emerges from the need to use many words to convey complex messages. Note that there is an acceleration of grammatical complexity that begins when children's vocabularies reach approximately 400 words. (From Bates, 1999.)

This broad conclusion is brought into question, however, by research on children who suffer from a rare genetic disorder called Williams syndrome. Children afflicted with Williams syndrome are also mentally retarded, yet their language is not as impaired as that of children with Down syndrome. Although initial language acquisition is often delayed, many Williams syndrome children eventually produce sentences that are grammatical, clearly pronounced, and understandable. They are also able to tell stories that are meaningful and display considerable subtlety in their portrayal of human feelings (Thomas & Karmiloff-Smith, 2003).

Overall, data on children who suffer some form of genetic disease indicate that children are capable of developing some degree of language competence even in the face of intellectual impairment and that at least some aspects of language develop independently of general cognitive functioning.

||||| █ APPLY ▬ CONNECT ▬ DISCUSS ▬▬▬▬▬▬▬▬▬▬▬▬▬▬▬▬▬▬▬▬▬▬▬

Review the discussion of primary and secondary intersubjectivity presented on p. 237. In what ways are they similar to Bruner's concept of a language acquisition support system (LASS)?

Reconsidering the Keys to Language

At the beginning of this chapter we argued that there are two keys to the world of language: normal human biological structures and processes, and active participation in a language-using community. With these two keys, the child enters a symbolic universe that is distinctively human. This new world of symbols is the place where music is made, mathematical equations are imagined and solved, cathedrals are built, books of poetry and law are written, and genetic codes are cracked and even changed (Jablonka & Lamb, 2007). Although communication research with nonhuman animals continues to raise the question of whether language is uniquely human, there is no doubt that humans are unique because of language.

Despite our clarity on the role of language in the ongoing evolution of human culture, a number of mysteries remain in understanding how language develops in children. Perhaps, as Jerome Bruner whimsically suggested, language is born from the union of the LAD (language acquisition device) and the LASS (language acquisition support system), the latter of which is apparent in the array of cultural routines—bath time, mealtime, bedtime—that define the interactional contexts of children's daily lives. Children acquire normal linguistic competence without special instruction if they can have access to language (either oral or sign) and if they participate in routine, culturally organized activity, which serves as a language-acquisition support system. Indeed, Goldin-Meadow's work with deaf children in hearing households suggests that participation in normal cultural routines can be sufficient for the rudiments of language to appear.

Although children 2½ to 3 years of age can properly be considered language-using human beings, their language development is obviously incomplete. Language continues to develop during childhood; indeed, some aspects of language develop into adulthood (Clark, 1995). Moreover, as children begin to acquire the specialized skills they will need to cope with adult life in their culture, deliberate teaching may begin to play a conspicuous role in language development. Such specialized activities as reciting nursery rhymes, acting in a play, and writing an essay are all forms of language activity that require practice and instruction. We shall return to examine some of the more specialized language developments associated with middle childhood in Chapter 11.

SUMMARY

The Power of Language

Language is a cultural tool, a symbolic system of enormous scope and power. As such, it profoundly affects development by mediating our activities, relationships, and thinking. Children are born predisposed to attend to language and to communicate. They move rapidly from cooing, babbling, and jargoning into the world of language.

Keys to the World of Language

- The two keys to language are the biological structures and systems that support language, and participation in a language-using community.

- Humans differ dramatically from nonhuman primates in their ability to acquire language. Bonobos and chimpanzees can be taught to understand and (with symbols and gestures) produce simple utterances, abilities at roughly the level of 2-year-old children.

- Studies of patients with aphasia have shown the importance for language of Broca's and Wernicke's areas, on the left frontal lobe. Neuroimaging studies confirm the involvement of Broca's area in the processing of complex speech. Although the left hemisphere appears to have evolved as the brain center for language, when infants suffer left hemisphere damage, the right hemisphere can take over language functions.

- A community of language users provides children with both models and opportunities for language acquisition, as is clear from studies of language-deprived environments. Deaf children of hearing parents who refuse to use sign develop home sign and reach but do not progress beyond early stages of producing complex sentences.

- Cultural variations in language environments—for example, whether and how much adults talk to infants, use motherese, and attempt deliberate instruction—generally do not much affect children's acquisition of language.

The Basic Domains of Language Acquisition

- As part of phonological development, young children learn to segment sequences of speech into meaning units of language and master the pronunciation and rules of their native sound system.

- Semantic development brings increasing understanding of the meaning of words and strings of words. With the help of adults, children learn to pair words to their referents, overcoming problems of overextension (using words too broadly) and underextension (using words too narrowly).

- Early words tend to be nouns, but these are soon supplemented by verbs, adjectives, and relational words. A vocabulary spurt occurs at about 2 or 3 years of age, when young children's new ability to understand speaker intent makes possible fast mapping, in which children form quick first-pass ideas of word meanings.

- With two-word utterances, the acquisition of grammar (or the rules for sequencing words) is evident. Children's utterances become increasingly long and complex, with more units of meaning, or morphemes, including grammatical morphemes.

- Pragmatic development enables children to understand and employ social and cultural conventions of language use, to use communications as conversational acts to achieve goals, and to use context to interpret communications.

- Young children increasingly understand and use figurative language such as metaphor and produce increasingly sophisticated narratives.

Explanations of Language Acquisition

- Biological explanations of language acquisition argue that children are able to acquire language on the basis of limited input because our brains are hardwired to learn a language that follows certain universal rules.

- Social and cultural explanations emphasize the role of the sociocultural environment, through, for example, formats (routine, patterned activities that adult and child do together) and through interactions generally.

- Cognitive approaches focus on the way emerging language abilities follow from children's increased ability to think and process information. For example, as egocentrism wanes, collective monologues give way to true dialogue.

Reconsidering the Keys to Language

- Questions about the specifics remain, but it is clear that with the two keys to the world of language—a brain for language and participation in a language-using community—young children enter a symbolic universe that is distinctively human.

Key Terms

infant-directed speech, p. 244

phonological development, p. 247

semantic development, p. 247

grammar, p. 247

pragmatic development, p. 247

morphemes, p. 248

overextension, p. 252

underextension, p. 253

fast mapping, p. 253

metaphor, p. 254

syntactic bootstrapping, p. 255

grammatical morphemes, p. 256

conversational acts, p. 257

protoimperatives, p. 257

protodeclaratives, p. 257

chronology, p. 258

cultural modeling, p. 259

language acquisition device (LAD), p. 260

formats, p. 262

language acquisition support system (LASS), p. 262

collective monologues, p. 263

true dialogue, p. 264

8

CHAPTER

Physical and Cognitive Development in Early Childhood

A group of 5-year-old children have been listening to their teacher read the folktale "Stone Soup," which tells the story of three hungry soldiers who trick some peasants into giving them food by making soup out of stones. "We've made some stone soup to share with everyone," say the soldiers, "but of course it would taste better with some cabbage and meat . . . ." Rose, one of the children listening to the story, asks, "Do stones melt?" The teacher, Vivian Paley, decides to help the children answer this question by making some stone soup of their own. Here is her report of the conversation surrounding their classroom experiment:

    "Do you think they melt, Rose?"

    "Yes."

    "Does anyone agree with Rose?"

    "They will melt if you cook them," said Lisa.

    "If you boil them," Eddie added.

    No one doubted that the stones in the story had melted and that ours, too, would melt.

    "We can cook them and find out," Mrs. Paley said. "How will we be able to tell if they've melted?"

    "They'll be smaller," said Deana.

    The stones are placed in boiling water for an hour and then put on the table for inspection.

    Ellen: They're much smaller.

    Fred: Much, much. Almost melted.

    Rose: I can't eat melted stones.

    Mrs. Paley: Don't worry, Rose. You won't. But I'm not convinced they've melted. Can we prove it?

    Ms. Paley suggests weighing the stones to see if they will lose weight as they boil. The children find that they weigh 2 pounds at the start. After they have been boiled again, the following conversation ensues:

    Eddie: Still 2 [pounds]. But they are smaller.

    Wally: Much smaller.

    Mrs. Paley: They weigh the same. Two pounds before and 2 pounds now. That means they didn't lose weight.

    Eddie: They only got a little bit smaller.

    Wally: The scale can't see the stones. Hey, once in Michigan there were three stones in a fire and they melted away. They were gone. We saw it.

    Deana: Maybe the stones in the story are magic.

    Wally: But not these.

(Adapted from Paley, 1981, pp. 16–18)

his discussion among a group of kindergarten children and their teacher illustrates both the fascination developmentalists feel and the challenges they face as they study the cognitive changes that occur in the years following infancy. When the teacher prompts the children to reconcile the world of the folktale and the world of their senses, the children exhibit a pattern of

AP Photo/Tom Uhlman

Like kindergartners everywhere, those in this Dayton, Ohio, class probably give their teacher, Celestine Scott, plenty of examples of how the young mind wobbles back and forth between logic and magic.

thinking that is typical for their age—a mixture of sound logic and magical thinking. The children correctly believe that when things are "cooked down," they grow smaller and that small stones should be lighter than big ones. At the same time, they are willing to believe that there really are such things as magical stones that melt, and so they miss the point of "Stone Soup." Their way of thinking appears to wobble back and forth between logic and magic, insight and ignorance, the reasonable and the irrational.

A similar mixture of cognitive competence and incompetence can be found in the youngsters' ability to remember objects and events. Young children can often recall the names and descriptions of their favorite dinosaurs, details of trips to the doctor's office, or where they last left their favorite toy with an accuracy that astounds their parents (Nelson & Fivush, 2000). But if an adult asks them to remember a short list of words or a set of toy objects—a task that is easy for older children and adults—they find it difficult to do so, even just a few minutes later (Tulving & Craik, 2000).

The variability of young children's intellectual performances highlights in a special way the unevenness of development, one of the key principles discussed in Chapter 3 (see p. 104 for the list of principles). At the same time, it raises important questions: Can early childhood be considered a distinct stage of development? If it can, then what explains the uneven and variable quality of thought during the years between 2 and 5?

As you probably expect from your reading thus far, theorists' answers to these questions depend on whether they view development as discontinuous and stage-like or continuous and gradual. Stage theorists see young children as being at a certain stage, at a certain level of cognitive *competence*, which they have attained as a result of general processes of change—physical maturation and the universal experiences children have with a variety of people, objects, and other features of their environments. In the view of these theorists, the unevenness of thought in early childhood is of little significance or consequence, largely a matter of variability in *performance* resulting from such factors as the variations in children's familiarity with a particular task or the specific way in which the task is presented (see also p. 181). In contrast, theorists who emphasize the continuity of development see the unevenness as consequential and as inconsistent with a stage view. These theorists tend to account for cognitive change and its unevenness by focusing either on gradual increases in various general psychological mechanisms such as short-term memory capacity or on changes within various isolated domains of psychological functioning, with changes in different domains occurring at different rates. In this chapter, we will examine each of these views in turn, looking at Piaget's preoperational stage, at information-processing approaches to cognitive development, and at cognitive development in privileged domains.

Physical and Motor Development

Growth rates of the body and brain are considerably slower during early childhood than they were in infancy. At the same time, children's ability to use and control their bodies grows by leaps and bounds. As you will see, these changes affect children's health and nutritional needs—needs that are not always met, for various cultural, social, and economic reasons.

motor drive The pleasure young children take in using their new motor skills.

Motor Development

Watching little children on a playground is a lesson in the extraordinary physical and motor developments that separate early childhood from infancy. As shown in the Table 8.1 column on gross motor skills, at 2 years of age, children can run, kick a ball, and climb the ladder of the slide, and at 3 years they can ride a tricycle. The ability to throw a ball overhand emerges at around age 4, as does skipping—that quintessentially childlike way of moving through the world. By the time they are 5, children have achieved a great deal of mastery over their bodies; they have good balance and can ride a scooter and climb nimbly on a jungle gym.

Just as impressive as these gains in motor development is the exuberance with which children practice them. Have you ever been at the grocery store or mall and noticed a young child hopping around or twitching goofily for no apparent reason other than the sheer joy of doing so? Indeed, young children seem to take great pleasure in their newfound abilities to control their bodies, an aspect of motor development described as **motor drive.**

In addition to advances in their gross motor skills, young children's fine motor skills improve notably—to the point that 5-year-olds can fully dress themselves and tie their shoes, use eating utensils effectively and pour water into a glass more or less reliably, and wield crayons with enough control to stay within the lines when they want to. Taken together, the growth and refinement of young children's gross and fine motor capacities markedly increase their abilities to explore their environments and add significantly to the variety of experiences they can have, providing ample occasions for the development of new ways to think and act.

Health

The slowed pace of physical growth during early childhood is reflected in the decreased and occasionally finicky appetites of young children (Dubois et al, 2006). Nevertheless, new levels of physical activity enabled by increased motor development and control place significant demands on the young body for appropriate

The enormous gains in gross motor development that characterize early childhood provide good reasons for South Korean parents to enroll their children in martial arts classes.

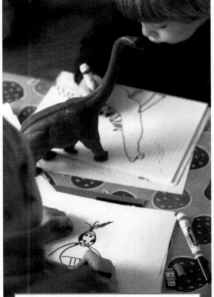

The drawings of these young boys demonstrate some of the remarkable advances in fine motor control that emerge in early childhood.

table **8.1**		
Motor Milestones of Early Childhood		
Age, in Years	Gross Motor Skills	Fine Motor Skills
2	Walks well Runs Goes up and down stairs alone Kicks ball	Uses spoon and fork Turns pages of a book Imitates circular stroke Builds tower of 6 cubes
3	Runs well Marches Rides tricycle Stands on one foot briefly	Feeds self well Puts on shoes and socks Unbuttons and buttons Builds tower of 10 cubes
4	Skips Standing broad jump Throws ball overhand High motor drive	Draws a person Cuts with scissors (not well) Dresses self well Washes and dries face
5	Hops and skips Good balance Skates Rides scooter	Dresses without help Prints simple letters Ties shoes

amounts of both sleep and nutrition. It is fairly well known that older children and adolescents often do not get enough sleep or eat as well as they should (see Chapter 11, p. 390, and Chapter 14, p. 509), but research indicates that this is often true for young children as well. As any parent can attest, children who do not get enough sleep or have not been eating well can be grumpy, overemotional, and easily frustrated, and can have trouble concentrating (Dahl & Lewin, 2002; El-Sheikh et al., 2006).

Sleep Despite pediatricians' recommendations that young children get 12 to 15 hours of sleep in a 24-hour period (naps included), a study conducted by Christine Acebo and her colleagues found that children between 2 and 5 years of age typically sleep only about 8.7 hours at night and less than 9.5 hours in the course of 24 hours (Acebo et al., 2005). The researchers collected their data by placing activity monitors on the children's ankles or wrists to record their sleep and by asking mothers to report their children's sleep habits in detailed diaries. In addition to finding that children sleep much less than recommended, the researchers discovered that more than 80 percent of the children in the study were not taking naps on some or all days. Furthermore, although most children woke frequently during the night, this was particularly true for children from low-income families, who also spent more time in bed compared to children from higher-income families. The effects of early sleep deprivation on later development have yet to be determined. However, the researchers expressed concern that the fast pace of modern life may be taking a toll on the sleep patterns of young children.

Nutrition In many parts of the world, breast-feeding continues well into the third and even fourth year of life (Whiting & Child, 1953; Konner, 2005). In most industrial societies, however, children usually have been fully weaned from the breast or bottle by the time they are 2 years of age. How parents meet the energy needs of young children has become a major source of concern for developmentalists, particularly in light of the obesity epidemic affecting developing children throughout the world (WHO, 2000). Indeed, a nationwide longitudinal study conducted in the United States found that children identified as overweight between 2 and 4 years of age were 5 times more likely than their normal-weight peers to be overweight as adolescents, placing them at risk for a variety of health problems, including diabetes, high blood pressure, and heart disease (Nader et al., 2006).

A similar national study of Finnish children found an interesting growth pattern associated with the emergence of heart disease in adulthood (Barker et al., 2006). Specifically, individuals most at risk for cardiovascular disease as adults were those who were actually underweight during the first 2 years of life and then underwent a period of rapid weight gain through early and later childhood. This

As these children enjoy their Happy Meals in Beijing, childhood obesity rates continue to rise throughout the world, due in part to increased access to diets high in fats and sugars.

Mark Leong/Redux

particular pattern has worrisome implications for children in Third World countries where globalization is creating major changes in access to food and in eating behavior, with an increase in calories and in fats and sugar in the diet. In fact, a study of children in China, India, Guatemala, Brazil, and the Philippines—all of which are experiencing the "nutrition transition" associated with globalization—found evidence for the pattern described in the Finnish study, that is, growth failure in the first few years of postnatal life followed by overweight in early and later childhood and elevated risk for diabetes and heart disease in adulthood (Stein et al., 2005).

Young children rely on parents to provide them with nutritious meals and snacks. For economic reasons, some parents may have difficulty meeting the nutritional needs of their children. In many regions of the world, more than 40 percent of all preschool-age children have stunted growth because their parents cannot afford to feed them adequately (WHO, 2008). Even in the United States, 11 percent of all families are considered **food insecure,** meaning that they do not have access to enough food to ensure good health for all family members, and 4 percent are considered "food insecure with hunger" (Figure 8.1).

Parental attitudes about food and eating can also take a toll on children's nutrition. A series of studies conducted by Thomas Joiner and his colleagues found that parents of 3-year-olds worried that their sons but not their daughters were underweight and did not eat enough, despite the fact that there was no difference in the actual average weight of boys and girls in the study (Holm-Denoma et al., 2005). This finding prompted the researchers to speculate that body-image stereotypes—specifically, that girls should be thin, and boys big and strong—may be affecting the diet of very young children and possibly increasing the risk of eating disorders in the future (see Chapter 14, p. 514). And, although parents today are increasingly concerned about early-childhood obesity, researchers have made the point that these concerns must be carefully balanced with the potential for children's undernutrition (Allen & Myers, 2006).

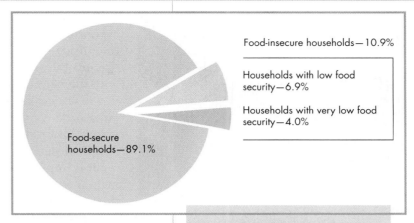

Food-insecure households—10.9%

Households with low food security—6.9%

Households with very low food security—4.0%

Food-secure households—89.1%

Figure 8.1 Food is surely at the top of the list of children's essential needs. Yet many parents across the globe have difficulty providing their children with enough food to ensure healthy growth and development. Even in the United States, one of the wealthiest countries in the world, 11 percent of families are food insecure, including 4 percent who are food insecure with hunger (Nord, Andrews & Carlson, 2007).

Brain Development

As we discussed in Chapter 5, after infancy the brain's development slows considerably until adolescence, when it undergoes another growth spurt. At the start of early childhood, the brain has attained about 80 percent of its adult weight; by age 5, it has grown to 90 percent of its full weight (Huttenlocher, 1994). Despite this modest growth rate, several noteworthy changes occur in the brain during early childhood (Lenroot & Giedd, 2006). For example, the overall enlargement in size results from the continuing process of *myelination,* which speeds the transmission of neural impulses within and among different areas of the brain (Sampaio & Truwitt, 2001). During early childhood, myelination is most prominent in brain areas such as the frontal cortex that are important for more advanced cognitive functions, including planning and regulating behavior (Pujol et al., 2006). In addition to increased myelination, there is an increase in the length and branching of neurons that connect different areas of the brain, as well as a continuation of *synaptic pruning,* in which nonfunctional synapses die off (see p. 116).

Even with these changes, the brain, of course, is still relatively immature, which may account for the limitations of children's problem-solving abilities. For example, myelination in parts of the brain that support memory (the hippocampus and frontal cortex) is still far from complete, which likely contributes to young children's difficulties in keeping several things in mind at once. In addition, various areas of the brain are developing, and connecting, at different times and at different rates, and this variability may account for the unevenness of cognitive development evident during this age period. When one part of the brain develops more rapidly than others, or when the neural pathways connecting a particular combination of cortical areas undergo a spurt in myelination, the psychological processes supported by the brain area or areas can be expected to undergo rapid change as well. High levels of performance are expected to occur when a given task calls upon brain systems that are highly developed, and, correspondingly, low levels of performance are expected to occur when a given task calls upon brain systems that are not yet mature.

food insecure Lacking enough food to ensure good health

all: DeLoache et al., 2004

Figure 8.2 Three examples of scale errors. (a) This 21-month-old child has committed a scale error by attempting to slide down a miniature slide; she has fallen off in this serious effort to carry out an impossible act. (b) This 24-month-old child has opened the door to the miniature car and is repeatedly trying to force his foot inside the car. (c) This 28-month-old child is looking between his legs to precisely locate the miniature chair that he is in the process of sitting on. (From DeLoache, Uttal, & Rosengren, 2005.)

A fascinating example of what happens when areas of the brain that will eventually communicate with each other are not yet connected is the *scale errors* made by toddlers. In older children and adults, the perception of the size, or scale, of an object is seamlessly integrated into the person's actions with the object. You would not, for example, try to put a really large peg in a really small hole. Children between 18 and 30 months of age, on the other hand, very well might. This is because they frequently commit **scale errors;** that is, they fail to integrate information about the size of an object into their decisions about how to use the object (Ware et. al, 2006). The result is serious and often amusing attempts to perform impossible actions, such as trying to sit in a dollhouse chair or get into a miniature toy car (Figure 8.2). On the basis of their research, Judy DeLoache and her colleagues argue that scale errors in young children involve a "disconnect" between children's use of visual information and their ability to plan and control their actions (2005). The dissociation of perception and action, they speculate, may be due to the immature cortical functioning of the brain, particularly in the prefrontal cortex (see also Barsalou, 2008, and Diamond et al., 2002).

Some of the changes that occur in brain development during early childhood are influenced by the cultural context; different culturally organized activities promote *experience-dependent* brain growth in the form of increased synaptic development and connections (see Chapter 4, p. 130). For example, if the young child lives in a culture that emphasizes hunting or weaving, both of which require concentrated and sustained processing of spatial relations, it can be expected that there will be increased growth of cells in the area of the brain responsible for processing spatial information (the parietal cortex). By contrast, if the child's culture places a heavy emphasis on verbal expression, the language centers of the brain are likely to undergo additional development. The influence of culturally organized activities on brain development is intriguingly illustrated in a recent study indicating that when children take music lessons between the ages of 4 and 6, brain processes associated with attention and memory become more active when they listen to music, and their general memory capacity and IQs improve compared with those of children who do not receive music training (Fujioka, Trainor, & Ross, 2008).

|||||| APPLY ■ CONNECT ■ DISCUSS

Armed with the information in Table 8.1, and your understanding of *motor drive,* visit a playground where you can observe young children engaged in motor play. What examples of motor skills and motor drive can you identify? Focusing on one or two children, can you guess their ages based on the motor skills they exhibit?

Preoperational Development

Adult: Why is it cold in winter?
Child: Because there is snow.
Adult: What is it that makes the cold?
Child: The snow.
Adult: If there were no snow would it be cold?
Child: No.
Adult: It is the snow which makes the cold, or the cold which makes the snow?

Child: The cold makes the snow.
Adult: And where does the cold come from?
Child: From the snow.
(Piaget, 1929/1979, p, 323)

As we discussed in Chapter 5, Piaget believed that when children complete the final sensorimotor substage of infancy, they are able to think symbolically, using one thing to stand for ("re-present") another. This newfound ability to use one thing to stand for another is the foundation for developing language. It is also the bridge to the next stage of intellectual development, which Piaget called *preoperational* and considered a transitional stage between the sensorimotor intelligence of infancy and the fully *operational* intelligence of middle childhood (Piaget & Inhelder, 1969). In order to explain what Piaget meant by *preoperational thinking,* we need first to say a bit about the meaning of operational thought (we will discuss it in more detail in Chapter 11).

According to Piaget, operational thinking involves **mental operations,** that is, mental "actions" in which children combine, separate, and transform information in a logical manner. Examples of mental operations include mathematical processes such as adding and subtracting, as well as arranging objects in particular orders (from smallest to largest, or alphabetically, and so on) or putting objects into categories based on some feature they have in common. The ability to engage in such mental actions and think operationally emerges around 7 to 8 years of age, making it possible for children to arrange their stamp collections according to country of origin and estimated value, for example, or to assemble a complex new toy right out of the box. They are better able to formulate explicit problem-solving strategies because they can think through alternative actions and modify them mentally before they actually act. Piaget believed that until children are able to engage in mental operations, their thinking is subject to fluctuations of the kind Ms. Paley's class demonstrated when answering questions about "Stone Soup," and to the type of circular reasoning in the above quotation of the child explaining the relationship between snow and the cold of winter.

Piaget's belief that young children often fall into error and confusion because they are still unable to engage in true mental operations is what led him to call the period of cognitive development in early childhood the **preoperational stage.** In his view, cognitive development during early childhood involves a process of overcoming the limitations that stand in the way of operational thinking. (These limitations, discussed in the next several sections, are outlined in Table 8.2.)

Although fluctuations and errors are typical of early childhood thought, Piaget insisted that preoperational thinking is not random or unsystematic. Indeed, as you will see below, the errors children make in the preoperational stage are remarkably consistent, and tell us much about the nature of cognition and its development. On the other hand, as you learned in Chapter 5, many developmentalists disagree with Piaget's conclusions, and argue that his interview methods make it difficult for children to demonstrate their competence on various tasks, thereby obscuring their level of actual understanding.

Centration

Imagine that we show you two beach balls. One is red with blue stripes; the other is red with yellow stripes. If we then ask you to point to the red ball, you would very likely want clarification: "Which red one? The one with yellow stripes or the one with blue stripes?" In contrast, a preoperational child would most likely point to one or the other of the balls with total confidence. According to Piaget,

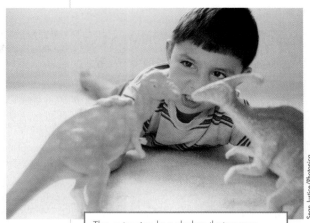

Sean Justice/Photonica

The extensive knowledge that young children acquire when they become engrossed in subjects like dinosaurs may only be a passing phase. But children's expertise about such matters is scientifically important because it shows that even young children, when they accumulate an extensive knowledge base in a specific domain, will display cognitive abilities more like those of adults.

scale errors Young children's inappropriate use of objects due to their failure to consider information about the object's size.

mental operations In Piaget's theory, the mental process of combining, separating, or transforming information in a logical manner.

preoperational stage According to Piaget, the stage of thinking between infancy and middle childhood in which children are unable to decenter their thinking or to think through the consequences of an action

table 8.2

Piaget's Stages of Cognitive Development: Preoperational

Age (years)	Stage	Description	Characteristics and Examples
Birth to 2	Sensorimotor	Infants' achievements consist largely of coordinating their sensory perceptions and simple motor behaviors. As they move through the 6 substages of this period, infants come to recognize the existence of a world outside of themselves and begin to interact with it in deliberate ways.	Centration, the tendency to focus (center) on the most salient aspect of whatever one is trying to think about. A major manifestation of this is egocentrism, or considering the world entirely in terms of one's own point of view. • Children engage in collective monologues, rather than dialogues, in each other's company. • Children have difficulty taking a listener's knowledge into account in order to communicate effectively. • Children fail to consider both the height and width of containers in order to compare their volumes. • Children confuse classes with subclasses. They cannot reliably say whether there are more wooden beads or more brown beads in a set of all wooden beads.
2 to 6	Preoperational	Young children can represent reality to themselves through the use of symbols, including mental images, words, and gestures. Objects and events no longer have to be present to be thought about, but children often fail to distinguish their point of view from that of others; become easily captured by surface appearances; and are often confused about causal relations.	Confusion of appearance and reality. • Children act as if a Halloween mask actually changes the identity of the person wearing it. • Children may believe that a straight stick partially submerged in water actually does become bent.
6 to 12	Concrete operational	As they enter middle childhood, children become capable of mental operations, internalized actions that fit into a logical system. Operational thinking allows children mentally to combine, separate, order, and transform objects and actions. Such operations are considered concrete because they are carried out in the presence of the objects and events being thought about.	Precausal reasoning, characterized by illogical thinking and an indifference to cause-and-effect relations. • A child may think a graveyard is a cause of death because dead people are buried there. A form of moral reasoning that sees morality as being imposed from the outside and that does not take intentions into account.
12 to 19	Formal operational	In adolescence, the developing person acquires the ability to think systematically about all logical relations within a problem. Adolescents display keen interest in abstract ideals and in the process of thinking itself.	

centration Young children's tendency to focus on only one feature of an object to the exclusion of all other features.

decentration The cognitive ability to pull away from focusing on just one feature of an object in order to consider multiple features.

objectivity The mental distancing made possible by decentration, and which Piaget believed to be the major goal of all cognitive development.

egocentrism In Piaget's terms, to "center on oneself," to consider the world entirely in terms of one's own point of view.

the source of such an error, and the greatest limitation to early childhood thinking, is **centration,** the tendency of young children to be "captured" by a single feature of whatever they are trying to think about and to focus on that one feature to the exclusion of all others. In the case of the beach balls, the child is captured by the color red and consequently ignores the other feature of stripes. The opposite of centration—and the key to cognitive growth beyond the preoperational stage—is **decentration,** that is, the ability to mentally pull away from focusing on just one aspect of an object or problem in order to consider multiple aspects of it. The *consequence* of the mental distancing enabled by decentration is **objectivity,** which Piaget believed to be the principal goal of cognitive development. Indeed, as you will see in later chapters, Piaget held that cognitive development from infancy through adolescence involves a steady march toward increasing objectivity, the hallmark of scientific reasoning.

Preoperational children, however, have just begun this journey toward objectivity. Their tendency to be captured by a single aspect or dimension of an object or event is the root of the three most common errors in early childhood reasoning: (1) egocentrism, (2) the confusion of appearance and reality, and (3) precausal reasoning. In the sections to follow, we will look at these three errors Piaget described; for each, we first summarize the evidence that led Piaget to his conclusions and then present findings that challenge his interpretations.

Egocentrism If we were to walk together down a road in the dark of night, we might notice that the moon seemed to follow us. We know, of course, that the moon does not *really* coordinate its movement with our own. If it did, how would we account for what would happen if we walked on but you decided suddenly to turn around and walk the other way? Now you are off in one direction, and we are off in another, yet all of us experience the moon following us around as if tethered to our wrists by an invisible string. There is a contradiction here: The moon cannot follow all of us. Preoperational children, on the other hand, have no sense of this contradiction. They will steadfastly maintain that the moon follows them around and fail to appreciate that it cannot possibly follow someone heading west at the same time it follows someone heading east.

In the context of Piaget's general concept of centration, **egocentrism** refers to the tendency to "center on oneself," or, in other words, to be captive to one's own point of view and unable to take another person's perspective. The child who wants to get daddy a Care Bear or an action hero for his birthday, and the child who maintains that the moon follows them around, are both demonstrating egocentrism.

A famous example of egocentrism as a failure to take another person's perspective is found in young children's performance on Piaget's classic "three-mountain problem." In this procedure, young children were shown a large diorama containing models of three mountains that were distinctively different in size, shape, and landmarks (Piaget & Inhelder, 1956) (Figure 8.3). First, the children were asked to walk around the diorama and become familiar with the landscape from all sides. Once the children had done this, they were seated on one side of the diorama. Next, a doll was placed on the opposite side of the diorama so that it had a "different view" of the landscape. The children were then shown pictures of the diorama from several perspectives and were asked to identify the picture that corresponded to the doll's point of view. Even though they had seen the diorama from the doll's location, the children almost always chose the picture corresponding to their own spatial perspective, not the doll's. Preoperational children's poor performance on Piaget's three-mountain problem has been widely replicated and long assumed to demonstrate the perspective-taking limitations of young children.

Speculating that the complexity of Piaget's task might affect children's performance, Helen Borke (1975) first replicated the classic three-mountain experiment with children between 3 and 4 years of age. She then presented the same children with an alternative form of the problem, a farm scene that included such landmarks as a small lake with a boat on it, a horse and a cow, ducks, people, trees, and a building (Figure 8.4). In this alternative version, Grover, a character from *Sesame Street,* drove around the landscape in a car, stopping from time to take a look at the view. The child's task was to indicate what that view looked like from Grover's perspective.

Children as young as 3 years old performed well on this perspective-taking problem, despite the fact that, as would be expected, their performance on the three-mountain version of the problem was poor. These contrasting levels of performance between the two forms of a logically identical

Figure 8.3 Preschool children shown this diorama of three mountains, each with a distinctive feature on its top, were unable to say how the scene might look from perspectives other than the one they had at the moment. (From Piaget & Inhelder, 1956.)

Figure 8.4 Borke's modification of Piaget's three-mountain perspective-taking task. When a diorama contains familiar objects, preschoolers are more likely to be able to say how it looks from a point of view other than their own.

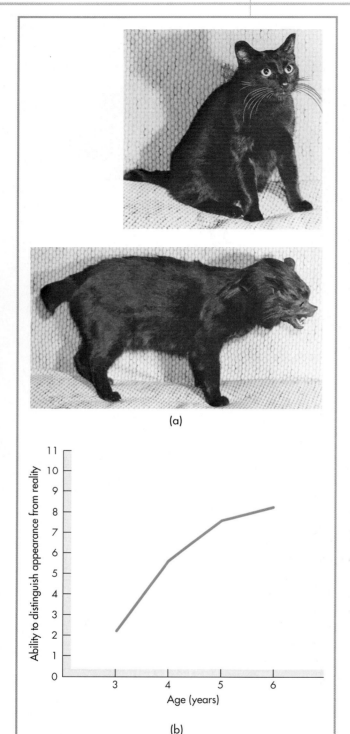

(a)

(b)

Figure 8.5 (a) Maynard the cat, without and with a dog mask. (b) A chart plotting the age-related increase in children's ability to understand that Maynard remains a cat even when his appearance is changed so that he looks like a dog. (Adapted from De Vries, 1969.)

problem led Borke to conclude that when perspective-taking tasks involve familiar, easily differentiated objects, and when care is taken to make it easy for young children to express their understanding, young children demonstrate that they are able to take spatial perspectives other than their own. In other words, young children have the *competence* to take the perspectives of others, but their *performance* may be affected by the demands of the task.

Confusing Appearance and Reality

First child: Pretend there's a monster coming, okay?
Second child: No. Let's don't pretend that.
First child: Okay. Why?
Second child: 'Cause it's too scary, that's why.
(Garvey & Berndt, 1977, p. 107)

The tendency to confuse appearance and reality is another common error of early childhood that Piaget attributed to centration. Difficulty distinguishing between appearance and reality would explain why 2½-year-olds often become frightened when someone puts on a mask at Halloween, as if the mask had actually changed the person into a witch or a dragon. In a classic study of this form of behavior, Rheta De Vries (1969) studied the development of the appearance–reality distinction with the help of Maynard, an unusually well-behaved black cat. At the start of the experiment, all the children said that Maynard was a cat. After they played with Maynard for a short while, De Vries hid Maynard's front half behind a screen while she strapped a realistic mask of a ferocious dog onto his head (Figure 8.5a). As she removed the screen, De Vries asked a set of questions to assess the children's ability to distinguish between the animal's real identity and its appearance: "What kind of animal is it now?" "Is it really a dog?" "Can it bark?"

By and large, the 3-year-olds focused almost entirely on Maynard's appearance (Figure 8.5b). They said he had actually become a ferocious dog, and some of them were afraid he would bite them. Most of the 6-year-olds scoffed at this idea, understanding that the cat only looked like a dog. The 4- and 5-year-olds showed considerable confusion. They did not believe that a cat could become a dog, but they did not always answer De Vries's questions correctly.

Similar confusions between appearance and reality have been reported by John Flavell and his colleagues, who showed young children various objects that appeared to be one thing but were really another: a sponge that appeared to be a rock, a stone that appeared to be an egg, and so on. The children were shown the objects and were asked, "What does that look like?" (the appearance question) and "What is it really?" (the reality question) (Flavell et al., 1986; Melot & Houde, 1998). The researchers found that 3-year-olds are likely to answer appearance–reality questions incorrectly. For example, it is to be expected that the children would initially think that the sponge "rock" was a rock because it was realistic enough to fool adults. But once children discover by touching it that the "rock" really is a sponge, they begin to insist that it not only feels like a sponge but also looks like a sponge! Four-year-olds seem to be in a transition state; they sometimes answer correctly, sometimes incorrectly. Five-year-olds have a much firmer grip on the appearance–reality distinction in these circumstances and usually answer the experimenters' questions in an adultlike manner. These findings have been replicated in several countries including China, Germany, and France (Huelsken et al., 2001; Melot & Houde, 1998). Thus, research like that of De Vries and Flavell would seem to confirm Piaget's view that centration can make it difficult for preschoolers to distinguish appearance from reality.

However, modifications of De Vries's and Flavell's experiments suggest otherwise. In an interesting variation of the experiment that turned Maynard, the cat, into a ferocious dog, Carl Huelsksen and his colleagues demonstrated that young children can make appearance–reality distinctions with regard to adults dressed up in a costume (Huelsken et al., 2001). In four out of five cases, 3- to 4-year olds indicated that they knew the person in the costume was the same as the person in his or her regular clothing, although a majority had difficulty providing an explicit verbal distinction between appearance and reality.

At 2 years of age, Riley can hardly be blamed for bursting into tears when she meets the Easter Bunny for the first time. Her age-typical confusion between appearance and reality can make such encounters truly scary.

Felicity Sapp and her colleagues also determined that the main difficulty experienced by 3-year-olds is to formulate the appearance–reality distinction in words (Sapp, Lee, & Muir, 2000). In a variation of Flavell's deceptive-objects experiment, the researchers found that when 3-year-olds were given the opportunity to distinguish between appearance and reality nonverbally, they were largely successful. For example, after the children had discovered the true nature of the sponge rock, they were presented with a number of items and asked to pick one to help the experimenter wipe up some water. Nearly all the children picked the sponge rock.

In a different approach, Catherine Rice and her colleagues (1997) repeated and extended Flavell's study by using a procedure that engaged 3-and 4-year-olds as coconspirators in the fake-object deception. After being tricked with a fake object such as a sponge rock, children were asked to help trick another adult with it. The experimenter and child displayed the trick object on a table, and then, while waiting for the adult to arrive, the experimenter asked the child several questions: What is the object, really; what does it appear to be; what will the absent adult think it is? In this playlike context, the children were able to say that the object was a sponge but that it looked like a rock—and that the adult would think it was a rock. Thus, they were clearly able to distinguish reality from appearance. The findings of the Sapp and Rice experiments illustrate just how careful experimenters must be to create appropriate versions of their tasks so that they are meaningful for young children and give them ample opportunity to reveal what they know (see Deák, 2006, for review).

Precausal Reasoning Nothing is more characteristic of 4- to 5-year old children than their love for asking questions. "Why is the sky blue?" "What makes clouds?" "Where do babies come from?" Clearly, children are interested in the causes of things. Piaget believed, however, that because young children are not yet capable of true mental operations, they cannot engage in genuine cause-and-effect reasoning. He claimed that instead of reasoning from general premises to particular cases (deduction) or from specific cases to general principles (induction), young children think *transductively,* from one particular to another. As an example, he described how his young daughter missed her customary nap one afternoon and remarked, "I haven't had a nap, so it isn't afternoon." As a consequence of such reasoning, young children are likely to confuse cause and effect. Because

precausal thinking Piaget's description of the reasoning of young children that does not follow the procedures of either deductive or inductive reasoning

he believed that transductive reasoning precedes true causal reasoning, Piaget referred to this aspect of young children's thinking as **precausal thinking** (Piaget, 1930).

One of our daughters gave a splendid demonstration of how transductive reasoning can lead a young child to confuse cause and effect. At the age of 3½, Jenny happened to walk with her parents through an old graveyard. Listening to her father read the inscriptions on the gravestones, she realized that somehow the old moss-covered stones represented people. "Where is she now?" she asked when he finished reading the inscription on one stone.

"She's dead," said her father.

"But where is she?"

Jenny's father tried to explain that when people die, they are buried in the ground, in cemeteries. After that, Jenny steadfastly refused to go into cemeteries and would become upset when she was near one. At bedtime every evening, she repeatedly asked about death, burial, and graveyards. Jenny's parents answered her questions as best they could, yet Jenny kept repeating the same questions and was obviously upset by the topic. The reason for her fear became clear when the family was moving to New York City. "Are there any graveyards in New York City?" she asked anxiously. Exhausted by her insistent questions, her parents' belief that they should be honest was crumbling.

"No," her mother lied. "There are no graveyards in New York City."

At this response, Jenny visibly relaxed. "Then people don't die in New York," she said.

Jenny had reasoned that since graveyards are places where dead people are found, graveyards must be the cause of death. This reasoning led her to the comforting but incorrect conclusion that if you can stay away from graveyards, you are not in danger of dying.

As with the other two errors we looked at, research on cause-and-effect reasoning suggests that under certain, carefully crafted conditions, young children are capable of greater cognitive sophistication than Piaget credited them with. Merry Bullock and Rochel Gelman, for example, used the apparatus shown in Figure 8.6 to demonstrate the causal reasoning abilities of 3- to 5-year-olds (Bullock, 1984; Bullock & Gelman, 1979). Children observed two sequences of events. First, a steel marble was dropped into one of two slots in a box, both of which were visible through the side of the box. Two seconds after the marble disappeared at the bottom of the slot, a Snoopy doll popped out of the hole in the middle of the apparatus. Then, at that moment, a second ball was dropped into the other slot. It too disappeared, with no further result. The children were then asked to say which of the balls had made Snoopy jump up and to provide an explanation.

Even children as young as 3 years old usually said that the first ball had caused Snoopy to jump up, and the 5-year-olds had no difficulty with the task at all. However, as we found in the case of young children's explanations for the difference between appearance and reality, there was a marked difference between the age groups in their ability to verbally explain what had happened. Many of the 3-year-olds could give no explanation or said something completely irrelevant ("It's got big teeth"). Almost all the 5-year-olds could provide an explanation related to the principle that causes precede effects. Subsequent research has shown that if the problem is slightly complicated, 3-year-olds become confused and can neither

Figure 8.6 The apparatus used by Bullock and Gelman to test preschoolers' understanding that cause precedes effect. (a) A marble was dropped into one of the slots. (b) Two seconds after the marble disappeared, a Snoopy doll popped out of the hole in the middle of the apparatus. At the same moment, a second marble was dropped into the other slot, where it disappeared, with no further result. Preschoolers are generally able to indicate which marble caused Snoopy to jump up. (Based on Bullock & Gelman, 1979.)

(a)

(b)

solve nor explain what appear to be relatively simple mechanical cause–effect relationships (Frye, 2000).

The Problem of Uneven Levels of Performance

The examples of preoperational thinking that we have provided thus far (summarized in Table 8.2 on page 276) are only a sample of the phenomena supporting the idea that there is a distinctive mode of thought associated with early childhood. But they are sufficient to give the flavor of the sorts of evidence collected by Piaget and others to argue that an inability to decenter one's thought pervades the preoperational stage of cognitive development, making it difficult for young children to consider multiple aspects of a situation simultaneously or to think through a problem systematically (for an example of the real-world challenges presented by young children's cognitive limitations, see the box "Bearing Witness: Can Young Children Tell the Truth?").

On the other hand, we have also discussed various studies that cast doubt on certain specifics of Piaget's tasks and on his reliance on interviews, which led him to judge young children as particularly vulnerable to errors of reasoning. Much of this new evidence indicates that early childhood cognitive development is a good deal more uneven than Piaget suggests. Under some circumstances, children show evidence of cognitive abilities well before Piaget believed possible (Goswami, 2002; Inagaki & Hatano, 2002; Rosengren & Brasswell, 2001).

Two kinds of approaches offer alternatives to Piaget's concept of a preoperational stage as characteristic of early childhood. These alternative approaches take different paths but share the twin goals of understanding the sources of unevenness in children's performance and the extent to which developmental change is general or piecemeal and stagelike or gradual (Case, 1998; Fischer & Pare-Blagoev, 2000; Goswami, 2008). As you will see in the next section, information-processing approaches propose general psychological mechanisms, such as increases in short-term memory capacity and knowledge, to account for the process of cognitive change and the unevenness of young children's cognitive performances. A competing set of theories, which we examine later, relegates general mechanisms to a secondary role and focuses on the ways in which cognitive development builds upon domain-specific psychological processes.

||||| APPLY ▪ CONNECT ▪ DISCUSS —

When young children are asked where they live, they often confuse the name of the city with the name of the state. How is this confusion an example of preoperational thinking?

Information-Processing Approaches to Cognitive Development

As discussed in Chapter 1, information-processing models of development depict the workings of the mind as analogous to the workings of a digital computer (Siegler, 2000). According to such models, the neural features of the human brain are analogous to the hardware of a computer—that is, its *structural* components—whereas the activities and practices that individuals engage in for the purpose of remembering and using information are analogous to the computer's software—that is, the programs that are written to *process* information through the system.

An overview of the essential components of this view of the mind is illustrated in Figure 8.7. The three boxes labeled "sensory register," "short-term storage,"

Bearing Witness: Can Young Children Tell the Truth?

T IS A SAD FACT THAT CHILDREN OF ALL ages are victims of crimes or witness crimes committed against others. Psychologists have traditionally viewed children's eyewitness testimony as unreliable—especially in cases involving sexual abuse and other traumatic events—because young children have been considered suggestible (Stern, 1910), incapable of distinguishing fantasy from reality (Piaget, 1926), and prone to fantasize sexual events (Freud, 1905/1953). Judges, lawyers, and prosecutors have also expressed reservations about children's reliability as witnesses (Bottoms et al., 2002; Goodman & Melinder, 2007). Legal rulings on the admissibility of children's testimony continue to reflect these longstanding doubts. In many states, for example, it is left up to the judge to determine whether a child below a certain age is competent to testify.

Owing to a growing concern about the prevalence of sexual and physical abuse of children in recent years, the scientific and legal communities are particularly interested in determining when and under what conditions young children can testify reliably about past events (Goodman, 2006; Quas et al., 2007). Children's behavior both in actual criminal trials and in experimental psychological studies reveals a complex picture in which memories and testimony are affected by the child's age, the nature of the event to be recalled, and a number of socioemotional factors.

A concern that has spurred considerable research is whether very young children may be unreliable witnesses because either their long-term memory is less reliable than older children's and adults' or they are particularly susceptible to misremembering events when they are coached or presented with misleading questions (Goodman & Melinder, 2007). Indeed, several studies have demonstrated that preschool-age children are more susceptible to false suggestions than are older children and adults (Poole & Lindsay, 2001). For example,

Three-year-old Amanda Conklin looks out at a crowded Van Nuys, California, courtroom as the judge questions her during the trial of her father for the murder of her mother.

Al Seib/Los Angeles Times

when researchers asked young children misleading, even strange questions about what happened when they went to the doctor's office ("Did the doctor cut off your hair?" or "Did the nurse lick your knee?"), the youngest children were much more likely than the older children to say that these things happened even though they did not (Ornstein et al., 1997).

On the other hand, Gail Goodman and her colleagues have found that children can be remarkably resistant to misleading questions if they are interviewed soon after an event, when it is still fresh in their minds (Quas et al., 2007; Malloy et al., 2004). Moreover, memory is improved when the event in question is emotionally intense. In one study, for example, when children were asked about their experiences getting vaccinated at the doctor's office, those who were more upset and cried more recalled more information (Goodman et al., 1991). In a long-term study of memory for child sexual abuse, it was found that sexual abuse victims who had more posttraumatic stress symptoms remembered the abuse particularly well, suggesting that such trauma leads to "fear networks" which foster hypervigilance to

trauma cues and reactivation of traumatic memories (Alexander et al., 2005).

Although a lot of research on children's eyewitness testimony has focused on how unreliable children can be, Gail Goodman has turned her attention to finding out how to help children tell the truth about the frightening events they have witnessed or personally experienced. She has, for example, identified techniques that help children make accurate face identifications in photo lineups and that limit their suggestibility in interviews (such as the interviewer's telling children things like "I may try to trick you" and "It's OK to say 'I don't know'"). As she has pointed out, "the legal system makes numerous assumptions about children's abilities and needs. For instance, the criminal justice system assumes that 'confrontation' of victims in open court is the best way to reach the truth—even if the victim is a young, traumatized child. Psychological science has the potential to test many of those assumptions and, in the process, to help create a more scientifically based jurisprudence concerning children" (Goodman, 2005, p. 873).

and "long-term storage" represent the basic system for attending to, interpreting, and storing information. The box at the top of the figure, labeled "control processes," represents the systems that, in effect, monitor and modify the results of the ongoing processes of the basic system.

You can follow the potential flow of information by starting at the left of the figure. The presumed starting point of any problem-solving process is the *sensory register,* which stores incoming information for a fraction of a second before it is attended to and selectively processed. Stimulation from the environment ("input,"

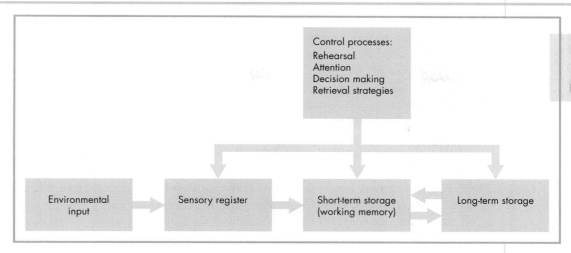

Figure 8.7 Major components of an information-processing model of mental actions. (Adapted from Atkinson & Schiffrin, 1968.)

in the language of computer programming) is detected by the sensory organs and is passed on to the sensory register. If the input is not attended to, it will disappear almost immediately. If it is attended to, it may be "read into" *short-term (working) memory,* where it can be retained for several seconds. Working memory is the part of the information-processing system where active thinking takes place. Working memory combines incoming information from the sensory register with memory of past experiences, or *long-term memory,* changing the information into new forms. If the information in working memory is not combined with information in long-term memory, it is easily forgotten.

Figure 8.7 also shows the way in which the flow of information between sensory register, working memory, and long-term memory is coordinated by *control processes.* These control processes determine how the information temporarily held in working memory is applied to the problem at hand. Important control processes include attention, rehearsal, and decision making. The "software" that implements the control processes determines the particular information that must be attended to, whether long-term memory must be searched more thoroughly, or whether a particular problem-solving strategy should be used. Control processes also determine whether a piece of information in short-term memory needs to be retained or can be forgotten.

You can get an overall idea of the information-processing approach by considering what occurs when a mother tries to teach her 4-year-old daughter to remember the family phone number. The mother sits with the child at the phone and shows her the sequence of buttons to push—say, 543-1234. The child watches what her mother does and hears what her mother is saying. First, the set of numbers enters the child's sensory register as images and a sequence of sounds and is transferred to working memory. Next, meanings corresponding to those images and sounds are retrieved from long-term memory and matched with the images and sounds in working memory. The child recognizes each number and applies control processes in order to "try to remember," perhaps by using the strategy of repeating each item to herself. Remembering occurs when the information concerning the numerical sequence enters long-term memory so that it is retrievable at a later time.

The young child in our example may experience difficulty at any phase of this process. She may pay insufficient attention to what her mother is saying, in which case the information will not enter her sensory register. Being young, she has a small (immature) working-memory capacity and may not be able to hold all the numbers in working memory as she tries to remember them. The speed with which she can transfer information from the sensory register to working memory

Although learning a telephone number can be good fun, it requires a fairly complex set of information-processing skills involving the sensory register, working memory, long-term memory, and retrieval processes.

elaborative style A form of talking with children about new events or experiences that enhances children's memories for those events and experiences.

privileged domains Cognitive domains that call upon specialized kinds of information, require specifically designated forms of reasoning, and appear to be of evolutionary importance to the human species.

and to long-term memory may be relatively slow, causing her to forget some of the numbers before they can be enduringly stored in long-term memory. Lastly, she may have little experience with intentional memorization and hence no repertoire of strategies for holding information in working memory for an extended period or for manipulating numbers in working memory.

Developmentalists who study children's memory find striking changes across the years of early childhood. To a large extent, the dramatic increase in young children's ability to remember is due to "software" changes, that is, changes in the way information flows through the memory system as a consequence of changes in the processes by which it is encoded, stored, and retrieved (Ornstein et al., 2006). Moreover, two factors can be key in contributing to children's increasing success: children's prior knowledge about the events or materials being remembered, and adults assisting children in remembering. In general, children are better at remembering when they have substantial prior knowledge on which to "hang" the new information. In the absence of prior knowledge, their memory can be greatly improved if adults talk with them about the new event or experience as it unfolds (Boland, Haden, & Ornstein, 2003; Haden et al., 2001). Studies of mother–child interactions (Ornstein, Haden, & Hendrick, 2004) have found that children's memories improve when mothers (and presumably other caregivers) use an **elaborative style,** including

- *wh- questions* (What's happening? Who is that?);
- *associations* that relate the new information to the child's prior knowledge;
- *follow-ins* that follow and discuss aspects of the events that the child finds interesting;
- *positive evaluations* that praise the child's verbal and nonverbal contributions to the interaction.

Intervention studies in which mothers were trained to use a more elaborative style when interacting with their children likewise found an increase in children's memory for specific events and experiences (Boland et al., 2003; Peterson et al., 1999).

In sum, from an information-processing perspective, young children's cognitive difficulties are caused by general cognitive factors including limitations in knowledge, memory, attentional control, and the speed of processing information, as well as by limited strategies for acquiring and using information (Siegler, 2000). Difficulties may be less in situations where children have prior knowledge or caregivers' elaborative style encourages remembering. As children grow older, their performance improves and its unevenness diminishes because the cognitive limitations are gradually reduced through maturation of their brains ("hardware") and the development of more effective information-processing strategies ("software").

▌▌▌▌ APPLY ▪ CONNECT ▪ DISCUSS

Suppose that two children are presented with the same set of unrelated pictures and told to remember the pictures because they will be given a memory test shortly.

Picture presented	Child 1 says	Child 2 says
Cat	cat, cat, cat	cat, cat
Shoe	shoe, shoe, shoe	cat, shoe, cat, shoe
Truck	truck, truck, truck	cat, shoe, truck
Pen	pen, pen, pen	cat, shoe, truck, pen

According to material presented in this section, why is child 2 likely to outperform child 1 on the memory test?

Cognitive Development in Privileged Domains

The teddy's arm fell off because you twisted it too far.

I talking very quiet because I don't want somebody to wake me up.

He needs more meat because he is growing long arms.

Each of these statements was made by a young child offering an explanation of an event encountered in daily life—a physical event (a broken object), a psychological event (an internal desire), and a biological event (physical growth) (Hickling & Wellman, 2001). In contrast to Piagetian and information-processing theorists, who emphasize how general intellectual processes such as centration or information storage and retrieval affect virtually all aspects of the young child's thinking, developmentalists taking another approach to cognition focus on changes within specific areas of knowledge acquisition, known as **privileged domains** (Chen & Siegler, 2000; Goswami, 2008). These domains are "privileged" in that they involve specific kinds reasoning that have evolutionary significance for our species. The most frequently studied privileged domains relevant to early childhood thinking are the domains of physics, psychology, and biology. Although these domains obviously are rudimentary in early childhood, they nevertheless direct children to attend to and respond to highly specific and important features of the environment, in particular, the way in which objects and people and other biological organisms behave under various conditions.

The Domain of Physics

In arguing that stones melt when they are boiled, the children in Vivian Paley's class seemed to demonstrate an intuitive understanding of the effect that intense heat has on physical materials. Of course, for stones to melt, much greater heat would be needed than that provided by a stove. Moreover, by the time the stones would start to melt, there would not be any water or pot left. Nevertheless, children's reasoning about melting stones indicates that they have ideas about the physical properties of objects. Indeed, Rose's question "Do stones melt?" indicates that children are interested in learning about such features of their environments. Because young children, like most adults, are not physicists but nevertheless harbor "everyday ideas" about how the physical world works—for example, about motion, the consequences of objects colliding, gravity, and changes of material state such as water turning into ice or stones melting—developmentalists refer to their reasoning as *naïve physics* (Baillargeon, 2002; Wellman & Gelman, 1998). As you saw in Chapter 5, it appears that within months after birth, children have some grasp of at least a few very basic physical principles, including expectations that two objects cannot occupy the same location at the same time and that an object cannot pass through physical obstructions. Clearly, the foundations of a naïve physics are laid down in infancy.

Much research on the naïve physics of young children has used the *violation-of-expectations* method—the "magic tricks" you learned about in Chapter 5 in our discussion of research on the cognitive capacities of infants (see pp. 185–186). For example, Kyong Kim and Elizabeth Spelke used the violation-of-expectations method to study developmental changes in children's understanding of gravity and inertia (Kim & Spelke, 1999). They showed infants and young children video sequences in which a ball rolled along a board and went off the end. The ball went off the end of the board in one of three ways: (1) moving in a straight line and at the same speed it had traversed the board, in defiance of the laws of gravity and

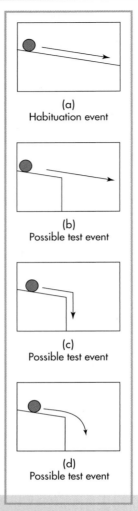

(a)
Habituation event

(b)
Possible test event

(c)
Possible test event

(d)
Possible test event

Figure 8.8 Test used by Kim and Spelke to explore children's knowledge of the physical principles of gravity and inertia. All the children saw the ball roll across a smooth surface (a) and then were tested with events such as those in (b)–(d), to see which of the test events violated their expectations and thus revealed awareness of the relevant physical laws. (Adapted from Kim & Spelke, 1999.)

inertia (Figure 8.8b); (2) plummeting straight down, in accordance with the law of gravity but not the law of inertia (Figure 8.8c); or (3) falling in a gradual arch, in accordance with the laws of both inertia and gravity (Figure 8.8d).

In these experiments, the infants showed no understanding of gravity or inertia, reacting no differently to one sequence than to another. The results for 2-year-olds were mixed: The 2-year-olds generally seemed unsurprised when the ball rolled off the end of the board and kept moving in a straight line or fell in a natural curve to the ground, but they stared longer when the ball fell straight down after leaving the end of the board, indicating that they were beginning to have some understanding of inertia. In contrast, 6-year-olds displayed sensitivity to both inertia and gravity, although they were not entirely consistent in their reactions, indicating that they had not fully mastered these concepts (Spelke, 2000).

Terry Au and her colleagues (1993) demonstrated that young children also have a reasonably good grasp of the physical makeup of objects. She showed middle- and working-class children as young as 3 years of age various natural and artificial substances, including wood and play dough, which she then transformed in one of three ways while they watched. Large chunks of a substance were broken into smaller chunks; chunks of the substance were broken down into a powder; the powder made from the substance was dissolved in water! Even when confronted with the most drastic transformation—a physical substance's being dissolved in water—the 3-year-olds correctly insisted that the substance continued to exist. As Wellman and Gelman (1998, p. 534) point out, "These data show that even quite young children know that larger objects are composed of smaller pieces and these pieces, even if invisible, have enduring physical existence and properties."

There is a great deal more to be learned about physical laws, as everyone who has taken an introduction to physics course knows. But by the age of 5 to 6 years, children have developed a serviceable set of ideas about the physical world that appear to be shared by people all over the world.

The Domain of Psychology

Just as children reason about their everyday physical world, they also reason about people, specifically, about how people's actions are affected by their internal mental states. Children's early understanding of the relationship between mental states and behavior is referred to as *naïve psychology.*

In the transition from infancy to early childhood, and all during early childhood, children gain a more comprehensive idea about how other people's desires, beliefs, and knowledge are related to how they act in the world. As you learned in Chapter 6, by the end of the first year, infants possess at least an intuitive understanding that other people's actions are caused by their goals and intentions. Even at the age of 2, children are able to distinguish between their own desires and those of others (Wellman, Cross & Watson, 2001). If the child's own preference is for strawberry ice cream but a character in a story prefers chocolate ice cream, the child will predict that, given a choice between the two, the storybook character would choose chocolate ice cream. Children's ability to reflect on and understand the mental states of others continues to develop throughout early childhood. As you will see, during this period children construct coherent *theories* about mental life and activity—that is, they develop a **theory of mind.**

To determine when children develop a mature theory of how people's beliefs and desires combine to shape their actions, developmentalists use a technique called the **false-belief task,** in which either a story character or the child him or herself is duped into believing something that is not true. In the first method, the child is presented with a brief story in which one of the characters comes to have a false belief. After hearing the story, the child is asked questions designed to reveal his or her understanding about what goes on in another person's mind. Here is a typical story and a follow-up question:

Story: Once there was a little boy who liked candy. One day he put a chocolate bar in a drawer and went out to play for a while. While he was gone, his mother came. She took the candy out of the drawer and put it in the kitchen. When the little boy came back he was hungry and went to get his candy.

Question: Where do you think the little boy will look for his candy?

When 3-year-olds are asked this question, they say that the boy will look in the kitchen, where they know the candy to be, and not in the drawer, where the boy in the story left it. In short, they respond as if the boy who left the room had the same information that they do. Five-year-olds are far more likely to say that the little boy will look in the drawer, presumably because they understand that the child who left the room has a false belief about the location of the candy.

In the second method, children themselves are tricked into a false belief. In this version of the task, children are shown a box covered with pictures of candy and are asked what they think is in the box. All, of course, answer, "Candy." Then they are shown that they are wrong—the box actually contains something else, such as a pencil. Next, the children are asked what a friend who has not yet seen inside the box would think it contains. Even though they have just gone through the process of being deceived themselves, most 3-year-olds say that the friend will think the box contains a pencil despite the fact that it has pictures of candy on it. Five-year-olds respond correctly (Astington, 1993).

In addition, 3-year-olds will often deny that they themselves have held a false belief just minutes earlier. If asked what they first thought was in the box, they will declare that they knew there were pencils there all along (Wimmer & Hartl, 1991). This kind of result supports the idea that young children still experience difficulty thinking of things separately from the way they have represented them mentally.

However, just as there is evidence that young children's performance on Piagetian tasks differs according to how the problem is posed for them, so there is evidence that in some circumstances 3-year-olds can appreciate the false-belief states of others (Carpenter, Call, & Tomasello, 2002). One way to induce such young children to solve false-belief tasks is to change the social role they play in the experiment. Using a variation of the pencil-in-the-candy-box task, Kate Sullivan and Ellen Winner (1993) arranged for an adult accomplice to be present together with the child while the experiment was in progress. In their procedure, the experimenter first pulls the standard candy-box trick on the child and then leaves the room. Next, the adult accomplice suggests that she and the child play a trick on the experimenter just like the trick that the experimenter has played on them. Making a great display of being a coconspirator in the plot to fool the experimenter, the adult takes a crayon box out of her purse and helps the child remove the crayons and replace them with something else. Then, while the experimenter is still out of the room, the adult, in a hushed, conspiratorial tone, asks the child what the experimenter will think is in the crayon box when she returns. In this gamelike situation, 75 percent of 3-year-olds predicted that the experimenter would mistakenly expect crayons. This result indicates that the children were, at least in these circumstances, able to think about the thought processes of others. By comparison, only 25 percent were correct in the standard false-belief task, a rate that was in line with the typically reported results. The researchers suggest that their version of the task engaged the children in the familiar scripted activity of fooling someone else, which primed the children to think about other people's mental states.

theory of mind The ability to think about other people's mental states and form theories of how they think

false-belief task A technique used to assess children's theory of mind that involves asking children about stories in which either the character or the child him or herself is fooled into believing something that is not true.

This and a range of corroborating evidence from false-belief tasks conducted in various industrialized countries indicates that although the exact timing of acquiring a theory of mind may vary from one culture to another, the child's developing theory of mind is in a transition around 3 years of age and becomes more-or-less solidified when children are 4 or 5 years old (Liu et al., 2008).

The Domain of Biology

Inquisitive developmentalist: How did the baby happen to be in your mommy's tummy?
Child: It just grows inside.
Developmentalist: How did it get there?
Child: It's there all the time. Mommy doesn't have to do anything. She waits until she feels it.
Developmentalist: You said the baby wasn't in there when you were there.
Child: Yeah, then he was in the other place. In . . . in America.
Developmentalist: America?
Child: Yeah, in somebody else's tummy.
Developmentalist: In somebody else's tummy?
Child: Yes, and then he went through somebody's vagina, then he went in, um, in my Mommy's tummy.
Developmentalist: In whose tummy was he before?
Child: Um, I don't know, who his, her name is. It's a her.
(Cowan, 1978, p. 86)

Young children's ideas about conception, as well as other biological processes are, well, different from ours, and arise in the privileged domain referred to as *naïve biology*.

An important starting point for developing biological understandings is making the distinction between animate and inanimate things. Christine Massey and Rochel Gelman (1988) demonstrated that 3- to 4-year-olds are able to make this distinction, associating self-initiated movement with living creatures. They showed the children photographs of unfamiliar animate and inanimate objects and, for each, asked if the object could walk uphill "all by itself" (Figure 8.9). The photographs included unfamiliar animals (for example, a marmoset, a tarantula) and artifacts (statues of animals; objects with wheels, such as a golf caddy; complex, rigid objects such as a camera).

Many of the 3-year-olds and most all of the 4-year-olds knew that only the animals, and not the artifacts, could move uphill on their own. Even though the animals were not seen in motion, the children's comments often focused on feet and "little legs" (Gelman, 1990). Especially interesting were their responses to photographs such as those in Figure 8.9: although no "little legs" are visible for the echidna, the children said that it could walk uphill but that the statue of the four-footed animal could not.

In addition to knowing that only living things can move themselves, young children know that living things grow and change their appearance, whereas artifacts may change in appearance due to wear or damage but do not grow. Moreover, as illustrated by the following quotes from interviews with Japanese children, they also recognize that if neglected, living things may die:

A boy (3 years old) [sees sweet potatoes drooping]: "Poor thing! Are you thirsty? I give lots of water (to you). So, cheer up."

Figure 8.9 Pictures of unfamiliar creatures and artifacts used by Massey and Gelman to determine if young children distinguish between animate things (which move on their own) and inanimate things (which do not). Children judged that the clay figure on the top would not move on its own but the echidna on the bottom would, even though its legs are hidden.

Drawings by Mary McManus; images courtesy of Dr. Rachel Gelman, Rutgers

A girl (5 years, 5 months old) [when asked what would happen to a tulip if it was not watered for a whole day]: "The tulip will wither. 'Cause if the tulip doesn't drink water, it won't become very lively." (Quoted in Inagaki & Hatano, 2002, p. 19.)

At present, developmentalists who support the idea of a privileged domain of naïve biology are uncertain about when and how it originates. Some believe that it slowly differentiates itself from naïve psychology, as young children gain greater experience with living things. Others believe that as children come into contact with different kinds of living creatures, they draw analogies between themselves and other living creatures to reason about the biological world. This tendency is clearly shown in the response of an almost-6-year-old Japanese boy interviewed by Kayoko Inagaki and Giyoo Hatano. Asked if it was inevitable that a baby rabbit would grow, the child replied, "We can't keep it [the rabbit] forever the same size. Because, like me, if I were a rabbit, I would be 5 years old and become bigger and bigger" (Inagaki & Hatano, 2002, p. 51). Drawing such analogies, however, must be balanced with understanding important differences between living things, including the fact that not all living things have goals and intentions (Figure 8.10).

Explaining Domain-Specific Cognitive Development

Although it is clear that young children have an intuitive understanding of physics, psychology, and biology, we are left with questions about where these privileged domains come from and how they develop. There are three major approaches to explaining the source and development of privileged domains. One, *modularity theory,* views each domain of reasoning as a distinct and separate set of mental processes that has evolved to handle domain-specific information and that changes very little over the course of development. The second approach, *theory theory,* holds that children are biologically endowed with basic notions about each domain but modify their ideas as they learn more about the world. Finally, the third approach emphasizes the special role of language and culture in weaving together the contributions of biological and general cognitive factors.

Modularity Theory Modularity theory's approach to understanding domain-specific intelligence is to conceive of it in terms of **mental modules,** innate mental faculties that are dedicated to receiving information from and processing information about particular types of objects in the environment, such as physical objects, people, and biological organisms (Atran, 1998; Fodor, 1983). Each module is distinct and separate from all others; there is very little interaction between them. In addition, because they are coded in the genes, such psychological processes do not need special tutoring in order to develop. They are present "at the beginning" in the normal human genome and only need to be "triggered" by the environment.

An intriguing line of research with autistic children provides strong evidence for modularity theory. **Autism** is a poorly understood, genetically induced condition that is defined primarily by an inability to relate normally to other people (Frith, 2003). Young autistic children rarely use language to communicate; they do not engage in symbolic, pretend play; and they engage in unusually repetitive movements such as rocking, spinning, or flapping their hands (see the box "In the Field: Supporting Siblings of Children with Autism").

What makes autism so interesting for modularity theorists is that autistic children routinely score poorly on false-belief tasks, such as the task described earlier in which children hear a story about a mother who, while her son was outside playing, moves a candy bar from the place the son put it to another place (pp. 286–287). Children are asked where the boy will look for the candy when he returns

Siegal & Peterson, 1999

Figure 8.10 Children often attribute humanlike properties, including goals and intentions, to all living things. This drawing of a germ depicts an organism with humanlike arms, legs, and eyes, as well as sharp fangs and spiky hair suggesting evil intent.

mental modules Innate mental faculties that receive inputs from particular classes of objects and produce corresponding information about the world.

autism A mental condition defined primarily by an inability to relate normally to other people and low scores on intelligence tests.

and how he will feel when he looks there. Autistic children of various ages perform like typical 3-year-olds, failing to realize that the absent child has a false belief about the location of the candy and that he will be disappointed when he looks in the wrong location. These same children may be very clever at solving mechanical puzzles such as putting together blocks to make a racing car, or they may have unusual abilities in music, art, math, memory, or some other specific area. The extreme difference in performance suggests that autism may affect a specific module—a theory-of-mind module, perhaps—leaving other modules unaffected.

In an early study to demonstrate the domain-specific nature of autism, Simon Baron-Cohen and his colleagues (1986) asked groups of 4-year-olds to arrange scrambled sequences of picture cards into stories. There were three types of stories, each depicted with four cards:

Mechanical sequences depicting physical interactions between people and objects—for example, a man kicks a rock, which rolls down a hill and then splashes in the water (Figure 8.11a).

Behavioral sequences depicting interactions among people—for example, a girl takes an ice cream cone from a boy and eats it, and the boy cries (Figure 8.11b).

Mentalistic sequences depicting stories that involve mental events—for example, a girl puts a toy down behind her while she picks a flower; another person sneaks up and takes the toy; the girl looks surprised when she turns around and finds the toy gone (Figure 8.11c).

Some of the children in this study were autistic; others were not autistic but were mentally retarded; and others were developing typically. The autistic children outperformed the typically developing children in arranging mechanical sequences and were just as proficient as typically developing children when arranging behavioral sequences in which the emotions of the figures in the story were obvious. But

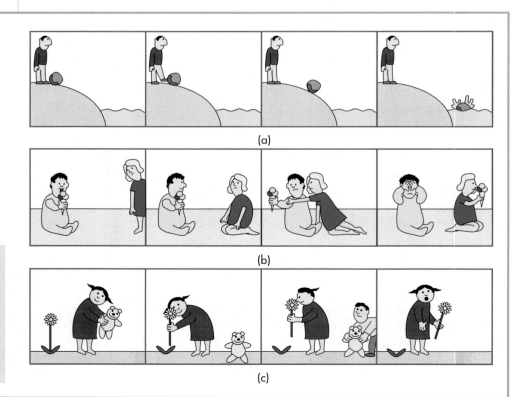

Figure 8.11 Stimuli used to assess autistic children's ability to think about mental states. At the top of the figure is a mechanical sequence (a) showing a man kicking a rock, which rolls down a hill; the middle behavioral sequence (b) shows a girl taking an ice cream cone from a boy; the bottom sequence (c) shows a boy taking a girl's teddy bear when her back is turned.

they were unable to create meaningful mentalistic sequences that reflected an understanding of thoughts or inner emotions, such as the surprise experienced by the girl whose toy disappeared in Figure 8.11c (see Figure 8.12). In addition, when asked to verbally tell the story of the mentalistic sequences, the autistic children's narratives tended to be purely descriptive, with no reference to mental states. Of the last card in Figure 8.11c, for example, they might say something like "The girl held the flower" rather than "The girl wondered where her toy went."

Studies of naïve physics and biology have also found evidence for the domain-specific nature of autism (Binnie & Williams, 2003; Peterson, 2005). For example, a study of Australian children conducted by Candida Peterson found that when asked questions about biological functions ("What does your heart do?" "What does your brain do?"), autistic children performed at least as well as typically developing children. On the other hand, most of the autistic children failed the false-belief task. Interestingly, in another study focused on the domains of physics and psychology, autistic children not only performed better than typically developing children in the physics domain, but they also tended to apply physical reasoning to psychological events (Binnie & Wiliams, 2003). Findings like this, along with the fact that autistic children perform very well in some privileged domains but routinely fail false-belief tasks, lead many developmentalists to argue for the existence of isolated modules, and to speculate that autism is due to a cognitive defect in a theory-of-mind module (Baron-Cohen, Leslie, & Frith, 2007).

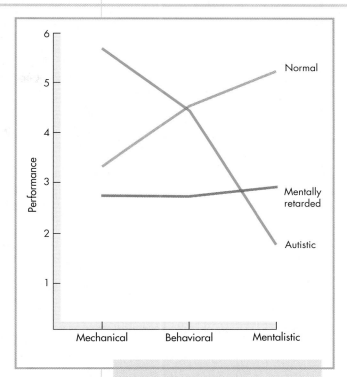

Figure 8.12 The level of performance achieved by normal, mentally retarded, and autistic children when asked to create meaningful mechanical, behavioral, and mentalistic sequences. Note that the autistic children are especially good at creating mechanical sequences but have even greater difficulty than retarded children when asked to create mentalistic sequences.

Theory Theory Despite the link between autism and having difficulty with the false-belief task, not all developmentalists agree that there is a theory-of-mind module that is present at birth and that a defect in this module explains autism (Tager-Flusberg, 2007). Those who disagree with modularity theory point out that, when placed in intensive therapeutic programs, many autistic children show significant improvement in their social behavior and communication skills. They can learn, for example, to interact with other children and to carry out simple household routines, and some are eventually able to hold jobs (Scheuermann, 2002). Such facts naturally raise a question that modularity theory does not address: How does experience influence domain-specific development?

An influential theory that does address this question is somewhat playfully referred to by developmentalists as the **theory theory.** According to this approach, young children, from birth or shortly thereafter, have primitive theories of how the world works. These theories direct the child's attention to domain-specific features of the environment and influence the child's actions in particular domains. Over time, the child modifies the theories in light of his or her experience (Kushnir & Gopnik, 2007; Gelman & Lucariello, 2002).

Children's thinking within privileged domains is like scientific theorizing in at least two important respects. First, children's ideas are accompanied by causal explanations. If asked why a little girl who climbs a tree and hangs from a branch soon falls to the ground, they provide a reasonable biological explanation: She is not strong enough, so her arms get tired and she eventually has to let go. If asked why a little boy who declares that he is going to step off a stool and float in the air actually falls to the ground, they provide explanations such as "He is too heavy to float in the air," or "Gravity brings him down." Second, their ideas generate reasonable predictions, as a theory should. They will predict that the little girl who

theory theory The theory that young children have primitive theories about how the world works, which influence how children think about and act within specific domains.

Name:	Charley Moskowitz
Education:	Master's of Social Work, Fordham University; additional experience at various agencies with infants with HIV, pediatric hospice, special needs preschoolers
Current Position:	Director of Special Needs Academic and Arts Center at the Jewish Community Center of Mid-Westchester, New York; private practice counseling children and families
Career Objectives:	Provide enrichment programs for children with disabilities and their families

"MY BROTHER'S BEEN HAVING A big problem," began 6-year-old Ruthie in a quiet and anxious voice. "He's been having a hard time with beeping noises. When he goes to school, there's a little beep, but you can hardly hear it, but he can hear it, but he still comes in the door and then he runs out of the other door and right into the classroom, and he's scared."

Ruthie continued to talk in sad pensive tones about her brother's terror of beeping noises until she was interrupted by Charley Moskowitz, a social worker who runs Sib Connection, a support group for siblings of children with disabilities: "Let me ask you a question, O.K.? Why are you so sad about this?"

"Because I don't want my brother to be like this, and it makes me feel sad that he has to be afraid of that."

"Can anybody help her?" Moskovitz asked the other children in the group.

Thomas raised his hand. "Well, a lot of times what autistic kids do, is like—my brother will go through a phase. This could just be, like, one month he might be afraid of beeps, and then next month he'll love beeps."

Then Nick chimed in. "The reason your brother might be doing that is because autistic kids, they have almost better senses. I know it sounds weird, but, like, my brother, he can hear things that are really low. It's nothing really bad; it's just something that happens." (Adapted from Olson, 2007.)

Most of the children in Ruthie's support group have siblings with an autism spectrum disorder (ASD). ASDs are a group of developmental disabilities that include autistic disorder, pervasive developmental disorder, and Asperger syndrome, all of which are characterized by significant impairments in social interaction and communication, and the presence of unusual behaviors and interests—a fear of beeps, or a fascination with the whirl of electric fans, for example (CDC, 2007). ASD usually appears before the age of 3, and it affects the person throughout life. While some individuals with ASD may have severe intellectual deficits, others may be highly gifted in certain areas of functioning. According to a recently released national study of prevalence rates in the United States, ASD is far more common that once supposed, affecting 1 out of every 150 children. It is four times more common in boys than girls.

The Autism Genome Project, a massive international study involving scientists who are collecting genetic data in 19 countries, is beginning to shed light on the chromosomal changes and mutations that contribute to ASD phenotypes (Ylisaukko-oja et al.,

Nick, who has an autistic sibling and participates in Sib Connection, designed this pin to help people better understand the behavior of autistic children.

2006; Karsten et al., 2006). In the meantime, children like Ruthie, Thomas, and Nick struggle to make sense of their siblings' behavior. Fortunately, some of them will do so with the help of peers who have similar experiences and of people like Charley Moskowitz who are aware of the unique issues and challenges facing siblings of special-needs children.

"Ruthie, you know what? There are some things that we can't change," Moskowitz said. "One of the things that we can't change is the way your brother reacts to things. What else is she doing, Nick?"

"Responsibility. You're having too much responsibility for your brother."

The sense of obligation weighs heavily on siblings of special-needs children. As Moskowitz says, "These are the kids who are going to be taking care of their siblings when their parents die. These are the kids that are going to have all the responsibility, and if they don't get help now, who's going to help them? They have to work through this before they graduate from high school so that they can have the courage to go off to college and have a life and still be connected to their sibling when it comes time to make a decision about what they have to do" (Olson, 2007, p. 46–47).

Charley Moscowitz

Mark Plage, 15, right, shares a quiet moment with his 13-year-old autistic brother, Derek. Sib Connection was designed to help children like Mark cope with the stress of having autistic siblings.

drops from the tree will hurt herself if the branch is high off the ground and that the little boy who fails to float will be disappointed. Although 3-year-olds may sometimes confuse biological and psychological explanations, by the time they are 4 years old, American children invoke the right kinds of theory to fit what it is that needs explaining (Wellman, Hickling, & Schult, 1997).

An important source of information for children's developing theories is their interactions and conversations with their parents (Hughes et al., 2005). For example, a study of Mexican-American parents and their children attending an agricultural science exhibition found that the context prompted children to ask questions that fall within the domain of biology and that parents offered domain-appropriate causal explanations. For instance, when one child asked, "Why can't I water the plants too much?" his mother answered, "Because they are going to drown; they don't need that much water." Another parent used an analogy to provide a basis for the child's theory development. When asked "Why do insects eat each other?" the mother answered, "Because insects are food for other animals just like other animals are food for us" (Tenenbaum, Callanan, Alba-Speyer, & Sandoval, 2002). Sometimes parents spontaneously offered up explanations of puzzling phenomena, providing a rich source of information that confirmed or denied children's initial theories. This study highlights the important role of parents in the process of theory testing; teachers, peers, and personal experience also contribute to children's construction of their knowledge base.

The Special Role of Language and Culture The third approach to explaining domain-specific development focuses primarily on how language and culture influence the emergence and growth of various domains. Considerations of language and culture are important for thinking about the nature of privileged domains because cultures vary dramatically in their use of domain-specific language. As an example, take the domain of psychology. Language, as Janet Astington and Eva Filippova point out, helps the young child figure out what other people might think, want, or feel (Astington & Filippova, 2005). Ample evidence from cultures around the world suggests that there is enormous variety in the extent and ways that mental states and actions are conceived (Lillard, 2006; Vinden, 2002). In terms of sheer number, English is at one extreme of the continuum, possessing more than 5000 words for emotions alone. By contrast, the Chewong people of Malaysia are reported to have only five terms to cover the entire range of mental processes, translated as "want," "want very much," "know," "forget," "miss or remember" (Howell, 1984).

At present, evidence from cultures where mental terminology is sparse does not give a clear picture of whether the lack of mental terms in a language slows down, or even eliminates altogether, the development of the kind of naïve psychology found in cultures where such language is prevalent. In some cases, there appears to be no lag in performance, for example, on standard false-belief tasks (Avis & Harris, 1991). In other cases, there does seem to be a significant delay, and in still other cases, it appears that the sort of theory of mind assumed to be universal by privileged-domain theorists does not appear at all (Vinden, 1998, 2002). Within countries where talk about minds and mental processes is prevalent, it has been shown that children whose parents engage in more conversation about mental processes in the course of their daily interactions acquire competence in the standardized tests for theory of mind more rapidly (Nelson et al., 2003).

The influence of language and cultural variation on privileged domains is not restricted to the domain of naïve psychology. Among the Tainae of Papua New Guinea, for example, Penelope Vinden found that it is common for people to believe that a person can literally change themselves into a pig or other animal, and that such changelings can, and occasional do, physically assault young children. Such beliefs defy the distinction we ordinarily make between human beings, other animals, and inanimate natural objects, calling into question the extent to which naïve biology and naïve psychology are distinct domains.

Indeed, the very idea that knowledge can be compartmentalized into distinct domains has been challenged by some developmentalists on the grounds that it represents a specifically Western perspective at odds with the belief systems of many non-Western cultures. It has been found, for example, that certain African societies have a more integrated view of knowledge. According to Bame Nsamenang, who studies African beliefs about knowledge, the knowledge, skills, and values children learn are not "compartmentalized into this or that activity, knowledge, or skill domain, but are massed together as integral to social interaction, cultural life, economic activity, and daily routines" (Nsamenang, 2006, p. 296).

||||| APPLY ▪ CONNECT ▪ DISCUSS

Of *modularity theory* and *theory theory*, which is more consistent with Piaget's understanding of development? Why?

Cognitive Development and Culture

As you may recall from Chapter 1, Vygotsky's sociocultural theory has had a significant impact on understanding how development in general and cognitive development in particular are influenced by the cultural contexts in which children live. As we have noted on several previous occasions, children's active participation in cultural activities, especially their interactions and communications with others, appears essential to their developing knowledge of the world (Nelson, 2003; Rogoff, 2003). *Cultural scripts* have received much attention as a specific feature of the environment that accounts for both the acquisition and unevenness of knowledge during early childhood.

Cultural Scripts

Katherine Nelson (1996) suggested that as a result of their participation in routine, culturally organized events, children acquire *generalized event representations,* or **scripts.** Scripts specify who participates in an event, what social roles they play, what objects they are to use during the event, and the sequence of actions that make up the event. Scripts exist both as external, material tools of culture—observable patterns of behavior expressed in the words, the customary procedures, the customs and routines that punctuate daily experience—and as internal representations of those tools (see Chapter 2, pp. 54–56). Scripts are, in both their internal and external aspects, *resources* for cognitive development that affect the child's thinking and reasoning skills.

Initially, scripts are a good deal more external than internal. Anyone who has made the attempt to bathe a 2-month-old knows that "taking a bath" is something the adult does to the baby. The adult fills a sink or appropriate basin with warm water, lays out a towel, a clean diaper, and clothing, and then slips the infant into the water, holding on tightly to keep the infant's head above water. The infant's contribution consists of squirming around. Gradually, however, as they become stronger and more familiar with the script of

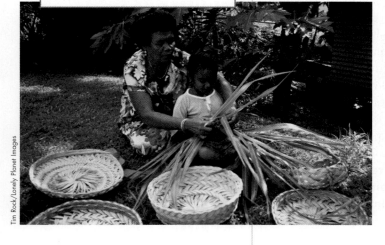

As she participates in basket weaving lessons over time, this young Palauan girl will develop a generalized script of what it means to "have a lesson," including the guidance of a teacher, the use of particular materials, and the sequence of activities performed.

Tim Rock/Lonely Planet Images

bath taking (and their caregivers perfect their role as bath givers), babies acquire more competence in parts of the activity and assume a greater role in the process.

By the age of 2 years, most children have "taken" many baths. Each time, roughly the same sequence is followed, the same kinds of objects are used, the same cast of characters participates, and the same kinds of talk accompany the necessary actions. Water is poured into a tub, clothes are taken off, the child gets into the water, soap is applied and rinsed off, and the child gets out of the water, dries off, and gets dressed. There may be variations—a visiting friend may take a bath with the child or the child may be allowed to play with her water toys after washing—but the basic sequence has a clear pattern to it.

During early childhood, adults still play the important role of "bath giver" in the scripted routine called "taking a bath." Adults initiate children's baths, scrub their ears, wash their hair, or help them dry off. Not until adulthood will the child be responsible for the entire event, including scouring the tub and worrying about clean towels, hot water, and the money to pay for them.

Nelson points out that, as in the "taking a bath" script, children grow up inside other people's scripts. As a consequence, human beings rarely, if ever, experience the natural environment "raw." Rather, they experience the world, including such simple activities as taking a bath and eating a meal, in a way that has been prepared (cooked up!) according to the scripts prescribed by their culture.

Nelson and her colleagues have studied the growth of scripted knowledge by interviewing children and by recording the conversations of children playing together. When Nelson asked children to tell her about "going to a restaurant," for example, she obtained reports like the following:

> Boy aged 3 years, 1 month: "Well, you eat and then go somewhere."
> Girl aged 4 years, 10 months: "Okay. Now, first we go to restaurants at nighttime and we, um, we, and we go and wait for a while, and then the waiter comes and gives us the little stuff with the dinners on it, and then we wait for a little bit, a half an hour or a few minutes or something, and, um, then our pizza comes or anything, and um, then when we're finished eating the salad that we order we get to eat our pizza when it's done, because we get the salad before the pizza's ready. So then when we're finished with all the pizza and all our salad, we just leave."
> (Nelson, 1981, p. 103)

Even these simple reports demonstrate that scripts represent generalized knowledge. For one thing, the children are describing general content: They are clearly referring to more than a single, unique meal. The 3-year-old uses the generalized form "you eat" rather than a specific reference to a particular time when he ate. The little girl's introduction ("First we go to restaurants at nighttime") indicates that she, too, is speaking of restaurant visits in general.

Besides containing general content, children's scripts are organized into a general structure, similar to that of adult scripts. Even very young children know that the events involved in "eating at a restaurant" do not take place haphazardly. Instead they describe a sequence: "First we do this, then we do that." Children evidently abstract the content of a script and its structure from many events and then use that knowledge to organize their behavior.

Scripts are guides to action. They are mental representations that children and adults use to figure out what is likely to happen next in familiar circumstances. Until children have acquired a large repertoire of scripted knowledge from which they can generalize in unfamiliar events, they must pay attention to the details of each new activity. As a consequence, they may be less likely to distinguish between the essential and the superficial features of a novel context. The little girl

"Taking a bath" as done to an infant.

Courtesy of Sheila Cole

Even a script such as "taking a bath" can vary considerably from one culture to another. This image shows a pilgrim and a child bathing in a sacred waterfall near a temple in India.

Micah Hanson/Alamy

scripts Event schemas that specify who participates in an event, what social roles they play, what objects they are to use during the event, and the sequence of actions that make up the event.

Participation in scripted activities, such as Caterina's birthday party in the Tuscany region of Italy, provide a context within which children can develop more complex understandings of their culture's basic concepts and ways of doing things.

interviewed by Nelson, for example, seemed to think that eating pizza is a basic part of the "going to a restaurant" script, whereas paying for the meal was entirely absent. However, because the little girl has grasped a small part of the restaurant script, and going to restaurants is a routine activity in her family, she will be free to attend to new aspects of the setting the next time she encounters it. Over time, she will gain a deeper understanding of the events she participates in and the contexts of which they are a part.

Scripts also allow people within a given social group to coordinate their actions with each other because scripts are in a very important sense *shared*. For this reason, Nelson argued that "the acquisition of scripts is central to the acquisition of culture" (Nelson, 1981, pp. 109, 110). Knowing the script, especially its variants and nuances, is an important marker of maturity and adaptation. For example, when children go to a "sit-down" restaurant in the United States, they learn that first you are seated by host or hostess and later you tell a waiter or waitress what you want to eat. However, a different script applies to fast-food establishments, where you first go to the counter and place your order and then seat yourself. If someone were to take the sit-down script to a fast-food establishment, they would go hungry. Likewise, someone who took the fast-food script to a sit-down restaurant would be viewed as very peculiar.

Cultural Context and the Unevenness of Development

Once children leave the confines of their cribs and their caregivers' arms, they begin to experience a great variety of contexts that compel them to acquire a variety of new scripts, as well as refine those with which they are already familiar. Thus it is natural that cognitive development during early childhood should appear to be so uneven. In familiar contexts, where they know the expected sequence of actions and can properly interpret the requirements of the situation, young children are most likely to behave in a logical way and adhere to adult standards of thought. But when the contexts are unfamiliar, they may apply inappropriate scripts and resort to magical or illogical thinking.

Overall, cultures influence the unevenness of children's development in several basic ways (Laboratory of Comparative Human Cognition, 1983; Rogoff, 2003; Super & Harkness, 2002):

1. *By making specific activities available:* One cannot learn about something without observing or hearing about it. A 4-year-old growing up among the !Kung of the Kalahari Desert is unlikely to learn about taking baths in bathtubs or pouring water from one glass to another. Children growing up in Seattle are unlikely to be skilled at finding water-bearing roots in a desert.

2. *By determining the frequency of basic activities:* Dancing is an activity found in all societies, but all societies do not focus equally on dancing. Owing to the importance placed on traditional dancing in Balinese culture, many children growing up in Bali become skilled dancers by the age of 4 (McPhee, 1970), while Norwegian children are more likely to become good skiers and skaters.

3. *By relating different activities to each other:* If pottery making is a valued activity, children are not only likely to become skilled pottery makers but also to learn a variety of related skills as well, such as digging clay from a

quarry, firing clay, glazing clay, painting designs, and selling the products. Molding clay as part of a nursery school curriculum will be associated with a distinctively different pattern of experiences, skills, and knowledge.

4. *By regulating the child's role in the activity:* Children enter most activities as novices who bear little responsibility for the outcome. As their roles and responsibilities change, so do the specialized abilities they develop.

|||||| APPLY ══ CONNECT ══ DISCUSS ‒

In arguing against the notion that knowledge can be compartmentalized into separate domains, Bame Nsamenang asserts that, according to African beliefs, knowledge is integrated into social life and daily routines. To what extent is this consistent with Katherine Nelson's theory of cultural scripts?

Reconciling Alternative Approaches

By this point, you should be convinced that the exceedingly uneven and complex picture that emerges from studies of childhood thought in the first few years following infancy cannot be explained by any single approach. Indeed, there have been a number of attempts to formulate more inclusive theories that are capable of accounting for both general and domain-specific changes in young children's competence and performance and for the fact that cognitive development sometimes appears to occur in discontinuous leaps and at other times as a process of gradual change. For example, Kurt Fischer has proposed that whether change appears continuous and gradual or abrupt and stagelike depends crucially upon the relationship between the specific cognitive process being investigated and the context in which it occurs (Fischer & Yan, 2002). Fischer has demonstrated that under conditions of optimal support from the context, increases in the level of children's performance go through a series of stagelike changes. But when support is low (and a child has many distracting problems to deal with simultaneously), change is continuous. Thus, the culturally organized context of children's developing competence and performance is an element that must always be taken into account.

Toshi Kawano/Getty Images

Whether she is pretending to be a monster, a character peering out from a television set, or both, this young Japanese girl has created an imaginary "play space" within a highly supportive cultural context that provides her with play materials, a play room, a vast variety of T.V. monster characters, and cultural expectations that pretend play is appropriate behavior for young children. According to Kurt Fischer, the specific cognitive processes used in such play, and supported by the culture, should result in stagelike changes in her development.

SUMMARY

Physical and Motor Development

- Early childhood is marked by impressive gains in both gross and fine motor skills.

- Young children's sleep needs often are not adequately met. Nutrition is also a common problem, with undernourishment and obesity both causes for concern.

- Brain development, although slower than in infancy, includes myelination of the frontal cortex as well as increases in the length and branching of neurons connecting different areas of the brain. Variability in the development of different areas may contribute to the unevenness of early childhood cognition.

Preoperational Development

- According to Piaget, children in the preoperational stage are in the process of overcoming limitations that stand in the way of mental operations, logical transformations of information. He considered the greatest limitation to be centration, focusing on one aspect of an object or problem to the exclusion of others. Centration explains three common early childhood errors:

  - Egocentrism, the tendency to be captive to one's own perspective and unable to take that of another;

  - The tendency to confuse appearance and reality;

  - Precausal reasoning, the tendency to reason from one particular to another, rather than engaging in cause-and-effect reasoning.

- Subsequent research suggests that under certain circumstances—for example, with tasks involving familiar objects—children do not commit these errors, showing evidence of cognitive abilities well before Piaget thought possible and hence more unevenness of cognitive development.

Information-Processing Approaches to Cognitive Development

- Information-processing approaches explore the workings of the mind through analogy to the digital computer, with the brain's neural features being like a computer's hardware and the practices that people engage in to process information like its software.

- Input from the environment goes to the sensory register and may be read into short-term (working) memory, where it may combine with information from long-term memory. The flow of information among these components is coordinated by control processes, which include attention, rehearsal, and decision making.

- As children grow older, their performance improves, as a result of both the maturation of their brains and the development of more effective information-processing strategies. Prior knowledge and caregivers' elaborative style in interactions with children can help children encode and store memories.

Cognitive Development in Privileged Domains

- Another approach to early childhood cognitive development focuses on changes within privileged domains, specific areas of knowledge that may have evolutionary significance.

  - Naïve physics traces to infancy and in early childhood extends to an understanding of laws such as gravity and inertia and of properties of objects.

  - Within naïve psychology, young children develop a theory of mind, as is reflected by their improving performance on false-belief tasks.

  - Naïve biology includes an understanding of differences between living things and inanimate objects.

- Several approaches seek to explain domain-specific cognitive development.

  - Modularity theory holds that distinct and separate mental modules—mental processes present from birth—are dedicated to the different privileged domains. Autistic children's difficulties in the psychology domain but not others is seen as support for this approach.

  - Theory theory holds that from birth or shortly thereafter, children have primitive theories about how the world works—theories that direct children's attention to domain-specific features of the environment and that children modify over time in light of their experience.

  - A third approach focuses on the influence of language and other aspects of culture on the emergence and development of domains. The idea of domains of knowledge may itself be a Western construct.

Cognitive Development and Culture

- As children participate in routine events of their culture, they acquire increasingly accurate scripts, or generalized representations, of these events.

- Cultures influence cognitive development by determining the frequency of basic activities, the specific activities that are available, and children's roles in activities.

Reconciling Alternative Approaches

- Studies of cognition in early childhood yield a picture, not of a homogeneous stage, but of complexity and unevenness. More inclusive theories are probably needed in order to account for processes that are both domain specific and general, and for developmental changes that are both continuous and discontinuous (stagelike).

Key Terms

motor drive, p. 271
food insecure, p. 273
scale errors, p. 274
mental operations, p. 274
preoperational stage, p. 274
centration, p. 276

decentration, p. 276
objectivity, p. 276
egocentrism, p. 277
precausal thinking, p. 280
elaborative style, p. 284
privileged domains, p. 285

theory of mind, p. 286
false-belief task, p. 286
mental modules, p. 289
autism, p. 291
theory theory, p. 291
scripts, p. 294

Social and Emotional Development in Early Childhood

There is a dark point in many children's lives when they realize that everyone else in the house stays up beyond the time that they are put to bed. In the case of one little girl, the realization brought with it a good deal of curiosity about what went on after her bedroom light went out—as well as a creeping sense of injustice. She imagined, her mother told us, that her family watched cartoons, ate ice cream, and had their friends over to play. The mother remembers one discussion on the subject particularly well. Like many similar conversations, it began with the little girl asking, as she was settled into bed, "What are you gonna do now?"

"Well," her mother replied, "maybe read a little or watch some TV."

"I want to do that, too," said the little girl.

"No, you need to go to bed."

"Why don't you go to bed?"

"I'm not sleepy yet."

"Well, I'm not sleepy, too."

"That may be," her mother conceded, "but you are a little girl, and little girls need lots of sleep so they can grow up big and strong like their mommies."

The mother believed her logic was unassailable. After all, mothers have been making exactly this argument for generations. The little girl, however, was unmoved. She looked at her mother and declared, matter-of-factly, "I am not a little girl anymore." Naturally, the mother was charmed to think that at the tender age of 3 her daughter had become, in her own eyes at least, a big girl.

"Oh?" said the mother, playing along, "So you're not a little girl anymore? Well then, what are you?"

And with the sobriety of a 3-year-old, the little girl replied, "I am a possum."

She was quite serious in her declaration, and even went on to remind her mother of the nocturnal habits of the species, this being their main attraction at the moment. It was around this time, too, that she became engaged to Chester, her cat. It was a drawn-out affair that she finally broke off in kindergarten when she met and fell head over heels in love with a classmate named Christine.

here is only a small window of time in children's development when identity feels so fluid that children can declare themselves a possum, for example, if it serves their purpose, and when there are no obstacles to true love and marriage. Over the course of early childhood, as you will discover in this chapter, children develop a relatively stable sense of their identities as boys or girls, as members of particular ethnic or racial groups, and as distinct individuals in their own right. This chapter will explore how children develop a sense of themselves in relation to the societies in which they live.

During early childhood, children's social and emotional lives develop along two closely connected paths. One is the path of **socialization,** which leads children

In addition to fulfilling a traditional role in a wedding ceremony, these little flower girls are learning about many important aspects of the social roles and behaviors expected of them when they grow up.

toward the standards, values, and knowledge of their society. The second is that of **personality formation,** on which children will develop their own unique patterns of feeling, thinking, and behaving in a wide variety of circumstances.

Children begin their trek down the paths of socialization and personality formation as soon as they are born, and with plenty of help from the significant people in their lives. It is not just idle talk when a father says of his newborn daughter, "She could be a concert pianist with these long fingers," and her mother adds, "Or a basketball player." The beliefs that give rise to such statements lead parents to shape their child's experience in a variety of ways, some obvious, others quite subtle. Socialization is apparent in the ways parents communicate to children how they should and should not behave ("You're a little girl and need lots of sleep so you can grow up big and strong like your mommy"). Socialization is also apparent in the ways parents—and their social and economic circumstances—influence the neighborhoods children live in, the day-care centers or preschools they attend, and a variety of other contexts in which they become conversant with their culture's funds of knowledge and rules of behavior.

But children do not automatically or passively absorb adults' lessons. They interpret and select from the many socializing messages they receive according to their budding and unique personalities. The early origins of personality formation are present in infancy. As we saw in Chapter 4 (p. 149), neonates display individual differences in characteristic levels of activity, responses to frustration, and readiness to engage in novel experiences. We referred to these patterns of responsivity and associated emotional states as *temperament,* and noted that it tends to be moderately stable over time: Children who draw back from novel experiences in infancy, for example, are more likely to behave shyly when they first enter a nursery school. Personality formation expands as children's initial temperamental styles of interacting with people and objects in their environments are integrated with their developing cognitive understanding, emotional responses, and habits (Sanson, Hamphill & Smart, 2002).

Thus, the paths of socialization and personality formation are closely connected. In traveling these paths, children, along with the significant others in their lives, play active roles in *coconstructing* the course of development (Hutto, 2008). That is, as we learned in Chapter 2, the behaviors, activities, and choices of both children and the people with whom they interact, shape, and modify the environments in which children develop. In this chapter, we will examine the social and emotional development of young children as they gain experience interacting with a variety of people, develop a more explicit sense of themselves and their abilities, and come to understand the ways in which they can (and cannot) use the rules and tools that society is attempting to press upon them. These changes in social and emotional development do not, of course, occur independently of the biological and cognitive changes discussed in Chapter 8. Socialization, personality formation, biological maturation, and cognitive development occur simultaneously.

Identity Development

Erik Erikson (1950) claimed that the path of identity takes a sharp and fateful turn in early childhood. In the previous stage of *autonomy versus shame and doubt* (associated with the "terrible twos"), children acquire, and confidently declare, their sense of free will and their ability to control their environments: "*I* do it!" "No!

I don't want that one; I want *that* one!" (see Chapter 6, p. 227). During early childhood, in contrast, children face the challenge of **initiative versus guilt**— that is, the challenge of continuing to declare their autonomy and existence as individuals, but in ways that begin to conform to the social roles and moral standards of society. According to Erikson, we see evidence of this in children's initiative and eagerness to join both peers and adults in constructing, planning, and making things. From building "forts" in which to play, to baking cookies or repairing broken toys, children of this age take special delight in cooperating with others for the purpose of accomplishing specific goals and tasks. In Erikson's words, "the child is at no time more ready to learn quickly and avidly, to become bigger in the sense of sharing obligation and performance" (1950, p. 258). Such enthusiasm during early childhood underscores identity development as a process by which children come to express and believe in their own value as social participants—as individuals who can contribute to the plans and goals of a group.

Developmentalists agree that one factor essential to socialization is **identification,** a psychological process in which children try to look, act, feel, and be like significant people in their social environment. They disagree, however, about the mechanisms by which identification is achieved.

The development of identification can be studied with respect to almost any social category—a family, a religious group, a neighborhood clique, or a nationality. We could ask, for example, how a boy goes about identifying with his father, his Hindu religion, his soccer team, or his country, India. The overwhelming majority of studies on identification in early childhood, however, focus on the acquisition of sex-role identity and ethnic identity. As the social categories and role expectations regarding gender and ethnicity become increasingly visible in our rapidly globalizing world, developmentalists are eager to understand the processes of identification through which children come to understand themselves as member of various social categories, and adopt behaviors consistent with various social roles. In this section we look at sex-role and ethnic identity in turn and then at the sense of self of which they are part.

Sex-role Identity

If an infant wearing nothing but a diaper and a bright-eyed smile were placed in your arms, you would probably have a hard time determining the baby's sex. Not so with the 3-year-old! In the short span of 3 years, children come to behave in ways that give clear signals about whether they are boys or girls (Golombok & Hines, 2002). For example, by the time they enter preschool, boys and girls differ in both what they play and how they play. They have distinctly different toy preferences, and boys are more active and rough-and-tumble, whereas girls tend to be more verbal and nurturing. Even their selection of playmates becomes gender-typed. By age 3, girls prefer to play with other girls, and boys prefer other boys, a phenomenon observed throughout the world and known as **gender segregation.**

Because sex-role identity is so central to adult experience, the question of how children acquire their sex-role identity and how they interpret that sex role* is of great interest to developmental psychologists (Eckes & Trautner, 2000). Here we

---

*Some psychologists recommend the use of the word "gender" instead of "sex" when this topic is discussed because they believe that the term "sex" implies that all sex-typed behavior is ultimately determined by biology. Others argue against the term "gender," which they think implies that sex-linked behavior is ultimately determined by the environment. We will use both "sex" and "gender" in contexts where they appear most appropriate, without implying either that sex/gender roles are basically biological or that they are basically environmental.

socialization The process by which children acquire the standards, values, and knowledge of their society.

personality formation The process through which children develop their own unique patterns of feeling, thinking, and behaving in a wide variety of circumstances.

initiative versus guilt According to Erikson's theory, the stage in early childhood during which children face the challenge of continuing to declare their autonomy and existence as individuals, but in ways that begin to conform to the social roles and moral standards of society.

identification A psychological process in which children try to look, act, feel, and be like significant people in their social environment.

gender segregation The term for the preference of girls to play with other girls, and boys to play with other boys.

phallic stage In Freudian theory, the period around the fourth year when children begin to regard their own genitals as a major source of pleasure.

Oedipus complex In Freudian theory, the fear, guilt, and conflict evoked by a little boy's desire to get rid of his father and take the father's place in his mother's affections.

Electra complex According to Freud's theory of sex-role development, the process by which girls blame their mother for their "castrated" condition, transfer their love to their father, and compete with their mother for their father's affection.

modeling The process by which children observe and imitate individuals of the same sex as themselves.

differential reinforcement The process by which girls and boys are differently rewarded for engaging in gender-appropriate behavior.

Table 9.1	
Paths to Sex-Role Identity	
View	**Process**
Psychodynamic	**Differentiation and identification:** Boys differentiate from their mothers and identify with their fathers through resolution of the Oedipus complex. Girls' resolution of the Electra complex results in identification with their mother, with the attempt to differentiate from her being short-circuited.
Social learning	**Modeling and differential reinforcement:** Boys and girls observe and imitate sex-typed behaviors of males and females, respectively, because they are rewarded for doing so.
Cognitive-developmental	**Conceptual development:** Children develop sex-role constancy (an understanding that their sex remains the same no matter what), and sex-role identity then begins to guide their thoughts and actions.
Gender schema	**Gender schemas *and* observation and imitation:** As in cognitive-developmental theory, children form concepts—gender schemas, which they use to process gender-relevant information. As in social learning theory, observation and imitation play a role.
Cultural	**Mediation:** The acquisition of gender roles occurs as children's activities are organized (mediated) by cultural conceptions and stereotypes of gender. This view is consistent with critical theories and feminist approaches.

will explore five major views of sex-role identity development—the psychodynamic, social learning, cognitive-developmental, gender schema, and cultural views (see Table 9.1 for a summary).

The Psychodynamic View By far the best known account of sexual identity formation is that of Sigmund Freud (1921/1949, 1933/1964). Although many of Freud's specific hypotheses about development have not been substantiated, he remains an influential theorist. Certainly, many parents can tell stories of "Freudian moments" when their own young children began to test the boundaries between their personal desires and culturally accepted behavior, as reflected in the following conversation:

> "When I grow up," says [4-year-old] Jimmy at the dinner table, "I'm gonna marry Mama."
> "Jimmy's nuts," says the sensible voice of 8-year-old Jane. "You can't marry Mama and anyway, what would happen to Daddy?" . . .
> "He'll be old," says [Jimmy], through a mouthful of string beans. "And he'll be dead."
> Then, awed by the enormity of his words, [Jimmy] adds hastily, "But he might not be dead, and maybe I'll marry Marcia instead."
> (Fraiberg, 1959, pp. 202–203)

By Freud's account, when Jimmy says that he wants to "marry Mama," he is playing out the universal predicament of boys around the age of 3 or 4, who have moved beyond the oral and anal stages to the **phallic stage** of development, at which children have become capable of deriving pleasure from their genitals. Jimmy's feelings toward his mother and father cause him a lot of mental anguish. He is old enough to know that feelings like wanting your father to die are bad, and he is young enough to believe that his parents, who are powerful figures in his life, are always aware of what he is thinking. So he lives in fear of being punished and feels guilty about his bad thoughts.

Freud called this predicament the **Oedipus complex,** referring to the ancient Greek tragedy in which Oedipus, King of Thebes, unknowingly kills his father

Many young boys are fascinated by their father's act of shaving, just as many young girls are fascinated by their mother's act of applying makeup. Seldom, however, do children become fascinated with the cosmetic rituals of the other-sex parent. Why this is the case would be explained differently by each of the major theoretical perspectives.

Lynn Johnson/Black Star

and marries his mother. To resolve these feelings, little boys, as they leave infancy and enter childhood, must mentally reorder their emotional attachments by *differentiating,* or distancing themselves, from their mothers and becoming closer to their fathers, identifying with them and taking on their characteristics, beliefs, and values. This process is driven by complex social emotions such as guilt and envy.

According to Freud, girls go through a very different process of sex-role identity development. The key event in the development of a girl's sex-role identity is her discovery that she does not have a penis: the girl is "mortified by the comparison with boys' far superior equipment" (Freud, 1933/1964, p. 126). She blames her mother for this "deficiency" and transfers her love to her father. Then she competes with her mother for her father's affection. This process was dubbed the **Electra complex** by Freud's student, Carl Jung (1970), in reference to another Greek tragedy, in which Electra persuades her brother to kill their mother in order to avenge the murder of their father.

As is the case with boys, the wish to replace the same-sex parent results in guilt. The girl is afraid that her mother knows what she is thinking and that she will be punished by loss of her mother's love. She overcomes her fear and guilt by repressing her feelings for her father and intensifying her identification with her mother. Freud believed that this pattern of identity formation, in which girls affiliate with their mothers, renders women "underdeveloped" versions of men because their attempts to differentiate themselves from their mothers were short-circuited.

Not surprisingly, Freud's argument has been strongly attacked, on various grounds. For example, critics reject Freud's belief that females are somehow underdeveloped compared to males. Indeed, if any priority were to be given to one sex, it would more plausibly be given to the female. As we saw in Chapter 3 (p. 89), the sex organs of all human embryos initially follow a female path of development, becoming male only if modified through the action of male hormones. Moreover, modern research indicates that there is more to children's achievement of sex-role identities than identifying with the same-sex parent around the age of 4 or 5, because aspects of identity formation can be discerned well before this age (Ruble & Martin, 1998). Freud's ideas, however criticized, continue to influence both popular and scholarly thinking about the acquisition of sex roles. The challenge facing those who dispute his theories is to provide a better account of the processes at work.

The Social Learning View
Freudian theories of identification assume that young children are caught in hidden conflicts between their fears and their desires. Identification with the same-sex parent is their way of resolving those conflicts. The social learning view differs from this in two fundamental ways. First, social learning theories emphasize entirely different developmental processes. Second, they assume that parents are not the only ones responsible for the child's sex-role development (Eagly & Koenig, 2006).

Whereas psychodynamic theory emphasizes the process of inner conflict, social learning theory emphasizes the processes of **modeling,** in which children observe and imitate individuals of the same sex as themselves, and **differential reinforcement,** in which girls and boys are differently rewarded for engaging in gender-appropriate behavior (Rust et al., 2000). According to this view, children observe that male behavior and female behavior differ. From this observation, they develop

Caring for others is an important component of socialization. Here, Michael and Sheila Cole's granddaughter (left) cuddles her doll in imitation of how her mother comforts the newest addition to the family.

Courtesy of Jennifer Cole

Dressed in a traditional costume, this little Swedish girl learns to clap and dance at a midsummer festival by observing and imitating the behavior of adults.

Anders Ryman/Alamy

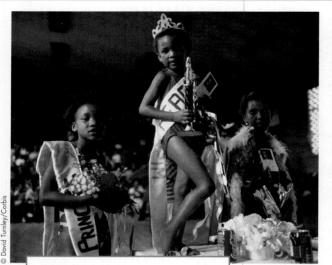

Figure 9.1 These South African girls have just won awards at a beauty pageant. They are learning that physical appearance in girls is valued and rewarded in their community.

hypotheses about appropriate male and female behaviors. Further, children learn that adults reward boys and girls for different kinds of behavior, so they choose to engage in sex-appropriate behaviors that will lead to rewards.

In addition to having a different view on the processes of sex-role development, social learning theorists believe that it is simplistic to think that children acquire gender-role identity primarily by imitating their same-sex parents. Instead, in coming to understand their gender role, children rely also on peers, siblings, and other adults in their lives, as well as on the gender stereotypes communicated in their cultures through television and other media (Sadovsky & Troseth, 2000) (Figure 9.1).

Siblings, for example, are known to be important resources in the child's construction of gender roles. In a major longitudinal study, John Rust and his colleagues (2000) examined the gender development of more than 5000 preschoolers. Some of the preschoolers had an older sister, some had an older brother, and some were only children. They found that boys with older brothers and girls with older sisters showed the greatest amount of sex-typed behavior, that is, behavior considered characteristic of one's gender. In contrast, boys with older sisters and girls with older brothers were the least sex-typed. Those without siblings were somewhere in the middle. Clearly, older siblings exert significant influence on the gender-role development of their little brothers and sisters.

The Cognitive-Developmental View The belief that a child's own conceptions are central to the formation of sex-role identity is implied by Piaget's theory of cognitive development and is the cornerstone of the *cognitive-developmental approach* to sex-role acquisition proposed by Lawrence Kohlberg (1966). In contrast to the social learning theorists' assumption that children passively absorb the gender-relevant information around them, Kohlberg argues that "the child's sex-role concepts are the result of the child's active structuring of his own experience; they are not passive products of social training" (p. 85). In contrast to Freud, Kohlberg claimed that the "process of forming a constant sexual identity depends less on guilt and fear than on the general process of conceptual development" (p. 85).

Kohlberg believed that sex-role development goes through three stages:

1. Basic sex-role *identity*. By the time children are 3 years old, they are able to label themselves as boys or girls.

2. Sex-role *stability*. During early childhood, children begin to understand that sex roles are stable over time—boys grow up to be men and girls grow up to be women.

3. Sex-role *constancy*. Young children may believe that their sex may be changed by altering their outward appearance in some way. Their sex-role development is completed when they understand that their sex remains the same no matter what the situation. They know that even if they dress up as a member of the opposite sex for Halloween, they will not turn into a member of the opposite sex.

There is a good deal of evidence that the development of sex-role identity goes through the general sequence proposed by Kohlberg (Szkrybalo & Ruble, 1999). However, psychologists remain divided about how this sequence interacts with the emergence of sex-role concepts and sex-appropriate behaviors. Kohlberg himself believed that sex-role identity begins to guide thoughts and actions only after children attain sex-role constancy, because only then are they "categorically certain" that their sex is unchangeable (Kohlberg, 1966, p. 95). Current data, however, do not support Kohlberg's strict idea of sex-role constancy as the critical turning point. For example, well before they attain sex-role constancy as defined by Kohlberg's criteria, children prefer the same toys as other members of their sex and imitate the behavior predominantly of same-sex models (Maccoby, 2003).

gender schema A mental model containing information about males and females that is used to process gender-relevant information.

The Gender Schema View To many psychologists it appears that an adequate explanation of how children's sex-role identity develops must include features of both social learning and cognitive-developmental theories. One approach that attempts this is *gender schema theory*.

Gender schema theory is similar in some respects to Kohlberg's cognitive-developmental theory. Adherents of both approaches believe that the environment affects the child's understanding indirectly, through a *schema,* or cognitive structure. Once formed, this schema guides the way the child selects and remembers information from the environment, and guides the child to act in gender-appropriate ways (Martin & Ruble, 2004). A **gender schema,** then, can be considered a mental model containing information about males and females that is used to process gender-relevant information, such as which types of toys, clothing, activities, and interests are "male" or "female" (Liben & Bigler, 2002).

Gary Levy and Robin Fivush (1993) point out that children form gender schemas not only for objects ("boy-things" and "girl-things") and people but also for familiar events, such as how daddy barbecues or how mommy shops for groceries. Accordingly, at the same time that they are discovering how to classify people and objects in terms of gender, gender information is becoming a part of the scripts that boys and girls will draw upon and apply—so that their barbecuing script features a male, for example, and their grocery shopping script a female.

Gender schema theorists depart from Kohlberg's cognitive-developmental theory in two ways. First, they believe that children's developing schematic knowledge motivates and guides their gender-linked interests and behavior even prior to the onset of Kohlberg's stages. Second, these theorists often employ an information-processing, rather than stage, approach to describe how the cognitive and learning elements of the system work together.

Figure 9.2 provides an illustration of how gender schemas work (Martin & Ruble, 2004). A little girl who can say that she is a girl and that her brother is a boy is presented with four objects with which to play. Two of the objects are gender-neutral—an orange and an artichoke—and two are stereotypically male or female—a truck and a doll. When the girl is presented with the doll, she must first

Figure 9.2 An example of an information-processing sequence associated with gender schema formation. In this case, the child is a girl who has been offered four objects with which to play. (Adapted from Martin & Halverson, 1981)

Trucks and little boys just seem to go together, as they do here in Indonesia. Understanding the source of gender-specific toy preferences is an important focus of developmental research.

decide if it is specifically relevant to her. She decides that "dolls are for girls" and that "I am a girl," so "dolls are relevant to me." As a result of this decision, write Martin and Halverson (1981), "she will approach the doll, explore it, ask questions about it, and play with it to obtain further information about it" (p. 1121). This sequence is depicted by the green line in the diagram. When the little girl is presented with a truck, by contrast, she will think, "trucks are for boys" and "I am a girl." This reasoning, in the sequence including the orange lines, will lead her to decide that "trucks are not relevant to me." As a result, she will avoid the truck and not be interested in knowing anything else about it. Asked about these toys later on, she will remember more about the doll than about the truck.

At this time no single theory appears to be able to encompass all the data concerning children's acquisition of sex-role identity. Recent cognitive-developmental approaches have confirmed the importance of such signposts as the ability to label one's own sex and the realization that one's sex remains constant over time and in different contexts (Ruble et al., 2007). Cognitive-developmental theory does not, however, explain the fact that young children's toy preferences and behaviors begin to fit the culture's notions of gender-appropriateness even before children can label their own sex. It seems plausible that this intuitive knowledge comes from the fact that children's behavior is *mediated* by gender categories from very early in development.

The Cultural View The acquisition of gender roles provides an excellent illustration of how the tools of culture (in this case, gender categories) organize children's activities and the way children relate to their environments. Evidence that such mediation may have significant consequences for children's gender-role development comes from studies of how children respond to contexts that vary in the extent to which gender is emphasized. For example, preschool teachers may differ widely in the extent to which they emphasize gender in their classroom activities. One preschool teacher may greet her class with an enthusiastic "Good morning, boys and girls!" During circle time, she may say, "All the boys with blue socks stand up! Now, all the girls wearing sweaters stand up!" Later, when it is time to go outside, she may say, "Okay, let's line up boy-girl-boy-girl." In her classroom, gender categories organize activities, and gender-typed language is used frequently. Children who spend time in preschool classrooms that emphasize gender in this way have higher levels of gender stereotyping compared with children in preschools that are more gender neutral (Biggler, 1995).

Children's behavior is mediated not only by the *content* of gender categories (what sorts of behaviors count as specifically "male" or "female") but also by the rigidness of the categories and the consequences of crossing category boundaries (Ruble & Martin, 2002). In many western cultures, the stereotype of the male is defined more clearly—and more rigidly—than the stereotype of the female. For example, this difference in rigidity in reflected in our culture's relative permissiveness when girls engage in typically malelike behaviors and much greater intolerance when boys engage in typically feminine behavior. One young mother told us of a time when her 2-year-old son snuggled up to her on the sofa while she was painting her fingernails. He put his hand out and said, "Me, too, Mommy." The mother took great pride in her efforts to raise a son who would be as affectionate and gentle as he was assertive and independent, and made sure that he had dolls as well as trucks with which to play. She painted one stubby fingernail a pearly pink. And then she stopped, unable to finish her task. It seems that crossing from male into female territory is difficult even for those who are trying hard to break down gender stereotypes. Thus, it is no surprise that while girls and women will admit to being "tomboys," very few boys and men will confess to being "sissies." Interestingly, the extent to which cultures tolerate (or fail to tolerate) in individuals behavior that is more typical of the other gender may influence children's developing knowledge about gender. For example, a study by Marion O'Brien and her colleagues (2000) found that preschool-age boys and girls are equally knowledgeable about male stereotypes but that girls are considerably more knowledgeable than boys about female stereotypes. It may be that the male stereotype, being more rigid than the female stereotype, is easier for boys and girls to learn. It is also possible that girls know both stereotypes well because they are allowed to experiment with both, whereas boys are confined to behaviors that are consistent with what society defines as the "male domain."

The notion that cultural conceptions and stereotypes of gender mediate children's activities is consistent with feminist approaches and other critical theories introduced in Chapter 1 (see pp. 29–30). According to these views, cultural expectations, beliefs, and values regarding gender infuse children's daily lives, affecting everything from the objects with which they play, the activities in which they engage, and the people with whom they interact. Critical theorists and feminist scholars argue that such thorough immersion in a world organized according to gender categories and stereotypes has a profound affect on children's development.

Ethnic Identity

Jean Phinney (2001) defines **ethnic identity** as "a subjective sense of belonging to an ethnic group, and the feelings and attitudes that accompany this sense of group membership" (p. 136). In a society populated by many ethnic groups, children's developing sense of their own ethnic identity has a host of social, psychological, and economic implications (Quintena et al., 2006). These implications range from whether ethnic grocery stores open in particular communities and whether ethnically relevant after-school clubs and activities are available for students to whether ethnic minority youth are at risk for suicide (see Chapter 15, pp. 566–568). As a consequence, researchers have studied how children identify their own ethnic group and how they form stable attitudes toward their own and other groups (Cross & Cross, 2008; Phinney, 2008). Studies have explored the different kinds of feelings and attitudes that can be associated with ethnic identity and possible effects on children's self-esteem.

Perhaps the most famous research on the development of ethnic identity was carried out by Kenneth and Mamie Clark (1939, 1950), who asked African American and European American children to indicate their preferences between pairs of dolls. The children, who were 3 years old and older, were presented with pairs of dolls representing the two ethnic groups and were asked to choose "which boy [doll] you would like to play with" or "which girl you don't like." The Clarks reported that most of the youngest children could distinguish between the categories of dolls and, more important, that African American children of all ages seemed to prefer the white dolls, a phenomenon that has come to be called "the white bias" (Justice et al., 1999). On the basis of this research, many psychologists concluded that African American children define themselves entirely in terms of the majority group, thereby denying the importance of their own families and communities in shaping their identities (Jackson, McCullough, & Gurin, 1997).

Studies conducted since the 1950s have confirmed the Clarks' findings (Justice et al., 1999; Spencer & Markstom-Adams, 1990) and have extended them to children of other minority groups, including Native Americans (Annis & Corenblum,

ethnic identity A sense of belonging to an ethnic group, and the feelings and attitudes that accompany the sense of group membership.

1987) and Bantu children in South Africa (Gregor & McPherson, 1966). However, these studies have also cast doubt on the notion that minority-group children acquire a negative ethnic self-concept (Spencer, 2006). Margaret Spencer (1988), for example, showed that while many of the 4- to 6-year-old African American children she interviewed said that they would prefer to play with a white doll, 80 percent of these children displayed positive self-esteem. Several other studies confirm that the "white bias" is not connected to the way that children think about and evaluate themselves (Justice et al., 1999). Ann Beuf (1977) reported incident after incident in which Native American children who chose white dolls made evident their understanding of the economic and social circumstances that make their lives difficult in contrast to the lives of white people. In one study, 5-year-old Dom was given several dolls representing Caucasians and Native Americans (whose skins were depicted as brown) to put into a toy classroom:

> Dom: (holding up a white doll) The children's all here and now the teacher's coming in.
> Interviewer: Is that the teacher?
> Dom: Yeah.
> Interviewer: (holding up a brown doll) Can she be the teacher?
> Dom: No way! Her's just an aide.
>
> (Beuf, 1977, p. 80)

In Beuf's view, the children's choices are less a reflection of their sense of personal self-worth than of their desire for the power and wealth of the white people with whom they had come in contact. Her views are echoed by James Jackson (2006), whose review of existing data provided little support for the idea that minority-group children's recognition that they are members of a relatively powerless group translates into a negative personal sense of themselves.

Other studies have shown that young children's expressed ethnic or racial preferences vary with the circumstances. Focusing on the interview situation itself, one study reported that Native American children show a greater preference for dolls representing their own group when they are tested in their native language (Annis & Corenblum, 1987). Harriette McAdoo (1985) reports that African American preschoolers' professed preference for white dolls has declined since the 1950s. She does not speculate on the reasons for this trend, but the end of racial segregation and several decades of political and cultural activism in the African American community are likely candidates. This conclusion is supported by Beuf's (1977) finding that young children of parents who were active in promoting Native American cultural awareness and social rights more often chose dolls representing Native Americans than did children whose parents took little interest in Native American affairs.

Developmentalists have become increasingly interested in how parents communicate with their children about issues of ethnicity. **Ethnic socialization** refers to the ethnic-related messages communicated to children. Several categories of messages have been identified, including (Hughes & Chen, 1999, p. 473):

1. *Cultural socialization,* which emphasizes ethnic heritage and pride.

2. *Preparation for bias,* which stresses ethnic discrimination and prejudice.

3. *Promotion of racial mistrust,* which encourages mistrust of the majority ethnicity.

4. *Egalitarianism,* which emphasizes the equality of members of all ethnicities.

In a study of African American preschoolers, Margaret Caughy and her colleagues (2002) discovered that the vast majority of parents in their sample routinely incorporated a variety of ethnic socialization messages when interacting with

Despite an early awareness that white Americans are more likely than black Americans to have wealth and power, African American children generally display positive self-esteem. These young girls are participating in an international parade in Florida that celebrates their African heritage, which may contribute to their sense of ethnic pride.

their young children. Nearly all of the parents (88 percent) communicated messages that emphasized cultural heritage and pride; the majority also had Afrocentric items in their homes. In contrast, messages promoting mistrust were less frequent, communicated by 65 percent of the parents. The greater emphasis placed on socializing ethnic pride over mistrust and bias has also been found in studies of Puerto Rican and Dominican parents in the United States (Hughes, 2003).

As discovered by Caughy and her colleagues, differences in the form of ethnic socialization bear importantly on children's cognitive abilities and behavioral adjustment. In their study, parents who promoted ethnic pride and provided a home that was rich in African American culture had children with stronger cognitive abilities and problem-solving skills, and fewer behavior problems, than children whose parents provided other forms of ethnic socialization, such as "preparation for bias" or "promotion of mistrust." Although similar findings have been reported in older school-age children (Johnson, 2001), Caughy's study indicates that the process of forming an ethnic identity is well underway in early childhood.

Personal Identity

I'm 3 years old and I live in a big house with my mother and father and my brother, Jason, and my sister, Lisa. I have blue eyes and a kitty that is orange and a television in my own room. I know all my ABC's, listen: A, B, C, D, E, F, G, H, L, K, O, M, P, Q, X, Z. I can run real fast. I like pizza and I have a nice teacher at preschool. I can count up to 100, want to hear me? I love my dog Skipper. I can climb to the top of the jungle gym, I'm not scared! I'm never scared! I'm always happy. I have brown hair and I go to preschool. I am really strong. I can lift this chair, watch me! (Harter, 1999, p. 37)

A sex-role and ethnic identity are just two aspects of the increasingly complex sense of self that develops during early childhood. Traditionally, developmentalists define **personal identity** as consisting of two parts: The *I-self* is the person's subjective sense of themselves as an individual who exists over time and who acts and experiences the world in a particular way; the *me-self,* in contrast, is the person's sense of their objective characteristics such as physical appearance and abilities and other things about themselves that can be objectively known ("I live in a big house.

ethnic socialization Ethnic-based messages communicated to children.

personal identity A person's sense of themselves as persisting over time (*I-self*), and their sense of personal characteristics such as appearance and abilities that can be objectively known (*me-self*).

I have blue eyes and a kitty.") The "I" and the "me" are two sides of the same coin; they shape each other continuously over the course of development (see also Chapter 15).

For reasons of cognitive immaturity, young children's descriptions of themselves focus on the objective self and are typically concrete, disconnected, and unrealistically positive. The highly specific and loosely connected behaviors, abilities, and preferences that children often list when defining themselves are rarely combined into generalized traits such as "being shy" or "being smart." That is, young children's self-descriptions are not well integrated into a *personality structure*. Instead, they tend to be disjointed, fluid, and shifting. As you learned in Chapter 8, this form of reasoning from particular to particular (transductive reasoning) is characteristic of preoperational thought. The integration of the self system is a gradual process that continues in step with cognitive development throughout childhood and adolescence (see Chapter 15, p. 560).

Cognitive limitations also contribute to young children's tendency to see themselves in the most favorable light. Their self-evaluations tend to be unrealistically positive because they have difficulty distinguishing between what they want to do and what they actually are able to do. For example, a child will say, "I know all my ABCs," and "I can swim the whole way across the pool," when he or she can do neither of these things. One reason young children describe themselves in such glowing and unrealistic terms is that they are not yet capable of distinguishing between a "real" self and an "ideal" self—a cognitive ability that won't emerge until middle childhood (Chapter 13, p. 488).

The continuing process of developing personal identity is greatly influenced in early childhood by children's increasingly sophisticated use of language (Gillespie, in press). Recall from Chapter 7 (p. 262) that language is acquired in routine, scripted activities during which young children interact with their caregivers. The same routine activities in family settings are crucial contexts for further development of the self. Not only do caregivers tell children that they are good or bad, boys or girls, black or white, Japanese or Irish, but they also help them acquire an enduring sense of themselves by helping them to create a personal narrative about themselves. This personal narrative is referred to as **autobiographical memory.**

Autobiographical memory is usually created in situations in which adults help children recall and interpret events in which they have participated (Fivush, Reese, & Haden, 2006; Fivush & Nelson, 2006). Initially, adults carry the burden of helping the child remember. Gradually, with increasing age and growing facility with language, the child assumes a more active role, as one of our daughters, Jenny, did when she was about 2 years old. "Tell me what Jenny did," she would say every night at bedtime, and her parents would oblige her by recounting the events of the day in a schematic way that highlighted events that were particularly interesting or worrisome to her. These conversations would go like this: "Do you remember this morning, when we went to pick up Michael, and Mandy [the dog] came running out?" and Jenny would say, "Doggie go wuff, wuff, wuff." "And what did Mandy do?" her parents would prompt. "Wagged her tail," Jenny would respond. "And what else did Mandy do?" they would ask, and she would laugh remembering, "She kissed me!" Although her parents continued to guide the narrative, as Jenny grew older, she increasingly corrected them and added details of her own until she stopped asking them to tell her what happened and started telling them the events of her day (or refusing to tell, as she often did).

Like all parents in such interactions, Jenny's parents were not simply mirrors reflecting their child's experiences. As participants in creating the stories of children's experience, parents strongly influence their children's autobiographical memories and are themselves influenced by the larger culture as well as by their own personal

autobiographical memory A personal narrative that helps children acquire an enduring sense of themselves.

histories, values, and interests. What is more, as illustrated in Jenny's case, parents are not necessarily objective in their contributions to the stories. Some parents may tend to embellish and exaggerate to heighten the stories and make them more exciting, or to play down children's incompetence or fears and exaggerate their capabilities and bravery. Other parents might stay closer to the objective facts in recounting the events in their children's lives. Yet others might tend to structure the stories of prior events so that they teach moral lessons. There are great variations among parents in what events they remember and include in these narratives as well as in how they structure the narratives (Nelson, 2003). Despite this variation, by the time most children are 4 years old they have internalized the narrative structures appropriate to their culture and can recount their personal experiences by themselves, a significant step in developing personal identity.

▐▐▐▐ **APPLY** ▪ **CONNECT** ▪ **DISCUSS**

Visit a major toy store and look for evidence of social categories of gender and ethnicity. What sorts of toys are marketed for boys, girls, or children of specific ethnic backgrounds? How might these toys mediate children's behavior?

Visit the children's section of a public library and look for similar evidence of social categories in books appropriate for 3- to 5-year-olds (you might enlist the help of the librarian). What similarities and differences do you note between books and toys?

A New Moral World

Eddie: Sometimes I hate myself.
Teacher: When?
Eddie: When I'm naughty.
Teacher: What do you do that's naughty?
Eddie: You know, naughty words. Like "shit." That one.
Teacher: That makes you hate yourself?
Eddie: Yeah, when my dad washes my mouth with soap.
Teacher: What if he doesn't hear you?
Eddie: Then I get away with it. Then I don't hate myself.

(Paley, 1981, p. 54)

Children's early ideas of what is good and bad come from the ways in which the significant people in their lives respond to their behavior. In the conversation above, it is clear that for Eddie, as for young children generally, "[b]ad and good depended on the adult response. . . . An angry parent denoted a naughty child" (Paley, 1981, p. 55). As you learned in Chapter 6, the seeds of this development are apparent at the end of infancy when children acquire sensitivity to adult standards and become frustrated or disappointed when they fail to meet them.

To get a sense of the vast territory between these early beginnings and fully mature moral reasoning, take a moment to think about your own moral standards—what you consider right, just, and fair. It is very likely that you believe these standards are not based on the dictates of authority. That is, although you may share your parents' or community's moral values, it is unlikely that you embrace your moral standards because you were told to do so or because you worry about what will happen if you get caught violating a moral standard. Instead, you probably have a deeply *personal* sense of right and wrong. Developmentalists are intent on discovering how such personally felt moral standards are acquired. In the sections below, we examine three perspectives that have dominated their research on children's moral development: psychodynamic theory, cognitive-developmental theory, and social domain theory.

id In Freudian theory, the mental structure present at birth that is the main source of psychological energy. It is unconscious and pleasure seeking and demands that bodily drives be satisfied.

ego In Freudian theory, this is the mental structure that develops out of the id as the infant is forced by reality to cope with the social world. The ego's primary task is self-preservation, which it accomplishes through voluntary movement, perception, logical thought, adaptation, and problem solving.

superego In Freudian terms, the conscience. It represents the authority of the social group and sits in stern judgment of the ego's efforts to hold the id in check. It becomes a major force in the personality in middle childhood.

heteronomous morality Piaget's term for young children's tendency to define morality in terms of objective consequences and externally imposed controls.

social domain theory The moral domain, the social conventional domain, and the personal domain have distinct rules that vary in how broadly the rules apply, and what happens when they are broken.

The Psychodynamic View

According to psychodynamic theory, we acquire a personal sense of what is right and wrong because we have *internalized* the moral standards of our parents, especially those of our same-sex parent. Indeed, our previous discussion of Freud's views on sexual identity development contains the kernel of his thinking about the development of moral reasoning.

According to Freud, the internalization of moral standards that occurs as a consequence of identifying with a same-sex parent is responsible for the creation of a new mental structure. He identified three mental structures that develop from early childhood. The **id,** which is present at birth, operates on the basis of the *pleasure principle;* it is unconscious, impulsive, and concerned with the immediate satisfaction of bodily drives (Freud, 1933/1964). Over the first few years of life, the id comes gradually to be held in check by the *ego,* a second mental structure, with which children become capable of controlling and regulating their behavior. Operating on the basis of the *reality principle*—that is, concerned with how bodily drives can be satisfied by taking reality into account—the **ego** is the intermediary between the demands of the id and the demands of the social world, which are often at odds with each other. Sometime later, around the age 5, children internalize adult standards, rules, and admonitions, resulting in the formation of the **superego.** In Freud's words, the superego "continues to carry on the functions which have hitherto been performed by the [parents]: it observes the ego, gives it orders, judges it and threatens it with punishments, exactly like the parents whose place it has [partially] taken" (1940/1964, p. 205). The emergence of the superego, and all its associated emotions of shame and guilt, is fundamental to children's abilities to regulate their behaviors according to their personal sense of right and wrong.

The Cognitive-Developmental View

Consider two scenes. In one, a young child named Luke is warned by his mother to stay away from the freshly baked cookies cooling on the kitchen counter. When she leaves the room, Luke snitches a cookie and, in his clumsy haste, knocks over a cup that falls to the floor and breaks. Now consider the second scene, in which young Zack is helping his mother set the dining room table for dinner. With hands full of napkins and silverware, he pushes open the door leading from the kitchen to the dining room. When the door swings open, it hits a tray on which are stacked a dozen cups, all of which fall to the floor and break. Who, in your judgment, is the naughtier child—Luke, who broke one cup while snitching a cookie, or Zack, who broke a dozen while helping his mother set the table?

When Piaget presented similar contrasts to children of different ages, he found that young, preoperational children considered Zack the naughtier of the two because he broke more cups. Older children, in contrast, chose Luke because he was deliberately violating his mother's order, whereas Zack was trying to do good and simply had an unfortunate accident.

As you might predict from previous discussions of preoperational thinking, when young children reason about moral issues, they tend to focus on objective consequences—how much damage is done (in the case of Luke and Zack) or whether the person gets caught and in trouble (as when Eddie's father washed his mouth with soap). Jean Piaget (1932/1965) called this pattern of thinking **heteronomous morality,** that is, morality defined in terms of externally imposed controls and objective consequences. According to Piaget, as children enter middle childhood and begin to interact increasingly with their peers outside of situations directly controlled by adults, heteronomous morality gives way to an *autonomous morality*, in which one's moral judgments are freely and personally chosen. (This idea and its extension in contemporary research will be discussed further in Chapter 14.)

As you can see, the cognitive-developmental and psychodynamic views both focus on how children move past their reliance on external authority and objective consequences to define right and wrong. But whereas the psychodynamic view emphasizes processes such as identification, internalization, and the development of the superego, the cognitive-developmental view links changes in moral reasoning to broader cognitive developments that are supported by the expansion of children's social lives.

The Social Domain View

The social domain view of moral development stands apart from the other two views we have considered because it emphasizes that there are different *types* of "right" and "wrong" (Killen & Smetana, 2007). For example, jaywalking is a very different type of transgression than pushing someone off a bridge. According to **social domain theory,** rules that dictate right and wrong fall into three domains, which are at different levels of generality: some rules are *moral rules,* others are *social conventions,* and yet others are rules within the *personal sphere* (Nucci, 2004; Turiel, 2008) (Table 9.2).

Moral rules are the most general; they are based on principles of justice and the welfare of others. Thus, moral rules specify, for example, that others be treated fairly, in a way that preserves their rights and avoids causing them harm. Often believed to derive from a divine source (e.g., to be God's law), and found in all societies, moral rules are obligations that are not to be transgressed.

At the next level of generality are social conventions—rules that are important for coordinating social behavior in a given society, such as rules about how men or women should act, or what constitutes appropriate dress at a house of worship or on the beach, or who has authority over whom. Social conventions are important aspects of the cultural scripts that young children are acquiring. Social conventions vary tremendously, not only among societies but also among subcultural groups within a society. This variation can contribute to difficulties children may have in knowing whether a rule they have broken is a moral rule or a social convention. For example, some families may treat cursing as violating a

table 9.2

Social Domain Theory Approach to Rules and Infractions	
Rule Type	**Sample Infractions**
Moral Rules—rules related to	
Physical harm	Hitting, pushing
Psychological harm	Hurting feelings, ridiculing
Fairness and rights	Refusing to take turns
Social Conventions—rules related to	
School behavior	Chewing gum in class, talking back to the teacher
Forms of address	Calling a physician "Mr." when he is working
Attire and appearance	Wearing pajamas to school
Sex roles	Boy wearing barrette to keep hair out of eyes while playing football
Personal Sphere—rules related to	
Personal habits	Making loud noises while eating
Hygiene	Not brushing teeth
Social events	Not sending a thank-you card for a gift

social convention ("That's not a nice word; you definitely shouldn't say it in front of your grandmother"), but when Eddie says "shit" and his mouth is washed out with soap, he might well believe that he has broken a moral rule!

At the most specific level are the rules that govern the personal sphere, in which children can make decisions on the basis of their personal preferences. They are allowed to choose whether to call or send a note to thank an uncle for a birthday gift. It is in the personal sphere that children are able to develop what is unique about the way they deal with the world (Nucci, 1996; Turiel, Killen, & Helwig, 1987).

Several studies have found that children as young as 3 or 4 years old from a variety of cultures can distinguish among moral, social, and personal rules (Yau & Smetana, 2003). For example, they respond quite differently to moral rule violations, such as hurting another child or taking another's favorite toy, than they do to violations of a social convention, such as wearing inappropriate clothes to school (Turiel, 2006).

As already suggested, the borders between the three levels of rules are not easy to learn and keep straight. Parents, for example, may treat their young children's wearing a bathing suit at the beach as a matter of social convention. Their young children, however, may treat wearing a bathing suit as a matter of personal choice, so they take it off to play naked in the water. It takes children many years to acquire their culture's normative separations, and even then, deciding which rules should be applied in which situations requires a good deal of negotiation (Nucci, 2004; Smetana, 2006).

||||| ▌ **APPLY ═ CONNECT ═ DISCUSS** ─ ─ ─ ─ ─ ─ ─ ─ ─ ─ ─ ─ ─ ─ ─ ─ ─ ─ ─

Erikson believed that identity development and moral development are closely related. Using material presented in this chapter, pull together evidence for his argument.

Developing Self-regulation

In the process of learning about basic social roles and rules and developing their sense of self, children are also learning to act in accordance with the expectations of their caregivers, even when they do not want to and are not being directly monitored. Learning to control one's thoughts, emotions, and behaviors, an ability referred to as **self-regulation,** spans various developmental stages and involves all the developmental domains (Kochanska & Aksan, 2006; Kochanska et al., 2007). Early in development, infants acquire the physiological capacity to maintain a constant body temperature, a capacity needed once they leave the womb. Later, they become capable of regulating their sleep/wake cycles and their crying. As they get older, children are increasingly able to tune out distractions in order to complete a task, thus regulating their attentional state; they can put aside hurt feelings in order to patch up a friendship; they can keep secrets.

Infants and young children require a great deal of assistance with regulation. They are soothed by caregivers when they cry; their interpersonal relationships are often orchestrated by others ("Tell him you're sorry and make up"); and their emotional expressions are monitored and managed ("No hitting!" "Use your words!"). Even the large and simple figures contained in young children's coloring books reflect the culture's response to children's need for assistance in regulating their attention and behavior (in this case, their fine motor behavior).

Because the ability to regulate one's own thoughts, emotions, behaviors, and attentional states is such an important part of what it means to function independently,

This girl's culture helps her regulate her immature motor skills by making extra big shovels for filling buckets with sand.

many developmentalists consider self-regulation to be a cornerstone of children's development (Ruff & Capozzoli, 2003; Shonkoff & Phillips, 2000).

Regulating Thought and Action

To intentionally focus one's attention, or remember to do something, or map out a plan to solve a problem involves the regulation of cognitive processes. Consider the preschooler who is stringing beads (after Shonkoff & Phillips, 2000, p. 116). Accomplishing this task requires that she regulate her thoughts in order to:

- Generate and maintain a mental representation that directs her behavior: "I need to hold up the string and put the end through the hole in the bead."

- Monitor her own progress: "I got one on; now I'll try another."

- Modify her problem-solving strategies: "This bead won't go on; I need one with a bigger hole."

The simple act of stringing beads calls on a host of skills that require the child to select certain actions (holding the bead to the string), eliminate actions that do not fit the goal (throwing the bead), and inhibit actions as the task requires (stop trying the bead with the too-small hole). The inhibition of an action that is already underway, also called **effortful control,** can be particularly difficult for young children, as anyone knows who has observed a game of "Red-Light Green-Light" or "Simon Says" (Shonkoff & Phillips, 2000). Once a behavior has been initiated, especially in a highly exciting situation, it can be difficult to stop.

In addition to exploring how children come to regulate their thought and action in solving problems and accomplishing tasks, developmentalists have asked how children regulate themselves in order to achieve social goals such as pleasing a parent or teacher. The most common way of studying this form of self-regulation is to examine children's ability to resist temptation and comply with adult norms. For example, Grazyna Kochanska and Nazan Aksan (1995) videotaped and analyzed the behavior of more than 100 children between the ages of 2 and 5 while they interacted with their mothers in two situations. In the first, the mother and child were given a large number of attractive toys to play with in their own home.

self-regulation The ability to control one's thoughts, emotions, and behaviors.

effortful control The inhibition of an action that is already underway.

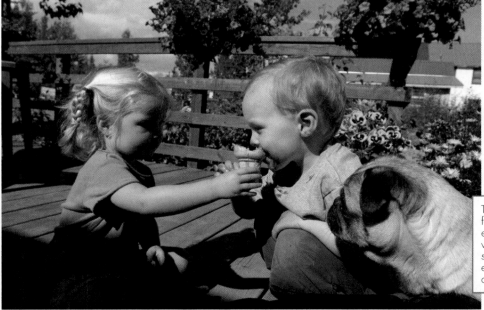

The expression on 2-year-old Riley's face (left) is ample evidence of the effort it takes to share her ice cream with Bjorn. It is likely that this form of self-regulation emerged with a lot of encouragement from parents and caregivers.

Rich Reid/Getty Images

Many adults have childhood memories about the difficulty of sitting quietly and respectfully during religious ceremonies that seemed to last forever. As illustrated by these Iranian children reading the Koran in a mosque, children are able to regulate their behavior to comply with adult expectations when consistently prompted to do so.

After the children played with the toys for a while, their mothers asked them to put them away. Only 10 percent of the children overtly disobeyed. Of the others, some exhibited what the researchers called "committed compliance," that is, they wholeheartedly embraced their mothers' agenda. Most, however, engaged in "situational compliance," meaning that they had to be continually prompted by their mothers to do as they were told. Consistent with what we know about effortful control, the children clearly found it difficult to put away the attractive toys with which they were still playing.

In the second situation, which took place in a laboratory, the mothers were instructed to tell their children not to touch a set of especially attractive toys on a shelf. After the children had been playing for a while, the researchers asked each mother to come to an adjoining room, to see if her child would continue to obey her even when she was not watching. The injunction not to touch the forbidden toys turned out to be easier to obey than the command to put the toys away, which required effortful control. That is, most of the children complied wholeheartedly. Some of the children were heard to talk to themselves, saying such things as "We don't touch these." Their use of the word "we" in such circumstances is a clear sign that they identified with their mothers and accepted their mothers' rules.

You have probably recognized that children's ability to control themselves in this manner is an example of internalization. In addition to being a key component of Freud's theory of moral development, internalization is central to the developmental theory of Lev Vygotsky. Vygotsky's view of the process was both broader and more benevolent than Freud's. For Freud, internalization is a response to an ongoing battle against parental authority, a battle that the child will ultimately lose. Vygotsky, in contrast, saw internalization as the process through which external social regulations, which may originate from parents, other adults, or even peers, are transferred to the child's internal psychological system. Once the social regulations are internalized, the child is capable of self-regulation without the assistance of others. A particularly interesting example of this process can be observed in children's play.

Self-regulation and Play

Play occupies a conspicuous role not only in young children's physical development but also in their cognitive and social development. According to Vygotsky and those who have followed in his footsteps, a crucial part of this role is in the development of self-regulation (Elias & Berk, 2002).

Key to Vygotsky's argument of how play leads to self-regulation is his idea regarding children's ability to separate the objects they play with from their thoughts about those objects. Remember that early in development, children have difficulty separating their thoughts and actions from the objects and situations that they think about and act upon. For example, prior to the age of 2, a child can pretend to talk on a telephone only if the toy really looks and acts like a telephone, complete with buttons to push and a handle to hold up to the mouth and ear. Not until age 2 can the child let one object substitute for another, for example, play "telephone" with a block. The ability to detach the *idea* of the telephone from the *object itself* increases through the next year, and by the age of 3, the attributes of the play symbol can be entirely independent of the object that it represents. So, for

Argus/Peter Arnold

Play provides an important opportunity for acquiring self-control. These young Tanzanian girls are regulating their behavior so that it is coordinated with that of their playmates.

example, the child can play "telephone" with a baby doll or a Tinker Toy or any other object. The ability to separate thought—which carries the *idea* or *meaning* of the object—from the object that is thought about means that the child is regulating her thoughts and actions. She is making herself imagine that the baby doll is a telephone, and she is making herself act on it accordingly. Vygotsky believed that the child's self-regulation is most required in, and hence most developed through, this type of imaginary play.

A particularly important and complex type of imaginary play is **sociodramatic play**—make-believe play in which two or more participants enact a variety of related social roles. Sociodramatic play requires a shared understanding of what the play situation involves, which often must be negotiated as part of the play. As an example, consider the following scene involving several children in preschool. The girls in the group have just agreed upon the roles they will play: mother, sister, baby, and maid.

> Karen: I'm hungry. Wa-a-ah!
> Charlotte: Lie down, baby.
> Karen: I'm a baby that sits up.
> Charlotte: First you lie down and sister covers you and then I make your cereal and then you sit up.
> Karen: Okay.
> Karen: (to Teddy, who has been observing) You can be the father.
> Charlotte: Are you the father?
> Teddy: Yes.
> Charlotte: Put on a red tie.
> Janie: (in the "maid's" falsetto voice) I'll get it for you, honey. Now don't that baby look pretty? This is your daddy, baby.
>   (Adapted from Paley, 1984, p. 1)

This transcript illustrates several features of young children's sociodramatic play. The children are enacting social roles and using scripts that they have encountered numerous times in their daily lives, on television, or in stories. Babies make stereotypic baby noises, maids get things for people, and fathers wear ties. At the same

sociodramatic play Make-believe play in which two or more participants enact a variety of related social roles.

The sociodramatic play of these two little girls involves enacting the roles of doctors or nurses. According to Vygotsky, such play is fundamental to the emergence of self-regulation.

time that they are playing their roles in the pretend world, the children are also outside it, giving stage directions to one another and commenting on the action. The "baby" who sits up has to be talked into lying down, and the boy is told what role he can play. The children here are clearly acting against immediate impulse and regulating their thoughts and behaviors according to the imaginary situation as it evolves in the course of interacting with their playmates.

Recently, developmentalists have sought empirical evidence for the link between sociodramatic play and the more general ability of children to regulate their actions. An example is a study conducted by Cynthia Elias and Laura Berk (2002), in which they observed 51 children aged 3 and 4 in their preschool classrooms. Elias and Berk recorded and assessed the children's involvement in sociodramatic play, and they assessed their level of self-regulation by observing how well they participated in cleanup and how attentive they were when they gathered in a circle to listen to the teacher. They used a short-term longitudinal design, assessing both play and self-regulation in the fall and assessing self-regulation again several months later.

The findings support Vygotsky's main idea regarding the role of play in facilitating self-regulation (see also the box "In the Field: Coping with Chronic Illness through Play"). In particular, children who engaged in a lot of sociodramatic play in the fall showed high levels of self-regulation several months later, even though there was no correlation between the two variables at the time of the first assessment. Interestingly, the correlation was especially strong for the most impulsive children, indicating that they benefited more than their less impulsive peers from opportunities to engage in sociodramatic play. Based on their findings, as well as what is known about the social and academic difficulties that go along with poor self-regulation skills (a matter that will be addressed below), Elias and Berk argued that sociodramatic play deserves an important place in preschool curricula and may be an important form of early intervention for highly impulsive children.

Both theory and research support the notion that sociodramatic play provides an important context for the development of self-regulation. It is, however, but one of many contexts through which children come to master themselves. Children encounter a vast array of social norms, parenting practices, school curricula, and work demands, which vary according to the child's culture, gender, and age. All provide possible contexts in support of the child's journey toward independence in thought and action.

Regulating Emotions

To be competent members of society, children must learn how to control their emotions in addition to controlling their thoughts and actions. As we noted in Chapter 6 (pp. 227–228), the development of qualitatively new emotions is one of the key changes associated with the transition from infancy to early childhood. Pride, shame, guilt, envy, and embarrassment—these *self-conscious emotions*—now join with anger, joy, and the other primary emotions to enable participation in new and more complex social relationships (Mascolo, Fischer, & Li, 2003). Children must learn to interpret the emotional states of others, manage their own emotions, and mask their true feelings when necessary.

Controlling Feelings Most of us know what it feels like to carry a chip on one's shoulder, stew over a negative experience, or react explosively to a frustrating situation. Such feelings present special challenges to children's developing self-regulation abilities. However, between 2 and 6 years of age, children develop a number of strategies to help them keep their emotions under control (Grolnick, McMenamy, & Kurowski, 1999; Saarni, 2007; Gross & Thompson, 2007). For example, they avoid or reduce emotionally charged information by closing their eyes, turning away, and putting their hands over their ears. They use their budding language and cognitive skills to help them reinterpret events to create a more acceptable version of what is occurring ("I didn't want to play with her anyway; she's mean"), to reassure themselves ("Mommy said she'll be right back"), and to encourage themselves ("I'm a big girl; big girls can do it"). At the age of 3, Jenny, one of our daughters, displayed a useful strategy for regulating her fright when hearing Maurice Sendak's tale *Where the Wild Things Are:* she hid the book so her parents could not read it to her.

The emerging ability to control emotions helps the preschool-age child deal with the disappointments, frustrations, and injured feelings that are so common at this stage. In addition, emotional regulation can be helpful in the increasingly important realm of social behavior. For example, when children observe a playmate falling down and getting hurt, they will likely feel anxious themselves. Children who can moderate their personal distress are more likely to show sympathy toward the playmate than are children who cannot manage their own emotional reactions (Eisenberg et al., 2007). Indeed, in order to sustain play, children must create and maintain a delicate balance of emotional expression and regulation (Halberstadt et al., 2001). As you will see, the skills associated with this balance are significantly related to children's altruistic, or *prosocial,* behaviors.

Controlling and Understanding Emotion Expressions Young children must learn not only to control their feelings but also to express their feelings in a socially appropriate way. Young infants display no such ability. They communicate their emotions directly, regardless of the circumstances. A 2-month-old who becomes upset during a wedding because he is hungry is not going to stop crying until he is fed. It takes several years for children to learn to control their emotional expressions.

In the United States, for example, it is considered socially inappropriate to act disappointed when someone gives you a present. You are expected to thank the giver and to say something nice about the present, whether or not you like it. Several researchers have studied the ability of children to understand the need to mask their real emotions and their ability to do so. In some studies, children were asked to interpret stories about a child who expects an exciting present and gets something undesirable instead. In other studies, the children themselves are put in situations where they expect a desirable object and experience disappointment (as when, for example, they are led to expect a toy car as a prize for playing a game but get a picture book instead).

Several general results come from this type of research in different cultures (summaries are provided in Saarni et al., 2006, and Thompson, 1998). First, during early childhood, children around the world appear to gain the ability to recognize when someone is masking his or her feelings. Second, girls tend to be better than boys at recognizing and displaying masked emotions. Third, there are wide cultural variations in the age at which children learn about masking emotion. For example,

Caught in the act of making a big mess, the signs of guilt are unmistakable on this girl's face. Self-conscious emotions, including guilt, first emerge during early childhood.

Misty Bedwell/drr.net

In the Field ┃ Coping with Chronic Illness through Play

Name:	Cindy Clark
Education:	B.A. in international relations, University of Pennsylvania; M.A. and Ph.D. in human development, University of Chicago
Current Position:	Associate Professor, Pennsylvania State University, Brandywine
Career Objectives:	Use research to learn about and reduce the stress and anxiety of children with chronic illnesses

T*he sight of a child unable to breathe carries unspeakable anxiety. Life begins with the first breath and ends when breathing does. Children's connection to life is only as reliable as inhaling and exhaling. Against this fact of life, asthma stalks, specterlike.*

—Cindy Clark, 2003, p. 89

A parent's letter to Mr. Rogers:

Our 5½-year-old daughter has an inoperable brain tumor. Our only hope to remove the tumor is radiation. On the first day of her radiation treatment, she screamed and cried when she found out that she would have to be in the room all by herself. . . . We kept saying that it would only take a minute . . . . Finally, she asked me, "What is a minute?" . . . I looked at my watch and started singing, "It's a beautiful day in this neighborhood, a beautiful day for a neighbor," and before I could finish the song I said "Oops, the minute's up. I can't even finish Mr. Rogers' song." Then Michelle said, "Is that a minute? I can do that." And she did. She laid perfectly still for the entire treatment; but there was a catch to it. I have to sing your song every time over the intercom.

From an interview with a child living with chronic asthma:

If I had a magic wand, all asthma medicine would taste good, not like the yucky stuff. And my inhaler and breathing machine would work as fast as I can snap my fingers, so I could start breathing and go play. My breathing machine takes 10,000 years. That's how slow it seems to me. Sometimes, I play games with myself when I do my breathing machine. I pretend I have a friend who is a dragon, and the dragon breathes smoke. You know the steam coming from the machine? That's dragon smoke. Another game is, I have a toy airplane. I fly my airplane through the steam. I pretend to fly away, to a place away from this. That's really fun to pretend, getting up and away.

Children afflicted with serious illness and disease face a number of challenges. The disease itself can be painful and physically

Cindy Clark

Bill Clark

exhausting—and terribly frightening. It can also be socially isolating, as when children need to stay home or in hospitals, away from their friends and schoolmates.

Beyond the physical, psychological, and social costs of the disease itself, chronically ill children pay a heavy toll as a consequence of the medical procedures required to heal them. As expressed in the stories above, the procedures can be scary and seem to make time stand still. Medical procedures can also unnerve the very people on whom sick children count for support, friendship, and comfort. That is, children with chronic illness are often shunned inadvertently by peers, and even family members, who may be squeamish in the face of the diabetic child's insulin shots and blood tests, the hair loss that typically accompanies chemotherapy, or the disfigurement of surgery.

How do children cope with chronic illness? According to Cindy Clark's intensive study (2003), they cope surprisingly well, particularly when they are allowed to play. In her interviews with children living with chronic severe asthma or diabetes, Clark found that play is an important means of altering the meanings of medical procedures and devices, and symbolically recasting what it means to be ill. Play provides children with a sense of control and empowerment over conditions and circumstances that are otherwise forced upon them by doctors and parents, and the medical regimens that keep them alive.

Thus, Clark found that parents and children often develop games and playful routines that transform unpleasant medical experiences into something fun, or at least endurable. The examples above of singing Mr. Rogers's song or imagining smoke-breathing dragons are cases in point. Parents of children with asthma described a variety of playful ways of counting to 10 while their children used their inhalers (inhalers are devices, also known as puffers, that deliver medicine; see figure)—they counted in French, in Pig Latin, in the voice of the Count from *Sesame Street*. Sometimes, the medical devices themselves were transformed into toys. Certain types of inhalers make a whistling sound to signal the patient that they are inhaling too quickly. As you might imagine, a lot of asthmatic children get the giggles by using their inhalers (improperly) as musical instruments. One mother recounted how her daughter played with a breathing mask used with the nebulizer (a breathing machine that delivers medicine, often to children too young to manipulate the more complicated puffer). The mother had intentionally acquired the second mask, thinking that using it in the context of play might facilitate her daughter's coping with asthma. Sure enough, the girl "played asthma" with her little friends, placing the mask on their faces, instructing them to sit quietly, and promising that mommy would read stories to pass the time.

At an "illness camp" for children with diabetes, syringes and paint are used to create art; at an asthma camp, some of the children put on a skit of "The Three Little Pigs," in which the big, bad wolf was unable to blow the houses down because he had life-threatening asthma. He was taken to the hospital, received a lung transplant, and was thereafter able to blow down just about anything. The audience laughed and laughed.

In her child-centered approach to understanding chronic illness, Clark attempts to reveal how children attach meaning to their illness, and the medical procedures and devices that they endure and use on a daily basis. What she found is a child's world in which fear, pain, embarrassment, and confusion are ordered and controlled through song, jokes, art, pranks, and funny stories. From a Vygotskian perspective, the blending of fantasy play and medical treatment creates a zone of proximal development through which the child gains a sense of control over the uncontrollable and frightening. Much of the play is spontaneously generated by children. However, some is encouraged by adults— parents in particular—who are sensitive to how children can regulate their thoughts and feelings in the context of play.

Increasingly, the therapeutic value of play is recognized by the medical community. At one hospital, the pediatric blood-testing machine is named "Herbie"; his most distinctive characteristic is his inclination to "suck your blood." One of Herbie's child "victims"

claimed that his encounter with blood-sucking Herbie was the best part of his hospital stay, and that Herbie made the procedure seem like it did not hurt quite so much. Other hospitals have systematically incorporated play into children's treatment regimens. Many now employ *child life specialists* whose primary duties involve familiarizing children with treatment and facilitating their coping and adjustment through the use of play and games.

Currently, developmentalists such as Clark are seeking new ways of using the functions of play to help children deal with debilitating diseases and medical procedures. Clark is now engaged in a study that incorporates inhalers that are shaped like toys, as in the figure. And you can bet that if they whistle, it is not when they are being used improperly.

Puffa Pals introduce a playful dimension to asthma inhalers, making them more attractive to the young children who must use them to manage the symptoms of their disease.

one study found that young English children acquired rules for masking negative emotions earlier than young Italian children did (Manstead, 1995), and another that 4–year–old girls from India were more sensitive to the need to mask negative emotions than were their English counterparts (Joshi & MacLean, 1994).

Children's increasing ability to read the emotions of others and to control their own emotional expression are considered forms of **socioemotional competence,** the ability to behave appropriately in social situations that evoke strong emotions. Carolyn Saarni (2007) proposed that socioemotional competence involves a variety of skills, most of which are acquired in early childhood. The skills include an awareness of one's own emotional state and the emotional states of others, and the realization that outward expressions do not necessarily reflect inner emotional states. It should come as no surprise that preschool children who display the characteristics of socioemotional competence are better liked by both their peers and their teachers (Eisenberg, Losoya, & Spinrad, 2003; Saarni, 1999).

The Influence of Culture on Emotion Regulation As you know from the previous section on regulating thought and action, the developmental task of self-regulation is not a solitary accomplishment. The child receives a great deal of social and cultural assistance. Developmentalists are just beginning to explore how

socioemotional competence The ability to behave appropriately in social situations that evoke strong emotions children's emotions and emotion regulation are affected by their culture's values, meanings, and belief systems.

For example, Michael Mascolo, Kurt Fischer, and Jin Li (2003) have explored differences in the emotional development of children growing up in China and the United States. The two cultures embrace vastly different values and beliefs. In the United States, great emphasis is placed on individualism and hence on personal achievement. Children are socialized to express themselves and take pleasure in their own accomplishments: "Good girl! You did it all by yourself!" Accordingly, American parents act to bolster their children's pride, and in this way their self-esteem, when they succeed, and to protect them from feelings of shame and failure, when they do not. In contrast, the Chinese embrace the philosophy of Confucianism, which emphasizes harmony with others as a principal goal. When a child succeeds at a task, the culturally appropriate response is not self-celebration, but modesty and praise for others: "You did all right, but now you need more practice. Play down your success." When a child fails, and thereby fails the group, Chinese parents often utilize a variety of "shaming techniques." Mascolo and his colleagues report that if a child does poorly in school, a parent might say, "Shame on you!" "You didn't practice hard enough!" "Everyone will laugh at you!" Because of the role shame plays, Mascolo and his colleagues argue, it emerges for Chinese children at an earlier point in development than it does for American children. As shown in Figure 9.3, children's emotional responses to their accomplishments follow radically different pathways as a consequence of their cultural traditions.

Figure 9.3 While children in the United States are socialized to strive for and take pride in personal achievements, children in China are encouraged to strive to meet social obligations and to feel honor in doing so. This figure shows the emotional outcomes for children who are successful or unsuccessful in meeting their culture's expectations.

©Yang Liu/Corbis

Consistent with the philosophy of Confucianism, Chinese parents commonly play down their children's successes and use "shaming techniques" when their children perform poorly.

▌▌▌▌▌ **APPLY ▪▪ CONNECT ▪▪ DISCUSS** ▪

We argued in Chapter 6 that one of the earliest purposes of emotion regulation was to maintain intersubjectivity. Review pages 205–209 and discuss the similarities and differences between infancy and early childhood in the purposes and consequences of emotion regulation.

Understanding Aggression

In order to be accepted as members of their social group, young children must learn not only to subordinate their personal desires to the good of the group when the situation demands it, but also to regulate their anger when their goals are thwarted. Such anger can lead to aggression, and learning to control aggression is one of the most basic tasks of young children's social development. Indeed, researchers have argued that early childhood holds the key to understanding both the origins of aggressive behavior and how to control it (Tremblay et al., 2005).

The Development of Aggression

During early childhood, two main categories of aggression are easily identified, each of which follows its own developmental path (Berkowitz, 2003). **Hostile aggression** is intended to injure the victim, physically or otherwise. **Instrumental aggression,** in contrast, is directed at achieving a particular goal—for example, threatening or hitting another child in order to obtain a toy or to gain peer approval. A study of sibling interactions found that instrumental aggression rose sharply between the ages of 1 and 2, just at the time when children typically begin to develop a distinctive sense of self and worry about "ownership rights" regarding their toys (Dunn, 1988).

Whether hostile or instrumental aggression, children's aggressive behavior can take a variety of forms. And, as with other types of behaviors, the particular form taken often depends on what may be occurring in specific developmental domains. For example, as children develop cognitive and language skills they become capable of teasing. Teasing is a subtle form of aggression requiring the ability to understand something about the mental states and desires of another—how destroying a favorite toy, or calling someone a name may be hurtful. Until the age of about 18 months, teasing and physical aggression occur with equal frequency. But as children approach their second birthdays, an increase in the amount of teasing

hostile aggression Aggression that is aimed at hurting another person as a way of establishing dominance, which may gain the aggressor advantages in the long run.

instrumental aggression Aggression that is directed at obtaining something.

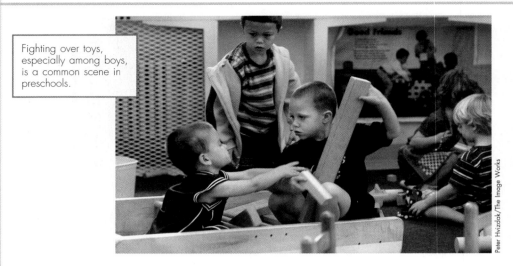

Fighting over toys, especially among boys, is a common scene in preschools.

Peter Hvizdak/The Image Works

means they are much more likely to tease their siblings than to hurt them physically (Figure 9.4).

Many studies of childhood aggression from around the world have reported that boys are more aggressive than girls in a wide variety of circumstances (Segall et al., 1999). Boys are more likely than girls to hit, push, hurl insults, and threaten to beat up other children (Dodge, Cole, and Lynham, 2006). When asked to pretend about conflict situations that might happen to them in preschool (e.g., a peer knocks over a block tower or refuses to share a toy), boys are more likely than girls to offer aggressive rather than positive solutions (Walker et al., 2002). This difference seems to emerge during the second and third years of life (Underwood, 2002). As you can see in Figure 9.5, direct aggression by girls drops markedly as they approach their second birthdays, while it increases slightly for boys. On the other hand, as we will discuss in detail in Chapter 13, preschool- and school-age girls are more likely than boys to engage in **relational aggression,** an indirect form of aggression intended to harm another child's friendships or exclude that child from the group (Ostrov & Crick, 2006).

Figure 9.4 Early in the second year of life, siblings are as likely to hurt each other physically as to tease each other, but as they approach their second birthdays teasing becomes much more frequent than physical aggression. (Adapted from Dunn, 1988)

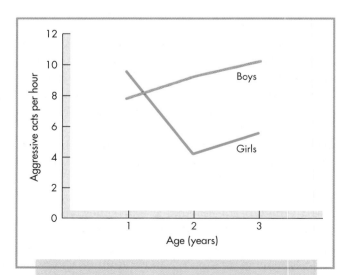

Figure 9.5 As children in a nursery school approach their second birthdays, acts of aggression decline significantly among girls but increase slightly among boys. (After Legault & Strayer, 1990)

What Causes and Controls Aggression?

Patterns of aggressive behavior often emerge during early childhood as personality becomes more defined. There is substantial evidence that 3-year-old children who behave defiantly and disobediently with adults, are aggressive toward their peers, and are impulsive and hyperactive are likely to still have these problems during middle childhood and adolescence (Campell et al., 2006). A number of longitudinal studies have found that, for boys in particular, the earlier the age at which children begin to exhibit such problem behaviors, the greater the likelihood that they will continue to behave in those ways later in life (Baillargeon et al., 2007). But what initiates these behaviors in young children? And how can such aggression be controlled? In studying aggression—problematic patterns of aggressive behaviors and aggression more generally—developmentalists have tended to focus on one of three sets of factors: biological, social and cultural, or emotional and cognitive factors.

Biological Contributions

Those who emphasize the role of biology in the development of aggression base their arguments on evolutionary and physiological factors (Ellis & Bjorklund, 2005). Noting that no group in the animal kingdom is free of aggression, many students of animal behavior have proposed that aggression is an important force in animal evolution (Lorenz, 1966). According to Darwin (1859/1958), a species gradually comes to assume the characteristics of its most successful individuals. Darwin defined as "successful" those individuals who manage to pass on their genetic characteristics to the next generation. Because each individual is, in some sense, competing with every other individual for the resources necessary for survival and reproduction, evolution would seem to favor individuals with competitive and selfish phenotypes. In many species, including our own, such phenotypic characteristics as defense of a territory, which ensures that a mating pair will have access to food, have been interpreted as survival-oriented competition (Wilson, 1975). According to this interpretation of evolution, aggression is natural and necessary; its appearance automatically accompanies the biological maturation of the young.

While aggression is widespread among animal species, so are mechanisms that limit it. The aggressive behavior in litters of puppies, for example, changes in accordance with a maturational timetable (James, 1951). At about 3 weeks, puppies begin to engage in rough-and-tumble play, mouthing and nipping one another. A week later the play has become rougher; the puppies growl and snarl when they bite, and the victims may yelp in pain. Once injurious attacks become really serious, however, a hierarchical social structure emerges, with some animals dominant and others subordinate. After such a dominance hierarchy is formed, the dominant puppy needs only to threaten in order to get its way; it has no need to attack. At this point, the frequency of fighting diminishes (Cairns, 1979). Throughout the animal kingdom one finds such hierarchies, which regulate interactions among members of the same species (Figure 9.6).

The developmental history of aggression and its control among puppies is similar in some interesting ways to development in human children. F. F. Strayer (1991) and his colleagues observed a close connection between aggression and the formation of dominance hierarchies among 3- and 4-year-olds in a nursery school. They identified a specific pattern of hostile interactions among children: When one child would behave aggressively, the other child would almost always submit by crying, running away, flinching, or seeking help from an adult. These dominance encounters led to an orderly pattern of social

relational aggression Indirect aggression intended to harm someone's friendships or exclude an individual from the group.

Figure 9.6 Many species of animals have innate behaviors for signaling defeat to allow the establishment of a social dominance hierarchy without bloodshed, in this photograph, the crouching posture of the wolf on the left.

Michael H. Francis

relationships within the group. Once children know their position in such a hierarchy, they challenge only those whom it is safe for them to challenge. They leave others alone, thereby reducing the amount of aggression within the group. As you will see in Chapter 13, a similar argument has been used to explain the increase in bullying that is associated with children's transitions into the new social environments of middle school.

Physiological factors also play an important role in the development of human aggression. For example, the hormone *testosterone* has often been cited as an explanation for the difference in the levels of aggression between boys and girls. There is a correlation between testosterone levels and aggression in both boys and girls during childhood (van Bokhoven et al., 2006). However, this correlation does not mean that testosterone directly causes aggressive behavior. Rather, researchers believe that testosterone may do so indirectly by increasing the child's activity level. In general, boys tend to have higher activity levels than girls and are more often involved in physical games that involve large groups of children. These differences might make physical aggression more functional, as well as more likely, for boys than for girls (Boulton, 1996; Coie & Dodge, 1998).

Social and Cultural Contributions

A second explanation for the causes of aggression, and for different levels of aggression, is that people learn to behave aggressively because aggression is sanctioned in their families, peer groups, or cultures. According to this perspective, children learn aggression by imitating the aggressive behaviors of others or because they are in some way rewarded for behaving aggressively (Cote et al., 2006). For example, in studies of aggression in nursery school children, Gerald Patterson and his colleagues found that in well over three-quarters of the cases, aggressive acts were followed by positive consequences for the aggressor: the victim either gave in or retreated (Patterson et al., 1967). Likewise, parents of aggressive children have been found to reward their children's aggressive behaviors by paying more attention to them, laughing, or otherwise signaling approval (Dishion et al., 2006).

Cross-cultural studies have yielded evidence both that children model the aggressive behavior of adults and that societies differ markedly in the levels of interpersonal violence they consider normal (Segall et al., 1997; see also the box, "The Spanking Controversy"). For example, Douglas Fry (1988) compared the levels of aggression of young children in two Zapotec Indian towns in central Mexico. On the basis of anthropological reports, Fry chose one town that was notable for the degree to which violence was controlled and a second town that was notable for the fact that people often fought at public gatherings, husbands beat their wives, and adults punished children by beating them with sticks.

Fry and his wife established residences in both towns so that they could get to know the people and develop enough rapport to be able to make their observations unobtrusively. They then collected several hours of observations of 12 children in each town as they played in their houses and around the neighborhood. When the researchers compared the aggressive acts of the children in the two towns, they found that those in the town with a reputation for violent behavior performed twice as many violent acts as the children in the other town.

Emotional and Cognitive Contributions

Another way to explore the development of aggression is to focus more particularly on how children feel and think about social situations that might provoke aggressive responses. Children's emotional reactions to events and their ability to regulate their emotional reactions depend importantly on how they interpret social contexts and on their ability to understand the emotions and intentions of others. It is known, for example, that

The Spanking Controversy

"This is gonna hurt me more than it hurts you."
— Prelude to a whuppin'

Two-year-old Mairin is starting to get the upper hand in her house—but not the kind of upper hand she had in mind. She throws her food across the kitchen, pitches tantrums when anyone touches "her" television, and recently got up and marched out the door when asked to sit still at the dinner table. So how's her mother responding? With a firm swat on the backside. "I know some people think it's awful," says her mother, "But how many of them have a 2-year-old?" (as reported by Costello, 2000).

Studies estimate that between 70 percent and 90 percent of parents in the United States spank their children at least occasionally. Punitive forms of discipline are more often associated with poverty. Surprisingly, as many as 75 percent of college-educated mothers spank their toddlers an average of 2.5 times per week (American Academy of Pediatrics, 1998). Recently, several states have passed laws explicitly granting parents the right to spank their children. The right to spank, moreover, extends well beyond the home front. Currently, 23 states currently permit the practice in public schools. A few years ago, a department-store Santa Claus was arrested in Boston for spanking a child who kept yanking his beard (Costello, 2000). He was quickly released to return to his duties and the admiring cheers of supporters who lined the streets to greet him.

In addition to being one of the more common forms of discipline in the United States, spanking is also one of the most controversial. Most parents do not like to hit their children and resort to spanking only after other tactics, such as reasoning and time-out, fail to produce the desired results. However, the argument made by those who oppose spanking is that it can damage children psychologically and emotionally. In fact, the practice has been outlawed in many European countries where public opinion takes a much dimmer view of its effectiveness. In Sweden, for example, only 11 percent of adults believe that spanking is an

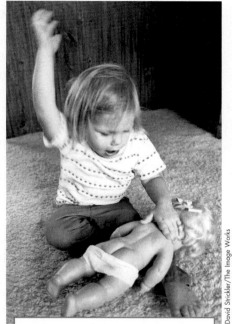

Spanking is outlawed in many countries because it is thought to contribute to the development of aggression in children.

David Strickler/The Image Works

appropriate method of discipline, whereas the vast majority of American parents endorse the practice (Day et al., 1998).

In the United States, most spanking is done by mothers, largely because they spend more time with their children compared with fathers (Dietz, 2000). Not surprisingly, individuals who were spanked as children are more likely to spank as parents (Rodriguez & Sutherland, 1999). In fact, the acceptability of spanking varies not only among families, but among geographic regions. In the United States, for example, spanking is more common and acceptable in the South compared with other regions (Straus & Stewart, 1999).

Spanking is also more common in African American families, perhaps because of the stigma attached to active African American children, particularly boys. According to Howard Stevenson and his colleagues (2001), African American parents may feel

pressure to limit the mobility of their children because it causes tension and anxiety in authority figures. There is added concern that if the African American child is not controlled at home, he or she will receive harsher discipline not only from the law but also from other authority figures who do not understand black culture and life experiences.

Is spanking an effective form of discipline? This question is at the heart of developmental research on the effects of spanking, as well as the advice given to parents by pediatricians and other child-care experts. In general, developmentalists discourage the practice. A host of studies link physical discipline to increased aggression and low self-esteem in children and adolescents. Vonnie McLoyd and Julia Smith (2002), for example, followed more than 2000 children from three different racial-ethnic groups over a period of 6 years, and found that spanking predicted an increase in children's problem behaviors over time. In addition, abusive parents are known to spank their children more than nonabusive parents, prompting speculation that relying on spanking may increase parents' risk for using more severe forms of punishment (Walsh, 2002).

On the other hand, some studies suggest that physical discipline does not inevitably place children at risk for later problems. The consequences of spanking seem to depend on other dimensions of parenting that tend to be associated with spanking. For example, many parents who spank are also more emotionally rejecting and less involved with their children. In the study described above, McLoyd and Smith (2002) found that the negative effects of spanking are particularly pronounced when parents provide low levels of emotional support. However, when parents provide high levels of warmth and emotional support, the negative effects typically associated with spanking disappear. Nevertheless, the bulk of research, as well as professional opinion, urges parents to seek alternatives to spanking. After many years of relative silence on the subject, the American Academy of Pediatrics has recently issued a statement indicating that the practice is harmful to both children and parents.

aggressive children often misinterpret social interactions in negative ways that lead them to respond aggressively (Coie & Dodge, 1998).

According to one view, aggression has its origins in the negative affect that arises in frustrating or otherwise unpleasant (aversive) situations (Berkowitz, 2003). These general negative feelings might result, for example, when a child fails to achieve

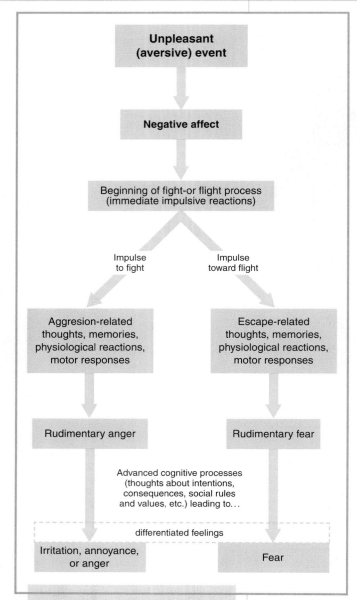

Figure 9.7 According to Len Berkowitz, aggression has its source in the negative feelings aroused by an unpleasant event but these feelings can be significantly modified by cognitive processes.

a goal, encounters a parent's disapproval, or is rejected by a peer. The negative feelings initiate a fight-or-flight process, an impulsive reaction to be aggressive or to withdraw. The impulse to fight is associated with aggression-related thoughts, memories, physiological reactions, and motor responses; the flight impulse has corresponding escape-related associations. In this way, the initial general negative feelings become the more specific emotions of rudimentary, or basic, anger or fear, for the fight-and-flight impulses, respectively. These rudimentary emotions can be significantly modified by cognitive processes, including the child's anticipation of consequences or thoughts about what he or she understands to be acceptable behavior. As a result, the child experiences more differentiated feelings—feelings different from and more complex than the rudimentary anger or fear—and the response of the child whose initial impulse was aggressive may or may not be aggression.

Suppose, for example, that a preschooler is playing with a toy and a playmate takes it away. According to the model shown in Figure 9.7, the child will experience negative feelings, and, depending on his temperament and past social experiences, he may be inclined to act aggressively. However, if he has internalized the "no hitting" rule of the classroom and knows that violating the rule carries the consequence of time-out, as a result of his thought processes he may, instead of furiously pushing his playmate in order to retrieve the toy, become annoyed and enlist the help of his teacher.

Developmentalists are building a strong case for the role of thought processes in children's aggressive behavior. A major influence on young children's aggressive tendencies is their understanding of their own and others' emotions, goals, and behaviors, and of how these are all linked together. The general argument is that children who have a more advanced understanding of emotions, including what causes them and how they are expressed, will be less likely to behave aggressively (Halberstadt et al., 2001; Lemerise & Arsenio, 2000; Arsenio, 2004).

Susanne Denham and her colleagues (Denham et al., 2002) tested this argument in a longitudinal study that followed 127 children between preschool and kindergarten. The researchers used puppets to assess children's emotional knowledge. The procedure involved asking children questions about a puppet's emotions in a variety of circumstances—its basic emotions ("What does she look like when she's sad?"), its emotions in particular situations ("What does she look like when she's had a nightmare?"), and its emotions in social situations that require masking emotions ("What does she look like if she's getting teased, but if she shows she's upset, she'll get teased even more?"). The children responded by choosing and attaching a face to the puppet. Children's anger and aggressive behaviors were assessed through both naturalistic observation of their play and through teacher reports. In general, the researchers found that both boys and girls who in preschool had less advanced knowledge of emotions and their expression were, in kindergarten, more likely to behave aggressively toward their peers.

Another study of preschoolers looked at how beliefs about aggression—specifically, the belief that aggression is an enduring trait of individuals rather than a changeable behavior—might contribute to children's use of aggression (Giles & Heyman, 2003). Jessica Giles and Gail Heyman argued that children who take an

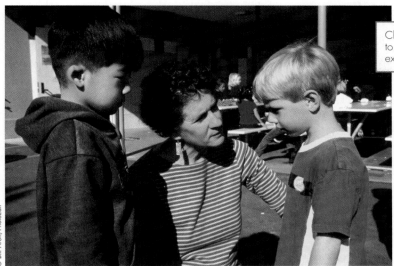

Children rely on adults to help them regulate the expression of emotions.

essentialist view of aggression—that is, believe that individuals who are aggressive in one situation will very likely be aggressive in the future—may be more likely to jump to conclusions about the hostile intention of a peer who behaves aggressively, and therefore be more likely to endorse the use of aggressive solutions.

To test preschoolers' essentialist beliefs about aggression, Giles and Heyman presented a group of 100 children with brief scenarios such as "Imagine there is a new girl in your class. She steals things from people, calls people mean names, and trips kids at recess. Do you think this new girl will always act this way?" Some children tended to believe that aggressiveness would endure over time, whereas others rejected this idea.

The children's endorsement of aggressive solutions was tested by presenting scenarios such as "Renee scribbled all over Belinda's art project. So Belinda hit Renee. What else could Belinda have done to solve the problem?" Some children said things such as "Well, she could kick her instead"; others, however, provided more socially appropriate solutions such as "She could tell the teacher." Consistent with their hypothesis, Giles and Heyman found that children who believed in aggressiveness as an enduring trait were more likely to endorse aggressive solutions.

Using testing methods such as those described above, developmentalists are amassing significant evidence that aggression must be understood in light of children's thoughts and beliefs about their own and others' emotional lives. This general idea suggests the possibility of controlling aggression by using reason. Though it is sometimes difficult to hold a rational discussion with a 4-year-old who has just grabbed a toy away from a playmate, discussions that emphasize how aggression hurts another person, and how conflicts can be resolved by sharing and taking turns, have been found to reduce aggression even at this early age (Erdley & Asher, 1999).

In contrast to employing cognitive strategies to help children select nonaggressive solutions, many people believe that aggression can best be controlled by providing children with harmless ways to be aggressive. This belief is based on the assumption that unless aggressive urges are "vented" in a safe way, they build up until they explode violently. There is little convincing evidence to support this belief (Bemak & Young, 1998). Nonetheless, the idea that venting releases negative emotions continues to be widely applied in psychotherapy with young, troubled children.

||||| APPLY ⬝ CONNECT ⬝ DISCUSS

Based on evidence presented in this section, design an activity for preschoolers that might reduce their aggressive behavior.

Developing Prosocial Behaviors

David: I'm a missile robot who can shoot missiles out of my fingers. I can shoot them out of everywhere—even out of my legs. I'm a missile robot.
Josh: (tauntingly) No, you're a fart robot.
David: (protestingly) No, I'm a missile robot.
Josh: No, you're a fart robot.
David: (hurt, almost in tears) No, Josh!
Josh: (recognizing that David is upset) And I'm a poo-poo robot.
David: (in good spirits again) I'm a pee-pee robot.

(From Rubin, 1980, p. 55)

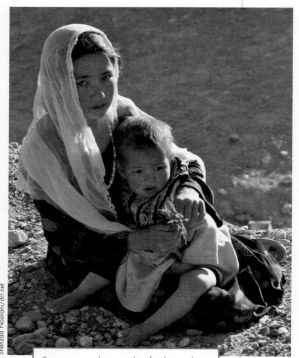

Sensitive to the needs of others, this girl from the Hazara ethnic group in Afghanistan provides care for her young sibling.

As suggested in the dialogue above, young children can be remarkably sensitive to the emotional needs of their playmates. Josh not only recognized his friend's distress at being teased but was able to remedy the situation by making similar deprecating remarks about himself. Such diplomacy becomes relatively common during early childhood as children acquire a number of sophisticated prosocial skills.

Prosocial behavior is defined as voluntary action intended to benefit others (Eisenberg et al., 2006). Sharing, helping, caregiving, and showing compassion are all examples of prosocial behaviors. The psychological states that corresponds to prosocial behavior in the way that anger corresponds to aggression are *empathy* and *sympathy*.

Empathy

Empathy, the sharing of another person's emotions and feelings, is widely believed to provide the essential foundations for prosocial behavior (Eisenberg & Fabes, 2006). According to Martin Hoffman, a child can feel empathy for another person at any age. As children develop, however, their ability to empathize broadens and they become better able to interpret and respond appropriately to the distress of others.

Hoffman has proposed that empathy develops in four stages significantly linked to stages in the child's self-development. The first stage occurs during the first year of life. As we noted earlier, babies as young as 2 days become stressed and cry at the sound of another infant's cries (Dondi, Simion, & Caltran, 1999). Hoffman calls this phenomenon *global empathy*. These early cries are akin to innate reflexes, since babies obviously can have no understanding of the feelings of others. Yet they respond as if they were having those feelings themselves.

During the second year of life, as children develop a sense of themselves as distinct individuals, their responses to others' distress change, and *egocentric empathy* emerges. Now when babies are confronted by someone who is distressed, they are capable of understanding that it is the other person who is upset. This realization allows children to turn their attention from concern for their own comfort to comforting others. Since they have difficulty keeping other people's points of view in mind, however, some of their attempts to help may be inappropriate and *egocentric* (see p. 277), such as giving a security blanket to an adult who looks upset.

The third stage of empathy occurs in early childhood when role-taking skills increase. Being able to distinguish one's own emotional needs from those of another allows the child to respond in a way that is less egocentric and more sensitive to the other. In addition, the increasing command of language vastly increases the contexts in which children can behave empathically. Language allows children to empathize with people who are expressing their feelings verbally, without visible emotions, as well as with people who are not present. Information gained indirectly through stories, pictures, or television permits children to empathize with people whom they have never met. (The fourth stage of empathy emerges in middle childhood, when the child understands that emotional responses may be tied to an individual's unique history of past experiences.)

Note that Hoffman's theory of empathy is linked to Piaget's theory of cognitive development. Each new stage of empathy corresponds to a new stage of cognitive ability in which decreasing egocentrism (and increasing *decentration*, see p. 276) allows children to understand themselves better in relation to others.

Perhaps because it is linked so closely to what children understand, Hoffman's explanation of the development of empathy tends to leave out how they feel. It is tacitly assumed that the more children understand, the more intensely they adopt the feelings of the person in distress. The catch, as Judy Dunn (1988) points out, is that children may understand perfectly well why another child is in distress and feel glad as a result.

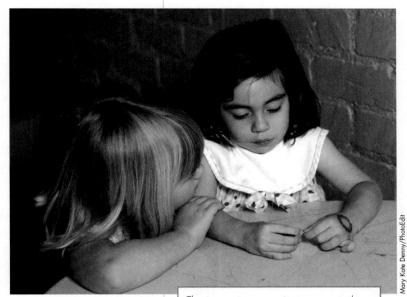

The increasing capacity to separate her own emotional state from that of others contributes to this preschooler's effectiveness in responding empathically to her distressed friend.

Sympathy

Other researchers have been more attentive to the emotional component of empathy, particularly regarding its role in prosocial behaviors. One of the best examples is the work of Nancy Eisenberg and her colleagues (Eisenberg et al., 2007). Similarly to Hoffman, Eisenberg sees empathy as an emotional reaction that stems from and is similar to what is experienced by another. However, she proposes that empathy often turns into sympathy and/or personal distress. **Sympathy** involves feelings of sorrow or concern for another person. A child who is being sympathetic is not feeling the same emotion as the other person. Instead, he or she feels "other-oriented concern." In contrast, **personal distress** is a self-focused emotional reaction in the face of another's distress.

Eisenberg argues that it is important to distinguish between sympathy and personal distress because they have entirely different consequences for prosocial behavior. For example, when shown films that depict characters who are distressed, children who exhibit concern or sadness are more likely to engage in prosocial behaviors than are children who exhibit personal distress (Eisenberg, Spinrad, & Sadovsky, 2006).

Personal distress, according to Eisenberg, stems from empathic overarousal in response to the negative emotions of another (Eisenberg & Fabes, 1992). When another person's distress generates too much negative emotion in the child, the result is a focus on the self, rather than the other-directed focus that underlies sympathy. Not surprisingly, personal distress is associated with poor social skills.

A deciding factor in whether the child's initial empathic response becomes personal distress or sympathy is the child's capacity to regulate his or her emotions. The relationship between emotional regulation and sympathy is illustrated in a series of studies involving 6- to 8-year olds. The studies focused on three variables: (1) general emotional intensity, the children's personal tendencies to respond to another's distress with strong feelings; (2) emotional regulation, the ability to modulate their negative feelings; and (3) sympathy, the expression of concern for the other. The first study found that children who were rated low in regulation were also low in sympathy, regardless of their general emotional

prosocial behavior Behavior such as sharing, helping, caregiving, and showing compassion.

empathy Sharing another person's emotions and feelings.

sympathy Feelings of sorrow or concern for another.

personal distress A self-focused emotional reaction to another person's distress.

intensity (Eisenberg et al., 1996). However, for those children who could regulate their emotions, greater emotional intensity was associated with greater levels of sympathy.

The second study went one step further and examined how attention focusing—another form of self-regulation—might enter into the picture (Eisenberg et al., 1998). The researchers argued that children who are more capable of focusing their attention may take in more information about other people and their circumstances, leading to increased perspective taking and, by extension, greater sympathy. They found that children who were low in emotional intensity and attention focusing were also low in sympathy. However, children who were low in emotional intensity but high in attention focusing were relatively high in sympathy.

All of this suggests that sympathy results from an optimal level of emotional arousal but that an optimal level can be achieved by different routes. Children who are inclined to extreme emotional reactions need to be able to regulate their emotions in order to be sympathetic. For children who are not as emotional, the ability to focus attention on others may enhance their understanding of others' needs.

APPLY ▪ CONNECT ▪ DISCUSS

From a Vygotskian perspective, what might account for whether children react to someone's distress with their own personal distress or with sympathy?

Taking One's Place in the Social Group

The kindergartners in Vivian Paley's classroom are discussing the story of Tico, a wingless bird who is cared for by his black-winged friends.

In the story, the wishingbird visits Tico one night and grants him a wish. Tico wishes for golden wings. When his friends see his golden wings in the morning, they are angry. They abandon him because he wants to be better than they are. Tico is upset by his friends' rejection and wants to gain readmission to the group. He discovers that he can exchange his golden feathers for black ones by performing good deeds. When at last he has replaced all the golden feathers with black ones, he is granted readmission by the flock, whose members comment, "Now you are just like us" (Leoni, 1964).

> Teacher: I don't think it's fair that Tico has to give up his golden wings.
> Lisa: It is fair. See, he was nicer when he didn't have any wings. They didn't like him when he had gold.
> Wally: He thinks he's better if he has golden wings.
> Eddie: He is better.
> Jill: But he's not supposed to be better. The wishingbird was wrong to give him those wings.
> Deana: She has to give him his wish. He's the one who shouldn't have asked for golden wings.
> Wally: He could put black wings on top of the golden wings and try to trick them.
> Deana: They'd sneak up and see the gold. He should just give every bird one golden feather and keep one for himself.
> Teacher: Why can't he decide for himself what kind of wings he wants?
> Wally: He has to decide to have black wings.

(Paley, 1981, pp. 25–26)

This conversation shows that the children understand that by wishing for golden wings, Tico has wished himself a vision of perfection. Each child has done the same thing countless times: "I'm the beautiful princess"; "I'm Superman; I'll save the world." For the blissful, magic moments when the world of play holds sway, perfection is attainable, even by a lowly bird or a preschool child. Wally and his friends also appreciate the dilemmas of perfection. In their eyes, Tico not only thinks he is better but is better—yet he is not supposed to be. Try as they may to conceive of a way for Tico to retain his prized possessions, the children realize that conformity is unavoidable. Wally's summary is difficult to improve upon: Tico has to choose to conform.

The children's discussion of Tico and his community of birds reveals more than an appreciation of the heavy hand of society as it is experienced by children everywhere. It also shows the children's awareness that individuals have a responsibility for regulating social relations. They understand that it is the wishingbird's job to grant wishes and therefore not the wishingbird's fault that Tico wished to be better than the others. Tico should have been able to control himself and make a reasonable wish.

This story returns us to the theme with which this chapter began—that socialization and personality development are two aspects of a single process. When children engage in acts of sharing and comforting, they reveal their ability to know another person's mental state. At the same time, they are displaying their own ways of thinking and feeling—in other words, their personalities.

Before we turn in Part IV to the wide range of new roles and rules that children encounter in middle childhood and the corresponding changes that take place in their sense of themselves, we need to round out the discussion of early childhood by investigating the range of contexts and social influences that make up the world of the young child. As we shall see in Chapter 10, even young children are exposed to a great variety of social influences and cultural prescriptions. It is in the course of dealing with the variety of concrete circumstances that structure their everyday experiences that children create the synthesis of cognition and emotion called personality and acquire their personal and social identities.

This little girl's ability to understand her brother's mental state helps her draw him into the storybook, providing an opportunity for sharing a happy emotional experience.

SUMMARY

- Children's social and emotional lives develop along two paths—that of socialization, through which they acquire the standards, values, and knowledge of their society, and that of personality formation, through which they develop their own unique patterns of feeling, thinking, and behaving in a wide variety of situations.

Identity Development

- Crucial to socialization is identification, a psychological process in which children try to look, act, feel, and be like significant people in their social environment. Identification includes acquisition of sex-role and ethnic identities.

- Sex-role identity development has been explained in various ways:

  - In Freud's psychodynamic view, children in the phallic stage experience the Oedipus complex (Electra complex in the case of girls), which they resolve by identifying with the same-sex parent, at around the age of 4 or 5.

  - According to the social learning view, identification occurs through modeling, in which children observe and imitate people of their sex, and through differential reinforcement, in which they are rewarded for gender-appropriate behavior.

  - In Kohlberg's cognitive-developmental approach, sex-role development goes through three stages—labeling oneself as a boy or girl, understanding the stability of sex roles, and, finally, understanding sex-role constancy—following which sex-role identity guides thoughts and actions.

  - According to gender schema theory, children form mental models with information about males and females (gender schemas), which then guide their interpretations and actions.

  - In the cultural view, gender categories are tools of culture, mediating children's behavior by their content and by the extent to which they are rigid.

- Ethnic identity is the sense of belonging to an ethnic group, and the associated feelings and attitudes. Young children show awareness of the status of their own and other groups. Parents can communicate different sorts of ethnic-related messages.

- Young children's personal identity, or sense of self, tends to be fluid and, as reflected in self-descriptions, focused on disconnected concrete attributes as well as unrealistically positive. Caregivers contribute to children's developing sense of self by helping them create an autobiographical memory, or personal narrative.

A New Moral World

- According to Freud's psychodynamic view, children's internalization of adult standards and rules results, at about age 5, in the formation of the superego, a third personality structure (along with the already existing id and ego), which then functions within the child to regulate the child's behavior.

- The cognitive-developmental view held by Piaget maintains that, as part of broader cognitive developments, children's moral reasoning moves from a focus on external authority and objective consequences to, in middle childhood, a sense of morality as personally chosen.

- According to social domain theory, young children can distinguish among three categories of rules—moral rules, social conventions, and personal sphere rules. The boundaries between these categories vary across and within cultures.

Developing Self-regulation

- The ability to control one's thoughts, behaviors, and emotions, referred to as self-regulation, is considered a cornerstone of children's development. Children must regulate myriad thoughts and actions to solve problems or achieve social goals.

- According to Vygotsky, play is important in the development of self-regulation, in part because it requires control of thoughts and actions. Sociodramatic play is particularly important, as children must negotiate a shared understanding of the evolving situation and control their thoughts and actions to enact their roles.

- To function socially, young children must learn to interpret the emotional states of others, manage their own emotions, and mask their feelings when necessary—all part of socioemotional competence, the ability to behave appropriately in social situations that evoke strong emotions.

- Cultures can influence the development of children's emotions and of their regulation of emotions.

Understanding Aggression

- Aggression may be hostile aggression, intended to hurt someone in some way, or instrumental aggression, intended to achieve a particular goal. Along with having different purposes, aggression can take different forms, for example, teasing and physical aggression.

- Boys' and girls' uses of aggression differs after age 2, with boys more likely to use direct, physical aggression but girls more likely to use relational aggression, a kind of indirect aggression aimed at excluding a child or harming their friendships.

- Developmentalists studying causes and control of aggression have focused on:

  - Biological contributions: Aggression is evident across animal species, a natural consequence of competition for resources. In groups of human children, as in other species, the development of dominance hierarchies can control aggression. Testosterone may indirectly increase aggression by increasing activity level.

  - Social and cultural contributions: Children learn aggression through imitation of adults or by being rewarded for aggressive behaviors. Cross-cultural studies have found a correlation between levels of adult violence and children's aggressive behaviors.

  - Emotional and cognitive contributions: Negative feelings in frustrating situations may or may not lead to violence, depending on factors including the child's cognitions. Children who have a better understanding of emotions and their expression are less likely to behave aggressively.

Developing Prosocial Behaviors

- Prosocial behavior, voluntary action intended to benefit others, may have as its foundation empathy, the sharing of another person's emotions and feelings. Development of empathy in early childhood may correspond to decreasing egocentrism.

- According to some developmentalists, empathic feelings may, depending on emotional regulation, become sympathy (feelings of sorrow or concern for another) or personal distress, with sympathy more likely to lead to prosocial behavior.

Taking One's Place in the Social Group

- Young children are increasingly able to understand others' mental states and to be aware that individuals have a responsibility for regulating social relations. They also increasingly display their own ways of thinking and feeling.

Key Terms

socialization, p. 301
personality formation, p. 302
initiative versus guilt, p. 303
identification, p. 303
gender segregation, p. 303
phallic stage, p. 304
Oedipus complex, p. 304
Electra complex, p. 305
modeling, p. 305
differential reinforcement, p. 305
gender schema, p. 307

ethnic identity, p. 309
ethnic socialization, p. 310
personal identity, p. 311
autobiographical memory, p. 312
id, p. 314
ego, p. 3xx, p. 314
superego, p. 314
heteronomous morality, p. 314
social domain theory, p. 315
self-regulation, p. 316
effortful control, p. 317

sociodramatic play, p. 319
socioemotional competence, p. 323
hostile aggression, p. 325
instrumental aggression, p. 325
relational aggression, p. 326
prosocial behavior, p. 332
empathy, p. 332
sympathy, p. 333
personal distress, p. 333

10

Contexts of Development

Africa is the continent of drums. Formed from the wood of special trees and animal skins, drums are slapped or beaten with sticks to celebrate birth, mourn the dead, and coronate kings. When beaten with special skill and grace, the drums of the Republic of Burundi resemble rolling thunderclaps; they are to be heard "not with your ear, but your heartbeat." For 13-year-old Thierry, beating the drums with his friends, all orphans of Burundi's genocidal war, is a source of pride and honor. Thierry and his friends are among 823,000 war orphans, 20,000 of whom lead desperate lives on the streets. Although such a dire existence places children at considerable risk for a number of physical, emotional, and intellectual problems, the lives of Thierry and his friends have taken a decided turn for the better. They have been recruited to a special program sponsored by UNICEF, which provides war orphans, including former child soldiers, with homes, education, and life skills, while also promoting Burundi's cultural traditions, such as beating the sacred drums. The newfound hope of young Thierry and his friends was apparent when they met with an international peace delegation and explained how young people must avoid the mistakes of their elders and work together in beating the drums and rebuilding their country. Education, Thierry emphasized, is essential to Burundi's children, as well as to its future as a nation.

t is hard to imagine what it might be like growing up on the street in Burundi, where "family" may be nothing more than a few other child associates with whom you steal food; where "education" involves learning how to avoid being captured by soldiers who would force you to fight in a war you do not understand; where "neighborhood" is a territory scarred by burned and abandoned buildings; and where "government"—including the policies and programs meant to provide a safety net in times of strife—has been brought to its knees by years of civil war. The importance of these contexts for children's health and well-being is recognized by developmental scientists and practitioners, and inspires the efforts of international organizations such as UNICEF to help children like Thierry by repairing the damaged contexts of their lives and development, or by creating new ones.

Families, neighborhoods, schools, governments, the media—these and other settings constitute the contexts of children's development. As we shift our attention to these contexts, it is helpful to remember Urie Bronfenbrenner's idea that children's development occurs within nested, interacting ecosystems (see Figure 1.4, p. 29). The innermost system is the *microsystem,* which includes the various settings children experience directly in their daily lives, such as the home, the church, the neighborhood, and the child-care center. The *mesosystem* comprises connections among these microsystem settings, for example, parents' involvement with their children's school. Elements of the *exosystem,* such as caregivers' workplaces, government agencies, and the mass media, may influence children either directly, as television does, or indirectly, through their impact on parents and other family

These Burundi children, displaced by genocidal violence, engage in the traditional practice of beating drums.

Danita Delimont/Alamy

members. The outermost *macrosystem* includes cultural values and beliefs that infuse the entire ecology, affecting everything from the content of television to educational programs and health-care policies to beliefs parents have about how to raise their children.

Our discussion of the major contexts of children's development begins with the more immediate and personal contexts of *family* and *child care*. We then move to consider the broader contexts of *neighborhoods and communities* before discussing what may be the broadest context that directly influences children—the *media*. As you read this chapter, you will come to appreciate how each context can provide children with resources for positive growth and development, or present significant challenges and risks to health and well-being.

The Family Context

According to an ancient Latin proverb, "the hand that rocks the cradle rules the world." Although each child's development is shaped by many hands—teachers, coaches, and playmates and other peers—the hand of the family is the first influence on the child and remains one of the most significant. Through their traditions, routines, stories, and cultural artifacts, families communicate their perceptions and values about the world to their children, and shape their children's behavior and how they relate to the world (Pratt & Fiese, 2004).

A classic study by Beatrice and John Whiting (1975) illustrates how differences in family life influence children's development. The Whitings organized teams of anthropologists to observe child rearing in six communities from vastly different cultures. A comparison of two of the groups, the Gusii of Nyansongo, Kenya, and Americans in a small New England town, demonstrates how cultural belief systems, practices, and economics are expressed in family contexts, affecting the way parents treat and socialize their children.

At the time of the Whitings' work, the 1950s, the Gusii were agriculturalists living in the fertile highlands of western Kenya. The basic family unit was large, commonly including three generations headed by a grandfather. Polygyny was the traditional marriage form, with several wives living in a compound that included a separate house for the husband. Women, who did most of the farm work, often left their infants and toddlers in the care of older siblings and elderly family members. As is typical of farming societies, children's labor was important in the production of food, in the care of younger children, and in household maintenance. Beginning at the age of 3 or 4, Gusii children were expected to start helping their mothers with simple domestic tasks. By the age of 7, their economic contributions to the family were indispensable.

The small New England town, referred to as "Orchard Town" by the researchers, represented the opposite extreme in family organization and social complexity. Most of the men of Orchard Town were wage earners who lived with their wives and children in single-family dwellings. A few of the mothers had part-time jobs, but most were full-time homemakers. The children of Orchard Town divided their time between playing at home (they were rarely asked to do chores) and attending school.

The Whitings' observations of children's behavior patterns in these two cultures documented notable overall differences. The Gusii children, for example, were more likely to offer help and support and make responsible suggestions to others. At the same time, they were more likely to reprimand and behave aggressively with other children. Both of these tendencies are consistent with their child-tending duties: They needed to be nurturing and responsible, but they also needed to exert high levels of control both for safety's sake and to communicate the cultural value of respecting one's elders.

Orchard Town children, in contrast, were more often observed seeking, rather than giving, help and attention, and were more often observed engaging in sociable horseplay, touching others, and joining groups in an amiable way. According to the Whitings, children of industrialized societies, such as those in Orchard Town, are less nurturing and responsible because they do not contribute economically to the family, and because they spend most days in school competing with other children rather than helping them. On the other hand, the higher level of intimacy shown by the Orchard Town children is likely a reflection of the close bonds that develop between individuals living in small families. Gusii, in contrast, socialize attachments to the broader group, consistent with a family living pattern that includes many members from several generations.

The Biocultural Origins of Family

Cultural comparisons like the one conducted by the Whitings show us that families can differ in many ways that affect children's lives and development. Take a moment to think about your own family. Were you raised by one parent, or two, or even three, or perhaps by a grandparent? Do you have brothers and sisters? Half-siblings or step-siblings? Did other people or relatives live with you while you were growing up? An important feature that defines your family is the members it includes and their relationships to you and each other. Developmentalists use the term **family structure** to refer to how a family is organized socially. There are two major forms of family structure—**nuclear families,** which consist of parents (including single parents) and their children, and **extended families,** which consist of parents (again including single parents) and their children as well as other kin, who may include grandparents, cousins, aunts and uncles, and others. Why are some families nuclear, while others are extended? And what difference does

In many cultures, children care for younger children. This responsibility requires both nurturance and control.

family structure The social organization of a family. Most commonly, nuclear or extended.

nuclear families Families consisting of parents (including single parents) and their children.

extended families A family in which not only parents and their children but other kin—grandparents, cousins, nephews, or more distant family relations—share a household.

family organization make in the lives and development of children? As you will see below, answers to these questions hinge on the cultural and evolutionary processes that influence how families are socially organized.

Family and Culture A major source for understanding the origins and significance of family is the historical work of Philippe Ariès (1962). According to Ariès, the nuclear family is a highly private structure unique to modern societies. Especially in the late eighteenth and early nineteenth centuries, large migrations from rural areas into newly industrialized cities contributed to a shift from extended family farm life to nuclear family patterns. In the relative isolation of nuclear families, close, intimate relationships between parents and children took on greater importance than the less personal relationships that bind children to their ancestral line, which had been central in the traditional extended family pattern. The greater isolation of nuclear families had other repercussions for children's lives. For example, Ariès contrasts the private nuclear family with the more sociable families of premodern times, in which "people lived on top of one another, masters and servants, children and adults, in houses open at all hours." Children reared in these conditions were exposed to an enormous diversity of roles, relationships, and patterns of interacting—experiences quite different from those of children growing up in nuclear families.

Despite the predominance of the nuclear family structure in the United States, the proportion of extended families has been steadily increasing in recent decades. According to the most recent U.S. Census report (Simmons & O'Connell, 2003), approximately 8 percent of all children live in a family that includes a grandparent; two-thirds of such families include one or more parents. This pattern is more likely to occur when a nuclear family cannot afford housing costs on its own, when the mother is young and single, or when cultural traditions and values are consistent with extended-family living arrangements, as they are among immigrants of Hispanic descent (Goodman & Satya, 2007). A strong grandparenting

This extended family from a remote Bhutan village in the Himalaya mountains gathers in the prayer room of their earthen house, around the food they will prepare and eat over the course of a week.

tradition is also apparent in African American families, in which grand-mothers have been esteemed as the "guardian of the generations" (Crewe, 2003; Goodman & Silverstein, 2006).

Many scholars see the extended family as a natural strategy for deal-ing with the combined handicaps of low income and low social stand-ing (Goodman & Silverstein, 2006). Young, economically disadvan-taged minority children are particularly likely to benefit from the problem-solving and stress-reducing resources provided by the extended family (Smith, 2002). Moreover, for children living in a single-parent nuclear family, grandparents and other members of the extended fam-ily often appear to be an important source of support. Indeed, a na-tionwide study conducted in Sweden found that in the absence of help from extended family members, children in single-parent homes are at heightened risk for injury and death (Weitoft et al., 2003). Interestingly, recent studies of hunter–gatherer societies in the Amazon forest of Peru and Tanzania found that children with only one biological parent were more likely to live with extended family than those with two parents (Sugiyama & Chacon, 2005; Marlowe, 2005).

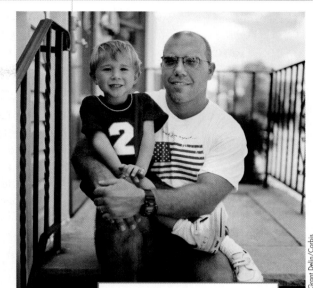

Eugene, a single father who lost his wife in the Sept. 11 tragedy, quit his job in order to care for his son, Jason.

Grant Delin/Corbis

Family and Evolution Extended kin make a difference in the lives of children because they provide essential *resources,* including food, income, child care, and help in maintaining the household, as well as less tangible assistance in the form of emotional support and counseling, and, in some cultures, opportunities for mothers to improve the family's economic situation by furthering their education (Jarrett, 2000). Such significant contributions to child and family well-being have been recognized by anthropologists and evolutionary theorists who study **allo-caregiving,** that is, child care and protection provided by group members other than the parents (Hewlitt & Lamb, 2005). Allocaregivers may include a child's siblings, uncles, aunts, and grandmothers, as well as nonkin such as foster children who live in the group. Several studies of highly diverse cultures have found that the help of allocaregivers increases the likelihood that mothers will have more children (see Hrdy, 2007, for review). Some of these studies have shown the ad-vantages of having a grandmother living with the family, others the importance of having a big sister. For example, in villages in Micronesia, the Caribbean, and Gambia, West Africa, it has been found that women whose firstborn child is a daughter tend to have more births, and more *surviving* children than women whose firstborn is a son.

Evidence that allocaregiving increases mothers' reproductive success has also been documented in nonhuman species. In addition to humans, many species of birds, as well as wild dogs, lions, and elephants, form networks of support in which nonparental individuals contribute resources toward rearing the young—that is, networks of allocaregivers—a practice referred to as **cooperative breeding** (Heinsohn & Double, 2004). Cooperative breeding is rather rare in the animal kingdom (estimates are that 8–17 percent of bird species, and only 3 percent of mammalian species, breed cooperatively). However, when it occurs it results not only in more numerous births and larger, healthier offspring but also in prolonged periods of childhood dependency as offspring can take longer to mature without becoming too burdensome to their mothers, who are busy producing new off-spring (Hrdy, 2007; McDonald, et al., 2008).

With respect to our own species, evidence regarding the consequences of co-operative breeding has ignited a fascinating controversy about why our children take so long to mature. According to the traditional view, an extended childhood evolved in our species because it provides the time necessary for the maturation

allocaregiving Child care and protection provided by group members other than the parents, usually other relatives.

cooperative breeding In humans and cer-tain other species, a system involving net-works of support in which individuals other than parents contribute resources toward rearing the young.

of our large and complex brains, and the development of cognitive, symbolic and linguistic skills, and other tools of culture important to our children's survival and success. In Darwinian terms, *natural selection* assures that individuals with *phenotypically* large and complex brains, and the spectacular cognitive, social, and linguistic skills that go along with them, are more likely to reproduce than individuals with less complex brains (presumably due to shorter childhoods; see Chapter 2, pp. 60–61). From this perspective delayed maturation is a by-product of brain evolution; we have long childhoods because we grow big brains. Evolutionary theorists who study cooperative breeding, however, have turned this perspective on its head, arguing that we grow big brains because we have long childhoods, and we have long childhoods because we have families. More specifically, the lengthy childhood enabled by the resources of extended family networks opened the door that allowed brain evolution to occur.

Parenting Practices

Regardless of who raised us, or how, there can be little doubt that the caregiving we received growing up has had a powerful impact on who we are today. As you will see below, virtually all individuals who raise children share a common set of goals. Efforts to reach these goals, however, vary considerably depending on the family's ecological context, cultural values, and beliefs about how children should behave.

Parenting Goals On the basis of his study of child-rearing practices in diverse cultures, the anthropologist Robert LeVine (1988) has proposed that three major goals are shared by parents the world over:

1. *The survival goal:* to ensure that their children survive, by providing for their health and safety.

2. *The economic goal:* to ensure that their children acquire the skills and other resources needed to be economically productive adults.

3. *The cultural goal:* to ensure that their children acquire the basic cultural values of the group.

These goals form a hierarchy. The most urgent goal for parents is their children's physical survival. It is not until the safety and health of their children appear secure that parents can focus on the other two goals, passing on the economically important skills and cultural values the children will need as adults to ensure the continued existence of their family and community.

LeVine found that the way parents raise their children reflects the extent to which any of these goals is threatened by the local ecology. For example, child-care practices in places with high infant mortality rates look fairly uniform throughout the world. In places as different as Africa, South America, and Indonesia, when there is a general threat to children's physical survival, parents tend to keep their infants on their bodies at all times, respond quickly to infants' cries, and nurse their babies often. Under such threat conditions, parents show little concern for the emotional and behavioral development of their infants and young children, rarely attempting, for example, to elicit smiles from their babies or engage them in vocal play. In contrast, in places where children's physical survival is more or less guaranteed, parents are more likely to focus on ensuring their children's future economic success. In industrialized societies, for example, where education is crucial to earning a living wage, many child-care practices are oriented toward enhancing cognitive development and supporting "school readiness" and children's achievement in the classroom. Indeed, as you may recall from Chapter 5, parents in the United States spend more than $1 billion each year on products designed to stimulate brain and intellectual development in their infants and young children.

Thus, LeVine's approach allows us to understand both the universality of parental goals and the diversity of parenting practices observed throughout the world. For example, it gives us insight into the "no-nonsense parenting" often practiced by African American single mothers (Brody & Murry, 2001; Steele et al., 2005). **No-nonsense parenting** is characterized by a mixture of high parental control, including physical restraint and punishment, and warm affection. Developmentalists who study no-nonsense parenting in African American families find that it is used more frequently by mothers living in urban areas than by those in rural areas, and by mothers who are better educated. This pattern is consistent with LeVine's approach, which would suggest that no-nonsense parenting, with its mix of control and warmth, is a protective response to the threats—social as well as physical—that urban life poses for children, especially in inner cities. Similarly, better-educated mothers may have higher aspirations for their children and consequently exert high levels of control over their behavior to see that they do what is needed to succeed.

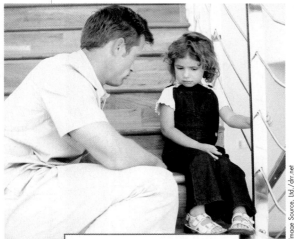

This father disciplines his daughter by attempting to explain why her behavior was wrong.

Parenting Styles Research in the United States has shown that while child-rearing practices vary widely, they can be analyzed using measures of parental warmth and control. This research addresses the question: What mix of control, autonomy, and expression of affection contributes most to healthy development?

In the early 1970s, Diana Baumrind (1971, 1980) launched what would become one of the best-known research programs on the developmental consequences of *parenting style*. On the basis of interviews and observations of predominantly white, middle-class preschoolers and their parents, Baumrind and her colleagues found that parenting behaviors in 77 percent of their families fit one of three patterns (see Table 10.1):

- **Authoritarian parenting pattern:** Parents who follow an authoritarian parenting pattern try to shape, control, and evaluate the behavior and attitudes of their children according to a set traditional standard. They stress the importance of obedience to authority and discourage their children from engaging them in verbal give-and-take. Comparatively lacking in the expression of warmth and responsiveness, they tend to favor punitive measures to curb their children's behavior whenever it conflicts with what they believe to be correct.

- **Authoritative parenting pattern:** Parents who follow an authoritative pattern set high standards for their children's behavior and expect them to respect established limits, but they also recognize that their children have needs and rights. They tend to be warm and also responsive, willing to consider their children's point of view, even if they do not always accept it. Authoritative parents are less likely than authoritarian parents to use physical punishment and less likely to stress obedience to authority as a virtue in itself. Instead, these parents attempt to control their children by explaining their rules or decisions and by reasoning with them. Authoritative parents encourage their children to be independent but socially responsible.

- **Permissive parenting pattern:** Parents who exhibit a permissive pattern exercise less explicit control over their children's behavior than do authoritarian and authoritative parents, either because they believe children

no-nonsense parenting Parenting characterized by a mix of high parental control, including punishment, and warmth, and associated especially with African American single mothers.

authoritarian parenting pattern Parenting style identified by Baumrind that focuses on enforcing obedience and conformity to traditional standards, including by use of punishment, and that is lacking in verbal give-and-take with children and in expression of warmth.

authoritative parenting pattern Parenting style identified by Baumrind in which parents set standards and limits for children but also encourage discussion and independence, and express warmth.

permissive parenting pattern Parenting style identified by Baumrind in which parents express warmth but do not exercise control over their children's behavior.

Authoritarian parents emphasize obedience, and tend to favor punitive measures in response to misbehaviors.

Randy Faris/Corbis

must learn how to behave through their own experience (permissive parenting) or because they do not take the trouble to provide discipline (*neglectful parenting*). They give their children a lot of leeway to determine their own schedules and activities, and often consult them about family policies. Although they tend to be warm, these parents do not demand the same levels of achievement and mature behavior that authoritative and authoritarian parents do.

Baumrind found that each parenting pattern tended to be associated with a different pattern of children's behavior in the preschool:

- *Children of authoritarian parents* tend to lack social competence in dealing with other children. They frequently withdraw from social contact and rarely take the initiative. In situations of moral conflict, they tend to look to outside authority to decide what is right. These children are often characterized as lacking spontaneity and intellectual curiosity.

- *Children of authoritative parents* appeared more self-reliant, self-controlled, and willing to explore than those raised by permissive or authoritarian parents. Baumrind believes that this difference is a result of the fact that authoritative parents explain the standards and limits they set for their children, and when they punish them, make clear why. Such explanations improve children's understanding and acceptance of social rules.

- *Children of permissive parents* tend to be relatively immature; they have difficulty controlling their impulses, accepting responsibility for social actions, and acting independently.

Baumrind's pioneering work inspired hundreds of studies on how parenting practices affect children's development. In more recent research, however, developmentalists have attempted to view the family from a more dynamic perspective that takes into account how children affect parents as well as how parents affect

table 10.1

Baumrind's Parenting Styles

Parenting Style	Description	Typical Children's Characteristics
Authoritarian	• Demanding and controlling • Favor punitive methods over reasoning • Stress obedience over independence	• Other-directed • Lack social competence • Lack curiosity • Withdrawn
Authoritative	• Demanding but reciprocal relationship • Favor reasoning over physical punishment • Encourage independence	• Self-reliant • Self-controlled • Display curiosity • Content
Permissive	• Undemanding and little control exercised • Allow children to learn through experience as a result of indulgence or neglect • Neither independence nor obedience stressed	• Dependent on others • Poor impulse control • Relative immaturity

children, and also how parenting styles and practices can have different effects on different children and can change over time (Collins, 2005; Maccoby, 2007). A variety of research, summarized by Avshalom Caspi (1998), suggests that it is just as likely that parenting style is influenced by the child's characteristics as it is that the child is shaped by the parenting style. For example, a particularly active and easily frustrated child may elicit authoritarian parenting from a parent while an easy-going or timid child elicits an authoritative style from that same parent. Research has also documented children's different responses to the same parenting style. For example, many African American children respond positively to no-nonsense parenting, which we discussed earlier, although it shares many features of the authoritarian style described by Baumrind.

The Role of Siblings

Our friend Laureen is the oldest of three. Reflecting on her experiences growing up with two younger brothers, she remembers a lot of fighting (but does not re-member why), babysitting (when she would rather have gone out with her friends), and sticking up for them when they got into trouble with peers or parents (which was often). In her words, "it was fine for *me* to push them around, but everyone else had better keep their hands off my little brothers!" Laureen also vividly re-members when her brothers overtook her in physical size and strength. "After that, my power as the 'big sister' was entirely psychological." Despite the fact that all three of them are now in their 50s and fairly good friends, Laureen still considers herself the big sister. Her relationships with her brothers, which have existed longer than any other relationships in her life, still bear the mark of their early experiences.

Of all the relationships an individual may ever have, those with siblings may be the longest lasting. Developmentalists are just beginning to understand the complexity of these relationships, and how they are affected by the ages and gender mix of the sibling pair.

Although parents are known to play significant roles in children's socialization (see the box "Fathers"), studies indicate that siblings are also influential in one another's development (Carpendale & Lewis, 2004; Whiteman, McHale, & Crouter, 2007). The socializing role of siblings is most obvious in agricultural societies, like the Gusii, discussed earlier in the chapter, in which much of the child care is performed by older siblings. It is through these child caretakers, who are some-times no more than 4 years older than their charges, that many of the behaviors and beliefs of the social group are passed on (Zukow-Goldring, 1995). In many industrialized societies, including the United States, the role of siblings as social-izers has become more prominent. With more mothers working, more children are being called upon to provide care for their younger siblings (McHale & Crouter, 1996). Within African American families, reliance on siblings for child care and socialization is commonplace, perhaps a reflection of African family traditions (Brody & Murry, 2001).

As suggested by Laureen, sibling relationships are often ambivalent, sometimes loving and supportive, sometimes hostile and competitive. The degree of intimacy and conflict in sibling relationships depends on a variety of factors, including the sex and age of the children. In a longitudinal study of siblings between 9 and 20 years of age, there appeared to be higher levels of intimacy between sisters than between brothers or between brothers and sisters (Kim et al., 2007). In addition, whereas the intimacy of same-sex sibling pairs remained fairly stable over time, that of mixed-sex pairs declined during middle childhood, perhaps as a conse-quence of *gender segregation* (see Chapter 9, p. 303), and then increased in mid-adolescence, when siblings may turn to each other for advice and support on mat-ters of peer and dating relationships (Figure 10.1).

Overall, and as Laureen recalls, sibling conflict declines throughout adolescence (Figure 10.2). One factor that reliably affects the siblings' relationship is the emo-tional climate of their family (Brody, 1998; Modry-Mandell, Gamble, & Taylor,

Figure 10.1 Intimacy between siblings varies depending on the age and gender mix of the sibling pair. Intimacy of same-sex sibling pairs is fairly constant over time, whereas the intimacy of mixed-sex pairs declines during middle childhood, then increases throughout adolescence and early adulthood.

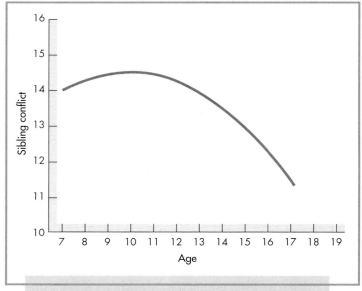

Figure 10.2 Conflicts between siblings peak during middle childhood, and decline throughout adolescence.

2007). Siblings are more likely to fight when their parents are not getting along well together, when their parents divorce, and when a stepfather enters the family, especially if one or both of the siblings are boys (Hetherington, 1988).

While most studies of siblings have focused on emotional factors such as intimacy and conflict, researchers have recently turned their attention to more cognitive issues, including the ways that the sibling relationship may provide a context for teaching and learning (Strauss & Ziv, 2004). For example, when Margarita Azmitia and Joanne Hesser (1993) had young children play with building blocks while their older sibling and an older friend, both of whom were approximately 9 years old, played with blocks nearby, the younger children spent more time imitating and consulting with their sibling than with the friend. Their older sibling, in turn, offered more spontaneous help than did the friend. When the older sibling and the friend were asked to help the younger sibling build a copy of a model out of blocks, the older sibling again provided more explanations and encouragement. Others studies find that older siblings are particularly helpful (provide more demonstrations and feedback) as tasks become more difficult or with siblings who are significantly younger (Howe, Brody, & Recchia, 2006). These findings suggest that close relationships encourage individuals to create a *zone of proximal development,* which, according to Lev Vygotsky, is key to the acquisition of new knowledge (see Chapter 1, pp. 23–24).

Family Diversity

Changes in values, politics, economies, and transportation technologies have altered the face of "family" in many parts of the globe, bringing to it a wide diversity of ethnic backgrounds, cultural heritages, and lifestyles. As immigrant populations swell across the globe, family ethnicity has become a special focus of developmentalists'

Fathers

I N "FATHER OF MINE," EVERCLEAR SINGS of desertion, when the whole world disappeared because "Father of mine . . . gave me a name . . . then walked away." In "Dance with My Father," Luther Vandross describes a different childhood, one colored by an image of his father lifting him high, dancing with him and his mother, spinning him around until he fell asleep: "Then up the stairs he would carry me; and I knew for sure I was loved."

Whether of loss and pain, or love and security, the lyrics by Everclear and Vandross capture the importance of fathers in the lives of their children. Nonetheless, research on fathers and fathering is just beginning to make a significant mark in the developmental sciences (McKinney & Renk, 2008). Part of the recent interest in fathers may be due to evidence of their increasing involvement in bringing up their children. In the past 30 or 40 years, for example, as mothers have gone to work, fathers have provided more child care. There has also been a rise in the number of single fathers raising children—in the United States between 1970 and 2000, an increase of nearly 510 percent, compared with a 330 percent increase in single mothers raising children (U.S. Bureau of the Census, 2002). Even in families in which the mother does not work, today's fathers appear to be interacting with their children in a way that distinguishes them from fathers of the past. Rather than being regarded primarily as the "breadwinner," the "new father" is expected to provide daily physical care, be emotionally connected to his children, and more attuned to their experiences and concerns (Yeung et al., 2001).

Indeed, one of the most significant new developments in research on fathers is an expanded notion of paternal involvement. Instead of focusing simply on the amount of time that dads spend with their children, contemporary researchers are looking in detail at the different types of activities in which they engage. It seems, in fact, that the sheer amount of time that fathers devote to their children is less important to children's well-being than how that time is spent. For example, going out together to dinner or to the movies is unrelated to children's levels of life satisfaction, whereas talking over problems and sharing and encouraging accomplishments are associated with high levels of satisfaction (Young et al., 1995). In general, fathering practices typically associated with authoritative parenting—providing emotional support, monitoring children's behaviors, and using noncoercive discipline—seem to be most beneficial to children (Marsiglio et al., 2000; Simons & Conger, 2007). Other research demonstrates that the influence of fathers extends well beyond the quality of their interactions with chil-

dren. Fathers who know their children's friends, maintain contact with teachers and coaches, and are generally connected to individuals and institutions in the community can help their children to develop and maintain important social networks. Fathers, in other words, can play a decisive role in developing their children's social ecologies (Furstenberg, 1998).

Interestingly, at the same time that fathers are gaining more attention, studies suggest that at least in some respects the proportion of men experiencing fatherhood may be diminishing (Eggebeen, 2002). In the mid-1960s, nearly 60 percent of men were living with children, compared with only 45 percent today. Developmentalists are beginning to ask questions regarding men's images of fathering and what it means to them to be fathers. Probing the identity issues surrounding the role of father, and the emotional and subjective experiences of fathering, may shed additional light on how much, and how well, fathers parent their children.

This father–son pair are clearly enjoying each other's company. Research indicates that fathers play an important role in children's development.

Andersen Ross/drr.net

attention. Likewise, research on families with single parents or sexual minority parents has increased in recent years owing to ever-growing numbers of single parents and of gay and lesbian couples raising children.

Immigrant Families

When I was in Korea, I did everything for my kids. But, since I came here, I had to completely change my parenting style; I make my kids take care of themselves. Well, when I was in Korea, I was not working, and I enjoyed my life. But, here in America, I have to do lots of physical work. It is very hard because my husband and I are not used to doing this kind of labor. My husband had a white-collar job [CPA] in Korea, so his doing this kind of labor is very hard for him as well. I can do very little for my kids. So, I asked them to do what they need. My daughter cooks for

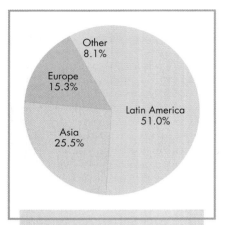

Figure 10.3 The wave of immigrants to the United States has led to sweeping changes in the racial and ethnic diversity of the country. Today, one in five children has immigrant parents. (Adapted from Suarez-Orozco, 2001.) This chart shows the percentage of immigrants to the United States from various parts of the globe.

us, and we eat the food that she made. Sometimes, she cooks special food for us, and she is taking care of her little brother very well. She prepares food for him, and she does whatever he asks. . . . She also comes to our shop on every Saturday and during the summer and winter breaks. She works at our shop. While she was in Korea, she was like a princess. She did not do anything that she does now before, but now she is different (Kim et al., 2006).

Ethnic diversity has been present in the United States throughout its history as a result of the colonization of Native Americans, the importation of slaves from Africa, and a continuous stream of immigrants, mostly from Europe. Moreover, in the past few decades, the United States has experienced an enormous influx of families from many parts of the globe. As shown in Figure 10.3, more than 50 percent of U.S. immigrants come from Latin America, 25 percent from Asia, 15 percent from Europe, and 8 percent from elsewhere. Currently, one in five children in the United States has immigrant parents, making immigrant children the fastest-growing group of children in the United States (Research Forum on Children, Families, and the New Federalism, 2002). Similar changes in the influx of immigrants have also occurred in Canada, Australia, and Germany and other European countries (United Nations Commission on Population and Development, 2005).

One of the most common ways of exploring diversity in families is to examine differences in parenting style. However, developmentalists have discovered that the patterns of parenting originally formulated by Baumrind on the basis of her research with middle-class parents may not apply to other ethnic populations, as we discovered in the case of African-American no-nonsense parenting. Indeed, the very categories and language that U.S. researchers use to describe differences in styles may be culturally specific (Parke & Buriel, 1998).

For example, research comparing Chinese American and European American parents has found that "authoritarian" does not have the same meanings for the two groups (Chao, 2001; Wu & Chao, 2005). Although Chinese American families might typically seem to have an authoritarian style, according to Ruth Chao the English word "authoritarian" carries many negative connotations—such as hostility, aggressiveness, mistrust, dominance—that render it inapplicable to the core methods of parenting in the Chinese family. While it is true that Chinese

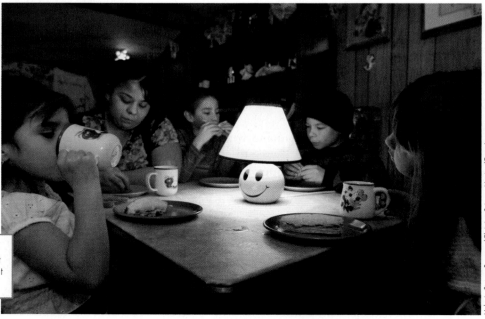

Enjoying dinner in their new mobile home, these five children from a migrant family are part of a large influx of recent immigrants to the United States.

parents place high value on controlling their children and on requiring their obedience, the preferred Chinese pattern of parenting is more aptly characterized by a Chinese notion that Chao translates as "training." Chao maintains that Chinese parents exercise control over their children and demand their obedience "in the context of a supportive, highly involved, and physically close mother–child relationship" (Chao, 1996, p. 112).

Just as parenting styles vary across cultures, so do the values that parents seek to instill in their children. Many recent immigrants to the United States come from cultures that place great value on education as a means to achieving a successful life. Indeed, immigrant parents tend to emphasize the importance of education more than do native-born Americans. In his ethnographic case study of a Hispanic immigrant family, Gerardo Lopez (2001) reported that the parents would often take their children with them as they worked in the fields in order to underscore important "life lessons" about how hard they worked and how poorly they were compensated. The most important lesson, however, was that education is the key to a better life.

What accounts for this difference in the valuing of education? Many developmentalists have pointed to the "ideologies of opportunity" and "cultures of optimism" that motivate families to migrate in the first place (Suárez-Orozco & Todorova, 2008). In short, parents believe that life in the new country will provide increased opportunities for their children. However, as with the family of the Korean mother quoted earlier, many immigrant families experience a significant drop in economic and social status when they arrive in the United States (Kim et al., 2007). Sadly, and perhaps counterintuitively, research indicates that, among immigrant Asian and Latino children alike, length of residence in the United States is associated with declines in health, school achievement, and aspirations (Portes & Rumbaut, 2001; Waters, 1999). Carola Suarez-Orozco and her colleagues (2008) suggests that the "Americanization" of foreign-born children often includes exposure to persistent forms of racism and to peer influence that together undermine their initial sense of optimism and regard for education.

Single-Parent Families It is estimated that half of all children born in the United States today will spend at least some portion of their childhood in a single-parent home. According to U.S. Census data, in the past 40 years there has been a 280 percent increase in single-parent families among European Americans and a 543 percent increase among African Americans (Kesner & McKenry, 2001). Indicative of this change, in 1999, female-headed households accounted for 14 percent of European American families, 23 percent of Latino families, and 45 percent of African American families (U.S. Bureau of the Census, 2002).

Studies of children from single-parent families report a number of behavioral, social, and academic problems. One explanation is that when a single parent has to assume the role of sole breadwinner, caregiver, and householder manager, that parent's contact with and supervision of the children is reduced, giving the children more unregulated time. According to this explanation, the very structure of the family places children at risk.

Other researchers argue that the presence of only one parent is not itself a problem; rather, other factors that often correlate strongly with single-parenthood are to blame. For example, with only one wage earner, single-parent families have fewer material resources and experience greater financial stress than do two-parent families. According to this view, whether there is one parent or two in the household is not the issue; exposure to poverty is what matters.

Yet another explanation associates the problems of children from single-parent families with the traumatic effects of divorce (you will learn more about the effects of divorce in Chapter 13). From this perspective as well, single-parent families are not a problem in and of themselves. Rather, the crisis of divorce generates behavioral, social, and academic problems for children, problems that can be expected to decline over time as the family learns to cope with the divorce and its effects.

In an effort to untangle these competing explanations, Gunilla Weitoft and her colleagues (2003) launched a nationwide study comparing health outcomes for children in single-parent and two-parent families in Sweden. They identified almost 1 million children who were living with the same single adult or the same two opposite-sex adults in both 1991 and 1999. Using national records of child deaths, social welfare benefits, and hospital discharges, they found that children in the single-parent homes fared less well than their two-parent-family peers on a variety of physical and mental health indicators. Although the researchers found that socioeconomic status was the most important factor in accounting for a number of differences between the two groups, children in single-parent families, regardless of socioeconomic status (SES), remained at greater risk for psychiatric disorders, suicide, injury, and addiction.

The results of such large-scale studies can provide important information about populations of individuals in general, as Weitoft and her colleagues suggest. However, they reveal little about family dynamics, family communication patterns, child-rearing practices, the reasons for single-parenthood, kin relationships outside the immediate family, and other factors that may influence the well-being of children in single-parent families.

Another problem with conclusions about children in single-parent families is that most of the relevant research has been conducted primarily with Caucasian families, raising the question of whether the results apply as well to ethnic-minority families. To address this question, John Kesner and Patrick McKenry (2001) studied 68 preschool children and their parents living in a large city in the southeastern United States. Most of the families were African American (66 percent) or Hispanic (10 percent). Sixty-six percent of the children lived with both parents, and 34 percent lived with their mothers who had never been married. There were no differences between the single- and two-parent families in terms of ethnicity or socioeconomic level.

Kesner and McKenry examined the children's social skills and conflict-management styles and found no differences between children from single-parent families and those from two-parent families. In discussing their results, the researchers note that compared with European Americans, African Americans are more supportive of single-parent families and attach less stigma to them. In addition, the extended-family pattern characteristic of the Hispanic and African American cultural traditions (as discussed earlier) may mean that children have a network of kin that provides additional support. Finally, Kesner and McKenry point out that because the single mothers in their study had never been married, their families were not exposed to the sudden emotional and financial changes typically experienced by divorced families. These mothers may also have stronger commitments to their nonconventional family structure than mothers who may have been divorced against their choice.

Gay and Lesbian Parents Another significant change in the nature of families is the increasing number of gay and lesbian parents. Research on gay- and lesbian-parent families has a number of limitations that require us to exercise caution in how we interpret it. Some of these limitations stem from parents' reluctance to discuss their families and sexual orientation for fear of discrimination. Other limitations, however, stem from a lack of reliable information regarding gay- and lesbian-parent families. For example, the 2000 U.S. Census reported that more than 250,000 children live with unmarried, same-sex partners, but did not collect data on how many of these partners were gay and lesbian, or how many single parents were gay and lesbian. Moreover, studies of gay- and lesbian-parent families have tended to involve small numbers of families that may or may not be representative.

Like families in general, those with gay and lesbian parents are diverse in size and structure, ethnicity, religion, and socioeconomic class. Some gay and lesbian co-parents come out after having their children in a heterosexual relationship. More recently, openly gay and lesbian couples and individuals are choosing to raise children that they have adopted or conceived by means of artificial insemination or surrogacy (Ariel & McPherson, 2000). In the United States, adoption is often a difficult procedure for gay and lesbian couples because traditional family law does not recognize such couples as constituting a legal marriage (Dalton & Bielby, 2000; Herek, 2006). Thus, co-parents who wish to adopt their partners' legal or biological children often must convince judges to reinterpret adoption statutes in ways that are inclusive of gay and lesbian unions (Ryan, 2000).

A number of studies have sought to determine whether children raised in gay and lesbian households are different from children raised in heterosexual families. Although most of these studies have been limited in size, they paint a generally positive picture of children's development and adjustment (Patterson, 2006). For example, although research suggests that children living in gay- and lesbian-parent families may be targets of teasing by peers and even shunned by their peers' parents (Morris et al., 2002), their emotional, social, and intellectual development is comparable to that of children raised by heterosexual parents (Ariel & McPherson, 2000; Patterson, 2008). Not surprisingly, children of gay- and lesbian-parents seem to be more tolerant of same-sex experimentation (Stacey, 1998), and may be somewhat more likely to develop a homosexual identity than children growing up with heterosexual parents (Stacey & Biblarz, 2001).

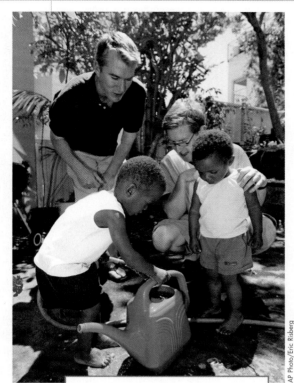

The families of gay and lesbian couples are diverse in size, ethnicity, religion, and socioeconomic status.

Distressed Families

Because the family is the first and perhaps the most important developmental context, *distressed families*—that is, families facing significant social, economic, and/or psychological challenges—are of special concern to those interested in children's well-being. According to developmentalists who study distressed families, the most significant family factors that impede children's development are poverty, parenthood in adolescence, and abuse. We look at each of these factors in turn (and at a fourth factor, divorce, in Chapter 13).

Families in Poverty One of the most consistent findings in research on families is the relationship between economic hardship and children's well-being. Because income level is highly associated with both education level and occupation, these three factors are usually folded into a single measure, called *socioeconomic status* (SES). Most research on children and economic distress relies on SES to establish the amount of hardship experienced by the family.

Poverty touches all aspects of family life: the quality of housing and health care, access to education and recreational facilities, and even one's safety as one walks along the street (Fauth, Leventhal & Brooks-Gunn, 2007; McLoyd, 1998a, 1998b). Interest in the influence of poverty on children's development has increased in recent years, owing in part to the rising rates of poor children in the United States.

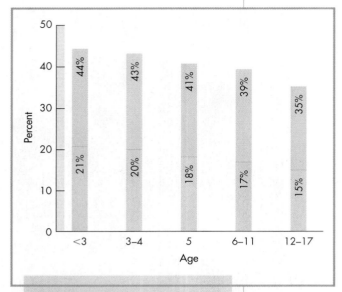

Figure 10.4 Percent of children in the United States living in low-income (green) or poor (peach) families. The National Center for Children in Poverty (NCCP) defines "poor" families as those with incomes below the federal poverty level ($20,000 for a family of 4 in 2006). Because research indicates that a family cannot meet its basic needs unless its income is at least 200% higher than the federal poverty level (Berstein, Brocht & Spade-Aguilar, 2000), the NCCP identifies such families as "low-income."

According to the National Center for Children in Poverty, approximately 18 percent of all children in the United States live in poverty, part of the approximately 40 percent who live in low-income families (NCCP, 2008) (Figure 10.4). As we discussed in Chapter 8, nearly 12 percent of all families in the United States are considered *food insecure,* meaning that they do not have access to enough food to ensure good health for all family members; nearly 4 percent are considered "food insecure with hunger," meaning that they have so little food that they are often hungry.

Contrary to popular belief, only half of all poor children and families in the United States are chronically and persistently poor. In a nationwide study, Duncan and his colleagues found that family income fluctuates significantly across the family's life cycle and tends to increase as children age (Duncan & Raudenbush, 1999). However, they also found that being poor during early childhood presents a greater challenge to children's well-being, particularly to their academic achievement, than does being poor during later stages of development. Considering that the family's SES is the most powerful predictor of intellectual skills when children enter school, and that early school success forecasts lifelong achievement and adjustment, the effects of poverty are particularly serious (Stipek, 2001).

Although research indicates that poverty in early childhood places individuals at risk for major depression in adulthood (Gilman et al., 2003), poverty-stricken children's mental health problems can be significantly reduced if their family's income rises above the poverty level. This was demonstrated by Jane Costello and her colleagues (2003) in an 8-year study of Native American children growing up on an Indian reservation. Some of the children lived in poverty; others did not. Halfway through the study, a casino opened on the reservation, moving many of the poor families out of poverty. Overall, children in these families subsequently showed a significant decrease in mental health disorders, whereas the children whose families remained in poverty showed no improvement in their mental health.

In addition to mental health problems, poverty is also associated with physical health problems and problems in intellectual development. Environmentally induced illnesses such as tuberculosis and asthma are all observed at higher rates in poor children than in nonpoor children (Books, 2000; Shonkoff & Phillips, 2000). Associated with learning disabilities and impaired intellectual functioning, lead poisoning is a significant threat to children living in deteriorating housing where they may be exposed to lead-based paint and dust.

Poverty may also affect parents' approach to child rearing. As discussed earlier in the chapter, studies in many parts of the world have found that in families experiencing economic hardship, parents are likely to be more harsh and controlling. Some researchers have suggested that poor minority mothers in the United States demand unquestioning obedience and discourage their children's curiosity because the dangerous circumstances of their daily life make independence on the part of their children too risky (McLoyd, 1998b).

Another important way in which poverty puts children at risk is by raising the level of their parents' stress. Low-income parents have higher rates of depression, negative feelings of self-worth, and negative beliefs about the extent to which they have control over their own life circumstances (summarized in Shonkoff & Phillips, 2000). Parents who are under stress are less nurturing, more likely to resort to physical punishment, and less consistent when they interact with their children (Sameroff et al., 1998).

The studies reviewed here indicate that poverty has far-reaching and long-lasting effects on children's development. Another risk associated with poverty arises in adolescence—that of becoming a teenage parent.

Families with Teen Mothers Many women who are raising children are still teenagers. As Figure 10.5 indicates, between 1990 and 2005 there was a dramatic drop in the proportion of adolescents giving birth in the United States. Nevertheless, the teen birth rate in the United States is among the highest in the industrialized world (Table 10.2). This situation is of grave concern because research has shown that children of unmarried teenage mothers suffer significant deficits in several developmental areas. In general, they tend to be more aggressive, less self-controlled, and less intellectually advanced than the children of older, married mothers (Jaffe et al., 2001). In one study of more than 100 children born to unmarried teenage mothers, less than one-third scored within normal ranges on tests of intelligence, language, and socioemotional functioning (Sommer et al., 2000).

Frank Furstenberg and his colleagues (1992) believe that two factors contribute to the negative developmental effect of being raised by a young unmarried mother. First, young mothers often are less prepared to bring up children and have little interest in doing so. One consequence is that they tend to vocalize less with their babies than older mothers do. As we discussed in Chapter 6, mother–infant communication is an important source of intellectual stimulation. Second, young mothers, especially those without husbands, are likely to have very limited financial resources. As a consequence, they are likely to be poorly educated, live in disadvantaged neighborhoods, lack quality health care, and be socially isolated.

It is important to recognize that not all children born to teenage mothers have equally grim outcomes. Tom Luster and his colleagues (2005) compared "more successful" and "less successful" children of adolescent mothers. Children who were most successful, as measured by a standardized test of intellectual and language functioning, were likely to live in environments that were more intellectually

table 10.2
Birth Rates for Teenagers (15–19 years old) in Selected Countries, 2000–2005

Country	Birth Rate (annual births per 1000 women)
Afghanistan	111
Bangladesh	125
Brazil	71
Canada	19
Colombia	80
Greece	10
Iraq	41
Kuwait	28
Lebanon	25
Mexico	64
Nicaragua	138
Poland	16
Romania	37
South Korea	3
Spain	6
Switzerland	5
Uganda	211
United States	49
Vietnam	20

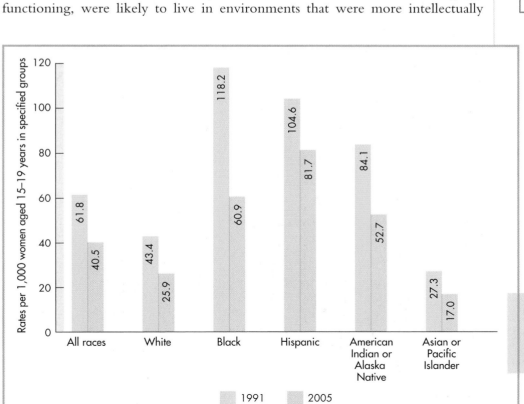

Figure 10.5 Proportion of adolescents giving birth in the United States. There has been a dramatic drop in the teen birth rate between 1990 and 2005, particular among black teens.

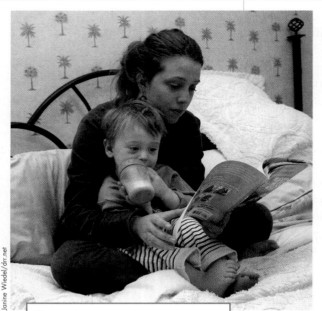

Despite the stresses of teen parenting, this young woman takes time to read to her baby.

stimulating and less stressful than those of their less successful peers. In addition, the mothers of the most successful children had received more years of education, were more likely to be employed, had fewer children, resided in more desirable neighborhoods, and lived with a male partner. Likewise, a study of adolescent mothers' participation in welfare-reform programs indicates that highly involved mothers— those who take advantage of center-based child care, educational opportunities, and job training programs—have children with more developed cognitive abilities than children whose mothers are less involved (Yoshikaw et al., 2001). Social programs for teen mothers, such as the one described in the box "In the Field: Louisiana Swamp Nurse," aim to decrease risks and increase protective factors for children by encouraging teen mothers to continue their education, pursue job opportunities, and read to their babies.

Abusive Families Scarcely a day goes by without a story in the media about a child who has been neglected, maltreated, or even murdered by a parent or other relative. Add to this the stories about children from around the world who are forced into prostitution, made to work long hours at grueling and sometimes dangerous tasks, commandeered to serve as soldiers, or killed simply because they are female or members of a particular ethnic group and you begin to get a sense of the enormity of child abuse and maltreatment across the globe.

Researchers interested in tracking the worldwide incidence of child maltreatment face a number of difficulties. One of the most common difficulties relates to how "maltreatment" is defined in different cultures. As you can see in Table 10.3, with the exception of extreme physical and sexual abuse, there is wide regional variation in the sorts of behaviors that are recognized as abusive (ISPCAN, 2006).

table 10.3

What Constitutes Abuse? Views from across the Globe

	Region			
	Africa	**Americas**	**Asia**	**Europe**
Sexual abuse (e.g., incest, sexual touching, pornography)	100.0	100.0	100.0	100.0
Physical abuse (e.g., beating, burning)	90.9	100.0	100.0	100.0
Failure to provide adequate food, clothing or shelter (neglect)	72.7	100.0	91.7	92.0
Abandonment by parent or caretaker	81.8	100.0	83.3	92.0
Emotional abuse (e.g., repeated belittling or insulting a child)	63.6	100.0	62.5	88.0
Failure to secure medical care for child based on religious beliefs	72.7	80.0	60.9	84.0
Psychological neglect (e.g., failure to provide emotional support/attention)	63.6	80.0	54.2	79.2
Parental substance abuse	63.6	70.0	45.8	88.0
Domestic violence	63.6	60.0	41.7	76.0
Parental mental illness	36.4	40.0	37.5	64.0
Physical discipline (e.g., spanking)	45.5	60.0	37.5	60.0
Non-organic failure to thrive (FTT)	36.4	50.0	37.5	56.0
Child prostitution	100.0	100.0	100.0	96.0
Children living on the street	100.0	100.0	83.3	92.0
Physical beating of a child by any adult	72.7	90.0	83.3	96.0
Forcing a child to beg	63.6	90.0	87.5	84.0
Female/child infanticide	72.7	70.0	82.6	88.0
Child labor	63.6	80.0	70.8	68.0
Abuse by another child	63.6	80.0	62.5	76.0
Children serving as soldiers	60.0	66.7	59.1	50.0
Female circumcision	60.0	60.0	45.0	60.9

This table reflects results from a mail survey of key informants identified by the International Society for the Prevention of Child Abuse as knowledgeable about child maltreatment issues within their respective countries. The number of informants from each region ranged from 10 (Americas) to 25 (Europe).

Definitional problems arise because what is deemed appropriate and inappropriate treatment of children, including the frequency and severity of physical punishment, varies dramatically from one family and community to the next (Holden, 2002). According to various surveys, for example, over 90 percent of all parents in the United States have spanked their children, a practice that is viewed as unacceptable in countries such as Sweden (see in Chapter 9, the box "The Spanking Controversy"). Clearly, the borders between culturally acceptable physical punishment and physical punishment that is defined as maltreatment depend very much on parents' beliefs about children and the modes of interaction sanctioned in the children's families and communities.

Why do parents abuse their own children? It is generally believed that parents who were physically abused by their parents are more likely to abuse their own children than are parents who were not themselves abused (Ammerman et al., 1999). However, only 30 percent of those who were abused become child abusers themselves; 70 percent do not (Kaufman & Zigler, 1989). Hence, a history of abuse may be associated with later abuse but cannot be considered a simple cause. Rather, a complex interplay of factors seems to set the stage for maltreatment (Zielinski & Bradshaw, 2006).

There is a good deal of evidence that one major contributor to abuse is stress on the family, including chronic poverty, recent job loss, marital discord, and social isolation (Gordon et al., 2003). The likelihood of abuse is also higher when the mother is very young, is poorly educated, abuses drugs or alcohol, or receives little financial support from the father (Goodman et al., 1998; Gordon et al., 2003).

Any child may be neglected or abused, but some characteristics seem to put children at greater risk (HHS, 2003). Factors that affect risk include the following:

- *Age:* infants and children under the age of 3 are at special risk.
- *Gender:* girls are slightly more likely than boys to be maltreated.
- *Ethnicity:* Pacific Islander, Native American, and African American children have higher rates of maltreatment. For example, the rate of maltreatment for European American children of 11.0 per 1000 compares to rates of 21.4 per 1000 for Pacific Islanders, 21.3 for Alaska Natives, and 20.4 for African Americans.

Many scholars who have studied the physical abuse of children in the United States see it as a social disease that accompanies the acceptance of violence in families, local communities, and society at large. Two kinds of evidence support this position. First, most child abuse occurs when parents set out to discipline their children by punishing them physically and then end up hurting them (Zigler & Hall, 1989). Second, countries in which the physical punishment of children is frowned upon, such as Sweden and Japan, have very low rates of physical abuse of children (Belsky, 1993; Cicchetti & Toth, 1993).

Although adults who have been maltreated as children are more likely to be depressed, abuse drugs and alcohol, have sexual problems, and engage in criminal behavior, nearly one-fourth of maltreated children show no long-term problems (McGloin & Widom, 2001). Factors that seem to buffer children from long-term consequences of abuse include having a warm relationship with at least one adult, having a fairly stable family residence (not moving around a lot), having positive experiences in school, and participating in extracurricular activities (Zielinski & Bradshaw, 2006). The multiple cultural, family, parent, and child factors that operate together in cases of child maltreatment suggest that broad-based, systematic intervention campaigns would offer the best hope for reducing the problem in the long run (Hughes, Graham-Bermann, & Gruber, 2001).

In the Field   Louisiana Swamp Nurse

Name:	Luwana Marts
Education:	B.S. in Nursing
Current position:	Nurse Visitor for the Nurse-Family Partnership of Louisiana

Luwana Marts is one of eight nurses who work with teen mothers living in a swampy, isolated region southwest of New Orleans. In Louisiana, 30 percent of all children are poor, almost half of all children are born to single mothers, and the proportion of people unable to read or write is among the highest in the nation. Myths about children and their development abound: formula is healthier than breast milk; babies held by menstruating women will become constipated; the baby's brain will be damaged if his or her hair is cut before the first birthday. In this context, a beautiful young woman named Alexis became pregnant with her first child, and became part of Luwana's caseload.

Until her eighth month of pregnancy, Alexis lived with her parents, but their constant fighting became more than she could bear, so she moved out. She made other changes as well. At Luwana's urging, Alexis gave up drinking and smoking, and had regular medical checkups. When her son, Daigan, was born, Luwana visited regularly to educate Alexis about her son's development, and how to be a good parent.

Alexis: One thing that I learned already is how he cries different when he's hungry than when he's wet.

Luwana, with a dazzling smile: Making that distinction is important. You're listening to him, and in his own way he's explaining what he needs. Pretty soon now he'll be making other sounds, and when he does you'll want to make that noise right back. He'll babble, and then you'll talk to him, and that's how you'll develop his language. Now, what you may also find, around 5 to 8 weeks, is that he'll be crying even more—it's a normal part of his development, but it can also stress out the mom, so we'll want to be prepared for it. The main things will be keeping calm—if you find yourself getting all worked up and frustrated—well, then what?

Alexis: Put him down? So I don't hurt him, shake him, make him brain-dead?

Luwana: Put him down and ?

Alexis: Call someone who isn't upset? Let the baby be, and get help.

Luwana, talking sweetly to Daigan: See, your mama is getting it. She's surely going to figure you out.

On Valentine's Day, Daigan's father, James, a tugboat worker on the Mississippi River, proposed to Alexis. Luwana was thrilled at the prospect that he would provide the family with some economic security and stability. Her hopes were later dashed when she went to visit at an appointed time, and Alexis failed to answer the door. As she drove back down the road, she encountered James, riding a bike.

Luwana: James!

James, tearfully: She broke my heart, Miss Luwana. After all what I did for her. She got a new guy. He got no job, on drugs, on parole, got warrants out for his arrest.

Luwana: Where's my baby? You have to work out some arrangements, James. Because whatever happens, Daigan still needs you to be the dad.

James, without heart or conviction: I know. I will.

(Adapted from Katherine Boo, 2006)

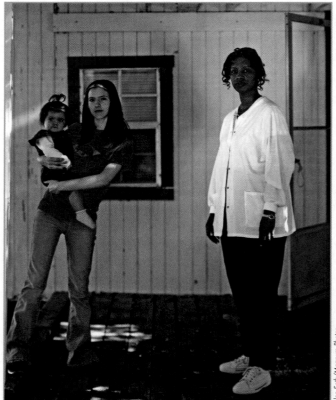

Luwana Marts, visiting nurse, with Maggie and her baby, Maia.

Alec Soth/Magnum Photos

Other Family Factors Although poverty, an adolescent mother, and abuse are some of the more obvious and significant factors that can impede development, a host of other family characteristics may put children at risk. There is evidence to suggest, for example, that children from wealthy families are at risk for behavioral and emotional problems. Suniya Luthar and Bronwyn Becker (2002) studied middle-school students living in one of the most affluent suburban communities in the United States. Their results showed high levels of depression, particularly among girls, as well as high levels of substance abuse. What might cause this pattern of distress among affluent young? According to the findings, many children of wealth feel themselves to be under a great deal of pressure to achieve—in school, in sports, socially, and financially. They also tend to be isolated from adults and feel emotionally distant from their mothers. Luthar and Becker's study supports recent concerns voiced in the popular press that wealthy families have become overly invested in performance and achievement issues and that their children are suffering as a consequence. Their children's time is overscheduled, especially with activities driven by the need to succeed. Such free time as children do have is often spent in the company of peers who endorse the use of drugs and alcohol as a means of "letting off steam." The study stands as a cautionary note against the assumption that children of means lack for nothing.

It is clear that families have pronounced effects on children's development. In addition to exerting influence through the ways they are structured (nuclear or extended) and the styles of care and interaction they provide, families influence children by linking them to other developmentally important contexts, including nonparental child-care settings.

APPLY ═ CONNECT ═ DISCUSS

Using Bronfenbrenner's model (Chapter 1, p. 28), analyze the ecology of Alexis and her baby as described in the box about the Louisiana swamp nurse. Describe features of the microsystems, exosystems, mesosystems, and macrosystems. If you lack specific information about the features of a system, try to speculate on the basis of features in the other systems.

Nonparental Child Care

Child care is a fact of life for nearly all children in the United States (Clarke-Stewart & Allhusen, 2005). By the time they reach 3 years of age, more than 90 percent will experience regular nonparental child care and more than 50 percent will be spending more than 30 hours per week in child care (NICHD, 2003b), numbers that in themselves suggest the importance of nonparental child care as a context for young children's development. In this section we focus on the varieties and general developmental consequences of nonparental care, leaving for Chapter 12 the more particular case of academically focused care such as preschools.

Varieties of Child Care

One of the most popular arrangements for children younger than 5 is **home child care**—care provided for children in their own homes, primarily by their grandmothers or other relatives, while their mothers are at work. Children cared for at home experience the least change from normal routine: They eat food provided by their parents and take naps in their own beds. They also come in contact with relatively few children their own age.

home child care Child care provided in the child's own home, primarily by a grandmother or other family member, while the parents are at work.

Child care offers children a variety of educational and social experiences.

Child care provided in someone else's home, that of either a relative or nonrelative, is called **family child care** (U.S. Bureau of the Census, 2003). Family child care often exposes children not only to caretakers from outside the family circle but also to new settings and to children of other families. The children in a family-child-care setting may range widely in age, forming a more diverse social group than is likely to exist at home. The routine of activities in family child care, however, is usually very similar to the routine at home.

Child-care centers—organized child-care facilities supervised by licensed professionals—have attracted the most public attention. The programs available vary in style and philosophy. Some offer an academic curriculum, emphasize discipline, and have a schoollike atmosphere. Others emphasize social development and allow children to exercise more initiative in their activities. Programs vary widely in quality as well. An important task many parents face is selecting the high-quality child-care facility or preschool that they feel best meets their children's needs (see Table 10.4 for questions that parents should ask regarding the quality of a child-care program they may be considering). Because licensed child-care centers often receive public financing, they have been more accessible than other nonparental care settings to researchers, who have studied both their characteristics and the way these characteristics affect children's development.

---

table **10.4**

Determining the Quality of Child-Care Centers

Questions about the Program:
- Is the program licensed by the state or local government?
- Is the program accredited by the National Association for the Education of Young Children or the National Association of Family Child Care?
- Does the program offer staff medical benefits and leave; does it support caregivers' continuing education through tuition reimbursement programs and/or sponsoring attendance at professional conferences and workshops?
- Does the staff-to-child ratio conform to state-regulated guidelines for the age group?
- Does the program encourage parent involvement through volunteering in the classroom, or participating on the board of directors or other committees?

Questions about the Environment:
- Is the environment safe and sanitary?
- Is the place appealing, with comfortable lighting and an acceptable noise level?
- Does the environment accommodate the child who may have special needs?
- Are toys and materials well organized so children can choose what interests them?

Questions about the Caregivers:
- Are the caregivers certified by the Council for Early Childhood Professional Recognition with a Child Development associate degree credential for infant/toddler caregivers or an equivalent credential that addresses comparable competencies (such as an A.A./A.S./B.A./B.S.)?
- Are the caregivers responsive, that is, are they:
  - Playful partners who introduce new ideas and games
  - Supportive of children in their social contacts with other children and adults
  - Respectful of the child's individual development, rhythms, style, strengths, and limitations
  - Respectful of the child's native culture or ethnicity

Source: Adapted from *Zero to Three*, 2003.

family child care Child care provided in someone else's home, that of either a relative or a stranger.

child-care center An organized child-care facility supervised by licensed professionals.

Preschool provides an important context for developing "children's culture." Handclapping games, like the one shown this Malaysian preschool, are but one example of the many games and rituals that children learn from other children.

Paul Chesley/Getty Images

Developmental Effects of Child Care

The effects of child care during the first 2 years of life depend primarily on the quality of the care provided and not on the mere fact of parent–child separation during the day. Nevertheless, concerns about the later effects of early child care continue to be raised, primarily regarding children's intellectual development, social development, and emotional well-being.

Physical and Intellectual Effects When children enter care outside the home, they enter a whole new world. There are new routines and expectations, new toys and children to play with, new adults who will provide care and comfort, and, as any parent will tell you—new germs. In fact, children under 3 years of age in care arrangements with more than six other children are at increased risk for upper respiratory infections, gastrointestinal illnesses, and ear infections (NICHD, 2003a). Although cold and flu bugs make regular rounds in child-care facilities, and often follow children home to their families, there is no evidence that increased illness takes a toll on children's overall development or school readiness (NICHD, 2003a).

Stress is another physical consequence of time spent in child care. Sarah Watamura and her colleagues (2003) measured levels of salivary cortisol (a hormone produced in response to stress) in groups of infants and toddlers who received care either in their homes or in child-care centers. Of those in child-care centers, 35 percent of the infants and 71 percent of the toddlers showed a rise in cortisol across the day. Of those receiving care in their homes, however, 71 percent of the infants and 64 percent of the toddlers showed *decreases* in cortisol levels. At this point, we can only speculate about the long-term consequences of elevated cortisol in infants and toddlers in child care. However, as you learned in Chapter 5 (p. 168), animal studies indicate that the quality of "mothering" can have both immediate and lasting effects on the stress levels of offspring and the way they respond to new and challenging environments (Brotman et al., 2003; Meaney, 2001). In these studies, stress levels associated with inadequate care early in life result in lowering exploratory behaviors and raising anxiety when faced with unfamiliar settings.

Despite the evidence that children in child care may experience higher levels of stress, research conducted in Europe as well as the United States indicates that intellectual development of children in high-quality child-care centers is at least as good as that of children raised at home by their parents (Campbell et al., 2001). Of special importance are the level of training received by the caregivers and appropriate child-to-staff ratios (NICHD, 2002b). In some cases, being in a high-quality child-care program lessens or prevents the decline in intellectual performance sometimes seen in children of low SES who remain at home with poorly educated parents after the age of 2 (NICHD, 2003b).

Impact on Social and Emotional Development Children who attend child-care centers in the United States tend to be more self-sufficient and more independent of parents and teachers, more verbally expressive, more knowledgeable about the social world, and more comfortable in new situations than children who do not attend child-care centers. Compared with children with no child-care experience, they are also happier and more enthusiastic about sharing toys and participating in fantasy play. However, the development of social competence is not simply a matter of children's learning how to get along by interacting with a variety of playmates. Caregivers play a crucial role. Children's social play and peer interactions become more complex and skilled when they are monitored and facilitated by warm, responsive caregivers (NICHD, 2001).

Not all the social and emotional effects of child care are positive, however. Children who attend child-care centers tend to be less polite, less agreeable, less compliant with adults, and more aggressive than those who do not. These effects seem to be related to the number of years a child spends in full-time nonparental care, with more extensive time being associated with more aggressive behavior and a greater likelihood of behavior problems in kindergarten (NICHD Early Child Care Research Network, 2003c). These negative behavioral effects, however, tend to be mild, particularly when compared with the effects of other factors such as the mother's sensitivity and the family's socioeconomic level.

Indeed, many developmentalists take strong issue with those who suggest that child care may adversely affect children's social behavior and emotional well-being. Some have argued that the quality, not the quantity, of out-of-home care exerts the biggest influence on children's adjustment. For example, an experimental study by John Love and his colleagues (2003) of children from low-income families (who would be expected to be at special risk for behavioral problems) found that those who received high-quality child care benefited in many ways and had less aggressive behavior problems than similar children who did not.

Others have argued that children's home life, including their preexisting relationship with parents, is more important in determining adjustment to child care. A study of middle-class German children in child care found that their mothers compensated for being away during the day with intense bouts of interaction and intimacy during the early morning and evening hours (Ahnert & Lamb, 2000). Likewise, Lieselotte Ahnert and Michael Lamb (2003) argue that one reason children in child care have trouble is because their working mothers are stressed and have little time and energy to engage them in high-quality interactions.

Child-care research that looks at such factors as family income, children's relationships with their parents, and parental stress goes well beyond the typical focus on parental versus nonparental care. In particular, this research alerts us to the ways in which other features of the ecology contribute to how children experience and adapt to different contexts of care.

An Ecological Approach to Child Care

An ecological approach is particularly important for understanding the child-care contexts of ethnic-minority and immigrant children. As Deborah Johnson and her colleagues have pointed out, much of the available research on child care does not include children of color, and when it does, it tends to ignore important variables—such as family structure and values, segregation and racism, and issues of cultural identity—that affect the type of care children have access to and how they respond to it (Johnson et al., 2003). For example, the very distinction between parental and nonparental care overlooks the fact that many African American and Hispanic families see parenting as a responsibility involving not only parents but a system of extended kin.

Figure 10.6 shows an ecological model for studying the contexts of child care and development in minority children. Following the arrows of the diagram reveals how the components of the model interact at a variety of levels—from the broadest social and cultural level (boxes #1–#3), through the more immediate community level (e.g., neighborhoods and schools; box #4), through family traditions, structures, and values (boxes #5–#6), to child characteristics and competencies (boxes #7–#8).

The model allows researchers to investigate the substantial racial and ethnic differences in the type of care that families need, prefer, and have access to. Racism and segregation, for example, have contributed to women of color being overrepresented in jobs that involve shift work, long hours, and layoffs. The childcare needs and resources of these women are very different from those who work in traditional 9-to-5 office jobs. In addition, the value systems of some families may lead them to seek child care that promotes positive racial or ethnic identity. Such "promoting environments" that are sensitive to children's native culture and language may enhance children's comfort and learning experiences. The fact that child-care outcomes are influenced by so many factors leads Johnson and her colleagues (2003) to conclude that "who cares for our children, how they are cared for, and the consequences of that care must be addressed in the appropriate ecological contexts, bringing to center the issues most relevant to the populations under study" (p. 1240).

Figure 10.6 An ecological approach to child care and development in minority children explores the interacting components of the macrosystem, exosystem, mesosystem, and microsystem. (Adapted from Johnson et al.,2003.)

By attending Head Start, these preschoolers from low-income families acquire learning skills and attitudes designed to help them succeed in school in the years ahead.

Laura Dwight

Imagine that you are preparing to have or adopt your first baby, and you are debating about when to return to work. To help you decide, outline the arguments for and against enrolling your baby in a child-care center. Based on the evidence of your arguments, what do you decide to do?

Neighborhoods and Communities

As children mature, their spheres of action expand beyond the microsystem settings of home and child care to include other developmentally important microsystem settings within the neighborhood and community. From the ecological perspective that we have been emphasizing throughout this chapter, these microsystem settings not only influence each other but also can be affected by other systems—for example, by local politics and the mass media (elements of the exosystem), as well as by the dominant beliefs and values of the culture (macrosystem).

Neighborhoods and communities differ substantially in the resources they provide to children and families. Who children interact with, the activities they engage in, the health services available to them, and even the food they eat are all strongly influenced by the particular location in which they live. Researchers use the term **social capital** to refer to such resources, which also include a community's social structures, its expectations for behavior, and the levels of trust and cooperation of its members (Franzini et al., 2006). These features of social capital are associated with children's quality of life and mental health outcomes (Drukker et al., 2003).

Community and Culture

Like families and other child-care settings, communities play an important role in transmitting the values and beliefs of culture. An excellent illustration of this is provided by Donna Marie San Antonio's (2004) study of children from two neighboring but vastly different communities in the rural northeastern United States. One community, Hillside, is a working-class community with one of the lowest levels of education and median family income in the state. The other, Lakeview, is more affluent, a white-collar community built around a thriving tourist industry.

social capital The resources that communities provide children and families, including not only schools, health services, and so on, but also social structures, expectations for behavior, and levels of trust and cooperation among community members.

Beyond social class differences, San Antonio found profoundly divergent perspectives on what constitutes a good life and how to secure it for one's children. For example, the people of Hillsdale cherish tradition, community, and family ties. Social status is determined "more by social and civic connections than by material wealth" (p. 87). In contrast, the people of Lakeview embrace the values of independence, family privacy, achievement, and upward mobility. San Antonio's study revealed that these two very different sets of beliefs and values are reflected in children's language and social interaction. Her observations of the children's behavior as she rode with them on school buses makes the point:

> [On Lakeview buses], most students spaced out in separate seats. Students were polite, but I was not drawn into conversations as I was on the Hillside–Two Rivers buses. The words spoken between students seemed fragmented; they were not conversations I could follow. Conversations between friends sitting together were whispered privately. In some instances, the communication seemed intended for power and position rather than for peer connection. On the Hillside bus, I heard students talk to each other in whole sentences—they included others, they said hello and good-bye to each other; on the Lakeview buses, I had an entirely different experience. (p. 170)

San Antonio's observations demonstrate how the values and beliefs of communities are expressed in children's behaviors and interactions. As we emphasized in Chapter 2, culture affects children's development so profoundly precisely because it is rooted in the everyday activities of families and peers.

Distressed Communities

Jasmine's elementary school is just two short blocks from home. Nevertheless, her mother walks her back and forth each day because she worries about Jasmine's safety. The street and sidewalk between the steps of their small row house and the school is strewn with garbage and litter; they pass a corner where mean-looking older kids hang out, harassing passersby for spare change. A few weeks ago, a boy was shot and killed in front of the school—an innocent victim caught in the crossfire of a drug-related shootout. How will Jasmine be affected by growing up in such a neighborhood?

The past several years have seen an explosion of research on the impact of distressed neighborhoods and communities on children's development (Franzini et al., 2008). This work has focused on economic disadvantage and physical and social disorder.

Economic Disadvantage You know from our previous discussion that children growing up in poverty-stricken families often suffer a variety of health, intellectual, social, and emotional problems. As you also know, most poverty-stricken families live in economically disadvantaged neighborhoods, which themselves contribute risk factors, including lack of decent housing and health care services, lack of grocery stores with fresh fruits and vegetables, and lack of recreational facilities. Plagued by excessive noise, crowding, and street traffic, economically disadvantaged neighborhoods generally have few parks or natural settings where children can play.

Research on communities indicates that neighborhood economic disadvantage profoundly affects children's development and well-being, over and above the effects of the income levels of their families. For example, a number of studies show that low-SES children living in substandard housing are at greater risk for emotional and academic problems, get sick and injured more often, and miss more school than low-SES children living in better housing (Evans, 2006; Shaw, 2004). Not surprisingly, children show significant improvements in school when their families move from substandard to better-quality housing.

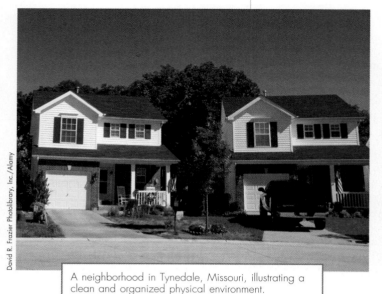

A neighborhood in Tynedale, Missouri, illustrating a clean and organized physical environment.

A neighborhood in Newburgh, New York, illustrating a disordered and deteriorating physical environment.

Physical and Social Disorder In addition to their poor economic conditions, distressed neighborhoods and communities are often ugly, congested, and confusing. One problem associated with such conditions is referred to as **neighborhood physical disorder,** which includes both *physical deterioration,* such as abandoned buildings and cars, garbage on the streets, broken windows, and graffiti on buildings, and *chaotic activity,* such as crowding, heavy street traffic, and high noise levels. Overall, children growing up in physically disordered environments are at risk for a variety of developmental problems. Compared with their peers in nondisordered environments, they are more likely to do poorly in school, be easily frustrated, and have less motivation to master difficult tasks (Haines et al., 2001; Maxwell & Evans, 2000).

Another problem associated with the conditions of distressed neighborhoods is **social disorganization** (Wen et al., 2005), which includes weak *social cohesion* (the sense of trust and connection between people), poor *neighborhood climate* (the level of fear related to crime and violence), and *perceived racism.* Children growing up in socially disorganized communities are at risk for a poor quality of life and poor mental health (Drukker et al., 2003).

Although most studies of physical and social disorganization have been conducted in North America, the effects of chaotic environments on children's development and well-being have no respect for national boundaries. For example, children living in a chaotic urban neighborhood in India were found to have a poor sense of personal control over their environments (Regani, 2000). Recently, researchers have turned their attention to a particularly troubling source of community disorganization that affects children in many parts of the world—the disruptive and destructive consequences of war (see the box "Children and War").

neighborhood physical disorder A problem in distressed communities, including both physical deterioration (garbage on the streets, rundown buildings, etc.) and chaotic activity (crowding, high noise levels, etc.).

social disorganization A problem in distressed communities, including weak social cohesion (lack of trust and connection among community members), poor neighborhood climate (fear related to crime and violence), and perceived racism.

media Forms of mass communication, including newspapers, magazines, books, comic books, radio, television, films, video games, and the Internet.

APPLY CONNECT DISCUSS

A newly elected mayor campaigned on promises to tackle the problems affecting a distressed community in his city. He has put you in charge of a task force and wants you to develop a plan for reducing social disorganization. Generate a list of possible community programs that you think might help reduce social disorganization, and explain why you think they would work and how they would improve the lives of children in the community.

The ways that families cope with misfortune can dramatically affect their children's risk for developmental problems. If the children living in this railroad car are cared for as well as their beautiful garden suggests, they may escape many of the usual consequences of poverty.

© Phil Schermeister/Corbis

Media Contexts

The term **media** refers to forms of mass communication, such as newspapers, books, magazines, comic books, radio, television, film, video games, and the Internet. Needless to say, children in technologically advanced societies are immersed in modern communications media to a staggering degree. On average, children in the United States are exposed to 8.33 hours of media each day (Table 10.5; Roberts, Foehr, & Rideout, 2005). It is clear that media matter to children. What children see on TV, read in books, and learn from video games influences their behavior in other contexts. Research from Germany, Israel, South Korea, and the United States indicates that children across cultures take themes and characters from media and fold them into their play and make-believe worlds (Gotz, Lemish, Aidman, & Moon, 2005). Our concerns about how children are affected by media are apparent in movie ratings and television V-chips and in the way parents worry about everything from fairy-tale-induced nightmares to Internet sexual predators.

Research on how the various media affect children's development focuses on two general issues. The first concerns whether the *physical form* of the medium

table 10.5

Children's Average Hourly Exposure per Day to Various Media

	Age (years)				
	0–3*	**4–6***	**8–10**	**11–14**	**15–18**
All screen media**	1:47	2:10	4:41	4:25	3:40
TV	1:01	1:10	3:17	3:16	2:36
Audio	1:03	0:49	0:59	1:42	2:24
Print	0:37	0:41	0:44	0:41	0:45
Computers	0:05	0:16	0:37	1:02	1:22
Video games	0:01	0:10	1:05	0:52	0:33

*For these age groups, audio media means listening to music, and print media means reading or being read to.

**Screen media includes TV, videotapes, DVDs, and movies.

Children and War

POLITICAL VIOLENCE HAS BEEN IDENtified as a major risk that threatens the lives and well-being of children across the globe (Kaslow, 2001). A United Nations (1996) report catalogs a list of horrifying traumas and rights violations suffered by children and their families. Children are recruited as soldiers and made to commit murder and other atrocities; they are exposed to disease and malnutrition when they are forced to flee their homes or while living in refugee camps; their access to education and health care is severely curtailed due to relocation, or because their schools and hospitals have been destroyed; children are injured, permanently disabled, or killed in conflict, often intentionally, sometimes by stumbling on unexploded land mines; they are raped and otherwise exploited sexually; they witness the murder of family members and neighbors; and they are orphaned. (See the table, which gives the experiences of 76 children during the war in Bosnia and Herzegovina, from 1992 to 1995.)

In light of these horrors, it is no surprise that children exposed to war often show symptoms of traumatic stress, including irritability, sleep difficulties, separation anxiety, and nightmares (Dybdahl, 2001). However, studies on the long-term effects of war on children present a complex picture. While some children suffer

War Experiences of Children and Families

Type of Event	n	%
Had to flee from my home	76	100
Thought I would die	70	92
Experienced war activities	68	90
Been shot at	64	84
Separated from close family	57	75
Family members missing	50	66
Family members wounded	49	65
Serious food deprivation	48	63
Seen dead bodies of victims	46	61
Family members killed	44	58
Witnessed home destroyed	23	30
Wounded	16	21
Forced to do things against own will	22	17
Witnessed torture	17	13
Abused, tortured	9	12
Been in concentration camp	6	8

Data were collected during the war in Bosnia and Herzegovia (1992–1995); n = 76.
Source: Dybdahl, 2001, p. 1221.

UNICEF/HG92-0587/I Dream of Peace

Children who experience the horrors of war firsthand often show psychological and emotional symptoms that are similar to those associated with post-traumatic stress syndrome. This child's drawing illustrates the frightening effects of war on home and village life.

affects development. For example, could the vivid images on television confuse young children regarding differences between reality and make-believe? Does excessive Internet use contribute to social isolation from one's peers and interfere with developing social skills? The second issue concerns whether the *content* of the medium affects development. Does Mr. Rogers really teach children that "you are special; you are the only one like you"? Does a steady diet of violent television teach children that aggression is an appropriate way to solve problems?

It is clear from the nature of these questions that considerable controversy surrounds the subject of media effects on children. Below we outline the controversies as they have surfaced in research on the effects of print media, television, and interactive media.

Print Media

As shown in Table 10.5, children's exposure to print media—books, comics, magazines, and newspapers—is relatively small, and fairly stable throughout childhood, greatly, become depressed, and develop psychosocial problems, the majority appear to be relatively resilient and cope reasonably well in everyday life despite the trauma they have experienced (Cairns & Dawes, 1996). Naturally, developmentalists are interested in identifying the factors that may contribute to children's successful coping. Two factors have received recent attention from researchers: the parenting that a child receives, and the cultural traditions in which the child develops.

Because political violence places families under significant stress, parenting may deteriorate. In the face of the pressures of war, parents often become more authoritarian and less emotionally positive in their interactions (Miller, 1996). They also tend to provide their children with less supervision. It seems, however, that parents and children may profit from intervention programs focused on supporting good parenting skills. In one study, refugee mothers were randomly assigned either to a control group or to an experimental group that was counseled on the importance of emotionally responsive communications with their children and of providing an emotionally warm and supportive environment (Dybdahl, 2001). Compared with the control group, mothers in the experimental group showed fewer trauma symptoms and greater life satisfaction. Based on the mothers' reports, the children of mothers in the experimental group appeared less anxious and sad, and had fewer nightmares compared with reports by mothers in the control group. In addition, children in the experi-

mental group gained more weight, showed higher levels of improvement on tests of cognitive reasoning, and perceived their mothers as more emotionally supportive compared with children in the control group.

Cultural traditions can also help children cope with the trauma of war. An example of this is provided in studies of child soldiers (Honwana, 2000; Summerfield, 1999). In many African nations torn by war over the years— including Zimbabwe, Mozambique, Angola, and Ethiopia, among others—children have been recruited to fight. Part of the process of recovering from war involves participating in

ritualized cleansing ceremonies. When young soldiers return home, they are symbolically cleansed of the contaminating ancestral spirits of their victims, which would otherwise spread from the soldiers to the entire social body (Honwana, 2000). The children are forbidden to speak of their war experiences, as this would "open a door" for the harmful spirits to infect the community. In contrast to Western traditions that view trauma as a personal problem, African traditions view it as a potential threat to the larger social group. It is therefore not only the individual who undergoes a process of recovery but also the entire community.

One of the most disturbing ways that children become victims of war is by being recruited as armed combatants into armies and other militant groups.

EPA/Stephen Morrison/AP Wide World

compared to their exposure to the other media forms (see Figure 10.7 for examples of print media for children). Nevertheless, we can reasonably conclude that children read, or are read to, just about every day (Comstock & Scharrer, 2007). Certainly, this is consistent with the fact that children's literature is a growing multimillion dollar industry. In general, developmentalists have approached children's literature from two directions. One direction explores why certain types of literature— adventures, mysteries, fantasies, and fairy tales, in particular—appeal to children and what functions they may serve in children's emotional development. The other direction, which we examine in Chapter 12, considers children's literature as a means of fostering intellectual development and "school readiness"—in particular, the development of language, reading, and writing skills.

One of the most famous analyses of the role of fairy tales in children's emotional development is that of the psychoanalyst Bruno Bettelheim (1977). Noting that many fairy tales include symbolic representations of universal childhood anxieties, such as abandonment and aggression, Bettelheim argued that children need fairy tales in order to find solutions to their own inner conflicts and fears.

The moon was out and we saw some sheep.
We saw some sheep take a walk in their sleep.
By the light of the moon, by the light of a star,
they walked all night, from near to far.
I would never walk. I would take a car.

—Dr. Seuss

There's a voice inside each of us that says, "Me first."
It tells us to please ourselves—to take what we want and
do what we like, never mind about anybody else. . . .
A girl who chooses to use good manners is telling the
world she believes that other people matter as much as
she does. She's saying that life isn't about what one
person does for herself but about what people can do
together for the common good.

—Nancy Holyoke, *A Smart Girl's*
Guide to Manners, p. 8, 2005.

Doraemon no Kokugo Omoshiro Koryaku © 2005 Fujiko-F-Fujio-Production/Shogakukan Inc.

Figure 10.7 From the playful wordplay of Dr. Seuss to the highly stylized world of Japanese *manga*, print media aimed at children vary widely in style and intention.

Consider, for example, Maurice Sendak's wonderful tale *Where the Wild Things Are*. You may remember that naughty Max is sent to his room, where he imagines sailing to an enchanted land and becoming king of the wild things. From a psychoanalytic perspective, the story traces Max's feelings of anger and aggression as they are projected into the forms of imaginary "wild things." When Max masters his emotions—that is, tames and becomes king of the wild things—he returns to the reality of his room, his mother, and his dinner, which is, comfortingly, "still hot."

In addition to serving as a tool of emotional control and development, children's literature has been used as a therapeutic device to help children cope with and communicate about a variety of emotionally troubling events, such as divorce, illness, and death, or even the birth of a sibling (Malchiodi & Grinns-Gruenberg, 2008).

Whether intended to delight, instruct, or comfort, children's literature reflects a centuries-old cultural belief that children's thoughts and emotions can be affected by exposure to specific types of print media.

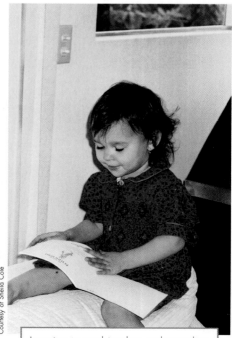

Learning to read involves understanding how to hold a book and turn pages, and what to look for on the page.

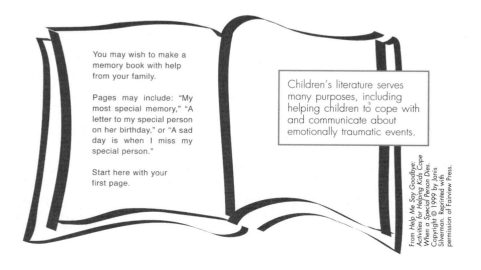

You may wish to make a memory book with help from your family.

Pages may include: "My most special memory," "A letter to my special person on her birthday," or "A sad day is when I miss my special person."

Start here with your first page.

Children's literature serves many purposes, including helping children to cope with and communicate about emotionally traumatic events.

From *Help Me Say Goodbye: Activities for Helping Kids Cope When a Special Person Dies.* Copyright © 1999 by Janis Silverman. Reprinted with permission of Fairview Press.

Television

Do you remember the airplanes slicing into the Twin Towers on 9/11, the plumes of smoke, the towers collapsing into clouds of dust? Do you remember the sight of people leaping from 80 floors up to escape the inferno and of the streets filled with people running in panic, or sitting, confused or hurt, on sidewalk curbs? Perhaps you also remember the flurry of concern about how children might be harmed by viewing—over and over again—the television replays of 9/11. In fact, research suggests that children who were exposed to extensive television replays of the World Trade Center attack were more likely to show symptoms of separation anxiety and posttraumatic stress disorders than were children who had less television exposure to the event (Gershoff & Aber, 2004; Hoven et al., 2004).

Television is powerful. It communicates information, sways our opinions, and moves us emotionally. And, clearly, young children are exposed more to television than to any other medium. On average, TV sets in American homes are on for 6 or more hours each day, and young children are in front of them for 2 or more of those hours (Schmidt et al., 2008). In addition, nearly 40 percent of 3- and 4-year-old children live in households in which the TV is on "always" or "most of the time," even when no one is watching it (Vandewater et al., 2005). Extensive research has focused on television as a potentially positive or destructive influence on children's development (Pecora, Murray, & Wartella, 2006).

The Muppet Kami is a newcomer to the cast of *Sesame Street* in South Africa. She likes nature, collecting stuff, and telling stories. She is also HIV positive.

Television Form

> The Count (with a bad Hungarian accent): I am the Count, and I *love* to count. Today I will count my bats. I see *one* bat. Now I see *two* bats. Now there is another. That makes how many bats?
>
> Tens of thousands of children watching the Count on TV respond as one: ***Three bats!!!!***
>
> The Count: Yes! There are *three bats*.

Before asking how television viewing affects children's thoughts, feelings, and behavior, we need to understand how children make sense of television sounds, images, and story plots. For example, a special concern about television viewing is that young children easily confuse TV make-believe and reality. Consistent with our earlier discussion of preoperational thinking (see Chapter 8, p. 275), research suggests that young children have little comprehension of the boundary between what they see on television and the rest of their perceptual environment (Troseth, 2003). They are likely to think, for example, that a bowl of popcorn shown on TV would spill if the TV set were turned upside down (Flavell et al., 1990). Even 4- and 5-year-olds may display such difficulty, believing that Sesame Street is a real place or that television characters can see and hear the people who are watching them. This no doubt contributes to the enthusiasm with which young children enter into conversations with TV characters such as the Count and to how special they may really feel when Mr. Rogers looks them right in the eye and says, "*You* are my special friend; I like you."

In addition to problems distinguishing between appearance and reality, young children often fail to comprehend what they watch, especially if understanding requires linking together fast-paced scenes (Juston et al., 2007). Consequently, they may fail to appreciate the overarching meaning of a TV story, not recognizing, for example, that the point of a typical police drama is that even if a character's bad behavior results in short-term gains, it does not pay off in the long run. Problems understanding the relationship between one scene and another may also contribute to the difficulty children have distinguishing between television programs and advertisements. Indeed, not until they are 7 or 8 years of age do children both

Television remains the most popular form of media among children.

ACE STOCK LIMITED/Alamy

distinguish between TV programs and advertisements and appreciate the persuasive intent of the latter (Gunter, Oates, & Blades, 2005). Concerns that children who do not understand the persuasive intent of advertising may be highly susceptible to it have led some countries, including Sweden, to ban television advertising to children under the age of 12 (Bjurstrom, 1994).

Television Content Television exposes children to a great range of content. The Count teaches counting; Mr. Rogers counsels on the importance caring for others; cartoon characters meet violent ends, sometimes more than once; prime-time dramas, as well as the evening news, depict sexuality, violence, and aggression, but also empathy and tenderness. For decades, developmentalists have been deeply interested in how television content affects children's behavior, attitudes, and development—both positively and negatively.

Violence. The aggressive and violent content of children's television in the United States has received considerable attention from researchers, as well as from society at large. Little wonder, given that nearly 70 percent of children's television shows contain acts of physical aggression, averaging 14 violent acts per hour, compared with fewer than 4 in programming not aimed at children (Wilson et al., 2002). Researchers estimate that by the age of 18, children have witnessed 200,000 acts of television violence and 16,000 television murders. To be sure, a large portion of these images are in the form of cartoons, in which the likes of Road Runner and Wile E. Coyote commit mayhem on each other, only to recover miraculously to fight another day. But there is a great deal of graphic and realistic violence as well.

Compared with children who watch less television violence, children who watch a lot of programs with fantasy violence, such as *Power Rangers,* or reality-based violent programs, such as *Cops,* tend to show lower levels of moral reasoning and are more likely to believe that violence is acceptable in certain circumstances (Krcmar & Vieira, 2005; Funk et al., 2004). Research into how violence is actually depicted in children's programming provides some clues as to why this might be the case. For one thing, violence goes unpunished 73 percent of the time and is executed by characters that may be attractive to children and with whom children might identify. In addition, the consequences of violence, such as pain and injury, are depicted unrealistically 58 percent of the time (Wilson et al., 2002). For the most part, violence takes the form of "good guys" combating "evil," conveying the moral lesson that violence is an acceptable means to a greater good.

As we have pointed out on many occasions, children are not passive recipients of what goes on around them but actively interpret messages and information from their environments, including their television sets. This was demonstrated by Jamie Ostrov and his colleagues, who conducted a longitudinal study of 78 preschoolers whose parents reported on their children's three favorite TV and video shows and assessed how violent and how educational they were (Ostrov, Gentile, & Crick, 2006). For this group of children, who were from families of relatively high SES, educational shows (mostly from PBS) were significantly preferred over violent shows. Interestingly, the children who watched the most television were rated by teachers and observers as engaging in more prosocial behaviors than children who watched less. Furthermore, although no gender differences were found in the type of programs watched by boys and girls, results suggested that boys and girls were learning different behaviors from the shows. In particular, for boys, greater exposure to violent shows predicted higher levels of future physical, verbal, and relational aggression. In girls, however, higher levels of exposure to violent shows were associated only with future verbal aggression. On the basis of this gender difference, the researchers speculated that boys and girls might be keying in on different forms of aggression depicted on TV. Additional support for this idea comes from the provocative finding that high levels of exposure to educational shows predict future relational aggression in girls but not in boys. These results suggest that even educational programs may be exposing children to relational aggression and, further, that gender socialization processes may be influencing how the content of television affects children's behavior (see Chapter 9, p. 305, to review gender socialization in young children).

Social Stereotypes. Another area of special concern to researchers and society is the social stereotypes in children's television programming, especially the stereotypes pertaining to gender and to ethnic minorities.

Regarding gender stereotyping, throughout the history of television in North America, the people who dominate the television screen have tended to be strong, powerful, and resourceful European American men, with women playing more passive and less visible roles. Although this is changing to some extent, gender stereotypes remain, even in children's programming. For example, a recent study of the gender content of such contemporary favorites as *Rugrats, Pokemon, Arthur,* and *CatDog,* indicates that male characters are still more likely than female characters to answer questions, boss or order others around, show initiative and ingenuity, achieve their goals, and eat (Aubrey & Harrison, 2004). Gender stereotypes also abound in music videos, and studies indicate that adolescents who watch a lot of music videos tend to hold more traditional attitudes toward gender roles than do peers who are less frequent viewers (Ward, Hansbrough, & Walker, 2005).

In light of the changing demographics of American society, developmentalists have become increasingly interested in TV ethnic stereotypes and their impact on the multicultural awareness of children (Berry & Asamen, 2001). The misrepresentation of ethnic minorities and foreigners is a significant problem, although there has been improvement for some groups (Children Now, 2003). Most promising are the changing depictions of African Americans. In the early days of television, African Americans did not appear on the screen often, and when they did appear, they were presented primarily as servants or criminals (Barcus, 1986). Today, in contrast, African Americans are likely to be portrayed more positively than European Americans are, including engaging in proportionally less violent or criminal behavior. Other ethnic groups have not fared as well, however. Hispanic Americans, for example, are even less visible than they were in the 1950s, and they are disproportionately portrayed in criminal roles (Lichter et al., 1997).

That children are keenly aware of these stereotypes is apparent in a study conducted with 1,200 children (300 African Americans, 300 European Americans, 300 Latinos, and 300 Asian Americans) between 10 and 17 years of age (Children Now, 1998; reported in Cortés, 2000, p. 126). Some of the major findings include the following:

1. Asian American children believed the news media provided fairer coverage of Asian Americans than did the entertainment media, whereas the opposite was true for African Americans.

2. Asian American, Latino, and African American children all chose black television figures as their favorite, most admired characters, whereas European American children chose white figures. No Latino or Asian American figures were selected as favorites.

3. Only about one-fifth of the participants felt that there were enough Latino or Asian American main characters. A majority of each ethnic group

Interactive video games draw these children every day to their neighborhood Internet cafe in Hue, Vietnam. Children throughout the world spend considerable amounts of time with interactive media, prompting researchers to examine the effects of such media on children's development.

believed it is important for young people to see those of their own racial or ethnic background on television.

4. Despite the recent changes in how black and white characters are depicted, the vast majority of each group believed that white characters were portrayed most positively, usually as wealthy, well educated, and in positions of leadership. Likewise, nearly 60 percent believed that black actors are most likely to be cast as criminals.

Stereotyping on television is of concern because it may (1) create or maintain negative attitudes toward minority groups, and (2) influence young minority children's attitudes about their own group and place in society.

Interactive Media

Although the television set continues to attract the lion's share of children's leisure time, interactive media, in which the actions of the user—clicking the mouse, turning the joystick, tapping the keyboard—are closing in quickly. The new media are attractive to children, owing both to their form and their content, and as you will see, many of the issues and controversies surrounding children's television viewing loom equally large in the case of children's use of interactive media.

The Form of Interactive Media

If you have watched children playing interactive video games or have played them yourself, you probably have a good sense of how exciting and intellectually challenging they can be. The amazing special effects of computer games provide children with highly sophisticated cartoonlike scenes that they can interact with, controlling the characters' actions and engaging in active problem solving at the same time. In general, computer games call upon a number of cognitive skills, including divided attention, spatial imagery, and representation (Subrahmanyam et al., 2001)

In addition to stimulating cognitive and intellectual processes, interactive media can stimulate emotional responses in children beyond excitement. An example is *Tamagotchi,* a game toy created in Japan. The *Tamagotchi* is an artificial life form that communicates its needs for food, sleep, or play by beeping its owner. The goal of the game is to keep the *Tamagotchi* alive as long as possible, which requires the child's constant attention. As you can imagine, *Tamagotchis* are dropping like flies; there are even virtual Internet "cemeteries" available in which to "bury" them. One researcher observed a young girl in a restaurant burst into tears when her own *Tamagotchi* bit the dust (Richards, 1998; reported in Subrahmanyam et al., 2001). The appearance–reality phenomenon associated with children's interpretation of television is clearly just as operative in the case of interactive media.

One concern about new media technologies—games, as well as e-mail, text-messaging, blogging, and so forth—is how they affect relationships with peers. In a report on the state of young people throughout the world, the United Nations addressed the argument that electronic networks have begun to replace face-to-face networks in many parts of the world, leading to an erosion of social cohesion and trust (U.N. Department of Economic and Social Affairs, 2005). It has been suggested, for example, that spending time on a machine necessarily cuts into time that otherwise would be spent interacting with friends. However, research does not entirely support this concern. Indeed, one study found that boys who play computer games often spend *more* time with their friends outside of school compared to boys who are infrequent users (Colwell, Brady, & Rhaiti, 1995).

A related concern is how the new interactive media affect family relationships. An early study found that new computer games brought families together for shared

This young Japanese girl shows the computer console that she uses several times a day to feed, play with, and generally care for her Tamagotchi.

HEART OF THE CITY   BY MARK TATULLI

email: heartofthecity@hotmail.com   www.ucomics.com/heartofthecity

Interactive computer games have introduced entirely new ways of playing ball.

play and interaction (Mitchell, 1985). However, now that games and computers are common, and children are often more knowledgeable than their parents about how to operate them, such sharing may be less frequent (Subrahmanyam et al., 2001). Indeed, most parents are fairly ignorant of the interactive games that appeal to their children, perhaps owing to the fact that many children play such games in their bedrooms, away from the watchful eyes of parents (Figure 10.8).

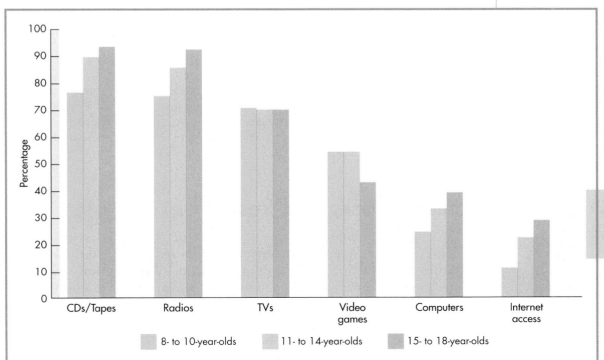

8- to 10-year-olds   11- to 14-year-olds   15- to 18-year-olds

Figure 10.8
Children's media use, according to age and media type.

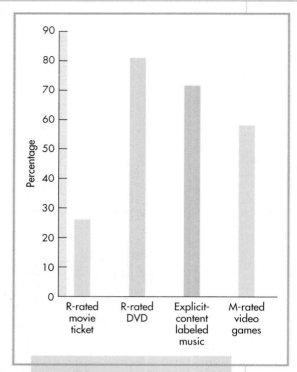

Figure 10.9 Use of adult media reported by junior high school students.

One survey found that only 1 in 50 parents had ever heard of *Duke Nukem,* a violent, M-rated (mature) game known to 8 in every 10 junior high school students (Oldberg, 1998). (Indeed, M-rated video games and other adult media are pervasive among young teens, as indicated in Figure 10.9.)

The Content of Interactive Media Like TV content, the content of the interactive media, particularly that of violent interactive games, has received a huge amount of attention in the popular press. Yet surprisingly few studies have examined the effects of violent video games on children's behavior (Kirsh, 2006). For the most part, research supports the conclusion that violent video game play is associated with an increase in aggressive, antisocial behavior. Interestingly, more recent studies find stronger associations than earlier research, perhaps reflecting the fact that video games have become increasingly graphic, explicit, and realistic (Comstock & Scharrer, 2007). In addition to their association with aggression and antisocial behavior, violent video games would appear to affect children's perceptions of real-world crime. For instance, a study of more than 300 third-through sixth-grade Flemish children found that children who played a lot of violent video games tended to overestimate the amount of violent crime occurring in the real world (Van Mierlo & Van den Bulck, 2004). This finding contributes to the concern that repeated exposure to video game violence may desensitize children to actual violence, making it seem normal and acceptable and reducing children's capacity to respond empathically to the emotional distress of others (Funk et al., 2004). Although this concern about effects of repeated exposure arises with other violent media as well, it is heightened in the case of interactive media because children are actively and constantly making violent choices and being rewarded (receiving more points, getting to the next level) for making these choices.

All told, research on the effects of media on children's development paints a consistent, if complex, picture. Children are immersed in media, and the media can have pronounced effects on how and what children think and feel. At the same time, however, children are active agents in the process; their individual differences and preferences shape how they are affected.

‖‖‖ APPLY ═ CONNECT ═ DISCUSS

Some argue that exposure to violent and aggressive interactive games causes children to be more aggressive. Others believe that such games are a symptom, not a cause, of the fact that our species and/or society is inherently aggressive, and that exposure is unlikely to make much difference. What is your own position on this classic chicken-or-egg debate? What evidence supports your position?

Contexts, Risk, and Resilience

Questions about the impact of different contexts on children's development are motivated by a desire to protect children from harm and promote their health and well-being. In recent years, a new area of research called **prevention science** has emerged to examine the biological and social processes that lead to maladjustment as well as those that are associated with healthy development (Wandersman & Florin, 2003).

Developmentalists working within this field are particularly interested in identifying **risk factors,** personal characteristics or environmental circumstances that increase the probability of negative outcomes for children. Risk is a statistic that

prevention science An area of research that examines the biological and social processes that lead to maladjustment as well as those that are associated with healthy development.

risk factors Personal characteristics or environmental circumstances that increase the probability of negative outcomes for children. Risk is a statistic that applies to groups, not individuals.

resilient The ability to recover quickly from the adverse effects of early experience or persevere in the face of stress with no apparent special negative psychological consequences.

protective factors Environmental and personal factors that are the source of children's resilience in the face of hardship.

applies to groups, not individuals. One can say, for example, that children who have parents who are depressed are more likely than the general population to become depressed themselves, but one cannot say that a particular child whose father or mother is depressed is necessarily at risk for becoming depressed. Most risk factors are not the direct cause of the developmental problems or disorders with which they are associated but, instead, interact in complex ways with other risk factors in contributing to a problem (Roosa, 2000). For example, having a poorly educated mother is a risk factor for school failure, but a mother's lack of education does not cause her children to fail in school. Instead, a child's school failure can be seen as a large puzzle in which one piece is the mother's lack of education and familiarity with the demands of school (for example, the need for the child to spend time at home studying) and other pieces may include a peer group that does not value academic achievement, a school with limited resources due to its location in an economically distressed community, as well as such risk factors as poor nutrition and exposure to environmental pollutants.

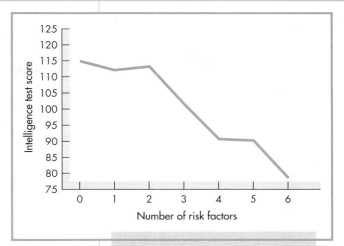

Figure 10.10 The average IQ scores for 13-year-olds decrease markedly when their development is affected by more than two risk factors. (From Sameroff et al., 1993.)

Many studies have demonstrated that most serious developmental problems are associated with a combination of biological, social, and environmental risk factors interacting over a considerable period of time (Cicchetti & Toth, 1998; Luthar et al., 2000; Sameroff et al., 1998; Shaw et al., 1998). Thus, an increase in the number of risk factors increases the likelihood of problems (see Figure 10.10 for a related example involving IQ scores). However, all of these studies have also demonstrated marked individual differences in outcome among children who live in highly stressful circumstances. Many children who grow up in the face of adversity—who are raised by alcoholic parents, attend substandard schools, have siblings who belong to gangs, experience dislocation due to war or homelessness due to poverty—are able to rise above their circumstances and lead healthy, productive lives. That is, they seem to be **resilient**—to have the ability to recover quickly from the adverse effects of early experience or to persevere in the face of stress with no apparent negative psychological consequences. Such cases have led developmentalists to search for the sources of children's resilience, referred to as **protective factors** (Luthar et al., 2000; Robinson, 2000). Table 10.6 summarizes risk and protective factors that have been identified.

At this point, you are well aware of how children's development can be impaired by risks present in family, community, and media contexts. When children are harmed by social chaos, poverty, abuse, hunger, or disease, responsible adults look for ways to reduce their suffering. This is, in fact, the goal of prevention science. A question that reaches deeply to address this goal is, What fundamental needs must be met to assure that children will develop into healthy, well-adjusted adults? In an effort to answer this question, the General Assembly of the United Nations in 1959 produced a document called "United Nations Declaration of the Rights of the Child" (see Table 10.7). This document reflected governments' recognition of the importance of coming together for the sake of protecting and nurturing the world's children (Colon & Colon, 2001). The declaration was followed, in 1989, by the "United Nations Convention on the

Now living in Jordan, this refugee family fled Iraq to escape poverty and hardship. The father, an amputee injured in the Iran–Iraq wars, was unable to accompany them. Despite their sad history, and the difficulty making ends meet with a low-paying job in their new community, this photograph captures a loving moment suggesting the family's resilience to difficult circumstances.

Chris Hondros/Getty Images

table **10.6**	
Examples of Risk and Protective Factors Associated with Childhood Problems	
Risk Factors	**Protective Factors**
Child Characteristics	
Difficult infant temperament	Easy infant temperament
Limited cognitive abilities	High intelligence
Insecure attachments	Secure attachments
Low self-esteem	High self-esteem
Poor peer relations	Positive peer relations
School difficulties	Positive adaptation to school
Psychopathology	Good mental health
Family	
Domestic violence	Good marital relations
Financial hardship	Consistent employment
Hostile family environment	Positive family relations
Parental psychopathology	Good parental mental health
Maladaptive child-rearing skills	Positive child-rearing skills
Neighborhood and Community	
High levels of community violence and crime	Low levels of community violence and crime
Impoverished community	Economically thriving community
Lack of community services	Extensive, easily accessed community services
Little or weak church presence	Supportive church
Society	
Lack of child-centered programs and policies	National support of education and children's rights
Social acceptance of violence	Social intolerance of violence
Physical punishment of children acceptable	Physical punishment unacceptable as a disciplinary practice
Economic recession	Strong economy with low unemployment

Source: Adapted from Cicchetti et al., 2000.

Rights of the Child," a binding resolution to provide children with specific protections. As of this writing, it has been ratified by all countries except two—Somalia and the United States.

In addition to international organizations such as the United Nations, individual governments have worked to develop programs to optimize children's development. **Public policies** are governmental laws and programs designed to promote the welfare of children and families. In the United States, public policies range from nutritional and education programs such as Women, Infants, and Children (WIC) and Head Start to policies regarding children's television programming and advertising and laws that govern the age at which children can be employed, married, vote, admitted to military service, or required to attend school.

This chapter has by no means surveyed all the contexts that influence the lives and development of children. Many children also spend considerable time in peer group contexts, and the special contexts created by religious or ethnic traditions and backgrounds. Indeed, children's ecologies include a vast variety of interacting systems which can be mutually supportive, mutually damaging, or present a mixture of risk and protective factors. Reducing all this complexity, however, is the individual child who interacts with, responds to, and finds meanings across the vast array of contexts according to his or her unique characteristics and past experiences.

public policies Governmental laws and programs such as those designed to promote the welfare of children and families.

table 10.7

United Nations Declaration of the Rights of the Child

Proclaimed by General Assembly Resolution 1386(XIV) of 20 November 1959

Principle 1

The child shall enjoy all the rights set forth in this Declaration. Every child, without any exception whatsoever, shall be entitled to these rights, without distinction or discrimination on account of race, color, sex, language, religion, political or other opinion, national or social origin, property, birth or other status, whether of himself or of his family.

Principle 2

The child shall enjoy special protection, and shall be given opportunities and facilities, by law and by other means, to enable him to develop physically, mentally, morally, spiritually and socially in a healthy and normal manner and in conditions of freedom and dignity. In the enactment of laws for this purpose, the best interests of the child shall be the paramount consideration.

Principle 3

The child shall be entitled from his birth to a name and a nationality.

Principle 4

The child shall enjoy the benefits of social security. He shall be entitled to grow and develop in health; to this end, special care and protection shall be provided both to him and to his mother, including adequate pre-natal and post-natal care. The child shall have the right to adequate nutrition, housing, recreation and medical services.

Principle 5

The child who is physically, mentally or socially handicapped shall be given the special treatment, education and care required by his particular condition.

Principle 6

The child, for the full and harmonious development of his personality, needs love and understanding. He shall, wherever possible, grow up in the care and under the responsibility of his parents, and, in any case, in an atmosphere of affection and of moral and material security; a child of tender years shall not, save in exceptional circumstances, be separated from his mother. Society and the public authorities shall have the duty to extend particular care to children without a family and to those without adequate means of support. Payment of State and other assistance towards the maintenance of children of large families is desirable.

Principle 7

The child is entitled to receive education, which shall be free and compulsory, at least in the elementary stages. He shall be given an education which will promote his general culture and enable him, on a basis of equal opportunity, to develop his abilities, his individual judgement, and his sense of moral and social responsibility, and to become a useful member of society. The best interests of the child shall be the guiding principle of those responsible for his education and guidance; that responsibility lies in the first place with his parents.

The child shall have full opportunity for play and recreation, which should be directed to the same purposes as education; society and the public authorities shall endeavor to promote the enjoyment of this right.

Principle 8

The child shall in all circumstances be among the first to receive protection and relief.

Principle 9

The child shall be protected against all forms of neglect, cruelty and exploitation. He shall not be the subject of traffic, in any form.

The child shall not be admitted to employment before an appropriate minimum age; he shall in no case be caused or permitted to engage in any occupation or employment which would prejudice his health or education, or interfere with his physical, mental or moral development.

Principle 10

The child shall be protected from practices which may foster racial, religious and any other form of discrimination. He shall be brought up in a spirit of understanding, tolerance, friendship among peoples, peace and universal brotherhood, and in full consciousness that his energy and talents should be devoted to the service of his fellow men.

APPLY ▪ CONNECT ▪ DISCUSS

Visit the Web site of the United Nations Children's Fund (UNICEF) at www.unicef.org. What are the priorities of the organization (see "What We Do")? Explore the most recent report of the State of the World's Children.

SUMMARY

- The contexts of children's development can be thought of as nested, interacting ecosystems. Each context can provide resources for positive growth or present significant challenges to health and well-being.

The Family Context

- Families are the first influence on development and one of the most important. The culture affects the way parents treat and socialize their children.

- The two major forms of family structure are nuclear families (parents and their children) and extended families (parents and their children and other kin), each with different implications for children's socialization. Although industrialization brought a shift to the nuclear family, the extended family prevailed for most of human history and remains important as a strategy for dealing with low income. From an evolutionary perspective, caregiving by extended kin may have made possible humans' extended childhood and large brain.

- Parents the world over have three goals: ensuring their children's survival, and if this goal is not threatened, ensuring they will be economically productive adults and will share the group's values. Parenting practices reflect this hierarchy of goals.

- Research initiated by Diana Baumrind found three patterns of parenting:

  - Authoritarian—parents focus on obedience and control, use physical punishment, and tend not to express warmth.

  - Authoritative—parents exert some control, use reasoning, and express warmth.

  - Permissive—parents express warmth but fail to set standards or exert control.

- The authoritative pattern was associated with more self-reliant and self-controlled child behavior.

- Siblings play important roles in one another's social and cognitive development, with their relationship influenced by culture and by factors such as age and gender and the family's emotional climate.

- In many of the world's countries, families are becoming increasingly diverse, through immigration and through changes in family composition.

  - One in five children in the United States has immigrant parents. Parenting styles and values vary across cultures, with, for example, education more highly valued by new immigrants.

  - About half of all children born in the United States today will spend at least some of their childhood in a single-parent home. Children from single-parent families have more behavioral, social, and academic problems. Various explanations have been offered, and it appears that cultural contexts may mitigate problems.

  - Research on the increasing number of children in gay and lesbian households, while limited, paints a generally positive picture of the children's development.

- Various family factors, including affluence, may impede children's development. The most significant of these factor are poverty, an adolescent parent, and abuse.

  - Poverty, affecting approximately 1 in 5 children in the United States, touches all aspects of life—housing, health care, education, even safety. Poverty in early childhood is associated with mental and physical health problems and problems in intellectual development.

  - Despite a recent dramatic drop, the teen birth rate in the United States remains among the highest in the industrialized world. Children of unmarried teenage mothers tend to be more aggressive, less self-controlled, and less intellectually advanced than other children.

  - Definitions of abuse vary widely across cultures. Causes of abuse by parents are not clear, but a parent's childhood experience of abuse, stresses on the family, certain maternal and child characteristics, and cultural acceptance of violence may increase its likelihood.

Nonparental Child Care

- By age 3, more than 90 percent of children in the United States experience regular nonparental care, which takes three forms: home child care (in the children's own home), family child care (in someone else's home), and care in child-care centers (organized facilities supervised by licensed professionals).

- The effects of early child care depend largely on the quality of the care. Children in child-care centers may experience higher levels of stress. Their intellectual development is at least as good as that of children not in child care. Social and emotional effects appear to be both positive (e.g., more self-sufficiency and verbal expressiveness) and negative (e.g., more aggressive behavior), with family factors playing a role. With ethnic minority children in particular, an understanding of the effects of child care requires an understanding of the larger context.

Neighborhoods and Communities

• Neighborhoods and communities differ substantially in the resources they provide children and families, with consequences for children's quality of life and mental health outcomes. Communities may also differ in the values and beliefs transmitted to children.

• Children are often adversely affected by living in distressed communities—communities characterized by economic disadvantage, physical disorder, and social disorganization.

Media Contexts

• Children in technologically advanced societies are extensively exposed to a wide range of media. Research has investigated how the form and content of different media affect development.

• Children's literature may help children with emotional control and development.

• Young children are exposed more to television than to any other medium. A concern about TV viewing is that young children have trouble distinguishing between appearance and reality. Other causes for concern are TV violence, which is especially common in children's shows, and stereotyping, evident in the somewhat limited roles of female and ethnic-minority characters.

• Increasingly important, interactive media such as video games help children develop cognitive skills. Like television, interactive media raise various concerns, including effects on relationships with peers and with family and effects of violent action that children themselves play at.

Contexts, Risk, and Resilience

• Prevention science seeks to protect children from harm and promote their well-being by identifying risk factors—personal and environmental characteristics that increase the probability of negative outcomes—as well as protective factors—factors that may be sources of children's resilience.

• International organizations such as the United Nations and individual governments through public policies seek to optimize children's development.

Key Terms

family structure, p. 341
nuclear families, p. 341
extended families, p. 341
allocaregiving, p. 343
cooperative breeding, p. 343
no-nonsense parenting, p. 345
authoritarian parenting pattern, p. 345

authoritative parenting pattern, p. 345
permissive parenting pattern, p. 345
home child care, p. 359
family child care, p. 360
child-care centers, p. 360
social capital, p. 364
neighborhood physical disorder, p. 366

social disorganization, p. 366
media, p. 367
prevention science, p. 376
risk factors, p. 376
resilient, p. 377
protective factors, p. 377
public policies, p. 378

Major Milestones of Middle Childhood

	Physical Domain	Cognitive Domain	Social and Emotional Domain	
What Develops...	• Increase in muscle mass results in greater strength for boys and girls. • Increase in fat tissue changes overall shape of the body. • Sex differences in motor skills increase, with boys excelling in strength and girls in agility. • Continued brain growth and synaptic pruning, especially in late-maturing areas of the brain (frontal and prefrontal cortex). • Electrical activity in different brain areas becomes more synchronous, suggesting greater coordination between areas.	• Emergence of mental operations allows sorting, classification, experimentation with variables. • Increased memory and attention. • Acquisition of memory strategies. • Increased memory due to greater efficiency in encoding, storing, and retrieving information. • Increased knowledge of cognition and memory and of own limitations in both.	• Stage of industry versus inferiority; success in coping with increased expectations for maturity result in positive self-esteem. • Emergence of playing games with rules. • Moral behavior regulated less by fear of authority, more by social relationships. • Emergence of clearly defined peer social structures. • Gender-typed behaviors increase. • Increasing proficiency at making and keeping friends and dealing with interpersonal conflicts. • Emergence of social comparison through which self is defined in relation to peers.	
Sociocultural Contributions and Consequences...	• Access to healthy food influences changes in height and weight • Different cultures provide different opportunities for boys and girls to engage in sports and physical activities.	• School is associated with development of specific intellectual skills and memory. • Different cultures may support the development of different memory and planning strategies. • Cultural and socioeconomic factors affect whether families encourage school-related activities. • Different instructional methods affect the rate and effectiveness of learning.	• Cultural differences in whether particular behaviors are seen as matters of morality or of convention. • Transition from elementary to middle school may contribute to increase in bullying as children reorganize social relationships. • Cultures may support development of different forms of aggression in girls and boys. • Sociocultural contexts may support development of cooperation or competition between children. • Cultural differences affect parental expectations for mature behavior and degree of parental supervision.	

part IV

Middle Childhood

Anthropological descriptions of a wide variety of cultures indicate that as children reach the ages of 5 to 7, they are no longer restricted to the home or to settings where they are carefully watched by adults. Instead, they become responsible for behaving themselves and are given responsibilities in a variety of new contexts, including contexts where they are alone or interacting with peers. The new activities they engage in vary from one society to the next. Among some of the Mayan people in the highlands of Guatemala, for example, boys go out to gather wood, a solitary activity that takes them well beyond the range of watchful adults, while girls spend more time doing domestic work in the company of their mothers and the older women of the village (Rogoff, 2003). In the United States, by contrast, boys and girls alike spend long hours in school receiving formal education; both in and out of school, their interactions with peers increase.

All these shifts prove important to children. Thus, solitary activities, such as gathering wood or chasing birds away from a growing rice crop, and peer interactions, such playing games, exchanging secrets, or simply hanging out, can be as significant for development as time spent in the classroom. Being in charge of the family cornfield or a younger sibling or engaging in informal interaction with peers provides children with important opportunities to learn what it means to take responsibility, to explore social relationships, and to develop moral understanding and personal identity.

The fact that cultures everywhere give children greater autonomy and responsibility as they enter middle childhood both reflects and supports the significant expansion of children's physical and cognitive capacities. For example, as you shall see, evidence from experiments, naturalistic observations, and clinical interviews makes it clear that during middle childhood children are increasingly able to think more deeply and logically, to follow through on a task once it is undertaken, and to keep track of several aspects of a situation at one time.

Our discussion of middle childhood is divided into three chapters. Chapter 11 focuses on the changes in children's physical and cognitive capacities between the ages of 6 and 12 that support the new freedoms and responsibilities that adults place upon them. Chapter 12 examines the influence of schooling on development, with particular attention to the organization of school activities and to the intellectual capacities that schooling both demands and fosters. Chapter 13 focuses on emotional development and on the significance of the new social relations that emerge during middle childhood, particularly among peers. The influence of physical, cognitive, and social factors, as they are woven together in different cultural contexts, creates the particular tapestry of middle childhood as it is encountered around the world.

11

Physical and Cognitive Development in Middle Childhood

A girl from Kukatja Community, a hunter-gatherer society in the desert of Western Australia, provides the following description of life in her camp:

Mothers and fathers gone out hunting and leave us kids in camp. When we got hungry we go hunting for little lizard, get him and cook it and eat him up. Me little bit big now, I go hunting myself, tracking goanna [a type of lizard] and kill him. . . . Soon as mother leave him, little ones go hunting, kill animals, blue tongue, mountain devil [both lizards], take them home before mother and father come back, cook and eat it. Mothers, they bring him goannas and blue tongue and father one still long way. Mother come back and feed all them kids. . . . After lunch mother and father go hunting for supper, all the little kids walk and kill little lizard, take him home, cook and eat him. . . .

Morning again, father one he go hunting. All little kids go hunting self. . . . . Mother go out separate from father and come back with big mob of animals. Me big enough to hunt around self. . . . Morningtime, father one bin for hunting long way way. He bin get and kill an emu, bring and cook him. Everyone happy, they bin say he good hunter. Mother and father sometime bin come back late from hunting. They bin go long way. (Kapanankga, 1995, p. 143).

Despite being a "little bit big now," and able to track, kill, and cook goanna, the Kukatja girl quoted above remains dependent on her mother and father to provide adequate nutrition and care throughout the years of middle childhood. As we have discussed in earlier chapters, our species is unique in its prolonged period of childhood dependency; once weaned, children in all societies rely on their elders for care and protection for well over a decade (Kaplan et al., 2003; Bird & Bird, 2005).

On the other hand, research conducted in many societies shows that adults begin to have new expectations when their children approach 6 years of age. Among the Ngoni of Malawi, in central Africa, for example, adults believe that the loss of milk teeth and the emergence of second teeth (starting around the age of 6) signal that children should begin to act more independently. They are supposed to stop playing childish games and start learning skills that will be essential when they grow up. They are also expected to understand their place and are held accountable for being discourteous. The boys leave the protection and control of women and move into dormitories, where they must adapt to a system of male dominance and male life. Margaret Read (1983) describes the difficulties that this transition to a new stage of life causes for Ngoni boys:

There was no doubt that this abrupt transition, like the sudden weaning [several years earlier], was a shock for many boys between six-and-a-half and seven-and-a-half. From having been impudent, well fed, self-confident, and spoiled youngsters among the women many of them quickly became skinny, scruffy, subdued, and had a hunted expression. (p. 49)

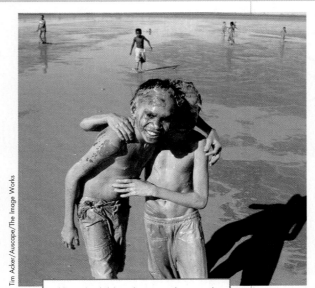

Tim Acker/Auscape/The Image Works

Although children begin to hunt and work at early ages in the Kukatja Community of Western Australia, they also have time to play together in the mud after a rare rainstorm in their desert home.

Observations of life among the Ifaluk of Micronesia provide a similar picture. The Ifaluk believe that at the age of 6 years, children gain "social intelligence," which includes the ability to acquire important cultural knowledge and skills, as well as the ability to work, to adhere to social norms, and to demonstrate compassion for others—all valued adult behaviors (Lutz, 1987). In Western Europe and the United States, this same transition has long been considered the beginning of the "age of reason" (White, 1996).

Adults' expectations that their children will begin to behave more maturely at around the age of 6 or 7 arise from a combination of cultural traditions, ecological circumstances and demands (for example, whether children must learn to cross busy streets or fast-moving streams), and their observations of how well their children now cope with new demands (Sameroff & Haith, 1996). At the age of 6, children are strong and agile enough to catch a runaway goat or to carry their little sisters on their hips. They become more proficient at hunting and gathering food, and know not to let a baby crawl near an open fire (Bock et al., 2005; Bird & Bird, 2005). They can wait for the school bus without wandering off. They can, sometimes under duress, sit still for several hours at a time while adults attempt to instruct them, and they are beginning to be able to carry out their chores in an acceptable manner. In short, they can perform tasks independently, formulate goals, and resist the temptation to abandon them.

As we discussed in Chapter 2, the duration of childhood in our species is one of the longest in the animal kingdom. Although there is considerable debate about whether we have long childhoods because we need to gain the experience, knowledge, and skills required to be fully functioning adults, or whether we gain so much experience and knowledge coincidentally because we have long childhoods, it is obvious to all that middle childhood involves significant changes to the size and functioning of the body and to ways of thinking and acting in the world. In this chapter we focus on the physical and cognitive changes that take place during middle childhood and might justify adults' new demands and expectations. The physical changes of middle childhood—continued growth, improved motor skills, and increased brain activity—are readily observable. Changes in children's cognitive functioning, however, are more difficult to measure and, as you might expect, have been addressed by different theoretical approaches.

The transition to middle childhood is often marked by new responsibilities, privileges, and rituals. Here, young girls participate in the Dasai Festival in Darjeeling, India.

Earl & Nazima Kowall/Corbis

Physical and Motor Development

An obvious reason that children can do more on their own is that they are bigger, are stronger, and have more endurance than they had when they were younger. Size and strength increase significantly during middle childhood, although more slowly than in earlier years. Motor development shows marked improvement as children perfect the skills needed for running, throwing, catching, and turning somersaults. In addition to changes in the size and functioning of the body are significant changes taking place in the brain that support the intellectual developments we will discuss later in this chapter.

Patterns of Growth

Children in the United States are on average about 39 inches tall and about 36 pounds at age 4; by the time they are 6 years old they are about 45 inches tall and weigh about 45 pounds. At the start of adolescence, 6 or 7 years later, their average height will have increased to almost 5 feet and their weight to approximately 90 pounds (Cameron, 2002). During middle childhood, increases in muscle mass contribute to increased strength for boys and girls (Figure 11.1). In addition, beginning at approximately age 7 for girls and age 8 for boys, there is a gradual increase in fat tissue that contributes to the changing appearance of the body (Figure 11.2). Like all aspects of development, children's growth during middle childhood continues to depend on the interaction of environmental and genetic factors.

Height Now fully grown, Amita just barely reaches the 5′3″ mark on the measuring stick. There would be nothing remarkable about her small stature except for the fact that she comes from a very tall family. Growing up with jokes that question her mother's relationship with the milkman, Amita is good-natured about defying what we know regarding how genetic factors influence one's height: tall parents tend to have tall children. Monozygotic twins reared together are very

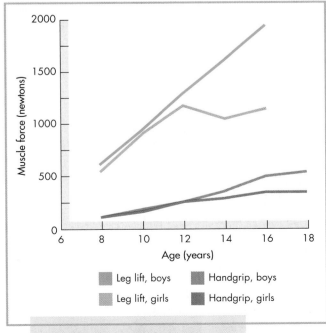

Figure 11.1 Developmental changes in strength for boys and for girls.

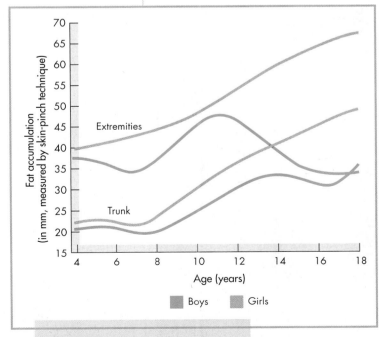

Figure 11.2 Developmental changes in fat distribution for boys and for girls.

similar in their patterns of growth, and those reared apart still tend to resemble each other more than do dizygotic twins, who share only 50 percent of their genes. Yet environmental conditions also play a significant role, as attested to by the existence of many cases in which one monozygotic twin is significantly smaller than the other because of the effects of illness (Amita attributes her shortness to several severe infections suffered during infancy) or a poor environment, as when one twin is raised in a healthy environment and the other develops in impoverished conditions.

The environmental contribution to size can also be seen in the variations in the height and rate of growth typical of populations that undergo changes in living conditions. From the late 1970s to the early 1990s, Mayan families from Guatemala migrated to the United States in record numbers (Bogin et al., 2002). Barry Bogin and his colleagues measured the height of more than four hundred 5- to 12-year-old Mayan American children in 1999 and 2000. These data were compared with data for a sample of more than 1000 Mayan children living in Guatemala at the time. The Mayan American children were about 4½ inches taller, on average, than Mayan children living in Guatemala. These results illustrate how the heights of human populations can be sensitive indicators of the quality of the environment for growth.

One of the key environmental factors that moderate genetic growth potential is nutrition. Poor children, who have less access to nutritious food and good health care, are usually smaller than children of the same age in well-off families. Problems are especially evident if lack of access is extreme. For example, Sunyoung Pak, an anthropologist at Seoul National University in South Korea, studied the physical development of children whose families sought refuge in South Korea from North Korea, where they had suffered from a chronic food shortage (Pak, 2004). The children's malnourishment was so severe that by the time they reached their 14th birthdays, the boys from North Korea were approximately 6 inches shorter than their South Korean counterparts; girls were approximately 3 inches shorter.

As indicated, health also plays a role in a child's growth. Growth slows during illnesses, even mild illnesses. When children are adequately nourished, this slowdown is usually followed by a period of rapid "catch-up growth," which quickly restores them to their genetically normative path of growth (Georgieff & Raghavendra, 2001). When nutritional intake is inadequate, however, the children never do catch up, and their growth is stunted (deRegnier et al., 2007).

Weight Body weight, like height, is influenced by genetic factors. A study of 540 Danish adoptees found a strong correlation between the adoptees' weight as adults and the weight of their biological parents, especially their mothers (Stunkard et al., 1986). Yet environmental factors—including the quantity and quality of food available—play a significant role in determining weight (Whitaker et al., 1997). For example, the number of calories consumed in an average day can have long-term effects for a child's growth. The consumption of as little as 50 extra calories a day can lead to an excess weight gain of 5 pounds over a course of a year (Kolata, 1986). Given that the average 12-ounce can of soda contains 180 calories and that soda has replaced bread as a major source of calories in the diets of American children and adults, you will not be surprised to learn that scores of studies have implicated soft drink consumption as a major contributor to childhood obesity (reviewed in Vartanian, Schwartz, & Brownell, 2007).

In recent years, increased attention has been focused on the issue of children's weight, and the factors that contribute to it, in light of the rising rates of obesity among American children (Eneli & Davies, 2008). (See the box "In the Field: The

Stockbyte/Alamy

Rising rates of obesity among children throughout the world have spurred developmentalists to identify factors that contribute to childhood overweight, and design programs that will prevent it.

Edible Schoolyard: Thinking outside the Lunchbox.") While obesity is commonly measured by weight, many researchers have argued that it can be diagnosed earlier and more accurately by measuring *body mass index* (*BMI*), the ratio of weight to height (American Academy of Pediatrics, 2003). BMI can be calculated by multiplying a person's weight (in pounds) by 705, and dividing by height (in inches) twice. The average BMI for 5-year-olds is 15.2 for girls and 15.4 for boys (Centers for Disease Control, 2000). Children whose BMI falls between the 85th and 95th percentile are considered at risk for obesity—roughly 15 percent of 6- to 11-year-olds now fit in this category (American Academy of Pediatrics, 2003).

Motor Development

Walking along the beach one day, we saw a girl about 7 years old and her little brother, who was about 4 years old, following their father and older brother, who was 10 or 11 years old. The father and older brother were tossing a ball back and forth as they walked. The girl was hopping along the sand on one foot, while her younger brother scrambled to keep up with her. Suddenly the little girl threw her arms up in the air, leaned over, threw her feet up, and did a cartwheel. She then did another cartwheel. Her younger brother stopped to watch her. Then he tried one. He fell in a heap in the sand, while she continued doing one perfect cartwheel after another. He picked himself up and ran ahead so that he was now between his father and his older brother. His father tossed the ball to him. He missed it, and when he picked it up and tried to throw it back, it flew off to the side. His older brother retrieved it and made a perfect throw.

In such everyday scenes you can see the increases in motor development that occur over the course of middle childhood (Figure 11.3). Children become stronger and more agile, and their balance improves. They run faster; they throw balls farther and with greater efficiency and are more likely to catch them. They also jump farther and higher than they did when they were younger, and they learn to skate, ride bikes, sail boats, dance, swim, and climb trees as well as acquire a host of other physical skills during this period. Nonetheless, studies indicate that about 10 percent of 9-year-olds fail to develop skills like kicking and throwing, indicating that such achievements require practice, and do not develop purely as a result of maturation (Haywood & Getchell, 2005).

As a general rule, boys and girls differ in their physical skills. By the time they are 5 years old, boys, on average, can jump a little farther, run a bit faster, and throw a ball about 5 feet farther than the average girl. Boys also tend to be better at batting, kicking, dribbling, and catching balls than most girls. Girls, on the other hand, tend to be more agile than boys. Over the course of middle childhood, these

Figure 11.3 The physical changes of childhood make possible a range of new activities. The ability to kick a ball, for example, improves dramatically. A young child learning to kick will simply push the leg forward (a), while an older child will step forward, cock the leg, and take a limited swing at the ball (b). By the end of middle childhood, the child is able to take a full swing at the ball while simultaneously moving arms and trunk to provide support and balance (c). (From Haywood & Getchell, 2005.)

(a)   (b)   (c)

In the field The Edible Schoolyard: Thinking outside the Lunchbox

Name:	Alice Waters
Education:	B.A. in French Cultural Studies from the University of California, Berkeley; additional education training at the Montessori School, London
Current Position:	Executive chef and owner of Chez Panisse Restaurant and Café, Berkeley, California
Career Objectives:	Instill life-long nutritious eating practices by involving children in the entire process of growing, preparing, and serving healthy food

Alice Waters is on a mission to transform children's lives by changing the way they eat. Her goal is to wean children from their three basic food groups—fat, sugar, and salt—and replace the practice of scarfing Happy Meals in the minivan with that of preparing and enjoying food in the family kitchen. In pursuit of this goal, the former schoolteacher and long-time advocate of hands-on learning has instigated a national movement to turn school blacktops into organic gardens tended by kids (Orenstein, 2004). Her logic is that if children are allowed to participate in growing and harvesting fruits and vegetables, they will be enticed to make healthy food choices and will avoid foods laden with fats, sugars, and salt, which, according to the Centers for Disease Control, have placed an entire generation of children at risk for obesity.

Since 1970 the incidence of childhood obesity has increased more than 50 percent among children between the ages of 6 and 11 years and nearly as much among adolescents age 12 to 17 (Ogden et al., 2006). The consequences of becoming obese during childhood and adolescence are severe. Obese children are often rejected by their peers, causing many of them to become withdrawn and suffer from a loss of self-esteem. Obese children are also more vulnerable to a variety of serious health problems such as asthma, heart disease, diabetes, respiratory disease, and orthopedic disorders (Davies & Fitzgerald, 2008). In recent years, there has been an alarming increase among obese minority children in the incidence of Type II diabetes, a serious condition that can lead to kidney disease, eye disorders, and nervous system problems as well as heart disease and stroke.

There appear to be three important periods during which there is an increased risk for developing obesity that persists into adulthood (Strauss, 1999). The first is the prenatal period, during which, it is believed, either maternal overnutrition or maternal undernutrition can cause metabolic changes in the fetus that permanently alter the child's appetite regulation. The second important period is related to what is known as the adiposity rebound period, during which children's body fat begins to increase again

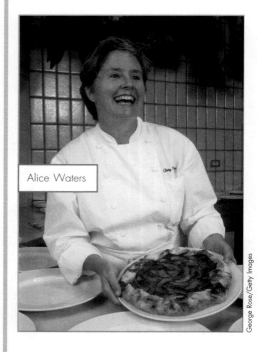

Alice Waters

George Rose/Getty Images

Alice Waters and friends tending their gardens in the Edible Schoolyard.

Justine Kurland

after a period of decreasing. Normally, the adiposity rebound period occurs at around age 6. Longitudinal studies have found that children whose body fat increases before the age of 5½ are significantly more likely than other children to become and remain obese. The third important period for the development of persistent obesity is adolescence, when there are changes in the quantity and location of body fat. This period is especially critical for girls. In boys the quantity of body fat normally decreases by about 40 percent, whereas in girls the quantity of body fat increases by about 40 percent, putting girls at elevated risk for becoming and staying obese.

Obviously, children's food choices are substantially influenced by the habits and preferences of the family. It is recognized increasingly, however, that social institutions, including schools, bear significant responsibility for children's eating behavior. For example, sugary drinks and snacks high in fat, sugar, and salt are readily available in school cafeterias and vending machines (Prentice & Jebb, 2003). To combat childhood obesity effectively, public attitudes must change to shift responsibility from children and families to include the schools and other social institutions that provide children with meals and snacks when they are away from home.

While many new school programs have tackled the obesity epidemic by changing cafeteria fare to include a greater variety of fresh fruits and vegetables, reducing the amount of soda and candy sold in vending machines, and educating children about the importance of a healthy diet, Alice Waters's Edible Schoolyard program takes a decidedly different approach. Reflecting her background as a renowned chef and founder of one of the most famous restaurants in the United States, Waters wants to influence children's eating behavior by changing their relationships with food. In the Edible Schoolyard, while tilling the garden, children graze from the strawberry patch or munch sugar snap peas. For those raised on frozen or canned peas, carrots, and corn, the Edible Schoolyard provides their first fresh-from-the-garden experience.

Waters envisions children's personal involvement in growing and harvesting their food expanding to include their involvement in meal preparation. Ultimately, the institutional cafeterias with which we all grew up—where food is served from stainless steel vats onto bland plates that are transported on trays from the lunch line to a line of narrow tables placed end to end—would be replaced by attractive dining rooms in which students have set tables with cloth and cutlery, and serve, family style, dishes that the children have helped to prepare using fresh ingredients, some of which were cultivated in the school yard. Educating children about the importance of eating well, making available healthy choices, and reducing access to foods high in fats, sugars, and salts are surely important to stemming the tide of childhood obesity. But these health-focused tactics are not enough to change children's eating habits. According to Waters, you must start with pleasure: "Kids need to find these foods to be delicious so they fall in love with them, and it changes their lives forever" (Orenstein, 2004, p. 32).

Since the late 1970s there have been dramatic increases in the percentages of children and adolescents in the United States who are overweight and obese.

In an example of how culture supports the development of fine motor skills, Michael carves a design in a clay turtle during a class focused on the pottery of Native Americans.

sex differences in motor skills become more pronounced (Malina, 1998). On average, boys tend to be slightly advanced in motor abilities that require power and force, while girls often excel in fine motor skills, such as drawing and writing, or in gross motor skills that combine balance and foot movement, such as skipping and hopping and the skills needed in gymnastics (Cameron, 2002).

Boys tend to have slightly greater muscle mass than most girls and are slightly bigger—until about the age of 10½, when girls spurt ahead in height for a few years—but these sex-related physical differences are not large enough in themselves to account for the superiority of boys in many motor skills during middle childhood. Cultural conceptions of the activities appropriate to boys and to girls also play a large role in shaping these differences in behavior. For example, being able to throw, catch, and hit a baseball is a valued set of skills for boys in American culture. American parents usually encourage their sons, much more than their daughters, to develop these skills by buying them balls and bats, taking them to ballgames, talking about baseball with them, playing with them, and enrolling them in Little League. And in all cultures, it is also much truer for boys than for girls that those who are considered to be good athletes are more popular with their peers than those who show no athletic ability. While the participation of girls in such sports as baseball, soccer, and tennis has increased significantly in a number of countries in recent decades, girls are still not given the amount of encouragement and coaching that boys receive in these sports, nor are they rewarded to the extent boys are for having the abilities these sports require (Horn, 2002). Nonetheless, both boys and girls appear to profit from being active in sports. As shown in Figure 11.4, children who are highly involved in sports are more likely than those who are not to have high self-esteem, a sense of belonging at school, and lower levels of depression (Simpkins et al., 2006).

Figure 11.4 Youths who are highly involved in sports report more positive friends, higher self-esteem, greater school belonging, fewer negative friends, and less depression, compared to youths who do not participate in sports. (Adapted from Simpkins, 2006, p. 298.)

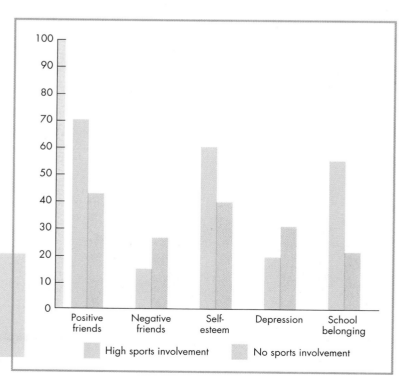

Brain Development

Middle childhood—particularly the early years, between ages 6 and 8—witnesses the continued growth of the brain and the development of specific kinds of brain functioning that are believed to underlie changes in cognitive skills:

1. Myelination, particularly in the frontal cortex, continues, and indeed will continue to adulthood (Janowsky & Carper, 1996; Sowell et al., 2007). (Recall from Chapter 4 that myelination provides the axon of cortical neurons with an insulating sheath of tissue that speeds transmission of nerve impulses.)

2. Synaptic pruning, the process by which nonfunctional synapses die off, continues for late-maturing areas of the brain (the frontal and prefrontal cortices), reducing the density of synapses among neurons. At the same time, more stable connections are found among remaining neurons (Sowell et al., 2002).

3. Brain activity patterns as measured by an EEG (electroencephalogram) undergo a dramatic change (Figure 11.5). Until the age of 5, EEGs recorded when children are awake display more theta activity (characteristic of adult sleep states) than alpha activity (characteristic of engaged attention). Between 5 and 7 years of age, the amounts of theta and alpha activity are about equal, but thereafter alpha activity (engaged attention) dominates (Corbin & Bickford, 1955).

4. The synchronization of electrical activity in different areas of the brain, called *EEG coherence,* increases significantly, reflecting the fact that different parts of the brain function more effectively as coordinated systems. Particularly important, according to Robert Thatcher (1994), is evidence of increased coordination between the electrical activity of the frontal lobes and the electrical activity in other parts of the brain.

This pattern of changes in brain structure and function—particularly in the frontal lobes and their connections to other parts of the brain—suggests that maturation of the brain plays an important role in the development of thinking during middle childhood, as in earlier periods. The pattern of brain changes following the onset of middle childhood permits the frontal lobes to coordinate the activities of other brain centers in a more complex way, enabling children to better control their attention, solve complex problems, form explicit plans, and engage in self-reflection, all behaviors that appear to undergo significant development in the transition to middle childhood. (The importance of the frontal lobes in these developments is supported by the fact that when the frontal lobes are damaged in humans and in other animals, individuals are unable to maintain goals, their actions become fragmentary and uncontrolled, they respond to irrelevant stimuli, and they are easily thrown off track by interruptions and pauses.)

One of the most convincing demonstrations that changes in brain functioning lead to changes in problem-solving processes comes from a study of changes in the brain activity of 5-year-old children being tested on a standard Piagetian task (conservation of quantity, which we will discuss later). The children wore caps that contained recording electrodes, allowing the researchers to track the changes in brain activity that accompanied their problem-solving endeavors. The children were tested three times, 1 year apart—first at the age of 5, then 6, and then 7. Initially the children did not succeed in solving the problem, but as they grew older, those who did succeed had a pattern of brain activity different from that of the children who failed at the task (Stauder et al., 1999), while the brain patterns

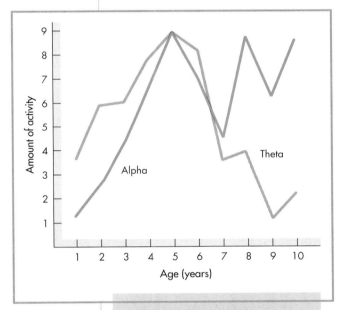

Figure 11.5 Changes in the amount of theta (sleeplike) and alpha (alert) EEG activity during development. Note that alpha waves come to predominate over theta waves around the age of 7. (From Corbin & Bickford, 1955.)

of those who failed were similar to those observed among young children. These findings seem to support the idea that certain behavioral changes of middle childhood are linked to changes in the organization and functioning of the brain.

Another interesting example of the relationship between brain and behavior comes from a study linking differences in brain development to individual differences in children's intelligence (Shaw et al., 2006). On the basis of standardized tests of intelligence (which we discuss in detail later in this chapter), more than 300 children and adolescents were classified as being of superior intelligence, high intelligence, or average intelligence. Neuroimaging techniques were used to measure the thickness of each child's cortex. Interestingly, the researchers found that intelligence test scores correlated, not with cortical thickness per se, but with a certain *developmental pattern* of cortical thickening and thinning over the course of childhood. Specifically, as shown in Figure 11.6, children with superior intelligence tended to have thinner cortexes at age 7 but then showed a marked increase in cortical thickness that peaked around 11 years of age, and then rapidly declined. In contrast, children with average intelligence showed a fairly steady decline in cortical thickening from age 7, while children with high intelligence demonstrated an intermediate pattern, but one more closely approximating that of the average

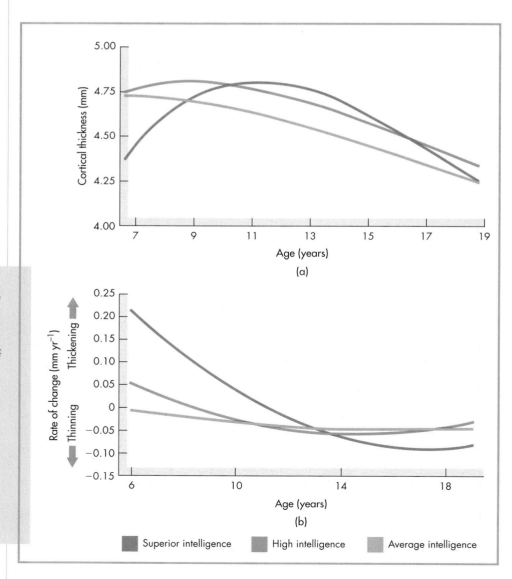

Figure 11.6 (a) Compared to children of high or average intelligence, at 7 years of age children with superior intelligence have thinner cortices, which then thicken dramatically (by synaptogenesis) until age 11, at which point they begin to thin gradually (by synaptic pruning). This pattern suggests that the brains of children of superior intelligence are more flexible and better able to respond to children's experiences. (The data shown are for the right superior frontal gyrus; similar patterns are found for other parts of the cortex.) (b) The rate of change in cortical thickening (indicated by positive values) and thinning (indicated by negative values) for children of superior, high, and average intelligence. Cortical thickening and thinning are much more dynamic in children of superior intelligence than in children of high or average intelligence, suggesting more responsive "experience-dependent" brain processes. (Adaption of Fig. 2a and Fig. 3 from Shaw et al., 2006, p. 677.)

intelligence group. Maximum cortical thickness occurred at 5.6 years for the average intelligence group, 8.5 years for the high intelligence group, and 11.2 years for the superior intelligence group.

What do we make of the waxing and waning of cortical thickness in these different groups of children? As the researchers point out, an increase in cortical thickness may be due to a proliferation of brain cells and synapses and/or an increase in myelin, the fatty substance that speeds the transmission of neural impulses. Cortical thinning, in contrast, takes place as a consequence of "pruning" nonfunctional synapses. The researchers speculate that cortexes of the "brainy" children, which thicken and then thin at a rapid rate through middle childhood and adolescence, are more flexible and dynamic compared to those of other children— that the pattern of cortical development provides a larger window in which neural circuitry can be laid down in response to learning experiences, a process of brain development we previously described as *experience dependent* (see Chapter 4). Thus, these children are not smarter because of the sheer amount of brain matter, but because of the dynamic properties of cortical development.

Despite these various research findings, we must be cautious about inferring direct causal links between particular changes in the brain and specific changes in behavior. The evidence we have cited is correlational: As children grow older, we observe changes in their brains and changes in their behavior, but the direction of causation remains uncertain. As explained in Chapter 4, the development and strengthening of neural pathways in the brain both affects and is affected by the individual's experience.

All of the biological changes of middle childhood—increased growth, improved motor skills, and continued brain development—enable children to meet the new expectations placed on them by adults. One major way in which they do so is by enabling greater cognitive achievements.

||||| **APPLY ● CONNECT ● DISCUSS** ‒

Discuss some of the ways that physical activity affects physical and psychological development of girls and boys during middle childhood. In your discussion, consider how the effects are similar for boys and girls, how they may differ, and the extent to which culture may contribute to any gender differences you identify.

Concrete-Operational Development

Piaget presented children of different ages with the apparatus shown below (Figure 11.7). The apparatus involves a toy wagon, suspended by a cable, that can be moved up and down a slope by manipulating three variables: the number of counterweights at the end of the cable; the weight of the load being carried by the wagon; and the angle of the track on which the wagon moves (Inhelder & Piaget, 1958, pp. 182–198). When a 6-year-old was asked how the wagon could be made to move, he pushed it down the track with his hand.

Experimenter: Can you do anything else?
Child: You drive in the train.
Experimenter tried a suggestion: And with the weights?
Child adds a counterweight to the cable: I put something on.
Experimenter: Why does it go up?
Child: I don't know. Because it's heavy.
Experimenter: And to make it go down?
Child: I don't know. You could push it.

A 10-year-old responded quite differently.

Child: To make it go up, you have to put a heavier weight here
[at the end of the cable].
Experimenter: What else could you do?
Child: Unload the wagon.
Experimenter tried a suggestion: Can you do something with the rail?
Child: Maybe you could lower it; it's easier for the wagon to go forward
because the track isn't as high.

In accounting for the vastly different ways in which these two children responded to the problem, Piaget points out that the 6-year-old is unable to identify the relevant variables (wagon load, counterweight, slope of incline); indeed, he is unable to separate the variables from his own actions of pushing, pulling, and "putting something on." The older child, in contrast, appreciates that the wagon's movement will depend on changes to the load, counterweight, and incline independent of the child's own actions on the apparatus.

In Chapter 8 we introduced you to Piaget's argument that the stages of cognitive development involve a process of increasing *decentration* through which thought becomes ever more *objective* (see p. 276). As we discussed, prior to middle childhood, children engage in *preoperational* thinking, and are vulnerable to *centration,* in which they become mentally "captured" by a single feature or attribute of experience. Centration interferes with the child's ability to engage in *mental operations,* or mental "actions" in which information is combined, separated, and transformed in a logical fashion. Emerging around 7 or 8 years of age, mental operations allow children to begin understanding how to experiment with several different variables to solve tasks such as the one described above. Mental operations also allow children to engage in activities such as sorting, collecting, and trading Pokemon cards according to category variables (whether they are character, energy, or trainer cards) and subcategory variables (whether they are Dark or Metal energy). **Concrete operations** is the term Piaget applied to the new stage of development in which

Figure 11.7 In this classic Piagetian task, a toy dump truck, suspended by a cable, is hauled up the inclined plane by the counterweights at the other end of the cable. The counterweights can be varied and the angle of the plane is adjustable; weights placed in the wagon provide the third variable. (Inhelder & Piaget, 1958, p. 183)

children begin to engage in mental operations. (See Table 11.1 for a summary of concrete operations in relation to other Piagetian stages.)

According to Piaget, in the transition from early to middle childhood, the advent of concrete operations transforms all aspects of psychological functioning. The physical world becomes more predictable because children come to understand that certain physical aspects of objects, such as size, density, length, and number, remain the same even when other aspects of the object's appearance have changed (recall from Chapter 8 that preoperational children confuse appearance and reality). Children's thinking also becomes more organized and flexible, and they become capable of thinking about alternative approaches and strategies for solving problems.

Piaget invented a number of problem-solving tasks, such as the one described above, to enable him to diagnose the presence or absence of concrete-operational thinking. In what follows, we look at some other examples of this key Piagetian concept, which demonstrate with special clarity why he believed that preoperational and concrete-operational thinking are characteristic of qualitatively different stages (Piaget & Inhelder, 1973).

concrete operations Coordinated mental actions that fit into a logical system in a way that creates greater unity of thinking.

table 11.1

Piaget's Stages of Cognitive Development: Concrete Operational

Age (years)	Stage	Description	Characteristics and Examples of Concrete Operations
Birth to 2	Sensorimotor	Infants' achievements consist largely of coordinating their sensory perceptions and simple motor behaviors. As they move through the 6 substages of this period, infants come to recognize the existence of a world outside of themselves and begin to interact with it in deliberate ways.	**New features of thinking** • Decentration: Children can notice and consider more than one attribute of an object at a time and form categories according to multiple criteria. • Conservation: Children understand that certain properties of an object will remain the same even when other, superficial ones are altered. They know that when a tall, thin glass is emptied into a short, fat one, the amount of liquid remains the same. • Logical necessity: Children have acquired the conviction that it is logically necessary for certain qualities to be conserved despite changes in appearance.
2 to 6	Preoperational	Young children can represent reality to themselves through the use of symbols, including mental images, words, and gestures. Objects and events no longer have to be present to be thought about, but children often fail to distinguish their point of view from that of others; become easily captured by surface appearances; and are often confused about causal relations.	• Identity: Children realize that if nothing has been added or subtracted, the amount must remain the same. • Compensation: Children can mentally compare changes in two aspects of a problem and see how one compensates for the other. • Reversibility: Children realize that certain operations can negate, or reverse, the effects of others.
6 to 12	Concrete operational	As they enter middle childhood, children become capable of mental operations, internalized actions that fit into a logical system. Operational thinking allows children mentally to combine, separate, order, and transform objects and actions. Such operations are considered concrete because they are carried out in the presence of the objects and events being thought about.	**Declining egocentrism** • Children can communicate more effectively about objects a listener cannot see. • Children can think about how others perceive them. • Children understand that a person can feel one way and act another.
12 to 19	Formal operational	In adolescence, the developing person acquires the ability to think systematically about all logical relations within a problem. Adolescents display keen interest in abstract ideas and in the process of thinking itself.	**Changes in social relations** • Children can regulate their interactions with each other through rules and begin to play rule-based games. • Children take intentions into account in judging behavior and believe the punishment must fit the crime.

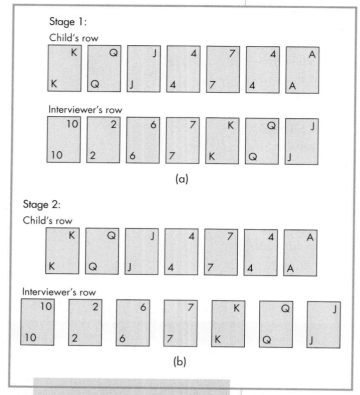

Figure 11.8 The procedure used to test for the conservation of number. (a) In stage 1, the child's and the interviewer's seven cards are arrayed at equal intervals. (b) In stage 2, the interviewer spreads out his or her cards and asks the child if he or she and the interviewer still have the same number of cards. (From Ginsburg, 1977.)

conservation of number Recognizing the one-to-one correspondence between sets of objects of equal number.

conservation of volume Understanding that the amount of liquid in a container remains the same despite being poured into a differently shaped container.

identity A mental operation in which the child realizes that a change limited to outward appearance does not change the substances involved.

compensation A mental operation in which the child realizes that changes in one aspect of a problem are compared with and compensated for by changes in another aspect.

reversibility A mental operation in which the child realizes that one operation can be negated, or reversed, by the effects of another.

Conservation

Conservation is Piaget's term for the understanding that some properties of an object or substance remain the same even when its appearance is altered in some superficial way. Consider, for example, the **conservation of number,** that is, the ability to recognize the one-to-one correspondence between two sets of objects of equal number, despite a difference in the sizes of the objects or in their spatial positions (Piaget, 1952a). To assess conservation of number, Piaget presented children with two rows of objects such as those shown in Figure 11.8a. Both the numbers of objects and the lengths of the two lines are equal, and the child is asked to affirm that they are. Then one of the rows is either spread out or compressed (Figure 11.8b), and the child is asked if the numbers of objects in the two rows are still equal. Children below the age of 6 or 7 rarely display conservation of number unless the total number of objects is very small, saying, for example, that the elongated row has more. In contrast, older children realize that on the grounds of *logic alone* the number must remain the same. They are able to say to themselves, in effect, "There must be the same number of cards, because if the experimenter moved the cards in his row back to where they were at the beginning, nothing would have changed." This understanding of *logical necessity*—that "it has to be that way"—is Piaget's key criterion of concrete operational thinking.

One of Piaget's most famous studies of conservation examines children's **conservation of volume,** the understanding that the amount of liquid in a container remains the same even though it is poured into a differently shaped flask. The task assessing conservation of volume involves presenting children with two identical glass beakers containing the same amounts of liquid (Figure 11.9). The experimenter begins by pouring the contents of one of the beakers into a third beaker that is taller and narrower. Naturally, the liquid rises higher in the new beaker. The experimenter then asks the child, "Does the new beaker contain more liquid than the old beaker, does it contain the same amount, or does it contain less?"

Ordinarily, 3- to 4-year-old children say that the taller beaker has more. When asked why, they explain, "There's more because it's higher," or "There's more because it's bigger," or even "There's more because you poured it." Consistent with the *centration* characteristic of preoperational thinking, they appear to focus their attention on a single aspect of the new beaker—its height. Even when the experimenter points out that no liquid was added or subtracted, and even after the liquid is poured back into the original beaker to demonstrate that the amount has not changed, 3- and 4-year-olds generally claim that there is more liquid in the taller, narrower beaker.

Piaget found that around the age of 5 or 6 years, children's understanding of conservation goes through a transitional stage. At this point, children seem to realize that it is necessary to consider both the height and the circumference of the beakers, but they have difficulty keeping both in mind simultaneously and coordinating the changes so that they can properly compare them.

According to Piaget, children fully master the principle of conservation around the age of 8, when they understand not only that the new beaker is both taller and narrower but also that a change in one dimension of the beaker (increasing height) is offset by a change in the other (decreasing circumference). Children who have mastered conservation recognize the logical necessity that the amount of liquid remains the same despite the change in appearance. When asked the reasons for their judgment, they offer arguments such as the following, showing that they understand the logical relationships involved:

- "They were equal to start with and nothing was added, so they're the same." This mental operation is called **identity;** the child realizes that a change limited to outward appearance does not change the actual amounts involved.

- "The liquid is higher, but the glass is thinner." This mental operation is called **compensation;** changes in one aspect of a problem are mentally compared with and compensated for by changes in another.

- "If you pour it back, you'll see that it's the same." This mental operation is called *negation* or **reversibility;** the child realizes that one operation can be negated, or reversed, by the effects of another.

Whether they are asked to reason about number or volume, children's ability to conserve leads to the logical conclusion that a change in visual *appearance* does not change the logical *reality* of amount.

Classification

Another significant change associated with concrete operations is the ability to understand the hierarchical structure of categories, in particular, the logical *relation of inclusion* that holds between a superordinate class and its subclasses (for example, the subclass of cats is included in the superordinate class of mammals; see Chapter 5, p. 191).

When 4- to 6-year-old children are shown a set of wooden beads including some brown beads and a smaller number of white beads and asked, "Are there more brown beads or more beads?" they are likely to say there are more brown beads than beads. According to Piaget, they answer this way because they cannot attend to the subclass (brown beads) and the superordinate class (beads) at the same time. Instead, they compare one subclass (brown beads) with another subclass (white beads). In middle childhood, subordinate–superordinate relations become more stable so the children realize that brown beads are a subset of the overall set of beads and answer correctly.

A more difficult classification ability that emerges during middle childhood is the capacity to categorize objects according to multiple criteria. This kind of logical classification can be seen when children begin to collect stamps, baseball cards, or Pokemon cards. Stamp collections, for example, can be organized according to multiple criteria. Stamps come from different countries. They are issued in different denominations and in different years. There are stamps depicting insects, animals, sports heroes, rock stars, and space exploration. Children who organize their stamps according to type of animal and country of origin (so that, for example, within their collection of stamps from France, all the birds are together, all the rabbits are together, and so on) are creating a multiple classification for their collections. The result is a marked increase in the number of relations among objects and events that children can think about and increased flexibility in the particular relations they choose to use in particular circumstances.

Planning

The abilities of decentering, considering multiple variables, and thinking flexibly in new situations are all cognitive prerequisites to efficient and effective planning.

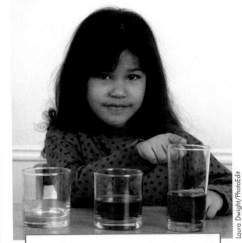

Figure 11.9 The procedure Piaget used to test for the conservation of quantity. First, present two beakers of equal size, with equal amounts of liquid. Second, present a taller, thinner beaker and pour the contents of one of the other beakers into it. Third, ask, "Which beaker has more liquid, or do they contain the same amount?" Did this girl display an understanding of conservation?

This young comic book collector is looking for a deal at an annual fair held at the Wolfson campus of Miami-Dade College. If he is a serious collector, he will have a fairly elaborate classification system that organizes his comic books according to multiple criteria.

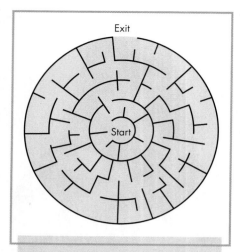

Figure 11.10 A maze of the kind used by Gardner and Rogoff (1990) to assess children's ability to plan ahead. Trace the route from start to finish to get a feel for how planning is needed to avoid encountering a dead end.

Preschoolers can be heard saying things to one another like "When you come over, we'll play house and have a party," but they have no plans to achieve their goal aside from informing their parents that they want to play with the other child. During middle childhood, children begin to plan in the sense that they form cognitive representations of the actions needed to achieve a specific goal. To make a plan, they have to keep in mind what is presently happening, what they want to happen in the future, and what they need to do in order to get from the present to the future. They must also have enough self-control to keep their attention on achieving the goal, a topic we address in more detail later in the chapter.

Take, for example, the kind of planning that is required in choosing a route to a destination. William Gardner and Barbara Rogoff (1990) asked groups of 4- to 6-year-olds and 7- to 10-year-olds to solve mazes such as the one shown in Figure 11.10. A glance at this maze quickly reveals that a child who simply begins to trace a path from the nearest opening, without first scanning the maze to see what barriers lie ahead, is certain to fail. To see how children's ability to plan a solution to the maze developed, Gardner and Rogoff gave different instructions to half the children in each age group. One subgroup was told that they should plan ahead from the start because it was most important to avoid making wrong turns. The other children were told the same thing but were also told that they had to go through the maze as quickly as possible.

When both speed and accuracy mattered, the children in both age groups planned out part of their route ahead of time and then planned only when they came to uncertain choice points. When accuracy in navigating the maze was the only factor that counted, many of the older children realized that a better strategy was to plan their entire set of moves before they began. In contrast, 4- to 6-year-olds did not change their planning when speed did not matter, either because they did not understand that they would make fewer errors if they planned ahead more systematically or because they could not keep this possibility in mind when they tackled a difficult maze.

Planning is also important in reasoning tasks. Games that require children to solve logical problems, like checkers or Mastermind, become popular in middle childhood. To play these games skillfully, children have to analyze both the goals and the means of attaining them. A good example of such a game is the Tower of Hanoi, the goal of which is to move a set of size-graded objects from one location to another. There are two rules: (1) only one object can be moved at a time; and (2) a larger object must go on top of a smaller one.

From Canada (left) to China (right), children enjoy the intellectual challenges of board games that call on newly-acquired cognitive skills.

Figure 11.11 To solve the Tower of Hanoi problem, the child must move the cans on the pegs before him and recreate the stack on the pegs opposite, on the side of the experimenter. The task requires careful planning, because it is illegal to place a small can on top of a large can as the cans are moved from peg to peg. (After Klahr, 1989.)

Child's side

Experimenter's side

In an experimental form of this game (Figure 11.11), the child is presented with three cans on a peg—the smallest on the bottom, the largest on the top—and is asked to move the cans to the peg opposite the experimenter's model. The problem depicted in Figure 11.11 requires a logical minimum of seven moves.

A variety of research (summarized in Siegler, 1998) shows that between the ages of 6 and 7 years, children become better at playing the game. This trend is not surprising, since, according to the evidence, older children are increasingly able to keep in mind both their current circumstances and the circumstances they want to create. Three-year-olds could not keep the rules in mind at all. Six-year-olds began to form subgoals that would take them part of the way to a solution, but they could not think the problem all the way through, and they still found it difficult to assemble their subgoals into an overall plan. If the problems require too many moves, even 9- and 10-year-olds fail to plan their solutions all the way through (Spitz, Minsky, & Besselieu, 1985). When, however, children are given opportunities to reflect on their planning by either watching videotapes of themselves working on the task, or being instructed in efficient problem strategies, their performance improves (Fireman & Kose, 2002).

Metacognition

The fact that children's problem solving can be enhanced by calling their attention to effective strategies and how to use them suggests that *knowledge* about how to think things through may facilitate problem-solving performance. Indeed, **metacognition,** the ability to think about and regulate one's own thoughts, allows one to assess how difficult a problem is likely to be and to choose strategies to solve it in a flexible way (Flavell, 2007). The development of metacognition has received considerable attention by researchers, who generally find large mismatches between young children's estimates of what they think they know about a problem and what they actually know. Preschoolers and kindergartners are especially prone to overestimating their knowledge. As metacognition develops over the course of middle childhood, children become more accurate in recognizing the limits of their knowledge and problem-solving skills.

metacognition The ability to think about one's own thought processes.

Grade	Explanation
Kindergarten	"You put something in it and then you press a button and then—you press the button. Push it down and leave it there. And then it heats and then it comes up too."
Second grade	"Well, you put the bread in and you push this little lever down so then there you go. It'll heat rays inside and it'll make the bread really really hard and stuff and it'll just pop out."
Fourth grade	"Ok. A toaster is made by electricity. You plug it in. There's a cord it comes electricity and then you put bread in. And then you press a button down. When you hit that button all the way down red lights which is heat comes out which is from the electricity and it heats the bread and when it comes out it's toast."

Figure 11.12 Examples of children's explanations of how a toaster works. (Mills & Keil, 2004, p. 13)

An example of metacognitive development is provided by Candice Mills and Frank Keil of Yale University, who asked kindergartners, second-graders, and fourth-graders to estimate their understanding of mechanical devices such as toasters, gum ball machines, and staplers (Mills & Keil, 2004). First, the children were trained to use a 5-point scale to show how much they thought they knew about how the device worked. At one end of the scale was one star, indicating very little understanding; at the other end was 5 stars, indicating a lot of understanding (there were, of course, 2, 3, and 4 stars in between). Next, the children were asked, for example, to estimate their knowledge of how a toaster works by pointing to the appropriate number of stars on the scale. Then they were asked to provide an explanation for how toasters toast, followed by once again using the scale to estimate their knowledge (some sample explanations from each age group are shown in Figure 11.12). The idea here is that the children might sense the holes in their own reasoning, and downgrade the estimates they initially provided. Finally, to really drive home the children's lack of knowledge, the researchers gave them an explanation of the workings of toasters as told by an expert "who knows five stars about how a toaster works," after which children had one last opportunity to rate their knowledge on the star scale.

As shown in Figure 11.13, the researchers found clear overall age differences in children's ratings of their toaster knowledge such that fourth-graders were significantly more conservative than kindergartners, with second-graders falling in between. Only the second- and fourth-graders significantly downgraded their estimates after they were asked to give an explanation of how the device works or were told of the "five star" expert's explanation. Indeed, at the end of the study, several of them remarked that they were surprised at how little they knew about toasters. Kindergartners' ratings, as you can see in the figure, actually *increased* after hearing the expert's account. Why? Apparently, the expert just reminded them of what they already knew but forgot to mention. This is a classic example of egocentrism: the youngsters have obvious difficulty separating their own perspective and knowledge from that of the expert.

Figure 11.13 Age differences in children's ratings of their own toaster knowledge. (Mills & Keil, 2004, p. 11, with modification.)

The growth of metacognitive skills provides children with important cognitive resources. As metacognitive skills increase, children are better able to keep track of how successfully they are accomplishing their goals, and this allows them to modify their strategies so that they are more successful.

Limitations of Concrete Operations

With the emergence of concrete operations, children take a significant step toward objectivity, and the ability to think logically and apply their knowledge flexibly to new problems and situations. However, as suggested by the term "concrete operations," children's intellectually functioning and problem solving is at its best when it involves concrete objects and events that children have experienced directly. As soon as children are asked to reason about abstract phenomena, their problem solving falters.

The difficulty children encounter when reasoning about abstract situations with which they have no direct experience is apparent in a study undertaken by Jason Low and Steve Hollis, two developmentalists at Victoria University in New Zealand (Low & Hollis, 2003). They asked groups of 6-, 9-, and 12-year-olds and college students to draw a portrait of themselves as they would look if they had three eyes instead of two and then to explain why they had placed the third eye where they had. Given good reasons for believing that no one in the sample had ever encountered a three-eyed person, the self-portrait task constituted a true challenge to abstract thinking.

Typical responses of each age group are shown in Figure 11.14. As you can see, all three groups of children tended to place the third eye close to the other two. In their concrete experience, this is, after all, where eyes belong. In addition to drawing similar portraits, children's reasons for their particular eye placements were fairly uniform—and concrete—emphasizing that a third eye on the forehead would help them see better or see farther. In contrast, the self-portraits of college students were much more imaginative and diverse, permitting not only better eyesight but an entirely different, 360-degree view.

▌▌▌▌▌ **APPLY ▪ CONNECT ▪ DISCUSS** ┈┈┈┈┈┈┈┈┈┈┈┈┈┈┈┈┈┈┈┈┈┈

Explain how Piaget's fundamental concepts of *decentration* and *objectivity* are apparent in the ability of children who are at the concrete-operational stage to solve conservation and classification tasks.

Figure 11.14 Age differences in drawings of where one would put a third eye. (Low & Hollis, 2003)

© 2003 International Society for the Study of Behavioral Development. International Journal of Behavioral Development, Vol. 27, No. 2, 97–108 (2003).

6-year-old
"Just felt the best place."

9-year-old
"So the person can see further away."

12-year-old
"So I could see sideways and straight ways."

18-year-old
"So I can see behind myself as well."

Information-Processing Approaches

In contrast to Piaget's focus on decentration as a source of increasing objectivity in reasoning, information-processing theorists account for cognitive changes during middle childhood by appealing to processes such as increased memory capacity and attention, more rapid and efficient mental operations, and the acquisition of a variety of mental strategies. According to these theorists, children's increased memory and attention abilities play a central role in allowing them to hold two or more aspects of a problem in mind while they are thinking. For example, a young soccer player racing for the goal can pay attention to and keep in mind the positions of her teammates, the goalie's well-known difficulty blocking low shots, and the special maneuver her coach taught her in practice. Younger players may have a difficult time simply remembering they are in a soccer game and may run after the ball only when it passes in front of them, or have their attention diverted by some irrelevant event taking place off the field.

The Role of Memory

Three factors, taken together, appear to bring about the memory changes characteristic of middle childhood (Schneider et al., 2004):

1. Increases in the speed and capacity of working memory
2. Increases in knowledge about the things one is trying to remember
3. The acquisition of more effective strategies for remembering

Increased Speed and Capacity of Working Memory *Working memory,* also known as *short-term memory,* has received a great deal of attention as a source of improved intellectual functioning during middle childhood because it is considered the "active" memory system that holds and manipulates information needed to reason about complex tasks and problems (Bayliss et al., 2005). Developmentalists have been particularly interested in the *capacity* of working memory to "hold" larger amounts of information, as well as the *speed* of working memory in manipulating (or processing) information.

A common behavioral method of measuring the changing capacity of working memory is to assess children's **memory span,** the number of randomly presented items of information children can repeat immediately after the items are presented. Most 4- and 5-year-olds can recall four digits presented one after another; most 9- and 10-year-olds can remember about six; most adults can remember about seven (Schneider & Pressley, 1997). Although it seems clear that the older child's memory capacity is larger than that of the younger child's, developmentalists are keenly aware that other factors also come into play. For example, in order to store into working memory several numbers presented at random, people must somehow represent each number to themselves, perhaps by silently repeating "10, 6, 8, 2." Young children take longer than older children simply to repeat a number such as 10 or 2. Because it takes them longer to say the numbers, memory for the numbers already presented is more likely to decay and be lost. Older children name individual numbers quite quickly, reducing the time interval between numbers and thereby increasing the likelihood of retaining the numbers in memory (Figure 11.15) (Case, Kurland, & Goldberg, 1982).

Cross-cultural research enriches these conclusions. When Chuansheng Chen and Harold Stevenson (1988) compared the memory

Figure 11.15 Relationship between memory span and speed of naming. (From Case et al., 1982.)

spans of U. S. and Chinese children age 4 to 6 years, they found that the Chinese children were able to recall more digits at each of the ages tested. At first, this finding might seem to suggest that the working memory of Chinese children was larger than that of the American children. However, as Chen and Stevenson pointed out, the Chinese words for the digits are shorter than the English words. Thus the task was easier for the Chinese children for the same reason that it was easier for the older North American children: There was a shorter interval between repeated items. This hypothesis was supported by a study in which Stevenson and his colleagues used lists of objects whose names were equal in length in English and Chinese. When these words were presented for remembering, Chinese and American children were found to have equal memory capacities (Stevenson et al., 1985).

Not surprisingly, developmentalists have looked increasingly at brain development as a source of change in working memory observed during middle childhood (Blair, 2006). Electrodes placed over different parts of the brain indicate that the speed with which children's brains can respond to complex stimuli increases gradually during middle childhood (Travis, 1998). As you know from our discussion above, increased speed of processing may help prevent information from being lost. In addition to processing speed, increases in the connections between brain regions have also been directly linked to memory performance in children aged 7 to 16 years (Sowell et al., 2001; Scherf, Sweeney, & Luna, 2006).

Expanded Knowledge Base The second factor that contributes to improved memory during childhood is the greater knowledge that older children are likely to have about any given topic simply because they have accumulated more experience (Ornstein, Haden, & Elischberger, 2006). This experience provides older children with a richer knowledge base, or store of information, with which to relate, and remember, new information.

A classic demonstration of how a rich knowledge base contributes to children's ability to remember was provided by Michelene Chi (1978), who studied college students' and 10-year-old chess buffs' memories for the arrangement of chess pieces. Compared to the college students who had little experience playing chess, the 10-year-old chess experts were much better at remembering the chess arrangements that occurred in the course of a game. However, when the two groups were compared on their ability to recall a random series of numbers, the college students' performances were far superior. A replication of this study by German researchers confirmed and extended these results by showing that when subjects were asked to remember random arrangements of chess pieces, rather than meaningful patterns that might plausibly occur during a game—thereby removing the importance of chess knowledge—the advantage of experts was greatly reduced (Schneider et al., 1993).

Improved Memory Strategies A third source of improved memory ability is children's increased use of **memory strategies,** that is, their deliberate use of actions to enhance remembering (Pressley & Hilden, 2006). A large number of studies have shown that children's spontaneous use of strategies for remembering undergoes a marked increase between early and middle childhood (Ornstein et al., 2006). Although memory strategies can take a vast variety of forms—from putting a book bag by the front door so we will remember to take it to school to writing *DF* on a yellow stickie so we will remember to pick up dog food on the way home—three memory strategies whose development has been intensively studied are rehearsal, organization, and elaboration.

Rehearsal is the process of repeating to oneself the material that one is trying to memorize, such as a word list, a song, or a phone number. In a classic

memory span The number of randomly presented items of information that can be repeated immediately after they are presented.

memory strategies Specific actions used deliberately to enhance remembering.

rehearsal The process of repeating to oneself the material that one is trying to memorize.

study of the development of rehearsal strategies in children, John Flavell and his colleagues (Keeney et al., 1967) presented 5- and 10-year-olds with seven pictures of objects to remember. The children were asked to wear a "space helmet" with a visor that was pulled down over their eyes during the 15-second interval between the presentation of the pictures and the test for recall. The visor prevented the children from seeing the pictures and allowed the experimenter to watch their lips to see if they repeated to themselves what they had seen. Few of the 5-year-olds were observed to rehearse, but almost all the 10-year-olds did. Within each age group, children who rehearsed the pictures recalled more than children who did not. When those who had not rehearsed were later taught to do so, they did as well on the memory task as those who had rehearsed on their own.

Marked changes are also found in **organizational strategies,** that is, strategies of mentally grouping the materials to be remembered in meaningful clusters of closely associated items so that it is necessary to remember only one part of a cluster to gain access to the rest. The use of organizational strategies is often studied by means of a procedure called *free recall*. In a free-recall task, children are shown a large number of objects or read a list of words one at a time and then asked to remember them. This kind of memory is called *free* recall because the children are free to recall the items in any order they choose.

Research has demonstrated that 7- and 8-year-olds are more likely than younger children to group the items they have to remember into easy-to-remember categories (Schlegmuller & Schneider, 2002). The kinds of groupings that children impose on lists of things to be remembered also change with age. Younger children often use sound features, such as rhyme ("cat," "sat"), or situational associations ("cereal," "bowl") to group words they are trying to remember. In middle childhood, children are more likely to link words according to categories such as animals ("cat," "dog," "horse"), foods ("cereal," "milk," "bananas"), or geometric figures ("triangle," "square," "circle"). The consequence of these changes is an enhanced ability to store and retrieve information deliberately and systematically.

Children who do not spontaneously use rehearsal and organizing strategies can be taught to do so (Pressley & Hilden, 2006). The effectiveness of this training indicates that there is no unbridgeable gap between the memory performance of 4- to 5-year-olds and that of 7- to 8-year-olds or between children who use strategies spontaneously and those who do not. Over the course of middle childhood, children become increasingly better at using various strategies to help them remember.

A third strategy, **elaboration,** is a process in which children identify or make up connections between two or more things they have to remember. Elaboration strategies have usually been studied in cases where children are presented with two words and asked to remember the second one when they hear the first. For example, they might be asked to remember the word "street" after hearing the word "tomato." An elaboration strategy for this word pair could be to think of a tomato squashed in the middle of a street.

Research with adults shows that elaboration strategies are effective when they are used (Schwenck, Bjorklund, & Schneider, 2007). However, it is only during middle childhood that children begin to use elaboration strategies spontaneously, and skill in the use of this kind of strategy continues to increase with age (Schlegmüller & Schneider, 2002).

Thinking about Memory

Most 7- and 8-year-olds not only know more about the world in general than do 3- to 5-year-olds, but also are likely to know more about memory itself—knowledge referred to as **metamemory,** which is a particular form of *metacognition*.

organizational strategies A memory strategy in which materials to be remembered are mentally grouped into meaningful categories.

elaboration A memory strategy that involves making connections between two or more things to be remembered.

metamemory The ability to think about one's memory processes.

Even 5-year-olds have some understanding of how memory works. In a study that has stimulated a great deal of the subsequent research on memory development, 5-year-olds said they knew that it was easier to remember a short list of words than a long one, to relearn something you once knew than to learn it from scratch, and to remember something that happened yesterday than something that happened last month (Kreutzer, Leonard, & Havell, 1975).

Nevertheless, most 8-year-olds have a better understanding of the limitations of their own memories than most 5-year-olds do. When shown a set of 10 pictures and asked if they could remember them all (something most children at these ages generally cannot do), most of the 5-year-olds—but only a few of the 8-year-olds—claimed that they could. The 5-year-olds also failed to evaluate correctly how much effort they would need to remember the pictures. Given unlimited time to master the set of pictures, the 5-year-olds announced that they were ready right away, even though they succeeded in remembering only a few of the items. The 8-year-olds, by contrast, knew enough to study the materials and to test themselves on their ability to remember (Flavell, Friedrichs, & Hoyt, 1970).

Interestingly, there seems to be a connection between children's metamemory and their use of memory strategies (Pressley & Hilden, 2006). In one memory study, William Fabricius and John Hagen (1984) created a situation in which 6- and 7-year-olds used an organizational strategy on some trials and not on others. When the children used the organizational strategy, they almost always remembered better. These researchers asked the children to tell them what they thought accounted for their better remembering efforts. Some of the children did not notice that the organizing strategy was helpful, even though they had just used it successfully. They attributed their better recall to slowing down and being more careful or to paying more attention to the stimuli. Other children attributed their better recall to the deliberate use of the organizing strategy. When the children were brought back for a second session, in which their ability to remember was tested in a slightly different situation, 99 percent of those who had understood the helpfulness of the organizing strategy in the first session used the same strategy the second time around. By contrast, only 32 percent of the children who attributed their better remembering efforts to some other factor used the organizing strategy. These and similar results indicate that children must acquire the ability to use metamemory knowledge in addition to acquiring useful strategies.

Increased Control of Attention

In addition to gaining greater control over memory strategies, during middle childhood children become better able to regulate their attention, staying focused on relevant aspects of a task and ignoring irrelevant distractions.

A classic study by Elaine Vurpillot (1968) illustrates the kinds of changes observed by many researchers. She recorded the eye movements of children age 3 to 10 while the children examined pairs of line drawings of houses such as those shown in Figure 11.16. In some trials, children were shown identical houses; in others, the houses differed in one or more relatively subtle ways. The children were asked to say whether or not the houses were identical.

Vurpillot found that all the children responded correctly when the houses were identical but that the younger children were more likely to make mistakes when the houses differed, especially if the houses differed in only one way. Her recordings of eye movements pinpointed the difficulty. Rather than systematically paying attention to each of the houses to see how they differed, the younger children scanned the houses in a haphazard order. By contrast, the older children paid attention to each of the houses, scanning, and sometimes rescanning, row by row

David Young-Wolff/PhotoEdit

Although children from traditional agricultural societies sometimes perform poorly on psychological tests, their cognitive abilities are often manifested in other ways. This Ugandan boy has constructed his toy car out of bits of wire and some wooden wheels.

Figure 11.16 Stimuli used by Vurpillot to assess the development of visual search strategies. It is not until middle childhood that children systematically compare the two houses of each pair so as to discover the subtle differences between them. (From Vurpillot, 1968)

or column by column. It seems from this that older children have a greater ability to select and execute an effective attentional strategy.

The ability to attend to the most important features of a situation is not the only aspect of children's attention that develops during early and middle childhood. More recent studies show that children also acquire the ability to ignore distractions and gain voluntary control over what they choose to pay attention to in order to obtain information more efficiently (Dossett & Burns, 2000; Huang-Pollack, Carr, & Nigg, 2002).

Combining Memory Development and Logical Stages

Thus far we have offered two explanations for children's increased mental abilities in middle childhood: a stagelike change in their ability to think through problems and the consequences of their actions logically, and increased memory and other information-processing capacities. Instead of pitting one explanation against the other, it seems more productive to many developmentalists to determine how these two sources of mental capacity might work together. This is the route taken by Robbie Case and his colleagues, who argued that when a child acquires a new cognitive scheme, working memory is stretched to capacity in applying the new scheme to new experiences (Case, 1998; Okamoto & Case, 1996). With practice over time, the scheme becomes automatic, freeing up space in working memory and permitting the child to attend other facets of experience. The ability to apply established schemes while also attending other facets of experience lays the groundwork for the child's ability to coordinate schemes and construct entirely new ones.

To illustrate their ideas, Case and his colleagues carried out a series of studies looking at children's understanding of such varied areas as numbers, storytelling, and drawing. In the case of number, for example, 6-, 8-, and 10-year-olds were given math problems of increasing complexity. The most simple problems (Category 1 and 2) required only thinking about a single number line, whereas the more complex problems required coordinating several number lines (Figure 11.17):

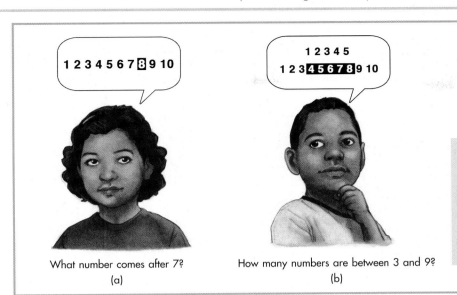

What number comes after 7?
(a)

How many numbers are between 3 and 9?
(b)

Figure 11.17 In studies with math problems, 6-, 8-, and 10-year-olds perform equally well on simple problems that require only the representation of a single number line (a). In contrast, there are clear age differences in performance on more complex problems that require the coordination of two or more number lines (b).

- Category 1: Problems required judgments only about whether specified numbers were more or less than other numbers.

- Category 2: In addition to requiring judgments of more or less, problems required more specific calculations such as "What number comes after 7?"

- Category 3: Problems required coordinating two number lines. For example, to answer the question "How many numbers are in between 3 and 9?" the child needs to imagine one number line that represents the position of the two numbers and a second number line that represents the difference between them.

- Category 4: Problems required that children compare the results of two problems like those in category 3 and calculate the difference. A typical problem was of the following kind: "Which difference is bigger, the difference between 6 and 9 or the difference between 8 and 3?"

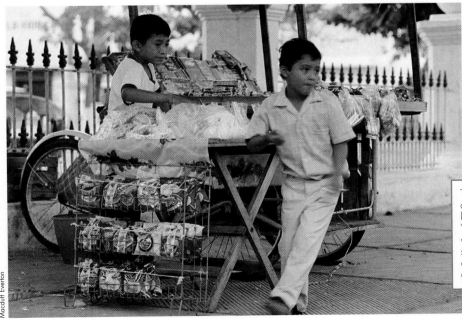

Macduff Everton

The kinds of work that children are assigned afford different kinds of learning opportunities. Young street vendors acquire a variety of arithmetic skills that sometimes surpass those of children of the same age who attend school.

table 11.2

Percentage of Correct Responses as a Function of Age and Problem Complexity

	6-Year-Olds	8-Year-Olds	10-Year-Olds
Category 1	100	100	100
Category 2	89	97	99
Category 3	28	66	86
Category 4	4	24	49

Source: Okamoto & Case, 1996.

The children were presented with several problems from each category. As shown in Table 11.2, when the problems were simple and only required the children to use one number line ("What number comes after 7?") there was little difference in the performance among the age groups. But the performance of 6-year-olds deteriorated markedly when they had to coordinate two number lines to answer such questions as "How many numbers are in between 2 and 7?" The 8-year-olds had less trouble with such problems, but they ran into serious difficulty when solving category 4 problems that required them to hold in mind two number lines as well as the results of their calculations on each and then to compare the two. The 10-year-olds had some difficulty when they were asked to solve category 4 problems, but they were successful half the time.

This pattern of results illustrates the researchers' claims of a close relationship between problem-solving ability and the capacity of working memory. Each time the demands on working memory were increased, fewer children at a given age level could manage the task.

Recently Andreas Demetriou and his colleagues extended Case's analysis to link speed of processing to working memory and to logical problem solving (Demetriou et al., 2005). They found that these three aspects of cognition build upon each other. Increased speed of processing leads to increases in working memory, which in turn lead to increases in the effectiveness of problem solving.

APPLY ▪ CONNECT ▪ DISCUSS

Many people believe that a really good memory involves the ability to store a lot of information for considerable periods of time. Memory, however, is not just about the *quantity* of information stored over time, but also about how the information is organized. In what specific ways does it seem that children's memories may be organized differently in middle childhood than in early childhood?

The Role of Social and Cultural Contexts

Thus far we have treated cognitive changes between early and middle childhood as if they were entirely determined by development of the brain and the specific internal, mental processes brought to bear on the task at hand. But as Usha Goswami cautions us, "The functioning of even these relatively specific developmental mechanisms . . . turns out to be influenced by the social . . . and cultural context in which learning takes place" (Goswami, 2002, p. 227). Cross-cultural research on developmental changes in cognitive ability underlines this point.

Is the Acquisition of Conservation Universal?

It was Piaget's (1966/1974) belief that the development of conservation is a universal achievement of human beings, regardless of the cultural circumstances in which they live. The only cultural variation he expected in the acquisition of conservation was that children in some cultures might acquire this form of reasoning earlier than children in others, because their culture provided them with more extensive relevant experiences.

However, cross-cultural research on the acquisition of conservation has provoked a great deal of controversy regarding its presumed universality and age of onset. Using Piaget's conservation tasks, several researchers found that children in traditional, nonindustrial societies who have not attended school lag a year or more behind the norms established by Piaget—and, in some cases, appear not to acquire this form of reasoning at all, even as adults. Reviewing the evidence available in the early 1970s, Pierre Dasen (1972) wrote, "It can no longer be assumed that adults of all societies reach the concrete operational stage" (p. 31).

This conclusion was quickly challenged because of its wide-reaching implication that traditional, nonliterate adults think like the preschool children of industrialized countries. For example, Gustav Jahoda (1980), a leading cross-cultural psychologist, rejected outright the possibility that in some cultures people never achieve the ability to think operationally. Jahoda pointed out that it is difficult to see how a society could survive if its members were indifferent to causal relations, incapable of thinking through the implications of their actions, or unable to adopt other people's points of view. He concluded that "no society could function at the preoperational stage, and to suggest that a majority of any people are at that level is nonsense almost by definition" (Jahoda, 1980, p. 116).

To resolve this issue, developmentalists who questioned nonschooled children's apparent failure to understand conservation designed new tests or otherwise modified research procedures. They sought to demonstrate that Piaget's research methods somehow misrepresented such children's mental capacities, either because the test situation was too unfamiliar to the children or because the experimenters, working in an unfamiliar culture and language, did not make their intentions clear. (Similarly, as you may recall from Chapter 8, researchers in early childhood cognition designed new tasks because they felt Piaget's tasks underestimated the thought processes of preschool-age children.) Dasen and his colleagues tackled the problem by training children to solve conservation tasks. They reasoned that if the children in traditional cultures did not seem to understand conservation because they were unfamiliar with the procedures, training on similar tasks should be sufficient to overcome their difficulties.

In a series of studies, these researchers demonstrated that by the end of middle childhood, relatively brief training in procedures similar to those used in the standard conservation task was sufficient to change the pattern of performance on the conservation task. One such result is shown in Figure 11.18, which compares the performance of children in the Australian city of Canberra with that of Inuit children living in the remote area of Cape Dorset in northern Canada. Without training, half the Inuit children seemed to fail to acquire the concept of conservation of quantity altogether. But when they were trained in the procedures used, their test results showed that they did understand the basic concept of conservation of quantity. Even with training, however, the Inuit children lagged behind the Canberra children by approximately 3 years, a situation suggesting that their nomadic, hunter–gatherer form of life does not provide the kinds of experiences that make for easier acquisition of this concept (Dasen, 1975).

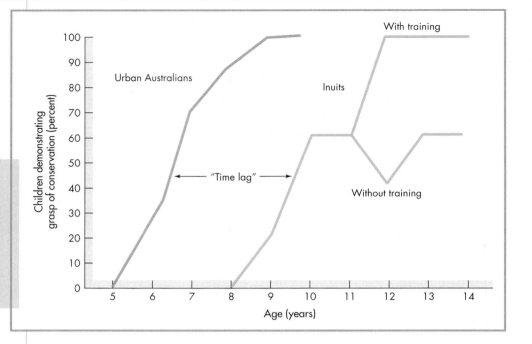

Figure 11.18 Curves representing the percentages of urban Australian and Inuit children who demonstrated a concept of conservation. Inuit children lagged behind Australian children by approximately 3 years. Without training, about 50 percent of Inuit children as old as 14 years failed to demonstrate an understanding of the concept of conservation. With training, all of that age accomplished the task. (From Dasen, 1975.)

A number of developmentalists subsequently suggested that if researchers know the local language and culture well so that children are able to follow the flexible questioning procedures that are the hallmark of Piaget's clinical interviews, the children will demonstrate conservation without any lags. Raphael Nyiti (1982), for example, compared the conservation performances of 10- and 11-year-old children of two cultural groups, both living on Cape Breton, Nova Scotia. Some of the children were of English-speaking European backgrounds, and some were of the Micmac Indian tribe. The Micmac children all spoke Micmac at home, but they had spoken English in school since the first grade. The children of European backgrounds were all interviewed in English by an English speaker of European background. The Micmac children were interviewed once in English and once in Micmac.

Nyiti found that when the children were interviewed on the conservation tasks in their native languages, there was no difference in the performances of the two cultural groups. But when the Micmac children were interviewed in English, only half as many seemed to understand the concept of conservation. Nyiti (1976) obtained similar results in a study of children in his native Tanzania, as did other researchers in the West African country of Sierra Leone (Kamara & Easley, 1977).

Taken as a whole, these studies, along with others, demonstrate that when Piaget's clinical procedures are applied appropriately, using contents with which people have extensive experience, conservation (and by extension, concrete operations) is a universal cognitive achievement of middle childhood, just as Piaget assumed it was (Segall et al., 1999). However, the evidence also shows that there are quite dramatic cultural variations in children's familiarity with the contents and procedures used in standard Piagetian tests of conservation and that these variations clearly influence children's performances on the tests.

Cultural Variations in the Use of Memory Strategies

Cross-cultural research has revealed striking variations in the use of organizational strategies in free-recall studies, but these results must be interpreted with great caution. For example, Michael Cole and his colleagues studied the development of memory among people living in rural Liberia (summarized in Cole, 1996). In one set of studies they presented groups of children of different ages with a set of 20 common objects that belonged to familiar and salient categories, such as food, clothing, and tools. Half the children at each age were attending school, while half were not because there were no schools in their villages.

The researchers found that children who had never gone to school improved their performance on these tasks very little after the age of 9 or 10. These children remembered approximately 10 items on the first trial, and managed to recall only 2 more items after 15 practice trials on the full set of 20 items. The Liberian children who were attending school, by contrast, learned the materials rapidly, much the way schoolchildren of the same age do in the United States.

Failure to use organizational strategies seemed to be the cause of the poor performance of the children who had not attended school. Schoolchildren in Liberia and the United States used categorical similarities among the items to aid their recall. After the first trial, they clustered their responses, recalling first, say, the items of clothing, then the items of food, and so on. The Liberians who had never attended school did very little clustering, an indication that they were not using the categorical relationships among the items to help them remember.

To track down the source of this difference, the researchers varied aspects of the task. They found that if, instead of presenting a series of objects in random order, they presented the same objects in a meaningful way as part of a story, their nonschooled Liberian subjects recalled them easily, clustering the objects according to the roles they played in the story. When memory for traditional children's stories was tested, cultural differences were also absent (Mandler et al., 1980). Similar results on tests of children's memorization skills have been obtained in research among Mayan people of rural Guatemala (Rogoff et al., 2005).

The implication of these cross-cultural memory studies differs from that of the cross-cultural studies of concrete-operational thinking. The latter studies probed basic mental operations presumed by Piaget and his followers to reflect the logic underlying everyday actions and reasoning in any culture. The ability to remember is also a universal intellectual requirement, but specific strategies for remembering are not universal. Indeed, many of them—the ones most often studied by psychologists—are associated with formal schooling.

As you will see in the next chapter, schooling presents children with specialized information-processing tasks—committing large amounts of information to memory in a short time, learning to manipulate abstract symbols in one's head and on paper, using logic to conduct experiments, and performing many more tasks that have few if any analogies in societies without formal schooling. The free-recall, random-order task that Cole and his colleagues initially used to assess memory among Liberian tribal people has no precise analogy in traditional Liberian cultures, so it is not surprising that subjects who had not attended school failed to show skill at such tasks.

Cultural Variations in Planning

A cross-cultural study by Shari Ellis and Bonnie Schneiders (reported in Ellis & Siegler, 1997) shows how differences in cultural values can shape the way and extent to which children will plan ahead (Figure 11.19). Using a schematic drawing of a maze representing a rural scene, Ellis and Schneiders studied the way that Navajo and European American children planned their routes to and from different parts of the maze. They were interested in contrasting these two groups because the two cultures place different values on doing things speedily. The Navajo emphasize doing things thoughtfully rather than quickly (John, 1972). By contrast,

Figure 11.19 Schematic drawing of the maze used in Ellis and Schneiders, 1989. Children were asked to find the shortest obstacle-free path from home to Grandmother's house, where they would pick up some money, and then go to the store. The dotted lines and open circles on this diagram indicate incorrect routes; solid lines and solid dots are acceptable routes. (From Ellis & Gauvain, 1992. Copyright 1992 by Lawrence Erlbaum Associates.)

speed of mental performance is often treated as an index of intelligence among Americans of European background (Sternberg, 1990). This cultural difference in values was expressed in the children's behavior as they planned their routes through the maze. The Navajo children spent almost 10 times as long planning their movements as the European-American children did—and as a result, they made significantly fewer errors.

||||| APPLY — CONNECT — DISCUSS

In what ways does Michael Cole's study of Liberian children suggest that culture contributes both to children's knowledge bases and to the type of memory strategies that children favor?

Individual Differences in Cognitive Development

If you are hungry and your parents are out hunting, how do you know where to go to find the edible goanna lizard? With all the various scratches and scuffs in the sand, how do you recognize the special tracks that will lead you to your prey? How will you catch and carry your lizards? How will you prepare them for cooking? Acquiring your afternoon snack obviously requires a good deal of knowledge and planning, characteristics of intelligent behavior. And if you nearly always return to camp with a goanna sack brimming with lizards, while your peers rarely do, we might even consider you the most intelligent child in the village.

But all those intelligent behaviors associated with successful goanna hunting are no guarantee against an empty stomach. They would, for example, get you nowhere at the corner store where you and your friends might stop for a snack on the way home from school. In this instance, your superior intelligence might be manifested by your having enough money in your pocket, being able to count your change, and knowing that a granola bar and an apple are better choices than a bag of chips and a soda.

The fact that intelligence is so securely anchored to the cultural contexts in which it is used has lead many developmentalists to argue that intelligence has no clear meaning outside its cultural context (Sternberg & Grigorenko, 2008). Indeed, although all languages have terms that describe individual differences in people's ability to solve various kinds of problems, the precise meanings of these terms vary among cultures, and it has proved difficult—some say impossible—to define intelligence so that individual differences in intelligence can be measured as precisely as weight or height, or the number of lizards in a goanna sack. Some cultures, including the Chewa of eastern Zambia, define intelligence largely in social terms, emphasizing cooperation and obedience (Serpell, 2000). Other cultures, including those of Europe and North America, define intelligence in mainly cognitive terms. Still others, including many Asian and African cultures, believe intelligence to include both social and cognitive features. A case in point is the conception of intelligence of rural Kenyans, studied by Elena Grigorenko and her colleagues (Grigorenko et al., 2001). These researchers report that among the Luo of rural Kenya, there are four words that people apply to different kinds of problem-solving abilities. One of these words appears to correspond to the notion of cognitive competence at the heart of European and North American conceptions of intelligence. The others refer to social qualities such as diligence or obedience, or personal qualities with social implications, such as a willingness to take initiative.

While cultural notions of intelligence vary, almost all children growing up today in industrialized countries can expect to take an intelligence test intended to assess their cognitive competence. Such tests are used to decide the kind of education they will receive and the kind of work they will do, which in turn will influence the lives they will lead as adults. It is thus important to understand the concept of intelligence these tests assume, as well as intelligence testing itself as a factor in children's development.

Measuring Intelligence

Interest in measuring intelligence became widespread at the beginning of the twentieth century, when mass education was becoming the norm in industrialized countries. Though most children seemed to profit from the instruction they were given, some had considerable difficulty learning, In France, the minister of public instruction named a commission to determine how to distinguish between what he termed "defective" children, who needed special educational treatment, and children who were failing to learn in school for other reasons. The commission asked Alfred Binet, a professor of psychology at the Sorbonne, and Théodore Simon, a physician, to create a means of identifying those children who needed special educational treatment. Binet and Simon set out to construct a test for diagnosing mental subnormality that would have all the precision and validity of a medical examination. They especially wanted to avoid incorrectly diagnosing children as "mentally subnormal" (Binet & Simon, 1916).

After considerable research on various test items presented to children of various ages, Binet and Simon concluded that they had succeeded in constructing a scale of intelligence. They called the basic index of intelligence for this scale *mental age (MA)*. A child who performed as well on the test as an average 7-year-old was said to have an MA of 7; a child who did as well as an average 9-year-old was said to have an MA of 9; and so on. The MA provided a convenient way to characterize mental subnormality. A "dull" 7-year-old child was one who performed like a normal child 1 or more years younger.

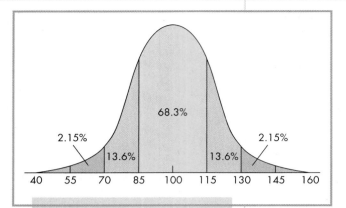

Figure 11.20 An idealized bell-shaped curve of the distribution of IQ scores. A bell-shaped curve is a distribution of scores on a graph in which the most frequent value, the mode, is in the center, and the less frequent values are distributed symmetrically on either side. By definition, the modal IQ score is 100.

Shortly after Binet and Simon introduced their scale, psychologist William Stern recognized a serious limitation in using MA as an index of intelligence. To get a sense of the limitation, consider two children, an 18-year-old with an MA of 16 and a 5-year-old with a MA of 3. Although both children are 2 years "behind" the average, we would be much more concerned about the intellectual development of the 5-year-old than we would about that of the 18-year-old. To overcome this limitation, Stern (1912) introduced a new way of calculating intelligence. He used the simple strategy of dividing children's mental age by their chronological age (CA) to obtain a measure of their intelligence. Thus was born the unit of measurement that we use today, the **intelligence quotient (IQ):**

$$IQ = (MA/CA)100$$

Calculation of IQ in this fashion ensures that when children are performing precisely as expected for their age, the resulting score will be 100; thus 100 is an "average IQ" by definition (Figure 11.20). Applied to the two children described above, the calculation generates an IQ score of 89 for the 18-year-old and 60 for the 5-year old.

Intelligence tests, along with the manner of calculating IQs, have undergone substantial refinement since the seminal work of Binet, Simon, and Stern. Despite various revisions, the logic of the procedures devised by Binet and Simon—to define "average" performance for each age and compare the scores of individual children against the average—is still the basis of standardized intelligence tests.

Persistent Questions about Intelligence

The adoption and refinement of their testing methods by later generations of developmentalists represent only part of Binet and Simon's legacy. Equally important have been the questions they brought to the fore, three of which have dominated research on intelligence ever since. The first question focuses on the nature of intelligence itself: Is it a general characteristic of a person's entire mental life, or is it a bundle of relatively specific abilities? Second is the nature–nurture question: How do biological and environmental factors contribute to variations among individuals and groups in test performance? The third question is about the nature of IQ tests and their relationship to culture: To what extent might tests be biased in their assessment of intelligence?

Despite persistent questions about the nature of intelligence and how to measure it, IQ tests are a routine part of many children's lives.

The Nature of Intelligence: General or Specific?

Although Binet and Simon (1916) were skeptical about the possibility of defining intelligence, they attempted to specify the quality of mind they were trying to test for:

> It seems to us that in intelligence there is a fundamental faculty, the alteration or lack of which is of the utmost importance for practical life. This faculty is judgment, otherwise called good sense, practical sense, initiative, the faculty of adapting oneself to circumstances. To judge well, to comprehend well, to reason well, these are the essential activities of intelligence. (p. 43)

By referring to intelligence as "a fundamental faculty" Binet and Simon signaled their belief that intelligence is a basic characteristic. Many others have followed this approach,

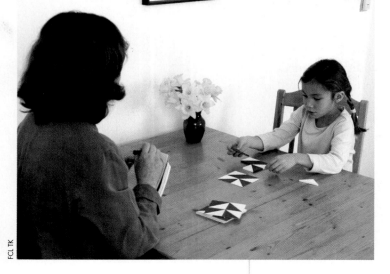

noting, for example, that an individual's performance tends to be similar across types of test items, a tendency consistent with the existence of a "general intelligence" (Spearman, 1927).

However, many psychologists now reject the idea of general intelligence, arguing instead that intelligence is composed of several distinct and separate abilities. Two approaches that depict intelligence in terms of distinctive capacities have been particularly influential. Howard Gardner (2006) has proposed a theory of *multiple intelligences*, each of which coincides with a different cognitive module and follows its own developmental path (Table 11.3). For example, musical intelligence often appears at an early age; logical mathematical intelligence seems to peak in late adolescence and early adulthood; and the kind of spatial intelligence on which artists rely may reach its peak much later. Gardner argues that the expression of each kind of intelligence depends upon a combination of three factors: (1) innate biological brain structures; (2) the extent to which the particular kind of intelligence is emphasized in a given culture; and (3) the extent to which a child is provided deliberate instruction in activities associated with the particular kind of intelligence.

Robert Sternberg (2007) has proposed what he calls a "triarchic" theory of intelligence, according to which there are three kinds of intelligence:

1. *Analytic,* the abilities we use to analyze, judge, evaluate, compare, and contrast

2. *Creative,* the abilities we use to create, invent, discover, and imagine or suppose

3. *Practical,* the abilities to apply knowledge by putting it into practice

Sternberg reports that an individual's performance level can vary from one kind of intelligence to another and argues that only analytic intelligence is measured by standard IQ tests.

What Explains Population Differences? Along with their disagreements about what intelligence means and whether it is specific or general, developmentalists disagree about the significance of differences across individuals and across groups in performance on tests. The debate dates back to the beginning of World

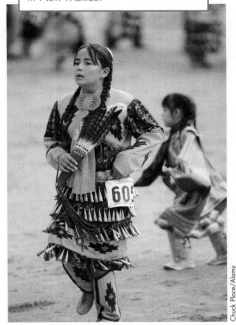

These talented young dancers display their creative intelligence in a dance competition at a ceremonial powwow in New Mexico.

Chuck Place/Alamy

intelligence quotient (IQ) The ratio of mental age to chronological age, calculated as IQ = (MA/CA)100. Calculation of IQ in this fashion ensures that when children are performing precisely as expected for their age, the resulting score will be 100; thus 100 is an "average IQ" by definition.

table **11.3**	
Gardner's Multiple Intelligences	
Kind of Intelligence	**Characteristics**
Linguistic	Special sensitivity to language, which allows one to choose precisely the right word or turn of phrase and to grasp new meanings easily
Musical	Sensitivity to pitch and tone, which allows one to detect and produce musical structure
Logical-mathematical	Ability to engage in abstract reasoning and manipulate symbols
Spatial	Ability to perceive relations among objects, to transform mentally what one sees, and to re-create visual images from memory
Bodily-kinesthetic	Ability to represent ideas in movement; characteristic of great dancers and mimes
Personal	Ability to gain access to one's own feelings and to understand the motivations of others
Social	Ability to understand the motives, feelings, and behaviors of other people

Source: Gardner, 1983.

War I, when Robert Yerkes proposed that all military recruits be given an intelligence test to determine their fitness to serve in military capacities. In addition to determining individual recruits' fitness, the testing was perceived as generating data about the U.S. population as a whole (Yerkes, 1921). Approximately 1.75 million men were given IQ tests—written tests for those who could read and write English, a picture-completion test for those who could not (Figure 11.21). Never before had IQ tests been administered to such large groups of people at one time or to people for whom the language of the tests was not their native language.

Yerkes's research began a controversy that continues to the present time. Two results appeared to be particularly provocative. First, the average mental age of native-born Anglo Americans was assessed to be 13 years. Since, by the standards of the time, a mental age of 8 to 12 years was considered subnormal for an adult, it appeared that a substantial part of the Anglo population consisted of "morons."

Figure 11.21 Items from the picture-completion test used by Robert Yerkes and his colleagues to test recruits during World War I. Each picture is incomplete in some way; the task is to identify what is missing. (From Yerkes, 1921.)

Second, there was a substantial difference between the scores obtained by recruits of European American and of African American origin. Overall, the average for recruits of European origin was a mental age of 13.7 years, whereas African Americans averaged slightly more than 10 years.

Several of the pioneer testers of intelligence interpreted such differences as the result of innate, immutable differences in natural intelligence ("nature"). According to this *innatist hypothesis of intelligence,* some people are born generally smarter than others, and no amount of training or variation in the environment can alter this fact. The generally lower test scores of members of ethnic minority groups and the poor (who often, but not always, are the same people) were widely interpreted to mean that such groups were innately and irrevocably inferior (Herrnstein & Murray, 1994).

During the 1930s and 1940s the general-intelligence, innatist position was countered by an *environmental hypothesis of intelligence,* which asserted that intelligence is both specific—that is, includes distinct and separate abilities—and heavily dependent on experience. It was demonstrated, for example, that after people had moved from rural areas to the city, their intelligence test scores rose (Klineberg, 1935), and that when orphans were removed from very restricted early environments, their intelligence test scores improved markedly.

One of the most striking new lines of evidence for the environmental hypothesis of intelligence is the fact that worldwide there has been a steady increase in IQ test performance since testing began roughly 100 years ago, a trend called the **Flynn effect,** named after the scientist who discovered it (Flynn, 2007). Although the amount of improvement differs somewhat according to the kind of test that is used and the particular country in which it is administered, the general result for the 20 countries where such testing has been widely carried out for many decades indicates that IQ scores have been going up an average of 10 to 20 points for every generation (Figure 11.22). This means, for example, that the average English person in 1900 would score at the level currently considered to indicate mental retardation.

Flynn effect The steady increase over the past 100 years in IQ test performance, believed to support the environmental hypothesis of intelligence.

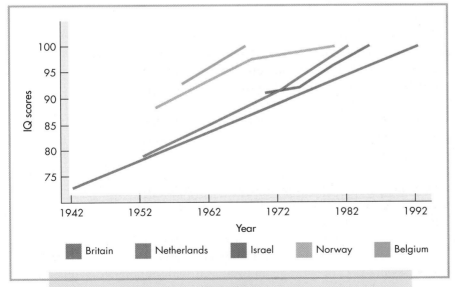

Figure 11.22 Countries that have been testing intelligence for decades, including the five illustrated here, find that IQ has been increasing by 10–20 points every generation, a phenomenon dubbed the "Flynn effect," after the scientist who discovered it. (Flynn, 1999, p. 7)

There is no clear consensus about what environmental factors are causing IQ scores to go up, but it is certain that the change must involve the environment, since rapid change in the genetic constitution of people all over the world has not taken place, but large changes in the environment have (Dickens & Flynn, 2006). As James Flynn points out, it is almost impossible to determine precisely how the environment contributes to the development of intelligence because all the possible causal factors are closely connected with each other, and all lead to changes that are in the same direction. The list of the possible causal factors ranges from improved nutrition and increasing years of education to an increase in the complexity of life, and even to the spread of interactive video games.

Are IQ Tests Culturally Biased? At the present time, no responsible scholar believes that the variation in intelligence test scores from person to person can be attributed entirely to either environmental or genetic factors. As we pointed out in Chapter 2, the attempt to tease apart the specific gene–environment interactions that shape human beings is especially difficult in relation to traits like intelligence that are *polygenic*—that is, traits that are shaped by several or many genes acting in combination in a given set of environmental conditions. Thus, even when it has been possible to estimate the genetic contribution to a trait, little can be said about precisely which genes are interacting with the environment in what way. Efforts to separate the various influences of nature and nurture on the phenotype are further complicated by the fact that parents contribute both to their children's genetic constitution and to the environment in which their children grow up. And then there is the final knot in the parsing of gene–environment interaction: Children actively shape their own environments in response to both genetic and environmental influences.

Attempts to understand how genetic and environmental factors combine to create the phenotypic behavior called "intelligence" face another, even greater difficulty. As we noted earlier, psychologists disagree profoundly about what, precisely, they are measuring when they administer an intelligence test. All they can say with any confidence is that these tests predict later school performance to a moderate degree.

At first glance, IQ tests may appear to be standard measures logically similar to a yardstick. But this appearance is an illusion. Precisely because intelligence tests derive their validity from their correlation with academic achievement, they are rooted in the schooled society in which they are developed and bound to the graphic systems of representation that are central to all schooling. But these modes of representation are generally absent in nonliterate societies. To be administered to a !Kung child, every existing intelligence test would thus require some modification—and not just translation from English to !Kung. If, for example, one of the test questions asks how many fingers are on two hands, the testers might assume that the test could be adapted to !Kung with only minimal modification—but that assumption would be wrong. The number system used by the !Kung is not the same as that used by Minnesotans, and it plays a different role in their lives. In !Kung society, the relative importance of knowing the number of fingers on a hand is less important than knowing how to tie knots with those fingers.

When it comes to the tests that require interpretation of pictures or some form of written answer, even more serious difficulties arise. The !Kung have no tradition of either drawing or writing, and research with nonliterate peoples in several parts of the world and with young children in the United States shows that people without such experience do not automatically interpret two-dimensional pictures of objects as they would the objects themselves (Pick, 1997; Serpell & Hanes,

2004). For them, interpreting the pictures requires additional mental work. As a result, tests that used pictures or required copying figures graphically would be inappropriate, as would any tests that depended on the ability to read. We thus cannot assume that an IQ test is like a yardstick, yielding equivalent measures in all cultural environments.

Various attempts have been made to create "culture-free" tests, but no generally satisfactory solution has yet been found: All tests of intelligence draw on a background of learning that is culture-specific (Serpell & Hanes, 2004). The fact that intelligence cannot be tested independently of the culture that gives rise to the test greatly limits the conclusions that can be drawn from IQ testing in different social and cultural groups.

|||||| APPLY • CONNECT • DISCUSS _____

IQ tests were first developed in order to identify children who needed special education. Today, the use of IQ tests in making decisions to place children on different "academic ability tracks" is hotly debated. Using concepts and research evidence presented in this section, describe the pros and cons of IQ testing and ability tracking in schools.

Reconsidering the Cognitive Changes in Middle Childhood

The changes in children's biological and cognitive abilities between early and middle childhood point to specific features of children's physical abilities and thought processes that are becoming more systematic and can be applied across a broader variety of settings. Particularly important is the extent to which children are gaining increasing understanding of, and control over, their new powers of thought and action. When we consider these changes as a whole, rather than as isolated achievements, we start to get a better idea of why adults begin to grant their children more independence during this developmental period.

However, the scant cross-cultural work available reminds us that we have not yet taken a direct look at the contexts where experience of the culturally organized environment exerts its effects. To address the issue properly, we need to reach beyond the relatively narrow range of tasks that has been featured in psychologists' studies of cognitive development and investigate the changes that children display in a variety of social contexts, especially in classrooms and peer groups, where many children in middle childhood begin to spend so much of their time. Many developmentalists believe that experiences in both of these contexts are crucial to the cognitive changes associated with middle childhood.

SUMMARY

- The beginning of middle childhood is recognized in cultures around the world, particularly in adults' new expectations of their 6- and 7-year-olds. These expectations relate to children's increased physical capacities and cognitive abilities.

Physical and Motor Development

- Size and strength increase significantly during middle childhood, although more slowly than in earlier years. Muscle mass and fat tissue both increase.

- Although height and weight are both influenced by genetic factors, environmental factors, such as nutrition and health, also play an important role. For example, in the United States changes in diet in recent decades have contributed to an increase in childhood obesity.

- Strength, agility, and balance all improve in middle childhood. Boys tend to be slightly advanced in motor abilities requiring power and force; girls often excel in fine motor skills and gross motor skills combining balance and foot movement.

- Brain development in the early years of middle childhood includes:

  - Continued myelination, especially in the frontal cortex.

  - Continued synaptic pruning in late-maturing brain areas, with more stable connections among remaining neurons.

  - A shift to more alpha activity (characteristic of engaged attention) than theta activity (characteristic of sleep states).

  - A significant increase in the synchronization of electrical activity between different brain areas, among them the frontal lobes, with the areas functioning more effectively as coordinated systems.

Concrete-Operational Development

- According to Piaget, as a result of increasing decentration, at about age 7 or 8, children become capable of mental operations—of logically combining, separating, and transforming information. With the advent of this stage of concrete operations, children can think in a more organized, flexible way and the world becomes more predictable to them.

- Concrete operational thinking is reflected in new abilities related to:

- Conservation, Piaget's term for the understanding that some properties of an object or substance remain the same even when its appearance is altered in some way.

- Classification, with children now able to understand the relation between a superordinate class and its subclasses and to categorize objects according to multiple criteria.

- Planning, which requires forming mental representations of actions needed to achieve a goal.

- Metacognition, with children better able to think about and regulate their thoughts.

- The limitations of concrete operations are apparent in the difficulty children encounter when reasoning about abstract, unfamiliar situations.

Information-Processing Approaches

- According to information-processing theorists, the cognitive changes in middle childhood are made possible by changes such as:

  - Improvements in memory, made possible by increased speed and capacity of working memory, increases in knowledge, and greater use of more effective strategies for remembering, such as rehearsal, organizational strategies, and elaboration.

  - Improvements in metamemory, or knowledge about memory including about memory limitations and strategies.

  - Increases in children's ability to regulate their attention, which enables them to stay focused and ignore distractions.

- Developmentalists have suggested that the mechanisms for cognitive change suggested in Piaget's stage approach and those suggested by information-processing theorists may in fact work together.

The Role of Social and Cultural Contexts

- Cross-cultural studies suggest the universality of concrete operations in middle childhood as well as significant cultural variations that influence performance.

- Across cultures, memory strategies used differ significantly depending on whether children have had schooling. Cross-cultural differences in planning relate to cultural differences in values.

Individual Differences in Cognitive Development

- Definitions of intelligence differ among cultures and may focus on social, rather than cognitive, competence.

- Intelligence tests, as they have been developed since their introduction by Binet and Simon, attempt to measure cognitive competence by producing an IQ score based on a child's performance compared to children of the same age.

- Research on intelligence has been dominated by three questions:

  1. Is intelligence a general characteristic or are there specific kinds of intelligence? Two approaches taking the second position are Gardner's theory of multiple intelligences and Sternberg's triarchic theory of intelligence.

  2. Are differences among individuals and among groups in performance on IQ tests the result of genetic or environmental factors? Evidence for an environmental role comes from the Flynn effect, the increase across generations in performance on IQ tests.

  3. To what extent might IQ tests be culturally biased? All tests draw on learning that is culture specific, limiting the conclusions that can be drawn.

Key Terms

concrete operations, p. 396

conservation of number, p. 398

conservation of volume, p. 398

identity, p. 399

compensation, p. 399

reversibility, p. 399

metacognition, p. 401

memory span, p. 404

memory strategies, p. 405

rehearsal, p. 405

organizational strategies, p. 406

elaboration, p. 406

metamemory, p. 406

intelligence quotient (IQ), p. 416

Flynn effect, p. 419

12

School as a Context for Development

Last month, I was sitting in the headmaster's office of a primary school in Samfya, in the heart of rural Zambia. Mr. Ben Charma leads 46 teachers in his school of 1,700 children, more than half of whom have been orphaned by AIDS. The son of a copper miner, Ben Charma worked hard at school and avoided the mining life that ruined his father's health. He knows what lies in store for children when educational chances are limited by poverty. The exam results were out and the final-year pupils at the primary school had done well. Yet this is the most heart-breaking time of all for school staff. They have worked so hard to achieve a good pass rate for their pupils, yet for many children—particularly girls—this will be their very last day at school, at the age of just 11 or 12. Without money for school clothing, shoes, books, stationery, and fees, these children have no chance of going on to secondary school. And so it is that parents come to beg. They know that, without the benefits of education, their daughters will be forced to marry young and face lives of back-breaking agricultural and domestic toil with babies born into families too poor to give them more than life.

It is a scandal that more than 24 million girls in sub-Saharan Africa are still not able to go to school. This has a devastating impact, particularly on rural communities. Children die younger when their mothers do not know about basic hygiene; HIV spreads more rapidly when uneducated women do not know how to protect themselves from the disease; and earnings are lower when women do not have access to education. Send a girl to school and the opportunities are multiplied across her whole community. When women farmers have the same access to education as their brothers and husbands, crop yields rise by 22 percent. In Africa, if mothers receive just 5 years of education, their children are 40 percent more likely to live to their fifth birthday. And educated women are 3 times more likely to protect themselves against AIDS than those with no education. Lamentably, the world has been slow to heed the urgent message that educating girls is the key to eradicating poverty. United Nations Secretary-General Kofi Annan has said: "Without achieving gender equity for girls in education, the world has no chance of achieving many of the ambitious health, social and development targets it has set for itself."

(adapted from Cotton, 2006)

n contrast to the students of Samfya, it is unlikely that at the tender age of 11 or 12 you worried about whether you would be able to continue your education, or thought about school in terms of its consequences for your future. But as Ann Cotton argues in her heartfelt plea to increase educational access for Africa's children, especially girls, going to school not only improves the life circumstances of individuals, it also contributes substantially to the health and economic well-being of local communities and to human society as a whole. Indeed, in the case of Africa, where children spend less time in school than do children

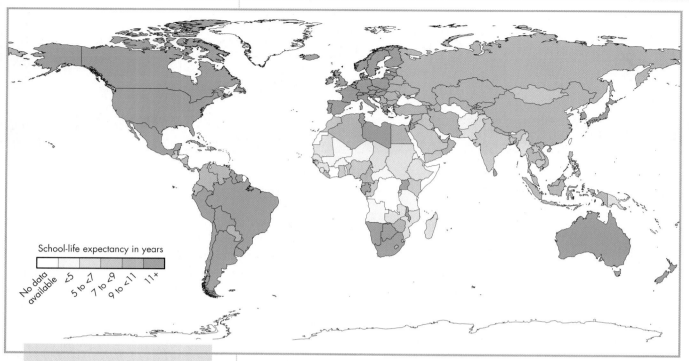

Figure 12.1 Compared to most other countries in the world, many African countries face significant challenges in providing education to their children.

These Ghanaian children are ready for school. Children in many other African countries tend to leave school at earlier ages compared to those living in Ghana, placing entire communities at greater risk for AIDS and poverty.

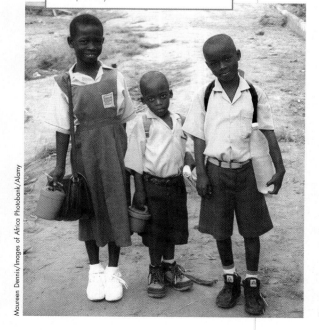

Maureen Dennis/Images of Africa Photobank/Alamy

anywhere else on earth (Figure 12.1), increasing access to education may provide countries with a powerful defense against the devastating epidemics of poverty and AIDS that are killing so many of their citizens.

Although access to education is not nearly as restricted in the United States and other wealthier nations as it is in Africa, disparities in who has access to quality education can be quite pronounced for a number of reasons. It is well known, for example, that educational quality suffers substantially in schools located in economically impoverished neighborhoods, where large numbers of ethnic minority children grow up. Yet conditions in such neighborhoods make educational quality all the more important. For example, living in poor neighborhoods makes it more likely not only that children will be exposed to environmental toxins that have been shown to harm cognitive development but also that they will be exposed to violence, which increases the likelihood of psychiatric disorders. To make matters more complicated, financing for schools in poor neighborhoods is often inadequate, and such schools are disproportionately assigned inexperienced teachers because experienced teachers, who often have more choice in where they teach, find such schools unpleasant to work in. A study of nearly 4000 African American families that moved from urban high-rise housing projects, where poverty and crime are pervasive, to new, private housing in a wealthier suburban school district found a marked improvement in several indicators of academic achievement, including a decrease in high school dropout rates and increased college attendance (Rubinowitz et al., 2000). Clearly, equal access to quality education remains an ideal to be struggled for rather than a reality for millions of American, as well as African, children.

This chapter is devoted to exploring the extraordinary impact of school as a context for children's development. We begin by discussing the unique features of school that set it apart from other contexts of learning and consider the particular contributions that school makes to intellectual development. We then examine *school readiness*, arising from the academic building blocks that children bring with them into the classroom, including those provided by family, community, and culture. Next, we examine the different ways of "doing school," that is, the various forms of classroom instruction and their implications for learning. Finally, we confront contemporary challenges to school access and school success in our rapidly globalizing world.

The Contexts of Learning

In Chapter 2 we introduced the idea that children acquire the material and symbolic tools of culture through three fundamental social processes: *social enhancement* (making use of resources present in the immediate environment), *imitation* (observing and copying the behaviors of others), and *explicit instruction* (deliberate teaching of knowledge and skills) (see p. 56). **Education** is a social process in which adults engage in explicit instruction of the young in order to transmit specialized knowledge and skills of their culture.

It is not known if education existed among the hunter–gatherer peoples who roamed the earth hundreds of thousands of years ago, but explicit instruction is not a conspicuous part of socialization in contemporary hunter–gatherer societies (Rogoff, 2003). Among the !Kung of Africa's Kalahari Desert, for example, basic training in the skills expected of adults is embedded in everyday activities, involving processes of social enhancement and imitation. The basic means by which adults ensure that children acquire culturally valued skills and knowledge is to include children in adult activities.

> There is . . . very little explicit teaching. . . . What the child knows, he learns from direct interaction with the adult community, whether it is learning to tell the age of the spoor left by a poisoned kudu buck, to straighten the shaft of an arrow, to build a fire, or to dig a spring hare out of its burrow. . . . It is all implicit. (Bruner, 1966, p. 59)

When societies achieve a certain degree of complexity and specialization in the roles people play, the tools they use, and the ways they secure food and housing, preparation for some occupations is likely to occur through **apprenticeship,** a form intermediate between learning through participation in family and community life and the explicit instruction of formal education. A young apprentice learns a craft or a skill by spending an extended period of time working for an adult master (Smits & Stromback, 2001). The settings in which apprentices learn are not organized solely for the purpose of teaching. Rather, instruction and productive labor are combined; from the beginning, apprentices contribute to the work process.

Researchers have found that novice apprentices receive relatively little explicit instruction but, instead, are given ample opportunity to observe skilled workers and to practice specific tasks (Rogoff, 2003). In many societies, the apprentice's relationship with the master is part of a larger web of family relationships. Often the apprentice lives with the master and does farm or household chores to help pay for his or her upkeep. In this way, the tasks of education and community building are woven together (Rogoff et al., 2007).

The earliest forms of formal schooling trace back to around 4000 B.C. in the Middle East, when innovations in technology made it possible for a segment of a population to grow enough food to support a large number of people besides

education A form of socialization in which adults engage in deliberate teaching of the young to ensure that they acquire specialized knowledge and skills.

apprenticeship A form of activity combining instruction and productive labor that is intermediate between the implicit socialization of family and community life and the explicit instruction of formal education.

Apprenticeship arrangements in which children learn by observing adults and working alongside them are still an important form of education despite the spread of formal schools.

MacDuff Everton

Figure 12.2 The earliest writings, which date from around 4000 B.C., were in the form of clay tablets etched with cuneiform symbols. This type of writing originated from pictograms, basic outline drawings of the objects being referred to. Over time and use, the pictograms became simplified and rendered as wedge-shaped (cuneiform) symbols that could convey sounds and abstract concepts, as well as objects. The tablet shown here, from Tello in ancient southern Mesopotamia, is a tallying of sheep and goats.

themselves. This shift made possible a substantial division of labor and the development of city-states. It also created a need for systems of writing (Figure 12.2) and arithmetic (Damerow, 1998). The places where young people were brought together to learn to read and write were the earliest schools.

As it has since developed, schooling differs from traditional apprenticeship training (and from informal instruction in the family) in four main ways (Lave & Wenger, 1991; Singleton, 1998):

1. *Motivation.* Apprentices get to practice their craft from the beginning and see the fruits of their labor. Students in schools must work for years to perfect their skills before they can put their knowledge to use in adult work. In the meantime, the tasks they are engaged in may seem pointless to them.

2. *Social relations.* Unlike masters of apprentices, schoolteachers are rarely kin or family acquaintances, and they may not even live in the community.

3. *Social organization.* Apprentices are most likely to learn in a work setting among people of diverse ages and skill levels, so they have more than one person to turn to for assistance. At school, children typically learn in the company of other children of about their age and one adult, who instructs them, and they are expected to work individually (in fact, asking for assistance from their peers may be considered cheating).

4. *Medium of instruction.* Apprenticeship instruction is usually conducted orally in the context of production. Oral instruction is important in formal schooling as well, but, as we will see later, it is speech of a special kind, closely associated with the use of written symbols as a means of acquiring skills and knowledge.

Not only does schooling differ from other learning contexts in these ways but the types of problems posed to children in school differ considerably from those they encounter in other learning contexts (Table 12.1). Consider, for example, a problem in which a child needs to figure out the distance between two locations. In a school context, the child might be asked to use a scientific instrument, such as a ruler, to precisely measure abstract units (centimeters, inches) between two

table 12.1

School Problems versus Everyday Problems

School Problems	Everyday Problems
• Tend to draw on analytic intelligence.	• Tend to draw on practical intelligence.
• Abstract in nature and goals.	• Concrete in nature and goals.
• Formulated for the learner by other people.	• Must be recognized or formulated by learners themselves.
• Generally have little or no intrinsic interest to the learner.	• Are intrinsically important to the learner.
• Are clearly defined.	• Generally are poorly defined.
• Usually have a single correct answer that can be reached by a single, generalizable method.	• Usually have several acceptable solutions that can be reached by a variety of routes.
• Include all the information needed to deal with them.	• Require people to seek new information.
• Are detached from ordinary experience.	• Are embedded in ordinary experience.

points. The goal of problem solving is to learn or demonstrate mastery over a mathematical system of measurement that can be applied to measure distances in any situation. In an everyday context, in contrast, the child might be faced with a problem of finding and cutting tree saplings of sufficient length to bridge a small stream so people can cross into crop fields without getting their feet wet. In this instance, problem solving is undertaken in the service of a highly specific goal that is important to the local community. In all likelihood, the child works with others to find saplings that are tall enough and strong enough to accomplish the task at hand. The measuring "tools" are specific to the particular, concrete problem at hand, and may be as variable as the sense that the saplings should be "taller than my house" or "young trees of at least 4 winters." The outcomes of such measuring will also be variable, lacking the precision of scientifically calibrated measurement instruments.

Thus, it appears that school problem solving supports the development and use of abstract reasoning whereas everyday problem solving supports reasoning based on particular concrete experience (Cole, 2005). Indeed, Alexander Luria, a Russian developmentalist who studied the cognitive effects of literacy, found evidence of this when he presented illiterate peasants with school-type problems that required the application of abstract reasoning, as in the following (adapted from Luria, 1976, pp. 108–109):

> Luria: In the North, where there is snow, all bears are white. Novaya Zemlya is in the Far North, and it always has snow. What color are the bears there?
> Peasant: I don't know. I've never been to Novaya Zemlya.
> Luria: But on the basis of my words [repeats the problem].
> Peasant: I've only seen black bears.
> Luria: But if you just think about my words [repeats the problem again].
> Peasant (becoming annoyed): Look . . . If a king or a czar had been to Novaya Zemlya and saw a bear and told about it, then maybe he could be believed. But I have never been there, and I have not seen the bears there, so I can't say. That's my last word!

Clearly, different contexts pose different types of intellectual challenges and support the development of different forms of reasoning. Formal education, according to Luria's research, encourages the development of abstract, hypothetical reasoning crucial to success in technologically advanced societies.

APPLY — CONNECT — DISCUSS

Using concepts presented in this section, explain some ways that going to school might contribute to the health and economic well-being of local communities and human society as a whole.

School Readiness

Four-year-olds Dawn and Heshan are coloring pictures when Dawn invites, "Let's play lieberry." "Okay," says Heshan, agreeably. Gesturing to a collection of books stacked on a toy shelf, Dawn suggests, "You can get some books over there." Heshan chooses several books while Dawn prepares a "check-out" by clearing toys from a space on the table and assembling some crayons and paper. "I'll take these," Heshan announces. Dawn takes the books he offers, looks at each one, gives them back, and warns, "They're due in 1 week." Heshan retreats to a corner of the room and begins "reading" a book about animal babies. Meanwhile, Dawn is scratching marks on small pieces of paper. After some minutes, she approaches Heshan and hands him a piece of paper. "You owe 5 dollars," she says. "What?" asks Heshan, clearly puzzled. Dawn explains,"You're overdue 1 week. If you don't pay 5 dollars that will be 5 weeks and you have to pay 100 dollars." "Oh," says Heshan, uncertainly. "Here," says Dawn, handing him another piece of paper. "This can be 5 dollars."

emergent literacy Knowledge, skills, and attitudes that provide the building blocks for learning to read and write.

emergent numeracy Knowledge, skills, and attitudes that provide the building blocks for learning how to do math.

decoding The process of establishing letter-sound correspondences when reading.

It is clear from our previous discussions of development during infancy and early childhood that by the time they start school, children already possess a number of building blocks relevant to literacy and math instruction. **Emergent literacy** and **emergent numeracy** include knowledge, skills, and attitudes that are precursors to learning to read, write, and do math. In the example above, it is clear that Dawn and Heshan have had experiences relevant to developing literacy and numeracy. They know about books and libraries and enjoy them well enough to include them in their play. Dawn pretends to write; Heshan pretends to read. And Dawn expresses the rudiments of mathematical knowledge. She not only uses number words—"one," "five," "one hundred"—but also demonstrates an understanding of which words reflect larger amounts (and higher library fines). When Dawn and Heshan start school, their emergent literacy and numeracy skills will provide an important foundation for academic success. In the following sections, we will examine several emergent literacy and numeracy skills associated with school readiness, as well as a number of factors known to contribute to the development of these skills, including experiences provided by families and preschools.

Precursors to Reading and Writing

The first step children must take in learning to read and write is to realize that there is a correspondence between the marks on the printed page and the spoken language. Once they understand that each word is represented by a cluster of graphic signs, they still have to figure out how each graphic sign is related to a linguistic sound. One of the most basic reading skills is **decoding** text, that is, translating units of print, or *graphemes,* to units of sound, or *phonemes* (Tolchinsky, 2006). Obviously, before this process of translation can occur, children must be able to distinguish between letters, as well as detect and manipulate phonemes (Thompson & Nicholson, 1999). As you learned in Chapter 4 (see pp. 132–133), the capacity to discriminate between phonemes occurs very early in life. However, this infant capacity is quite different from the ability to detect and manipulate the phonemes that make up words. So, for example, your own capacity to detect and manipulate phonemes makes it easy for you to fill in the blanks below, each of which represents a phoneme:

Fuzzy Wu_y wa_ a bear.
Fuzzy Wu_y had no h_ _.
Fuzzy Wu_y wa_ n't fuzzy, wa_ he?

Research suggests that the *phonological awareness* you used to fill in the blanks of the "Fuzzy Wuzzy" ditty—your ability to detect and manipulate the phonemes in words—does not occur without deliberate instruction: nonliterate adults in various parts of the world do not seem able to identify the phonemic units that make up individual words (Scholes, 1998).

A wealth of research conducted by Peter Bryant and his colleagues in different countries has demonstrated that children who find it difficult to break words into their constituent syllables and phonemes in a purely oral task have difficulty linking sounds and letters (Bryant & Nunes, 1998). This research has spawned special educational programs that provide children with enriched experiences in oral language analysis before they are taught to read or when they experience difficulty in reading (Sunseth & Bowers, 2002). The lessons include practice in rhyming, breaking words down into syllables, and special language games such as pig Latin, in which the first phoneme of each word is moved to the end of the word and then followed by an "ay" (as in "igpay atinlay"). Such special instruction has been found to increase the literacy skills of poor readers substantially (Blachman et al., 2004).

Ramos reads to his teddy bear, clearly demonstrating his interest and enjoyment of books. His positive attitude will contribute to his success learning to read in school.

Precursors to Learning Mathematics

Like learning to read and write, learning mathematics involves a process of translation. In the case of mathematics, however, children must learn to translate their culture's number words and symbols (e.g., Arabic numerals) into an understanding of specific quantities (Geary, 2006). Although very young babies, as well as a wide variety of nonhuman species, demonstrate the ability to discriminate between different amounts—distinguishing, for example, between a set containing 6 objects and a set containing 12 objects—the vastly more complex process of mapping symbols to quantities does not begin in earnest until 2 to 3 years of age (Gilmore & Spelke, 2008; Beran & Beran, 2004; Gordon, 2004).

As we all know, early counting efforts are prone to error, as when Jasmine says "three, five" when asked to count two crayons, and "three, five, six" when asked to count three crayons. However, errors like Jasmine's actually reveal several competencies that are central to mathematics learning. First, when Jasmine is asked to count, she responds with number words, not color words, demonstrating her awareness of the special language of mathematics. Furthermore, she uses each count word only once, suggesting an understanding that different number words correspond to different quantities. Finally, her word order—"three, five" and "three, five, six"—indicates her awareness that the sequence of words matters in counting (Sarnecka & Gelman, 2004).

With increasing age, Jasmine will become more proficient at mapping number words onto specific quantities. Interestingly, research indicates that this developmental process would unfold more quickly if Jasmine spoke Chinese rather than English (Geary et al., 1996). Mapping number words onto the base-10 number system can be troublesome for English-speaking children because the language includes some irregular number words such as "eleven" and "twelve" that do not carry the same structural information as words like "thirteen," "fourteen," and "fifteen." Chinese, in contrast, does not include irregular number words. Moreover, Chinese number words map very clearly onto the base-10 number system. The Chinese word for "twelve," for example, translates as "ten two," making the tens value of 1 and units value of 2 much more transparent than they are in English (Geary, 2006). It is easy to see why English-speaking first-graders make such errors as writing "203" when they mean to write "23": this representation corresponds to the way the number is said ("20-3").

Despite the challenges presented by her native tongue, as Jasmine gains mathematical experience during elementary school, she will become able to envision quantities in terms of a mental number line. That is, she will be able to imagine an abstract number line composed of discrete units and to identify the placement of a particular number on the line (Figure 12.3). Interestingly, as we found with children's abilities to identify and manipulate the phonemic units of words, the ability to identify and manipulate numeric units seems to emerge only in the context of school (Siegler & Opfer, 2003). Later in the chapter we will examine other ways in which formal education fosters the development of abstract thinking.

Figure 12.3 The ability to locate a specific number on an abstract number line emerges during middle childhood.

The Role of Family

The family's important role in supporting the child's emergent literacy and numeracy skills has long been recognized by teachers and researchers alike. In many cultures, parents provide their children with special toys, games, and activities designed to promote learning mathematics, reading, and writing (Ginsburg, 2008;

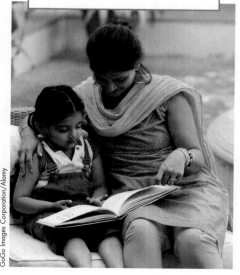

Figure 12.4 Ethnographic studies find that families prepare their children for school in a number of ways, emphasizing academic lessons, world lessons, and/or academic play. The extent to which a family may stress one or more of these ways depends on the specific culture and socioeconomic status of the family.

It is now well documented that children who are read to on a daily basis will develop larger vocabularies and, in turn, have even more reading experiences compared to children who are read to less often.

Tudge et al., 2006). When Jonathan Tudge and his colleagues conducted an ethnographic study of 3-year-olds growing up in the United States, Kenya, and Brazil, they found important differences in children's school-readiness activities depending on the children's culture and socioeconomic status (Tudge et al., 2006). For example, as shown in Figure 12.4, in all cultures, children from middle-class families were more likely than their working-class counterparts to engage with their parents in academically oriented play and academically oriented lessons such as counting, spelling, and learning shapes and colors. Interestingly, in Kenya, but not in the other cultures, children from working-class families were more likely than their middle-class counterparts to be engaged with their parents in "world lessons," such as learning how things work, why things happen, and how to be safe. Interestingly, Kenyan working-class children also spent considerably more time than children in any of the other cultural/socioeconomic groups engaged in work-related activities, such as cleaning, shopping, and repairing. As the researchers suggest, it is likely that the concentration on "world lessons" and work-related activities helps move Kenyan working-class children "on a trajectory more to do with the world of work than the world of school" (2006, p. 1463). In contrast, Kenyan middle-class children spent more time than any other group engaged in academically oriented play and academic lessons with parents. In Kenyan society, children must pass school-readiness tests to be admitted to the more prestigious schools. In preparation for these tests, most middle-class families enroll their children in preschools that provide substantial school-relevant content.

Taken together, results from Tudge's exhaustive analysis of children's everyday activities underscore the importance of family in creating contexts for children to engage in activities relevant to school readiness. There is, in fact, a wealth of research indicating that such activities have a significant bearing on children's intellectual development and academic success. Strong relationships have been found, for example, between being read to at 14 months of age and language comprehension, vocabulary size, and cognitive functioning at 2 years (Raikes et al., 2006).

In addition, it seems that such early reading experience and emergent literacy skills enhance one another. Thus, when young children are read to on a daily basis, their vocabularies increase, and as their vocabularies increase, so too do their daily reading experiences. Helen Raikes, who discovered this relationship in a study involving more than 2500 children and families, described it as a "snowball" effect in which reading and vocabulary lead to more opportunities to use and learn language.

Preschools

With the recognition of the importance of school readiness to academic success, and of education in general to the well-being of children, their communities, and society as a whole, enrollment in preschools throughout the world has tripled since 1970. Nevertheless, consistent with our earlier discussion about children's access to education, significant cross-national disparities exist in preschool enrollments (Figure 12.5). Sadly, according to a recent report issued by the United Nations (UNESCO, 2007), the children most likely to benefit from preschool education—for example, those at highest risk for malnourishment and contracting preventable diseases—are the least likely to be enrolled in a preschool program.

In addition to cross-national differences in preschool enrollments, there are differences within countries. Several studies conducted in the United States, for example, have found that children of ethnic-minority immigrant families are less likely than their native-born ethnic-majority peers to participate in preschool (Brandon, 2004; Crosnoe, 2006). Knowing that immigrant families are overrepresented among the poor, undereducated, and underemployed (Magnuson et al., 2006; Capps et al., 2004), we might speculate that immigrant children are more likely to stay home because unemployed adult family members are available to care for them and because their families lack financial resources to pay for such things as transportation, clothing, and supplies, not to mention any preschool costs. Although this may well be the case for some immigrant families, research suggests that cultural factors, including cultural norms regarding whether and how to prepare children for school, may influence whether or not immigrant children attend preschool (Bainbridge et al., 2005; Liang, Fuller, & Singer, 2000). Supporting the notion that cultural norms affect preschool participation, one study found that even when family income and maternal employment are held constant, children whose families speak Spanish at home remain less likely to be enrolled in preschool, perhaps because of the cultural value placed on family care (Liang et al., 2000).

As Magnuson and her colleagues (2006) point out, studies on the effects of preschool participation on school readiness rarely undertake comparative analyses of the effects for immigrant children and those for native-born, ethnic-majority children, but when they do, they find generally that preschool experience is at least as beneficial for the former as for the latter. Indeed, similar to findings that preschool participation is more effective for children who are economically disadvantaged, or demonstrate lower levels of intellectual development, research indicates that children of immigrant families profit significantly from preschool

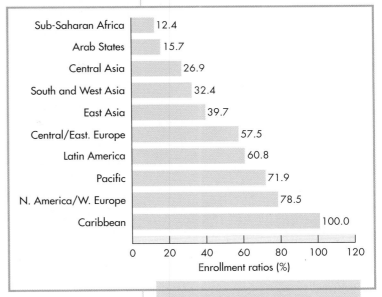

Region	Enrollment ratio (%)
Sub-Saharan Africa	12.4
Arab States	15.7
Central Asia	26.9
South and West Asia	32.4
East Asia	39.7
Central/East. Europe	57.5
Latin America	60.8
Pacific	71.9
N. America/W. Europe	78.5
Caribbean	100.0

Enrollment ratios (%)

Figure 12.5 There are vast differences in preschool enrollments throughout the world. Children who are most at risk for malnourishment and disease are least likely to be enrolled in preschool.

Preschool programs can boost children's readiness for primary school, especially when children are from immigrant families.

Arthur Bakker/Freudenthal Institute at Universiteit Utrecht

experiences (e.g., NICHD Early Child Care Research Network, 2004; Magnuson & Waldfogel, 2005). In particular,

- preschool enrollment has a larger impact on the language skills of Hispanic children than it does on those of non-Hispanic white children (Gormley & Gayer, 2005);
- Hispanic children who participate in Head Start preschools show significant gains in reading and math skills and diminished risk for having to repeat grades (Lee & Burkam, 2003; Magnuson et al., 2006);
- participation in preschool improves the English proficiency of immigrant children, especially those whose mothers have less than a high school education (Magnuson et al., 2006).

Taken as a whole, this research presents a strong case for the role of preschool programs in boosting a variety of school-readiness indicators for children of immigrant families. This would seem to suggest that the more immigrant children enrolled in preschool, the better. But accomplishing this goal requires knowledge of whatever barriers may exist to preschool participation and how to remove them.

||||| APPLY ▪ CONNECT ▪ DISCUSS

Both phonemic awareness and the ability to identify and manipulate numeric units appear to emerge only in the context of formal education. What do these two developments have in common, and how might formal schooling stimulate their development?

In the Classroom

When Alice fell down the rabbit hole into Wonderland, she met a number of interesting creatures, including the Mock Turtle, a tearful fellow who never quite got over his experiences in the classroom. Whereas most of us remember early lessons in reading and writing, ancient and modern history, and addition, subtraction, multiplication, and division, the Mock Turtle remembers reeling and writhing, ancient and modern mystery, and ambition, distraction, uglification, and derision.

At this point in your life, you have been in school long enough to appreciate the vastly different ways in which school can be experienced by students. Students come to have different feelings about school and put more or less energy into doing well. Students also experience different types of instruction according to the educational philosophy of the particular school or teacher. In your own extensive experience, you have surely encountered some teachers who rely on workbooks and tests and others who emphasize hands-on projects and papers. In this section we explore various factors that shape students' school experience, including the social organization of classroom instruction and personal and cultural barriers to school success.

Social Organization of the Classroom and Instructional Design

From the earliest schools of the ancient Middle East to neighborhood schools throughout the modern world, there has been controversy about how to design instruction more effectively. Opinion seems to oscillate back and forth between two extreme approaches. One approach begins with the assumption that instruction should proceed from the simple to the complex. Emphasizing what is known

bottom-up processing An approach to education that starts with teaching basic skills and, once they have been mastered, moves on to more complex tasks.

top-down processing An approach to education that focuses on using skills to accomplish specific, meaningful tasks.

instructional discourse A distinctive way of talking and thinking that is typical in school but rarely encountered in everyday interactions in the community or home.

initiation–reply–feedback sequence An instructional discourse pattern in which the teacher initiates an exchange, usually by asking a question; a student replies; and then the teacher provides feedback.

as **bottom-up processing,** this approach starts with teaching basic skills, and after these have been mastered, moves on to teaching skills to solve a variety of more complicated tasks. The other approach emphasizes **top-down processing.** Those taking this approach argue that an exclusive focus on the acquisition of basic skills causes children to lose sight of the larger goal—using reading, writing, and arithmetic to accomplish interesting, important purposes—and, thus, in many cases, to lose motivation and fail to thrive in school. This fundamental difference of opinion about the appropriate organization of school-based instruction can be clearly seen in the different ways that classroom instruction is organized.

The Standard Classroom Format Classrooms from antiquity that have been excavated bear a striking resemblance to the typical classroom found in schools today in the United States and throughout the world. Today, as in the past, far and away the most common arrangement is for the teacher to sit at a desk or stand at a blackboard facing the children who sit in parallel rows facing front (Gallego, Cole, & LCHC, 2000). These physical circumstances reflect the assumption that the teacher is an authority figure who is there to talk to and teach children who are there to listen and learn. This assumption is also reflected in the routine use of **instructional discourse,** a unique way of talking that is typical in school but rarely encountered in everyday interactions in the community or home. The central goals of instructional discourse are (1) to give students information stipulated by the curriculum, and (2) to give students and teachers feedback on students' efforts to learn this information (Wells, 2001).

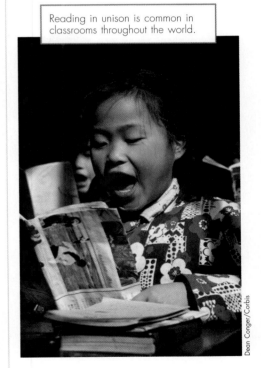

Reading in unison is common in classrooms throughout the world.

Dean Conger/Corbis

The most common pattern for instructional discourse is the "recitation script," which follows the **initiation–reply–feedback sequence,** as exemplified in Table 12.2 (Mehan, 1998). In this pattern, the teacher initiates an exchange, usually by asking a question; a student replies; and then the teacher provides feedback, in this case, an evaluation. The initiation–reply–feedback sequence uses the "known-answer question"—a form of questioning that is rarely encountered in everyday conversation. When the teacher asks Beth, "What does this word say?" the teacher already knows the answer (as Beth fully understands) and is actually seeking information about Beth's progress in learning to read. Learning to respond easily to known-answer questions, in addition to learning the academic content of the curriculum, is an important early lesson of schooling (Mehan, 1979).

The initiation–reply–feedback sequence can be quite flexible. In the discourse shown in Table 12.2, when Ramona hesitates, the teacher immediately calls on Kim, who provides the answer. This variation of the sequence allows Ramona to learn from Kim's answer and the teacher's response to it at the same time that it allows the teacher to assess Ramona's need for more instruction. On other occasions, the teacher might use the feedback part of the sequence as a means to open up new aspects of the topic at hand or to involve another child in the discussion (Nassaji & Wells, 2000).

table 12.2

Initiation–Reply–Feedback Sequence

Initiation	Reply	Feedback
T [Teacher]: What does this word say? Beth.	Beth: One.	T: Very good.
T: What does this word say? Jenny.	Jenny: One.	T: Okay.
T: Now look up here. What does this word say? Ramona.	Ramona: Umm.	
T: Kim.	Kim: First.	T: Okay.

Source: Mehan, 1979.

table 12.3

Lesson on Use of Prepositions

Initiation	Reply
T [Teacher]: Make a red flower under the tree. [pause] Okay, let's look at the red flower. Can you tell me where the red flower is?	Children: Right here, right here.
T: Dora?	Dora: Under the tree.
T: Tell me in a sentence.	Dora: It's under the tree.
T: What's under the tree, Dora?	Children: The flower.
T: Tell me, the flower . . .	Dora: The flower is under the tree.
T: Where is the red flower, Richard?	Richard: Under the tree.
T: Can you tell me in a sentence?	Richard: The flower is under the tree.
T: Cindy, where is the red flower?	Cindy: The red flower is under the tree. Richard [noticing that Cindy actually drew the "red" flower with a yellow crayon]: Hey, that's not red.

Source: Mehan, 1979.

Another special characteristic of instructional discourse is the emphasis that is often placed on the linguistic form of students' replies, particularly, of course, in language arts instruction, as shown in the lesson on the use of prepositions in Table 12.3. When you read this exchange, note that the teacher uses the recitation script to get students to respond with the particular linguistic form that she wants (a full sentence with a preposition). (Also note that for the purposes of this lesson, the truth of what the children say may be less important than the way they say it—Cindy gave her answer in the form the teacher was looking for, but, as Richard noticed, she had actually used the wrong color in her drawing.)

Alternative Forms of Classroom Instruction Although use of the recitation script is widespread in classrooms around the world, many developmentalists argue that it is not the best way of organizing instruction. Among other shortcomings, children taught in this manner are placed in the role of passive recipients of predigested information and therefore gain very little practice in formulating and solving problems for themselves. In contrast, the instructional alternatives we will consider next make children active participants in the educational process—a strategy that is closely aligned with the developmental theories of Piaget and Vygotsky.

Reciprocal Teaching One alternative to the recitation script is **reciprocal teaching,** which was designed by Ann Brown and Annemarie Palincsar as a way to integrate bottom-up and top-down processing, through small-group discussion at the time of reading. It was targeted at the many children who have learned to read in the sense that they can decode simple texts but who have difficulty making sense of what they read (Brown, Palincsar, & Armbruster, 1994).

In the reciprocal-teaching procedure, a teacher and a small group of students read silently through segments of text and take turns leading discussions of their meaning (Palincsar et al., 2007). The discussion leader (teacher or child) begins by asking a question about the main idea of the segment and then answers the question by summarizing the content in his or her own words. If members of the group disagree with the summary, the group rereads the segment and discusses its con-

reciprocal teaching A method of teaching reading in which teachers and children take turns reading text in a manner that integrates decoding and comprehension skills.

tents to clarify what it says. Finally, the leader asks for predictions about what will come next.

Note that each of the key elements in reciprocal teaching —asking questions about content, summarizing it, clarifying it, and predicting narrative progression—presupposes that the purpose of the activity is comprehension, that is, figuring out what the text means. And because these strategies involve talking about (and arguing over) textual meaning, children are able to see and hear the teacher and other children model metacognitive behaviors that aid comprehension. For example, as a way of making sense of what is being read, the teacher might point to relevant information in a prior paragraph that needs to be taken into account, or might relate an idea in the text to some common experience that all the children have had. As Brown (1997) points out, reciprocal teaching is an application of Vygotsky's notion of the "zone of proximal development" (Chapter 1, pp. 23–24) that allows children to participate in the act of reading for meaning even before they have acquired the full set of abilities that independent reading requires. A number of studies (summarized in Brown, 1997) have found that reciprocal teaching can produce rapid and durable increases in children's reading skills. Figure 12.6 shows the findings of a study in which reciprocal teaching was being used in a science class and a social studies class, not as a "reading lesson" but as a way to foster mastery of the course material. Used in this manner, the reciprocal-teaching activity increases knowledge of important subject matter at the same time that it improves reading skills.

In this second grade reading group in Oakland, California, it is likely that the teacher uses discourse patterns, such as initiation–reply–feedback or reciprocal teaching, that draw a number of students into the learning process, and allow her to track her students' understanding of the material.

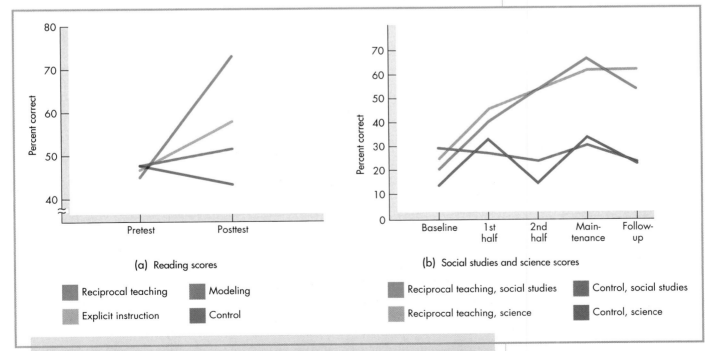

(a) Reading scores

Reciprocal teaching   Modeling

Explicit instruction   Control

(b) Social studies and science scores

Reciprocal teaching, social studies   Control, social studies

Reciprocal teaching, science   Control, science

Figure 12.6 (a) Reciprocal teaching proved to be more effective than traditional strategies such as explicit instruction and modeling: all three led to improved reading, but by far the greatest improvement was obtained through reciprocal teaching. (b) Reciprocal teaching also led to large and sustained improvement in social studies and science classes; students in a control group showed no improvement. (From Brown et al., 1992.)

Realistic Mathematics Education Recognizing the limitations of recitation scripts and the bottom-up approach, the National Council of Teachers of Mathematics adopted a set of standards for improving mathematics education that shifts the focus of mathematics instruction from training in basic skills, procedures, and memorization toward conceptual understanding and linkages between mathematics and real-world problems (National Council of Teachers of Mathematics, 2000). An example of a mathematics program that seeks to implement these goals is provided by the work of Paul Cobb and his colleagues, who draw upon "realistic mathematics education," which is widely used in the Netherlands (Cobb et al., 1997). According to these researchers, **realistic mathematics education** should do the following:

1. *Use meaningful activities.* For example, a first-grade teacher might introduce counting up to 20 by creating a make-believe situation in which a bus conductor has to keep track of how many people are on a double-decker bus that has 10 seats on each deck. As we have learned from the experimental research on children's problem solving discussed in previous chapters, such stories help to provide a meaningful context for carrying out cognitive operations.

2. *Support basic mathematical skills.* In the case of the double-decker bus, for example, the teacher wants children to learn how to group numbers for calculation, to realize that there are 8 people on the bus if there are 4 on top and 4 on the bottom, or 6 on the top and 2 on the bottom, or 2 on the top and 6 on the bottom, and so on. Each configuration is a different way of representing a total of 8.

3. *Employ models in educational activity.* Cobb describes a number of studies that use an "arithmetic rack," with two rows containing 10 beads each. For the conductor-on-the-bus context, the arithmetic rack provides a rather precise spatial model with each of its rows corresponding to a deck of the bus. But the beads on the rack can also be used to represent the number of cookies put in or taken out of a cookie jar and a variety of other story contexts involving similar mathematical concepts.

Over time, children gradually master the conceptual structures that the stories and models initially support, and they can carry out the needed calculations without such aids.

As in the case of reciprocal teaching, a social organization of the classroom that supports the mixing of bottom-up knowledge with top-down conceptual and utilization knowledge is key. Teachers work to establish a classroom culture in which children are expected to justify their reasoning when they answer a question and to try to understand the reasoning behind other children's answers. In addition, children are expected to be helpful to the group, to solicit help from others, and to share what they have learned.

"Problem-oriented" approaches that emphasize the processes of reasoning about mathematical problems have been found to be successful well beyond the elementary school years (Boaler, 2001; Lampert & Blunk, 1998). Jo Boaler observed students in two secondary school classrooms in England. One class followed a traditional recitation-script approach to learning mathematics, while the other used a small-group, problem-oriented approach. In the traditional classroom, the teacher began lessons by presenting a standard problem and the standard method for solving it ("Here is how to determine the area of a parallelogram"). After observing the solution method, the students practiced it on their own. The teacher did not

realistic mathematics instruction An approach to mathematics education that focuses on developing the student's understanding of how math can be used to solve real-world problems.

playworld practice Used in several European countries, and based on theories regarding the importance of play in intellectual development, it involves students performing and discussing various themes in children's literature.

explain why the method worked and did not encourage students to invent their own methods. In the activity-centered classroom, the teacher would begin a lesson by presenting students with a problem designed to intrigue them. In one such problem, a fence with 36 planks was depicted, and the students were asked to figure out all the different shapes that could be made with the planks. After the problem was introduced, the students were encouraged to ask questions as a way of orienting themselves to the task. Then they worked in small groups while the teacher moved around the room; providing help when it was requested.

The teachers in both classrooms believed strongly that their approach was superior, and they passed their enthusiasm for it on to their students. They also reported that discipline problems were virtually nonexistent, but the researchers noted that the project-oriented classroom was somewhat noisier than the traditional classroom and that the students in it more often engaged in "off-task" activities such as chatting with their friends.

When the students were tested at the end of the year on both standard tests and tests that assessed their ability to apply mathematics to new problems, there were striking differences between students in the two classrooms. Students who participated in the traditional instructional format scored better on knowledge of prespecified mathematical procedures, but students in the project-based class were significantly better on conceptual questions and on questions that required them to apply their knowledge to a novel problem, such as designing an apartment.

In this classroom in the Netherlands, children are engaged in realistic mathematics education that tries to link mathematics to real-world problems.

Playworld Practice In contrast to recent trends in the United States that emphasize teaching content that will help students pass mandatory statewide tests, several European countries are moving in the direction of integrating play and art into classroom activities. Devised on the basis of developmental theory regarding the importance of play in children's understanding and representation of the world (see Chapter 9, p. 322), **playworld practice** involves enacting, discussing, making art, and playing with themes based on works of children's literature. Although playworld practice has for some years been featured in Swedish and Finnish classrooms (Sandberg & Samuelsson, 2003; Hakkarainen, 2004), only recently have efforts been made to compare playworld practice with other instructional formats experimentally. In one such study, Sonja Baumer and her colleagues identified two classrooms of 5- to 7-year-olds who were learning about *The Lion, the Witch, and the Wardrobe* (Baumer, Ferholt, & Lecusay, 2005). In the playworld-practice classroom, the children, teacher, and researchers enacted scenes from the story, drew pictures of the scenes, and played with costumes and props used in the enactments. In the standard-instruction classroom, in contrast, the teacher read from the book, guided the students in a discussion of the story, and had the children draw pictures or write stories. Results from the study indicated that compared to standard instruction, the playworld practice format generated significantly larger increases in children's language skills, especially their abilities to tell and understand stories. (For another example of the use of play in instruction, this time in an after-school program designed to promote computer literacy and cognitive and other skills, see the box "In the Field: Learning after School in the Fifth Dimension.")

Overall, the evidence indicates that when properly organized, instructional methods that induce students to be active contributors to classroom discourse can be quite effective. But such methods are more complex to organize than the recitation script and are still encountered in only a minority of classrooms.

Name:	Michael Cole
Education:	B.A. in psychology, University of California, Los Angeles; Ph.D. in psychology, Indiana University
Current Position:	Professor of Communication and Psychology, University of California, San Diego
Career Objectives:	Explore relationships between development and culture, and use understanding to improve contexts of children's learning

The early 1980s saw the invention of computers that were affordable and accessible enough to be used beyond the high-tech, professional, and academic contexts to which they previously had been restricted. Michael Cole, a professor of communication and psychology at the University of California, San Diego, remembers the time as one of "enormous optimism about the potential of new technology to provide opportunities for individual instruction" (Rich, 2004). It was also a time that allowed him to bring into alignment three areas that interested him deeply: his research on the acquisition of literacy and its effect on cognitive development; his concern about the poor literacy skills in the growing population of immigrant children attending San Diego schools; and his conviction that undergraduate programs focused on children, education, and development should provide hands-on experience with kids. Seizing the moment, Professor Cole created the Fifth Dimension, an after-school program that is based on computer and other games, and that has been elaborated and extended by a number of developmentalists working with school children throughout the world (Cole & Distributed Literacy Consortium, 2006).

Although the Fifth Dimension program is intentionally flexible so it can be fitted to the needs of the particular children enrolled—their ages, academic skill levels, languages spoken, and so on—it includes several key features. One is the use of a model wooden maze composed of 20 rooms that helps the children organize their play. Children move through the maze by advancing a token after they complete a game (usually, but not always, a computer game). Many games are structured to foster progressive skill devel-

opment, from basic, through intermediate, to advanced levels. For example, at the basic level, the computer game *Space Adventure* presents the child with the following challenge: *The alien council wants to know what Earthlings know about the moon. Find out when the first men landed on the moon and what they found there.* Once children navigate through the program and discover answers to the challenge, they are presented with an "adventure task," such as, *Pretend you are walking on the moon. Draw what you see, and then make a list of the things that you see or don't see.* An advanced challenge might include using Internet and video equipment to research and make a video "telling everything you know about space." Other games such as *Candy Land* and *Where in the World Is Carmen Sandiego?* reinforce counting and reasoning skills. Indeed, research on the Fifth Dimension indicates that participants score higher than nonparticipants on math and reading exams, and show improved basic language skills.

Another key feature of the Fifth Dimension is its use of undergraduate college students as mentors for the children. Each child is linked with a college student whose main role is to help the child define and meet his or her own challenges and game goals. Not only do the college students gain insight into how developmental principles can be applied in interacting with children, but the children seem to profit tremendously from interacting with their mentors. In particular, spending hours and hours with college students seems to increase the children's interest in attending college someday themselves.

Cole attributes the enormous success of the Fifth Dimension to its capacity for scaffolding children's intellectual development by creating a context that engages children's curiosity and imagination. Allowing children to choose their own game activities and pursue their goals with the assistance of college student mentors creates a zone of proximal development for the acquisition of literacy skills. Ismael Castanon, a high school junior who has participated in the program for more than a decade, writes, "At first I didn't think that the program would have such a big impact on my life, but boy was I wrong. Through this program I learned most of my English and math, and about computers in general." Like many other Fifth Dimension "success stories," Ismael is on his way to college.

The Fifth Dimension program is used in Brazil (above) and throughout the world to scaffold children's intellectual development by providing a context that fosters creativity and imagination.

Courtesy of the SARAH Network of Rehabilitation Hospitals, Brazil

Michael Cole

Courtesy Michael Cole

Barriers to School Success

There is, of course, more to children's school experience than the ways classroom instruction is organized and designed. Many students experience difficulty in school, regardless of instructional organization and design, often because they have learning disabilities or because they lack motivation to learn.

Specific Learning Disabilities **Specific learning disabilities** is a term used to refer to the academic difficulties of children who fare poorly in school despite normal IQ test performance. The U.S. government defines specific learning disabilities as follows:

> Children with special learning disabilities exhibit a disorder in one or more of the basic psychological processes involved in understanding or in using spoken or written language. These may be manifested in disorders of listening, thinking, talking, reading, writing, spelling, or arithmetic. They include conditions which have been referred to as perceptual handicaps, brain injury, minimal brain dysfunction, dyslexia, developmental aphasia, etc. They do not include learning problems which are due primarily to visual, hearing, or motor handicaps, to mental retardation, emotional disturbance, or to environmental disadvantage. (U.S. Office of Education, 1977)

Identifying children with learning disabilities presents special challenges to developmentalists. Unlike physical disabilities such as blindness or deafness, specific learning disabilities are generally not apparent until children enter school, and in some cases not apparent until they begin to use graphic symbols. Further difficulties in identifying learning-disabled children are reflected in the official definition of learning disability. Not only are many conditions included, but ruling out excluded conditions is not a simple matter. How do we know, for example, if a learning problem arises from features of the brain or is the consequence of living in a "disadvantaged environment"? All these complications have made it difficult to estimate the number of children who suffer from specific learning disabilities (Warner et al., 2002).

Although it has been repeatedly criticized as imprecise, the most widely used method to distinguish children with a specific learning disability is to analyze their performance both on an intelligence test and on an academic achievement test that covers many parts of the curriculum (D'Angiulli & Siegel, 2003). According to this approach, to qualify as specifically learning disabled (and not retarded), a child should have an overall IQ test score in the normal range but show a large discrepancy between different parts of the test (for example, a low score on a subtest that taps verbal ability but a high score on a subtest that taps quantitative ability). The profile of the child's academic performance should correspond to the pattern in the IQ test. That is, we would expect a child with a low verbal ability score and a high quantitative ability score to have difficulty in learning to read but not in learning arithmetic. This pattern of performance, called *dyslexia,* is the most frequent form of specific learning disability. Other children display a pattern of performance called *dyscalculia,* in which verbal IQ is high and quantitative IQ is low and, correspondingly, children do not have difficulty learning to read but have difficulty learning arithmetic. Yet another pattern characterizes *dysgraphia,* or special difficulties in learning to write; and so on. We focus our discussion on dyslexia, which is the most frequently encountered specific learning disability and the one about which the most is known.

Why do children who are considered dyslexic have difficulty reading? As we saw earlier, phonological awareness—the ability to detect and manipulate the phonemes in words—is crucial to learning to decode text, or relate graphemes (symbols of the writing system) to phonemes. More directly, phonological awareness is

specific learning disabilities A term used to refer to the academic difficulties of children who fare poorly in school despite having normal intelligence.

a crucial part of *phonological processing*—of understanding and applying the rules relating phonemes and graphemes. Like problems with phoneme awareness, delays in the development of phonological processing skills may indicate that a child has dyslexia (Helland et al., 2008).

The leading test of phonological processing skills employs *pseudowords*, pronounceable combinations of letters that are not real words—for example, "shum," "laip," and "cigbet"—but can be read by following the rules for converting graphemes into phonemes. Because they are not real words, they cannot simply be recognized but require phonological processing.

To demonstrate the link between deficient phonological processing and dyslexia, Linda Siegel and her colleagues have compared normal and dyslexic readers in their ability to read pseudowords (Siegel, 2008; Gottardo et al., 1999). By 9 years of age, the normal readers were quite proficient in reading the pseudowords, but 14-year-old dyslexic readers were no better at reading pseudowords than normal 7-year-old readers. Even when dyslexic readers and normal readers were matched for reading level on a standardized test (the dyslexic readers being considerably older than the normal readers), the dyslexic readers performed more poorly on the pseudowords task.

Current theories about the causes of dyslexia assume that the difficulties arise because of anomalies in brain development, but there is uncertainty about how specific reading difficulties are linked to specific abnormalities in specific areas of the brain. In line with evidence pinpointing difficulties in phonological processing, Paula Tallal and her colleagues report that, when asked to identify whether letter names rhymed or did not rhyme (D–B versus M–T, for example), children diagnosed with dyslexia had much greater difficulty than did normal readers. They showed slower neural processing, with less activation in just those areas of the brain that are specialized for language (Figure 12.7a, b), supporting the idea that the difficulties of the dyslexic children had a specific brain location (Tallal, 2003).

To help children who have this phonological processing difficulty, Tallal has created computer games that provide rich practice in making accurate discriminations between very brief, rapidly changing sounds—and in some cases, children become capable of such discriminations with as few as 16 hours of this therapy (Tallal et al., 1998). Moreover, as a result of this training, the brain activation patterns of the dyslexic children on tasks such as identifying rhyming letter names appears to be similar to those of normal readers (Figure 12.7c).

Motivation to Learn As we noted earlier, a distinctive aspect of formal education is that children are expected to pay attention and try to master material that may be difficult to learn and that may hold little interest for them. They must also learn to cope with the fact that they will not always be successful in their schoolwork. In such circumstances, a significant proportion of children lose their

Figure 12.7 Brain activation of normal and dyslexic readers. The children were given the task of providing a rhyming sound when they heard a letter pronounced. Comparison of the two groups shows significant differences in left-hemisphere activity (brightness of red indicates degree of activation) for normal and dyslexic children. (a) While the normal children display heightened activity in both the visual cortex and Broca's area (specialized for language), the dyslexic readers do not (b). However, after intense training in discriminating between phonemes, the dyslexic children display activity in the same areas as do the normal children (c).

(a) Normal

(b) Learning disabled

(c) Learning disabled; after training

Temple et al., 2003

academic motivation—the ability to try hard and persist at school tasks in the face of difficulties. On the other hand, many children seem to thrive on the challenges presented by formal education.

What accounts for these differences? Researchers who study this question distinguish between two ways in which children approach school tasks (Anderman, Austin, & Johnson, 2001; Martin et al., 2008): **mastery orientation,** in which children are motivated to learn, to try hard, and to improve; and **performance orientation,** in which children are motivated by their level of performance, ability, and incentives for trying.

Mastery and performance orientations have consistently been associated with two different outcomes in terms of children's academic success. Children who adopt a mastery orientation are more likely to succeed in the long run, to use more advanced learning strategies, and to relate what they are trying to accomplish at the moment to relevant prior knowledge. Even if these children have just done poorly or failed at a task, they remain optimistic and tell themselves "I can do it if I try harder next time." As a result of this kind of thinking, they tend to persist in the face of difficulties and to seek out new intellectual challenges. Over time, this kind of motivational pattern allows these children to improve their academic performance. By contrast, children who adopt a performance orientation are more likely, on failing at a task, to tell themselves, "I can't do that." They may give up trying altogether, and when they encounter similar tasks in the future, tend to avoid them.

It might be thought that more able students would typically display the mastery-oriented pattern and that less able students would be the ones to adopt a performance orientation, quickly giving up in the face of difficulty and avoiding challenges. However, the evidence concerning motivational orientation and school achievement is mixed. Carol Dweck and her colleagues report that these two patterns were not related to children's IQ scores or their academic achievement: Many able students give up in the face of difficulty, and many weaker students show a mastery orientation (Dweck, 1999). But a large-scale review of many recent studies reports that mastery motivation does promote cognitive development (Jennings & Dietz, 2003).

In an extensive series of studies looking at factors that might lead to the two different motivational patterns, Carol Dweck has related the patterns to two different conceptions of ability, conceptions that children develop as they progress through school (Dweck, 2001). According to Dweck, children as young as 2½ years old are sensitive to success or failure in their problem-solving attempts and are vulnerable to becoming discouraged and unmotivated when they fail. But it is not until the onset of formal schooling, when, through grading practices, children's academic abilities are directly compared with those of their peers, that the notion of ability becomes a distinctive category that children use to evaluate themselves and their relationship to academic challenges. Children's conceptions of ability continue to change during the elementary school years, with children increasingly less likely to engage in wishful thinking about problems they can solve and increasingly more likely to see ability as a fixed characteristic of people.

Around the age of 12, when children make the transition from elementary to middle school, North American children begin to articulate theories about what it means to "be intelligent." Some children adopt an **entity model of intelligence;** that is, they see intelligence as a quality of which each person has a certain fixed amount. Other children, by contrast, adopt an **incremental model of intelligence;** they see intelligence as something that can grow as one learns and has new experiences. These theories about intelligence include ideas about how effort is related to outcome. Children who adopt the entity model see academic

academic motivation The ability to try hard and persist at school tasks in the face of difficulties.

mastery orientation A way that children approach school tasks in which they are motivated to learn, to try hard, and to improve their performance.

performance orientation A way of approaching school tasks in which students are motivated by their level of performance, ability, and incentives for trying.

entity model of intelligence The belief that intelligence is a quality of which each person has a certain fixed amount.

incremental model of intelligence The belief that intelligence is something that can grow over time as one learns.

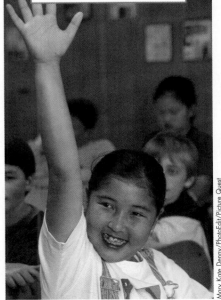

This student seems to be the personification of academic motivation: If she happens to give an incorrect answer this time, she will not give up and is likely to work harder to get it right the next time.

Mary Kate Denny/PhotoEdit/Picture Quest

success as depending primarily on fixed ability and thus remaining relatively un-affected by effort; children who adopt the incremental model see academic success, along with ability, as depending on the effort expended. Dweck has found that children who adopt an entity model of intelligence are likely to develop a performance orientation to problems. When they fail, they believe that it is because they lack ability and that nothing they can do will change this. Because they view intelligence as a fixed entity, they try to avoid situations that put them at risk for failure and feel hopeless when they are confronted with challenging tasks. Children who adopt an incremental model of intelligence, on the other hand, tend to develop a mastery orientation to challenging situations. They believe that if they apply themselves and try hard enough, they will succeed and become more intelligent; and when they fail at a particular task, their response is to try harder the next time. As children encounter the more challenging environment of middle school, their particular ways of interpreting and responding to failure cause notable achievement gaps between students who have one or the other of the basic motivational patterns.

Findings such as these challenge developmentalists to devise ways to assist children who develop a helpless motivational pattern. One approach has been to train teachers to provide feedback to students in ways that foster a mastery orientation. Another has been to retrain the children themselves so that they attribute their failures to a lack of effort rather than a lack of ability (Dweck, 1999).

‖‖‖ APPLY ⸺ CONNECT ⸺ DISCUSS ‒ ‒ ‒ ‒ ‒ ‒ ‒ ‒ ‒ ‒ ‒ ‒ ‒ ‒ ‒ ‒ ‒ ‒

Write a letter to the best or worst teacher you ever had. Using concepts presented in this section, explain how the format of the classroom and method of instruction affected your motivation.

The Cognitive Consequences of Schooling

Because formal schooling is so widely available throughout the world, it is difficult to do research that directly compares groups of schooled and nonschooled children for the purpose of assessing the cognitive consequences of formal education. Given this limitation, three research strategies have generally been found useful:

1. *The school-cutoff strategy* compares 6-year-olds who have experienced formal schooling with 6-year-olds who have not yet experienced it.

2. *School–nonschool comparisons* take advantage of circumstances in which schooling has been introduced unevenly into a society, providing formal education for some children but not for others.

3. *Second-generation studies* focus on differences between children whose mothers have attended school and children whose mothers have not, looking for effects that the mothers' schooling might have on their children.

The School-Cutoff Strategy

In many countries, school boards require that children be a certain age by a particular date to begin attending school. To enter grade 1 in September of a given year, children in Edmonton, Alberta, Canada, for example, must have passed their sixth birthday by March 1 of that year. Six-year-olds born after that date must attend kindergarten instead, so their formal education is delayed for a year. Such policies allow researchers to assess the impact of early schooling while holding age virtually constant: They simply compare the intellectual performances of children who

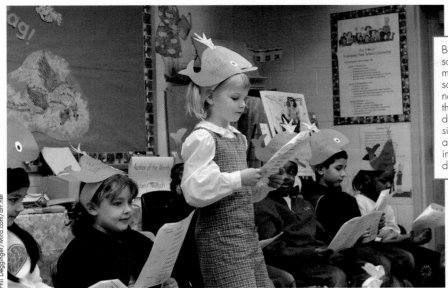

Because of the school-cutoff strategy, some children in this first-grade class may be just a month or so older than some children in the kindergarten class next door. Research shows that over the course of the school year, memory development of the first-graders will significantly surpass that of similar-aged kindergarteners, illustrating the importance of schooling to intellectual development.

turn 6 in January or February with those who turn 6 in March or April, testing both groups at the beginning and at the end of the school year. This procedure is known as the **school-cutoff strategy** (Morrison et al., 1995; Christian et al., 2001).

Researchers who have used the school-cutoff strategy find that the first year of schooling brings about a marked increase in the sophistication of some cognitive processes but not others. Frederick Morrison and his colleagues (1995), for example, compared the ability of first-graders and kindergartners to recall pictures of nine common objects. The first-graders were, on average, only a month older than the kindergartners. The performances of the two groups were virtually identical at the start of the school year. At the end of the school year, however, the first-graders could remember twice as many pictures as they did at the beginning of the year, whereas the kindergartners showed no improvement in memory at all. Significantly, the first-graders engaged in active rehearsal (a memory strategy you encountered in Chapter 11, pp. 405–406) during the testing, but the kindergartners did not. Clearly, one year of schooling had brought about marked changes in their strategies and performance. The same pattern of results was obtained in tasks such as recognizing the names of the letters of the alphabet, in standardized reading and mathematics tests, and in a variety of deliberate remembering tests. But no effects of attending a year of school were found when children were administered a standard Piagetian test of conservation (see Chapter 11, pp. 398–399), or assessed for the coherence of their storytelling or for the number of vocabulary words they understood (Christian et al., 2001). Performance in these latter tasks improved largely as a consequence of children's age. These findings both confirm the importance of schooling in promoting a variety of relatively specific cognitive abilities and support Piaget's belief that the ability to understand the conservation of quantity develops without any special instruction at some time between the ages of 5 and 7.

Comparing Schooled and Nonschooled Children

Although the school-cutoff strategy provides an excellent way to assess the cognitive consequences of small amounts of schooling, it is, by definition, limited to only the first year. For a longer-range picture of the contribution of formal education to cognitive development, researchers have conducted studies in societies in which

school-cutoff strategy A means of assessing the impact of education while controlling for age by comparing children who are almost the same age but begin schooling a year apart because of school rules that set a specific cutoff birthday date for starting school.

schooling is available to only a part of the population. We will summarize evidence from three cognitive domains that have figured heavily in our earlier discussions of cognitive development: logical thinking, memory, and metacognitive skills.

Logical Thinking A large number of cross-cultural studies have been conducted to determine if participation in formal schooling enhances performance on Piagetian conservation tasks and other tasks created to reveal concrete-operational thinking (Segall et al., 1999). In terms of results, the studies have split more or less evenly between those that found enhanced performance among schooled children and those that did not. Consistent with the evidence presented in Chapter 11 (p. 413), when schoolchildren do better than their unschooled peers on the standard Piagetian tests, their greater success appears to have less to do with more rapid achievement of concrete-operational thinking than with their greater familiarity with the circumstances of test taking. Such specialized test-taking knowledge includes familiarity with the forms in which questions are asked, greater ease in speaking to unfamiliar adults, and fluency in the language in which the test is given when the testing is not conducted in the child's native language. When these factors are taken into account, the overall pattern of results indicates that the development of concrete-operational thinking increases with age and is relatively unaffected by schooling.

Memory In Chapter 11 (p. 412) you saw that, unlike North American children, children in some cultures do not show an increase in free-recall memory performance as they grow older and that the difference related to the fact that the children did not attend school. Indeed, research comparing schooled and non-schooled children in other societies, like the research on first-graders and kinder-gartners presented here, has shown that schooling is the crucial experience underlying differences in performance on free-recall tasks. The performance of children in other cultures who attended school is more similar to that of their North American counterparts in the same grade than it is to that of their age-mates in the same village who have not been to school (Rogoff, 2003).

A study by Daniel Wagner (1974) suggests the kind of memory-enhancing information-processing skills that children acquire as a consequence of schooling. Wagner conducted his study among Mayans in Yucatán, Mexico, who had completed different amounts of schooling. He asked 248 people ranging in age from 6 years to adulthood to recall the positions of picture cards laid out in a line (Figure 12.8). (To ensure that the items pictured on the cards would be familiar

(a) Take a good look and turn the page

Figure 12.8 (a) Cards used to test short-term memory. Seven cards are selected and then turned facedown one at a time. The person being tested is then shown a duplicate of one of the cards (see p. 448) and asked to select the card that corresponds to it from the seven that are face down. (b) Which card has matching pictures? (From Wagner, 1978) to all the participants, the pictures were taken from a local version of bingo called *Lotería,* which uses pictures instead of numbers.) On each trial, each of seven cards was displayed for 2 seconds and then turned face down. As soon as all seven cards had been presented, a duplicate of one of the cards was shown and the participant was asked to point to its twin. By selecting different duplicate cards, Wagner manipulated the length of time between the presentation of a card and the moment its location was to be recalled.

For participants who attended school, performance improved markedly with age (Figure 12.9), as in similar research in the United States. In contrast, among those who did not attend school, older children and adults remembered no better than young children, leading Wagner to conclude that it was schooling that made the difference. Additional analyses of the data revealed that increasingly efficient use of the memory strategy of rehearsal (discussed in Chapter 11, p. 405) by those who attended school was largely responsible for the improvement in their performance.

Evidence such as this does not mean that memory simply fails to develop among children who have not attended school. The difference between schooled and nonschooled children's performance in cross-cultural memory experiments is most noticeable when the items to be remembered are not related to one another according to any everyday script. When the items are part of a meaningful setting, such as the animals found in a barnyard or the furniture placed in a toy house, the effects of schooling on memory performance disappear (Rogoff & Wadell, 1982). Similarly, we saw in Chapter 11 that a story context for recall eliminated differences evident in a free-recall task for which schooled but not unschooled children used the strategy of clustering. It appears that schooling helps children to develop specialized strategies for remembering and thereby enhances their ability to commit arbitrary material to memory for purposes of later testing. There is no evidence to support the conclusion that schooling increases memory capacity per se.

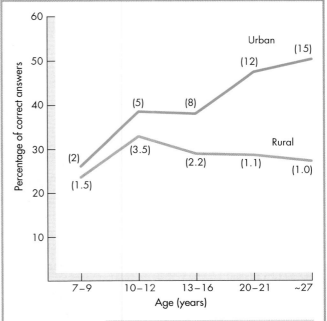

Figure 12.9 Short-term memory performance as a function of age and number of years of education. In the absence of further education (as among the rural people tested in this study), performance does not improve with age. Thus, schooling appears to be a key factor in one's ability to do well at this task. (Numbers in parentheses represent the average number of years of education for the designated group.) (From Wagner, 1974.)

Metacognitive Skills Schooling appears to influence the ability to reflect on and talk about one's own thought processes (Rogoff, 2003; Tulviste, 1991). When children have been asked to explain how they arrived at the answer to a logical problem or what they did to make themselves remember something, those who have not attended school are likely to say something like "I did what my sense told me" or to offer no explanation at all. Schoolchildren, on the other hand, are likely to talk about the mental activities and logic that underlie their responses. The same results apply to metalinguistic knowledge. Sylvia Scribner and Michael Cole (1981) asked schooled and unschooled Vai people in Liberia to judge the grammatical correctness of several sentences spoken in Vai. Some of the sentences were grammatical, some not. Education had no effect on the interviewees' ability to identify the ungrammatical sentences, but schooled people could generally explain just what it was about a sentence that made it ungrammatical whereas unschooled people could not.

Assessing the Second-Generation Impact of Schooling

The evidence from both school-cutoff and cross-cultural research supports the conclusion that the cognitive consequences of schooling are quite specific to the particular skill being tested. The clearest evidence for a general cognitive impact

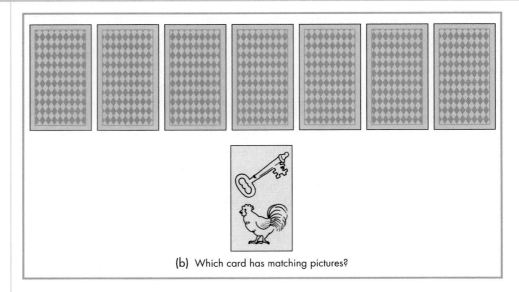

(b) Which card has matching pictures?

of schooling comes from studies of the child-rearing practices of mothers who have, or have not, gone to school and the subsequent school achievement of their children.

Based on evidence collected in many countries over several decades, Robert LeVine and his colleagues emphasize that maternal education is linked to three major differences for children: Compared with children whose mothers had no formal schooling, children whose mothers attended elementary school have a lower level of infant mortality, better health during childhood, and greater academic achievement (LeVine, LeVine, & Schnell, 2001). These researchers propose a set of habits, preferences, and skills that mothers acquired in school that might help account for these differences. Beyond rudimentary literacy and numeracy skills, this set includes the mothers'

1. ability to understand written texts, and engage in discussion about, health and educational issues involving their children;
2. use of teaching and learning models based on the scripted activities and authority structure of schooling, which they then employ in the home, talking more to their children and using less-directive child-rearing methods;
3. ability and willingness to acquire and accept information from governmental agencies and the mass media regarding their children's health and development.

LeVine and his colleagues hypothesized that girls who have been to school retain these habits of mind into adulthood and apply them in the course of raising their own children. The work of these researchers has been supported by direct observations of the teaching styles of Mayan mothers who have, or have not, been to school. Pablo Chavajay and Barbara Rogoff found that mothers who had had 12 years of schooling used school-like teaching styles when asked to teach their young children to complete a puzzle, whereas mothers who had had 2 years or less of schooling participated with their children in completing the puzzle but did not explicitly teach them (Chavajay & Rogoff, 2002). There is nothing wrong with the unschooled mothers' teaching style, but it does not prepare their children well for schools, which rely heavily on the recitation script as the mode of instruction.

When we consider how school affects health-related behaviors, including mothers' use of modern social welfare institutions and ways of interacting with their children, it is clear that schooling can have profound consequences for society.

Overall, extensive research on the cognitive consequences of schooling has produced a mixed picture. The idea that schooling is directly responsible for broad changes in the way the mind works is, at best, only minimally supported. When schooling has been found to improve cognitive performance, the effect appears to work in one of three ways: (1) by increasing children's knowledge base, including ways of using language; (2) by teaching specific information-processing strategies that are relevant primarily to school itself; and (3) by changing children's overall life situations and attitudes, which they pass on to their children in the form of new child-rearing practices that promote school achievement. As we emphasized at the beginning of the chapter, it may be that the most important consequences of schooling for the majority of the world's people are not simply cognitive. Schooling is a gateway to health and nutrition, to economic power and social status.

||||||| APPLY ▪ CONNECT ▪ DISCUSS _

Your local government has earmarked a special pool of money to support services for the rising population of immigrant families in your community. Concerned about the school readiness of immigrant children, officials plan to apply most of the money to a vast preschool expansion project. You believe this focus would be too narrow, and want to convince the officials to divert funds to support adult education for immigrant parents. Map out the evidence that you will use to persuade the officials to your point of view.

Contemporary Challenges in a Globalizing World

As we pointed out earlier, access to quality education continues to be a major challenge for educators and policy makers. There are vast disparities among countries in the proportions of children who are able to go to school. Within many countries, there are also vast disparities among children in the amount of schooling received and the quality of schools attended. As we discussed previously, a child's gender, ethnicity, and socioeconomic status all can profoundly affect both the amount and the quality of schooling. (Another disparity among countries is in children's school achievement; for a discussion of some differences and possible explanations, see the box "Comparing Mathematics Achievement across Cultures.")

In addition to the challenge of access, schools are challenged by the increasing cultural and linguistic diversity of the students they serve. Throughout the world, large numbers of families are moving away from their native lands and cultures, seeking new lives in places where the language, cultural practices, and values and beliefs are radically different from their own. Indeed, children of immigrant families are the fastest-growing group of children in the United States (Research Forum on Children, Families, and the New Federalism, 2002). In 2000, 20 percent of children below the age of 18 had at least one foreign-born parent, a threefold increase from 1970 (U.S. Census Bureau, 2003).

Although some areas in the United States, especially border states, attract a preponderance of Spanish-speaking immigrants, an increasing number of school districts are seeing an enormous rise in the cultural and linguistic diversity of their immigrant students (for an example, see

Children of immigrant families are the fastest-growing group of children in the United States.

Steve Skjold / Alamy

table 12.4

Languages Spoken Head Start Classrooms near Philadelphia

Akan
Albanian
American Sign Language (ASL)
Arabic
Bambara
Bassa
Bengali
Cantonese
Cherokee
Creole
Dutch
Edo
English
French
French Creole
Fulani
Greek
Gujarati
Haitian Creole
Igbo
Indonesian
Jamaican Patwa
Kirio
Krahn
Krio
Laotian
Liberian English
Limba
Loman
Mandarin
Mandingo
Mende
Nigerian
Oromo
Pali
Pashto
Portuguese
Punjabi
Spanish
Swahili
Tagalog
Temne
Twi
Urdu
Vietnamese
West African Creole
Yoruba
West African

Source: Delaware County Intermediate Unit Head Start, personal communication

Table 12.4). Given that studies routinely find that children of immigrant families are overrepresented among students who experience academic difficulties and school failure (Schmitt-Rodermund & Silbereisen, 2008; Conchas, 2001; Capps et al., 2004), schools face a particularly difficult challenge in identifying and responding to the unique academic needs of immigrant students who vary so widely in native language and heritage culture. Indeed, as we will see, many immigrant children and their families must adjust not only to a new culture and language but also to the unique culture and language of school.

The Culture of School

A number of scholars have proposed that every culture can be described in terms of its own particular worldview, a dominant way of thinking about and relating to the world that arises from a people's common historical experience. This dominant pattern of interpreting events is called a **cultural style** (Greenfield, Keller, Fuligni, & Maynard, 2003; Kagitçabasi, 1997). An important dimension of cultural style is that of independence–interdependence: an *independent,* or *individualistic,* cultural style emphasizes the individual and the individual's personal choices and goals; an *interdependent,* or *collectivist,* style emphasizes the group and group harmony, downplaying individual achievement (see Table 12.5 for a summary of the differences between the two styles).

Patricia Greenfield and her colleagues have proposed that, given the competitive nature of the American education system, the cultural practices of standard American classrooms favor children who come from homes that promote the prevailing American cultural style of independence, with the goal of socializing children to become autonomous individuals who enter into social relations by personal choice (an individualistic orientation). They also propose that the standard culture of American schools is correspondingly disadvantageous to children from homes that promote a cultural style of interdependence, that is, children whose parents have been socializing them to place a strong value on social networks and downplay personal achievement. To help reduce this possible disadvantage, Greenfield and her colleagues have conducted special training programs that sensitize teachers to work effectively with children and their families from cultures with an interdependent style (Turnbull, Rothstein-Fisch, Greenfield, & Quiroz, 2001).

Other researchers emphasize the point that many children who come from families with an interdependent orientation thrive in the standard American classroom. The success of these children appears to be due in large measure to the positive role the parents play in their schooling. For example, Nathan Caplan and his colleagues studied the children of refugees who fled to the United States from Vietnam, Cambodia, and Laos during the 1970s and 1980s. These children, whose home cultures are characterized by an interdependent cultural style, have been

table 12.5

Cultural Styles: Independent (Individualistic) versus Interdependent (Collectivist)

Independent	Interdependent
Emotional detachment from group; personal goals have primacy over group goals	Self is defined in terms of group; personal goals relate to group goals
Behavior regulated by attitudes and by analysis of cost and benefits to self	Behavior regulated by group norms and analysis of costs and benefits to group
Confrontation considered OK	Harmony within the group considered important

Source: Adapted from Triandis et al., 1990.

conspicuously successful in educational pursuits (Caplan, Choy, & Whitmore, 1991). Although they had lost from 1 to 3 years of formal education in refugee camps and most were unable to speak English when they entered school in the United States, 8 out of 10 students surveyed had a B average or better within 3 to 6 years. Almost half received A's in mathematics. These achievements are all the more noteworthy because they were attained in schools in low-income, inner-city areas traditionally associated with fewer resources and less motivated, more disruptive students.

In trying to account for the spectacular success of these children, Caplan and his colleagues found parents' involvement to be crucial. Almost half of the parents surveyed said that they read to their children, many in their native language. That the parents didn't know English well evidently mattered less to the children's school performance than did the children's positive emotional associations of being read to and the connection to their culture. Indeed, it has been found that children across a variety of ethnic-minority groups profit when their families make explicit efforts to pass on to them their native language and cultural heritage: They do better in school, are more likely to attend college, have higher academic and occupational aspirations, and are less at risk for certain psychiatric disorders and behaviors, including suicide (Portes & Rumbaut, 2001; Farver, Eppe, & Ballon, 2006; Chandler et al., 2003).

Aspects of culture other than an interdependent cultural style can prove to be poorly supported by, and disadvantageous in the context of, the standard American classroom culture. According to Wade Boykin, African American children inherit a rich tradition of using expressive movement as a part of their everyday communicative behavior—a tradition they are required to suppress in classrooms that emphasize sitting quietly while learning. Hypothesizing that this suppression of an important cultural asset has a negative impact on their learning, Boykin conducted experiments with African American children in which some of the children were presented with stories to remember and problems to solve under conditions that allowed them to dance, run, and jump, while other children were presented with the same stories and problems under conditions that required them to be still or, at most, move in a "school-like" manner. The children who were allowed to express themselves with high levels of movement significantly outperformed their counterparts, supporting Boykin's idea about the importance of this cultural factor for the children's learning (Boykin & Cunningham, 2001).

Taken together, these different studies strongly implicate home cultural values and modes of behavior as important factors in children's school success. But they also indicate that there is no "one right way" to incorporate such differences into classroom practices.

Developmentalists point out that schools have different cultural styles that influence classroom practices and the assumptions and attitudes of teachers and students. Because of the increasing number of students from immigrant families, some schools are training their teachers to be sensitive to the possibility of "culture clashes" between the cultural style of the school and the children's culture of origin.

The Language of School

Even when people speak the same language, they do not necessarily use language in the same way. As we have seen, language is used in schools in rather distinctive ways, and children's experience of oral and written language in the home will differ to some extent not only from language practices at school but from those of other homes within the community.

cultural style A dominant way of thinking about and relating to the world that arises from a people's common historical experience.

Comparing Mathematics Achievement across Cultures

F YOU WERE SOMEHOW ABLE TO VISIT schools throughout the world, you would find that—for all the vast differences in geographic location, languages spoken, economic resources available, religious beliefs adhered to, and so on—the world's classrooms and curricula are in many ways remarkably similar. Despite these fundamental similarities, studies of classroom life and academic performance in different societies reveal that both the process and the products of schooling vary markedly from one culture to the next (Serpell & Hatano, 1997; Kim & Park, 2006). One noteworthy difference is the exceptionally high level of mathematics achievement in many Asian countries; for example, on standardized international tests of mathematics achievement given every 4 years to fourth- and eighth-graders, children from Asian countries consistently outperform their peers in other countries (see the figure for mathematics results for the 2003 TIMSS, or Trends in International Mathematics and Science Study).

Not surprisingly, developmentalists concerned with educational issues have been interested in discovering the source of such exceptional achievement and, more generally, factors responsible for variation in children's achievement from one society to the next. A series of studies initiated by psychologist Harold Stevenson in the 1980s provided a good deal of insight into the ways in which cultural differences in elementary school education may contribute to variations in children's performance (Stevenson & Stigler, 1992; Stigler, Gallimore, & Hiebert, 2000). These studies used videotapes of actual classroom lessons in three countries—the United States, Japan, and Taiwan—to discover how differences in modes of instruction were related to overall test performance (the list of participating countries has now swelled to 38). Several results stood out when comparing the ways classroom behaviors differed among the three countries.

First, the researchers found that compared to children in other countries, including the United States, Asian children attended school more days each year and spent more hours in school each week. At the fifth-grade level, for example, Japanese children went to school 44 hours a week; Chinese students, 37 hours week; and American children, 30 hours a week. Furthermore, on each school day the two Asian groups spent as much time on mathematics as they did on reading and writing, while the American group spent almost 3 times as much on language arts. As James Stigler and Michelle Perry (1990, p. 336) note, the disparity in the sheer number of hours spent on mathematics lessons was large enough to "go a long way toward explaining the differences in mathematics achievement."

Second, the Asian classrooms were organized quite differently from classrooms in the United States. By and large, classrooms in the two Asian countries were centrally organized, with the teacher instructing the whole class at once. In contrast, classrooms in the United States were generally more decentralized, with the teacher often devoting attention to one group at a time while the other children worked independently. As a result of this classroom organization, children in the United States spent a good deal of time being instructed by no one. This might not have mattered much if the children had been absorbed by their workbooks and truly working independently. But here another difference came into play: the children in the United States did not use their independent study time well, spending almost half of it out of their seats or engaged in inappropriate behavior such as gossiping with friends or causing mischief; Asian children spent far more time attending to schoolwork.

Recent studies of cultural differences in mathematical achievement have expanded their focus from the amount of time spent on math and the organization of math instruction, to explore cultural beliefs about education and the process of learning. An example is a study of Korean beliefs about academic achievement, conducted by Uichol Kim and Young-Shin Park (Kim & Park, 2006). Noting that Korea, compared to most Western countries, spends considerably less money per student and has larger class sizes, Kim and Park argue that the exceptional academic achievement of Korean students is due to Korean cultural values and family relationships. For instance, Koreans tend to believe that achievement is a consequence of personal effort rather than innate ability—a

In order to gain insight into how language used in the home may differ from language practices associated with school and school success, Shirley Heath (1983) conducted an ethnographic study of three populations of children and their families over a period of years. The populations she studied, all from the same geographical locale, included the families of a group of European American schoolteachers, a group of European American textile workers, and a group of African Americans engaged in farming and textile jobs.

Conducting observations both in homes and in classrooms, Heath found that the families of European American teachers experienced the least mismatch with the school. About half of the conversations she recorded in the teachers' homes included the "instructional discourse" that is a prominent feature of classrooms. In addition, these parents involved their children in labeling objects, naming letters, and reading. When reading with their children, they went well beyond the text itself to make clear the relationships between what was in the book and experiences the child might have had or might have in the future. In a sense, the teachers were being teachers at home as well as at school. Perhaps as a result, their children tended to do well in school.

belief conducive to academic success, as discussed earlier in the chapter. Furthermore, they view education as an important aspect of self-growth that should be pursued for its own sake in order to be successful in life. Finally, parents are expected to play a key role in their children's academic success, largely by providing emotional (rather than informational) support, which is thought to foster a sense of indebtedness in children and a desire to repay parents by doing well in school.

Such findings underscore the fact that classroom learning is a cultural activity in which many different factors are always at work (Heibert et al., 2005). Thus, as sociologist Merry White (1987) noted, cross-cultural research cannot provide a blueprint for improving the education of children. Rather, it provides a mirror that sharpens our awareness of our own cultural practices and provides some hints about how they might be changed to make teaching and learning more effective.

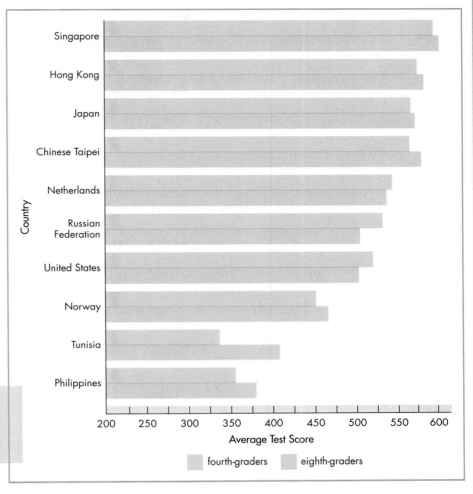

Average mathematics scores from eighth graders in ten countries from different parts of the world. (Adapted from the National Center for Education Statistics, 2001)

In the homes of European American textile workers, a major departure from the pattern in schools and in the teachers' homes was that, although parents read to their children, they limited their storybook conversations to the text itself. Parents asked their children questions about the characters and events in stories they were read but did not encourage them to imaginatively link the stories to the world around them. Overall, the children from these working-class European American families tended not to do well in school. More precisely, in what may have been a reflection of the language-use pattern in their homes, they tended to perform well in the early grades of school, where a focus on the literal meaning of a text fits most tasks, but less well in the higher grades, where it becomes necessary to draw inferences from complex texts.

Unlike the two groups of European American parents, the African American parents rarely used the known-answer questions of instructional discourse ("What color is your jacket?"). Rather, parents most often asked children questions that encouraged them to think about similarities across situations related to the children's own experience ("Do you think you can get along with your cousin on this visit?"). Such questions often served as the pretext for discussing some interesting event and helped children think about their shifting roles and responsibilities in different situations. Heath also documented many inventive uses of language in teasing and storytelling. But the children's language experience generally did not expose them to the kinds of language patterns they would be expected to use in school. Again, perhaps in part because of the mismatch, these African American working-class children tended not to perform well in school. Similar findings have been reported for Latino children (Vasquez, 2002).

These differences in academic success among the children from the three groups are understandable in terms of the relative fit between school and home language use and culture. At the same time, it is the goal of teachers to be successful with all children. So the question becomes one of how to design educational interventions to make it possible for everyone to learn effectively.

Culturally Responsive Classroom Strategies

In recognition of the importance of children's home language and culture to their success in the classroom, schools have begun to make a place for them in academic curricula and to host special events to explore and celebrate the cultural heritages of the young people they serve. Common programs such as English as a second language (ESL), bilingual education programs, and heritage language classes are intended to help immigrant students make the transition to an all-English curriculum. The overarching goal is to foster assimilation while valuing cultural diversity (Padilla, 2006).

An early and influential example of the culturally responsive approach to education occurred in a classroom of students from the Odawa Indian tribe in Canada taught by an expert Odawa teacher (Erickson & Mohatt, 1982). On the surface, the teacher appeared to adhere to a recitation-script approach, talking for most of the lessons, asking many known-answer questions, and limiting the students' role to answering her questions. But she did so in a special way consistent with the language use and cultural patterns employed in Odawa homes. When she was giving instruction, she organized students into small groups instead of rows, approximating the way the children interacted in groups at home. She generally addressed the children as a group and did not single out individual children. Instead of saying "good" when she was giving the children feedback on their responses to her questions, she signaled her acceptance of students' answers by moving on to the next question. She praised but did not reprimand students in public, in accordance with Odawa norms against public criticism. This culture-sensitive way of implementing classroom lessons worked well to improve children's academic performance.

Another example of the importance of culture-sensitive instruction was provided by an experiment conducted by Carol Lee, who drew upon African American high school students' familiarity with, and appreciation of, the linguistic form called signifying (Lee, 1995). Within the African American community, to signify means to speak in a manner that uses innuendo and words with double meanings, to play with the sounds and meanings of words, and to be quick-witted and funny, all at the same time. According to Lee, African American adolescents use signifying for a wide variety of speech functions including:

- To challenge someone in a verbal duel, but remain friendly
- To persuade someone by driving home a message in a distinctive way
- To criticize someone in a way that is difficult to pin down

Lee began by presenting students examples of signifying dialogues of the sort they were familiar with and getting the students to analyze and explain how each example of signifying worked to achieve a specific goal. Then she had them read stories and novels by African American writers that included signifying and asked them to apply the rules, which they knew intuitively, to the interpretation of complex inferential questions from the literary texts.

When Lee compared the performance of students who engaged in this kind of culturally responsive instruction with that of students who took the regular literature course, she found they demonstrated a significantly higher level of literary understanding and active engagement with the problem of literary interpretation.

On the basis of available research, these examples could be multiplied to encompass a wide variety of ethnic and social-class groups—wide enough to make a convincing case that it is possible to organize effective contexts for education by taking into account local variations in culture and social class (Tharp & Yamauchi, 2000). At the same time, it needs to be recognized that there is no single "right way" to connect classroom instruction to home culture. Research on this topic makes it clear that a wide variety of specific classroom strategies can successfully engage students from the vast variety of backgrounds characteristic of American society. However, culturally specific strategies are likely to be applicable only when there is a culturally homogeneous classroom (Gallego & Cole, 2000).

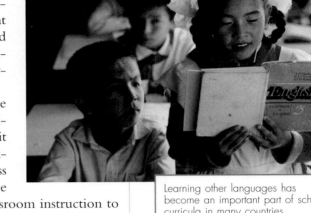

Learning other languages has become an important part of school curricula in many countries.

||||| ▌ APPLY ▬ CONNECT ▬ DISCUSS

In her research with African American children, Carol Lee found that, compared to traditional instruction, culturally responsive instruction results both in a higher level of literary understanding (of how to analyze and interpret texts) and in increased engagement. Review the curriculum she developed around the concept of "signifying," and explain how it led to both these results.

Outside the School

As important as schooling is to middle childhood, it is not the only context beyond the family that influences children. Especially important is the time spent in new kinds of activities with friends and one's peer group. On weekday afternoons and evenings, on weekends and holidays, elementary-school-age children are likely to be found among other children their own age, engaged in activities of their own choosing. Some of these settings have an adult or two present, but in many cases, adults are not on the scene.

Participation in these peer groups provides a kind of preparation for adult life that is quite different from that organized by adults in classrooms or at home. At the same time, peer-group experiences influence life at home and in school. Consequently, a full understanding of the nature of middle childhood requires investigation of peer contexts as well, so we turn to this important topic in Chapter 13.

SUMMARY

The children of the world have vastly unequal access to education, yet school can have an extraordinary impact as a context for children's development.

The Contexts of Learning

- Education refers to explicit instruction of children in order to transmit a culture's knowledge and skills.

- Early hunter–gatherer societies transmitted cultural knowledge and skills through social enhancement and imitation as children participated in everyday activities, rather than through explicit instruction. Increasing specialization led to the emergence of apprenticeship— an intermediate form involving some explicit instruction but relying mainly on participation—and to the emergence of education, or schooling.

- Schooling differs from traditional apprenticeship training in dimensions including motivation, social relations, social organization, and mediums of instruction. Its problems are abstract, in contrast to those of everyday life.

School Readiness

- Children often start school with knowledge, skills, and attitudes that serve as building blocks for learning to read and write and to do math.

- A basic reading skill is decoding text—translating graphemes (units of print) to phonemes (units of sound). This in turn requires the ability to detect and manipulate the phonemes in words, an ability that comes only with instruction.

- To learn math, children must be able to relate number words and symbols to quantities. Children learn to envision the placement of numbers on an abstract number line and to manipulate numeric units.

- Families play a key role in promoting school readiness by creating contexts for children to engage in relevant activities. School readiness promotes academic success.

- Preschools also promote school readiness. Although world-wide preschool enrollment has tripled in recent decades, there are significant disparities in enrollment across and within countries, with lower enrollments among many groups of children who might most benefit from pre-school, including immigrant children in the United States.

In the Classroom

- Educators have debated the merits of a bottom-up approach, which initially focuses on basic skills, versus a top-down approach, which focuses on the big picture of which the basic skills are part.

- The standard classroom format features a teacher at the head of the class instructing students who sit in rows and the use of a special instructional discourse, including the initiation–reply–feedback sequence and known-answer questions.

- Alternative forms of classroom instruction seek to counter the passivity of students in the standard format and make them active participants in their education. Examples include:

  - Reciprocal teaching, in which a teacher and a small group of students read segments of text and take turns leading discussions of their meaning.

  - Realistic mathematics education, which encourages development of conceptual understanding as well as basic skills through the use of models and meaningful, problem-oriented activities.

  - Playworld practice, which involves enacting, making art, and playing with themes based on children's literature.

- For many children, specific learning disabilities pose a barrier to school success. Such children have normal IQs but fare poorly in at least some academic areas. The most common specific learning disability is dyslexia, reading difficulty often involving difficulties detecting phonemes and with the rules that relate graphemes and phonemes.

- While some students thrive on the challenges of schooling, others lose their academic motivation. Researchers exploring the reasons have found two patterns:

  - Children who adopt an incremental model of intelligence see intelligence as something that can grow as one learns. They tend to have a mastery motivation that motivates them to learn and improve.

  - Children who adopt an entity model of intelligence see intelligence as fixed. They tend to develop a performance orientation that motivates them to perform well, but to give up when they experience failure.

The Cognitive Consequences of Schooling

- The cognitive consequences of schooling have been assessed through three research strategies for comparing schooled and nonschooled children.

- The school-cutoff strategy, which compares 6-year-olds in first grade with those in kindergarten, finds that schooling makes a difference mainly to a range of relatively specific cognitive abilities.

- School–nonschool comparisons show few clear differences other than increased use of specialized memory strategies and increased metacognitive skills.

- Second-generation studies, comparing schooled and unschooled mothers, suggest that habits and skills acquired in school may influence child-rearing practices in such a way as to lead to better health and educational outcomes for children. Thus, school's greatest impact may be other than cognitive.

Contemporary Challenges in a Globalizing World

- A major challenge is to increase access to quality education, reducing disparities across and within countries, including disparities related to gender, ethnicity, and socioeconomic status.

- Another major challenge in many countries is to serve student populations that are increasingly diverse in terms of language and culture.

- Home cultural values are important to children's school success. A good match between home and school language also favors success. Although the culture of U.S. schools reflects the dominant cultural style, classroom practices can be sensitive to other cultural styles, thereby benefitting a wider range of children.

Key Terms

education, p. 427
apprenticeship, p. 427
emergent literacy, p. 430
emergent numeracy, p. 430
decoding, p. 430
bottom-up processing, p. 435
top-down processing, p. 435

instructional discourse, p. 435
initiation–reply–feedback sequence, p. 435
reciprocal teaching, p. 436
realistic mathematics education, p. 438
playworld practice, p. 439
specific learning disabilities, p. 441
academic motivation, p. 443

mastery orientation, p. 443
performance orientation, p. 443
entity model of intelligence, p. 443
incremental model of intelligence, p. 443
school-cutoff strategy, p. 445
cultural style, p. 450

13

CHAPTER

Social and Emotional Development in Middle Childhood

Cassie and Becca had been best friends since first grade. When the girls were in fifth grade, Kelly moved into town. At first, the three of them were quite close. But something happened a few weeks ago. According to 10-year-old Cassie:

Becca kind of forgot me. They started to get really close and they just forgot me. And then they started ganging up on me and stuff. Like, after lunch we have a place where we meet and stuff. We get in a circle and just talk. And they'd put their shoulders together and they wouldn't let me, you know, in the circle. They would never talk to me, and they would never listen to what I had to say. I don't think I've ever done anything to them. I've always been nice to them. I feel like I don't want to go to school, because I don't know what they'll do every day. I talk to my mom but it kind of makes her mad because she says I should ignore them. But I can't. And I can't concentrate. They're like—they look at me and stuff like that. They stare at me. I can hear them saying stuff and whispering and they look right at me.

(Adapted from Simmons, 2002)

ery few of us pass through middle childhood without experiencing the sting of peer rejection. As children between the ages of 6 and 12 spend more time in the company of age-mates, and correspondingly less time with parents, peers begin to assume a more prominent place in their lives and exert more influence on their behavior and development. Indeed, one of the most significant changes of middle childhood is the emergence of peer influence as a form of social control, with considerable power to shape behavior. Sometimes the rule of "might makes right" prevails, as when an especially strong child dominates group activity. At other times, the complexity of social relationships, including popularity, sets the tone, as Cassie came to experience.

The emergence of new forms of social control is also apparent in the changing nature of children's relations with their parents. Parents can no longer successfully demand blind obedience from their children, nor can they easily just pick them up and remove them from danger or from situations in which they are behaving badly. Parents can still monitor their children's whereabouts, but they must rely on their children's greater understanding of the consequences of their actions and on their desire to conform to adult standards to keep them out of harm's way and behaving in ways that are socially appropriate and morally acceptable. As a result, parents' socialization techniques become more indirect, and they rely increasingly on discussion and explanation to influence their children's behavior.

As their relationships with others change, so, too, does children's sense of themselves. As long as they spend their time primarily among family members, their social roles and sense of self are more or less predefined and determined. They are little brothers or older sisters, with all the expectations and privileges that go along with those roles. When children spend more time among their peers, however,

During middle childhood, peers become increasingly important to social and emotional development, as illustrated in the joyful interaction of these girls as they play together on a beach in South Africa.

the sense of self they acquired in their families no longer suffices, and they must form new identities appropriate to the new contexts they inhabit. The child who seems fearless at home and who dominates her younger siblings may find that she needs to be more restrained on the playground with her peers.

This chapter focuses on how new forms of social control, that is, new ways of organizing behavior in relation to group life and society, are manifested in children's moral development, peer interactions and friendships, relationships with parents, and changing sense of self.

Moral Development

One of the most significant changes in moral development, as in social development generally, is the child's new ability to internalize society's rules and standards. Remember from Chapter 9 that as children develop, their reasoning and behaviors become less dependent on external rewards and punishments, and more dependent on an internal, personal sense of right and wrong. According to Freud's *psychodynamic theory* (see Chapter 9, p. 314), this transition occurs with the development of the superego. The *superego,* remember, is the part of the personality that monitors and evaluates whether the individual's actions are morally appropriate. It is the individual's conscience—the *internalization* of society's moral codes. Once the superego has formed, the child is able to draw upon his or her own internal notions of right and wrong in making moral judgments, rather than be driven by hope of reward or fear of reprisal.

Interest in the shift from external to internal control is also apparent in the *cognitive-developmental* view of moral development held by Piaget and those who followed in his footsteps (see Chapter 9, p. 314). Much of their work has focused on exploring children's reasoning about what is morally right or wrong, and the relationship between moral reasoning and moral behavior.

Piaget's Theory of Moral Development

In Chapter 9 we explained that for Piaget, moral development involves a shift from *heteronomous morality,* in which right and wrong are defined according to objective consequences (whether 1 cup or 10 cups were broken; whether dad got angry), to **autonomous morality** in which right and wrong are defined according to the person's internal motives and intentions (see pp. 314–315). An important question for Piaget, as well as the rest of us, is what, exactly, triggers the shift from heteronomous to autonomous moral reasoning? How is it that children who must always be told what is right and wrong come to reason it out for themselves? Piaget's answer is that the shift in moral reasoning takes place in the context of peer activities—playing *games,* in particular.

Like 4- and 5-year-olds, children who have entered middle childhood engage in fantasy role play, with each child taking a part in an imaginary situation: cops chase robbers, shipwrecked families take up residence in tree houses, runaway children hide in secret forts (Singer, 2006). But about the age of 7 or 8, children also engage in a new form of play—

In Jamaica (here) and throughout the world, children will begin in middle childhood to organize their behavior according to the dictates of their peer groups.

games based on rules. As you saw in Chapter 9, preschool fantasy role play may involve rules, but these rules can change on a whim. In contrast, in the rule-based fantasy role play and other games characteristic of middle childhood, the rules must be agreed upon ahead of time and consistently followed; anyone who changes the rules without common consent is cheating.

Piaget conducted some of the most famous and influential studies of the development of games with rules by observing changes in how children play the game of marbles. He found that young children (6–8 years) have a "mystical respect" for the rules of the game. Children believe that rules are "eternal and unchangeable" because they have been handed down by authority figures such as parents, grandparents, or even God (Piaget, 1995, pp. 206–207) (see the box "Children's Ideas about God"). This way of thinking about rules corresponds, of course, to heteronomous morality. Older children (10–12 years), in contrast, recognize that the rules have been agreed upon by the players and can be modified if everyone agrees to it. Consistent with the onset of autonomous morality, rules are no longer mystical, but rational.

Piaget (1932/1965) believed that games are models of society—that rule-based games have several fundamental characteristics of social institutions in general. First, rule-based games remain basically the same as they are passed from one generation to the next. Thus, like other social institutions—a church service, for example—rule-based games provide an existing structure of rules about how to behave in specific social circumstances. Second, rule-based games can exist only if people agree to participate in them. There would be no religions if there were no practicing believers; there would be no hopscotch if children stopped playing it. In order to participate in social institutions, including games, people must subordinate their immediate desires and behavior to a socially agreed-upon system, be it a religious ceremony or the rules of hopscotch. Piaget (1932/1965) linked this ability to play within a framework of rules to children's acquisition of respect for rules and a new level of moral understanding.

In Piaget's (1932/1965) view, it is through game-playing—that is, through the give-and-take of negotiating plans, settling disagreements, making and enforcing rules, and keeping and breaking promises—that children come to understand that social rules make cooperation with others possible. As a consequence of this understanding, peer groups can be self-governing, and their members capable of autonomous moral thinking.

autonomous morality The second and final stage of Piaget's theory of moral development in which right and wrong are defined according to internal motives and intentions rather than objective consequences.

These members of the Long Island Gulls hockey team know that breaking the rules is cheating. According to Piaget, participating in rule-governed games such as hockey contributes to children's moral development.

Bruce Bennett/Getty Images

Children's Ideas about God

CAREN, AGE 9:
Once upon a time in Heaven. . . .
God woke up from his nap. It was his
birthday. But nobody knew it was his
birthday but one angel. . . . And this angel rounds up all these other angels, and
when he gets out of the shower, they have
a surprise party for him. (Heller, 1986,
cited in Barrett, 2001)

An adult:
God is infinite, pervasive, and man finite
and limited to a locality. Man cannot
comprehend God as he can other things.
God is without limits, without dimensions.
(Ullah, 1984, cited in Barrett, 2001)

The quotes above would seem to support the
conclusion shared by many developmentalists
that children's understanding of God moves
from primitive, anthropomorphic conceptions—
God has birthdays, naps, and showers—to
abstract concepts that refer to God's infinite
knowledge and power, formlessness, and existence beyond the realm of physical and natural laws.

This was certainly the view held by both
Freud and Piaget, who believed that, early on,
children's conceptions of God are similar to
their conceptions of parents. Freud, for example, argued that the idea of God is a projec-
tion of our need for a protective parent figure.
Piaget, as you have come to expect, adopted
an approach that links changing conceptions
of God to changing cognitive systems. In particular, children initially attribute godlike properties to God and their parents. Once they
realize that their parents are, indeed, fallible—
vulnerable to errors in judgment and knowledge—they differentiate the divine from the
merely human, granting ultimate supremacy to
God alone. Not until adolescence and the advent of abstract reasoning do children begin
to understand God in terms of "infinite knowledge," and "formlessness."

Children's developing conceptions of God
have been studied using a variety of methods.
Children have been asked to describe God,
or to draw pictures of God, or the house that
God lives in. In general, the studies suggest
that major cognitive shifts occur across childhood. For example, Dimitris Pnevmatikos
(2002) asked first- through fifth-grade Catholic
and Greek Orthodox children living in Luxem-
bourg to draw the house where God lives. He
found a tendency for first- and second-graders
to draw real houses or churches on earth,
sometimes next door to their own homes. Many
third-graders, however, located the buildings
in clouds, suggesting a more heavenly neighborhood. With increasing age, material buildings became less frequent in the drawings,
which began to include symbolic elements, including Heaven's gates, angels, and planets.
Not until fourth grade did a very few children,
perhaps on the threshold of adolescent abstract reasoning, begin to depict God as co-

existing with qualities such as goodness, love,
peace, and so on, rather than as residing in
tangible structures.

On the other hand, some developmentalists
have argued that the differences between
younger and older children, or between children and adults, are not as robust or dramatic
as once believed, and depend greatly on the
demands of the task. Some studies have found
evidence that under certain circumstances,
adults are prone to anthropomorphize God,
much as children do. In one such study, adults
of several faith traditions in the United States
and India were told a story in which a boy
was swimming in a swift and rocky river. His
leg became caught between two rocks, and
he began to struggle and pray. Although God
(or Vishnu, Shiva, Brahman, or Krishna, depending on the child's faith) was answering
another prayer in another part of the world
when the boy started praying, before long
God responded by pushing one of the rocks
so the boy could get his leg out. The boy then
struggled to the riverbank and fell over exhausted (Barrett, 2001).

When asked to interpret the story, most
adults reported that God had been busy answering another prayer and attended to the
drowning boy as soon as business allowed.
Attributing such qualities as divided or limited
attention suggests that adults, like children, are
quite capable of anthropomorphizing God. (Interestingly, when God was replaced in the

Kohlberg's Theory of Moral Development

The most influential attempt to build on Piaget's approach to moral development
was carried out by Lawrence Kohlberg (Turiel, 2002). Whereas Piaget argued for
the existence of two stages, heteronomous and autonomous moral reasoning,
Kohlberg proposed a sequence of six stages extending from childhood into adolescence and adulthood. These six stages are grouped into three levels of moral
reasoning: *preconventional*, *conventional*, and *postconventional* (Colby & Kohlberg,
1987; Kohlberg, 1969, 1976, 1984). We will focus here on the application of
Kohlberg's ideas to middle childhood and postpone an overall evaluation of his
approach until the discussion of adolescent moral development in Chapter 14. The
stages are characterized by ideas about what is right and reasons for doing right,
all of which evolve over time as egocentrism declines and is replaced by social
perspective taking. (Table 13.1 shows all six stages, and gives greater details on the
first three, which we discuss below.)

Kohlberg's method for studying moral reasoning was to present children with
stories about people faced with dilemmas involving the value of human life and
property, people's obligations to each other, and the meaning of laws and rules.

story by a space alien named Mog, who had godlike properties, most adults believed that Mog could handle both problems simultaneously.) It would seem that adults' conceptions of God are complex, and depend at least in part on the context of reasoning.

Yet another challenge to the idea of a dramatic shift in conceptions of God comes from evidence that very young children, like adults, think of God in abstract terms. Using a version of the "false-belief task" (see Chapter 8, p. 286), Justin Barrett and his colleagues showed 3- to 6-year-old children a closed cracker box which, when opened, revealed rocks. The children were asked what their mother, in another room, would think was in the closed box if she were to come in and see it on the table. Consistent with much of the theories-of-mind research, the youngest children replied "rocks," not appreciating that their mother could have a different point of view, whereas the 5 and 6 year olds replied "crackers." However, when asked what God would think was in the box, children of all ages were equally likely to say "rocks." Thus, the 5- and 6-year-olds seemed to understand that a "God's-eye view" is much different, and less limited, than their mother's.

Based on his review of the research described here, Justin Barrett (2001) suggested that conceptions of God for children and adults depend importantly on the context and may not be as different as once supposed. It may be that anthropomorphic and abstract conceptions of God are not mutually exclusive, but interact, and remain relevant to the ways in which individuals try to make sense of the divine.

Young children's drawings of the house where God lives often depict real houses (a and b), whereas older children's drawings link God's house to abstract ideas such as "goodness," "love," and "peace" (c).

  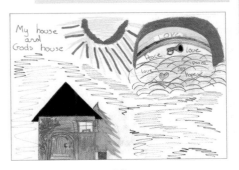

All drawings courtesy of Dr. Dimitris Prevmatikos, 2002

(a)   (b)   (c)

In the manner of Piaget's clinical interview technique, after reading the story, Kohlberg would ask the child's opinion about how the protagonist should behave in response to the dilemma and then probe the reasoning behind the opinion. Kohlberg's (1969) most famous story is the "Heinz dilemma":

> In Europe, a woman was near death from cancer. One drug might save her, a form of radium that a druggist in the same town had recently discovered. The druggist was charging $2,000, ten times what the drug cost him to make. The sick woman's husband, Heinz, went to everyone he knew to borrow the money, but he could get together only about half of what it cost. He told the druggist that his wife was dying and asked him to sell it cheaper or let him pay later. But the druggist said no. The husband got desperate and broke into the man's store to steal the drug for his wife. Should the husband have done that? Why? (p. 379)

In Kohlberg's theory of moral development, individuals who are at the *preconventional level* see right and wrong in terms of external consequences for the individual of following or not following the rules. This level comprises stages 1 and 2.

Stage 1, *heteronomous morality*, coincides with the end of the preschool period and the beginning of middle childhood. The social perspective of children at stage 1 is egocentric: In making judgments about right and wrong, they do not recognize the

table 13.1
Kohlberg's Six Moral Stages

Level and Stage	What Is Right	Reasons for Doing Right	Social Perspective
Level I—Preconventional			
Stage 1—Heteronomous morality	• Adherence to rules backed by punishment. • Obedience for its own sake. • Avoidance of physical damage to persons and property.	• Avoidance of punishment. • Superior power of authorities.	Egocentric perspective: doesn't consider the interests of others or recognize that they differ from one's own. Actions are considered in terms of physical consequences, not psychological consequences for others. Confusion of authority's perspective with one's own.
Stage 2—Instrumental morality	• Following rules when doing so is in one's immediate interest. • Acting to meet one's own interests and needs and letting others do the same. • Fairness, seen as an equal exchange.	• To serve one's own needs or interests in a world where other people have their own interests.	Concrete individualistic perspective: aware that all people have their own interests to pursue and these interests conflict, so that right is relative.
Level II—Conventional			
Stage 3—Good-child morality	• Living up to what is expected by people close to you. • Having good motives, and showing concern about others. • Keeping mutual relationships by such means as trust, loyalty, respect, and gratitude.	• The need to be a good person in one's own eyes and those of others. • Caring for others. • Belief in the Golden Rule. • Desire to maintain rules and authority that support stereotypical good behavior.	Perspective of an individual in relationships with other individuals: aware of shared feelings, agreements, and expectations. Ability to relate points of view through the Golden Rule.
Stage 4—Law-and-order morality	• Upholding the law.	• To keep the institution going as a whole.	Perspective of an individual in relation to the social group.
Level III—Postconventional, or Principled			
Stage 5—Social-contract reasoning	• Being aware that people hold a variety of values and opinions.	• A sense of obligation to law because of one's social contract to act for the welfare of the group.	Prosocial perspective: perspective of a rational individual aware of others' values and rights.
Stage 6—Universal ethical principles	• Following self-chosen ethical principles.	• A belief in the validity of universal moral principles.	Perspective of a moral point of view from which social arrangements derive.

Source: Adapted from Kohlberg, 1976.

interests of others as distinct from their own. What is right or wrong for them must be right or wrong for others. Moreover, their judgments about the rightness and wrongness of an action are based on its objective outcome, which in this case is how powerful authorities would respond to it. In stage 1, children might assert that Heinz must not steal the medicine because he will be put in jail.

Stage 2 ordinarily is reached at around the age of 7 or 8, with a shift in children's social perspective: Children can now recognize that different people have different perspectives and interests, and that these may conflict with their own. Consequently, they believe that what is morally right is highly individualistic, that is, it depends on the specific perspective and situation of the person who is dealing with the moral issue. In keeping with this *concrete individualistic* social perspective, morality is seen as serving one's immediate interests and needs and letting others do the same. Similarly, fairness is understood in the context of an exchange system, of giving as much as you receive. Kohlberg referred to the moral reasoning of children at this stage as *instrumental morality* because it assumes that what serves one's own interests is moral. Children at this stage might respond to the Heinz dilemma by saying that Heinz should steal the drug because someday he might have cancer and would want someone to steal it for him.

Stage 2 is the key transition associated with school-age children's ability to get along without adult supervision. Children no longer depend on a strong external source to define right and wrong; instead, their behavior is regulated by reciprocal relations between group members. Sometimes the resulting behaviors are desirable ("I'll help you with your model, if you help me with mine"); other times, they are less so ("I won't tell Mom you went to the arcade, if you don't tell her I got in a fight at school"). In either case, this form of thinking allows children to regulate their actions with each other.

At the *conventional level,* the focus of moral reasoning shifts from external consequences to society's standards and rules. In stage 3, *good-child morality,* which children begin to reach around the age of 10 or 11, moral judgments are made from the social perspective of *relationships with other individuals.* Children at this stage have come to see shared feelings and agreements, especially with people close to them, as more important than individual self-interest. One child quoted by Kohlberg (1984) said, "If I was Heinz, I would have stolen the drug for my wife. You can't put a price on love, no amount of gifts make love" (p. 629). Stage 3 is often equated with the golden rule (treat others as you wish to be treated), a moral rule of reciprocity found in scriptures in all major religions.

Kohberg's theory and interview method have been extremely influential in studies of children's moral development, although, as you will see in Chapter 14, some of his conclusions about the stages have been questioned, especially from feminist and cross-cultural perspectives. The lion's share of contemporary research continues to present children with hypothetical stories or dilemmas for the purpose of identifying stagelike changes in different areas of moral reasoning. A good example is found in studies of prosocial moral reasoning.

Prosocial Moral Reasoning

Prosocial moral reasoning refers to the thinking that is involved in deciding whether to share with, help, or take care of other people (whether to engage in *prosocial behavior*) when doing so may prove costly to oneself (Eisenberg, Spinrad, & Sadovsky, 2006). According to Nancy Eisenberg (1992; Eisenberg & Fabes, 2006), prosocial moral reasoning goes through stagelike developmental changes similar to those proposed by Kohlberg for moral reasoning.

In her research on prosocial moral reasoning, Eisenberg used story dilemmas that generally included a conflict between immediate self-interest and the interest of others. For example, in one such story, a child is having a good time playing in his yard and sees a bully hurting another child when no adults are around. In another, the child has to choose between going to a birthday party or stopping to help a child who has injured his leg. The contrasts between a 5-year-old and a 10-year-old responding to the latter story illustrate the changes in reasoning typically observed between early and middle childhood:

Age 5 years
Interviewer: What do you think [Eric, the story protagonist] should do?
Child: Go to the party.
Interviewer: Why is that?
Child: Because he doesn't want to be late.
Interviewer: Why doesn't he want to be late?
Child: 'Cause then it'd be over.

prosocial moral reasoning The thinking that is involved in deciding whether to share with, help, or take care of other people when doing so may prove costly to oneself.

Age 10 years
Interviewer: What do you think Eric should do?
Child: Go get the boy's parents.
Interviewer: Why do you think he would want to get his parents for him?
Child: Because he doesn't want him to have a broken leg and he wants him to get to the hospital real fast because he doesn't want him to get a broken leg or anything worse.
(Eisenberg, 1992, p. 29)

Although many factors are involved in determining the sophistication of children's prosocial moral reasoning, reviews of the large amount of literature on this topic show that as children get older, their reasoning reflects the trend in these two examples. Young children focus on themselves, and their decisions to help others are based on what is to be gained personally. With increasing age, children express more empathy for the person in difficulty and a greater consideration of social norms.

As you recall from our discussion in Chapter 9 regarding the link between prosocial behavior and feelings of empathy and sympathy, developmentalists are interested in understanding how children's actions toward others relate to their thoughts and feelings about others. It should come as no surprise that the relationship between prosocial moral reasoning and prosocial behavior has been a focus for research in this area. For example, are children who reason at advanced levels about hypothetical stories more likely to exhibit higher levels of morality in their actual behavior? In an extensive survey of studies on children's prosocial moral reasoning, Nancy Eisenberg and her colleagues (2003) found that higher levels of reasoning are indeed positively related to higher levels of prosocial behavior. Studies of cheating, for example, find that children who score at higher levels on tests of prosocial reasoning are less likely to cheat than children who score at lower levels. However, even children with advanced reasoning will succumb to temptation if it seems that they can get away with it (Alencar, de Oliveira, & Yamamoto, 2008; Subbotsky, 1993). Apparently, there is no guarantee that a person will engage in high levels of prosocial behavior, even though he or she may have the intellectual means of doing so.

As children acquire more advanced forms of prosocial reasoning, they show higher levels of prosocial behavior.

Jeff Isaac Greenberg/Photo Researchers

Social Domain Theory

As you have learned, Freud, Piaget, and Kohlberg all shared the view that young children rely on external consequences and authority for deciding right and wrong. However, as we indicated in Chapter 9 (see p. 316), research within the social domain perspective has suggested that children may demonstrate a relatively strong sense of fairness and others' welfare, as well as an ability to question the legitimacy of authority, at earlier ages than developmentalists once thought (Turiel, 2002). This research often presents children with stories that create a conflict between authority on the one hand and fairness or others' welfare on the other. For example, children might be told of a situation in which two children are fighting on the school playground. A peer tells the two to stop fighting; however, a teacher says that it is okay for the fight to continue. Researchers find that children as young as 5 or 6 years of age will insist that the peer's position to stop the fight is more legitimate than the teacher's position to allow it to continue (Laupa et al., 1995).

The priority that children give to the morality of the act over the status of the authority figure has been found even in cultures, such as Korea, that are assumed to attach great weight to authority (Kim, 1998). This suggests that instead of deferring to rules and authority, children rely on concepts of harm and welfare in judging moral behavior. This fact led Elliot Turiel and his colleagues to conclude that reasoning about moral issues is quite different from reasoning about authority and social conventions (Turiel, 2002).

Consider the following example, in which children from 5 to 11 years of age are presented with two different stories about school rules (Turiel, 1983, p. 62). In one story, the school allows children to take off their clothes when the weather is hot (a social conventional issue); in the other, the school permits children to hit each other (a moral issue). A child in the study gave this response when asked whether it is appropriate to allow children to remove their clothes:

> Yes, because that is the rule. (*Why can they have that rule?*) If that's what the boss wants to do, he can do that. (*How come?*) Because he's the boss, he is in charge of the school.

On the other hand, the child was much less likely to recognize the principal's authority to dictate whether children can hurt each other:

> No, it is not okay. (*Why not?*) Because that is like making other people unhappy. You can hurt them that way. It hurts other people, hurting is not good.

Despite their behavior, even young children know that fighting is generally wrong. This suggests that they are able to use concepts of harm and welfare in judging moral behavior.

Over the course of the past 20 years, more than 100 studies have supported the claim that children distinguish between the moral domain and the social conventional domain when they judge how people should and should not behave (reviewed in Killen, McGlothin, & Lee-Kim, 2002; Nucci, 2001). Consequently, researchers have begun to look at the development of children's reasoning in the two separate domains. They have found that, while the bases for reasoning are different in the two domains, in both cases there is development from more concrete to more abstract reasoning.

In the moral domain, research indicates that young children's judgments are based on concepts of harm or welfare, whereas the judgments of older children and adolescents make use of the more abstract concepts of justice and rights. Children of all ages, however, are unlikely to judge moral transgressions, such as hitting or stealing, according to rules, the dictates of authority, or common practices. Hitting, for example, is wrong even if there is no rule against it, even if the school principal says it is okay, and even if hitting is a common behavior in a particular context.

In contrast to judgments in the moral domain, reasoning about social conventions takes into account rules, authority, and custom. However, whereas young children's reasoning about social conventions tends to emphasize social rules, that of older children tends to emphasize more abstract concepts such as social roles and the social order. For example, a young child might argue that it is wrong to call a teacher by her first name because there is a rule against it, but an older child might express concern that the students would begin to treat the teacher as a peer rather than as someone in authority (Turiel, 1983). Over the course of middle childhood, children become increasingly concerned with social group roles and effective group functioning (Killen & Stangor, 2001). As you will discover later in this chapter, age-related changes in reasoning in the social conventional domain influence children's interpretations of peer rejection and social exclusion.

A current controversy among the developmental psychologists who study moral reasoning concerns cultural variations in distinguishing between the moral and social conventional domains. Using culturally appropriate versions of Turiel's stories, researchers have replicated his basic findings in a wide variety of societies (summarized in Turiel, 1998). Other researchers, using slightly different methods to elicit judgments, have concluded that certain issues North Americans tend to see as matters of social convention may in some other cultures tend to be considered moral issues (Shweder et al., 2006). We will discuss the question of cross-cultural variation again in Chapter 14, because most of the relevant data have been collected from adolescents and adults.

Moral Reasoning and Theories of Mind

Yet another way to look at moral reasoning is to ask how it relates to other areas of development. You learned in Chapter x that around 4 to 5 years of age, children develop a *theory of mind*, that is, the ability to think about other people's mental states. Indeed, when judges and juries deliberate a criminal case, a lot of time is devoted to understanding the mental state of the accused: Did he or she intend to commit the crime? Was it premeditated? What was the motive? Research indicates that the way that children judge someone's moral behavior may depend on their ability to understand the person's mental state. Bryan Sokol and Michael Chandler (2004) have explored this in a series of studies that involve a *Punch and Judy* puppet theater. *Punch and Judy* is a famous slapstick puppet show that can be found at carnivals, beaches, amusement parks, and other places frequented by children. If you have ever seen it, you probably remember that Punch and Judy are comically and literally at each other's throats, each trying unsuccessfully to "off" the other.

Two of the scenarios devised for Sokol and Chandler's studies unfolded as follows:

> *Scenario 1:* Punch and Judy are on stage with two large boxes. One is orange. The other is some other, non-orange color, and Punch and Judy are busily filling it with oranges. At some point Punch is made to leave the stage briefly. In his absence Judy trips and falls into the box containing the oranges. "Help!" she cries, "I have fallen into the orange box!" Punch rushes on stage and, seeing this as his golden opportunity to be rid of Judy forever, pushes the orange colored box—the empty one— off the edge of the stage.

> *Scenario 2:* Punch and Judy are again on stage with boxes. One is green. The other is white with a large, green number "1" painted on it. Again Punch leaves briefly, and again, in his absence, Judy accidentally falls into one of the boxes—the green-colored box. Shouting for help, she cries, "Check the green one!" This time Punch really and truly tries to rescue Judy. However, misinterpreting her cry to mean that she is in the box with the green "1", he inadvertently pushes the green box— the one that Judy fell into—off the edge in a frenzied effort to reach her in the other box.

When children were asked to rate the "badness" of Punch's behavior in the two scenes, the youngest commonly claim that he behaves more badly in scenario 2 because it ends with Judy jettisoned off stage. The children maintain what Sokol

Punch and Judy, a famous slapstick puppet show in which the characters are continually trying to kill each other, provides a context for studying the relationship between developing theories of mind, and how children reason about moral issues.

Courtesy of Dr. Michael J. Chandler

and Chandler describe as an **objective view of responsibility,** in that they assess responsibility based on objective consequences alone. Older children and adults, in contrast, demonstrate a **subjective view of responsibility** in that they consider Punch's intentions. They therefore rate the failed attempted murder of scenario 1 much more negatively than the accidental manslaughter of scenario 2.

Thus, with increasing age, children become more competent at interpreting a person's objective behavior in light of his or her subjective mental state. In suggesting that moral deliberations are tied importantly to children's developing theories of mind, Sokol and Chandler offer an alternative explanation for the shift, documented by Piaget and Kohlberg, from children's reliance on external consequences to internal motives.

||||||| APPLY ▪ CONNECT ▪ DISCUSS ─

Academic integrity is a "hot button" issue on many high school and college campuses. Review your school's definition of academic integrity.

- To what extent does it emphasize academic integrity as a moral issue as compared to a social conventional issue?
- Do you think middle school children are more or less likely to view cheating as a moral or social conventional issue? Why?
- Drawing on the theoretical insights of Piaget and Kohlberg, describe how middle schools might encourage the development of academic integrity in their students.

Peer Relationships

Once children begin to spend significant amounts of time among their peers, they must learn to create a satisfying place for themselves within the social group. Their greater appreciation of social rules and their increased ability to consider other people's points of view are essential resources for this developmental task. But no matter how sensitive or sophisticated they may be about social relations, there is no guarantee that they will be accepted by other children. In creating a life for themselves among peers, all children must learn to compete for social status, come to terms with the possibility that they may not be liked, and deal with the conflicts that inevitably arise.

Peer Relations and Social Status

Whenever a group of children exists over a period of time, a social structure emerges. **Social structures** are complex organizations of relationships between individuals. Developmentalists describe children's social structures in a couple of ways, one of which focuses on degree of *dominance* (who does and does not hold power over others), the other of which focuses on degree of *popularity* (who is liked or disliked).

Dominance As is true for many other species, dominance hierarchies contribute to the functioning of human social groups, including those of children (see Chapter 9, pp. 327–328). Dominance hierarchies are usually established through a repeated pattern of fighting or arguing and then making up (Pellegrini, 2006). Over time, individuals who are skilled at managing the conflict–reconciliation pattern establish dominance within the group (Hawley, Little, & Card, 2007). **Dominant children** are those who control "resources"—toys, play spaces, the determination of group activities, and so forth.

Although dominance hierarchies are evident even in preschool social groups (Pelligrini et al., 2007), there are critical moments in development when children work hard to negotiate their positions with each other. One such moment is the transition between elementary and middle school, when new social groupings are being formed. In a longitudinal study that followed more than 100 students from fifth through seventh grades, Andrew Pellegrini and Jeffrey Long (2002) found that, while bullying is used by elementary and middle school children to influence the dominance hierarchy, its incidence peaks during the sixth grade, the first year of middle school, when children are working to establish dominance in new social groups, and then diminishes significantly during the seventh grade, once the dominance patterns have been fully formed (see the box "Bullies and Their Victims").

objective view of responsibility An understanding that responsibility depends on objective consequences alone.

subjective view of responsibility An understanding that responsibility depends on both intentions and consequences.

social structures Complex organizations of relationships between individuals.

dominant children In reference to social hierarchies, those children who control "resources" such as toys, play spaces, and decisions about group activities.

Bullies and Their Victims

N APRIL OF 1999, TWO TEEN-agers with automatic weapons entered their high school, massacred 15 individuals, and then killed themselves. It was widely speculated that they were social outcasts and may have been teased and taunted by their peers. The tragedy at Columbine turned a national spotlight on school violence. There has since been a flood of research directed toward identifying different forms of aggression, the factors that contribute to schoolchildren's aggressive behaviors, and the social and emotional consequences of being either the agent or the victim of violent acts.

Bullies and their victims have received a great deal of attention from developmentalists (Pellegrini & Long, 2002). Bullies engage in unprovoked aggression intended to harm, intimidate, and/or dominate. Their attacks can be physical—pushing and hitting, for example—or verbal, as in teasing and name-calling. Children's access to communication technologies—cell phones and e-mail, in particular—creates a whole new world for bullies who can now intimidate through text messages, anytime, anywhere. Because bullying is instrumental, that is, a means of controlling other people and getting one's way, developmentalists consider it a form of *proactive aggression*. Proactive aggression is distinguished from *reactive aggression*, which is usually impulsive and displayed in response to a per-

Anna Hassan, a teacher at a large, inner-city school in London, England, deals with a playground bullying incident. Because children in England do not change schools during middle childhood, they do not experience the sixth-grade bullying peak observed in countries that transition children from elementary to middle schools.

ceived threat or provocation (Polman et al., 2007). Research on aggression in middle childhood finds that proactive aggression may even be valued in some peer groups, and a basis for friendship and group formation among middle school boys (Poulin & Boivin, 2000). In the same vein, some researchers argue that bullies often have quite well-developed social skills (Crick & Dodge, 1999; Sutton et al., 1999), and are sometimes among

the boys considered to be most popular by their 11- to 12-year-old classmates (Rodkin et al., 2000).

A nationwide survey of school children conducted by the U.S. Department of Justice (2000/2000) yielded several findings (see figure). As you can see, boys are somewhat more inclined than girls to report bullying; bullying is reported more often by children from rural communities than by those from urban or suburban communities; and reports of bullying are highest among sixth-graders (the youngest group sampled for this study), and then drop off dramatically between seventh and eighth grade. This last finding is consistent with the results of longitudinal studies showing that bullying reaches a peak during the transition between the elementary and middle school years, perhaps due to children's need to establish dominance in their new peer groups (Pellegrini & Long, 2002). Interestingly, in Ireland and England, where children do not change schools at this age, bullying simply declines without interruption (Smith et al., 1999).

Bullies often target the same children in their attacks. In middle childhood, victims of chronic bullying are known by other children as the kids most often teased, bullied, and "picked on" (Goodman et al., 2001). *Peer victimization* is the term used by developmentalists to describe the experiences of children who are chronically harassed, teased, and bullied at

Our usual stereotype about bullies and dominance hierarchies is that they belong to the world of boys. However, recent research calls this bias into question. Whereas boys may tend to engage in direct, physical aggression such as hitting, kicking, and pushing, girls often practice *relational aggression,* actions that threaten the relationships and social standing of their peers (Simmons, 2002). Common forms of relational aggression include making mean and derogatory comments, spreading rumors, or gossiping in ways intended to tarnish a peer's reputation (Crick, Ostrov, & Kawabata, 2007). Nicki Crick and her colleagues found that relational aggression, like more familiar forms of bullying, peaks during the sixth and seventh grades. It also seems to be used as a way of raising one's status within the peer system. Thus, girls who are particularly well-practiced in the art of relational aggression tend to be among the most popular. They have been called *alpha girls* in tribute to their position at the top of the dominance hierarchy. Crick and her colleagues suggest that relational aggression can be at least as damaging as more direct forms of aggression, and should be taken just as seriously (Murray-Close, Ostrov, & Crick, 2007).

school. Studies indicate that boys are more often victimized than girls, probably because they tend to hang out with other boys, and boys are more likely to bully. And while bullies engage in proactive aggression, their victims are most likely to engage in reactive aggression (Boivin, Vitaro, & Poulin, 2005; Poulin & Boivin, 2000). Victimized children experience a variety of social difficulties in addition to the mistreatment they receive directly from their peers: in general, they lose their tempers easily, have difficulty regulating their attention, and act in an immature and dependent way (Craig, 1998; Finnegan, Hodges, & Perry, 1998; Schwartz et al., 1998). Peer victimization decreases from the middle school years through adolescence, in part because bullying decreases, but also because children learn to ignore, avoid, and/or retaliate against their aggressors (Pellegrini & Long, 2003; Smith & Marks, 2008).

The longitudinal research on bullies and victims has important implications for the timing and the content of prevention and intervention efforts. It would seem that the early elementary school years are a ripe time to introduce prevention measures that help children to recognize and respond to bullying behaviors. However, intervention efforts may be most effective if applied during that part of middle childhood when children experience the major social transition from primary to secondary schools (Goodman et al., 2001). With the understanding that a major function of bullying is to establish status and relationships in the peer group, some researchers have suggested that schools devise ways to help children foster more varied and closer peer relationships as they move from the socially more intimate context of elementary school to the larger, hard-to-navigate social scene of secondary school.

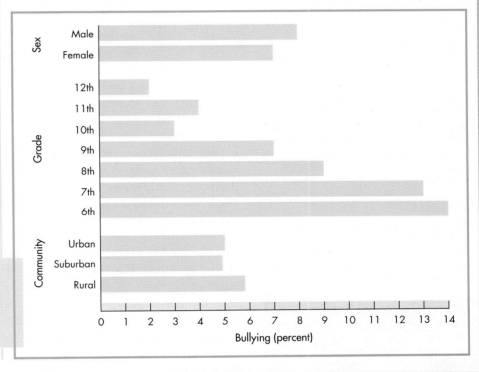

Bullying decreases dramatically between sixth and twelfth grades, as indicated by the percentages of students who reported being bullied at school in the previous 6 months.

Popularity Beyond their relative position in a dominance hierarchy, children acquire social status as a consequence of how well they are liked by their peers. Who are the popular children? Who are the outcast or excluded children? Researchers who study the relative social status of group members usually begin in one of two ways. Using a *nomination procedure*, they may ask children to name their friends or to name children who they would like to sit near, play with, or work with. Using a *rating procedure*, they may ask children to rank every child in the group according to a specific criterion, such as popularity, or desirability as a friend or as a teammate in sports. Data obtained through these techniques can then be used to construct *sociograms*, graphic representations of each child's relationship to all others in the group (Figure 13.1).

As you can imagine, there has been an enormous amount of research on children's social status and its implications for development. What follows is a summary of that work, grouped according to the four main *popularity statuses* that have been identified (Asher & Coie, 1990; Ladd, 1999; Rubin et al., 2006a).

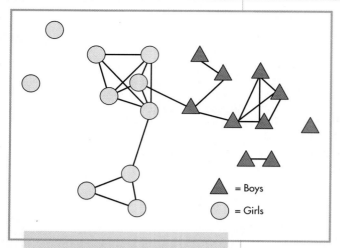

Figure 13.1 A sociogram of the relationships among a group of fifth-grade boys and girls. Notice that the one boy who has a friendship with a girl has a friendship with two other boys but is not part of a group of boys, whereas the girl in this friendship is part of a group of girls. Two girls and one boy are social isolates. (Adapted from Gronlund, 1959.)

▲ = Boys

○ = Girls

Peer rejection is not only emotionally painful, but associated with a number of difficulties that can extend well into the future, including delinquency, substance abuse, and psychological disturbances.

Popular children. *Popular children* are those who receive the highest numbers of positive nominations, or highest rankings, from their peers. In general, popular children tend to be rated as more physically attractive (Boyatzis et al., 1998; Langlois, 1986), and seem more skilled at initiating and maintaining positive relationships. Kenneth Rubin and his colleagues comment that when popular children attempt to enter a group, "it is as if they ask themselves, 'What's going on?' and then, 'How can I fit in?'" They are also good at compromising and negotiating. Overall, their behavior appears to be socially competent (Rubin et al., 2006a).

Rejected children. *Rejected children* are those who receive few positive nominations, or receive low rankings, from their peers. They are actively disliked. Studies conducted in the United States, the Netherlands, and Korea find that some children are rejected because they are shy and withdrawn (Parke et al., 1997; Shin, 2007). These children are often aware of their social failure, an awareness that makes them lonelier and more distressed about their social relationships (Asher, Rose, & Gabriel, 2001, Crick & Ladd, 1993). The most common reason for rejection, however, is aggressive behavior; children quite naturally do not like to be around others who behave unpleasantly or hurt them (Dodge et al., 2003). Aggressive rejected children overestimate their social skills and competence and underestimate how much their peers dislike them (Bellmore & Cillessen, 2006; Hymel et al., 2002). They are also more likely to misinterpret an accidental injury from another as deliberate, which may contribute to a desire to retaliate.

Once children are rejected, they may acquire a reputation as being someone that no one likes and have a difficult time gaining acceptance by their peer group even if their behavior changes. Shelley Hymel and her colleagues found that when negative opinions about a child become general in a group, the child's reputation ("He is always hitting"; "She never gives anyone else a turn") can become self-perpetuating (Hymel et al., 1990). These researchers described a number of cases in which a peer group's expectations caused the members to interpret a child's behavior as aggressive or unfriendly even when, by objective standards, it was not. Such biased interpretations make the rejected child's task of winning acceptance more difficult and may even evoke the very behaviors (grabbing, hitting, tattling, or crying) that led to the child's being rejected in the first place.

Rejected children experience difficulties that extend beyond the classroom into everyday life. They show higher levels of delinquency, substance abuse, and psychological disturbances compared to children who are accepted by their peers. Not surprisingly, they are almost twice as likely to be arrested as juvenile delinquents (Kupersmidt et al., 2004).

Neglected Children. *Neglected children* are those who receive few nominations of any kind. These children seem to be ignored by their peers rather than disliked. Neglected children, like rejected children, are less sociable than their peers, but they are neither aggressive nor overly shy and appear less concerned about their social status. A study conducted in Holland found that neglected children are more likely than rejected children to improve their social status among their classmates over the course of the school year (Cillessen et al., 1992). Neglected children also perform better academically than rejected children, are more compliant in school, and are better liked by their teachers (Wentzel & Asher, 1995).

Controversial Children. *Controversial children,* as the label suggests, are those who receive both positive and negative nominations. Controversial children tend to behave even more aggressively than rejected children. However, they compensate for their aggression by joking about it or by using other social and cognitive skills to keep their social partners from becoming angry enough to break off the relationship (Newcomb, Bukowski, & Pattee, 1993). Children who engage in high levels of relational aggression often generate a mixture of liking and dislike in their peers (Cillessen & Mayeux, 2004; Rose, Swenson, & Carlson, 2004). Like neglected children, controversial children tend not to be particularly distressed by their relative lack of social success. The reason may be that such children are usually liked by at least one other child—these relationships may be sufficient to prevent loneliness. As we discuss below, chronically friendless children are at risk for a variety of psychosocial problems (Ladd & Troop-Gordon, 2003).

Competition and Cooperation among Peers

Spending significant time with one's peers creates conditions for both competition and cooperation, facets of social life that bear importantly on our relationships with others. As you will see below, the extent to which children are competitive or cooperative in their interactions, and the effects of such interactions on peer relationships, depend on both the contexts and cultures in which they occur.

The Role of Context A classic series of studies by Muzafer and Carolyn Sherif (1956) provides the best evidence to date about the role of context in fostering cooperation and competition in children's social groups. In the most famous of these studies, 11-year-old boys from similar backgrounds but all strangers to one another, were divided into two groups and brought to two separate summer camps in Robbers Cave State Park in Oklahoma. To ensure that the boys at each encampment formed a cohesive group, the adults arranged for them to encounter problems they could solve only by cooperating. They provided the ingredients for each day's dinner, for example, but left it to the boys themselves to prepare and apportion the food. By the end of the week, friendships had formed and leaders had emerged within each group. Each group had adopted a name: the *Rattlers* and the *Eagles*.

When it was clear that both groups had formed a stable pattern of interactions, the adults let each group know about the other. The two groups soon expressed a keen desire to compete against each other, and the adults arranged for a tournament between the two, with prizes for the winners. On the first day of competition, the Eagles lost a tug-of-war with the Rattlers. Stung by their defeat, they burned the Rattlers' flag. In retaliation, the Rattlers seized the Eagles' flag. Scuffling and name-calling ensued. After 5 days in which hostility escalated, the experimenters took steps to reverse it by introducing a series of problems requiring cooperation between the groups. For example, they arranged for the food delivery truck to get stuck in mud (imagine kids at summer camp without food!). When efforts to push the truck failed, the boys came up with the idea of using their tug-of-war rope to pull the truck out, resulting in what the Sherifs (1956) described as "jubilation over the common success" (p. 323). After the two groups had banded together to solve several other problems requiring cooperation, the boys' opinions of each other changed significantly. Mutual respect largely replaced hostility, and several of the boys formed intergroup friendships.

As developmentalists interested in peer group relations, the Sherifs intentionally manipulated the contexts of children's interactions in ways that encouraged competitive or cooperative behavior. But as a moment's reflection will no doubt reveal, such context manipulations by adults are far from unusual in children's lives. Take your own educational experiences as an example. If you attended school in a Western culture, it is likely that you experienced educational practices that foster interpersonal comparisons and competition in which children who show themselves better than their peers are publicly praised and rewarded; their papers and tests are showcased on classroom bulletin boards, they make honor roll, and their parents display car bumper stickers proclaiming their academic excellence. Recently, however, in a deliberate effort to bolster cooperation over competition, some schools have manipulated the contexts of children's learning through *cooperative learning programs*. These programs are meant to foster children's appreciation for their peers' successes as well as their own. In a review of research on cooperative learning, Barry Schneider (2000) found evidence that when children care about each other's learning, they do better in school, engage in more prosocial behavior, and show improved relations with teachers and peers. It has been suggested that cooperative learning is particularly beneficial in classrooms where students have diverse cultural origins or ability levels (Klinger et al., 1998).

The Sherifs' classic experiment and the research on cooperative learning environments carry an important lesson. Cooperation and competition are not fixed characteristics of individuals or of groups, but are heavily influenced by the context in which they occur. The research also carries an important but controversial message, namely, that competition is detrimental to peer group relationships, whereas cooperation nurtures relationships and children's sense of belonging. This message has been called into question, however, by research documenting cultural differences in the extent to which competition is valued and rewarded (Schneider et al., 2006).

The Role of Culture Most studies of cultural differences in children's tendencies to behave competitively or cooperatively with peers involve bringing children together to play games that have been specifically designed to distinguish between children's use of competitive or cooperative game strategies. Playing such games, children can, for example, play competitively, maximizing their own "wins" at other children's expense and even choosing to suffer personal losses as long as the other does not win. Alternatively, children can play cooperatively, suffering some personal losses but distributing "wins" more equally across players.

Using such experimentally designed games, researchers find that North American children tend to adopt competitive strategies, whereas children from Asia, Latin America, and other cultures that emphasize interdependence, and the well-

Kairibi Dede, who plays for the Auburn, Alabama, football team, is leading Spirit Day at Ogletree Elementary School, and emphasizing the importance of getting a good education. When children take pride in their peers' educational successes, as well as their own, they do better in school and engage in more prosocial behavior with peers and teachers.

AP Photo/Todd J. Van Ernst

being of the group over individual success, tend to adopt cooperative strategies (Kagan & Madsen, 1971; Shapira & Madsen, 1969; Domino, 1992).

At present there is no overarching explanation for what cultural factors in particular foster cooperation over competition. One leading possibility is that societies that value interdependence over independence also foster collaboration over competition (Kagitçibasi, 2003). However, a recent study of more than 1000 preadolescent seventh-graders in Canada, Costa Rica, Cuba, and Spain suggests a more complicated picture. In their study, Barry Schneider and his colleagues reasoned that a cultural emphasis on interdependence or independence would tend to be reflected at the individual level in children's *basic social goals,* and that these goals would influence the extent to which children were inclined to be competitive in peer interactions. The researchers divided goals into three types, using a questionnaire to assess how strong these each were for the children in the study:

1. *Ego-oriented goals:* ("I feel really successful when I can do better than my friends.")

2. *Task-oriented goals:* ("I feel really successful when I keep practicing hard.")

3. *Cooperation goals:* ("I feel really successful when my friends and I help each other do our best.")

The researchers also distinguished between two forms of competition, which they assessed through a second questionnaire:

1. *Hypercompetitiveness*—the desire to win at any cost as a means of maintaining feelings of self-worth, often with manifestations of aggressiveness: ("[Friend's name] and I often compare our school marks to see who did better, and he [she] gets upset if I do better in our tests or assignments.")

2. *Nonhostile social comparison*—friendly competition with little emotional investment in who wins: ("[Friend's name] and I often play sports or games against each other; we see who's better, but we don't really care who wins.")

As shown in Figure 13.2, there was much more hypercompetitiveness in the friendships of Spanish and Canadian children compared to the Costa Rican and Cuban children. The researchers also found significant gender differences, with boys of all cultures scoring significantly higher than girls in hypercompetitiveness. On the other hand, there were no cultural differences in nonhostile social comparison. As expected, competitive behavior correlated strongly with children's social goals. Across all four cultures, children with high ego orientation also tended to be more hypercompetitive and less cooperative. Importantly, the researchers found significant cultural differences in effects of hypercompetition on children's relationships (Schneider et al., 2006). In particular, friendly competition seemed to enhance the closeness of Latin American boys, whereas hypercompetition correlated with friendship termination in Canadian girls, as well as all Latin American children. In the case of Canadian boys, a moderate amount of hypercompetition was associated with closer relationships, although higher levels threatened friendship bonds.

Figure 13.2 Hypercompetitiveness, that is, the desire to win at any cost, is significantly more common in the friendships of Canadian and Spanish children, compared to Costa Rican and Cuban children. In contrast, nonhostile comparison, that is, friendly competition, is not significantly different across the four cultures.

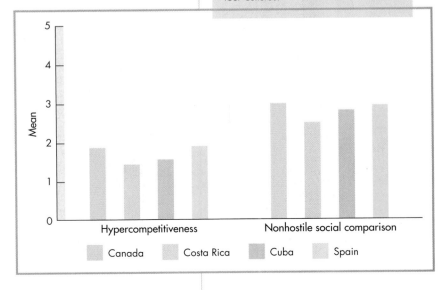

In short, this research suggests that certain kinds of competition among children are common across cultures and are not detrimental to peer relationships and that even hypercompetitiveness may not necessarily be detrimental, depending in part on the culture in which it occurs.

Clearly, the types of competitive and cooperative activities that children engage in affect the organization of their social groups and relationships. Often times, such activities are influenced by cultural values and practices, or by adults who want to manipulate children's social experiences. However, children's social relationships are also affected by factors that extend well beyond cooperation and competition. For example, children are known to sort into groups based on ethnicity, socio-economic status, and as you will see below, gender.

Relations between Boys and Girls

During middle childhood, children of all cultures spend a great deal of time in sexually segregated groups (Pellegrini & Long, 2003). Studies in the United States have found that when children are 6 years of age, roughly 68 percent choose a child of the same sex as a "best friend"; by the time children are 12, the figure has grown to about 90 percent (Graham et al., 1998), prompting Eleanor Maccoby to propose that there are "two cultures of childhood" (Maccoby, 1998, p. 32). As shown in Figure 13.3, similar age differences have been found in non-Western cultures as well.

According to Maccoby, the tendency to aggregate with peers of the same sex strengthens throughout middle childhood because of gender differences in activity preferences. In particular, the *male-style play* preferred by boys includes high levels of physical activity, such as horseplay and play fighting, whereas the *female-style play* preferred by girls includes more nurturing, prosocial play. Over the course of middle childhood, as boys play increasingly with other boys, and girls with other girls, they amplify each other's gender-typed behavior, further socializing gender-typed activity preferences. Maccoby points out, however, that these two styles of play can be moderated depending on the extent of gender differentiation in the culture. That is, gender-typed play styles may be more subtle in children growing up in cultures that make few distinctions between males and females in terms of work, activities, and status, but more evident in children in cultures that draw strict lines around male and female behavior (see the box "In the Field: Gender Politics on the Playground").

Although middle childhood is a time when children increasingly seek out same-sex companions, the boundaries between boys and girls are far from impermeable. Boys and girls do interact with each other, sometimes in very amusing ways. Calling a boy on the telephone and leaving a pseudoromantic message on the family answering machine is one favorite border-crossing technique. Interactions with, or even proximity to, a member of the other sex can result in elaborate shows of having been contaminated and needing to engage in "cleansing rituals" to get rid of the "girl cooties" or the "boy germs." Alan Sroufe and his colleagues (1993) report that a boy

Figure 13.3 In many cultures throughout the world, the tendency to aggregate with peers of the same sex increases during middle childhood, perhaps because boys and girls develop different preferences for styles of play.

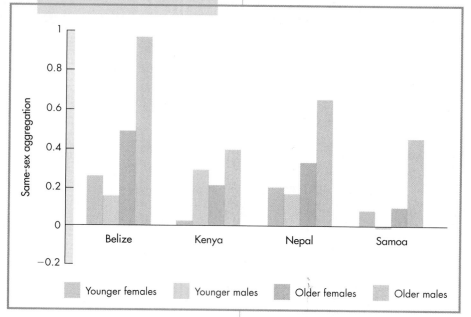

table **13.2**	
Knowing the Rules: In What Circumstances Is It Permissible to Have Contact with the Other Gender in Middle Childhood?	
Rule:	The contact is accidental.
Example:	You're not looking where you are going and you bump into someone.
Rule:	The contact is incidental.
Example:	You go to get some lemonade and wait while two children of the other gender get some. (There should be no conversation.)
Rule:	The contact is in the guise of some clear and necessary purpose.
Example:	You may say, "Pass the lemonade," to persons of the other gender at the next table. No interest in them is expressed.
Rule:	An adult compels you to have contact.
Example:	"Go get that map from X and Y and bring it to me."
Rule:	You are accompanied by someone of your own gender.
Example:	Two girls may talk to two boys, though physical closeness with your own partner must be maintained and intimacy with the others is disallowed.
Rule:	The interaction or contact is accompanied by disavowal.
Example:	You say someone is ugly or hurl some other insult or (more commonly for boys) push or throw something at the person as you pass by.

Source: Sroufe et al., 1993.

at a day camp was seen leaving the girls' tent (where he had gone to retrieve his radio) and was bombarded with taunts from his peers like "Uuh, he's with the girls!" and "Did you kiss anyone, Charlie?" He had to chase and hit each taunter in turn to reestablish his place in the group.

From their own and others' observations of children in a variety of contexts in this same day camp, Sroufe and his coworkers abstracted a number of rules under which school-age children find it permissible to have contact with members of the other sex (Table 13.2). The researchers found that most children observed the rules for cross-sex contact; those who did not were generally unpopular with the other children, and also judged by their counselors to be less socially competent than their peers. On occasion, the rules could be broken with social approval, with the rule breaking usually taking the form of "raids" into enemy territory, accompanied by a lot of excitement. From time to time, for example, the boys would run through an area where the girls were playing and try to get the girls to chase them, or a couple of girls, shrieking with laughter, would threaten to kiss a boy.

During middle childhood, children of all cultures begin to spend a great deal of time in sexually segregated groups.

Ellen Senisi/The Image Works

the field ▎ Gender Politics on the Playground

Name:	Marjorie Goodwin
Education:	B.A. in Spanish (junior year in Spain), Lake Erie College; Ph.D. in anthropology, University of Pennsylvania
Current Position:	Professor of Anthropology, University of California, Los Angeles
Career Objectives:	Study the culture and development of girls in the contexts of their relationships with each other, and their position in society

Marjorie Goodwin, who teaches anthropology at the University of California, Los Angeles, and does research on language, gender, and children's social organization, is taking notes during lunchtime at an elementary school in Southern California. The children are gulping down their food in order to rush off to play. They understand that whichever group is first to occupy a particular area—the soccer field, the jungle gym, the basketball courts—is the group allowed to use the space. But the competition for space isn't overwhelming; this is no free-for-all. Although girls might argue over who gets the hopscotch area first, and boys might quarrel over the basketball court, there are traditions about which groups gain access to different play areas. Research on children's play (Thorne, 1993), as well as our personal memories of our elementary school days, indicate that boys and girls occupy different territories on elementary school playgrounds. Boys control large spaces intended for team sports. They occupy the grassy soccer fields, baseball diamonds, and basketball courts. In contrast, the space controlled by girls is only one-tenth of that controlled by boys, and tends to be cemented and closer to the school building.

But as Goodwin is about to discover, today is different. A group of fifth-grade girls who like to play soccer is beginning to challenge the idea that the playing fields are an exclusively male space (Goodwin, 2002). Today these girls have rushed through lunch in order to beat the boys to the soccer field. Once they have secured the space, they begin to organize their teams. Soon, however, two boys arrive, demanding their right to the field.

Amy: We have it today.
Paulo: We play soccer every day, okay?
Mark: It's more boys than girls.
Amy: So? Your point?
Mark: This is our field.
Amy: It's not your field. Did you pay for it? No. Your name is not written on this land.
Kathy: Mine is. K-A-T-H-Y [as she writes her name].

The boys move away, but return moments later with the male playground aide who confronts the girls:

Male aide: Girls. Go somewhere else! The boys are coming to play and you took over their field. I think I'm gonna go and tell the vice principal. . . . When the boys are coming out here to play soccer, okay? You have no right to kick them off the field. Listen, I've seen it happen more than once. . . . You can go over there and play soccer [pointing to the jungle gym area]. You girls can go anywhere to do what you're doing.
Laura: Why can't they go anywhere.
Male aide: They can't go on the blacktop and play soccer. Somebody's gonna fall and hurt their knee.
Kathy: Well neither can we!

In her analysis of the dispute presented above, Goodwin argued that in negotiating access to the territory the girls resisted and challenged not only the arguments of the boys ("Your name is not written on this land") and those of the male aide ("Why can't they go

Friendship: A Special Type of Relationship

Harry Stack Sullivan (1953), an American psychiatrist, proposed that the formation of close, one-on-one relationships, which he called *chumships,* is key to the development of social skills and competencies during middle childhood. In Sullivan's words:

If you will look very closely at one of your children when he finally finds a chum . . . you will discover something very different in the relationship—namely, that your child begins to develop a new sensitivity to what matters to another person. And this is not in the sense of "what should I do to get what I want," but instead "what should I do to contribute to the happiness or to support the prestige and feeling of worth-whileness of my chum." So far as I have been ever able to discover, nothing remotely like this appears before the age of, say, 8½, and sometimes it appears decidedly later. (pp. 245–246)

Marjorie Goodwin

Courtesy of Marjorie Goodman

anywhere"), but the very social structure of the playground. Historically the field had indeed belonged to boys. In all probability, this had been the case for generations of children attending the school.

True to his word, the aide summoned the vice principal, who, after hearing from all parties, formulated the problem in terms of exclusion, asking, "At school do we exclude anyone?" The girls responded with a long list of exclusionary practices typical of the boys' behavior: "they hog the ball"; "boys are always team captains"; "they always pick boys first and then girls last." Apparently taking the girls' complaints to heart, the following year the school administrators instituted a rotating system for using the fields that allowed boys and girls equal access. Yet, despite the changes, "boys continued to favor passing the ball to other boys; when they did pass to girls they did it with such force that girls often stopped playing. In addition, during the sixth grade girls had to contend with boys grabbing their breasts in the midst of the game." The playground aides responsible for supervising the children's activities often looked on such behavior as part of a natural order. One even suggested that it prepared girls for their "appropriate" and "eventual" adult sex roles as sports spectators rather than participants.

Traditions by definition resist change. However, Goodwin's research indicates that some girls on some playgrounds are staging microrevolutions, challenging the status quo, and working to define

a new moral order on their own terms. In addition to inviting us to think about the sources of social and political transformation, Goodwin's research is provocative in another sense. In particular, it challenges current thinking that girls, compared with boys, are less concerned about matters of justice and fairness, and instead tend to be more cooperative and focused on preserving harmony and cohesion (Gilligan, 1982; Maccoby, 1998; see Chapter 14). Goodwin argues that a narrow view of girls and women as nurturing and noncompetitive prevents us all—developmental scientists included—from seeing and studying girls and women as wielders of power and instruments of change. In contrast, a broader view permits an understanding that "we can not only obtain a better picture of children's worlds but also attempt to implement equity policies which promote children's fundamental democratic rights to be spared oppression and humiliation in school" (Goodwin, 2006).

Photofusion Picture Library/Alamy

At many schools, including this one in the United Kingdom, girls tend to play on small, paved places close to the school building, whereas boys tend to occupy large fields.

Sullivan believed that children's tendency to pick out one or a few other children with whom they feel this kind of special affinity is the childhood precursor of the need for interpersonal intimacy that will be called love when it is encountered again in adolescence. He further claimed that the failure to form such friendships in childhood creates a social deficit that is difficult to remedy later.

Sullivan's general view of the importance of friendships is widely shared by developmentalists who find that children with best friends score higher on measures of self-esteem and positive feelings of self-worth, whereas children with no friends tend to be timid, overly sensitive, and at risk for later psychological problems (Rubin et al., 2006; Ladd & Troop-Gordon, 2003). Expanding on Sullivan's early work, researchers have identified several developmental functions of friendships (Hartup, 1992; Parker et al., 2006). These functions include providing children with

1. contexts in which to develop many basic social skills, including communication, cooperation, and the ability to resolve conflicts;

2. information about themselves, others, and the world;

3. companionship and fun that relieve the stress of everyday life; and

4. models of intimate relationships characterized by helping, caring, and trust.

Given the importance of friendships for children's feelings of well-being and social success, developmentalists are naturally interested in understanding the processes through which children form and maintain close relationships with their peers.

Making Friends The old saying that "birds of a feather flock together" applies especially well to children's friendship choices. Children tend to pick friends who are similar to themselves in age, ethnicity, sex, SES, and general skill level in various activities. Friends are also likely to feel the same way about school (a child who likes school and gets good grades is likely to have a friend who also likes school and gets good grades) and to like the same sports, music, movies, books, and so on (Rose & Asher, 2000). But other than noticing that certain peers are similar to themselves in appearance and background, and have compatible interests, how, exactly, do children become close friends?

In a classic study of friendship formation, John Gottman (1983) arranged for pairs of children of the same age to meet and play together in one of the children's homes for three sessions within the space of a month. Each session was videotaped. The children, who were strangers to each other at the start of the study, ranged from 3 to 9 years in age. In order to find out if the children became friends during the experiment, Gottman asked the host mothers to fill out a questionnaire at the end of the sessions that probed the strength and quality of the children's relationship. He then analyzed the tapes of the play sessions, comparing children who became friends with those who did not. Five aspects of the children's social interaction appeared to distinguish pairs who became friendly from those who did not:

Children tend to pick friends who are similar to themselves in sex, age, race, and general skill level.

© Ron Fehling/Masterfile

1. *Common-ground activity.* The children who became friends were those who quickly found something they could do together. In addition, they explored their similarities and differences.

2. *Clear communication.* Children who became friends were likely to listen to each other, request clarification when they did not understand, and speak in ways that were relevant to the task at hand.

3. *Exchange of information.* Children who became friends both asked their partners for relevant information and provided such information to them.

4. *Resolution of conflicts.* Children who became friends gave good reasons when they disagreed, and they were able to bring conflicts to a quick resolution.

5. *Reciprocity.* Children who became friends were likely to respond to their partner's positive behaviors with an appropriate positive contribution of their own.

Gottman's study sheds considerable light on how children become friends. Other developmentalists, in contrast, have focused on how children maintain their friendships over time.

Keeping Friends As we discussed above, having close friends is critically important to children's development and well-being. Research indicates, however, that only about one-half of all close friendships are stable over the course of a school year (Bowker, 2004). What characteristics distinguish between friendships that endure over time and those that fall apart? And is the ability to keep friends any more or less important than the ability to make friends?

It makes sense that one's initial choice of friends would have a bearing on whether the relationship is likely to endure. Indeed, a key characteristic of a lasting relationship is the degree to which two new friends are similar to each other at the start of their friendship. Developmentalists find that similarity promotes equality in the relationship, positive reinforcement, and cooperative interactions— all factors associated with friendship stability (Poulin & Bovin, 2000). Thus, keeping friends is enhanced when children share similar behavioral characteristics, even when those characteristics are maladaptive. For example, the stability of shy, withdrawn children's friendships is as high as that of nonshy peers *if* their friends are also shy and withdrawn (Rubin et al., 2006b).

The role of behavioral similarity in friendship stability is further illuminated in a short-term longitudinal study conducted by Wendy Ellis and Lynne Zarbatany (2007), involving more than 600 children in fifth through eighth grades. Over the course of the first 3 months of a school year, the researchers collected information on the children's friendships, as well as on behavioral characteristics such as engaging in overt aggression (harming through physical or verbal actions such as hitting or threatening), engaging in relational aggression (harming by disrupting social relationships or self-esteem), and being bullied by peers. They found that behavioral similarity tended to predict friendship stability and that some of the most unstable relationships were those in which the children were behaviorally mismatched. As shown in Figure 13.4, for example, children's relationships were more stable when both friends scored either high or low on a measure of relational aggression than when friends were mismatched on this measure. The same was true when the characteristic was that of being bullied. Relationships faltered when girls who had been bullied by peers began friendships with girls who had not been bullied. The researchers speculated that girls face dire social consequences for hanging out with unpopular (bullied) peers, and may abandon their new friends at the first signs of their own social status suffering as a consequence of the friendship. In contrast, if both girls are bullied they can provide each other with much-needed comfort and support and, with little risk of further drop in social status, establish a relatively stable relationship.

Importantly, the one exception Ellis and Zarbatany found to the pattern involved children who were high in measures of overt aggression. That is, when an aggressive child became friends with another aggressive child, the relationship was no more likely to endure than when the aggressive child became friends with a nonaggressive child. Although aggressive children had no trouble making new friends, they were at a distinct disadvantage in holding on to them for any length of time (Figure 13.5).

A Cognitive-Developmental Approach
In addition to becoming skilled at making and keeping friends, during middle childhood, children develop a more sophisticated understanding of their friendships, and the unique needs, motives,

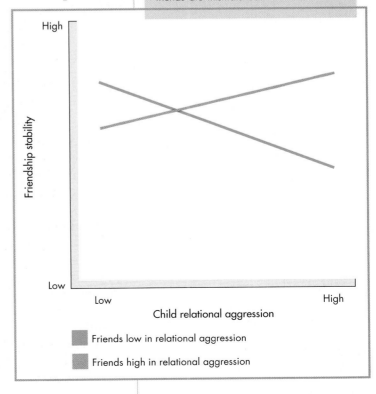

Figure 13.4 Children's relationships tend to be more stable when both friends score either high or low on a measure of relational aggression, compared to when friends are mismatched.

Friends low in relational aggression

Friends high in relational aggression

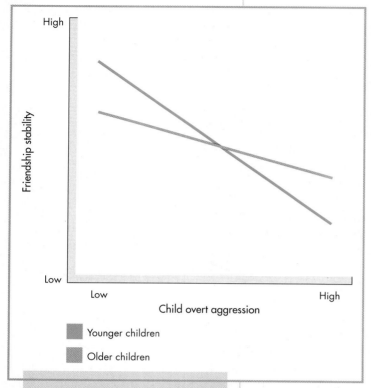

Figure 13.5 Although aggressive children are capable of making friends, they have great difficulty maintaining friendships over time.

and goals of their friends. According to Robert Selman and his colleagues, this more complex understanding, a crucial ingredient for successful relationships, arises as a consequence of the higher levels of *perspective taking* and declining *egocentrism* associated with the transition from preoperational to concrete-operational thinking (see Chapter 11, pp. 396–397). Based on extensive studies of children with and without friendship problems, Selman (1997) proposed that friendship involves three general spheres of influence, each of which is affected by the development of perspective taking: friendship understanding, friendship skills, and friendship valuing.

Friendship understanding refers to the child's developing knowledge of the nature of friendship. Selman describes children as young philosophers who have theories about how to make friends, sustain relationships, and manage conflicts. For example, an immature friendship philosophy, typical of preschoolers, is "A friend is someone who gives me toys." Somewhat more mature, and typical of the early elementary school years, is the idea that "A friend is someone who always does what you want." With increasing interpersonal understanding and decreasing egocentrism, children will eventually come to define friendships with reference to balancing and even cherishing different perspectives as a means of ensuring both personal autonomy and intimacy in relationships, as we discuss further in Chapter 15.

The second influence on friendships, *friendship skills,* refers to the specific action strategies that children use in developing their relationships. Like friendship understanding, friendship skills become increasingly sophisticated over time. The action strategies used by preschoolers are often impulsive and focused on getting immediate needs met. In a conflict over a toy, for example, there may be grabbing and crying. In just a few years, however, children develop a capacity to take turns. Later, they manage conflicts using complex strategies such as compromise, with each side agreeing to give up something in order to achieve a goal.

The final influence, *friendship valuing,* is the child's ability to make a personal commitment to a relationship and be emotionally invested and motivated to maintain it. As Selman (1997) writes, "to know friendship and practice friendship one must be involved in the process of being a good friend—one must take the risk of investing oneself in meaningful friendship experiences" (p. 44). To see the development of friendship valuing, consider a girl who breaks a play date with a close friend because a new girl invited her to go to the circus. If the girl is in the early years of middle childhood, she may defend her decision in a way that is dismissive of the relationship, saying something like "Well, I love the circus." An older child would be more likely to consider her action in light of her relationships and the needs of her friend, and reason, "Alex's feelings may be hurt if I go to the circus with Janine, so I'll invite her for a sleepover this weekend." Selman argues that friendship valuing depends on children's increasing capacity to take responsibility for their own contributions to the friendship, and to see the personal consequences of their actions for the relationship.

Overall, middle childhood is a time during which children acquire a variety of resources for managing their relationships. This is particularly apparent when friends argue and fight. Whereas younger children rely on coercion to resolve their conflicts, as children progress through middle childhood they become aware of several alternatives. In a major review of research on children's conflict resolutions,

Danielle Popp and her colleagues (2008) found that in middle childhood children are more aware of the importance of **social repair mechanisms,** strategies that allow friends to remain friends even when serious differences temporarily drive them apart. Examples of social repair mechanisms include negotiation, disengaging before a disagreement escalates into a fight, staying nearby after a fight to smooth things over, and minimizing the importance of a conflict once it is over. Each of these strategies increases the likelihood that when the conflict is over, the children will still be friends. Social repair mechanisms take on importance in middle childhood because of children's changed social circumstances. When no caregiver is present, children must settle conflicts on their own.

social repair mechanisms Strategies that allow friends to remain friends even when serious differences temporarily drive them apart.

||||| **APPLY ⊨ CONNECT ⊨ DISCUSS** –

Refer to the story of Cassie and Becca, at the beginning of the chapter. Using concepts presented in this section, explain what might have motivated Becca's and Kelly's behavior toward Cassie.

The Influence of Parents

In addition to monumental shifts in the nature and influence of peer relations and friendships, middle childhood is a time of significant change in the relationship between children and their parents. As you will see, the new patterns of interaction that emerge in the family are felt also in other social arenas, including children's peer relationships.

Changing Expectations

As children grow older, the nature of parent–child interactions changes in a number of ways. For one thing, there is an overall decrease in overt affection (Collins et al., 1997). Parents no longer act as if their children are adorable; they expect them to behave themselves and perform appropriately. The children, for their part, are often embarrassed when their parents do show them open affection in public because they do not want to be "treated like a baby." For another, children are less likely to use coercive behaviors such as whining, yelling, or hitting; now they argue with their parents and point out their parents' inconsistencies.

In addition, parents are more severe with older children and are more critical of the mistakes they make (Maccoby, 1984). Two related factors combine to account for this change in parental standards and behavior as children enter middle childhood. First, parents all over the world believe that the children should now be more capable and responsible. Second, the strategies parents adopt to influence their children's good behavior and correct their bad behavior change as children's competence increases (Lamb & Lewis, 2005).

The precise ages at which parents expect children to be able to display behavioral competence in different areas vary across cultures. Jacqueline Goodnow and her colleagues asked Japanese, American, Australian, and Lebanese-born Australian mothers at what approximate age—before 4 years, between 4 and 6 years, or after 6 years—they expected children to be capable of each of 38 kinds of behavior (Goodnow et al., 1984). They found that Japanese mothers expected their children to display emotional maturity, compliance, and ritual forms of politeness at an earlier age than mothers in the other three groups. The American and Australian mothers, in contrast, expected their children to develop social skills and the ability to assert themselves verbally at a relatively early age. Finally, the Lebanese Australian mothers were distinctive in their willingness to let the children attain

Although parent–child relationships will change dramatically during the middle childhood years, parents will continue to play an important and influential role in their children's lives and development.

Peter Cavanagh/Alamy

This girl is being taught by her grandmother to weave in the tradition of her Padaung culture of Thailand. Given children's importance to the economy of Padaung families and communities, it is likely that parents, grandparents, and other adults raise their expectations for work performance when their children reach middle childhood.

the needed competencies in their own good time; their developmental timetables were usually later than those of the other groups. Despite cultural variations in the ages at which the various competencies were expected to be achieved, all the parents expected their children to master these basic competencies sometime during middle childhood.

For children growing up in economically developed countries, school achievement is a major target of parental expectations and attention. Parents worry about how involved they should become in their child's schoolwork, what they should do if a child has academic problems, and how they should deal with school behavior problems. Other matters of concern to parents during middle childhood include the extent to which they should monitor their children's social life and whether they should require their children to do chores around the house and, if so, what standards of performance to expect of them and whether to pay them (Goodnow, 1998). In less developed countries, where a family's survival often depends on putting children to work as early as possible, parents may be more likely to worry instead about their children's ability to take care of younger kin in the absence of adult supervision and to help with important economic tasks such as caring for livestock or hoeing weeds (Weisner et al., 2005).

As children grow older and are increasingly held responsible for themselves, parents attempt to influence their behavior by reasoning with them, appealing to their self-esteem ("You wouldn't do anything that stupid") or to their sense of humor, and arousing their sense of guilt. In many societies, when school-age children break rules, their parents are less likely to spank them than to deprive them of privileges or ground them (Lamb et al., 1999).

In sum, parents increasingly share their control over their children's lives with the children themselves (Collins & van Dulmen, 2006). Maccoby (1984) terms this sharing of responsibility **coregulation.** Coregulation is built on parent–child cooperation. It requires that parents work out methods of monitoring, guiding, and supporting their children when adults are not present, using the time they are together to reinforce their children's understandings of right and wrong, what is safe and unsafe, and when they need to come to adults for help. For coregulation to succeed, children must be willing to inform their parents of their whereabouts, their activities, and their problems.

Parents and Peers

While family life and peer relationships sometimes appear to be two separate social worlds, they are linked in several important ways. As we explained in our discussion of parents' role in constructing children's *ecological niches* (see Chapter 2, p. 76), parents have considerable power in determining the contexts in which their children spend their time. They choose, for example, the neighborhood in which they live and where their children go to school (and, hence, who their children have as potential playmates and schoolmates). They also provide or deny their children opportunities to interact with other children in specific activities during nonschool hours (Parke & Ladd, 1992), although this form of managing their children's social contacts with peers begins to decline during middle childhood (Schneider, 2000). The influence of parents on children's peer relations is also apparent in the way parents monitor where their children are, whom they are with, and what they are doing (Pettit et al., 2007). Children whose parents do not know where they are or whom they are with are more likely to engage in antisocial behavior and to face rejection by their peers (see Ladd, 1999, for a review of this evidence).

coregulation A form of indirect social control in which parents and children cooperate to reinforce the children's understandings of right and wrong, what is safe and unsafe, when they are not under direct adult control.

In addition to these very direct ways of organizing their children's social lives, parents affect peer relationships indirectly by providing working models for how people should interact with each other. There is ample evidence that interactional patterns established between parents and children influence peer relations (Rubin et al., 2003). Aggressive behavior is a good case in point. As you saw in Chapter 9, parents may unwittingly encourage their children to behave aggressively when they themselves engage in coercive, power-assertive modes of socialization. Since aggressive behavior in children is associated with rejection by their peers, a number of researchers have focused on *coercive family interaction patterns* as a possible source of low social status in middle childhood (Granic, Hollenstein, Dishion, & Patterson, 2003).

In one such study, Thomas Dishion (1990) collected information on the social status of over 200 boys aged 9 and 10 by interviewing their teachers and classmates. Through interviews with the parents and the boys themselves, as well as home observations, he also obtained information about the children's family socialization patterns and their behavior in the family setting. Dishion found that the boys who were exposed to more coercive family experiences at home were the ones most likely to be rejected by their peers at school. These boys not only were more aggressive with their peers but also behaved badly in the classroom. Although boys from lower-income homes were more likely to fall within the rejected category, Dishion's data showed that socioeconomic class was not a direct cause of lower peer status or aggressive behavior. Rather, in accord with findings discussed in Chapter 10 (p. 353), he found that poverty affected social status and behavior indirectly by increasing the general level of stress within the family. When parents coped well enough with the pressures of poverty to treat their children in a non-coercive way, the children were less likely to have low social status among their peers. These results were replicated and supplemented in a study conducted in the People's Republic of China (Chen & Rubin, 1994).

Children who have been maltreated are also at risk for peer rejection (Bolger & Patterson, 2001). In an effort to understand why, Kerry Bolger and Charlotte Patterson (2001) followed two groups of children across the elementary and middle school years. One group included a representative sample of more than 100 maltreated children; the other included an equal number of nonmaltreated children. Bolger and Patterson's results showed that children who are chronically maltreated, through either abuse or neglect, are at greater risk for becoming aggressive, which, as we have seen, places children at risk for peer rejection. In other words, maltreatment per se does not cause peer rejection. Instead, and as shown in Figure 13.6, children's aggression mediates between maltreatment and rejection.

Alan Sroufe and his colleagues have argued that children's relations with parents and peers are linked by a "cascade effect wherein early family relationships

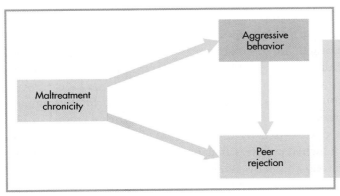

Figure 13.6 Researchers have established that children who are chronically maltreated are often rejected by their peers. In their study, Bolger and Patterson found no direct relationship between maltreatment and peer rejection, as indicated by the orange arrow in this diagram. However, they found a significant relationship between maltreatment and aggressive behavior, and between aggressive behavior and peer rejection, as indicated by solid lines, and thus concluded that maltreatment is an indirect cause of rejection that acts through the influence of aggressive behavior. (Adapted from Bolger & Patterson, 2001.)

provide the necessary support for effectively engaging the world of peers, which, in turn, provides the foundation for deeper and more extensive and complex peer relationships. Each phase supports the unfolding of subsequent capacities" (Sroufe et al., 1999a, p. 258). Whether or not this developmental cascade actually takes place depends critically on the stability of the environmental conditions and the extent to which they permit or disrupt parent–child interaction patterns. One very common example of such instability is the case of divorce.

Divorce

Between 40 and 50 percent of all marriages in the United States end in divorce, affecting more than 1 million children annually (U.S. Census Bureau, 2002; Centers for Disease Control and Prevention, 2006). While the divorce rate in the United States is by far the highest in the world, the rate of divorce is rising rapidly in many places throughout the world, including in Asian, Eastern European, and other nations undergoing major social and economic transitions associated with globalization (Antonov & Medkov, 2007; Becker, 2007).

A range of problems has been associated with divorce. Children whose parents have divorced are twice as likely as children whose parents are still together to have problems in school, to act out, to be depressed and unhappy, to have lower self-esteem, and to be less socially responsible and competent (Amato, 2006; Sun & Li, 2002).

Divorce leads to several changes in children's life experiences that might be expected to contribute to these negative outcomes. First, divorce often brings changes in children's economic status. In the United States, the average income of single-parent families created by divorce or separation falls by 37 percent within 4 months of the breakup (U.S. Census Bureau, 2002). Moreover, only 73 percent of the custodial parents who are due child support receive any money at all from their former spouses, and most receive only a portion of what is owed to them (U.S. Census Bureau, 2002). As a consequence, about 30 percent of all custodial parents find themselves living below the poverty threshold. (In 2008, the Census Bureau defined a family of four as poor if its annual income fell below $21,200.) The changes in economic status often mean that after their parents divorce, children have to move away from their friends and neighbors to poorer neighborhoods with different schools and lower-quality child care. These changes are difficult for children to deal with.

Second, parents raising children alone are trying to accomplish by themselves what is usually a demanding job for two adults. Both fathers and mothers who have sole custody of their children complain that they are overburdened by the necessity of juggling child care and household and financial responsibilities by themselves (Amato, 2006). Divorce forces many mothers to enter the workforce at the same time that they and their children are adapting to a new family configuration. In the United States, approximately 80 percent of divorced mothers are in the labor force; most of them work full-time (Burtless, 2004). Because of the many demands on their mothers' time, children of divorce not only receive less guidance and assistance but tend to lose out on important kinds of social and intellectual stimulation (Hetherington, Collins, & Laursen, 1999).

In studying the consequences of divorce, some developmentalists employ a *crisis model* in which divorce is viewed as a specific disturbance to which parents and children adjust over time. Recently, however, developmentalists have created a *chronic strain model,* which recognizes that ongoing hardships, including financial insecurity and continuing conflict between parents, may affect children's lives and adjustments for many years to come. Paul Amato (2006) has attempted to capture the insights of both models—representing both the short-term trauma associated with divorce and its long-term effects—with the *divorce-stress-adjustment perspective*. This more inclusive model views marital dissolution not as a discrete event, but as a complex process that varies depending on the specific stressors and protective factors influencing the short- and long-term adjustment of the family as a whole and its individual members.

Although it makes intuitive sense that the losses associated with the breakup of a family are the cause of the various behavioral and social problems experienced by children of divorce, a number of studies that collected data about children before their parents divorced have cast doubt on this idea.

An alternative to the divorce-stress-adjustment perspective, in which child problems begin with the divorce itself, is the *selection perspective*. According to this model, most of the negative effects of family disruption may be accounted for by problems that predate the divorce (Sun & Li, 2008). Several large longitudinal studies indicate that long-standing dysfunctional family patterns and inherent characteristics of parents, such as antisocial personality traits, create unhealthy environments for children, thereby contributing to their adjustment problems (Hetherington, 2006; Sun & Li, 2008).

One consequence of high rates of divorce is high rates of remarriage, resulting in "blended families." This photograph includes children that were blended from their parents' previous marriages.

Interestingly, the similarity in divorce rates among twin pairs is higher for monozygotic twins than for dizygotic twins, suggesting that a genetic component may be at work (Jocklin, McGue, & Lykken, 1996). That is, children from divorced families might be more troubled than those from intact families because they have inherited predispositions from their troubled parents that place them at greater risk for a variety of problems, including divorce (Vangelisti, Reis, & Fitzpatrick, 2002). According to these studies, the divorce itself has negligible effects on children's adjustments.

There is, of course, a range of individual differences in how children adjust to divorce. In his comprehensive review of research in the area, Paul Amato identified factors that have been found to affect adjustment (Amato, 2000; Amato & Hohmann-Marriott, 2007). Factors that facilitate adjustment include active coping skills such as seeking social support; support from peers; and access to therapeutic interventions, including school-based support programs. Factors that impede adjustment include avoidant coping mechanisms, a tendency toward self-blame, and feelings of lack of control.

Amato, among others, realizes that research on the consequences of divorce fuels a contentious debate. Some see divorce as a source of a variety of social ills and child problems. Others, however, see it as a benign force that allows parents to seek happiness in new relationships and provides an escape for children otherwise trapped in dysfunctional families. On the strength of several decades of research, Amato concludes that "divorce benefits some individuals, leads others to experience temporary decrements in well-being that improve over time, and forces others on a downward cycle from which they might never fully recover" (Amato, 2000, p. 1285). Given the rising divorce rates in the United States and other countries, continued research on the consequences of divorce remains a high priority.

|||||| APPLY ▪▪ CONNECT ▪▪ DISCUSS –

This section has presented evidence that coercive parenting practices are associated with the development of aggressive behavior and peer rejection in children. Review the previous section on peer relationships, and suggest how parents might interact with children in ways that promote their ability to form successful friendships.

A New Sense of Self

The significant rearrangement of children's social lives that takes place in the transition from early to middle childhood is accompanied by equally striking developments in how children think about themselves, the emergence of a new level of sensitivity to their personal standing among their peers, and their resulting efforts to maintain their self-esteem.

Changing Conceptions of the Self

A sizeable body of evidence suggests that as children move from early childhood to middle childhood and then to adolescence, their sense of self undergoes marked changes that parallel the changes occurring in their cognitive and social processes (Harter, 2006b; Mascolo & Fischer, 1998).

To understand how children's conceptions of themselves change as they grow older, William Damon and Daniel Hart (1988) asked children between 4 and 15 years of age to describe themselves. They found that all of the children referred to their appearance, their activities, their relations to others, and their psychological characteristics, but both the importance they attached to these various characteristics and the complexity of their self-concepts changed with age. As Table 13.3 shows, children between the ages of 4 and 7 years make categorical statements about aspects of themselves that place them in socially recognized categories ("I'm 6 years old"), but comparative judgments relating one's own characteristics to those of others ("I'm bigger than most kids") seldom occur until sometime between the ages of 8 and 11 years. (Descriptions of personal characteristics as significant to interpersonal relationships are uncommon until adolescence, as also shown in the table.)

Subsequent research has supported the picture of a general trend from self-concepts based on limited, concrete characteristics to more abstract and stable conceptions arrived at through **social comparison,** the process of defining oneself in relation to one's peers (Pomerantz et al., 1995).

There is no mystery as to why social comparison begins to play a significant role in children's sense of themselves during middle childhood. The increased time they spend with their peers and their greater ability to understand others' points

table 13.3

A Developmental Model of Self-Concept

Typical Organizing Principle for Self-Concepts	Area of Evaluation			
	Physical	Activity-Based	Social	Psychological
1. Categorical identification (4–7 years)	I have blue eyes. I'm 6 years old.	I play baseball. I play and read a lot.	I'm Catholic. I'm Sarah's friend.	I get funny ideas sometimes. I'm happy.
2. Comparative assessments (8–11 years)	I'm bigger than most kids. I have really light skin, because I'm Scandinavian.	I'm not very good at school. I'm good at math, but I'm not so good at art.	I'm one of the best players on my baseball team. I don't do as well in school as my sister does.	I'm not as smart as most kids. I get upset more easily than other kids.
3. Interpersonal implications (12–15 years)	I am a four-eyed person. Everyone makes fun of me. I have blonde hair, which is good because boys like blondes.	I play sports, which is important because all kids like athletes. I treat people well so I'll have friends when I need them.	I am an honest person, so people trust me. I'm very shy, so I don't have many friends.	I understand people, so they come to me with their problems. I'm the kind of person who loves being with my friends; they make me feel good about being me.

Source: After Damon & Hart, 1988.

of view lead children to engage in a new kind of questioning about themselves. They must decide on answers to such questions as "Am I good at sports?" "Am I a good friend?" "Do the other kids like me?" and "Am I good at math?" Such questions have no absolute answer because there are no absolute criteria of success. Rather, success is measured in relation to the performance of others in the social group. The many comparisons children make in a wide variety of settings provide them with a new overall sense of themselves.

Children's use of social comparison becomes increasingly complex and subtle over time. When deliberate and pervasive social comparison becomes important at around 8 years of age, children are initially inclined to make overt social comparisons in interaction with their peers, saying such things as "My picture is the best one." But they soon discover that this kind of comparison is perceived as bragging and is likely to evoke negative reactions. As a consequence, they begin to develop more subtle ways of making social comparisons: Instead of telling another child that they are faster at doing math or better at a video game, they will ask the other child, "What problem are you on?" or "What was your highest score?" (Pomerantz et al., 1995). Overt expressions of superiority are more likely to be used intentionally to make another child feel bad.

Social comparison often takes the form of asking how one's friends are doing on a school assignment.

Sometime around the age of 7 or 8, children also begin to describe themselves in terms of more general, stable traits. Instead of saying "I can kick a ball far" or "I know my ABCs," they begin to say "I am a good athlete" or "I am smart." At the same time, they begin to assume more consistently that other people also have stable traits that can be used to anticipate what they will do in a variety of contexts (Dweck, Higgins, & Grant-Pillow, 2003). Studies indicate that children begin to attribute stability to the psychological states of others at about the same time they begin to think about themselves as having stable traits.

Self-esteem

Erik Erikson (1963) thought of middle childhood as the time during which children have to resolve the crisis of **industry versus inferiority.** If children judge themselves (and are judged by others) as being industrious and meeting the new responsibilities and challenges they are given by adults at home and at school, then they are able to maintain positive **self-esteem**—that is, they make a positive evaluation of their own worth. If, however, they fail to demonstrate to themselves and others that they are capable, they feel "inferior" and, as a result, their self-esteem suffers. Research over the past half-century has built upon Erikson's early insights, finding evidence that in many cultures, self-esteem is associated with a variety of mental health indicators, and has its foundation in experiences and interactions that confer a sense of control and mastery over one's environment.

Changes in Children's Self-evaluations Susan Harter, a developmental researcher and clinician, has been intrigued for more than 20 years by the question of children's evaluations of themselves and their development of self-esteem. Her research has shown that self-esteem is an important index of mental health. High self-esteem during childhood has been linked to satisfaction and happiness in later life, while low self-esteem has been linked to depression, anxiety, and maladjustment both in school and in social relations.

social comparison The process of defining oneself in relation to one's peers.

industry versus inferiority According to Erikson's theory, the stage during which children judge themselves to be industrious and successfully meeting the new challenges posed by adults at home and school, or inferior and incapable of meeting such challenges.

self-esteem One's evaluation of one's own self-worth.

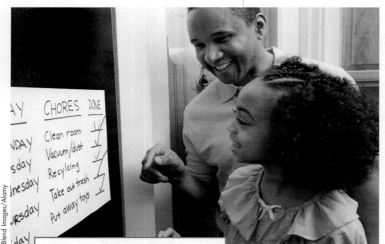

The positive feedback this African girl receives from her father for completing her chores will have an important impact on her developing self-esteem.

To study the basis on which children's evaluations of themselves change in the transition from early to middle childhood, Harter and Robin Pike (1984) presented 4-, 5-, 6-, and 7-year-olds with pairs of pictures and asked them to say whether each picture was a lot or a little like them. Each pair of pictures was selected to tap the children's judgments in one of four domains important to self-esteem: cognitive competence, physical competence, peer acceptance, and maternal acceptance. The younger and older children were given comparable but age-appropriate items. For example, an item such as "Knows the alphabet" used to assess judgments of cognitive competence in the 4- and 5-year-olds corresponded to the item "Can read alone" for the 6- and 7-year-olds.

The pattern of children's responses to these self-evaluation tasks revealed that they judged their own worth in terms of two broad categories—competence and acceptance. That is, statistical analysis revealed that the children lumped cognitive and physical competence together in a single category of competence and combined peer and maternal acceptance in the single category of acceptance. Nevertheless, the scale seemed to tap children's feelings of self-worth in a realistic way. Harter and Pike found, for example, that, as might be expected, the picture selections of children who had been held back a grade reflected a self-evaluation of low competence while the picture selections of newcomers to a school reflected a self-evaluation of low acceptance.

In research on somewhat older children (8 to 12 years old), Harter (1982) assessed self-esteem using the written format shown in Figure 13.7. She found that these older children made more differentiated self-evaluations; for example, they distinguished between cognitive, social, and physical competence (Harter, 1987). At the same time that older children's self-evaluations become more differentiated, a new level of integration in the components of self-esteem appears, enabling children to form an overall sense of their general self-worth (Harter, 2006b). (Table 13.4 shows the content of sample items in each area of self-esteem included in Harter's scale for 8- to 12-year-olds.)

Another aspect of children's changing ideas about themselves in middle childhood is that they begin to form representations of the kind of person they would like to be—an "ideal self" against which they measure their "actual self," that is, the person they believe they actually are. The fact that there is likely to be a discrepancy between children's actual and ideal selves can be either a source of motivation toward self-improvement or a source of distress and discouragement, depending on the perceived degree of discrepancy.

Of course, not all discrepancies between the actual and ideal selves are equally important. If, for example, being athletic is not important to a child, then her self-worth will not be much affected by her feelings that she is not a good athlete and

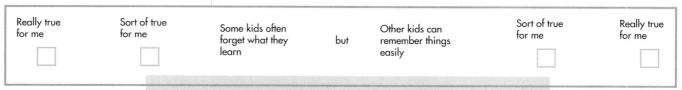

Really true for me	Sort of true for me	Some kids often forget what they learn	but	Other kids can remember things easily	Sort of true for me	Really true for me
☐	☐				☐	☐

Figure 13.7 A sample item from Harter's scale of self-esteem. Choices to the left of center indicate degrees of poor self-esteem. Choices to the right indicate degrees of positive self-esteem. (From Harter, 1982.)

table **13.4**	
Harter Self-Esteem Scale for 8- to 12-Year-Olds	
Area of Self-Evaluation	Content of Sample Items
Cognitive competence	Good at schoolwork, can figure out answers, remembers easily, remembers what is read
Social competence	Have a lot of friends, popular, do things with kids, easy to like
Physical competence	Do well at sports, good at games, chosen first for games
General self-worth	Sure of myself, do things fine, I am a good person, I want to stay the same

Source: Harter, 1982.

will never become one. In contrast, if her athletic ability is a core part of her sense of self, then the child might be devastated by the knowledge that she will never be much good at sports (Harter, 2006a).

Harter and others also report that there is an age-related change in the extent to which children's self-evaluations fit the views of others (Harter, 1999). Younger children's rating of their peers' "smartness" at school generally agrees with teachers' evaluations. Their ratings of their own smartness, however, do not correlate with either their teachers' or their peers' ratings, tending generally to be unrealistically high. Around the age of 8, children's self-evaluations begin to fit with the judgments of both their peers and their teachers. This pattern of results fits nicely with the conclusion presented earlier that an overall sense of oneself in relation to others arises around the age of 8.

Foundations of Self-esteem Self-esteem has been linked to patterns of child rearing (Coopersmith, 1967; Hughes et al., 2006). In an extensive study of 10- to 12-year-old boys, Stanley Coopersmith found that parents of boys with high self-esteem (as determined by their answers to a questionnaire and their teachers' ratings) employed a style of parenting strikingly similar to the *authoritative parenting pattern* described by Diana Baumrind (see Chapter 10, p. 345). Recall that authoritative parents are distinguished by their mixture of firm control, promotion of high standards of behavior, encouragement of independence, and willingness to reason with their children. Coopersmith's data suggest that three parental characteristics combine to produce high self-esteem in late middle childhood:

1. *Parents' acceptance of their children.* The mothers of sons with high self-esteem had closer, more affectionate relationships with their children than did mothers of children with low self-esteem. The children seemed to appreciate this approval and to view their mothers as supportive. They also tended to interpret their mothers' interest as an indication of their personal importance, as a consequence of which they came to regard themselves favorably. "This is success in its most personal expression—the concern, attention, and time of significant others" (Coopersmith, 1967, p. 179).

2. *Parents' setting of clearly defined limits.* Parents' imposition and enforcement of strict limits on their children's activities appeared to give the children a sense that norms are real and significant, and contributed to their self-definition.

3. *Parents' respect for individuality.* Within the limits set by the parents' sense of standards and social norms, the children with high self-esteem were allowed a great deal of individual self-expression. Parents showed respect for these children by reasoning with them and considering their points of view.

Taken together, contemporary evidence suggests that the key to high self-esteem is the feeling, transmitted in large part by the family, that one has some ability to control one's own future by controlling both oneself and one's environment (Chirkov & Ryan, 2001; Harter, 2006a). This feeling of control is not without bounds. As Coopersmith's data suggest, children who have a positive self-image know their boundaries, but this awareness does not detract from their feeling of effectiveness. Rather, it sets clear limits within which the person feels considerable assurance and freedom.

While several decades of study on the relationship between parenting practices and children's self-esteem provides a fairly consistent picture, most of this work has been conducted on European American families. It has recently been pointed out that other cultures and ethnic groups attach much less weight to the importance of self-esteem in their children's development and are consequently less inclined to organize their parenting practices in ways that explicitly promote it. Peggy Miller and her colleagues (2002) conducted interviews about child rearing with European American and Taiwanese mothers. For the American mothers, self-esteem played a prominent role in child-rearing practices and children's development. The Taiwanese mothers, in contrast, rarely mentioned the role of "self-respect–heart/mind" (the nearest Chinese word to "self-esteem"). When they did, they expressed concern that it would create psychological vulnerabilities.

Additional support for the idea that self-esteem is a culture-specific concept comes from a comparative study of European American and Mexican American families. In this case, the research suggests that the link between self-esteem and parenting practices may depend on culture: Researchers found that the relationship between parenting practices and children's self-esteem was strong in the European American families but comparatively weak in the Mexican American families (Ruiz, Roosa, & Gonzales, 2002). That is, in Mexican American families, parenting practices appeared to have less influence on the child's level of self-esteem.

Developmentalists are thus taking a closer look both at the possibility that the concept of self-esteem may be not a universal feature of children's sense of self, but, rather, specific to particular cultural contexts, and at the possibility that parenting practices and the associated outcomes are also less general than has been thought. As you saw earlier, the authoritative parenting style, in which parents are firm, warm, and willing to negotiate, has been associated with a variety of positive social and intellectual outcomes in European American families. In contrast, a study of Korean American families found that only 25 percent could be classified into Baumrind's categories and that, for those that could be so classified, children thrived (as measured by academic achievement) with both authoritative and permissive fathers (Kim & Rohner, 2002). This finding suggests that parental warmth, characteristic of both styles, is the critical factor underlying children's well-being, not firmness or control.

|||||| ▌ APPLY ▬ CONNECT ▬ DISCUSS ▬

- In what ways do changing conceptions of self appear as related to cognitive developments characteristic of middle childhood (see Chapter 11)?

- How might self-esteem be related to developing self-regulation discussed in Chapter 9 (see pp. 316–324)?

Reconsidering Middle Childhood

Sigmund Freud described the years of middle childhood as a period of *latency,* during which the sexual instincts that drive development lay dormant and the child experiences relative stability. Freud's idea that not much happens during middle childhood no doubt accounts for the lack of attention he devoted to the period. As documented in this and the previous two chapters, however, a host of significant changes occur between the ages of 6 and 12. Surveys of the world's cultures make it clear that adults everywhere assign 6- and 7-year-olds to a new social category, characterized by new responsibilities and by expectations for higher levels of independence, autonomy, and self-control.

Another universal characteristic of middle childhood is the rise of the peer group as a major context for development. For the first time, children must define their status within a group of relative equals without the intervention of adults. In many cultures, interactions with peers become coordinated, with games governed by rules serving as substitutes for adult control. The experience of negotiating these interactions and comparing themselves with peers contributes to children's mastery of the social conventions and moral rules that regulate their communities. Peer interactions also provide crucial contexts within which children arrive at a new, more complex, and global sense of themselves.

The new cognitive capacities that develop at this time are less obvious than changes in the social domain but are no less important. As you saw in Chapters 11 and 12, thought processes in middle childhood become more logical, deliberate, and consistent. Children become more capable of thinking through actions and their consequences; they are able to engage in concentrated acts of deliberate learning in the absence of tangible rewards; they keep in mind the points of view of other people in a wider variety of contexts; and they learn to moderate their emotional reactions in order to facilitate smooth relations with their parents and their peers. As we have emphasized several times, these cognitive changes must be considered as both cause and effect of the social changes discussed in this chapter.

Least visible are the biological changes that underpin children's apparent new mental capacities and modes of social interaction. The fact that children are bigger, stronger, and better coordinated is obvious enough. But only recently has modern anatomical and neurophysiological research provided evidence of such subtle changes as the proliferation of brain circuitry, changing relations between different kinds of brain-wave activity, and the greatly expanded influence of the brain's frontal lobes. Without such biological changes, the cognitive and social changes we have reviewed would not be possible. By the same token, when children are severely deprived of experience, such biological changes are disrupted.

The existence of a universal pattern of changes associated with middle childhood in no way contradicts the fact that there are significant cultural variations in the particular ways that 6- to 12-year-old children's lives are organized. The beliefs and values of a culture shape and are transmitted through parenting practices and school curricula, as well as particular expectations for age-appropriate behavior, duties, and responsibilities. Both interpersonal (family and peers) and institutional (schools) practices contribute to the *niche construction* of middle childhood, and position children for their next developmental step: adolescence.

SUMMARY

Moral Development

- According to Piaget, in middle childhood there is a shift to autonomous morality, in which judgments of right and wrong are based on people's intentions rather than objective consequences. Experience with rule-based games makes possible this shift and the emergence of self-governing peer groups.

- Kohlberg proposed six stages of moral reasoning, with children moving in middle childhood from heteronomous morality, based on authority and objective consequences, to instrumental morality, based on one's own and others' self-interests and equal exchange, and then good-child morality, characterized by concern about others and their expectations and needs.

- Prosocial moral reasoning also becomes more sophisticated in middle childhood, with children showing more empathy and greater consideration of social norms.

- Social domain theory suggests that even young children distinguish between moral and social conventional domains, basing moral judgments on concepts of harm and welfare, a basis that shifts, over time, to more abstract concepts of justice and rights.

- The shift in moral reasoning from external consequences to internal motives may be made possible by children's developing theories of mind, especially by an increasing ability to interpret other people's behaviors in light of their mental states.

Peer Relationships

- Whenever a peer group forms, a social structure emerges. These structures are often described in one of two ways:

    - In terms of dominance hierarchies, which are often influenced by bullying.

    - In terms of relative popularity, with children often falling into one of four popularity statuses—popular, rejected, neglected, or controversial.

- Contexts may promote cooperation or competition in children's interactions. The extent, nature, and effects of competition may be influenced by culture.

- In middle childhood, gender differences in play style increase gender segregation, although the boundaries between boys and girls are far from impermeable.

- Friendship becomes important in middle childhood, and close friendships may contribute to self-esteem, providing models and contexts for developing social skills.

- Children tend to choose friends who are similar to themselves and with whom they interact well.

- Friendship stability is promoted by similarity, including in behavioral characteristics. Overly aggressive children have difficulty maintaining friendships.

- The changes in friendship of middle childhood may be possible because declining egocentrism and increased perspective taking lead to increases in children's understanding of friendship, friendship skills, and commitment to friendships.

The Influence of Parents

- Parent–child interactions change in middle childhood, with parents expecting their children to display new behavioral competencies and increasingly sharing their control over their children's lives with the children themselves.

- Parents affect their children's peer relationships both directly, by choosing neighborhoods, schools, and activities, and monitoring their children, and indirectly, by providing working models for interactions.

- Children whose parents divorce are more likely than other children to have problems in a range of areas. According to the divorce-stress-adjustment perspective, these stem from both the short-term trauma of divorce and its long-term effects. The selection perspective attributes problems not to divorce but to long-standing family patterns and to parents' characteristics that children have inherited.

A New Sense of Self

- In middle childhood, there is a shift from self-concepts based on limited, concrete characteristics to more abstract, stable conceptions arrived at through social comparison.

- For Erikson, the crisis of middle childhood is that of industry versus inferiority. Positive self-esteem is associated with a sense of self as industrious.

- According to Harter, in middle childhood self-evaluations become more differentiated, more integrated into an overall sense of self-worth, and more in keeping with judgments made by others. Children measure themselves against an "ideal self."

- High self-esteem may be linked to an authoritative parenting style. However, cross-cultural research suggests a more complicated picture of both self-esteem and the role of parenting practices.

Reconsidering Middle Childhood

- Around the world, despite considerable cultural variations, the ages of 6 and 7 mark the beginning of new responsibilities and expectations. Closely associated with these changes are the rise of the peer group as a context for development and new cognitive capacities.

Key Terms

autonomous morality, p. 460

prosocial moral reasoning, p. 465

objective view of responsibility, p. 468

subjective view of responsibility, p. 468

social structures, p. 469

dominant children, p. 469

social repair mechanisms, p. 483

coregulation, p. 484

social comparison, p. 488

industry versus inferiority, p. 489

self-esteem, p. 489

Major Milestones of Adolescence

	Physical Domain	Cognitive Domain	Social and Emotional Domain	
What Develops...	• Rapid increase in height and weight, changing the requirements for food and sleep. • For boys, increase in muscle tissue, decrease in body fat. • For girls, increase in both muscle tissue and body fat. • Influx of hormones stimulates growth and functioning of reproductive organs. • Significant changes in brain regions associated with impulse control, decision-making, and ability to multitask.	• Emergence of new forms of mental operations associated with scientific reasoning abilities. • Increased ability to think hypothetically. • Increase in working memory enables higher-level problem-solving strategies. • Increased decision-making skills. • Increased ability to use reasoning in making moral judgments.	• Compared to childhood, daily experience of positive emotions decreases and daily experience of negative emotions increases. • Increased ability to regulate emotions. • New bases for friendships, which, ideally, balance intimacy and autonomy. • Peer groups provide opportunities for exploring identity possibilities. • Gender-typed behaviors increase. • Increase in parent-child conflict in some but not all domains. • Emergence of a more coherent, stable sense of identity. • Emergence of sexual orientation and ethnic identities.	
Sociocultural Contributions and Consequences...	• Access to nutritious food and health care lowers the age of pubertal onset for general populations. • Diets excessively high in fat that result in overweight and obesity may further lower the age of pubertal onset, as in low-income minority populations in the United States • Physical changes marking sexual maturity (breast development, facial hair, etc.) affect how peers, parents, and others interact with the child. • Cultural stereotypes regarding ideal body types may burden girls' experience of normal weight gain and contribute to the development of eating disorders. • Some cultures mark pubertal onset with special rites and ceremonies.	• Emergence of various forms of reasoning and problem-solving skills is highly variable across cultures. • Social and emotional aspects of a context can substantially affect decision-making • Cultures vary in the extent to which they support the emergence of different moral standards and values. • Both parent and peer relationships and interaction styles can affect moral development.	• Parental warmth and behavior affect adolescent's developing emotion-regulation ability. • Cultural expectations affect gender differences in the regulation and expression of emotion. • Cultural variation in support of developing autonomy. • Cultural differences in support of developing sexual-orientation and ethnic-minority identities.	

Adolescence

Most of us look back on our adolescence and see it as a special time in our lives—a time that we still associate with intense friendships, dramatic and often embarrassing bodily changes, parents who were as maddening as they were supportive, experimentation with everything from sports and drama to drugs and alcohol, a feeling of freedom derived from such simple things as driving around in a car with friends. For some, adolescence was especially wonderful; for others, it was downright awful. But however we remember it, it is unlikely that any of us feel neutral about those few years that included such momentous events as the onset of reproductive maturity and the first, sexually charged kiss.

Puberty begins around the end of the first decade of life, with a cascade of biochemical events that alters the body's size, shape, and functioning. The most revolutionary of these alterations is the emergence of the ability to produce offspring—new human beings to carry forward the genetic and cultural heritages of the species. This biological fact has profound interpersonal implications. As their reproductive organs reach maturity, boys and girls begin to engage in new forms of social behavior because of emerging sexual attractions.

Although reproductive maturity is the biological signal of adulthood, most societies attempt to delay many social changes associated with adulthood, including marriage and parenting. In the United States and other industrialized countries, a gap of seven to nine years typically separates the biological changes of sexual maturity from the social roles that confer adult status. This lengthy period is necessary because it takes young people many years to acquire the knowledge and skills they will need to achieve independence and to contribute to their society. Nonetheless, some societies have only a brief delay between the beginnings of sexual maturity and adulthood (Whiting et al., 1986). These are usually societies in which biological maturity occurs late by Western standards and in which the level of technology is relatively low. In such societies, by the time biological reproduction becomes possible, at about the age of 14 or 15, young people already know how to perform the basic tasks of their culture, such as farming, weaving cloth, preparing food, and caring for children.

In Chapter 14 we examine the advent of biological maturity and its intimate links with sexual behavior and health. We also explore the changes in intellectual functioning and moral reasoning that underpin the adolescent's ability to be an effective member of society. Chapter 15 concentrates on aspects of emotional and social life, including new abilities to regulate the intense emotions of adolescence, changing relationships with parents and peers, and a changing sense of personal identity related to the sexual and social changes of adolescence. Throughout, we will address the many ways that adolescence is a unique and essential time for acquiring the tools, practices, and traditions of culture.

14

CHAPTER

Physical and Cognitive Development in Adolescence

oni, a nurse at a program that provides support and counseling to pregnant and parenting teenagers, is all about condoms. She has a goldfish bowl full of them on her office desk, and to further make her point, at one of the program's annual Halloween parties, she wrapped herself in plastic and sprayed whipped cream on her head. Toni monitors the health of young women during their pregnancies and, after they have delivered, provides well-baby checkups, along with contraceptive and family-planning counseling. Well aware of the educational and financial challenges created by early parenthood and also concerned about young women's sexual health, Toni encourages young women to delay subsequent pregnancies and to protect themselves from STIs (sexually transmitted infections) by engaging in sexually responsible behavior. Hence, her enthusiasm for condoms.

Toni has a son, Ryan, who grew up in an atmosphere of free and open discussion about sex and contraception. Toni felt confident that she had prepared her son well for adolescence, especially with regard to the onset of sexual desire, the responsibilities that accompany romantic relationships, and the importance of thoughtful decision making and planning in the area of sexual behavior. However, it seemed that all that preparation went out the window when Ryan was 16 and fell in love with Nikki. This is the story Toni told us:

> I was in the kitchen, getting dinner ready, and saw a letter laying open on the table. I picked it up, and saw that it was from Nikki to Ryan. The first line was, "Last night with you was so special." I couldn't put it down. Basically, it described their wonderful first sexual experience the night before in our basement. Now you know how I am. I'm open about these things—always have been with Ryan. I knew it was just a matter of time, so I'm basically okay with it. But I'm wondering why Ryan left the letter on the table, in plain view, like maybe he wanted me to see it or something. So when he gets home I hand it to him. He shrugs, and puts it in his pocket. I ask him if he wants to talk about it—tell him I've read enough to know what it's about. He says, No, that's okay. So I ask him, well, did you at least use a condom? He says, No. I couldn't believe it! My own son didn't use a condom! I asked if Nikki is on birth control. He doesn't even know if she is or isn't!

Ryan was probably better prepared than most children for the onset of puberty, sexual feelings, and sexual relationships. Nevertheless, the vast store of information conveyed over the years by his mother was insufficient to guarantee his practicing safe sex. What happened? In this chapter, we will examine the complex and often confusing changes that are typical of adolescence—and that sometimes lead to poor judgment and risky behavior. First, the biological changes of puberty not only transform the size and shape of young people's bodies but also evoke new, intense, and initially strange feelings. In addition, peers, teachers, siblings, parents—even complete strangers—interact with young people differently once they show signs of sexual maturity. Adolescents will encounter many, sometimes conflicting

499

Recognizing that some teens may engage in risky sexual behavior, many countries, including Mexico (here) provide family planning classes in which adolescents learn about sexual health and pregancy prevention.

expectations about how they should and should not behave in their new bodies, and how they should and should not relate to others.

The complex developments of puberty are associated with major changes in the way young people think. New cognitive abilities launch adolescents into a world of complex problem solving, abstract thinking, and fantasy that affects everything from their schoolwork to the way they imagine themselves in their uncertain futures. At the same time, however, adolescents have a reputation for exercising poor judgment and taking unreasonable risks, sometimes placing their health—and, on occasion, their lives—in great jeopardy.

This chapter focuses on the unique and remarkable changes in physical and intellectual development that converge in adolescence. As you know from previous chapters, the challenges facing individuals at any given period in development, and the challenges facing those who want to study and understand development, are deeply rooted in the views of society at a particular moment in history. So we begin our discussion of the physical and cognitive changes of adolescence by tracing the roots of current conceptions of adolescence. As you will see, many beliefs about adolescence have endured for thousands of years, whereas others relate to the issues and concerns of the modern world. These beliefs reflect the relationship between adolescents and society and influence the efforts of researchers and practitioners who want to understand adolescent development and devise strategies for promoting healthy developmental outcomes.

Adolescents and Society

The relationship between adolescents and society is no less complex than adolescent development itself. One source of this complexity is the fact that adolescents inhabit a gray, transitional area in between childhood and maturity. In some ways, adolescents are pressed to be responsible, knowledgeable, independent, and adult-like; in other ways, they are encouraged to remain childlike and immature. For example, in some societies, adolescents may be hurried toward financial independence but discouraged from mature sexual behavior. Societies guide their children through adolescence in various ways, depending on such factors as cultural beliefs and values and economic structures. However, virtually all societies recognize adolescence as an important transition that requires special attention.

Historical Views

The idea of a transitional period between childhood and adulthood is an ancient one, and many contemporary views of the problems and turmoil of adolescents, as well as of how to keep young people out of trouble, are strikingly similar to views expressed millennia ago. In about 350 B.C., for example, the Greek philosopher Plato warned that youth and alcohol were a particularly bad combination and advocated a minimum drinking age:

> [B]oys shall not taste wine at all until they are eighteen years of age . . . fire must not be poured upon fire, whether in the body or in the soul, until they begin to go to work—this is a precaution which has to be taken against the excitableness of youth; afterwards they may taste wine in moderation up to the age of thirty, but while a man is young he should abstain altogether from intoxication and from excess of wine. (*Laws, Book 2*)

Not surprisingly, interest in youth, and the idea that the period of adolescence is a dangerous one, extended well beyond the gates of philosophy. Literature from the Middle Ages onward is filled with images of young people as passionate, sensual, and impulsive (Kiell, 1959; Violato & Wiley, 1990). In Chaucer's *Canterbury Tales,* for example, young squires are portrayed as seekers of high adventure, willing to take risks in love as well as in battle; Shakespeare's *Romeo and Juliet* depicts what is probably the most famous literary example of a teenage romance and suicide.

Plato's student Aristotle also wrote about youthful passions and impulses and the unfortunate consequences they could lead to. However, he also viewed the period of adolesecence as an especially fertile one for the development of new powers of thought, and suggested that individuals are not able to profit from "the education of reason" until they reach puberty.

The notion that adolescence is a period of both peril and promise—of emotional conflict and instability, as well as higher intellectual functioning—persisted into modern times. We will now consider how this notion intensified in the industrial age and captured the attention of the public and the scientific community.

Adolescents in the Industrial Age

In the late eighteenth and early nineteenth centuries, widespread scientific and public interest in adolescence was sparked by two trends stemming from industrialization. One trend was increased urbanization and related problems; the other was increased education.

Because industrialization generated wage-paying job opportunities, a great many young people flocked to the cities. Once in the cities, as child welfare advocates among others noted, many of these youths were not only joining the workforce, they were getting into trouble (Addams, 1910; Kett, 1977). Adolescent drinking, sexual promiscuity, and card-playing were identified as major social problems (Mintz, 2004). In response to the rising social problems created by adolescents, efforts were made to provide teenagers with organized services and structured activities that would occupy them during their leisure hours. Jane Addams, a founder of the famous Hull House of Chicago, which provided a wide range of services for the working class, initiated several programs designed specifically to deal with problems of youth—programs that were among the first of their type in United

Hull House of Chicago, founded by Jane Addams, was one of the first settlement houses in the nation to provide programs for adolescents experiencing a variety of problems.

States. The Juvenile Protective Association, for example, was designed to prevent juvenile delinquency and was associated with the campaign that led to the establishment of the nation's first juvenile court (Polikoff, 1999). Addams also spearheaded the creation of the Juvenile Psychopathic Institute for the purpose of determining the degree to which juvenile delinquency is influenced by mental disorders.

Although increased industrialization is thought to have led to an increase in youth problems, it also created demands for more educated workers. Children were staying in school longer to prepare for the ever-increasing number of jobs that were available in the new

Bettmann/Corbis

growth spurt A rapid change in height and weight that signals the onset of puberty.

industrial age. The massive expansion of education that took place during this period meant that high school attendance soared by over 700 percent between 1890 and 1918, and a new high school opened on average every day between 1900 and 1930 (Mintz, 2004). As education for adolescents became more extensive, educators were faced with the need to develop new ways of teaching that were appropriate to adolescents' advanced mental capacities, and they turned to the scientific community for recommendations and guidance.

At the same time that counselors and educators were pondering the challenges of adolescents in the age of industrialization, the scientific community was developing theories of the factors that drive and shape adolescent development. Several important theories focused mainly on the biological aspects of adolescent development. In the next section, we begin with the contributions of two of these theorists—G. Stanley Hall and Sigmund Freud—and then turn our attention to the evolutionary and ethological approaches that they helped to inspire.

||||| APPLY ═ CONNECT ═ DISCUSS ─

Provide some personal examples of how social and cultural pressures to be both childlike and adultlike affected your adolescence. To what extent might these examples be associated with contemporary social and cultural issues facing adolescents and their families?

Biological Theories of Adolescent Development

In Chapter 1, we explained that early theories of children's development were heavily influenced by Darwin's theory of evolution. In the case of adolescence, this influence is readily apparent in the attention that developmentalists paid to the relationship between adolescent behavior and the survival of the species.

G. Stanley Hall

G. Stanley Hall, the first president of the American Psychological Association and a major figure in the shaping of developmental psychology, was instrumental in promoting the idea that understanding the unique qualities of adolescence was essential to understanding the proper education and counseling of adolescents, as well as to understanding the evolution of the species (Cairns, 1998; Hall, 1904). Two key features of his theory continue to influence modern thinking and research (Arnett & Cravens, 2006; White, 1991).

The most influential feature of Hall's theory is the notion that adolescence is a time of heightened emotionality and oppositions: stratospheric highs and deep depressions, boundless self-confidence and nagging insecurity, astounding generosity and equally astounding selfishness. In Hall's view, adolescence is a time of "storm and stress," attributable to "raging hormones" associated with the biological processes of puberty. Although contemporary research indicates that the relationship between adolescent hormonal levels and emotions is more complex than Hall suggested, there is compelling evidence that the increase in major depression during adolescence is driven at least in part by hormonal changes (Angold, 2003).

The second key feature of Hall's theory that remains influential is the idea that the stage of adolescence is the consequence of evolutionary processes. Consistent with most other theorists of his time, Hall believed that the developing child passes through stages that correspond to the evolutionary steps of the species, beginning with the primitive, animal-like stage of infancy, and progressing toward the civilized,

Bettmann/Corbis

G. Stanley Hall (1844–1924).

mature stage of modern adults. According to Hall, middle childhood corresponds to an ancient period of human evolution when reason, morality, feelings of love toward others, and religion were underdeveloped. He believed that it is only when they reach adolescence that young people go beyond the biologically predetermined past to create new ways of thinking and feeling. As a consequence, Hall believed, adolescence is more flexible and creative than any other period of development. It is also why Hall believed (as many others do) that adolescents are literally the future of our species.

Sigmund Freud

You may recall from Chapter 1 (p. 18) that Freud's psychodynamic theory reflects a largely biological position with respect to the sources of development. Freud viewed adolescence as a distinctive stage because it is the time during which human beings become capable of fulfilling the biological imperative to reproduce themselves and sexual intercourse becomes a major motive of behavior. Accordingly, he considered adolescence to be the beginning of the *genital stage,* the final stage in his theory of psychosexual development.

Like Hall, Freud emphasized both storm and stress and evolutionary processes as major features of the stage. In Freud's theory, the emotional storminess associated with adolescence is the culmination of a psychological struggle among the three components of personality—the id, the ego, and the superego (see Chapter 9, p. 314). As Freud saw it, the upsurge in sexual excitation that accompanies puberty reawakens primitive instincts, increases the power of the id, and upsets the psychological balance achieved during middle childhood. This imbalance produces psychological conflict and erratic behavior. The main developmental task of adolescence is therefore to reestablish the balance of psychological forces by reintegrating them in a new and more mature way that is compatible with the individual's new sexual capacities.

The theoretical perspectives of Hall and Freud have had a lasting impact on developmental science, particularly on the study of the biological and social foundations of adolescence. Although there is currently some dispute regarding the extent to which adolescence is necessarily a period of stress and conflict (McKinney, 1998), it is widely accepted that adolescents are especially prone to argue with their parents, engage in risky and rebellious behaviors, experience mood fluctuations, and generally think and act in creative, imaginative ways.

Modern Theories of Biological Development

Modern biological approaches to adolescence emphasize how development is influenced by the evolutionary history of our species. A feature of adolescence that has received a lot of recent attention is the **growth spurt,** the rapid change in height and weight that marks the onset of puberty. Interestingly, it seems that human beings are the only primate species that experience a spurt of growth after early childhood (Locke & Bogin, 2006; Leigh, 2001). Figure 14.1 shows the speed of growth from birth to maturity for females in the United States and for captive female chimpanzees (Walker et al., 2006). It is easy to identify the *takeoff velocity* for girls, beginning around 7½ years of age, when

These African Masai adolescents have painted their faces white as a part of the initiation ceremony marking their passage from childhood to adulthood.

Figure 14.1 Compared to other primate species, the human species is markedly delayed in reaching physical maturity, and in experiencing an adolescent growth spurt.

Differences in the physical sizes of these fifth-graders from Schenectady, New York, illustrate the amazing variability in the timing of pubertal onset.

Ellen Senisi/The Image Works

the growth spurt starts (for boys, takeoff velocity is closer to 10½ years of age). In contrast, the speed of growth of the female chimpanzees continues to decline in a relatively straight line over the course of time.

Figure 14.1 illustrates another interesting species difference that has captured the attention of developmentalists: the slow rate of growth of humans relative to that of other primate species (Charnov, 2004). As you can see in the figure, although the speed of growth decreases substantially in both species, it remains dramatically slower in humans than in chimpanzees, until the adolescent growth spurt. Thus, in our species, the onset of puberty and the capacity to reproduce is radically delayed compared to its onset in our evolutionarily closest relatives.

Given that evolution operates to maximize species survival through reproduction, it would seem to follow that the sooner human beings started producing offspring, the better. So why the delay in reaching reproductive maturity? Evolutionary theorists have argued that delayed maturation in humans actually contributes to our reproductive success. Energy that would be spent on rapid physical development is instead diverted to disease prevention (McDade, 2003) and to other functions that give humans time to develop the complex brain associated with capacities such as language, sophisticated problem solving, and an extraordinary ability to make and use the tools of culture. Moreover, from a biocultural perspective, the phenotype of delayed maturation confers significant reproductive advantages to our species "by allowing the adolescent to learn and practice adult economic, social, and sexual behavior before reproducing" (Bogin, 1999, p. 216). In the following section, we will examine changes to the human body as it responds to the physical events of puberty.

||||| APPLY ⬤ CONNECT ⬤ DISCUSS _ _ _ _ _ _ _ _ _ _ _ _ _ _ _ _

From a biocultural perspective, why might it be advantageous to develop advanced social, economic, and cognitive skills and abilities prior to, rather than after reaching, sexual maturity?

Puberty

Puberty refers to the series of biological developments that transforms individuals from a state of physical immaturity into a state in which they are biologically mature and capable of sexual reproduction. Generally taking 3 to 4 years to complete, puberty begins with a chemical signal from the hypothalamus, which "tells" the pituitary gland to make more growth hormones (Traggiai & Stanhope, 2003; Grumbach & Styne, 2002). These hormones will stimulate the growth throughout the body, with some of them stimulating the development and functioning of the *gonads,* or ovaries and testes. In the following discussion, we will first look at the physical changes of puberty and will then turn our attention to how adolescents react to these radical changes affecting their bodies.

The Growth Spurt

As noted, one of the first visible signs of puberty is the onset of the growth spurt, during which boys and girls grow more quickly than at any other time since they were babies (Kontulainen et al., 2007). Over the 2 to 3 years that the growth spurt lasts, up to 45 percent of skeletal growth takes place, and up to 37 percent of total bone mass may be accumulated (Whiting et al., 2004; Ballabriga, 2000). A boy

puberty The series of biological developments that transforms individuals from a state of physical immaturity into one in which they are biologically mature and capable of sexual reproduction.

primary sex characteristics The organs directly involved in reproduction.

secondary sex characteristics The anatomical and physiological signs that outwardly distinguish males from females.

menarche The first menstrual period.

may grow as much as 9 inches taller, and a girl, as much as 6 to 7 inches taller. Although adolescents continue to grow throughout puberty, they reach 98 percent of their adult height by the end of their growth spurt (Sinclair & Dangerfield, 1998).

The rate of growth during adolescence varies for different parts of the body, prompting James Tanner (1978) to quip, "A boy stops growing out of his trousers (at least in length) a year before he stops growing out of his jackets" (p. 69). As a result of asynchronous growth patterns, many adolescents develop a gangly appearance and become awkward in their movements.

Changes in physical size are accompanied by changes in overall shape. Girls develop breasts, and their hips expand. Boys undergo a marked increase in muscle development and shoulder width, and a decrease in body fat, giving them a more muscular and angular appearance than girls, who continue to have a higher ratio of fat to muscle and hence continue to have a rounder, softer look (Bogin, 1999).

Most boys not only appear to be stronger than girls at the end of puberty but are stronger. Before puberty, boys and girls of similar size differ little in strength. But by the end of puberty, boys can exert more force per ounce of muscle than girls of the same size. Boys can also exercise for longer periods. They develop relatively larger hearts and lungs, which give them higher blood pressure when their heart muscles contract, a lower resting heart rate, and a greater capacity for carrying oxygen in the blood (oxygen in the blood neutralizes the chemicals that lead to fatigue during physical exercise) (Weisfeld & Janisse, 2005). In general, the aerobic power associated with the cardiovascular and muscular systems peaks earlier for females, but is of greater magnitude in males (Geithner et al., 2004).

The physiological differences between males and females may help to explain why males have traditionally been the warriors, hunters, and heavy laborers throughout human history. They also help to explain why most superior male athletes can outperform superior female athletes. In some important respects, however, females exhibit greater physical prowess than males: On average, they are healthier, live longer, and are better able to tolerate long-term stress (Weisfield & Janisse, 2005).

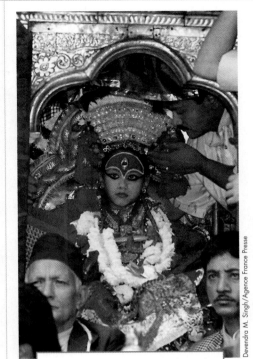

When she reaches puberty, this girl from Kathmandu, Nepal, will face a dramatic change in life. Since she was 4, she has been the personification of the goddess Kumari and, except for religious festivals, she has spent her entire childhood secluded in a temple. But as soon as she reaches puberty, another 4-year-old girl will be chosen and this one will return to her family.

Sexual Development

Human sexual development includes both the development of the gonads and other reproductive organs (including the uterus and vagina in females, and the penis, scrotum, and prostate in males), known as **primary sex characteristics,** and the outward bodily changes such as breasts in females and broad shoulders in males, known as **secondary sex characteristics** (Figure 14.2).

Development of Primary Sex Characteristics During puberty, the reproductive organs enlarge and become functionally mature, due to the action of specific hormones, chiefly *testosterone* and *estrogen*. Testosterone in boys increases to 18 times its level in middle childhood, while estrogen undergoes an eightfold increase in girls (Malina & Bouchard, 1991). Although these two hormones are generally referred to, respectively, as "the male hormone" and "the female hormone," both are present in each sex, even before the onset of puberty, although in different amounts.

During female sexual development, the ovaries are stimulated to manufacture additional estrogen and to release mature ova into the fallopian tubes. Typically the release of ova, or ovulation, does not begin until about 12 to 18 months after **menarche,** the first menstrual period, which usually occurs about 18 months after the growth spurt has reached its peak velocity (Bogin, 1999). Over the course of this development, the uterus grows and the vaginal lining thickens. The pelvic inlet, the bony opening of the birth canal, grows more slowly and does not reach

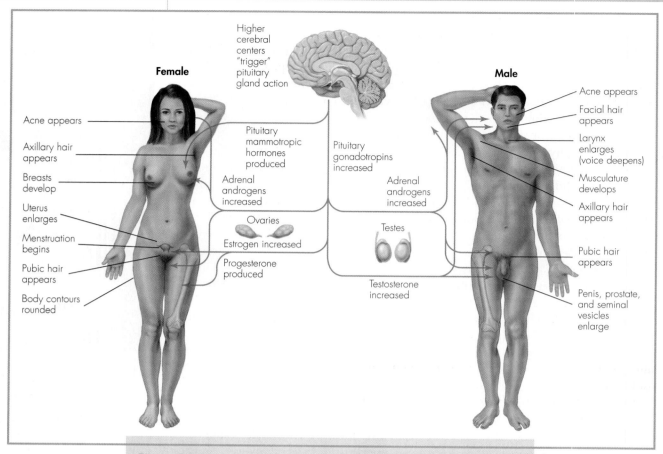

Figure 14.2 The hormonal changes that accompany puberty cause a wide variety of physical changes in both males and females. (Adapted from Netter, 1965).

its full size until about 18 years of age, which means that childbirth is more difficult and potentially more dangerous for young adolescents (Bogin, 1999).

In males, the testes are stimulated to produce additional testosterone and as a result begin to manufacture sperm cells, and the prostate begins to produce semen, the fluid that carries the sperm cells (Bogin, 1999). **Semenarche,** the first ejaculation, often occurs as a nocturnal emission, that is, spontaneously during sleep. For the first year or so after semenarche, the sperm in the semen are less numerous and less fertile than sperm in adult males (Katchadourian, 1977).

Among the first changes of puberty in males are an enlargement of the testes and a thickening and reddening of the skin of the scrotum. Soon after, at about the time that the growth spurt gets underway, the penis begins to grow; growth of the penis continues for about 2 years. It is approximately a year after the penis begins to grow that semenarche occurs.

Development of Secondary Sex Characteristics The anatomical and physiological signs that outwardly distinguish males and females appear at the same time that the reproductive organs are maturing, as is evident from Figure 14.2. Secondary sex characteristics play an essential role in communicating to the adolescent, and to others, that sexual maturation is underway. Ethologists have suggested that secondary sex characteristics are highly significant to the reproductive process of our species because they signal that individuals are capable of reproducing and trigger sexually relevant responses in others—flirting, for example.

semenarche The first ejaculation. Ejaculation often occurs spontaneously during sleep and is called a nocturnal emission.

The first visible sign that a girl is beginning to mature sexually is often the appearance of a small rise around the nipples called the breast bud. Pubic hair usually appears a little later, just before the growth spurt begins. Girls' secondary sex characteristics develop throughout puberty. The breasts continue to grow with the development of the mammary glands, which allow for lactation (milk production), and with the accumulation of adipose (fatty) tissue, which gives the breasts their adult shape.

The appearance of pubic hair in boys is, along with the enlargement of the testes, an early sign of puberty. The appearance of facial hair follows the peak height spurt, as does another noticeable change—the gradual deepening of the voice as the larynx expands and the vocal cords lengthen, a process during which sudden high-pitched cracks in a boy's voice announce to the world the changes that are taking place in his body.

Clearly, the sexual development of the human body is a dramatic and complex process. Less obvious, but just as important, are the radical changes that take place in the adolescent brain.

Brain Development

Until fairly recently, it was believed that most changes in the brain take place well before adolescence. However, new technologies such as magnetic resonance imaging (MRI) provide evidence that the brain remains a work in progress through adolescence.

Although the brain, which has attained 90 percent of its adult weight by the age of 5, grows very little in size during adolescence (Sinclair & Dangerfield, 1998), recent longitudinal MRI studies point to complex changes in its organization and functioning (Figure 14.3; Durston & Casey, 2006; Gogtay et al., 2004). There are, for example, significant changes in the frontal lobes of the cerebral cortex, which continue to develop until late adolescence (Luciana et al., 2005). The frontal lobes, part of the evolutionarily recent neocortex, are associated with a number of advanced behaviors and processes, including memory, decision making, reasoning, impulse control, and the ability to multitask. Results from MRI studies show that these changes in the brain including the frontal lobes are of two kinds. One concerns the amount of white matter; the other, the amount of gray matter.

White matter is made up of dense concentrations of myelin, the insulating substance that coats axons and thereby enhances communication between neurons. Longitudinal studies indicate that white matter increases fairly steadily from childhood to early adulthood (Shaw et al., 2008), suggesting that during adolescence the brain is continuing on its course toward greater efficiency.

The story regarding gray matter is a bit more complicated. In contrast to the steady increase of white matter throughout adolescence, gray matter first increases and then decreases. Since the amount of gray matter is believed to reflect the number of neural connections, or synapses, these changes in gray matter during adolescence suggest a spurt of synapse production in early puberty followed by a reduction in synapses in late adolescence. Neuroscientists believe that pubertal hormones may trigger the overproduction of synapses in adolescents (Giedd et al., 1999b). They base their speculation on the fact that peak amounts of gray matter occur in early puberty, when hormone production is at its peak, and that gray matter reaches a peak rate of growth in females about 1 year before it peaks in males, consistent with the pattern of pubertal hormonal activity.

This spurt of *synaptogenesis,* or synapse formation, followed by a period of *synaptic pruning,* or reduction in the number of synapses, parallels the pattern of brain development during infancy (see Chapter 4, p. 129). As you may recall from our earlier

(a)

(b)

Both images courtesy of Dr. Elizabeth Sowell/UCLA/Laboratory of Neuro Imaging

Figure 14.3 These images are composites derived from brain scans of normally developing children and adolescents (a) and adolescents and adults (b). The red areas indicate where there is both an increase in the size of the brain and a decrease in gray matter. As you can see, there are substantially more areas of red in the adolescent and adult image, most of which are concentrated in the frontal area of the brain associated with complex cognitive processes. The fact that areas of the brain are growing even though their gray matter is decreasing suggests that the growth is most likely due to an increase in white matter.

"Young man, go to your room and stay there until your cerebral cortex matures."

Some developmentalists, as well as parents, speculate that immaturities in the adolescent cerebral cortex contribute to risky behavior and poor decision-making.

discussion, far from reflecting a less capable brain, synaptic pruning actually improves functioning. The decrease in synapses reflects the consolidation of neural pathways, presumably the result of specific experiences.

Given that the adolescent brain undergoes a process of synaptogenesis followed by synaptic pruning, how might its development be affected by particular experiences? Researchers speculate that the adolescent brain may be particularly vulnerable to the effects of drugs and alcohol, in much the same way that the fetus's developing systems are vulnerable to the effects of teratogens (see Chapter 4). That is, in the same way that the fetus is more vulnerable to teratogens at certain periods of its development than at others, the brain may be more susceptible to drugs and alcohol during times of rapid structural and functional developments, such as those that are occurring during adolescence. Compounding this physical susceptibility in adolescence is the fact that many young people may be particularly prone to experimentation with drugs and alcohol and to exercising poor judgment.

The Timing of Puberty

A glance around a seventh-grade classroom is sufficient to remind even the most casual observer of the wide variations in the age at which puberty begins. Some of the 12- and 13-year-old boys look much as they did at the age of 9 or 10, whereas others have the gangly look that often characterizes the growth spurt. Girls, on average, begin to mature sexually somewhat earlier, so some of the 12- and 13-year-olds look like mature women with fully developed breasts and rounded hips; others still have the stature and shape of little girls, and yet others are somewhere in between.

Like all significant milestones in development, the timing of puberty depends on complex interactions between genetic and environmental factors. Figure 14.4 displays the average age of menarche for adolescents growing up in urban and rural environments in several different countries. The differences are dramatic, and more so in some countries than in others. Cross-national differences raise several important questions: Why does menarche occur earlier in some countries rather than others? Why are the rural/urban differences relatively small in some countries (in Finland, for example), but quite large in others (such as India and South Africa)? Identifying the genetic and environmental factors that affect the onset of puberty would help developmentalists understand these national differences, and might help policy makers identify areas of the world in need of greater levels of health care.

Twin studies have provided important information regarding the influence of genetic factors on the timing of puberty. For example, a study of nearly 2000 Finnish twins found that the timing of a variety of pubertal changes was more highly correlated in identical twins than in fraternal twins (Mustanski et al., 2004). Genetic contributions also appear to underlie timing differences across ethnic groups in the United States. For example, African American boys and girls tend to reach puberty at earlier ages than do boys and girls of European descent (Herman-Giddens et al., 1997; Herman-Giddens et al., 2001).

Several studies have indicated that environmental factors are also important in the timing of puberty. One critical factor is caloric intake (Bénéfice et al., 2003). The onset of menstruation, for instance, is associated with certain levels in body fat, and when calorie intake is insufficient to reach those levels, menstruation is delayed (or may cease if it has begun). This is why many lean

Figure 14.4 Complex interactions between genetic and environmental factors result in large regional differences in the average age of pubertal onset. In general, puberty begins earlier in urban compared with rural areas.

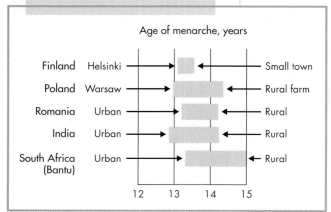

Age of menarche, years

Finland	Helsinki	Small town
Poland	Warsaw	Rural farm
Romania	Urban	Rural
India	Urban	Rural
South Africa (Bantu)	Urban	Rural

12   13   14   15

adolescent dancers, gymnasts, and other girls who participate in a high level of physical exercise reach menarche later than most girls do (Calabrese et al., 1983; Warren et al., 1991); it is also why many overweight girls reach puberty earlier than their average-weight peers (Kaplowitz et al., 2001; Kaplowitz, 2008).

A variety of other environmental factors—such as health and nutrition, to which caloric intake is tied, as well as stress and psychological depression—also influence the age of puberty (Romans et al., 2003). One important contributor to stress is family conflict. Studies in the United States and New Zealand have found that adolescents who experience a high level of family conflict go through menarche earlier than do those who live in more harmonious families (Graber, Brooks-Gunn, & Warren, 1995; Moffit et al., 1992). Although there is broad agreement that environmental stress affects children's developing hormonal systems, the exact mechanisms of these effects remain uncertain.

The age at which puberty is reached has also undergone striking historical changes. The **secular trend** refers to a pattern of decline in the average age of puberty which has occurred in industrialized countries among all social groups and has occurred to a lesser extent in developing countries as well (Graham, Larsen, & Xu, 1999). In the 1840s, the average age of menarche among European women was between 14 and 15 years, whereas by the 1960s it had dropped to between 12 and 13 years of age (Eveleth & Tanner, 1990), and the drop has continued (Figure 14.5). Developmentalists speculate that the secular trend was the consequence of better nutrition and access to health care. Although research results from more recent decades are inconsistent, developmentalists agree that they indicate a continued drop in the average age of breast development and menarche for girls in the United States (results regarding an ongoing secular trend for boys are too mixed to draw conclusions) (Euling et al., 2008). Moreover, compared to white girls, African American girls appear to be affected by the trend to a greater extent, reaching menarche, on average, 3 months earlier than white girls (Freedman et al., 2002).

Developmentalists speculate that higher levels of body fat account for both the secular trend (contemporary adolescents have more body fat than those of several decades ago) and ethnic differences (African American adolescents have more body fat than white adolescents) (Styne, 2004; Slyper, 2006). Interestingly, in contrast to the early years for which the secular trend was associated with improving health in the general population, the continued fall in age of pubertal onset in the recent past has been interpreted as a sign of worsening health (Euling et al., 2008). In particular, early pubertal onset, presumably due to its association with high levels of body fat, is now linked to risk for obesity, breast cancer, and other diseases (see Freedman et al., 2002, for review).

Puberty and Health

Worldwide, adolescence is a period of relatively good health. Compared with children and older people, adolescents experience fewer infections, chronic diseases, and life-threatening illnesses (WHO, 2008). Nevertheless, the astronomical growth

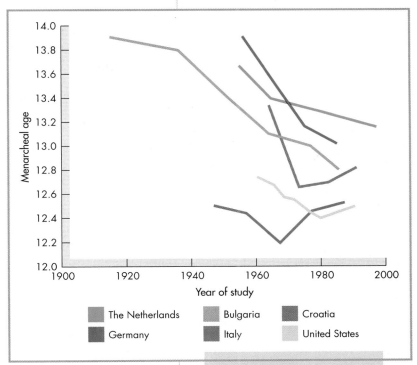

Figure 14.5 In general, the average age of menarche in industrialized nations has declined substantially over the past several decades, a phenomenon referred to as the "secular trend."

secular trend Observed in industrialized countries, a pattern in which the average age of puberty declines across decades.

rates of adolescence place new demands on the body, and developmentalists have recently begun to focus attention on the unique needs of adolescents for adequate nutrition, sleep, and physical activity.

Nutrition The body's total nutrient needs are greater during adolescence than at any other time in life. These needs are especially great during the growth spurt; in fact, it has been estimated that at the peak of the growth spurt, the body needs twice the nutrients that it needs at other points during adolescence. Optimal nutrition during adolescence is essential not only for achieving full growth potential but also for preventing a number of diseases in later life, including heart disease, cancer, and osteoporosis (Stang & Story, 2005). Unfortunately, as shown in Table 14.1, the average diet of adolescents, in the United States, at least, is low in essential vitamins and minerals and high in fats and sugars.

The importance of a healthy diet to adolescent development cannot be overemphasized. Vitamins and minerals, for instance, are known to influence essential physiological processes. Here are just a few examples:

- *Zinc* is vital for gene expression, and plays a role in sexual maturation. Only two-thirds of adolescents in the United States get enough zinc. Major sources include red meat, shellfish, and whole grains.

- *Vitamin A* contributes to reproduction, general growth, and the functioning of the immune system. It is also important to normal vision. In the United States, only two-thirds of adolescents consume the recommended amount of Vitamin A. In developing countries, as many as 500,000 children go blind each year because of Vitamin A deficiencies (Russell, 2001). Major sources of this nutrient include milk, cheese, and carrots.

- *Folate* is a mineral that plays a significant role in biological processes affecting DNA. Nationwide studies indicate that 90 percent of young women, and nearly 60 percent of young men 14 to 18 years of age, do not consume the recommended amount of folate (Suitor & Gleason, 2002). Women who have folate deficiencies and become pregnant are at risk for having babies with birth defects (Institute of Medicine, 1990). Men with low folate levels often have chromosomal abnormalities in their sperm (Young et al., 2008). Common sources of folate include cereal, orange juice, milk, and bread.

table 14.1

Nutrients of Concern in the Average Diet of Adolescents in the United States

Nutrient Intakes		Females	Males
Lower than Recommended Intakes	**Vitamins**		
	Folate	✔	✔
	Vitamin A	✔	
	Vitamin E	✔	✔
	Vitamin B₆	✔	
	Minerals		
	Calcium	✔	✔
	Iron	✔	
	Zinc	✔	
	Magnesium	✔	✔
	Other		
	Fiber	✔	✔
Higher than Recommended Intakes	Total fat	✔	✔
	Saturated fat	✔	✔
	Sodium	✔	✔
	Cholesterol		✔
	Total sugars		✔

Source: Data from Stang & Story, 2005.

Hooker Middle School in New Haven, Connecticut, has launched an initiative that provides students with healthy choices in the cafeteria.

Peter Hvizdak/The Image Works

Naturally, developmentalists are interested in identifying the sources of adolescents' poor diets and dietary choices. In many parts of the world, of course, adolescents simply do not have access to healthy food. This is obviously true in economically poor, developing nations, but it is also true in many communities in wealthy countries. In the United States, for example, people in poor, urban neighborhoods have far fewer grocery stores, and fewer means of transportation to them, than do those in more affluent neighborhoods (Cotterill & Franklin, 1995).

As shown in Figure 14.6, limited access to food is just one of a variety of social, psychological, and cultural factors that contribute to nutritional problems in adolescence. You are no doubt well aware of the fast-food "super-size me" craze

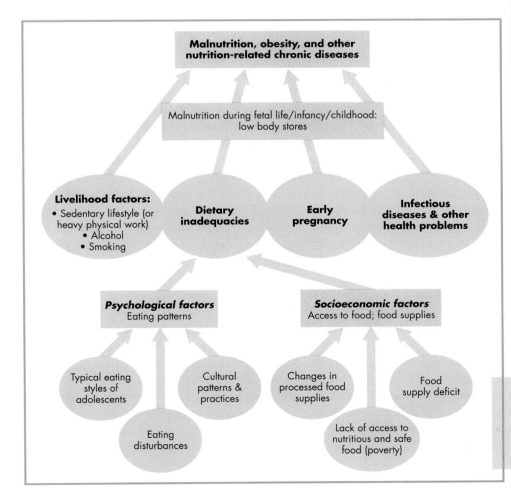

Figure 14.6 Nutrition-related diseases and problems can be caused by a number of interacting psychological and socioeconomic factors. (Adapted from WHO, 2008.)

in the United States, and the sharp criticism it drew for encouraging consumption of excessive quantities of food, particularly of food high in fats, salts, and "empty" calories. Unfortunately, while poor, urban communities lack adequate grocery stores, they have a plethora of fast-food outlets, nearly twice the number found in wealthier neighborhoods. This combination of factors may help account for the higher levels of obesity found in African Americans and other ethnic minority populations in the United States (Block, Scribner, & DeSalvo, 2004).

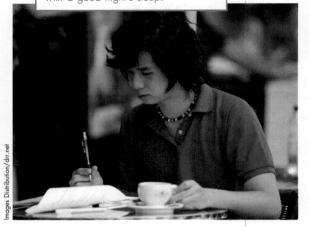

In a Montreal coffee shop, this 17-year-old Vietnamese boy is doing his homework under the influence of caffeine, a practice that may interfere with a good night's sleep.

Images Distribution/drr.net

Sleep In addition to not getting enough nutrients, many adolescents do not get enough sleep. Adolescents are night-owls, tending to stay up later at night than they did as children and, when their schedule permits, to sleep later in the morning (Laberge et al., 2001). This shift in the sleep–wake pattern may not be particularly problematic on weekends, when adolescents are not required to rise early for school. However, during the school week, late bedtimes, combined with early rising, create morning classrooms full of bleary-eyed teens who are less prepared to learn than if they had had a good night's rest (not to mention a nutritious breakfast!). There is also concern that adolescents are inclined to use chemical stimulants, including caffeine and nicotine, to cope with sleep deprivation.

Concerns about the effects of sleep deprivation on academic performance are not new. Over a century ago, G. Stanley Hall argued that adolescents should not be allowed to go to school at all without 9 hours of sleep (1904). His recommendation is not far from that of contemporary developmentalists who believe that 8 hours of sleep is optimal for most adolescents (Carskadon et al., 2004). However, during the school week, the average bedtime for high school students in the United States is later than 11 P.M., and the average high school senior rises (or tries to, at least) before 6:15 A.M., resulting in *chronic sleep deprivation* for a large portion of students (Dahl & Hariri, 2005).

Sleep researchers recognize that the sleep–wake shift results from an interaction of biological and environmental influences. It is known to occur earlier in girls than boys, and has been linked to hormones that affect the brain's biological clock, suggesting that pubertal status may play a role (Laberge et al., 2001; Lee et al., 2004). However, the later bedtime of teenagers has also been linked to decreased parental control, increased schoolwork, and other social pressures (Gau & Soong, 2003). For example, researchers at the National Taiwan University studied sleep patterns in nearly 1600 Taiwanese students between fourth and eighth grade (Gau & Soong, 2003). In Taiwan, only a limited number of students are admitted to senior high school (beginning in tenth grade), and academic competition and parental pressure to achieve in school are both extremely intense. The researchers found that the increased academic demands of the higher grade levels were more strongly associated with the sleep–wake shift than pubertal status.

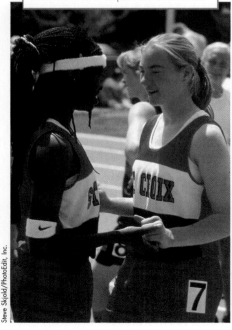

Girls who are involved in team sports may feel more confidence in themselves, and show higher levels of admiration and respect for each other.

Steve Skjold/PhotoEdit, Inc.

Physical Activity As you have been advised for years, in addition to eating and sleeping well, it is important to get plenty of exercise. Indeed, adolescents who engage in higher levels of physical activity experience greater well-being than less physically active adolescents. Studies indicate that high levels of athletic activity are generally associated with less depression, less drug use, better relationships with parents, and higher academic performance, for adolescent girls and boys alike (Field et al., 2001). On the basis of intensive interviews with adolescent girls and boys on issues of sexuality and pubertal development, Karin Martin concluded that girls who are involved in sports feel confidence in themselves and their bodies, and show a good deal of admiration and respect for each other (Martin, 1996).

Despite the importance of physical activity to body, mind, and social relationships, many adolescents get woefully little of it. There is growing concern about a
rising tide of adolescent couch potatoes who spend far too much time engaged in
sedentary activities such as watching TV, playing computer games, and electronic
surfing. It is well known that excessive sedentary behavior increases the risk for
obesity in children and adolescents (Berkey et al., 2000) and becomes more prevalent during puberty (Bradley et al., 2000). A recent large-scale study of British
11- and 12-year-olds documents a significant relationship between low levels of
emotional well-being and high levels of sedentary behavior (Brodersen et al., 2005).

On the basis of current evidence, it seems likely that both biology and culture
play significant roles in whether, and how, adolescents get enough nutrition, sleep,
and exercise to support the dramatic physical changes of puberty. We turn now
to the special role played by culture in pubertal development.

Puberty and Culture

In all societies, the biological changes associated with puberty have profound social and psychological significance, both to the young people themselves and to
their community. Some cultures have elaborate ceremonies that celebrate the onset of puberty and formally mark the transition to membership in the adult community. During these ceremonies, adolescents are often instructed in a variety of
"adult" behaviors and provided with specific "adult" knowledge. Other cultures
have events that, while less formal and less specifically tied to puberty, are nevertheless important milestones of maturity. Some familiar examples include getting
a driver's license, registering to vote, and consuming alcoholic beverages to mark
the attainment of the legal drinking age.

Ceremonial and institutional ways of marking the transition to adulthood are
coupled with changing expectations of how adolescents should behave in their
new, sexually mature bodies. These expectations are tied to a variety of broader
cultural and social beliefs and values, and influence adolescents' experiences of
their own development. In the sections that follow, we explore how such beliefs, values, and expectations affect adolescents' experiences of their own pubertal development.

Culture and Gender It is well documented that boys and girls experience puberty in very different ways psychologically. Although some amount of anxiety
and uncertainty about one's changing body is common for both sexes, puberty
seems to be more difficult subjectively for girls than it is for boys—that is, girls
more often than boys report having mixed feelings or negative feelings about puberty. Several studies have examined adolescents' **emotional tone,** or their sense
of well-being versus depression and anxiety (reviewed in Petersen
et al., 1998). In general, findings show that for adolescents in the
United States, positive emotional tone increases throughout adolescence for boys but plateaus after early adolescence for girls. Similar trends have been found, for example, in Mexican adolescents
(Benjet & Hernandez-Guzman, 2001). Some developmentalists
believe that cultural values and stereotypes contribute to the girls'
greater ambivalence toward their changing bodies. In particular,
girls' maturing bodies tend to be viewed as sexual objects to a
greater extent than boys' bodies do, making girls feel more self-
conscious (Brooks-Gunn & Warren, 1989; Martin, 1996; Thorne,
1993). It may be that the sexualization of the female body also accounts for the different reactions that parents have to their sons'

emotional tone The degree to which a
person experiences a sense of well-being
versus depression and anxiety.

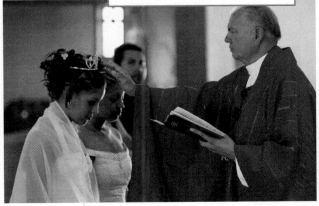

These Hispanic twins celebrate their
fifteenth birthdays—the quinceaños—
with a special Catholic mass to mark
their transition from girlhood to
womanhood.

Spencer Grant/PhotoEdit, Inc.

Although the average developing girl gains as much as 10 pounds each year during her puberty, she is surrounded by media messages that glamorize bodies that are grossly underweight.

and daughters' development. In contrast to boys, who report that their parents grant them greater freedom as they become sexually mature, many girls report that their parents become more restrictive (Martin, 1996).

One of the pubertal changes that carries significant psychological consequences is the increase in weight. For boys, this increase comes largely from a gain in muscle mass. For girls, the increase is largely the result of the addition of body fat, estimated to be, on average, a little more than 24 pounds over the course of adolescence (Bogin, 1999). These changes are perfectly normal but can carry very different psychological consequences for boys and girls, depending on cultural values and beliefs. For boys in many cultures, bulking up is valued—as an athletic advantage and as a step toward becoming "buff" and sexy. For girls, in contrast, the increase in fat can deviate from cultural ideals and thus be a source of significant psychological distress (Polivy & Herman, 2004). In the United States, for example, a thin, prepubertal body shape is the current ideal for women, an ideal reflected in everything from television, movie, and magazine images to dolls given to young girls (Botta, 1999). As a consequence, many adolescent girls are dissatisfied with their new, more mature bodies, and go on fad diets that may cut out entire classes of food such as fats or carbohydrates, or take drugs to suppress their appetite, or induce vomiting and take laxatives to avoid gaining weight. All these practices endanger their health and, in extreme forms, can lead to eating disorders such as **anorexia nervosa,** or intentional self-starving, and **bulimia nervosa,** or cycles of "binge eating" followed by self-induced vomiting (Keel et al., 2003; Keel & Klump, 2003).

Culture and the Timing of Puberty For many girls, getting the first bra is a major milestone. It is also material for social comparison and gossip. Some girls may be proud of this sign of maturity, even wearing bras before they need them. Other girls, however, may wear baggy shirts for several years to conceal their advanced development. Whether positive or negative, adolescents' responses to the changes of puberty are strongly influenced by the age at which they undergo these changes. Some children enter puberty well before most of their peers, whereas others experience significant delays. *Early maturation* is defined as the development of sex characteristics before 8 years of age for girls and 9 years of age for boys. *Late maturation,* on the other hand, is defined as the absence of sex characteristics at 13.4 years of age for girls and 14 years of age for boys (Traggiai & Stanhope, 2003).

Several studies have sought to determine how pubertal timing might affect young people's peer relations, personality, and social adjustment. Early maturation, especially in girls, has been identified as a *risk factor* (see Chapter 10, pp. 376–378) that contributes to a long list of problems, including depression, eating disorders, delinquency, suicide attempts, and early drug and alcohol use and sexual behavior (Graber, Brooks-Gunn, & Archibald, 2003; Felson & Haynie, 2002; Lanza & Collins, 2002; Wiesner & Ittel, 2002).

Developmentalists have proposed two main explanations for the link between pubertal timing and problem behavior (Haynie & Piquero, 2006). According to the first explanation, problems arise because of a mismatch between the adolescent's physical maturity and his or her social and cognitive maturity. Eric, for example, matured early physically and began hanging out with a group of older boys (early maturers often hang out with older peers) who liked to party. Although in physical appearance Eric "fit" with his partying friends, he lacked their social and

anorexia nervosa A condition in which girls (and only rarely boys) starve themselves, losing up to 25 percent or more of their body weight.

bulimia nervosa An eating disorder characterized by "binge eating" followed by self-induced vomiting.

cognitive maturity. As a consequence, he, unlike his older friends, usually drank too much and either made a fool of himself in front of his friends or got into trouble with authority figures.

The second explanation linking maturational timing to problem behavior is that early maturers are reacting to their being out of synch—with their peers and with the broader culture. As you will learn in Chapter 15, belonging to a peer group is important to identity development and emotional well-being. Becoming obviously different from one's peers can threaten one's sense of belonging, leading to psychological distress and problem behavior (Moffitt et al., 2001). The lack of fit with the broader culture comes because early maturing adolescents reach physical maturity well before many cultures are prepared to grant them the autonomy, freedom, and status of adulthood. Some developmentalists argue that the problem behavior of early maturers may constitute a form of rebellion against social and parental restrictions (Agnew, 2003; Moffitt et al., 2001).

Now that we have seen how the effects of puberty are influenced by the social context in which it takes place and by the way others respond to the physical changes young people are experiencing, let us look at how biology and culture interact in the emergence of adolescents' sexual behavior.

||||||■ APPLY ■ CONNECT ■ DISCUSS _

There is evidence that early maturation is a greater risk factor for girls than for boys. Why might this be so?

The Emergence of Sexual Behavior

Your virginity is what determines whether you're a man or a boy in the eyes of every teenage male. Teenage men see sex as a race: the first one to the finish line wins. In high school, virginity is a self-demeaning label that you want nothing more than to get rid of. . . . It is much tougher for women. . . . A woman who has lots of sex at a young age is considered a slut. Women who don't have sex at all are considered prudes. The double standard is a trap for females.
—Jeff, 16, in W. Pollack, *Real Boys' Voices,* 2000

The step from being a virgin to being sexually active is a significant one. As expressed in Jeff's commentary on the relationship between sexual behavior and gender, the emergence of sexual behavior extends far beyond the physical act to include a host of social influences and cultural meanings (Peplau et al., 1999). In many cultures, sexuality is not a frequent topic of conversation between adolescents and their parents, peers, or school counselors. Nor are adolescents openly provided with opportunities to explore their sexualities. Martha Nussbaum (2001) argues that Western culture, including its scholars, associates strong feelings of shame with the body and its sexual behaviors and desires and is therefore reluctant to have sexuality addressed in an open manner. (It was the state of affairs that Nussbaum describes—the inherent conflict between the human body's sexual drives and appetites and society's sanctions against their expression—that inspired Freud's theory.) According to some developmentalists, cultural ambivalence about sex may also account for why researchers have neglected to explore adolescent sexual experiences and sexual identity development as a normal part of growing up, focusing only on problems of adolescent sexuality (Savin-Williams, 2008). Indeed, as we discuss below, much of the information that adolescents receive regarding sexual behavior is delivered in the form

Cuddling on the steps of a cathedral in Peru, this couple demonstrates a universal feature of adolescence: romance.

of warnings about unwanted pregnancy and STIs (sexually transmitted infections). As you will see, there are enormous cultural and historical differences in how adolescents are educated about sex, including when they are expected to become sexually active, how they should have sex, and with whom.

Learning about Sex

Q: how do u kno if u hve a sti?
A: if u hve sex u can get a sti chlamydia gonorrhea=no symptoms most of the time dropin get chcked

Yes, adolescents can now use their cell phones to learn about sex and their sexual health. San Francisco's Department of Public Health has set up a text messaging service for teens with questions, such as "my bf wnts 2 hve sex wht shld I do?" and "condom brok is ths a prblm?"

Adolescents learn about sexuality from a variety of sources—from parents, peers, media, and through special educational and counseling programs that have been devised by schools and public health institutions (Sutton et al., 2002). Likewise, adolescents learn about sexuality through several social processes, including observation and imitation and explicit instruction (see Chapter 2, p. 56). Like contexts of learning in general, the contexts of learning about sex can range from casual and subtle to rigorous and formal. Family conventions regarding touching and nudity, depictions of sexual behavior on television, sex-education courses, debates in the popular press regarding "abstinence only" versus "comprehensive" sex education—all provide young people with resources for constructing an understanding of themselves as a sexual beings.

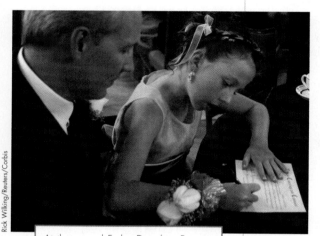
At the annual Father-Daughter Purity Ball in Colorado Springs (U.S.), Hannah signs a contract promising to remain a virgin until she marries, while her father, who promises to defend her virginity, looks on.

In some cultures, like the Kaguru of Tanzania, knowledge of sexual behavior is communicated in the course of elaborate initiation ceremonies (Beidelman, 1997). Beidelman's extensive ethnographic studies indicate that direct communication between Kaguru parents and their children about sexual matters is strictly forbidden. However, the stories, riddles, and songs that young children are taught are very often colored with allusions to sex and sexuality, and most of the songs taught to pubescent boys and girls at initiation involve instruction about sexual organs and sexual relations, communicated mainly through metaphor. Here are two examples (from Beidelman, 1997, p. 198):

Chimudodo chilimo, chidodo cilenga dilenga chitunge ne dikami.
Translation: The small, small mouth makes milk and water.
Explanation: This song explains that the penis is capable of both urinating and ejaculating semen. Kaguru sometimes describe semen as a kind of nurturant milk. Semen not only produces children but is thought to foster the maturation of girls, who should have frequent intercourse if they want to develop a full, feminine figure.

Mang'ina sena mahusi-husi, galonda mbolo gabaka mafuta.
Translation: Your mothers are conniving to take a penis and anoint it with oil.
Explanation: Women are said to lubricate men's penises with oil before intercourse. Some Kaguru say that a woman should pass down her oil container to her daughter. It is as much a material embodiment of her personhood as a bow and arrow or a shotgun is for a man. Castor oil facilitates the receptivity of women. It is also a means of blessing a person, as in bestowing a name. Any part of the body that is well oiled is thought to be more sexually attractive. At dances women often oil much of their bodies so that they glisten alluringly.

Although information about sexuality is often transmitted more explicitly in technologically advanced societies, there is a great deal of family, ethnic, and cultural variability in the nature of information taught and the manner in which it is transmitted. Studies of how mothers in the United States communicate with their adolescent children about sexuality and AIDS, for example, find significant differences that affect adolescents' knowledge of sexual matters. In one study it was found that adolescents whose mothers dominated conversations with them about AIDS were less knowledgeable about AIDS 2 years later than were adolescents whose mothers had been more interactive in their conversations (Boone et al., 2003).

Research has also uncovered interesting ethnic differences in family communication patterns about sexual matters. For example, Lefkowitz and her colleagues (Lefkowitz et al., 2000) discovered that in their discussions with their children about sexuality and AIDS, Hispanic American mothers were more likely to dominate the conversation than were European American mothers, who demonstrated greater responsiveness to their children's comments and questions. The tendency of the Hispanic American mothers to dominate the discussions is consistent with cultural expectations that children will be respectful and obedient toward their parents (Huynh & Fuligni, 2008).

There are also striking cultural differences among technologically advanced societies in the way sexuality is taught. In many European countries, adolescent sex is considered a normal part of development rather than a problem to be prevented. Adolescents in such countries as Switzerland, Sweden, the Netherlands, and New Zealand have easy access to contraceptives, confidential health care, and comprehensive (rather than abstinence-only) sex education. According to a recent study of more than 30 countries in Western and Eastern Europe, societal acceptance of sexual activity among young people, combined with comprehensive and balanced information about sexuality, pregnancy, and prevention of STIs, as well as an emphasis on teenage relationships and responsibility, are hallmarks of countries with low levels of adolescent pregnancy, childbearing, and STIs (Guttmacher Institute, 2006).

In contrast, teenage sex is considered by many in the United States to be risky and potentially harmful as a source of unintended pregnancies and STIs. This view is reflected in the rise of abstinence-only programs and the "virginity pledge" movement, which encourage youth to remain virgins until marriage. Approximately 23 percent of adolescent females and 16 percent of adolescent males are estimated to have taken this pledge (Bearman & Brückner, 2001). However, research indicates that pledgers are no different from nonpledgers in the ages at which they begin genital play, oral sex, and vaginal intercourse (Bersamin et al., 2005).

The Sexual Debut

As you can see in Figure 14.7, the average age at which adolescents first engage in sexual intercourse varies considerably across the globe. There are also some interesting cultural differences between boys' and girls' sexual debut. For example, in the United States and most Western European cultures, boys tend to first have sexual intercourse at slightly earlier ages than girls do. However, the situation is reversed in many other countries, sometimes radically so. In Ethiopia, the median age of first intercourse is 18 years for girls and 21½ years

Figure 14.7 Median age at first intercourse (age by which half of the population becomes sexually active).

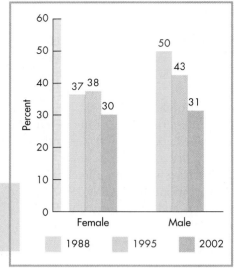

Figure 14.8 Percent of never-married females and males 15–17 years of age who have ever had sexual intercourse (U.S. 1988–2002 data).

for boys; in Peru, it is 16½ for girls and 19 for boys (Centers for Disease Control [CDC], 2004). Cross-cultural variations in the adolescent sexual debut are likely due to a variety of biological and cultural factors, including the age of pubertal onset, social norms, and cultural practices regarding sexuality. Adolescents' sexual debut can also vary across decades. For example, a nationwide study of adolescents in the United States found a significant decrease from 1988 to 2002 in the numbers of sexually active adolescents, especially among males, although it is not clear whether this is the beginning of a downward trend or merely a statistical fluke (Figure 14.8; CDC, 2004).

Developmentalists have been particularly interested in how adolescents feel about their first experience of sexual intercourse. In the United States, research on this question has found that boys tend to report more positive feelings about first intercourse than do girls (Figure 14.9). According to the nationwide survey cited above, for example, very few boys said that they really did not want to have intercourse at the time; in contrast, girls were much more likely to report either that they had not wanted to have sex at the time or that they had had mixed feelings about it (CDC, 2004). Many girls are less positive about their initial experience of intercourse for a good reason: they were coerced into having sex. About 60 percent of the girls who had sex before they were 15 years old say that they did so involuntarily (Guttmacher Institute, 2006). Cultural attitudes, such as those expressed by Jeff at the start of this section, likely also play a role in adolescents' feelings about their early sexual experiences.

Beyond such findings, researchers' knowledge of adolescents' first sexual experiences is remarkably thin. Only recently have developmentalists begun to explore such aspects as sexual desire (Tolman & Diamond, 2001), social motives for engaging in sexual activity (O'Sullivan & Meyer-Bahlberg, 2003), and the sexual experiences of sexual minority youth (lesbians, gays, bisexuals; Savin-Williams & Diamond, 2004). One explanation for this is that sexuality research reflects the biases of the larger culture. In particular, the belief that has prevailed, at least in the United States, that teen sex is categorically problematic because it can lead to such negative outcomes as pregnancy, STIs, abortions, school dropout, and so forth may lead researchers to focus their attention on identifying risk and protective factors associated with having sex, and the consequences to adolescents who become pregnant or who contract sexually transmitted infections (Savin-Williams & Diamond, 2004). Some research findings on pregnancy are discussed in the box "Teenage Pregnancy." We now turn to sexually transmitted infections.

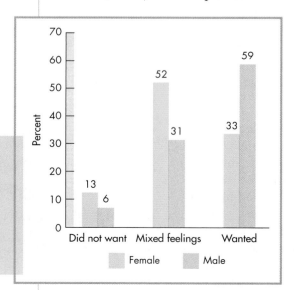

Figure 14.9 Percent of males and females who reported intercourse before age 20, according to whether they wanted intercourse, did not want intercourse, or had mixed feelings. More females than males either did not want intercourse or had mixed feelings, whereas more males than females reported that they wanted intercourse. (From CDC, 2004)

Sexual Behavior and Reproductive Health

According to a recent report from the Centers for Disease Control and Prevention (2008), about 25 percent of all 14- to 19-year-old girls in the United States have at least one sexually transmitted infection. Furthermore, of the approximately 19 million new infections that occur each year, nearly 50 percent are to young people ages 15–24, and the infection rates are on the rise for the age group (Weinstock et al., 2004). The statistics are even more alarming in the case of ethnic minority groups, all of which have higher STI rates than whites, with the exception of Asian-Pacific Islanders. For example, it is estimated that fully half of African American adolescent girls are infected with an STI. The costs of STIs are high. Apart from their consequences for individuals' physical and psychological well-being, the direct medical costs associated with their diagnosis and treatment are estimated to be $14.7 billion annually (Chesson et al., 2006).

Chlamydia With more than 1 million cases reported in 2006, chlamydia is among the most commonly reported infectious diseases in the United States. As shown in Figure 14.10, among females the rate of infection is higher for 15- to 19-year-olds than for any other age group. Estimates are that chlamydia affects 1 in 7 adolescent females and 1 in 10 adolescent males. The infection rate for African American women is particularly startling—more than twice that of Hispanic women and more than 7 times that of European American women. Chlamydia often goes unreported, placing women at increased risk for pelvic inflammatory disease and infertility. Complications among infected men are rare, and include painful inflammation of the urethra.

Human Papillomavirus There are more than 40 different types of human papillomavirus (HPV), which affects skin and mucus membranes in the genital areas of males and females. It is the most common sexually transmitted infection, with at least 50 percent of all men and women acquiring a form of the disease at some point in their lives. However, because HPV usually has no symptoms, it often goes undiagnosed. Thus, although it is the most common STI, it is far from being the most commonly *reported* disease.

Figure 14.10 Infection rates of chlamydia, one of the most commonly reported infectious diseases in the U.S., peaks during the adolescent and early adulthood years. (From CDC, 2008)

Teenage Pregnancy

EACH YEAR, ABOUT 7.5 PERCENT OF all American teenage females—roughly 700,000—become pregnant, giving the United States the highest teenage pregnancy rate among developed countries (Guttmacher Institute, 2006). Teenagers in the United States are no more sexually active than those in the other countries surveyed, so it seems clear that American adolescents use contraception far less often than do adolescents in other developed countries. Indeed, when asked whether they had used contraceptives during their last sexual intercourse, 20 percent of teens in the United States responded negatively, compared to 12 percent of French teens, 7 percent of Swedish, and 4 percent of teens from Great Britain. One reason for the difference in the use of contraceptives may be that adults in many other industrialized countries have a more realistic view of the likelihood of teenage sexual activity and thus better prepare their adolescent children for dealing with their sexuality, whereas in the United States, sex education, for example, is still controversial in many communities (Blinn-Pike et al., 2008).

Researchers have identified a number of risk factors that increase the probability of teen pregnancy, including living in a low-SES home or in a disorganized or dangerous neighborhood, or having a mother who also became pregnant during her teen years (Miller et al., 2001). Risk is also associated with ethnicity. Pregnancy rates for African American and Hispanic teens, for example, are 2 to 3 times higher than that of white teens (Guttmacher Institute, 2006). Biological factors, including timing of pubertal development, also affect teen pregnancy risk.

One of the most significant risk factors for teen pregnancy is the age difference between sexual partners (Manlove et al., 2007). Indeed, more than one in four babies born to 15- to 17-year-old mothers were fathered by men who were at least 5 years older than the mothers.

The vast majority of teen pregnancies that occur in the United States are unintended, and nearly one-third end in voluntary abortions (National Center for Health Statistics, 2003). However, researchers point out that "unintended" can have several meanings. For teenage girls who are mired in poverty, grow up in communities in which teen pregnancy is common, and see few opportunities to advance themselves in other ways, pregnancy may be a means of establishing a role for themselves. As one teen mother reported, "Most of my friends do have their babies. It seems like most of them are lost and that seems like the only thing—they feel needed, and I figure that is why they get pregnant, because they want to be needed" (Moran, 2000, p. 225).

Race, social class, education, and the strength of religious beliefs all affect a teenager's decision about whether or not to

Despite its steady decline in recent years, the adolescent pregnancy rate in the United States continues to be among the highest in the industrialized world.

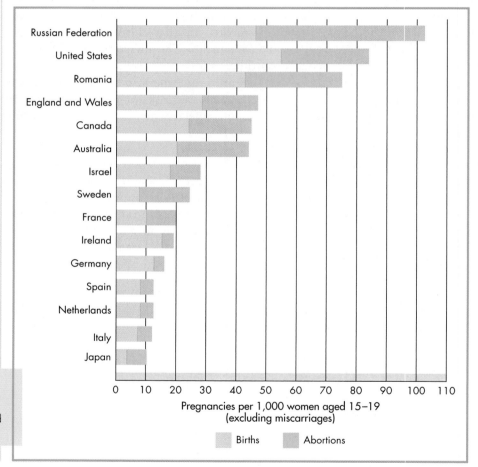

There are two general categories of HPV: "low risk" (wart causing), and "high risk" (cancer causing). Most infections are low risk, and are successfully eliminated within 2 years by the individual's immune system. Although both genital warts and cancers can be treated, there is no current treatment for the virus itself.

LaTanya, 19, and her daughter Jameelah, 10 months, attend a rally to support teen pregnancy prevention programs, and education programs for teen mothers.

AP Photo/Patricia McDonnell

have and keep her child (Coley & Chase-Lansdale, 1998). African American teenagers are more likely than European American teenagers to become single mothers. According to government statistics, 83 percent of the teenagers who give birth come from poor or low-income families (National Center for Health Statistics, 2003). The more education a pregnant teenager's mother has (which is an indirect measure of her social class) and the better the teenager is doing in school, the more likely she is to decide to terminate the pregnancy. However, teenagers with strong religious convictions are likely to have and keep their babies, no matter what their race or social class (Eisen et al., 1983).

While many of the negative outcomes that follow from teenage pregnancy, such as poverty and low educational achievement, also precede pregnancy (as many as one-third of all teen mothers drop out of school *before* they become pregnant; Aber et al., 1995), teenage childbearing serves to further limit the futures of girls who are already disadvantaged. Compared with women who delay their childbearing, women who give birth while in their teens are, on the average, more likely to drop out of school, to divorce, to continue to have children outside of marriage, to change jobs more frequently, to be on welfare, and to have health problems (Coley & Chase-Lansdale, 1998). They are also more likely to have low-birth-weight babies who are susceptible to illness and infant mortality.

Despite these grim findings, not every girl who bears a child while still in her teens ends up quitting school or living in poverty. Longitudinal studies of mothers who became pregnant as teenagers have found that some of these women eventually complete high school and become economically self-sufficient. Long-term success for these women was predicted by their being at grade level when they become pregnant, coming from smaller families that were not on welfare, and knowing that their family had high expectations for their future (Furstenberg et al., 1992).

There have been a number of efforts to reduce the probability of teenage pregnancy.

Responding to the disproportionately high rates of teen pregnancy among economically disadvantaged African Americans, several Afrocentric educational programs have been developed. The aim of these programs is to instill pride and a sense of self-determination in girls of African descent. One such program, A Journey Toward Womanhood, encourages African American teenagers to explore different cultures and the role of women in history, and develop interpersonal communication skills, job skills, self-confidence, and self-respect. Teens who participated in the program were more likely than nonparticipants to delay the onset of sexual behavior and to use contraception when they did engage in sexual intercourse (Dixon et al., 2000). Research on the effectiveness of these programs indicates that a focus on reproductive education alone is insufficient to affect adolescents' behaviors. To be effective, programs must examine the meaning of sexual behavior and pregnancy within broader social and economic contexts of adolescents' lives.

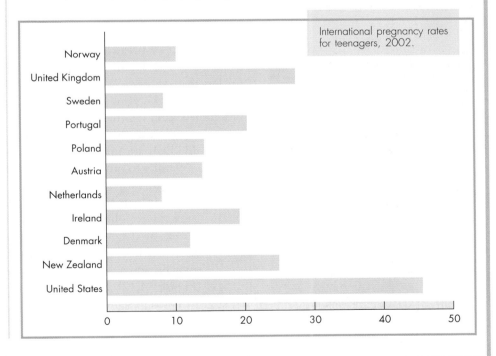

International pregnancy rates for teenagers, 2002.

Recently, however, a vaccine has been developed that protects girls and women from the HPV types that most often cause cancers and warts. It is recommended that girls be vaccinated when they reach 11 or 12 years of age, although all females under the age of 26 may profit from completing the vaccination series.

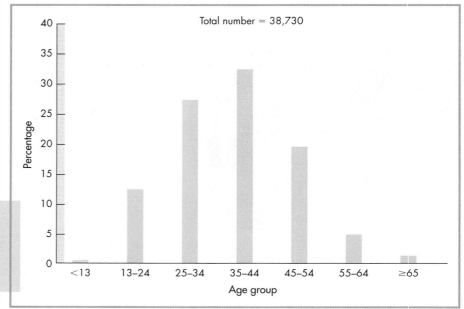

Figure 14.11 Because it can take many years before an HIV/AIDS-infected person shows symptoms of the disease, many teens who contract the disease may not be diagnosed until their 20s or 30s. (From CDC, 2004.)

Figure 14.12 African American and Hispanic adolescents are more likely to report having first intercourse before age 13 compared to their white counterparts. Early intercourse is known to be a risk factor for sexually transmitted infections. (From CDC, 2004.)

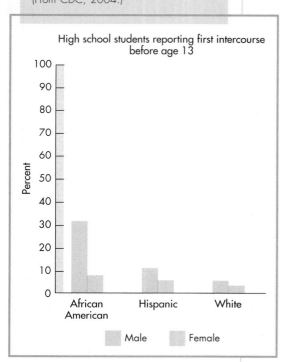

HIV/AIDS Human immunodeficiency virus (HIV) is the virus that causes acquired immunodeficiency syndrome (AIDS), a deadly disease that attacks the immune system, preventing it from combating infections. HIV is generally found in the blood and semen or vaginal fluid of infected individuals. Most HIV is contracted through anal, oral, or vaginal sex, or by sharing needles or syringes with an infected person, or prenatally or in infancy, by exposure through the uterine environment or breast milk,

As shown in Figure 14.11, in the United States those under 25 years account for less than 15 percent of new HIV/AIDS cases diagnosed in a given year. However, because the virus has a long incubation period before symptoms occur, many individuals who contracted the infection during their teen years may not be diagnosed until their 20s or 30s. It is estimated that 25 percent of infected individuals are unaware that they have contracted the virus.

Similar to other STIs, HIV/AIDS is especially prevalent in African American and Hispanic populations in the United States (Kaiser Foundation, 2008). In part this may be because the disease is concentrated primarily in large metropolitan areas in the United States, where there are large populations of ethnic minority groups. Ethnic minority groups may also be at greater risk because more African American and Hispanic youth become sexually active at earlier ages than their European American counterparts (Figure 14.12) and the age of first intercourse itself predicts infection risk.

To date, there is no cure for AIDS, although significant strides have been made in managing symptoms of the disease and prolonging the lives of infected individuals. Consequently, health care professionals and educators focus their attention on communicating the importance of disease prevention, for HIV/AIDS as well as for all other STIs. For sexually active youth, the consistent use of condoms is the most reliable means of STI prevention.

The dramatic changes of puberty are obvious to all. Sexual maturation places new demands on the body for sleep and good nutrition, opens new possibilities for relationships and experiences, and requires attention to special matters of health and well-being. Equally important, although perhaps less evident, are the substantial changes in reasoning and cognition that occur during adolescence.

_ _

Your school board is once again seeking your assistance, this time to revamp its sex education program, which is considered outdated and out of touch with issues facing today's youth. The goal is to develop programs aimed at seventh graders (12-year-olds) and tenth graders (15-year-olds). Outline a general plan for each program. What topics should each program include? What "issues facing today's youth" should be addressed? Should boys and girls participate in the program together or separately? Explain how the program would take into account differences between 12- and 15-year-olds.

Cognitive Development

How adolescents interpret and react to their changing bodies, as well as to their changing social life and relationships, is influenced by their developing intellectual abilities—that is, the ways in which they reason about themselves and their development and about the world around them. Indeed, some of the most fascinating developments of the adolescent period are those that concern the workings of the mind. When G. Stanley Hall argued that adolescents are the future of our species, he was thinking in particular of their newly acquired capacities for reasoning, planning, deciding, and imagining—intellectual ingredients that are essential to our species' proudest accomplishments, as well as to the individual's success in the world. As in earlier chapters, we look at various approaches to cognition—at Piaget's theory and then at information processing and sociocultural approaches.

Advances in cognitive development and reasoning played an important part in Herbert Hedberg's high school science project on cancer diagnosis, for which he won top honors and a $100,000 scholarship.

Piaget's Theory of Formal Operations

It was Piaget's contention that changes in the way adolescents think about themselves, their personal relationships, and the nature of their society have a common source: the emergence of **formal operations** (Table 14.2). As you may recall, an "operation" in Piaget's terminology is a mental action that fits into a logical system. Examples of *concrete operations,* typically achieved in middle childhood, include the mathematical operations of adding and subtracting, as well as other logical operations such as placing items in a serial order—say, from shortest to tallest. The concrete-operational child is able to apply operations to the real world. What distinguishes the formal-operational adolescent is the ability to apply operations to operations—that is, to systematically relate relationships to each other. For this reason, formal operations are also called *second-order operations.* David Moshman provides the following illustration (Moshman, 1999, p. 13):

Consider the following proportion:

$$10/5 = 4/2$$

To comprehend the logic of this proportion, it must be understood that the relation of 10 to 5 is equal to the relation of 4 to 2 (that is, that in both cases, the first number is twice as great as the second). The focus is on a relation (of equality, in this case) between two relations. A proportion, in other words, is a relation between two relations, a second-order relation.

Formal-operational thinking is the kind of thinking needed by anyone who has to solve problems systematically. To give two examples from the adult world of work, the ability to use formal-operational thinking is needed by the owner of a gasoline station who, to make a profit, has to take into account the wholesale price of gasoline, the kinds of customers who pass by the station, the types of services

formal operations In Piaget's terms, a kind of mental operation in which all possible combinations are considered in solving a problem. Consequently, each partial link is grouped in relation to the whole; in other words, reasoning moves continually as a function of a structured whole.

table 14.2

Piaget's Stages of Cognitive Development: Formal Operational

Age (years)	Stage	Description	Characteristics of Formal-Operational Thinking
Birth to 2	Sensorimotor	Infants' achievements consist largely of coordinating their sensory perceptions and simple motor behaviors. As they move through the 6 substages of this period, infants come to recognize the existence of a world outside themselves and begin to interact with it in deliberate ways.	Formal-operational reasoning, in which each partial link in a chain of reasoning is related to the problem as a whole • Young people solve the combination-of-chemicals problem by systematically testing all possible combinations. • In forming a personal identity, young people take into account how they judge others, how others judge them, how they judge the judgment process of others, and how all this corresponds to social categories available in the culture. Application of formal-operational thinking to a wide variety of life's problems • Young people think about politics and law in terms of abstract principles, and are capable of seeing the beneficial, rather than just the punitive, side of laws. • Young people are interested in universal ethical principles and critical of adults' hypocrisies.
2 to 6	Preoperational	Young children can represent reality to themselves through the use of symbols, including mental images, words, and gestures. Objects and events no longer have to be present to be thought about, but children often fail to distinguish their point of view from that of others', become easily captured by surface appearances, and are often confused about causal relations.	
6 to 12	Concrete operational	As they enter middle childhood, children become capable of mental operations, internalized actions that fit into a logical system. Operational thinking allows children mentally to combine, separate, order, and transform objects and actions. Such operations are considered concrete because they are carried out in the presence of the objects and events being thought about.	
12 to 19	Formal operational	In adolescence, the developing person acquires the ability to think systematically about all logical relations within a problem. Adolescents display keen interest in abstract ideas and in the process of thinking itself.	

the station needs to offer, the hours it needs to stay open, and the cost of labor, supplies, rent, and utilities; or by a lawyer who must consider a wide variety of alternative strategies, legal precedents, and possible consequences in deciding how best to present a case and counter the arguments of the attorney on the opposing side.

Reasoning by Manipulating Variables Inhelder and Piaget's studies of formal-operational thinking focused on very basic versions of the kinds of problems encountered in scientific laboratories. Typically, these problems require subjects to hold one variable of a complex system constant while systematically searching mentally through all the other variables. To illustrate, suppose you remembered the first two digits of your combination lock (2, 5) but could not remember the last two. Thus, you need to solve the problem: $2 - 5 - x - y$, where x and y are variables that can vary from 0 to 9. Solving the problem without formal operations, you might plug in values randomly, or insert your brother's age, the number of times you have given blood, and so on. This strategy is obviously flawed. For one thing, it would be very difficult for you to keep track of all your previous entries and separate the "tried" from the "to be tried." A formal-operational strategy, on the other hand, would systematically test every possible pair of digits—0-0, 0-1, 0-2 . . . 1-0, 1-1, 1-2 . . . all the way through to 9-0, 9-1 . . . 9-9 if necessary.

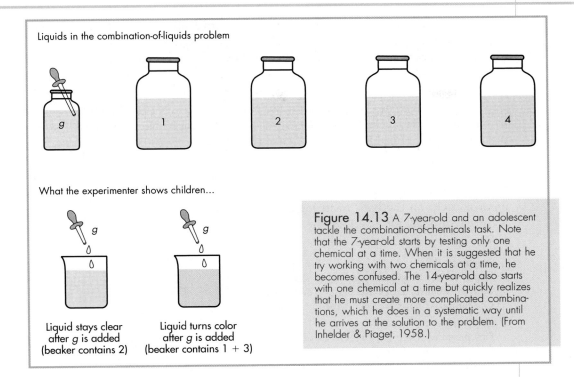

Liquids in the combination-of-liquids problem

g   1   2   3   4

What the experimenter shows children...

g   *g*

Liquid stays clear
after *g* is added
(beaker contains 2)

Liquid turns color
after *g* is added
(beaker contains 1 + 3)

Figure 14.13 A 7-year-old and an adolescent tackle the combination-of-chemicals task. Note that the 7-year-old starts by testing only one chemical at a time. When it is suggested that he try working with two chemicals at a time, he becomes confused. The 14-year-old also starts with one chemical at a time but quickly realizes that he must create more complicated combinations, which he does in a systematic way until he arrives at the solution to the problem. (From Inhelder & Piaget, 1958.)

Perhaps the most widely cited Piagetian test of formal operations is the combination-of-liquids problem, which basically is the combination lock problem with a twist. At the start of the task, the individual is shown four large bottles, numbered 1–4, along with a smaller bottle containing an eye dropper and labeled *g* (Figure 14.13). Each bottle contains a clear liquid. The experimenter then draws the individual's attention to two beakers, explaining that each contains liquid from one, some, or all of the four bottles. Then comes the critical moment: The experimenter puts a drop of the liquid from the small bottle into each beaker. The liquid in one beaker stays clear; the liquid in the other turns a brilliant yellow. (The first beaker contains liquid from bottle 2; the second beaker—the one that changes color— contains liquid from bottles 1 and 3.) The individual's task is to figure out how to produce the color change by putting the liquids (alone and in combination) into new beakers, and adding to each beaker a drop from the *g* bottle.

Drawing on the combination lock problem, you can imagine how a formal-operational individual might set about systematically testing all possibilities—adding *g* first to each of the four liquids separately, then to all two-way combinations, all three-way combinations and, finally, the four-way combination. Systematic testing is especially crucial because this problem involves a twist: the liquid in bottle 4 is a neutralizer, which will keep the color clear, no matter what. A formal-operational individual will figure this out, based on the following evidence:

$$1 - 3 \rightarrow \text{yellow}$$
$$1 - 2 - 3 \rightarrow \text{yellow}$$
$$1 - 3 - 4 \rightarrow \text{clear}$$
$$1 - 2 - 3 - 4 \rightarrow \text{clear}$$

As you can see, this is a very difficult problem, and concrete-operational children and formal-operational adolescents tend to solve it in much the same way that they might solve the combination lock problem. That is, concrete-operational children are unable to grasp the system of relations that logically specify all possible solutions to the problem and are likely to go about the task unsystematically, combining the liquids willy-nilly. In contrast, formal-operational-adolescents will begin with the simplest possibility (that one of the liquids in the numbered bottles, when combined with *g,* might turn yellow) and then proceed to the other levels of complexity—systematically adding combinations of two, three, and all four of the liquids. Interestingly, a child's success on this, as well as Piaget's other tests of formal operations, seems critically connected to whether the child has had extensive experience in Western-style schools that emphasize systematically testing hypotheses, as in high school science classes (Rogoff, 2003).

Hypothetical-Deductive Reasoning

A central feature of scientific thinking is **hypothetical-deductive reasoning**, which involves the ability to judge an argument entirely on the basis of its logical form, regardless of whether the argument is true. Consider, for example, the following arguments (adapted from Moshman, 1999):

Argument 1
First premise: Elephants are bigger than mice.
Second premise: Dogs are bigger than mice.
Conclusion: Therefore, elephants are bigger than dogs.

Argument 2
First premise: Mice are bigger than dogs.
Second premise: Dogs are bigger than elephants.
Conclusion: Therefore, mice are bigger than elephants.

Because all the statements in the first argument are true, the concrete-operational child will judge it to be more logical than the second argument, for which all of the statements are false. The formal-operational individual, on the other hand, will understand that the second argument is logical—that is, the conclusion follows from the premises—whereas the first argument is not. Correctly solving this task demonstrates the ability of formal thinkers to distinguish between truth and logic, an ability of vital importance in thinking beyond actual experience to consider and evaluate the possible.

In general, research (summarized by Müller et al., 1999) finds a steady increase in logical reasoning between the fourth and twelfth grades (roughly, between 10 and 18 years of age). In fact, formal-deductive reasoning is very rare before the sixth grade (11 to 12 years of age).

Promoting Formal-Operational Thinking through Sociocognitive Conflict

Particularly because of evidence that formal operational thinking flourishes better in some contexts than in others, developmentalists have worked to understand the nature of experience that promotes its development. Recall that according to Piaget's theory, developmental change takes place when the processes of *assimilation* and *accommodation* lead to *equilibration*—that is, to a new balance in the person's understanding of the world achieved by the person's finding a fit between his or her previous understanding and new experiences (Chapter 1, pp. 22–23). Thus, new experiences disrupt an existing balance, producing a type of cognitive conflict, and with the resolution of the conflict and restoration of equilibration, the individual moves to a higher, more inclusive level of understanding.

Cognitive conflict is in this way key to development and, Piaget argued, social interaction is an important source of cognitive conflict (Piaget, 1928, 1995). This is because social interaction exposes children to points of view and ways of understanding the world that are different from their own, and these new ideas upset the balance reflected in their current level of understanding. **Sociocognitive conflict** is the term used by developmentalists to describe cognitive conflict that is rooted in social experience (Bearison & Dorval, 2002).

hypothetical-deductive reasoning The ability to formulate and evaluate the logical implications of a set of premises, even if it is imaginary or contradicts the real world.

sociocognitive conflict Cognitive conflict that is rooted in social experience.

Insight into the nature of sociocognitive conflict is provided in a study of changes in how college students solve formal-operational tasks. Rose Dimant and David Bearison (1991) had college students work through six sessions of increasingly difficult problems that were similar to the combinations-of-liquids task. In some cases the students worked alone, and in others, they worked with another student. Analysis of videotapes of the sessions in which two students worked together revealed that the quality of the students' conversation about the problems was the key to their exhibiting formal-operational abilities on this task. Students who actively engaged in the task and worked cooperatively showed significantly greater gains when retested than did students who worked alone or who worked in pairs but did not engage in collaborative problem-solving actions. Interactions that included disagreements, contradictions, and alternative solutions—the interactions with the potential to trigger sociocognitive conflict—were the most effective in promoting higher levels of functioning (see the box "ICONS: Peacekeeping in a Virtual Classroom" for an example of a program designed to induce sociocognitive conflict).

Variability in Formal-Operational Thinking Cross-cultural evidence that people failed to reach formal operations without extensive schooling led Piaget to conclude that the stage of formal operations is not universal but depends on certain types of experience. In fact, even extensive schooling does not guarantee the attainment of formal operations. For example, studies find that as few as 30 to 40 percent of well-educated Americans in their late teens and early twenties are able to solve the combination-of-liquids and other formal-operational problems (Moshman, 1998). In addition, formal operations show a high degree of variability within individuals; that is, many individuals who are capable of formal-operational thought do not employ formal-operational strategies in all situations (Markovits & Barrouillet, 2002). Thus, a car mechanic who uses formal-operational thought to troubleshoot an engine problem may use concrete-operational thinking in most other domains of life. Indeed, there is mounting evidence that most decisions in everyday contexts, whether by adolescents or adults, do not employ the strategies of formal-operational thinking (Klaczynski & Cottrell, 2004; Kokis et al., 2002; Keating, 2004).

In light of the high degree of variability of formal-operational thinking both between and within cultures, modern researchers have argued that the study of advanced intellectual development should shift from focusing on a general stage, of formal operations, to looking at specific forms of reasoning associated with particular types of tasks and cultural practices.

Information-Processing Approaches

Whereas in the Piagetian view the advances in adolescents' cognition result from global, qualitative change, information-processing theorists believe that adolescents' expanded cognitive abilities are better explained as the result of the continuing development of various cognitive structures and processes. In particular, information-processing approaches emphasize how adolescents' ability to think systematically arises from the increased capacity of their working memory and from their ability to apply more powerful problem-solving strategies with increasing reliability (Case, 1998; Markovits, 2006). In problem solving, increased memory capacity makes it possible to coordinate several different factors at once, keep intermediate results in mind, and come up with a solution that is comprehensive and consistent.

Adolescent decision making is an area of special interest to developmentalists because it has far-reaching consequences for adolescents' health and well-being. Knowledge of how adolescents make decisions regarding risk-taking behavior, for example, may help educators, policy makers, and child advocates in addressing

ICONS: Peacekeeping in a Virtual Classroom

IMAGINE THAT YOU AND A TEAM OF classmates are representing Nigeria at a conference table that includes teams of delegates from 10 other countries. This international committee is meeting to develop guidelines for how the United Nations should respond to outbreaks of genocide and politicide—that is, to mass murder committed against members of, respectively, an ethnic or political group. In the past, as with the present massacres occurring in Darfur, the international community has responded slowly and unsystematically, often simply standing by while brutal campaigns against a targeted group continued unchecked. Your committee is charged with proposing answers to the following questions: What guidelines should dictate when it is appropriate for the international community to commit peacekeeping forces to a specific conflict? How should a decision about when and how to commit such forces be made? Should international forces be involved in ending conflicts or limited to only keeping an existing peace?

The scenario described above is typical of the hypothetical situations given to high school and college students involved in a special project created at the University of Maryland. The International Communications and Negotiation Project (ICONS) uses computer networks and peer collaboration to create learning environments in which students reason about deep political issues concerning human rights and the global environment. In ICONS, students pretend to be diplomats from different countries and negotiate solutions to problems with other student-diplomats. Students on the same team (Nigeria, for example), meet face-to-face, but they interact with the other teams through computers. Each team needs to present a "unified front" when it negotiates with the other teams, which encourages team members to works toward a common perspective and fosters identification with the country they represent.

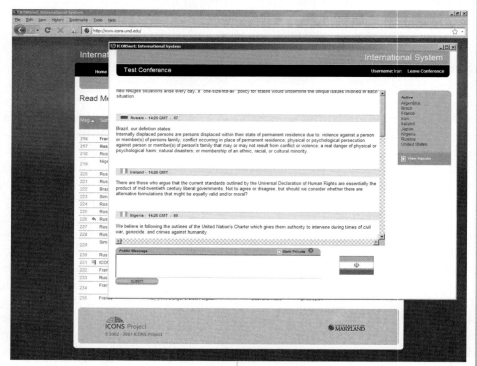

Courtesy of Icons Project

Although ICONS was originally designed simply to engage students in simulated international negotiation about political issues, it has captured the attention of developmentalists interested in how knowledge is coconstructed in social contexts. Developmentalists have examined how students build political expertise on an issue in the course of interacting with teammates and other student teams (Torney-Purta, 1996). In general, they find that over time students generate increasingly sophisticated problem solutions. In the course of discussion—agreeing, disagreeing, clarifying goals, suggesting revisions, and justifying positions—students are increasingly able to take into account multiple political, economic, and humanitarian variables and the perspectives of different countries. In the terms of Vygotsky's sociocultural approach, this sort of collaborative problem solving serves to scaffold the development of knowledge and contributes to a process through which student-diplomats are transformed from novices to experts. A central feature of the process is the creation of a "community of learners" (Rogoff et al., 2005) in which members feel responsibility toward each other and toward their common goals. Indeed, a survey tapping into the student-diplomats' sense of community found that 90 percent of the project participants reported moderate or high levels of identification with the country they represented. On the final day of her involvement on the project, one student remarked sadly, "It's really too bad; next week there won't be any [computer] messages for us as Nigerian diplomats. We'll have to go back to just being students" (Torney-Purta, 1996; p. 216).

such problems as juvenile crime, suicide, pregnancy, and HIV infection (Miller & Byrnes, 2001). Likewise, the complexity of adolescent thinking is relevant to important legal issues. It is, for example, at the heart of debates about whether adolescents who commit crimes should be tried as adults (Grisso et al., 2003) and about whether adolescents should be allowed to undergo medical procedures, including abortions, without the consent of a parent. The decision-making abilities of adolescents are also relevant to the question of whether they are capable of giving *informed consent* (see Chapter 1, p. 44) to participate in research projects (Halpern-Felsher & Cauffman, 2001).

In their review of research on decision-making competence, Bonnie Halpern-Felsher and Elizabeth Cauffman (2001) identified five steps that are commonly associated with effective decision making:

1. Identify possible decision options.

2. Identify possible risks and benefits associated with each option.

3. Evaluate the desirability of each consequence.

4. Assess the likelihood of each consequence.

5. Decide on the best course of action by combining the information obtained in the previous steps according to a decision rule.

In an effort to examine variation in decision-making in children's daily lives, Halpern-Felsher and Cauffman presented sixth- to twelfth-graders and young adults with decision-making scenarios in which they were asked to help a peer solve a problem. The problems included whether the peer should undergo a medical procedure (medical domain), should participate in a research project (informed consent domain), or should live with the mother or father after a divorce (family domain). For example, the following dilemma was presented for the medical domain: "I've been thinking about having this operation. It won't make me healthier or anything, but I'd like to have it because it would make me look better since I've always had this ugly thing like a bump on my cheek. I could have an operation to remove it. I'm trying to decide whether to have the operation, and I can't decide. Do you think I should have the operation?" (p. 262).

The participants were played a tape of the dilemmas and instructed to respond out loud with their advice. The researchers then coded their responses, looking for whether or not the participants mentioned options (e.g., "Are there treatments other than surgery?"), risks (e.g., "You could be scarred by the operation"), benefits (e.g., "You could be happy with the results of the surgery"), long-term consequences (e.g., "In the long run, you might feel better about yourself"), and applying a decision rule ("Have you gotten a second opinion?").

Overall, the researchers found that adults demonstrate significantly higher levels of decision-making competence than do adolescents, being more likely than adolescents, especially sixth- to eighth-graders, to employ all five of the decision-making steps listed above. However, noting that many adolescents in the study displayed high levels of competence, the researchers argue that it is difficult to identify an age boundary between immature and mature decision making, and they caution against making hard-and-fast legal or social policies based solely on age or (in)competence. It is particularly difficult, they contend, to justify withholding certain medical treatments (for HIV infection, for example) because adolescents do not fully understand the implications of the treatment. "In such cases," the researchers believe, "the benefits of extending health-care access may outweigh the risks" (Halpern-Felsher & Cauffman, 2001, p. 272).

In the work described above, adolescents were presented with hypothetical problems in artificial settings. As we will discuss in Chapter 15, making decisions in a laboratory can be quite different from making them in emotionally charged and socially meaningful "real life" settings. The contexts of decision making, and the consequences of good and bad decisions, are quite different for adolescents and adults.

Sociocultural Approaches

Like information-processing theorists, developmentalists who examine adolescent thinking from a sociocultural perspective focus mainly on specific forms of thinking

Sociocultural approaches focus on how social interactions, relationships, and cultural norms contribute to intellectual development and learning. It is likely that these boys, thoroughly engrossed in their books, recieve a lot of support from family, teachers, and peers for excelling at school.

GoGo Images Corporation/Alamy

used in particular problem-solving situations. In addition, however, sociocultural theorists emphasize how the means of solving problems are influenced and guided by the social interactions of the participants (Greenfield et al., 2003; Rogoff, 2003).

From a sociocultural perspective, games provide an ideal setting for exploring the development of complex reasoning skills in adolescence. As you may recall from our discussion in Chapter 13 (pp. 460–461), games typically include material and symbolic tools of culture, provide a means of transmitting cultural values and norms, and often involve quite sophisticated forms of reasoning. In addition, many games are highly social, requiring players to coordinate goals and strategies with each other. Using a Vygotskian sociocultural approach, Na'ilah Nasir has explored adolescents' reasoning in the context of a game of strategy popular in many African American communities—dominoes (Nasir, 2005).

In Nasir's study, pairs of individuals played in teams against one another. Each player selects 7 dominoes from the total set of 28 tiles (all are placed face down). Whoever draws the double 6 tile places it on the board, and the game begins. Players take turns matching the end of one of their dominoes to the end of a tile on the board. In the version of dominoes involved, if, after a domino is played, the sum of all the end dominoes is a multiple of five, then the player receives those points; if the sum is not a multiple of five, no points are scored. Playing the game well involves scoring points by making the right sorts of matches (resulting in multiples of five) and assisting one's partner while blocking the opposing team from scoring.

Nasir's analysis documents fascinating transformations in domino play by children, adolescents, and adults. As we would expect from Piagetian research, adolescents were much more adept at generating and evaluating the point value of possible moves—for themselves, as well as for their partner and opponents—than were younger children, who were primarily concerned with the matching of ends. However, the Vygotskian approach adopted by Nasir emphasized how individuals sought and received help from other players in ways that scaffolded their developing knowledge of the game and their mastery of various scoring, blocking, and partner-assisting strategies. Consider the following examples, the first involving elementary school students, the second high school students (Nasir, 2005, pp. 13, 20):

> It's David's turn and he's not sure which domino to play. He holds out the 6-0 toward his partner, Tyrell, saying, "Man, put that down there, dog." An opponent responds with "Where?" Tyrell says, "It goes right there!" and plays the domino for David.

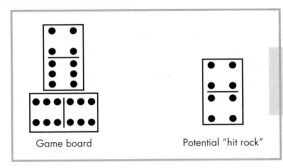

Figure 14.14 Popular in many African American communities, the game of dominoes calls on complex formal-operational reasoning skills.

Game board

Potential "hit rock"

Latrisha and Deondre are playing against James and Aaron. Deondre begins the game with the double 6. Aaron follows the play with the 6-4 (Figure 14.14). James immediately criticizes this play by saying, "What you doin' over there, man?" criticizing Aaron for leaving open the possibility of the other team playing the 4-4 (known as the "hit rock") and scoring 20 points. Latrisha chimes in, affirming James's criticism, "He lucky I ain't got the hit rock. I sho' would tax your butt."

From these examples it is clear that forms of reasoning change substantially from childhood to adolescence and that this intellectual development is not a solitary process but emerges in the course of social participation (Cole, 1996). Just as social participation contributes to intellectual development, intellectual development, as we will see below, contributes to the adolescent's social participation, by affecting moral reasoning and behavior.

||||| **APPLY** ▪ **CONNECT** ▪ **DISCUSS** _

Present evidence for and against the argument that it is appropriate for adolescents to be tried in court as adults. What is your own opinion on this matter? Why? Defend your position using research presented in this section.

Moral Development

Regardless of their theoretical orientation, developmentalists agree that adolescence is a time during which issues of moral behavior take on special importance for young people, typified by such questions as: What is right? What is wrong? What principles should I base my behavior on and use to judge the behavior of others? Evidence suggests that the processes used to think about such questions, like those used to think about science problems, undergo important changes between the ages of 12 and 19 years (Moshman, 1999; Turiel, 2002).

Kohlberg's Theory of Moral Reasoning

As we noted in Chapter 13 (pp. 462–465), the study of moral development has been greatly influenced by Lawrence Kohlberg, who proposed that moral reasoning may progress across three broad levels, each consisting of two stages (Table 14.3 summarizes these levels and stages). As they develop from one stage to the next, children make more complex analyses both of moral obligations among individuals and of moral obligations between individuals and their social groups.

Recall that, according to Kohlberg, at the start of middle childhood moral reasoning is at the *preconventional level* (stages 1 and 2), with children judging the rightness or

Their increased understanding of the social order motivates adolescents to question authority and challenge the status quo. This Turkish student is being arrested for protesting against a political council that strictly controls Turkish universities.

Tarik Tinazoy/AFP/Getty Images

table 14.3

Kohlberg's Six Moral Stages

Level and Stage	What Is Right	Reasons for Doing Right	Social Perspective
Level I—Preconventional			
Stage 1—Heteronomous morality	• Adherence to rules backed by punishment; obedience for its own sake.	• Avoidance of punishment.	Egocentric point of view.
Stage 2—Instrumental morality	• Acting to meet one's own interests and needs and letting others do the same.	• To serve one's own needs or interests.	Concrete individualistic perspective: right is relative, an equal exchange.
Level II—Conventional			
Stage 3—Good-child morality	• Living up to what others expect.	• The need to be a good person in one's own eyes and those of others.	Perspective of the individual sharing feelings, agreements, and expectations with others.
Stage 4—Law-and-order morality	• Fulfilling the actual duties to which one has agreed. • Upholding laws except in extreme cases when they conflict with other fixed social duties • Contributing to society, group, or institution.	• To keep the institution going as a whole. • What would happen "if everyone did it"? • The imperative of conscience to meet one's defined obligations (easily confused with stage 3 belief in rules and authority).	Perspective of an individual in relation to the social group: takes the point of view of the system that defines roles and rules.
Level III—Postconventional, or Principled			
Stage 5—Social-contract reasoning	• Being aware that people hold a variety of values and opinions, most of which are relative to the group that holds them. • Upholding rules in the interest of impartiality and because they are the social contract. • Upholding universal values and rights, such as life and liberty, regardless of majority opinion.	• A sense of obligation to law because of one's social contract to make and abide by laws for the welfare of all and for the protection of all people's rights. • A feeling of contractual commitment, freely entered upon, to family, friendship, trust, and work obligations. • Concern that laws and duties be based on rational calculation of overall utility, "the greatest good for the greatest number."	Prior-to-society perspective: perspective of a rational individual aware of values and rights prior to social attachments and contracts.
Stage 6—Universal ethical principles	• Following self-chosen ethical principles because they are universal principles of justice: the equality of human rights and respect for the dignity of human beings as individual persons. • Judging laws or social agreements by the extent to which they rest on such principles. • When laws violate principles, acting in accordance with the principle.	• A belief in the validity of universal moral principles. • A sense of personal commitment to those principles.	Perspective of a moral point of view from which social arrangements derive: perspective is that of any rational individual recognizing the nature of morality or the fact that persons are ends in themselves and must be treated as such.

Source: Adapted from Kohlberg, 1976.

wrongness of actions purely in light of their own wants and fears, and that toward the end of middle childhood, children attain the first stage of the *conventional level*, stage 3, in which they begin to take social conventions into account and to recognize shared standards of right and wrong. Thus, in response to the famous "Heinz

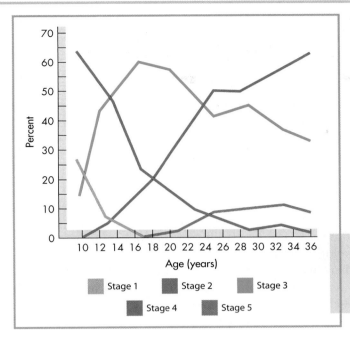

Figure 14.15 Mean percentage of U.S. citizens at each of Kohlberg's stages of moral reasoning at different ages. (Adapted from Colby et al., 1983.)

dilemma" (see p. 463), a younger child, at the preconventional level, might argue that Heinz should steal the expensive drug to save his wife because if she dies, he would get into trouble and be punished, whereas a child who has reached stage 3 might argue that he should steal the drug because if she dies, the family would blame him and he would be ashamed. Kohlberg called stage 3 reasoning "good-child morality" because he believed that for individuals in this stage, being moral means living up to the expectations of one's family and other significant people in one's life.

In adolescence moral reasoning at stage 4, the second stage of the conventional level, begins to appear, although stage 3 remains the dominant mode of moral reasoning until people reach their mid-20s (Figure 14.15) (Colby et al., 1983). Reasoning at stage 4 is like that at stage 3 except that its focus—the social perspective from which judgments are made—shifts from relations between individuals to relations between the individual and the larger society. People who reason at stage 4 believe that society has legitimate authority over individuals, and they feel an obligation to accept its laws, customs, and standards of decent behavior. Moral behavior from this point of view is behavior that upholds the law, maintains the social order, and contributes to the group. For this reason, stage 4 reasoning is also called "law-and-order morality" (Brown & Herrnstein, 1975, p. 289).

Kohlberg believed that moral thinking at stages 3 and 4 depends on a partial ability to engage in formal-operational reasoning—specifically, it requires the ability to consider simultaneously the various existing factors relevant to moral choices (Kohlberg, 1984). People who are reasoning at stages 3 and 4, however, are still reasoning concretely insofar as they do not yet simultaneously consider all possible relevant factors or form abstract hypotheses about what is moral.

With the transition from stage 4 to stage 5 comes another basic shift in the level of moral judgment. Reasoning at the *postconventional* (or *principled*) level requires people to go beyond existing social conventions to consider more abstract principles of right and wrong. Reasoning at stage 5, called *social contract reasoning,* is based on the idea of a society as bound by a social contract designed and agreed upon by the group to serve the needs of its members. People still accept and value the social system, but instead of insisting on maintaining society as it is, they are open to democratic processes of change and to continual exploration of possibilities for improving on the existing social order. Recognizing that laws are sometimes in conflict with moral principles, they become creators as well as maintainers of laws. Kohlberg found that stage 5 moral reasoning never appears before early adulthood and then only rarely.

People reach stage 6 in Kohlberg's system, the stage of *universal ethical principles,* when they make moral judgments in accordance with ethical principles that they believe transcend the rules of individual societies—principles of the equality of human rights and respect for the dignity of human beings as individuals. Laws are valid only insofar as they rest on these principles. Kohlberg and his colleagues failed to observe stage 6 reasoning in their research on moral dilemmas, and Kohlberg eventually concluded that this stage is more usefully thought of as a philosophical ideal than as a psychological reality. Nonetheless, there are examples of people who have put their lives at risk because of moral beliefs guided by stage 6 reasoning. Such was the case during World War II, when many European gentiles attempted to protect Jews from the Nazi efforts to exterminate them, even though being caught would have resulted in their own execution. According to Samuel and Pearl Oliner (1988), most of these individuals were motivated by ethical principles that they believed apply to all of humanity, the hallmark of stage 6 moral reasoning.

By and large, research confirms that children and adolescents progress through the sequence of moral reasoning proposed by Kohlberg (Rest et al., 1999). However, Kohlberg's approach is not without its difficulties (Moshman, 1999; Turiel, 2002). Two important critiques relate to gender and to culture.

Feminist Approaches to Moral Reasoning

Since her car accident, Tara had been in a persistent vegetative state, kept alive by sophisticated medical machinery. Her case became headline news in Canada when doctors refused the request of Tara's family to disconnect her life-support system and allow Tara to die. Emotionally charged arguments emerged on both sides of the issue as the case went to court. Some insisted that acceding to the family's request would violate Tara's right to life; others insisted that failing to do so would violate her right to die with dignity. At one point in the hotly debated and highly publicized drama, Tara's older sister, Kim, was interviewed by the press. "Everyone is talking about rights—the right to life; the right to die. It's become a big legal thing," said Kim. "But this isn't about rights at all. It's about my sister, and about our family, and how we take care of each other. I wish people could see that, and feel some compassion for what we're going through."

One of the most strident criticisms of Kohlberg's theory is that its conception of the nature of morality is too narrow. Taking a feminist approach to moral reasoning, Carol Gilligan (1982) asserted that Kohlberg's theory reflects a **morality of justice**—that is, a morality that emphasizes issues of rightness, fairness, and equality. As Kim illustrated in her comments to the press, the debate regarding her sister's right to life, or right to die with dignity, reflects a morality of justice orientation. However, from Carol Gilligan's feminist perspective on moral development, Kohlberg's emphasis on justice neglects a key dimension of moral reasoning and action: the importance of our duties and responsibilities to others. This other dimension, the **morality of care,** focuses on relationships, compassion, and social obligations—just the sort of issues that Kim said were being overlooked in the case of her sister.

These students were arrested on suspicion of planning an attack on their school. Despite evidence that teenagers lack adult decision-making and reasoning skills, they are often tried as adults in U.S. courts of law.

morality of justice A morality that emphasizes issues of rightness, fairness, and equality.

morality of care A morality that stresses relationships, compassion, and social obligations.

Gilligan's work inspired a great deal of debate, not because of her conception of a morality of care but because of her claim, based on largely anecdotal evidence, that girls and women are oriented to the morality of care, whereas boys and men are oriented toward the morality of justice (Moshman, 1999). More systematic research has found few gender differences in levels of moral reasoning in predominantly white or African American adolescents (Turiel, 1998; Walker et al., 1995; Weisz & Black, 2003). Despite the lack of evidence for strong gender differences, Gilligan's conception of a morality of care provides a broader, more inclusive view of moral reasoning than Kohlberg's original formulation, and has helped to orient researchers to the broader contexts of moral development and judgment.

Parent and Peer Contributions to Moral Development

Kohlberg maintained that parents have a minimal role in the moral development of their children, whereas peer interactions are essential to promoting moral growth (Walker et al., 2000). This is due, he argued, to the differences in power inherent in the two types of relationships. Because parents have unilateral authority over their offspring, children are not inclined to try to understand their parents' point of view when it differs from their own, or to negotiate and compromise on issues of disagreement. As you know from the previous discussion of sociocognitive conflict, intense engagement with alternative points of view can be a strong impetus to attaining higher levels of reasoning. Kohlberg believed that the more mutual and cooperative nature of peer relationships would provide a more fertile context for moral development. Indeed, research indicates that both the quantity and quality of peer relationships, including the number of close friendships, amount of participation in social activities, and leadership status, are significantly related to moral reasoning in adolescence (Schonert-Reichl, 1999).

Be that as it may, developmentalists have challenged Kohlberg's idea that parents have little impact in the moral realm (Pratt et al., 2003; Walker, 2007). Research finds that, in general, authoritative, democratic, responsive parenting is associated with higher levels of moral maturity (Pratt et al., 2003). Lawrence Walker and his colleagues conducted a rare longitudinal study comparing both parent and peer contexts (2000). Compared with peers, parents provided a higher level of cognitive functioning in discussions of moral issues and, when a "gentle Socratic method" was employed, children's moral maturity was advanced. However, consistent with the notion of sociocognitive conflict, peer interactions that were more turbulent and conflict-ridden were associated with the development of higher moral levels. The upshot is that both parent and peer relationships were highly influential in moral development, but each type of relationship contributed in distinctive ways.

Cultural Variations in Moral Reasoning

Like studies showing cross-cultural variability in formal-operational reasoning, studies using Kohlbergian dilemmas (such as the Heinz dilemma) reveal significant differences between cultural groups in moral reasoning (Kohlberg, 1969; Turiel, 2008). Although there are some exceptions (Shweder et al., 1987), most studies show that people who live in relatively small, technologically unsophisticated communities, have primarily face-to-face interactions with others, and have not received extensive schooling that exposes them to ways of life other than their own rarely reason beyond stage 3 on Kohlberg's scale (Figure 14.16). Most often they justify their moral decisions at the level of stage 1 or 2, although people in roles of special responsibility may reason at stage 3 (Snarey, 1995).

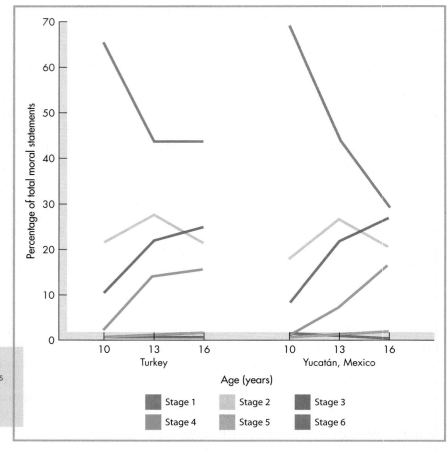

Figure 14.16 Age trends in the moral judgments of boys in small, isolated villages in two nations. Note the continuing high incidence of stage 1 responses even by 16-year-olds. (From Kohlberg, 1969)

Kohlberg suggested that cultural differences in social stimulation produce differences in moral reasoning. However, several developmentalists have argued that Kohlberg's stage sequence, particularly the higher stages, contains built-in value judgments that reflect the moral views of Western culture and democracy. Are we really to believe, such critics ask, that people who grow up in a traditional village in a developing country and reason at stage 2 of Kohlberg's sequence are less moral than the residents of a city in an industrially advanced country (Shweder et al., 2002)?

Kohlberg (1984) denied that cultural differences in performance on his dilemmas leads to the conclusion that some societies are more moral than others. He echoed the classical position of modern anthropology, that cultures should be thought of as unique configurations of beliefs and institutions that help the social group adapt to both local conditions and universal aspects of life on earth (Boas, 1911; Geertz, 1984). In this view, a culture in which stage 3 is the height of moral reasoning would be considered "morally equivalent" to a culture in which some people reason at stage 5 or 6, even though the specific reasoning practices could be scored as less "developed" according to Kohlberg's criteria.

Nevertheless, other approaches to moral reasoning have produced results that depart markedly from those obtained using Kohlberg's methods. Cross-cultural studies have reported that by adulthood, a shift from conventional to postconventional moral reasoning is quite widespread if not universal (Gielen & Markoulis, 2001). In cases in which differences appear between countries, the level of education provided to the populations in question appears to be the critical factor.

Using their *social domain theory,* which emphasizes the need to separate moral issues from issues involving social convention and personal choice (see Chapter

And as we discuss in Chapter 15, moral behavior is also tied to identity issues and the degree to which individuals are motivated to lead exemplary moral lives.

Yet another way to examine the relationship between moral reasoning and behavior is to approach it from the perspective of social domain theory. In the same way that this theory has proved useful in accounting for cross-cultural variability in moral reasoning, it provides insight into the relationship between adolescents' moral reasoning and their moral actions. In particular, the behaviors that researchers (and parents, as we discuss in Chapter 15) define as "moral" may not be defined as such by adolescents. An example comes from a study of the relationship between moral reasoning and risky behavior. Tara Kuther and Ann Higgins-D'Alessandro (2000) found that compared to adolescents who report lower levels of drugs and alcohol use, those who report higher levels are more likely to see their risky behaviors as personal decisions rather than as moral or conventional decisions. The researchers suggested that directors of drug and alcohol intervention programs take heed of this tendency and encourage youth to explore their views of the personal choice, social convention, and moral realms, and examine their behavior in light of each realm.

▌▌▌▌ APPLY ▬ CONNECT ▬ DISCUSS

Suppose you want to facilitate moral development in juvenile delinquents participating in a counseling program. How would you go about this from a Kohlbergian perspective? How would you do this from the perspective of social domain theory? In each case, consider whether your intervention programs would work with the teens one-on-one, or in family or peer groups.

Implications

Bodily changes that signal sexual maturity; wholly new ways of thinking, deciding, and processing information; a new sense of what constitutes morally appropriate behavior—all of these are significant changes that are part of the transitions of adolescence. But however private and personal these changes may be, the expectations, technologies, and institutions of an adolescent's culture provide maps for the journey toward maturity. In the following chapter, we explore the social and emotional developments that interweave with the physical and cognitive changes we have been examining.

SUMMARY

Adolescence is characterized by remarkable changes in physical and intellectual development, presenting challenges whose specifics depend on the particular society.

Adolescents and Society

- Virtually all societies recognize adolescence as an important transition requiring special attention. In philosophy and literature through the ages, adolescence has been seen as a period of unique peril and promise.

- Industrialization led to increased attention to adolescence, because it led to urban youth problems and to a need for a more educated workforce.

Biological Theories of Adolescent Development

- G. Stanley Hall saw adolescence as a time of "storm and stress" and as evolutionarily corresponding to a period beyond the biologically predetermined past, with adolescents thus representing the future of the species.

- Sigmund Freud saw adolescence as the beginning of the genital stage of psychosexual development and its main task as reestablishing the balance among the id, ego, and superego that was upset by the upsurge of sexual excitation at puberty.

- Modern biological approaches focus on evolutionary implications of such aspects as delayed maturation followed by the growth spurt at puberty, a pattern unique to humans and evolutionarily advantageous.

Puberty

- Puberty refers to the biological developments that lead to physical maturity and capacity for reproduction.

- The growth spurt is one of the first signs of puberty.

- In girls, the development of primary sex characteristics, or reproductive organs, includes the maturation of the ovaries, which leads to ovulation, typically beginning after menarche, the first menstrual period. In boys, it includes the maturation of the testes, which leads to sperm production and to semenarche, the first ejaculation. Development of secondary sex characteristics, beginning with breast buds in girls and pubic hair in both sexes, provides evidence that puberty is underway.

- Significant brain development in adolescence, particularly of the frontal lobes, includes further myelination and a spurt of synaptogenesis following by synaptic pruning.

- The timing of puberty, earlier for girls than for boys, varies widely as a result of complex interactions between genetic and environmental factors. Caloric intake may be among the crucial environmental factors, as a certain level of body fat may be required for the onset of puberty; thus, nutritional improvements may have led to the secular trend of decline over the decades in the average age of puberty.

- Although adolescence is generally a time of good health, its astronomical growth rates place new demands on the body, creating special needs for nutrition, sleep, and physical activity—needs that all too often are not fully met.

- Whether or not a society marks puberty with special ceremonies, puberty has profound social and psychological consequences, which are influenced by cultural beliefs and values. For cultural reasons, puberty may tend to be more psychologically difficult for girls than for boys and early pubertal timing may tend to be more psychologically difficult than late timing.

The Emergence of Sexual Behavior

- The step from virginity to sexual activity is a significant one and is treated in different ways from culture to culture.

- Adolescents learn about sexuality from various sources—parents, peers, media, and educational programs—and there is great variability in what is taught and how it is taught. Greater societal acceptance of teenage sexuality may be linked to lower levels of teen pregnancy and STIs.

- Age at first intercourse varies considerably across countries and over time. Boys tend to report more positive feelings about first intercourse than do girls.

- Rates of STIs, including chlamydia and, especially, HPV (human papillomavirus), are high among adolescents in the United States. Relatively low HIV/AIDS rates might reflect the disease's incubation period.

Cognitive Development

- According to Piaget, adolescence is marked by the emergence of a capacity for formal operational thinking, for relating relationships to each other. Formal-operational thinkers can reason by systematically manipulating variables and can use hypothetical-deductive reasoning, judging an argument based on logical form alone.

- Sociocognitive conflict—cognitive conflict rooted in social experience—may be particularly useful for promoting formal-operational thinking. Rather than being a universal stage, formal-operational thinking appears to depend on certain experiences and to not be consistently used by those who do use it.

- Information-processing approaches attribute adolescents' more systematic thinking to increased working memory capacity and to the use of more powerful problem-solving strategies.

- Sociocultural approaches to adolescent thinking demonstrate the role of social interactions in scaffolding its development.

Moral Development

- According to Lawrence Kohlberg, moral reasoning at stage 4 ("law-and-order morality") appears during adolescence, although reasoning at stage 3 ("good-child morality") remains more typical. Kohlberg believed that postconventional reasoning (based on principles) is relatively rare.

- Carol Gilligan, taking a feminist approach, argued that Kohlberg had emphasized a morality of justice at the expense of a morality of care.

- Although Kohlberg's approach showed significant differences between cultures in members' moral reasoning, cross-cultural studies taking other approaches suggest that differences between cultures are few and that the shift to postconventional reasoning is widespread. Social domain theory, one such approach, shows the importance of separating issues of morality from issues of social convention and personal choice.

- Parents and peers make important but distinct contributions to adolescents' moral development.

- Adolescents' actions do not always accord with their morals, perhaps reflecting inconsistent societal standards, as well as adolescents' different definitions of issues as belonging to moral versus personal choice and social convention domains. Perspective taking and prosocial reasoning encourage moral behavior.

Key Terms

growth spurt, p. 503
puberty, p. 504
primary sex characteristics, p. 505
secondary sex characteristics, p. 505
menarche, p. 505

semenarche, p. 506
secular trend, p. 509
emotional tone, p. 513
anorexia nervosa, p. 514
bulimia nervosa, p. 514

formal operations, p. 503
hypothetical-deductive reasoning, p. 526
sociocognitive conflict, p. 526
morality of justice, p. 534
morality of care, p. 534

Social and Emotional Development in Adolescence

Kelly, Anna, and Hope are high school juniors who have been good friends since middle school. They have been through a lot together—algebra, swim team, the divorce of Kelly's parents and, of course, puberty. But of all the experiences they have shared, Jamborees stand out as especially important to their friendship. They started the Jamboree tradition when they were freshmen and decided to have a party in the woods. It was a complicated affair, requiring a great deal of organization and planning. Tents and sleeping bags were needed, as well as excuses for staying out all night. The centerpiece of the event—the keg of beer—was acquired through sensitive, high-powered negotiations with Anna's older brother; getting it to the designated place in the woods involved "borrowing" a three-wheeler in the wee hours of the morning, after its owner (Kelly's dad) had gone to bed. The first Jamboree was such a success that the girls went on to organize about two every year. Each Jamboree was a unique adventure, but the girls agree that the first one was special, a "sacred" event.

> Kelly: We reminisce about it now.
> Anna: . . . the most embarrassing things . . .
> Hope: Yeah, like you and Ryan!
> Anna: I didn't kiss him or anything.
> Kelly: That was the third [Jamboree].
> Anna: No, that was the second, when Elliot came looking for Hope, while you were out with Tyler.
> Kelly: All of our new friends, like, feel so out of place because when anyone brings up a Jamboree, we talk about it like we're in our own little world.
> Hope: A lot of people comment that we seem really close.
> Kelly: That's true, how close we are. And because of that, because we always seem like we have fun, and because it's noticeable, we seem so close that people will assume that, "Oh, they must not want us to talk to them."
> Anna: We don't try to; it's not intentional. It's just 'cause if you'd seen it . . . it wasn't like a normal party, 'cause people spend the night, and it's like a mile walk . . .
> Hope: And remember how, at the first one, Kelly lost her shoe in the river, and cut her foot, and had to walk barefoot?
> Anna: And that guy, that ex-convict that was hiding in the woods, and how the police came and we thought that they caught us?

(Adapted from Lightfoot, 1997.)

Social and emotional lives undergo significant changes when children enter adolescence. This is apparent in the closeness shared by Kelly, Hope, and Anna; in

Dennis MacDonald/PhotoEdit Inc

David R. Frazier/The Image Works

Whether they grow up in Michigan, U.S., or Tierra del Fuego, Argentina, adolescents increasingly turn to each other to share ideas, feelings, and experiences.

their belief that their closeness affects those around them; and in their sense that their friendship deepened through the Jamboree experiences that they organized on their own, in opposition to authority—their parents, as well as the law.

In this chapter, we examine the new feelings, relationships, and ways of interacting with family and friends that are typical of adolescence and that mark a new beginning in adolescents' sense of themselves and their place in the world. Adolescence is a time of seeking answers to fundamental questions of identity: Who am I? Who will I become? What do I want? How do I fit in?

We begin this chapter by exploring adolescents' emotional development, asking about the different types of feelings that adolescents experience and how they come to express and control them. We then focus our attention on adolescents' changing relationships—first with friends, then with family. Our third topic is identity development, and its relationship to adolescents' social lives and cultures. We also look at some social and emotional problems of adolescence. Finally, we examine how the complex emotional, social, and identity developments of adolescence converge in the period of "emerging adulthood" and position individuals at the threshold of maturity. Throughout our discussion, you will see evidence of how culture and biology are interwoven in the fabric of adolescent development.

Emotional Development in Adolescence

Adolescence is widely regarded as a period fraught with emotional highs and lows, in which behavior is often driven by impulse rather than rational thought. You know from Chapter 14 that adolescents' reputation for emotional intensity, instability, and flaming passion was well established as early as Plato's day. Recall his warning against adolescents' consumption of wine: "fire must not be poured upon fire." Two thousand years later, Freud described the adolescent as a "boiling cauldron of desire." Needless to say, these images of adolescence are as vivid today as they ever were.

In this section we take the age-old notion of adolescence as an emotional roller coaster ride punctuated with impulse-driven behavior and hold it up to the light of scientific analysis. Is it true that adolescents experience especially intense emotions and dramatic mood swings? If so, why, and how is emotional stability achieved as adolescents mature? Is it true that adolescents' behavior is exceptionally impulsive? If it is, how can behavioral impulsivity be reconciled with what we know about the significant strides adolescents make in the area of cognitive development and reasoning? As you saw in our discussions of emotional development during infancy and childhood, developmentalists have found it useful to distinguish between how emotions are experienced and how they are controlled and regulated (see Chapters 6, 9, and 13).

The Experience of Emotions

Many believe that peaks and valleys of emotional experience are a defining feature of adolescence. However, as you know from our discussions regarding infants and children, the study of emotional experiences poses significant challenges for researchers. Consequently, it is difficult to document whether, and to what extent, adolescence is the emotional roller coaster that so many believe it to be.

The effective study of emotional development in adolescence requires research tools that provide access to adolescents' emotional lives. One of the tools developmentalists most commonly use is the **experience sampling method (ESM),** in which research participants carry electronic pagers that beep at random intervals, signaling that it is time for them to fill out a brief report on their current feelings (Csikszentmihalyi & Larson, 1987). Although the ESM is time intensive and disruptive for participants (typically, the pager beeps every 1 to 2 hours, 15 hours per day, for a week or more), it has been praised for its *ecological validity* (see Chapter 1, p. 37) (Silk, Steinberg, & Morris, 2003). It has also generated a wealth of information about the types and intensities of adolescents' emotions, the situations in which they occur, and the extent to which they are related to gender, age, pubertal status, and psychological problems (Eisenberg et al., 2005; Larson & Richards, 2000; Silk et al., 2003).

In general, ESM studies find strong evidence for the idea that emotional states change in type and intensity throughout the adolescent years. Reed Larsen and his colleagues conducted a comprehensive, longitudinal study using ESM data collected from 220 participants over a period spanning early to late adolescence (Larson et al., 2002). When the participants were signaled by their pagers, they rated their emotional states (happy–unhappy; cheerful–irritable, friendly–angry) on a 7-point scale. Twice a year, they also filled out questionnaires about whether they had experienced major life events, including stressful events, during the past 6 months. The researchers found that more than 70 percent of the time, adolescents reported experiencing positive emotions. However, they also found some interesting changes in emotional life between early and late adolescence:

- On average, daily emotions become less positive between early adolescence and middle adolescence (10th grade) and remain relatively low through late adolescence; in other words, average happiness decreases during adolescence (Figure 15.1).

- The decline in average happiness is due in part to a decrease in intense positive emotions but due mostly to an increase in negative emotions.

experience sampling method (ESM) Tool used by developmentalists in which study participants, when signaled by electronic pagers at random intervals, fill out brief reports on their feelings. ESM has been used to study adolescents' emotional lives.

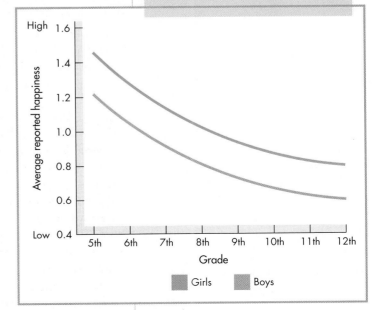

Figure 15.1 In general, girls report higher levels of happiness than do boys, although happiness declines for both girls and boys over the course of adolescence. (From Larson et al., 2002.)

- Throughout adolescence, girls tend to have more positive average emotions than do boys, as shown in the figure.

- Stressful life events were associated with equal amounts of negative emotion throughout adolescence, suggesting that there is no time during which adolescents are particularly emotionally sensitive or reactive to major life events.

- Over the course of adolescence, emotions become less intense and emotional ups and downs become less frequent.

In general, research suggests that an emotional roller coaster may be a poor metaphor for adolescent emotional life. There does not seem to be a particular time when adolescents are hypersensitive to stressful events, and the intensity and fluctuations of emotion seem to decrease over time.

Regulating Emotions

One of the primary explanations for why emotions become less intense and more stable over the course of adolescence is that teenagers become better able to control and regulate them, as well as the behaviors they might inspire (Steinberg, 2005). When her mom complains yet again that Shelley's tongue-piercing looks trashy and makes her sound like she has a speech impediment, Shelley may retreat to fume in her room rather than lash out in fury, "It's my @#$#% tongue, and I'll do what I want to it!" Or when Marisha's friends are heading out to party, she may stay home to study chemistry, not because she is passionate about the subject (she hates it, actually), but because she wants to do well on tomorrow's exam.

Both Shelley and Marisha are acting against impulse and inhibiting certain behaviors that would very likely lead to unsatisfying consequences. In addition, Marisha is persisting on a task (studying chemistry) despite a total lack of desire to do so, and in the face of a much more attractive alternative (partying). *Impulse control, inhibition,* and *persistence* are among the main features of emotion regulation, and they underlie the abilities to "down-regulate" negative emotions (as Shelley did when she cooled her fury) and "up-regulate" positive ones (as Marisha did when she mustered enthusiasm for studying). Adolescents who have difficulty regulating their emotions, especially negative emotions, are more likely to experience depression, anger, and a variety of social and behavior problems (Silk et al., 2003; Cooper et al., 2003).

As you may recall from earlier chapters, regulating emotions involves a complex interplay of biological and sociocultural processes. In adolescence, these processes interact in a unique way that has recently become of considerable interest to developmentalists.

Biological Processes As we discussed in Chapter 14, adolescence includes two significant biological events that occur on different timetables: (1) an influx of pubertal hormones during early adolescence, and (2) a spurt in brain growth that begins in early adolescence (possibly triggered by hormones) but is not complete until late adolescence. Several studies suggest that pubertal hormones are associated with emotional intensity and may account for adolescents' **sensation seeking,** or desire to participate in highly arousing activities (Martin et al., 2002). The infusion of hormones occurs at a time when the brain is undergoing considerable development, especially in regions of the frontal lobes associated with higher mental processes such as decision-making, judgment, and impulse control (see p. 507). Some developmentalists, including Laurence Steinberg, have speculated that in early adolescence there is a gap between intense emotions triggered by pubertal

sensation seeking Desire to participate in highly arousing activities, especially common in early and mid-adolescence.

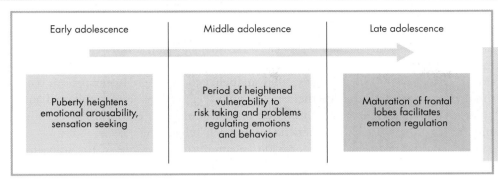

Figure 15.2 The influx of pubertal hormones may contribute to the sensation-seeking and risk taking characteristic of early and middle adolescence. The decline of these behaviors in late adolescence may be due to maturation of the frontal cortex, an area of the brain associated with decision making and higher cognitive functions. (From Steinberg, 2005.)

hormones and the brain's ability to regulate them (Figure 15.2). As a consequence, until the maturation of the frontal lobes is complete, the adolescent is especially vulnerable to risk taking, recklessness, and emotional problems (Steinberg, 2005).

The possible link between brain development and adolescents' unique vulnerability to risky decision making was explored in a recent study comparing adolescents' and adults' decisions under different social conditions (Gardner & Steinberg, in press). The study involved a computerized driving game that presented opportunities for taking risks, such as driving through a yellow light in order to get more points for getting the car farther down the road. In one condition, participants played alone. In the other condition, participants played while two friends were watching and giving advice. The adults played similarly in both conditions. In contrast, adolescents who played with friends present were much more likely than those who played alone to risk crashing the car by driving through yellow lights.

It seems, then, that compared with those of adults, adolescents' judgments may be more easily swayed by the social and emotional features of decision-making contexts. This is consistent with the argument that adolescents are hormonally "primed" for emotionally intense experiences but lack commensurate emotion-regulation abilities due to the fact that their brains—the frontal lobes in particular—are not yet fully mature.

Social Processes While biological processes may very well influence the maturity of adolescents' emotional responses, most developmentalists agree that the ways adolescents regulate their emotions depend importantly on the social contexts in which the adolescents develop. In particular, they depend on family interaction patterns and on social expectations regarding the expression of emotion.

Families play a critical role in how adolescents learn to manage their feelings. Consistent with research conducted on younger children (see Chapter 10, p. 345), studies of adolescents find that warm, supportive parenting is associated with the ability to regulate one's feelings, whereas a family history of emotional negativity increases adolescents' negative emotions and aggressive behaviors, which can spill over into their peer relationships and contribute to social rejection (Kim et al., 2001).

In a longitudinal study that followed children from 9 to 13 years of age, Nancy Eisenberg and her colleagues explored the relationships between the emotional quality of parent–child interactions, adolescents' abilities to regulate their emotions, and adolescents' behavioral problems such as aggression (Eisenberg et al., 2005). The longitudinal design allowed the researchers to discover an interesting pattern: parents' emotional warmth and expression of positive emotions during their children's mid-elementary school years (when the children were about 9 years old) predicted higher levels of children's emotion regulation 2 years later (early adolescence), which in turn predicted fewer externalizing behaviors 2 years after that (middle adolescence).

In addition to examining the role of family, developmentalists have explored how the adolescent's gender affects their regulation of emotion. It is widely believed that males and females are socialized to manage their emotional expressions in vastly different ways. In particular, girls and women are considered "more emotional" than boys and men—that is, they are believed to experience emotions more intensely and to communicate them more willingly, presumably due to social conventions and cultural expectations that represent females as emotionally nurturing and expressive and males as independent and self-reliant.

Gender differences in crying provide an interesting example of the impact of sociocultural factors on adolescents' emotion regulation. Although boy and girl babies cry with equal frequency, gender differences in crying emerge in early childhood and become larger over the course of childhood and throughout adolescence (Brody, 2000; Jansz, 2000; Tilburg, Unterberg, & Vingerhoets, 2002). The ever-widening gender gap, particularly during adolescence, is due to boys' crying much less frequently (girls' crying is relatively stable through adolescence; Tilburg et al., 2002). Several studies suggest that expectations, and sociocultural factors generally, underpin gender differences in crying. For example, one study of adolescents found that on measurements of shame, boys scored higher than girls on only one item: "I feel shame when I cry" (Truijers & Vingerhoets, 1999; cited in Tilburg et al., 2002). Another study found that boys are more likely to cry if their parents are accepting of emotional expression and therefore less likely to reinforce cultural stereotypes (Bronstein et al., 1996).

To investigate the complex interplay between emotion and social expectations regarding its expression in boys and girls, Archana Singh-Manoux studied 9th- and 11th-grade adolescents in India and England (Singh-Manoux, 2000). The adolescents were asked to describe a situation that led to an experience of fear, shame, or sadness. They were then asked a series of questions regarding the intensity of the emotion, whether they shared their emotional experience with others, and for how long the experience had preoccupied them. In both cultures, girls were more likely than boys to share their emotional experiences with others and to be preoccupied with them longer. However, the intensity of the emotions was greater for girls than for boys only in England; in India, boys reported more intense emotions than did girls. Furthermore, on most measures, the differences between boys and girls were much greater in England than in India. This may be due to different cultural conceptions of adolescence: In India, adolescents are considered older children rather than young men and women. Consequently, social pressures to act

The extent to which boys and girls differ in the expression of emotions depends importantly on their culture's conceptions of what is appropriate behavior for males and females.

David R. Frazier/The Image Works

Dennis MacDonald/PhotoEdit, Inc.

masculine or feminine may emerge later for Indian teenagers than for their Western European counterparts.

Altogether, research provides ample evidence that the experience and regulation of emotions undergo substantial change over the course of adolescence and are influenced by both biological and sociocultural factors. These changes have important implications for adolescents' relationships with peers and family, topics that we address below.

||||| APPLY ▪ CONNECT ▪ DISCUSS -

In general, girls are considered "more emotional" than boys. Evaluate this belief in light of research on gender differences in emotional experience and emotion regulation.

Relationships with Peers

As children enter adolescence, their social activities and relationships with peers undergo several major changes. First, the sheer amount of time spent with peers increases dramatically, to the point where high school students spend twice as much time with their friends as they do with their parents or other adults (Csikszentmihalyi & Larson, 1984; Fuligni & Stevenson, 1995). Second, compared with younger children, adolescents are more mobile and better able to avoid the watchful eyes of parents and other authorities, so their peer activities are more likely to go unsupervised. As you will see, not only does the amount of time spent with peers change but so, too, does the nature of peer interactions and relationships. Peer groups increase in size and diversity during adolescence, and friendships and other close relationships increase in intensity. When exploring the nature of these changes and the implications they have for other areas of adolescent growth and adjustment, developmentalists tend to distinguish between adolescents' *close relationships* with friends and romantic partners and their *peer networks,* that is, their connections to groups of teens that may include casual acquaintances as well as good friends. As we discuss below, each type of relationship has different functions and fulfills different needs in adolescents' social and emotional development.

Friendships

In general, a **friendship** refers to a close relationship between two individuals. As you saw in previous chapters, the friendships of young children are often based on such shifting and transitory factors as playing with the same toys or being on the same sports team. Several large-scale studies conducted in the United States and other industrialized countries document the changing basis of friendships as children enter adolescence (Berndt, 2007; Schneider et al., 2005). In contrast to the apparently superficial characteristics that bind younger children together, the characteristics that adolescents see as fundamental to their friendships are reciprocity, commitment, and equality (Hartup, 1993; Larsen, 1996). *Reciprocity,* the give-and-take of close relationships, includes emotional sharing as well as the sharing of interests and activities; *commitment* refers to the loyalty and trust between friends, and *equality* to the equal distribution of power among them.

Developmental Functions of Friendships
The dyadic friendships of adolescence serve two significant developmental functions: intimacy and autonomy—the yin and yang of social life (Selman et al., 1997). When we reflect on the importance of friendship, what probably comes most readily to mind is **intimacy,**

friendship A close relationship between two individuals. Friendships may have different bases.

intimacy A sense of close connection between two individuals, resulting from shared feelings, thoughts, and activities.

or "the gratifying connection between two individuals through some combination of shared feelings, thoughts, and activities" (Selman et al., 1997, p. 32). However, as Selman and his colleagues have demonstrated in numerous studies of normally developing and psychosocially disturbed children and adolescents, in healthy relationships intimacy is balanced with **autonomy**—the ability to govern the self and assert one's own needs. Indeed, unhealthy friendships can place a child at significant risk, depending on whether the scales tip more toward intimacy or autonomy. Selman and his colleagues point out, for example, that the inability to assert one's needs without jeopardizing friendship intimacy contributes to a child's willingness to bow to peer pressure. On the other hand, an excess of autonomy can also be problematic, for example, bullying one's peers into risky behaviors.

Evidence from various studies indicates that close, well-balanced friendships have a positive influence on adolescents' social and personality development (Eccles, Brown, & Templeton, 2008). Adolescents who perceive their friends as supportive report fewer school-related and psychological problems, greater confidence in their social acceptance by peers, and less loneliness. Difficulty in making friends during adolescence is usually part of a broader syndrome of poor social adjustment often first apparent in early childhood (Pedersen et al., 2007).

Friendships and Gender

While friends are important to both boys and girls during adolescence, there are differences in the quality of their friendships. In particular, research finds that girls' friendships are more intense and intimate (Brown, 2004). Several explanations have been offered. Thomas Berndt and Lonna Murphy (2002), for example, suggest that male adolescent friendships are less intimate because, compared with teenage girls, teenage boys are less trusting of their friends and, consequently, less likely to share the emotional details of their lives with them. Indeed, the study of Indian and English adolescents described earlier indicates that boys in both cultures tend to share more superficial aspects of emotionally charged experiences with friends, whereas girls are more likely to share their feelings (Singh-Manoux, 2000). Consider, for example, 13-year-old Michael's description of how boys discuss sex and sexual arousal "more openly" than girls:

> I think guys can speak about it [sex] more openly with each other from what I've seen from the girls in my school. They usually keep to themselves about it instead of talking about it, whereas guys can be more open with it. We talk about girls and wet dreams. . . . With guys you can just say, "Oh, I saw this really good looking chick on TV and I cracked a boner."

Although Michael describes boys as more open with each other regarding these highly sensitive subjects, his language suggests that humor may be used to diffuse the emotional intensity of shared events. Indeed, Michael goes on to suggest that his friends keep some of their most deeply significant emotional experiences to themselves:

> [But] I've got a friend of mine whose mom died a few years ago and he never brought it up in school and even now he rarely talks about it. I've got another friend of mine whose dad is in the hospital with a disease and he never talks about that. (Martino & Pallotta-Chiarolli, 2003, p. 65)

Yet another explanation proposed for why the friendships of boys are less intimate than those of girls is that **homophobia**—a fear of homosexuality—prevents adolescent males from demonstrating or admitting to strong feelings of intimacy toward their male friends (Raymond, 1994). An ethnographic study of Australian boys and young men found evidence that they carefully monitored and policed the levels of intimacy in their relationships in order to avoid being perceived as homosexual (Martino & Pallotta-Chiarolli, 2003). Consider the following discus-

autonomy The ability to assert one's own needs in a relationship.

homophobia A fear of homosexuality. Homophobia may diminish intimacy among adolescent males.

clique A group of several young people that remains small enough to enable its members to be in regular interaction with one another and to serve as the primary peer group.

crowd A large, reputation-based and mixed-gender social network observed when cliques interact.

sion between a researcher (Maria) and 16-year-old Darren who, although hetero-sexual, had been called gay because of the perceived closeness of his male friend-ships (p. 67):

> Maria: How do you feel about that [being labeled gay for having close friendships with other boys]?
> Darren: It's weird but I wouldn't know how to explain it. It [being called "gay"] gives you a shock.
> Maria: And do you find that you change the way you talk to some guys?
> Darren: Yes, exactly. I wouldn't bring up some subjects, I would just try and keep away from it.

In addition to differences in intimacy, the friendships of boys and girls differ in their degree of competition (Schneider et al., 2005), with girls' friendships tending to be less competitive. Among boys, friendly competition (as opposed to hyper-competitiveness, which is marked by higher levels of aggression) is usually enjoyed and may even increase the closeness of relationships. The higher level of competition in boys' friendships is consistent with the widely held idea that boys and girls have different relationship "goal orientations": Girls tend to focus more on *communal goals,* which emphasize relationship-enhancement and cooperation, whereas boys tend to focus more on *agentic goals,* which emphasize dominance and self-interest (Saragovi et al., 2002; Rudolph & Conley, 2005). Such gender dif-ferences in goal orientation, of course, fit Western cultural stereotypes of females as oriented more toward connectedness and intimacy and males more toward independence and autonomy.

Cliques and Crowds

A friendship is the smallest unit of peer interaction, a group of two. As children move into adolescence, two additional, more inclusive kinds of peer groups be-come prominent—*cliques* and *crowds*. Adolescent cliques and crowds are significant social groups in societies that group children by age for the purpose of education. In such societies, adolescents spend a lot of time with each other, and consequently learn to establish and maintain relationships with groups of peers. Cliques and crowds differ in size as well as in the developmental functions that they serve.

In general, **cliques** are small and intimate and have the function of serving ado-lescents' emotional and security needs (Henrich et al., 2006). A clique typically includes five to seven members who are relatively good friends (Brown, 2004). Dexter Dunphy (1963), one of the first researchers to study cliques and crowds, noted that cliques are about the size of a family and serve a similar emotional func-tion as an "alternative center of security" (p. 233). Fur-thermore, cliques have an internal structure that usually includes a leader who tends to be more mature and more socially connected. In early adolescence, clique members are usually of the same gender, but by middle adolescence, mixed-gender cliques are common. Most adolescents be-long to several different cliques, associated with different times of the day or different settings. For example, an ado-lescent may be a member of one clique in science class, another during gymnastics practice, and still another in the neighborhood on the weekends.

A **crowd** is a larger group of friends and acquaintances that emerges when cliques interact, as they might at a big party or get-together. In contrast to the emotional func-tions of cliques, crowds appear to provide opportunities to

This crowd of Oxide and Neutrino fans probably includes a number of cliques—smaller groups of good friends who came to the concert together and will depart together. According to Dunphy, the crowd serves the important function of providing opportunities for ado-lescents to meet new people and develop new relationships.

S.IN./Corbis

meet new people, explore one's social identity (Barber, Eccles, & Stone, 2001), and develop new relationships, especially romantic relationships.

The importance of crowds to adolescents' exploration of identity comes especially from the fact that crowds typically have public identities of their own, that is, reputations for engaging in certain types of behaviors and having particular values, norms, and goals (Brown, 1999; Barber, Eccles, & Stone, 2001). Crowd reputations are apparent in stereotyped labels such as "jocks," "brains," "loners," "druggies," and "nerds" (Brown & Huang, 1995; Eckert, 1995). In schools with a diverse ethnic population, ethnic labels ("African Americans," "Latinos," "Asians," etc.) are also common (Brown & Huang, 1995). As names such as "jocks," "brains," and "druggies" indicate, crowds vary in the extent to which their norms and values conform to those of the adult community. Other labels, such as "normal" and "outcast," indicate how the crowd's norms and values adhere to those of the adolescent community.

Being identified as a member of a particular crowd may have a significant impact on an adolescent's social status, depending on the local peer culture. For example, as a rule, "brains" occupy a status somewhere between the elite groups and groups that are unpopular. However, in some peer cultures, poor academic achievement is associated with high levels of popularity—as is the case where aggressive, low-achieving individuals are highly popular (Rodkin et al., 2000; Estell et al., 2002)—and "brains" are disparaged. Similarly, in some working-class African American communities, being labeled as a "brain" can lead to being ostracized, and many academically able young people try to mask their abilities (Ogbu, 1997). In general, crowds and the way they are categorized help adolescents learn about the alternative social identities that are available to them, and strongly influence whom they are likely to meet and spend time with (Brown et al., 1994).

Romantic Relationships

In many cultures, a key function of the peer group is to provide an avenue to romantic relationships (Connolly, Furman, & Konarski, 2000; Furman & Simon, 2008). It has been noted, in fact, that romantic relationships are central to adolescents' sense of belonging and group status (Collins, 2003). Dexter Dunphy argued that the process of developing romantic relationships takes place through a series of stages, as shown in Figure 15.3: The same-sex cliques of early adolescence give way to the mixed-sex crowds of mid-adolescence, which gradually disintegrate as members become involved in romantic relationships. Contemporary work generally supports the stages that Dunphy proposed and also marks mid-adolescence as a major turning point during which nearly 50 percent of adolescents report involvement in relatively intense romantic relationships (Feiring, 1996; Kuttler & La Greca, 2004; but see the box "Friends with Benefits" for an exception to this pattern).

Although these studies provide convincing evidence of a stagelike process, there are important cultural and historical variations in adolescent romantic relationships (Berndt & Savin-Williams, 1993; Brown et al., 1994). On the basis of the data he collected in the late 1950s, Dunphy reported that the crowd disintegrated into couples who were going steady or were engaged to get married. Fifty years later, this pattern may continue in some parts of the world, but it does not appear to be generally characteristic of contemporary industrialized societies. Instead, marriage is often postponed until several years after the initiation of sexual activity. In addition, adolescents typically do not stop hanging out with their friends once they become involved in romantic relationships (Connolly et al., 2004). Thus, romantic relationships take

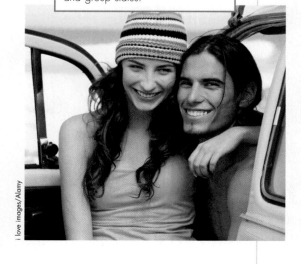

Romantic relationships become increasingly important during the adolescent years. In addition to providing opportunities for exploring intimacy and identity, romantic relationships are important to adolescents' sense of belonging and group status.

i love images/Alamy

place alongside other peer relationships, creating a context in which adolescents must maneuver between relationships with their friends and their romantic partners. Developmentalists have found that adolescents often feel neglected when their friends start dating, particularly in the early phases of new romantic relationships (Roth & Parker, 2001; Shulman & Seiffge-Krenke, 2001).

Ami Kuttler and Annette La Greca explored the complications of managing romantic and friend relationships in an ethnically diverse sample of adolescent girls (2004). They found that casual dating may actually enhance feelings of closeness with best friends because it provides opportunities to share and discuss intimate subjects regarding romance and sexuality. In addition, casual daters generally relied more on their best friends than on their dating partners for companionship, affection, and support. In contrast, girls who indicated that they were involved in "serious" romantic relationships reported less companionship with best friends, presumably because they spent less time with friends than with their romantic partners and tended to rely more on their romantic partners for their emotional needs. However, all girls, regardless of the seriousness of their romantic relationships, reported higher levels of conflict and pressure with their romantic partners than with their best friends.

Romantic relationships may evolve differently within different cultural subgroups. Anderson (1990), for example, found evidence that male gangs in economically depressed neighborhoods actively discourage involvement in significant relationships and often ridicule members who have them. And given that most adolescent peer groups generally disapprove of homosexual relationships, as we will discuss below, it is likely that peer influences are quite different in the formation of gay and lesbian relationships.

In addition, cultures vary widely in the extent to which they support and provide opportunities for the development of romantic relationships. In many Middle Eastern cultures, particularly those influenced by Islamic religious traditions, dating is either carefully monitored by adults or actively discouraged (Mahdi, 2003). In Iraq, for example, even casual contact between adolescent boys and girls can have dire social consequences, as 16-year-old Samira reports:

> Yes, of course I would like to be able to speak with boys and get to know how they think about girls, but this is getting more and more difficult. I have heard some cases where a boy tried to drag a girl to speak with him by claiming that he was in love with her. But the truth is that he just wanted to show his friends that he had "a sexual affair" with her. This is a very dangerous thing to say about a girl in Iraq. Such incidents would mean that the girl has desecrated her family's honor—something for which she might be severely punished by her father or her brother. It would also mean that her chances of getting a husband become very slim. (Al-Ali & Hussein, 2003, p. 48)

Peer Pressure and Conformity

An aspect of adolescent social relationships that has been extensively examined is peer pressure and conformity (Brown et al., 2008). Conformity, also known as **homophily,** refers to the degree to which friends are similar to each other in their behavior, their taste in clothes and music, and their goals and aspirations for the

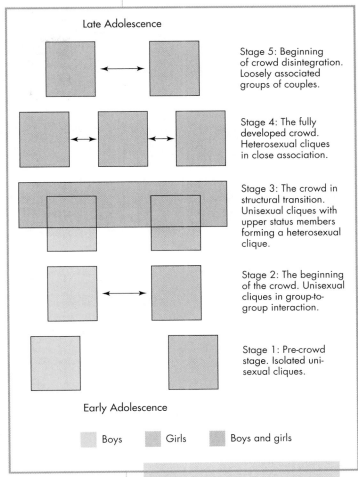

Late Adolescence

Stage 5: Beginning of crowd disintegration. Loosely associated groups of couples.

Stage 4: The fully developed crowd. Heterosexual cliques in close association.

Stage 3: The crowd in structural transition. Unisexual cliques with upper status members forming a heterosexual clique.

Stage 2: The beginning of the crowd. Unisexual cliques in group-to-group interaction.

Stage 1: Pre-crowd stage. Isolated unisexual cliques.

Early Adolescence

Boys   Girls   Boys and girls

Figure 15.3 Stages of adolescents' social relationships from early to late adolescence, according to Dexter Dunphy.

homophily The degree to which friends are similar to each other.

Name:	Benoit Denizet-Lewis
Education:	B.A. from the Medill School of Journalism, Northwestern University
Current Position:	Book author; contributing writer to the *New York Times Magazine*
Career Objectives:	Publish books and articles on youth culture, addiction, sex, and sexuality

"Being in a real relationship just complicates everything," says 16-year-old Brian. "You feel obligated to be all, like, couple-y. And that gets really boring after a while. When you're friends with benefits, you go over, hook up, then play video games or something. It rocks."

According to Benoit Denizet-Lewis, Brian is part of a growing number of mostly white, suburban teens, for whom "hooking up" is more common than dating (Denizet-Lewis, 2004). With an educational background in journalism and sociology, and a keen interest in cultural issues, Denizet-Lewis spent several months hanging out and communicating online with nearly 100 high school students. What he found sent parents, teachers, counselors, and researchers scrambling to catch up with what appeared to be a new trend in adolescent sexual relationships. Although it can encompass anything from kissing to sexual intercourse, and is often associated with oral sex, for most adolescents, "hooking up" refers to sexual encounters with a partner who is no more than a friend. Friends with whom one hooks up regularly are "friends with benefits."

Denizet-Lewis first met his teen informants online, at Internet sites popular with high school and college students, such as sites for placing personal profiles and chat rooms for flirting and, on occasion, arranging hook ups. (Many informants claimed that hooking up with someone from your own school can be risky, and sought out partners from neighboring schools and towns.) Two of the more popular sites, hotornot.com and facethejury.com, have more than 5 million members combined. Through online and face-to-face interviews with teens, Denizet-Lewis examined the world of adolescent casual sex in a way that has thus far eluded the questionnaire and survey efforts of researchers. In addition to documenting the increasing popularity of hooking up, he found, for example, that although many teens have had romantic rela-

tionships, they find them complicated, often painful, and not at all necessary when one has close friends of the opposite sex that can be counted on for "benefits." As one teen explained, "A lot of guys get in relationships just so they can get steady [expletive]. But now that it's easy to get sex outside of relationships, guys don't need relationships." According to another informant, however, the relationship between friends with benefits can be a bit more complicated than it appears. On the day that Denizet-Lewis met Melissa, she was distressed because her friend with benefits had just broken up with her. "How is that even possible?" she asked. "The point of having a friend with benefits is that you won't get broken up with, you won't get hurt. He told me online that he met a girl that he really likes, so now, of course, we can't hook up anymore."

Despite the apparent enthusiasm for no-strings-attached sex, Denizet-Lewis found plenty of evidence that hooking up may have a downside. For one thing, it can jeopardize one's reputation and interfere with developing more serious relationships: "You have to be careful," said one boy. "I have this huge crush on this girl who knows a lot of the girls I know, and I don't want her to find out that I hook up a lot and think I'm dirty." Indeed, feeling "dirty," disappointed, confused, and guilty were common consequences of hooking up, especially for teens who wanted or expected more from the relationship. Another significant issue is the possible gender asymmetry in who actually benefits from friends with benefits. Denizet-Lewis pointed out that a recurrent theme in his interviews was whether the sexual desires and satisfactions of boys overshadowed those of girls. The girls he spoke with voiced different opinions. One said, "If I ask a guy to come over to my house and hook up, I'm the one benefiting because I'm the one who wants to. . . . . It's not just about pleasing the guy." But another girl disagreed: "I feel like women have less power today. It's not just that the guy often doesn't respect the girl or the girl's sexuality, but the girl sometimes doesn't really respect and validate herself. . . . I think a lot of times girls are really self-destructive."

The adolescents interviewed by Denizet-Lewis make it abundantly clear that norms regarding sexual behavior and relationships are undergoing significant changes within the peer group. They also reveal the extent to which such changes invite reflection on other aspects of their lives, including how they think and feel about themselves.

In addition to its many other uses, the computer provides teens with Web sites where they can post personal profiles, chat, flirt and, on occasion, arrange to "hook up."

Image Source Ltd./drr.net

Benoit Denizet-Lewis.

Benoit Denizet-Lewis/Patrick Lentz

future (Kandel, 1978; Kandel & Chen, 2000; Furman & Simon, 2008). Although adolescents in the United States are more mobile than younger children, attend larger schools, and have more opportunities to meet peers of other social classes and ethnic backgrounds, their close friends tend to be even more similar to them than they were in elementary school, a trend that continues throughout adolescence (Berndt & Keefe, 1995). High school friends tend to be similar in their views of school, their academic achievement, and their dating and other leisure-time activities (Berndt & Murphy, 2002; Patrick et al., 2002). They also tend to feel the same way about drug use, drinking, and delinquency (Akers, Jones, & Coyl, 1998; Tani et al., 2001; Urberg et al., 1998).

Selection and Socialization

Selection and Socialization A seminal study by Denise Kandel and her colleagues (1978) focused on the developmental processes through which homophily is established. In this 1-year-long longitudinal study of drug use, educational goals, and delinquency, the researchers determined that two processes are involved: selection and socialization. Through *selection,* adolescents target others as potential friends, seeking out teenagers who seem similar to them in important traits and behaviors, especially those that are relevant to the adolescent's social reputation. Hockey players are more likely to hang out with other hockey players; delinquents, with other delinquents; and so on. Once selection has done its job, socialization comes into play. Through *socialization,* socially significant behaviors are modeled and reinforced, in the course of ongoing interactions. Socialization accounts for the tendency of individuals to become increasingly more alike—to show higher levels of behavioral agreement—as their relationships develop over time. For example, studies have found that children who are at risk for antisocial behavior and who become friendly with delinquent peers are likely to become delinquent themselves (Rodkin et al., 2000).

Conformity and Deviance

Conformity and Deviance For decades, developmentalists have worried that it may be unhealthy for adolescents to spend excessive time with their peers, removed from the observation and control of adults. Frederic Thrasher (1927) argued as much in his classic study of more than 1300 Chicago gangs in existence during the early years of the 1900s. The problem, he argued, was not due to the nature of the boys who joined the gangs, many of which began as neighborhood play groups. Gangs became problematic only when they functioned without supervision and opportunities to participate in socially acceptable activity. More recently, Urie Bronfenbrenner (1970) made the point that "if children have contact only with their own age-mates, there is no possibility for learning culturally-established patterns of cooperation and mutual concern" (p. 121).

It is an open question whether adolescents, left entirely to their own devices, would create a "Lord of the Flies" society, in which cooperation and concern for others would be overshadowed by self-interested, deviant behavior. There is, however, plenty of evidence to support the notion that deviancy can be socialized in the context of peer relationships (Blanton & Burkley, 2008). For example, Thomas Berndt and Keunho Keefe (1995) asked a large group of seventh- and eighth-graders in the fall and the spring of the school year to identify their friends and to describe any disruptive behaviors they engaged in. They found that boys and girls whose friends engaged in a high level of disruptive behavior in the fall reported an increase in the level of their own disruptive behavior in the spring, with the girls being more susceptible to such influence. Other studies show that if an adolescent's close friends smoke cigarettes, drink alcohol, use illegal drugs, are sexually active, or break the law, sooner or later the adolescent is likely to do these things, too (Kandel & Chen, 2000; Reed & Roundtree, 1997).

These girls were photographed inhaling air freshener in the bathroom of their high school. Inexpensive and readily available, inhalants are an increasingly popular avenue to drug abuse among adolescents.

AP Photo/The Daily Oklahoman, Jim Beckel

Adolescent gangs have been studied since the early 1900s. Modern developmentalists have focused on understanding the risk factors associated with gang involvement, as well as the social processes involved in deviant behavior.

Thomas Dishion and his colleagues proposed the concept of *deviancy training* to account for the homophily of antisocial behavior among adolescent peers (Piehler & Dishion, 2007). **Deviancy training** occurs when friends respond to talk about rule breaking and other deviant forms of behavior by laughing or reacting in other positive ways. In a series of longitudinal studies, boys were videotaped as they engaged in discussions with friends. The researchers coded the discussion sessions for "deviant talk" and whether it was reinforced. It was found that deviancy training in discussions at age 13 or 14 predicted increased violent behavior, as well as the initiation of tobacco, alcohol, and marijuana use, by age 15 or 16 (Dishion et al., 1999).

Peer processes similar to deviancy training have been blamed for the surprising finding that group counseling and therapy for delinquent adolescents may actually do more harm than good (Dishion et al., 1999). In two experimentally controlled intervention studies, peer-group interventions actually increased adolescents' problem behaviors, suggesting that the teens reinforced positive attitudes about delinquent behavior. The adolescents involved in group counseling had higher rates of delinquency and deviant behavior up to 3 years after the termination of the counseling sessions (Dishion et al., 1999). This is a good lesson in the importance of scientific research in planning and understanding counseling and intervention practices. It also underscores the importance of designing and using developmentally appropriate therapies. Therapeutic strategies that are effective with adults may backfire when used with adolescents.

|||||| APPLY ▪ CONNECT ▪ DISCUSS

How does Dunphy's distinction between cliques and crowds fit your own adolescent experience of peer groups? Reflect on the social structure of your high school and try to map out the different crowd types and the different cliques within them. How do the concepts of homophily, selection, and socialization apply?

Relationships with Parents

The increasing time that adolescents spend with their peers and romantic partners and the increasing importance they place on these relationships inevitably change the relationships between adolescents and their parents. In fact, the amount of time that adolescents in the United States spend with their families drops by approximately 50 percent between the fifth and ninth grades (Larson & Richards, 1991). At the most general level, adolescents become more distant from their parents and more likely to turn to peers than to parents for support and advice on questions about how to conduct themselves in a wide range of contexts (Figure 15.4; Steinberg & Silk, 2002; Meeus, 2003). Furthermore, parents of adolescents are likely to be undergoing significant life changes of their own. They are reaching an age when they probably have increased responsibilities at work; their own parents are aging and may need special care; and their physical powers are beginning to decline. Given the stress that both parents and their adolescent children feel, it is not surprising that conflicts arise between them (Steinberg & Duncan, 2002). However, extensive research shows that the specifics of such conflicts, and, more generally, the ways in which parent–child relationships change, depend on a host of factors.

Adolescent–Parent Conflicts

When developmentalists describe adolescence as a period of "storm and stress," they are usually thinking about the conflicts between adolescents and their parents.

deviancy training Positive reactions to discussions of rule breaking.

Indeed, the parent–adolescent relationship is thought by many to reflect the basic dilemma of adolescence. Teenagers are caught between two worlds, one of childhood dependence, the other of adult responsibility.

On the basis of a review of a large number of studies carried out over the past several decades, Brett Laursen and his colleagues found that the pattern of conflict between parents and their children changes over the course of adolescence (Laursen et al., 1998). In particular, they found that both the frequency and the intensity of conflict between parents and adolescents are highest early in adolescence and then decrease.

Interestingly, a recent longitudinal study found that this pattern depended importantly on the family context (Shanahan et al., 2007). Following siblings who were relatively close in age as they moved from middle childhood to adolescence, the researchers found the expected pattern for the older child—conflict peaked during early adolescence and then declined. For the younger sibling, however, conflict peaked during middle childhood—that is, as their older sibling transitioned to adolescence, not as they themselves transitioned. The researchers speculate that the younger sibling may be caught in the middle between the older sibling and the parents—swept up in conflict while trying to support or protect the older brother or sister.

When conflicts do arise, they can evoke strong feelings (Csikszentmihalyi & Larson, 1984). Very often, however, adolescent–parent conflict is inspired by seemingly trivial matters such as household responsibilities and privileges, dating and curfews, involvement in athletics, and financial independence. Arguments over "big issues," such as religion and politics, are much less common (Holmbeck, 1996).

Interestingly, research suggests that parents and adolescents can be of very different minds when it comes to defining a "big issue." For example, a lot of parent–adolescent conflicts emerge when parents and adolescents differ in their understanding of what constitutes the domain of "personal space" (Nucci, 1996; Turiel, 1998). As you may remember from the discussion in Chapter 9 of social domain theory, people distinguish among three domains—the moral, the social conventional, and the personal—and may differ in how one domain is distinguished from another. Research on social domain theory indicates that conflicts between parents and adolescents, in particular, may relate to differences in where they draw boundaries between the social conventional and personal domains. A parent who insists that an adolescent dress in a socially appropriate way, and an adolescent who insists that dress is a matter of personal choice, are disputing the boundaries of the social conventional and the personal. Larry Nucci and his colleagues (Milnitsky-Sapiro, Turiel, & Nucci, 2006; Smetana, 2006) have discovered that parents in both Brazil and the United States recognize the importance of providing adolescents with a personal sphere in which to exercise personal freedom and develop independence and autonomy, but that conflicts arise over exactly what qualifies as "personal," as illustrated in this interview excerpt:

> Even now, like at Easter, when I went to Church, my Mom was real concerned with what I was going to wear. And I finally just said, "Look, I'm going to wear what I am going to wear, Mom." I didn't wear anything outrageous, just a skirt and a blouse. But here I am 20 years old, and it was such a concern about what I was going to wear. (Nucci, 1996, p. 51)

Research on parent–adolescent relationships in different ethnic groups shows broad cultural differences in where the boundaries between domains are drawn (Smetana, 2000; Smetana & Gettman, 2006). Judith Smetana has found, for example, that compared with middle-class European American families, middle-class African American families have relatively restricted definitions of what constitutes

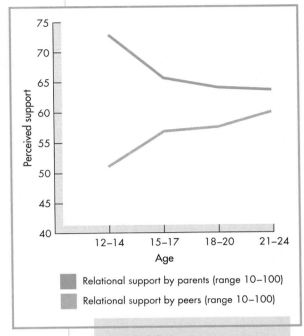

Figure 15.4 Although parents are perceived as highly supportive throughout adolescence and early adulthood, perceived parental support declines across these years, while perceived peer support increases. (From Meeus, 2003.)

This mother is helping her son prepare for his Bar Mitzvah, a Jewish ritual celebrating coming of age. Although she may continue to play an important role in her son's adolescence, her sphere of influence may shrink as he spends more time away from home with his peers.

Mark Richards/PhotoEdit, Inc.

the adolescent's personal jurisdiction. Even so, negotiating the boundary of authority is still a significant source of parent–adolescent conflict for African American families. It seems that conflicts over "little things" represent deeper disagreements about the major issues of growing up—the power to decide for oneself and to take responsibility for oneself.

Smetana argues that African American families' parenting practices can be better described in terms of social domain theory than by such global terms as authoritarian or parent centered. According to social domain theory, parents' expectations for obedience will vary from one domain of action to the next. This also suggests that parent–adolescent conflict need not characterize the entire relationship; rather, it is confined to certain areas where the authority to have one's way in the face of contentious issues is in dispute. Few adolescents take issue with parents' authority in the domain of moral action, but will challenge it when it is applied to how they dress or color their hair.

Parental Influences beyond the Family

Although conflicts between parents and their adolescent children may be stormy, they rarely lead to a serious breakdown in relations (Schneider & Stevenson, 1999). It seems clear that parents continue to play a very important role in their children's lives. This continuing influence extends well beyond providing shelter, food, and advice. For example, a major study of more than 600 German adolescents and their parents indicated that adolescents whose parents demonstrate warmth, engage in discussions concerning academic and intellectual matters, and have high expectations for academic performance do better in school than peers whose parents are less warm and involved (Juang & Silbereisen, 2002). Similarly, a study of parents' role in shaping adolescents' occupational aspirations indicated that positive identification with parents was strongly related to adolescents' valuing of academics, for both African American and European American samples (Jodl et al., 2001). Parents also influence with whom their adolescent children interact, including the kinds of crowds with which their children are likely to become associated (Brown & Huang, 1995; Holmbeck, Paikoff, & Brooks-Gunn, 1995).

In a study of sixth- and seventh-graders, Andrew Fuligni and Jacqueline Eccles (1993) asked young adolescents to answer a questionnaire about their parents' strictness, their opportunities to make decisions on their own, and the extent to which their parents monitored their behavior (Table 15.1). The questionnaire also included questions about the extent to which the adolescents turned to peers rather than to their parents for support, as well as about their adjustment to junior high school.

Fuligni and Eccles found that the extent to which the adolescents spent time with their peers and turned to them for advice depended on how their parents' behavior toward them changed in response to their growing up. Children who perceived their parents as becoming stricter as they progressed into adolescence turned to their peers to a greater extent than did those who felt their parents included them in family decisions and encouraged them to express their ideas. At the same time, a certain degree of monitoring appeared to reduce adolescents' tendency to turn to peers: Children whose parents set a curfew for them and asked them to call if they were going to be late coming home were less peer-oriented than those whose parents did not monitor their behavior. Similarly, adolescents in both the United States and China report experiencing more positive emotions, and better academic performance, when they perceive their parents as supporting their developing autonomy (Wang & Chen, 2007).

Studies of family communication patterns tell a similar story. In intensive clinical studies into the family dynamics of both normally developing and troubled

---

table 15.1

Sample Items Measuring Relationships between 6th- and 7th-Graders and Their Parents

How does each of the following questions and statements apply to your situation?

Parental Strictness

My parents want me to follow their directions even if I disagree with them.

I have to ask my parents' permission to do most things.

My parents worry that I am up to something they won't like.

Decision-Making Opportunities

How often do you take part in family decisions concerning yourself?

My parents encourage me to give my ideas and opinions even if we might disagree.

Parental Monitoring

When you go out at night, do you have a curfew?

When you are late getting home, do you have to call home?

Do your parents warn you it is dangerous to go out alone?

Source: Fuligni & Eccles, 1993.

adolescents, Hauser and colleagues (1991) identified two patterns of family inter-actions. *Constraining interactions* limit and restrict communication through detach-ment, lack of curiosity, and other forms of discouragement. In contrast, *enabling interactions* facilitate and enhance communication through explaining, empathizing, expressing curiosity, and encouraging mutual problem solving. The researchers argue that parents who promote enabling interactions enhance healthy psycho-logical and identity development in their adolescents by "making the family en-vironment safe for the adolescent to risk 'trying out' new ideas and perspectives, or expressing new feelings" (p. 27).

In a comprehensive review of research on the influence of parenting styles on adolescent behavior, Grayson Holmbeck and his colleagues (Holmbeck et al., 1995) report that the developmental outcomes for adolescents are most favorable when parents:

1. Set clear standards for behavior.

2. Enforce rules in ways that are firm but not coercive.

3. Discipline their children in a consistent way.

4. Explain the basis for their decisions.

5. Permit real discussion of contentious issues.

6. Monitor their adolescents' whereabouts without being overprotective.

7. Foster a warm family environment.

8. Provide information and help their adolescents develop social skills.

9. Respond flexibly to their children as they develop.

You may recognize this pattern as consistent with the authoritative parenting style described in Chapter 10 (p. 345). Indeed, the analysis presented above paral-lels the findings of other studies showing that adolescent children of authoritative parents are more competent in school and less likely to get into trouble than are their peers from authoritarian or permissive families (Steinberg, 2001). Moreover, these positive effects of authoritative parenting apply whether the adolescents in question are classified as "jocks," "druggies," "nerds," or "brains" (Brown & Huang, 1995). These effects even extend to the adolescents' friends, who are likely to ex-perience improved school performance and behavior as an indirect result of the effective parenting of their friends' parents (Fletcher et al., 1995).

On the whole, current evidence strongly supports the notion that adolescents' conflicts with their parents increase relative to middle childhood, while their feel-ings of family solidarity and warmth decrease (Collins & Laursen, 2006). Some adolescents really do break away and establish relationships outside the family that remove them from their parents both physically and emotionally, but the more common pattern is for adolescents and their parents to negotiate a new form of interdependence that grants the adolescent increasingly equal rights and more nearly equal responsibilities.

|||||| **APPLY ▪▪ CONNECT ▪▪ DISCUSS** ▪

Your 16-year-old daughter announces that she intends to leave home and school in order to join a spiritual community that encourages its members to "find themselves" by working toward the common good. As an informed and sensitive parent, you recognize this as an expression of developing autonomy but, for obvious reasons, believe it would be a terrible mistake for her to pursue such a plan at this point in her life. Keeping in mind the evidence presented in this section on effective parenting, write your daughter a letter about what you think of her plan.

identity development The process through which individuals achieve a sense of who they are and of their moral and political beliefs, their career preferences, and their relationship to their culture and community.

me-self Includes all of the things that people know about themselves.

I-self The part of the system that reflects on, guides, and directs the self.

saturated self A self full to the brim with multiple "me's" that have emerged as a consequence of needing to conform to social roles and relationships that demand different, and sometimes contradictory, selves.

Identity Development

Forming a coherent and stable identity is considered one of the most challenging tasks and significant accomplishments of adolescence. **Identity development** is the process through which individuals achieve a sense of who they are, what moral and political beliefs they embrace, the sort of occupation they wish to pursue, and their relationship to their communities and culture. In this section, we will explore various paths of identity development and their relations to adolescents' families, friends, and culture.

The "I" and the "Me"

In order to understand the full scope of what an identity is, and the processes through which it is formed, developmentalists have found it useful to distinguish between two, interlocking components of the self: the "I" and the "me." Defined originally by William James (1842–1910), a famous American philosopher and psychologist, the **me-self** is the *object self*; it includes social roles and relationships ("I am a student"; "I am Tenisha's fiancé"), material possessions ("I drive a late-model Chevy"), traits ("I am ambitious"), and other features that can be objectively known (age, family, school, religion, and so forth). In contrast, the **I-self,** as defined by James, is the *subject self*, the part of the system that reflects on, guides, and directs the object self. According to Harter (1999, p. 6), the I-self includes

- *self-awareness,* an appreciation of one's internal states, needs, thoughts, and emotions;
- *self-agency,* the sense of authorship over one's thoughts and actions;
- *self-continuity,* the sense that one remains the same person over time;
- *self-coherence,* the sense that one is a single, integrated, and bounded entity.

Some contemporary developmentalists maintain that the self is a story about who one is. If so, then the me-self is the character in that story, and the I-self is the author and storyteller (Nakkula & Toshalis, 2006).

Identity theorists have long maintained that social and historical contexts play a pivotal role in how a person's self develops. A child growing up in a traditional society isolated from the modern world, for example, may have a relatively clearly defined path of identity development as a consequence of the limited number of social role possibilities. In contrast, aspects of the modern world have created new challenges and opportunities for understanding oneself in relation to one's society and culture. Kenneth Gergen has suggested that self-coherence is difficult to achieve in technologically advanced societies in which mass communications have dramatically accelerated and multiplied our relations to each other and to our communities. According to Gergen, modern society has resulted in a **saturated self**—a self full to the brim with multiple "me's" that have emerged as a consequence of needing to conform to a dizzying whirl of social roles and relationships that demand different, and sometimes contradictory, selves. The appearance of "multiple selves" in the self-descriptions of adolescents makes it necessary for them to deal with the fact that they are, in some sense, different people in different contexts. It is at this point that the question of personal authenticity—"Who is the real me?"—becomes particularly compelling, and, perhaps, anxiety provoking (Harter, 2006).

Adolescents often seek out heroes to adulate and imitate. In the United States, many identify with popular musicians. These young people are waiting outside a funeral home to pay tribute to the platinum-selling rapper known as Big Pun.

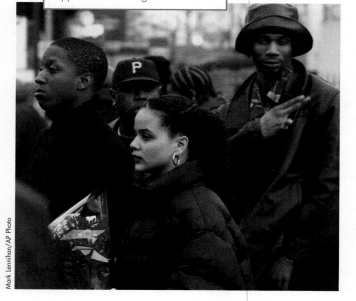

Mark Lennihan/AP Photo

Achieving a Mature Identity

The possibility that adolescents may be troubled by the feeling of multiple selves makes the search for one's "true self" one of the dominant developmental themes of adolescence (Meeus & de Wied, 2007). As we discussed in Chapter 1, Erik Erikson believed that the quest for identity is a lifelong task through which individuals achieve a coherent understanding of themselves in relation to their societies. Although the identity quest is lifelong, its challenges come to a climax during adolescence, when young people must deal with biological pressures to become sexually active and social pressures to adopt culturally valued roles and beliefs. According to Erikson (1968a), in order to successfully navigate these multiple pressures (regarding, for example, occupational goals, intimate relationships, social and political values, and religious beliefs) the adolescent has to integrate a stable sense of self across various roles and responsibilities, creating a unified sense of identity. Adolescents who fail this developmental task suffer from "identity confusion." For Erikson, then, the crisis of adolescence is one of *identity versus role confusion*.

In many cultures, adolescent identity development is complicated by the multiple identity possibilities that exist within the peer group and the larger culture.

The popularity of Erikson's ideas created a demand for an assessment method that could both depict an identity in the process of being formed and provide quantitative measures of the different states of identity formation (Grotevant, 2001; Marcia, 2002) (for a description of another assessment method, see the box "From Diaries to Blogs"). In an early and influential effort at such an assessment method, James Marcia (1966) focused on two factors identified by Erikson as essential to achieving a mature identity: exploration and commitment. **Exploration** refers to the process through which adolescents actively examine their possible future roles and paths in life, think about the choices their parents have made, and begin to search for alternatives that they find personally satisfying. **Commitment** refers to individuals' personal involvement in, and allegiance to, the goals, values, beliefs, and future occupation that they have adopted for themselves.

Based on interviews with male college students about choice of occupation and beliefs about politics and religion, Marcia (1966, 2002) identified four patterns of coping with the task of identity formation that arise from four possible patterns of exploration and commitment (Figure 15.5):

Figure 15.5 When the combinations of Erikson's two factors in identity formation—exploration and commitment—are considered together, the result is the four patterns of adolescent identity formation proposed by Marcia.

1. *Identity achievement.* Adolescents who display this pattern have gone through a period of decision making about their choice of occupation, their political commitment, their religious beliefs, and so on, and are now actively pursuing their own goals. When asked about their political commitment, for example, they might respond with such answers as "I've thought it over, and I've decided to support the _____ party. Their program is the most sensible one for the country to be following."

2. *Foreclosure.* Young people who display this pattern are also committed to occupational and ideological positions, but they show no signs of having gone through a period of exploration. Instead, they have just taken over patterns of identity from their parents. They respond to questions about their political beliefs with such answers as "I really never gave politics much thought. Our family always votes for the _____ party, so that's how I vote."

3. *Moratorium.* This pattern is displayed by adolescents actively engaged in a process of exploration. They might answer questions about their political

exploration According to Marcia, the process through which adolescents actively examine their possible future roles and paths.

commitment According to Marcia, individuals' sense of allegiance to the goals, values, beliefs, and occupation they have chosen.

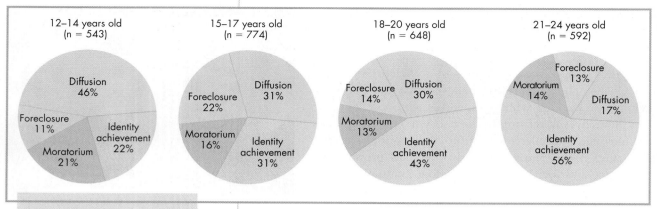

Figure 15.6 The proportion of identity statuses change across the adolescent years such that most individuals in the U.S. have an achieved identity by the time they reach their early 20s. (From Meeus, 2003.)

beliefs by saying, "I'm not sure. Both parties have their good points, but neither one seems to offer a better chance for my economic future."

4. *Identity diffusion.* Adolescents who manifest this pattern have neither explored nor committed to identity possibilities. They are likely to take a cynical attitude toward the issues confronting them, so they may answer questions about political commitment by declaring, "I stopped thinking about politics ages ago. There are no parties worth supporting."

Other researchers have extended Marcia's methods to incorporate additional domains of experience, including family life, friendships, dating, and sex roles (Goosens, 2001; Grotevant, 1998). In general, the research has shown that identity achievement increases with age, whereas diffusion and moratorium decrease (Figure 15.6; Meeus, 2003). The increase in achievement and the decrease in diffusion are both steady trends over the period from the years before high school to the late college years (Grotevant & Cooper, 1998; Kroger, 2003; Moshman, 1998).

Because identity achievement is considered so important to normal adolescent development, researchers have given special effort to identifying factors that facilitate or complicate identity formation for adolescents growing up in different contexts and cultures.

Family and Identity

Research has shown that family relations exert significant influence on an adolescent's identity formation (Sartor & Youniss, 2002; Reis, Youniss, McIntosh, & Eisermann, 2007). In particular, families can be fertile ground for identity development when they create contexts that are open and accepting of change and provide a high level of support (Bosma & Kunnen, 2001). Harold Grotevant and Catherine Cooper have demonstrated this in several studies focusing on the special role that social relationships within families play in shaping identity formation (Grotevant & Cooper, 1998). In one study, they constructed a "family interaction task" to evaluate the way that patterns of family interaction influence the process of identity exploration (Grotevant & Cooper, 1985). In this task, a mother, a father, and their adolescent are asked to make plans for a 2-week vacation together. They have 20 minutes to arrive at a day-by-day plan that covers both the location and the activity for each day. The discussions are scored according to the extent to which the family members express their individuality (for example, by stating their own point of view or by disagreeing with another family member) and their connectedness (for example, by their responsiveness and sensitivity to others' points of view). In this and subsequent studies, Grotevant and Cooper found that adolescents who scored higher on measures of identity exploration lived in families that supported their right to express their own points of view (Grotevant, 1998).

It seems, then, that families that are most effective in promoting identity development are those that offer adolescents support and security while encouraging them to create a distinct identity. This is also suggested in research showing that secure attachment is positively related to identity achievement, whereas insecure attachment correlates with identity diffusion (Zimmermann & Becker-Stoll, 2002).

Forming a Sexual Identity

I was truly happy before my mind understood what it was to be sexual at all. My troubles began when my body began changing and when my intellect began understanding those changes and the feelings they caused. Parties were great in middle school until I became sexual. An innocent game of spin-the-bottle among friends was a lot of fun. . . . Things got tougher, however, when one of my oversexed and underexperienced adolescent friends would suggest that we play a game of "French" spin-the-bottle. It sent a shiver up my spine and caused my stomach to contract to the size of a pea. When we entered high school . . . I wasn't comfortable. I just couldn't bring myself to talk about girls and all of the other stuff that high school guys talked about. I did, however, more often than not, awkwardly participate in the talks about girls and sex. However, in the back of my mind was the ever-present feeling that I wasn't normal, and that I must change. (Anonymous, reflecting on his growing awareness of his homosexuality, in A. Garrod et al., 1999)

If identity can be defined as an answer to the question "Who am I?", then sexual identity development can be defined as answering the question "Who am I as a sexual being?" More specifically, **sexual identity** refers to an individual's understanding of himself or herself as heterosexual, homosexual (gay or lesbian), or bisexual. However, as you might imagine, it simply does not happen that young heterosexual people discover and declare to the world (or themselves), "I'm straight!" (Striepe & Tolman, 2003). Instead, as is clearly suggested by the young man quoted above, developing a sexual identity can be particularly pressing and complicated for **sexual minority youth,** that is, adolescents who develop identities as gays, lesbians, or bisexuals. A large national sample of adolescents revealed that over 8 percent of boys and 6 percent of girls have had same-sex attractions or relationships (Russell & Joyner, 2001), although fewer than 2 percent of adolescents "identify" themselves as gay, lesbian, or bisexual (Garofalo et al., 1999).

Adolescents seem to go through a series of stages in the process of defining themselves as gay, lesbian, or bisexual (Ferrer-Wreder et al., 2002; Troiden, 1993). Richard Troiden developed the following stage model of forming a sexual minority identity. As you read through the stage descriptions, notice how the questions of personal authenticity, self-continuity, and self-coherence that are key to identity formation are additionally complicated for sexual-minority youths:

Stage 1: Sensitization; feeling different Like the young man quoted at the start of this section, during early adolescence many sexual minority youths begin to experience a feeling of being "different."

Stage 2: Self-recognition; identity confusion With puberty, they may realize that they are attracted to members of the same sex and begin to label such feelings as homosexual. This recognition can be the source of considerable inner turmoil and identity confusion:

sexual identity An individual's understanding of himself or herself as heterosexual, homosexual, or bisexual.

sexual minority youth Adolescents who develop identities as gays, lesbians, or bisexuals.

More than 6000 high school students participated in the Annual Gay/Straight Youth Pride March that took place in Massachusetts.

Marilyn Humphries/The Image Works

From Diaries to Blogs

IF YOU HAVE EVER KEPT A DIARY OR online journal or written intimate letters to a close friend or lover, then you can probably appreciate how such personal documents can provide researchers with unique and important insights into the identity development of adolescents, as well as allowing them to "witness" emotions and issues of a personal nature that adolescents seldom reveal to adults. Probably the most well-known teenage diary is the one written by Anne Frank over the 2-year period that she and her family, who were Jewish, hid in secret attic rooms to escape Nazi persecution during World War II. In the diary, Anne describes her puberty, her sexual awakening, and her changing relationships with family and peers. Viewed though the lens of developmental theory, diaries such as hers can provide a record of adolescents' cognitive and emotional growth (Haviland & Kramer, 1991; Magai & Haviland-Jones, 2002).

In addition to being viewed as a record of experience and development, diary and journal writing can be viewed as an experience in its own right—one that may be helpful in dealing with the identity issues and complex feelings that accompany adolescence. Would Anne have kept such a detailed account of her most personal thoughts and feelings if she had had easy access to friends with whom she could easily talk and share secrets? Did her regular retreat into the privacy of her diary provide her with much-needed personal "space" in the cramped quarters of the attic? On the basis of her analysis of diaries written between the late 1950s and early 1970s by 10- to 14-year-old girls, Barbara Crowther (1999) suggested that writing in a private diary can make a very public statement about inde-

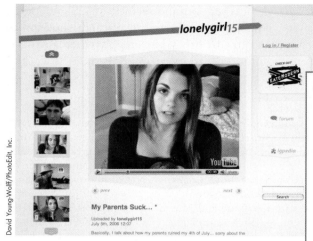

David Young-Wolff/PhotoEdit, Inc.

Although eventually revealed as a hoax, "lonelygirl15" was the screen name for a teenage video blogger on YouTube, whose postings attracted the attention of millions. The fictional blogger, 15-year-old Bree, began by posting details of personal experiences typical of adolescence. When the video blogs took a turn towards soap-opera drama, the blog was investigated and found to be a fake, with Bree being played by the actress, Jessica Lee Rose.

pendence and individuality. She noted, for example, that the keeping of a diary is rarely kept secret, and that girls will often make a big deal about it, putting warnings such as "Strictly Private—No Entry" on the diary covers. Such warnings, while appearing to be about ensuring privacy, are also a declaration: "I have ideas, feelings, opinions that are my own." Writing a diary, from Crowther's perspective, can be a way of establishing a sense of personal autonomy.

It is interesting to speculate about how the study of personal documents will change as a consequence of technological advances. The Internet has already enabled the construction of entirely new types of personal documents: the personal Web page and its most recent offspring, the blog, Facebook, and MySpace. Unlike diaries, which can be intensely private, these new electronic documents are radically public and interactive, accessible to literally billions of people, any of whom may comment on the document's contents. And whereas diaries are evolving records that preserve past entries, contributing to, or at least reflecting, a continuous self, Web pages may reflect something closer to Gergen's saturated self. That is, personal Web pages can be entirely rewritten to present an entirely different self—or selves—to the world.

According to a new report by the Pew Internet & American Life Project, Internet content creation by teenagers continues to grow (Lenhart et al., 2007). Perhaps surprisingly, girls are responsible for most of this activity, with some 34 percent of U.S. teen girls blogging, compared to 20 percent of boys. Given the explosion of blogging, we might reasonably ask what purpose it serves. Based on her interviews with adolescent bloggers, Emily

You are confused about what sort of person you are and where your life is going. You ask yourself the questions "Who am I? Am I a homosexual? Am I really a heterosexual?" (Cass, 1984, p. 156)

By middle or late adolescence, they begin to believe that they are probably homosexual because they are uninterested in the heterosexual activities of their peers. Many homosexual adults recall adolescence as a time when they were loners and social outcasts.

Stage 3: Identity assumption Some young people who have had homosexual experiences and who recognize that they prefer sexual relations with members of their own sex do not openly acknowledge their preference. Many others, however, move from private acknowledgment of their homosexual orientation to admitting it publicly, at least to other homosexuals. Young people who have achieved this level of homo-

Nussbaum concludes that blogging provides a means of self-expression, as well as a sense of community with other teens (Nussbaum, 2004). The postings of bloggers chronicle their authors' loneliness and insecurities; and they seek and offer advice on everything from finding a mate to getting rid of a mate to surviving inept and unreasonable parents. "I need your help," one poster wrote. "Yes, your help. You, the one reading this . . . what am i supposed to do when the dynamic of a once-romantic relationship sort of changes but sort of doesn't, and the next week i continually try to get in touch with the girl but she is either not there or can't talk very long, and before

this change in the dynamic she was always available?" A string of responses suggested a variety of options, including "don't call her so much" and "confront her . . . what she's doing isn't fair to you" (Nussbaum, 2004, p. 35). Although most comments tend to be sympathetic one-liners or wisecracks, some are hurtful and hostile, placing the blogger in a peculiar position relative to the audience of on-line onlookers. As noted by one of the bloggers interviewed by Nussbaum, "If I get a really mean comment and I go back and look at it again, and again, it starts to bother me. But then I think, if I delete it, everyone will know this bothers me. But if I respond, it'll

mean I need to fight back. So it turns into a conflict, but it's fun. It's like a soap opera, kind of" (p. 35).

In addition to the drama, such public displays clearly encourage a high degree of self-reflection that developmentalists consider the hallmark of the I-self. Unfortunately, these new electronic diary forms are ephemeral, making it difficult for developmentalists to find and analyze them after they have served their authors' adolescent purposes.

sexual identity deal with it in a variety of ways. Some try to avoid homosexual contacts and attempt to pass as heterosexual because they are afraid of being stigmatized. Others begin to align themselves with the homosexual community.

Stage 4: Commitment; identity integration This final stage is reached by those who have come to terms with their homosexuality and are "out" in their communities. Identity integration is indicated by a fusion of one's sexuality and emotional commitments, by expressions of satisfaction with one's orientation, and by public disclosure of one's homosexual identity.

Troiden notes that commitment to a homosexual identity may vary from weak to strong, depending on such factors as the individual's success in forging satisfying personal relationships, being accepted by family members, and functioning well

table 15.2

Milestones of Sexual Minority Development (Mean Age)

Milestone	Gay (n = 53)	Lesbian (n = 34)	Bisexual (n = 25)
Became aware	9.6	10.9	13.2
Sexual contact	14.7	14.3	14.9
Same-sex contact	14.9	16.4	16.7
Disclosure	16.8	16.0	16.8

Source: Maguen et al., 2002.

at work or in a career. Indeed, the social stigma and oppression facing sexual minority youth, along with fear of being rejected by parents, can make public disclosure of sexual identity, or coming out, a major challenge (Heights, 1999). Retrospective accounts of gay men indicate that "living a lie," "alienation and isolation," and "telling others" were significant issues in their adolescent experiences (Flowers & Buston, 2002). Table 15.2 illustrates the average age of first disclosure in a sample of 117 young adults who were approximately 20 years of age at the time of the study and who self-identified as gay, lesbian, or bisexual (Maguen et al., 2002).

Two noteworthy patterns emerge from the data in Table 15.2: First, the average age of disclosure is similar across the subgroups; second, the subgroups are significantly different in the average age both of awareness of same-sex attractions and of acting on these attractions. These age differences are consistent with distinct patterns of experience found for the different subgroups. For example, lesbians are more likely than gay men to report sexual contacts with both males and females; moreover, they are more likely than gay men to have had their first sexual contact with a person of the other sex. The distinctive pattern that characterizes lesbians is consistent with arguments that sexual minority women may be more likely than men to be attracted to both sexes, and that girls may be under more social pressure to date (Ellis et al., 2002; Savin-Williams & Diamond, 2004).

It has been pointed out that in most respects, the needs and concerns of youths with same-sex attractions are simply those of all youths: "Regardless of sexual orientation youths need the love and respect of their parents, must negotiate their ongoing relationships as they move toward adulthood, are concerned with peer status, desire love and sex, and wonder about their future" (Savin-Williams, 2001, p. 6).

Forming an Ethnic Identity

In the same way that sexual identity refers to counting oneself as a member of a particular sexual orientation group, **ethnic identity** refers to counting oneself as a member of a particular ethnic group. And, as with sexual minority youth, the process of identity formation can be complicated for ethnic minority and immigrant children (Phinney & Haas, 2003; Phinney, 2008). First, in cases in which the values, beliefs, and customs of the minority group differ from those of the majority population, ethnic minority youth face the task of reconciling two different identities—one based on their own cultural heritage, the other on the cultural heritage of the majority group. In effect, they have at least twice as much psychological work to do. Second, these young people often face prejudice, discrimination, and accompanying barriers to economic opportunity, all of which further complicate their task.

As you saw in Chapter 9 (p. 310), ethnic identity development is well underway by middle childhood when ethnic minority children know particular characteristics of their ethnic group and have developed basic attitudes about their ethnicity. During middle childhood and adolescence, children in ethnic minority groups move through three additional stages of ethnic identity formation (Cross, 2003; Phinney & Haas,

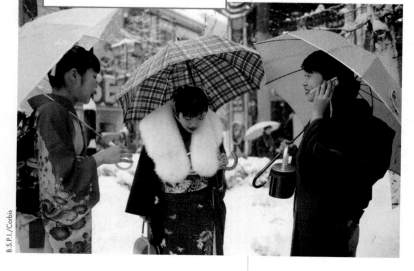

Multicultural influences are pervasive in many parts of the world, creating a special challenge for adolescents who may feel the tug of both traditional and modern beliefs, values, and expectations of behavior.

2003). Although researchers apply different labels to these stages, they agree on the basic content of each stage and the general kinds of experiences associated with movement from one stage to the next. In this discussion, we have adopted the labels suggested by Jean Phinney (2008) because she explicitly links the stages to the processes of exploration and commitment discussed above.

Stage 1: Unexamined ethnic identity In this stage, children tend to accept and show a preference for the cultural values of the majority culture in which they find themselves. This acceptance may include a negative evaluation of their own group (see Chapter 9, p. 310–311). In some cases, this stage appears to correspond to Marcia's category of foreclosure, because the person refuses to consider the relevant issues and adopts the views of others unquestioningly. One Mexican American boy told Phinney, "I don't go looking for my culture. I just go by what my parents say and do, and what they tell me to do, the way they are" (p. 68). In other cases, the failure to examine questions of ethnic identity is more similar to identify diffusion. For example, an African American girl remarked, "Why do I need to learn about who was the first black woman to do this or that? I'm just not too interested" (p. 68).

Stage 2: Ethnic identity search Movement beyond stage 1 is often initiated by a shocking experience in which the young person is rejected or humiliated because of his or her ethnic background. The specifics of such encounters are quite varied (Cross, 2003; Fordham & Ogbu, 1986). A minority student may be accused of cheating when he or she does outstanding work, simply because the teacher assumes that members of the student's ethnic group are incapable of such work; or a boy and girl who have been friends for years may be forbidden to socialize with each other romantically because they have different skin colors, ethnic backgrounds, or religious affiliations. However, a shocking encounter is not necessary for young people to begin pondering their ethnic identity: for some, this move into stage 2 is precipitated simply by a growing awareness that the values of the dominant group may not be beneficial to ethnic minorities.

In stage 2, young people show an intense concern for the personal implications of their ethnicity and often engage in an active search for information about their group. They are likely to become involved in social and political movements in which ethnicity is a core issue. They may also experience intense anger at the majority group and glorify their own ethnic heritage.

Signithia Fordham and John Ogbu (1986) describe cases in which African American adolescents go through a process of *oppositional identity formation*, rejecting the patterns of dress, speech, mannerisms, and attitudes associated with European American society and adopting an identity that opposes them. These researchers believe that the process of oppositional identity formation provides one of the major explanations for the school failure of African American children. For many of these young people, who feel automatically shut out of the economic opportunities of the majority culture, successful identity formation requires that they look upon the academic activities of school as irrelevant to their lives. Evidence suggests that similar identity processes are at work in the development of adolescents of many minority groups in the United States (Phinney, 2008).

Stage 3: Ethnic identity achievement Individuals who achieve a mature ethnic identity have resolved the conflicts characteristic of stage 2 and

ethnic identity Individuals' sense of themselves as a member of a particular ethnic group.

Faced with an increasingly multiethnic population, schools and communities provide opportunities to celebrate the cultural heritage of young people. This girl is demonstrating Korean drumming at her school's "International Day."

Michael J. Doolittle/The Image Works

now have a secure self-confidence in their ethnicity and a positive self-concept (Cross, 2003). Researchers have found that mature ethnic identity may be a protective factor against particular risks (LaFromboise et al., 2006). An example comes from a study of 434 seventh-grade students living in a large Southwestern city who self-identified as American Indian: students who had a greater sense of ethnic pride also had stronger antidrug norms (Kulis, Napoli, & Marsiglia, 2002).

Naturally, developmentalists have been interested in identifying the factors that may facilitate ethnic identity formation. In a study of immigrant Armenian, Vietnamese, and Mexican families, Jean Phinney and her colleagues found that identity formation is strongest when the native language is maintained in the home and when adolescents spend significant amounts of time with peers who share their ethnic heritage (Phinney & Ong, 2002). Positive ethnic identity formation also seems to be fostered when parents deliberately uphold cultural traditions in the home and instruct their children in them.

Many families that immigrate to the United States settle in established communities that share their ethnic heritage. For example, families who move from Mexico to the Southwest may become part of a Mexican American community that has existed for generations. In such communities, it may be relatively easy for children, including in immigrant families, to develop a positive ethnic identity, if their peers, family, and community embrace Mexican cultural traditions. Increasingly, however, Mexican and other Latino immigrants are settling in areas without established Latino communities—for example, in Maine, Indiana, Arkansas, and North Carolina (Hamann, 2002). This situation creates new identity challenges both within the developing Latino community and within the settled community of long-time residents who have little understanding of Latino cultures.

In an ethnographic study, Karen Grady (2002) documents how a group of Latino students, predominantly Mexican, whose families had recently settled in rural Indiana came to develop a sense of shared identity. The students had been marginalized and isolated in the high school, when English proficiency tests had placed most of them together in lower-track and ESL classes with limited bilingual resources and teaching personnel. Most of the "instruction" involved doing unchallenging worksheets. After a while, the students established their own routines for occupying the day. Specifically, they worked on lowrider art, a contemporary art form that combines a variety of ethnic themes (religious symbols, pre-Columbian motifs, symbols of the Mexican revolution) into a celebration of Mexican and Latino heritage (Figure 15.7). One girl, Xochitl, told Grady that she got her ideas for her art from *Lowrider* magazine, commenting, "I like to read that magazine because it talks about my culture and I feel so proud when I read that my people are doing good things and not going out in the streets and selling drugs or getting into trouble" (p. 176). The students' artwork was soon the talk of the school, and the art teacher incorporated the art form into her curriculum in much the same way that she included Greco-Roman art and Impressionism, requiring students to learn the symbolic meanings of its images. Grady argues that through lowrider art, the students were able to make themselves visible to the rest of the students, and to others in the dominant culture, as members of an ethnic group with its sources of pride and a remarkable history. Her study offers an example of how adolescents can use art and music in the process of identity formation (for another example, see the box "The Hip-Hop Generation").

Figure 15.7 Popular among U.S. adolescents of Hispanic descent, lowrider art often includes symbols of both American and Mexican culture.

Danny Villescas/The Castro Collection, www.castrocollection.com

The Hip-Hop Generation

REGARDLESS OF YOUR OWN ETHNIC background or social status, it is highly likely that you know that B-boying is break dancing, MC'ing is rapping, and that these activities, along with DJ'ing and graffiti, are key features of hip hop. And it is just as likely that the adults in your life are only dimly, if at all, aware of these terms. Hip hop, which emerged during the 1970s from urban, lower-income African American youth, has swept through North America to such an extent that many developmentalists believe it defines a large segment of contemporary youth culture, hence the label: the hip-hop generation (Chang, 2005).

Wherever youth culture exists, the music, dance, books, styles of dress, and speech that have defined it, while changing from one decade to the next, have consistently been accused of poisoning the minds and bodies of otherwise innocent adolescents, and eroding the social and moral standards of the day. Those who speak against hip hop argue that it encourages and glamorizes violence, consumerism, and sexism. You do not need to look hard for examples to support this view.

Others point out, however, that from its infancy, hip hop has expressed the damage and injustice of growing up poor—especially black and poor. According to many researchers, hip hop—rap music in particular—is a form of social commentary on police brutality, drugs, sex, and poverty (Dyson, 1996; Richardson & Scott, 2002). When Niggas With Attitude (N.W.A.) released their 1988 album *Straight Outta Compton*, their lyrics of violence, death, drugs, and despair—all a part of the experience of many poor urban youth—marked the birth of gangsta rap (Richardson & Scott, 2002).

Beyond providing commentary on social conditions through its music, dance, and graffiti, as well as through film and video and particular styles of dress and speech, hip hop also communicates particular values, most notably being authentic, or "keeping it real." As you know from Chapter 1, art, language, and values are all aspects of culture as it is usually defined. Researchers of hip hop argue that it constitutes a genuine culture that impacts the formation of identity among adolescents (Lloyd, 2002), particularly those of African and Latino descent (Richardson & Scott, 2002; Watts et al., 2002). A striking example of this is Murray Forman's (2002) ethnographic study of Somali immigrant adolescents, which documents how these minority youth expand the frontiers of their

Philadelphia Daily News/Jennifer Midberry/The Image Works

Music and dance play important roles in adolescent identity development and peer culture. Originated by African American teenagers in the 1970s, break dancing swept the North American continent and crossed the ocean to Asia.

own identity through the medium of music. Since the early 1990s, Somalis have immigrated to the United States in unprecedented numbers to escape the political violence and oppression of their homeland. Uprooted from their traditional way of life and transplanted to an entirely foreign environment, Somali adolescents face a clash of cultures. Forman notes that as they learn to negotiate their new surroundings—new schools, neighborhoods, language, and customs—these adolescents often begin to drift away from core values of the family and their traditional Islamic religion. An important means of coping with this cultural transition is to try to find a sense of self and belonging in peer groups. According to Forman, "Somali teens often stake out deliberately rebellious positions, in which hip hop is strategically influential . . . in doing so they are also signaling to their peers that they are 'cool,' unafraid of possible repercussions, and willing to test the system for flaws or weaknesses" (Forman, 2002, p. 100). Hip hop is thus a means of expressing authenticity and connecting with peers.

Interestingly, it is only upon their arrival in North America that "being black" becomes an issue for these Somali youth: Cultural codes of race are simply not relevant in Somalia, where virtually the entire population is black. Hip hop, Forman argues, provides an important vehicle by which the adolescents can understand the racial basis of their new social status because the music generates an awareness of blackness and of the situation of black, urban youth. Forman writes

that "there is a sense of comfort—even a sense of security—in the students' identification with hip hop" (Forman, 2002, p. 110).

Whereas Forman focused on why Somali immigrant youth may be drawn to hip hop, other researchers have sought to use the music as a teaching tool. For example, Stephens and his colleagues (1998) have argued that hip hop can provide a culturally relevant and peer-endorsed medium for teaching teens about HIV/AIDS prevention (today, AIDS is the leading cause of death for African American men, ages 25 to 44, and the third-leading cause of death for African American women of the same age). Focusing on the social commentary inherent in much of hip-hop music and film, Roderick Watts and his colleagues (2002) used hip hop as part of a youth program intended to foster the development of "critical consciousness," that is, adolescents' understanding of the social forces and oppression that challenge African Americans.

Thus, hip hop seems to play several roles in the lives and development of black adolescents. Shared with peers, it provides a sense of belonging and social identification built upon the core value of authenticity—"keeping it real." It also provides raw commentary and insight on the prejudices, economic inequities, and political oppression of blacks in contemporary America. As the noted author James Baldwin (1992) pointed out, it is often the role of artists and musicians to give voice to injustice, and "disturb the peace."

independent sense of self The sense of self encouraged by individualistic cultures, characterized by an orientation to being unique, promoting one's individual goals, and expressing one's thoughts and opinions.

interdependent sense of self The sense of self encouraged by collectivist cultures, characterized by an orientation to fitting into the group, promoting group goals, and developing the ability to understand the thoughts of others.

Identity and Culture

Adolescents' perceptions of themselves as members of particular ethnic groups clearly affect their sense of identity. Might, then, their sense of identity develop in radically different ways depending on the particular culture in which they live? Many researchers have answered this question in the affirmative, claiming that a culture's values, beliefs, and patterns of life profoundly affect the identity development of its members (Adams & Markus, 2001; Miller, 1997; Shweder et al., 2002). For example, it is common for cultures to be considered along a continuum that describes the degree to which concepts of the self and identity are rooted either in the individual or in the social group (Greenfield et al., 2006; Kagitçibasi, 2003). At one end are cultures whose members see themselves primarily as individuals, as most middle-class Americans do. At the other end are cultures, such as Japan's, whose members see themselves primarily in relation to the larger social group. Members of the first kind of culture are said to perceive themselves as *independent*; members of the second kind, to perceive themselves as *interdependent*.

According to Hazel Markus and Shinobu Kitayama, people whose cultures encourage an **independent sense of self,** or individualistic cultures, are oriented to being unique, to promoting their individual goals, and to expressing their own thoughts and opinions. People whose cultures emphasize an **interdependent sense of self,** or collectivist cultures, by contrast, seek to fit into the group, to promote the goals of others (that is, of the group), and to develop the ability to "read" the minds of others.

As Markus and Kitayama point out, this difference in orientation to the self creates different sets of problems for the young person who is forging a unified sense of identity. For example, the American emphasis on the autonomous, independent self presupposes that identity formation is an individual, personal process. By contrast, in collectivist societies, an integral part of identity formation is conformance to, and acceptance by, the group. Thus adolescents in collectivist societies—particularly highly traditional collectivist societies—do not have to make many of the decisions and choices that American adolescents must face in order to resolve their identity. It makes little sense to assert that healthy identity formation requires adolescents to make a "commitment to a sexual orientation, an ideological stance, and a vocational choice" (Marcia, 1980, p. 160) in traditional collectivist societies in which marriages are arranged by the family, one's vocation is whatever one's father or mother does, and strict subordination to one's elders is a moral imperative (Grotevant, 1998). The most distinctive fact about identity formation in such

In Balinese society, tooth filing is a significant ceremony that marks the age of puberty. The ceremony involves a slight filing of the upper canine teeth, and is meant to eradicate symbolically the "wild" nature of the individual.

Arnie Hodalic/Corbis

societies is that it involves little of the cognitive deliberation and personal choice that play such large roles in accounts of identity formation in Western cultures. In societies with few distinct adult roles, a young person has few decisions to make.

In response to this view, Elliot Turiel (2002) has cautioned against grouping cultures into two broad categories—those that foster an independent sense of self versus those that foster interdependence. He argues that cultures, and the people who live them, are much more diverse in their practices, struggles, and ambitions than can be captured by a two-category system. Even in America, it is unlikely that the "rugged individualist" could ever have "won the West"—much less survived it—in the absence of collectivist practices such as barn raising. Nevertheless, as discussed in the box "Suicide among Native American Adolescents," cultural traditions and beliefs can play a substantial role in how adolescents understand themselves, which, in turn, has important implications for adolescent mental health.

Following Erikson's influential theory, many contemporary developmentalists believe that identity is one of the most complex areas of adolescent development because it is so importantly tied to the child's developing relationship to community and culture. As such, identity development is influenced by the society's roles and categories, norms and moral codes, as well as the adolescent's emerging ability to make sense of them. For some adolescents, this process is further complicated by social and emotional problems, as we discuss below.

||||■■ APPLY ▬ CONNECT ▬ DISCUSS ▬ ▬ ▬ ▬ ▬ ▬ ▬ ▬ ▬ ▬ ▬ ▬ ▬ ▬ ▬ ▬ ▬

How does the distinction between an independent and an interdependent sense of self apply to your own sense of self?

Social and Emotional Problems of Adolescence

One of the most extensively studied topics of adolescence is the increase of social and emotional problems during this period (Steinberg, 2008). In general, developmentalists distinguish between two categories of emotional problems: internalizing problems and externalizing problems. **Internalizing problems,** which are more common in girls, include disturbances in emotion or mood such as depression, worry, guilt, and anxiety. **Externalizing problems,** which are more common in boys, include social and behavioral problems such as aggression and delinquency—ranging from the violation of age-appropriate social norms, such as skipping school and running away, to law-breaking behaviors such as drug use and vandalism (Graber, 2004; Farrington, 2004). Developmentalists seeking to understand and help adolescents with social and emotional problems have focused on three broad questions: Why do these problems seem to erupt during adolescence? What are the differences between adolescents who develop these problems and those who do not? Why is it that when problems do arise, girls tend to have internalizing problems and boys externalizing problems?

Internalizing Problems

Based on decades of research conducted throughout the world, it is now widely accepted that there is a surge during adolescence in feelings of depression, sadness, and anxiety, and that it mostly affects girls (Costello et al., 2008; Twenge & Nolen-Hoeksema, 2002). Figure 15.8 reflects results from a study conducted with several thousand Scottish children at 11, 13, and 15 years of age (Sweeting & West, 2003).

internalizing problems Disturbances in emotion or mood such as depression, worry, guilt, and anxiety; more common in girls than boys.

externalizing problems Social and behavioral problems such as aggression and delinquency; more common in boys than girls.

The age and gender trends shown in the figure are fairly typical in indicating an increase in emotional distress for both boys and girls along with an ever-widening gender difference such that by the age of 15, girls are about twice as likely as boys to experience serious depression (Keenan & Hipwell, 2005).

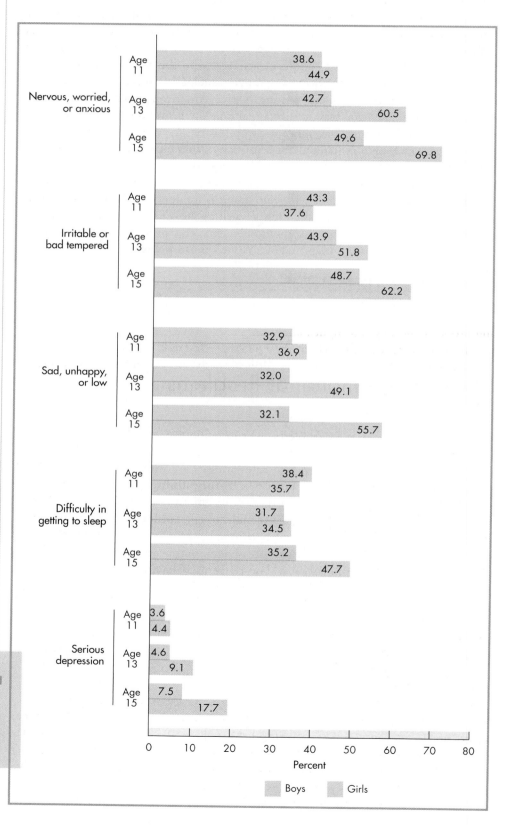

Figure 15.8 Consistent with research done in many other countries, results from a large national study of Scottish children found an increase in emotional distress for boys and girls between the ages of 11 and 15, as well as an ever-widening gender gap such that among 15-year-olds, girls are twice as likely as boys to experience serious depression. (From Sweeting & West, 2003.)

A number of explanations have been offered to account for the adolescent surge in internalizing problems, as well as for the large gender difference in their incidence. Accounting for the surge, some developmentalists point to the stresses associated with the host of biological and social changes we have previously noted, including with the chemistry of puberty, transitions to different schools, new friends and peer groups, increased family conflict, and increased pressures to achieve from parents and teachers (Compas, 2004). In light of our earlier discussions of gender differences in regulation of emotion (girls appear to be more preoccupied with their negative emotions than boys are) and intimacy orientations (girls appear to be more focused on achieving and maintaining emotional closeness in their relationships), it is perhaps predictable that girls might react more negatively than boys to the stressful events of adolescence, especially when they involve conflict in relationships with parents, peers, and romantic partners (Rudolph, 2002). A second, related explanation is that compared to boys, girls are more concerned about how they are evaluated by others, worry more about how they are judged by their peers, and are generally more apprehensive about relationships. Such "social-evaluative concerns" contribute to girls' being more competent in their interpersonal relationships but also more vulnerable to feelings of depression and anxiety (Rudolph & Conley, 2005).

Externalizing Problems

Like internalizing problems, externalizing problems seem to peak in adolescence. For both boys and girls, behaviors such as skipping school, stealing and destroying property, getting into fights, and taking illegal drugs rise sharply between early and mid-adolescence, after which they decline (Dodge & Pettit, 2003; Storvoll & Wichstrom, 2002; Steinberg, 2008). However, the gender differences, which, as noted, are reversed, are much greater (Lahey et al., 2000). In fact, it has been estimated that over 25 percent of all 16- to 17-year-old males have been involved in at least one serious violent offense (Elliot, 1994).

The incidence of externalizing problems during adolescence poses an important question: Is the increase due to the fact that a larger proportion of teens are involved, perhaps minimally, in behaviors such as skipping school, drinking alcohol, smoking pot, getting into fights, and so forth, or is it the case that a small number of teens become increasingly active in such behavior? Studies indicate that the increase reflects both factors—an increase in the number of teens involved, and an increase in the involvement of specific individuals (Maccoby, 2004). For example, in a nationwide longitudinal study of Norwegian adolescents, more than 75 percent of all 15- to 16-year-old boys and girls reported some involvement in externalizing behaviors (with the percentage being somewhat higher for boys than for girls), but only 25 percent of boys and 15 percent of girls reported high levels of involvement (Storvoll & Wichstrom, 2002). This is consistent with other research indicating that over 50 percent of all violent behaviors are perpetrated by only 6 percent of all adolescents, most of whom are also involved in other externalizing behaviors such as theft and the frequent use of drugs and alcohol (Dodge & Pettit, 2003; Moffitt et al., 2002).

Naturally, developmentalists are especially concerned about this small minority of adolescents who show high levels of externalizing behaviors. Indeed, the more serious, chronic forms of externalizing problems account for the majority of referrals to outpatient adolescent mental health clinics and the largest proportion of placements in special education classes (reviewed in Dodge & Pettit, 2003). To shed light on this minority group, a team of researchers studied approximately 1000 individuals growing up in New Zealand, following them from birth to

Suicide among Native American Adolescents

NATIVE AMERICAN ADOLESCENTS ARE at greater risk for killing themselves than are members of any other group in the world (Kermayer, 1994). Michael Chandler, Chris Lalonde, and their colleagues are working to understand why (Chandler et al., 2003; Lalonde, 2003). Their efforts have led them to evaluate suicide risk in light of the complex relationship between identity development and cultural change.

One identity issue that all adolescents must face is the problem of self-continuity. *Self-continuity* is understanding oneself as the same person throughout time, despite obvious internal or external changes. According to Chandler and his colleagues, without some way to understand that the self will continue in time regardless of change, it is difficult for adolescents to imagine themselves in the future and to work toward, or be invested in, their own future selves, and suicide might thus seem a more reasonable course of action than it would be otherwise.

In the process of studying adolescents of Western European and Native American descent, the research team identified cultural differences in the ways that adolescents solved the problem of self-continuity (Chandler et al., 2003). In particular, most adolescents of Western European descent gave *essentialist* accounts of self-continuity. That is, they believed that they were the same person across time and situations because some essential feature of their identity remained unchanged—their fingerprints, or basic personality structure, for example: "I have always been competitive. When I was little I wanted to win races, now I want to get the best grades" (p. 35). Native American adolescents, in contrast, gave *narrative* accounts of self-continuity, arguing that

Children who grow up in tribes that preserve their cultural ceremonies and practices may be less vulnerable to suicide risk in adolescence.

Jack Kurtz/The Image Works

they were the same person across time because they were able to tell a story that linked together their past, present, and future selves: "I used to be quiet and stuff . . . but I had a change . . . I just realized that . . . okay . . . I don't know how to explain it . . . I guess it would be a shock to others. . . . It is not as much of a shock to me because I know my life . . . and if they want to know out of curiosity, they could ask me . . . and I could tell them" (Chandler et al., 2003, p. 41).

These two distinct ways of understanding self-continuity reflect the two different cultural traditions. Western European culture tends to emphasize individual characteristics of the self, whereas Native American culture is based on a storytelling tradition. What is particularly interesting in light of adolescent mental health issues is that the two ways of understanding self-continuity may result in profoundly different levels of suicidal risk, especially under conditions of radical social change such as those affecting Native American communities.

Over the course of just a few generations, Native American culture has been crushed. Tribal lands have been taken, hunting and fishing practices have been outlawed, families have been broken up and relocated to reservations, and many Native American languages and cultural practices have disappeared. In a manner of speaking, Native American stories have been silenced. For adolescents struggling to establish a narrative-based account of self-continuity, the consequences of having no cultural stories can be dire.

Given the current statistical trends, 1 out of every 20 Native American adolescents will die by his or her own hand (Chandler et al., 2003). But how can we be sure that the suicides are due to the devastation of Native American culture and not to some other factor, such as genetic vulnerability to depression, for example? As it happens, Native American suicides are not equally distributed throughout all tribes. In many tribes, suicides are quite rare—in fact, much less common than the national average. In other tribes, in contrast, suicide rates are astoundingly high.

What accounts for these differences? According to Chandler and his colleagues, the answer lies in differences in the extent to which tribes have attempted to reconstruct their culture and reclaim their heritage. The researchers

adulthood (Moffitt et al., 2002; Moffitt, 2007). The researchers identified two, highly distinctive developmental patterns. In one, called *adolescent onset*, externalizing problems emerged in adolescence and had a fairly brief time course, declining significantly in young adulthood. In the other, called *childhood onset*, or *life-course persistent*, high levels of aggression emerged in preschool and persisted throughout childhood and adolescence and into adulthood. Although boys outnumbered girls in both groups, the boy/girl ratio was much smaller (1.5 to 1) in the adolescent-onset group than in the childhood–onset group, in which boys outnumbered girls by a ratio of 10 to 1. Note that these results are similar to those of the Norwegian study described previously, in which gender differences were much greater identified six *cultural continuity* factors that are present in the tribes with lower suicide rates and lacking in tribes with higher suicide rates. As shown in the first figure, suicide rates are greatly reduced if the tribe is self-governing, fights legal battles to win back traditional lands, exercises some control over its own public health services, schools, and police and fire departments, and has built a facility for cultural activities. It appears, moreover, that the effects of these cultural continuity factors are cumulative. That is, the presence of each additional factor further decreases suicide risk, as shown in the second figure.

Chandler's work demonstrates that tribal efforts to reclaim a cultural heritage can help to provide adolescents with a safety net while they work through the developmental task of establishing a sense of self-continuity. It also underscores the importance of understanding development in the context of culture and history.

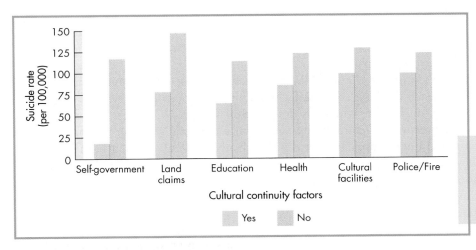

Native American tribes that engage in forms of cultural continuity and efforts to be self-determining have lower adolescent suicide rates than tribes whose cultural traditions have been eroded or lost.

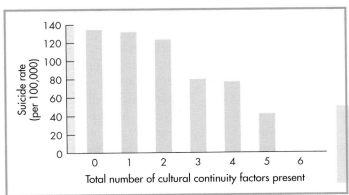

The effects of cultural continuity factors are cumulative; as the number of continuity factors rise, so does adolescents' protection from suicide risk.

for reports of "highly involved" externalizing behaviors than for overall reports of involvement.

The developmental histories of adolescents who exhibit childhood-onset problems are strikingly different from those of their adolescent-onset peers (Patterson et al., 1989). As shown in Figure 15.9, boys who go on to develop life-course persistent problems typically have difficult temperaments and receive inconsistent parenting during early childhood (the developmental histories of life-course persistent girls have not yet been well studied). In essence, by virtue of their difficult temperaments, these young boys are hard to handle, and their parents, lacking the skills necessary to cope effectively with their behaviors, tend to respond in two

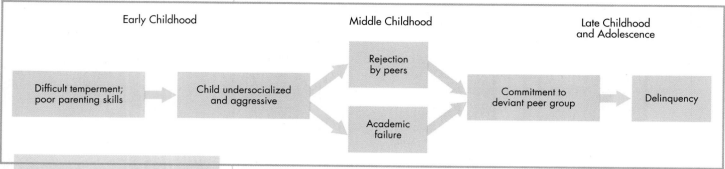

Figure 15.9 Boys who develop life-course persistent problems often have difficult temperaments as young children. Such children often receive ineffective parenting, which contributes to poor socialization, and sets them up for social and academic failures at school. These failure experiences, in turn, push these children into deviant peer groups in which they are further socialized into deviant and delinquent behavior. (From Patterson et al., 1989.)

ways: They ignore the boys' inappropriate and often aggressive behaviors, which fails to teach the boys social skills, including self-control, or they respond with excessive punishment, which, as described in Chapter 9, creates a family system in which parents and children are caught in a dynamic of escalating negative interactions. Either approach increases the chances that when such boys begin school they are both aggressive and undersocialized. As a consequence, by middle childhood they are often rejected by peers and performing poorly in school. By late childhood and adolescence, they typically form alliances with other deviant peers, who further reinforce their externalizing behaviors.

As noted above, there has been little research into how and why some girls develop externalizing problems. On the other hand, there has been a great deal of speculation as to why such problems are less common in girls than in boys. In general, most developmentalists maintain that the gender differences are largely due to an interaction of biological and sociocultural processes. As discussed in Chapter 9 (p. 326), boys and girls may have different biological predispositions to behave aggressively (Maccoby, 2004). Coupled with this are the considerable differences in the socialization of boys and girls, by parents as well as peers (Zahn-Waxler & Polanichka, 2004). In particular, norm-violating behaviors are less tolerated in girls, and more often ignored in boys. Moreover, the *communal orientation* of girls discussed earlier would seem to further diminish their involvement in externalizing behaviors.

All told, evidence indicates that adolescence is a vulnerable period for the onset of social and emotional problems, and that these problems are significantly affected by sociocultural norms and expectations.

||||| APPLY ▪ CONNECT ▪ DISCUSS -----------------------------

How might our knowledge of gender differences in internalizing versus externalizing problems influence efforts to prevent the occurrence of such problems?

Emerging Adulthood

In technologically advanced societies in which prolonged education and delayed marriage and childbearing are common, young people who are adults chronologically often continue to rely on their parents for support, engage in an extended period of identity exploration, and feel unprepared for the roles and responsibilities typically associated with adulthood. Does this description capture how you see yourself? If so, are you experiencing a prolonged adolescence or an entirely new stage of development? If you resist describing yourself as an "adolescent," you are not alone. Based in part on how college students and slightly older young adults feel about themselves, some developmentalists have argued for the existence of a new stage of development. This stage carries the name **emerging adulthood,** which is meant to capture the unique developmental challenges facing many individuals between the ages of 18 and 25 in technologically advanced societies (Jensen, 2008; Eccles et al., 2003; Nelson, Badger, & Wu, 2004). Although the term is relatively recent, the idea behind it—that changing social conditions have set the stage for the emergence of a distinctive new period in the life cycle—was suggested decades ago (Keniston, 1963; Parsons, 1963).

Kenneth Keniston, for example, proposed that we adopt the term "youth" to describe individuals in their late teens and early 20s who are coming of age in rapidly changing societies (1963). He argued that societies undergoing fast-paced technological change also experience a high degree of social, political, and cultural change as they adapt to these new technologies. Such societies tend to value innovation over tradition. As a consequence, the connections that once bound generations together are weakened: The knowledge and values of the parent generation feel less relevant to their children's interests and concerns. According to Keniston, under such conditions, youth turn to each other, rather than to their elders, to sort out fundamental identity issues. They create their own "youth culture" separate and distinct from the culture of the prior generation. The cultural discontinuity between generations contributes to a number of attitudes and behaviors that Keniston observed in youth, including their sense of powerlessness to make a personal difference in their societies and their lack of interest and involvement in politics.

More recently, developmentalists have explored how young people between the ages of 18 and 25 are oriented toward achieving self-sufficiency, stable romantic relationships, and adult work roles. For example, several studies report that in defining what it means to be mature, emerging adults place considerable weight on accepting responsibility for oneself, making independent decisions, and becoming financially independent (Jensen, 2008). In the area of romantic relationships, Jeffrey Arnett suggests that whereas adolescents are largely concerned with finding partners for the purpose of sharing good times and company, emerging adults are involved in a process that merges romantic concerns with identity issues in order to answer the question, "Given the kind of person I am, what kind of person do I wish to have as a partner through life?" (Arnett, 2000, p. 473).

emerging adulthood According to some developmentalists, a stage that in industrial societies now comes between adolescence and adulthood, reflecting the new challenges faced by people of about 18 to 25.

Some developmentalists believe that the demand for prolonged education found in most industrialized societies, including the U.S. (left), has created a new developmental phase, emerging adulthood. For societies in which adult roles and responsibilities have changed little over recent generations, as in a community in Darjiling, India (right), where many adults work to harvest tea, the new phase does not exist.

epistemic development Changes in the individuals' reasoning about the nature of knowledge.

objectivist theory of knowledge The view of knowledge as involving an accumulation of objective facts and definite answers.

subjectivist theory of knowledge The view that there is no absolute truth, as truth shifts and changes depending on the perspective.

evaluativist theory of knowledge The view that truth can shift and change but is nevertheless subject to particular standards of evaluation.

While some developmentalists have focused on the social and identity issues of emerging adulthood (Phinney, 2008), others have addressed intellectual changes of the period. One of the most interesting and productive areas of research has examined changes in how individuals reason about the nature of knowledge, known also as **epistemic development** (Perry, 1970; Magolda, 2008; Hofer, 2008). Here are a few examples taken from college students who were interviewed about their experiences in school (Perry, 1970):

I feel rather insecure thinking about these philosophical things all the time and not coming up with any definite answers. Definite answers are, well, they're sort of my foundation point. In physics you get definite answers to a point. Beyond that point you know there *are* definite answers, but you can't reach them (yet).

The instructor kept trying to force her ideas about the poem on us. . . . I mean, what makes her ideas any better than mine, anyway?

So here were all these theorists and theories and stuff—and hell, I said, "These are *games,* just *games* and everybody makes up their own rules! So it's gotta be bullshit." But then I realized "What else have we got?" and now every time I get into a thing I set out to learn all its rules, 'cause that's the only way I can tell whether *I'm* talking bullshit.

Each of the examples above reflects a very different view of the nature of knowledge. The first example reflects an **objectivist theory of knowledge,** that is, a belief that knowledge involves an accumulation of objective facts and "definite answers." In contrast, the second example reflects a **subjectivist theory of knowledge,** according to which there is no absolute truth, as truth can shift and change depending on one's perspective. Finally, the third example expresses an **evaluativist theory of knowledge,** in which is it recognized that although truth can shift and change, it is nevertheless subject to particular standards of evaluation, the "rules of the game" (Hallett, Chandler, & Krettenauer, 2002; Gottlieb & Mandel Leadership Institute, 2007).

Most studies of epistemic development in emerging adulthood find that these three epistemologies form a developmental hierarchy such that an objectivist theory of knowledge emerges first, followed by a subjectivist theory, and finally, an evaluativist theory. However, recent studies have found cultural as well as developmental differences in epistemic development, suggesting that cultures may emphasize one or another theory of knowledge (Hofer, 2008; Tabak & Weinstock, 2008). Cultures that value tradition, for example, may believe that knowledge resides in, and is transmitted by, authority figures (real or spiritual), thereby tending to support the objectivist theory of knowledge. Other cultures, in contrast, may believe that knowledge must be evaluated in terms of scientific standards, thereby supporting the evaluativist theory of knowledge.

In general, developmentalists see emerging adulthood, not as a universal stage, but rather as depending on the cultural context in which children develop. As your own experience will tell, in technologically advanced societies success in the adult world requires increasing levels of education. This has the effect of delaying the individual's entry into adult work and family roles, permitting a longer period of *moratorium* in which to explore an ever-widening array of identity possibilities and different theories of knowledge.

APPLY ■ CONNECT ■ DISCUSS

In what ways does the concept of emerging adulthood fit your own experience? Do you think that your theory of knowledge has changed since adolescence? If so, how?

Reconsidering Adolescence

Evidence presented in this chapter, as well as in Chapter 14, indicates that the bio-cultural transition of adolescence universally involves dramatic transformation across the physical, cognitive, social, and emotional domains, and is often accompanied by conflict, anxiety, and uncertainty.

Compared to all other primate species, humans are radically delayed in reaching reproductive maturity. Many have argued that the delay is to allow the brain to develop areas associated with advanced processes—language, reasoning, decision making—required to make and use the sophisticated tools of human culture. Even so, at the onset of puberty, the frontal lobes are not sufficiently mature for the effective regulation of the surge of emotional intensity associated with the release of hormones, and poorly regulated emotions make the adolescent vulnerable to risk taking, recklessness, and emotional problems.

While the onset and course of adolescence are heavily influenced by such biological factors, the many contexts of development—from the physical environment to cultural values and practices—also play significant roles in adolescent development. Thus, culture has played a role in the timing of the onset of puberty, as evidenced by the secular trend—the increasingly early pubertal onset, associated with changes in the contexts of development. In centuries past, the secular trend was attributed to increased access to nutritious food and health care. The continuing downward trend of the past few decades, however, has been associated with the rising tide of obesity and poor health, particularly among low-income minority populations in the United States, providing an unfortunate illustration of how phenotypic development is constrained by both biological and cultural processes.

Similarly, research provides strong evidence that the adolescent experience—how individuals navigate the passage to adulthood—is to a large extent structured by families, communities, and institutions, and dependent on cultural beliefs, values, and practices. For example, many of the questions that concern adolescents—Who am I? Who will I become? Who will be my mate? What is right and just?—may be less significant in cultures where identity, career, and social role possibilities are mapped out in advance according to long-standing cultural traditions, and where traditional beliefs and values are rarely open to question.

And then there is the issue of whether the cumulative cultural evolution of technologically advanced societies has created a context for the emergence of yet another way station between childhood and adulthood, a new stage of "emerging adulthood," in which the developing individual comes to terms with a kaleidoscopic array of possibilities—for identity, relationships, education, and ways of understanding the nature of truth and knowledge. But regardless of whether emerging adulthood proves to be a specific stage in the life course, we can be sure that the transition to adulthood reflects a special relationship between developing individuals and the cultures they will transform and carry into the future.

SUMMARY

Emotional Development in Adolescence

- Contrary to perceptions of adolescence as an emotional roller coaster, research indicates that over adolescence, ups and downs become less frequent and emotions less intense, although average happiness decreases.

- Decreased emotional intensity is in large part explained by increased emotional regulation. In early adolescence, immature frontal lobes may be unable to deal with hormonally triggered emotions, leaving adolescents vulnerable to risk taking; frontal lobe maturation facilitates emotional regulation. Emotional regulation also appears to be promoted by parental warmth and to be shaped by social expectations related to gender.

Relationships with Peers

- With adolescence, time spent with peers increases dramatically, peer groups become larger, and relationships become more important and intense.

- Adolescents seek friendships marked by reciprocity, commitment, and equality. Close friendships serve the functions of intimacy and autonomy and thus promote social and personality development. Girls' friendships are more intense and intimate than boys', with expressions of intimacy between boys curtailed perhaps by lack of trust, perhaps by homophobia; gender differences in relationship goals may also explain friendship differences.

- In addition to friendships, adolescent peer relations take the form of cliques—small, intimate peer groups that serve emotional and security needs—and crowds—larger groups, which provide opportunities to meet people, to develop romantic relationships and, because different crowds have different reputations, to explore their social identity.

- According to classic research by Dexter Dunphy, romantic relationships develop from other peer groups in a stagelike process, in which same-sex cliques of early adolescence give way to mixed-sex crowds, which gradually give way to romantic relationships. Significant cultural variations exist, however, and in contemporary industrialized societies marriage is postponed and romantic relationships take place alongside other peer relationships.

- Adolescent peer relationships tend to be characterized by high levels of homophily, or similarity in behaviors, tastes, views, and goals. A study by Denise Kandel showed homophily as resulting from two successive processes: Selection—in which adolescents target as potential friends teens who seem similar—and socialization—in which friends model and reinforce significant behavior. Thus, deviancy can be socialized in the context of peer relationships, in a process that has been labeled deviancy training.

Relationships with Parents

- In intensity and frequency, parent–child conflict reaches a peak in early adolescence and then decreases. Conflicts tend to focus on such matters as responsibilities and curfews—seemingly trivial but related to major issues of growing up. They often reflect differences between parents' and adolescents' understanding of what belongs to the personal, as opposed to the social conventional, domain.

- Parents of adolescents generally continue to be an important influence in their children's lives and to be sought for advice, particularly if parents provide a safe environment for communication and have an authoritative parenting style. Over adolescence, parents and child typically negotiate a new form of interdependence.

Identity Development

- A key challenge of adolescence is that of forming a coherent, stable identity, through the process of identity development. The self can be seen as consisting of a me-self—or object self, including roles and relationships, possessions, and characteristics—and an I-self—or subject self, reflecting on and guiding the object self. Contexts play a role in development of self, and according to Kenneth Gergen, modern society has resulted in a saturated self—multiple me's, making the question of authenticity more pressing for adolescents.

- For Erik Erikson, the quest for identity, although lifelong, is particularly the task of adolescence. Focusing on exploration and commitment, the factors Erikson considered essential to achieving a mature identity, James Marcia identified four patterns young people fell into: identity achievement, with commitment following exploration; foreclosure, or commitment without exploration; moratorium, or active exploration with commitment not yet reached; and identity diffusion, with neither commitment nor exploration. Over adolescence, there is an increase in achievement and a decrease in diffusion.

- Families can effectively promote identity development if they offer support and encourage exploration.

- The development of sexual identity—individuals' understanding of themselves as heterosexual, gay or lesbian, or bisexual—can be especially pressing and complicated for sexual minority youth. According to Richard Troiden's stage model, sexual minority youth move from sensitization and feeling different, generally in early adolescence, through self-recognition and identity confusion and then identity assumption, before finally reaching, in many cases, commitment and identity integration.

- The development of an ethnic identity can be more complicated for ethnic minority youth, especially if the group's culture differs significantly from the majority culture or the group faces prejudice. Jean Phinney has identified a process that leads from unexamined ethnic identity through an identity search to ethnic identity achievement. Positive ethnic formation is easiest when families uphold cultural traditions and the ethnic group is well established in the community.

- According to many developmentalists, identity development may be profoundly affected by cultural factors. For example, people whose culture encourages an independent sense of self may be oriented to promoting their individual goals and expressing their opinions; those whose culture is collectivist may be oriented to seeking to fit in and promoting group goals.

Social and Emotional Problems of Adolescence

- Social and emotional problems, which increase during adolescence, are of two types:
  - Internalizing problems, more common in girls, include disturbances in emotion or mood such as depression, worry, guilt, and anxiety.
  - Externalizing problems, more common in boys, include social and behavioral problems such as aggression and delinquency—skipping school, stealing, vandalizing, getting into fights, using drugs, and so on. Researchers distinguish two patterns—adolescent onset, emerging in adolescence and having a fairly brief time course, and childhood onset, emerging in preschool and persisting into adulthood.

Emerging Adulthood

- Today young people who are chronologically adults may have a period of continued exploration of identity and reliance on parents, in what is sometimes seen as a new stage—emerging adulthood. Emerging adulthood is dependent on context, occurring in technologically advanced societies, where success requires increasing levels of education and entry into the work world is delayed.

Key Terms

experience sampling method (ESM), p. 545
sensation seeking, p. 546
friendship, p. 549
intimacy, p. 549
autonomy, p. 550
homophobia, p. 550
clique, p. 551
crowd, p. 551
homophily, p. 553
deviancy training, p. 556

identity development, p. 560
me-self, p. 560
I-self, p. 560
saturated self, p. 560
exploration, p. 561
commitment, p. 561
sexual identity, p. 563
sexual minority youth, p. 563
ethnic identity, p. 566
independent sense of self, p. 570

interdependent sense of self, p. 570
internalizing problems, p. 571
externalizing problems, p. 571
emerging adulthood, p. 577
epistemic development, p. 578
objectivist theory of knowledge, p. 578
subjectivist theory of knowledge, p. 578
evaluativist theory of knowledge, p. 578

Guide to Discussions of Specific Aspects of Development

Guide 1 Discussions of Physical Development		
Period	**Characteristic**	**Page Numbers**
Early Infancy	Physical development in the first three months	124–126
	Maturation of the nervous system	126–130
	Brain development in first three months	129–130
	Infant sensory capacity	131–140
	Reflexes present at birth	141
	Development of reaching and grasping	144
	Maturation of sleeping patterns	150–153
Later infancy	Physical growth in the first two years	162–164
	Brain development in the first two years	165–168
	Fine motor skills	168–171
	Gross motor skills	171–175
	Control during elimination	175–177
Early childhood	The biological key to language	238–241
	Biological explanations of language acquisition	239–241
	Motor development	270–271
	Health and nutrition	271–273
	Brain maturation	273–274
Middle childhood	Patterns of growth	387–389
	Motor development	389–392
	Brain development	393–395
Adolescence	Biological theories	502–504
	Puberty	504–515

Guide 2 Discussions of Social Development

Period	Characteristic	Page Numbers
Early Infancy	Infant's preference for facelike figures	136–137
	Emergence of social smiling	205–206
	Infant sleeping arrangements	151–153
	Crying	155–156
	Coordination of infant's needs and caretaker's responses	141–143, 151, 153
Later infancy	Intersubjectivity	205–209
	Infant-caregiver relationship	209–210
	Self-recognition	226–227
	Self-reference	227
Early childhood	The environmental key to language	241–246
	Social explanations of language development	262
	Scripts	294–297
	Acquiring a sex-role identity	303–309
	Acquiring an ethnic or racial identity	309–311
	Personal identity	311–313
	Self-regulation	316–321
	Aggression	325–331
	Prosocial behavior	332–334
	Family origins and structure	341–344
	Parenting styles	345–347
	Relations with siblings	347–348
	Family diversity	348–353
	Distressed families	353–359
	Child care	359–363
	Effects of media	367–376
Middle childhood	Sociodramatic play	319–320
	Social organization of classroom instruction	434–437
	Rule-based games	397, 461
	Morality	460–469
	Peer relationships	469–483
	Influence of parents	483–487
	Sense of self	488–492
Adolescence	Peer relationships	549–552
	Romantic Relationships	552–553
	Relations with parents	556–559
	Identity development	560–570
	Social problems of adolescence	571–576

Guide 3 Discussions of Language Development

Period	Characteristic	Page Numbers
General	Biological key to language	238–241
	Environmental key to language	241–246
	Domains of language acquisition	247–254
	Explanations of language acquisition	260–265
Infancy	Language preferences at birth	224–225
	Intersubjectivity and social referencing	222–223
	Pointing	224
	Beginnings of speech: cooing, babbling, jargoning	224–225
Early childhood	Phonological development	248
	Semantic development and first words	248–250
	Earliest vocabulary	251–253
	Pragmatic development	257–260
Middle childhood	The language of school	451–455

Guide 4 Discussions of Emotional Development

Period	Characteristic	Page Numbers
Early infancy	Evidence of temperament differences at birth	148–150
	Emotion in the first three months	203–207
	Crying and parents' responses	155–156
Later infancy	Theories of emotional development	203–210
	The onset of wariness	209–212
	Beginnings of attachment	209
	Explanations of attachment	210–212
	Patterns of attachment	212, 217, 222
	Self-conscious emotions	227–228
Early childhood	Regulation of emotions	320–325
	Aggression	325–331
	Empathy and understanding others	332–334
Middle childhood	Emotions and friendship	478–483
Adolescence	Experience of emotions	544–546
	Regulating emotions	546–549
	Emotional problems	571–576

Guide 5 Discussions of Cultural Influences on Development

Period	Characteristic	Page Numbers
General	Cultural explanations of language	252–253
	Family organization	340–344, 349–351
	Influence on community	364–366
Early infancy	Motor skills	168–175
	Sleeping arrangements	151
	Sleep schedules	152–153
	Nursing behaviors	153–154
Later infancy	Attachment	209–222
	Language	224–225
Early childhood	Role of language	238–253
	Scripts	294–297
	Unevenness of development	270, 296–297
	Acquiring a sex-role identity	303–309
	Acquiring ethnic and racial identity	309–311
	Internalization of adult standards	318–320
	Regulation of emotion	320–325
	Causes of aggression	325–331
	Family structure and roles	340–348
Middle childhood	Concrete operations	395–403
	Information processing and memory	404–410
	Intelligence	415–421
	Intelligence testing	415–421
	Schooling	428–431, 433–440
	Moral reasoning	460–468
	Competition and cooperation among peers	473–476
Adolescence	Formal operations	523–527
	Formal operations and adolescent thinking	523–527
	Moral reasoning	531–539
	Friendships	549–551
	Romantic relationships	552–553
	Parent-child relations	556–559
	Identity formation	560–569
	Cultural Identity	570–571

Guide 6 Discussions of Cognitive Development

Period	Characteristic	Page Numbers
Early Infancy	Intermodal perception	136–139
	Piagetian substages 1 and 2	145, 146, 178
	Learning	146–148
	Piagetian substages 3 and 4	178–181
	Criticisms/challenges of Piaget's theory	177–178
	Appearance/stages of object permanence	182–188
	Perception of number	189–190
	Categorizing by perceptual features	191–193
	Memory	194–197
	Imitation	146, 180, 208
Later infancy	Piagetian substages 5 and 6	180–181
	Mastery of object permanence	182–184
	Generalized imitation	208
	Categorizing by conceptual features	191–193
	Attention and memory	194–197
Early childhood	Maturation of the brain	273–274
	Preoperational thinking	274–276
	Egocentrism	277–278
	Confusing appearance and reality	278–286
	Precausal reasoning	271–280
	Uneven levels of performance	281
	Information processing and memory	281–284
	Privileged domains	285–294
	Role of cultural context	294–299
	Empathy	332–333
Middle childhood	Brain development	393–395
	Concrete operations	395–403
	Information processing and memory	404–410
	Logical problem solving	408–410
	Strategies	405–407
	Intelligence	415–421
	Culture and cognition	411, 414
	Learning to read	430, 434–437
	Learning mathematics	431, 438–439
	Learning disabilities	441–444
	Moral reasoning	460–468
	Peer relationships	473–476
Adolescence	Puberty brain development	507
	Formal operations and reasoning	523–527
	Morality	531–534

A-not-B error In an object permanence task, when the child looks in location A, where the object had been previously found, even though the child just observed the object hidden at location B.

academic motivation The ability to try hard and persist at school tasks in the face of difficulties.

action Complex, coordinated behaviors.

adoption study A study in which genetically related individuals who are raised in different family environments or genetically unrelated individuals living in the same family are compared to determine the extent to which heredity or environment controls a given trait.

allele The specific form of a gene coded for a particular trait.

allocaregiving Child care and protection provided by group members other than the parents, usually other relatives.

amnion A thin, tough, transparent membrane that holds the amniotic fluid.

anorexia nervosa A condition in which girls (and only rarely boys) starve themselves, losing up to 25 percent or more of their body weight.

avoidant attachment The attachment pattern in which infants are indifferent to where their mothers are sitting, may or may not cry when their mothers leave, are as likely to be comforted by strangers as by their mothers, and are indifferent when their mothers return to the room.

Apgar Scale A quick, simple test used to diagnose the physical state of newborn infants.

apprenticeship A form of activity combining instruction and productive labor that is intermediate between the implicit socialization of family and community life and the explicit instruction of formal education.

attachment The emotional bond that children form with their caregivers at about 7 to 9 months.

autobiographical memory A personal narrative that helps children acquire an enduring sense of themselves.

authoritarian parenting pattern Parenting style identified by Baumrind that focuses on enforcing obedience and conformity to traditional standards, including by use of punishment, and that is lacking in verbal give-and-take with children and in expression of warmth.

authoritative parenting pattern Parenting style identified by Baumrind in which parents set standards and limits for children but also encourage discussion and independence and express warmth.

autism A mental condition defined primarily by an inability to relate normally to other people and low scores on intelligence tests.

autonomous morality The second and final stage of Piaget's theory of moral development in which right and wrong are defined according to internal motives and intentions rather than objective consequences.

autonomy The ability to assert one's own needs in a relationship.

autonomy versus shame and doubt For Erikson, the second stage of infancy, during which children develop a sense of themselves as competent to accomplish tasks or as not competent.

axon The main protruding branch of a neuron that carries messages to other cells in the form of electrical impulses.

babbling A form of vocalizing, beginning at around 7 months, in which infants utter strings of syllables that combine a consonant sound and a vowel sound.

basic emotions Joy, fear, anger, surprise, sadness, disgust—universal emotions, expressed similarly in all cultures and present at birth or in the early months.

basic trust versus mistrust For Erikson, the first stage of infancy, during which children come to trust others as reliable and kind and to regard the world as safe or else come to mistrust others as insensitive and hurtful and to regard the world as unpredictable and threatening.

biological drives Impulses to attempt to satisfy essential physiological needs.

bottom-up processing An approach to education that starts with teaching basic skills and, once they have been mastered, moves on to more complex tasks.

brain stem The base of the brain, which controls such elementary reactions as blinking and sucking, as well as such vital functions as breathing and sleeping.

Brazelton Neonatal Assessment Scale A scale used to assess the newborn's neurological condition.

bulimia nervosa An eating disorder characterized by "binge eating" followed by self-induced vomiting.

canalized A trait that is canalized follows a strictly defined path, regardless of most environmental and genetic variations.

carriers Individuals who are heterozygous for a trait with a dominant and recessive allele and thus express only the characteristics associated with the dominant allele but may pass the recessive allele, including for a recessive disorder, on to their offspring.

causation When the occurrence of one event depends upon the occurrence of a prior event.

centration Young children's tendency to focus on only one feature of an object to the exclusion of all other features.

cephalocaudal pattern The pattern of development that proceeds from the head down.

cerebral cortex The brain's outermost layer. The networks of neurons in the cerebral cortex integrate information from several sensory sources with memories of past experiences, processing them in a way that results in human forms of thought and action.

child-care center An organized child-care facility supervised by licensed professionals.

chorion One of the membranes that develops out of the trophoblast. It forms the fetal component of the placenta.

chromosome A threadlike structure made up of genes. In humans, there are 46 chromosomes in every cell, except sperm and ova.

chronology A simple story structure used by young children, in which they present a sequence of concrete events.

classical conditioning Learning in which previously existing behaviors come to be elicited by new stimuli.

cleavage The series of mitotic cell divisions that transform the zygote into the blastocyst

clinical method A research method in which questions are tailored to the individual, with each question depending on the answer to the preceding one.

clique A group of several young people that remains small enough to enable its members to be in regular interaction with one another and to serve as the primary peer group.

co-construction The shaping of environments through interactions between children and their caregivers, siblings, neighbors, and friends.

codominance Outcome in which a trait that is determined by two alleles is different from the trait produced by either of the contributing alleles alone.

coevolution The combined process that emerges from the interaction of biological evolution and cultural evolution.

cohort A group of persons born about the same time who are therefore likely to share certain experiences.

cohort sequential design An experimental design in which the longitudinal method is replicated with several cohorts.

collective monologues Communications in which young children each voice their own thoughts without attending to what the others are saying.

commitment According to Marcia, individuals' sense of allegiance to the goals, values, beliefs, and occupation they have chosen.

compensation A mental operation in which the child realizes that changes in one aspect of a problem are compared with and compensated for by changes in another aspect.

concrete operations Coordinated mental actions that fit into a logical system in a way that creates greater unity of thinking.

conditional response (CR) In classical conditioning, a response to the conditional stimulus (CS).

conditional stimulus (CS) In classical conditioning, a stimulus that elicits a behavior that is dependent on the way it is paired with the unconditional stimulus (UCS).

conservation of number Recognizing the one-to-one correspondence between sets of objects of equal number.

conservation of volume Understanding that the amount of liquid in a container remains the same despite being poured into a differently shaped container.

constructivist theory Piaget's theory, in which cognitive development results from children's active construction of reality based on their experiences with the world.

control group The group in an experiment that is treated as much as possible like the experimental group except that it does not participate in the experimental manipulation.

conversational acts Actions that achieve goals through language.

cooperative breeding In humans and certain other species, a system involving networks of support in which individuals other than parents contribute resources toward rearing the young

coregulation A form of indirect social control in which parents and children cooperate to reinforce the children's understandings of right and wrong, what is safe and unsafe, when they are not under direct adult control.

correlation The condition that exists between two factors when changes in one factor are associated with changes in the other.

correlation coefficient The degree of association between factors, symbolized as r and ranging between -1.0 and $+1.0$.

critical period A period during which specific biological or environmental events are required for normal development to occur.

critical theories Theories that address cultural biases that may be present in traditional developmental theories and that examine power relations between groups and the influence on development of gender, race, ethnicity, and socioeconomic class.

cross-sectional design A research design in which children of various ages are studied at the same time.

crowd A large, reputation-based and mixed-gender social network observed when cliques interact.

cultural modeling Culturally specific ways of telling stories.

cultural style A dominant way of thinking about and relating to the world that arises from a people's common historical experience.

decentration The cognitive ability to pull away from focusing on just one feature of an object in order to consider multiple features.

decoding The process of establishing letter-sound correspondences when reading.

dendrite The protruding part of a neuron that receives messages from the axons of other cells.

detachment For Bowlby, the state of indifference toward others experienced by children who have been separated from their caregiver for an extended time and have not formed a new stable relationship.

developmental science The field of study that focuses on the physical, intellectual, social, and emotional changes that children undergo from conception onward.

developmental stage A qualitatively distinctive, coherent pattern of behavior that emerges during the course of development.

deviancy training Positive reactions to discussions of rule breaking.

differential emotions theory The view that basic emotions are innate and emerge in their adult form, either at birth or on a biologically determined timetable.

differential reinforcement The process by which girls and boys are differently rewarded for engaging in gender-appropriate behavior.

dishabituation The term used to describe the situation in which an infant's interest is renewed after a change in the stimulus.

disorganized attachment The insecure attachment pattern in which infants seem to lack a coherent method for dealing with stress. They may behave in seemingly contradictory ways, such as screaming for their mother but moving away when she approaches. In extreme cases, they may seem dazed.

dizygotic twins Twins that come from two zygotes.

DNA (deoxyribonucleic acid) A long double-stranded molecule that makes up chromosomes.

dominant allele The allele that is expressed when an individual possesses two.

dominant children In reference to social hierarchies, those children who control "resources" such as toys, play spaces, and decisions about group activities.

dynamic systems theory Theory that addresses how new complex systems of behavior develop from the interaction of less complex parts.

ecological inheritance Environmental modifications, as a result of niche construction, that affect the development of offspring and descendants.

ecological systems theory Theory focusing on the organization and interactions of the multiple environmental contexts within which children develop.

ecological validity The extent to which behavior studied in one environment (such as a psychological test) is characteristic of behavior exhibited by the same person in a range of other environments.

ectoderm Cells of the inner cell mass that develop into the outer surface of the skin, the nails, part of the teeth, the lens of the eye, the inner ear, and the central nervous system.

education A form of socialization in which adults engage in deliberate teaching of the young to ensure that they acquire specialized knowledge and skills.

effortful control The inhibition of an action that is already underway.

ego In Freudian theory, this is the mental structure that develops out of the id as the infant is forced by reality to cope with the social world. The ego's primary task is self-preservation, which it accomplishes through voluntary movement, perception, logical thought, adaptation, and problem solving.

egocentrism In Piaget's terms, to "center on oneself," to consider the world entirely in terms of one's own point of view.

elaboration A memory strategy that involves making connections between two or more things to be remembered.

elaborative style A form of talking with children about new events or experiences that enhances children's memories for those events and experiences.

Electra complex According to Freud's theory of sex-role development, the process by which girls blame their mothers for their "castrated" condition, transfer their love to their fathers, and compete with their mothers for their fathers' affection.

embryonic period The period that extends from the time the organism becomes attached to the uterus until the end of the 8th week of pregnancy, when all the major organs have taken primitive shape.

emergent literacy Knowledge, skills and attitudes that provide the building blocks for learning to read and write.

emergent numeracy Knowledge, skills and attitudes that provide the building blocks for learning how to do math.

emerging adulthood A developmental stage describing the unique developmental challenges facing individuals between the ages of 18 and 25 in technologically advanced societies.

emotion A feeling state that involves distinctive physiological reactions and cognitive evaluations, and motivates action.

emotion regulation Ways of acting to modulate and control emotions.

emotional tone The degree to which a person experiences a sense of well-being versus depression and anxiety.

empathy Sharing another person's emotions and feelings.

endoderm Cells of the inner cell mass that develop into the digestive system and the lungs.

entity model of intelligence The belief that intelligence is a quality of which each person has a certain fixed amount.

epigenesis The process by which a new form emerges through the interactions of the preceding form and its current environment.

epistemic development Changes in the individuals' reasoning about the nature of knowledge.

equilibration The main source of development, consisting of a process of achieving a balance between the child's present understanding and the child's new experiences.

ethnic identity A sense of belonging to an ethnic group, and the feelings and attitudes that accompany the sense of group membership.

ethnography The study of the cultural organization of behavior.

ethnic socialization Ethnic-based messages communicated to children.

ethology An interdisciplinary science that studies the biological and evolutionary foundations of behavior.

evaluativist theory of knowledge The view that truth can shift and change but is nevertheless subject to particular standards of evaluation.

evolutionary theories Theories that explain human behavior in terms of how it contributed to the survival of the species and that look at how our evolutionary past influences individual development.

experience-dependent Development of neural connections that is initiated in response to experience.

experience-expectant Development of neural connections under genetic controls that occurs in any normal environment.

experience sampling method (ESM) Tool used by developmentalists in which study participants, when signaled by electronic pagers at random intervals, fill out brief reports on their feelings. ESM has been used to study adolescents' emotional lives.

experiment In psychology, research in which a change is introduced in a person's experience and the effect of that change is measured.

experimental group The persons in an experiment whose experience is changed as part of the experiment.

explicit memory The ability to recall absent objects and events without any clear reminder.

exploration According to Marcia, the process through which adolescents actively examine their possible future roles and paths.

extended family A family in which not only parents and their children but other kin—grandparents, cousins, nephews, or more distant family relations—share a household.

externalizing problems Social and behavioral problems such as aggression and delinquency; more common in boys than girls.

exuberant synaptogenesis A rapid growth in synaptic density that prepares the brain for a vast range of possible experiences.

false belief task A technique used to assess children' theory of mind that involves asking children about stories in which either the character or the child him- or herself is fooled into believing something that is not true.

family child care Child care provided in someone else's home, that of either a relative or a stranger.

family structure The social organization of a family, most commonly, nuclear or extended.

family study A study that compares members of the same family to determine how similar they are on a given trait.

fast mapping The way in which children quickly form an idea of the meaning of an unfamiliar word they hear in a familiar and highly structured social interaction.

fetal alcohol syndrome A syndrome found in babies whose mothers were heavy consumers of alcohol while pregnant. Symptoms include an abnormally small head and underdeveloped brain, eye abnormalities, congenital heart disease, joint anomalies, and malformations of the face.

fetal growth retardation The term for newborns who are especially small for their gestational age.

fetal period This period begins the 9th week after conception, with the first signs of the hardening of the bones, and continues until birth.

fine motor skills Motor skills related to the development and coordination of small muscles, such as those that move the fingers and eyes

Flynn effect The steady increase over the past 100 years in IQ test performance, believed to support the environmental hypothesis of intelligence.

fontanels "Soft spots," or spaces separating the bones of the skull prenatally and in early infancy.

food insecure Lacking enough food to ensure good health.

formal operations In Piaget's terms, a kind of mental operation in which all possible combinations are considered in solving a problem. Consequently, each partial link is grouped in relation to the whole; in other words, reasoning moves continually as a function of a structured whole.

format Recurrent socially patterned activities in which adult and child do things together.

friendship A close relationship between two individuals. Friendships may have different bases.

gender schema A mental model containing information about males and females that is used to process gender-relevant information.

gender segregation The term for the preference of girls to play with other girls, and boys to play with other boys.

gene pool The total variety of genetic information possessed by a sexually reproducing population.

genes The segments on a DNA molecule that act as hereditary blueprints for the organism's development.

genotype The genetic endowment of an individual

germ cells The sperm and ova, which are specialized for sexual reproduction and have half the number of chromosomes normal for a species.

germinal period The period that begins at conception and lasts until the developing organism becomes attached to the wall of the uterus about 8 to 10 days later.

gestational age The time that has passed between conception and birth. The normal gestational age is between 37 and 43 weeks.

grammar The rules of a given language for the sequencing of words in a sentence and the ordering of parts of words.

grammatical morphemes Words and parts of words that create meaning by showing the relations between other elements within the sentence.

gross motor skills Motor skills related to the development and coordination of large muscles, important for locomotion

growth charts Charts showing average values of height, weight, and other measures of growth, based on large samples of normally developing infants and used to evaluate an infant's development.

growth spurt One of the first signs of puberty during which boys and girls undergo rapid changes in height and weight.

habituation The process in which attention to novelty decreases with repeated exposure.

heritability A measure of the degree to which a variation in a particular trait among individuals in a specific population is related to genetic differences among those individuals.

heterochrony Variability in the rates of development of different parts of the organism.

heterogeneity Variability in the levels of development of different parts of the organism at a given time.

heteronomous morality Piaget's term for young children's tendency to define morality in terms of objective consequences and externally imposed controls.

heterozygous Having inherited two genes of different allelic forms for a trait.

home child care Child care provided in the child's own home, primarily by the father or a grandmother, while the mother is at work.

homophily The degree to which friends are similar to each other.

homophobia An exaggerated fear of homosexuality. Homophobia may diminish intimacy among adolescent males.

homozygous Having inherited two genes of the same allelic form for a trait.

hostile aggression Aggression that is aimed at hurting another person as a way of establishing dominance, which may gain the aggressor advantages in the long run.

hypothesis A possible explanation based on theory and precise enough to be shown true or false.

hypothetical-deductive reasoning The ability to formulate and evaluate the logical implications of a set of premises, even if it is imaginary or contradicts the real world.

I-self The part of the system that reflects on, guides, and directs the self.

id In Freudian theory, the mental structure present at birth that is the main source of psychological energy. It is unconscious and pleasure-seeking and demands that bodily drives be satisfied.

identification A psychological process in which children try to look, act, feel, and be like significant people in their social environment.

identity A mental operation in which the child realizes that a change limited to outward appearance does not change the substances involved.

identity development The process through which individuals achieve a sense of who they are and of their moral and political beliefs, their career preferences, and their relationship to their culture and community.

incremental model of intelligence The belief that intelligence is something that can grow over time as one learns.

industry versus inferiority According to Erikson's theory, the stage during which children judge themselves to be industrious and successfully meeting the new challenges posed by adults at home and school, or inferior and incapable of meeting such challenges.

implantation The process by which the blastocyst becomes attached to the uterus.

implicit memory The ability to recognize objects and events that have been previously experienced.

independent sense of self The sense of self encouraged by individualistic cultures, characterized by an orientation to being unique, promoting one's individual goals, and expressing one's thoughts and opinions.

infant-directed speech (or motherese or baby-talk) Speech adults use with infants, characterized by high pitch, exaggerated intonation, clear boundaries between parts, and simplified vocabulary.

information-processing theories Theories that look at cognitive development in terms of how children come to process, store, organize, retrieve, and manipulate information in increasingly efficient ways.

initiation–reply–feedback sequence An instructional discourse pattern in which the teacher initiates an exchange, usually by asking a question; a student replies; and then the teacher provides feedback.

initiative versus guilt According to Erikson's theory, the stage in early childhood during which children face the challenge of continuing to declare their autonomy and existence as individuals, but in ways that begin to conform to the social roles and moral standards of society.

institutional review boards (IRBs) Groups responsible for evaluating and overseeing the ethical soundness of research practices at an institution.

instrumental aggression Aggression that is directed at obtaining something.

Intelligence Quotient (IQ) The ratio of mental age to chronological age, calculated as IQ = (MA/CA)100. Calculation of IQ in this fashion ensures that when children are performing precisely as expected for their age, the resulting score will be 100; thus 100 is an "average IQ" by definition.

intentionality The ability to engage in behaviors directed toward achieving a goal.

interdependent sense of self The sense of self encouraged by collectivist cultures, characterized by an orientation to fitting in to the group, promoting group goals, and developing the ability to understand the thoughts of others.

intermodal perception The understanding that a certain object or event can be simultaneously perceived by more than one sensory system.

internal working model A mental model that children construct as a result of their experiences with their caregivers and that they use to guide their interactions with their caregivers and others.

instructional discourse A distinctive way of talking and thinking that is typical in school but rarely encountered in everyday interactions in the community or home.

internalizing problems Disturbances in emotion or mood such as depression, worry, guilt, and anxiety; more common in girls than boys.

intimacy A sense of close connection between two individuals, resulting from shared feelings, thoughts, and activities.

kinship studies The use of naturally occurring conditions provided by kinship relations to estimate genetic and environmental contributions to a phenotypic trait.

kwashiorkor A potentially fatal form of malnutrition in which the diet is extremely low in protein.

language acquisition device (LAD) Chomsky's term for an innate language-processing capacity that is programmed to recognize the universal rules that underlie any particular language that a child might hear.

language acquisition support system (LASS) Bruner's term for the parental behaviors and formatted events within which children acquire language. It is the environmental complement to the innate, biologically constituted LAD.

learning A relatively permanent change in behavior brought about by experience of events in the environment.

locomotion The ability to move around on one's own.

longitudinal design A research design in which data are gathered about the same group of children as they grow older over an extended period of time.

low birth weight The term used to describe babies weighing 5 pounds, 8 ounces (2500 grams) or less at birth whether or not they are premature.

mastery orientation A way that children approach school tasks in which they are motivated to learn, to try hard, and to improve their performance.

material tools Cultural tools including physical objects and observable patterns of behavior such as family routines and social practices.

me-self Includes all of the things that people know about themselves.

media Forms of mass communication, including newspapers, magazines, books, comic books, radio, television, films, video games, and the Internet.

meiosis The process that produces sperm and ova, each of which contains only half of the parent cell's original complement of 46 chromosomes.

memory span The number of randomly presented items of information that can be repeated immediately after they are presented.

memory strategies Specific actions used deliberately to enhance remembering.

menarche The first menstrual period.

mental modules Innate mental faculties that receive inputs from particular classes of objects and produce corresponding information about the world.

mental operations In Piaget's theory, the mental process of combining, separating, or transforming information in a logical manner.

mesoderm The cells of the inner cell mass that give rise to the muscles, the bones, the circulatory system, and the inner layers of the skin

metacognition The ability to think about one's own thought processes.

metaphor Use of a word in a way that draws a comparison between the thing the word usually refers to and some other, unrelated thing.

microgenetic design A research method in which children's development is studied intensively over a relatively short period of time.

mirror neurons Special brain cells that fire when an individual sees or hears another perform an action, just as they would fire if the individual were performing the same action.

mitosis The process of cell duplication and division that generates all the individual's cells except sperm and ova.

metamemory The ability to think about one's memory processes.

modeling The process by which children observe and imitate individuals of the same sex as themselves.

monozygotic twins Twins that come from one zygote and therefore have identical genotypes.

morality of care A morality that stresses relationships, compassion, and social obligations.

morality of justice A morality that emphasizes issues of rightness, fairness, and equality.

morpheme The smallest unit of meaning in the words of a language.

motor drive The pleasure young children take in using their new motor skills.

mutation An error in the process of gene replication that results in a change in the molecular structure of the DNA.

myelin A sheath of fatty cells that insulates axons and speeds transmission of nerve impulses from one neuron to the next.

naturalistic observation Observation of the actual behavior of people in the course of their everyday lives.

natural selection The process through which species survive and evolve, in which individuals with phenotypes that are more adaptive to the environmental conditions survive and reproduce with greater success than individuals with phenotypes are that less adaptive.

nature The inherited biological predispositions of the individual.

neighborhood physical disorder A problem in distressed communities, including both physical deterioration (garbage on the streets, rundown buildings, etc.) and chaotic activity (crowding, high noise levels, etc.).

neural tube An embryonic structure that will develop into the brain and spinal cord.

neuron A nerve cell.

neurotransmitter A chemical secreted by a cell sending a message that carries the impulse across the synaptic gap to the receiving cell.

niche construction The active shaping and modification of individuals' environments by the individuals' own behaviors, activities, and choices.

no-nonsense parenting Parenting characterized by a mix of high parental control, including punishment, and warmth, and associated especially with African American single mothers.

nuclear families Families consisting of a husband, wife, and their children.

nurture The influences of the social and cultural environment on the individual.

object permanence The understanding that objects have substance, maintain their identities when they change location, and ordinarily continue to exist when out of sight.

objectivist theory of knowledge The view of knowledge as involving an accumulation of objective facts and definite answers.

objective view of responsibility An understanding that responsibility depends on objective consequences alone.

objectivity The requirement that scientific knowledge not be distorted by the investigator's preconceptions.

Oedipus complex In Freudian theory, the fear, guilt, and conflict evoked by a little boy's desire to get rid of his father and take the father's place in his mother's affections.

ontogenetic adaptation Something that has evolved because it contributes to survival and normal development; in one view, infant emotions are ontogenetic adaptations.

operant conditioning Learning in which changes in behavior are shaped by the consequences of that behavior, thereby giving rise to new and more complete behaviors.

organizational strategies A memory strategy in which materials to be remembered are mentally grouped into meaningful categories.

overextension A term for the error of applying verbal labels too broadly.

perceptual scaffolding The way in which a familiar word serves as an anchor for learning new words that come immediately before or after it.

performance orientation A way of approaching school tasks in which students are motivated by their level of performance, ability and incentives for trying.

permissive parenting pattern Parenting style identified by Baumrind in which parents express warmth but do not exercise control over their children's behavior.

personal distress A self-focused emotional reaction to another person's distress.

personal identity A person's sense of themselves as persisting over time (*I-self*), and their sense of personal characteristics such as appearance and abilities that can be objectively known (*me-self*).

personality formation The process through which children develop their own unique patterns of feeling, thinking, and behaving in a wide variety of circumstances.

phallic stage In Freudian theory, the period around the fourth year when children begin to regard their own genitals as a major source of pleasure

phenotype The organism's observable characteristics that result from the interaction of the genotype with the environment.

phenotypic plasticity The degree to which the phenotype is open to influence by the environment, rather than determined by the genotype.

phonemes The smallest sound categories in human speech that distinguish meanings. Phonemes vary from language to language.

phonological development Learning to segment speech into meaningful units of sound.

placenta An organ made up of tissue from both the mother and the fetus that serves as a barrier and filter between their bloodstreams.

plasticity The degree to which, and the conditions under which, development is open to change and intervention.

playworld practice Used in several European countries, and based on theories regarding the importance of play in intellectual development, it involves students performing and discussing of various themes in children's literature.

pragmatic development Learning the conventions that govern the use of language in particular social contexts.

precausal thinking Piaget's description of the reasoning of young children that does not follow the procedures of either deductive or inductive reasoning.

prefrontal area Part of the cortex located directly behind the forehead, and important to the development of voluntary behaviors.

preoperational stage According to Piaget, the stage of thinking between infancy and middle childhood in which children are unable to decenter their thinking or to think through the consequences of an action.

preterm The term for babies born before the 37th week of pregnancy.

prevention science An area of research that examines the biological and social processes that lead to maladjustment as well as those that are associated with healthy development.

primary circular reaction The term Piaget used to describe the infant's tendency to repeat pleasurable bodily actions for their own sake.

primary intersubjectivity Organized, reciprocal interaction between an infant and caregiver with the interaction itself as the focus.

privileged domains Cognitive domains that call upon specialized kinds of information, require specifically designated forms of reasoning, and appear to be of evolutionary importance to the human species.

prosocial behavior Behavior such as sharing, helping, caregiving, and showing compassion.

prosocial moral reasoning The thinking that is involved in deciding whether to share with, help, or take care of other people when doing so may prove costly to oneself

protective factors Environmental and personal factors that are the source of children's resilience in the face of hardship.

proximodistal pattern The pattern of development that proceeds from the middle of the organism out to the periphery.

puberty The series of biological developments that transforms individuals from a state of physical immaturity into one in which they are biologically mature and capable of sexual reproduction.

public policies Governmental laws and programs such as those designed to promote the welfare of children and families.

primary sex characteristics The organs directly involved in reproduction.

protodeclaratives Early conversational acts whose purpose is to establish joint attention and sustain a dialogue.

protoimperatives Early conversational acts whose purpose is to get another person to do something.

psychodynamic theories Theories, such as those of Freud and Erikson, exploring the influence on development and developmental stages of universal biological drives and the life experiences of individuals.

realistic mathematics education An approach to mathematics education that focuses on developing the student's understanding of how math can be used to solve real-world problems.

recessive allele The allele that is not expressed when an individual possesses two different alleles for the same trait.

reciprocal teaching A method of teaching reading in which teachers and children take turns reading text in a manner that integrates decoding and comprehension skills.

reflex A specific, well-integrated, automatic (involuntary) response to a specific type of stimulation.

rehearsal The process of repeating to oneself the material that one is trying to memorize.

relational aggression Indirect aggression intended to harm someone's friendships or exclude an individual from the group.

reliability The scientific requirement that when the same behavior is measured on two or more occasions by the same or different observers, the measurements be consistent with each other.

replicability The scientific requirement that other researchers can use the same procedures as an initial investigator did and obtain the same results.

representations The ability to form mental symbols and present experiences to oneself mentally, according to Piaget, emerges during sensorimotor substage 6.

research design The overall plan describing how a study is put together; it is developed before conducting research.

resilient The ability to recover quickly from the adverse effects of early experience or persevere in the face of stress with no apparent special negative psychological consequences.

resistant attachment The attachment pattern in which infants stay close to their mothers and appear anxious even when their mothers are near. They become very upset when their mothers leave but are not comforted by their return. They simultaneously seek renewed contact with their mothers and resist their mothers' efforts to comfort them.

reversibility A mental operation in which the child realizes that one operation can be negated, or reversed, by the effects of another

risk factors Personal characteristics or environmental circumstances that increase the probability of negative outcomes for children. Risk is a statistic that applies to groups, not individuals.

saturated self A self full to the brim with multiple "me's" that have emerged as a consequence of needing to conform to social roles and relationships that demand different, and sometimes contradictory, selves.

scale errors Young children's inappropriate use of objects due to their failure to consider information about the object's size.

school-cutoff strategy A means of assessing the impact of education while controlling for age by comparing children who are almost the same age but begin schooling a year apart because of school rules that set a specific cutoff birthday date for starting school.

scripts Event schemas that specify who participates in an event, what social roles they play, what objects they are to use during the event, and the sequence of actions that make up the event.

secondary circular reactions The behavior characteristic of the third substage of Piaget's sensorimotor stage, in which babies repeat actions to produce interesting changes in their environment.

secondary intersubjectivity A form of interaction between infant and caregiver, emerging at about 9–12 months, with communication and emotional sharing focused not just on the interaction but on the world beyond.

secondary sex characteristics The anatomical and physiological signs that outwardly distinguish males from females.

secular trend Most typical of industrialized countries, a historical pattern in which the age of pubertal onset declines across generations.

secure attachment A pattern of attachment in which children play comfortably and react positively to a stranger as long as their mothers are present. They become upset when their mothers leave and are unlikely to be consoled by a stranger, but they calm down as soon as their mothers reappear.

secure base Bowlby's term for the people whose presence provides the child with the security that allows him or her to make exploratory excursions.

self-conscious emotions Emotions such as embarrassment, pride, shame, guilt, and envy, which emerge after 8 months with infants' growing consciousness of self.

self-esteem One's evaluation of one's own self-worth.

self regulation The ability to control one's thoughts, emotions, and behaviors.

semantic development Learning meanings of words and of combinations of words.

semenarche The first ejaculation. Ejaculation often occurs spontaneously during sleep and is called a nocturnal emission.

sensation seeking Desire to participate in highly arousing activities, especially common in early and mid-adolescence.

sensitive period A time in an organism's development when a particular experience has an especially profound effect.

sensorimotor stage Piaget's term for the stage of infancy during which the process of adaptation consists largely of coordinating sensory perceptions and simple motor behaviors to acquire knowledge of the world.

separation anxiety The distress that babies show when the person to whom they are attached leaves.

small for gestational age Newborns whose birth weight falls in the lowest 10 percent for their gestational age because they have not grown at the normal rate.

sexual identity An individual's understanding of himself or herself as heterosexual, homosexual, or bisexual.

sexual minority youth Adolescents who develop identities as gays, lesbians, or bisexuals.

social capital The resources that communities provide children and families, including not only schools, health services, and so on, but also social structures, expectations for behavior, and levels of trust and cooperation among community members.

social comparison The process of defining oneself in relation to one's peers.

social disorganization A problem in distressed communities, including weak social cohesion (lack of trust and connection among community members), poor neighborhood climate (fear related to crime and violence), and perceived racism.

social domain theory The moral domain, the social conventional domain, and the personal domain have distinct rules that vary in how broadly the rules apply, and what happens when they are broken.

social learning theories Theories that focus on development as the result of learning, changes in behavior as a result of forming associations between behavior and its consequences.

social repair mechanisms Strategies that allow friends to remain friends even when serious differences temporarily drive them apart.

social referencing A form of secondary intersubjectivity in which infants look to their caregiver for an indication of how to feel and act on encountering an unfamiliar object or event.

social structures Complex organizations of relationships between individuals.

socialization The process by which children acquire the standards, values, and knowledge of their society.

sociocognitive conflict Cognitive conflict that is rooted in social experience.

sociocultural theory The theory associated with Vygotsky and emphasizing the influence of culture on development.

sociodramatic play Make-believe play in which two or more participants enact a variety of related social roles.

socioemotional competence The ability to behave appropriately in social situations that evoke strong emotions.

somatic cells All the cells in the body except for the germ cells (ova and sperm).

specific learning disabilities A term used to refer to the academic difficulties of children who fare poorly in school despite having normal intelligence.

spinal cord The part of the central nervous system that extends from below the waist to the base of the brain.

strange situation A procedure designed to assess children's attachment on the basis of their responses to a stranger when they are with their mothers, when they are left alone, and when they are reunited with their mothers.

subjective view of responsibility An understanding that responsibility depends on both intentions and consequences.

subjectivist theory of knowledge The view that there is no absolute truth, as truth shifts and changes depending on the perspective.

superego In Freudian terms, the conscience. It represents the authority of the social group and sits in stern judgment of the ego's efforts to hold the id in check. It becomes a major force in the personality in middle childhood.

symbolic tools Cultural tools, such as abstract knowledge, beliefs, and values.

sympathy Feelings of sorrow or concern for another.

synapse The tiny gap between axons and dendrites.

synaptic pruning The process of selective dying off of nonfunctional synapses.

synaptogenesis The process of synapse formation.

syntactic bootstrapping Use of knowledge of grammar to figure out the meaning of new words.

system theories Theories that envision development in terms of complex wholes made up of parts and that explore how these wholes and their parts are organized and interact and change over time.

temperament The term for the individual modes of responding to the environment that appear to be consistent across situations and stable over time. Typically included under the rubric of temperament are such characteristics as children's activity level, their intensity of reaction, the ease with which they become upset, their characteristic responses to novelty, and their sociability.

teratogens Environmental agents that cause deviations from normal development and can lead to abnormalities or death.

theory A broad framework or set of principles that can be used to guide the collection and interpretation of a set of facts.

theory of gradual differentiation The view that infants are born only with general emotional reactions, which differentiate into basic emotions over the first two years.

theory of mind The ability to think about other people's mental states and form theories of how they think

theory theory The theory that young children have primitive theories about how the world works, which influence how children think about and act within specific domains.

top-down processing An approach to education that focuses on using skills to accomplish specific, meaningful tasks.

totipotent stem cells Cells that have the potential to grow into a complete embryo and, ultimately, a normal, healthy infant.

true dialogue A communication in which each person's utterances take into account the utterances of others.

twin study A study in which groups of monozygotic (identical) and dizygotic (fraternal) twins of the same sex are compared to each other and to other family members for similarity on a given trait.

umbilical cord A soft tube containing blood vessels that connects the developing organism to the placenta.

unconditional response (UCR) In classical conditioning, the response, such as salivation, that is invariably elicited by the unconditional stimulus (UCS).

unconditional stimulus (UCS) In classical conditioning, the stimulus, such as food in the mouth, that invariably causes the unconditional response (UCR).

underextension A term used for applying verbal labels in a narrower way than adults do.

validity The scientific requirement that the data being collected actually reflect the phenomenon being studied.

violation of expectations method A test of mental representation in which the child is habituated to an event, and then presented with possible and impossible variants of the event.

visual acuity Sharpness of vision.

X chromosome One of the two chromosomes that determine sex; in females, both members of the twenty-third pair of chromosomes and in males one member of the twenty-third pair.

Y chromosome One of the two chromosomes that determine sex; in males, one member of the twenty-third pair of chromosomes.

zone of proximal development For Vygotsky, the gap between what children can accomplish independently and what they can accomplish when interacting with others who are more competent.

zygote The single cell formed at conception from the union of the sperm and the ovum.

Abbott, S. (1992). Holding on and pushing away: Comparative perspectives on an Eastern Kentucky child rearing practice. *Ethos, 20,* 33–65.

Abebe, T., & Aase, A. (2007). Children, AIDS and the politics of orphan care in Ethiopia: The extended family revisited. *Social Science & Medicine, 64*(10), 2058–2069.

Aber, J. L., Brooks-Gunn, J., & Maynard, R. A. (1995). Effects of welfare reform on teenage parents and their children. *Future of Children, 5*(2), 53–71.

Abrams, R., Gerhardt, K., & Antonelli, P. J. (1998). Fetal hearing. *Developmental Psychobiology, 33*(1), 1–3.

Acebo, C., Sadeh, A., Seifer, R., Tzischinsky, O., Hafer, A., & Carskadon, M. A. (2005). Sleep/wake patterns derived from activity monitoring and maternal report for healthy 1- to 5-year-old children. *Sleep, 28,* 1568–1577.

Adams, G., & Markus, H. R. (2001, September). Culture as patterns: An alternative approach to the problem of reification. *Culture & Psychology. Special Issue: Culture and the dialogical self: Theory, method and practice, 7*(3), 283–296.

Adamson, L. B. (1995). *Communication development during infancy.* Madison, WI: Brown & Benchmarks.

Addams, J. (1910). *The spirit of youth and the city streets.* New York: Macmillan.

Adolph, K. E., & Eppler, M. A. (2002). Flexibility and specificity in infant motor skill acquisition. In J. W. Fagen & H. Hayne (Eds.), *Progress in infancy research: Vol. 2* (pp. 121–167). Mahwah, NJ: Lawrence Erlbaum Associates.

Agnew, R. (2003). An integrated theory of the adolescent peak in offending. *Youth and Society, 34,* 263–299.

Ahadi, S. A., & Rothbart, M. K. (1993). Children's temperament in the U.S. and China: Similarities and differences. *European Journal of Personality, 7,* 359–377.

Ahnert, L., & Lamb, M. (2000). The East German child care system: Associations with caretaking and caretaking beliefs, children's early attachment and adjustment. *American Behavioral Scientist, 44,* 1843–1863.

Ahnert, L., & Lamb, M. (2003). Shared care: Establishing a balance between home and child care settings. *Child Development, 74,* 1044–1049.

Ahnert, L., Pinquart, M., & Lamb, M. E. (2006). Security of children's relationships with nonparental care providers: A meta-analysis. *Child Development, 77*(3), 664–679.

Ainsworth, M. D. S. (1967). *Infancy in Uganda: Infant care and the growth of love.* Baltimore, MD: Johns Hopkins University Press.

Ainsworth, M. D. S. (1982). Attachment: Retrospect and prospect. In C. M. Parkes & J. Stevenson-Hinde (Eds.), *The place of attachment in human behavior.* New York: Basic Books.

Ainsworth, M. D. S., & Bell, S. M. (1969). Some contemporary patterns of mother-infant interaction in the feeding situation. In A. Ambrose (Ed.), *Stimulation in early infancy.* New York: Academic Press.

Ainsworth, M. D. S., Bell, S. M., & Stayton, D. J. (1971). Individual differences in strange-situation behavior of one-year-olds. In H. R. Schaffer (Ed.), *The origins of human social relations.* New York: Academic Press.

Ainsworth, M. D. S., Blehar, M. C., Waters, E., & Wall, S. (1978). *Patterns of attachment: A psychological study of the strange situation.* Mahwah, NJ: Lawrence Erlbaum Associates.

Akers, J. F., Jones, R. M., & Coyl, D. D. (1998). Adolescent friendship pairs: Similarities in identity status development, behaviors, attitudes, and intentions. *Journal of Adolescent Research, 13*(2), 178–201.

Al-Ali, N., & Hussein, Y. (2003). Iraq. In A. Mahdi (Ed.), *Teen life in the Middle East.* Westport, CT: Greenwood Press.

Aldrich, C. A., & Hewitt, E. S. (1947). A self-regulating feeding program for infants. *Journal of the American Medical Association, 35,* 341.

Alencar, A. I., de Oliveira Siqueira, J., & Yamamoto, M. E. (2008, January). Does group size matter? Cheating and cooperation in Brazilian school children. *Evolution and Human Behavior, 29*(1), 42–48.

Alexander, K., Quas, J., Goodman, G., Ghetti, S., Edelstein, R., Redlich, A. D., et al. (2005). Traumatic impact predicts long-term memory of documented child sexual abuse. *Psychological Science, 16,* 33–40.

Allen, R. E., & Myers, A. L. (2006). Nutrition in toddlers. *American Family Physician 74*(9), 1527–1532.

Amato, P. (2000). The consequences of divorce for adults and children. *Journal of Marriage and the Family, 62,* 1269–1287.

Amato, P. R. (2006). Marital discord, divorce, and children's well-being: Results from a 20-year longitudinal study of two generations. In A. Clarke-Stewart & J. Dunn (Eds.), *Families count: Effects on child and adolescent development. The Jacobs Foundation series on adolescence* (pp. 179–202). New York: Cambridge University Press.

Amato, P. R., & Hohmann-Marriott, B. (2007, August). A comparison of high- and low-distress marriages that end in divorce. *Journal of Marriage and Family. 69*(3), 621–638.

American Academy of Pediatrics. (2003). Policy statement. *Pediatrics 112*(2), 424–430.

American Academy of Pediatrics Committee on Psychosociological Aspects of Child and Family Health. (1998). Guidance for effective discipline. *Pediatrics, 101,* 723–728.

American Psychiatric Association. (2000). *Diagnostic and statistical manual of mental disorders* (Rev. 4th ed.). Washington, DC: Author.

Ammerman, R. T., Kolko, D. J., Kirisci, L., Blackson, T. C., & Dawes, M. A. (1999). Child abuse potential in parents with histories of substance use disorder. *Child Abuse and Neglect, 23,* 1225–1238.

Anderman, E. M., Austin, C. C., & Johnson, D. (2001). The development of goal orientation. In A. Wigfield & J. S. Eccles (Eds.), *Development of achievement orientation* (pp. 197–221). San Diego: Academic Press.

Anderman, E. M., Griesinger, T., & Westerfield, G. (1998). Motivation and cheating during early adolescence. *Journal of Educational Psychology, 90,* 84–93.

Anderson, D., & Kirkorian, H. (2006). Attention and television. In J. Bryant & P. Vorderer (Eds.), *Psychology of entertainment* (pp. 35–54). Mahwah, NJ: Lawrence Erlbaum Associates.

Anderson, E. (1990). *Streetwise: Race, class, and change in an urban community.* Chicago: University of Chicago Press.

Anderson, S. W., Damasio, H., & Damasio, A. R. (2005). A neural basis for collecting behaviour in humans. *Brain: A Journal of Neurology, 128*(1), 201–212.

Anglin, J. M. (1993). Vocabulary development: A morphological analysis. *Monographs of the Society for Research in Child Development, 58*(10, Serial No. 238).

Angold, A. (2003). Adolescent depression, cortisol and DHEA. *Psychological Medicine, 33,* 573–581.

Annis, R. C., & Corenblum, B. (1987). Effect of test language and experimenter race on Canadian Indian children's racial and self-identity. *Journal of Social Psychology, 126,* 761–773.

Antonov, A. I., & Medkov, V. M. (2007). Demographic processes in the countries of Eastern Europe, the CIS, and the Baltic: Trends in the 1990s and what we should expect in the next decade. In A. S. Loveless & T. B. Holman (Eds.), *The family in the new millennium: World voices supporting the "natural" clan: Vol. 1. The place of family in human society* (pp. 296–315). Westport, CT: Praeger Publishers/Greenwood Publishing Group.

Antonov, A. N. (1947). Children born during the siege of Leningrad in 1942. *Journal of Pediatrics, 30*, 250.

Apgar, V. (1953). A proposal for a new method of evaluation of the newborn infant. *Current Researches in Anesthesia and Analgesics, 32*, 260–267.

Apple, R. (2006). *Perfect motherhood: Science and childrearing in America.* New Brunswick, NJ: Rutgers University Press.

Ariel, J., & McPherson, D. (2000). Therapy with lesbian and gay parents and their children. *Journal of Marital and Family Therapy, 26*, 421–432.

Ariès, P. (1962). *Centuries of childhood.* Translated from the French by Robert Baldick. London: Cape.

Ariès, P. (1965). *Centuries of childhood: A social history of family life.* Oxford, England: Vintage Books.

Arnett, J. J. (2000). Emerging adulthood: A theory of development from the late teens through the twenties. *American Psychologist, 55*, 469–480.

Arnett, J. J., & Cravens, H. (2006, August). G. Stanley Hall's adolescence: A centennial reappraisal: Introduction. *History of Psychology, 9*(3), 165–171.

Arsenio, W. F. (2004). The stability of young children's physical aggression: Relations with child care, gender, and aggression subtypes. *Monographs of the Society for Research in Child Development, 69*(4), 130–143.

Arterberry, M. E., & Yonas, A. (2000). Perception of three-dimensional shape specified by optic flow by 8-week-old infants. *Perception and Psychophysics, 62*(3), 550–556.

Asendorph, J. (2002). Self-awareness, other-awareness, and secondary representation. In A. Meltzoff & W. Prinz (Eds.), *The imitative mind: Development, evolution, and brain bases.* Cambridge, England: Cambridge University Press.

Asher, S. R., & Coie, J. D. (Eds.). (1990). *Peer rejection in childhood.* New York: Cambridge University Press.

Asher, S. R., Rose, A. J., & Gabriel, S. W. (2001). Peer rejection in everyday life. In M. R. Leary (Ed.), *Interpersonal rejection* (pp. 105–142). London: Oxford University Press.

Aslin, R. N., Jusczyk, P. W., & Pisoni, D. B. (1998). Speech and auditory processing during infancy: Constraints on and precursors to language. In D. Kuhn & R. S. Siegler (Eds.), *Handbook of child psychology: Vol. 2* (pp. 147–198). New York: Wiley.

Astington, J. W. (1993). *The child's discovery of the mind.* Cambridge, MA: Harvard University Press.

Astington, J. W., & Filippova, E. (2005). Language as the route into other minds. In B. F. Malle & S. D. Hodges (Eds.), *Other minds: How humans bridge the divide between self and others* (pp. 209–222). New York: Guilford Press.

Atkinson, J. (1998). The "where and what" or "who and how" of visual development. In F. Simion & G. Butterworth (Eds.), *The development of sensory, motor and cognitive capacities in early infancy: From perception to cognition.* Hove, England: Psychology Press/Lawrence Erlbaum Associates.

Atkinson, R. C., & Shiffrin, R. M. (1968). Human memory: A proposed system and its control processes. In K. W. Spence & J. T. Spence (Eds.), *The psychology of learning and motivation: Advances in research and theory: Vol. 2.* Orlando, FL: Academic Press.

Atran, S. (1998). Folk biology and the anthropology of science: Cognitive universals and cultural particulars. *Behavioral & Brain Sciences, 21*(4), 547–609.

Au, T. K., Sidle, A. L., & Rollins, K. B. (1993). Developing an intuitive understanding of conservation and contamination: Invisible particles as a plausible mechanism. *Developmental Psychology, 29*(2), 286–299.

Aubrey, J. S., & Harrison, K. (2004, May). The gender-role content of children's favorite television programs and its links to their gender-related perceptions. *Media Psychology, 6*(2), 111–146.

Avis, J., & Harris, P. L. (1991). Belief-desire reasoning among Baka children: Evidence for a universal conception of mind. *Child Development, 62*, 460–467.

Aylward, G. P. (2005). Neurodevelopmental outcomes of infants born prematurely. *Journal of Developmental & Behavioral Pediatrics, 26*(6), 427–440.

Azmitia, M., & Hesser, J. (1993). Why siblings are important agents of cognitive development: A comparison of siblings and peers. *Child Development, 64*, 430–444.

Baillargeon, R. (1993). The object concept revisited: New directions in the investigation of infants' physical knowledge. In C. E. Granrud (Ed.), *Visual perception and cognition in infancy.* Hillsdale, NJ: Lawrence Erlbaum Associates.

Baillargeon, R. (2000). Reply to Bogartz, Shinskey, and Schilling; Schilling; and Cashon and Cohen. *Infancy, 1*(4), 447–462.

Baillargeon, R. (2001). Infants' physical knowledge: Of acquired expectations and core principles. In E. Dupoux (Ed.), *Language, brain, and cognitive development: Essays in honor of Jacques Mehler* (pp. 341–361). Cambridge, MA: The MIT Press.

Baillargeon, R. (2002). The acquisition of physical knowledge in infancy: A summary of eight lessons. In U. Goswami (Ed.), *Blackwell's handbook of childhood cognitive development* (pp. 47–83). Oxford, England: Blackwell Publishing.

Baillargeon, R. (2004). Infants' physical world. *Current Directions in Psychological Science, 13*, 89–94.

Baillargeon, R., Zoccolillo, M., Keenan, K., Côté, S., Pérusse, D., Wu, H., et al. (2007). Gender differences in physical aggression: A prospective population-based survey of children before and after 2 years of age. *Developmental Psychology, 43*(1), 13–26.

Bainbridge, J., Meyers, M. K., Tanaka, S., & Waldfogel, J. (2005, September). Who gets an early education? Family income and the enrollment of three- to five-year-olds from 1968 to 2000. *Social Science Quarterly, 86*(3), 724–745.

Bajanowski, T., Vege, Å., Byard, R., Krous, H., Arnestad, M., Bachs, L., et al. (2007). Sudden infant death syndrome (SIDS)—Standardised investigations and classification: Recommendations. *Forensic Science International, 165*(2–3), 129–143.

Baker, S. A., Golinkoff, R. M., & Petitto, L.-A. (2006). New insights into old puzzles from infants' categorical discrimination of soundless phonetic units. *Language Learning and Development, 2*(3), 147–162.

Bakker, E., & Wyndaele, J. J. (2000). Changes in the toilet training of children during the last 60 years: The cause of an increase in lower urinary tract dysfunction? *BJU International, 86*, 248.

Baldwin, J. (1992). Letter: Luanne. In N. Phillip (Ed.), *Frontiers: Essays and writings on racism and culture.* Stratford, Canada: Mercury.

Bale, J. F. J. (2002). Congenital infections. *Neurological Clinic, 20*(4), 1039–1060.

Ballabriga, A. (2000, March). Morphological and physiological changes during growth: An update. *European Journal of Clinical Nutrition, 54*(Suppl. 1), S1–S6.

Bandstra, E. S., Morrow C. E., Anthony J. C., Accornero V. H., & Fried, P. A. (2001). Longitudinal investigation of task persistence and sustained attention in children with prenatal cocaine exposure. *Neurotoxicology and Teratology, 23*(6), 545–559.

Bandura, A. (1997). Behavior theory and the models of man (1974). In J. M. Notterman (Ed.), *The evolution of psychology: Fifty years of the American Psychologist* (pp. 154–172). Washington, DC: American Psychological Association.

Barber, B., Eccles, J., & Stone, M. (2001). Whatever happened to the jock, the brain, and the princess? Young adult pathways linked to adolescent activity involvement and social identity. *Journal of Adolescent Research, 16,* 429–455.

Barcus, F. E. (1986). The nature of television advertising to children. In E. L. Palmer & A. Dorr (Eds.), *Children and the faces of television* (pp. 273–285). New York: Academic Press.

Bard, K. (2004). What is the evolutionary basis for colic? *Behavioral and Brain Sciences, 27,* 459.

Bargelow, P., Vaughn, B. E., & Molitor, N. (1987). Effects of maternal absence due to employment on the quality of infant-mother attachment in a low-risk sample. *Child Development, 58,* 945–953.

Barker, D.J.P., Osmond, C., Forsén, T.J., Kajantie, E., Eriksson, J.G. (2005). Trajectories of growth among children who later develop coronary heart disease or its risk factors. *New England Journal of Medicine, 353,* 1802-9.

Baron-Cohen, S., Leslie, A. M., & Frith, U. (1986) Mechanical, behavioural, and intentional understanding of picture stories in autistic children. *British Journal of Developmental Psychology, 4,* 113–125.

Baron-Cohen, S., Leslie, A. M., & Frith, U. (2007). Does the autistic child have a 'theory of mind'? In B. Gertler & L. Shapiro (Eds.), *Arguing about the mind* (pp. 310–318). New York: Routledge/Taylor & Francis Group.

Barr, R. G., Konner, M., Bakeman, R., & Adamson, L. (1991). Crying in pKung San infants: A test of the cultural specificity hypothesis. *Developmental Medicine & Child Neurology, 33*(7), 601–610.

Barrett, J. (2001). Do children experience God as adults do? In J. Andressen (Ed.), *Religion in mind: Cognitive perspectives on religious belief, ritual, and experience.* Cambridge, England: Cambridge University Press.

Barrett, M. (1995). Early lexical development. In P. Fletcher & B. McWhinney (Eds.), *The handbook of child language* (pp. 362–392). Cambridge, MA: Blackwell Publishing.

Barsalou, L. W. (2008, April). Cognitive and neural contributions to understanding the conceptual system. *Current Directions in Psychological Science, 17*(2), 91–95.

Bartlett, E. (1977). The acquisition of the meaning of color terms. In P. T. Smith & R. N. Campbell (Eds.), *Proceedings of the Sterling Conference on the psychology of language.* New York: Plenum Press.

Basow, S. A. (2006). Gender role and gender identity development. In J. Worell & C. D. Goodheart (Eds.), *Handbook of girls' and women's psychological health: Gender and well-being across the lifespan. Oxford series in clinical psychology* (pp. 242–251). New York: Oxford University Press.

Bates, E. (1999). On the nature and nurture of language. In E. Bizzi, P. Calissano, & V. Volterra (Eds.), *Frontiere della biologia* [Frontiers of biology]. Rome: Giovanni Trecanni.

Bates, E. (2005). Plasticity, localization, and language development. In S. T. Parker, J. Langer, & C. Milbrath (Eds.), *Biology and knowledge revisited: From neurogenesis to psychogenesis. The Jean Piaget symposium series* (pp. 205–253). Mahwah, NJ: Lawrence Erlbaum Associates.

Bates, E., Benigni, L., Bretherton, I., Camaioni, L., & Volterra, V. (1979). *The emergence of symbols: Cognition and communication in infancy.* New York: Academic Press.

Bates, E., Camaioni, L., & Volterra, V. (1975). The acquisition of performatives prior to speech. *Merrill Palmer Quarterly, 21,* 205–226.

Bates, E., O'Connell, B., & Shore, C. (1987). Language and communication. In J. D. Osofsky (Ed.), *Handbook of infant development* (2nd ed.). New York: Wiley.

Bates, E., & Roe, K. (2001). Language development in children with unilateral brain injury. In C. A. Nelson & M. Luciana (Eds.), *Handbook of developmental cognitive neuroscience.* Cambridge, MA: The MIT Press.

Bauer, I. (2001). *Diaper free! The gentle wisdom of natural infant hygiene.* Saltspring Is., BC, Canada: Natural Wisdom Press.

Bauer, P. J., Wiebe, S. A., Carver, L. J., Waters, J. M., & Nelson, C. (2003). Developments in long-term explicit memory late in the first year of life: Behavioral and electrophysiological indices. *Psychological Science, 14*(6), 629–635.

Baumer, S., Ferholt, B., & Lecusay, R. (2005). Promoting narrative competence through adult-child joint pretense: Lessons from the Scandinavian educational practices of playworld. *Cognitive Development, 20*(4), 576–590.

Baumrind, D. (1971). Current patterns of parental authority. *Developmental Psychology Monographs, 4(1, Part 2).*

Baumrind, D. (1980). New directions in socialization research. *American Psychologist, 35,* 639–652.

Bayley, N. (1993). *The Bayley scales of infant development.* San Antonio, TX: Psychological Corporation.

Bayliss, D. M., Jarrold, C., Baddeley, A. D., Gunn, D. M., & Leigh, E. (2005, July). Mapping the developmental constraints on working memory span performance. *Developmental Psychology, 41*(4), 579–597.

Bearce, K., & Rovee-Collier, C. (2006) Repeated priming increases memory accessibility in infants. *Journal of Experimental Child Psychology, 93,* 357–376.

Bearison, D. J., & Dorval, B. (2002). *Collaborative cognition: Children negotiating ways of knowing. (Advances in discourse processes).* Westport, CT: Ablex Publishing.

Bearman, P., & Brückner, H. (2001). Promising the future: Virginity pledges and first intercourse. *American Journal of Sociology, 106,* 859–911.

Becker, G. S. (2007). The role of the family in modern economic life. In A. S. Loveless & T. B. Holman (Eds.), *The family in the new millennium: World voices supporting the "natural" clan: Vol. 1. The place of family in human society* (pp. 3–11). Westport, CT: Praeger Publishers/Greenwood Publishing Group.

Beidelman, T. (1997). *The cool knife: Imagery of gender, sexuality, and moral educaion in Kaguru initiation ritual.* Washington, DC: Smithsonian Institution Press.

Belkin, L. (2005, November 6). A doctor for the future. *New York Times Magazine.*

Bellmore, A. D., & Cillessen, A. H. N. (2006). Reciprocal influences of victimization, perceived social preference, and self-concept in adolescence. *Self and Identity 5*(3), 209–229.

Belsky, J. (1993). Etiology of child maltreatment: A developmental-ecological analysis. *Psychological Bulletin, 114,* 413–434.

Belsky, J. (1999). Interactional and contextual determinants of attachment security. In J. Cassidy & P. R. Shaver (Eds.), *Handbook of attachment: Theory, research, and clinical applications* (pp. 249–264). New York: Guilford Press.

Belsky, J. (2005). Attachment in ecological context. In K. Grossmann, K. Grossmann, & E. Waters (Eds.), *Attachment from infancy to adulthood.* New York: Guilford Press.

Belsky, J., Burchinal, M., McCartney, K., Vandell, D. L., Clarke-Stewart, K. A., & Owen, M. T. (2007). Are there long-term effects of early child care? *Child Development, 78*(2), 681–701.

Bemak, F., & Young, M. E. (1998). Role of catharsis in group psychotherapy. *International Journal of Action Methods, 50*(4), 166–184.

Bendersky, M., & Lewis, M. (1998). Arousal modulation in cocaine-exposed infants. *Developmental Psychology, 3,* 555–564.

Bénéfice, E., Caïus, N., & Garnier, D. (2003). Cross-cultural comparison of growth, maturation and adiposity indices of two contrasting adolescent populations in rural Senegal (West Africa) and Martinique (Caribbean). *Public Health Nutrition, 7,* 479–485.

Bengtson, V. L. (2005). *Sourcebook of family theory and research.* Thousand Oaks, CA: Sage Publications.

Benjet, C., & Hernandez-Guzman, L. (2001). Gender differences in psychological well-being of Mexican early adolescents. *Adolescence, 36,* 47–65.

Beran, M., & Beran, M. (2004). Chimpanzees remember the results of one-by-one addition of food items to sets over extended time periods. *Psychological Science, 15*, 94–99.

Berger, S. E., & Adolph, K. E. (2003). Infants use handrails as tools in a locomotor task. *Developmental Psychology, 39*(3), 594–605.

Berkey, C., Rockett, H., & Field, A. (2000) Activity, dietary intake, and weight changes in a longitudinal study of preadolescent and adolescent boys and girls. *Pediatrics, 105*, E56.

Berkowitz, L. (2003). Affect, aggression and antisocial behavior. In R. Davidson, K. Scherer, & H. Goldsmith (Eds.), *Handbook of affective sciences.* Oxford, England: Oxford University Press.

Berland, J. (1982) *No five fingers are alike.* Cambridge, MA: Harvard University Press.

Bernal, J. F. (1972). Crying during the first few days and maternal responses. *Developmental Medicine and Child Neurology, 14*, 362–372.

Berndt, T. J. (2007). Children's friendships: Shifts over a half-century in perspectives on their development and their effects. In G. Ladd, *Appraising the human development sciences: Essays in honor of Merrill-Palmer Quarterly (Landscapes of childhood series).* Detroit, MI: Wayne State University Press.

Berndt, T. J., & Keefe, K. (1995). Friend's influence on adolescent's adjustment in school. *Child Development, 66*, 1312–1329.

Berndt, T. J., & Murphy, L. M. (2002). Influences of friends and friendships: Myths, truths, and research recommendations. In R. V. Kail (Ed.), *Advances in child development and behavior: Vol. 30* (pp. 275–310). San Diego: Academic Press.

Berndt, T. J., & Savin-Williams, R. C. (1993). Peer relations and friendships. In P. H. Tolan & B. J. Cohler (Eds.), *Handbook of clinical research and practice with adolescents.* New York: Wiley.

Berry, G., & Asamen, J. (2001). Television, children, and multicultural awareness. In D. Singer & J. Singer (Eds.), *Handbook of children and the media.* Thousand Oaks, CA: Sage.

Bersamin, M., Walker, S., Waiters, E., Fisher, D., & Grube, J. (2005). Promising to wait: Virginity pledges and adolescent sexual behavior. *Journal of Adolescent Health, 36*, 428–436.

Berstein, J., Brocht, C., & Spade-Aguilar, M. (2000). *How much is enough? Basic family budgets for working families.* Washington, DC: Economic Policy Institute.

Bettelheim, B. (1977). *The uses of enchantment: The meaning and importance of fairytales.* New York: Vintage Books.

Beuf, A. H. (1977). *Red children in white America.* Philadelphia: University of Pennsylvania Press.

Bialystok, E. (2001). *Bilingualism in development: Language, literacy, and cognition.* Cambridge, England: Cambridge University Press.

Bialystok, E., & Shapero, D. (2005). Ambiguous benefits: the effect of bilingualism on reversing ambiguous figures. *Developmental Science, 8*, 595–604.

Biemiller, A., & Slonim, N. (2001). Estimating root word vocabulary growth in normative and advantaged populations: Evidence for a common sequence of vocabulary acquisition. *Journal of Educational Psychology, 93*(3), 498–520.

Bigelow, A. E. (1998). Infants' sensitivity to familiar imperfect contingencies in social interaction. *Infant Behavior and Development, 21*(1), 149–161.

Biggler, R. (1995). The role of classification skill in moderating environmental influences on children's gender stereotyping: A study of the functional use of gender in the classroom. *Child Development, 66*, 1440–1452.

Binet, A., & Simon, T. (1916). *The development of intelligence in children.* Vineland, NJ: Publications of the Training School at Vineland (reprinted by Williams Publishing Co., Nashville, TN, 1980.).

Binnie, L., & Williams, J. (2003). Intuitive psychology and physics among children with autism and typically developing children. *Autism, 7*, 173–193.

Bird, D., & Bird, R. (2005). Martu children's hunting strategies in the Western desert, Australia. In B. Hewlett & M. Lamb (Eds.), *Hunter-gatherer childhoods.* New Brunswick, NJ: Adeline Publishers.

Bjorklund, D. F., & Pellegrini, A. D. (2002). *The origins of human nature: Evolutionary developmental psychology.* Washington, DC: American Psychological Association.

Bjurstrom, E. (1994). *Children and television advertising.* Vallingby, Sweden: Konsumentverket.

Blachman, B. A., Schatschneider, C., Fletcher, J. M., Francis, D. J., Clonan, S. M., Shaywitz, B A., & Shaywitz, S. E. (2004, September). Effects of intensive reading remediation for second and third graders and a 1-year follow-up. *Journal of Educational Psychology, 96*(3), 444–461.

Blair, C. (2006, April). How similar are fluid cognition and general intelligence? A developmental neuroscience perspective on fluid cognition as an aspect of human cognitive ability. *Behavioral and Brain Sciences, 29*(2), 109–160.

Blair, P., Sidebotham, P., Berry, P., Evans, M., & Fleming, P. (2006). Major epidemiological changes in sudden infant death syndrome: A 20-year population-based study in the UK. *Lancet, 367*, 314–319.

Blake, J., & De Boysson-Bardies, B. (1992). Patterns in babbling: A cross-linguistic study. *Journal of Child Language, 19*, 51–74.

Blakeslee, S. (2006, January 6). Cells that read minds. *New York Times.*

Blanton, H., & Burkley, M. (2008). Deviance regulation theory: Applications to adolescent social influence. In M. J. Prinstein & K. A. Dodge (Eds.), *Understanding peer influence in children and adolescents. Duke series in child development and public policy* (pp. 94–121). New York: Guilford Press.

Blinn-Pike, L. (2008, February). Sex education in rural schools in the United States: Impact of rural educators' community identities. *Sex Education, 8*(1), 77–92.

Block, J., Scribner, R., & DeSalvo, K. (2004). Fast food, race/ethnicity, and income: A geographic analysis. *American Journal of Preventive Medicine, 27*, 211–217.

Bloom, L. (1973). *One word at a time: The use of single word utterances before syntax.* The Hague: Mouton.

Boaler, J. (2001). Mathematical modelling and new theories of learning. *Teaching Mathematics and Its Applications 20*(3), 121–127.

Boas, F. (1911). *The mind of primitive man.* New York: Macmillan.

Bock, J. (2005). Farming, foraging, and children's play in the Okavango Delta, Botswana. In A. D. Pellegrini & P. K. Smith (Eds.), *The nature of play: Great apes and humans* (pp. 254–281). New York: Guilford Press.

Bogin, B. (1999). *Patterns of human growth* (2nd ed.). New York: Cambridge University Press.

Bogin, B. (2001). *The growth of humanity.* New York: Wiley-Liss.

Bogin, B., Smith, P., Orden, A. B., Varela Silva, M. I., & Loucky, J. (2002). Rapid change in height and body proportions of Maya American children. *American Journal of Human Biology, 14*(6), 753–761.

Boivin, M., Vitaro, F., & Poulin, F. (2005). Peer relationships and the development of aggressive behavior in early childhood. In R. E. Tremblay, W. W. Hartup, & J. Archer (Eds.), *Developmental origins of aggression* (pp. 376–397). New York: Guilford Press.

Boland, A., Haden, C., & Ornstein, P. (2003). Boosting children's memory by training mothers in the use of an elaborative conversational style as an event unfolds. *Journal of Cognition and Development, 4*, 39–65.

Bolger, K., & Patterson, C. (2001). Developmental pathways from child maltreatment to peer rejection. *Child Development, 72*, 549–568.

Boo, K. (2006, February 6). A reporter at large: Swamp Nurse. *The New Yorker*, p. 54.

Boone, T. L., Lefkowitz, E. S., Romo, L., Corona, R., Sigman, M., & Au, T. K. F. (2003). Mothers' and adolescents' perceptions of AIDS vulnerability. *International Journal of Behavioral Development, 27*(4), 347–354.

Borke, H. (1975). Piaget's mountains revisited: Changes in the egocentric landscape. *Developmental Psychology, 11,* 240–443.

Bornstein, M. H., Cote, L. R., Maital, S., Painter, K., Park, S.,-Y., Pascual, L., et al. (2004). Cross-linguistic analysis of vocabulary in young children: Spanish, Dutch, French, Hebrew, Italian, Korean, and American English. *Child Development, 75*(4), 1115–1139.

Bortfeld, H., Morgan, J., Golinkoff, R., & Rathburn, K. (2005). Mommy and me: Familiar names help launch babies into speech-stream segmentation. *Psychological Science, 16,* 298–304.

Bosma, H., & Kunnen, S. (2001). Determinants and mechanisms in ego identity development: A review and synthesis. *Developmental Review, 21,* 39–66.

Botta, R. A. (1999). Television images and adolescent girls' body image disturbance, *Journal of Communication, 49*(2), 22–41.

Bottoms, B. L., Goodman, G. S., Schwartz-Kenney, B. M., & Thomas, S. N. (2002). Understanding children's use of secrecy in the context of eyewitness reports. *Law & Human Behavior, 26*(3), 285–314.

Boulton, M. J. (1996). A comparison of 8- and 11-year-old girls' and boys' participation in specific types of rough and tumble play and aggressive fighting: Implications for functional hypotheses. *Aggressive Behavior, 22*(4), 271–287.

Bower, T. G. R. (1979). *Human development.* San Francisco: W. H. Freeman.

Bower, T. G. R. (1982). *Development in human infancy.* New York: W. H. Freeman.

Bowker, A. (2004). Predicting friendship stability during early adolescence. *Journal of Early Adolescence, 24,* 85–112.

Bowlby, J. (1969). *Attachment and loss: Vol. 1. Attachment.* New York: Basic Books.

Bowlby, J. (1973). *Attachment and loss: Vol. 2. Separation.* New York: Basic Books.

Bowlby, J. (1980). *Attachment and loss: Vol. 3. Loss, sadness, and depression.* New York: Basic Books.

Boyatzis, C. J., Baloff, P., & Durieux, C. (1998). Effects of perceived attractiveness and academic success on early adolescent peer popularity. *Journal of Genetic Psychology, 159*(3), 337–344.

Boyer, L. A., Lee, T. I., Cole, M. F., Johnstone, S. E., Levine, S. S., Jacob P. Zucker, J. P., et al. (2005, September 23). Core transcriptional regulatory circuitry in human embryonic stem cells *Cell, 122*(6), 947–956.

Bradley, C., McMurray, R., Harrell, J., & Deng, S. (2000). Changes in common activities of 3rd through 10th graders: The CHIC study. *Medicine and Science in Sports and Exercise, 32,* 2071–2078.

Brandon, P. (2004). The child care arrangements of preschool age children in immigrant families in the United States. *International Migration Review, 42,* 65–88.

Brazelton, T. B. (1984). *Neonatal behavioral assessment scale* (2nd ed.). London: Spastics International Medical Publications.

Bremner, J., Johnson, S., Slater, A., Mason, U., Foster, K., & Cheshire, A. (2005). Conditions for young infants' perception of object trajectories. *Child Development, 76,* 1029–1043.

Bretherton, I. (2005). In pursuit of the internal working model construct and its relevance to attachment relationships. In K. E. Grossmann, K. Grossmann, & E. Waters (Eds.), *Attachment from infancy to adulthood: The major longitudinal studies* (pp. 13–47). New York: Guilford Press.

Bretherton, I., & Munholland, K. (1999). Internal working models in attachment relationships: A construct revisited. In J. Cassidy and P. Shaver (Eds.), *Handbook of attachment: Theory, research and clinical applications.* New York: Guilford Press.

Bridges, K. (1932). Emotional development in early infancy. *Child Development, 3,* 324–334.

Brodersen, N., Steptie, A., Williamson, S., & Wardle, J. (2005). Sociodemographic, developmental, environmental, and psychological correlates of physical activity and sedentary behavior at age 11 to 12. *Annals of Behavioral Medicine, 29,* 2–11.

Brody, G. H. (1998). Sibling relationship quality: Its causes and consequences. *Annual Review of Psychology, 49,* 1–24.

Brody, G. H., & Murry, V. M. (2001). Sibling socialization of competence in rural, single-parent African American families. *Journal of Marriage and the Family 63*(4), 996–1008.

Brody, L. (2000). The socialization of gender differences in emotional expression: Display rules, infant temperament, and differentiation. In A. H. Fischer (Ed.), *Gender and emotion: Social psychological perspectives* (pp. 24–47). Cambridge, England: Cambridge University Press.

Bronfenbrenner, U. (1970). *Two worlds of childhood: U.S. and U.S.S.R.* New York: Russell Sage Foundation.

Bronson, G. W. (1991). Infant differences in rate of visual encoding. *Child Development, 62,* 44–54.

Bronson, G. W. (1994). Infants' transitions toward adult-like scanning. *Child Development, 65,* 1243–1261.

Bronson, G. W. (1997). The growth of visual capacity: Evidence from infant scanning patterns. *Advances in Infancy Research, 11,* 109–141.

Bronstein, P., Briones, M., Brooks, T., & Cowan, B. (1996). Gender and family factors as predictors of late adolescent emotional expressiveness and adjustment: A longitudinal study. *Sex Roles, 34,* 739–765.

Brooke, J. (1991, June 15). Cubato journal: Signs of life in Brazil's industrial valley of death. *New York Times,* Pt. 1, p. 2.

Brooks-Gunn, J., & Warren, M. (1989). Biological and social contributions to negative affect in young adolescent girls. *Child Development, 60,* 40–55.

Brotman, L., Gouley, K., Klein, R., Castellanos, F., & Pine, D. (2003). Children, stress and context: Integrating basic, clinical, and experimental prevention research. *Child Development, 74,* 1053–1057.

Brown, A. L. (1997). Transforming schools into communities of thinking and learning about serious matters. *American Psychologist, 52*(4), 399–413.

Brown, A. L., Campione, J. C., Reeve, R. A., Ferrara, R. A., & Palincsar, A. S. (1992). Interactive learning and individual understanding: The case of reading and mathematics. In L. T. Landsmann (Ed.), *Culture, schooling, and psychological development.* Mahwah, NJ: Lawrence Erlbaum Associates.

Brown, A. L., Palincsar, A. S., & Armbruster, B. B. (1994). Instructing comprehension-fostering activities in interactive learning situations. In R. B. Ruddell & N. J. Unrau (Eds.), *Theoretical models and processes of reading* (pp. 757–787). Newark, DE: International Reading Association.

Brown, B. B. (1999). Measuring the peer environment of American adolescents. In S. L. Friedman & T. D. Wachs (Eds.), *Measuring environment across the life span.* Washington, DC: American Psychological Association.

Brown, B. B. (2004). Adolescents' relationships with peers. In R. M. Lerner & L. Steinberg (Eds.), *Handbook of adolescent psychology* (2nd ed., pp. 363–394). Hoboken, NJ: John Wiley & Sons.

Brown, B. B., Bakken, J. P., Ameringer, S. W., & Mahon, S. D. (2008). A comprehensive conceptualization of the peer influence process in adolescence. In M. J. Prinstein & K. A. Dodge (Eds.), *Understanding peer influence in children and adolescents. Duke series in child development and public policy* (pp. 17–44). New York: Guilford Press.

Brown, B. B., & Huang, B. (1995). Examining parenting practices in different peer contexts: Implications for adolescent trajectories. In L. J. Crockett & A. C. Crouter (Eds.), *Pathways through adolescence: Individual development in relation to social contexts* (pp. 151–174). Mahwah, NJ: Lawrence Erlbaum Associates.

Brown, B. B., Mory, M. S., & Kinney, D. (1994). Casting adolescent crowds in a relational perspective: Caricature, channel, and context. In R. Montemayor, G. Adams, & T. Gullotta (Eds.), *Personal relationships in adolescence: Advances in adolescent development, Vol. 6.* Thousand Oaks, CA: Sage.

Brown, G. L, McBride, B. A., Shin, N., & Bost, K. K. (2007). Parenting predictors of father-child attachment security: Interactive effects of father involvement and fathering quality. *Fathering, 5*(3), 197–219.

Brown, P. (2002). Everyone has to lie in Tzeltal. In S. Blum-Kulka & C. E. Snow (Eds.), *Talking to adults: The contribution of multiparty discourse to language acquisition* (pp. 241–275). Mahwah, NJ: Lawrence Erlbaum Associates.

Brown, R. (1973). *A first language: The early stages.* Cambridge, MA: Harvard University Press.

Brown, R., & Bellugi, U. (1964). Three processes in the child's acquisition of syntax. *Harvard Educational Review, 34,* 133–151.

Brown, R., & Herrnstein, R. J. (1975). *Psychology.* Boston: Little, Brown.

Bruer, J. T. (2001). A critical and sensitive period primer. In D. B. J. Bailey, J. T. Bruer, F. J. Symons, & J. W. Lichtman (Eds.), *Critical thinking about critical periods.* Baltimore, MD: Paul H. Brookes.

Bruer, J. T., & Greenough, W. T. (2001). The subtle science of how experience affects the brain. In D. B. Bailey, Jr., J. T. Bruer, F. J. Symons, & J. W. Lichtman (Eds.), *Critical thinking about critical periods* (pp. 209–232). Baltimore, MD: Paul H. Brookes.

Bruner, J. S. (1982). Formats of language acquisition. *American Journal of Semiotics, 1,* 1–16.

Brunet, M., Guy, F., Pilbeam, D., Mackaye, H. T., Likius, A., et al. (2002). A new hominid from the Upper Miocene of Chad, Central Africa. *Nature, 418,* 145–151.

Bryant, P., & Nunes, T. (1998). Learning about the orthography: A cross-linguistic approach. In S. G. Paris & H. M. Wellman (Eds.), *Global prospects for education: Development, culture, and schooling* (pp. 171–191). Washington, DC: American Psychological Association.

Bullock, M. (1984). Preschool children's understandings of causal connections. *British Journal of Developmental Psychology, 2,* 139–142.

Bullock, M., & Gelman, R. (1979). Preschool children's assumptions about cause and effect: Temporal ordering. *Child Development, 50,* 89–96.

Burtless, G. (2004). *The labor force status of mothers who are most likely to receive welfare.* Brookings Institute. Retrieved April 25, 2006, from http://www.brookings.edu/~/media/Files/rc/opinions/2004/0330children families_burtless/20040330.pdf

Bushnell, I. W. R. (2001). Mother's face recognition in newborn infants: Learning and memory. *Infant and Child Development, 10*(1–2), 67–74.

Buttelmann, D., Call, J., & Tomasello, M. (2008). Behavioral cues that great apes use to forage for hidden food. *Animal Cognition, 11*(1), 117–128.

Butterworth, G. (2001). Joint visual attention in infancy. In G. Bremner & A. Fogel (Eds.), *Blackwell handbook of infant development. Handbooks of developmental psychology* (pp. 213–240). Malden, MA: Blackwell Publishers.

Butterworth, G., & Morissette, P. (1996). Onset of pointing and the acquisition of language in infancy. *Journal of Reproductive & Infant Psychology, 14*(2), 219–231.

Cairns, E., & Dawes, A. (1996). Children: Ethnic and political violence—A commentary. *Child Development, 67,* 129–139.

Cairns, R. B. (1979). *Social development: The origins of interchanges.* New York: W. H. Freeman.

Cairns, R. B. (1998). The making of developmental psychology. In W. Damon & R. M. Lerner (Eds.), *Handbook of child psychology: Vol. 1. Theoretical models of human development* (5th ed.). New York: Wiley.

Calabrese, L. H., Kirkendall, D. T., Floyd, M., Rapoport, S., Williams, G. W., Weiker, G. F., & Bergfeld, J. A. (1983). Menstrual abnormalities, nutritional patterns and body composition in female classical ballet dancers. *Physician and Sports Medicine, 11,* 86–98.

Caldwell, M. B., Brotman, L. M., Coard, S. I., Wallace, S. A., Stellabotte, D. J., & Calzada, E. J. (2005, September). Community involvement in adapting and testing a prevention program for preschoolers living in urban communities: ParentCorps. *Journal of Child and Family Studies, 14*(3), 373–386.

Calkins, S., & Degnan, K. (2005). Temperament in early development. In R. T. Ammerman (Ed.), *Comprehensive handbook of personality and psychopathology: Vol. 3. Child psychopathology.* Hoboken, NJ: John Wiley & Sons.

Cameron, N. (Ed.). (2002). *Human growth and development.* New York: Academic Press.

Campbell, D. (1997). *The Mozart effect: Tapping the power of music to heal the body, strengthen the mind, and unlock the creative spirit.* New York: Avon.

Campbell, F., Pungello, E., Miller-Johnson, S., Burchinal, M., & Ramey, C. (2001). The development of cognitive and academic abilities: Growth curves from an early childhood educational experiment. *Developmental Psychology, 37,* 231–242.

Campbell, S., Spieker, S., Burchinal, M., & Poe, M. (2006). Trajectories of aggression from toddlerhood to age 9 predict academic and social functioning through age 12. *Journal of Child Psychology and Psychiatry, 47*(8), 791–800.

Campos, J. J., Anderson, D. I., Barbu-Roth, M. A., Hubbard, E. M., Hertenstein, M. J., & Witherington, D. (2000). Travel broadens the mind. *Infancy, 1*(2), 149–219.

Camras, L., A., Oster, H., Bakeman, R., Meng, Z., Ujiee, T., & Campos, J. J. (2007). Do infants show distinct negative facial expressions for fear and anger?: Emotional expression in 11-month-old European-American, Chinese, and Japanese infants. *Infancy, 11*(2), 131–155.

Caplan, N., Choy, M. H., & Whitmore, J. K. (1991). *Children of the boat people: A study of educational success.* Ann Arbor: University of Michigan Press.

Capps, R., Fix, M., Murray, J., Ost, J., Herwantoro, S., Zimmerman, W., et al. (2004). *Promise or peril: Immigrants, LEP students, and the No Child Left Behind Act.* Washington, DC: Urban Institute.

Carey, S. (1978). The child as word learner. In M. Halle, J. Bresnan, & G. A. Miller (Eds.), *Linguistic theory and psychological reality.* Cambridge, MA: The MIT Press.

Carlson, S., Davis, A., & Leach, J. (2005). Less is more: Executive function and symbolic representation in preschool children. *Psychological Science, 16,* 609–616.

Carlson, V. J., & Harwood, R. L. (2003). Attachment, culture, and the caregiving system: The cultural patterning of everyday experiences among Anglo and Puerto Rican mother-infant pairs. *Infant Mental Health Journal, 24*(1), 53–73.

Carpendale, J. (2000). Kohlberg and Piaget on stages and moral reasoning. *Developmental Review, 20,* 181–205.

Carpendale, J., & Lewis, C. (2004). Constructing an understanding of mind: The development of children's social understanding within social interaction. *Behavioral and Brain Sciences, 27,* 79–151.

Carpenter, M., Call, J., & Tomasello, M. (2002). A new false belief test for 36-month-olds. *British Journal of Developmental Psychology, 20*(3), 393–420.

Carpenter, M., Nagell, K., & Tomasello, M. (1998). Social cognition, joint attention, and communicative competence from 9 to 15 months of age. *Monographs of the Society for Research in Child Development, 63*(4), 176.

Carskadon, M., Acebo, C., & Jenni, O. (2004). Regulation of adolescent sleep: Implications for behavior. *Annals of the New York Academy of Sciences, 1021,* 276–291.

Case, R. (1998). The development of conceptual structures. In D. Kuhn & R. S. Siegler (Eds.), *Handbook of child psychology: Vol. 2. Cognition, perception and language* (5th ed., pp. 745–800). New York: Wiley.

Case, R., Kurland, D. M., & Goldberg, J. (1982). Operational efficiency and growth of short-term memory span. *Journal of Experimental Child Psychology, 33*, 386–404.

Casper, R. C. (1996). Carbohydrate metabolism and its regulatory hormones in anorexia nervosa. *Psychiatry Research, 62*(1), 85–96.

Caspi, A. (1998). Personality development across the life course. In W. Damon & N. Eisenberg (Eds.), *Handbook of child psychology: Vol. 3. Social, emotional, and personality development* (5th ed., pp. 311–388). New York: Wiley.

Caspi, A., Roberts, B. W., & Shiner, R. L. (2005). Personality development: Stability and change. *Annual Review of Psychology, 56*, 453–484.

Cass, V. C. (1984, May). Homosexual identity formation: Testing a theoretical model. *Journal of Sex Research, 20*(2), 143–167.

Cassidy, J., & Shaver, P. R. (Eds.). (1999). *Handbook of attachment.* New York: Guilford Press.

Cassidy, T. (2005, December 4). Special care of early babies; New studies of neotatal brain development are changing the way hospitals manage premature births. *The Boston Globe,* p. 34.

Caughy, M., Campo, P., Randolph, S., & Nickerson, K. (2002). The influence of racial socialization practices on the cognitive and behavioral competence of African American preschoolers. *Child Development, 73,* 1611–1625.

Cazden, C. B. (1965). *Environmental assistance to the child's acquisition of grammar.* Unpublished doctoral dissertation, Harvard University.

Centers for Disease Control and Prevention. (2000). Trends in the attendant, place, and timing of births and in the use of obstetric interventions in the United States, 1989–1997. *Mortality and Morbidity Weekly Report, 49.*

Centers for Disease Control and Prevention. (2004). *National vital statistics report* (Vol. 52, No. 3, 9/18/2003). Washington, DC: Department of Health and Human Services.

Centers for Disease Control and Prevention. (2006a, September 29). *Births: Final data for 2004.* National Vital Statistics Report, 55.

Centers for Disease Control and Prevention. (2006b). *Births, marriages, divorces, and deaths: Provisional data for 2005.* National Vital Statistics Report, 54(20). Retrieved April 4, 2007, from http://www.cdc.gov/nchs/data/nvsr/nvsr54/nvsr54_20.pdf

Centers for Disease Control and Prevention. (2007). *Autism spectrum disorders overview.* Retrieved October 10, 2008, from http://www.cdc.gov/ncbddd/autism/overview.htm

Centers for Disease Control and Prevention. (2008). *National Center for HIV/AIDS, viral hepatitis, STD, and TB prevention. 2006 disease profile.* Retrieved September 10, 2008, from http://www.cdc.gov/nchhstp/Publications/docs/2006_Disease_Profile_508_FINAL.pdf

Chaffin, M., Hanson, R., Saunders, B., Nichols, T., Barnett, D., Zeanah, C., Berliner, L., Egeland, B., Newman, E., et al. (2006). Report of the APSAC task force on attachment therapy, reactive attachment disorder, and attachment problems. *Child Maltreatment, 11,* 76–89.

Chan, A., Keane, R. J., & Robinson, J. S. (2001). The contribution of maternal smoking to preterm birth, small for gestational age and low birthweight among Aboriginal and non-Aboriginal births in South Australia. *Medical Journal of Australia, 174*(8), 389–393.

Chandler, M. J., Lalonde, C. E., Sokol, B. W., & Hallett, D. (2003, June). Personal persistence, identity development, and suicide: A study of Native and non-Native North American adolescents. *Monographs of the Society for Research in Child Development, 68*(2), vii–130.

Chang, F., Dell, G., & Bock, K. (2006). Becoming syntactic. *Psychological Review, 113,* 234–272.

Chang, J. (2005). Can't stop won't stop: A history of the hip-hop generation. New York: St Martins Press.

Chang, J. C., Ye, L., & Kan, Y. W. (2006). Correction of the sickle cell mutation in embryonic stem cells. *Proceedings of the National Academy of Sciences, 103*(4), 1036–1040.

Chao, R. K. (1996). Chinese and European American mothers' beliefs about the role of parenting in children's school success. *Journal of Cross-Cultural Psychology, 27*(4), 403–423.

Chao, R. K. (2001). Extending research on the consequences of parenting style for Chinese Americans and European Americans. *Child Development, 72*(6), 1832–1843.

Charnov, E. (2004). The optimal balance between growth rate and survival in mammals. *Evolution and Ecological Research, 6,* 307–313.

Charpak, N., Ruiz-Pelaez, J. G., Figueroa de Calume, Z., & Charpak, Y. (2001). A randomized, controlled trial of kangaroo mother care: Results of follow-up at 1 year of corrected age. *Pediatrics, 108*(5), 1072–1079.

Chavajay, P., & Rogoff, B. (2002). Schooling and traditional collaborative social organization of problem solving by Mayan mothers and children. *Developmental Psychology, 38*(1), 55–66.

Chen, C., & Stevenson, H. W. (1988). Cross-linguistic differences in digit span of preschool children. *Journal of Experimental Child Psychology, 46,* 150–158.

Chen, X., & Rubin, K. H. (1994). Family conditions, parental acceptance, and social competence and aggression in Chinese children. *Social Development, 3*(3), 269–290.

Chen, Z., & Siegler, R. S. (2000). Intellectual development in childhood. In R. J. Sternberg (Ed.), *Handbook of intelligence* (pp. 92–116). New York: Cambridge University Press.

Chess, S., & Thomas, A. (1982). Infant bonding: Mystique and reality. *American Journal of Orthopsychiatry, 52,* 213–221.

Chess, S., & Thomas, A. (1996). *Temperament: Theory and practice.* New York: Brunner-Mazel.

Chesson, H. W., Gift, T. L., & Pulver, A. L. S. (2006, November). The economic value of reductions in gonorrhea and syphilis incidence in the United States, 1990–2003. *Preventive Medicine: An International Journal Devoted to Practice and Theory, 43*(5), 411–415.

Chi, M. T. H. (1978). Knowledge structures and memory development. In R. S. Siegler (Ed.), *Children's thinking: What develops?* Mahwah, NJ: Lawrence Erlbaum Associates.

Chicz-DeMet, A., Barbaro, T. G., Doan, P. H., Glynn, L. M., Garite, T., Wadhwa, P. D., et al. (2001). Maternal stress hormone changes during pregnancy associated with preterm births. *Society for Neuroscience Abstracts, 27*(2), 1942.

Children Now. (1998). *A different world: Children's perceptions of race and class in the media.* Oakland, CA: Children Now.

Children Now. (2003). *Fall colors: Prime-time diversity report, 2003–2004.* Retrieved October 10, 2007, from http://publications.childrennow.org/assets/pdf/cmp/fall-colors-03/fall-colors-03-v5.pdf

Chirkov, V., & Ryan, R. (2001). Parent and teacher autonomy–support in Russian and U.S. adolescents. *Journal of Cross-Cultural Psychology, 32,* 618–635.

Chisholm, K. (1998). A three-year follow-up of attachment and indiscriminate friendliness in children adopted from Romanian orphanages. *Child Development, 69*(4), 1092–1106.

Chomsky, N. (1959). Review of verbal behavior by B. F. Skinner. *Language, 35,* 26–58.

Chomsky, N. (1980). Initial states and steady states. In M. Piatelli-Palmerini (Ed.), *Language and learning: The debate between Jean Piaget and Noam Chomsky.* Cambridge, MA: Harvard University Press.

Chomsky, N. (1988). *Language and problems of knowledge.* Cambridge, MA: The MIT Press.

Chomsky, N. (2006). *Language and mind* (3rd ed.). New York: Cambridge University Press.

Chouinard, M. M., & Clark, E. V. (2003). Adult reformulations of child errors as negative evidence. *Journal of Child Language, 30,* 637–669.

Christian Aid. (2001). *No excuses: Facing up to sub-Saharan Africa's AIDS orphans crisis.* London: Christian Aid.

Christian, K., Bachman, H. J., & Morrison, F. J. (2001). Schooling and cognitive development. In R. J. Sternberg & E. L. Grigorenko (Eds.), *Environmental effects on cognitive abilities* (pp. 287–336). Mahwah, NJ: Lawrence Erlbaum Associates.

Christian, P. (2002). Maternal nutrition, health, and survival. *Nutritional Review, 60,* S59–S63.

Chugani, H., Behen, M., Muzik, O., Juhász, C., Nagy, F., & Chugani, D. (2001). Local brain functional activity following early deprivations: A study of postinstitutionalized Romanian orphans. *NeuroImage, 14,* 1290–1301.

Cicchetti, D., & Toth, S. L. (1993). Child maltreatment research and social policy: The neglected nexus. In D. Cicchetti & S. L. Toth (Eds.), *Advances in applied developmental psychology series: Vol. 8. Child abuse, child development, and social policy.* Norwood, NJ: Ablex.

Cicchetti, D., & Toth, S. L. (1998). The development of depression in children and adolescents. *American Psychologist, 53*(2), 221–241.

Cicchetti, D., Toth, S. L., & Maughm, A. (2000). An ecological-transactional model of child maltreatment. In A. Sameroff, M. Lewis, & J. Miller (Eds.), *Handbook of developmental psychology* (2nd ed.). New York: Plenum.

Cillessen, A. H. N., Van IJzendoorn, H. W., Van Lieshorst, C. F. M., & Hartup, W. W. (1992). Heterogeneity among peer-rejected boys: Subtypes and stabilities. *Child Development, 63,* 893–905.

Cillessen, A., & Mayeux, L. (2004). From censure to reinforcement: Developmental changes in the association between aggression and social status. *Child Development, 75*(1), 147–163.

Clark, C. (2003). *In sickness and in play: Children coping with chronic illness.* New Brunswick, NJ: Rutgers University Press.

Clark, E. (2004). How language acquisition builds on cognitive development. *Trends in Cognitive Sciences, 8,* 472–478.

Clark, E. V. (1995). Later lexical development and word formation. In P. Fletcher & B. MacWhinney (Eds.), *The handbook of child language* (pp. 393–412). Oxford, England: Blackwell Publishing.

Clark, E. V. (2006). Color, reference, and expertise in language acquisition. *Journal of Experimental Child Psychology, 94,* 339–343.

Clark, E. V., & Wong, A. D.-W. (2002). Pragmatic directions about language use: Words and word meanings. *Language in Society, 31,* 181–212.

Clark, H. H. (2003). Pointing and placing. In S. Kita (Ed.), *Pointing: Where language, culture, and cognition meet* (pp. 243–268). Mahwah, NJ: Lawrence Erlbaum Associates.

Clark, K. B., & Clark, M. P. (1939). The development of consciousness of self and the emergence of racial identity in Negro pre-school school-children. *Journal of Social Psychology, 10,* 591–599.

Clark, K. B., & Clark, M. P. (1950). Emotional factors in racial identification and preference in Negro children. *Journal of Negro Education, 19,* 341–350.

Clarke, A. M., & Clarke, A. D. B. (2000). *Early experience and the life path.* London: Jessica Kingsley.

Clarke-Stewart, A., & Allhusen, V. D. (2005). *What we know about childcare.* Cambridge, MA: Harvard University Press.

Clarke-Stewart, A., & Koch, J. B. (1983). *Children: Development through adolescence.* New York: Wiley.

Clausson, B., Granath, F., Ekbom A., Lundgren, S., Nordmark, A., Signorello, L. B., et al. (2002). Effect of caffeine exposure during pregnancy on birth weight and gestational age. *American Journal of Epidemiology, 155*(5), 429–436.

Clearfield, M. W., Diedrich, F. J., Smith, L. B., & Thelen, E. (2006). Young infants reach correctly in A-not-B tasks: On the development of stability and perseveration. *Infant Behavior & Development, 29*(3), 435–444.

Cobb, P., Gravemeijer, K., Yackel, E., McClain, K., & Whitenack, J. (1997). Mathematizing and symbolizing: The emergence of chains of signification in one first-grade classroom. In D. Kirshner & J. A. Whitson (Eds.), *Situated cognition: Social, semiotic, and psychological perspectives* (pp. 151–234). Mahwah, NJ: Lawrence Erlbaum Associates.

Coghlan, D., & Jacobs, C. (2005, December). Kurt Lewin on reeducation: Foundations for action research. *Journal of Applied Behavioral Science, 41*(4), 2005, 444–457.

Cohen, L. B. (2002). Extraordinary claims require extraordinary controls: Reply. *Developmental Science, 5*(2), 210–212.

Cohen, L. B., & Cashon, C. H. (2006). Infant cognition. In D. Kuhn, R. S. Siegler, W. Damon, & R. M. Lerner (Eds.), *Handbook of child psychology: Vol. 2. Cognition, perception, and language* (6th ed., pp. 214–251). Hoboken, NJ: John Wiley & Sons.

Cohen, L. B., Chaput, H. H., & Cashon, C. H. (2002). A constructivist model of infant cognition. *Cognitive Development, 17,* 1323–1343.

Cohen, L. B., & Marks, K. S. (2002). How infants process addition and subtraction events. *Developmental Science, 5*(2), 186–201.

Coie, J. D., & Dodge, K. A. (1998). Aggression and antisocial behavior. In N. Eisenberg (Ed.), *Handbook of child psychology: Vol. 3. Social, emotional, and personality development* (5th ed., pp. 779–882). New York: Wiley.

Colby, A., & Kohlberg, L. (1987). *The measurement of moral judgment.* New York: Cambridge University Press.

Colby, A., Kohlberg, L., Gibbs, J., & Lieberman, M. (1983). A longitudinal study of moral development. *Monographs of the Society for Research in Child Development, 48* (1–2, Serial No. 200).

Cole, M. (1996). *Cultural psychology: A once and future discipline.* Cambridge, MA: The Belknap Press of Harvard University Press.

Cole, M. (2005). Cross-cultural and historical perspectives on the developmental consequences of education. *Human Development, 48*(4), 195–216.

Cole, M. (2006). Culture and cognitive development in phylogenetic, historical and ontogenetic perspective. In W. Damon & R. M. Lerner (Eds.), *Handbook of child psychology: Vol. 2* (pp. 636–683). Hoboken, NJ: Wiley.

Cole, M., & The Distributed Literacy Consortium. (2006). *The fifth dimension: An after-school program built on diversity.* New York: Russell Sage.

Coley, R. L., & Chase-Lansdale, P. L. (1998). Adolescent pregnancy and parenthood. *American Psychologist, 53*(2), 152–166.

Collins, W. A. (2003). More than myth: The developmental significance of romantic relationships during adolescence. *Journal of Research on Adolescence, 13,* 1–24.

Collins, W. A. (2005, December). Commentary: Parsing parenting: Refining models of parental influence during adolescence. *Monographs of the Society for Research in Child Development, 70*(4), 138–145.

Collins, W. A., & Laursen, B. (2006). Parent-adolescent relationships. In P. Noller & J. A. Feeney (Eds.), *Close relationships: Functions, forms and processes* (pp. 111–125). Hove, England: Psychology Press/Taylor & Francis (UK).

Collins, W. A., Laursen, B., Mortensen, N., Luebker, C., & Ferreira, M. (1997). Conflict processes and transitions in parent and peer relationships: Implications for autonomy and regulation. *Journal of Adolescent Research, 12*(2), 178–198.

Collins, W. A., & van Dulmen, M. (2006). The significance of middle childhood peer competence for work and relationships in early adulthood. In A. C. Huston & M. N. Ripke (Eds.), *Developmental contexts in middle childhood: Bridges to adolescence and adulthood. Cambridge studies in social and emotional development* (pp. 23–40). New York: Cambridge University Press.

Colon, A., & Colon, P. (2001). *A history of children.* Westport, CT: Greenwood Press.

Colwell, J., Grady, C., & Rhaiti, S. (1995). Computer games, self-esteem, and gratification of needs in adolescents. *Journal of Community and Applied Social Psychology, 5,* 195–206.

Compas, B. E. (2004). Processes of risk and resilience during adolescence: Linking contexts and individuals. In R. M. Lerner & L. Steinberg (Eds.), *Handbook of adolescent psychology* (2nd ed., pp. 263−296). Hoboken, NJ: John Wiley & Sons.

Comstock, G., & Scharrer, E. (2007). *Media and the American child.* New York: Elsevier.

Conchas, G. Q. (2001). Structuring failure and success: Understanding the variability in Latino school engagement. *Harvard Educational Review. Special Issue: Immigration and education, 71*(3), 475−504.

Condry, K. F., Smith, W. C., & Spelke, E. S. (2000). Development of perceptual organization. In F. Lacerda, C. von Hofsten, & M. Heiman (Eds.), *Emerging cognitive abilities in early infancy.* Mahwah, NJ: Lawrence Erlbaum Associates.

Conel, J. L. (1939/1967). *The postnatal development of the human cerebral cortex* (8 vols.). Cambridge, MA: Harvard University Press.

Connolly, J., Craig, W., Goldberg, A., & Pepler, D. (2004). Mixed-gender groups, dating, and romantic relationships in early adolescence. *Journal of Research on Adolescence, 14*, 185−207.

Connolly, J., Furman, W., & Konarski, R. (2000). The role of peers in the emergence of heterosexual romantic relationships in adolescence. *Child Development, 71*, 1395−1408.

Connolly, K., & Dalgleish, M. (1989). The emergence of a tool using skill in infancy. *Developmental Psychology, 25*, 539−549.

Connor, J. M., & Ferguson-Smith, M. A. (1993). *Essential medical genetics* (3rd ed.). Oxford, England: Blackwell Publishing.

Cooper, M., Wood, P., Orcutt, H., & Albino, A. (2003). Personality and the predisposition to engage in risky or problem behaviors during adolescence. *Journal of Personality and Social Psychology, 84*, 390−410.

Coopersmith, S. (1967). *The antecedents of self-esteem.* New York: W. H. Freeman.

Corbin, P. F., & Bickford, R. G. (1955). Studies of the electroencephalogram of normal children. *Electroencephalography and Clinical Neurology, 7*, 15−28.

Cormier, K., Mauk, C., & Repp, A. (1998). Manual babbling in deaf and hearing infants: A longitudinal study. In E. V. Clark (Ed.), *The Proceedings of the Twenty-Ninth Annual Child Language Research Forum* (pp. 55−61). Chicago: Center for the Study of Language and Information.

Cortés, C. (2000). *The children are watching: How the media teach about diversity.* New York: Teachers College Press.

Costello, D. (2000, June 9). Spanking makes a comeback. *Wall Street Journal.*

Costello, D. M., Swendsen, J., Rose, J. S., & Dierker, L. C. (2008, April). Risk and protective factors associated with trajectories of depressed mood from adolescence to early adulthood. *Journal of Consulting and Clinical Psychology, 76*(2), 173−183.

Costello, E. J., Compton, S. N., Keeler, G., & Angold, A. (2003, October). Relationships between poverty and psychopathology: A natural experiment. *Journal of the American Medical Association, 290*(15), 2023−2029.

Côté, S., Vaillancourt, T., LeBlanc, J., Nagin, D., & Tremblay, R. (2006). The development of physical aggression from toddlerhood to pre-adolescence: A nation wide longitudinal study of Canadian children. *Journal of Abnormal Child Psychology, 34*(1), 68−82.

Cotterill, R. W., & Franklin, A. W. (1995). *The urban grocery store gap* (Food Marketing Policy Issue Paper No. 8). Storrs, CT: Food Marketing Policy Center, University of Connecticut.

Cotton, A. (2006). Camfed founder receives Women of the Year award. Retrieved October 10, 2008, from http://uk.camfed.org/news/2006/03/08/marking-international-womens-day/#more-71

Courage, M. L., Reynolds, G. D., & Richards, J. E. (2006) Infants' attention to patterned stimuli: Developmental change from 3 to 12 months of age. *Child Development 77*(3), 680−695.

Cowan, P. A. (1978). *Piaget: With feeling: Cognitive, social, and emotional dimensions.* New York: Holt, Rinehart and Winston.

Cowan, W. M. (1979). The development of the brain. *Scientific American, 241*, 112−133.

Craig, W. M. (1998). The relationship among bullying, victimization, depression, anxiety, and aggression in elementary school children. *Personality & Individual Differences, 24*(1), 123−130.

Crewe, S. (2003). African-American grandparent caregivers: Eliminating double jeopardy in social policy. In T. Bent-Goodley (Ed.), *African-American social workers and social policy.* Binghamton, NY: Harworth Social Work Practice Press.

Crick, N. R., & Dodge, K. A. (1999). "Superiority" is in the eye of the beholder: A comment on Sutton-Smith and Swettenham. *Social Development, 8*(1), 128−131.

Crick, N. R., & Ladd, G. W. (1993). Children's perceptions of their peer experiences: Attributions, loneliness, social anxiety and social avoidance. *Developmental Psychology, 29*, 244−254.

Crick, N. R., Ostrov, J. M., & Kawabata, Y. (2007). Relational aggression and gender: An overview. In D. J. Flannery, A. T. Vazsonyi, & I. D. Waldman (Eds.), *The Cambridge handbook of violent behavior and aggression* (pp. 245−259). New York: Cambridge University Press.

Crosnoe, R. (2006, March). Health and the education of children from racial/ethnic minority and immigrant families. *Journal of Health and Social Behavior, 47*(1), 77−93.

Cross, W. E. (2003). Tracing the historical origins of youth delinquency and violence: Myths and realities about black culture. *Journal of Social Issues, 59*(1), 67−82.

Cross, W. E., & Cross, T. B. (2008). Theory, research, and models. In S. M. Quintana & C. McKown (Eds.), *Handbook of race, racism, and the developing child* (pp. 154−181). Hoboken, NJ: John Wiley & Sons.

Crowther, B. (1999). Writing as performance: Young girls' diaries. In R. Josselson & A. Lieblich (Eds.), *Making meaning in the narrative study of lives.* Thousand Oaks, CA: Sage Publications.

Csaba, A. (2003). Ethical dimensions of genetic counseling. *Clinics in Perinatology, 30*, 81−93.

Csikszentmihalyi, M., & Larson, R. (1984). *Being adolescent: Conflict and growth in the teenage years.* New York: Basic Books.

Csikszentmihalyi, M., & Larson, R. (1987). The experience sampling method. *Journal of Nervous and Mental Disease, 175*, 526−536.

Cunningham, F. G., MacDonald, P. C., Gant, N. F., Leveno, K. J., Gilstrap, L. C., III, Hankins, G. D. V., & Clark, S. L. (2001). *Williams obstetrics* (21st ed.). Stamford, CT: Appleton & Lange.

Curtis, H. (1979). *Biology.* New York: Worth.

D'Angiulli, A., & Siegel, L. S. (2003). Cognitive functioning as measured by the WISC-R: Do children with learning disabilities have distinctive patterns of performance? *Journal of Learning Disabilities, 36*(1), 48−58.

Dahl, R. E., & Hariri, A. R. (2005, November). Lessons from G. Stanley Hall: Connecting new research in biological sciences to the study of adolescent development. *Journal of Research on Adolescence, 15*(4), 367−382.

Dahl, R., & Lewin, D. (2002). Pathways to adolescent health: Sleep regulation and behavior. *Journal of Adolescent Health, 31*, 175−184.

Daiute, C. (2004). Creative uses of cultural genres. In C. Daiute & C. Lightfoot (Eds.), *Narrative analysis: Studying the development of individuals in society.* Thousand Oaks, CA: Sage.

Dalton, S., & Bielby, D. (2000). "That's our kind of constellation": Lesbian mothers negotiate institutionalized understandings of gender within the family. *Gender & Society, 14*, 36−61.

Damerow, P. (1998). Prehistory and cognitive development. In J. Langer & M. Killen (Eds.), *Piaget, evolution, and development* (pp. 247−270). Mahwah, NJ: Lawrence Erlbaum Associates.

Damon, W., & Hart, D. (1988). *Self-understanding in childhood and adolescence.* Cambridge, England: Cambridge University Press.

Darwin, C. (1859/1958). *The origin of species.* New York: Penguin.

Darwin, C. (1872). *The expression of emotion in man and animals.* London: John Murray.

Dasen, P. R. (1972). Cross-cultural Piagetian research: A summary. *Journal of Cross-Cultural Psychology, 3,* 29–39.

Dasen, P. R. (1973). Preliminary study of sensori-motor development in Baoule children. *Early Child Development & Care, 2*(3), 345–354.

Dasen, P. R. (1975, June). Concrete operational development in three cultures. *Journal of Cross-Cultural Psychology, 6*(2), 156–172.

David, H. P. (1981). Unwantedness: Longitudinal studies of Prague children born to women twice denied abortions for the same pregnancy and matched controls. In P. Ahmed (Ed.), *Pregnancy, childbirth, and parenthood.* New York: Elsevier.

Davidov, M., & Grusec, J. E. (2006). Untangling the links of parental responsiveness to distress and warmth to child outcomes. *Child Development, 77,* 44–58.

Davies, H. D., & Fitzgerald, H. E. (Eds.). (2008). *Obesity in childhood and adolescence: Vol. 1. Medical, biological, and social issues. Praeger perspectives: Child psychology and mental health.* Westport, CT: Praeger Publishers/ Greenwood Publishing Group.

Davis, B.L., MacNeilage, P.F., Matyear, C.L., & Powell, J.K. (2000). Prosodic correlates of stress in babbling: An acoustical study. *Child Development, 71*(5), 1258-1275

Day, R., Peterson, G., & McCracken, C. (1998). Predicting spanking of younger and older children by mothers and fathers. *Journal of Marriage and the Family, 60,* 79–94.

de Lemos, C. (2000). Questioning the notion of development: The case of language acquisition. *Culture & Psychology, 6*(2), 169–182.

De Villiers, J. G., & de Villiers, P. A. (1978). *Language acquisition.* Cambridge, MA: Harvard University Press.

De Vries, J. I., Hay V. G., & Prechtl, H. F. (1982). The emergence of fetal behaviour. I. Qualitative aspects. *Early Human Development, 7*(4), 301–322.

de Vries, M. W, & de Vries, M. R. (1977). Cultural relativity of toilet training readiness: A perspective from East Africa. *Pediatrics 60,* 170.

De Vries, R. (1969). Constancy of genetic identity in the years three to six. *Monographs of the Society for Research in Child Development, 34* (Serial No. 127).

de Vrijer, B., Harthoorn-Lasthuizen, E. J., & Oosterbaan, H. P. (1999). The incidence of irregular antibodies in pregnancy: a prospective study in the region of the 's-Hertogenbosch. *Nederlands Tijdschrift voor Geneeskunde, 143*(5), 2523–2527.

De Wolff, M., & van IJzendoorn, M. H. (1997). Sensitivity and attachment: A meta-analysis on parental antecedents of infant attachment. *Child Development, 68*(4), 571–591.

Deák, G. O. (2006). Do children really confuse appearance and reality? *Trends in Cognitive Sciences, 10*(12), 546–550.

DeCasper, A. J., & Spence M. J. (1986). Prenatal maternal speech influences newborn's perceptions of speech sounds. *Infant Behavior and Development, 3,* 133–150.

Delaney, C. (2000). Making babies in a Turkish village. In J. S. DeLoache & A. Gottlieb (Eds.), *A world of babies: Imagined childcare guides for seven societies.* Cambridge, England: Cambridge University Press.

della Cava, M. R. (2002, June 25). The race to raise a brainier baby. *USA Today.*

DeLoache, J., Uttal, D., & Rosengren, K. (2005). Scale errors offer evidence for a perception-action dissociation early in life. *Science, 304,* 1027–1029.

Demetriou, A., Kui, Z. X., Spanoudis, G., Christou, C., Kyriakides, L., & Platsidou, M. (2005, March–April). The architecture, dynamics, and development of mental processing: Greek, Chinese, or Universal? *Intelligence, 33*(2), 109–141.

Denham, S., Caverly, S., Schmidt, M., Blair, K., DeMulder, E., Caal, S., Hamada, H., & Mason, T. (2002). Preschool understanding of emotions: Contributions to classroom anger and aggression. *Journal of Child Psychology and Psychiatry, 43,* 901–916.

Denizet-Lewis, B. (2004, May 30). Friends, friends with benefits and the benefits of the local mall. *New York Times Magazine.*

Dennis, W., & Dennis, M. (1940). The effect of cradling practices upon the onset of walking in Hopi children. *Journal of Genetic Psychology, 56,* 77–86.

Dent-Read, C. (1997). A naturalistic study of metaphor development: Seeing and seeing as. In C. Dent-Read & P. Zukow-Goldring (Eds.), *Evolving explanations of development* (pp. 255–296). Washington, DC: American Psychological Association.

deRegnier, R.-A., Long, J. D., Georgieff, M. K., & Nelson, C. A. (2007). Using event-related potentials to study perinatal nutrition and brain development in infants of diabetic mothers. *Developmental Neuropsychology, 31*(3), 379–396.

Devescovi, A., Caselli, M. C., Marchione, D., Pasqualetti, P., Reilly, J., & Bates, E. (2005). A cross-linguistic study of the relationship between grammar and lexical development. *Journal of Child Language, 32*(4), 759–786.

Diamond, A. (1991). Neuropsychological insights into the meaning of object concept development. In R. Gelman (Ed.), *The epigenesis of mind: Essays on biology and cognition* (pp. 67–110). Mahwah, NJ: Lawrence Erlbaum Associates.

Diamond, A. (2000). Close interrelation of motor development and cognitive development and of the cerebellum and prefrontal cortex. *Child Development, 71*(1), 44–56.

Diamond, A. (2002a). A model system for studying the role of dopamine in prefrontal cortex during early development in humans. In M. H. Johnson & Y. Munakata (Eds.), *Brain development and cognition: A reader* (pp. 441–493). Malden, MA: Blackwell Publishing.

Diamond, A. (2002b). Normal development of prefrontal cortex from birth to young adulthood: Cognitive functions, anatomy, and biochemistry. In D. Stuss & R. Knight (Eds.), *Principles of frontal lobe functioning* (466–503). New York: Oxford University Press.

Dickens, W. T., & Flynn, J. R. (2006, October). Black Americans reduce the racial IQ gap: Evidence from standardization samples. *Psychological Science, 17*(10), 913–920.

Diener, M. L., Nievar, M. A., & Wright, C. (2003). Attachment security among mothers and their young children living in poverty: Associations with maternal, child, and contextual factors. *Merrill-Palmer Quarterly, 49*(2), 154–182.

Dietz, T. (2000). Disciplining children: Characteristics associated with the use of corporal punishment. *Child Abuse and Neglect, 24,* 1529–1542.

Dimant, R. J., & Bearison, D. J. (1991). Development of formal reasoning during successive peer interactions. *Developmental Psychology, 27*(2), 277–284.

Dishion, T. J. (1990). The family ecology of boys' peer relations in middle childhood. *Child Development, 61,* 874–892.

Dishion, T. J., McCord, J., & Poulin, F. (1999). When interventions harm. *American Psychologist, 54*(9), 755–764.

Dishion, T. J., & Patterson, G. R. (2006). The development and ecology of antisocial behavior in children and adolescents. In D. Cicchetti & D. J. Cohen (Eds.), *Developmental psychopathology: Vol. 3. Risk, disorder, and adaptation* (2nd ed., pp. 503–541). Hoboken, NJ: John Wiley & Sons.

Dissanayake, E. (2000). Antecedents of the temporal arts in early mother-infant interaction. In N. Wallin, B. Merker, & S. Brown (Eds.), *The origins of music* (pp. 389–410). Cambridge, MA: The MIT Press.

Dixon, A. C., Schoonmaker, C. T., & Philliber, W. W (2000). A journey toward womanhood: Effects of an Afrocentric approach to pregnancy prevention among African-American adolescent girls. *Adolescence, 35,* 425–429.

Do, J. T., Han, D. W., & Schöler, H. R. (2006). Reprogramming somatic gene activity by fusion with pluripotent cells. *Stem Cell Reviews, 2*(4), 257–264.

Dodge, K. A. (1990). Developmental psychopathology in children of depressed mothers. *Developmental Psychology, 26,* 3–6.

Dodge, K. A., Coie, J., & Lynam, D. (2006) Aggression and antisocial behavior in youth. In N. Eisenberg, W. Damon, & R. M. Lerner (Eds.), *Handbook of child psychology: Vol. 3. Social, emotional, and personality development* (6th ed., pp. 719–788). Hoboken, NJ: John Wiley & Sons.

Dodge, K. A., Lansford, J. E., Burks, V. S., Bates, J. E., Pettit, G. S., Fontaine, R., & Price, J. M. (2003). Peer rejection and social information-processing factors in the development of aggressive behavior problems in children. *Child Development, 74*(2), 374–393.

Dodge, K. A., & Pettit, G. S. (2003, March). A biopsychosocial model of the development of chronic conduct problems in adolescence. *Developmental Psychology. Special Issue: Violent children, 39*(2), 349–371.

Domino, G. (1992). Cooperation and competition in Chinese and American children. *Journal of Cross-Cultural Psychology, 23*(4), 456–467.

Dondi, M., Simion, F., & Caltran, G. (1999). Can newborns discriminate between their own cry and the cry of another newborn infant? *Developmental Psychology, 35*(3), 323–334.

Dore, J. (1979). Conversational acts and the acquisition of language. In E. Ochs & B. B. Schieffelin (Eds.), *Developmental Pragmatics.* New York: Academic Press.

Dossett, D., & Burns, B. (2000). The development of children's knowledge of attention and resource allocation in single and dual tasks. *The Journal of Genetic Psychology 16*(2), 216–234.

Draganova, R., Eswaran, H., Murphy, P., Lowery, C., & Preissl, H. (2007, March). Serial magnetoencephalographic study of fetal and newborn auditory discriminative evoked responses. *Early Human Development, 83*(3), 199–207.

Dromi, E. (1999). Early lexical development. In M. Barrett (Ed.), *The development of language* (pp. 99–131). Philadelphia: Psychology Press/Taylor & Francis.

Drucker, M., Kaplan, C., Feron, F., & van Os, J. (2003). Children's health-related quality of life, neighborhood socio-economic deprivation and social capital: A contextual analysis. *Social Science & Medicine, 57*(5), 825–841.

Dubois, L., Farmer, A., Girard, M., & Peterson, K. (2006). Preschool children's eating behaviors are related to dietary adequacy and body weight. *European Journal of Clinical Nutrition, 61,* 846–855.

Duncan, G., & Raudenbush, W. (1999). Assessing the effects of context in studies of children and youth development. *Educational Psychology, 34,* 29–41.

Dunn, J. (1988). *The beginnings of social understanding.* Cambridge, MA: Harvard University Press.

Dunphy, D. C. (1963). The social structure of urban adolescent peer groups. *Sociometry, 26,* 230–246.

Durham, W. (1991). *Coevolution: Genes, culture, and human diversity.* Palo Alto, CA: Stanford University Press.

Durston, S., & Casey, B. J. (2006). What have we learned about cognitive development from neuroimaging? *Neuropsychologia. Special Issue: Advances in developmental cognitive neuroscience, 44*(11), 2149–2157.

Dweck, C. S. (1999). *Self-theories: Their role in motivation, personality, and development.* Philadelphia, PA: Psychology Press/Taylor & Francis.

Dweck, C. S. (2001). The development of ability conceptions. In A. Wigfield & J. S. Eccles (Eds.), *The development of achievement motivation* (pp. 57–91). San Diego: Academic Press.

Dweck, C. S., Higgins, E. T., & Grant-Pillow, H. (2003). Self-systems give unique meaning to self variables. In M. R. Leary & J. P. Tangney (Eds.), *Handbook of self and identity* (pp. 239–252). New York: Guilford Press.

Dybdahl, R. (2001). A psychosocial support programme for children and mothers in war. *Clinical Child Psychology and Psychiatry, 6,* 425–436.

Dyson, M. E. (1996). *Between God and gangsta rap: Bearing witness to black culture.* New York: Oxford University Press.

Eagly, A. H., & Koenig, A. M. (2006). Social role theory of sex differences and similarities: Implication for prosocial behavior. In K. Dindia & D. J. Canary (Eds.), *Sex differences and similarities in communication* (2nd ed., 161–177). Mahwah, NJ: Lawrence Erlbaum Associates.

Eccles, J., Brown, B. V., & Templeton, J. (2008). A developmental framework for selecting indicators of well-being during the adolescent and young adult years. In B. V. Brown (Ed.), *Key indicators of child and youth well-being: Completing the picture* (pp. 197–236). Mahwah, NJ: Lawrence Erlbaum Associates.

Eccles, J., Templeton, J., Barber, B., & Stone, M. (2003). Adolescence and emerging adulthood: The critical passageways to adulthood. In M. H. Bornstein, L. Davidson, C. L. Keyes, K. A. Moore, & the Center for Child Well Being (Eds.), *Well-being: Positive development across the life course. Crosscurrents in contemporary psychology* (pp. 383–406). Mahwah, NJ: Lawrence Erlbaum Associates.

Eckert, P. (1995). Trajectory and forms of institutional participation. In L. J. Crockett & A. C. Crouter (Eds.), *Pathways through adolescence: Individual development in relation to social contexts* (pp. 175–195). Mahwah, NJ: Lawrence Erlbaum Associates.

Eckes, T., & Trautner, H. (Eds.). (2000). *The developmental social psychology of gender.* Mahwah, NJ: Lawrence Erlbaum Associates.

Edvardsen, J., Torgersen, S., Roysamb, E., Lygren, S., Skre, I., Onstad, S., et al. (2008, March). Heritability of bipolar spectrum disorders. Unity or heterogeneity? *Journal of Affective Disorders, 106*(3), 229–240.

Eggebeen, D. J. (2002). The changing course of fatherhood: Men's experiences with children in demographic perspective. *Journal of Family Issues, 23,* 486–505.

Eimas, P. D. (1985). The perception of speech in early infancy. *Scientific American, 252*(1), 66–72.

Eisen, M., Zellman, G. I., Leibowitz, A., Chow, W. K., & Evans, J. R. (1983). Factors discriminating pregnancy resolution decisions of unmarried adolescents. *Genetic Psychology Monographs, 108,* 69–95.

Eisenberg, N. (1992). *The caring child.* Cambridge, MA: Harvard University Press.

Eisenberg, N., & Fabes, R. A. (1992). Emotion, regulation, and the development of social competence. *Review of Personality and Social Psychology, 14,* 119–150.

Eisenberg, N., & Fabes, R. A. (2006). Emotion regulation and children's socioemotional competence. In L. Balter & C. S. Tamis-LeMonda (Eds.), *Child psychology: A handbook of contemporary issues* (2nd ed., pp. 357–381). New York: Psychology Press.

Eisenberg, N., Fabes, R. A., Murphy, B., Karbon, M., Smith, M., & Maszk, P. (1996). The relations of children's dispositional empathy-related responding to their emotionality, regulation, and social functioning. *Developmental Psychology, 32,* 195–209.

Eisenberg, N., Fabes, R. A., Shepard, S., Murphy, B., Jones, J., & Guthrie, I. (1998). Contemporaneous and longitudinal prediction of children's sympathy from dispositional regulation and emotionality. *Developmental Psychology, 34,* 910–924.

Eisenberg, N., Hofer, C., & Vaughan, J. (2007). Effortful control and its socioemotional consequences. In J. J. Gross (Ed.), *Handbook of emotion regulation* (pp. 287–306). New York: Guilford Press.

Eisenberg, N., Losoya, S., & Spinrad, T. (2003). Affect and prosocial responding. In R. Davidson, K. Scherer, & H. Goldsmith (Eds.), *Handbook of affective sciences*. Oxford, England: Oxford University Press.

Eisenberg, N., Spinrad, T. L., & Sadovsky, A. (2006a). Empathy-related responding in children. In M. Killen & J. G. Smetana (Eds.), *Handbook of moral development* (pp. 517–549). Mahwah, NJ: Lawrence Erlbaum Associates.

Eisenberg, N., Zhou, Q., & Koller, S. (2001). Brazilian adolescents' prosocial moral judgement and behavior: Relationships to sympathy, perspective taking, gender-role orientation, and demographic characteristics. *Child Development, 72,* 518–534.

Eisenberg, N., Zhou, Q., Liew, J., Champion, C., & Pidada, S. (2006b). Emotion, emotion-related regulation, and social functioning. In X. Chen, D. C. French, & B. H. Schneider (Eds.), *Peer relationships in cultural context. Cambridge studies in social and emotional development* (pp. 170–197). New York: Cambridge University Press.

Eisenberg, N., Zhou, Q., Spinrad, T., Valiente, C., Fabes, R., & Liew, J. (2005). Relations among positive parenting, children's effortful control, and externalizing problems: A three-way longitudinal study. *Child Development, 76,* 1055–1071.

Ekman, P. (1999). Facial expressions. In T. Dalgleish & M. J. Power (Eds.), *Handbook of cognition and emotion* (pp. 301–320). Chichester, England: Wiley.

Elder, G. H. J. (1998). The life course and human development. In W. Damon & R. M. Lerner (Eds.), *Handbook of child psychology: Vol. 1. Theoretical models of human development* (5th ed., pp. 939–992). New York: Wiley.

Elias, C., & Berk, L. (2002). Self-regulation in young children: Is there a role for sociodramatic play? *Early Childhood Research Quarterly, 17,* 216–238.

Elliot, D. S. (1994). Serious violent offenders: Onset, developmental course, and termination. The American Society of Criminology 1993 presidential address. *Criminology, 32,* 1–21.

Ellis, B., & Bjorklund, D. (Eds.). (2005). *Origins of the social mind: Evolutionary psychology and child development.* New York: Guilford Press.

Ellis, S. A., & Gauvain, M. (1992). Social and cultural influences on children's collaborative interactions. In L. T. Winegar & J. Valsiner (Eds.), *Children's development within social context* (pp. 155–180). Mahwah, NJ: Lawrence Erlbaum Associates.

Ellis, S., & Siegler, R. S. (1997). Planning as a strategy choice, or why don't children plan when they should? In S. L. Friedman & E. K. Scholnick (Eds.), *The developmental psychology of planning: Why, how, and when do we plan?* (pp. 183–208). Mahwah, NJ: Lawrence Erlbaum Associates.

Ellis, S. J., Kitzinger, C., & Wilkinson, S. (2002). Attitudes towards lesbians and gay men and support for lesbian and gay human rights among psychology students. *Journal of Homosexuality, 44*(1), 121–138.

Ellis, W. E., & Zarbatany, L. (2007, January). Explaining friendship formation and friendship stability. The role of children's and friends' aggression and victimization. *Merrill-Palmer Quarterly, 53*(1), 79–104.

Elman, J. L., Bates, E. A., Johnson, M. J., Karmilof-Smith, A., Parsi, D., & Plunkett, K. (1996). *Rethinking innateness: A connectionist perspective on development.* Cambridge, MA: The MIT Press.

El-Sheikh, M., Buckhalt, J., Mize, J., & Acebo, C. (2006). Marital conflict and disruption of children's sleep. *Child Development, 77,* 31–43.

Emde, R. N., & Hewitt, J. K. (Eds.). (2001). *Infancy to early childhood: Genetic and environmental influences on developmental change.* New York: Oxford University Press.

Eneli, I., & Davies, H. D. (2008). Epidemiology of childhood obesity. In H. D. Davies & H. E. Fitzgerald (Eds.), *Obesity in childhood and adolescence: Vol. 1. Medical, biological, and social issues. Praeger perspectives: Child psychology and mental health* (pp. 3–23). Westport, CT: Praeger Publishers/Greenwood Publishing Group.

Enfield, N. J., & Levinson, S. C. (2006). *Roots of human sociality: Culture, cognition and interaction* (Wenner-Gren International Symposium Series). Oxford, England: Berg Publishers.

Erdley, C., & Asher, S. (1999). A social goals perspective on children's social competence. *Journal of Emotional and Behavioral Disorders, 7*(3), 156–167.

Erickson, F., & Mohatt, G. (1982). Cultural organization of participation structures in two classrooms of Indian students. In G. Spindler (Ed.), *Doing the ethnography of schooling: Educational anthropology in action* (pp. 132–175). Prospect Heights, IL: Waveland Press.

Erikson, E. H. (1950). *Childhood and society.* New York: W. W. Norton.

Erikson, E. H. (1963a). *Childhood and society* (2nd ed.) New York: W. W. Norton.

Erikson, E. H. (1963b). *The challenge of youth.* New York: Doubleday.

Erikson, E. H. (1968a). *Identity: Youth and crisis.* New York: W. W. Norton.

Erikson, E. H. (1968b). Life cycle. In D. L. Sills (Ed.), *International encyclopedia of the social sciences: Vol. 9.* New York: Crowell, Collier.

Erikson, M. F., Sroufe, L. A., & Egeland, B. (1985). The relationship between the quality of attachment and behavior problems in preschool in a high-risk sample. *Monographs of the Society for Research in Child Development, 50,* 1–2, No. 209.

Eshleman, L. (2003) *Becoming a family: Promoting healthy attachments with your adopted child.* Dallas, TX: Taylor Publishing Company.

Estell, D. B., Farmer, T. W., Cairns, R. B., & Cairns, B. D. (2002). Social relations and academic achievement in inner-city early elementary classrooms. *International Journal of Behavioral Development, 26*(6), 518–528.

Estevez, P. A., Held, C. M., Holtzmann, C. A., Perez, C. A., Perez, J. P., Heiss, J., Garrido, M., & Peirano, P. (2002). Polysomnographic pattern recognition for automated classification of sleep-waking states in infants. *Medical and Biological Engineering and Computing, 40*(1), 105–113.

Euling, S. Y., Herman-Giddens, M. E., Lee, P. A., Selevan, S. G., Juul, A., Sorensen, T. I. A., et al. (2008). Examination of US puberty-timing data from 1940 to 1994 for secular trends: Panel findings. *Pediatrics, 121,* S172–S191.

Evans, G. W. (2006.) Child development and the physical environment. *Annual Review of Psychology, 57,* 423–451.

Eveleth, P., & Tanner, J. (1990). *Worldwide variation in human growth* (2nd ed.). Cambridge, England: Cambridge University Press.

Fabricius, W. V., & Hagen, J. W. (1984). Use of casual attributions about recall performance to assess metamemory and predict strategic memory behavior in young children. *Developmental Psychology, 20*(5), 975–987.

Fadiman, A. (1998). *The spirit catches you and you fall down : A Hmong child, her American doctors, and the collision of two cultures.* New York: Farrar, Straus & Giroux.

Falk, D. (2004). Prelinguistic evolution in early hominids: Whence motherese? *Behavioral and Brain Sciences, 27,* 491–541.

Fan, G. X., Qing, L. X., Jun, Y., & Mei, Z. (1999). Molecular studies and prenatal diagnosis of phenylkletonuria in Chinese patients. *Southeast Asian Journal of Tropical Medicine & Public Health, 30* (Suppl. 2), 63–65.

Fanaroff, A. A., & Martin, R. J. (Eds.). (1997). *Neonatal-perinatal medicine: Diseases of the fetus and infant.* St. Louis, MO: Mosby.

Fantz, R. L. (1961). The origins of form perception. *Scientific American, 204*(5) 66–72.

Fantz, R. L. (1963). Pattern vision in newborn infants. *Science, 140,* 296–297.

Farrington, D. (2004). Conduct disorder, aggression, and delinquency. In R. M. Lerner & L. Steinberg (Eds.), *Handbook of adolescent psychology* (2nd ed.). Hoboken, NJ: John Wiley & Sons.

Farver, J., Eppe, S., & Ballon, D. (2006). Acculturation and family characteristics that facilitate literacy development among Latino children.

In M. Bornstein & L. Cole (Eds.), Acculturation and parent-child relationships: Measurement and development. Mahwah, NJ: Lawrence Erlbaum Associates.

Fauth, R. C., Leventhal, T., & Brooks-Gunn, J. (2007, May). Welcome to the neighborhood? Long-term impacts of moving to low-poverty neighborhoods on poor children's and adolescents' outcomes. *Journal of Research on Adolescence, 17*(2), 249–284.

Feiring, C. (1996). Lovers as friends: Developing couscious views of romance in adolescence. *Journal of Research on Adolescence, 7*, 214–224.

Felson, R., & Haynie, D. (2002). Pubertal development, social factors, and delinquency among adolescent boys. *Criminology, 40*, 967–988.

Fenson, L., Dale, P. S., Reznick, J. S., Bates, E., Thal, O. J., & Pettnick, S. J. (1994). Variability in early communicative development. *Monographs for Research in Child Development, 59*(5, Serial No. 242).

Fernald, A. (1991). Prosody in speech to children: Prelinguistic and linguistic functions. In R. Vasta (Ed.), *Annals of child development: Vol. 8.* London: Kingley.

Fernald, A. (2001). Hearing, listening, and understanding: Auditory development in infancy. In G. Bremner & A. Fogel (Eds.), *Blackwell handbook of infant development* (pp. 35–70). Malden, MA: Blackwell Publishing.

Fernald, A., Perfors, A., & Marchman, V. (2006). Picking up speed in understanding: Speech processing efficiency and vocabulary growth across the 2nd year. *Developmental Psychology, 42*(1), 98–116.

Fernandez, M., Blass, E., Hernandez-Reif, M., Field, T., & Miguel, S. (2003). Sucrose attenuates a negative electroencephaliographic response to aversive stimulus for newborns. *Journal of Developmental and Behavioral Pediatrics, 24*, 261–266.

Ferrer-Wreder, L., Lorente, C. C., Kurtines, W., Briones, E., Bussell, J., Berman, S., & Arrufat, O. (2002). Promoting identity development in marginalized youth. *Journal of Adolescent Research, 17*(2), 168–187.

Field, T. M., Diego, M., Hernandez-Reif, M., & Fernandez, M. (2007a). Depressed mothers' newborns show less discrimination of other newborns' cry sounds. *Infant Behavior & Development, 30*(3), 431–435.

Field, T. M., Diego, M., & Sanders, C. (2001). Exercise is positively related to adolescents' relationships and academics. *Adolescence, 36*, 106–110.

Field, T., M. Hernandez-Reif, M., Diego, M., Feijo, L., Vera, Y., Gil, K., et al. (2007b). Responses to animate and inanimate faces by infants of depressed mothers. *Early Child Development and Care, 177*(5), 533–539.

Fields, W. M., Segerdahl, P., & Savage-Rumbaugh, S. (2007). The material practices of ape language research. In J. Valsiner & A. Rosa (Eds.), *The Cambridge handbook of sociocultural psychology* (pp. 164–186). New York: Cambridge University Press.

Fifer, W. P., & Moon, C. M. (1995). The effects of fetal experience with sound. In J. P. Lecanuet, W. P. Fifer, N. A. Krasnegor, & W. P. Smotherman (Eds.), *Fetal development: A psychobiological perspective.* Mahwah, NJ: Lawrence Erlbaum Associates.

Finnegan, R. A., Hodges, E. V. E., & Perry, D. G. (1998). Victimization by peers: Associations with children's reports of mother-child interaction. *Journal of Personality & Social Psychology, 75*(4), 1076–1086.

Fireman, G., & Kose, G. (2002, December). The effect of self-observation on children's problem solving. *Journal of Genetic Psychology, 163*(4), 410–423.

Fischer, K. W., & Pare-Blagoev, J. (2000). From individual differences to dynamic pathways of development. *Child Development 71*(4), 850–853.

Fischer, K. W., & Yan, Z. (2002). The development of dynamic skill theory. In R. Lickliter & D. Lewkowicz (Eds.), *Conceptions of development: Lessons from the laboratory.* Hove, England: Psychology Press.

Fishbein, H. D. (1976). *Evolution, development and children's learning.* Pacific Palisades, CA: Goodyear.

Fisher, C., Klingler, S., & Song, H. (2006). What does syntax say about space? 2-year-olds use sentence structure to learn new prepositions. *Cognition, 101*(1), b19–b29.

Fivush, R., & Nelson, K. (2006, March) Parent-child reminiscing locates the self in the past. *British Journal of Developmental Psychology, 24*(1), 235–251.

Fivush, R., Reese, E., & Haden, C. (2006, November). Elaborating on elaborations: Role of maternal reminiscing style in cognitive and socio-emotional development. *Child Development, 77*(6), 1568–1588.

Flavell, J. H. (1971). Stage-related properties of cognitive development. *Cognitive Psychology, 2*, 421–453.

Flavell, J. H. (2007). Theory-of-mind development: Retrospect and prospect. In G. W. Ladd (Ed.), *Appraising the human developmental sciences. Landscapes of childhood series* (pp. 38–55). Detroit, MI: Wayne State University Press.

Flavell, J. H., Flavell, E. R., Green, F. L., & Korfmacher, J. E. (1990). Do young children think of television images as pictures or real objects? *Journal of Broadcasting & Electronic Media, 34*, 339–419.

Flavell, J. H., Friedrichs, A. G., & Hoyt, J. D. (1970). Developmental changes in memorization processes. *Cognitive Psychology, 1*, 324–340.

Flavell, J. H., Green, F. L., & Flavell, E. R. (1986). Development of knowledge about the appearance-reality distinction. *Monographs of the Society for Research in Child Development, 51*(1, Serial No. 212).

Fletcher, A. C., Darling, N. E., Steinberg, L., & Dornbusch, S. (1995). The company they keep: Relation of adolescents' adjustment and behavior to their friends; perceptions of authoritative parenting in the social network. *Developmental Psychology, 31*, 300–310.

Flowers, P., & Buston, K. (2002). "I was terrified of being different": Exploring gay men's accounts of growing up in a heterosexist society. *Journal of Adolescence, 24*, 51–65.

Flynn, J. R. (1999). Searching for justice: The discovery of IQ gains over time. *American Psychologist, 54*(1), 5–20.

Flynn, J. R. (2007). *What is intelligence? Beyond the Flynn effect.* New York: Cambridge University Press.

Fodor, J. (1983). *The modularity of mind.* Cambridge, MA: The MIT Press.

Fonagy, P. (2001). *Attachment theory and psychoanalysis.* New York: Other Press.

Fordham, S., & Ogbu, J. U. (1986). Black students' school success: Coping with the "burden of 'acting white.'" *Urban Review, 18*(3), 176–206.

Foreman, N., Fielder, A., Minshell, C., Hurrion, E., & Sergienko, E. (1997). Visual search, perception, and visual-motor skill in "healthy" children born at 27–32 weeks' gestation. *Journal of Experimental Child Psychology, 64*(1), 27–41.

Forman, M. (2002). Keeping it real: African youth identities and hip hop. In R. Young (Ed.), *Critical Studies, 19, Music, popular culture, identities.* New York: Rodopi.

Forsyth, B. W. C. (1989). Colic and the effect of changing formulas: A double-blind, multiple crossover study. *Journal of Pediatrics, 115*, 521–552.

Fraga, M. F., Ballestar, E., Paz, M. F., Ropero, S., Setien, F., Ballestar, M. L., et al. (2005). Epigenetic differences arise during the lifetime of monozygotic twins. *Proceedings of the National Academy of Sciences, 102*(30), 10604–10609.

Fraiberg, S. H. (1959). *The magic years: Understanding and handling the problems of early childhood.* New York: Scribner.

Frankel, K., & Bates, J. (1990). Mother-toddler problem solving: Antecedents in attachment, home behavior, and temperament. *Child Development, 61*, 810–819.

Franzini, L., Caughy, M. O., Nettles, S. M., & O'Campo, P. (2008, March). Perceptions of disorder: Contributions of neighborhood characteristics to subjective perceptions of disorder. *Journal of Environmental Psychology, 28*(1), 83–93.

Freed, K. (1983, March 14). Cubatao—a paradise lost to pollution. Los Angeles *Times,* pp. 1, 12, 13.

Freedman, D., Khan, L., Serdula, M., Dietz, W., Srinivasan, S., & Berenson, G. (2002). Relation of age at menarche to race, time period, and anthropometric dimensions: The Bogalusa heart study. *Pediatrics, 110,* 1–7.

Freud, S. (1905/1953). Three essays on the theory of sexuality. In J. Strachey (Ed.), *The standard edition of the complete psychological works of Sigmund Freud: Vol. 7.* London: Hogarth Press.

Freud, S. (1920/1955). Beyond the pleasure principle. In J. Strachey (Ed.), *The standard edition of the complete psychological works of Sigmund Freud: Vol. 18.* London: Hogarth Press.

Freud, S. (1921/1949). Group psychology—The analysis of the ego. In J. Strachey (Ed.), *The standard edition of the complete psychological works of Sigmund Freud: Vol. 18.* London: Hogarth Press.

Freud, S. (1933/1964). *New introductory lectures in psychoanalysis.* New York: W. W. Norton.

Freud, S. (1940/1964). An outline of psychoanalysis. In J. Strachey (Ed.), *The standard edition of the complete psychological works of Sigmund Freud: Vol. 32.* London: Hogarth Press.

Friederici, A. D., Bahlmann, J., Heim, S., Schubotz, R. I., & Anwander, A. (2006). The brain differentiates human and non-human grammars: Functional localization and structural connectivity. *Proceedings of the National Academy of Sciences, 103*(7), 2458–2463.

Frith, U. (1989). *Autism.* Oxford, England: Oxford University Press.

Frith, U. (2003). *Autism: Explaining the enigma* (2nd ed.). Oxford, England: Blackwell Publishing.

Fromkin, V., Krashen, S., Curtiss, S., Rigler, D., & Rigler, M. (1974, January). The development of language in Genie: A case of language acquisition beyond the "critical period." *Brain and Language, 1*(1), 81–107.

Fry, D. P. (1988). Intercommunity differences in aggression among Zapotec children. *Child Development, 59,* 1008–1018.

Frye, D. (2000). Theory of mind, domain specificity, and reasoning. In K. J. Riggs & P. Mitchell, *Children's reasoning and the mind* (pp. 149–167). Hove, England: Psychology Press/Taylor & Francis.

Fujioka, T., Trainor, L. J., & Ross, B. (2008, February). Simultaneous pitches are encoded separately in auditory cortex: An MMNm study. *Neuroreport: For Rapid Communication of Neuroscience Research, 19*(3), 361–366.

Fuligni, A. J., & Eccles, J. S. (1993). Perceived parent–child relationships and early adolescents' orientation toward peers. *Developmental Psychology, 29,* 622–632.

Fuligni, A. J., & Stevenson, H. W. (1995). Time use and mathematics achievement among American, Chinese, and Japanese high school students. *Child Development, 66*(3), 830–842.

Fullard, W., & Reiling, A. M. (1976). An investigation of Lorenz's babyness. *Child Development, 47,* 1191–1193.

Funk, J. B., Baldacci, H. B., Pasold, T., & Baumgardner, J. (2004, February). Violence exposure in real-life, video games, television, movies, and the internet: Is there desensitization? *Journal of Adolescence, 27*(1), 23–39.

Furman, W., & Simon, V. A. (2008). Homophily in adolescent romantic relationships. In M. J. Prinstein & K. A. Dodge (Eds.), *Understanding peer influence in children and adolescents. Duke series in child development and public policy* (pp. 203–224). New York: Guilford Press.

Furstenberg, F. F., Jr. (1998). Social capital and the role of fathers in the family. In A. Booth & A. C. Crouter (Eds.), *Men in families: When do they get involved? What difference does it make? (pp. 295–301).* Mahwah, NJ: Lawrence Erlbaum Associates.

Furstenberg, F. F., Jr., Hughes, M. E., & Brooks-Gunn, J. (1992). The next generation: The children of teenage mothers grow up. In M. Rosenheim & M. F. Testa (Eds.), *Early parenthood and coming of age in the 1990's.* New Brunswick, NJ: Rutgers University Press.

Gallego, M. A., & Cole, M. (2000, May). Success is not enough: Challenges to sustaining new forms of educational activity. *Computers in Human Behavior. Special Issue: Afterschool computer programs for children, 16*(3), 271–286.

Gallego, M. A., Cole, M., & Laboratory of Comparative Human Cognition. (2000). Classroom culture and culture in the classroom. In V. Richardson (Ed.), *The Handbook of Research on Teaching.* Washington, DC: American Educational Research Association.

Gallup, G. G. J. (1970). Chimpanzees: Self-recognition. *Science, 167,* 86–87.

Gammage, J. (2003, June 14). Bringing Jin Yu home. *The Philadelphia Inquirer.*

Garciaguirre, J. S., Adolph, K. E., & Shrout, P. (2007). Baby carriage: Infants walking with loads. *Child Development 78*(2), 664–680.

Gardner, H. (1983). *Frames of mind: The theory of multiple intelligences.* New York: Basic Books.

Gardner, H. (2006, September–October). On failing to grasp the core of MI theory: A response to Visser et al. *Intelligence, 34*(5), 503–505.

Gardner, M., & Steinberg, L. (in press). Risk-taking among adolescents, young adults, and adults: The role of peer influence. *Developmental Psychology.*

Gardner, W., & Rogoff, B. (1990). Children's deliberateness of planning according to task circumstances. *Developmental Psychology, 26,* 480–487.

Garofalo, R., Wolf, R., Wissow, L., Woods, E., & Goodman, E. (1999). Sexual orientation and risk of suicide attempts among a representative sample of youth. *Archives of Pediatrics and Adolescent Medicine, 153,* 487–493.

Garrod, A., Smulyan, L., Powers, S., & Kilkenny, R. (Eds.). (1999). *Adolescent portraits: Identity, relationships, and challenges.* Boston: Allyn & Bacon.

Garrow, I., & Werne, J. (1953). Sudden apparently unexplained death during infancy: III. Pathological findings in infants dying immediately after violence, contrasted with those after sudden apparently unexplained death. *American Journal of Pathology, 29*(5), 833–851.

Garvey, C., & Berndt, R. (1977). Organization of pretend play. *Catalog of Selected Documents in Psychology, 7,* 107.

Gaskins, S. (1999). Children's daily lives in a Mayan village: A case study of culturally constructed roles and activities. In A. Göncü (Ed.), *Children's engagement in the world: Sociocultural perspectives* (pp. 25–61). New York: Cambridge University Press.

Gau, S., & Soong, W. (2003). The transition of sleep-wake patterns in early adolescence. *Sleep, 26,* 449–454.

Geary, D. (2006). Development of mathematical understanding. In D. Kuhn & R. S. Siegler (Eds.), *Handbook of child psychology: Vol. 2. Cognition, perception, and language* (6th ed., pp. 777–810). New York: Wiley.

Geary, D., Bow-Tomas, C., Lui, F., & Siegler, R. (1996). Development of arithmetical competencies in Chinese and American children: Influence of age, language, and schooling. *Child Development, 67,* 2022–2044.

Geers, A., Spehar, B., & Sedey, A. (2002, February). Use of speech by children from total communication programs who wear cochlear implants. *American Journal of Speech-Language Pathology, 11*(1), 50–58.

Geertz, C. (1984). From the native's point of view: On the nature of anthropological understanding. In R. Shweder & R. Levine (Eds.), *Culture theory.* Cambridge, England: Cambridge University Press.

Geiger, B. (1996). *Fathers as primary caregivers.* Westport, CT: Greenwood.

Geithner, C. A., Thomis, M. A., Vanden Eynde, B., Maes, H. H., Loos, R. J., Peeters, M., et al. (2004, September). Growth in peak aerobic power during adolescence. *Medicine & Science in Sports & Exercise, 36*(9), 1616–1624.

Gelis, J. (1991). *History of childbirth.* Cambridge, England: Polity Press.

Gelman, R. (1990). First principles affect learning and transfer in children. *Cognitive Science, 14,* 79–107.

Gelman, R., & Lucariello, J. (2002). Role of learning in cognitive development. In R. Gallistel (Ed.), *Stevens' handbook of experimental psychology: Vol. 3* (pp. 395–444). New York: Wiley.

Georgieff, M. K., & Raghavendra, R. (2001). The role of nutrition in cognitive development. In C. A. Nelson and M. Luciana (Eds.), *Handbook of developmental cognitive neuroscience* (pp. 491–504). Cambridge, MA: The MIT Press.

Gershoff, E. T., & Aber, J. L. (2004, July). Editors' introduction: Assessing the impact of September 11th, 2001, on children, youth, and parents: Methodological challenges to research on terrorism and other non-normative events. *Applied Developmental Science, 8*(3), 106–110.

Gertner, Y., Fisher, C., & Eisengart, J. (2006). Learning words and rules: Abstract knowledge of word order in early sentence comprehension. *Psychological Science, 17,* 684–691.

Geschwind, D. H., & Dykens, E. (2004). Neurobehavioral and psychosocial issues in Klinefelter syndrome. *Learning Disabilities Research & Practice, 19*(3) 166–173.

Giacoman, S. L. (1971). Hunger and motor restraint on arousal and visual attention in the infant. *Child Development, 42*(2), 605–614.

Gibson, E. J. (1988). Exploratory behavior in the development of perceiving, acting, and the acquiring of knowledge. *Annual Review of Psychology, 39,* 1–41.

Gibson, E. J., & Pick, A. D. (2000). *An ecological approach to perceptual learning and development.* London: Oxford University Press.

Giedd, J. N., Blumenthal, J., Jeffries, N. O., Castellanos, F. X., Liu, H., Zijdenbos, A., et al. (1999a). Brain development during childhood and adolescence: A longitudinal MRI study. *Nature Neuroscience, 2*(10), 861–863.

Giedd, J. N., Blumenthal, J., Jeffries, N. O., Rajapakse, J. C., Vaituzis, A. C., Liu, H., et al. (1999b). Development of the human corpus collosum during childhood and adolescence: A longitudinal MRI study. *Progress in Neuro-Psychopharmacology & Biological Psychiatry, 23,* 571–588.

Gielen, U. P., & Markoulis, D. C. (2001). Preference for principled moral reasoning: A developmental and cross-cultural perspective. In L. L. Adler & U. P. Gielen (Eds.), *Cross-cultural topics in psychology* (2nd ed., pp. 81–101). Westport, CT: Praeger.

Gilbert, S. F. (2001). Ecological developmental biology: Developmental biology meets the real world. *Developmental Biology, 233*(1), 1–12.

Giles, J., & Heyman, G. (2003). Preschoolers' beliefs about the stability of antisocial behavior: Implications for navigating social challenges. *Social Development, 12,* 182–197.

Gillespie, A. (in press). Position exchange: The social development of agency. *New Ideas in Psychology.*

Gilligan, C. (1982). *In a different voice: Psychological theory and women's development.* Cambridge, MA: Harvard University Press.

Gilman, S., Kawachi, I., Fitzmaurice, G., & Buka, S. (2003). Family disruption in childhood and risk of adult depression. *The American Journal of Psychiatry, 160,* 939–946.

Gilmore, C. K., & Spelke, E. S. (2008, June). Children's understanding of the relationship between addition and subtraction. *Cognition, 107*(3), 932–945.

Ginsburg, H. (1977). *Children's arithmetic.* New York: Van Nostrand.

Ginsburg, H. P. (2008). Challenging preschool education: Meeting the intellectual needs of all children. In B. Z. Presseisen (Ed.), *Teaching for intelligence* (2nd ed., pp. 212–229). Thousand Oaks, CA: Corwin Press.

Godfrey, K. M., & Barker, D. J. P. (2000). Fetal nutrition and adult disease. *American Journal of Clinical Nutrition, 71*(Suppl. 5), 1344S–1352S.

Gogtay, N., Giedd, J., Lusk, L., Hayashi, K. I., Sreenstein, D., & Vaituzis, A. (2004). Dynamic mapping of human cortical development during childhood through early adulthood. *Proceedings of the National Academy of Sciences of the United States of America, 101,* 8174–8179.

Goldin-Meadow, S., & Mylander, C. (1998). Spontaneous sign systems created by deaf children in two cultures. *Nature, 391,* 279–281.

Goldin-Meadow, S., Mylander, C., & Franklin, A. (2007). How children make language out of gesture: Morphological structure in gesture systems developed by American and Chinese deaf children. *Cognitive Psychology, 55*(2), 87–135.

Goldman, J., & Salus, M. K. (2003). A coordinated response to child abuse and neglect: The foundation for practice. User Manual Series. Washington, DC: U.S. Department of Health and Human Services.

Goldsmith, H. H., & Campos, J. J. (1982). Toward a theory of infant temperament. In R. N. Emde & R. Harmon (Eds.), *The development of attachment and affiliative systems.* New York: Plenum Press.

Golinkoff, R., & Hirsh-Pasek, K. (2006). Baby wordsmith: From associationist to social sophisticate. *Current Directions in Psychological Science, 15*(1), 30–33.

Golinkoff, R. M., Hirsh-Pasek, K., & Schweisguth, M. A. (1999). A reappraisal of young children's knowledge of grammatical morphemes. In J. Weissenborn & B. Hoehle (Eds.), *Approaches to bootstrapping: Phonological, syntactic, and neurophysiological aspects of early language acquisition.* Amsterdam and Philadelphia: John Benjamins.

Golinkoff, R. M., Mervis, C. B., & Hirsh-Pasek, K. (1994). Early object labels: The case for a developmental lexical principles framework. *Journal of Child Language, 21,* 125–155.

Golombok, S., & Hines, M. (2002). Sex differences in social behavior. In P. Smith & C. Hart (Eds.), *Blackwell handbook of childhood social development.* Malden, MA: Blackwell Publishing.

Goodman, C., & Silverstein, M. (2006). Grandmothers raising grandchildren: Ethnic and racial differences in well-being among custodial and coparenting families. *Journal of Family Issues, 27,* 1605–1626.

Goodman, G. S. (2005). Wailing babies in her wake. *American Psychologist, 60*(8), 872–881.

Goodman, G. S. (2006). Children's eyewitness memory: A modern history and contemporary commentary. *Journal of Social Issues, 62*(4), 811–832.

Goodman, G. S., Emery, R. E., & Haugaard, J. J. (1998). Developmental psychology and the law: Divorce, child maltreatment, foster care, and adoption. In I. E. Sigel & K. A. Renninger (Eds.), *Handbook of child psychology: Vol. 4. Child psychology in practice* (5th ed., pp. 775–876). New York: Wiley.

Goodman, G. S., Hirschman, J. E., Hepps, D., & Rudy, L. (1991, January). Children's memory for stressful events. *Merrill-Palmer Quarterly, 37*(1), 109–157.

Goodman, G. S., & Melinder, A. (2007). Child witness research and forensic interviews of young children: A review. *Legal and Criminological Psychology 12*(1), 1–19.

Goodman, M. R., & Rao, S. P. (2007, October). Grandparents raising grandchildren in a US-Mexico border community. *Qualitative Health Research, 17*(8), 1117–1136.

Goodman, M. R., Stormshak, E., & Dishion, T. (2001). The significance of peer victimization at two points in development. *Applied Developmental Psychology, 22,* 507–526.

Goodnow, J. J. (1998). Beyond the overall balance: The significance of particular tasks and procedures for perceptions of fairness in distributions of household work. *Social Justice Research, 11*(3), 359–376.

Goodnow, J. J., Cashmore, J., Cotton, S., & Knight, R. (1984). Mothers' developmental timetables in two cultural groups. *International Journal of Psychology, 19,* 193–205.

Goodwin, M. H. (2002). Exclusion in girls' peer groups: Ethnographic analysis of language practices on the playground. *Human Development, 45*(6), 392–415.

Goodwin, M. H. (2006). *The hidden life of girls: Games of stance, status, and exclusion.* Oxford, England: Blackwell Publishing.

Goossens, L. (2001). Global versus domain-specific statuses in identity research: A comparison of two self-report measures. *Journal of Adolescence, 24,* 681–699.

Gopnik, A., & Rosati, A. (2001). Duck or rabbit? Reversing ambiguous figures and understanding ambiguous representations, *Developmental Science, 4,* 175–183.

Gopnik, A., & Meltzoff, A. N. (1997). *Words, thoughts, and theories.* Cambridge, MA: The MIT Press.

Gordon, P. (2004, October 15). Numerical cognition without words: Evidence from Amazonia. *Science, 306,* 496–499.

Gordon, R. A., Savage, C., Lahey, B. B., Goodman, S. H., Jensen, P. S., Rubio-Stipic, M., et al. (2003). Family and neighborhood income: Additive and multiplicative associations with youths' well-being. *Social Science Research, 32,* 191–219.

Gormley, W., & Gayer, T. (2005). Promoting school readiness in Oklahoma: An evaluation of Tulsa's pre-K program. *Journal of Human Resources, 40*(3), 533–558.

Goswami, U. (2008). *Cognitive development: The learning brain.* New York: Psychology Press.

Goswami, U. (Ed.). (2002). Blackwell handbook of childhood cognitive development. Oxford, England: Blackwell Publishing.

Gottardo, A., Chiappe, P., Siegel, L. S., & Stanovich, K. E. (1999). Patterns of word and nonword processing in skilled and less-skilled readers. *Reading & Writing, 11*(5–6), 465–487.

Gottlieb, A. (2000). Luring your child into this life: A Beng path for infant care. In J. S. DeLoache & A. Gottlieb (Eds.), *A world of babies: Imagined childcare guides for seven societies* (55–88). Cambridge, England: Cambridge University Press.

Gottlieb, A. (2005). *The afterlife is where we come from: The culture of infancy in West Africa.* Chicago: University of Chicago Press.

Gottlieb, E., & Mandel Leadership Institute. (2007) Learning how to believe: Epistemic development in cultural context. *Journal of the Learning Sciences, 16*(1), 5–35.

Gottlieb, G. (2002). Developmental-behavioral initiation of evolutionary change. *Psychological Review, 109*(2), 211–218.

Gottlieb, G., & Lickliter, R. (2007, January). Probabilistic epigenesis. *Developmental Science, 10*(1), 1–11.

Gottman, J. M. (1983). How children become friends. *Monographs of the Society for Research in Child Development, 48*(3, Serial No. 201).

Gotz, M., Lemish, D., Aidman, A., & Moon, H. (2005). *Media and the make-believe worlds of children.* Mahwah, NJ: Lawrence Erlbaum Associates.

Graber, J. A. (2004). Internalizing problems during adolescence. In R. M. Lerner & L. Steinberg (Eds.), *Handbook of adolescent psychology* (2nd ed.). Hoboken, NJ: John Wiley & Sons.

Graber, J. A., Brooks-Gunn, J., & Archibald, A. (2003). Links between girls' puberty and externalizing and internalizing behaviors: Moving from demonstrating effects to identifying pathways. In D. Stoff & E. Susman (Eds.), *Developmental psychobiology of aggression.* New York: Cambridge University Press.

Graber, J. A., Brooks-Gunn, J., & Warren, M. (1995). The antecedents of menarcheal age: Heredity, family environment, and stressful life events. *Child Development, 66,* 346–359.

Grady, K. (2002). Lowrider art and Latino students in the rural Midwest. In S. Wortham, E. Murillo, & E. Hamann (Eds.), *Education in the new Latino diaspora.* Westport, CT: Ablex.

Graham, J. A., Cohen, R., Zbikowski, S. M., & Secrist, M. E. (1998). A longitudinal investigation of race and sex as factors in children's classroom friendship choices. *Child Study Journal, 28*(4), 245–266.

Graham, M. J., Larsen, U., & Xu, X. (1999). Secular trend in age at menarche in China: A case study of two rural counties in Anhui province. *Journal of Biosocial Science, 31*(2), 257–267.

Granic, I., Hollenstein, T., Dishion, T. J., & Patterson, G. R. (2003). Longitudinal analysis of flexibility and reorganization in early adolescence: A dynamic systems study of family interactions. *Developmental Psychology, 39*(3), 606–617.

Greenfield, P. M., Brazelton, T. B., & Childs, C. P. (1989). From birth to maturity in Zinacantan: Ontogenesis in cultural context. In V. Bricker & G. Gossen (Eds.), *Ethnographic encounters in southern Mesoamerica: Celebratory essays in honor of Evon Z. Vogt.* Albany: Institute of Mesoamerican Studies, State University of New York.

Greenfield, P. M., Keller, H., Fuligni, A., & Maynard, A. (2003). Cultural pathways through universal development. *Annual Review of Psychology, 54,* 461–490.

Greenfield, P. M., & Lyn, H. (2007). Symbol combination in *Pan:* Language, action, and culture. In D. A. Washburn (Ed.), *Primate perspectives on behavior and cognition* (pp. 255–267). Washington, DC: American Psychological Association.

Greenfield, P. M., Suzuki, L., & Rothstein-Fisch, C. (2006). Cultural pathways through human development. In K. Renninger, I. Sigel, W. Damon, & R. Lerner (Eds.), *Handbook of child psychology: Vol. 4. Child psychology in practice* (6th ed.). Hoboken, NJ: Wiley.

Greenough, W., Black, J., & Wallace, C. (1987). Experience and brain development. *Child Development, 58,* 539–559.

Greenspan, S. I. (2003). Child care research: A clinical perspective. *Child Development, 74*(4), 1064–1068.

Greenspan, S. I., & Shanker, S. (2004). *The first idea: How symbols, language and intelligence evolved from our primate ancestors to modern humans.* Cambridge, MA: Da Capo Press.

Gregor, J. A., & McPherson, D. A. (1966). Racial preference and ego identity among White and Bantu children in the Republic of South Africa. *Genetic Psychology Monographs, 73,* 218–253.

Griffin, P. (1983). Personal communication.

Grigorenko, E. L., Geissler, P., Wenzel, P. R., Okatcha, F., Nokes, C., Kenny, D. A., et al. (2001). The organization of Luo conceptions of intelligence: A study of implicit theories in a Kenyan village. *International Journal of Behavioral Development, 25*(4), 367–378.

Grisso, T., Steinberg, L., Woolard, J., Cauffman, E., Scott, E., Graham, S., et al. (2003). Juveniles' competence to stand trial: A comparison of adolescents' and adults' capacities as trial defendants. *Law and Human Behavior, 27*(4), 333–363.

Grolnick, W. S., McMenamy, J. M., & Kurowski, C. O. (1999). Emotional self-regulation in infancy and toddlerhood. In L. Balter & C. S. Tamis-LeMonda (Eds.), *Child psychology: A handbook of contemporary issues.* Philadelphia: Psychology Press/Taylor & Francis.

Gronlund, N. E. (1959). *Sociometry in the classroom.* New York: Harper Brothers.

Gross, J. J., & Thompson, R. A. (2007). Emotion regulation: Conceptual foundations. In J. J. Gross (Ed.), *Handbook of emotion regulation* (pp. 3–24). New York: Guilford Press.

Grossmann, K. E., & Grossmann, K. (2005). Universality of human social attachment as an adaptive process. In C. S. Carter, L. Ahnert, K. E. Grossmann, S. B. Hrdy, M. E. Lamb, S. W. Porges, et al. (Eds.), *Attachment and bonding: A new synthesis* (pp. 199–228). Cambridge, MA: The MIT Press.

Grotevant, H. D. (1998). Adolescent development in family contexts. In W. Damon & N. Eisenberg (Eds.), *Handbook of child psychology: Vol. 3. Social, emotional, and personality development* (5th ed., pp. 1097–1150). New York: Wiley.

Grotevant, H. D. (2001). Developing new insights from a process approach to adolescent development. *Human Development, 44*(1), 55–58.

Grotevant, H. D., & Cooper, C. R. (1985). Patterns of interaction in family relationships and the development of identity exploration in adolescence. *Developmental Psychology, 56*, 415–428.

Grotevant, H. D., & Cooper, C. R. (1998). Individuality and connectedness in adolescent development: Review and prospects for research on identity, relationships, and context. In E. E. A. Skoe & A. L. von der Lippe (Eds.), *Personality development in adolescence: A cross national and life span perspective* (pp. 3–37). New York: Routledge.

Grumbach, M., & Styne, D. (2002). Puberty: Ontogeny, neuroendocrinology, physiology, and disorders. In P. Larsen, H. Kronenberg, S. Melmed, & K. Polonsky (Eds.), *Williams textbook of endocrinology* (10th ed., pp. 1509–1625). Philadelphia: Saunders.

Gunter, B., Oates, C., & Blades, M. (2005). *Advertising to children on TV: Content, impact and regulation.* Mahwah, NJ: Lawrence Erlbaum Associates.

Guralnick, M. J. (2005) Early intervention for children with intellectual disabilities: Current knowledge and future prospects. *Journal of Applied Research in Intellectual Disabilities, 18*(4), 313–324.

Guttler, F. (1988). Epidemiology and natural history of phenylketonuria and other hyperphenylalaninemias. In R. J. Wurtman & E. Ritter-Walker (Eds.), *Dietary phenylaline and brain function.* Boston: Birkhauser.

Guttmacher Institute. (2006). *Abortion in women's lives.* Retrieved April 25, 2007, from http://www.guttmacher.org/pubs/2006/05/04/AiWL.pdf

Haden, C. A., Ornstein, P. A., Eckerman, C. O., & Didow, S. M. (2001). Mother–child conversational interactions as events unfold: Linkages to subsequent remembering. *Child Development, 72*(4), 1016–1031.

Haines, M. M., Stansfeld, S. A., Brentnall, S., Head, J., Berry, B., Jiggins, M., & Hygge, S. (2001, November). The West London Schools Study: The effects of chronic aircraft noise exposure on child health. *Psychological Medicine, 31*(8), 1385–1396.

Haith, M. M. (1980). *Rules that babies look by: The organization of newborn visual activity.* Mahwah, NJ: Lawrence Erlbaum Associates.

Hakkarainen, P. (2004). Narrative learning in the fifth dimension. *Outlines: Critical Social Studies, 6*, 5–20.

Halberstadt, A., Denham, S., & Dunsmore, J. (2001). Affective social competence. *Social Development, 10*, 79–119.

Hall, G. S. (1904). *Adolescence.* New York: Appleton.

Hallett, D., Chandler, M. J., & Krettenauer, T. (2002). Disentangling the course of epistemic development: Parsing knowledge by epistemic content. *New Ideas in Psychology. Special Issue: Folk epistemology, 20*(2–3), 285–307.

Halpern-Felsher, B., & Cauffman, E. (2001). Costs and benefits of a decision: Decision-making competence in adolescents and adults. *Applied Developmental Psychology, 22*, 257–273.

Halverson, H. M. (1931). An experimental study of prehension in infants by means of systemic cinema records. *Genetic Psychology Monographs, 10*, 107–286.

Hamann, E. (2002). *Un paso adelante?* The politics of bilingual education, Latino student accommodation, and school district management in Southern Appalachia. In S. Wortham, E. Murillo, & E. Hamann (Eds.), *Education in the new Latino diaspora.* Westport, CT: Ablex.

Hanawalt, B., & Kobialka, M. (Eds.). (2000). *Medieval practices of space.* Minneapolis: University of Minnesota Press.

Harden, K. P., Turkheimer, E., & Loehlin, J. C. (2007, March). Genotype by environment interaction in adolescents' cognitive aptitude. *Behavior Genetics, 37*(2), 273–283.

Harlow, H. F. (1959). Love in infant monkeys. *Scientific American, 200*(6), 68–74.

Harlow, H. F., & Harlow, M. K. (1962). Social deprivation in monkeys. *Scientific American, 207*(5), 136–146.

Harlow, H. F., & Harlow, M. K. (1969). Effects of various mother-infant relationships on rhesus monkey behaviors. In B. M. Foss (Ed.), *Determinants of infant behavior: Vol. 4* (4th ed.). London: Methuen.

Hart, B., & Risley, T. R. (1999). *The social world of children learning to talk.* Baltimore: Brookes.

Hart, C., Young, C., Nelson, D., Jin, S., Bazarskaya, N., Nelson, L., et al. (1999). Peer contact patterns, parenting practices, and preschoolers' social competence in China, Russia, and the United States. In P. Slee & K. Rigby (Eds.), *Children's peer relationships* (pp. 3–30). London: Routledge.

Harter, S. (1982). The perceived competence scale for children. *Child Development, 53*, 87–97.

Harter, S. (1987). The determinants and mediational role of global self-worth in children. In N. Eisenberg (Ed.), *Contemporary topics in developmental psychology.* New York: Wiley.

Harter, S. (1998). The development of self-representation. In N. Eisenberg (Ed.), *Handbook of child psychology: Vol. 3. Social, emotional, and personality development* (5th ed., pp. 553–617). New York: Wiley.

Harter, S. (1999). *The construction of the self: A developmental perspective.* New York: Guilford Press.

Harter, S. (2006a). Developmental and individual difference-perspectives on self-esteem. In D. K. Mroczek & T. D. Little (Eds.), *Handbook of personality development* (311–334). Mahwah, NJ: Lawrence Erlbaum Associates.

Harter, S. (2006b). The development of self-esteem. In M. H. Kernis (Ed.), *Self-esteem issues and answers: A sourcebook of current perspectives* (pp. 144–150). New York: Psychology Press.

Harter, S., & Pike, R. (1984). The pictorial scale of perceived competence and social acceptance for young children. *Child Development, 55*, 1969–1982.

Hartshorn, K., Rovee-Collier, C., Gerhardstein, P., Bhatt, R. S., Wondoloski, T. L., Klein, P., Gilch, J., et al. (1998). The ontogeny of long-term memory over the first year-and-a-half of life. *Developmental Psychobiology, 32*(2), 69–89.

Hartup, W. W. (1992). Friendships and their developmental significance. In H. McGurk (Ed.), *Childhood social development: Contemporary perspectives.* London: Lawrence Erlbaum Associates.

Hartup, W. W. (1993). Adolescents and their friends. In B. Laursen (Ed.), *Close friendships in adolescence* (pp. 3–22). San Francisco: Jossey-Bass.

Hauck, F. R., Herman, S. M., Donovan, M., Iysau, S., Moore, C. M., Donoghue, E., et al. (2003). Sleep environment and the risk of sudden infant death syndrome in an urban population: The Chicago Infant Mortality Study. *Pediatrics, 111*(5, Part 2), 1207–1214.

Hauser, G., Chitayat, D., Berbs, L., Braver, D., & Mulbauer, B. (1985). Peculiar odors in newborns and maternal pre-natal ingestion of spicy foods. *European Journal of Pediatrics, 144,* 403.

Hauser, M. D., & Chomsky, N. (2002). The faculty of language: What is it, who has it, and how did it evolve? *Science, 298*, 1569–1579.

Hauser, S., Powers, S., & Noam, G. (1991). *Adolescents and their families: Paths of ego development.* New York: Free Press.

Haviland, J. M., & Kramer, D. A. (1991). Affect-cognition relationships in adolescent diaries: The case of Anne Frank. *Human Development, 34*(3), 143–159.

Hawkins, A. J., Lovejoy, K. R., Holmes, E. K., Blanchard, V. L., & Fawcett, E. (2008). Increasing fathers' involvement in child care with a couple-focused intervention during the transition to parenthood. *Family Relations, 57*(1), 49–59.

Hawley, P. H., Little, T. D., & Card, N. A. (2007, March). The allure of a mean friend: Relationship quality and processes of aggressive adolescents with prosocial skills. *International Journal of Behavioral Development, 31*(2), 170–180.

Hayes, K., & Hayes, C. (1951). The intellectual development of a home-raised chimpanzee. *Proceedings of the American Philosophical Society, 95*, 105–109.

Haynie, D., & Piquero, A. (2006). Pubertal development and physical victimization in adolescence. *Journal of Research in Crime and Delinquency, 43,* 3–35.

Haywood, K. M., & Getchell, N. (2005). *Life span motor development* (4th ed.). Champaign, IL: Human Kinetics.

Heath, S. B. (1983). *Ways with words: Language, life, and work in communities and classrooms.* Cambridge, England: Cambridge University Press.

Heights, R. (1999). Identity development of homosexual youth and parental and familiar influences on the coming out process. *Adolescence, 34,* 597–601.

Heinrich, C. C., Brookmeyer, K. A., Shrier, L. A., & Shahar, G. (2006, April). Supportive relationships and sexual risk behavior in adolescence: An ecological–transactional approach. *Journal of Pediatric Psychology, 31*(3), 286–297.

Heinsohn, R., & Double, M. (2004). Cooperate or speciate: New theory for the distribution of passerine birds. *Trends in Ecology and Evolution, 19,* 55–60.

Helland, T., Asbjornsen, A. E., Hushovd, E., & Hugdahl, K. (2008, February). Dichotic listening and school performance in dyslexia. *Dyslexia: An International Journal of Research and Practice, 14*(1), 42–53.

Henrich, J., & Henrich, N. (2006). Culture, evolution and the puzzle of human cooperation. *Cognitive Systems Research. Special Issue: Cognition, Joint Action and Collective Intentionality, 7*(2–3), 220–245.

Herek, G. M. (2006, September). Legal recognition of same-sex relationships in the United States: A social science perspective. *American Psychologist, 61*(6), 607–621.

Herman-Giddens, M., Slora, E., Wasserman, R., Bourdony, C., Bhapkar, M., Koch, G., & Hasemeier, C. (1997). Secondary sex characteristics and menses in young girls seen in office practice: A study from the Pediatric Research in Office Settings network. *Pediatrics, 99,* 505–512.

Herman-Giddens, M., Wang, L., & Koch, G. (2001). Secondary sex characteristics in boys: Estimates from the National Health and Nutrition Examination Survey III, 1988–1994. *Archives of Pediatric and Adolescent Medicine, 155,* 1022–1028.

Hernàndez Blasi, C., & Bjorklund, D. F. (2003). Evolutionary developmental psychology: A new tool for better understanding human ontogeny. *Human Development, 46,* 259–281.

Herrmann, E., Call, J., Hernández-Lloreda, M. V., Hare, B., & Tomasello, M. (2007). Humans have evolved specialized skills of social cognition: The cultural intelligence hypothesis. *Science, 317*(5843), 1360–1366.

Herrnstein, R. J., & Murray, C. (1994). *The bell curve: Intelligence and class structure in American life.* New York: Free Press.

Hespos, S., & Baillargeon, R. (2006). Decalage in infants' knowledge about occlusion and containment events: Converging evidence from action tasks. *Cognition, 99,* 31–41.

Hetherington, E. M. (1988). Parents, children, and siblings: Six years after divorce. In R. A. Hinde & J. Stevenson-Hinde (Eds.), *Relationships within families: Mutual influences.* Oxford, England: Oxford University Press.

Hetherington, E. M. (2006). The influence of conflict, marital problem solving and parenting on children's adjustment in nondivorced, divorced and remarried families. In A. Clarke-Stewart & J. Dunn (Eds.), *Families count: Effects on child and adolescent development. The Jacobs Foundation series on adolescence* (pp. 203–237). New York: Cambridge University Press.

Hetherington, E. M., Collins, W. A., & Laursen, E. (1999). Social capital and the development of youth from nondivorced, divorced and remarried families. In W. A. Collins (Ed.), *Relationships as developmental contexts* (pp. 177–209). Mahwah, NJ: Lawrence Erlbaum Associates.

Hewlett, B. S. (1992). The parent-infant relationship and socio-emotional development among Aka pygmies. In J. L. Roopnarine & D. B. Carter (Eds.), *Parent-child socialization in diverse cultures: Vol. 5* (pp. 223–244). Norwood, NJ: Ablex.

Hewlett, B., & Lamb, M. (2005). Emerging issues in the study of hunter-gatherer children. In B. Hewlitt & M. Lamb (Eds.), *Hunter-gatherer childhoods: Evolutionary, cultural and developmental perspectives.* New Brunswick, NJ: Transaction Publishers.

Hewlett, B. S., Lamb, M. E., Shannon, D., Leyendecker, B., & Schölmerich, A. (1998). "Culture and early infancy among central African foragers and farmers": Correction to Hewlett et al. (1998). *Developmental Psychology, 34*(5), 891.

Heywood, C. (2001). *A history of childhood: Children and childhood from medieval to modern times.* Malden, MA: Polity Press.

Hickling, A. K., & Wellman, H. M. (2001). The emergence of children's causal explanations and theories: Evidence from everyday conversation. *Developmental Psychology, 37*(5), 668–683.

Hicks, L. E., Langham, R. A., & Takenaka, J. (1982). Cognitive and health measures following early nutritional supplementation: A sibling study. *American Journal of Public Health, 72,* 1110–1118.

Hiebert, J., Stigler, J. W., Jacobs, J. K., Givvin, K. B., Garnier, H., Smith, M., et al. (2005). Mathematics teaching in the United States today (and tomorrow): Results from the TIMSS 1999 Video Study. *Educational Evaluation and Policy Analysis, 27*(2), 111–132.

Hindman, H. D. (2002). *Child labor: An American history.* Armonk, NY: Sharpe.

Hindmarsh, P. C., Geary, M. P., Rodeck, C. H., Kingdom, J. C., & Cole, T. J. (2008). Factors predicting ante- and postnatal growth. *Pediatric Research, 63*(1), 99–102.

Hodges, J., & Tizard, B. (1989a). IQ and behavioral adjustments of ex-institutional adolescents. *Journal of Child Psychology and Psychiatry, 30,* 53–75.

Hodges, J., & Tizard, B. (1989b). Social and family relationships of ex-institutional adolescents. *Journal of Child Psychology and Psychiatry, 30,* 77–97.

Hofer, B. (2008). Personal epistemology and culture. In M. Khine (Ed.), *Knowing, knowledge and beliefs: Epistemological studies across diverse cultures* (pp. 3–22). New York: Springer Science + Business Media.

Hoff, E. (2001). *Language development.* Belmont, CA: Wadsworth.

Hoff, E. (2006, March). How social contexts support and shape language development. *Developmental Review, 26*(1), 55–88.

Hoff-Ginsberg, E., & Tardiff, T. (1995). Socioeconomic status and parenting. In M. H. Bornstein (Ed.), *Handbook of parenting: Biology and ecology of parenting: Vol. 2* (pp. 161–188). Mahwah, NJ: Lawrence Erlbaum Associates

Holcroft, C. J., Blakemore, K. J., Allen, M. A., & Graham, E. M. (2003). Prematurity and neonatal infection are most predictive of neurologic morbidity in very low birthweight infants. *Obstetrics & Gynecology, 101*(6), 1249–1254.

Holden, G. W. (2002). Perspectives on the effects of corporal punishment: Comment on Gershoff (2002). *Psychological Bulletin, 128,* 590–595.

Holmbeck, G. N. (1996). A model of family relational transformations during the transition to adolescence: Parent-adolescent conflict and adaptation. In J. A. Graber & J. Brooks-Gunn (Eds.), *Transitions through adolescence: Interpersonal domains and context* (pp. 167–199). Mahwah, NJ: Lawrence Erlbaum Associates.

Holmbeck, G. N., Paikoff, R. L., & Brooks-Gunn, J. (1995). Parenting adolescents. In M. H. Bornstein (Ed.), *Handbook of parenting: Children and parenting: Vol. 1* (pp. 91–118). Mahwah, NJ: Lawrence Erlbaum Associates.

Holm-Denoma, J. M., Lewinsohn, P. M., Gau, J. M., Joiner, T. E., Jr., Striegel-Moore, R., & Otamendi, A. (2005, November). Parents' reports of the body shape and feeding habits of 36-month-old children: An investigation of gender differences. *International Journal of Eating Disorders, 38*(3), 228–235.

Holowka, S., & Petitto, L. A. (2002). Left hemisphere cerebral specialization for babies while babbling. *Science, 297*(5586).

Holsti, L., Grunau, R. V. E., & Whitfield, M. F. (2002). Developmental coordination disorder in extremely low birth weight children at nine years. *Journal of Developmental and Behavioral Pediatrics, 23*(1), 9–15.

Holyoke, N. (1997). *A smart girl's guide to manners.* Middleton, WI: Pleasant Co.

Honwana, A. (2000). Children of war: Understanding war and war cleansing in Mozambique and Angola. Retrieved April 25, 2006, from http://cas.uchicago.edu/workshops/African/papers/honwana.htm

Hopkins, B., & Westen, T. (1988). Maternal handling and motor development: An intracultural study. *Genetic Psychology Monographs, 14,* 377–420.

Horn, T. S. (Ed.). (2002). *Advances in sport psychology.* Champaign, IL Human Kinetics.

Hoshower, L. M., Buikstra, J. E., Goldstein, P. S., & Webster, A. D. (1995). Artificial cranial deformation at the Omo M10 site: A Tiwanaku complex from the Moquegua Valley, Peru. *Latin American Antiquity, 6,* 145–164.

Hossain, Z., Roopnarine, J. L., Ismail, R., Hashmi, S., & Sombuling, A. (2007). Fathers' and mothers' reports of involvement in caring for infants in Kadazan families in Sabah, Malaysia. *Fathering, 5*(1), 58–72.

Hoven, C. W., Duarte, C. S., Wu, P., Erickson, E. A., Musa, G. J., & Mandell, D. J. (2004, October). Exposure to trauma and separation anxiety in children after the WTC attack. *Applied Developmental Science. 8*(4), 172–183.

Howe, N., Brody, M.-H., & Recchia, H. (2006). Effects of task difficulty on sibling teaching in middle childhood. *Infant and Child Development, 15*(5), 455–470.

Howell, S. (1984). Equality and hierarchy in Chewong classification. *Journal of the Anthropological Society of Oxford, 15*(1), 30–44.

Howes, C. (1999). Attachment relationships in the context of multiple caregivers. In J. Cassidy & P. R. Shaver (Eds.), *Handbook of attachment: Theory, research, and clinical applications* (pp. 671–687). New York: Guilford Press.

Hrdy, S. B. (2007). Evolutionary context of human development: The cooperative breeding model. In C. A. Salmon & T. D. Shackelford (Eds.), *Family relationships: An evolutionary perspective* (pp. 39–68). New York: Oxford University Press.

Huang-Pollack, C. L., Carr, T. H., & Nigg, J. T. (2002). Development of selective attention: Perceptual load influences early versus late attentional selection in children and adults. *Developmental Psychology, 38*(3), 363–375.

Hubel, D., & Wiesel, T. (2004). *Brain and visual perception: The story of a 25-year collaboration.* New York: Oxford University Press.

Huelsken, C., Sodian, B., & Pickel, G. (2001). Distinguishing between appearance and reality in a dressing-up game—a problem of dual coding or preserving identity? *Zeitschrift für Entwicklungspsychologie und Paedagogische Psychologie, 33*(3), 129–137.

Hughes, C., Jafee, S., Happe, F., Taylor, A., Caspi, A., & Moffitt, T. (2005). Origins of individuals differences in theory of mind: From nature to nurture. *Child Development, 76*(2), 356–370.

Hughes, D. (2003). Correlates of African American and Latino parents' messages to children about ethnicity and race: A comparative study of racial socialization. *American Journal of Community Psychology, 31,* 15–33.

Hughes, D., & Chen, L. (1999). The nature of parents' race-related communications to children: A developmental perspective. In L. Balter & C. S. Tamis-LeMonda (Eds.), *Child psychology: A handbook of contemporary issues* (pp. 467–490). Philadelphia: Psychology Press.

Hughes, D., Rodriguez, J., Smith, E., Johnson, D. J., Stevenson, H. C., & Spicer, P. (2006, September). Parents' ethnic-racial socialization practices: A review of research and directions for future study. *Developmental Psychology, 42*(5), 747–770.

Hughes, H., Graham-Bermann, S., & Gruber, G. (2001). Resilience in children exposed to domestic violence. In S. Graham-Bermann & J. Edleson (Eds.), *Domestic violence in the lives of children: The future of research, intervention and social policy.* Washington, DC: American Psychological Association.

Huizink, A. C., & Mulder, E. J. (2006). Maternal smoking, drinking or cannabis use during pregnancy and neurobehavioral and cognitive functioning in human offspring. *Neuroscience & Biobehavioral Reviews, 30*(1), 24–41.

Hulbert, A. (2003). *Raising America: Experts, parents, and a century of advice about children.* New York: Knopf.

Hunsley, M., & Thoman, E. B. (2002). The sleep of co-sleeping infants when they are not co-sleeping: Evidence that co-sleeping is stressful. *Developmental Psychobiology, 40*(1), 14–22.

Hussong, A. M., Zucker, R. A., Wong, M. M., Fitzgerald, H. E., & Puttler, L. I. (2005, September). Social competence in children of alcoholic parents over time. *Developmental Psychology, 41*(5), 747–759.

Huttenlocher, P. R. (1994). Synaptogenesis in human cerebral cortex. In G. Dawson & K. W. Fischer (Eds.), *Human behavior and the developing brain.* New York: Guilford Press.

Hutto, D. D. (2008, April). *Folk psychological narratives: The sociocultural basis of understanding reasons.* Cambridge, MA: The MIT Press.

Huynh, V. W., & Fuligni, A. J. (2008, July). Ethnic socialization and the academic adjustment of adolescents from Mexican, Chinese, and European backgrounds. *Developmental Psychology, 44*(4), 1202–1208.

Hymel, S., Vaillancourt, T., McDougall, P., & Renshaw, P. D. (2002). Peer acceptance and rejection in childhood. In P. K. Smith & C. H. Hart (Eds.), *Blackwell handbook of childhood social development* (pp. 265–284). Malden, MA: Blackwell Publishing.

Hymel, S., Wagner, E., & Butler, L. J. (1990). Reputational bias: View from the peer group. In S. R. Asher & J. D. Coie (Eds.), *Peer rejection in childhood.* Cambridge, England: Cambridge University Press.

Inagaki, K., & Hatano, G. (2002). *Young children's naive thinking about the biological world.* New York: Psychology Press.

Inhelder, B., & Piaget, J. (1958). *The growth of logical thinking from childhood to adolescence.* New York: Basic Books.

Inoue-Nakamura, N. (2001). Mirror self-recognition in primates: An ontogenetic and a phylogenetic approach. In T. Matsuzawa (Ed.), *Primate origins of human cognition and behavior* (pp. 297–312). New York: Springer-Verlag.

Institute of Medicine. (1990). *Nutrition during pregnancy: Part I, weight gain; Part II, nutrient supplements.* Washington, DC: National Academy Press.

ISPCAN. (2006). *World perspectives on child abuse* (7th ed.). Chicago: National Society for the Prevention of Child Abuse and Neglect.

Itard, J. M. G. (1801/1982). *The wild boy of Aveyron.* New York: Appleton-Century-Crofts.

Ivey, P. (2000). Cooperative reproduction in Ituri Forest huntergatherers: Who cares for Efe infants? *Current Anthropology, 41,* 856–866.

Izard, C. E., & Abe, J. (2004). Developmental changes in facial expressions of emotions in the strange situation during the second year of life. *Emotion, 4,* 251–265.

Izard, C. E., Huebner, R. R., Risser, D., McGinnes, G. C., & Dougherty, L. M. (1980). The young infant's ability to produce discrete emotion expressions. *Developmental Psychology, 16,* 132–140.

Izawa, E.-I., Yanagihara, S., Atsumi, T., & Matsushima, T. (2001). The role of basal ganglia in reinforcement learning and imprinting in domestic chicks. *Neuroreport: For Rapid Communication of Neuroscience Research, 12*(8), 1743–1747.

Jablonka, E., & Lamb, M. (2005). *Evolution in four dimensions.* Cambridge, MA: The MIT Press.

Jablonka, E., & Lamb, M. J. (2007). Precis of evolution in four dimensions. *Behavioral and Brain Sciences, 30*(4), 353–365.

Jackson, J. P., Jr. (2006). The historical context of the African American social scientist. *Monographs of the Society for Research in Child Development, 71*(1), 218–223.

Jackson, J. S., McCullough, W. R., & Gurin, G. (1997). Family, socialization environment, and identity development in Black Americans. In H. P. McAdoo (Ed.), *Black families* (3rd ed., pp. 251–266). Thousand Oaks, CA: Sage.

Jaeger, J. (2005). *Kids' slips: What young children's slips of the tongue reveal about language development.* Mahwah, NJ: Lawrence Erlbaum Associates.

Jaffe, J., Beebe, B., Feldstein, S., Crown, C. L., & Jasnow, M. D. (2001, April). *Monographs of the Society for Research in Child Development, 66*(2), vii–131.

Jahoda, G. (1980). Theoretical and systematic approaches in cross-cultural psychology. In H. C. Triandis & W. W. Lambert (Eds.), *Handbook of cross-cultural psychology: Vol. 1.* Boston: Allyn & Bacon.

James, D., Pillai, M., & Smoleniec, J. (1995). Neurobehavioral development in the human fetus. In J. P. Lecanuet & W. P. Fifer (Eds.), *Fetal development: A psychobiological perspective* (pp. 101–128). Mahwah, NJ: Lawrence Erlbaum Associates.

James, W. T. (1890). *The principles of psychology.* New York: Holt, Rinehart and Winston.

James, W. T. (1951). Social organization among dogs of different temperaments: Terriers and beagles reared together. *Journal of Comparative and Physiological Psychology, 44,* 71–77.

Janowsky, J. S., & Carper, R. (1996). Is there a neural basis for cognitive transitions in school-age children? In Arnold J. Sameroff & M. M. Haith (Eds.), *The five to seven year shift: The age of reason and responsibility.* Chicago: University of Chicago Press.

Jansz, J. (2000). Masculine identity and restrictive emotionality. In A. H. Fischer (Ed.), *Gender and emotion: Social psychological perspectives* (pp. 24–47). Cambridge, England: Cambridge University Press.

Jarrett, R. (2000). Voices from below: The use of ethnographic research for informing public policy. In J. Mercier, S. Garasky, & M. Shelly (Eds.), *Redefining family policy: Implications for the 21st century.* Ames, IA: Iowa State University Press.

Jason, L. A., Keys, C. B., Suarez-Balcazar, Y., Taylor, R. R., & Davis, M. I. (Eds.). (2004). *Participatory community research: Theories and methods in action (APA decade of behavior).* Washington, DC: American Psychological Association.

Jenkins, H. (Ed.). (1998). *The children's culture reader.* New York: New York University Press.

Jenni, O., Deboer, T., & Achermann, P (2006). Development of the 24-h rest-activity pattern in human infants. *Infant Behavior & Development, 29,* 143–152.

Jennings, K. D., & Dietz, L. J. (2003). Mastery motivation and goal persistence in young children. In M. H. Bornstein, L. Davidson, C. L. Keyes, K. A. Moore, & the Center for Child Well Being (Eds.), *Well-being: Positive development across the life course. Crosscurrents in contemporary psychology* (pp. 295–309). Mahwah, NJ, Lawrence Erlbaum Associates.

Jensen, L. A. (2008). Coming of age in a multicultural world: Globalization and adolescent cultural identity formation. In D. L. Browning (Ed,), *Adolescent identities: A collection of readings. Relational perspectives book series* (pp. 3–17). New York: The Analytic Press/Taylor & Francis Group.

Jocklin, V., McGue, M., & Lykken, D. (1996). Personality and divorce: A genetic analysis. *Journal of Personality and Social Psychology, 71*(2), 288–299.

Jodl, K. M., Michael, A., Malanchuk, O., Eccles, J., & Sameroff, A. (2001). Parents' roles in shaping early adolescents' occupational aspirations. *Child Development, 72,* 1247–1265.

Joh, A., Sweeney, B., & Rovee-Collier, C. (2002). Minimum duration of reactivation at 3 months of age. *Developmental Psychobiology, 40*(1), 23–32.

John, V. P. (1972). Styles of learning—styles of teaching: Reflections on the education of Navajo children. In C. Cazden, V. P. John, & D. Hymes (Eds.), *Functions of language in the classroom* (pp. 331–343). New York: Teachers College Press.

Johnson, D. (2001). Parental characteristics, racial stress, and racial socialization processes as predictors of racial coping in middle childhood. In A. M. Neal-Barnett, J. Contreras, & K. Kerns (Eds.), *Forging links: African American children—clinical and developmental perspectives.* Westport, CT: Praeger.

Johnson, D., Jaeger, E., Randolph, S., Cauce, A., Ward, J., & NICHD (2003). Studying the effects of early child care experiences on the development of children of color in the United States: Toward a more inclusive research agenda. *Child Development, 74,* 1227–1244.

Johnson, S., Amso, D., & Slemmer, J. (2003). Development of object concepts in infancy: Evidence for early learning in an eye-tracking paradigm. *Proceedings of the National Academy of Science, USA, 100,* 10568–10573.

Jolly, A. (1999). *Lucy's legacy: Sex and intelligence in human evolution.* Cambridge, MA: Harvard University Press.

Jones, H. E. (2006). Drug addiction during pregnancy: Advances in maternal treatment and understanding child outcomes. *Current Directions in Psychological Science, 15*(3), 126–130.

Jones, M., Yonezawa, S., Ballesteros, E., & Mehan, H. (2002). Shaping pathways to higher education. *Educational Researcher, 3,* 3–17.

Jones, R. E. (1997). *Human reproductive biology.* San Diego: Academic Press.

Jones, S. M., & Zigler, E. (2002). The Mozart effect: Not learning from history. *Journal of Applied Developmental Psychology, 23*(3), 355–372.

Jordan, B. (1993). *Birth in four cultures: A cross-cultural investigation of childbirth in Yucatan, Holland, Sweden, and the United States.* Prospect Heights, IL: Waveland Press.

Jordan, K., & Brannon, E. (2006). The multisensory representation of number in infancy. *Proceedings of the National Academy of Sciences, 103,* 3486–3489.

Joseph, J. (2001). Separated twins and the genetics of personality differences: A critique. *American Journal of Psychology, 114*(1), 1–30.

Joseph, K. S., Liston, R. M., Dodds, L., Dahlgren, L., & Allen, A. C. (2007). Socioeconomic status and perinatal outcomes in a setting with universal access to essential health care services. *Canadian Medical Association Journal, 177*(6), 583–590.

Joshi, M. S., & MacLean, M. (1994). Indian and English children's understanding of the distinction between real and apparent emotion. *Child Development, 65*(5), 1372–1384.

Juang, L. P., & Silbereisen, R. K. (2002). The relationship between adolescent academic capability beliefs, parenting and school grades. *Journal of Adolescence, 25,* 3–18.

Jung, C. (1970). *Psychoanalysis and neurosis.* Princeton, NJ: Princeton University Press.

Jusczyk, P. W. (2001). Finding and remembering words: Some beginnings by English-learning infants. In E. Bates (Ed.), *Language development: The essential readings* (pp. 19–25). Malden, MA: Blackwell Publishing.

Justice, E., Lindsey, L., & Morrow, S. (1999). The relation of self-perceptions to achievement among African American preschoolers. *Journal of Black Psychology, 25,* 48–60.

Juston, A., Bickham, D., Lee, J., & Wright, J. (2007). From attention to comprehension: How children watch and learn from television. In N. Pecora, J. Murray, & E. Wartella (Eds.), *Children and television: Fifty years of research.* Mahwah, NJ: Lawrence Erlbaum Associates.

Kagan, J. (2000). Human morality is distinctive. *Journal of Consciousness Studies, 7*(1–2), 46–48.

Kagan, J. (2001). Biological constraint, cultural variety, and psychological structures. In A. Harrington (Ed.), *Unity of knowledge: The convergence of natural and human science* (pp. 177–190). New York: New York Academy of Sciences.

Kagan, S., & Madsen, M. C. (1971). Cooperation and competition of Mexican, Mexican-American, and Anglo-American children of two ages under four instructional sets. *Developmental Psychology, 5,* 32–39.

Kagitçibasi, C. (1997). Individualism and collectivism. In J. Berry, M. H. Segall, & C. Kagitçibasi (Eds.), *Handbook of cross-cultural psychology: Vol. 3* (pp. 1–50). Needham Heights, MA: Allyn & Bacon.

Kagitçibasi, C. (2003). Autonomy, embeddedness and adaptability in immigration contexts. *Human Development, 46*(2–3), 145–150.

Kaiser Foundation. (2008, March). *HIV/AIDS policy fact sheet 2008.* Retrieved October 10, 2008, from http://www.kff.org/hivaids/upload/3029-09.pdf

Kaltenbach, K., Berghella, V., Finnegan, L., & Woods, J. R., Jr. (1998). Opioid dependence during pregnancy: effects and management in substance abuse in pregnancy. *Obstetrics and Gynecology Clinics of North America, 25*(1), 139–152.

Kamara, A. I., & Easley, J. A. (1977). Is the rate of cognitive development uniform across cultures? A methodological critique with new evidence from Themne children. In P. R. Dasen (Ed.), *Piagetian psychology: Cross-cultural contributions.* New York: Gardner.

Kandel, D. (1978). Homophily, selection, and socialization in adolescent friendships. *American Journal of Sociology, 84,* 427–436.

Kandel, D. B., & Chen, K. (2000, May). Types of marijuana users by longitudinal course. *Journal of Studies on Alcohol, 61*(3), 367–378.

Kaplan, H., & Dove, H. (1987). Infant development among the Ache of Eastern Paraguay. *Developmental Psychology, 23,* 190–198.

Kaplan, H., Lancaster, J., Hill, K., Hurtado, M., & Robson, A. (2003). Embodied capital and the evolutionary economics of the human life span. *Population and Development Review 29*(3) Suppl., 152–182.

Kaplowitz, P. B. (2008, February). Link between body fat and the timing of puberty. *Pediatrics, 121*(Suppl. 3), S208–S217.

Kaplowitz, P. B., Slora, E., Wasserman, R., Pedlow, S., Herman-Giddens, M. (2001). Earlier onset of puberty in girls: Relations to increased body mass index and race. *Pediatrics, 108,* 347–353.

Karmiloff, K., & Karmiloff-Smith, A. (2001). *Pathways to language: From fetus to adolescent.* Cambridge, MA: Harvard University Press.

Karsten, S. L., Sang, T.-K., Gehman, L. T., Chatterjee, S., Liu J., Lawless, G. M., et al. (2006). A genomic screen for modifiers of tauopathy identifies puromycin-sensitive aminopeptidase as an inhibitor of tau-induced neurodegeneration. *Neuron, 51*(5), 549–560.

Kaslow, F. (2001). Families and family psychology at the millennium. *American Psychologist, 56,* 37–46.

Katchadourian, H. A. (1977). *The biology of adolescence.* San Francisco: Freeman.

Kaufman, J., & Zigler, E. (1989). The intergenerational transmission of child abuse. In D. Cicchetti & V. Carlson (Eds.), *Child maltreatment: Theory and research on the causes and consequences of child abuse and neglect.* Cambridge, England: Cambridge University Press.

Kaye, K. (1982). *The mental and social life of babies.* Chicago: University of Chicago Press.

Keating, D. (2004). Cognitive and brain development. In R. M. Lerner & L. Steinberg (Eds.), *Handbook of adolescent psychology* (2nd ed.). Hoboken, NJ: John Wiley & Sons.

Keel, P. K., Dorer, D. J., Eddy, K. T., Franko, D., Charatan, D. L., & Herzog, D. B. (2003). Predictors of mortality in eating disorders. *Archives of General Psychiatry, 60*(2), 179–183.

Keel, P. K., & Klump, K. L. (2003). Are eating disorders culture-bound syndromes? Implications for conceptualizing their etiology. *Psychological Bulletin, 129*(5), 747–769.

Keenan, K., & Hipwell, A. (2005). Preadolescent clues to understanding depression in girls. *Clinical Child and Family Psychology Review, 8,* 89–105.

Keeney, T. J., Cannizzo, S. D., & Flavell, J. H. (1967). Spontaneous and induced verbal rehearsal in a recall task. *Child Development, 38,* 935–966.

Keller, H. (2003). Socialization for competence: Cultural models of infancy. *Human Development, 46*(5), 228–311.

Kelley, T. (2005, October 9). Toilet training at 6 months? Better take a seat. *New York Times.*

Kellman, P. J., & Banks, M. S. (1998). Infant visual perception. In R. Siegler & D. Kuhn (Eds.), *Handbook of child psychology: Vol. 2* (5th ed., pp. 103–146). New York: Wiley.

Kellogg, W. N., & Kellogg, L. A. (1933). *The ape and the child: A study of environmental influences upon early behavior.* New York: Whittlesey House.

Keniston, K. (1963). Social change and youth in America. In E. Erikson (Ed.), *Youth: Change and challenge.* New York: Basic Books.

Kermayer, L. (1994). Suicide among Canadian aboriginal people. *Transcultural Psychiatric Research Review, 31,* 3–57.

Kesmodel, U. (2001). Binge drinking in pregnancy: Frequency and methodology. *American Journal of Epidemiology, 154*(8), 777–782.

Kesner, J., & McKenry, P. (2001). Single parenthood and social competence in children of color. *Families in Society, 82,* 136–144.

Kett, J. F. (1977). *Rites of passage: Adolescence in America 1790 to the present.* New York: Basic Books.

Kiell, N. (1959). *The adolescent through fiction: A psychological approach.* New York: International Universities Press.

Killen, M., McGlothlin, H., & Lee–Kim, J. (2002). Between individuals and culture: Individuals' evaluations of exclusion from social groups. In H. Keller, Y. Poortinga, & A. Schoelmerich (Eds.), *Between biology and culture: Perspectives on ontogenetic development.* Cambridge, England: Cambridge University Press.

Killen, M., & Smetana, J. (2007, September). The biology of morality: Human development and moral neuroscience. *Human Development, 50*(5), 241–243.

Killen, M., & Stangor, C. (2001). Children's social reasoning about inclusion and exclusion in gender and race peer group contexts. *Child Development, 72*(1), 174–186.

Kim, E., Han, G., & McCubbin, M. A. (2007). Korean American maternal acceptance-rejection, acculturation, and children's social competence. *Family & Community Health, 30*(Suppl. 2), S33–S45.

Kim, I. J., Kim, L. I. C., Kelly, J. G. (2006, March). Developing cultural competence in working with Korean immigrant families. *Journal of Community Psychology. Special Issue: Addressing mental health disparities through culturally competent research and community-based practice, 34*(2), 149–165.

Kim, I.-K., & Spelke, E. S. (1999). Perception and understanding of effects of gravity and inertia on object motion. *Developmental Science 2*(3), 339–362.

Kim, J. M. (1998). Korean children's concepts of adult and per authority and moral reasoning. *Developmental Psychology, 34,* 947–955.

Kim, J.-Y., McHale, S. M., Crouter, A. C., & Osgood, D. W. (2007, July). Longitudinal linkages between sibling relationships and adjustment from middle childhood through adolescence. *Developmental Psychology, 43*(4), 960–973.

Kim, K., Conger, R., Lorenz, F., & Elder, G. (2001). Parent-adolescent reciprocity in negative affect and its relation to early adult social development. *Developmental Psychology, 37,* 775–790.

Kim, K., & Rohner, R. (2002). Parental warmth, control and involvement in schooling: Predicting academic achievement in Korean American adolescents. *Journal of Cross-Cultural Psychology, 33,* 127–140.

Kim, U., & Park, Y.-S. (2006). The scientific foundation of indigenous and cultural psychology: The transactional approach. In U. Kim, K.-S. Yang, & K.-K. Hwang (Eds.), *Indigenous and cultural psychology: Understanding people in context* (pp. 27–48). New York: Springer Science + Business Media.

Kirsh, S. (2006). *Children, adolescence and media violence: A critical look at research.* New York: Sage.

Kirsten, G. F., Bergman, N. J., & Hann, F. M. (2001). Kangaroo mother care in the nursery. *Pediatric Clinics of North America, 48*(2), xvi, 443–452.

Kisilevsky, B. S., Hains, S. M., Lee, K. Muir, D. W., Xu, F., Fu, G., et al. (1998). The still-face effect in Chinese and Canadian 3- to 6-month-old infants. *Child Developmental Psychology, 34,* 629–639.

Kisilevsky, B. S., Hains, S. M., & Low, J. A. (2001). Maturation of fetal heart rate and body movement in 24–33-week-old fetuses threatening to deliver prematurely. *Developmental Psychobiology, 38*(1), 78–86.

Kisilevsky, B. S., & Low, J. A. (1998). Human fetal behavior: 100 years of study. *Developmental Review, 18,* 1–29.

Kitamura, C., Thanavishuth, C., Luksaneeyanawin, S., & Burnham, D. (2002). Universality and specificity in infant-directed speech: Pitch modifications as a function of infant age and sex in a tonal and non-tonal language. *Infant Behavior & Development, 24*(4), 372–392.

Klaczynski, P. A., & Cottrell, J. M. (2004, March). A dual-process approach to cognitive development: The case of children's understanding of sunk cost decisions. *Thinking & Reasoning, 10*(2), 147–174.

Klahr, D. (1989). Information-processing approaches. In R. Vasta (Ed.), *Annals of child development: Vol. 6. Six theories of child development: Revised formulations and current issues.* Greenwich, CT: JAI Press.

Klaus, M. H., Kennell, J. H., & Klaus, P. H. (1995). *Bonding: Building the foundations of secure attachment and independence.* Reading, MA: Addison-Wesley.

Klebanoff, M. A., Levine, R. J., Clemens, J. D., & Wilkins, D. G. (2002). Maternal serum caffeine metabolites and small-for-gestational-age birth. *American Journal of Epidemiology, 155*(1), 32–37.

Klineberg, O. (1935). *Race differences.* New York: Harper & Row.

Klinger, J., Vaughn, B., & Schumm, J. (1998). Collaborative strategic reading during social studies and heterogeneous fourth-grade classrooms. *The Elementary School Journal, 96,* 275–293.

Klumpp, A., Domingos, M., & Klumpp, G. (2002). Foliar nutrient contents in tree species of the Atlantic rain forest as influenced by air pollution from the industrial complex of Cubatao, SE-Brazil. *Water Air and Soil Pollution, 133*(1–4), 315–333.

Kochanska, G., & Askan, N. (1995). Mother-child mutually positive affect, the quality of child compliance to requests, and prohibitions, and maternal control as correlates of early internalization. *Child Development, 66,* 236–254.

Kochanska, G., & Aksan, N. (2006, December). Children's conscience and self-regulation. *Journal of Personality, 74*(6), 1587–1617.

Kochanska, G., Aksan, N., Penney, S. J., & Doobay, A. F. (2007, December). Early positive emotionality as a heterogenous trait: Implications for children's self-regulation. *Journal of Personality and Social Psychology, 93*(6), 1054–1066.

Kochukhova, O., & Gredebäck, G. (2007). Learning about occlusion: Initial assumptions and rapid adjustments. *Cognition, 105*(1), 26–46.

Kohlberg, L. (1966). A cognitive-developmental analysis of children's sex role concepts and attitudes. In E. E. Maccoby (Ed.), *The development of sex differences.* Palo Alto, CA: Stanford University Press.

Kohlberg, L. (1969). Stage and sequence: The cognitive-developmental approach to socialization. In D. A. Goslin (Ed.), *Handbook of socialization theory and research.* Chicago: Rand McNally.

Kohlberg, L. (1976). Moral stages and moralization: The cognitive-developmental approach. In J. Lickona (Ed.), *Moral development behavior: Theory, research and social issues.* New York: Holt, Rinehart and Winston.

Kohlberg, L. (1984). *The psychology of moral development: The nature and validity of moral stages: Vol. 2.* New York: Harper & Row.

Kokis, J., Macpherson, R., Toplak, M., West, R., & Stanovich, K. (2002). Heuristic and analytic processing: Age trends and associations with cognitive ability and cognitive styles. *Journal of Experimental Child Psychology, 83,* 26–52.

Kolata, G. (1986). Obese children: A growing problem. *Science, 232,* 20–21.

Konner, M. (1977). Evolution in human behavior development. In P. H. Leiderman, S. Tulkin, & A. Rosenfeld (Eds.), *Culture and infancy: Variations in human experience.* New York: Academic Press.

Konner, M. (2005). Hunter-gatherer infancy and childhood: The !Kung and others. In B. S. Hewlett & M. E. Lamb (Eds.), *Hunter-gatherer childhoods.* New Brunswick, NJ: Aldine Transaction.

Kontulainen, S. A., Hughes, J. M., Macdonald, H. M., & Johnston, J. D. (2007). The biomechanical basis of bone strength development during growth. *Medicine and Sport Science, 51,* 13–32.

Koopmans-van Beinum, F. J., Clement, C. J., & van den Dikkenberg-Pot, I. (2001). Babbling and the lack of auditory speech perception: A matter of coordination? *Developmental Science, 4*(1), 61–70.

Korner, A. F., & Constantinou, J. C. (2001). The neurobehavioral assessment of the preterm infant: Reliability and developmental and clinical validity. In L. T. Singer & P. S. Zeskind (Eds.), *Biobehavioral assessment of the infant* (pp. 381–397). New York: Guilford Press.

Koyama, R., Takahashi, Y., & Mori, K. (2006). Assessing the cuteness of children: Significant factors and gender differences. *Social Behavior and Personality, 34*(9), 1087–1100.

Krasnogorski, N. I. (1907/1967). The formation of artificial conditioned reflexes in young children. In Y. Brackbill & G. G. Thompson (Eds.), *Behavior in infancy and early childhood: A book of readings.* New York: Free Press.

Krcmar, M., & Vieira, E. T., Jr. (2005, June). Imitating life, imitating television: The effects of family and television models on children's moral reasoning. *Communication Research, 32*(3), 267–294.

Kreutzer, M. A., Leonard, S. C., & Flavell, J. H. (1975). An interview study of children's knowledge about memory. *Monographs of the Society for Research in Child Development, 40*(1, Serial No. 159).

Kroger, J. (2003). What transits in an identity status transition? *Identity, 3*(3), 197–220.

Kuhl, P. K. (2001). Speech, language, and developmental change. In F. Lacerda, C. von Hofsten, & M. Heimann (Eds.), *Emerging cognitive abilities in early infancy* (pp. 111–133). Mahwah, NJ: Lawrence Erlbaum Associates.

Kuhl, P. K., Stevens, E., Hayashi, A., Deguchi, T., Kiritani, S., & Iverson, P. (2006). Infants show a facilitation effect for native language phonetic perception between 6 and 12 months. *Developmental Science, 9*(2), F13–F21.

Kulis, S., Napoli, M., & Marsiglia, F. (2002). Ethnic pride, biculturalism, and drug use norms of urban American Indian adolescents. *Social Work Research, 26,* 101–112.

Kumra, S., Giedd, J., Vaituzis, A., & Jacobsen, L. (2000). Childhood-onset psychotic disorders: Magnetic resonance imaging of volumetric differences in brain structure. *American Journal of Psychiatry, 157,* 1467–1474.

Kupersmidt, J. B., Coie, J. D., & Howell, J. C. (2004). Resilience in children exposed to negative peer influences. In K. I. Maton, C. J. Schellenbach, B. J. Leadbeater, & A. L. Solarz (Eds.), *Investing in children, youth, families, and communities: Strengths-based research and policy* (pp. 251–268). Washington, DC: American Psychological Association.

Kushnir, T., & Gopnik, A. (2005, September). Young children infer causal strength from probabilities and interventions. *Psychological Science, 16*(9), 678–683.

Kushnir, T., & Gopnik, A. (2007). Conditional probability versus spatial contiguity in causal learning: Preschoolers use new contingency evidence to overcome prior spatial assumptions. *Developmental Psychology, 43*(1), 186–196.

Kusiako, T., Ronsmans, C., & Van der Paal, L. (2000). Perinatal mortality attributable to complications of childbirth in Matlab, Bangladesh. *Bulletin of the World Health Organization, 78*(5), 621–627.

Kuther, T., & Higgins-D'Alessandro, A. (2000). Bridging the gap between moral reasoning and adolescent engagement in risky behavior. *Journal of Adolescence, 23,* 409–422.

Kuttler, A., & La Greca, A. (2004). Linkages among adolescent girls' romantic relationships, best friendships, and peer networks. *Journal of Adolescence, 27,* 395–414.

Laberge, L., Petit, D., Simard, C., Vitaro, F., Tremblay, R., & Montplaisir, J. (2001). Development of sleep patterns in early adolescence. *Journal of Sleep Research, 10,* 59–67.

Laboratory of Comparative Human Cognition. (1983). Culture and cognitive development. In P. Mussen (Ed.), *Handbook of child psychology: Vol. 1. History, theory, and methods* (4th ed.). New York: Wiley.

Ladd, G. W. (1999). Peer relationships and social competence during early and middle childhood. *Annual Review of Psychology, 50,* 333–359.

Ladd, G. W., & Troop-Gordon, W. (2003). The role of chronic peer difficulties in the development of children's psychological adjustment problems. *Child Development, 74*(5), 1344–1367.

LaFromboise, T., Hoyr, D., Oliver, L., & Whitbeck, L. (2006). Family, community, and school influences on resilience among American Indian adolescents in the upper Midwest. *Journal of Community Psychology, 34,* 193–209.

Lagercrantz, H., & Slotkin, T. A. (1986). The "stress" of being born. *Scientific American, 254,* 100–107.

Lahey, B. B., Schwab-Stone, M., Goodman, S. H., Waldman, I. D., Canino, G., Rathouz, P. J.; et al. (2000, August). Age and gender differences in oppositional behavior and conduct problems: A cross-sectional household study of middle childhood and adolescence. *Journal of Abnormal Psychology, 109*(3), 488–503.

Laland, K., Odling-Smee, J., & Feldman, M. (2000). Niche construction, biological evolution, and cultural change. *Behavioral and Brain Sciences, 23,* 131–175.

Lalonde, C. E. (2003). Counting the costs of failures of personal and cultural continuity. *Human Development, 46*(2–3), 137–144.

Lamb, M. E., & Ahnert, L. (2006). Nonparental child care: Context, concepts, correlates, and consequences. In K. A. Renninger, I. E. Sigel, W. Damon, & R. M. Lerner (Eds.), *Handbook of child psychology: Vol. 4. Child psychology in practice* (6th ed., pp. 950–1016). Hoboken, NJ: John Wiley & Sons.

Lamb, M. E., Hwang, C. P., Ketterlinus, R. D., & Fracasso, M. P. (1999). Parent-child relationships: Development in the context of the family. In M. H. Bornstein & M. E. Lamb (Eds.), *Developmental psychology: An advanced textbook* (pp. 411–450). Mahwah, NJ: Lawrence Erlbaum Associates.

Lamb, M. E., & Lewis, C. (2005). The role of parent-child relationships in child development. In M. H. Bornstein & M. E. Lamb (Eds.), *Developmental science: An advanced textbook* (5th ed., pp. 429–468). Mahwah, NJ: Lawrence Erlbaum Associates.

Lampert, M., & Blunk, M. L. (Eds.). (1998). *Talking mathematics in school: Studies of teaching and learning.* Cambridge, England: Cambridge University Press.

Landau, B., & Gleitman, L. R. (1985). *Language and experience: Evidence from the blind child. Cognitive science series, 8.* Cambridge, MA: Harvard University Press.

Lane, H. (1976). *The wild boy of Aveyron.* Cambridge, MA: Harvard University Press.

Langlois, J. H. (1986). From the eye of the beholder to behavioral reality: Development of social behaviors and social relations as a function of physical attractiveness. In C. P. Herman, M. P. Zanna, & E. T. Higgins (Eds.), *Physical appearance, stigma, and social behavior: The Ontario Symposium: Vol. 3.* Mahwah, NJ: Lawrence Erlbaum Associates.

Langlois, J. H., Kalakanis, L., Rubenstein, A. J., Larson, A., Hallam, M., & Smoot, M. (2000). Maxims or myths of beauty? A meta-analytic and theoretical review. *Psychological Bulletin, 126*(3), 390–423.

Langlois, J. H., Ritter, J. M., Casey, R. J., & Sawin, D. B. (1995). Infant attractiveness predicts maternal behaviors and attitudes. *Developmental Psychology, 31,* 464–472.

Lanza, S. T., & Collins, L. M. (2002, March). Pubertal timing and the onset of substance use in females during early adolescence. *Prevention Science, 3*(1), 69–82.

Largo, R. H., Molinari, L., von Siebenthal, K., & Wolfensberger, U. (1996). Does a profound change in toilet-training affect development of bowel and bladder control? *Developmental Medicine and Child Neurology, 38,* 1106–1116.

Larsen, B. (1996). Closeness and conflict in adolescent peer relationships: Interdependence with friends and romantic partneter. In W. Bukowski, A. Newcomb, & W. Hartup (Eds.), *The company they keep: Friendship in childhood and adolescence.* New York: Cambridge University Press.

Larson, R., Moneta, G., Richards, M., & Wilson, S. (2002). Continuity, stability, and change in daily emotional experience across adolescence. *Child Development, 73,* 1151–1165.

Larson, R., & Richards, M. (1991). Daily companionship in late childhood and early adolescence: Changing developmental contexts. *Child Development, 62,* 284–300.

Larson, R., & Richards, M. (2000, July). *Changes in daily emotions associated with entry into adolescence for urban African Americans.* Paper presented at the biannual meeting of the International Society for the Study of Behavioral Development, Beijing, China.

Laupa, M., Turiel, E., & Cowan, P. (1995). Obedience to authority in children and adults. In M. Killen & D. Hart (Eds.), *Morality in everyday life: Developmental perspectives* (pp. 131–165). Cambridge, England: Cambridge University Press.

Laursen, B., Coy, K. C., & Collins, W. A. (1998). Reconsidering changes in parent-child conflict across adolescence: A meta-analysis. *Child Development (Chicago), 69*(3), 817–832.

Lave, J., & Wenger, E. (1991). *Situated learning: Legitimate peripheral practice.* New York: Cambridge University Press.

Lawrence, J. A., & Valsiner, J. (2003, December). Making personal sense: An account of basic internalization and externalization processes. *Theory & Psychology, 13*(6), 723–752.

Leakey, M. D., & Hay, R. L. (1979). Pliocene footprints in the laetolil beds at Laetoli, northern Tanzania. *Nature 278*(5702), 317–323.

Lecanuet, J.-P., Granier-Deferre, C., & DeCasper, A. (2005). Are we expecting too much from prenatal sensory experiences? In B. Hopkins & S. P. Johnson (Eds.), *Prenatal development of postnatal functions (Advances in infancy research)* (pp. 31–49). Westport, CT: Praeger Publishers/Greenwood Publishing Group.

Lecanuet, J. P., Graniere-Deferre, C., Jacquet, A-Y., & DeCasper, A. J. (2000). Fetal discrimination of low-pitched musical notes. *Developmental Psychobiology, 36*(1), 29–39.

Lecanuet, J. P., & Schaal, B. (1996). Fetal sensory competencies. *European Journal of Obstetrics, Gynecology, and Reproductive Biology, 68,* 1–23.

Lee, B. H., Stoll, B. J., McDonald, S. A., Higgins, R. D., & National Institute of Child Health and Human Development Neonatal Research Network. (2006, May). Adverse neonatal outcomes associated with antenatal dexamethasone versus antenatal betamethasone. *Pediatrics, 117*(5), 1503–1510.

Lee, C. D. (1995). Signifying as a scaffold for literary interpretation. *Journal of Black Psychology, 21*(4), 357–381.

Lee, C. D., Rosenfeld, E., Mendenhall, R., Rivers, A., & Tynes, B. (2004). Cultural modeling as a frame for narrative analysis. In C. Daiute & C. Lightfoot (Eds.), *Narrative analysis: Studying the development of individuals in society.* Thousand Oaks, CA: Sage.

Lee, T., Hummer, D., Jechura, T., & Mahoney, M. (2004, June). Pubertal development of sex differences in circadian function: An animal model. *Annals of the New York Academy of Sciences, 1021,* 262–275.

Lee, V. E., & Burkam, D. T. (2003). Dropping out of high school: The role of school organization and structure. *American Educational Research Journal, 40*(2), 353–393.

Lefeber, Y., & Voorhoeve, H. W. A. (1998). *Indigenous customs in childbirth and child care.* Assen, Netherlands: Von Gocum.

Lefkowitz, E., Romo, L., Corona, R., Au, T., & Sigman, M. (2000). How Latino American and European American adolescents discuss conflicts, sexuality, and AIDS with their mothers. *Developmental Psychology, 36,* 315–325.

Legault, F., & Strayer, F. F. (1990). The emergence of sex-segregation in preschool peer groups. In F. F. Strayer (Ed.), *Social interaction and behavioral development during early childhood.* Montreal: La Maison D'Ethologie de Montreal.

Leigh, S. (2001). Evolution of human growth. *Evolutionary Anthropology, 10,* 223–236.

Leighton, D., & Kluckhohn, C. (1947/1969). *Children of the people; the Navaho individual and his development.* Cambridge, MA: Harvard University Press.

Lemerise, E., & Arsenio, W. (2000). An integrated model of emotion processes and cognition in social information processing. *Child Development, 71,* 107–118.

Lenhart, A., Madden, M., Macgill, A. R., & Smith, A. (2007, December 19). *Teens and social media: The use of social media gains a greater foothold in teen life as they embrace the conversational nature of interactive online media.* Pew Internet & American Life Project, Research Report.

Lenneberg, E. H. (1967). *Biological foundations of language.* Hoboken, NJ: Wiley.

Lenroot, R., & Giedd, J. (2006). Brain development in children and adolescents: Insights from anatomical magnetic resonance imaging. *Neuroscience and Biobehaviorial Reviews, 30,* 718–729.

Leoni, L. (1964). *Tico and the golden wings.* New York: Pantheon.

Lerner, R. M., Anderson, P. M., Balsano, A. B., Dowling, E. M., & Bobek, D. L. (2003). Applied developmental science of positive human development. In R. M. Lerner, M. A. Easterbrooks, & J. Mistry (Eds.), *Handbook of psychology: Vol. 6. Developmental psychology* (pp. 535–558). New York: Wiley.

Leslie, A. M. (1994). To MM, to BY, and agency: Core architecture and domain specificity. In L. A. Hirschfeld & S. Gelman (Eds.), *Mapping the mind: Domain specificity in cognition and culture.* New York: Cambridge University Press.

Leslie, A. M. (2002). Pretense and representation revisited. In N. L. Stein, P. J. Bauer, & M. Rabinowitz (Eds.), *Representation, memory, and development: Essays in honor of Jean Mandler* (pp. 103–114). Mahwah, NJ: Lawrence Erlbaum Associates.

Lester, B. M., Boukydis, C. Z., Garcia-Coll, C. T., Hole, W., & Peucker, M. (1992). Infantile colic: Acoustic cry characteristics, maternal perception of cry, and temperament. *Infant Behavior & Development, 15*(1), 15–26.

Lester, B. M., & Tronick, E. Z. (1994). The effects of prenatal cocaine exposure and child outcome. Special issue: Prenatal drug exposure and child outcome. *Infant Mental Health Journal, 15,* 107–120.

LeVine, R. A. (1988). Human parental care: Universal goals, cultural strategies, individual behavior. *New Directions for Child Development, 40,* 3–12.

LeVine, R. A., Dixon, S., LeVine, S., Richman, A., Leiderman, P. H., Keefer, C. H., & Brazelton, T. B. (1994). *Child care and culture: Lessons from Africa.* New York: Cambridge University Press.

LeVine, R. A., LeVine, S. E., & Schnell, B. (2001). "Improve the women": Mass schooling, female literacy, and worldwide social change. *Harvard Educational Review, 71*(1), 1–50.

Levy, E. (1989). Monologue as development of the text-forming function of language. In K. Nelson (Ed.), *Narratives from the crib.* Cambridge, MA: Harvard University Press.

Levy, G. D., & Fivush, R. (1993). Scripts and gender: A new approach for examining gender-role development. *Developmental Review, 13,* 126–146.

Lewis, M. (2001). Origins of the self-conscious child. In W. R. Crozier & L. E. Alden (Eds.), *International handbook of social anxiety: Concepts, research and interventions relating to the self and shyness* (pp. 101–118). New York: Wiley.

Lewontin, R. (2001). *The triple helix: Gene, organism, and environment.* Cambridge, MA: Harvard University Press.

Liang, X., Fuller, B., & Singer, J. D. (2000). Ethnic differences in child care selection: The influence of family structure, parental practices, and home language. *Early Childhood Research Quarterly, 15*(3), 357–384.

Liaw, F.-R., Meisels, S. J., & Brooks-Gunn, J. (1995). The effects of experience of early intervention on low birth weight, premature children: The Infant Health and Development Program. *Early Childhood Research Quarterly, 10*(4), 405–431.

Liben, L., & Bigler, R. (2002). The developmental course of gender differentiation. *Monographs for the Society for Research in Child Development, 67,* 1–147.

Lichter, S. R., Lichter, L. S., & Amundson, D. (1997). Does Hollywood hate business or money? *Journal of Communication, 47*(1), 68–84.

Liddell, C. (2002). Emic perspectives on risk in African childhood. *Developmental Review, 22,* 97–116.

Lightfoot, C. (1997). *The culture of adolescent risk taking.* New York: Guilford Press.

Lillard, A. (2006). The socialization of theory of mind: Cultural and social class differences in behavior explanation. In A. Antonietti, O. Sempio-Liverta, & A. Marchetti (Eds.), *Theory of mind and language in developmental contexts* (pp. 65–76). New York: Springer Science + Business Media.

Lipsitt, L. P. (2003). Crib death: A biobehavioral phenomenon. *Current Directions in Psychological Science, 12*(5), 164–170.

Liu, D., Wellman, H. M., Tardif, T., & Sabbagh, M. A. (2008). Theory of mind development in Chinese children: A meta-analysis of false-belief understanding across cultures and languages. *Developmental Psychology, 44*(2), 523–531.

Lloyd, B. T. (2002). A conceptual framework for examining adolescent identity, media influence, and social development. *Review of General Psychology, 6*(1), 73–91.

Locke, J. L., & Bogin, B. (2006, June). Language and life history: A new perspective on the development and evolution of human language. *Behavioral and Brain Sciences, 29*(3), 259–325.

Loehlin, J. C. (1992). *Genes and environment in personality development: Vol. 2.* Newbury Park, CA: Sage Publications.

Lonsdorf, E. V. (2007). The role of behavioral research in the conservation of chimpanzees and gorillas. *Journal of Applied Animal Welfare Science, 10*(1), 71–78.

Lopez, G. (2001). The value of hard work: Lessons on parent involvement from an (im)migrant household. *Harvard Educational Review, 71,* 416–437.

Lorenz, J. M. (2001). The outcome of extreme prematurity. *Seminars in Perinatology* (Philadelphia), *25*(5), 348–359.

Lorenz, K. (1943). Die Angebornen Formen mogicher Erfahrung. *Zeitschrift fur Tierpsychologie, 5,* 233–409.

Lorenz, K. (1966). *On aggression.* New York: Harcourt, Brace & World.

Love, J., Harrison, L., Sagi-Schwartz, A., van IJzendoorn, M., Ross, C., Ungerer, J., et al. (2003). Child care quality matters: How conclusions may vary with context. *Child Development, 74,* 1021–1033.

Low, J., & Hollis, S. (2003, March). The eyes have it: Development of children's generative thinking. *International Journal of Behavioral Development, 27*(2), 97–108.

Luciana, M., Conklin, H., Hooper, C., & Yarger, R. (2005). The development of nonverbal working memory and executive control processes in adolescents. *Child Development, 76,* 697–712.

Lundqvist, C., & Sabel, K.-G. (2000). Brief report: The Brazelton Neonatal Behavioral Assessment Scale detects differences among newborn infants of optimal health. *Journal of Pediatric Psychology, 25*(8), 577–582.

Luo, Y., & Baillargeon, R. (2005). Can a self-propelled box have a goal? Psychological reasoning in 5-month-olds. *Psychological Science, 16,* 601–608.

Luria, A. R. (1973). *The waking brain.* New York: Basic Books.

Luria, A. R. (1976). *Cognitive development: Its cultural and social foundations* (Trans M. Lopez-Morillas & L. Solotaroff). London: Harvard University Press.

Luria, A. R. (1981). *Language and cognition.* New York: Wiley.

Luster, T., & Haddow, J. L. (2005). Adolescent mothers and their children: An ecological perspective. In T. Luster & L. Okagaki (Eds.), *Parenting: An ecological perspective. Monographs in parenting* (2nd ed., pp. 73–101). Mahwah, NJ: Lawrence Erlbaum Associates.

Luthar, S., & Becker, B. (2002). Privileged but pressured? A study of affluent youth. *Child Development, 73,* 1593–1610.

Luthar, S., Cicchetti, D., & Becker, B. (2000). The construct of resilience: A critical evaluation and guidelines for future research. *Child Development, 71*(3), 543–562.

Lutz, C. (1987). Goals, events, and understanding Ifaluk emotion theory. In D. Holland & N. Quinn (Eds.), *Cultural models in language and thought.* Cambridge, England: Cambridge University Press.

Lyons-Ruth, K., & Jacobvitz, D. (1999). Attachment disorganization. In J. Cassidy & P. R. Shaver (Eds.), *Handbook of attachment: Theory, research, and clinical applications* (pp. 520–554). New York: Guilford Press.

Lyra, M. C. D. P. (2007). Modeling the dynamics of meaning construction: Appropriation of the home environment. *Culture & Psychology, 13*(2), 179–188.

Maccoby, E. E. (1984). Middle childhood in the context of the family. In W. A. Collins (Ed.), *Development during middle childhood: The years from six to twelve.* Washington, DC: National Academy Press.

Maccoby, E. E. (1998). *The two sexes.* Cambridge, MA: Havard University Press.

Maccoby, E. E. (2003). The gender of child and parent as factors in family dynamics. In A. C. Crouter & A. Booth (Eds.), *Children's influence on family dynamics: The neglected side of family relationships* (pp. 191–206). Mahwah, NJ: Lawrence Erlbaum Associates.

Maccoby, E. E. (2004). Aggression in the context of gender development. In M. Putallaz & K. Bierman (Eds.), *Aggression, antisocial behavior, and violence among girls.* New York: Guilford Press.

Maccoby, E. E. (2007). Historical overview of socialization research and theory. In J. E. Grusec & P. D. Hastings (Eds.), *Handbook of socialization: Theory and research* (pp. 13–41). New York: Guilford Press.

MacFarlane, A. (1977). *The psychology of childbirth.* Cambridge, MA: Harvard University Press.

Magai, C., & Haviland-Jones, J. (2002). *The hidden genius of emotion: Lifespan transformations of personality.* Cambridge, England: Cambridge University Press.

Magnuson, K. A., Lahaie, C., & Waldfogel, J. (2006). Preschool and school readiness of children of immigrants. *Social Science Quarterly, 87,* 1241–1262.

Magnuson, K. A., & Waldfogel, J. (2005). Early childhood care and education: Effects on ethnic and racial gaps in school readiness. *The Future of Children, 15*(1), 169–196.

Magolda, M. (2008). The evolution of self-authorship. In M. Khine (Ed.), *Knowing, knowledge and beliefs: Epistemological studies across diverse cultures* (pp. 45–64). New York: Springer Science + Business Media.

Maguen, S., Floyd, F., Bakeman, R., & Armistead, L. (2002). Developmental milestones and disclosure of sexual orientation among gay, lesbian, and bisexual youths. *Applied Developmental Psychology, 23.*

Mahdi, A. (2003). *Teen life in the Middle East.* Westport, Connecticut: Greenwood Press.

Main, M., Hesse, E., & Kaplan, N. (2005). Predictability of attachment behavior and representational processes at 1, 6, and 19 years of age: The Berkeley Longitudinal Study. In K. E. Grossmann, K. Grossmann, & E. Waters (Eds.), *Attachment from infancy to adulthood: The major longitudinal studies* (pp. 245–304). New York: Guilford Press.

Main, M., & Solomon, J. (1990). Procedures for identifying infants as disorganized/disoriented during the Ainsworth strange situation. In M. Greenberg, D. Cicchetti, & E. M. Cummings (Eds.), *Attachment in the preschool years: Theory, research, and intervention* (pp. 121–160). Chicago: University of Chicago Press.

Majnemer, A., & Barr, R. G. (2005). Influence of supine sleep positioning on early motor milestone acquisition. *Developmental Medicine & Child Neurology, 47*(6), 370–376.

Malchiodi, C. A., & Ginns-Gruenberg, D. (2008). Trauma, loss, and bibliotherapy: The healing power of stories. In C. A. Malchiodi (Eds.), *Creative interventions with traumatized children* (pp. 167–185). New York: Guilford Press.

Maleta, K., Virtanen, S., Espo, M., Kulmala, T., & Ashorn, P. (2003). Timing of growth faltering in rural Malawi. *Archives of Disease in Childhood, 88,* 574–578.

Malina, R. M. (1998). Motor development and performance. In S. J. Ulijaszek, F. E. Johnston, & M. A. Preece (Eds.), *The Cambridge encyclopedia of human growth and development* (pp. 247–250). Cambridge, England: Cambridge University Press.

Malina, R. M., & Bouchard, C. (1991). *Growth, maturation and physical activity.* Champaign, IL: Human Kinetics Books.

Malloy, L. C., Mitchell, E., Block, S., Quas, J. A., & Goodman, G. S. (2007). Children's eyewitness memory: Balancing children's needs and defendants' rights when seeking the truth. In M. P. Toglia, J. D. Read, D. F. Ross, & R. C. L. Lindsay, R. C. L. (Eds.), *The handbook of eyewitness psychology: Vol. 1. Memory for events* (pp. 545–574). Mahwah, NJ: Lawrence Erlbaum Associates.

Mandler, J. M. (1998). Representation. In D. Kuhn & R. S. Siegler (Eds.), *Handbook of child psychology: Vol. 2. Cognition, perception and language* (5th ed., pp. 255–308). New York: Wiley.

Mandler, J. M. (2004). *The foundations of mind: Origins of conceptual thought.* Oxford, England: Oxford University Press.

Mandler, J. M. (2006). Actions organize the infant's world. In K. Hirsh-Pasek & R. M. Golinkoff (Eds.), *Action meets word: How children learn verbs.* New York: Oxford University Press.

Mandler, J. M., & McDonough, L. (1993). Concept formation in infancy. *Cognitive Development, 8,* 291–318.

Mandler, J. M., & McDonough, L. (1998, November). On developing a knowledge base in infancy. *Developmental Psychology, 34*(6), 1274–1288.

Mandler, J. M., Scribner, S., Cole, M., & de Forest, M. (1980). Cross-cultural invariance in story recall. *Child Development, 51,* 19–26.

Manlove, J. S., Ryan, S., & Franzetta, K. (2007, February). Risk and protective factors associated with the transition to a first sexual relationship with an older partner. *Journal of Adolescent Health, 40*(2), 135–143.

Manstead, A. S. R. (1995). Children's understanding of emotion. In J. A. Russell & J. M. Fernandez-Dols (Eds.), *Everyday conceptions of emotion: An introduction to the psychology, anthropology and linguistics of emotion.* Boston: Kluwer Academic Publishers.

Mappes, T. A., & DeGrazia, D. (Eds.). (2001). *Biomedical ethics.* Boston: McGraw-Hill.

Marcia, J. E. (1966). Development and validation of ego identity status. *Journal of Personality and Social Psychology, 3,* 551–558.

Marcia, J. E. (1980). Identity in adolescence. In J. Adelson (Ed.), *Handbook of adolescent psychology.* New York: Wiley.

Marcia, J. E. (2002). Identity and psychosocial development in adulthood. *Identity, 2*(1), 7–28.

Margulies, S., & Thibault, K. (2000). Infant skull and suture properties: Measurements and implications for mechanisms of pediatric brain injury. *Journal of Biomechanical Engineering, 122,* 364–371.

Markovits, H. (2006). Making conditional inferences: The interplay between knowledge and logic. In L. Smith & J. Vonèche (Eds.), *Norms in human development* (pp. 237–252). New York: Cambridge University Press.

Markovits, H., & Barrouillet, P. (2002). The development of conditional reasoning: A mental model account. *Developmental Review, 22,* 5–36.

Marlowe, F. (2005). Who tends Hadza children? In B. Hewlitt & M. Lamb (Eds.), *Hunter-gatherer childhoods: Evolutionary, cultural and developmental perspectives.* New Brunswick, NJ: Transaction Publishers.

Marsiglio, W., Amato, P., Day, R., & Lamb, M. (2000). Scholarship on fatherhood in the 1990s and beyond. *Journal of Marriage and the Family, 62*(1), 1173–1191.

Martin, A. J., Marsh, H. W., Debus, R. L., & Malmberg, L.-E. (2008, June). Performance and mastery orientation of high school and university/college students: A Rasch perspective. *Educational and Psychological Measurement, 68*(3), 464–487.

Martin, C. A., Kelly, T. H., Rayens, M. K., Brogli, B. R., Brenzel, A., Smith, W. J., et al. (2002). Sensation seeking, puberty, and nicotine, alcohol and marijuana use in adolescence. *Journal of the American Academy of Child and Adolescent Psychiatry, 41,* 1495–1502.

Martin, C. B., Jr. (1998). Electronic fetal monitoring: A brief summary of its development, problems and prospects. *European Journal of Obstetrics & Gynecology and Reproductive Biology, 78,* 133–140.

Martin, C. H., & Halverson, C. F. (1981). A schematic processing model of sextyping and stereotyping in children. *Child Development, 52,* 1119–1134.

Martin, C. L., & Ruble, D. (2004). Children's search for gender cues: Cognitive perspectives on gender development. *Current Directions in Psychological Science, 13*(2), 67–70.

Martin, K. (1996). *Puberty, sexuality and the self: Boys and girls at adolescence.* New York: Routledge.

Martino, W., & Pallotta-Chiarolli, M. (2003). *So what's a boy?: Addressing issues of masculinity in Education.* London: Open University Press

Mascolo, M. F., & Fischer, K. W. (1998). The development of self through the coordination of component systems. In M. D. Ferrari & R. J. Sternberg (Eds.), *Self-awareness: Its nature and development* (pp. 332–384). New York: Guilford Press.

Mascolo, M., Fischer, K., & Li, J. (2003). Dynamic development of component systems of emotions: Pride, shame and guilt in China and the United States. In R. Davidson, K. Scherer, & H. Goldsmith (Eds.), *Handbook of affective sciences.* Oxford, England: Oxford University Press.

Massey, C. M., & Gelman, R. (1988). Preschooler's ability to decide whether a photographed unfamiliar object can move itself. *Developmental Psychology, 24*(3), 307–317.

Matturri, L., Biondo, B., Suarez-Mier, M. P., & Rossi, L. (2002). Brain stem lesions in the sudden infant death syndrome: Variability in the hypoplasia of the arcuate nucleus. *Acta Neuropathology* (Berlin), *104,* 12–20.

Maxwell, L. E., & Evans, G. W. (2000, March). The effects of noise on pre-school children's pre-reading skills. *Journal of Environmental Psychology, 20*(1), 91–97.

McAdoo, H. P. (1985). Racial attitude and self-concept of young black children over time. In H. P. McAdoo & J. L. McAdoo (Eds.), *Black children: Social, educational, and parental environments.* Beverly Hills, CA: Sage.

McCabe, D. (1999). Academic dishonesty among high school students. *Adolescence, 34,* 681–687.

McCarty, M. E., Clifton, R. K., Ashmead, D. H., Lee, P., & Goubet, N. (2001). How infants use vision for grasping objects. *Child Development, 72*(4), 973–987.

McDade, T. (2003). Life history theory and the immune system: Steps toward a human ecological immunology. *Yearbook of Physical Anthropology, 46,* 100–125.

McDonald, P. G., te Marvelde, L., Kazem, A. J. N., & Wright, J. (2008, April). Helping as a signal and the effect of a potential audience during provisioning visits in a cooperative bird. *Animal Behaviour, 75*(4), 1319–1330.

McElwain, N. L., & Booth-LaForce, C. (2006). Maternal sensitivity to infant distress and nondistress as predictors of infant-mother attachment security. *Journal of Family Psychology, 20*(2), 247–255.

McGloin, J. M., & Widom, C. S. (2001). Resilience among abuse and neglected children grown up. *Development and Psychopathology, 13*(4), 1021–1038.

McGraw, M. B. (1975). *Growth: A study of Johnny and Jimmy.* New York: Arno Press. (Original work published 1935)

McGuire, S. (2002). Nonshared environment research: What is it and where is it going? *Marriage & Family Review, 33*(1), 31–56.

McHale, S., & Crouter, A. (1996). The family contexts of children's sibling relationships. In G. H. Brody (Ed.), *Sibling relationships: Their causes and consequences.* Norwood, NJ: Ablex.

McKelvie, P., & Low, J. (2002). Listening to Mozart does not improve children's spatial ability: Final curtains for the Mozart effect. *British Journal of Developmental Psychology, 20,* 241–258.

McKenna, J. J. (1996) Sudden infant death syndrome in cross-cultural perspective: Is infant-parent cosleeping protective? *Annual Review of Anthropology, 25,* 201–216.

McKinney, C., & Renk, K. (2008, June). Differential parenting between mothers and fathers: Implications for late adolescents. *Journal of Family Issues, 29*(6), 806–827.

McKinney, M. L. (1998). Cognitive evolution by extending brain development: On recapitulation, progress, and other heresies. In J. Langer & M. Killer (Eds.), *Piaget, evolution, and development.* Mahwah, NJ: Lawrence Erlbaum Associates.

McLeod, N. M. H., Arana-Urioste, M. L., & Saeed, N. R. (2004, March). Birth prevalence of cleft lip and palate in Sucre, Bolivia. *The Cleft Palate—Craniofacial Journal, 41*(2), 195–198.

McLoughlin, G., Ronald, A., Kuntsi, J., Asherson, P., & Plomin, R. (2007, December). Genetic support for the dual nature of attention deficit hyperactivity disorder: Substantial genetic overlap between the inattentive and hyperactive-impulsive components. *Journal of Abnormal Child Psychology. 35*(6), 999–1008.

McLoyd, V. C. (1998a). Children in poverty: Development, public policy, and practice. In I. E. Sigel & K. A. Renninger (Eds.), *Handbook of child psychology: Vol. 4. Child psychology in practice* (5th ed., pp. 135–210). New York: Wiley.

McLoyd, V. C. (1998b). Socioeconomic disadvantage and child development. *American Psychologist, 53*(2), 185–204.

McLoyd, V. C., & Smith, J. (2002). Physical discipline and behavior problems in African American, European American, and Hispanic children: Emotional support as a moderator. *Journal of Marriage and Family, 64,* 40–53.

McNeill, D. (1966). Developmental psycholinguistics. In S. Smith & G. A. Miller (Eds.), *The genesis of language: A psycholinguistic approach.* Cambridge, MA: The MIT Press.

McPhee, C. (1970). Children and music in Bali. In J. Belo (Ed.), *Traditional Balinese culture* (pp. 212–239). New York: Columbia University Press.

Meaney, M. (2001). Maternal care, gene expression, and the transmission of individual differences in stress reactivity across generations. *Annual Review of Neuroscience, 24,* 1161–1192.

Meara, E. (2001). *Why is health related to socioeconomic status? The case of pregnancy and low birth weight.* Cambridge, MA: National Bureau of Economic Research.

Meeus, W. (2003). Parental and peer support, identity development and psychological well-being in adolescence. *Psychology: The Journal of the Hellenic Psychological Society, 10*(2–3), 192–201.

Meeus, W., & de Wied, M. (2007). Relationships with parents and identity in adolescence: A review of 25 years of research. In M. Watzlawik & A. Born Aristi (Eds.), *Capturing identity: Quantitative and qualitative methods* (pp. 131–147). Lanham, MD: University Press of America.

Mehan, H. (1998). The study of social interaction in educational settings: Accomplishments and unresolved issues. *Human Development, 41*(4), 245–268.

Meléndez, L. (2005). Parental beliefs and practices around early self-regulation: The impact of culture and immigration. *Infants & Young Children, 18*(2), 136–146.

Melot, A.-M., & Houde, O. (1998). Categorization and theories of mind: The case of the appearance/reality distinction. *Cahiers de Psychologie Cognitive/Current Psychology of Cognition 17*(1), 71–93.

Meltz, B. (2004, January 29). Nurturing an adopted child. *Boston Globe,* p. H1.

Meltzoff, A. N. (1988). Imitation of televised models by infants. *Child Development, 59,* 1221–1229.

Meltzoff, A. N. (2007). The 'like me' framework for recognizing and becoming an intentional agent. *Acta Psychologica. Special Issue: Becoming an intentional agent, 124*(1), 26–43.

Meltzoff, A., & Borton, R. (1979). Intermodal matching by human neonates. *Nature, 282,* 403–403.

Meltzoff, A., & Decety, J. (2003). What imitation tells us about social cognition: A rapprochement between developmental psychology and cognitive neuroscience. *The Royal Society, 358,* 491–500.

Mennella, J., & Beauchamp, C. (1999). Experience with a flavor in mother's milk modifies the infant's acceptance of flavored cereal. *Developmental Psychobiology, 35,* 197–203.

Mennella, J., & Beauchamp, G. (2005). Understanding the origin of flavor preferences. *Chemical Senses, 30*(Suppl. 1), 242–243.

Mennella, J., Jagnow, C., & Beauchamp, G. (2001). Prenatal and postnatal flavor learning by human infants. *Pediatrics, 107,* 88–94.

Meyers, S. (2001). *Everywhere babies.* San Diego: Harcourt.

Miller, B. C., Bgenson, B., & Galbraith, K. (2001). Family relationships and adolescent pregnancy risk: A research synthesis. *Developmental Review, 21,* 1–38.

Miller, D., & Byrnes, J. (2001). Adolescents' decision making in social situations: A self-regulation perspective. *Journal of Applied Developmental Psychology, 22,* 237–256.

Miller, J. G. (1997). Theoretical issues in cultural psychology. In J. W. Berry & Y. H. Poortinga (Eds.), *Handbook of cross-cultural psychology: Theory and method* (pp. 85–128). Boston: Allyn & Bacon.

Miller, J. G., & Schaberg, L. (2003). Cultural perspectives on personality and social psychology. In T. Millon, & M. J. Lerner (Eds.), *Handbook of psychology: Vol. 5. Personality and social psychology* (pp. 31–56). New York: Wiley.

Miller, K. (1996). The effects of state terrorism and exile on the indigenous Guatemalan refugee children: A mental health assessment and an analysis of children's narratives. *Child Development, 67,* 89–106.

Miller, P. (1982). *Amy, Wendy and Beth: Learning language in south Baltimore.* Austin: University of Texas Press.

Miller, P. (2002). *Theories of developmental psychology* (4th ed.). New York: Worth.

Miller, P., Wang, W., Sandel, T., & Cho, G. (2002). Self-esteem as folk theory: A comparison of European American and Taiwanese mothers' beliefs. *Parenting, 2,* 209–239.

Mills, C. M., & Keil, F. C. (2004, January). Knowing the limits of one's understanding: The development of an awareness of an illusion of explanatory depth. *Journal of Experimental Child Psychology, 87*(1), 1–32.

Milnitsky-Sapiro, C., Turiel, E., & Nucci, L. (2006). Brazilian adolescents' conceptions of autonomy and parental authority. *Cognitive Development, 21*(3), 317–331.

Mintz, S. (2004). *Huck's raft: A history of American childhood.* Cambridge, MA: Cambridge University Press.

Mitchell, E. (1985). The dynamics of family interaction around home video games. *Marriage & Family Review. Special Issue: Personal computers and the family, 8*(1–2), 121–135.

Modell, J., & Elder, G. H. (2002). Children develop in history: So what's new? In W. Hartup & R. A. Weinberg (Eds.), *Child psychology in retrospect and prospect: In celebration of the 75th anniversary of the Institute of Child Development. The Minnesota symposia on child psychology* (Vol. 32, pp. 173–205). Mahwah, NJ: Lawrence Erlbaum Associates.

Modry-Mandell, K. L., Gamble, W. C., & Taylor, A. R. (2007, February). Family emotional climate and sibling relationship quality: Influences on behavioral problems and adaptation in preschool-aged children. *Journal of Child and Family Studies, 16*(1), 61–73.

Moffitt, T. E. (2007). A review of research on the taxonomy of life-course persistent versus adolescence-limited antisocial behavior. In D. J. Flannery, A. T. Vazsonyi, & I. D. Waldman (Eds.), *The Cambridge handbook of violent behavior and aggression* (pp. 49–74). New York: Cambridge University Press.

Moffitt, T. E., Caspi, A., Belsky, J., & Silva, P. A. (1992). Childhood experience and the onset of menarche: A test of a sociobiological model. *Child Development, 63,* 47–58.

Moffitt, T. E., Caspi, A., Rutter, M., & Silva, P. A. (2001). *Sex differences in antisocial behavior: Conduct disorder, delinquency and violence in the Dunedin Longitudinal Study.* New York: Cambridge University Press.

Moffitt. T. E., Caspi, A., Rutter, M., & Silva, P. A. (2002, November). Review of sex differences in antisocial behaviour: Conduct disorder, delinquency and violence in the Dunedin Longitudinal Study. *Psychological Medicine, 32*(8), 1475–1476.

Molina, J. C., Spear, N. E., Spear, L. P., Mennella, J. A., & Lewis, M. J. (2007). The International Society for Developmental Psychobiology 39th annual meeting symposium: Alcohol and development: Beyond fetal alcohol syndrome. *Developmental Psychobiology, 49*(3), 227–242.

Mondloch, C. J., Lewis, T. L., Budreau, D. R., Maurer, D., Dannemiller, J. L., Stephens, B. R., & Kleiner-Gathercoal, K. A. (1999). Face perception during early infancy. *Psychological Science, 10*(5), 419–422.

Moon, C., Cooper, R. P., & Fifer, W. P. (1993). Two-day-olds prefer their native language. *Infant Behavior Development, 16,* 495–500.

Moore, K. L., & Persaud, T. V. N. (1993). *The developing human: Clinically oriented embryology* (5th ed.). Philadelphia: Saunders.

Moore, K. L., & Persaud, T. V. N. (1998). *The developing human: Clinically oriented embryology.* Philadelphia: Saunders.

Moore, K. M., & Meltzoff, A. N. (2008, April). Factors affecting infants' manual search for occluded objects and the genesis of object permanence. *Infant Behavior & Development, 31*(2), 168–180.

Mora, J. O., & Nestel, P. S. (2000). Improving prenatal nutrition in developing countries: Strategies, prospects, and challenges. *American Journal of Clinical Nutrition, 71*(Suppl. 5), 1353S–1363S.

Moran, J. P. (2000). *Teaching sex: The shaping of adolescence in the 20th century.* Cambridge, MA: Harvard University Press.

Morelli, G. A., Rogoff, B., Oppenheim, D., & Goldsmith, D. (1992). Cultural variation in infants sleeping arrangements: Questions of independence. *Developmental Psychology, 28,* 604–613.

Morelli, G. A., Tronick, E., & Beeghly, M. (1999). *Is there security in numbers? Child care in a hunting and gathering community and infants' attachment relationships.* Albuquerque, NM: Society for Research in Child Development.

Morgan, G., & Woll, B. (Eds.). (2002). *Directions in sign language acquisition.* Philadelphia: John Benjamins.

Morris, J. F., Balsam, K. F., & Rothblum, E. D. (2002, June). Lesbian and bisexual mothers and nonmothers: Demographics and the coming-out process. *Journal of Family Psychology, 16*(2), 144–156.

Morrison, F. J., Smith, L., & Dow-Ehrensberger, M. (1995). Education and cognitive development: A natural experiment. *Developmental Psychology, 31,* 789–799.

Morrongiello, B. A., Fenwick, K. D., Hillier, L., & Chance, G. (1994). Sound localization in newborn human infants. *Developmental Psychobiology, 27*(8), 519–538.

Morrow, C. E., Bandstra, E. S., Anthony, J. C., Ofir, A. Y., Xue, L., & Reyes, M. B. (2003). Influence of prenatal cocaine exposure on early language development: Longitudinal findings from four months to three years of age. *Journal of Developmental and Behavioral Pediatrics, 24*(1), 39–50.

Morton, S. M. B. (2006). Maternal nutrition and fetal growth and development. In P. Gluckman & M. Hanson (Eds.), *Developmental origins of health and disease* (pp. 98–129). New York: Cambridge University Press.

Moshman, D. (1998). Cognitive development beyond childhood. In D. Kuhn & R. S. Siegler (Eds.), *Handbook of child psychology: Vol. 2. Cognition, perception, and language* (5th ed., pp. 947–978). New York: Wiley.

Moshman, D. (1999). *Adolescent psychological development: Rationality, morality and identity.* Mahwah, NJ: Lawrence Erlbaum Associates.

Moss, N. E., & Carver, K. (1998). The effect of WIC and Medicaid on infant mortality—the United States. *American Journal of Public Health, 88,* 1354–1361.

Müller, U., Sokol, B., & Overton, W. F. (1999). Developmental sequences in class reasoning and propositional reasoning. *Journal of Experimental Child Psychology, 74,* 69–106.

Munakata, Y., Casey, B., & Diamond, A. (2004). Developmental cognitive neuroscience: Progress and potential. *Trends in Cognitive Sciences, 8,* 122–128.

Murray, L., & Trevarthen, C. (1986, February). The infant's role in mother-infant communications. *Journal of Child Language,* 13(1), 1529.

Murray-Close, D., Ostrov, J. M., & Crick, N. R. (2007). A short-term longitudinal study of growth of relational aggression during middle childhood: Associations with gender, friendship intimacy, and internalizing problems. *Development and Psychopathology, 19*(1), 187–203.

Mustanski, B., Viken, R., Pullkinen, L., Kaprio, J., & Rose, R. (2004). Genetic and environmental influences on pubertal development: Longitudinal data from Finnish twins at ages 11 and 14. *Developmental Psychology, 40,* 1188–1198.

Nadel, J. (2002). Imitation and imitation recognition: functional use in preverbal infants and nonverbal children with autism. In A. Meltzoff & W. Prinz (Eds.), *The imitative mind: Development, evolution, and brain bases.* Cambridge, England: Cambridge University Press.

Nader, P., O'Brien, M., Houts, R., Bradley, R., Belsky, J., Crosnoe, R., et al. (2006). Identifying risk for obesity in early childhood. *Pediatrics, 118,* 594–601.

Nagler, J. (2002). Sudden infant death syndrome. *Current Opinion in Pediatrics, 14*(2), 247–250.

Nakkula M., & Toshalis, E. (2006). *Understanding youth: Adolescent development for educators.* Cambridge, MA: Harvard Education Press.

Napanangka, Y. (1995). Kid left behind in camp. In J. Crugnale (Ed.), *Footprints across our land.* Broome, Western Australia: Magabala.

Nasir, N. (2005). Individual cognitive structuring and the sociocultural context: Strategy shifts in the game of dominoes. *Journal of the Learning Sciences, 14,* 5–34.

National Center for Educational Statistics. (2001). *Statistics and assessment: Annual report.* Retrieved April 25, 2008, from http://www.ed.gov/about/reports/annual/2001report/edlite-261.html

National Center for Health Statistics. (2003). *Healthy people, 2000, review.* Hyattsville, MD: National Center for Health Statistics.

National Council of Teachers of Mathematics. (2000). *Principles and standards for school mathematics.* Reston, VA: National Council of Teachers of Mathematics.

Nazzi, T., Kemler Nelson, D. G., Jusczyk, P. W., & Jusczyk, A. M. (2000). Six-month-olds' detection of clauses embedded in continuous speech: Effects of prosodic well-formedness. *Infancy, 1*(1), 123–147.

NCCP. (2008). *Basic facts about low income children, birth to age 18.* Retrieved August 20, 2008, from http://www.nccp.org/publications/pub_845.html

Needham, A., & Baillargeon, R. (1993). Intuitions about support in 4.5-month-old infants. *Cognition, 47*(2), 121–148.

Needham, A., Barrett, T., & Peterman, K. (2002). A pick-me-up for infants' exploratory skills: Early stimulated experiences reaching for objects using "sticky mittens" enhances young infants' object exploration skills. *Infant Behavior and Development, 25,* 279–295.

Nelson, C. A. (2001). The development and neural bases of face recognition. *Infant and Child Development, 10*(1–2), 3–18.

Nelson, C. A. (2006). Neurobehavioral development in the context of biocultural co-constructivism. In P. B. Baltes, P. A. Reuter-Lorenz, & F. Rösler (Eds.), *Lifespan development and the brain: The perspective of biocultural co-constructivism* (pp. 61–81). New York: Cambridge University Press.

Nelson, C. A., & Bloom, F. E. (1997). Child development and neuroscience. *Child Development, 68,* 970–987.

Nelson, C. A., & Luciana, M. (Eds.). (2001). *Handbook of developmental cognitive neuroscience.* Cambridge, MA: The MIT Press.

Nelson, C. A., Zeanah, C. H., Fox, N. A. (2007). The effects of early deprivation on brain-behavioral development: The Bucharest Early Intervention Project. In D. Romer & E. F. Walker (Eds.), *Adolescent psychopathology and the developing brain: Integrating brain and prevention science* (pp. 197–215). New York: Oxford University Press.

Nelson, K. (1981). Social cognition in a script framework. In J. H. Flavell & L. Ross (Eds.), *Social cognitive development.* Cambridge, MA: Cambridge University Press.

Nelson, K. (1996). *Language in cognitive development.* New York: Cambridge University Press.

Nelson, K. (2003). Co-constructing the cultural person through narratives in early childhood. In C. Daiute & C. Lightfoot (Eds.), *Narrative analysis: Studying the development of individuals in society.* New York: Sage Press.

Nelson, K., & Fivush, R. (2000). Socialization of memory. In E. Tulving & F. I. M. Craik (Eds.), *The Oxford handbook of memory* (pp. 283–295). London: Oxford University Press.

Nelson, K., & Shaw, L. (2002). Developing a socially shared symbolic system. In E. Amsel & J. Byrnes (Eds.), *Language, literacy, and cognitive development.* Mahwah, NJ: Lawrence Erlbaum Associates.

Nelson, K., Skwerer, D. P., Goldman, S., Henseler, S., Presler, N., & Walkenfeld, F. F. (2003). Entering a community of minds: An experimental approach to "theory of mind." *Human Development, 46*(1), 24–46.

Nelson, L., Badger, S., & Wu, B. (2004). The influence of culture in emerging adulthood: Perspectives of Chinese college students. *International Journal of Behavioral Development, 28*(1), 26–36.

Netter, F. H. (1965). *The CIBA collection of medical illustrations.* Summit, NJ: CIBA Pharmaceutical Products.

Neville, H. J. (2005). Development and plasticity of human cognition. In U. Mayr, E. Awh, & S. W. Keele (Eds.), *Developing individuality in the human brain: A tribute to Michael I. Posner. Decade of behavior* (pp. 209–235). Washington, DC: American Psychological Association.

Newcomb, A. F., Bukowski, W. M., & Pattee, L. (1993). Children's peer relations: A meta-analytic review of popular, rejected, controversial and average sociometric status. *Psychological Bulletin, 113*, 99–128.

Newport, E. L., Bavelier, D., & Neville, H. J. (2001). Critical thinking about critical periods: Perspectives on a critical period for language acquisition. In E. Dupoux (Ed.), *Language, brain, and cognitive development: Essays in honor of Jacques Mehler* (pp. 481–502). Cambridge, MA: The MIT Press.

Newton, N., & Newton, M. (1972). Lactation: Its psychological component. In J. G. Howells (Ed.), *Modern perspectives in psycho-obstetrics*. New York: Brunner/Mazel.

NICHD Early Child Care Research Network. (2001). Child care and children's peer interaction at 24 and 36 months: The NICHD Study of Early Child Care. *Child Development, 72*, 1478–1500.

NICHD Early Child Care Research Network. (2002). Structure, process, outcome: Direct and indirect effects of caregiving quality on young children's development. *Psychological Science, 13*, 199–206.

NICHD Early Child Care Research Network. (2003a). Child care and common communicable illnesses in children aged 37 to 54 months. *Archives of Pediatrics and Adolescent Medicine, 157*, 196–201.

NICHD Early Child Care Research Network. (2003b). Does amount of time spent in child care predict socioemotional adjustment during the transition to kindergarten? *Child Development, 74*, 976–1005.

NICHD Early Child Care Research Network. (2003c). Does quality of care affect child outcomes at age 4? *Developmental Psychology, 39*, 451–469.

NICHD Early Child Care Research Network. (2004, January). Are child developmental outcomes related to before- and after-school care arrangements? Results from the NICHD study of early child care. *Child Development 75*(1) 280–295.

Nkata, M. (2001). Perinatal mortality in breech delivery. *Tropical Doctor, 31*(4), 222–223.

Noland, J. S., Singer, L. T., Arendt, R. E., Minnes, S., Short, E. J., & Bearer, C. F. (2003). Executive functioning in preschool-age children prenatally exposed to alcohol, cocaine, and marijuana. *Alcohol and Clinical Experimental Research, 27*(4), 647–656.

Nord, M., Andrews, M., & Carlson, S. (2007). *Household food security in the United States, 2006* (Economic Research Report No. 49). Washington, DC: U.S. Department of Agriculture.

Nsamenang, A. (2006). Human ontogenesis: An indigenous African view on development and intelligence. I*nternational Journal of Psychology. Special Issue: The indigenous psychologies, 41*(4), 293–297.

Nucci, L. (1996). Morality and the personal sphere of actions. In E. Reed, E. Turiel & T. Brown (Eds.), *Values and knowledge* (pp. 41–60). Mahwah, NJ: Lawrence Erlbaum Associates.

Nucci, L. (2001). *Education in the moral domain*. Cambridge, England: Cambridge University Press.

Nucci, L. (2004a). Social interaction and the construction of moral and social knowledge In J. I. M. Carpendale & U. Muller (Eds.), *Social interaction and the development of knowledge* (pp. 195–213). Mahwah, NJ: Lawrence Erlbaum Associates.

Nucci, L. (2004b). The promise and limitations of the moral self construct. In C. Lightfoot, C. LaLonde, & M. Chandler (Eds.), *Changing conceptions of psychological life*. Mahwah, NJ: Lawrence Erlbaum Associates.

Nussbaum, M. (2001). *Upheavals of thought*. Cambridge, England: Cambridge University Press.

Nussbaum, M. (2004, January 11). My so-called blog. *The New York Times Magazine.*

Nyiti, R. M. (1976). The development of conservation in the Meru children of Tanzania. *Child Development, 47*, 1122–1129.

Nyiti, R. M. (1982). The validity of "cultural differences explanations" for cross-cultural variation in Piagetian cognitive development. In D. A. Wagner & H. W. Stevenson (Eds.), *Cultural perspectives on child development*. San Francisco, CA: Freeman.

O'Brien, M., Peyton, V., Mistry, R., Hruda, L., Jacobs, A., Caldera, Y., et al. (2000). Gender-role cognition in three-year-old boys and girls. *Sex Roles, 42*, 1007–1025.

O'Sullivan, L. F., & Meyer-Bahlberg, H. F. L. (2003, April). African American and Latina inner-city girls' reports of romantic and sexual development. *Journal of Social and Personal Relationships. Special Issue: Race/ethnicity and interpersonal relationships, 20*(2), 221–238.

Oakes, L. M., & Cohen, L. B. (1990). Infant perception of a causal event. *Cognitive Development, 5*, 193–207.

Ochs, E. (1982). Talking to children in Western Samoa. *Language in Society, 11*, 77–104.

Ochs, E., & Schieffelin, B. (1995). The impact of language socialization or grammatical development. In P. Fletcher & B. MacWhinney (Eds.), *The handbook of child language*. Cambridge, MA: Blackwell Publishing.

Ogbu, J. U. (1997). Understanding the school performance of urban Blacks: Some essential background knowledge. In H. J. Walberg & O. Reyes (Eds.), *Children and youth: Interdisciplinary perspectives* (pp. 190–222). Thousand Oaks, CA: Sage.

Ogden, C. L., Carroll, M. D., Curtin, L. R., McDowell, M. A., Tabak, C. J., & Flegal, K. M. (2006). Prevalence of overweight and obesity in the United States, 1999–2004. *Journal of the American Medical Association, 295*, 1549–1555.

Oh, S. Y., Romero, R., Shim, S. S., Park, J. S., Jun, J. K., & Yoon, B. H. (2006). Fetal plasma cortisol and dehydroepiandrosterone sulfate concentrations in pregnancy and term parturition. *Journal of Maternal-Fetal and Neonatal Medicine, 19*(9), 529–536.

Okami, P., Weisner, T., & Olmstead, R. (2002). Outcome correlates of parent-child bedsharing: An eighteen-year longitudinal study. *Journal of Developmental and Behavioral Pediatrics, 23*, 244–253.

Okamoto, Y., & Case, R. (1996). Exploring the microstructure of children's central conceptional structures on the domain of numbers. *Monographs of the Society for Research on Child Development, 61*(1–2), 27–58.

Oldberg, C. (1998, December 15). Children and violent video games: A warning. *New York Times*, p. 6.

Oliner, S. B., & Oliner, P. (1988). *The altruistic personality: Rescuers of Jews in Nazi Germany*. New York: Macmillan.

Olson, K. (2007, February 18). Her autistic brothers. *New York Times Magazine*, 42–47.

Orenstein, P. (2004, March 7). Food fighter Alice Waters. *New York Times Magazine*, pp. 30–33.

Orioli, I. M., & Castilla, E. E. (2000). New associations between prenatal exposure to drugs and malformations. *American Journal of Human Genetics, 67*(4, Suppl. 2), 175.

Ornstein, P. A., Baker-Ward, L., Gordon, B. N., Pelphrey, K. A., Tyler, C. S., & Gramzow, E. (2006). The influence of prior knowledge and repeated questioning on children's long-term retention of the details of a pediatric examination. *Developmental Psychology, 42*, 332–344.

Ornstein, P. A., Haden, C. A., & Elischberger, H. B. (2006). Children's memory development: Remembering the past and preparing for the future. In *E. Bialystok & F. I. M. Craik (Eds.), Lifespan cognition: Mechanisms of change* (pp. 143–161). New York: Oxford University Press.

Ornstein, P. A., Haden, C., & Hendrick, A. (2004). Learning to remember: Social-communicative exchanges and the development of children's memory skills. *Developmental Review, 24*, 374–395.

Ornstein, P. A., Shapiro, L. R., Clubb, P. A., Follmer, A., & Baker-Ward, L. (1997). The influence of prior knowledge on children's memory for salient medical experiences. In N. Stein, P. A. Ornstein, B. Tversky, & C. J. Brainerd (Eds.), *Memory for everyday and emotional events* (pp. 83–112). Mahwah, NJ: Lawrence Erlbaum Associates.

Osofsky, J., & Fitzgerald, H. (Eds.). (2000). *Handbook of infant mental health. World Association for Infant Mental Health.* New York: Wiley.

Oster, H. (2005). The repertoire of infant facial expressions: An ontogenetic perspective. In J. Nadel & D. Muir (Eds.), *Emotional development*. Oxford, England: Oxford University Press.

Ostrer, H., Huang, H. Y., Masch, R. J., & Shapiro, E. (2007). A cellular study of human testis development. *Sexual Development 1*(5), 286–292.

Ostrov, J., & Crick, N. (2006). How recent developments in the study of relational aggression and close relationships in early childhood advance the field. *Journal of Applied Developmental Psychology, 27*(3), 189–192.

Ostrov, J., Gentile, D., & Crick, N. (2006). Media exposure, aggression and prosocial behavior during early childhood: A longitudinal study. *Social Development, 15*, 612–627.

Padilla, A. (2006). Bicultural social development. *Hispanic Journal of Behavioral Sciences, 28*, 467–497.

Page-Goertz, S., McCamman, S., & Westdahl, C. (2001). Breastfeeding promotion. Top tips for motivating women to breastfeed their infants. *AWHONN Lifelines, 5*(1), 41–43.

Pak. S. (2004). The biological standard of living in the two Koreas. *Economics and Human Biology, 2*, 511–521.

Paley, V. G. (1981). *Wally's stories.* Cambridge, MA: Harvard University Press.

Paley, V. G. (1984). *Boys & girls: Superheroes in the doll corner.* Chicago: The University of Chicago Press.

Palincsar, A. S., Spiro, R. J., Kucan, L., Magnusson, S. J., Collins, B., Hapgood, S., et al. (2007). Designing a hypermedia environment to support comprehension instruction. In D. S. McNamara (Ed.), *Reading comprehension strategies: Theories, interventions, and technologies* (pp. 441–462). Mahwah, NJ: Lawrence Erlbaum Associates.

Pan, B. A., & Snow, C. E. (1999). The development of conversational and discourse skills. In M. Barrett (Ed.), *The development of language* (pp. 229–250). Hove, England: Psychology Press.

Panksepp, J. (2003). At the interface of affective, behavioral and cognitive neurosciences. Decoding the emotional feelings of the brain. *Brain and Cognition, 52*, 4–14.

Panksepp, J., & Smith-Pasqualini, M. (2005). The search for fundamental brain/mind sources of affective experience. In J. Nadel and D. Muir (Eds.), *Emotional Development*. Oxford, England: Oxford University Press.

Parke, R. D., & Buriel, R. (1998). Socialization in the family: Ethnica and ecological perspectives. In W. Damon & N. Eisenberg (Eds.), *Handbook of child development: Vol. 3. Social, emotional, and personality development* (5th ed., pp. 463–552). New York: Wiley.

Parke, R. D., & Ladd, G. W. (1992). Family-peer relationships. *Merrill-Palmer Quarterly, 40*, 1–20.

Parke, R. D., O'Neil, R., Spitzer, S., Isley, S., Welsh, M., Wang, S., et al. (1997). A longitudinal assessment of sociometric stability and the behavioral correlates of children's social acceptance. *Merrill-Palmer Quarterly, 43*, 635–662.

Parker, J. G., Rubin, K. H., Erath, S. A., Wojslawowicz, J. C., & Buskirk, A. A. (2006). Peer relationships, child development, and adjustment: A developmental psychopathology perspective. In D. Cicchetti & D. J. Cohen (Eds.), *Developmental psychopathology: Vol. 1. Theory and method* (2nd ed., pp. 419–493). Hoboken, NJ: John Wiley & Sons.

Parker, S. T. (2005). Piaget's legacy in cognitive constructivism, niche construction, and phenotype development and evolution. In S. T. Parker,

J. Langer, & C. Milbrath (Eds.), *Biology and knowledge revisited: From neurogenesis to psychogenesis.* Mahwah, NJ: Lawrence Erlbaum Associates.

Parker, S. T., & McKinney, M. L. (1999). *Origins of intelligence: The evolution of cognitive development in monkeys, apes, and humans.* Baltimore, MD: Johns Hopkins University Press.

Parsons, T. (1963). Youth in the context of American society. In E. Erikson (Ed.), *Youth: Change and challenge.* New York: Basic Books.

Patrick, H., Anderman, L. H., & Ryan, A. M. (2002). Social motivation and the classroom social environment. In C. Midgley (Ed.), *Goals, goal structures, and patterns of adaptive learning* (pp. 85–108). Mahwah, NJ: Lawrence Erlbaum Associates.

Patterson, C. J. (2006, October). Children of lesbian and gay parents. *Current Directions in Psychological Science, 15*(5), 241–244.

Patterson, C. J. (2008). Sexual orientation across the life span: Introduction to the special section. *Developmental Psychology, 44*(1), 1–4.

Patterson, G. R., Littman, R. A., & Bricker, W. (1967). Assertive behavior in young children: A step toward a theory of aggression. *Monographs of the Society for Research for Child Development, 32*(Serial No. 113).

Patterson, G. R., DeBaryshe, B. D., & Ramsey, E. (1989). A developmental perspective on antisocial behavior. *American Psychologist, 44*(2), 329–335.

Pavlov, I. P. (1927). *Conditioned reflexes.* Oxford, England: Oxford University Press.

Pecora, N., Murray, J. P., & Wartella, E. A. (Eds.). (2006). *Children and television: Fifty years of research.* Mahwah, NJ: Lawrence Erlbaum Associates.

Pedersen, S., Vitaro, F., Barker, E. D., & Borge, A. I. H. (2007, July). The timing of middle-childhood peer rejection and friendship: Linking early behavior to early-adolescent adjustment. *Child Development, 78*(4), 1037–1051.

Pelaez, M., Field, T., Pickens, J., & Hart, S. (2008). Disengaged and authoritarian parenting behavior of depressed mothers with their toddlers. *Infant Behavior & Development, 31*(1), 145–148.

Pellegrini, A. D. (2006). The development and function of rough-and-tumble play in childhood and adolescence: A sexual selection theory perspective. In A. Göncü & S. Gaskins (Eds.), *Play and development: Evolutionary, sociocultural, and functional perspectives. The Jean Piaget symposium series* (pp. 77–98). Mahwah, NJ: Lawrence Erlbaum Associates.

Pellegrini, A. D., & Long, J. (2002). A longitudinal study of bullying, dominance, and victimizationduring the transition from primary through secondary school. *British Journal of Developmental Psychology, 20*, 259–280.

Pellegrini, A. D., & Long, J. D. (2003). A sexual selection theory longitudinal analysis of sexual segregation and integration in early adolescence. *Journal of Experimental Child Psychology, 85*(3), 257–278.

Pellegrini, A. D., Roseth, C. J., Mliner, S., Bohn, C. M., Van Ryzin, M., Vance, N., et al. (2007, February). Social dominance in preschool classrooms. *Journal of Comparative Psychology, 121*(1), 54–64.

Penchaszadeh, V. B. (2001). Genetic counseling issues in Latinos. *Genetic Testing, 5*(3), 193–200.

Peplau, L. A., DeBro, S. C., Veniegas, R. C., & Taylor, P. L. (1999). *Gender, culture, and ethnicity: Current research about women and men.* Mountain View, CA: Mayfield.

Perrizo, K., & Pustilnik, S. (2006). Association between sudden death in infancy and co-sleeping. *American Journal of Forensic Medicine and Pathology, 27*, 169–172.

Perry, W. G., Jr. (1970) *Forms of intellectual and ethical development in the college years: A scheme.* New York: Holt, Rinehart, and Winston.

Persaud, T. V. N. (1977). *Problems of birth defects: From Hippocrates to thalidomide and after.* Baltimore, MD: University Park Press.

Petersen, A., Sarigiani, P., Leffert, N., & Camarena, P. (1998). Resilience in adolescence. In A. Schwartzberg (Ed.), *The adolescent in turmoil.* Westport, CT: Praeger.

Peterson, C. (2005). Mind and body: Concepts of human cognition, physiology and false belief in children with autism or typical development. *Journal of Autism and Developmental Disorders, 35,* 487–497.

Peterson, C., Jesso, B., & McCabe, A. (1999). Encouraging narratives in preschoolers: An intervention study. *Journal of Child Language, 26,* 49–67.

Peterson, C., & McCabe, A. (2004). Echoing our parents: Parental influences on children's narration. In M. W. Pratt & B. H. Fiese (Eds.), *Family stories and the life course: Across time and generations* (pp. 27–54). Mahwah, NJ: Lawrence Erlbaum Associates.

Petitto, L. A, Katerlos, M., Levy, B. G., Gauna, K., Tétreault, K., & Ferraro, V. (2001). Bilingual signed and spoken language acquisition from birth: Implications for the mechanisms underlying early bilingual language acquisition. *Journal of Child Language, 28,* 453–496.

Pettit, G. S., Keiley, M. K., Laird, R. D., Bates, J. E., & Dodge, K. A. (2007, June). Predicting the developmental course of mother-reported monitoring across childhood and adolescence from early proactive parenting, child temperament, and parents' worries. *Journal of Family Psychology. 21*(2), 206–217.

Phinney, J. S. (2005). Ethnic identity in late modern times: A response to Rattansi and Phoenix. *Identity, 5*(2), 187–194.

Phinney, J. S. (2008). Ethnic identity exploration in emerging adulthood. In D. L. Browning (Ed.), *Adolescent identities: A collection of readings. Relational perspectives book series* (pp. 47–66). New York: The Analytic Press/Taylor & Francis Group.

Phinney, J. S., & Haas, K. (2003). The process of coping among ethnic minority first-generation college freshmen: A narrative approach. *Journal of Social Psychology, 143*(6), 707–726.

Phinney, J. S., & Ong, A. D. (2002). Adolescent-parent disagreements and life satisfaction in families from Vietnamese- and European-American backgrounds. *International Journal of Behavioral Development, 26*(6), 556–561.

Piaget, J. (1926). *The language and thought of the child.* New York: Meridian Books.

Piaget, J. (1928). *Judgment and reasoning in the child.* London: Routledge & Kegan Paul.

Piaget, J. (1929/1979). *The child's conception of the world.* New York: Harcourt Brace.

Piaget, J. (1930). *The child's conception of physical causality.* New York: Harcourt Brace.

Piaget, J. (1932/1965). *The moral judgment of the child.* New York: Free Press. (Original work published 1932)

Piaget, J. (1952a). *The child's conception of number.* New York: W. W. Norton.

Piaget, J. (1952b). *The origins of intelligence in children.* New York: International Universities Press.

Piaget, J. (1954). *The construction of reality in the child.* New York: Basic Books.

Piaget, J. (1966/1974). Need and significance of cross-cultural studies in genetic psychology. In J. W. Berry & P. R. Dasen (Eds.), *Culture and cognition: Readings in cross-cultural psychology.* London: Metheun.

Piaget, J. (1973). *The psychology of intelligence.* Totowa, NJ: Littlefield & Adams.

Piaget, J. (1977). *The development of thought: Equilibration of cognitive structure.* New York: Viking.

Piaget, J. (1995). *Sociological studies.* New York: Routledge.

Piaget, J., & Inhelder, B. (1956). *The child's conception of space.* London: Routledge & Kegan Paul.

Piaget, J., & Inhelder, B. (1969). *The psychology of the child.* New York: Basic Books.

Piatt, J. H., Jr. (2003). *Infant heads: Too big, too small, misshapen.* Retrieved July 29, 2006, from http://www.drexelmed.edu/documents/ped_neurosurgery/about_heads.pdf

Pick, A. D. (1997). Perceptual learning, categorizing, and cognitive development. In C. Dent-Read & P. Zukow-Golding (Eds.), *Evolving explanations of development: Ecological approaches to organism environment systems* (pp. 335–370). Washington, DC: American Psychological Association.

Piehler, T. F., & Dishion, T. J. (2007, September). Interpersonal dynamics within adolescent friendships: Dyadic mutuality, deviant talk, and patterns of antisocial behavior. *Child Development, 78*(5), 1611–1624.

Pigliucci, M. (2001). *Phenotypic plasticity: Beyond nature and nurture.* Baltimore, MD: Johns Hopkins University Press.

Pinelli, J., & Symington, A. (2001). Non-nutritive sucking for the promotion of physiologic stability and nutrition in preterm infants. *Cochrane Database of Systematic Reviews, 3,* CD001071.

Pinker, S. (2002). *The blank slate: The modern denial of human nature.* New York: Viking.

Pinker, S. (2007). *The stuff of thought: Language as a window into human nature.* New York: Viking.

Pittman, R., & Oppenheim, R. W. (1979). Cell death of motoneurons in the chick embryo spinal cord. *Journal of Comparative Neurology, 187,* 425–446.

Pizzuto, E., Ardito, B., Caselli, M. C., & Volterra, V. (2001). Cognition and language in Italian deaf preschoolers of deaf and hearing families. In M. D. Clark, M. Marschark, & M. Karchmer (Eds.), *Context, cognition, and deafness* (pp. 49–70). Washington, DC: Gallaudet University Press.

Pleck, J. H., & Masciadrelli, B. P. (2003). Paternal involvement in U.S. residential fathers: Levels, sources, and consequences. In M. Lamb (Ed.), *The role of the father in development.* New York: Wiley.

Plomin, R., De Fries, J. C., McClearn, G. E., & Rutter, M. (2001). *Behavioral genetics: A primer* (4th ed.). New York: Worth.

Pnevmatikos, D. (2002). Conceptual changes in religious concepts of elementary schoolchildren: The case of the house where God lives. *Educational Psychology, 22*(1), 93–112.

Polikoff, B. (1999). *With one bold act: The story of Jane Addams.* Chicago: Boswell Books.

Polivy, J., & Herman, C. P. (2004). Sociocultural idealization of thin female body shapes: An introduction to the special issue on body image and eating disorders. *Journal of Social and Clinical Psychology, 23*(1), 1–6.

Pollack, H. A., & Frohna, J. G. (2002). Infant sleep placement after the back to sleep campaign. *Pediatrics, 109*(4), 608–614.

Pollack, W. S. (2000). *Real boys' voices.* New York: Random House.

Pollitt, E. (2001). Statistical and psychobiological significance in developmental research. *American Journal of Clinical Nutrition, 74*(3), 281–282.

Pollitt, E., Saco-Pollitt, C., Jahari, A., Husaini, M. A., & Huang, J. (2000). Effects of an energy and micronutrient supplement on mental development and behavior under natural conditions in undernourished children in Indonesia. *European Journal of Clinical Nutrition, 54*(Suppl. 2), S80–S90.

Pollock, D. (1999). *Telling bodies performing birth: Everyday narratives of childbirth.* New York: Columbia University Press.

Polman, H., de Castro, B. O., Koops, W., van Boxtel, H. W., & Merk, W. W. (2007, August). A meta-analysis of the distinction between reactive and proactive aggression in children and adolescents. *Journal of Abnormal Child Psychology. 35*(4), 522–535.

Pomerantz, E. M., Ruble, D. N., Frey, K. S., & Greulich, F. (1995). Meeting goals and confronting conflict: Children's changing perceptions of social comparison. *Child Development, 66,* 723–738.

Pontius, K., Aretz, M., Griebel, C., Jacobs, C., LaRock, K., et al. (2001). Back to sleep—Tummy time to play. *Newsletter of the Children's Hospital, 4*(4), 1–3.

Poole, D., & Lindsay, D. (2001). Children's eyewitness reports after exposure to misinformation from parents. *Journal of Experimental Psychology: Applied, 7,* 27–50.

Popp, D., Laursen, B., Kerr, M., Stattin, H., & Burk, W. K. (2008, July). Modeling homophily over time with an actor-partner interdependence model. *Developmental Psychology, 44*(4), 1028–1039.

Porter, R., & Winberg, J. (1999). Unique salience of maternal breast odors for newborn infants. *Neuroscience and Biobehavioral Reviews, 23,* 439–449.

Portes, A., & Rumbaut, R. (2001). *Legacies: The story of the second generation.* Berkeley: University of California Press.

Posada, G., Carbonell, O. A., Alzate, G., & Plata, S. J. (2004). Through Colombian lenses: Ethnographic and conventional analyses of maternal care and their associations with secure base behavior. *Developmental Psychology, 40*(4), 508–518.

Posner, M. I., Rothbart, M. K., Sheese, B. E., & Tang, Y. (2007). The anterior cingulate gyrus and the mechanism of self-regulation. *Cognitive, Affective, & Behavioral Neuroscience, 7*(4), 391–395.

Poulin, F., & Boivin, M. (2000). The formation and development of friendship in childhood: The role of proactive and reactive aggression. *Developmental Psychology, 36,* 233–240.

Poulin-Dubois, D., & Forbes, J. (2006). Word, intention, and action: A two-tiered model of action word learning. In K. Hirsh-Pasek & R. M. Golinkoff (Eds.), *Action meets word: How children learn verbs* (pp. 262–285). New York: Oxford University Press.

Pratt, M. W., & Fiese, B. H. (Eds.). (2004). *Family stories and the life course: Across time and generations.* Mahwah, NJ: Lawrence Erlbaum Associates.

Pratt, M. W., Hunsberger, B., Pancer, S. M., & Alisat, S. (2003, November). A longitudinal analysis of personal values socialization: Correlates of a moral self-ideal in late adolescence. *Social Development, 12*(4), 563–585.

Prechtl, H. (1977). *The neurological examination of the full-term newborn infant* (2nd ed.). Philadelphia: Lippincott.

Preisser, D. A., Hodson, B. W., & Paden, E. P. (1988). Developmental phonology: 18–29 months. *Journal of Speech and Hearing Disorders, 53,* 125–130.

Prentice, A. M., & Jebb, S. A. (2003). Fast foods, energy density and obesity: A possible mechanistic link. *Obesity Review 4*(4), 187–194.

Pressley, M., & Hilden, K. (2006). Cognitive strategies. In D. Kuhn, R. S. Siegler, W. Damon, & R. M. Lerner (Eds.), *Handbook of child psychology: Vol. 2. Cognition, perception, and language* (6th ed., pp. 511–556). Hoboken, NJ: John Wiley & Sons.

Preyer, W. T. (1890). *The mind of the child . . . observations concerning the mental development of the human being in the first years of life.* New York: Appleton.

Pruden, S., Hirsh-Pasek, K., Golinkoff, R., & Hennon, E. (2006). The birth of words; Ten-month-olds learn words through perceptual salience. *Child Development, 77,* 266.

Pujol, J., Soriano-Mas, C., Ortiz, H., Sebastián-Gallés, N., Losilla, J., M., & Deus, J. (2006). Myelination of language-related areas in the developing brain. *Neurology, 66,* 339–343.

Pujol, J., Soriano-Mas, C., Ortiz, H., Sebastián-Gallés, N., Losilla, J., & Deus, J. (2006). Myelination of language-related areas in the developing brain. *Neurology, 66*(3), 339–343.

Quas, J. A., Davis, E. L., Goodman, G. S., & Myers, J. E. B. (2007). Repeated questions, deception, and children's true and false reports of body touch. *Child Maltreatment, 12*(1), 60–67.

Quas, J. A., Malloy, L. C., Melinder, A., Goodman, G. S., D'Mello, M., & Schaaf, J. (2007, July). Developmental differences in the effects of repeated interviews and interviewer bias on young children's event memory and false reports. *Developmental Psychology, 43*(4), 823–837.

Quinn, P. C. (2002). Early categorization. In U. Goswami (Ed.), *Blackwell handbook of childhood cognitive development* (pp. 85–101). Oxford, England: Blackwell Publishing.

Quinn, P. C., & Eimas, P. D. (1996). Perceptual organization and categorization in young infants. In C. Rovee-Collier & L. P. Lipsitt (Eds.), *Advances in infancy research: Vol. 10* (pp. 1–36). Norwood, NJ: Ablex.

Quinn, P. C., Eimas, P. D., & Rosenkrantz, S. L. (1993). Evidence for representations of perceptually similar natural categories by 3-month-old and 4-month-old infants. *Perception, 22,* 463–475.

Quinn, P. C., Westerlund, A., & Nelson, C. A. (2006) Neural markers of categorization in 6-month-old infants. *Psychological Science 17*(1), 59–66.

Quintana, S., Aboud, F., Chao, R., Contreras-Grau, J., Cross, W., Hudley, C., et al. (2006). Race, ethnicity, and culture in child development: Contemporary research and future directions. *Child Development, 77*(5) 1129–1141.

Raeburn, P. (2005, August 14). A second womb. *New York Times Magazine,* p. 37

Raikes, H., Luze, G., Brooks-Gunn, J., Raikes, H. A., Pan, B. A., Tamis-LeMonda, C. S, et al. (2006). Mother-child bookreading in low-income families: Correlates and outcomes during the first three years of life. *Child Development, 77*(4), 924–953.

Rauscher, F. H., Shaw, G. L., & Ky, K. N. (1993). Music and spatial task performance. *Nature, 365,* 611.

Raymond, D. (1994). Homophobia, identity, and the meanings of desire: Reflections on the culture construction of gay and lesbian adolescent sexuality. In J. Irvine (Ed.), *Sexual cultures and the construction of adolescent identities* (pp. 115–150). Philadelphia: Temple University Press.

Read, M. (1960/1968). *Children of their fathers: Growing up among the Ngoni of Malawi.* New York: Holt, Rinehart & Winston.

Read, M. (1983). *Children of their fathers: Growing up among the Ngoni of Malawi.* New York: Irvington.

Reddy, V. (2005). Feeling shy and showing-off: Self-conscious emotions must regulate self-awareness. In J. Nadel and D. Muir (Eds.), *Emotional development* (pp. 183–204). Oxford, England: Oxford University Press.

Reed, M. D., & Roundtree, P. W. (1997). Peer pressure and adolescent substance abuse. *Journal of Quantitative Criminology, 13*(2), 143–180.

Regani, R. (2000). Living in urban environment and leaning toward external locus of control orientation. *Journal of the Indian Academy of Applied Psychology, 26*(1–2), 129–133.

Reichel-Domatoff, G., & Reichel-Domatoff, A. (1961). *The people of Aritama.* London: Routledge & Kegan Paul.

Reis, O., Youniss, J., McIntosh, H., & Eisermann, J. (2007). Continuity, change and mechanisms of identity development. In M. Watzlawik & A. Born (Eds.), *Capturing identity: Quantitative and qualitative methods* (pp. 163–177). Lanham, MD: University Press of America.

Relier, J.-P. (2001). Influence of maternal stress on fetal behavior and brain development. *Biology of the Neonate, 79*(3–4), 168–171.

Renz-Polster, H., & Buist, A. S. (2002). Being born by cesarean section increases the risk of asthma and hay fever as a child. *Journal of Investigative Medicine, 50*(1), 29a.

Repacholi, B. M., Meltzoff, A. N., & Olsen, B. (2008). Infants' understanding of the link between visual perception and emotion: "If she can't see me doing it, she won't get angry." *Developmental Psychology, 44*(2), 561–574.

Research Forum on Children, Families, and the New Federalism. (2002, February). Lack of appropriate research leads to gaps in knowledge about children in immigrant families. *The Forum, 5.* Retrieved August 22, 2008, from http://www.researchforum.org/media/forum51.pdf

Rest, J., Narvaez, D., Bebeau, M. l. J., & Thoma, S. J. (1999). *Postconventional moral thinking: A neo-Kohlbergian approach.* Mahwah, NJ: Lawrence Erlbaum Associates.

Rice, C., Koinis, D., Sullivan, K., & Tager-Flusberg, H. (1997). When 3-year-olds pass the appearance-reality test. *Developmental Psychology, 33*(1), 54–61.

Rich, J. L. (2004, March). Play school. *Teacher Magazine, 15*(5), 40–45.

Richards, J. E. (2003). Attention affects the recognition of briefly presented visual stimuli in infants: An ERP study. *Developmental Science, 6*(3), 312–328.

Richardson, J., & Scott, K. (2002). Rap music and its violent progency: America's culture of violence in context. *The Journal of Negro Education, 71*(3), 175–192.

Richerson, P., & Boyd, R. (2005). *Not by genes alone: How culture transformed human evolution.* Chicago: University of Chicago Press.

Richmond, J., & Nelson, C. A. (2007, September). Accounting for change in declarative memory: A cognitive neuroscience perspective. *Developmental Review, 27*(3), 349–373.

Ritz, B., Wilhelm, M., & Zhao Y. (2006). Air pollution and infant death in southern California, 1989–2000. *Pediatrics, 118*(2), 493–502.

Rizzolatti, G., Fadiga, L., Gallese, V., & Fogassi, L. (1996). Premotor cortex and the recognition of motor actions. *Cognitive Brain Opinion, 3,* 131–141.

Robbins, W. J., Brody, S., Hogan, A. G., Jackson, C. M., & Greene, C. W. (Eds.). (1929). *Growth.* New Haven, CT: Yale University Press.

Roberts, D., Foehr, U., & Rideout, V. (2005, March). *Generation M: Media in the lives of 8– 18 year-olds. A Kaiser Family Foundation study.* Menlo Park, CA: Henry J. Kaiser Family Foundation.

Robinson, J. L. (2000). Are there implications for prevention research from studies of resilience? *Child Development, 71*(3), 570–572.

Robinson, J. L., Emde, R. N., & Corley, R. P. (2001). Dispositional cheerfulness: Early genetic and environmental influences. In R. N. Emde & J. K. Hewitt (Eds.), *Infancy to early childhood: Genetic and environmental influences on developmental change* (pp. 163–177). New York: Oxford University Press.

Robinson, S. R., & Kleven, G. A. (2005). Learning to move before birth. In B. Hopkins & S. P. Johnson (Eds.), *Prenatal development of postnatal functions (Advances in infancy research)* (pp. 131–175). Westport, CT: Praeger Publishers/Greenwood Publishing Group.

Rochat, P. (2000). *The infant world: Self, objects, people.* Cambridge, MA: Harvard University Press.

Rodkin, P. C., Farmer, T. W., Pearl, R., & Van Acker, R. (2000). Heterogeneity of popular boys: Antisocial and prosocial configurations. *Developmental Psychology, 36*(1), 14–24.

Rodriguez, C., & Sutherland, D. (1999). Predictors of parents' physical disciplinary practices. *Child Abuse and Neglect, 23,* 651–657.

Rogoff, B. (2003). *The cultural nature of human development.* Oxford, England: Oxford University Press.

Rogoff, B., & Waddell, K. J. (1982). Memory for information organized in a scene by children from two cultures. *Child Development, 53,* 1224–1228.

Rogoff, B., Correa-Chávez, M., & Cotuc, M. N. (2005). A cultural/historical view of schooling in human development. In D. B. Pillemer & S. H. White (Eds.), *Developmental psychology and social change: Research, history and policy* (pp. 225–263). New York: Cambridge University Press.

Rogoff, B., Moore, L., Najafi, B., Dexter, A., Correa-Chávez, M., & Solís, J. (2007). Children's development of cultural repertoires through participation in everyday routines and practices. In J. E. Grusec & P. D. Hastings (Eds.), *Handbook of socialization: Theory and research* (pp. 490–515). New York: Guilford Press.

Romans, S. E., Martin, M., Gendall, K., & Herbison, G. P. (2003). Age of menarche: The role of some psychosocial factors. *Psychological Medicine, 33*(5), 933–939.

Roosa, M. (2000). Some thoughts about resilience versus positive development, main effects versus interactions, and the value of resilience. *Child Development, 71,* 567–569.

Rose, A. J., & Asher, S. R. (2000) Children's friendships. In C. Hendrick & S. S. Hendrick (Eds.), *Close relationships: A sourcebook* (pp. 47–57). Thousand Oaks, CA: Sage Publications.

Rose, A. J., Swenson, L., & Carlson, W. (2004). Friendships of aggressive youth: Considering the influence of being disliked and of being perceived popular. *Journal of Experimental Child Psychology, 88,* 25–45.

Rose, S. A., Feldman, J. F., & Jankowski, J. J. (2004). Infant visual recognition memory. *Developmental Review, 24*(1), 74–100.

Rosen, W. D., Adamson, L. B., & Bakeman, R. (1992). An experimental investigation of infant social referencing: Mothers' messages and gender differences. *Developmental Psychology, 28*(6), 1172–1178.

Rosenblatt, R. A., Dobie, S. A., Hart, L. G., Schneeweiss, R., Gould, D., Raine, T. R., et al. (1997). Interspecialty differences in the obstetric care of low-risk women. *American Journal of Public Health, 87*(3), 344–351.

Rosengren, K. S., & Brasswell, G. S. (2001). Variability in children's reasoning. In H. W. Reese and R. Kail (Eds.), *Advances in child development and behavior: Vol. 28* (pp. 2–41). New York: Academic Press.

Rosenstein, D., & Oster, H. (1988). Differential facial responses to four basic tastes in newborns. *Child Development, 59,* 1555–1568.

Rosenzweig, M. R. (1984). Experience, memory, and the brain. *American Psychologist, 39,* 365–376.

Rosso, P. (1990). *Nutrition and metabolism in pregnancy.* Oxford, England: Oxford University Press.

Roth, M., & Parker, J. (2001). Affective and behavioral responses to friends who neglect their friends for dating partners: Influences of gender, jealousy and perspective. *Journal of Adolescence, 24,* 281–296.

Rothbart, M. K., Ahadi, S. A., & Evans, D. E. (2000). Temperament and personality: Origins and outcomes. *Journal of Personality and Social Psychology, 78*(1), 122–135.

Rothbaum, F., & Kakinuma, M. (2004). Amae and attachment: Security in cultural context. (2004). *Human Development, 47*(1), 34–39.

Rothbaum, F., Weisz, J., Pott, M., & Morelli, G. (2000). Attachment and culture: Security in the United States and Japan. *American Psychologist, 55*(10), 1093–1104.

Rovee-Collier, C. (1997). Dissociations in infant memory: Rethinking the development of implicit and explicit memory. *Psychological Review, 104*(3), 467–498.

Rovee-Collier, C., & Barr, R. (2001). Infant learning and memory. In G. Bremner & A. Fogel (Eds.), *Blackwell handbook of infant development* (pp. 139–168). Malden, MA: Blackwell Publishing.

Rovee-Collier, C., Hartshorn, K., & DiRubbo, M. (1999). Long-term maintenance of infant memory. *Developmental Psychobiology, 35*(2), 91–102

Rubin, J. Z., Provezano, F. J., & Luria, Z. (1974). The eye of the beholder: Parents' view on sex of newborns. *American Journal of Orthopsychiatry, 44,* 512–519.

Rubin, K. H., Bukowski, W. M., & Parker, J. G. (2006a). Peer interactions, relationships, and groups. In N. Eisenberg, W. Damon, & R. M. Lerner (Eds.), *Handbook of child psychology: Vol. 3. Social, emotional, and personality development* (6th ed., pp. 571–645). Hoboken, NJ: John Wiley & Sons.

Rubin, K. H., Burgess, K. B., Kennedy, A. E., & Stewart, S. L. (2003). Social withdrawal in childhood. In E. J. Mash & R. A. Barkley (Eds.), *Child psychopathology* (2nd ed., pp. 372–406). New York: Guilford Press.

Rubin, K. H., Wojslawowicz, J. C., Rose-Krasnor, L., Booth-LaForce, C., & Burgess, K. B. (2006b). The best friendships of shy/withdrawn children: Prevalence, stability, and relationship quality. *Journal of Abnormal Child Psychology, 34*(2), 143–157.

Rubin, Z. (1980). *Children's friendships.* Cambridge, MA: Harvard University Press.

Rubinowitz, L. S., Rosenbaum, J. E., Dvorin, S., Kulieke, M., McCareins, A., & Popkin, S. (2000). *Crossing the class and color lines: From public housing to white suburbia.* Chicago: University of Chicago Press.

Ruble, D. N., & Martin, C. L. (1998). Gender development. In W. Damon & N. Eisenberg (Eds.), *Handbook of child development: Social, emotional, and personality development: Vol. 5* (pp. 933–1016). New York: Wiley.

Ruble, D. N., & Martin, C. L. (2002). Conceptualizing, measuring and evaluating the developmental course of gender differentiation. *Monographs of the Society for Research in Child Development, 67,* 148–166.

Ruble, D. N., Taylor, L. J., Cyphers, L., Greulich, F. K., Lurye, L. E., & Shrout, P. E. (2007). The role of gender constancy in early gender development. *Child Development, 78*(4), 1121–1136.

Rudolph, K. (2002). Gender differences in emotional responses to interpersonal stress during adolescence. *Journal of Adolescent Health, 30,* 3–13.

Rudolph, K., & Conley, C. (2005). The socioemotional costs and benefits of social-evaluative concerns: Do girls care too much? *Journal of Personality, 73*(1), 115–138.

Ruel, M. T., & Menon, P. (2002). Child feeding practices are associated with child nutritional status in Latin America: Innovative uses of the demographic and health surveys. *Journal of Nutrition, 132*(6), 1180–1187.

Ruff, H. A., & Capozzoli, M. C. (2003). Development of attention and distractibility in the first 4 years of life. *Developmental Psychology, 39*(5), 877–890.

Ruffman, T., Slade, L., & Redman, J. (2005). Young infants' expectations about hidden objects. *Cognition, 97,* 35–43.

Ruiz, S., Roosa, M., & Gonzales, N. (2002). Predictors of self-esteem for Mexican American and European American youths: A reexamination of the influence of parenting. *Journal of Family Psychology, 16,* 70–80.

Rumbaugh, D. M., Savage-Rumbaugh, E. S., & Sevcik, R. A. (1994). Biobehavioral roots of language: A comparative perspective on chimpanzee, child, and culture. In R. W. Wrangham, W. C. McGrew, F. B. M. de Waal, & P. G. Helthe (Eds.), *Chimpanzee cultures.* Cambridge, MA: Harvard University Press.

Rumbaugh, D. M., & Washburn, D. A. (2003). *Intelligence of apes and other rational beings.* New Haven, CT: Yale University Press.

Russell, R. (2001). New nicronutrient dietary reference intakes from the National Academy of Sciences. *Nutrition Today, 36,* 163–171.

Russell, S., & Joyner, K. (2001). Adolescent sexual orientation and suicide risk: Evidence from a national study. *American Journal of Public Health, 91,* 1276–1281.

Rust, J., Golombok, S., Hines, M., & Johnston, K. (2000). The role of brothers and sisters in the gender development of preschool children. *Journal of Experimental Child Psychology, 77,* 292–303.

Rutter, M. (2006). The psychological effects of early institutional rearing. In P. Marshall & N. Fox (Eds.), *The development of social engagement: Neurobiological perspectives* (pp. 355–391). New York: Oxford University Press.

Ryan, R. R., Martin, A., & Brooks-Gunn, J. (2006). Is one good parent good enough? Patterns of mother and father parenting and child cognitive outcomes at 24 and 36 months. *Parenting: Science and Practice, 6,* 211–228.

Ryan, S. (2000). Examining social workers' placement recommendations of children with gay and lesbian adoptive parents. *Families in Society, 81,* 517–528.

Saarni, C. (1999). *The development of emotional competence.* New York: Guilford Press.

Saarni, C. (2007). The development of emotional competence: Pathways for helping children to become emotionally intelligent. In R. Bar-On, J. G. Maree, & M. J. Elias (Eds.), *Educating people to be emotionally intelligent* (pp. 15–35). Westport, CT: Praeger Publishers/ Greenwood Publishing Group.

Saarni, C., Campos, J. J., Camras, L. A., & Witherington, D. (2006). Emotional development: Action, communication, and understanding. In N. Eisenberg, W. Damon, & R. M. Lerner (Eds.), *Handbook of child psychology: Vol. 3. Social, emotional, and personality development* (6th ed., pp. 226–299). Hoboken, NJ: John Wiley & Sons.

Sachs, J., Bard, B., & Johnson, M. (1981). Language learning with restricted input: Case studies of two hearing children of deaf parents. *Applied Psycholinguistics, 2,* 33–54.

Sadovsky, A., & Troseth, G. (2000). Aspects of young children's perceptions of gender-typed occupations. *Sex Roles, 42,* 993–1006.

Sagi, A., van IJzendoorn, M. H., Aviezer, O., Donnell, F., Koren-Karie, N., Joels, T., et al. (1995). Attachments in a multiple-caregiver and multiple-infant environment: The case of the Israeli kibbutzim. *Monographs of the Society for Research in Child Development, 60*(2–3), 71–91.

Sagi-Schwartz, A., & Aviezer, O. (2005). Correlates of attachment to multiple caregivers in kibbutz children from birth to emerging adulthood: The Haifa Longitudinal Study. In K. E. Grossmann, K. Grossmann, & E. Waters (Eds.), *Attachment from infancy to adulthood: The major longitudinal studies* (pp. 165–197). New York: Guilford Press.

Sai, F. Z. (2005). The role of the mother's voice in developing mother's face preference: Evidence for intermodal perception at birth. *Infant and Child Development, 14,* 29–50.

Saltvedt, S., Almstrom, H., Kublickas, M., Valentin, L., Bottinga, R., Bui, T. H., et al. (2005). Screening for Down syndrome based on maternal age or fetal nuchal translucency: a randomized controlled trial in 39,572 pregnancies. *Ultrasound in Obstetrics and Gynecology, 25*(6), 537–545.

Salzarulo, P., & Ficca, G. (Eds.). (2002). *Advances in consciousness research: Vol. 38. Awakening and sleep-wake cycle across development.* Amsterdam: John Benjamins.

Sameroff, A. J. (1983). Developmental systems: Contexts and evolutions. In P. H. Mussen (Ed.), *Handbook of child psychology: Vol. 1. History, theory and methods.* New York: Wiley.

Sameroff, A. J., Bartko, W. T., Baldwin, A., Baldwin, C., & Seifer, R. (1998). Family and social influences on the development of child competence. In M. Lewis & C. Feiring (Eds.), *Families, risk, and competence* (pp. 161–186). Mahwah, NJ: Lawrence Erlbaum Associates.

Sameroff, A. J., & Haith, M. M. (1996). *The five to seven year shift: The age of reason and responsibility.* Chicago: University of Chicago Press.

Sameroff, A. J., Seifer, R., Baldwin, A., & Baldwin, C. (1993). Stability of intelligence from preschool to adolescence: The influence of social and family risk factors. *Child Development, 64,* 80–97.

Sampaio, R. C., & Truwitt, C. L. (2001). Myelination in the developing human brain. In C. Nelson and M. Luciana (Eds.), *Handbook of developmental cognitive science* (pp. 35–44). Cambridge, MA: The MIT Press.

San Antonio, Donna Marie. (2004). Adolescent lives in transition: How social class influences the adjustment to middle school. Albany, NY: State University of New York Press,

Sandberg, A., & Samuelsson, I. P. (2003). Preschool teachers' play experiences then and now. *Early childhood research and practice, 5*(1).

Sanson, A., Hamphill, S., & Smart, D. (2002). Temperament and social development. In P. Smith & C. Hart (Eds.), *Blackwell handbook of childhood social development.* Malden, MA: Blackwell Publishing.

Sapp, F., Lee, K., & Muir, D. (2000). Three-year-olds' difficulty with the appearance-reality distinction: Is it real or is it apparent? *Developmental Psychology, 36*(5), 547–560.

Saragovi, C., Aube, J., Koestner, R., & Zuroff, D. (2002). Traits, motives, and depressive styles as reflections of agency and communion. *Personality and Social Psychology Bulletin, 28,* 563–577.

Sarnecka, B., & Gelman, S. (2004). Six does not just mean a lot: Preschoolers see number words as specific. *Cognition, 92,* 329–352.

Sartor, C., & Youniss, J. (2002). The relationship between positive parental involvement and identity achievement during adolescence. *Adolescence,* 221–234.

Savage-Rumbaugh, E. S. (1993). How does evolution design a brain capable of learning language? *Monographs of the Society for Research in Child Development 58*(3–4), 243–252.

Savage-Rumbaugh, E. S., Toth, N., & Schick, K. (2007). Kanzi learns to knap stone tools. In D. A. Washburn (Ed.), *Primate perspectives on*

behavior and cognition (pp. 279–291). Washington, DC: American Psychological Association.

Savage-Rumbaugh, E. S., & Fields, W. (2000). Linguistic, cultural and cognitive capacities of bonobos. *Culture & Psychology, 6*(2), 131–153.

Savin-Williams, R. C. (2001). A critique of research on sexual-minority youths. *Journal of Adolescence, 24,* 5–13.

Savin-Williams, R. C. (2008, January). Then and now: Recruitment, definition, diversity, and positive attributes of same-sex populations. *Developmental Psychology, 44*(1), 135–138.

Savin-Williams, R. C., & Diamond, L. (2004). Sex. In R. M. Lerner & L. Steinberg (Eds.), *Handbook of adolescent psychology* (2nd ed.). Hoboken, NJ: John Wiley & Sons.

Saxe, G. B. (2002). Children's developing mathematics in collective practices: A framework for analysis. *Journal of the Learning Sciences, 11*(2–3), 275–300.

Saxon, T. F., Gollapalli, A., Mitchell, M. W., & Stanko, S. (2002). Demand feeding or schedule feeding: Infant growth from birth to 6 months. *Journal of Reproductive and Infant Psychology, 20*(2), 89–100.

Saxton, M. (1997). The contrast theory of negative input. *Journal of Child Language, 24*(1), 139–161.

Scarr, S., & Salapatek, P. (1970). Patterns of fear development during infancy. *Merrill-Palmer Quarterly, 16*(1), 53–90.

Schack-Nielsen, L., Larnkjaer, A., & Michaelsen, K. F. (2005). Long term effects of breastfeeding on the infant and mother. *Advances in Experimental Medicine and Biology, 569,* 16–23.

Schafer, G., & Plunkett, K. (1998). Rapid word learning by fifteen-month-olds under tightly controlled conditions. *Child Development, 69*(2), 309–320.

Scherf, K. S., Sweeney, J. A., & Luna, B. (2006, July). Brain basis of developmental change in visuospatial working memory. *Journal of Cognitive Neuroscience, 18*(7), 1045–1058.

Scheuermann, B. (2002). *Autism: Teaching does make a difference.* Belmont, CA: Wadsworth Thomson Learning.

Schick, B. (2006). Acquiring a visually motivated language: Evidence from diverse learners. In B. Schick, M. Marschark & P. Spencer (Eds.), *Advances in the sign language development of deaf children.* New York: Oxford University Press.

Schlagmuller, M., & Schneider, W. (2002). The development of organizational strategies in children: Evidence from a microgenetic longitudinal study. *Journal of Experimental Child Psychology, 81*(3), 298–319.

Schmidt, M. E., Pempek, T. A., Kirkorian, H. L., Lund, A. F., & Anderson, D. R. (2008). The effects of background television on the toy play behavior of very young children. *Child Development, 79*(4), 1137–1151.

Schmitt-Rodermund, E., & Silbereisen, R. K (2008, March). Well-adapted adolescent ethnic German immigrants in spite of adversity: The protective effects of human, social, and financial capital. *European Journal of Developmental Psychology, 5*(2), 186–209.

Schneider, B. H. (2000). *Friends and enemies: Peer relations in childhood.* New York: Oxford University Press.

Schneider, B. H., del Pilar Soteras de Toro, M., Woodburn, S., Fulop, M., Cervino, C., Bernstein, S., et al. (2006). Cross-cultural differences in competition among children and adolescents. In X. Chen, D. C. French, & B. H. Schneider (Eds.), *Peer relationships in cultural context. Cambridge studies in social and emotional development* (pp. 310–338). New York: Cambridge University Press.

Schneider, B. H., & Stevenson, D. (1999). *The ambitious generation: America's teenagers, motivated, but directionless.* New Haven, CT: Yale University Press.

Schneider, B. H., Woodburn, S., del Pilar Soteras del Toro, M., & Udvari, S. J. (2005, April). Cultural and gender differences in the impli-cations of competition for early adolescent friendship. *Merrill-Palmer Quarterly, 51*(2), 163–191.

Schneider, W., & Bjorklund, D. F. (1998). Memory. In D. Kuhn & R. S. Siegler (Eds.), *Handbook of child psychology: Vol. 2. Cognition, perception, and language* (5th ed., pp. 467–522). New York: Wiley.

Schneider, W., Gruber, H., Gold, A., & Opwis, K. (1993). Class expertise and memory for chess positions in children and adults. *Journal of Experimental Child Psychology, 56,* 328–349.

Schneider, W., Kron, V., Hünnerkopf, M., & Krajewski, K. (2004, June). The development of young children's memory strategies: First findings from the Würzburg Longitudinal Memory Study. *Journal of Experimental Child Psychology, 88*(2), 193–209.

Schneider, W., & Pressley, M. (1997). *Memory development between two and twenty* (2nd ed.). Mahwah, NJ: Lawrence Erlbaum Associates.

Scholes, R. J. (1998). The case against phonemic awareness. *Journal of Research in Reading, 21*(3), 177–218.

Schonert-Reichl, K. A. (1999). Relations of peer acceptance, friendship adjustment, and social behavior to moral reasoning during early adolescence. *Journal of Early Adolescence, 19,* 249–279.

Schuetze, P., Eiden, R. D., & Coles, C. D. (2007, April). Prenatal cocaine and other substance exposure: Effects on infant autonomic regulation at 7 months of age. *Developmental Psychobiology, 49*(3), 276–289.

Schuler, M. E., & Nair, P. (1999). Frequency of maternal cocaine use during pregnancy and infant neurobehavioral outcome. *Journal of Pediatric Psychology, 24*(6), 511–514.

Schum, T. R., Kolb, T. M., McAuliffe, T., Simms, M. D., Underhill, R. L., & Marla, L. (2002). Sequential acquisition of toilet-training skills: A descriptive study of gender and age differences in normal children. *Pediatrics, 109*(3), e48.

Schwartz, D., McFadyen-Ketchum, S. A., Dodge, K. A., & Pettit, G. S. (1998). Peer group victimization as a predictor of children's behavior problems at home and in school. *Development & Psychopathology, 10*(1), 87–99.

Schwenck, C., Bjorklund, D. F., & Schneider, W. (2007, November). Factors influencing the incidence of utilization deficiencies and other patterns of recall/strategy-use relations in a strategic memory task. *Child Development, 78*(6), 1771–1787.

Scribner, S., & Cole, M. (1981). *The psychology of literacy.* Cambridge, MA: Harvard University Press.

Sears, R. (1975). Your ancients revisited: A history of child development. In E. M. Hetherington (Ed.), *Review of child development research: Vol. 5.* Chicago: University of Chicago Press.

Segal, N. L. (1999). *Entwined lives: Twins and what they tell us about human behavior.* New York: Dutton/Penguin Books.

Segall, M. H., Dasen, P., Berry, J. W., & Poortinga, Y. (1999). *Human behavior in global perspective: An introduction to cross-cultural psychology* (2nd ed.). Needham Heights, MA: Allyn & Bacon.

Segall, M. H., Ember, C., & Ember, M. (1997). Aggression, crime, and warfare. In J. W. Berry, M. H. Segall, & C. Kagitçibasi (Eds.), *Handbook of cross-cultural psychology: Vol. 3. Social and behavioral applications* (pp. 213–254). Boston: Allyn & Bacon.

Selman, R., Levitt, M., & Schultz, L. (1997). The friendship framework: Tools for the assessment of psychosocial development. In R. Selman, C. Watts, & L. Schultz (Eds.), *Fostering friendship: Pair therapy for treatment and prevention.* New York: Aldine de Gruyter.

Senghas, A., & Coppola, M. (2001). Children creating language: How Nicaraguan sign language acquired a spatial grammar. *Psychological Science, 12*(4), 323–328.

Senghas, R., Senghas, A., & Pyers, J. (2005). The emergence of Nicaraguan sign language: Questions of development, acquisition, and evolution. In S. T. Parker, J. Langer, & C. Milbrath (Eds.), *Biology and* *knowledge revisited: From neurogenesis to psychogenesis* (pp. 287–306). Mahwah, NJ: Lawrence Erlbaum Associates.

Serjeant, G. R., & Serjeant, B. E. (2001). *Sickle cell disease* (3rd ed.). Oxford, England: Oxford University Press.

Serpell, R. (2000). Intelligence and culture. In R. J. Sternberg and E. L. Grigorenko (Eds.), *Handbook of intelligence.* New York: Cambridge University Press.

Serpell, R., & Hatano, G. (1997). Education, schooling, and literacy. In J. W. Berry, P. R. Dasen, & T. S. Saraswathi (Eds.), *Handbook of cross-cultural psychology: Vol. 2.* Boston: Allyn & Bacon.

Serpell, R., & Haynes, B. P. (2004). The cultural practice of intelligence testing: Problems of international export. In R. J. Sternberg & E. L. Grigorenko (Eds.), *Culture and competence: Contexts of life success* (pp. 163–185). Washington, DC: American Psychological Association.

Shanahan, L., McHale, S. M., Osgood, D. W., & Crouter, A. C. (2007, May). Conflict frequency with mothers and fathers from middle childhood to late adolescence: Within- and between-families comparisons. *Developmental Psychology, 43*(3), 539–550.

Shapira, A., & Madsen, M. C. (1969). Cooperative and competitive behavior of kibbutz and urban children in Israel. *Child Development, 4,* 609–617.

Shapka, J. D., & Keating, D. P. (2005, April). Structure and change in self-concept during adolescence. *Canadian Journal of Behavioural Science, 37*(2), 83–96.

Sharpe, N., & Carter, R. (2006). *Genetic testing: Care, consent, and liability.* Hoboken, NJ: John Wiley.

Shatz, M. (1978). Children's comprehension of question-directives. *Journal of Child Language, 5,* 39–46.

Schonberg, M. A., & Shaw, D. S. (2007, October). Risk factors for boy's conduct problems in poor and lower-middle-class neighborhoods. *Journal of Abnormal Child Psychology, 35*(5), 759–772.

Shaw, D. S., Winslow, E. B., Owens, E. B., & Hood, N. (1998). Young children's adjustment to chronic family adversity: A longitudinal study of low-income families. *Journal of the American Academy of Child and Adolescent Psychiatry, 37*(5), 545–553.

Shaw, P., Greenstein, D., Lerch, J., Clasen, L., Lenroot, R., Gogtay, N., et al. (2006, March). Intellectual ability and cortical development in children and adolescents. *Nature, 440*(7084), 676–679.

Shaw, P., Kabani, N. J., Lerch, J. P., Eckstrand, K., Lenroot, R. Gogtay, N., et al. (2008, April). Neurodevelopmental trajectories of the human cerebral cortex. *Journal of Neuroscience, 28*(14), 3586–3594.

Sherif, M., & Sherif, C. W. (1956). *An outline of social psychology.* New York: Harper & Row.

Shin, Y. (2007). Peer relationships, social behaviors, academic performance and loneliness in Korean primary school children. *School Psychology International, 28*(2), 220–236.

Shinskey, J., & Munakata, Y. (2005). Familiarity breeds searching: Infants reverse their novelty preferences when reaching for hidden objects. *Psychological Science, 16,* 596–600.

Shonkoff, J., & Phillips, D. (Eds.). (2000). *From neurons to neighborhoods: The science of early childhood development.* Washington, DC: National Academy Press.

Shopen, T. (1980). How Pablo says "love" and "store." In T. Shopen & J. M. Williams (Eds.), *Standards and dialects in English.* Cambridge, MA: Winthrop.

Shostak, M. (1981). *Nissa: The life and words of a !Kung Woman.* Cambridge, MA: Harvard University Press.

Shulman, S., & Seiffge-Krenke, I. (2001). Adolescent romance: Between experience and relationships. *Journal of Adolescence, 24,* 417–428.

Shweder, R. A., Goodnow, J. J., Hatano, G., LeVine, R. A., Markus, H. R., & Miller, P. J. (1998). The cultural psychology of development: One mind, many mentalities. In R. M. Lerner (Ed.), *Handbook of child psy-*

chology: Vol. 1. Theoretical models of human development (5th ed., pp. 865–938). Hoboken, NJ: Wiley.

Shweder, R. A., Goodnow, J. J., Hatano, G., LeVine, R. A., Markus, H. R., & Miller, P. J. (2006). The cultural psychology of development: One mind, many mentalities. In R. M. Lerner & W. Damon (Eds.), *Handbook of child psychology: Vol. 1. Theoretical models of human development* (6th ed., pp. 716–792). Hoboken, NJ: John Wiley & Sons.

Shweder, R. A., Mahapatpa, M., & Miller, J. G. (1987). Culture and moral development. In J. Kagan & S. Lamb (Eds.), *The emergence of morality in young children.* Chicago: University of Chicago Press.

Shweder, R. A., Minow, M., & Markus, H. R. (Eds.). (2002). *Engaging cultural differences: The multicultural challenge in liberal democracies.* New York: Russell Sage Foundation.

Siegal, M., & Peterson, C. (Eds.). (1999). *Children's understanding of biology and health. Cambridge studies in cognitive and perceptual development.* Cambridge, England: Cambridge University Press.

Siegel, L. S. (2008, January–March). Morphological awareness skills of English language learners and children with dyslexia. *Topics in Language Disorders, 28*(1), 15–27.

Siegler, R. S. (1998). *Children's thinking* (3rd ed.). Upper Saddle River, NJ: Prentice Hall.

Siegler, R. S. (2000). The rebirth of children's learning. *Child Development, 71*(1), 26–35.

Siegler, R. S. (2005, November). Children's learning. *American Psychologist, 60*(8), 769–778.

Siegler, R. S., & Opfer, J. (2003). The development of numerical estimation: Evidence for multiple representations of numerical quantity. *Psychological Science, 14*(3), 237–243.

Silk, J., Steinberg, L., & Morris, A. (2003). Adolescents' emotion regulation in daily life: Links to depressive symptoms and problem behavior. *Child Development, 74,* 1869–1800.

Simmons, R. (2002). *Odd girl out: The hidden culture of aggression in girls.* New York: Harcourt.

Simmons, T., & O'Connell, M. (2003) *Married couple and unmarried partner households: 2000. Census 2000 Special Reports.* Retrieved April 25, 2008, from http://www.census.gov/prod/2003pubs/censr-5.pdf

Simons, L. G., & Conger, R. D. (2007, February). Linking mother-father differences in parenting to a typology of family parenting styles and adolescent outcomes. *Journal of Family Issues, 28*(2), 212–241.

Simpkins, S. D., Fredricks, J. A., Davis-Kean, P. E., & Eccles, J. S. (2006). Healthy mind, healthy habits: The influence of activity involvement in middle childhood. In A. C. Huston & M. N. Ripke (Eds.), *Developmental contexts in middle childhood: Bridges to adolescence and adulthood. Cambridge studies in social and emotional development* (pp. 283–302). New York: Cambridge University Press.

Simpson, J. A., Collins, W. A., Tran, S., & Haydon, K. C. (2007). Attachment and the experience and expression of emotions in romantic relationships: A developmental perspective. *Journal of Personality and Social Psychology, 92*(2), 355–367.

Sinclair, D. C., & Dangerfield, P. (1998). *Human growth after birth.* New York: Oxford University Press.

Singer, J. L. (2006). Epilogue: Learning to play and learning through play. In D. G. Singer, R. M. Golinkoff, & K. Hirsh-Pasek (Eds.), *Play = learning: How play motivates and enhances children's cognitive and social-emotional growth* (pp. 251–262). New York: Oxford University Press.

Singer, L. T., & Zeskind, P. S. (Eds.). (2001). *Biobehavioral assessment of the infant.* New York: Guilford Press.

Singh-Manoux, A. (2000). Culture and gender issues in adolescence: Evidence from studies on emotion. *Psicothema, 12*(Suppl. 1), 93–100.

Singleton, J. (Ed.). (1998). *Learning in likely places: Varieties of apprenticeship in Japan.* New York: Cambridge University Press.

Siqueland, E. R. (1968). Reinforcement patterns and extinction in human newborns. *Journal of Experimental Child Psychology, 6,* 431–432.

Sizun, J., & Westrup, B. (2004). Early developmental care for preterm neonates: A call for more research. *Archives of Disease in Childhood: Fetal and Neonatal Edition, 89,* 384–388.

Skinner, B. F. (1938). *The behavior of organisms.* New York: Appleton-Century-Crofts.

Skinner, B. F. (1953). *Science and human behavior.* New York: Macmillan.

Slaughter, V., & McConnell, D. (2003). Emergence of joint attention: Relationships between gaze following, social referencing, imitation, and naming in infancy. *Journal of Genetic Psychology, 164*(1), 54–71.

Slobin, D. (2005). From ontogenesis to phylogenesis: What can child language tell us about language evolution? In S. T. Parker, J. Langer, & C. Milbrath (Eds.), *Biology and knowledge revisited: From neurogenesis to psychogenesis* (pp. 287–306). Mahwah, NJ: Lawrence Erlbaum Associates.

Slyper, A. H. (2006, July). The pubertal timing controversy in the USA, and a review of possible causative factors for the advance in timing of onset of puberty. *Clinical Endocrinology (Oxford), 65*(1), 1–8.

Smetana, J. G. (2000). Middle class African American adolescents' and parents' conceptions of parental authority and parenting practices: A longitudinal investigation. *Child Development, 71,* 1672–1686.

Smetana, J. G. (2006). Social-cognitive domain theory: Consistencies and variations in children's moral and social judgments. In M. Killen & J. G. Smetana (Eds.), *Handbook of moral development* (pp. 119–153). Mahwah, NJ: Lawrence Erlbaum Associates.

Smetana, J. G., & Gettman, D. C. (2006, November). Autonomy and relatedness with parents and romantic development in African American adolescents. *Developmental Psychology, 42*(6), 1347–1351.

Smith, A. M., Fried, P. A., Hogan, M. J., & Cameron, I. (2004). Effects of prenatal marijuana on response inhibition: An fMRI study of young adults. *Neurotoxicology and Teratology, 26*(4), 533–542.

Smith, K. (2002). *Who's minding the kids? Child care arrangements: Spring 1997.* Current Population Reports, P70–86, U.S. Census Bureau. Washington, DC: U.S. Government Printing Office.

Smith, P. K., & Monks, C. P. (2008). Concepts of bullying: Developmental and cultural aspects. *International Journal of Adolescent Medicine and Health, 20*(2), 101–112.

Smith, P. K., Morita, Y., Junger-Tas, J., Olweus, D., Catalano, R., & Slee, P. (1999). *The nature of school bullying: A cross-national perspective.* London: Routledge.

Smits, W., & Stromback, T. (2001). *The economics of the apprenticeship system.* Cheltenham, England: E. Elgar.

Smitsman, A. W. (2001). Action in infancy—Perspectives, concepts, and challenges: The development of reaching and grasping. In A. Fogel (Ed.), *Blackwell handbook of infant development* (pp. 71–98). Malden, MA: Blackwell Publishing.

Smotherman, W. P., & Robinson, S. R. (1996). The development of behavior before birth. *Developmental Psychology, 32* (3), 425–434.

Smyth, C. M., & Bremner, W. J. (1998). Klinefelter syndrome. *Archives of Internal Medicine, 158,* 1309–1314.

Snarey, J. R. (1995). Cross-cultural universality of social moral development: A critical review of Kohlbergian research. *Psychological Bulletin, 97,* 202–232.

Snow, C. E. (1972). Mother's speech to children learning language. *Child Development, 43,* 549–565.

Snow, C. E. (1995). Issues in the study of input: Fine-tuning, universality, individual and developmental differences, and necessary causes. In P. Fletcher & B. MacWhinney (Eds.), *The handbook of child language.* Oxford, England: Blackwell Publishing.

Sokol, B. W., & Chandler, M. J. (2004). A bridge too far: On the relations between moral and secular reasoning. In J. I. M. Carpendale & U. Muller (Eds.), *Social interaction and the development of knowledge* (pp. 155–174). Mahwah, NJ: Lawrence Erlbaum Associates.

Solomon, S. G. (2005). *American playgrounds: Revitalizing community space.* Lebanon, NH: University Press of New England.

Somerset, D. A., Moore, A., Whittle, M. J., Martin, W., & Kilby, M. D. (2006). An audit of outcome in intravascular yransfusions using the intrahepatic portion of the fetal umbilical vein compared to cordocentesis. *Fetal Diagnosis and Therapy, 21*(3), 272–276.

Sommer, K., Whitman, T., Gorkowski, J., & Gondoli, D. (2000). Prenatal maternal predictors of cognitive and emotional delays in children of adolescent mothers. *Adolescence, 35,* 87–112.

Sowell, E. R., Delis, D., Stiles, J., & Jernigan, T. L. (2001). Improved memory functioning and frontal lobe maturation between childhood and adolescence: A structural MRI study. *Journal of the International Neuropsychological Society, 7*(3), 312–322.

Sowell, E. R., Thompson, P. M., & Toga, A. W. (2007). Mapping adolescent brain maturation using structural magnetic resonance imaging. In D. Romer & E. F. Walker (Eds.), *Adolescent psychopathology and the developing brain: Integrating brain and prevention science* (pp. 55–84). New York: Oxford University Press.

Sowell, E. R., Trauner, D. A., Gamst, A., & Jernigan, T. L. (2002). Development of cortical and subcortical brain structures in childhood and adolescence: A structural magnetic resonance imaging study. *Developmental Medical Child Neurology, 44,* 4–16.

Spearman, C. (1927). *The abilities of man.* New York: Macmillan.

Spelke, E. S. (2000). Core knowledge. *American Psychologist, 35,* 1233–1234.

Spelke, E. S., Breinlinger, K., Macomber, J., & Jacobson, K. (1992). Origins of knowledge. *Psychological Review, 99*(4), 605–632.

Spencer, M. B. (1988). Self-concept development. *New Directions for Child Development, 42,* 59–72.

Spencer, M. B. (2006). Revisiting the 1990 special issue on minority children: An editorial perspective 15 years later. *Child Development, 77*(5), 1149–1154.

Spencer, M. B., & Markstrom-Adams, C. (1990). Identity processes among racial and ethnic minority children in America. *Child Development, 61,* 290–310.

Spencer, P. E., & Harris, M. (2006). Patterns and effects of language input to deaf infants and toddlers from deaf and hearing mothers. In B. Schick, M. Marschark, & P. E. Spencer (Eds.), *Advances in the sign language development of deaf children. Perspectives on deafness* (pp. 71–101). New York: Oxford University Press.

Spitz, H. H., Minsky, S. K., & Besselieu, C. L. (1985). Influence of planning time and first move strategy on Tower of Hanoi problem solving performance of mentally retarded young adults and nonretarded children. *American Journal of Mental Deficiency, 90*(1), 46–56.

Sreeramareddy, C. T., Joshi, H. S., Sreekumaran, B. V., Giri, S., & Chuni, N. (2006). Home delivery and newborn care practices among women in western Nepal: A questionnaire survey. BMC Pregnancy and Childbirth, 6, 27.

Sroufe, L. A. (2005). *Emotional development: The organization of emotional life in the early years.* New York: Cambridge University Press

Sroufe, L. A., Carlson, E. A., Levy, A. K., & Egeland, B. V. (1999). Implications of attachment theory for developmental psychopathology. *Development & Psychopathology, 11*(1), 1–13.

Sroufe, L. A., Carlson, E., & Shulman, S. (1993). Individuals in relationships: Development from infancy through adolescence. In D. C. Funder, R. D. Parke, C. Tomlinson-Keasey, & K. Widaman (Eds.), *Studying life through time: Personality and development.* Washington, DC: American Psychological Association.

Sroufe, L. A., Egeland, B., Carlson, E., & Collins, W. A. (2005). Placing early attachment experiences in developmental context. In K. E. Grossmann,

K. Grossmann, & E. Waters (Eds.), *Attachment from infancy to adulthood: The major longitudinal studies* (pp. 48-70). New York: Guilford Publications.

Sroufe, L. A., & Fleeson, J. (1986). Attachment and the construction of relationships. In W. W. Hartup & Z. Rubin (Eds.), *Relationships and development*. Mahwah, NJ: Lawrence Erlbaum Associates.

St. James-Roberts, I., Alvarez, M., Csipke, E., Abramsky, T., Goodwin, J., & Sorgenfrei, E. (2006). Infant crying and sleeping in London, Copenhagen, and when parents adopt a "proximal" form of care. *Pediatrics, 117,* 1146–1155.

St. James-Roberts, I., Conroy, S., & Wilshir, K. (1996). Bases for maternal perceptions of infant crying and colic behavior. *Archives of Disease in Childhood, 75,* 375–381.

Stacey, J. (1998). Gay and lesbian families: Queer like us. In M. A. Mason, A. Skolnick, & S. D. Sugarman (Eds.), *All our families: New policies for a new century* (pp. 117–143). New York: Oxford University Press.

Stallings, J., Fleming, A., Corter, C., Worthman, C., & Steiner, M. (2001). The effects of infant cries and odors on sympathy, cortisol, and autonomic responses in new mothers and nonpostpartum women. *Parenting: Science and Practice, 1*(1–2), 71–100.

Stang, J., & Story, M. (Eds.). (2005). *Guidelines for adolescent nutrition services.* Retrieved June 15, 2006, from http://www.epi.umn.edu/let/pubs/adol_book.shtm

Stauder, J. E., Molenaar, P. C., & Van Der Molen, M. W. (1999). Brain activity and cognitive transition during longitudinal event-related brain potential study. *Child Neuropsychology, 5,* 44–59.

Stearns, P. (2006). *Childhood in world history.* New York: Routledge.

Steele, R. G., Nesbitt-Daly, J. S., Daniel, R. C., & Forehand, R. (2005, December). Factor structure of the Parenting Scale in a low-income African American sample *Journal of Child and Family Studies, 14*(4), 535–549.

Stein, A., Thompson, A., & Waters, A. (2005). Childhood growth and chronic disease: Evidence from countries undergoing the nutrition transition. *Maternal and Child Nutrition, 3,* 177–184.

Steinberg, L. (2001). We know some things: Parent-adolescent relationships in retrospect and prospect. *Journal of Research on Adolescence, 11,* 1–19.

Steinberg, L. (2005, February). Cognitive and affective development in adolescence. *Trends in Cognitive Sciences 9*(2), 69–74.

Steinberg, L. (2008, March). A social neuroscience perspective on adolescent risk-taking. *Developmental Review, 28*(1), 78–106.

Steinberg, L., & Duncan, P. (2002). Work group IV: Increasing the capacity of parents, families, and adults living with adolescents to improve adolescent health outcomes. *Journal of Adolescent Health, 31*(Suppl. 6), 261–263.

Steinberg, L., & Silk, J. S. (2002). Parenting adolescents. In M. H. Bornstein (Ed.), *Handbook of parenting: Vol. 1. Children and parenting* (2nd ed., pp. 103–133). Mahwah, NJ: Lawrence Erlbaum Associates.

Steiner, M., Attarbaschi, A., Konig, M., Nebral, K., Gadner, H., Haas, O. A., Mann, G., & Austrian Berlin-Frankfurt-Munster Group. (2005). Equal frequency of TEL/AML1 rearrangements in children with acute lymphoblastic leukemia with and without Down syndrome. *Journal of Pediatric Hematology/Oncology, 22*(1), 11–16.

Stern, D. N. (1977). *The first relationship.* Cambridge, MA: Harvard University Press.

Stern, D. N. (2002). *The first relationship: Infant and mother.* Cambridge, MA: Harvard University Press.

Stern, W. (1910). Abstracts of lectures on the psychology of testimony and on the study of individuality. *American Journal of Psychology, 21,* 273–282.

Stern, W. (1912). *Psychologische methoden der intelligenz-prufung.* Leipzig: Barth.

Sternberg, R. J. (1990). *Metaphors of mind: Conceptions of the nature of intelligence.* New York: Cambridge University Press.

Sternberg, R. J. (2007, January). A systems model of leadership: WICS. *American Psychologist. Special Issue: Leadership, 62*(1), 34–42.

Sternberg, R. J., & Grigorenko, E. L. (2008). Ability testing across cultures. In L. A. Suzuki & J. G. Ponterotto (Eds.), *Handbook of multicultural assessment: Clinical, psychological, and educational applications* (pp. 449–470). San Francisco, CA: Jossey-Bass.

Stevens, J., Quittner, A. L., Zuckerman, J. B., & Moore, S. (2002). Behavioral inhibition, self-regulation of motivation, and working memory in children with attention deficit hyperactivity disorder. *Developmental Neuropsychology, 21*(2), 117–140.

Stevenson, H. C., Davis, G., & Abdul-Kabir, S. (2001). *Stickin' to, watchin' over, and gettin' with: An African American parent's guide to discipline.* San Francisco: Jossey Bass.

Stevenson, H. W., & Stigler, J. W. (1992). *The learning gap: Why our schools are failing and what we can learn from Japanese and Chinese education.* New York: Summit.

Stevenson, H. W., Stigler, J. W., Lee, S., Lucker, G. W., Kitamura, S., & Hsu, C. (1985). Cognitive performance and academic achievement of Japanese, Chinese, and American children. *Child Development, 56,* 718–734.

Stevenson, R. (1977). *The fetus and newly born infant: Influence of the prenatal environment* (2nd ed.). St. Louis: Mosby.

Stigler, J. W., & Perry, M. (1990). Mathematics learning in Japanese, Chinese, and American classrooms. In J. W. Stigler, R. A. Shweder, & G. Herdt (Eds.), *Cultural psychology: Essays on comparative human development.* New York: Cambridge University Press.

Stigler, J. W., Gallimore, R., & Hiebert, J. (2000). Using video surveys to compare classrooms and teaching across cultures: Examples and lessons from the TIMSS video studies. *Educational Psychologist, 35*(2), 87–100.

Stipek, D. (2001). Pathways to constructive lives: The importance of early school success. In A. C. Bower & D. J. Stipek (Eds.), *Constructive & destructive behavior: Implications for family, school, & society* (pp. 291–315). Washington, DC: American Psychological Association.

Stoltz, H. E., Barber, B. K., & Olsen, J. A. (2005). Toward disentangling fathering and mothering: An assessment of relative importance. *Journal of Marriage and Family, 67,* 1076–1092.

Stoltzfus, R. J., Kvalsvig, J. D., Chwaya, H. M., Montresor, A., Albonico, M., Tielsch, J. M., et al. (2001). Effects of iron supplementation and anthelmintic treatment on motor and language development of preschool children in Zanzibar: Double blind, placebo controlled study. *British Medical Journal, 323*(7326), 1389–1393.

Stone, J. L., & Church, J. (1957). *Childhood and adolescence: A psychology of the growing person.* New York: Random House.

Storvoll, E. E., & Wichstrom, L. (2002, April). Do the risk factors associated with conduct problems in adolescents vary according to gender? *Journal of Adolescence 25*(2), 182–202.

Strathearn, L., Gray, P. H., O'Callaghan, M. J., & Wood, D. O. (2001). Childhood neglect and cognitive development in extremely low birth weight infants: A prospective study. *Pediatrics, 108*(1), 142–151.

Stratton, K., Howe, C., & Battaglia, F. (1996). *Fetal alcohol syndrome: Diagnosis, epidemiology, prevention, and treatment.* Washington, DC: National Academy Press.

Straus, M., & Stewart, J. (1999). Corporal punishment by American parents: National data on prevalence, chronicity, severity, and duration, in relation to child and family characteristics. *Clinical Child and Family Psychology Review, 2,* 55–70.

Strauss, R. (1999). Childhood obesity. *Current Problems in Pediatrics, 29*(1), 1–29.

Strauss, S., & Ziv, M. (2004). Teaching: Ontogenesis, culture, and education. *Cognitive Development, 19,* 451–456.

Strayer, F. F. (1991). The development of agonistic and affiliative structures in preschool play groups. In J. Silverberg & P. Gray (Eds.), *To fight or not to fight: Violence and peacefulness in humans and other primates.* Oxford, England: Oxford University Press.

Striano, T., & Rochat, P. (2000). Emergence of selective social referencing in infancy. *Infancy, 1*(2), 253–264.

Striepe, M., & Tolman, D. (2003). Mom, Dad, I'm straight: The coming out of gender ideologies in adolescent sexual-identity development. *Journal of Clinical Child and Adolescent Psychology, 32*, 523–530.

Stunkard, A. J., Sorenson, T. I., Hanis, C., Teasdale, T. W., Chakraborty, R., Schull, W. J., & Schulsinger, F. (1986). An adoption study of human obesity. *New England Journal of Medicine, 314*, 193–198

Styne, D. M. (2004, December). Puberty, obesity and ethnicity. *Trends in Endocrinology and Metabolism, 15*(10), 472–478.

Suárez-Orozco, C, Suárez-Orozco, M. M.& Todorova, I. (2008) *Learning a new land: Immigrant students in American society*. Cambridge, MA: The Belknap Press of Harvard University Press.

Suarez-Orozco, M. (2001). Globalization, immigration, and education: The research agenda. *Harvard Educational Review, 71*, 345–365.

Subbotsky, E. V. (1993). *The birth of personality: The development of independent and moral behavior in preschool children*. New York: Harvester Wheatsheaf.

Subrahmanyam, K., Kraut, R., Greenfield, P., & Gross, E. (2001). New forms of electronic media: The impact of interactive games and the Internet on cognition, socialization, and behavior. In D. Singer & J. Singer (Eds.), *Handbook of children and the media*. Thousand Oaks, CA: Sage.

Sugiyama, L., & Chacon, R. (2005). Juvenile responses to household ecology among the Yora of Peruvian Amazonia. In B. Hewlitt & M. Lamb (Eds.), *Hunter-gatherer childhoods: Evolutionary, cultural and developmental perspectives*. New Brunswick, NJ: Transaction Publishers.

Suitor, C. W., & Gleason, P. M. (2002, April). Using dietary reference intake-based methods to estimate the prevalence of inadequate nutrient intake among school-aged children. *Journal of the American Dietetic Association, 102*(4), 530–536.

Sullivan, H. S. (1953). *The interpersonal theory of psychiatry*. New York: W. W. Norton.

Sullivan, K., & Winner, E. (1993). Three-year-olds' understanding of mental states: The influence of trickery. *Journal of Experimental Child Psychology, 56*(2), 135–148.

Summerfield, D. (1999). A critique of seven assumptions behind psychological trauma programmes in war-affected areas. *Social Science and Medicine, 48*, 1449–1462.

Sun, Y., & Li, Y. (2002). Children's well-being during parents' marital disruption process: A pooled time-series analysis. *Journal of Marriage and Family, 64*, 472–488.

Sun, Y., & Li, Y. (2008, February). Stable postdivorce family structures during late adolescence and socioeconomic consequences in adulthood. *Journal of Marriage and Family 70*(1), 129–143.

Sunseth, K., & Bowers, P. G. (2002). Rapid naming and phonemic awareness: Contributions to reading, spelling, and orthographic knowledge. *Scientific Studies of Reading, 6*(4), 401–429.

Suomi, S. (1995). Influences of attachment theory on ethological studies of biobehavioral development in nonhuman primates. In S. Goldberg, R. Muir, & J. Kerr (Eds.), *Attachment theory: Social, developmental, and clinical perspectives* (pp. 185–202). Mahwah, NJ: Analytic Press.

Suomi, S. J. (2000). A biobehavioral perspective on developmental psychopathology: Excessive aggression and serotonergic dysfunction in monkeys. In A. Sameroff, M. Lewis, & S. M. Miller (Eds.), *Handbook of developmental psychopathology* (2nd ed., pp. 237–256). Dordrecht, Netherlands: Kluwer Academic.

Super, C. M. (1976). Environmental effects on motor development: A case of African infant precocity. *Developmental Medicine and Child Neurology, 18*, 561–567.

Super, C. M., & Harkness, S. (1972). The infant's niche in rural Kenya and metropolitan America. In L. Adler (Ed.), *Issues in cross-cultural research*. New York: Academic Press.

Super, C. M., & Harkness, S. (2002). Culture structures the environment for development. *Human Development, 45*, 270–274.

Susman, E. J. (2006). Psychobiology of persistent antisocial behavior: Stress, early vulnerabilities and the attenuation hypothesis. *Neuroscience & Biobehavioral Reviews, 30*(3), 376–389.

Susman, E. J., Schmeelk, K. H., Ponirakis, A., & Gariepy, J. L. (2001). Maternal prenatal, postpartum, and concurrent stressors and temperament in 3-year-olds: A person and variable analysis. *Development and Psychopathology, 13*(3), 629–652.

Sutton, J., Smith, P. K., & Swettenham, J. (1999). Bullying and "theory of mind": A critique of the "social skills deficit" view of anti-social behavior. *Social Development, 8*(1), 117–127.

Sutton, M., Brown, J., Wilson, K., & Klein, J. (2002). Shaking the tree of knowledge for forbidden fruit: Where adolescents learn about sexuality and contraception. In J. Brown, J. Steele, & K. Walsh-Childers (Eds.), *Sexual teens, sexual media*. Mahwah, NJ: Lawrence Erlbaum Associates.

Suzuki, K., Minai, J., & Yamagata Z. (2007). Maternal negative attitudes towards pregnancy as an independent risk factor for low birthweight. *Journal of Obstetrics and Gynaecology Research 33*(4), 438–444.

Sweeney, J., & Bradbard, M., R. (1988). Mothers' and fathers' changing perceptions of their male and female infants over the course of pregnancy. *Journal of Genetic Psychology, 149*(3), 393–404.

Sweeting, H., & West, P. (2003, December). Young people's leisure and risk-taking behaviours: Changes in gender patterning in the west of Scotland during the 1990s. *Journal of Youth Studies, 6*(4), 391–412.

Symington, A., & Pinelli, J. (2003). Developmental care for promoting development and preventing morbidity in preterm infants. *Cochrane Database of Systematic Reviews, 4*, CD001814.

Szkrybalo, J., & Ruble, D. N. (1999). "God made me a girl": Sex-category constancy judgments and explanations revisited. *Developmental Psychology, 35*(2), 392–402.

Tabak, I., & Weinstock, M. (2008). A sociocultural exploration of epistemological beliefs. In M. S. Khine (Ed.), *Knowing, knowledge and beliefs: Epistemological studies across diverse cultures* (pp. 177–195). New York: Springer Science + Business Media.

Tager-Flusberg, H. (2007, December). Evaluating the theory-of-mind hypothesis of autism. *Current Directions in Psychological Science, 16*(6), 311–315.

Tallal, P. (2003). Language learning disabilities: Integrating research approaches. *Current Directions in Psychological Science, 12*(6), 206–211.

Tallal, P., Merzenich, M., Miller, S., & Jenkins, W. (1998). Language learning impairment: Integrating research and remediation. *Scandinavian Journal of Psychology, 39*(3), 197–199.

Tani, C. R., Chavez, E. L., & Deffenbacher, J. L. (2001). Peer isolation and drug use among while non-Hispanic and Mexican American adolescents. *Adolescence, 36*, 127–139.

Tanner, J. M. (1978). *Fetus into man: Physical growth from conception to maturity*. Cambridge, MA: Harvard University Press.

Tanner, J. M. (1990). *Fetus into man: Physical growth from conception to maturity* (Rev. ed.). Cambridge, MA: Harvard University Press.

Tanner, J. M. (1998). Sequence, tempo, and individual variation in growth and development of boys and girls aged twelve to sixteen. In D. P. Harriet (Ed.), *Adolescent behavior and society: A book of readings* (5th ed., pp. 34–46). New York: McGraw-Hill.

Temple, C. M., & Sanfilippo, P. M. (2003). Executive skills in Klinefelter's syndrome. *Neuropsychologia, 41*, 1547–1559.

Tenenbaum, H. R., Callanan, M., Alba-Speyer, C., & Sandoval, L. (2002). The role of educational background, activity, and past experiences in Mexican-descent families' science conversations. *Hispanic Journal of Behavioral Sciences, 24*(2), 225–248.

Tharp, R., & Yamauchi, L. (2000). Instructional conversations in Native American classrooms: Rural, urban and minority education. *Journal of Early Education and Family Review,* 7(5), 33–37.

Thatcher, R. W. (1994). Cyclic cortical reorganization. In G. Dawson & K. W. Fischer (Eds.), *Human behavior and the developing brain.* New York: Guilford Press.

Thelen, E. (1995). Motor development: A new synthesis. *American Psychologist, 50,* 79–95.

Thelen, E. (2002). Self-organization in developmental processes: Can systems approaches work? In M. H. Johnson & Y. Munakata (Eds.), *Brain development and cognition: A reader* (2nd ed., pp. 336–374). Malden, MA: Blackwell Publishing.

Thelen, E., Fisher, D. M., & Ridley-Johnson, R. (2002). The relationship between physical growth and a newborn reflex. *Infant Behavior and Development, 25*(1), 72–85.

Thelen, E., Schoener, G., Scheier, C., & Smith, L. B. (2001). The dynamics of embodiment: A field theory of infant perseverative reaching. *Behavioral and Brain Sciences, 24*(1), 1–86.

Thelen, E., & Smith, L. B. (1998). Dynamic systems theory. In W. Damon & R. M. Lerner (Eds.), *Handbook of child psychology: Vol. 12* (5th ed., pp. 563–634). New York: Wiley.

Thiessen, E. D., Hill, E. A., & Saffran, J. R. (2005). Infant-directed speech facilitates word segmentation. *Infancy, 7*(1), 53–71.

Thoman, E. B., & Whitney, M. P. (1989). Sleep states of infants monitored in the home: Individual differences, developmental trends, and origins of diurnal cyclicity. *Infant Behavior & Development, 12*(1), 59–75.

Thomas, M., & Karmiloff-Smith, A. (2003). Modeling language acquisition in atypical phenotypes. *Psychological Review, 110,* 647–682.

Thompson, G. B., & Nicholson, T. (Eds.). (1999). *Learning to read: Beyond phonics and whole language.* New York: Teachers College Press.

Thompson, R. A. (1998). Early sociopersonality development. In N. Eisenberg (Ed.), *Handbook of child psychology: Vol. 3. Social, emotional, and personality development* (5th ed., pp. 25–104). New York: Wiley.

Thorne, B. (1993). *Gender play: Girls and boys in school.* New Brunswick, NJ: Rutgers University Press.

Thrasher, F. (1927). *The gang: A study of 1,313 gangs in Chicago.* Chicago: University of Chicago Press.

Tilburg, M., Unterberg, M., & Vingerhoets, A. (2002). Crying during adolescence: The role of gender, menarche, and empathy. *British Journal of Developmental Psychology, 20,* 77–87.

Tizard, B., & Hodges, J. (1978). The effect of early institutional rearing on the development of eight-year-old children. *Journal of Child Psychology and Psychiatry, 19,* 99–118.

Tizard, B., & Rees, J. (1975). The effect of early institutional rearing on the behavioral problems and affectional relationship of four-year-old children. *Journal of Child Psychology and Psychiatry, 16,* 61–73.

Tokita, M., Kiyoshi, T., & Armstrong, K. N. (2007). Evolution of craniofacial novelty in parrots through developmental modularity and heterochrony. *Evolution & Development, 9*(6), 590–601.

Tolchinsky, L. (2006). The emergence of writing. In C. A. MacArthur, S. Graham, & J. Fitzgerald (Eds.), *Handbook of writing research* (pp. 83–95). New York: Guilford Press.

Tolman, D. L., & Diamond, L. M. (2001). Desegregating sexuality research: Cultural and biological perspectives on gender and desire. *Annual Review of Sex Research, 12,* 33–74.

Tomasello, M. (1999). *The cultural origins of human cognition.* Cambridge, MA: Harvard University Press.

Tomasello, M. (2000). First steps toward a usage-based theory of language acquisition. *Cognitive Linguistics. Special Issue: Language Acquisition* 11(1–2), 61–82.

Tomasello, M. (2003). *Constructing a language: A usage-based theory of language acquisition.* Cambridge, MA: Harvard University Press.

Tomasello, M., Carpenter, M., Call, J., Behne, T., & Moll, H. (2005). In search of the uniquely human. *Behavioral and Brain Sciences, 28*(5), 721.

Torney-Purta, J. (1996). Conceptual change among adolescents using computer networks and peer collaboration in studying international political issues. In S. Vosniadou, E. De Corte, R. Glaser, & H. Mandl (Eds.), *International perspectives on the design of technology-supported learning environments.* Mahwah, NJ: Lawrence Erlbaum Associates.

Traggiai, C., & Stanhope, R. (2003, February). Disorders of pubertal development. *Best Practice and Research Clinical Obstetrics and Gynaecology, 17*(1), 41–56.

Travis, F. (1998). Cortical and cognitive development in 4th, 8th and 12th grade students: The contribution of speed of processing and executive functioning to cognitive development. *Biological Psychology, 48*(1), 37–56.

Tremblay, R., Nagin, D., Séguin, J., Zoccolillo, M., Zelazo, P., Boivin, M., et al. (2005). Physical aggression during early childhood: Trajectories and predictors. *Canadian Child and Adolescent Psychiatry Review, 14*(1), 3–9.

Trevarthen, C. (1998). The concept and foundations of infant intersubjectivity. In S. Braten (Ed.), *Intersubjective communication and emotion in early ontogeny* (pp. 15–46). New York: Cambridge University Press.

Trevarthan, C. (2005). Action and emotion in development of cultural intelligence: Why infants have feelings like ours. In J. Nadel and D. Muir (Eds.), *Emotional development.* Oxford, England: Oxford University Press.

Trevarthen, C., & Reddy, V. (2007). Consciousness in infants. In M. Velmans & S. Schneider (Eds.), *The Blackwell companion to consciousness* (pp. 41–57). Malden, MA: Blackwell Publishing.

Triandis, H. C., McCusker, C., & Hui, C. H. (1990, November). Multimethod probes of individualism and collectivism. *Journal of Personality and Social Psychology, 59*(5), 1006–1020.

Troiden, R. R. (1993). The formation of homosexual identities. In L. D. Garnets & D. C. Kimmel (Eds.), *Psychological perspectives on lesbian and gay male experiences* (pp. 191–217). New York: Columbia University Press.

Tronick, E. (2005). Why is connection with others so critical? The formation of dyadic states of consciousness and the expansion of individuals' states of consciousness: Coherence governed selection and the co-creation of meaning out of messy meaning making. In J. Nadel and D. Muir (Eds.), *Emotional development* (pp. 293–315). Oxford, England: Oxford University Press.

Tronick, E. (2007). *The neurobehavioral and social-emotional development of infants and children (The Norton series on interpersonal neurobiology).* New York: W. W. Norton.

Tronick, E. Z., Messinger, D. S., Weinberg, M. K., Lester, B. M., LaGasse, L., Seifer, R., et al. (2005, September). Cocaine exposure is associated with subtle compromises of infants' and mothers' social-emotional behavior and dyadic features of their interaction in the face-to-face still-face paradigm. *Developmental Psychology, 41*(5), 711–722.

Troop-Gordon, W., & Ladd, G. W. (2005, September–October). Trajectories of peer victimization and perceptions of the self and schoolmates: Precursors to internalizing and externalizing problems. *Child Development, 76*(5), 1072–1091.

Troseth, G. L. (2003). Getting a clear picture: Young children's understanding of a televised image. *Developmental Science, 6,* 247–253.

Tuchmann-Duplessis, H. (1975). *Drug effects on the fetus.* Acton, MA: Publishing Science Group.

Tuchmann-Duplessis, H., David, G., & Haegel, P. (1971). *Illustrated human embryology: Vol. 1.* New York: Springer-Verlag.

Tucker, G. R. (1999). *A global perspective on bilingualism and bilingual education.* Washington, DC: ERIC Clearinghouse on Languages and Linguistics.

Tudge, J., Odero, D., Piccinini, C., Doucet, F., Sperb, T., & Lopes, R. (2006). A window into different cultural worlds: Young children's everyday activities in the United States, Brazil, and Kenya. *Child Development, 77,* 1446–1469.

Tulving, E., & Craik, F. I. M. (Eds.). (2000). *The Oxford handbook of memory.* London: Oxford University Press.

Tulviste, P. (1991). *The cultural-historical development of verbal thinking.* Commack, NY: Nova Science.

Turati, C., Simion, F., Milani, I., & Umilta, C. (2002). Newborn's preference for faces: What is crucial? *Developmental Psychology, 38*(6), 875–882.

Turiel, E. (1983). *The development of social knowledge: Morality and convention.* Cambridge, England: Cambridge University Press.

Turiel, E. (1998). The development of morality. In W. Damon & N. Eisenberg (Eds.), *Handbook of child psychology: Vol.3. Social, emotional, and personality development* (5th ed., pp. 863–932). New York: Wiley.

Turiel, E. (2002). *The culture of morality.* Cambridge, England: Cambridge University Press.

Turiel, E. (2006). The development of morality. In N. Eisenberg, W. Damon, & R. M. Lerner (Eds.), *Handbook of child psychology: Vol. 3. Social, emotional, and personality development* (6th ed., pp. 789–857). Hoboken, NJ: John Wiley & Sons.

Turiel, E. (2008, January). Thought about actions in social domains: Morality, social conventions, and social interactions. *Cognitive Development, 23*(1), 136–154.

Turiel, E., Killen, M., & Helwig, C. C. (1987). Morality: Its structure, functions, and vagaries. In J. Kagan & S. Lamb (Eds.), *The emergence of morality.* Chicago: Chicago University Press.

Turnbull, E., Rothstein-Fisch, C., Greenfield, P. M., & Quiroz, B. (2001). *Bridging cultures between home and school.* Mahwah, NJ: Lawrence Erlbaum Associates.

Twenge, J. M., & Nolen-Hoeksema, S. (2002, November). Age, gender, race, socioeconomic status, and birth cohort difference on the children's depression inventory: A meta-analysis. *Journal of Abnormal Psychology, 111*(4), 578–588.

UNAIDS. (2004). *Children on the brink 2004: A joint report of new orphan estimates and a framework for action.* New York: United Nations Children's Fund.

Underwood, M. (2002). Aggression among boys and girls. In P. Smith & C. Hart (Eds.), *Blackwell handbook of childhood social development.* Malden, MA: Blackwell Publishing.

UNESCO. (2007). EFA Global Monitoring Report: Strong foundations: Early childhood care and education. Retrieved January 9, 2007, from http://unesdoc.unesco.org/images/0014/001477/147794E.pdf

UNICEF. (2003). *Prevention of mother-to-child transmission of HIV.*

UNICEF. (2006). *State of the world's children: 2006.* Retrieved October 10, 2007, from http://www.unicef.org/sowc06/pdfs/sowc06_fullreport.pdf

UNICEF/United Nations Children's Fund. (1999). *The state of the world's children.* Oxford, England: Oxford University Press.

UNICEF/United Nations Children's Fund. (2008). *State of the world's children, 2008: Child survival.* Retrieved September 9, 2008, from http://www.unicef.org/lac/The_State_of_the_Worlds_Children_2008.pdf

United Nations Commission on Population and Development. (1996). *Report of the Secretary-General on world population monitoring, focusing on international migration, with special emphasis on the linages between migration and development on gender issues and the family.* United Nations: Official Records of the Economic and Social Council, Suppl. 5 (E/1996/25).

United Nations Commission on Population and Development. (2005). *Trends in total migrant stock: The 2005 revision.* Retrieved October 18, 2008, from http://www.un.org/esa/population/publications/migration/UN_Migrant_Stock_Documentation_2005.pdf

United Nations Department of Economic and Social Affairs. (2005). *World youth report 2005.* Retrieved October 18, 2008, from http://www.un.org/esa/socdev/unyin/wpayinformation.htm#WYR2005

Urberg, K. A., Degirmencioglu, S. M., & Tolson, J. M. (1998). Adolescent friendship selection and termination: The role of similarity. *Journal of Social & Personal Relationships, 15*(5), 703–710.

Ursitti, F., Klein, J., & Koren, G. (2001). Confirmation of cocaine use during pregnancy: A critical review. *Therapeutic Drug Monitoring, 23*(4), 347–353.

U.S. Census Bureau. (2002). *Statistical abstract of the United States: 2002* (122nd ed.). Washington, DC: U.S. Government Printing Office.

U.S. Census Bureau. (2003). *The foreign-born population: 2000.* Retrieved December 1, 2008, from http://www.census.gov/prod/2003pubs/c2kbr-34.pdf

U.S. Department of Health and Human Services. (1999). *Trends in the well-being of America's children and youth: 1999.*

U.S. Department of Justice. (2002/2000). *Sourcebook of criminal justice statistics, 2000.* Washington, DC: Congressional Information Service.

U.S. Office of Education. (1977). Federal Register, 42(250), 65083. Washington, DC: U.S. Government Printing Office.

U.S. Department of Labor. (2007). *Employment characteristics of families.* Retrieved April 2008 from http://www.bls.gov/news.release/famee.toc.htm

Uzgiris, I. C., & Hunt, J. (1975). *Assessment in infancy: Ordinal scales of psychological development.* Champaign: University of Illinois Press.

Valentin, S. (2005). Commentary: Sleep in German infants: The cult of independence. *Pediatrics, 115,* 269–271.

Valian, V. (1999). Input and language acquisition. In W. C. Ritchie & T. K. Bhatia (Eds.), *Handbook of child language acquisition* (pp. 497–530). San Diego: Academic Press.

Valsiner, J. (1998). Editorial: Culture and psychology on the move. *Culture & Psychology, 4,* 5–9.

Valsiner, J. (2005). Transformations and flexible forms: where qualitative psychology begins. *Qualitative Research in Psychology, 4*(4), 39–57.

Valsiner, J. (2006). Developmental epistemology and implications for methodology. In R. M. Lerner & W. Damon (Eds.), *Handbook of child psychology: Vol. 1. Theoretical models of human development* (6th ed., pp. 166–209). Hoboken, NJ: John Wiley & Sons.

Valsiner, J. (2007). *Culture in minds and societies.* New York: Sage.

Valsiner, J., & Rosa, A. (2007). *The Cambridge handbook of sociocultural psychology.* New York: Cambridge University Press.

van Bokhoven, I., van Goozen, S., van Engeland, H., Schaal, B., Arseneault, L., Séguin, J., et al. (2006). Salivary testosterone and aggression, delinquency, and social dominance in a population-based longitudinal study of adolescent males. *Hormones and Behavior, 50*(1), 118–125.

van der Put, N. M. J., van Straaten, H. W. M., Trijbels, F. J. M., & Blom, H. J. (2001). Folate homocysteine and neural tube defects: An overview. *Experimental Biology and Medicine, 226*(4), 243–270.

van IJzendoorn, M. H., & Sagi, A. (2001). Cross-cultural patterns of attachment: Universal and contextual dimensions. In J. Cassidy & P. R. Shaver (Eds.), *Handbook of attachment: Theory, research, and clinical applications* (pp. 713–734). New York: Guilford Press.

Van Mierlo, J., & Van den Bulck, J. (2004). Benchmarking the cultivation approach to video game effects: A comparison of the correlates of TV viewing and game play. *Journal of Adolescence, 27,* 97–111.

Vandewater, E. A., Lee, J. H., & Shim, M.-S. (2005, February). Family conflict and violent electronic media use in school-aged children. Media Psychology, 7(1), 73–86.

Vangelisti, A., Reis, H., & Fitzpatrick, M. (Eds.). (2002). *Stability and change in relationships.* Cambridge, England: Cambridge University Press.

Vartanian, L. R., Schwartz, M. B., & Brownell, K. D. (2007, April). Effects of soft drink consumption on nutrition and health: A systematic review and meta-analysis. *American Journal of Public Health, 97*(4), 667–675.

Vasquez, O. (2002). *La classe magica.* Mahwah, NJ, Lawrence Erlbaum Associates.

Viding, E., Jones, A. P., Frick, P. J., Moffitt, T. E., & Plomin, R. (2008, January). Heritability of antisocial behaviour at 9: Do callous-unemotional traits matter? *Developmental Science, 11*(1), 17–22.

Vinden, P. G. (1998). Imagination and true belief: A cross-cultural perspective. In J. de Rivera & T. R. Sarbin (Eds.), *Believed-in imaginings: The narrative construction of reality.* Memory trauma, dissociation, and hypnosis series (pp. 73–85). Washington, DC: American Psychological Association.]

Vinden, P. G. (2002). Understanding minds and evidence for belief: A study of Mofu children in Cameroon. *International Journal of Behavioral Development, 26*(5), 445–452.

Vintzileos, A. M., Ananth, C. V., Smulian, J. C., Scorza, W. E., & Knuppel, R. A. (2001). Do maternal-fetal medicine practice characteristics influence high-risk referral decisions by general obstetrician-gynecologists? *Journal of Maternal-Fetal Medicine, 10,* :112–115.

Vintzileos, A. M., Ananth, C. V., Smulian, J. C., Scorza, W. E., & Knuppel, R. A. (2002). Prenatal care black-white fetal death disparity in the United States: Heterogeneity by high-risk conditions. *Obstetrics and Gynecology, 99*(3), 483–489.

Violato, C., & Wiley, A. (1990). Images of adolescence in English literature: The middle ages to the modern period. *Adolescence, 25,* 253–264.

Volterra, V., Iverson, J., & Castrataro, M. (2006). The development of gesture in hearing and deaf children. In B. Schick, M. Marschark, & P. Spencer (Eds.), *Advances in the sign language development of deaf children* (pp. 46–70). New York: Oxford University Press.

von Hofsten, C. (1982). Eye-hand coordination in the newborn. *Developmental Psychology, 18*(3), 450–461.

von Hofsten, C. (1984). Developmental changes in the organization of prereaching movements. *Developmental Psychology, 20*(3), 378–388.

von Hofsten, C. (2001). On the early development of action, perception, and cognition. In F. Lacerda, C. von Hofsten, & M. Heimann (Eds.), *Emerging cognitive abilities in early infancy* (pp. 73–89). Mahwah, NJ: Lawrence Erlbaum Associates.

Vurpillot, E. (1968). The development of scanning strategies and their relation to visual differentiation. *Journal of Experimental Child Psychology, 6,* 632–650.

Vygotksy, L. S. (1978). *Mind in society.* Cambridge, MA: Harvard University Press.

Wachs, T. D. (2000). *Necessary but not sufficient: The respective roles of single and multiple influences on individual development* (pp. 69–96). Washington, DC: American Psychological Association.

Wachs, T. D., & Bates, J. E. (2001). *Temperament.* In G. Bremmer & A. Fogel (Eds.), *Blackwell handbook of infant development: Vol. 12. Handbooks of developmental psychology* (pp. 465–501). Malden, MA: Blackwell Publishing.

Wagner, D. A. (1974). The development of short-term and incidental memory: A cross cultural study. *Child Development, 48,* 389–396.

Wagner, D. A. (1978). Memories of Morocco: The influence of age, schooling, and environment on memory. *Cognitive Psychology, 10,* 1–28.

Wagner, V., Epoo, B., Nastapoka, J., & Harney, E. (2007). Reclaiming birth, health, and community: Midwifery in the Inuit villages of Nunavik, Canada. *Journal of Midwifery and Women's Health, 52,* 384–391.

Wainryb, C. (1995). Reasoning about social conflicts in different cultures: Druze and Jewish children in Israel. *Child Development, 66*(2), 390–401.

Walker, L. J. (2007). Progress and prospects in the psychology of moral development. In G. W. Ladd (Ed.), *Appraising the human developmental sciences: Essays in honor of Merrill-Palmer Quarterly. Landscapes of childhood series.* Detroit, MI: Wayne State University Press.

Walker, L. J., Hennig, K., & Krettenauer, T. (2000). Parent and peer contexts for children's moral reasoning development. *Child Development, 71,* 1033–1048.

Walker, L. J., Pitts, R. C., Henning, K. H., & Matsuba, M. K. (1995). Reasoning about morality and real-life moral problems. In M. Killen & D. Hart (Eds.), *Morality in everyday life: Developmental perspectives.* New York: Cambridge University Press.

Walker, R., Hill, K., Burger, O., & Hurtado, M. (2006). Life in the slow lane revised: Ontogenetic separation between chimpanzees and humans. *American Journal of Physical Anthropology, 129,* 577–583.

Walker, S., Irving, K., & Berthelsen, D. (2002). Gender influences on preschool children's social problem-solving strategies. *The Journal of Genetic Psychology, 163,* 197–209.

Walsh, W. (2002). Spankers and nonspankers: Where they get information on spanking. *Family Relations, 51,* 81–88.

Wandersman, A., & Florin, P. (2003). Community interventions and effective prevention. *American Psychologist, 58*(6–7), 441–448.

Wang, A. O. (2001). Multicultural genetic counseling: Then, now, and in the 21st century. *American Journal of Medical Genetics, 106*(3), 208–215.

Wang, Q., Pomerantz, E. M., & Chen, H. (2007, September). The role of parents' control in early adolescents' psychological functioning: A longitudinal investigation in the United States and China. *Child Development, 78*(5), 1592–1610.

Wang, S., Baillargeon, R., & Brueckner, L. (2004). Young infants' reasoning about hidden objects: Evidence from violation-of-expectation tasks with test trials only. *Cognition, 93,* 167–198.

Wang, X., Zuckerman, B., Pearson, C., Kaufman, G., Chen, C., Wang, G., et al. (2002). Maternal cigarette smoking, metabolic gene polymorphism, and infant birth weight. *Journal of the American Medical Association, 287*(2), 195–202.

Ward, K. (1994). Genetics and prenatal diagnosis. In J. R. Scott, P. J. DiSaia, C. B. Hammond, & W. N. Spellacy (Eds.), *Dansforth's obstetrics and gynecology* (7th ed.). Philadelphia: J. B. Lippincott.

Ward, L. M., Hansbrough, E., & Walker, E. (2005, March). Contributions of music video exposure to black adolescents' gender and sexual schemas. *Journal of Adolescent Research, 20*(2), 143–166.

Ware, E. A., Uttal, D. H., Wetter, E. K., & DeLoache, J. S. (2006). Young children make scale errors when playing with dolls. *Developmental Science, 9*(1), 40–45.

Warner, T. D., Dede, D. E., Garvan, C. W., & Conway, T. W. (2002). One size still does not fit all in specific learning disability assessment across ethnic groups. *Journal of Learning Disabilities, 35*(6), 501–509.

Washburn, S. L. (2004). *Classification and human evolution.* New York: Routledge.

Watamura, S., Donzella, B., Alwin, J., & Gunnar, M. (2003). Morning-to-afternoon increases in cortisol concentrations for infants and toddlers at child care: Age differences and behavioral correlates. *Child Development, 74,* 1006–1020.

Waters, E., Hamilton, C., & Weinfield, N. (2000a) The stability of attachment security from infancy to adolescence and early adulthood: General introduction. *Child Development, 71,* 678–683.

Waters, E., Merrick, S., Treboux, D., Crowell, J., & Albersheim, L. (2000b). Attachment security in infancy and early adulthood: A twenty-year longitudinal study. *Child Development, 71,* 684–689.

Waters, H. S., & Waters, E. (2006). The attachment working models concept: Among other things, we build script-like representations of secure base experiences. *Attachment & Human Development. Special Issue: Script-like Attachment Representations and Behavior in Families and Across Cultures, 8*(3), 185–197.

Waters, M. (1999). Black identities: West Indian immigrant dreams and American realities. Cambridge, England: Cambridge University Press.

Watson, J. B. (1930). *Behaviorism.* Chicago: University of Chicago Press.

Watts, R. J., Abdul-Adil, J. K., & Pratt, T. (2002). Enhancing critical consciousness in young African American men: A psychoeducational approach. *Psychology of Men and Masculinity, 3*(1), 41–50.

Webb, S. J., Monk, C. S., & Nelson, C. A. (2001). Mechanisms of postnatal neurobiological development: Implications for human development. *Developmental Neuropsychology, 19*(2), 147–171.

Weinstock, H., Berman, S., & Cates, W., Jr. (2004). Sexually transmitted diseases among American youth: Incidence and prevalence estimates, 2000. *Perspectives on Sexual and Reproductive Health, 36*(1), 6–10.

Weinstock, M. (2005, July). The potential influence of maternal stress hormones on development and mental health of the offspring. *Brain, Behavior, and Immunity, 19*(4), 296–308.

Weisfeld, G. E., & Janisse, H. C. (2005). Some functional aspects of human adolescence. In B. J. Ellis & D. F. Bjorklund (Eds.), *Origins of the social mind: Evolutionary psychology and child development* (pp. 189–218). New York: Guilford Press.

Weisner, T. S., Matheson, C., Coots, J., & Bernheimer, L. P. (2005). Sustainability of daily routines as a family outcome. In A. E. Maynard & M. I. Martini (Eds.), *Learning in cultural context: Family, peers, and school. International and cultural psychology series* (pp. 41–73). New York: Kluwer Academic/Plenum Publishers.

Weiss, D., & Newport, E. (2006). Mechanisms underlying language acquisition: Benefits from a comparative approach. *Infancy, 92*, 241–257.

Weisz, A. N., & Black, B. M. (2003). Gender and moral reasoning: African American youths respond to dating dilemmas. *Journal of Human Behavior in the Social Environment, 6*(3), 17–34.

Weitoft, G., Hern, A., Haglunk, B., & Rosen, M. (2003). Mortality, severe morbidity, and injury in children living with single parents in Sweden: A population-based study. *Lancet, 361,* 289–295.

Wellman, H. M., & Gelman, S. A. (1998). Knowledge acquisition in foundational domains. In D. Kuhn & R. S. Siegler (Eds.), *Handbook of child psychology: Vol. 2. Cognition, perception, and language* (5th ed., pp. 523–574). New York: Wiley.

Wellman, H. M., Cross, D., & Watson, J. (2001). Meta-analysis of theory of mind development: The truth about false beliefs. *Child Development, 72,* 655–684.

Wellman, H. M., Hickling, A. K., & Schult, C. A. (1997). Young children's psychological, physical, and biological explanations. In H. M. Wellman & K. Inagaki (Eds.), *The emergence of core domains of thought: Children's reasoning about physical, psychological, and biological phenomena* (pp. 7–26). San Francisco: Jossey-Bass.

Wells, G. (2001). *Action, talk, and text: Learning and teaching through inquiry.* New York: Teachers College Press.

Wells, G. (2007). The mediating role of discoursing in activity. *Mind, Culture, and Activity, 14*(3), 160–177.

Wen, M., Cagney, K. A., & Christakis, N. A. (2005, September). Effect of specific aspects of community social environment on the mortality of individuals diagnosed with serious illness. *Social Science & Medicine, 61*(6), 1119–1134.

Wentzel, K. R., & Asher, S. R. (1995). The academic level of neglected, rejected, popular, and controversial children. *Child Development, 66,* 754–763.

Werker, J. F., Pegg, J. E., & McLeod, P. J. (1994). A cross-language investigation of infant preference for infant-directed communication. *Infant Behavior and Development, 17*(3), 323–333.

West-Eberhard, J. (2003). *Developmental plasticity and evolution.* Oxford, England: Oxford University Press.

Whitaker, R. C., Wright , J. A., Pepe, M. S., Seidel, K. D., & Dietz, W. H. (1997). Predicting obesity in young adulthood from childhood and parental obesity. *New England Journal of Medicine, 337*(13), 869–873.

White, M. (1987). *The Japanese education challenge: A commitment to children.* New York: Free Press.

White, S. H. (1991). Three visions of educational psychology. In L. Tolchinsky-Landsmann (Ed.), *Culture, schooling and psychological development* (pp. 1–38). Norwood, NJ: Ablex.

White, S. H. (1996). The relationship of developmental psychology to social policy. In E. F. Zigler & S. L. Kagan (Eds.), *Children, families, and government: Preparing for the twenty-first century* (pp. 409–426). New York: Cambridge University Press.

Whiteman, S. D., McHale, S. M., & Crouter, A. C. (2007, November). Competing processes of sibling influence: Observational learning and sibling deidentification. Social Development, 16(4), 642–661.

Whiting, B. B., & Whiting, J. W. M. (1975). *Children of six cultures: A psycho-cultural analysis.* Cambridge, MA: Harvard University Press.

Whiting, J. W. M., & Child, I. L. (1953). *Child training and personality.* New Haven, CT: Yale University Press.

Whiting, S. J., Vatanparast, H., Baxter-Jones, A., Faulkner, R. A, Mirwald, R., & Bailey, D. A. (2004, March). Factors that affect bone mineral accrual in the adolescent growth spurt. *The Journal of Nutrition, 134*(3), 696S–700S.

WHO. (2006a). WHO child growth standards based on length/height, weight and age. *Acta Paediatrica, 95*(Suppl. 450), 76–85.

WHO. (2008). *World health report 2008.* Retrieved April 25, 2008, from http://www.who.int/whr/2008/en/index.html

WHO, & de Onis, M. (2006b). Motor Development Study. Windows of achievement for six gross motor development milestones. *Acta Pædiatrica, 95*(Suppl. 450), 86–95.

Wiesner, M., & Ittel, A. (2002). Relations of pubertal timing and depressive symptoms to substance use in early adolescence. *Journal of Early Adolescence, 22,* 5–23.

Wigle, D. T., Arbuckle, .T. E., Walker, M., Wade, M. G., Liu, S., & Krewski, D. (2007). Environmental hazards: evidence for effects on child health. *Journal of Toxicology and Environmental Health Part B: Critical Reviews, 10*(1–2), 3–39.

Wilcox, A. J., Baird, D. D., & Weinberg, C. R. (1999). Time of implantation of the conceptus and loss of pregnancy. *New England Journal of Medicine, 340*(23), 1796–1799.

Wilson, B. J., Smith, S. L., Potter, W. J., Kunkel, D., Linz, D., Colvin, C. M., et al. (2002, March). Violence in children's television programming: Assessing the risks. *Journal of Communication, 52*(1), 5–35.

Wilson, E. O. (1975). *Sociobiology: The new synthesis.* Cambridge, MA: Harvard University Press.

Wilson, J. D. (1995). Editorial: Sex hormones and sexual behavior. *New England Journal of Medicine, 300*(22), 121–134.

Wilson, S. M., Olver, R. E., & Walters, D. V. (2007). Developmental regulation of lumenal lung fluid and electrolyte transport. *Respiratory Physiology and Neurobiology, 159*(3), 247–255.

Wimmer, H., & Hartl, M. (1991). Against the Cartesian view on mind: Young children's difficulty with own false beliefs. *British Journal of Developmental Psychology, 9,* 125–138.

Winner, E. (1998). *The point of words: Children's understanding of metaphor and irony.* Cambridge, MA: Harvard University Press.

Winnicott, D. W. (1971). *Playing and reality.* London: Tavistock.

Wolfenstein, M. (1953). Trends in infant care. *American Journal of Orthopsychiatry, 23,* 120–130.

Wolff, P. H. (1966). The causes, controls, and organization of behavior in the neonate. *Psychological Issues, 5,* 1–105.

Woodruff-Pak, D. S., Logan, C. G., & Thompson, R. F. (1990). Neurobiological substrates of classical conditioning across the life-span. *Annals of the New York Academy of Sciences, 608,* 150–178.

Worchel, F. F., & Allen, M. (1997). Mothers' ability to discriminate cry types in low-birthweight premature and full-term infants. *Children's Health Care, 26*(3), 183–195.

World Health Organization. (2000). *Obesity: Preventing and managing the global epidemic* (World Health Organization Technical Support Series 894). Geneva, Switzerland: WHO.

World Health Organization. (2002). *HIV/AIDS statistics and features by world region.* UNAID. Retrieved April 25, 2007, from www.unaids.org

World Health Organization. (2008). *World health report.* Retrieved August 20, 2008, from http://www.who.int/whr/2008/whr08_en.pdf

Wu, C., & Chao, R. K. (2005, November). Intergenerational cultural conflicts in norms of parental warmth among Chinese American immigrants. *International Journal of Behavioral Development, 29*(6), 516–523.

Wynn, K. (1992). Addition and subtraction by human infants. *Nature, 358,* 749–750.

Yanai, J., Dotan, S., Goz, R., Pinkas, A., Seidler, F. J., Slotkin, T. A., & Zimmerman, F. (2008). Exposure of developing chicks to perfluorooctanoic acid induces defects in prehatch and early posthatch development. *Journal of Toxicology and Environmental Health, Part A, 71*(2), 131–133.

Yanai, J., Steingart, R. A., Snapir, N., Gvaryahu, G., Rozenboim, I., & Katz, A. (2000). The relationship between neural alterations and behavioral deficits after prenatal exposure to heroin. *Annals of the New York Academy of Sciences, 914,* 402–411.

Yang, C., & Hahn, H. (2002). Cosleeping in young Korean children. *Journal of Developmental & Behavioral Pediatrics, 23,* 151–157.

Yang, Q., Carter, H., Mulinare, J., Berry, R., Friedman, J., & Erickson, J. (2007). Race-ethnicity differences in folic acid intake in women of childbearing age in the United States after folic acid fortification: Findings from the National Health and Nutrition Examination Survey, 2001–2002. *American Journal of Clinical Nutrition, 85,* 1409–1416,

Yau, J., & Smetana, J. (2003). Conceptions of moral, social-conventional, and personal events among Chinese preschoolers in Hong Kong. *Child Development, 74*(3), 647–658.

Yerkes, R. M. (Ed.). (1921). *Psychological examining in the United States Army. Memoirs of the National Academy of Sciences, 15,* 1–890.

Yeung, W., Sandberg, J., Davis-Dean, P., & Hofferth, S. (2001). Children's time with fathers in intact families. *Journal of Marriage and the Family, 63*(1), 136–154.

Ylisaukko-oja, T., Alarcón, M., Cantor, R. M., Auranen, M., Vanhala, R., Kempas, E., et al. (2006). Search for autism loci by combined analysis of Autism Genetic Resource Exchange and Finnish families. *Annals of Neurology, 59*(1), 145–155.

Yoshikawa, H., Rosman, E., & Hsueh, J. (2001). Variation in teenage mothers' experiences of child care and other components of welfare reform: Selection processes and developmental outcomes. *Child Development, 72,* 299–317.

Young, M., Miller, B., Norton, M., & Hill, E. (1995). The effect of parental supportive behaviors on life satisfaction of adolescent offspring. *Journal of Marriage and the Family, 57,* 813–822.

Young, S. S., Eskenazi, B., Marchetti, F. M., Block, G., & Wyrobek, A. J. (2008, May). The association of folate, zinc and antioxidant intake with sperm aneuploidy in healthy non-smoking men. *Human Reproduction, 23*(5), 1014–1022.

Zafeiriou, D. I., Tsikoulas, I. G., Kremenopoulos, G. M., & Kontopoulos, E. E. (1999). Moro reflex profile in high-risk infants at the first year of life. *Brain and Development, 21*(3), 216–217.

Zahn-Waxler, C., & Polanichka, N. (2004). All things interpersonal: Socialization and female aggression. In M. Putallaz & K. Bierman (Eds.), *Aggression, antisocial behavior, and violence among girls.* New York: Guilford Press.

Zeanah, C. (Ed.). (2000). *Handbook of infant mental health.* New York: Guilford Press.

Zeifman, D. M. (2001). An ethological analysis of human infant crying: Answering Tinbergen's four questions. *Developmental Psychobiology, 39*(4), 265–285.

Zelazo, P. R. (1983). The development of walking: New findings and old assumptions. *Journal of Motor Behavior, 15,* 99–137.

Zero to Three. (2003). *Choosing quality child care.* Retrieved April 4, 2007, from http://www.zerotothree.org/choosecare.htm

Zeskind, P. S., & Lester, B. M. (2001). Analysis of infant crying. In L. T. Singer & P. S. Zeskind (Eds.), *Biobehavioral assessment of the infant* (pp. 149–166). New York: Guilford Press.

Zielinski, D. S., & Bradshaw, C. P. (2006, February). Ecological influences on the sequelae of child maltreatment: A review of the literature. *Child Maltreatment: Journal of the American Professional Society on the Abuse of Children, 11*(1), 49–62.

Zigler, E. F., & Hall, N. W. (1989). Physical child abuse in America: Past, present, and future. In D. Cicchetti & V. Carlson (Eds.), *Child maltreatment: Theory and research on the causes and consequences of child abuse and neglect.* New York: Cambridge University Press.

Zimmermann, P., & Becker-Stoll, F. (2002). Stability of attachment representations during adolescence: The influence of ego-identity status. *Journal of Adolescence, 25,* 107–124.

Zukow-Goldring, P. (1995). Sibling caregiving. In M. Bornstein (Ed.), *Handbook of parenting: Vol. 3. Status and social conditions of parenting.* Mahwah, NJ: Lawrence Erlbaum Associates.